LITERATURE

LITERATURE

SECOND EDITION

OPTIONS FOR READING AND WRITING

Donald A. Daiker
Mary Fuller
Jack E. Wallace

Miami University of Ohio

HARPER & ROW, PUBLISHERS, New York
Cambridge, Philadelphia, San Francisco,
London, Mexico City, São Paulo,
Singapore, Sydney

Sponsoring Editor: Lucy Rosendahl
Project Editor: Steven Pisano
Text Design Adaptation: Maria Carella
Cover Design: Jean Wyckoff
Cover Illustration: "The Jack Pine," Tom Thomson (1877–1917), oil on canvas National
   Gallery of Canada, Ottawa
Production Manager: Jeanie Berke
Production Assistant: Paula Roppolo
Compositor: ComCom Division of Haddon Craftsmen, Inc.
Printer and Binder: R. R. Donnelley & Sons Company
Cover Printer: Lehigh Press

Literature: Options for Reading and Writing, Second Edition

Library of Congress Cataloging in Publication Data

Daiker, Donald A., 1938–
   Literature: options for reading and writing / Donald A. Daiker, Mary
Fuller, Jack E. Wallace.—2nd ed.
      p.   cm.
   Includes indexes.
   1. College readers.   2. English language—Rhetoric.   I. Fuller,
Mary, 1951– . II. Wallace, Jack E., 1928– . III. Title.
PE1417.D18   1989
808'.0427—dc19   88–10207
                                                                                      CIP

   ISBN 0-06-041483-9 (Student Edition)
   ISBN 0-06-041484-7 (Teacher's Edition)

88 89 90 91 9 8 7 6 5 4 3 2 1

In gratitude to our colleagues:

Frank Jordan, Jr.

Marc Britt
Richard S. Donnell
Roland A. Duerksen
Alice Fannin
Alice Fox
Robert C. Johnson
Robert R. Kettler
Rebecca J. Lukens
S. Allison McCormack
Jerome H. Rosenberg
C. Gilbert Storms
Randolph Wadsworth

who tested in their composition classrooms the methodology and much of the material in this book.

CONTENTS

PART TWO

Writing Assignments for Selected Novels

PART THREE

Poetry

(Each poem is followed by a series of suggestions for writing.)

1 / Poems about Youth and Self-Revelation   561

2 / Poems about Nature   623

5 / Poems about Husbands, Wives, and Lovers   719

PART FOUR

Drama   (Each play is followed by a series of suggestions for writing.)

PREFACE

In this second edition of *Literature: Options for Reading and Writing,* we have made several changes which provide greater variety and richness in both reading and writing assignments. Additions to the reading selections include Shakespeare's *Hamlet,* Tom Stoppard's *The Real Thing,* and a series of stories: new tales by the nineteenth-century masters Edgar Allan Poe and Nathaniel Hawthorne; new science fiction by Ray Bradbury and Ursula K. Le Guin; and, most prominently, new contemporary stories by Ann Beattie, Raymond Carver, Gail Godwin, and David Quammen. The poetry unit has been changed in several ways. We have added poems by Margaret Atwood, Gwendolyn Brooks, Emily Dickinson, Mona Van Duyn, W.S. Merwin, Lorraine Karafel, Erica Jong, Sylvia Plath, Robert Penn Warren, and David Wagoner. The new poems offer greater breadth and depth to the poetry unit. For instance, Erica Jong's "On the First Night," David Wagoner's "The Best Slow Dancer," and Mona Van Duyn's "Late Loving" are more upbeat than many of the current selections, providing balance for Gwendolyn Brook's "The Mother," which grimly recounts a mother's message to her aborted children, and Lorraine Karafel's "Heroines," which tells of Medea and Judith's murderous sacrifices. By adding additional poems by David Wagoner and Emily Dickinson, we provide poem "clusters," which allow teachers to assign four or five poems from one writer to show that artist's growth over a period of time. Additions to the writing assignments include prereading topics as well as a series of questions based on actual passages from student writing. These additions better enable us to attain our original aim: to provide a text for instructors who are as strongly committed to the teaching of writing as to the teaching of literature.

This book originated in our attempt to answer objections to conventional courses in literature and composition. The most common objection is that literature has a way of overwhelming composition; instructors typically schedule five or six reading assignments for every one writing assignment and spend five or six class periods interpreting literature for every one class period examining student writing. As a result, students are often made to feel that what they write is not as important as what they read. We wanted, therefore, to design a course that reasserted the importance of writing and that encouraged students to see their writing as a means of discovery: discovery about their own tastes and values, discovery about the meaning of a particular story or poem, discovery about the nature of literary experience.

With support from the National Endowment for the Humanities, we constructed a course that demonstrated that the process of writing and the process of interpreting literature can become mutually reinforcing activities. One basic strategy in this course was to design a number of brief writing assignments for every reading assignment. Sample student papers about each work were typically shared with the class, either by having them read aloud or, more often, duplicated and distributed. These samples not only provided revision practice and initiated class discussion but in many cases became partial drafts for longer papers. Because of our increased emphasis on student writing and revision, we assigned fewer literary works (for example, one story a week instead of one story per class meeting) and we selected works that were readily accessible—on at least one important level of meaning—to college freshmen.

This course was class-tested at Miami University during the 1982 Spring semester. It was tested in 22 sections of freshman English taught by 15 different instructors and involving 550 students. The testing was conducted by Donald J. Gray, a former director of composition and department chair at Indiana University and then editor of *College English.* On the basis of his extensive evaluation, Gray wrote in his final report to the National Endowment for the Humanities that the integrated course had been "markedly successful" both in improving students' writing and in increasing students' literary understanding. According to Gray, "faculty members thought that they had never before been so successful in connecting the teaching of literature to the teaching of writing, and that they had never before taught literature or writing so effectively." Gray concluded that the course had successfully demonstrated that the study of literature is not only compatible with the study of writing but that, properly integrated, the two activities are mutually sustaining and reinforcing. Since then we have continued to construct and test different kinds of writing assignments and to adapt them to a wide range of literary works. This book is the product of both the NEH course and our subsequent work.

The main feature of this text, the feature that distinguishes it from others of its kind, is the number and diversity of writing assignments. While the second edition retains many of these assignments, we have made certain improvements based on our own experience in the classroom and the council of colleagues who have used this text in other schools. In the first edition we followed the usual practice of putting the writing assignments after a particular reading. In the second edition we additionally provide prereading topics that ask students to write about issues and situations that they will encounter in their reading. Before reading Marvell's "To His Coy Mistress," for example, students are asked to explore their views on sexual freedom, and before reading Miller's *Death of a Salesman,* they are asked to discuss the meaning of success in America. These papers will help students to see how different beliefs and attitudes might influence their reading of a text. After reading a story or poem students are provided a choice of prewriting activities—free writing, looping, listing, and brainstorming—which help them in the discovery process.

Several sorts of more formal exercises provide steady practice in all phases of critical activity. Although we no longer classify writing assignments as explanation, argument, and personal response, there are for each reading a number of topics that stress each of these rhetorical patterns. Some topics are primarily explanatory—asking students to recognize, select, and organize evidence in a particular work. These assignments provide practice in familiar strategies for development—especially illustration, comparison and contrast, and cause and effect. One aim of these assignments is to establish in the class some basic agreement about "what happens" in a story or poem. But students, in giving what they assume to be a factual account of what happens, are likely to reveal their tastes and values in ways that indicate at least a preliminary interpretation of the work.

Another type of assignment provides practice in the strategies of argument, asking students to defend an interpretation against another one of equal or nearly equal validity. In order to do this, students must learn to recognize and anticipate objections to their argument—a valuable exercise in improving both their persuasive writing and their literary understanding. A third kind of assignment asks students to show how their personal response to a particular character or event affects their perception and evaluation of a work. While these assignments seem to encourage the "affective fallacy," students who begin by asking, "How does this affect me?" usually discover the need to generalize their personal experience and to assume that they do not speak simply for themselves but for typical readers. The students' concern about the role of the reader is also reinforced when they share their personal responses with other members of the class.

Additional writing practice is provided by sentence-combining exercises which vary in both length and function. One such exercise is designed to help students understand and use important critical terms such as irony, symbol, setting, point of view, rhythm, and metaphor. Another kind asks students to select from a group of sentences only those most relevant to their purpose and then to organize them into an effective whole.

Together, the prewriting activities and the short paper assignments provide a learn-as-you-write introduction to literary method and practice. More importantly, they provide the foundation for full-length compositions and thus encourage students to view their writing as a coherent sequence of writing tasks. Because we have found that student essays about literature are more effective when they grow out of the class's unmediated response and discussion, we have not interposed expert opinion on "How to Write about Literature" or prescriptive definitions of such literary terms as plot, setting, theme, irony, and the like. Students come to a better understanding of these terms by discovering how their own writing must inevitably take them into account.

In creating *Literature: Options for Reading and Writing* we have had invaluable help. We owe special thanks to our colleague Frank Jordan, Jr., who was one of the co-directors of the NEH grant that enabled us to develop and test a series of literature-based composition assignments. We have dedicated this book to Frank and to twelve other colleagues who class-tested our approach and our materials in their freshman English courses: Marc Britt, Dick Donnell, Roland Duerksen, Alice Fannin, Alice Fox, Bob Johnson, Rob Kettler, Becky Lukens, Allison McCormack, Jerry Rosenberg, Gil Storms, and Randolph Wadsworth. We are deeply grateful as well to our NEH consultant and evaluator Donald J. Gray. Don worked with characteristic intelligence, insight, and diligence in helping us to design and then to evaluate the project.

For their perceptive comments on our manuscript, we are indebted to ten skilled and sensitive readers: Harold Ackerman of Bloomsburg University; John Clifford of the University of North Carolina at Wilmington; Millicent Garcia of Creighton University; Donald J. Gray of Indiana University; Jim Holte of East Carolina University; Richard L. Larson of Herbert H. Lehman College of the City University of New York; Elizabeth McPherson, formerly of Forest Park Community College; Jack Selzer of The Pennsylvania State University; William L. Stull of the University of Hartford; and Robert E. Yarber of San Diego Mesa Community College. We also thank these additional reviewers: Glenn Reed of Northern Arizona University; Jeannette Bouchard of Northeastern University; D'Ann Madewell of North Lake College; Brian Best of Brigham Young University; and Ronald Trouse of College of San Mateo. We thank Jim Flavin and Karl Schnapp for expertly managing permissions. Betty Marak is still the best typist we know. Finally, we are grateful to our editors at Harper & Row for encouraging us to develop a book that integrates composition and literature, and for supporting us throughout with their generosity and wisdom.

Donald A. Daiker
Mary Fuller
Jack E. Wallace

PART ONE

SHORT
STORIES

JOHN STEINBECK

The Murder

Before Reading

Do you think that a husband is ever justified in beating his wife? Free write on this question for 5 or 10 minutes.

This happened a number of years ago in Monterey County, in central California. The Cañon del Castillo is one of those valleys in the Santa Lucia range which lie between its many spurs and ridges. From the main Cañon del Castillo a number of little arroyos cut back into the mountains, oak-wooded canyons, heavily brushed with poison oak and sage. At the head of the canyon there stands a tremendous stone castle, buttressed and towered like those strongholds the Crusaders put up in the path of their conquests. Only a close visit to the castle shows it to be a strange accident of time and water and erosion working on soft, stratified sandstone. In the distance the ruined battlements, the gates, the towers, even the arrow slits, require little imagination to make out.

Below the castle, on the nearly level floor of the canyon, stand the old ranch house, a weathered and mossy barn and a warped feeding-shed for cattle. The house is deserted; the doors, swinging on rusted hinges, squeal and bang on nights when the wind courses down from the castle. Not many people visit the house. Sometimes a crowd of boys tramp through the rooms, peering into empty closets and loudly defying the ghosts they deny.

Jim Moore, who owns the land, does not like to have people about the house. He rides up from his new house, farther down the valley, and chases the boys away. He has put "No Trespassing" signs on his fences to keep curious and morbid people out. Sometimes he thinks of burning the old house down, but then a strange and powerful relation with the swinging doors, the blind and desolate windows, forbids the destruction. If he should burn the house he would destroy a great and important piece of his life. He knows that when he goes to town with his plump and still pretty wife, people turn and look at his retreating back with awe and some admiration.

Jim Moore was born in the old house and grew up in it. He knew every grained and weathered board of the barn, every smooth, worn manger-rack. His mother and father were both dead when he was thirty. He celebrated his majority by raising a beard. He sold the pigs and decided never to have any more. At last he bought a fine Guernsey bull to improve his stock, and he began

THE MURDER First published in 1938. John Steinbeck (1902–1968) was born in Salinas, California, the setting of many of his stories. He is the author of *The Grapes of Wrath, Of Mice and Men,* and *East of Eden.*

to go to Monterey on Saturday nights, to get drunk and to talk with the noisy girls of the Three Star.

Within a year Jim Moore married Jelka Sepic, a Jugo-Slav girl, daughter of a heavy and patient farmer of Pine Canyon. Jim was not proud of her foreign family, of her many brothers and sisters and cousins, but he delighted in her beauty. Jelka had eyes as large and questioning as a doe's eyes. Her nose was thin and sharply faceted, and her lips were deep and soft. Jelka's skin always startled Jim, for between night and night he forgot how beautiful it was. She was so smooth and quiet and gentle, such a good housekeeper, that Jim often thought with disgust of her father's advice on the wedding day. The old man, bleary and bloated with festival beer, elbowed Jim in the ribs and grinned suggestively, so that his little dark eyes almost disappeared behind puffed and wrinkled lids.

"Don't be big fool, now," he said. "Jelka is Slav girl. He's not like American girl. If he is bad, beat him. If he's good too long, beat him too. I beat his mama. Papa beat my mama. Slav girl! He's not like a man that don't beat hell out of him."

"I wouldn't beat Jelka," Jim said.

The father giggled and nudged him again with his elbow, "Don't be big fool," he warned. "Sometime you see." He rolled back to the beer barrel.

Jim found soon enough that Jelka was not like American girls. She was very quiet. She never spoke first, but only answered his questions, and then with soft short replies. She learned her husband as she learned passages of Scripture. After they had been married a while, Jim never wanted for any habitual thing in the house but Jelka had it ready for him before he could ask. She was a fine wife, but there was no companionship in her. She never talked. Her great eyes followed him, and when he smiled, sometimes she smiled too, a distant and covered smile. Her knitting and mending and sewing were interminable. There she sat, watching her wise hands, and she seemed to regard with wonder and pride the little white hands that could do such nice and useful things. She was so much like an animal that sometimes Jim patted her head and neck under the same impulse that made him stroke a horse.

In the house Jelka was remarkable. No matter what time Jim came in from the hot dry range or from the bottom farm land, his dinner was exactly, steamingly ready for him. She watched while he ate, and pushed the dishes close when he needed them, and filled his cup when it was empty.

Early in the marriage he told her things that happened on the farm, but she smiled at him as a foreigner does who wishes to be agreeable even though he doesn't understand.

"The stallion cut himself on the barbed wire," he said.

And she replied, "Yes," with a downward inflection that held neither question nor interest.

He realized before long that he could not get in touch with her in any way. If she had a life apart, it was so remote as to be beyond his reach. The barrier in her eyes was not one that could be removed, for it was neither hostile nor intentional.

At night he stroked her straight black hair and her unbelievably smooth golden shoulders, and she whimpered a little with pleasure. Only in the climax of his embrace did she seem to have a life apart, fierce and passionate. And then immediately she lapsed into the alert and painfully dutiful wife.

"Why don't you ever talk to me?" he demanded. "Don't you want to talk to me?"

"Yes," she said. "What do you want me to say?" She spoke the language of his race out of a mind that was foreign to his race.

When a year had passed, Jim began to crave the company of women, the chattery exchange of small talk, the shrill pleasant insults, the shame-sharpened vulgarity. He began to go again to town, to drink and to play with the noisy girls of the Three Star. They liked him there for his firm, controlled face and for his readiness to laugh.

"Where's your wife?" they demanded.

"Home in the barn," he responded. It was a never-failing joke.

Saturday afternoons he saddled a horse and put a rifle in the scabbard in case he should see a deer. Always he asked, "You don't mind staying alone?"

"No. I don't mind."

At once he asked, "Suppose someone should come?"

Her eyes sharpened for a moment, and then she smiled. "I would send them away," she said.

"I'll be back about noon tomorrow. It's too far to ride in the night." He felt that she knew where he was going, but she never protested nor gave any sign of disapproval. "You should have a baby," he said.

Her face lighted up. "Some time God will be good," she said eagerly.

He was sorry for her loneliness. If only she visited with the other women of the canyon she would be less lonely, but she had no gift for visiting. Once every month or so she put horses to the buckboard and went to spend an afternoon with her mother, and with the brood of brothers and sisters and cousins who lived in her father's house.

"A fine time you'll have," Jim said to her. "You'll gabble your crazy language like ducks for a whole afternoon. You'll giggle with that big grown cousin of yours with the embarrassed face. If I could find any fault with you, I'd call you a damn foreigner." He remembered how she blessed the bread with the sign of the cross before she put it in the oven, how she knelt at the bedside every night, how she had a holy picture tacked to the wall in the closet.

One Saturday of a hot dusty June, Jim cut oats in the farm flat. The day was long. It was after six o'clock when the mower tumbled the last band of oats. He drove the clanking machine up into the barnyard and backed it into the implement shed, and there he unhitched the horses and turned them out to graze on the hills over Sunday. When he entered the kitchen Jelka was just putting his dinner on the table. He washed his hands and face and sat down to eat.

"I'm tired," he said, "but I think I'll go to Monterey anyway. There'll be a full moon."

Her soft eyes smiled.

"I'll tell you what I'll do," he said. "If you would like to go, I'll hitch up a rig and take you with me."

She smiled again and shook her head. "No, the stores would be closed. I would rather stay here."

"Well, all right, I'll saddle the horse then. I didn't think I was going. The stock's all turned out. Maybe I can catch a horse easy. Sure you don't want to go?"

"If it was early, and I could go to the stores—but it will be ten o'clock when you get there."

"Oh, no—well, anyway, on horseback I'll make it a little after nine."

Her mouth smiled to itself, but her eyes watched him for the development of a wish. Perhaps because he was tired from the long day's work, he demanded, "What are you thinking about?"

"Thinking about? I remember, you used to ask that nearly every day when we were first married."

"But what are you?" he insisted irritably.

"Oh—I'm thinking about the eggs under the black hen." She got up and went to the big calendar on the wall. "They will hatch tomorrow or maybe Monday."

It was almost dusk when he had finished shaving and putting on his blue serge suit and his new boots. Jelka had the dishes washed and put away. As Jim went through the kitchen he saw that she had taken the lamp to the table near the window, and that she sat beside it knitting a brown wool sock.

"Why do you sit there tonight?" he asked. "You always sit over here. You do funny things sometimes."

Her eyes arose slowly from her flying hands. "The moon," she said quietly. "You said it would be full tonight. I want to see the moon rise."

"But you're silly. You can't see it from that window. I thought you knew direction better than that."

She smiled remotely. "I will look out of the bedroom window, then."

Jim put on his black hat and went out. Walking through the dark empty barn, he took a halter from the rack. On the grassy sidehill he whistled high and shrill. The horses stopped feeding and moved slowly in towards him, and stopped twenty feet away. Carefully he approached his bay gelding and moved his hand from its rump along its side and up and over its neck. The halter-strap clicked in its buckle. Jim turned and led the horse back to the barn. He threw his saddle on and cinched it tight, put his silver-bound bridle over the stiff ears, buckled the throat latch, knotted the tie-rope about the gelding's neck and fastened the neat coil-end to the saddle string. Then he slipped the halter and led the horse to the house. A radiant crown of soft red light lay over the eastern hills. The full moon would rise before the valley had completely lost the day-light.

In the kitchen Jelka still knitted by the window. Jim strode to the corner of the room and took up his 30-30 carbine. As he rammed cartridges into the magazine, he said, "The moon glow is on the hills. If you are going to see it rise, you better go outside now. It's going to be a good red one at rising."

"In a moment," she replied, "when I come to the end here." He went to her and patted her sleek head.

"Good night. I'll probably be back by noon tomorrow." Her dusky black eyes followed him out of the door.

Jim thrust the rifle into his saddle-scabbard, and mounted and swung his horse down the canyon. On his right, from behind the blackening hills, the great red moon slid rapidly up. The double light of the day's last afterglow and the rising moon thickened the outlines of the trees and gave a mysterious new perspective to the hills. The dusty oaks shimmered and glowed, and the shade under them was black as velvet. A huge, long-legged shadow of a horse and half a man rode to the left and slightly ahead of Jim. From the ranches near and distant came the sound of dogs tuning up for a night of song. And the roosters crowed, thinking a new dawn had come too quickly. Jim lifted the gelding to a trot. The spattering hoof-steps echoed back from the castle behind him. He thought of blond May at the Three Star in Monterey. "I'll be late. Maybe someone else'll have her," he thought. The moon was clear of the hills now.

Jim had gone a mile when he heard the hoofbeats of a horse coming towards him. A horseman cantered up and pulled to a stop. "That you, Jim?"

"Yes. Oh, hello, George."

"I was just riding up to your place. I want to tell you—you know the springhead at the upper end of my land?"

"Yes, I know."

"Well, I was up there this afternoon. I found a dead campfire and a calf's head and feet. The skin was in the fire, half burned, but I pulled it out and it had your brand."

"The hell," said Jim. "How old was the fire?"

"The ground was still warm in the ashes. Last night, I guess. Look, Jim, I can't go up with you. I've got to go to town, but I thought I'd tell you, so you could take a look around."

Jim asked quietly, "Any idea how many men?"

"No. I didn't look close."

"Well, I guess I better go up and look. I was going to town too. But if there are thieves working, I don't want to lose any more stock. I'll cut up through your land if you don't mind, George."

"I'd go with you, but I've got to go to town. You got a gun with you?"

"Oh yes, sure. Here under my leg. Thanks for telling me."

"That's all right. Cut through any place you want. Good night." The neighbour turned his horse and cantered back in the direction from which he had come.

For a few moments Jim sat in the moonlight, looking down at his stilted shadow. He pulled his rifle from its scabbard, levered a cartridge into the chamber, and held the gun across the pommel of his saddle. He turned left from the road, went up the little ridge, through the oak grove, over the grassy hogback and down the other side into the next canyon.

In half an hour he had found the deserted camp. He turned over the heavy, leathery calf's head and felt its dusty tongue to judge by the dryness how

long it had been dead. He lighted a match and looked at his brand on the
half-burned hide. At last he mounted his horse again, rode over the bald grassy
hills and crossed into his own land.

A warm summer wind was blowing on the hilltops. The moon, as it
quartered up the sky, lost its redness and turned the colour of strong tea. Among
the hills the coyotes were singing, and the dogs at the ranch houses below joined
them with broken-hearted howling. The dark green oaks below and the yellow
summer grass showed their colours in the moonlight.

Jim followed the sound of the cowbells to his herd, and found them eating
quietly, and a few deer feeding with them. He listened for the sound of hoofbeats or the voices of men on the wind.

It was after eleven when he turned his horse towards home. He rounded
the west tower of the sandstone castle, rode through the shadow and out into
the moonlight again. Below, the roofs of his barn and house shone dully. The
bedroom window cast back a streak of reflection.

The feeding horses lifted their heads as Jim came down through the
pasture. Their eyes glinted red when they turned their heads.

Jim had almost reached the corral fence—he heard a horse stamping in the
barn. His hand jerked the gelding down. He listened. It came again, the
stamping from the barn. Jim lifted his rifle and dismounted silently. He turned
his horse loose and crept towards the barn.

In the blackness he could hear the grinding of the horse's teeth as it
chewed hay. He moved along the barn until he came to the occupied stall. After
a moment of listening he scratched a match on the butt of his rifle. A saddled
and bridled horse was tied in the stall. The bit was slipped under the chin and
the cinch loosened. The horse stopped eating and turned its head towards the
light.

Jim blew out the match and walked quickly out of the barn. He sat on the
edge of the horse trough and looked into the water. His thoughts came so slowly
that he put them into words and said them under his breath.

"Shall I look through the window? No. My head would throw a shadow
in the room."

He regarded the rifle in his hand. Where it had been rubbed and handled,
the black gun finish had worn off, leaving the metal silvery.

At last he stood up with decision and moved towards the house. At the
steps, an extended foot tried each board tenderly before he put his weight on
it. The three ranch dogs came out from under the house and shook themselves,
stretched and sniffed, wagged their tails and went back to bed.

The kitchen was dark, but Jim knew where every piece of furniture was.
He put out his hand and touched the corner of the table, a chair back, the towel
hanger, as he went along. He crossed the room so silently that even he could
hear only his breath and the whisper of his trouser legs together, and the beating
of his watch in his pocket. The bedroom door stood open and spilled a patch
of moonlight on the kitchen floor. Jim reached the door at last and peered
through.

The moonlight lay on the white bed. Jim saw Jelka lying on her back, one soft bare arm flung across her forehead and eyes. He could not see who the man was, for his head was turned away. Jim watched, holding his breath. Then Jelka twitched in her sleep and the man rolled his head and sighed—Jelka's cousin, her grown, embarrassed cousin.

Jim turned and quickly stole back across the kitchen and down the back steps. He walked up the yard to the water-trough again, and sat down on the edge of it. The moon was white as chalk, and it swam in the water, and lighted the straws and barley dropped by the horses' mouths. Jim could see the mosquito wigglers, tumbling up and down, end over end, in the water, and he could see a newt lying in the sun moss in the bottom of the trough.

He cried a few dry, hard, smothered sobs, and wondered why, for his thought was of the grassed hilltops and of the lonely summer wind whisking along.

His thought turned to the way his mother used to hold a bucket to catch the throat blood when his father killed a pig. She stood as far away as possible and held the bucket at arms'-length to keep her clothes from getting spattered.

Jim dipped his hand into the trough and stirred the moon to broken, swirling streams of light. He wetted his forehead with his damp hands and stood up. This time he did not move so quietly, but he crossed the kitchen on tiptoe and stood in the bedroom door. Jelka moved her arm and opened her eyes a little. Then the eyes sprang wide, then they glistened with moisture. Jim looked into her eyes; his face was empty of expression. A little drop ran out of Jelka's nose and lodged in the hollow of her upper lip. She stared back at him.

Jim cocked the rifle. The steel click sounded through the house. The man on the bed stirred uneasily in his sleep. Jim's hands were quivering. He raised the gun to his shoulder and held it tightly to keep from shaking. Over the sights he saw the little white square between the man's brows and hair. The front sight wavered a moment and then came to rest.

The gun crash tore the air. Jim, still looking down the barrel, saw the whole bed jolt under the blow. A small, black, bloodless hole was in the man's forehead. But behind, the hollow-point took brain and bone and splashed them on the pillow.

Jelka's cousin gurgled in his throat. His hands came crawling out from under the covers like big white spiders, and they walked for a moment, then shuddered and fell quiet.

Jim looked slowly back at Jelka. Her nose was running. Her eyes had moved from him to the end of the rifle. She whined softly, like a cold puppy.

Jim turned in panic. His boot heels beat on the kitchen floor, but outside, he moved slowly towards the water-trough again. There was a taste of salt in his throat, and his heart heaved painfully. He pulled his hat off and dipped his head into the water. Then he leaned over and vomited on the ground. In the house he could hear Jelka moving about. She whimpered like a puppy. Jim straightened up, weak and dizzy.

He walked tiredly through the corral and into the pasture. His saddled horse came at his whistle. Automatically he tightened the cinch, mounted and rode away, down the road to the valley. The squat black shadow traveled under him. The moon sailed high and white. The uneasy dogs barked monotonously.

At daybreak a buckboard and pair trotted up to the ranch yard, scattering the chickens. A deputy sheriff and a coroner sat in the seat. Jim Moore half reclined against his saddle in the wagon-box. His tired gelding followed behind. The deputy sheriff set the brake and wrapped the lines around it. The men dismounted.

Jim asked, "Do I have to go in? I'm too tired and wrought up to see it now."

The coroner pulled his lip and studied. "Oh, I guess not. We'll tend to things and look around."

Jim sauntered away towards the water-trough. "Say," he called, "kind of clean up a little, will you? You know."

The men went on into the house.

In a few minutes they emerged, carrying the stiffened body between them. It was wrapped up in a comforter. They eased it up into the wagon-box. Jim walked back towards them. "Do I have to go in with you now?"

"Where's your wife, Mr. Moore?" the deputy sheriff demanded.

"I don't know," he said wearily. "She's somewhere around."

"You're sure you didn't kill her too?"

"No. I didn't touch her. I'll find her and bring her in this afternoon. That is, if you don't want me to go in with you now."

"We've got your statement," the coroner said. "And by God, we've got eyes, haven't we, Will? Of course there's a technical charge of murder against you, but it'll be dismissed. Always is in this part of the country. Go kind of light on your wife, Mr. Moore."

"I won't hurt her," said Jim.

He stood and watched the buckboard jolt away. He kicked his feet reluctantly in the dust. The hot June sun showed its face over the hills and flashed viciously on the bedroom window.

Jim went slowly into the house, and brought out a nine-foot, loaded bull whip. He crossed the yard and walked into the barn. And as he climbed the ladder to the hayloft, he heard the high, puppy whimpering start.

When Jim came out of the barn again, he carried Jelka over his shoulder. By the water-trough he set her tenderly on the ground. Her hair was littered with bits of hay. The back of her shirtwaist was streaked with blood.

Jim wetted his bandana at the pipe and washed her bitten lips, and washed her face and brushed back her hair. Her dusty black eyes followed every move he made.

"You hurt me," she said. "You hurt me bad."

He nodded gravely. "Bad as I could without killing you."

The sun shone hotly on the ground. A few blowflies buzzed about, looking for the blood.

Jelka's thickened lips tried to smile. "Did you have any breakfast at all?"

"No," he said. "None at all."

"Well, then, I'll fry you up some eggs." She struggled painfully to her feet.

"Let me help you," he said. "I'll help you get your shirtwaist off. It's drying stuck to your back. It'll hurt."

"No. I'll do it myself." Her voice had a peculiar resonance in it. Her dark eyes dwelt warmly on him for a moment, and then she turned and limped into the house.

Jim waited, sitting on the edge of the water-trough. He saw the smoke start out of the chimney and sail straight up into the air. In a very few moments Jelka called him from the kitchen door.

"Come, Jim. Your breakfast."

Four fried eggs and four thick slices of bacon lay on a warmed plate for him. "The coffee will be ready in a minute," she said.

"Won't you eat?"

"No. Not now. My mouth's too sore."

He ate his eggs hungrily and then looked up at her. Her black hair was combed smooth. She had on a fresh white shirtwaist. "We're going to town this afternoon," he said. "I'm going to order lumber. We'll build a new house farther down the canyon."

Her eyes darted to the closed bedroom door and then back to him. "Yes," she said. "That will be good." And then, after a moment, "Will you whip me any more—for this?"

"No, not any more, for this."

Her eyes smiled. She sat down on a chair beside him, and Jim put out his hand and stroked her hair and the back of her neck.

Writing Assignments for "The Murder"

I. Brief Papers

A. 1. Show that Jim thinks of Jelka as an animal.

2. Explain what goes on at the Three Star. Is the place merely a saloon?

3. Show that the murder is deliberate and premeditated, not a spontaneous "crime of passion."

4. Show that Jim does not kill Jelka's cousin dispassionately but that he is emotionally affected by the killing.

5. Explain why, after the murder, Jim decides to build a new house but decides against tearing down the old one.

B. Choose one assertion below and argue for or against it:

1. Jim treats Jelka as an animal primarily because she behaves like one.

2. Jelka knows her cousin will be coming to see her on the night of the murder.

3. Jim will be tried and convicted and imprisoned for the murder of Jelka's cousin.

4. Jim's and Jelka's marriage improves as a result of the murder and the beating.

C. 1. How is your response to the story affected by Jim's efforts to communicate with Jelka? (Suppose, instead, that Jim had never tried to reach out to her.)

2. How effective and how well written is the following student response to the previous question?

> Jim's efforts to communicate with Jelka show that Jim does try to make the marriage work. This proves the outcome of the story is not entirely Jim's fault. When Jim first marries Jelka, he repeatedly tries to make small talk with her: "The stallion cut himself on the barbed wire" (p. 4). Jelka, however, only responds, " 'Yes,' with a downward inflection that held neither question nor interest" (p. 4). Many times Jim insists that Jelka tell him what is on her mind. Her thoughts are never volunteered but are forever coaxed by Jim. No matter how he tried he could not get in touch with her. "The barrier in her eyes was not one that could be removed, for it was neither hostile nor intentional" (p. 4). Jelka is responsible for the lack of communication in the marriage, and therefore Jim cannot be entirely blamed.

3. How is your response to the story affected by Jim's plan to meet "blond May" at the Three Star on the night of the murder? (Suppose, instead, he was going to the hardware store.)
4. Do you find Jelka's father sympathetically portrayed? Why or why not?
5. What is left out of a story is sometimes as important as what is included. How do you think your response is affected by the omission of a detailed description of Jim's whipping Jelka? (Suppose, instead, the beating was described in vivid detail.)
6. Do you, like the people of Monterey, look upon Jim "with awe and some admiration?" (p. 3). Why or why not?

II. Longer Papers
A. Develop one of your brief papers into a longer one.
B. Explain in convincing detail whether you think "The Murder" has a happy ending.
C. Do you think that "The Murder" demonstrates that Jim's murdering the cousin and whipping Jelka result in a revitalized marriage?
D. Do you believe that Jim should be tried and convicted and imprisoned for the murder of Jelka's cousin? Why or why not?
E. Expand and develop one of the following assertions:
  1. "The Murder" is anti-feminist: it shows the necessity and justice of the double standard, and it approves a code beyond the law that permits killing and wife beating.
  2. "The Murder" is pro-feminist: it condemns the injustice and brutality of a sexist code that assumes a wife, like cattle, is a husband's property.
  3. "The Murder" is neither pro-feminist nor anti-feminist; it does not attempt to characterize women at all but rather to show that all human behavior—Jim's as well as Jelka's—is determined by forces over which the individual has no control.

SUSAN GLASPELL
A Jury of Her Peers

Before Reading

Do you think that, aside from relative physical strength, men are in any way superior to women? Do you think that women are in any way superior to men? Free write on one or both of these questions for about 10 minutes.

When Martha Hale opened the storm-door and got a cut of the north wind, she ran back for her big woolen scarf. As she hurriedly wound that round her head her eye made a scandalized sweep of her kitchen. It was no ordinary thing that called her away—it was probably farther from ordinary than anything that had ever happened in Dickson County. But what her eye took in was that her kitchen was in no shape for leaving: her bread all ready for mixing, half the flour sifted and half unsifted.

She hated to see things half done; but she had been at that when the team from town stopped to get Mr. Hale, and then the sheriff came running in to say his wife wished Mrs. Hale would come too—adding, with a grin, that he guessed she was getting scarey and wanted another woman along. So she had dropped everything right where it was.

"Martha!" now came her husband's impatient voice. "Don't keep folks waiting out here in the cold."

She again opened the storm-door, and this time joined the three men and the one woman waiting for her in the big two-seated buggy.

After she had the robes tucked around her she took another look at the woman who sat beside her on the back seat. She had met Mrs. Peters the year before at the county fair, and the thing she remembered about her was that she didn't seem like a sheriff's wife. She was small and thin and didn't have a strong voice. Mrs. Gorman, sheriff's wife before Gorman went out and Peters came in, had a voice that somehow seemed to be backing up the law with every word. But if Mrs. Peters didn't look like a sheriff's wife, Peters made it up in looking like a sheriff. He was to a dot the kind of man who could get himself elected sheriff—a heavy man with a big voice, who was particularly genial with the law-abiding, as if to make it plain that he knew the difference between criminals and non-criminals. And right there it came into Mrs. Hale's mind, with a stab, that this man who was so pleasant and lively with all of them was going to the Wrights' now as a sheriff.

"The country's not very pleasant this time of year," Mrs. Peters at last ventured, as if she felt they ought to be talking as well as the men.

A JURY OF HER PEERS   First published in 1917. Susan Glaspell (1882–1948) grew up in Iowa, and the events of this short story were suggested to her when she was working for a newspaper in Des Moines.

Mrs. Hale scarcely finished her reply, for they had gone up a little hill and could see the Wright place now, and seeing it did not make her feel like talking. It looked very lonesome this cold March morning. It had always been a lonesome-looking place. It was down in a hollow, and the poplar trees around it were lonesome-looking trees. The men were looking at it and talking about what had happened. The county attorney was bending to one side of the buggy, and kept looking steadily at the place as they drew up to it.

"I'm glad you came with me," Mrs. Peters said nervously, as the two women were about to follow the men in through the kitchen door.

Even after she had her foot on the door-step, her hand on the knob, Martha Hale had a moment of feeling she could not cross that threshold. And the reason it seemed she couldn't cross it now was simply because she hadn't crossed it before. Time and time again it had been in her mind, "I ought to go over and see Minnie Foster"—she still thought of her as Minnie Foster, though for twenty years she had been Mrs. Wright. And then there was always something to do and Minnie Foster would go from her mind. But *now* she could come.

The men went over to the stove. The women stood close together by the door. Young Henderson, the county attorney, turned around and said, "Come up to the fire, ladies."

Mrs. Peters took a step forward, then stopped. "I'm not—cold," she said.

And so the two women stood by the door, at first not even so much as looking around the kitchen.

The men talked for a minute about what a good thing it was the sheriff had sent his deputy out that morning to make a fire for them, and then Sheriff Peters stepped back from the stove, unbuttoned his outer coat, and leaned his hands on the kitchen table in a way that seemed to mark the beginning of official business. "Now, Mr. Hale," he said in a sort of semi-official voice, "before we move things about, you tell Mr. Henderson just what it was you saw when you came here yesterday morning."

The county attorney was looking around the kitchen.

"By the way," he said, "has anything been moved?" He turned to the sheriff. "Are things just as you left them yesterday?"

Peters looked from cupboard to sink; from that to a small worn rocker a little to one side of the kitchen table.

"It's just the same."

"Somebody should have been left here yesterday," said the county attorney.

"Oh—yesterday," returned the sheriff, with a little gesture as of yesterday having been more than he could bear to think of. "When I had to send Frank to Morris Center for that man who went crazy—let me tell you, I had my hands full *yesterday*. I knew you could get back from Omaha by to-day, George, and as long as I went over everything here myself—"

"Well, Mr. Hale," said the county attorney, in a way of letting what was past and gone go, "tell just what happened when you came here yesterday morning."

Mrs. Hale, still leaning against the door, had that sinking feeling of the mother whose child is about to speak a piece. Lewis often wandered along and got things mixed up in a story. She hoped he would tell this straight and plain, and not say unnecessary things that would just make things harder for Minnie Foster. He didn't begin at once, and she noticed that he looked queer—as if standing in that kitchen and having to tell what he had seen there yesterday morning made him almost sick.

"Yes, Mr. Hale?" the county attorney reminded.

"Harry and I had started to town with a load of potatoes," Mrs. Hale's husband began.

Harry was Mrs. Hale's oldest boy. He wasn't with them now, for the very good reason that those potatoes never got to town yesterday and he was taking them this morning, so he hadn't been home when the sheriff stopped to say he wanted Mr. Hale to come over to the Wright place and tell the county attorney his story there, where he could point it all out. With all Mrs. Hale's other emotions came the fear now that maybe Harry wasn't dressed warm enough—they hadn't any of them realized how that north wind did bite.

"We come along this road," Hale was going on, with a motion of his hand to the road over which they had just come, "and as we got in sight of the house I says to Harry, 'I'm goin' to see if I can't get John Wright to take a telephone.' You see," he explained to Henderson, "unless I can get somebody to go in with me they won't come out this branch road except for a price *I* can't pay. I'd spoke to Wright about it once before; but he put me off, saying folks talked too much anyway, and all he asked was peace and quiet—guess you know about how much he talked himself. But I thought maybe if I went to the house and talked about it before his wife, and said all the women-folks liked the telephones, and that in this lonesome stretch of road it would be a good thing—well, I said to Harry that that was what I was going to say—though I said at the same time that I didn't know as what his wife wanted made much difference to John—"

Now, there he was!—saying things he didn't need to say. Mrs. Hale tried to catch her husband's eye, but fortunately the county attorney interrupted with:

"Let's talk about that a little later, Mr. Hale. I do want to talk about that, but I'm anxious now to get along to just what happened when you got here."

When he began this time, it was very deliberately and carefully:

"I didn't see or hear anything. I knocked at the door. And still it was all quiet inside. I knew they must be up—it was past eight o'clock. So I knocked again, louder, and I thought I heard somebody say 'Come in.' I wasn't sure—I'm not sure yet. But I opened the door—this door," jerking a hand toward the door by which the two women stood, "and there, in that rocker"—pointing to it—"sat Mrs. Wright."

Every one in the kitchen looked at the rocker. It came into Mrs. Hale's mind that that rocker didn't look in the least like Minnie Foster—the Minnie Foster of twenty years before. It was a dingy red, with wooden rungs up the back, and the middle rung was gone, and the chair sagged to one side.

"How did she—look?" the county attorney was inquiring.

"Well," said Hale, "she looked—queer."

"How do you mean—queer?"

As he asked it he took out a note-book and pencil. Mrs. Hale did not like the sight of that pencil. She kept her eye fixed on her husband, as if to keep him from saying unnecessary things that would go into that note-book and make trouble.

Hale did speak guardedly, as if the pencil had affected him too.

"Well, as if she didn't know what she was going to do next. And kind of—done up."

"How did she seem to feel about your coming?"

"Why, I don't think she minded—one way or other. She didn't pay much attention. I said, 'Ho' do, Mrs. Wright? It's cold, ain't it?' And she said, 'Is it?'—and went on pleatin' at her apron.

"Well, I was surprised. She didn't ask me to come up to the stove, or to sit down, but just set there, not even lookin' at me. And so I said: 'I want to see John.'

"And then she—laughed. I guess you would call it a laugh.

"I thought of Harry and the team outside, so I said, a little sharp, 'Can I see John?' 'No,' says she—kind of dull like. 'Ain't he home?' says I. Then she looked at me. 'Yes,' says she, 'he's home.' 'Then why can't I see him?' I asked her, out of patience with her now. 'Cause he's dead,' says she, just as quiet and dull—and fell to pleatin' her apron. 'Dead?' says I, like you do when you can't take in what you've heard.

"She just nodded her head, not getting a bit excited, but rockin' back and forth.

" 'Why—where is he?' says I, not knowing *what* to say.

"She just pointed upstairs—like this"—pointing to the room above.

"I got up, with the idea of going up there myself. By this time I—didn't know what to do. I walked from there to here; then I says: 'Why, what did he die of?'

" 'He died of a rope around his neck,' says she; and just went on pleatin' at her apron."

Hale stopped speaking, and stood staring at the rocker, as if he were still seeing the woman who had sat there the morning before. Nobody spoke; it was as if every one were seeing the woman who had sat there the morning before.

"And what did you do then?" the county attorney at last broke the silence.

"I went out and called Harry. I thought I might—need help. I got Harry in, and we went upstairs." His voice fell almost to a whisper. "There he was—lying over the—"

"I think I'd rather have you go into that upstairs," the county attorney interrupted, "where you can point it all out. Just go on now with the rest of the story."

"Well, my first thought was to get that rope off. It looked—"

He stopped, his face twitching.

"But Harry, he went up to him, and he said, 'No, he's dead all right, and we'd better not touch anything.' So we went downstairs.

"She was still sitting that same way. 'Has anybody been notified?' I asked. 'No,' says she, unconcerned.

" 'Who did this, Mrs. Wright?' said Harry. He said it business-like, and she stopped pleatin' at her apron. 'I don't know,' she says. 'You don't *know?*' says Harry. 'Weren't you sleepin' in the bed with him?' 'Yes,' says she, 'but I was on the inside.' 'Somebody slipped a rope round his neck and strangled him, and you didn't wake up?' says Harry. 'I didn't wake up,' she said after him.

"We may have looked as if we didn't see how that could be, for after a minute she said, 'I sleep sound.'

"Harry was going to ask her more questions, but I said maybe that weren't our business; maybe we ought to let her tell her story first to the coroner or the sheriff. So Harry went fast as he could over to High Road—the Rivers' place, where there's a telephone."

"And what did she do when she knew you had gone for the coroner?" The attorney got his pencil in his hand all ready for writing.

"She moved from that chair to this one over here"—Hale pointed to a small chair in the corner—"and just sat there with her hands held together and looking down. I got a feeling that I ought to make some conversation, so I said I had come in to see if John wanted to put in a telephone; and at that she started to laugh, and then she stopped and looked at me—scared."

At the sound of a moving pencil the man who was telling the story looked up.

"I dunno—maybe it wasn't scared," he hastened; "I wouldn't like to say it was. Soon Harry got back, and then Dr. Lloyd came, and you, Mr. Peters, and so I guess that's all I know that you don't."

He said that last with relief, and moved a little, as if relaxing. Every one moved a little. The county attorney walked toward the stair door.

"I guess we'll go upstairs first—then out to the barn and around there."

He paused and looked around the kitchen.

"You're convinced there was nothing important here?" he asked the sheriff. "Nothing that would—point to any motive?"

The sheriff too looked all around, as if to re-convince himself.

"Nothing here but kitchen things," he said, with a little laugh for the insignificance of kitchen things.

The county attorney was looking at the cupboard—a peculiar, ungainly structure, half closet and half cupboard, the upper part of it being built in the wall, and the lower part just the old-fashioned kitchen cupboard. As if its queerness attracted him, he got a chair and opened the upper part and looked in. After a moment he drew his hand away sticky.

"Here's a nice mess," he said resentfully.

The two women had drawn nearer, and now the sheriff's wife spoke.

"Oh—her fruit," she said, looking to Mrs. Hale for sympathetic understanding. She turned back to the county attorney and explained: "She worried about that when it turned so cold last night. She said the fire would go out and her jars might burst."

Mrs. Peters' husband broke into a laugh.

"Well, can you beat the woman! Held for murder, and worrying about her preserves!"

The young attorney set his lips.

"I guess before we're through with her she may have something more serious than preserves to worry about."

"Oh, well," said Mrs. Hale's husband, with good-natured superiority, "women are used to worrying over trifles."

The two women moved a little closer together. Neither of them spoke. The county attorney seemed suddenly to remember his manners—and think of his future.

"And yet," said he, with the gallantry of a young politician, "for all their worries, what would we do without the ladies?"

The women did not speak, did not unbend. He went to the sink and began washing his hands. He turned to wipe them on the roller towel—whirled it for a cleaner place.

"Dirty towels! Not much of a housekeeper, would you say, ladies?"

He kicked his foot against some dirty pans under the sink.

"There's a great deal of work to be done on a farm," said Mrs. Hale stiffly.

"To be sure. And yet"—with a little bow to her—"I know there are some Dickson County farm-houses that do not have such roller towels." He gave it a pull to expose its full length again.

"Those towels get dirty awful quick. Men's hands aren't always as clean as they might be."

"Ah, loyal to your sex, I see," he laughed. He stopped and gave her a keen look. "But you and Mrs. Wright were neighbors. I suppose you were friends, too."

Martha Hale shook her head.

"I've seen little enough of her of late years. I've not been in this house—it's more than a year."

"And why was that? You didn't like her?"

"I liked her well enough," she replied with spirit. "Farmers' wives have their hands full, Mr. Henderson. And then"—She looked around the kitchen.

"Yes?" he encouraged.

"It never seemed a very cheerful place," said she, more to herself than to him.

"No," he agreed; "I don't think any one would call it cheerful. I shouldn't say she had the home-making instinct."

"Well, I don't know as Wright had, either," she muttered.

"You mean they didn't get on very well?" he was quick to ask.

"No; I don't mean anything," she answered, with decision. As she turned a little away from him, she added: "But I don't think a place would be any the cheerfuler for John Wright's bein' in it."

"I'd like to talk to you about that a little later, Mrs. Hale," he said. "I'm anxious to get the lay of things upstairs now."

He moved toward the stair door, followed by the two men.

"I suppose anything Mrs. Peters does'll be all right?" the sheriff inquired. "She was to take in some clothes for her, you know—and a few little things. We left in such a hurry yesterday."

The county attorney looked at the two women whom they were leaving alone there among the kitchen things.

"Yes—Mrs. Peters," he said, his glance resting on the woman who was not Mrs. Peters, the big farmer woman who stood behind the sheriff's wife. "Of course Mrs. Peters is one of us," he said, in a manner of entrusting responsibility. "And keep your eye out, Mrs. Peters, for anything that might be of use. No telling; you women might come upon a clue to the motive—and that's the thing we need."

Mr. Hale rubbed his face after the fashion of a show man getting ready for a pleasantry.

"But would the women know a clue if they did come upon it?" he said; and, having delivered himself of this, he followed the others through the stair door.

The women stood motionless and silent, listening to the footsteps, first upon the stairs, then in the room above them.

Then, as if releasing herself from something strange, Mrs. Hale began to arrange the dirty pans under the sink, which the county attorney's disdainful push of the foot had deranged.

"I'd hate to have men comin' into my kitchen," she said testily—"snoopin' round and criticizin'."

"Of course it's no more than their duty," said the sheriff's wife, in her manner of timid acquiescence.

"Duty's all right," replied Mrs. Hale bluffly; "but I guess that deputy sheriff that come out to make the fire might have got a little of this on." She gave the roller towel a pull. "Wish I'd thought of that sooner! Seems mean to talk about her for not having things slicked up, when she had to come away in such a hurry."

She looked around the kitchen. Certainly it was not "slicked up." Her eye was held by a bucket of sugar on a low shelf. The cover was off the wooden bucket, and beside it was a paper bag—half full.

Mrs. Hale moved toward it.

"She was putting this in there," she said to herself—slowly.

She thought of the flour in her kitchen at home—half sifted, half not sifted. She had been interrupted, and had left things half done. What had interrupted Minnie Foster? Why had that work been left half done? She made a move as if to finish it,—unfinished things always bothered her,—and then she glanced around and saw that Mrs. Peters was watching her—and she didn't want Mrs. Peters to get that feeling she had got of work begun and then—for some reason—not finished.

"It's a shame about her fruit," she said, and walked toward the cupboard that the county attorney had opened, and got on the chair, murmuring: "I wonder if it's all gone."

It was a sorry enough looking sight, but "Here's one that's all right," she said at last. She held it toward the light. "This is cherries, too." She looked again. "I declare I believe that's the only one."

With a sigh, she got down from the chair, went to the sink, and wiped off the bottle.

"She'll feel awful bad, after all her hard work in the hot weather. I remember the afternoon I put up my cherries last summer."

She set the bottle on the table, and, with another sigh, started to sit down in the rocker. But she did not sit down. Something kept her from sitting down in that chair. She straightened—stepped back, and, half turned away, stood looking at it, seeing the woman who had sat there "pleatin' at her apron."

The thin voice of the sheriff's wife broke in upon her: "I must be getting those things from the front room closet." She opened the door into the other room, started in, stepped back. "You coming with me, Mrs. Hale?" she asked nervously. "You—you could help me get them."

They were soon back—the stark coldness of that shut-up room was not a thing to linger in.

"My!" said Mrs. Peters, dropping the things on the table and hurrying to the stove.

Mrs. Hale stood examining the clothes the woman who was being detained in town had said she wanted.

"Wright was close!" she exclaimed, holding up a shabby black skirt that bore the marks of much making over. "I think maybe that's why she kept so much to herself. I s'pose she felt she couldn't do her part; and then, you don't enjoy things when you feel shabby. She used to wear pretty clothes and be lively—when she was Minnie Foster, one of the town girls, singing in the choir. But that—oh, that was twenty years ago."

With a carefulness in which there was something tender, she folded the shabby clothes and piled them at one corner of the table. She looked up at Mrs. Peters, and there was something in the other woman's look that irritated her.

"She don't care," she said to herself. "Much difference it makes to her whether Minnie Foster had pretty clothes when she was a girl."

Then she looked again, and she wasn't so sure; in fact, she hadn't at any time been perfectly sure about Mrs. Peters. She had that shrinking manner, and yet her eyes looked as if they could see a long way into things.

"This all you was to take in?" asked Mrs. Hale.

"No," said the sheriff's wife; "she said she wanted an apron. Funny thing to want," she ventured in her nervous little way, "for there's not much to get you dirty in jail, goodness knows. But I suppose just to make her feel more natural. If you're used to wearing an apron—. She said they were in the bottom drawer of this cupboard. Yes—here they are. And then her little shawl that always hung on the stair door."

She took the small gray shawl from behind the door leading upstairs, and stood a minute looking at it.

Suddenly Mrs. Hale took a quick step toward the other woman.

"Mrs. Peters!"

"Yes, Mrs. Hale?"

"Do you think she—did it?"

A frightened look blurred the other things in Mrs. Peters' eyes.

"Oh, I don't know," she said, in a voice that seemed to shrink away from the subject.

"Well, I don't think she did," affirmed Mrs. Hale stoutly. "Asking for an apron, and her little shawl. Worryin' about her fruit."

"Mr. Peters says—." Footsteps were heard in the room above; she stopped, looked up, then went on in a lowered voice: "Mr. Peters says—it looks bad for her. Mr. Henderson is awful sarcastic in a speech, and he's going to make fun of her saying she didn't—wake up."

For a moment Mrs. Hale had no answer. Then, "Well, I guess John Wright didn't wake up—when they was slippin' that rope under his neck," she muttered.

"No, it's *strange*," breathed Mrs. Peters. "They think it was such a—funny way to kill a man."

She began to laugh; at sound of the laugh, abruptly stopped.

"That's just what Mr. Hale said," said Mrs. Hale, in a resolutely natural voice. "There was a gun in the house. He says that's what he can't understand."

"Mr. Henderson said, coming out, that what was needed for the case was a motive. Something to show anger—or sudden feeling."

"Well, I don't see any signs of anger around here," said Mrs. Hale. "I don't—"

She stopped. It was as if her mind tripped on something. Her eye was caught by a dish-towel in the middle of the kitchen table. Slowly she moved toward the table. One half of it was wiped clean, the other half messy. Her eyes made a slow, almost unwilling turn to the bucket of sugar and the half empty bag beside it. Things begun—and not finished.

After a moment she stepped back, and said, in that manner of releasing herself:

"Wonder how they're finding things upstairs? I hope she had it a little more red up up there. You know,"—she paused, and feeling gathered,—"it seems kind of *sneaking:* locking her up in town and coming out here to get her own house to turn against her!"

"But, Mrs. Hale," said the sheriff's wife, "the law is the law."

"I s'pose 'tis," answered Mrs. Hale shortly.

She turned to the stove, saying something about that fire not being much to brag of. She worked with it a minute, and when she straightened up she said aggressively:

"The law is the law—and a bad stove is a bad stove. How'd you like to cook on this?"—pointing with the poker to the broken lining. She opened the oven door and started to express her opinion of the oven; but she was swept into her own thoughts, thinking of what it would mean, year after year, to have that stove to wrestle with. The thought of Minnie Foster trying to bake in that oven—and the thought of her never going over to see Minnie Foster—.

She was startled by hearing Mrs. Peters say: "A person gets discouraged—and loses heart."

The sheriff's wife had looked from the stove to the sink—to the pail of water which had been carried in from outside. The two women stood there silent, above them the footsteps of the men who were looking for evidence against the woman who had worked in that kitchen. That look of seeing into things, of seeing through a thing to something else, was in the eyes of the sheriff's wife now. When Mrs. Hale next spoke to her, it was gently:

"Better loosen up your things, Mrs. Peters. We'll not feel them when we go out."

Mrs. Peters went to the back of the room to hang up the fur tippet she was wearing. A moment later she exclaimed, "Why, she was piecing a quilt," and held up a large sewing basket piled high with quilt pieces.

Mrs. Hale spread some of the blocks on the table.

"It's log-cabin pattern," she said, putting several of them together. "Pretty, isn't it?"

They were so engaged with the quilt that they did not hear the footsteps on the stairs. Just as the stair door opened Mrs. Hale was saying:

"Do you suppose she was going to quilt it or just knot it?"

The sheriff threw up his hands.

"They wonder whether she was going to quilt it or just knot it!"

There was a laugh for the ways of women, a warming of hands over the stove, and then the county attorney said briskly:

"Well, let's go right out to the barn and get that cleared up."

"I don't see as there's anything so strange," Mrs. Hale said resentfully, after the outside door had closed on the three men—"our taking up our time with little things while we're waiting for them to get the evidence. I don't see as it's anything to laugh about."

"Of course they've got awful important things on their minds," said the sheriff's wife apologetically.

They returned to an inspection of the block for the quilt. Mrs. Hale was looking at the fine, even sewing, and preoccupied with thoughts of the woman who had done that sewing, when she heard the sheriff's wife say, in a queer tone:

"Why, look at this one."

She turned to take the block held out to her.

"The sewing," said Mrs. Peters, in a troubled way. "All the rest of them have been so nice and even—but—this one. Why, it looks as if she didn't know what she was about!"

Their eyes met—something flashed to life, passed between them; then, as if with an effort, they seemed to pull away from each other. A moment Mrs. Hale sat there, her hands folded over that sewing which was so unlike all the rest of the sewing. Then she had pulled a knot and drawn the threads.

"Oh, what are you doing, Mrs. Hale?" asked the sheriff's wife, startled.

"Just pulling out a stitch or two that's not sewed very good," said Mrs. Hale mildly.

"I don't think we ought to touch things," Mrs. Peters said, a little helplessly.

"I'll just finish up this end," answered Mrs. Hale, still in that mild, matter-of-fact fashion.

She threaded a needle and started to replace bad sewing with good. For a little while she sewed in silence. Then, in that thin, timid voice, she heard:

"Mrs. Hale!"

"Yes, Mrs. Peters?"

"What do you suppose she was so—nervous about?"

"Oh, *I* don't know," said Mrs. Hale, as if dismissing a thing not important enough to spend much time on. "I don't know as she was—nervous. I sew awful queer sometimes when I'm just tired."

She cut a thread, and out of the corner of her eye looked up at Mrs. Peters. The small, lean face of the sheriff's wife seemed to have tightened up. Her eyes had that look of peering into something. But the next moment she moved, and said in her thin, indecisive way:

"Well, I must get those clothes wrapped. They may be through sooner than we think. I wonder where I could find a piece of paper—and string."

"In that cupboard, maybe," suggested Mrs. Hale, after a glance around.

One piece of the crazy sewing remained unripped. Mrs. Peters' back turned, Martha Hale now scrutinized that piece, compared it with the dainty, accurate sewing of the other blocks. The difference was startling. Holding this block made her feel queer, as if the distracted thoughts of the woman who had perhaps turned to it to try and quiet herself were communicating themselves to her.

Mrs. Peter's voice roused her.

"Here's a bird-cage," she said. "Did she have a bird, Mrs. Hale?"

"Why, I don't know whether she did or not." She turned to look at the cage Mrs. Peters was holding up. "I've not been here in so long." She sighed. "There was a man round last year selling canaries cheap—but I don't know as she took one. Maybe she did. She used to sing real pretty herself."

Mrs. Peters looked around the kitchen.

"Seems kind of funny to think of a bird here." She half laughed—an attempt to put up a barrier. "But she must have had one—or why would she have a cage? I wonder what happened to it."

"I suppose maybe the cat got it," suggested Mrs. Hale, resuming her sewing.

"No; she didn't have a cat. She's got that feeling some people have about cats—being afraid of them. When they brought her to our house yesterday, my cat got in the room, and she was real upset and asked me to take it out."

"My sister Bessie was like that," laughed Mrs. Hale.

The sheriff's wife did not reply. The silence made Mrs. Hale turn round. Mrs. Peters was examining the bird-cage.

"Look at this door," she said slowly. "It's broke. One hinge has been pulled apart."

Mrs. Hale came nearer.

"Looks as if some one must have been—rough with it."

Again their eyes met—startled, questioning, apprehensive. For a moment neither spoke nor stirred. Then Mrs. Hale, turning away, said brusquely:

"If they're going to find any evidence, I wish they'd be about it. I don't like this place."

"But I'm awful glad you came with me, Mrs. Hale." Mrs. Peters put the bird-cage on the table and sat down. "It would be lonesome for me—sitting here alone."

"Yes, it would, wouldn't it?" agreed Mrs. Hale, a certain determined naturalness in her voice. She had picked up the sewing, but now it dropped in her lap, and she murmured in a different voice: "But I tell you what I *do* wish, Mrs. Peters. I wish I had come over sometimes when she was here. I wish—I had."

"But of course you were awful busy, Mrs. Hale. Your house—and your children."

"I could've come," retorted Mrs. Hale shortly. "I stayed away because it weren't cheerful—and that's why I ought to have come. I"—she looked around—"I've never liked this place. Maybe because it's down in a hollow and you don't see the road. I don't know what it is, but it's a lonesome place, and always was. I wish I had come over to see Minnie Foster sometimes. I can see now—" She did not put it into words.

"Well, you mustn't reproach yourself," counseled Mrs. Peters. "Somehow, we just don't see how it is with other folks till—something comes up."

"Not having children makes less work," mused Mrs. Hale, after a silence, "but it makes a quiet house—and Wright out to work all day—and no company when he did come in. Did you know John Wright, Mrs. Peters?"

"Not to know him. I've seen him in town. They say he was a good man."

"Yes—good," conceded John Wright's neighbor grimly. "He didn't drink, and kept his word as well as most, I guess, and paid his debts. But he was a hard man, Mrs. Peters. Just to pass the time of day with him—." She stopped, shivered a little. "Like a raw wind that gets to the bone." Her eye fell upon the cage on the table before her, and she added, almost bitterly: "I should think she would've wanted a bird!"

Suddenly she leaned forward, looking intently at the cage. "But what do you s'pose went wrong with it?"

"I don't know," returned Mrs. Peters; "unless it got sick and died."

But after she said it she reached over and swung the broken door. Both women watched it as if somehow held by it.

"You didn't know—her?" Mrs. Hale asked, a gentler note in her voice.

"Not till they brought her yesterday," said the sheriff's wife.

"She—come to think of it, she was kind of like a bird herself. Real sweet and pretty, but kind of timid and—fluttery. How—she—did—change."

That held her for a long time. Finally, as if struck with a happy thought and relieved to get back to everyday things, she exclaimed:

"Tell you what, Mrs. Peters, why don't you take the quilt in with you? It might take up her mind."

"Why, I think that's a real nice idea, Mrs. Hale," agreed the sheriff's wife, as if she too were glad to come into the atmosphere of a simple kindness. "There couldn't possibly be any objection to that, could there? Now, just what will I take? I wonder if her patches are in here—and her things."

They turned to the sewing basket.

"Here's some red," said Mrs. Hale, bringing out a roll of cloth. Underneath that was a box. "Here, maybe her scissors are in here—and her things." She held it up. "What a pretty box! I'll warrant that was something she had a long time ago—when she was a girl."

She held it in her hand a moment; then, with a little sigh, opened it.

Instantly her hand went to her nose.

"Why—!"

"Mrs. Peters drew nearer—then turned away.

"There's something wrapped up in this piece of silk," faltered Mrs. Hale.

"This isn't her scissors," said Mrs. Peters, in a shrinking voice.

Her hand not steady, Mrs. Hale raised the piece of silk. "Oh, Mrs. Peters!" she cried. "It's—"

Mrs. Peters bent closer.

"It's the bird," she whispered.

"But, Mrs. Peters!" cried Mrs. Hale. *"Look* at it! It's neck—look at its neck! It's all—other side *to.*"

She held the box away from her.

The sheriff's wife again bent closer.

"Somebody wrung its neck," said she, in a voice that was slow and deep.

And then again the eyes of the two women met—this time clung together in a look of dawning comprehension, of growing horror. Mrs. Peters looked from the dead bird to the broken door of the cage. Again their eyes met. And just then there was a sound at the outside door.

Mrs. Hale slipped the box under the quilt pieces in the basket, and sank into the chair before it. Mrs. Peters stood holding to the table. The county attorney and the sheriff came in from outside.

"Well, ladies," said the county attorney, as one turning from serious things to little pleasantries, "have you decided whether she was going to quilt it or knot it?"

"We think," began the sheriff's wife in a flurried voice, "that she was going to—knot it."

He was too preoccupied to notice the change that came in her voice on that last.

"Well, that's very interesting, I'm sure," he said tolerantly. He caught sight of the bird-cage. "Has the bird flown?"

"We think the cat got it," said Mrs. Hale in a voice curiously even.

He was walking up and down, as if thinking something out.

"Is there a cat?" he asked absently.

Mrs. Hale shot a look up at the sheriff's wife.

"Well, not *now,*" said Mrs. Peters. "They're superstitious, you know; they leave."

She sank into her chair.

The county attorney did not heed her. "No sign at all of any one having come in from outside," he said to Peters, in the manner of continuing an interrupted conversation. "Their own rope. Now let's go upstairs again and go over it, piece by piece. It would have to have been some one who knew just the—"

The stair door closed behind them and their voices were lost.

The two women sat motionless, not looking at each other, but as if peering into something and at the same time holding back. When they spoke now it was as if they were afraid of what they were saying, but as if they could not help saying it.

"She liked the bird," said Martha Hale, low and slowly. "She was going to bury it in that pretty box."

"When I was a girl," said Mrs. Peters, under her breath, "my kitten—there was a boy took a hatchet, and before my eyes—before I could get there—" She covered her face an instant. "If they hadn't held me back I would have"—she caught herself, looked upstairs where footsteps were heard, and finished weakly—"hurt him."

Then they sat without speaking or moving.

"I wonder how it would seem," Mrs. Hale at last began, as if feeling her way over strange ground—"never to have had any children around?" Her eyes made a slow sweep of the kitchen, as if seeing what that kitchen had meant through all the years. "No, Wright wouldn't like the bird," she said after that—"a thing that sang. She used to sing. He killed that too." Her voice tightened.

Mrs. Peters moved uneasily.

"Of course we don't know who killed the bird."

"I knew John Wright," was Mrs. Hale's answer.

"It was an awful thing was done in this house that night, Mrs. Hale," said the sheriff's wife. "Killing a man while he slept—slipping a thing round his neck that choked the life out of him."

Mrs. Hale's hand went out to the bird-cage.

"His neck. Choked the life out of him."

"We don't *know* who killed him," whispered Mrs. Peters wildly. "We don't *know*."

Mrs. Hale had not moved. "If there had been years and years of—nothing, then a bird to sing to you, it would be awful—still—after the bird was still."

It was as if something within her not herself had spoken, and it found in Mrs. Peters something she did not know as herself.

"I know what stillness is," she said, in a queer, monotonous voice. "When we homesteaded in Dakota, and my first baby died—after he was two years old—and me with no other then—"

Mrs. Hale stirred.

"How soon do you suppose they'll be through looking for the evidence?"

"I know what stillness is," repeated Mrs. Peters, in just that same way.

Then she too pulled back. "The law has got to punish crime, Mrs. Hale," she said in her tight little way.

"I wish you'd seen Minnie Foster," was the answer, "when she wore a white dress with blue ribbons, and stood up there in the choir and sang."

The picture of that girl, the fact that she had lived neighbor to that girl for twenty years, and had let her die for lack of life, was suddenly more than she could bear.

"Oh, I *wish* I'd come over here once in a while!" she cried. "That was a crime! That was a crime! Who's going to punish that?"

"We mustn't take on," said Mrs. Peters, with a frightened look toward the stairs.

"I might 'a' *known* she needed help! I tell you, it's *queer*, Mrs. Peters. We live close together, and we live far apart. We all go through the same things— it's all just a different kind of the same thing! If it weren't—why do you and I *understand*? Why do we *know*—what we know this minute?"

She dashed her hand across her eyes. Then, seeing the jar of fruit on the table, she reached for it and choked out:

"If I was you I wouldn't *tell* her her fruit was gone! Tell her it *ain't*. Tell her it's all right—all of it. Here—take this in to prove it to her! She—she may never know whether it was broke or not."

She turned away.

Mrs. Peters reached out for the bottle of fruit as if she were glad to take it—as if touching a familiar thing, having something to do, could keep her from something else. She got up, looked about for something to wrap the fruit in, took a petticoat from the pile of clothes she had brought from the front room, and nervously started winding that round the bottle.

"My!" she began, in a high, false voice, "it's a good thing the men couldn't hear us! Getting all stirred up over a little thing like a—dead canary." She hurried over that. "As if that could have anything to do with—with—My, wouldn't they *laugh*?"

Footsteps were heard on the stairs.

"Maybe they would," muttered Mrs. Hale—"maybe they wouldn't."

"No, Peters," said the county attorney incisively; "it's all perfectly clear, except the reason for doing it. But you know juries when it comes to women. If there was some definite thing—something to show. Something to make a story about. A thing that would connect up with this clumsy way of doing it."

In a covert way Mrs. Hale looked at Mrs. Peters. Mrs. Peters was looking at her. Quickly they looked away from each other. The outer door opened and Mr. Hale came in.

"I've got the team round now," he said. "Pretty cold out there."

"I'm going to stay here awhile by myself," the county attorney suddenly announced. "You can send Frank out for me, can't you?" he asked the sheriff. "I want to go over everything. I'm not satisfied we can't do better."

Again, for one brief moment, the two women's eyes found one another.

The sheriff came up to the table.

"Did you want to see what Mrs. Peters was going to take in?"

The county attorney picked up the apron. He laughed.

"Oh, I guess they're not very dangerous things the ladies have picked out."

Mrs. Hale's hand was on the sewing basket in which the box was concealed. She felt that she ought to take her hand off the basket. She did not seem able to. He picked up one of the quilt blocks which she had piled on to cover the box. Her eyes felt like fire. She had a feeling that if he took up the basket she would snatch it from him.

But he did not take it up. With another little laugh, he turned away, saying:

"No; Mrs. Peters doesn't need supervising. For that matter, a sheriff's wife is married to the law. Ever think of it that way, Mrs. Peters?"

Mrs. Peters was standing beside the table. Mrs. Hale shot a look up at her; but she could not see her face. Mrs. Peters had turned away. When she spoke, her voice was muffled.

"Not—just that way," she said.

"Married to the law!" chuckled Mrs. Peters' husband. He moved toward the door into the front room, and said to the county attorney:

"I just want you to come in here a minute, George. We ought to take a look at these windows."

"Oh—windows," said the county attorney scoffingly.

"We'll be right out, Mr. Hale," said the sheriff to the farmer, who was still waiting by the door.

Hale went to look after the horses. The sheriff followed the county attorney into the other room. Again—for one final moment—the two women were alone in that kitchen.

Martha Hale sprang up, her hands tight together, looking at that other woman, with whom it rested. At first she could not see her eyes, for the sheriff's wife had not turned back since she turned away at that suggestion of being married to the law. But now Mrs. Hale made her turn back. Her eyes made her turn back. Slowly, unwillingly, Mrs. Peters turned her head until her eyes met the eyes of the other woman. There was a moment when they held each other in a steady, burning look in which there was no evasion nor flinching. Then Martha Hale's eyes pointed the way to the basket in which was hidden the thing that would make certain the conviction of the other woman—that woman who was not there and yet who had been there with them all through that hour.

For a moment Mrs. Peters did not move. And then she did it. With a rush forward, she threw back the quilt pieces, got the box, tried to put it in her handbag. It was too big. Desperately she opened it, started to take the bird out. But there she broke—she could not touch the bird. She stood there helpless, foolish.

There was the sound of a knob turning in the inner door. Martha Hale snatched the box from the sheriff's wife, and got it in the pocket of her big coat just as the sheriff and the county attorney came back into the kitchen.

"Well, Henry," said the county attorney facetiously, "at least we found out that she was not going to quilt it. She was going to—what is it you call it, ladies?"

Mrs. Hale's hand was against the pocket of her coat.

"We call it—knot it, Mr. Henderson."

Writing Assignments for "A Jury of Her Peers"

I. Brief Papers

A. 1. Show that the men in "A Jury of Her Peers" believe themselves to be superior to the women.

   2. Characterize John Wright. What kind of a man was he?

   3. Show how the relationship between Mrs. Hale and Mrs. Peters changes during the story.

   4. A story's first and last sentences are often especially important. Show how either the first or last sentence of "A Jury of Her Peers" relates to the story as a whole.

   5. Explain the significance of the story's title. Who is the jury? Why are the jury members "her peers"? In what sense do they behave like a jury?

B. 1. The story's first paragraph ends with Martha Hale's leaving her kitchen with things "half done." Argue for or against the assertion that the story itself ends with things only "half done."

   2. Argue for or against the assertion that the story demonstrates that women are more intelligent than men.

   3. Argue for or against the assertion that the story makes clear that Minnie Wright will subsequently be convicted for the murder of her husband.

C. 1. How is your response to the story affected by Mrs. Hale's saying that Minnie Foster was "kind of like a bird herself"?

   2. How do you react to John Wright? Do you like or dislike the man? Why? How has Susan Glaspell written her story so as to guide your response to him?

   3. How do you feel about the other men in the story and how do these feelings affect your overall response to the story and your interpretation of it?

   4. In responding to this question (C.3), one student wrote this:

> The other men in "A Jury of Her Peers" are all arrogant, closed-minded, chauvinistic, and just plain stupid. Their continued harassment of the women in the story can be nothing but third grade behavior. After he was told that Mrs. Wright was worried about her fruit while she was sitting in jail, Mrs. Peters' husband laughed and said, "Well, can you beat the woman! Held for murder, and worrying about her preserves!", which shows what arrogance he has because he's a man. A little later on Mr. Hale found only a small crumb of humor when he added, "But would the women know a clue if they did come about it?" This dry, humorless question only strengthens my argument by showing the flat-

out chauvinistic attitude carried by the men in this story. To top all of this off, the women stay in the kitchen, while the men head upstairs, only to find all the necessary clues to convict Mrs. Wright. This irony not only proves that the women are pretty keen on detective work but also how stupid the men are.

Are you convinced by the student's assertion that the men are "stupid"? Why or why not?

II. Longer Papers

A. Explain why Mrs. Hale and Mrs. Peters are finally able to see and understand more than the men. What does the story say about seeing and understanding and knowing?

B. Sheriff Peters is described as a man who acted as if he "knew the difference between criminals and noncriminals" (p. 13). Does the story as a whole indicate that it is easy to separate criminals from noncriminals?

C. Irony usually involves a discrepancy—between what we say and what we mean; between what we think is true and what is actually true; or between what we expect to happen and what in fact happens. Explain how the use of irony in "A Jury of Her Peers" relates to one or more meanings of the story.

D. Explain whether you agree or disagree with the verdict reached by Mrs. Hale and Mrs. Peters.

E. Pretend that you are either the prosecuting attorney or the defense attorney in the murder trial of Minnie Wright. Either way, you have access—as does the other side—to all the evidence uncovered in the story, including both the evidence discovered by the women as well as the evidence discovered by the men. Present your closing argument to the the all-male jury that will decide whether Minnie Wright is guilty or not guilty.

III. Comparative Papers

A. Both "The Murder" and "A Jury of Her Peers" invite us to consider the question of extralegal killing and whether it is ever justified. Argue that one of the two stories provides the more intelligent and more comprehensive exploration of the question.

B. Taken together, what do "The Murder" and "A Jury of Her Peers" have to say about marriage in early twentieth-century America?

C. Taken together, what do "The Murder" and "A Jury of Her Peers" have to say about the situation of American women in the early twentieth century?

WILLIAM CARLOS WILLIAMS
The Use of Force

Before Reading

Try to remember the last time you were physically forced to do something against your will or the last time you used force on another person. Explain, in as much detail as you can, exactly what happened.

They were new patients to me, all I had was the name, Olson. Please come down as soon as you can, my daughter is very sick.

When I arrived I was met by the mother, a big startled looking woman, very clean and apologetic who merely said, Is this the doctor? and let me in. In the back, she added. You must excuse us, doctor, we have her in the kitchen where it is warm. It is very damp here sometimes.

The child was fully dressed and sitting on her father's lap near the kitchen table. He tried to get up, but I motioned for him not to bother, took off my overcoat and started to look things over. I could see that they were all very nervous, eyeing me up and down distrustfully. As often, in such cases, they weren't telling me more than they had to, it was up to me to tell them; that's why they were spending three dollars on me.

The child was fairly eating me up with her cold, steady eyes, and no expression to her face whatever. She did not move and seemed, inwardly, quiet; an unusually attractive little thing, and as strong as a heifer in appearance. But her face was flushed, she was breathing rapidly, and I realized that she had a high fever. She had magnificent blonde hair, in profusion. One of those picture children often reproduced in advertising leaflets and the photogravure* sections of the Sunday papers.

She's had a fever for three days, began the father and we don't know what it comes from. My wife has given her things, you know, like people do, but it don't do no good. And there's been a lot of sickness around. So we tho't you'd better look her over and tell us what is the matter.

As doctors often do I took a trial shot at it as a point of departure. Has she had a sore throat?

Both parents answered me together. No . . . No, she says her throat don't hurt her.

Does your throat hurt you? added the mother to the child. But the little girl's expression didn't change nor did she move her eyes from my face.

Have you looked?

*photogravure: The illustrated "magazine" section of a newspaper.

THE USE OF FORCE   First published in 1938. William Carlos Williams (1883–1963) was born and lived in northern New Jersey, where he was both a full-time doctor (a pediatrician) and a writer, primarily a poet.

I tried to, said the mother, but I couldn't see.

As it happens we had been having a number of cases of diphtheria* in the school to which this child went during that month and we were all, quite apparently, thinking of that, though no one had as yet spoken of the thing.

Well, I said, suppose we take a look at the throat first. I smiled in my best professional manner and asking for the child's first name I said, come on, Mathilda, open your mouth and let's take a look at your throat.

Nothing doing.

Aw, come on, I coaxed, just open your mouth wide and let me take a look. Look, I said opening both hands wide. I haven't anything in my hands. Just open up and let me see.

Such a nice man, put in the mother. Look how kind he is to you. Come on, do what he tells you to. He won't hurt you.

At that I ground my teeth in disgust. If only they wouldn't use the word "hurt" I might be able to get somewhere. But I did not allow myself to be hurried or disturbed but speaking quietly and slowly I approached the child again.

As I moved my chair a little nearer suddenly with one cat-like movement both her hands clawed instinctively for my eyes and she almost reached them too. In fact she knocked my glasses flying and they fell, though unbroken, several feet away from me on the kitchen floor.

Both the mother and father almost turned themselves inside out in embarrassment and apology. You bad girl, said the mother, taking her and shaking her by one arm. Look what you've done. The nice man . . .

For heaven's sake, I broke in. Don't call me a nice man to her. I'm here to look at her throat on the chance that she might have diphtheria and possibly die of it. But that's nothing to her. Look here, I said to the child, we're going to look at your throat. You're old enough to understand what I'm saying. Will you open it now by yourself or shall we have to open it for you?

Not a move. Even her expression hadn't changed. Her breaths however were coming faster and faster. Then the battle began. I had to do it. I had to have a throat culture for her own protection. But first I told the parents that it was entirely up to them. I explained the danger but said that I would not insist on a throat examination so long as they would take the responsibility.

If you don't do what the doctor says you'll have to go to the hospital, the mother admonished her severely.

Oh yeah? I had to smile to myself. After all, I had already fallen in love with the savage brat, the parents were contemptible to me. In the ensuing struggle they grew more and more abject, crushed, exhausted while she surely rose to magnificent heights of insane fury of effort bred of her terror of me.

The father tried his best, and he was a big man but the fact that she was his daughter, his shame at her behavior and his dread of hurting her made him release her just at the critical moment several times when I had almost achieved

*diphtheria: A highly contagious and sometimes fatal disease; one of its symptoms is an inflamed throat.

success, till I wanted to kill him. But his dread also that she might have diphtheria made him tell me to go on, go on though he himself was almost fainting, while the mother moved back and forth behind us raising and lowering her hands in an agony of apprehension.

Put her in front of you on your lap, I ordered, and hold both her wrists.

But as soon as he did the child let out a scream. Don't, you're hurting me. Let go of my hands. Let them go I tell you. Then she shrieked terrifyingly, hysterically. Stop it! Stop it! You're killing me!

Do you think she can stand it, doctor! said the mother.

You get out, said the husband to his wife. Do you want her to die of diphtheria?

Come on now, hold her, I said.

Then I grasped the child's head with my left hand and tried to get the wooden tongue depressor between her teeth. She fought, with clenched teeth, desperately! But now I also had grown furious—at a child. I tried to hold myself down but I couldn't. I know how to expose a throat for inspection. And I did my best. When finally I got the wooden spatula behind the last teeth and just the point of it into the mouth cavity, she opened up for an instant but before I could see anything she came down again and gripping the wooden blade between her molars she reduced it to splinters before I could get it out again.

Aren't you ashamed, the mother yelled at her. Aren't you ashamed to act like that in front of the doctor?

Get me a smooth-handled spoon of some sort, I told the mother. We're going through with this. The child's mouth was already bleeding. Her tongue was cut and she was screaming in wild hysterical shrieks. Perhaps I should have desisted and come back in an hour or more. No doubt it would have been better. But I have seen at least two children lying dead in bed of neglect in such cases, and feeling that I must get a diagnosis now or never I went at it again. But the worst of it was that I too had got beyond reason. I could have torn the child apart in my own fury and enjoyed it. It was a pleasure to attack her. My face was burning with it.

The damned little brat must be protected against her own idiocy, one says to one's self at such times. Others must be protected against her. It is social necessity. And all these things are true. But a blind fury, a feeling of adult shame, bred of a longing for muscular release are the operatives. One goes on to the end.

In a final unreasoning assault I overpowered the child's neck and jaws. I forced the heavy silver spoon back of her teeth and down her throat till she gagged. And there it was—both tonsils covered with membrane. She had fought valiantly to keep me from knowing her secret. She had been hiding that sore throat for three days at least and lying to her parents in order to escape just such an outcome as this.

Now truly she *was* furious. She had been on the defensive before but now she attacked. Tried to get off her father's lap and fly at me while tears of defeat blinded her eyes.

Writing Assignments for "The Use of Force"

I. Brief Papers

    A. 1. Explain the changes that occur, as the examination progresses, within the doctor, or within the child, or within the parents.

        2. Explain an instance within the story of a character's ambivalence—that is, his or her simultaneous conflicting feelings.

        3. Explain why the doctor comes to view the parents as "contemptible."

        4. Many short stories lead to a final revelation. Explain what is revealed by the story's conclusion besides the fact that the child has diphtheria.

    B. Argue for or against any one of these assertions:

        1. The doctor is characterized as perceptive and sensitive.

        2. The doctor is characterized as a competent professional.

        3. It is absolutely necessary for the doctor to use the force he does against the child.

        4. The story would be more appropriately titled "The Diagnosis" or "The Examination."

    C. Suppose any one of the following details in the story had been changed. How do you think the change would affect your reaction to the story and your interpretation of it?

        1. The child turns out to have a cold instead of diphtheria.

        2. The doctor is characterized as stupid, unprofessional, and mean.

        3. The Olsons are a wealthy, upper-class family.

        4. Mathilda is unattractive, and the doctor dislikes her from the start.

II. Longer Papers

    A. 1. Take the story's title as your subject ("The use of force . . ."), complete the sentence, and use it as the governing idea of an interpretive essay.

        2. Explain what the story has to say about human rationality.

        3. Explain how the doctor's language—the way he talks and writes—helps to characterize him and to define his values.

        4. Write an interpretation of the story as a commentary on the nature and consequences of war.

        5. In the story's last sentence, the child has become "blinded" by the tears of defeat. According to the story, what is the connection between seeing and the use of force?

HUGH NISSENSON
Forcing the End

Before Reading

Do you think it will ever be possible to achieve lasting world peace? If so, what will it take? If not, why not? Explain your thoughts in 10 minutes of free writing.

Having refused a chair, Rabbi Jacobi stands in front of my desk, pulling the tuft of white beard that sprouts beneath his underlip.

"All I want," he says, "is your permission to leave the city, go to Yavneh,* open up a school there, and teach."

"Yes, I understand, Rabbi, but unfortunately, under the circumstances, I must refuse you permission."

"What circumstances?"

"For one thing, you'll be safer here."

"Really?" he asks. "Look out the window and tell me what you see."

"Jaffa Road."†

"Look again."

I rise to my feet. The street, the entire city has vanished. We are in a wilderness, where a white haze has effaced the boundary between the earth and the azure sky. Mount Scopus is a barren rock, illuminated on its eastern slope by the morning sun. Huge, yellowish limestone boulders, tinged with red, reflect the glaring light. The ruins of buildings? It's impossible to tell. They seem to have been strewn indiscriminately on the parched ground shimmering from the rising heat. Only an ancient, twisted oak, with shriveled leaves, grows there, just below my window, and as I watch, a jackal which has been sleeping in the shade rises unsteadily, its pink tongue lolling from its jaws, and pisses against the tree trunk: a short spurt of urine, in which, suddenly dropping from the cloudless sky, a starling immerses itself for an instant, fluttering its wings and catching a few drops in its gaping beak.

And twisting the tuft of hair below his mouth, Jacobi says, "You're looking at the Holy City through my eyes."

"The past?"

He shrugs. "The future, too. What's the difference? They're one and the same."

*Yavneh: A village west of Jerusalem and not far from the Mediterranean Sea.
†Jaffa Road: The road leading from Jerusalem, where the story is set, to the Israeli capital city of Tel Aviv.

FORCING THE END   First published under the title "On Jaffa Road" in 1968 and later included in a volume of Nissenson short stories ironically titled *In the Reign of Peace* (1972). Hugh Nissenson, born in New York in 1933, worked on a border kibbutz, a collective farm, in Israel for two years. Since Israel gained its independence in 1948, armed conflicts between Jews and Arabs have been frequent, especially in 1948–1949, 1956, and 1967 (the Six-Day War).

"That's impossible."

"Nevertheless, God help us, it's true," he says, covering his face with his hands. As he has been speaking, a Sammael, one of our new, self-propelled rocket launchers, roars up Jaffa Road in the direction of the Russian compound. Its two rockets, capable of carrying nuclear warheads, are covered by canvas.

Jacobi twists that tuft of beard between the thumb and forefinger of his right hand. Is he a hypnotist, or what? I read over his dossier, open on my desk, once again. He was born in Jerusalem in 1917 and was ordained at the age of nineteen. After that, for twelve years, he was the rabbi of the small town of Arav in the southern Galilee, where he also worked as a clerk in the local post office because he refused any remuneration for teaching Torah.* His wife died last year, and he lost his only son at the age of sixteen to nephritis. The boy was also a precociously brilliant scholar, of whom his father said at his death, "I am consoled by the fact that my son, may his memory be blessed, fulfilled the purpose for which man was created—the study of the Holy Law."

For the last eight years, Jacobi has lived in Jerusalem, teaching a select group of students in a small Talmud Torah† on Adani Street. He has been in constant conflict with the rabbinate over its acquisition of extensive property, and with the government over its policy of retaliatory raids for terrorist attacks.

My secretary, Dora, whose husband was killed two years ago by an Arab grenade while serving on reserve duty in Gaza, comes into my office and whispers excitedly in my ear, "Sunday, at dawn."

"How do you know?"

"Yoram's sister heard it from her husband."

"Who's her husband?"

"The pilot."

"What's the matter with you? You know how tight security is. It's just another rumor."

She adds without conviction, "Yoram's sister swears it's the truth," and sighs. She has aged extraordinarily in the last two years; her lips are as wrinkled as an old woman's.

"No, there's still time," Jacobi says. "Not much, but enough. At least enough for me to go to Yavneh, open my school, and plant a few lemon trees. They're very delicate, you know, but I love the odor of the blossoms, don't you? Sweet but spicy. An unusual combination." He goes to the door and says, "Tell me the truth. Do you honestly believe that this time we'll achieve a lasting peace?"

"Absolutely."

"By force of arms?"

"Of course."

"Really? How I admire your faith. Let me tell you something, my friend. A secret. When I'm in Yavneh, and if one day I'm planting a sapling and I hear

---

*Torah: The first five books of the Bible, the Pentateuch, but also the whole body of Jewish religious literature, including the Scriptures and the Talmud.
†Talmud Torah: Hebrew school.

that the Messiah himself has arrived, do you know what I'll do? Finish planting the sapling, and then go to welcome him." He opens the door. "Did you know that lemons turn yellow only after they've been picked? It's a fact. They remain green and bitter on the tree. You have to store them for months before they turn yellow and ripen."

"Not any more," Dora says. "A specially heated storage plant forces them to ripen in four or five days."

"Is that so? How hot?"

"I'm not sure."

"As hot as this?" he asks, and in the sweaty palm of his right hand he holds up a yellow lemon. "From the new storage plant in Yavneh, by the way, and fully ripe, as you can see; juicy too, with a wonderful smell . . ."

He passes it under Dora's nose.

"Right?" And closing his eyes and inhaling deeply, he recites the traditional benediction, " 'Blessed art Thou—the Eternal, our God, King of the Universe—who hath given fragrance unto fruit.' " Then he smiles, and says, "This one, for your information, was picked from a tree four and a half days ago and then stored at exactly 22° C." He twirls it in the air. "Why, one could almost imagine it's the world: cut off from its source, mercifully ignorant of its state; and just think: some minute malfunction of some machine in that storage plant, for example, or more likely some human error, and the temperature rises only three or four degrees, and look at it now! That marvelous color splotched brown. See? This whole side has changed its color; faintly, but changed, nevertheless, and it's gotten soft—feel it—rotten . . ."

"Where is it?" Dora cries out. "I know. Up your sleeve." But, shaking his head, Jacobi replied, "No, it was only a trick. Well, not exactly that, but . . ."

"What?" she asks, in a peculiar, strident voice that makes Jacobi stare at her. She looks him straight in the eye.

"It's true about you and your brother, isn't it?" he asks, but she says nothing. She and her brother Menachem are reputed to be important members of the Knives, a new, illegal organization allegedly responsible for the murders of a prominent writer who advocated trying to make peace with the Arabs by restoring to them all their territory which we now occupy, and an eighteen-year-old pacifist who, last fall, refused to register for the draft.

Leaving the door open, she goes into the outer office and, with an unlit cigarette dangling from her wrinkled lips, sits down at her desk and pecks away with one finger at some official form, in triplicate, stuffed into her old Remington typewriter. Jacobi follows her. Six of his students from the Talmud Torah on Adani Street crowd around him, speaking Yiddish in hushed, agitated voices. One boy, not more than fifteen, fixes his dark eyes on me and grimaces. He's deformed in a way I've never seen. His right arm is normal, but the left, hanging loose, reaches his knee.

Two days later, at about four, while I'm having my afternoon glass of tea and a butter cookie, I idly glance out of the window again. Four soldiers, in battle dress and armed with submachine guns, are patrolling the street. Each one has inserted a thirty-round magazine into his weapon, behind the trigger guard, and has taped another magazine at right angles to the first, to facilitate rapid reloading. Their footfalls, I notice, are muffled by the sandbags which last night were heaped up, waist high, against the walls of the buildings.

Then, at a command from their sergeant, they break rank, to allow a funeral procession to pass down the center of the street. Four bearded men, dressed in black kaftans, are carrying an unpainted pine coffin on their shoulders. Behind them, three women, with fringed black shawls over their heads, are howling at the top of their lungs. In spite of the sandbags, the din is terrific. About to shut the window, I notice that the boy with the long arm is also following the coffin. With his good hand, he rhythmically pounds his chest, and his narrow face is twisted by the same grimace he gave me—a grimace that bares his yellow upper teeth to the gums.

"Who is it?" I shout down. "Who's died?" But the howling women, who are now scratching their cheeks with their fingernails, drown me out.

"Answer me," I yell louder, and the boy with the long arm raises his face.

"Our master," he yells back. "The Light of the World."

"Rabbi Jacobi?"

He nods, and Dora, who has been standing behind me, rushes down to the street, where I can see her arguing with one of the pallbearers who has trouble balancing the coffin and rummaging in his pocket for some papers at the same time. When she returns, she says, "They've gotten permission to bury him in Arav."

"Arav?"

"Next to his kid."

"What about transportation?"

"Two horse-drawn carts, if you can believe it."

"Who authorized them to leave the city?"

"What's-his-name. Oh, you know who I mean. That Litvak from the Ministry of Interment who dyes his hair. Kovner."

"Are you sure?"

"Yes," she says. "I'm sure." And she glances at her briefcase, on the filing cabinet, in which she keeps the yellowing document, signed by Kovner, which authorized the burial of her husband, with full military honors, on Mount Herzl.

The next morning, Shmelke Kalb, who works in an office across the street, throws open my door, waving a newspaper in my face. As usual, he's wearing a steel helmet; not because he's the air-raid warden in charge of the block, but because he suffers from skin cancer, a discolored blotch on his forehead, and puts on the helmet whenever he has to go outside, to protect himself from the sun.

"Have you read about Jacobi?" he asks.

"No, but I'm sorry, in a way."

"What're you talking about? Are you crazy? He's deserted the city. And five or six more of his students have already joined him in Yavneh."

"But that's impossible. The man's dead. I saw his funeral procession."

"A sealed coffin?"

"Yes."

"It was a trick to smuggle him out of the city."

"What're you saying?"

"Some of his students nailed him into a coffin and smuggled him out of the city two days ago. It's all here, in this morning's paper, along with some kind of manifesto for some new kind of school he wants to start."

"Let me see that," I tell him, and then read aloud:

We shall be as the disciples of Aaron, loving peace, pursuing peace, and teaching Torah which alone sustains the Jews who, if they faithfully follow its Holy Principles, will be redeemed by them, and then redeem all mankind, in God's good time . . .

Dora has come to the door; Kalb lowers his voice: "They say Kovner has disappeared without a trace."

At one—during critical times like these, we grab a sandwich for lunch at the office—I turn on the radio for the latest news.

". . . which will demand from each of us the greatest sacrifice . . . credence, which, although . . . New York . . ."

I can catch only a word now and then because of the noise: columns of Sammaels, rattling the windowpanes, have been roaring up the street for the last two hours. I twist the knob, and unexpectedly, in a perfectly audible voice, the announcer says that Rabbi Jacobi's body, spattered with dried blood, was discovered in Yavneh early this morning in front of a vegetarian restaurant on the Rishon-Lezion road. A preliminary coroner's report has established that the distinguished religious leader was stabbed once through the heart with a penknife, and died instantly, between 2 and 3 a.m. The district superintendent of police reports that no fingerprints were found on the weapon, but he has been quoted that he is confident that the criminal or criminals will soon be apprehended because of a peculiar aspect of the case. The distinguished rabbi's jaws were pried open after his death, and a yellow lemon inserted in his mouth . . .

Another Sammael, which makes it impossible for me to hear Dora shouting from the outer office, where she's been pecking away at the Remington.

"What?" I ask.

"Green," she says. "The idiot. Not yellow, green."

Writing Assignments for "Forcing the End"

I. Brief Papers

    A. 1. Write a clear, concise summary of "Forcing the End": what happens and why?

2. Explain what you think has happened to Kovner—he is reported to have "disappeared without a trace"—and why you think so.
3. Explain how Rabbi Jacobi and Dora react in different ways to the death of someone they love.
4. As fully as you can in a single paragraph, characterize the narrator of "Forcing the End." What are his traits and values?
5. Summarize the major beliefs and values of Rabbi Jacobi.

B. Choose one assertion below and argue for or against it:
1. "Forcing the End" is a more effective and appropriate title than the story's original title, "On Jaffa Road."
2. The story is at least in part an attack on governmental bureaucracy.
3. The story implicitly endorses the philosophy of pacifism.
4. The tricks and deceptions of Rabbi Jacobi prove that he is a fraud, that he really doesn't believe what he says he believes.

C. 1. How do you feel toward Dora at the end of the story?
2. How do you feel about humanity as the story ends? You may want to differentiate between the way you felt after your first reading and the way you feel now.
3. How do you think the inclusion of the last paragraphs affects your response to the story? Suppose it had ended, instead, with "a yellow lemon inserted in his mouth"?

II. Longer Papers

A. The story's narrator says that he is absolutely certain that lasting peace will be achieved, but Rabbi Jacobi is skeptical. At the end of the story, whose position is more plausible?
B. How hopeful is the story that machines and technology will help humanity to achieve a happier and more fulfilling existence?
C. Compare and contrast Dora and Rabbi Jacobi in order to argue that one is more sympathetically portrayed than the other.
D. The *setting* of a story includes not only its time and place but also the general situation and circumstances—the total environment within which the characters move and events take place. Explain how the setting of "Forcing the End" contributes to the story's meaning and experience.

III. Comparative Papers

A. Argue that either "The Use of Force" or "Forcing the End" is more clearly and intensely a story endorsing pacifism.
B. What do "The Use of Force" and "Forcing the End" together say about the consequences of using force and violence?
C. What do "The Use of Force" and "Forcing the End" together say about human rationality?

ERNEST HEMINGWAY
Indian Camp

Before Reading

Do you think that pain is an inevitable and unavoidable part of human experience? Why or why not? Free write on this question for about 10 minutes.

At the lake shore there was another rowboat drawn up. The two Indians stood waiting.

Nick and his father got in the stern of the boat and the Indians shoved it off and one of them got in to row. Uncle George sat in the stern of the camp rowboat. The young Indian shoved the camp boat off and got in to row Uncle George.

The two boats started off in the dark. Nick heard the oarlocks of the other boat quite a way ahead of them in the mist. The Indians rowed with quick choppy strokes. Nick lay back with his father's arm around him. It was cold on the water. The Indian who was rowing them was working very hard, but the other boat moved further ahead in the mist all the time.

"Where are we going, Dad?" Nick asked.

"Over to the Indian camp. There is an Indian lady very sick."

"Oh," said Nick.

Across the bay they found the other boat beached. Uncle George was smoking a cigar in the dark. The young Indian pulled the boat way up on the beach. Uncle George gave both the Indians cigars.

They walked up from the beach through a meadow that was soaking wet with dew, following the young Indian who carried a lantern. Then they went into the woods and followed a trail that led to the logging road that ran back into the hills. It was much lighter on the logging road as the timber was cut away on both sides. The young Indian stopped and blew out his lantern and they all walked on along the road.

They came around a bend and a dog came out barking. Ahead were the lights of the shanties where the Indian bark-peelers lived. More dogs rushed out at them. The two Indians sent them back to the shanties. In the shanty nearest the road there was a light in the window. An old woman stood in the doorway holding a lamp.

Inside on a wooden bunk lay a young Indian woman. She had been trying to have her baby for two days. All the old women in the camp had been helping her. The men had moved off up the road to sit in the dark and smoke out of range of the noise she made. She screamed just as Nick and the two Indians followed his father and Uncle George into the shanty. She lay in the lower bunk,

INDIAN CAMP   First published in 1924. Ernest Hemingway (1899–1961) wrote a series of short stories about Nick Adams; many of them, like "Indian Camp," are set in northern Michigan.

very big under a quilt. Her head was turned to one side. In the upper bunk was her husband. He had cut his foot very badly with an ax three days before. He was smoking a pipe. The room smelled very bad.

Nick's father ordered some water to be put on the stove, and while it was heating he spoke to Nick.

"This lady is going to have a baby, Nick," he said.

"I know," said Nick.

"You don't know," said his father. "Listen to me. What she is going through is called being in labor. The baby wants to be born and she wants it to be born. All her muscles are trying to get the baby born. That is what is happening when she screams."

"I see," Nick said.

Just then the woman cried out.

"Oh, Daddy, can't you give her something to make her stop screaming?" asked Nick.

"No. I haven't any anæsthetic," his father said. "But her screams are not important. I don't hear them because they are not important."

The husband in the upper bunk rolled over against the wall.

The woman in the kitchen motioned to the doctor that the water was hot. Nick's father went into the kitchen and poured about half of the water out of the big kettle into a basin. Into the water left in the kettle he put several things he unwrapped from a handkerchief.

"Those must boil," he said, and began to scrub his hands in the basin of hot water with a cake of soap he had brought from the camp. Nick watched his father's hands scrubbing each other with the soap. While his father washed his hands very carefully and thoroughly, he talked.

"You see, Nick, babies are supposed to be born head first but sometimes they're not. When they're not they make a lot of trouble for everybody. Maybe I'll have to operate on this lady. We'll know in a little while."

When he was satisfied with his hands he went in and went to work.

"Pull back that quilt, will you, George?" he said. "I'd rather not touch it."

Later when he started to operate Uncle George and three Indian men held the woman still. She bit Uncle George on the arm and Uncle George said, "Damn squaw bitch!" and the young Indian who had rowed Uncle George over laughed at him. Nick held the basin for his father. It all took a long time.

His father picked the baby up and slapped it to make it breathe and handed it to the old woman.

"See, it's a boy, Nick," he said. "How do you like being an interne?"

Nick said, "All right." He was looking away so as not to see what his father was doing.

"There. That gets it," said his father and put something into the basin. Nick didn't look at it.

"Now," his father said, "there's some stitches to put in. You can watch this or not, Nick, just as you like. I'm going to sew up the incision I made."

Nick did not watch. His curiosity had been gone for a long time.

His father finished and stood up. Uncle George and the three Indian men stood up. Nick put the basin out in the kitchen.

Uncle George looked at his arm. The young Indian smiled reminiscently.

"I'll put some peroxide on that, George," the doctor said.

He bent over the Indian woman. She was quiet now and her eyes were closed. She looked very pale. She did not know what had become of the baby or anything.

"I'll be back in the morning," the doctor said, standing up. "The nurse should be here from St. Ignace* by noon and she'll bring everything we need."

He was feeling exalted and talkative as football players are in the dressing room after a game.

"That's one for the medical journal, George," he said. "Doing a Caesarian with a jack-knife and sewing it up with nine-foot, tapered gut leaders."

Uncle George was standing against the wall, looking at his arm.

"Oh, you're a great man, all right," he said.

"Ought to have a look at the proud father. They're usually the worst sufferers in these little affairs," the doctor said. "I must say he took it all pretty quietly."

He pulled back the blanket from the Indian's head. His hand came away wet. He mounted on the edge of the lower bunk with the lamp in one hand and looked in. The Indian lay with his face toward the wall. His throat had been cut from ear to ear. The blood had flowed down into a pool where his body sagged the bunk. His head rested on his left arm. The open razor lay, edge up, in the blankets.

"Take Nick out of the shanty, George," the doctor said.

There was no need of that. Nick, standing in the door of the kitchen, had a good view of the upper bunk when his father, the lamp in one hand, tipped the Indian's head back.

It was just beginning to be daylight when they walked along the logging road back toward the lake.

"I'm terribly sorry I brought you along, Nickie," said his father, all his post-operative exhilaration gone. "It was an awful mess to put you through."

"Do ladies always have such a hard time having babies?" Nick asked.

"No, that was very, very exceptional."

"Why did he kill himself, Daddy?"

"I don't know, Nick. He couldn't stand things, I guess."

"Do many men kill themselves, Daddy?"

"Not very many, Nick."

"Do many women?"

"Hardly ever."

"Don't they ever?"

"Oh, yes. They do sometimes."

"Daddy?"

"Yes."

*St. Ignace: A village on the southern tip of Michigan's upper peninsula.

"Where did Uncle George go?"

"He'll turn up all right."

"Is dying hard, Daddy?"

"No, I think it's pretty easy, Nick. It all depends."

They were seated in the boat, Nick in the stern, his father rowing. The sun was coming up over the hills. A bass jumped, making a circle in the water. Nick trailed his hand in the water. It felt warm in the sharp chill of the morning.

In the early morning on the lake sitting in the stern of the boat with his father rowing, he felt quite sure that he would never die.

Writing Assignments for "Indian Camp"

I. Brief Papers
   A. 1. Explain why Nick's father takes Nick to the Indian camp.
      2. Explain what Nick's father means when he says that the woman's "screams are not important. I don't hear them because they are not important" (p. 42).
      3. Explain how the opening three paragraphs of the story (the boat ride to the camp) compare to the closing two paragraphs (the boat ride home)?
      4. Explain why Nick at times calls his father "Dad" but at other times calls him "Daddy" and why Nick is usually called "Nick" but on one occasion is called "Nickie."

   B. Choose one assertion below and either develop it or refute it:
      1. Nick's father is depicted as a callous, cruel person and an insensitive, unloving father.
      2. The story has a happy ending.
      3. Uncle George has no real function in "Indian Camp" and so Hemingway should never have included him in the story.

   C. 1. How did you respond to the last sentence of the story the first time you read it: "In the early morning on the lake sitting in the stern of the boat with his father rowing, he felt quite sure he would never die"? How do you respond to it now?
      2. Do you find "Indian Camp" unnecessarily graphic in its depiction of violence and pain? Why or why not?

II. Longer Papers
   A. Has Nick been changed in any way by his experience at the Indian Camp? Is the Nick who leaves camp in the morning the same person who arrived there the previous night?
   B. What does "Indian Camp" have to say about pain and how to deal with pain?
   C. Nick's father suggests that the Indian husband killed himself because he "couldn't stand things." According to the story, what are the "things" one must learn to stand in order to go on living?

D. Hemingway wrote over 25 stories about Nick. One reader thinks that these stories characteristically move from loss or trauma to recovery and fortification. Explain whether "Indian Camp" follows this movement.

E. You are a college literature instructor who has assigned "Indian Camp" in your freshman course. One day the college president sends you a letter she has received together with the request that you answer it and forward her a copy of your answer. Here is the letter:

> Dear President Edwards:
>
> Are you aware of what's going on in the literature courses at your college? Students are being forced to read trash like Hemingway's "Indian Camp." It is a story filled with violence, from biting and ax injuries to throat slitting. With all the violence on TV and the movies, why do we need more of it in college literature courses? Especially from someone like Hemingway who blew his own brains out? Why aren't students reading stories that are more wholesome, more realistic, more useful, and more American? As a loyal contributor to the Alumni Fund, I would appreciate hearing from you.
>
> Sincerely yours,
> Kenneth L. Albright
> *Class of '59*

III. Irony of Situation in "Indian Camp"

Combine the following sentences (inserting transitions and deleting material where appropriate) into a short essay that defines *irony of situation* and illustrates its use in "Indian Camp."

1. Irony of situation occurs when what happens turns out to be quite different from what is expected.
2. What happens is sometimes the opposite of what is expected.

3. Here is an example of irony of situation.
4. The luxury liner *Titanic* was thought to have been unsinkable.
5. The *Titanic* struck an iceberg and sank on its maiden voyage.

6. Here is another example of irony of situation.
7. Many Americans, including government officials and military leaders, believed that the Vietnam conflict could be ended quickly.
8. Vietnam turned out to be the longest war in American history.

9. In "Indian Camp" there are several instances of situational irony.
10. That is, there are several instances of discrepancy between expectation and fulfillment.

11. Here is one instance of situational irony in "Indian Camp."
12. It is the Indian wife, not the husband, who suffers excruciating physical pain.
13. Yet it is the husband, not the wife, who commits suicide.

14. Here is another instance of situational irony in "Indian Camp."
15. Nick's father brings Nick to the Indian camp so that Nick can watch the birth of a child.
16. But Nick is far more interested in the death of a man.

17. Here is a final instance of situational irony in "Indian Camp."
18. Nick watches a man die.
19. But afterwards Nick feels quite sure that he himself will live forever.

20. Irony of situation involves a conflict between what is anticipated and what actually occurs.
21. Since this is so, perhaps one of the functions of irony of situation in "Indian Camp" is to suggest the mystery and unpredictability of life.

KATHERINE ANNE PORTER

The Downward Path to Wisdom

Before Reading

Explain in 100 to 150 words what the phrase "The Downward Path to Wisdom" means to you and what, judging from the title, you think the story will be about.

In the square bedroom with the big window Mama and Papa were lolling back on their pillows handing each other things from the wide black tray on the small table with crossed legs. They were smiling and they smiled even more when the little boy, with the feeling of sleep still in his skin and hair, came in and walked up to the bed. Leaning against it, his bare toes wriggling in the white fur rug, he went on eating peanuts, which he took from his pajama pocket. He was four years old.

"Here's my baby," said Mama. "Lift him up, will you?"

He went limp as a rag for Papa to take him under the arms and swing him up over a broad tough chest. He sank between his parents like a bear cub in a warm litter, and lay there comfortably. He took another peanut between his teeth, cracked the shell, picked out the nut whole, and ate it.

"Running around without his slippers again," said Mama. "His feet are like icicles."

"He crunches like a horse," said Papa. "Eating peanuts before breakfast will ruin his stomach. Where did he get them?"

"You brought them yesterday," said Mama, with exact memory, "in a

THE DOWNWARD PATH TO WISDOM   First published in 1939. Katherine Anne Porter (1890–1980), American author of short stories, essays, and the novel *Ship of Fools,* often wrote of childhood experiences.

grisly little cellophane sack. I have asked you dozens of times not to bring him things to eat. Put him out, will you? He's spilling shells all over me."

Almost at once the little boy found himself on the floor again. He moved around to Mama's side of the bed and leaned confidingly near her and began another peanut. As he chewed he gazed solemnly in her eyes.

"Bright-looking specimen, isn't he?" asked Papa, stretching his long legs and reaching for his bathrobe. "I suppose you'll say it's my fault he's dumb as an ox."

"He's my little baby, my only baby," said Mama richly, hugging him, "and he's a dear lamb." His neck and shoulders were quite boneless in her firm embrace. He stopped chewing long enough to receive a kiss on his crumby chin. "He's sweet as clover," said Mama. The baby went on chewing.

"Look at him staring like an owl," said Papa.

Mama said, "He's an angel and I'll never get used to having him."

"We'd be better off if we never *had* had him," said Papa. He was walking about the room and his back was turned when he said that. There was silence for a moment. The little boy stopped eating, and stared deeply at his Mama. She was looking at the back of Papa's head, and her eyes were almost black. "You're going to say that just once too often," she told him in a low voice. "I hate you when you say that."

Papa said, "You spoil him to death. You never correct him for anything. And you don't take care of him. You let him run around eating peanuts before breakfast."

"You gave him the peanuts, remember that," said Mama. She sat up and hugged her only baby once more. He nuzzled softly in the pit of her arm. "Run along, my darling," she told him, in her gentlest voice, smiling at him straight in the eyes. "Run along," she said, her arms falling away from him. "Get your breakfast."

The little boy had to pass his father on the way to the door. He shrank into himself when he saw the big hand raised above him. "Yes, get out of here and stay out," said Papa, giving him a little shove toward the door. It was not a hard shove, but it hurt the little boy. He slunk out, and trotted down the hall trying not to look back. He was afraid something was coming after him, he could not imagine what. Something hurt him all over, he did not know why.

He did not want his breakfast, he would not have it. He sat and stirred it round in the yellow bowl, letting it stream off the spoon and spill on the table, on his front, on the chair. He liked seeing it spill. It was hateful stuff, but it looked funny running in white rivulets down his pajamas.

"Now look what you're doing, dirty boy," said Marjory. "You dirty little old boy."

The little boy opened his mouth to speak for the first time. "You're dirty yourself," he told her.

"That's right," said Marjory, leaning over him and speaking so her voice would not carry. "That's right, just like your Papa. Mean," she whispered, "mean."

The little boy took up his yellow bowl full of cream and oatmeal and sugar with both hands and brought it down with a crash on the table. It burst and some of the wreck lay in chunks and some of it ran all over everything. He felt better.

"You see?" said Marjory, dragging him out of the chair and scrubbing him with a napkin. She scrubbed him as roughly as she dared until he cried out. "That's just what I said. That's exactly it." Through his tears he saw her face terribly near, red and frowning under a stiff white band, looking like the face of somebody who came at night and stood over him and scolded him when he could not move or get away. "Just like your Papa, *mean.*"

The little boy went out into the garden and sat on a green bench dangling his legs. He was clean. His hair was wet and his blue woolly pull-over made his nose itch. His face felt stiff from the soap. He saw Marjory going past a window with the black tray. The curtains were still closed at the window he knew opened into Mama's room. Papa's room. Mommanpoppasroom, the word was pleasant, it made a mumbling snapping noise between his lips; it ran in his mind while his eyes wandered about looking for something to do, something to play with.

Mommanpoppas' voices kept attracting his attention. Mama was being cross with Papa again. He could tell by the sound. That was what Marjory always said when their voices rose and fell and shot up to a point and crashed and rolled like the two tomcats who fought at night. Papa was being cross, too, much crosser than Mama this time. He grew cold and disturbed and sat very still, wanting to go to the bathroom, but it was just next to Mommanpoppasroom, he didn't dare think of it. As the voices grew louder he could hardly hear them any more, he wanted so badly to go to the bathroom. The kitchen door opened suddenly and Marjory ran out making the motion with her hand that meant he was to come to her. He didn't move. She came to him, her face still red and frowning, but she was not angry; she was scared just as he was. She said, "Come on, Honey, we've got to go to your gran'ma's again." She took his hand and pulled him. "Come on quick, your gran'ma is waiting for you." He slid off the bench. His mother's voice rose in a terrible scream, screaming something he could not understand, but she was furious, he had seen her clenching her fists and stamping in one spot, screaming with her eyes shut; he knew how she looked. She was screaming in a tantrum, just as he remembered having heard himself. He stood still, doubled over, and all his body seemed to dissolve, sickly, from the pit of his stomach.

"Oh my God," said Marjory. "Oh my God. Now look at you. Oh my God. I can't stop to clean you up."

He did not know how he got to his Grandma's house, but he was there at last, wet and soiled, being handled with disgust in the big bathtub. His grandma was there in long black skirts saying, "Maybe he's sick, maybe we should send for the doctor."

"I don't think so, m'am," said Marjory. "He hasn't et anything; he's just scared."

The little boy couldn't raise his eyes, he was so heavy with shame. "Take this note to his mother," said Grandma.

She sat in a wide chair and ran her hands over his head, combing his hair with her fingers; she lifted his chin and kissed him. "Poor little fellow," she said.

"Never you mind. You always have a good time at your grandma's, don't you? You're going to have a nice little visit, just like the last time."

The little boy leaned against the stiff, dry-smelling clothes, and felt horribly grieved about something. He began to whimper and said, "I'm hungry. I want something to eat." This reminded him. He began to bellow at the top of his voice; he threw himself upon the carpet and rubbed his nose in a dusty woolly bouquet of roses. "I want my peanuts," he howled. "Somebody took my peanuts."

His grandma knelt beside him, and gathered him up so tightly he could hardly move. She called in a calm voice above his howls to Old Janet in the doorway, "Bring me some bread and butter with strawberry jam."

"I want peanuts," yelled the little boy, desperately.

"No, you don't, darling," said his grandma. "You don't want horrid old peanuts to make you sick. You're going to have some of Grandma's nice fresh bread with good strawberries on it. That's what you're going to have." He sat afterward very quietly and ate and ate. His grandma sat near him and Old Janet stood by, near a tray with a loaf and a glass bowl of jam upon the table at the window. Outside there was a trellis with tube-shaped red flowers clinging all over it, and brown bees singing.

"I hardly know what to do," said Grandma, "it's very . . ."

"Yes, m'am," said Old Janet, "it certainly is . . ."

Grandma said, "I can't possibly see the end of it. It's a terrible . . ."

"It certainly is bad," said Old Janet, "all this upset all the time and him such a baby."

Their voices ran on soothingly. The little boy ate and forgot to listen. He did not know these women, except by name. He could not understand what they were talking about, their hands and their clothes and their voices were dry and far away; they examined him with crinkled eyes without any expression that he could see. He sat there waiting for whatever they would do next with him. He hoped they would let him go out and play in the yard. The room was full of flowers and dark red curtains and big soft chairs, and the windows were open, but it was still dark in there, somehow; dark, and a place he did not know, or trust.

"Now drink your milk," said Old Janet, holding out a silver cup.

"I don't want any milk," he said, turning his head away.

"Very well, Janet, he doesn't have to drink it," said Grandma quickly. "Now run out in the garden and play, darling. Janet, get his hoop."

A big strange man came home in the evenings, who treated the little boy very confusingly. "Say 'please,' and 'thank you,' young man," he would roar, terrifyingly, when he gave any smallest object to the little boy. "Well, fellow, are you ready for a fight?" he would say, again, doubling up huge hairy fists and making passes at him. "Come on now, you must learn to box." After the first few times this was fun.

"Don't teach him to be rough," said Grandma. "Time enough for all that."

"Now, Mother, we don't want him to be a sissy," said the big man. "He's got to toughen up early. Come on now, fellow, put up your mitts." The little boy liked this new word for hands. He learned to throw himself upon the strange big man, whose name was Uncle David, and hit him on the chest as hard as he could; the big man would laugh and hit him back with his huge loose fists. Sometimes, but not often, Uncle David came home in the middle of the day. The little boy missed him on the other days, and would hang on the gate looking down the street for him. One evening he brought a large square package under his arm.

"Come over here, fellow, and see what I've got," he said, pulling off quantities of green paper and string from the box, which was full of flat, folded colors. He put something in the little boy's hand. It was limp and silky and bright green with a tube on the end. "Thank you," said the little boy, nicely, but not knowing what to do with it.

"Balloons," said Uncle David in triumph. "Now just put your mouth here and blow hard." The little boy blew hard and the green thing began to grow round and thin and silvery.

"Good for your chest," said Uncle David. "Blow some more." The little boy went on blowing and the balloon swelled steadily.

"Stop," said Uncle David, "that's enough." He twisted the tube to keep the air in. "That's the way," he said. "Now I'll blow one, and you blow one, and let's see who can blow up a big balloon the fastest."

They blew and blew, especially Uncle David. He puffed and panted and blew with all his might, but the little boy won. His balloon was perfectly round before Uncle David could even get started. The little boy was so proud he began to dance and shout, "I beat, I beat," and blew in his balloon again. It burst in his face and frightened him so he felt sick. "Ha ha, ho ho ho," whooped Uncle David. "That's the boy. I bet I can't do that. Now let's see." He blew until the beautiful bubble grew and wavered and burst into thin air, and there was only a small colored rag in his hand. This was a fine game. They went on with it until Grandma came in and said, "Time for supper, now. No, you can't blow balloons at the table. Tomorrow, maybe." And it was all over.

The next day, instead of being given balloons, he was hustled out of bed early, bathed in warm soapy water, and given a big breakfast of soft-boiled eggs with toast and jam and milk. His grandma came in to kiss him good morning. "And I hope you'll be a good boy and obey your teacher," she told him.

"What's teacher?" asked the little boy.

"Teacher is at school," said Grandma. "She'll tell you all sorts of things and you must do as she says."

Mama and Papa had talked a great deal about School, and how they must send him there. They had told him it was a fine place with all kinds of toys and other children to play with. He felt he knew about School. "I didn't know it was time, Grandma," he said. "Is it today?"

"It's this very minute," said Grandma. "I told you a week ago."

Old Janet came in with her bonnet on. It was a prickly-looking bundle held with a black rubber band under her back hair. "Come on," she said. "This is my busy day." She wore a dead cat slung around her neck, its sharp ears bent over under her baggy chin.

The little boy was excited and wanted to run ahead. "Hold to my hand like I told you," said Old Janet. "Don't go running off like that and get yourself killed."

"I'm going to get killed, I'm going to get killed," sang the little boy, making a tune of his own.

"Don't say that, you give me the creeps," said Old Janet. "Hold to my hand, now." She bent over and looked at him, not at his face but at something on his clothes. His eyes followed hers.

"I declare," said Old Janet, "I did forget. I was going to sew it up. I might have known. I *told* your grandma it would be that way from now on."

"What?" asked the little boy.

"Just look at yourself," said Old Janet, crossly. He looked at himself. There was a little end of him showing through the slit in his short blue flannel trousers. The trousers came halfway to his knees above, and his socks came halfway to his knees below, and all winter long his knees were cold. He remembered now how cold his knees were in cold weather. And how sometimes he would have to put the part of him that came through the slit back again, because he was cold there, too. He saw at once what was wrong, and tried to arrange himself, but his mittens got in the way. Janet said, "Stop that, you bad boy," and with a firm thumb she set him in order, at the same time reaching under his belt to pull down and fold his knit undershirt over his front.

"There now," she said, "try not to disgrace yourself today." He felt guilty and red all over, because he had something that showed when he was dressed that was not supposed to show then. The different women who bathed him always wrapped him quickly in towels and hurried him into his clothes, because they saw something about him he could not see for himself. They hurried him so he never had a chance to see whatever it was they saw, and though he looked at himself when his clothes were off, he could not find out what was wrong with him. Outside, in his clothes, he knew he looked like everybody else, but inside his clothes there was something bad the matter with him. It worried him and confused him and he wondered about it. The only people who never seemed to notice there was something wrong with him were Mommanpoppa. They never called him a bad boy, and all summer long they had taken all his clothes off and let him run in the sand beside a big ocean.

"Look at him, isn't he a love?" Mama would say and Papa would look, and say, "He's got a back like a prize fighter." Uncle David was a prize fighter when he doubled up his mitts and said, "Come on, fellow."

Old Janet held him firmly and took long steps under her big rustling skirts. He did not like Old Janet's smell. It made him a little quivery in the stomach; it was just like wet chicken feathers.

School was easy. Teacher was a square-shaped woman with square short hair and short skirts. She got in the way sometimes, but not often. The people around him were his size; he didn't have always to be stretching his neck up to faces bent over him, and he could sit on the chairs without having to climb. All the children had names, like Frances and Evelyn and Agatha and Edward and Martin, and his own name was Stephen. He was not Mama's "Baby," nor Papa's "Old Man"; he was not Uncle David's "Fellow" or Grandma's "Darling," or even Old Janet's "Bad Boy." He was Stephen. He was learning to read, and to sing a tune to some strange-looking letters or marks written in chalk on a blackboard. You talked one kind of lettering, and you sang another. All the children talked and sang in turn, and then all together. Stephen thought it a fine game. He felt awake and happy. They had soft clay and paper and wires and squares of colors in tin boxes to play with, colored blocks to build houses with. Afterward they all danced in a big ring, and then they danced in pairs, boys with girls. Stephen danced with Frances, and Frances kept saying, "Now you just follow me." She was a little taller than he was, and her hair stood up in short shiny curls, the color of an ash tray on Papa's desk. She would say, "You can't dance." "I can dance, too," said Stephen, jumping around holding her hands, "I can, too, dance." He was certain of it. *"You* can't dance," he told Frances, "you can't dance at all."

Then they had to change partners, and when they came round again, Frances said, "I don't *like* the way you dance." This was different. He felt uneasy about it. He didn't jump quite so high when the phonograph record started going dumdiddy dumdiddy again. "Go ahead, Stephen, you're doing fine," said Teacher, waving her hands together very fast. The dance ended, and they all played "relaxing" for five minutes. They relaxed by swinging their arms back and forth, then rolling their heads round and round. When Old Janet came for him he didn't want to go home. At lunch his grandma told him twice to keep his face out of his plate. "Is that what they teach you at school?" she asked. Uncle David was at home. "Here you are, fellow," he said, and gave Stephen two balloons. "Thank you," said Stephen. He put the balloons in his pocket and forgot about them. "I told you that boy could learn something," said Uncle David to Grandma. "Hear him say 'thank you'?"

In the afternoon at school Teacher handed out big wads of clay and told the children to make something out of it. Anything they liked. Stephen decided to make a cat, like Mama's Meeow at home. He did not like Meeow, but he thought it would be easy to make a cat. He could not get the clay to work at all. It simply fell into one lump after another. So he stopped, wiped his hands on his pull-over, remembered his balloons, and began blowing one.

"Look at Stephen's horse," said Frances. "Just look at it."

"It's not a horse, it's a cat," said Stephen. The other children gathered around. "It looks like a horse, a little," said Martin.

"It is a cat," said Stephen stamping his foot, feeling his face turning hot. The other children all laughed and exclaimed over Stephen's cat that looked like a horse. Teacher came down among them. She sat usually at the top of the room before a big table covered with papers and playthings. She picked up Stephen's lump of clay and turned it round and examined it with her kind eyes. "Now children," she said, "everybody has the right to make anything the way he pleases. If Stephen says this is a cat, it *is* a cat. Maybe you were thinking about a horse, Stephen?"

"It's a *cat*," said Stephen. He was aching all over. He knew then he should have said at first "Yes, it's a horse." Then they would have let him alone. They would never have known he was trying to make a cat. "It's Meeow," he said, in a trembling voice, "but I forgot how she looks."

His balloon was perfectly flat. He started blowing it up again, trying not to cry. Then it was time to go home, and Old Janet came looking for him. While Teacher was talking to other grown-up people who came to take other children home, Frances said, "Give me your balloon, I haven't got a balloon." Stephen handed it to her. He was happy to give it. He reached in his pocket and took out the other. Happily, he gave her that one, too. Frances took it, then handed it back. "Now you blow up one and I'll blow up the other, and let's have a race," she said. When their balloons were only half filled, Old Janet took Stephen by the arm and said, "Come on here, this is my busy day."

Frances ran after them, calling, "Stephen, you give me back my balloon," and snatched it away. Stephen did not know whether he was surprised to find himself going away with Frances' balloon, or whether he was surprised to see her snatching it as if it really belonged to her. He was badly mixed up in his mind, and Old Janet was hauling him along. One thing he knew, he liked Frances, he was going to see her again tomorrow, and he was going to bring her more balloons.

That evening Stephen boxed a while with his Uncle David, and Uncle David gave him a beautiful orange. "Eat that," he said, "it's good for your health."

"Uncle David, may I have some more balloons?" asked Stephen.

"Well, what do you say first?" asked Uncle David, reaching for the box on the top bookshelf.

"Please," said Stephen.

"That's the word," said Uncle David. He brought out two balloons, a red and a yellow one. Stephen noticed for the first time they had letters on them, very small letters that grew taller and wider as the balloon grew rounder. "Now that's all, fellow," said Uncle David. "Don't ask for any more because that's all." He put the box back on the bookshelf, but not before Stephen had seen that the box was almost full of balloons. He didn't say a word, but went on blowing, and Uncle David blew also. Stephen thought it was the nicest game he had ever known.

He had only one left, the next day, but he took it to school and gave it to Frances. "There are a lot," he said, feeling very proud and warm, "I'll bring you a lot of them."

Frances blew it up until it made a beautiful bubble, and said, "Look, I want to show you something." She took a sharp pointed stick they used in working the clay, she poked the balloon, and it exploded. "Look at that," she said.

"That's nothing," said Stephen, "I'll bring you some more."

After school, before Uncle David came home, while Grandma was resting, when Old Janet had given him his milk and told him to run away and not bother her, Stephen dragged a chair to the bookshelf, stood upon it, and reached into the box. He did not take three or four as he believed he intended; once his hands were upon them he seized what they could hold and jumped off the chair, hugging them to him. He stuffed them into his reefer pocket, where they folded down and hardly made a lump.

He gave them all to Frances. There were so many, Frances gave most of them away to the other children. Stephen, flushed with his new joy, the lavish pleasure of giving presents, found almost at once still another happiness. Suddenly he was popular among the children; they invited him specially to join whatever games were up, they fell in at once with his own notions for play, and asked him what he would like to do next. They had festivals of blowing up the beautiful globes, fuller and rounder and thinner, changing as they went from deep color to lighter, paler tones, growing glassy thin, bubbly thin, then bursting with a thrilling loud noise like a toy pistol.

For the first time in his life, Stephen had almost too much of something he wanted, and his head was so turned he forgot how this fullness came about, and no longer thought of it as a secret. The next day was Saturday, and Frances came to visit him, with her nurse. The nurse and Old Janet sat in Old Janet's room drinking coffee and gossiping, and the children sat on the side porch, blowing balloons. Stephen chose an apple-colored one and Frances a pale green one. Between them on the bench lay a tumbled heap of delights still to come.

"I once had a silver balloon," said Frances, "a beyootiful silver one, not round like these, it was a long one. But these are even nicer I think," she added quickly, for she did want to be polite.

"When you get through with that one," said Stephen, gazing at her with the pure bliss of giving added to loving, "you can blow up a blue one and then a pink one and a yellow one and a purple one." He pushed the heap of limp objects toward her. Her clear-looking eyes, with fine little rays of brown in them like the spokes of a wheel, were full of approval for Stephen. "I wouldn't want to be greedy, though, and blow up all your balloons."

"There'll be plenty more left," said Stephen, and his heart rose under his thin ribs. He felt his ribs with his fingers and discovered with some surprise that they stopped somewhere in front, while Frances sat blowing balloons rather half-heartedly. The truth was, she was tired of balloons. After you blow six or seven, your chest gets hollow and your lips feel puckery. She had been blowing balloons steadily for three days now. She had begun to hope they were giving out. "There's boxes and boxes more of them, Frances," said Stephen, happily. "Millions more. I guess they'd last and last if we didn't blow too many every day."

Frances said, somewhat timidly, "I tell you what. Let's rest a while and fix some liquish water. Do you like liquish?"

"Yes, I do," said Stephen, "but I haven't got any."

"Couldn't we buy some?" asked Frances, "it's only a cent a stick, the nice rubbery, twisty kind. We can put it in a bottle with some water, and shake it and shake it, and it makes foam on top like soda pop and we can drink it. I'm kind of thirsty," she said in a small weak voice, "blowing balloons all the time makes you thirsty, I think."

Stephen, in silence, realized a dreadful truth and a numb feeling crept over him. He did not have a cent to buy licorice for Frances and she was tired of his balloons. This was the first real dismay of his whole life, and he aged at least a year in the next minute, huddled, with his deep serious blue eyes focused down his nose in intense speculation. What could he do to please Frances that would not cost money? Only yesterday Uncle David had given him a nickel, and he had thrown it away on gumdrops. He regretted that nickel so bitterly his neck and forehead were damp. He was thirsty, too.

"I tell you what," he said, brightening with a splendid idea, lamely trailing off on second thought, "I know something we can do, I'll—I . . ."

"I *am* thirsty," said Frances, with gentle persistence. "I think I'm so thirsty maybe I'll have to go home." She did not leave the bench, though, but sat, turning her grieved mouth toward Stephen.

Stephen quivered with the terrors of the adventure before him, but he said boldly, "I'll make some lemonade. I'll get sugar and lemon and some ice and we'll have lemonade."

"Oh, I love lemonade," cried Frances. "I'd rather have lemonade than liquish."

"You stay right here," said Stephen, "and I'll get everything."

He ran around the house, and under Old Janet's window he heard the dry chattering voices of the two old women whom he must outwit. He sneaked on tiptoe to the pantry, took a lemon lying there by itself, a handful of lump sugar, and a china teapot, smooth, round, with flowers and leaves all over it. These he left on the kitchen table while he broke a piece of ice with a sharp metal pick he had been forbidden to touch. He put the ice in the pot, cut the lemon, and squeezed it as well as he could—a lemon was tougher and more slippery than he had thought—and mixed sugar and water. He decided there was not enough sugar, so he sneaked back and took another handful. He was back on the porch in an astonishingly short time, his face tight, his knees trembling, carrying iced lemonade to thirsty Frances with both his devoted hands.

A pace distant from her, he stopped, literally stabbed through with a thought. Here he stood in broad daylight carrying a teapot with lemonade in it, and his grandma or Old Janet might walk through the door at any moment.

"Come on, Frances," he whispered loudly. "Let's go round to the back behind the rosebushes where it's shady." Frances leaped up and ran like a deer beside him, her face wise with knowledge of why they ran; Stephen ran stiffly, cherishing his teapot with clenched hands.

It was shady behind the rosebushes, and much safer. They sat side by side on the dampish ground, legs doubled under, drinking in turn from the slender spout. Stephen took his just share in large cool delicious swallows. When Frances drank, she set her round pink mouth daintily to the spout and her throat beat steadily as a heart. Stephen was thinking he had really done something pretty nice for Frances. He did not know where his own happiness was, it was mixed with the sweet-sour taste in his mouth and a cool feeling in his bosom because Frances was there, drinking his lemonade, which he had got for her with great danger.

Frances said, "My, what big swallows you take," when his turn came next.

"No bigger than yours," he told her, downrightly. "You take awfully big swallows."

"Well," said Frances, turning this criticism into an argument for her rightness about things, "that's the way to drink lemonade, anyway." She peered into the teapot. There was quite a lot of lemonade left and she was beginning to feel she had enough. "Let's make up a game and see who can take the biggest swallows."

This was such a wonderful notion they grew reckless, tipping the spout into their opened mouths above their heads until lemonade welled up and ran over their chins in rills down their fronts. When they tired of this, there was still lemonade left in the pot. They played first at giving the rosebush a drink and ended by baptizing it. "Name father son holygoat," shouted Stephen, pouring. At this sound, Old Janet's face appeared over the low hedge, with the tan, disgusted-looking face of Frances' nurse hanging over her shoulder.

"Well, just as I thought," said Old Janet. "Just as I expected." The bag under her chin waggled.

"We were thirsty," he said, "we were awfully thirsty." Frances said nothing, but she gazed steadily at the toes of her shoes.

"Give me that teapot," said Old Janet, taking it with a rude snatch. "Just because you're thirsty is no reason," said Old Janet. "You can ask for things. You don't have to steal."

"We didn't steal," cried Frances suddenly. "We didn't. We didn't!"

"That's enough from you, Missy," said her nurse. "Come straight out of there. You have nothing to do with this."

"Oh, I don't know," said Old Janet, with a hard stare at Frances' nurse. "*He* never did such a thing before, by himself."

"Come on," said the nurse to Frances, "this is no place for you." She held Frances by the wrist and started walking away so fast Frances had to run to keep up. "Nobody can call *us* thieves and get away with it."

"You don't have to steal, even if others do," said Old Janet to Stephen, in a high carrying voice. "If you so much as pick up a lemon in somebody else's house, you're a little thief." She lowered her voice then, and said, "Now I'm going to tell your grandma and you'll see what you get."

"He went in the icebox and left it open," Janet told Grandma, "and he got into the lump sugar and split it all over the floor. Lumps everywhere underfoot. He dribbled water all over the clean kitchen floor, and he baptized the rosebush, blaspheming. And he took your Spode teapot."

"I didn't, either," said Stephen, loudly, trying to free his hand from Old Janet's big hard fist.

"Don't tell fibs," said Old Janet, "that's the last straw."

"Oh, dear," said Grandma. "He's not a baby any more." She shut the book she was reading and pulled the wet front of his pull-over toward her. "What's this sticky stuff on him?" she asked and straightened her glasses.

"Lemonade," said Old Janet. "He took the last lemon."

They were in the big dark room with the red curtains. Uncle David walked in from the room with the bookcases, holding a box in his uplifted hand. "Look here," he said to Stephen. "What's become of all my balloons?"

Stephen knew well that Uncle David was not really asking a question.

Stephen, sitting on a footstool at his grandma's knee, felt sleepy. He leaned heavily and wished he could put his head on her lap, but he might go to sleep, and it would be wrong to go to sleep while Uncle David was still talking. Uncle David walked about the room with his hands in his pockets, talking to Grandma. Now and then he would walk over to a lamp and leaning, peer into the top of the shade, winking in the light, as if he expected to find something there.

"It's simply in the blood, I told her," said Uncle David. "I told her she would simply have to come and get him, and keep him. She asked me if I meant to call him a thief and I said if she could think of a more exact word I'd be glad to hear it."

"You shouldn't have said that," commented Grandma, calmly.

"Why not? She might as well know the facts. . . . I suppose he can't help it," said Uncle David, stopping now in front of Stephen and dropping his chin into his collar, "I shouldn't expect too much of him, but you can't begin too early——"

"The trouble is," said Grandma, and while she spoke, she took Stephen by the chin and held it up so that he had to meet her eye; she talked steadily in a mournful tone, but Stephen could not understand. She ended. "It's not just about the balloons, of course."

"It *is* about the balloons," said Uncle David, angrily, "because balloons now mean something worse later. But what can you expect? His father—well, it's in the blood. He——"

"That's your sister's husband you're talking about," said Grandma, "and there is no use making things worse. Besides, you don't really *know.*"

"I *do* know," said Uncle David. And he talked again very fast, walking up and down. Stephen tried to understand, but the sounds were strange and floating just over his head. They were talking about his father, and they did not like him. Uncle David came over and stood above Stephen and Grandma. He hunched over them with a frowning face, a long, crooked shadow from him falling across them to the wall. To Stephen, he looked like his father, and he shrank against his grandma's skirts.

"The question is, what to do with him now?" asked Uncle David. "If we keep him here, he'd just be a—— I won't be bothered with him. Why can't they take care of their own child? That house is crazy. Too far gone already, I'm afraid. No training. No example."

"You're right, they must take him and keep him," said Grandma. She ran her hands over Stephen's head, tenderly she pinched the nape of his neck between thumb and forefinger. "You're your Grandma's darling," she told him, "and you've had a nice long visit, and now you're going home. Mama is coming for you in a few minutes. Won't that be nice?"

"I want my Mama," said Stephen, whimpering, for his grandma's face frightened him. There was something wrong with her smile.

Uncle David sat down. "Come over here, fellow," he said, wagging a forefinger at Stephen. Stephen went over slowly, and Uncle David drew him between his wide knees in their loose rough clothes. "You ought to be ashamed of yourself," he said, "stealing Uncle David's balloons when he had already given you so many."

"It wasn't that," said Grandma quickly. "Don't say that. It will make an impression——"

"I hope it does," said Uncle David, in a louder voice, "I hope he remembers it all his life. If he belonged to me I'd give him a good thrashing."

Stephen felt his mouth, his chin, his whole face jerking. He opened his mouth to take a breath, and tears and noise burst from him. "Stop that, fellow, stop that," said Uncle David, shaking him gently by the shoulders, but Stephen could not stop. He drew his breath again and it came back in a howl. Old Janet came to the door.

"Bring me some cold water," called Grandma. There was a flurry, a commotion, a breath of cool air from the hall, the door slammed, and Stephen heard his mother's voice. His howl died away, his breath sobbed and fluttered, he turned his dimmed eyes and saw her standing there. His heart turned over within him and he bleated like a lamb, "Maaaaama," running toward her. Uncle David stood back as Mama swooped in and fell on her knees beside Stephen. She gathered him to her and stood up with him in her arms.

"What are you doing to my baby?" she asked Uncle David in a thickened voice. "I should never have let him come here. I should have known better——"

"You always should know better," said Uncle David, "and you never do. And you never will. You haven't got it here," he told her, tapping his forehead.

"David," said Grandma, "that's your——"

"Yes, I know, she's my sister," said Uncle David. "I know it. But if she must run away and marry a——"

"Shut up," said Mama.

"And bring more like him into the world, let her keep them at home. I say let her keep——"

Mama set Stephen on the floor, and holding him by the hand, she said to Grandma all in a rush as if she were reading something, "Good-bye, Mother. This is the last time, really the last. I can't bear it any longer. Say good-bye to Stephen, you'll never see him again. You let this happen. It's your fault. You know David was a coward and a bully and a self-righteous little beast all his life and you never crossed him in anything. You let him bully me all my life and you let him slander my husband and call my baby a thief, and now this is the end. . . . He calls my baby a thief over a few horrible little balloons because he doesn't like my husband. . . ."

She was panting and staring about from one to the other. They were all standing. Now Grandma said: "Go home, daughter. Go away, David. I'm sick of your quarreling. I've never had a day's peace or comfort from either of you. I'm sick of you both. Now let me alone and stop this noise. Go away," said Grandma, in a wavering voice. She took out her handkerchief and wiped first one eye and then the other, and said, "All this hate, hate—what is it for? . . . So this is the way it turns out. Well, let me alone."

"You and your little advertising balloons," said Mama to Uncle David, "the big honest businessman advertises with balloons and if he loses one he'll be ruined. And your beastly little moral notions. . . ."

Grandma went to the door to meet Old Janet, who handed her a glass of water. Grandma drank it all, standing there.

"Is your husband coming for you, or are you going home by yourself?" she asked Mama.

"I'm driving myself," said Mama, in a far-away voice as if her mind had wandered. "You know he wouldn't set foot in this house."

"I should think not," said Uncle David.

"Come on, Stephen darling," said Mama. "It's far past his bedtime," she said, to no one in particular. "Imagine keeping a baby up to torture him about a few miserable little bits of colored rubber." She smiled at Uncle David with both rows of teeth, as she passed him on the way to the door, keeping between him and Stephen. "Ah, where would we be without high moral standards?" she said, and then to Grandma, "Good night, Mother," in quite her usual voice. "I'll see you in a day or so."

"Yes, indeed," said Grandma cheerfully, coming out into the hall with Stephen and Mama. "Let me hear from you. Ring me up tomorrow. I hope you'll be feeling better."

"I feel very well now," said Mama, brightly, laughing. She bent down and kissed Stephen. "Sleepy, darling? Papa's waiting to see you. Don't go to sleep until you've kissed your Papa good night."

Stephen woke with a sharp jerk. He raised his head and put out his chin a little. "I don't want to go home," he said, "I want to go to school. I don't want to see Papa, I don't like him."

Mama laid her palm over his mouth softly. "Darling, don't."

Uncle David put his head out with a kind of snort. "There you are," he said. "There you've got a statement from headquarters."

Mama opened the door and ran, almost carrying Stephen. She ran across the sidewalk, jerking open the car door and dragging Stephen in after her. She spun the car around and dashed forward so sharply Stephen was almost flung out of the seat. He sat braced, then, with all his might, hands digging into the cushions. The car speeded up and the trees and houses whizzed by all flattened out. Stephen began suddenly to sing to himself, a quiet inside song so Mama would not hear. He sang his new secret, it was a comfortable, sleepy song: "I hate Papa, I hate Mama, I hate Grandma, I hate Uncle David, I hate Old Janet, I hate Marjory, I hate Papa, I hate Mama . . ."

His head bobbed, leaned, came to rest on Mama's knee, eyes closed. Mama drew him closer and slowed down, driving with one hand.

Writing Assignments for "The Downward Path to Wisdom"

I. Brief Papers

A. 1. Explain why Stephen feels confused by Uncle David's behavior.
  2. Account for Stephen's mother telling Grandma at one moment that their relationship is over yet saying soon afterward that "I'll see you in a day or so."
  3. Take a pair of characters—Mama and Grandma, Papa and Uncle David, or Marjory and Janet—and explain whether the two characters are essentially like or unlike each other.
  4. Explain the difference between Frances's saying, "You can't dance" and "I don't like the way you dance" (p. 52).
  5. Does Stephen like school? How do you know?
  6. A student wrote the following paragraph in response to the previous question. How effective a piece of writing is it?

> There are clues in "The Downward Path to Wisdom" by Katherine Anne Porter which lead me to believe that Stephen essentially likes school. From the first moment school is mentioned, Stephen appears anxious and excited. "Is it today?" (p. 50) The whole way to school he sings and chants and runs ahead. "The little boy was excited and wanted to run ahead." (p. 51) Once finally there, Stephen finds many things to like about school. To him, school is easy. It is also the first time someone actually calls him by his first name instead of "my darling" or "my angel". This is also the first time that Stephen is among his peers. "The people around him were his size, he didn't have always to be stretching his neck up to faces bent over him" (p. 51). Stephen finds himself learning to read, sing, dance, and most importantly to share and play with other children. All of these things make Stephen feel "awake and happy" (p. 52). This new, happy experience for Stephen is what essentially makes Stephen enjoy and like school.

B. Choose one assertion below, and argue either for it or against it:
  1. The opening scene in Mama's and Papa's bedroom makes clear that, as Papa says, Stephen is "dumb as an ox."
  2. The scene at the breakfast table shows that Marjory is right in calling Stephen "mean."
  3. Stephen's taking the balloons proves that Uncle David is correct in labeling him a thief.
  4. Uncle David is "a coward and a bully and a self-righteous little beast" (p. 58), just as Mama says.

C. 1. Do you sympathize with Stephen even though the adults find him to be stupid or mean or bad? Explain why or why not.
   2. Explain how your feelings for Stephen affect the way you understand the meanings of the story.
   3. Tell a childhood story about a time either when you felt guilty for something that was not your fault or when adults sent you mixed signals. Compare your experience with Stephen's.

II. Longer Papers

A. Stephen is described at one point as "badly mixed up in his mind." Is he still badly mixed up at the end of the story?
B. What does the story say about the human capacity for accepting responsibility for our faults and shortcomings?
C. What does the story say about the causes of shame?
D. What does the story say about the reasons for hating others?
E. Explain the significance of the next-to-last paragraph, especially of Stephen's "new secret," his "comfortable, sleepy song."
F. Explain the meanings of the story's title.

III. Comparative Papers

A. In most initiation stories, a young protagonist matures as a result of new experiences. Write a comparison of "Indian Camp" and "The Downward Path to Wisdom" that focuses on the growth and development of Nick and Stephen.
B. Both "Indian Camp" and "The Downward Path to Wisdom" begin with the protagonist at home, center on scenes spent away from home, and conclude with a journey back home. Does this common narrative pattern mean that Nick and Stephen have also moved in identical psychological and emotional directions?
C. Argue that either "Indian Camp" or "The Downward Path to Wisdom" is the more optimistic and affirmative story.
D. Argue that the fictional world of either "Indian Camp" or "The Downward Path to Wisdom" is more uncertain and more unpredictable than in the other story, that its events are less easily foreseen and the conduct of its characters less easily anticipated.

IV. Allusions to the Garden of Eden in "The Downward Path to Wisdom"

Combine the following sentences (inserting transitions and deleting material where appropriate) into a short essay that defines *allusion* and illustrates its use in "The Downward Path to Wisdom."

1. An allusion is a reference to an event in history.
2. An allusion is a reference to a work of art or literature.
3. Sometimes the reference is openly stated.
4. Sometimes the reference is merely implied.

5. Suppose we say that a thoroughly defeated politician has "met her Waterloo."
6. Then we are alluding to a historical event.
7. The event is Napoleon's final, crushing military defeat.
8. The defeat occurred in 1815.
9. The defeat occurred at Waterloo.
10. Waterloo is in Belgium.

11. And suppose we say that a successful friend has "the Midas touch."
12. Then we are alluding to a literary work.
13. The literary work is a Greek myth.
14. In the Greek myth King Midas is granted the power to turn any object he touches into gold.

15. The major allusion in Katherine Anne Porter's "The Downward Path to Wisdom" is implied rather than stated.
16. The major allusion is to the Biblical story of the Garden of Eden.

17. This is according to the Bible.
18. Adam and Eve are expelled from Eden.
19. Eden is a paradise.
20. Adam and Eve are expelled after they have been tempted by Satan.
21. Adam and Eve are expelled because they disobey God's commandment.
22. God commanded them not to eat fruit from the forbidden tree of knowledge.

23. Here is an example.
24. It comes from the garden scene.
25. Stephen is tempted by Frances.
26. Stephen steals a piece of fruit.
27. Stephen uses a pick he had been forbidden to touch.
28. Stephen and Frances are like Adam and Eve in the following three ways:
29. They hide together.
30. They are caught.
31. They are punished.

32. Sometimes it is easier to recognize an allusion than to explain its function in a story.
33. But perhaps the allusion to Eden suggests this.
34. The Porter story is like the Biblical story.
35. Both deal with the loss of innocence.

36. Another function may be to reinforce this view of humanity.
37. From almost the very beginning humanity has been imperfect.
38. From almost the very beginning humanity has been flawed.
39. From almost the very beginning humanity has fallen.

SHERWOOD ANDERSON
I'm a Fool

Before Reading

Can you think of a time when you were a fool or at least behaved like one? Write for 10 minutes about that experience in such a way that your reader senses you are different now than you used to be.

It was a hard jolt for me, one of the most bitterest I ever had to face. And it all came about through my own foolishness, too. Even yet sometimes, when I think of it, I want to cry or swear or kick myself. Perhaps, even now, after all this time, there will be a kind of satisfaction in making myself look cheap by telling of it.

It began at three o'clock one October afternoon as I sat in the grand stand at the fall trotting and pacing meet at Sandusky, Ohio.

To tell the truth, I felt a little foolish that I should be sitting in the grand stand at all. During the summer before I had left my home town with Harry Whitehead and, with a nigger named Burt, had taken a job as swipe with one of the two horses Harry was campaigning through the fall race meets that year. Mother cried and my sister Mildred, who wanted to get a job as a schoolteacher in our town that fall, stormed and scolded about the house all during the week before I left. They both thought it something disgraceful that one of our family should take a place as a swipe with race horses. I've an idea Mildred thought my taking the place would stand in the way of her getting the job she'd been working so long for.

But after all I had to work, and there was no other work to be got. A big lumbering fellow of nineteen couldn't just hang around the house and I had got too big to mow people's lawns and sell newspapers. Little chaps who could get next to people's sympathies by their sizes were always getting jobs away from me. There was one fellow who kept saying to everyone who wanted a lawn mowed or a cistern cleaned that he was saving money to work his way through college, and I used to lay awake nights thinking up ways to injure him without being found out. I kept thinking of wagons running over him and bricks falling on his head as he walked along the street. But never mind him.

I got the place with Harry and I liked Burt fine. We got along splendid together. He was a big nigger with a lazy sprawling body and soft, kind eyes,

I'M A FOOL   First published in 1922. Sherwood Anderson (1876–1941) grew up in northern Ohio near Sandusky, the setting of "I'm a Fool" and many of his other stories. The events of "I'm a Fool" take place some time before Prohibition, the period from 1920 to 1933 when the manufacture and sale of liquor was forbidden by federal law, but the narrator tells his story some time after Prohibition has begun.

and when it came to a fight he could hit like Jack Johnson.* He had Bucephalus, a big black pacing stallion that could do 2.09 or 2.10 if he had to, and I had a little gelding named Doctor Fritz that never lost a race all fall when Harry wanted him to win.

We set out from home late in July, in a box car with the two horses and after that, until late November, we kept moving along to the race meets and the fairs. It was a peachy time for me, I'll say that. Sometimes now I think that boys who are raised regular in houses, and never have a fine nigger like Burt for best friend, and go to high schools and college, and never steal anything, or get drunk a little, or learn to swear from fellows who know how, or come walking up in front of a grand stand in their shirt sleeves and with dirty horsy pants on when the races are going on and the grand stand is full of people all dressed up—What's the use of talking about it? Such fellows don't know nothing at all. They've never had no opportunity.

But I did. Burt taught me how to rub down a horse and put the bandages on after a race and steam a horse out and a lot of valuable things for any man to know. He could wrap a bandage on a horse's leg so smooth that if it had been the same color you would think it was his skin, and I guess he'd have been a big driver, too, and got to the top like Murphy and Walter Cox and the others if he hadn't been black.

Gee whizz! it was fun. You got to a county-seat town, maybe say on a Saturday or Sunday, and the fair began the next Tuesday and lasted until Friday afternoon. Doctor Fritz would be, say, in the 2.25 trot on Tuesday afternoon and on Thursday afternoon Bucephalus would knock 'em cold in the "free-for-all" pace. It left you a lot of time to hang around and listen to horse talk, and see Burt knock some yap cold that got too gay, and you'd find out about horses and men and pick up a lot of stuff you could use all the rest of your life, if you had some sense and salted down what you heard and felt and saw.

And then at the end of the week when the race meet was over, and Harry had run home to tend up to his livery-stable business, you and Burt hitched the two horses to carts and drove slow and steady across country, to the place for the next meeting, so as to not overheat the horses, etc., etc., you know.

Gee whizz! Gosh amighty! the nice hickory-nut and beechnut and oaks and other kinds of trees along the roads, all brown and red, and the good smells, and Burt singing a song called "Deep River," and the country girls at the windows of houses and everything. You can stick your colleges up your nose for all me. I guess I know where I got my education.

Why, one of those little burgs of towns you came to on the way, say now on a Saturday afternoon, and Burt says, "Let's lay up here." And you did.

And you took the horses to a livery stable and fed them, and you got your good clothes out of a box and put them on.

And the town was full of farmers gaping, because they could see you were racehorse people, and the kids maybe never see a nigger before and was afraid and run away when the two of us walked down their main street.

*Jack Johnson: First black heavyweight champion of the world (1908–1915).

And that was before prohibition and all that foolishness, and so you went into a saloon, the two of you, and all the yaps come and stood around, and there was always some one pretended he was horsy and knew things and spoke up and began asking questions, and all you did was to lie and lie all you could about what horses you had, and I said I owned them, and then some fellow said, "Will you have a drink of whisky?" and Burt knocked his eye out the way he could say, offhand like, "Oh, well, all right, I'm agreeable to a little nip. I'll split a quart with you." Gee whizz!

But that isn't what I want to tell my story about. We got home late in November and I promised mother I'd quit the race horses for good. There's a lot of things you've got to promise a mother because she don't know any better.

And so, there not being any work in our town any more than when I left there to go to the races, I went off to Sandusky and got a pretty good place taking care of horses for a man who owned a teaming and delivery and storage and coal and real-estate business there. It was a pretty good place with good eats, and a day off each week, and sleeping on a cot in a big barn, and mostly just shoveling in hay and oats to a lot of big good-enough skates of horses that couldn't have trotted a race with a toad. I wasn't dissatisfied and I could send money home.

And then, as I started to tell you, the fall races come to Sandusky and I got the day off and I went. I left the job at noon and had on my good clothes and my new brown derby hat I'd bought the Saturday before, and a stand-up collar.

First of all I went downtown and walked about with the dudes. I've always thought to myself, "Put up a good front," and so I did it. I had forty dollars in my pockets and so I went into the West House, a big hotel, and walked up to the cigar stand. "Give me three twenty-five cent cigars," I said. There was a lot of horsemen and strangers and dressed-up people from other towns standing around in the lobby and in the bar, and I mingled amongst them. In the bar there was a fellow with a cane and a Windsor tie on, that it made me sick to look at him. I like a man to be a man and dressed up, but not to go put on that kind of airs. So I pushed him aside, kind of rough, and had me a drink of whisky. And then he looked at me, as though he thought maybe he'd get gay, but he changed his mind and didn't say anything. And then I had another drink of whisky, just to show him something, and went out and had a hack out to the races, all to myself, and when I got there I bought myself the best seat I could get up in the grand stand, but didn't go in for any of these boxes. That's putting on too many airs.

And so there I was, sitting up in the grand stand as gay as you please and looking down on the swipes coming out with their horses, and with their dirty horsy pants on and the horseblankets swung over their shoulders, same as I had been doing all the year before. I liked one thing about the same as the other, sitting up there and feeling grand and being down there and looking up at the yaps and feeling grander and more important, too.

One thing's about as good as another, if you take it just right. I've often said that.

Well, right in front of me, in the grand stand that day, there was a fellow with a couple of girls and they was about my age. The young fellow was a nice guy, all right. He was the kind maybe that goes to college and then comes to be a lawyer or maybe a newspaper editor or something like that, but he wasn't stuck on himself. There are some of that kind are all right and he was one of the ones.

He had his sister with him and another girl and the sister looked around over his shoulder, accidental at first, not intending to start anything—she wasn't that kind—and her eyes and mine happened to meet.

You know how it is. Gee, she was a peach! She had on a soft dress, kind of a blue stuff and it looked carelessly made, but was well sewed and made and everything. I knew that much. I blushed when she looked right at me and so did she. She was the nicest girl I've ever seen in my life. She wasn't stuck on herself and she could talk proper grammar without being like a schoolteacher or something like that. What I mean is, she was O.K. I think maybe her father was well-to-do, but not rich to make her chesty because she was his daughter, as some are. Maybe he owned a drug store or a dry-goods store in their home town, or something like that. She never told me and I never asked.

My own people are all O.K. too, when you come to that. My grandfather was Welsh and over in the old country, in Wales he was—But never mind that.

The first heat of the first race come off and the young fellow setting there with the two girls left them and went down to make a bet. I knew what he was up to, but he didn't talk big and noisy and let everyone around know he was a sport, as some do. He wasn't that kind. Well, he come back and I heard him tell the two girls what horse he'd bet on, and when the heat trotted they all half got to their feet and acted in the excited, sweaty way people do when they've got money down on a race, and the horse they bet on is up there pretty close at the end, and they think maybe he'll come on with a rush, but he never does because he hasn't got the old juice in him, come right down to it.

And then, pretty soon, the horses came out for the 2.18 pace and there was a horse in it I knew. He was a horse Bob French had in his string but Bob didn't own him. He was a horse owned by a Mr. Mathers down at Marietta, Ohio.

This Mr. Mathers had a lot of money and owned some coal mines or something and he had a swell place out in the country, and he was stuck on race horses, but was a Presbyterian or something, and I think more than likely his wife was one, too, maybe a stiffer one than himself. So he never raced his horses hisself, and the story round the Ohio race tracks was that when one of his horses got ready to go to the races he turned him over to Bob French and pretended to his wife he was sold.

So Bob had the horses and he did pretty much as he pleased and you can't blame Bob, at least, I never did. Sometimes he was out to win and sometimes he wasn't. I never cared much about that when I was swiping a horse. What I did want to know was that my horse had the speed and could go out in front, if you wanted him to.

And, as I'm telling you, there was Bob in this race with one of Mr.

Mathers' horses, was named "About Ben Ahem"* or something like that, and was fast as a streak. He was a gelding and had a mark of 2.21, but could step in .08 or .09.

Because when Burt and I were out, as I've told you, the year before, there was a nigger Burt knew, worked for Mr. Mathers and we went out there one day when we didn't have no race on at the Marietta Fair and our boss Harry was gone home.

And so everyone was gone to the fair but just this one nigger and he took us all through Mr. Mathers' swell house and he and Burt tapped a bottle of wine Mr. Mathers had hid in his bedroom, back in a closet, without his wife knowing, and he showed us this Ahem horse. Burt was always stuck on being a driver but didn't have much chance to get to the top, being a nigger, and he and the other nigger gulped the whole bottle of wine and Burt got a little lit up.

So the nigger let Burt take this About Ben Ahem and step him a mile in a track Mr. Mathers had all to himself, right there on the farm. And Mr. Mathers had one child, a daughter, kinda sick and not very good looking, and she came home and we had to hustle to get About Ben Ahem stuck back in the barn.

I'm only telling you to get everything straight. At Sandusky, that afternoon I was at the fair, this young fellow with the two girls was fussed, being with the girls and losing his bet. You know how a fellow is that way. One of them was his girl and the other his sister. I had figured that out.

"Gee whizz," I says to myself, "I'm going to give him the dope."

He was mighty nice when I touched him on the shoulder. He and the girls were nice to me right from the start and clear to the end. I'm not blaming them.

And so he leaned back and I give him the dope on About Ben Ahem. "Don't bet a cent on this first heat because he'll go like an oxen hitched to a plow, but when the first heat is over go right down and lay on your pile." That's what I told him.

Well, I never saw a fellow treat any one sweller. There was a fat man sitting beside the little girl, that had looked at me twice by this time, and I at her, and both blushing, and what did he do but have the nerve to turn and ask the fat man to get up and change places with me so I could set with his crowd.

Gee whizz, craps amighty. There I was. What a chump I was to go and get gay up there in the West House bar, and just because that dude was standing there with a cane and that kind of a necktie on, to go and get all balled up and drink that whisky, just to show off.

Of course she would know, me setting right beside her and letting her smell of my breath. I could have kicked myself right down out of that grand stand and all around that race track and made a faster record than most of the skates of horses they had there that year.

Because that girl wasn't any mutt of a girl. What wouldn't I have give right then for a stick of chewing gum to chew, or a lozenger, or some licorice, or most

---

*About Ben Ahem: "Abou Ben Adhem" is the title of a once well-known poem by the nineteenth-century British writer Walter Savage Landor. The first line of the poem is "Abou Ben Adhem (may his tribe increase!)."

anything. I was glad I had those twenty-five cent cigars in my pocket and right away I gave that fellow one and lit one myself. Then that fat man got up and we changed places and there I was, plunked right down beside her.

They introduced themselves and the fellow's best girl, he had with him, was named Miss Elinor Woodbury, and her father was a manufacturer of barrels from a place called Tiffin, Ohio. And the fellow himself was named Wilbur Wessen and his sister was Miss Lucy Wessen.

I suppose it was their having such swell names that got me off my trolley. A fellow, just because he has been a swipe with a race horse, and works taking care of horses for a man in the teaming, delivery, and storage business isn't any better or worse than any one else. I've often thought that, and said it too.

But you know how a fellow is. There's something in that kind of nice clothes, and the kind of nice eyes she had, and the way she had looked at me, awhile before, over her brother's shoulder, and me looking back at her, and both of us blushing.

I couldn't show her up for a boob, could I?

I made a fool of myself, that's what I did. I said my name was Walter Mathers from Marietta, Ohio, and then I told all three of them the smashingest lie you ever heard. What I said was that my father owned the horse About Ben Ahem and that he had let him out to this Bob French for racing purposes, because our family was proud and had never gone into racing that way, in our own name, I mean, and Miss Lucy Wessen's eyes were shining, and I went the whole hog.

I told about our place down at Marietta, and about the big stables and the grand brick house we had on a hill, up above the Ohio River, but I knew enough not to do it in no bragging way. What I did was to start things and then let them drag the rest out of me. I acted just as reluctant to tell as I could. Our family hasn't got any barrel factory, and since I've known us, we've always been pretty poor, but not asking anything of any one at that, and my grandfather, over in Wales—but never mind that.

We sat there talking like we had known each other for years and years, and I went and told them that my father had been expecting maybe this Bob French wasn't on the square, and had sent me up to Sandusky on the sly to find out what I could.

And I bluffed it through I had found out all about the 2.18 pace, in which About Ben Ahem was to start.

I said he would lose the first heat by pacing like a lame cow and then he would come back and skin 'em alive after that. And to back up what I said I took thirty dollars out of my pocket and handed it to Mr. Wilbur Wessen and asked him, would he mind, after the first heat, to go down and place it on About Ben Ahem for whatever odds he could get. What I said was that I didn't want Bob French to see me and none of the swipes.

Sure enough the first heat come off and About Ben Ahem went off his stride, up the back stretch, and looked like a wooden horse or a sick one, and come in to be last. Then this Wilbur Wessen went down to the betting place under the grand stand and there I was with the two girls, and when that Miss

Woodbury was looking the other way once, Lucy Wessen kinda, with her shoulder you know, kinda touched me. Not just tucking down, I don't mean. You know how a woman can do. They get close, but not getting gay either. You know what they do. Gee whizz.

And then they give me a jolt. What they had done, when I didn't know, was to get together, and they had decided Wilbur Wessen would bet fifty dollars, and the two girls had gone and put in ten dollars each, of their own money, too. I was sick then, but I was sicker later.

About the gelding, About Ben Ahem, and their winning their money, I wasn't worried a lot about that. It came out O.K. Ahem stepped the next three heats like a bushel of spoiled eggs going to market before they could be found out, and Wilbur Wessen had got nine to two for the money. There was something else eating at me.

Because Wilbur come back, after he had bet the money, and after that he spent most of his time talking to that Miss Woodbury, and Lucy Wessen and I was left alone together like on a desert island. Gee, if I'd only been on the square or if there had been any way of getting myself on the square. There ain't any Walter Mathers, like I said to her and them, and there hasn't ever been one, but if there was, I bet I'd go to Marietta, Ohio, and shoot him tomorrow.

There I was, big boob that I am. Pretty soon the race was over, and Wilbur had gone down and collected our money, and we had a hack downtown, and he stood us a swell supper at the West House, and a bottle of champagne beside.

And I was with the girl and she wasn't saying much, and I wasn't saying much either. One thing I know. She wasn't stuck on me because of the lie about my father being rich and all that. There's a way you know . . . Craps amighty. There's a kind of girl you see just once in your life, and if you don't get busy and make hay, then you're gone for good and all, and might as well go jump off a bridge. They give you a look from inside of them somewhere, and it ain't no vamping, and what it means is—you want that girl to be your wife, and you want nice things around her like flowers and swell clothes, and you want her to have the kids you're going to have, and you want good music played and no ragtime. Gee whizz.

There's a place over near Sandusky, across a kind of bay, and it's called Cedar Point. And after we had supper we went over to it in a launch, all by ourselves. Wilbur and Miss Lucy and that Miss Woodbury had to catch a ten o'clock train back to Tiffin, Ohio, because, when you're out with girls like that you can't get careless and miss any trains and stay out all night, like you can with some kinds of Janes.

And Wilbur blowed himself to the launch and it cost him fifteen cold plunks, but I wouldn't never have knew if I hadn't listened. He wasn't no tin horn kind of a sport.

Over at the Cedar Point place, we didn't stay around where there was a gang of common kind of cattle at all.

There was big dance halls and dining places for yaps, and there was a beach you could walk along and get where it was dark, and we went there.

She didn't talk hardly at all and neither did I, and I was thinking how glad

I was my mother was all right, and always made us kids learn to eat with a fork at the table, and not swill soup, and not be noisy and rough like a gang you see around a race track that way.

Then Wilbur and his girl went away up the beach and Lucy and I sat down in a dark place, where there was some roots of old trees the water had washed up, and after that the time, till we had to go back in the launch and they had to catch their trains, wasn't nothing at all. It went like winking your eye.

Here's how it was. The place we were setting in was dark, like I said, and there was the roots from that old stump sticking up like arms, and there was a watery smell, and the night was like—as if you could put your hand out and feel it—so warm and soft and dark and sweet like an orange.

I most cried and I most swore and I most jumped up and danced, I was so mad and happy and sad.

When Wilbur come back from being alone with his girl, and she saw him coming, Lucy she says, "We got to go to the train now," and she was most crying too, but she never knew nothing I knew, and she couldn't be so all busted up. And then, before Wilbur and Miss Woodbury got up to where we was, she put her face up and kissed me quick and put her head up against me and she was all quivering and—Gee whizz.

Sometimes I hope I have cancer and die. I guess you know what I mean. We went in the launch across the bay to the train like that, and it was dark, too. She whispered and said it was like she and I could get out of the boat and walk on water, and it sounded foolish, but I knew what she meant.

And then quick we were right at the depot, and there was a big gang of yaps, the kind that goes to the fairs, and crowded and milling around like cattle, and how could I tell her? "It won't be long because you'll write and I'll write to you." That's all she said.

I got a chance like a hay barn afire. A swell chance I got.

And maybe she would write me, down at Marietta that way, and the letter would come back, and stamped on the front of it by the U.S.A. "there ain't any such guy," or something like that, whatever they stamp on a letter that way.

And me trying to pass myself off for a big-bug and a swell—to her, as decent a little body as God ever made. Craps amighty—swell chance I got!

And then the train come in, and she got on it, and Wilbur Wessen, he come and shook hands with me, and that Miss Woodbury was nice too and bowed to me, and I at her, and the train went and I busted out and cried like a kid.

Gee, I could have run after the train and made Dan Patch* look like a freight train after a wreck but, socks amighty, what was the use? Did you ever see such a fool?

I'll bet you what—if I had an arm broke right now or a train had run over my foot—I wouldn't go to no doctor at all. I'd go set down and let her hurt and hurt—that's what I'd do.

---

*Dan Patch: Famous harness horse that set a record time for the mile in 1905 which was not broken until 1938.

I'll bet you what—if I hadn't a drunk that booze I'd never been such a boob as to go tell such a lie—that couldn't never be made straight to a lady like her.

I wish I had that fellow right here that had on a Windsor tie and carried a cane. I'd smash him for fair. Gosh darn his eyes. He's a big fool—that's what he is.

And if I'm not another you just go find me one and I'll quit working and be a bum and give him my job. I don't care nothing for working, and earning money, and saving it for no such boob as myself.

Writing Assignments for "I'm a Fool"

I. Brief Papers

A. 1. What does the narrator mean when he says that he lies to Lucy Wessen because "I couldn't show her up for a boob, could I?"?

2. What are the real reasons the narrator becomes so angry when he sees the man with the cane and Windsor tie?

3. Since the narrator tells us that he got his education at the race track, explain what kind of education he received there. What has the race track taught him?

4. Show that even if the narrator hadn't told us that he never attended college, we could infer it from his language.

5. Is Wilbur Wessen essentially like or unlike the narrator?

B. Choose one assertion below and argue for or against it:

1. The horse races in "I'm a Fool" are fixed.

2. The narrator's lying to Lucy Wessen is the only instance of dishonesty or deception in his entire life.

3. The narrator is a snob: he feels contempt for those he considers his inferiors, and he admires and seeks to associate with those he considers his superiors.

C. 1. Tell a story about a time when you pretended you were better or different than you really were, and then compare your motivation for doing so with the narrator's.

2. Free write for 10 minutes beginning with either the sentence, "I feel sorry for the narrator because . . ." or "I do not feel sorry for the narrator because. . . ." When you are done, look back over what you have written to pick out the idea that seems most promising for a paper. Then briefly explain why the idea is promising.

II. Longer Papers

A. Develop either your free writing or a brief paper into a full-length essay.

B. Support or refute the assertion that the narrator finally understands neither why he is a fool nor how great a fool he is.

C. Is "I'm a Fool" a story about growing up or the failure to grow up?

  D. Explain the relevance of either the scene at Cedar Point or the earlier trip to the country home of Mr. Mathers.
  E. You just received "I'm a Fool" as a letter from an old friend. Write a return letter that either (1) helps him to understand his experience more fully or (2) helps him to realize he still has a lot more to learn about himself and his values.

III. Dramatic Irony in "I'm a Fool"

Combine the following sentences (inserting transitions and deleting material where appropriate) into a short essay that defines *dramatic irony* and illustrates its use in "I'm a Fool."

  1. "I'm a Fool" is a story.
  2. "I'm a Fool" is enriched with dramatic irony.
  3. Sherwood Anderson wrote "I'm a Fool."

  4. All irony depends upon a contrast.
  5. Or all irony depends upon a discrepancy.
  6. In verbal irony, it is a contrast between what a person says and what she means.
  7. In irony of situation, it is a discrepancy between what is expected and what actually occurs.
  8. But the dramatic irony of "I'm a Fool" depends upon the difference between two things.
  9. One is what the story's narrator thinks is true.
 10. The other is what is in fact true.

 11. Here is an example.
 12. It is ironic that the swipe dislikes people who put on airs.
 13. The swipe is the narrator of "I'm a Fool."
 14. Yet the swipe fails to realize that he puts on airs himself.
 15. His brown derby is a sign that he puts on airs.
 16. His stand-up collar is a sign that he puts on airs.
 17. His expensive cigars are a sign that he puts on airs.

 18. Here is another example.
 19. It is ironic that the swipe blames his lies on the man with the cane and Windsor tie.
 20. It is clear that the swipe would have lied under any circumstances.

 21. Here is a final example.
 22. It is ironic that the swipe believes this.
 23. He would not have lied except for the whiskey.

 24. But this is a fact.
 25. The swipe's practice "was to lie and lie all you could" (p. 65).
 26. The swipe did so whenever he was among strangers.

27. All these are instances of dramatic irony.
28. All these are instances of contrasts.
29. The contrasts are between two things.
30. One is the truth as the swipe sees it.
31. The other is the truth as seen by the reader.
32. These instances suggest that the swipe never fully understands himself.
33. These instances suggest that the swipe never fully understands his painful experience.

JAMES JOYCE
Araby

Before Reading

Do you have more or less imagination now than when you were in grade school? Free write on that question for about 10 minutes.

North Richmond Street, being blind,* was a quiet street except at the hour when the Christian Brothers' School set the boys free. An uninhabited house of two storeys stood at the blind end, detached from its neighbours in a square ground. The other houses of the street, conscious of decent lives within them, gazed at one another with brown imperturbable faces.

The former tenant of our house, a priest, had died in the back drawing-room. Air, musty from having been long enclosed, hung in all the rooms, and the waste room behind the kitchen was littered with old useless papers. Among these I found a few paper-covered books, the pages of which were curled and damp: *The Abbot,* by Walter Scott,† *The Devout Communicant*‡ and *The Memoirs of Vidocq.* § I liked the last best because its leaves were yellow. The wild garden behind the house contained a central apple-tree and a few straggling bushes under one of which I found the late tenant's rusty bicycle-pump. He had been a very charitable priest; in his will he had left all his money to institutions and the furniture of his house to his sister.

*North Richmond Street, being blind: A dead-end street in Dublin.
†*The Abbot,* by Walter Scott: A historical romance about Catholic Mary Stuart (Mary, Queen of Scots), Queen of Scotland from 1542 to 1567 and beheaded in 1587 on the order of Protestant Queen Elizabeth I of England.
‡*The Devout Communicant:* A Catholic religious tract with the subtitle *Pious Meditations and Aspirations for the Three Days Before and the Three Days After Receiving the Holy Eucharist* (1813).
§*The Memoirs of Vidocq:* Francois Vidocq (1775–1857) was a French criminal who became chief of detectives.

ARABY   First published in 1916 in Joyce's collection of short stories *Dubliners* but written about 11 years earlier. James Joyce (1882–1941), born in Dublin, Ireland, and educated at Catholic schools there, wrote about his homeland in his short stories and in novels like *A Portrait of the Artist as a Young Man* and *Ulysses.*

When the short days of winter came dusk fell before we had well eaten
our dinners. When we met in the street the houses had grown sombre. The
space of sky above us was the colour of ever-changing violet and towards it
the lamps of the street lifted their feeble lanterns. The cold air stung us and
we played till our bodies glowed. Our shouts echoed in the silent street. The
career of our play brought us through the dark muddy lanes behind the
houses where we ran the gauntlet of the rough tribes from the cottages, to the
back doors of the dark dripping gardens where odours arose from the ashpits,
to the dark odorous stables where a coachman smoothed and combed the
horse or shook music from the buckled harness. When we returned to the
street light from the kitchen windows had filled the areas. If my uncle was
seen turning the corner we hid in the shadow until we had seen him safely
housed. Or if Mangan's sister came out on the doorstep to call her brother in
to his tea we watched her from our shadow peer up and down the street. We
waited to see whether she would remain or go in and, if she remained, we left
our shadow and walked up to Mangan's steps resignedly. She was waiting for
us, her figure defined by the light from the half-opened door. Her brother
always teased her before he obeyed and I stood by the railings looking at her.
Her dress swung as she moved her body and the soft rope of her hair tossed
from side to side.

Every morning I lay on the floor in the front parlour watching her door.
The blind was pulled down to within an inch of the sash so that I could not be
seen. When she came out on the doorstep my heart leaped. I ran to the hall,
seized my books and followed her. I kept her brown figure always in my eye
and, when we came near the point at which our ways diverged, I quickened my
pace and passed her. This happened morning after morning. I had never spoken
to her, except for a few casual words, and yet her name was like a summons to
all my foolish blood.

Her image accompanied me even in places the most hostile to romance.
On Saturday evenings when my aunt went marketing I had to go to carry some
of the parcels. We walked through the flaring streets, jostled by drunken men
and bargaining women, amid the curses of labourers, the shrill litanies of
shop-boys who stood on guard by the barrels of pigs' cheeks, the nasal chanting
of street-singers, who sang a *come-all-you* about O'Donovan Rossa,* or a ballad
about the troubles in our native land. These noises converged in a single
sensation of life for me: I imagined that I bore my chalice safely through a
throng of foes. Her name sprang to my lips at moments in strange prayers and
praises which I myself did not understand. My eyes were often full of tears (I
could not tell why) and at times a flood from my heart seemed to pour itself
out into my bosom. I thought little of the future. I did not know whether I
would ever speak to her or not or, if I spoke to her, how I could tell her of my

*a *come-all-you* about O'Donovan Rossa: A nationalistic song that begins "Come, all you Irishmen"
named for the nineteenth-century Irish patriot Jeremiah O'Donovan, popularly known as
O'Donovan Rossa.

confused adoration. But my body was like a harp and her words and gestures were like fingers running upon the wires.

One evening I went into the back drawing-room in which the priest had died. It was a dark rainy evening and there was no sound in the house. Through one of the broken panes I heard the rain impinge upon the earth, the fine incessant needles of water playing in the sodden beds. Some distant lamp or lighted window gleamed below me. I was thankful that I could see so little. All my senses seemed to desire to veil themselves and, feeling that I was about to slip from them, I pressed the palms of my hands together until they trembled, murmuring: *"O love! O love!"* many times.

At last she spoke to me. When she addressed the first words to me I was so confused that I did not know what to answer. She asked me was I going to *Araby.* * I forgot whether I answered yes or no. It would be a splendid bazaar, she said she would love to go.

"And why can't you?" I asked.

While she spoke she turned a silver bracelet round and round her wrist. She could not go, she said, because there would be a retreat that week in her convent. Her brother and two other boys were fighting for their caps and I was alone at the railings. She held one of the spokes, bowing her head towards me. The light from the lamp opposite our door caught the white curve of her neck, lit up her hair that rested there and, falling, lit up the hand upon the railing. It fell over one side of her dress and caught the white border of a petticoat, just visible as she stood at ease.

"It's well for you" she said.

"If I go," I said, "I will bring you something."

What innumerable follies laid waste my waking and sleeping thoughts after that evening! I wished to annihilate the tedious intervening days. I chafed against the work of school. At night in my bedroom and by day in the classroom her image came between me and the page I strove to read. The syllables of the word *Araby* were called to me through the silence in which my soul luxuriated and cast an Eastern enchantment over me. I asked for leave to go to the bazaar on Saturday night. My aunt was surprised and hoped it was not some Freemason affair.† I answered few questions in class. I watched my master's face pass from amiability to sternness; he hoped I was not beginning to idle. I could not call my wandering thoughts together. I had hardly any patience with the serious work of life which, now that it stood between me and my desire, seemed to me child's play, ugly monotonous child's play.

On Saturday morning I reminded my uncle that I wished to go to the bazaar in the evening. He was fussing at the hallstand, looking for the hat-brush, and answered me curtly:

---

*Araby: The name of an actual bazaar held in Dublin in 1894; it was advertised as a "Grand Oriental Fête."
†Freemason affair: The Masons, or Freemasons, an international secret fraternal organization, were considered enemies of the Catholics.

"Yes, boy, I know."

As he was in the hall I could not go into the front parlour and lie at the window. I left the house in bad humour and walked slowly towards the school. The air was pitilessly raw and already my heart misgave me.

When I came home to dinner my uncle had not yet been home. Still it was early. I sat staring at the clock for some time and, when its ticking began to irritate me, I left the room. I mounted the staircase and gained the upper part of the house. The high cold empty gloomy rooms liberated me and I went from room to room singing. From the front window I saw my companions playing below in the street. Their cries reached me weakened and indistinct and, leaning my forehead against the cool glass, I looked over at the dark house where she lived. I may have stood there for an hour, seeing nothing but the brown-clad figure cast by my imagination, touched discreetly by the lamplight at the curved neck, at the hand upon the railings and at the border below the dress.

When I came downstairs again I found Mrs. Mercer sitting at the fire. She was an old garrulous woman, a pawnbroker's widow, who collected used stamps for some pious purpose. I had to endure the gossip of the tea-table. The meal was prolonged beyond an hour and still my uncle did not come. Mrs. Mercer stood up to go: she was sorry she couldn't wait any longer, but it was after eight o'clock and she did not like to be out late, as the night air was bad for her. When she had gone I began to walk up and down the room, clenching my fists. My aunt said:

"I'm afraid you may put off your bazaar for this night of Our Lord."

At nine o'clock I heard my uncle's latchkey in the halldoor. I heard him talking to himself and heard the hallstand rocking when it had received the weight of his overcoat. I could interpret these signs. When he was midway through his dinner I asked him to give me the money to go to the bazaar. He had forgotten.

"The people are in bed and after their first sleep now," he said.

I did not smile. My aunt said to him energetically:

"Can't you give him the money and let him go? You've kept him late enough as it is."

My uncle said he was very sorry he had forgotten. He said he believed in the old saying: "All work and no play makes Jack a dull boy." He asked me where I was going and, when I had told him a second time he asked me did I know *The Arab's Farewell to his Steed.* * When I left the kitchen he was about to recite the opening lines of the piece to my aunt.

I held a florin† tightly in my hand as I strode down Buckingham Street towards the station. The sight of the streets thronged with buyers and glaring

---

*The Arab's Farewell to his Steed: A sentimental poem by Caroline Elizabeth Sarah Norton (1808–1877) that begins, "A soldier of the Legion lay dying in Algiers, / There was a lack of woman's nursing, there was a dearth of woman's tears. . . ."

†florin: A two-shilling coin and therefore worth four times the entrance fee of six pennies.

with gas recalled to me the purpose of my journey. I took my seat in a third-class carriage of a deserted train. After an intolerable delay the train moved out of the station slowly. It crept onward among ruinous houses and over the twinkling river. At Westland Row Station a crowd of people pressed to the carriage doors; but the porters moved them back, saying that it was a special train for the bazaar. I remained alone in the bare carriage. In a few minutes the train drew up beside an improvised wooden platform. I passed out on to the road and saw by the lighted dial of a clock that it was ten minutes to ten. In front of me was a large building which displayed the magical name.

I could not find any sixpenny entrance and, fearing that the bazaar would be closed, I passed in quickly through a turnstile, handing a shilling to a weary-looking man. I found myself in a big hall girdled at half its height by a gallery. Nearly all the stalls were closed and the greater part of the hall was in darkness. I recognised a silence like that which pervades a church after a service. I walked into the centre of the bazaar timidly. A few people were gathered about the stalls which were still open. Before a curtain, over which the words *Café Chantant** were written in coloured lamps, two men were counting money on a salver. I listened to the fall of the coins.

Remembering with difficulty why I had come I went over to one of the stalls and examined porcelain vases and flowered tea-sets. At the door of the stall a young lady was talking and laughing with two young gentlemen. I remarked their English accents and listened vaguely to their conversation.

"O, I never said such a thing!"

"O, but you did!"

"O, but I didn't!"

"Didn't she say that?"

"Yes. I heard her."

"O, there's a . . . fib!"

Observing me the young lady came over and asked me did I wish to buy anything. The tone of her voice was not encouraging; she seemed to have spoken to me out of a sense of duty. I looked humbly at the great jars that stood like eastern guards at either side of the dark entrance to the stall and murmured:

"No, thank you."

The young lady changed the position of one of the vases and went back to the two young men. They began to talk of the same subject. Once or twice the young lady glanced at me over her shoulder.

I lingered before her stall, though I knew my stay was useless, to make my interest in her wares seem the more real. Then I turned away slowly and walked down the middle of the bazaar. I allowed the two pennies to fall against the sixpence in my pocket. I heard a voice call from one end of the gallery that the light was out. The upper part of the hall was now completely dark.

Gazing up into the darkness I saw myself as a creature driven and derided by vanity; and my eyes burned with anguish and anger.

Café Chantant: A café with music.

Writing Assignments for "Araby"

I. Brief Papers

A. 1. Are the boy and the narrator approximately the same age? How do you know?
   2. Go through the story and circle any words or images related to light and darkness. Can you see any pattern?
   3. Explain the meaning of the sentence, "I imagined that I bore my chalice safely through a throng of foes" (p. 74).
   4. What does the last sentence of the story mean to you?
   5. How convincing and informative do you find the following student paragraph on the story's symbolic setting?

> The boy finds himself trapped in a cold, insensitive world. Symbolically, it is a place where houses gaze "with brown, imperturbable faces" at one another without seeing, and a "very charitable priest," a salvation figure, dies in a back drawing room. Even a threatening Eden symbol, which is "the wild garden behind the house," barely sustains life, containing only "a central apple tree and a few straggling bushes." Through symbolism, Joyce creates the boy's inner conflict—the sensuous struggle against a dark world.

B. Argue for or against either assertion below:
   1. The adults in "Araby" are dull and insensitive.
   2. The boy in "Araby" is highly imaginative.

C. 1. Would you characterize the boy's affection for Mangan's sister as "puppy love"? Why or why not?
   2. Do you think Mangan's sister is aware of the boy's feelings for her? Why or why not?
   3. Do you identify or empathize with the boy? Or do you feel superior to him? Explain your response.

II. Longer Papers

A. Develop one of your brief papers into a full-length essay.
B. The story begins, "North Richmond Street, being blind, was a quiet street. . . ." Explain how blindness relates to "Araby" as a whole.
C. James Joyce wrote a novel called *A Portrait of the Artist as a Young Man.* Is the young man in "Araby" likely to become a poet or an artist?
D. What does "Araby" say about the differences between youth and adulthood?
E. Underline every reference in "Araby" to church and religion. Why are there so many religious references in a story about a boy's affection for a girl?
F. Take any one detail or group of related details and explain its connection to the story as a whole. Here are some suggestions: (1) the dead priest; (2) the setting of the story; (3) the wild garden; (4) Mrs. Mercer; and (5) the conversation at the bazaar.

G. Argue for or against the assertion that "Araby" is an affirmative and optimistic story.

III. Comparative Papers

A. Develop or refute the assertion that "I'm a Fool" is just as appropriate a title for "Araby" as for Sherwood Anderson's story.
B. Compare the language of "I'm a Fool" to the language of "Araby" in order to reach some conclusions about the differences between the two narrators.
C. What do "I'm a Fool" and "Araby," taken together, say about self-deception?
D. Relate "I'm a Fool" to "Araby" in any way that seems interesting and important to you.

JOYCE CAROL OATES
Four Summers

Before Reading

Do you believe that a human being can become whatever he or she chooses—that there are no limitations of any kind to what we can achieve in life? Free write for 10 minutes in response to this quesion.

I

It is some kind of special day. "Where's Sissie?" Ma says. Her face gets sharp, she is frightened. When I run around her chair she laughs and hugs me. She is pretty when she laughs. Her hair is long and pretty.

We are sitting at the best table of all, out near the water. The sun is warm and the air smells nice. Daddy is coming back from the building with some glasses of beer, held in his arms. He makes a grunting noise when he sits down.

"Is the lake deep?" I ask them.

They don't hear me, they're talking. A woman and a man are sitting with us. The man marched in the parade we saw just awhile ago; he is a volunteer fireman and is wearing a uniform. Now his shirt is pulled open because it is hot. I can see the dark curly hair way up by his throat; it looks hot and prickly.

A man in a soldier's uniform comes over to us. They are all friends, but I can't remember him. We used to live around here Ma told me, and then we moved away. The men are laughing. The man in the uniform leans back against the railing, laughing, and I am afraid it will break and he will fall into the water.

"Can we go out in a boat, Dad?" says Jerry.

He and Frank keep running back and forth. I don't want to go with them, I want to stay by Ma. She smells nice. Frank's face is dirty with sweat. "Dad," he says, whining, "can't we go out in a boat? Them kids are going out."

A big lake is behind the building and the open part where we are sitting. Some people are rowing on it. This tavern is noisy and everyone is laughing; it is too noisy for Dad to think about what Frank said.

"Harry," says Ma, "the kids want a boat ride. Why don't you leave off drinking and take them?"

"What?" says Dad.

He looks up from laughing with the men. His face is damp with sweat and he is happy. "Yeah, sure, in a few minutes. Go over there and play and I'll take you out in a few minutes."

FOUR SUMMERS   First published in 1967. Joyce Carol Oates was born in Lockport, New York, in 1938, has taught at the University of Windsor and at Princeton University, and writes about ordinary people in the modern world.

The boys run out back by the rowboats, and I run after them. I have a bag of potato chips.

An old man with a white hat pulled down over his forehead is sitting by the boats, smoking. "You kids be careful," he says.

Frank is leaning over and looking at one of the boats. "This here is the best one," he says.

"Why's this one got water in it?" says Jerry.

"You kids watch out. Where's your father?" the man says.

"He's gonna take us for a ride," says Frank.

"Where is he?"

The boys run along, looking at the boats that are tied up. They don't bother with me. The boats are all painted dark green, but the paint is peeling off some of them in little pieces. There is water inside some of them. We watch two people come in, a man and a woman. The woman is giggling. She has on a pink dress and she leans over to trail one finger in the water. "What's all this filthy stuff by the shore?" she says. There is some scum in the water. It is colored a light brown, and there are little seeds and twigs and leaves in it.

The man helps the woman out of the boat. They laugh together. Around their rowboat little waves are still moving; they make a churning noise that I like.

"Where's Dad?" Frank says.

"He ain't coming," says Jerry.

They are tossing pebbles out into the water. Frank throws his sideways, twisting his body. He is ten and very big. "I bet he ain't coming," Jerry says, wiping his nose with the back of his hand.

After awhile we go back to the table. Behind the table is the white railing, and then the water, and then the bank curves out so that the weeping willow trees droop over the water. More men in uniforms, from the parade, are walking by.

"Dad," says Frank, "can't we go out? Can't we? There's a real nice boat there—"

"For Christ's sake, get them off me," Dad says. He is angry with Ma. "Why don't you take them out?"

"Honey, I can't row."

"Should we take out a boat, us two?" the other woman says. She has very short, wet-looking hair. It is curled in tiny little curls close to her head and is very bright. "We'll show them, Lenore. Come on, let's give your kids a ride. Show these guys how strong we are."

"That's all you need, to sink a boat," her husband says.

They all laugh.

The table is filled with brown beer bottles and wrappers of things. I can feel how happy they all are together, drawn together by the round table. I lean against Ma's warm leg and she pats me without looking down. She lunges forward and I can tell even before she says something that she is going to be loud.

"You guys're just jealous! Afraid we'll meet some soldiers!" she says.

"Can't we go out, Dad? Please?" Frank says. "We won't fight. . . ."

"Go and play over there. What're those kids doing—over there?" Dad says, frowning. His face is damp and loose, the way it is sometimes when he drinks. "In a little while, okay? Ask your mother."

"She can't do it," Frank says.

"They're just jealous," Ma says to the other woman, giggling. "They're afraid we might meet somebody somewhere."

"Just who's gonna meet this one here?" the other man says, nodding with his head at his wife.

Frank and Jerry walk away. I stay by Ma. My eyes burn and I want to sleep, but they won't be leaving for a long time. It is still daylight. When we go home from places like this it is always dark and getting chilly and the grass by our house is wet.

"Duane Dorsey's in jail," Dad says. "You guys heard about that?"

"Duane? Yeah, really?"

"It was in the newspaper. His mother-in-law or somebody called the police, he was breaking windows in her house."

"That Duane was always a nut!"

"Is he out now, or what?"

"I don't know, I don't see him these days. We had a fight," Dad says.

The woman with the short hair looks at me. "She's a real cute little thing," she says, stretching her mouth. "She drink beer, Lenore?"

"I don't know."

"Want some of mine?"

She leans toward me and holds the glass by my mouth. I can smell the beer and the warm stale smell of perfume. There are pink lipstick smudges on the glass.

"Hey, what the hell are you doing?" her husband says.

When he talks rough like that I remember him: we were with him once before.

"Are you swearing at me?" the woman says.

"Leave off the kid, you want to make her a drunk like yourself?"

"It don't hurt, one little sip. . . ."

"It's okay," Ma says. She puts her arm around my shoulders and pulls me closer to the table.

"Let's play cards. Who wants to?" Dad says.

"Sissie wants a little sip, don't you?" the woman says. She is smiling at me and I can see that her teeth are darkish, not nice like Ma's.

"Sure, go ahead," says Ma.

"I said leave off that, Sue, for Christ's sake," the man says. He jerks the table. He is a big man with a thick neck; he is bigger than Dad. His eyebrows are blond, lighter than his hair, and are thick and tufted. Dad is staring at something out on the lake without seeing it. "Harry, look, my goddam wife is trying to make your kid drink beer."

"Who's getting hurt?" Ma says angrily.

Pa looks at me all at once and smiles. "Do you want it, baby?"

I have to say yes. The woman grins and holds the glass down to me, and it clicks against my teeth. They laugh. I stop swallowing right away because it is ugly, and some of the beer drips down on me. "Honey, you're so clumsy," Ma says, wiping me with a napkin.

"She's a real cute girl," the woman says, sitting back in her chair. "I wish I had a nice little girl like that."

"Lay off of that," says her husband.

"Hey, did you bring any cards?" Dad says to the soldier.

"They got some inside."

"Look, I'm sick of cards," Ma says.

"Yeah, why don't we all go for a boat ride?" says the woman. "Be real nice, something new. Every time we get together we play cards. How's about a boat ride?"

"It better be a big boat, with you in it," her husband says. He is pleased when everyone laughs, even the woman. The soldier lights a cigarette and laughs. "How come your cousin here's so skinny and you're so fat?"

"She isn't fat," says Ma. "What the hell do you want? Look at yourself."

"Yes, the best days of my life are behind me," the man says. He wipes his face and then presses a beer bottle against it. "Harry, you're lucky you moved out. It's all going downhill, back in the neighborhood."

"You should talk, you let our house look like hell," the woman says. Her face is blotched now, some parts pale and some red. "Harry don't sit out in his back yard all weekend drinking. He gets something done."

"Harry's younger than me."

Ma reaches over and touches Dad's arm. "Harry, why don't you take the kids out? Before it gets dark."

Dad lifts his glass and finishes his beer. "Who else wants more?" he says.

"I'll get them, you went last time," the soldier says.

"Get a chair for yourself," says Dad. "We can play poker."

"I don't want to play poker, I want to play rummy," the woman says.

"At church this morning Father Reilly was real mad," says Ma. "He said some kids or somebody was out in the cemetery and left some beer bottles. Isn't that awful?"

"Duane Dorsey used to do worse than that," the man says, winking.

"Hey, who's that over there?"

"You mean that fat guy?"

"Isn't that the guy at the lumberyard that owes all that money?"

Dad turns around. His chair wobbles and he almost falls; he is angry.

"This goddamn place is too crowded," he says.

"This is a real nice place," the woman says. She is taking something out of her purse. "I always liked it, didn't you, Lenore?"

"Sue and me used to come here a lot," says Ma. "And not just with you two, either."

"Yeah, we're real jealous," the man says.

"You should be," says the woman.

The soldier comes back. Now I can see that he is really a boy. He runs to the table with the beer before he drops anything. He laughs.

"Jimmy, your ma wouldn't like to see you drinking!" the woman says happily.

"Well, she ain't here."

"Are they still living out in the country?" Ma says to the woman.

"Sure. No electricity, no running water, no bathroom—same old thing. What can you do with people like that?"

"She always talks about going back to the Old Country," the soldier says. "Thinks she can save up money and go back."

"Poor old bastards don't know there was a war," Dad says. He looks as if something tasted bad in his mouth. "My old man died thinking he could go back in a year or two. Stupid old bastards!"

"Your father was real nice. . . ." Ma says.

"Yeah, real nice," says Dad. "Better off dead."

Everybody is quiet.

"June Dieter's mother's got the same thing," the woman says in a low voice to Ma. "She's had it a year now and don't weigh a hundred pounds—you remember how big she used to be."

"She was big, all right," Ma says.

"Remember how she ran after June and slapped her? We were there— some guys were driving us home."

"Yeah. So she's got it too."

"Hey," says Dad, "why don't you get a chair, Jimmy? Sit down here."

The soldier looks around. His face is raw in spots, broken out. But his eyes are nice. He never looks at me.

"Get a chair from that table," Dad says.

"Those people might want it."

"Hell, just take it. Nobody's sitting on it."

"They might—"

Dad reaches around and yanks the chair over. The people look at him but don't say anything. Dad is breathing hard. "Here, sit here," he says. The soldier sits down.

Frank and Jerry come back. They stand by Dad, watching him. "Can we go out now?" Frank says.

"What?"

"Out for a boat ride."

"What? No, next week. Do it next week. We're going to play cards."

"You said—"

"Shut up, we'll do it next week." Dad looks up and shades his eyes. "The lake don't look right anyway."

"Lots of people are out there—"

"I said shut up."

"Honey," Ma whispers, "let him alone. Go and play by yourselves."

"Can we sit in the car?"

"Okay, but don't honk the horn."

"Ma, can't we go for a ride?"

"Go and play by yourselves, stop bothering us," she says. "Hey, will you take Sissie?"

They look at me. They don't like me, I can see it, but they take me with them. We run through the crowd and somebody spills a drink—he yells at us. "Oops, got to watch it!" Frank giggles.

We run along the walk by the boat. A woman in a yellow dress is carrying a baby. She looks at us like she doesn't like us.

Down at the far end some kids are standing together.

"Hey, lookit that," Frank says.

A blackbird is caught in the scum, by one of the boats. It can't fly up. One of the kids, a long-legged girl in a dirty dress, is poking at it with a stick.

The bird's wings keep fluttering but it can't get out. If it could get free it would fly and be safe, but the scum holds it down.

One of the kids throws a stone at it. "Stupid old goddamn bird," somebody says. Frank throws a stone. They are all throwing stones. The bird doesn't know enough to turn away. Its feathers are all wet and dirty. One of the stones hits the bird's head.

"Take that!" Frank says, throwing a rock. The water splashes up and some of the girls scream.

I watch them throwing stones. I am standing at the side. If the bird dies, then everything can die, I think. Inside the tavern there is music from the jukebox.

II

We are at the boathouse tavern again. It is a mild day, a Sunday afternoon. Dad is talking with some men; Jerry and I are waiting by the boats. Mommy is at home with the new baby. Frank has gone off with some friends of his, to a stock-car race. There are some people here, sitting out at the tables, but they don't notice us.

"Why doesn't he hurry up?" Jerry says.

Jerry is twelve now. He has pimples on his forehead and chin.

He pushes one of the rowboats with his foot. He is wearing sneakers that are dirty. I wish I could get in that boat and sit down, but I am afraid. A boy not much older than Jerry is squatting on the boardwalk, smoking. You can tell he is in charge of the boats.

"Daddy, come on. Come on," Jerry says, whining. Daddy can't hear him.

I have mosquito bites on my arms and legs. There are mosquitoes and flies around here; the flies crawl around the sticky mess left on tables. A car over in the parking lot has its radio on loud. You can hear the music all this way. "He's coming," I tell Jerry so he won't be mad. Jerry is like Dad, the way his eyes look.

"Oh, that fat guy keeps talking to him," Jerry says.

The fat man is one of the bartenders; he has on a dirty white apron. All these men are familiar. We have been seeing them for years. He punches Dad's arm, up by the shoulder, and Dad pushes him. They are laughing, though. Nobody is mad.

"I'd sooner let a nigger—" the bartender says. We can't hear anything more, but the men laugh again.

"All he does is drink," Jerry says. "I hate him."

At school, up on the sixth-grade floor, Jerry got in trouble last month. The principal slapped him. I am afraid to look at Jerry when he's mad.

"I hate him, I wish he'd die," Jerry says.

Dad is trying to come to us, but every time he takes a step backward and gets ready to turn, one of the men says something. There are three men beside him. Their stomachs are big, but Dad's isn't. He is wearing dark pants and a white shirt; his tie is in the car. He wears a tie to church, then takes it off. He has his shirt sleeves rolled up and you can see how strong his arms must be.

Two women cross over from the parking lot. They are wearing high-heeled shoes and hats and bright dresses—orange and yellow—and when they walk past the men look at them. They go into the tavern. The men laugh about something. The way they laugh makes my eyes focus on something away from them—a bird flying in the sky—and it is hard for me to look anywhere else. I feel as if I'm falling asleep.

"Here he comes!" Jerry says.

Dad walks over to us, with his big steps. He is smiling and carrying a bottle of beer. "Hey, kid," he says to the boy squatting on the walk, "how's about a boat?"

"This one is the best," Jerry says.

"The best, huh? Great." Dad grins at us. "Okay, Sissie, let's get you in. Be careful now." He picks me up even though I am too heavy for it, and sets me in the boat. It hurts a little where he held me, under the arms, but I don't care.

Jerry climbs in. Dad steps and something happens—he almost slips, but he catches himself. With the wet oar he pushes us off from the boardwalk.

Dad can row fast. The sunlight is gleaming on the water. I sit very still, facing him, afraid to move. The boat goes fast, and Dad is leaning back and forth and pulling on the oars, breathing hard, doing everything fast like he always does. He is always in a hurry to get things done. He has set the bottle of beer down by his leg, pressed against the side of the boat so it won't fall.

"There's the guys we saw go out before," Jerry says. Coming around the island is a boat with three boys in it, older than Jerry. "They went on the island. Can we go there too?"

"Sure," says Dad. His eyes squint in the sun. He is suntanned, and there are freckles on his forehead. I am sitting close to him, facing him, and it surprises me what he looks like—he is like a stranger, with his eyes narrowed. The water beneath the boat makes me feel funny. It keeps us up now, but if I fell over the side I would sink and drown.

"Nice out here, huh?" Dad says. He is breathing hard.

"We should go over that way to get on the island," Jerry says.

"This goddamn oar has splinters in it," Dad says. He hooks the oar up and lets us glide. He reaches down to get the bottle of beer. Though the lake and some trees and the buildings back on shore are in front of me, what makes me look at it is my father's throat, the way it bobs when he swallows. He wipes his forehead. "Want to row, Sissie?" he says.

"Can I?"

"Let me do it," says Jerry.

"Naw, I was just kidding," Dad says.

"I can do it. It ain't hard."

"Stay where you are," Dad says.

He starts rowing again, faster. Why does he go so fast? His face is getting red, the way it does at home when he has trouble with Frank. He clears his throat and spits over the side; I don't like to see that but I can't help but watch. The other boat glides past us, heading for shore. The boys don't look over at us.

Jerry and I look to see if anyone else is on the island, but no one is. The island is very small. You can see around it.

"Are you going to land on it, Dad?" Jerry says.

"Sure, okay." Dad's face is flushed and looks angry.

The boat scrapes bottom and bumps. "Jump out and pull it in," Dad says. Jerry jumps out. His shoes and socks are wet now, but Dad doesn't notice. The boat bumps; it hurts me. I am afraid. But then we're up on the land and Dad is out and lifting me. "Nice ride, sugar?" he says.

Jerry and I run around the island. It is different from what we thought, but we don't know why. There are some trees on it, some wild grass, and then bare caked mud that goes down to the water. The water looks dark and deep on the other side, but when we get there it's shallow. Lily pads grow there; everything is thick and tangled. Jerry wades in the water and gets his pants legs wet. "There might be money in the water," he says.

Some napkins and beer cans are nearby. There is part of a hot-dog bun, with flies buzzing around it.

When we go back by Dad, we see him squatting over the water doing something. His back jerks. Then I see that he is being sick. He is throwing up in the water and making a noise like coughing.

Jerry turns around right away and runs back. I follow him, afraid. On the other side we can look back at the boathouse and wish we were there.

III

Marian and Betty went to the show, but I couldn't. She made me come along here with them. "And cut out that snippy face," Ma said, to let me know she's watching. I have to help her take care of Linda—poor fat Linda, with her runny nose! So here we are inside the tavern. There's too much smoke, I hate smoke. Dad is smoking a cigar. I won't drink any more root beer, it's flat, and I'm sick of potato chips. Inside me there is something that wants to run away, that hates them. How loud they are, my parents! My mother spilled something on the front of her dress, but does she notice? And my aunt Lucy and uncle Joe, they're here. Try to avoid them. Lucy has false teeth that make everyone stare at her. I know that everyone is staring at us. I could hide my head in my arms and turn away, I'm so tired and my legs hurt from sunburn and I can't stand them any more.

"So did you ever hear from them? That letter you wrote?" Ma says to Lucy.

"I'm still waiting. Somebody said you got to have connections to get on the show. But I don't believe it. That Howie Masterson that's the emcee, he's a real nice guy. I can tell."

"It's all crap," Dad says. "You women believe anything."

"I don't believe it," I say.

"Phony as hell," says my uncle.

"You do too believe it, Sissie," says my mother. "Sissie thinks he's cute. I know she does."

"I hate that guy!" I tell her, but she and my aunt are laughing. "I said I hate him! He's greasy."

"All that stuff is phony as hell," says my Uncle Joe. He is tired all the time, and right now he sits with his head bowed. I hate his bald head with the little fringe of gray hair on it. At least my father is still handsome. His jaws sag and there are lines in his neck—edged with dirt, I can see, embarrassed—and his stomach is bulging a little against the table, but still he is a handsome man. In a place like this women look at him. What's he see in *her?* they think. My mother had her hair cut too short last time; she looks queer. There is a photograph taken of her when she was young, standing by someone's motorcycle, with her hair long. In the photograph she was pretty, almost beautiful, but I don't believe it. Not really. I can't believe it, and I hate her. Her forehead gathers itself up in little wrinkles whenever she glances down at Linda, as if she can't remember who Linda is.

"Well, nobody wanted you, kid," she once said to Linda. Linda was a baby then, one year old. Ma was furious, standing in the kitchen where she was washing the floor, screaming: "Nobody wanted you, it was a goddamn accident! An accident!" That surprised me so I didn't know what to think, and I didn't know if I hated Ma or not; but I kept it all a secret . . . only my girl friends know, and I won't tell the priest either. Nobody can make me tell. I narrow my eyes and watch my mother leaning forward to say something—it's like she's going to toss something out on the table—and think that maybe she isn't my mother after all, and she isn't that pretty girl in the photograph, but someone else.

"A woman was on the show last night that lost two kids in a fire. Her house burned down," my aunt says loudly. "And she answered the questions right off and got a lot of money and the audience went wild. You could see she was a real lady. I love that guy, Howie Masterson. He's real sweet."

"He's a bastard," Dad says.

"Harry, what the hell? You never even seen him," Ma says.

"I sure as hell never did. Got better things to do at night." Dad turns to my uncle and his voice changes. "I'm on the night shift, now."

"Yeah, I hate that, I—"

"I can sleep during the day. What's the difference?"

"I hate those night shifts."

"What's there to do during the day?" Dad says flatly. His eyes scan us at the table as if he doesn't see anything, then they seem to fall off me and go behind me, looking at nothing.

"Not much," says my uncle, and I can see his white scalp beneath his hair. Both men are silent.

Dad pours beer into his glass and spills some of it. I wish I could look away. I love him, I think, but I hate to be here. Where would I rather be? With Marian and Betty at the movies, or in my room, lying on the bed and staring at the photographs of movie stars on my walls—those beautiful people that never say anything—while out in the kitchen my mother is waiting for my father to come home so they can continue their quarrel. It never stops, that quarrel. Sometimes they laugh together, kid around, they kiss. Then the quarrel starts up again in a few minutes.

"Ma, can I go outside and wait in the car?" I say. "Linda's asleep."

"What's so hot about the car?" she says, looking at me.

"I'm tired. My sunburn hurts."

Linda is sleeping in Ma's lap, with her mouth open and drooling on the front of her dress. "Okay, go on," Ma says. "But we're not going to hurry just for you." When she has drunk too much there is a struggle in her between being angry and being affectionate; she fights both of them, as if standing with her legs apart and her hands on her hips, bracing a strong wind.

When I cross through the crowded tavern I'm conscious of people looking at me. My hair lost its curl because it was so humid today, my legs are too thin, my figure is flat and not nice like Marian's—I want to hide somewhere, hide my face from them. I hate this noisy place and these people. Even the music is ugly because it belongs to them. Then, when I'm outside, the music gets faint right away and it doesn't sound so bad. It's cooler out here. No one is around. Out back, the old rowboats are tied up. Nobody's on the lake. There's no moon, the sky is overcast, it was raining earlier.

When I turn around, a man is standing by the door watching me.

"What're you doing?" he says.

"Nothing."

He has dark hair and a tanned face, I think, but everything is confused because the light from the door is pinkish—there's a neon sign there. My heart starts to pound. The man leans forward to stare at me. "Oh, I thought you were somebody else," he says.

I want to show him I'm not afraid. "Yeah, really? Who did you think I was?" When we ride on the school bus we smile out the windows at strange men, just for fun. We do that all the time. I'm not afraid of any of them.

"You're not her," he says.

Some people come out the door and he has to step out of their way. I say to him, "Maybe you seen me around here before. We come here pretty often."

"Who do you come with?" He is smiling as if he thinks I'm funny. "Anybody I know?"

"That's my business."

It's a game. I'm not afraid. When I think of my mother and father inside, something makes me want to step closer to this man—why should I be afraid? I could be wild like some of the other girls. Nothing surprises me.

We keep on talking. At first I can tell he wants me to come inside the tavern with him, but then he forgets about it; he keeps talking. I don't know what we say, but we talk in drawling voices, smiling at each other but in a secret, knowing way, as if each one of us knew more than the other. My cheeks start to burn. I could be wild like Betty is sometimes—like some of the other girls. Why not? Once before I talked with a man like this, on the bus. We were both sitting in the back. I wasn't afraid. This man and I keep talking and we talk about nothing, he wants to know how old I am, but it makes my heart pound so hard that I want to touch my chest to calm it. We are walking along the old boardwalk and I say: "Somebody took me out rowing once here."

"Is that so?" he says. "You want me to take you out?"

He has a hard, handsome face. I like that face. Why is he alone? When he smiles I know he's laughing at me, and this makes me stand taller, walk with my shoulders raised.

"Hey, are you with somebody inside there?" he says.

"I left them."

"Have a fight?"

"A fight, yes."

He looks at me quickly. "How old are you anyway?"

"That's none of your business."

"Girls your age are all alike."

"We're not all alike!" I arch my back and look at him in a way I must have learned somewhere—where?—with my lips not smiling but ready to smile, and my eyes narrowed. One leg is turned as if I'm ready to jump away from him. He sees all this. He smiles.

"Say, you're real cute."

We're walking over by the parking lot now. He touches my arm. Right away my heart trips, but I say nothing, I keep walking. High above us the tree branches are moving in the wind. It's cold for June. It's late—after eleven. The man is wearing a jacket, but I have on a sleeveless dress and there are goosepimples on my arms.

"Cold, huh?" he says.

He takes hold of my shoulders and leans toward me. This is to show me he's no kid, he's grown-up, this is how they do things; when he kisses me his grip on my shoulders gets tighter. "I better go back," I say to him. My voice is queer.

"What?" he says.

I am wearing a face like one of those faces pinned up in my room, and what if I lose it? This is not my face. I try to turn away from him.

He kisses me again. His breath smells like beer, maybe, it's like my father's breath, and my mind is empty; I can't think what to do. Why am I here? My legs feel numb, my fingers are cold. The man rubs my arms and says, "You should have a sweater or something. . . ."

He is waiting for me to say something, to keep on the way I was before. But I have forgotten how to do it. Before, I was Marian or one of the older girls; now I am just myself. I am fourteen. I think of Linda sleeping in my mother's lap, and something frightens me.

"Hey, what's wrong?" the man says.

He sees I'm afraid but pretends he doesn't. He comes to me again and embraces me, his mouth presses against my neck and shoulder, I feel as if I'm suffocating. "My car's over here," he says, trying to catch his breath. I can't move. Something dazzling and icy rises up in me, an awful fear, but I can't move and can't say anything. He is touching me with his hands. His mouth is soft but wants too much from me. I think, What is he doing? Do they all do this? Do I have to have it done to me too?

"You cut that out," I tell him.

He steps away. His chest is heaving and his eyes look like a dog's eyes, surprised and betrayed. The last thing I see of him is those eyes, before I turn and run back to the tavern.

IV

Jesse says, "Let's stop at this place. I been here a few times before."

It's the Lakeside Bar. That big old building with the grubby siding, and a big pink neon sign in front, and the cinder driveway that's so bumpy. Yes, everything the same. But different too—smaller, dirtier. There is a custard stand nearby with a glaring orange roof, and people are crowded around it. That's new. I haven't been here for years.

"I feel like a beer," he says.

He smiles at me and caresses my arm. He treats me as if I were something that might break; in my cheap linen maternity dress I feel ugly and heavy. My flesh is so soft and thick that nothing could hurt it.

"Sure, honey. Pa used to stop in here too."

We cross through the parking lot to the tavern. Wild grass grows along the sidewalk and in the cracks of the sidewalk. Why is this place so ugly to me? I feel as if a hand were pressing against my chest, shutting off my breath. Is there some secret here? Why am I afraid?

I catch sight of myself in a dusty window as we pass. My hair is long, down to my shoulders. I am pretty, but my secret is that I am pretty like everyone is. My husband loves me for this but doesn't know it. I have a pink mouth and plucked darkened eyebrows and soft bangs over my forehead; I know everything, I have no need to learn from anyone else now. I am one of those girls younger girls study closely, to learn from. On buses, in five-and-tens, thirteen-year-old girls must look at me solemnly, learning, memorizing.

"Pretty Sissie!" my mother likes to say when we visit, though I told her how I hate that name. She is proud of me for being pretty, but thinks I'm too thin. "You'll fill out nice, after the baby," she says. Herself, she is fat and veins have begun to darken on her legs; she scuffs around the house in bedroom slippers. Who is my mother? When I think of her I can't think of anything—do I love her or hate her, or is there nothing there?

Jesse forgets and walks ahead of me, I have to walk fast to catch up. I'm wearing pastel-blue high heels—that must be because I am proud of my legs. I have little else. Then he remembers and turns to put out his hand for me, smiling to show he is sorry. Jesse is the kind of young man thirteen-year-old girls stare at secretly; he is not a man, not old enough, but not a boy either. He is a year older than I am, twenty. When I met him he was wearing a navy uniform and he was with a girl friend of mine.

Just a few people sitting outside at the tables. They're afraid of rain—the sky doesn't look good. And how bumpy the ground is here, bare spots and little holes and patches of crab grass, and everywhere napkins and junk. Too many flies outside. Has this place changed hands? The screens at the windows don't fit right; you can see why flies get inside. Jesse opens the door for me and I go in. All bars smell alike. There is a damp, dark odor of beer and something indefinable—spilled soft drinks, pretzels getting stale? This bar is just like any other. Before we were married we went to places like this, Jesse and me and other couples. We had to spend a certain amount of time doing things like that—and going to movies, playing miniature golf, bowling, dancing, swimming—then we got married, now we're going to have a baby. I think of the baby all the time, because my life will be changed then; everything will be different. Four months from now. I should be frightened, but a calm laziness has come over me. It was so easy for my mother. . . . But it will be different with me because my life will be changed by it, and nothing ever changed my mother. You couldn't change her! Why should I think? Why should I be afraid? My body is filled with love for this baby, and I will never be the same again.

We sit down at a table near the bar. Jesse is in a good mood. My father would have liked him, I think; when he laughs Jesse reminds me of him. Why is a certain kind of simple, healthy, honest man always destined to lose everything? Their souls are as clean and smooth as the muscular line of their arms. At night I hold Jesse, thinking of my father and what happened to him—all that drinking, then the accident at the factory—and I pray that Jesse will be different. I hope that his quick, open, loud way of talking is just a disguise, that really he is someone else—slower and calculating. That kind of man grows old without jerks and spasms. Why did I marry Jesse?

Someone at the bar turns around, and it's a man I think I know—I have known. Yes. That man outside, the man I met outside. I stare at him, my heart pounding, and he doesn't see me. He is dark, his hair is neatly combed but is thinner than before; he is wearing a cheap gray suit. But is it the same man? He is standing with a friend and looking around, as if he doesn't like what he sees. He is tired too. He has grown years older.

Our eyes meet. He glances away. He doesn't remember—that frightened girl he held in his arms.

I am tempted to put my hand on Jesse's arm and tell him about that man, but how can I? Jesse is talking about trading in our car for a new one. . . . I can't move, my mind seems to be coming to a stop. Is that the man I kissed, or someone else? A feeling of angry loss comes over me. Why should I lose everything? Everything? Is it the same man, and would he remember? My heart bothers me, it's stupid to be like this: here I sit, powdered and sweet, a girl safely married, pregnant and secured to the earth, with my husband beside me. He still loves me. Our love keeps on. Like my parents' love, it will subside someday, but nothing surprises me because I have learned everything.

The man turns away, talking to his friend. They are weary, tired of something. He isn't married yet, I think, and that pleases me. Good. But why are these men always tired? Is it the jobs they hold, the kind of men who stop in at this tavern? Why do they flash their teeth when they smile, but stop smiling so quickly? Why do their children cringe from them sometimes—an innocent upraised arm a frightening thing? Why do they grow old so quickly, sitting at kitchen tables with bottles of beer? They are everywhere, in every house. All the houses in this neighborhood and all neighborhoods around here. Jesse is young, but the outline of what he will be is already in his face; do you think I can't see it? Their lives are like hands dealt out to them in their innumerable card games. You pick up the sticky cards, and there it is: there it is. Can't change anything, all you can do is switch some cards around, stick one in here, one over here . . . pretend there is some sense, a secret scheme.

The man at the bar tosses some coins down and turns to go. I want to cry out to him, "Wait, wait!" But I cannot. I sit helplessly and watch him leave. Is it the same man? If he leaves I will be caught here, what can I do? I can almost hear my mother's shrill laughter coming in from outside, and some drawling remark of my father's—lifting for a moment above the music. Those little explosions of laughter, the slap of someone's hand on the damp table in anger, the clink of bottles accidentally touching—and there, there, my drunken aunt's voice, what is she saying? I am terrified at being left with them. I watch the man at the door and think that I could have loved him. I know it.

He has left, he and his friend. He is nothing to me, but suddenly I feel tears in my eyes. What's wrong with me? I hate everything that springs upon me and seems to draw itself down and oppress me in a way I could never explain to anyone. . . . I am crying because I am pregnant, but not with that man's child. It could have been his child, I could have gone with him to his car; but I did nothing, I ran away, I was afraid, and now I'm sitting here with Jesse, who is picking the label off his beer bottle with his thick squarish fingernails. I did nothing. I was afraid. Now he has left me here and what can I do?

I let my hand fall onto my stomach to remind myself that I am in love: with this baby, with Jesse, with everything. I am in love with our house and our life and the future and even this moment—right now—that I am struggling to live through.

Writing Assignments for "Four Summers"

I. Brief Papers
  A. 1. What do we know about the social, economic, and religious background of
        Sissie's family?
     2. How do we know, without ever being told, that Sissie is a small child during
        the first summer (Part I)?
     3. Why can't Sissie believe that the photograph of her mother (Part III) is genu-
        ine?
     4. When Sissie meets the young man during the third summer, she says, "It's a
        game." Explain the purpose of the game and the rules for playing it.
     5. When does the game become more than a game?
     6. What makes Sissie afraid when she and Jesse stop at the Lakeside Bar during
        the fourth summer?
     7. How convincing and well written is the following student response to the
        previous question?

> Sissie sees at the Lakeside Bar, all the things she has hated as a child
> and vowed to break free from. Sissie knows she has made a choice. It
> is quite evident in the fact that she is married and pregnant. She has
> chosen a life she believes will be safe and happy. A life with a hand-
> some strong man who will love her and their children. Why then does
> Sissie become afraid? When she realizes the choice she has made she
> feels trapped like the bird in the water during the first summer. She
> knows that "If it could get free it could fly and be safe," but she also
> realizes that "the scum holds it down." She wonders if the choice she
> has made is really as great as she had thought. She thinks back to the
> summer of the boat trip to the island and how they could "look back
> at the boathouse and wish we were there." When she sees the man in
> the bar she realizes that she has indeed given up her freedom, and with
> it her chance for the life she dreamed about. She looks at her husband
> and sees the same helpless person she saw in her father. She begins to
> realize that she has made the same safe choice as her mother.

  B. Choose one assertion below and argue for or against it:
     1. Sissie is probably right in thinking that "everything will be different" in her life
        once her baby is born.
     2. Sissie lost a genuine chance for happiness during the third summer when she
        decided not to go off with the young man.
     3. The lives of Sissie's parents and brothers all follow the same pattern.

  C. 1. What would you do if you found yourself in Sissie's position?
     2. In what fundamental ways do you think your own life differs from Sissie's?
     3. Do you find Sissie to be an essentially likable and sympathetic character?
     4. Compare your reaction to the story after a first reading with your reaction after
        a second or third reading. Did subsequent readings of the story lead you to
        interpret it differently?

II. Longer Papers

A. Why do characters in "Four Summers" drink beer, and how does their beer drinking affect our experience and interpretation of the story?

B. Does the trip to the island during the second summer correspond to the pattern and meaning of the story as a whole?

C. Explain the significance of the fourth summer. How does its inclusion change the meaning and experience of the first three summers?

D. Explain how Sissie's fears change from summer to summer and how these changes contribute to the meaning and experience of the story.

E. Argue for or against the assertion that "Four Summers" ends affirmatively.

F. Develop or refute the argument that "Four Summers" endorses the view that human beings are free to control their own lives.

G. Toward the end of the story Sissie asks herself, "What's wrong with me?" Write Sissie a personal letter answering her question as honestly but as tactfully as you know how.

III. Symbolism in "Four Summers"

Using the sentences below, construct a short essay that defines *symbol* and briefly illustrates its use in "Four Summers."

1. A symbol is something that stands for or represents something else.
2. A symbol is usually an object or an action.

3. Here are some examples of symbols.
4. The dove is a symbol of peace.
5. The cross is a symbol of suffering.
6. And the cross is a symbol of salvation for Christians.

7. Banging one's head against the wall symbolizes attempting the impossible.
8. Going around in circles suggests motion that gets nowhere.

9. This is true in literature.
10. Symbols are a concise way of creating and enhancing meaning.

11. Here is an example from "Four Summers."
12. The bird seems to be symbolic.
13. So does the boys' throwing stones at the bird.

14. The bird is caught in the scum of the lake.
15. The bird may represent anyone trapped by his or her environment.
16. The boys' throwing stones may stand for the forces of life.
17. The forces of life include other people.
18. The forces of life prevent her from escaping.

19. Sissie seems to sense the bird's symbolic importance.
20. Sissie thinks, "If the bird dies, then everything can die."

21. That the bird is a symbol is an interpretation.
22. This interpretation gains plausibility when we realize this.
23. "Four Summers" focuses on a young woman.
24. The young woman is like the bird.
25. The young woman is trapped by circumstances.
26. The young woman struggles unsuccessfully to free herself from them.

WILLIAM FAULKNER
Barn Burning

Before Reading

Do you believe that it is possible for a young girl or boy to grow up with moral values substantially different from her or his parents'? Do your own moral values differ substantially from your parents'? Free write on one or both questions for 10 minutes.

The store in which the Justice of the Peace's court was sitting smelled of cheese. The boy, crouched on his nail keg at the back of the crowded room, knew he smelled cheese, and more: from where he sat he could see the ranked shelves close-packed with the solid, squat, dynamic shapes of tin cans whose labels his stomach read, not from the lettering which meant nothing to his mind but from the scarlet devils and the silver curve of fish—this, the cheese which he knew he smelled and the hermetic meat which his intestines believed he smelled coming in intermittent gusts momentary and brief between the other constant one, the smell and sense just a little of fear because mostly of despair and grief, the old fierce pull of blood. He could not see the table where the Justice sat and before which his father and his father's enemy (*our enemy* he thought in that despair; *ourn! mine and hisn both! He's my father!*) stood, but he could hear them, the two of them that is, because his father had said no word yet:

"But what proof have you, Mr. Harris?"

"I told you. The hog got into my corn. I caught it up and sent it back to him. He had no fence that would hold it. I told him so, warned him. The next time I put the hog in my pen. When he came to get it I gave him enough wire to patch up his pen. The next time I put the hog up and kept it. I rode down to his house and saw the wire I gave him still rolled on to the spool in his yard. I told him he could have the hog when he paid me a dollar pound fee. That evening a nigger came with the dollar and got the hog. He was a strange nigger. He said, 'He say to tell you wood and hay kin burn.' I said, 'What?' 'That whut

BARN BURNING   First published in 1939. William Faulkner (1897–1962) was born and grew up in northern Mississippi. The events of "Barn Burning" take place in Mississippi during the 1890s.

he say to tell you,' the nigger said. 'Wood and hay kin burn.' That night my barn burned. I got the stock out but I lost the barn."

"Where is the nigger? Have you got him?"

"He was a strange nigger, I tell you. I don't know what became of him."

"But that's not proof. Don't you see that's not proof?"

"Get that boy up here. He knows." For a moment the boy thought too that the man meant his older brother until Harris said, "Not him. The little one. The boy," and, crouching, small for his age, small and wiry like his father, in patched and faded jeans even too small for him, with straight, uncombed, brown hair and eyes gray and wild as storm scud, he saw the men between himself and the table part and become a lane of grim faces, at the end of which he saw the Justice, a shabby, collarless, graying man in spectacles, beckoning him. He felt no floor under his bare feet; he seemed to walk beneath the palpable weight of the grim turning faces. His father, stiff in his black Sunday coat donned not for the trial but for the moving, did not even look at him. *He aims for me to lie,* he thought, again with that frantic grief and despair. *And I will have to do hit.*

"What's your name, boy?" the Justice said.

"Colonel Sartoris Snopes," the boy whispered.

"Hey?" the Justice said. "Talk louder. Colonel Sartoris? I reckon anybody named for Colonel Sartoris* in this country can't help but tell the truth, can they?" The boy said nothing. *Enemy! Enemy!* he thought; for a moment he could not even see, could not see that the Justice's face was kindly nor discern that his voice was troubled when he spoke to the man named Harris: "Do you want me to question this boy?" But he could hear, and during those subsequent long seconds while there was absolutely no sound in the crowded little room save that of quiet and intent breathing it was as if he had swung outward at the end of a grape vine, over a ravine, and at the top of the swing had been caught in a prolonged instant of mesmerized gravity, weightless in time.

"No!" Harris said violently, explosively. "Damnation! Send him out of here!" Now time, the fluid world, rushed beneath him again, the voices coming to him again through the smell of cheese and sealed meat, the fear and despair and the old grief of blood:

"This case is closed. I can't find against you, Snopes, but I can give you advice. Leave this country and don't come back to it."

His father spoke for the first time, his voice cold and harsh, level, without emphasis: "I aim to. I don't figure to stay in a country among people who . . ." he said something unprintable and vile, addressed to no one.

"That'll do," the Justice said. "Take your wagon and get out of this country before dark. Case dismissed."

His father turned, and he followed the stiff black coat, the wiry figure walking a little stiffly from where a Confederate provost's man's musket ball had taken him in the heel on a stolen horse thirty years ago, followed the two backs

---

*Colonel Sartoris: Commander of the Mississippi Civil War regiment in which Abner Snopes claims membership.

now, since his older brother had appeared from somewhere in the crowd, no taller than the father but thicker, chewing tobacco steadily, between the two lines of grim-faced men and out of the store and across the worn gallery and down the sagging steps and among the dogs and half-grown boys in the mild May dust, where as he passed a voice hissed:

"Barn burner!"

Again he could not see, whirling; there was a face in a red haze, moonlike, bigger than the full moon, the owner of it half again his size, he leaping in the red haze toward the face, feeling no blow, feeling no shock when his head struck the earth, scrabbling up and leaping again, feeling no blow this time either and tasting no blood, scrabbing up to see the other boy in full flight and himself already leaping into pursuit as his father's hand jerked him back, the harsh, cold voice speaking above him: "Go get in the wagon."

It stood in a grove of locusts and mulberries across the road. His two hulking sisters in their Sunday dresses and his mother and her sister in calico and sunbonnets were already in it, sitting on and among the sorry residue of the dozen and more movings which even the boy could remember—the battered stove, the broken beds and chairs, the clock inlaid with mother-of-pearl, which would not run, stopped at some fourteen minutes past two o'clock of a dead and forgotten day and time, which had been his mother's dowry. She was crying, though when she saw him she drew her sleeve across her face and began to descend from the wagon. "Get back," the father said.

"He's hurt. I got to get some water and wash his . . ."

"Get back in the wagon," his father said. He got in too, over the tail-gate. His father mounted to the seat where the older brother already sat and struck the gaunt mules two savage blows with the peeled willow, but without heat. It was not even sadistic; it was exactly that same quality which in later years would cause his descendants to over-run the engine before putting a motor car into motion, striking and reining back in the same movement. The wagon went on, the store with its quiet crowd of grimly watching men dropped behind; a curve in the road hid it. *Forever* he thought. *Maybe he's done satisfied now, now that he has . . .* stopping himself, not to say it aloud even to himself. His mother's hand touched his shoulder.

"Does hit hurt?" she said.

"Naw," he said. "Hit don't hurt. Lemme be."

"Can't you wipe some of the blood off before hit dries?"

"I'll wash to-night," he said. "Lemme be, I tell you."

The wagon went on. He did not know where they were going. None of them ever did or ever asked, because it was always somewhere, always a house of sorts waiting for them a day or two days or even three days away. Likely his father had already arranged to make a crop on another farm before he . . . Again he had to stop himself. He (the father) always did. There was something about his wolflike independence and even courage when the advantage was at least neutral which impressed strangers, as if they got from his latent ravening ferocity not so much a sense of dependability as a feeling that his ferocious conviction in the rightness of his own actions would be of advantage to all whose interest lay with his.

That night they camped, in a grove of oaks and beeches where a spring ran. The nights were still cool and they had a fire against it, of a rail lifted from a nearby fence and cut into lengths—a small fire, neat, niggard almost, a shrewd fire; such fires were his father's habit and custom always, even in freezing weather. Older, the boy might have remarked this and wondered why not a big one; why should not a man who had not only seen the waste and extravagance of war, but who had in his blood an inherent voracious prodigality with material not his own, have burned everything in sight? Then he might have gone a step farther and thought that that was the reason: that niggard blaze was the living fruit of nights passed during those four years in the woods hiding from all men, blue or gray, with his strings of horses (captured horses, he called them). And older still, he might have divined the true reason: that the element of fire spoke to some deep mainspring of his father's being, as the element of steel or of powder spoke to other men, as the one weapon for the preservation of integrity, else breath were not worth the breathing, and hence to be regarded with respect and used with discretion.

But he did not think this now and he had seen those same niggard blazes all his life. He merely ate his supper beside it and was already half asleep over his iron plate when his father called him, and once more he followed the stiff back, the stiff and ruthless limp, up the slope and on to the starlit road where, turning, he could see his father against the stars but without face or depth—a shape black, flat, and bloodless as though cut from tin in the iron folds of the frockcoat which had not been made for him, the voice harsh like tin and without heat like tin:

"You were fixing to tell them. You would have told him."

He didn't answer. His father struck him with the flat of his hand on the side of the head, hard but without heat, exactly as he had struck the two mules at the store, exactly as he would strike either of them with any stick in order to kill a horse fly, his voice still without heat or anger: "You're getting to be a man. You got to learn. You got to learn to stick to your own blood or you ain't going to have any blood to stick to you. Do you think either of them, any man there this morning, would? Don't you know all they wanted was a chance to get at me because they knew I had them beat? Eh?" Later, twenty years later, he was to tell himself, "If I had said they wanted only truth, justice, he would have hit me again." But now he said nothing. He was not crying. He just stood there. "Answer me," his father said.

"Yes," he whispered. His father turned.

"Get on to bed. We'll be there tomorrow."

Tomorrow they were there. In the early afternoon the wagon stopped before a paintless two-room house identical almost with the dozen others it had stopped before even in the boy's ten years, and again, as on the other dozen occasions, his mother and aunt got down and began to unload the wagon, although his two sisters and his father and brother had not moved.

"Likely hit ain't fitten for hawgs," one of the sisters said.

"Nevertheless, fit it will and you'll hog it and like it," his father said. "Get out of them chairs and help your Ma unload."

The two sisters got down, big, bovine, in a flutter of cheap ribbons; one of them drew from the jumbled wagon bed a battered lantern, the other a worn broom. His father handed the reins to the older son and began to climb stiffly over the wheel. "When they get unloaded, take the team to the barn and feed them." Then he said, and at first the boy thought he was still speaking to his brother: "Come with me."

"Me?" he said.

"Yes," his father said. "You."

"Abner," his mother said. His father paused and looked back—the harsh level stare beneath the shaggy, graying, irascible brows.

"I reckon I'll have a word with the man that aims to begin tomorrow owning me body and soul for the next eight months."

They went back up the road. A week ago—or before last night, that is—he would have asked where they were going, but not now. His father had struck him before last night but never before had he paused afterward to explain why; it was as if the blow and the following calm, outrageous voice still rang, repercussed, divulging nothing to him save the terrible handicap of being young, the light weight of his few years, just heavy enough to prevent his soaring free of the world as it seemed to be ordered but not heavy enough to keep him footed solid in it, to resist it and try to change the course of its events.

Presently he could see the grove of oaks and cedars and the other flowering trees and shrubs where the house would be, though not the house yet. They walked beside a fence massed with honeysuckle and Cherokee roses and came to a gate swinging open between two brick pillars, and now, beyond a sweep of drive, he saw the house for the first time and at that instant he forgot his father and the terror and despair both, and even when he remembered his father again (who had not stopped) the terror and despair did not return. Because, for all the twelve movings, they had sojourned until now in a poor country, a land of small farms and fields and houses, and he had never seen a house like this before. *Hit's big as a courthouse* he thought quietly, with a surge of peace and joy whose reason he could not have thought into words, being too young for that: *They are safe from him. People whose lives are a part of this peace and dignity are beyond his touch, he no more to them than a buzzing wasp: capable of stinging for a little moment but that's all; the spell of this peace and dignity rendering even the barns and stable and cribs which belong to it impervious to the puny flames he might contrive . . .* this, the peace and joy, ebbing for an instant as he looked again at the stiff black back, the stiff and implacable limp of the figure which was not dwarfed by the house, for the reason that it had never looked big anywhere and which now, against the serene columned backdrop, had more than ever that impervious quality of something cut ruthlessly from tin, depthless, as though, sidewise to the sun, it would cast no shadow. Watching him, the boy remarked the absolutely undeviating course which his father held and saw the stiff foot come squarely down in a pile of fresh droppings where a horse had stood in the drive and which his father could have avoided by a simple change of stride. But it ebbed only for a moment, though he could not have thought this into words either, walking on in the spell of the house, which he could even want but without envy, without sorrow, certainly never with that ravening and jealous rage which unknown to him walked in the ironlike black coat before him: *Maybe he will feel it too. Maybe it will even change him now from what maybe he couldn't help but be.*

They crossed the portico. Now he could hear his father's stiff foot as it came down on the boards with clocklike finality, a sound out of all proportion to the displacement of the body it bore and which was not dwarfed either by the white door before it, as though it had attained to a sort of vicious and ravening minimum not to be dwarfed by anything—the flat, wide, black hat, the formal coat of broadcloth which had once been black but which had now that friction-glazed greenish cast of the bodies of old house flies, the lifted sleeve which was too large, the lifted hand like a curled claw. The door opened so promptly that the boy knew the Negro must have been watching them all the time, an old man with neat grizzled hair, in a linen jacket, who stood barring the door with his body, saying, "Wipe yo foots, white man, fo you come in here. Major ain't home nohow."

"Get out of my way, nigger," his father said, without heat too, flinging the door back and the Negro also and entering, his hat still on his head. And now the boy saw the prints of the stiff foot on the doorjamb and saw them appear on the pale rug behind the machinelike deliberation of the foot which seemed to bear (or transmit) twice the weight which the body compassed. The Negro was shouting "Miss Lula! Miss Lula!" somewhere behind them, then the boy, deluged as though by a warm wave by a suave turn of the carpeted stair and a pendant glitter of chandeliers and a mute gleam of gold frames, heard the swift feet and saw her too, a lady—perhaps he had never seen her like before either—in a gray, smooth gown with lace at the throat and an apron tied at the waist and the sleeves turned back, wiping cake or biscuit dough from her hands with a towel as she came up the hall, looking not at his father at all but at the tracks on the blond rug with an expression of incredulous amazement.

"I tried," the Negro cried. "I tole him to . . ."

"Will you please go away?" she said in a shaking voice. "Major de Spain is not at home. Will you please go away?"

His father had not spoken again. He did not speak again. He did not even look at her. He just stood stiff in the center of the rug, in his hat, the shaggy iron-gray brows twitching slightly above the pebble-colored eyes as he appeared to examine the house with brief deliberation. Then with the same deliberation he turned; the boy watched him pivot on the good leg and saw the stiff foot drag round the arc of the turning, leaving a final long and fading smear. His father never looked at it, he never once looked down at the rug. The Negro held the door. It closed behind them, upon the hysteric and indistinguishable woman-wail. His father stopped at the top of the steps and scraped his boot clean on the edge of it. At the gate he stopped again. He stood for a moment, planted

stiffly on the stiff foot, looking back at the house. "Pretty and white, ain't it?"
he said. "That's sweat. Nigger sweat. Maybe it ain't white enough yet to suit
him. Maybe he wants to mix some white sweat with it."

Two hours later the boy was chopping wood behind the house within
which his mother and aunt and the two sisters (the mother and aunt, not the
two girls, he knew that; even at this distance and muffled by walls the flat loud
voices of the two girls emanated an incorrigible idle inertia) were setting up the
stove to prepare a meal, when he heard the hooves and saw the linen-clad man
on a fine sorrel mare, whom he recognized even before he saw the rolled rug
in front of the Negro youth following on a fat bay carriage horse—a suffused,
angry face vanishing, still at full gallop, beyond the corner of the house where
his father and brother were sitting in the two tilted chairs; and a moment later,
almost before he could have put the axe down, he heard the hooves again and
watched the sorrel mare go back out of the yard, already galloping again. Then
his father began to shout one of the sisters' names, who presently emerged
backward from the kitchen door dragging the rolled rug along the ground by
one end while the other sister walked behind it.

"If you ain't going to tote, go on and set up the wash pot," the first said.

"You, Sarty!" the second shouted. "Set up the wash pot!" His father
appeared at the door, framed against that shabbiness, as he had been against that
other bland perfection, impervious to either, the mother's anxious face at his
shoulder.

"Go on," the father said. "Pick it up." The two sisters stopped, broad,
lethargic; stooping, they presented an incredible expanse of pale cloth and a
flutter of tawdry ribbons.

"If I thought enough of a rug to have to git hit all the way from France
I wouldn't keep hit where folks coming in would have to tromp on hit," the
first said. They raised the rug.

"Abner," the mother said. "Let me do it."

"You go back and git dinner," his father said. "I'll tend to this."

From the woodpile through the rest of the afternoon the boy watched
them, the rug spread flat in the dust beside the bubbling wash pot, the two sisters
stooping over it with that profound and lethargic reluctance, while the father
stood over them in turn, implacable and grim, driving them though never
raising his voice again. He could smell the harsh homemade lye they were using;
he saw his mother come to the door once and look toward them with an
expression not anxious now but very like despair; he saw his father turn, and
he fell to with the axe and saw from the corner of his eye his father raise from
the ground a flattish fragment of field stone and examine it and return to the
pot, and this time his mother actually spoke: "Abner. Abner. Please don't.
Please, Abner."

Then he was done too. It was dusk; the whippoorwills had already begun.
He could smell coffee from the room where they would presently eat the cold
food remaining from the mid-afternoon meal, though when he entered the
house he realized they were having coffee again probably because there was a
fire on the hearth, before which the rug now lay spread over the backs of the

two chairs. The tracks of his father's foot were gone. Where they had been were now long, water-cloudy scoriations resembling the sporadic course of a Lilliputian mowing machine.

It still hung there while they ate the cold food and then went to bed, scattered without order or claim up and down the two rooms, his mother in one bed, where his father would later lie, the older brother in the other, himself, the aunt, and the two sisters on pallets on the floor. But his father was not in bed yet. The last thing the boy remembered was the depthless, harsh silhouette of the hat and coat bending over the rug and it seemed to him that he had not even closed his eyes when the silhouette was standing over him, the fire almost dead behind it, the stiff foot prodding him awake. "Catch up the mule," his father said.

When he returned with the mule his father was standing in the black door, the rolled rug over his shoulder. "Ain't you going to ride?" he said.

"No. Give me your foot."

He bent his knee into his father's hand, the wiry, surprising power flowed smoothly, rising, he rising with it, on to the mule's bare back (they had owned a saddle once; the boy could remember it though not when or where) and with the same effortlessness his father swung the rug up in front of him. Now in the starlight they retraced the afternoon's path, up the dusty road rife with honeysuckle, through the gate and up the black tunnel of the drive to the lightless house, where he sat on the mule and felt the rough warp of the rug drag across his thighs and vanish.

"Don't you want me to help?" he whispered. His father did not answer and now he heard again that stiff foot striking the hollow portico with that wooden and clocklike deliberation, that outrageous overstatement of the weight it carried. The rug, hunched, not flung (the boy could tell that even in the darkness) from his father's shoulder struck the angle of wall and floor with a sound unbelievably loud, thunderous, then the foot again, unhurried and enormous; a light came on in the house and the boy sat, tense, breathing steadily and quietly and just a little fast, though the foot itself did not increase its beat at all, descending the steps now; now the boy could see him.

"Don't you want to ride now?" he whispered. "We kin both ride now," the light within the house altering now, flaring up and sinking. *He's coming down the stairs now,* he thought. He had already ridden the mule up beside the horse block; presently his father was up behind him and he doubled the reins over and slashed the mule across the neck, but before the animal could begin to trot the hard, thin arm came around him, the hard, knotted hand jerking the mule back to a walk.

In the first red rays of the sun they were in the lot, putting plow gear on the mules. This time the sorrel mare was in the lot before he heard it at all, the rider collarless and even bareheaded, trembling, speaking in a shaking voice as the woman in the house had done, his father merely looking up once before stooping again to the hame he was buckling, so that the man on the mare spoke to his stooping back:

"You must realize you have ruined that rug. Wasn't there anybody here, any of your women . . ." he ceased, shaking, the boy watching him, the older brother leaning now in the stable door, chewing, blinking slowly and steadily at nothing apparently. "It cost a hundred dollars. But you never had a hundred dollars. You never will. So I'm going to charge you twenty bushels of corn against your crop. I'll add it in your contract and when you come to the commissary you can sign it. That won't keep Mrs. de Spain quiet but maybe it will teach you to wipe your feet off before you enter her house again."

Then he was gone. The boy looked at his father, who still had not spoken or even looked up again, who was now adjusting the logger-head in the hame.

"Pap," he said. His father looked at him—the inscrutable face, the shaggy brows beneath which the gray eyes glinted coldly. Suddenly the boy went toward him, fast, stopping as suddenly. "You done the best you could!" he cried. "If he wanted hit done different why didn't he wait and tell you how? He won't git no twenty bushels! He won't git none! We'll gether hit and hide hit! I kin watch . . ."

"Did you put the cutter back in that straight stock like I told you?"

"No, sir," he said.

"Then go do it."

That was Wednesday. During the rest of that week he worked steadily, at what was within his scope and some which was beyond it, with an industry that did not need to be driven nor even commanded twice; he had this from his mother, with the difference that some at least of what he did he liked to do, such as splitting wood with the half-size axe which his mother and aunt had earned, or saved money somehow, to present him with at Christmas. In company with the two older women (and on one afternoon, even one of the sisters), he built pens for the shoat and the cow which were a part of his father's contract with the landlord, and one afternoon, his father being absent, gone somewhere on one of the mules, he went to the field.

They were running a middle buster now, his brother holding the plow straight while he handled the reins, and walking beside the straining mule, the rich black soil shearing cool and damp against his bare ankles, he thought *Maybe this is the end of it. Maybe even that twenty bushels that seems hard to have to pay for just a rug will be a cheap price for him to stop forever and always from being what he used to be;* thinking, dreaming now, so that his brother had to speak sharply to him to mind the mule: *Maybe he even won't collect the twenty bushels. Maybe it will all add up and balance and vanish—corn, rug, fire; the terror and grief; the being pulled two ways like between two teams of horses—gone, done with for ever and ever.*

Then it was Saturday; he looked up from beneath the mule he was harnessing and saw his father in the black coat and hat. "Not that," his father said. "The wagon gear." And then, two hours later, sitting in the wagon bed behind his father and brother on the seat, the wagon accomplished a final curve, and he saw the weathered paintless store with its tattered tobacco- and patent-medicine posters and the tethered wagons and saddle animals below the gallery. He mounted the gnawed steps behind his father and brother, and there again was the lane of quiet, watching faces for the three of them to walk through. He saw the man in spectacles sitting at the plank table and he did not need to be told this was a Justice of the Peace; he sent one glare of fierce, exultant, partisan defiance at the man in collar and cravat now, whom he had seen but twice before in his life, and that on a galloping horse, who now wore on his face an expression not of rage but of amazed unbelief which the boy could not have known was at the incredible circumstance of being sued by one of his own tenants, and came and stood against his father and cried at the Justice: "He ain't done it! He ain't burnt . . ."

"Go back to the wagon," his father said.

"Burnt?" the Justice said. "Do I understand this rug was burned too?"

"Does anybody here claim it was?" his father said. "Go back to the wagon." But he did not, he merely retreated to the rear of the room, crowded as that other had been, but not to sit down this time, instead, to stand pressing among the motionless bodies, listening to the voices:

"And you claim twenty bushels of corn is too high for the damage you did to the rug?"

"He brought the rug to me and said he wanted the tracks washed out of it. I washed the tracks out and took the rug back to him."

"But you didn't carry the rug back to him in the same condition it was in before you made the tracks on it."

His father did not answer, and now for perhaps half a minute there was no sound at all save that of breathing, the faint, steady suspiration of complete and intent listening.

"You decline to answer that, Mr. Snopes?" Again his father did not answer. "I'm going to find against you, Mr. Snopes. I'm going to find that you were responsible for the injury to Major de Spain's rug and hold you liable for it. But twenty bushels of corn seems a little high for a man in your circumstances to have to pay. Major de Spain claims it cost a hundred dollars. October corn will be worth about fifty cents. I figure that if Major de Spain can stand a ninety-five dollar loss on something he paid cash for, you can stand a five-dollar loss you haven't earned yet. I hold you in damages to Major de Spain to the amount of ten bushels of corn over and above your contract with him, to be paid to him out of your crop at gathering time. Court adjourned."

It had taken no time hardly, the morning was but half begun. He thought they would return home and perhaps back to the field, since they were late, far behind all other farmers. But instead his father passed on behind the wagon, merely indicating with his hand for the older brother to follow with it, and crossed the road toward the blacksmith shop opposite, pressing on after his father, overtaking him, speaking, whispering up at the harsh, calm face beneath the weathered hat: "He won't git no ten bushels neither. He won't git one. We'll . . ." until his father glanced for an instant down at him, the face absolutely calm, the grizzled eyebrows tangled above the cold eyes, the voice almost pleasant, almost gentle:

"You think so? Well, we'll wait till October anyway."

The matter of the wagon—the setting of a spoke or two and the tightening of the tires—did not take long either, the business of the tires accomplished by driving the wagon into the spring branch behind the shop and letting it stand

there, the mules nuzzling into the water from time to time, and the boy on the
seat with the idle reins, looking up the slope and through the sooty tunnel of
the shed where the slow hammer rang and where his father sat on an upended
cypress bolt, easily, either talking or listening, still sitting there when the boy
brought the dripping wagon up out of the branch and halted it before the door.

"Take them on to the shade and hitch," his father said. He did so and
returned. His father and the smith and a third man squatting on his heels inside
the door were talking, about crops and animals; the boy, squatting too in the
ammoniac dust and hoof-parings and scales of rust, heard his father tell a long
and unhurried story out of the time before the birth of the older brother even
when he had been a professional horsetrader. And then his father came up
beside him where he stood before a tattered last year's circus poster on the other
side of the store, gazing rapt and quiet at the scarlet horses, the incredible
poisings and convolutions of tulle and tights and the painted leers of comedians,
and said, "It's time to eat."

But not at home. Squatting beside his brother against the front wall, he
watched his father emerge from the store and produce from a paper sack a
segment of cheese and divide it carefully and deliberately into three with his
pocket knife and produce crackers from the same sack. They all three squatted
on the gallery and ate, slowly, without talking; then in the store again, they
drank from a tin dipper tepid water smelling of the cedar bucket and of living
beech trees. And still they did not go home. It was a horse lot this time, a tall
rail fence upon and along which men stood and sat and out of which one by
one horses were led, to be walked and trotted and then cantered back and forth
along the road while the slow swapping and buying went on and the sun began
to slant westward, they—the three of them—watching and listening, the older
brother with his muddy eyes and his steady, inevitable tobacco, the father
commenting now and then on certain of the animals, to no one in particular.

It was after sundown when they reached home. They ate supper by lamplight, then, sitting on the doorstep, the boy watched the night fully accomplish,
listening to the whippoorwills and the frogs, when he heard his mother's voice:
"Abner! No! No! Oh, God. Oh, God. Abner!" and he rose, whirled, and saw
the altered light through the door where a candle stub now burned in a bottle
neck on the table and his father, still in the hat and coat, at once formal and
burlesque as though dressed carefully for some shabby and ceremonial violence,
emptying the reservoir of the lamp back into the five-gallon kerosene can from
which it had been filled, while the mother tugged at his arm until he shifted the
lamp to the other hand and flung her back, not savagely or viciously, just hard,
into the wall, her hands flung out against the wall for balance, her mouth open
and in her face the same quality of hopeless despair as had been in her voice.
Then his father saw him standing in the door.

"Go to the barn and get that can of oil we were oiling the wagon with,"
he said. The boy did not move. Then he could speak.

"What . . ." he cried. "What are you . . ."

"Go get that oil," his father said. "Go."

Then he was moving, running, outside the house, toward the stable: this the old habit, the old blood which he had not been permitted to choose for himself, which had been bequeathed him willy nilly and which had run for so long (and who knew where, battening on what of outrage and savagery and lust) before it came to him. *I could keep on,* he thought. *I could run on and on and never look back, never need to see his face again. Only I can't. I can't,* the rusted can in his hand now, the liquid sploshing in it as he ran back to the house and into it, into the sound of his mother's weeping in the next room, and handed the can to his father.

"Ain't you going to even send a nigger?" he cried. "At least you sent a nigger before!"

This time his father didn't strike him. The hand came even faster than the blow had, the same hand which had set the can on the table with almost excruciating care flashing from the can toward him too quick for him to follow it, gripping him by the back of his shirt and on to tiptoe before he had seen it quit the can, the face stooping at him in breathless and frozen ferocity, the cold, dead voice speaking over him to the older brother who leaned aginst the table, chewing with that steady, curious, sidewise motion of cows:

"Empty the can into the big one and go on. I'll catch up with you."

"Better tie him up to the bedpost," the brother said.

"Do like I told you," the father said. Then the boy was moving, his bunched shirt and the hard, bony hand between his shoulder-blades, his toes just touching the floor, across the room and into the other one, past the sisters sitting with spread heavy thighs in the two chairs over the cold hearth, and to where his mother and aunt sat side by side on the bed, the aunt's arms about his mother's shoulders.

"Hold him," the father said. The aunt made a startled movement. "Not you," the father said. "Lennie. Take hold of him. I want to see you do it." His mother took him by the wrist. "You'll hold him better than that. If he gets loose don't you know what he is going to do? He will go up yonder." He jerked his head toward the road. "Maybe I'd better tie him."

"I'll hold him," his mother whispered.

"See you do then." Then his father was gone, the stiff foot heavy and measured upon the boards, ceasing at last.

Then he began to struggle. His mother caught him in both arms, he jerking and wrenching at them. He would be stronger in the end, he knew that. But he had no time to wait for it. "Lemme go!" he cried. "I don't want to have to hit you!"

"Let him go!" the aunt said. "If he don't go, before God, I am going up there myself!"

"Don't you see I can't?" his mother cried. "Sarty! Sarty! No! No! Help me, Lizzie!"

Then he was free. His aunt grasped at him but it was too late. He whirled, running, his mother stumbled forward on to her knees behind him, crying to the nearer sister: "Catch him, Net! Catch him!" But that was too late too, the sister (the sisters were twins, born at the same time, yet either of them now gave the impression of being, encompassing as much living meat and volume and weight as any other two of the family) not yet having begun to rise from the chair, her head, face, alone merely turned, presenting to him in the flying instant an astonishing expanse of young female features untroubled by any surprise even, wearing only an expression of bovine interest. Then he was out of the room, out of the house, in the mild dust of the starlit road and the heavy rifeness of honeysuckle, the pale ribbon unspooling with terrific slowness under his running feet, reaching the gate at last and turning in, running, his heart and lungs drumming, on up the drive toward the lighted house, the lighted door. He did not knock, he burst in, sobbing for breath, incapable for the moment of speech; he saw the astonished face of the Negro in the linen jacket without knowing when the Negro had appeared.

"De Spain!" he cried, panted. "Where's . . ." then he saw the white man too emerging from a white door down the hall. "Barn!" he cried. "Barn!"

"What?" the white man said. "Barn?"

"Yes!" the boy cried "Barn!"

"Catch him!" the white man shouted.

But it was too late this time too. The Negro grasped his shirt, but the entire sleeve, rotten with washing, carried away, and he was out that door too and in the drive again, and had actually never ceased to run even while he was screaming into the white man's face.

Behind him the white man was shouting, "My horse! Fetch my horse!" and he thought for an instant of cutting across the park and climbing the fence into the road, but he did not know the park nor how high the vine-massed fence might be and he dared not risk it. So he ran on down the drive, blood and breath roaring; presently he was in the road again though he could not see it. He could not hear either: the galloping mare was almost upon him before he heard her, and even then he held his course, as if the very urgency of his wild grief and need must in a moment more find him wings, waiting until the ultimate instant to hurl himself aside and into the weed-choked roadside ditch as the horse thundered past and on, for an instant in furious silhouette against the stars, the tranquil early summer night sky which, even before the shape of the horse and rider vanished, stained abruptly and violently upward: a long, swirling roar incredible and soundless, blotting the stars, and he springing up and into the road again, running again, knowing it was too late yet still running even after he heard the shot and an instant later, two shots, pausing now without knowing he had ceased to run, crying "Pap! Pap!", running again before he knew he had begun to run, stumbling, tripping over something and scrabbling up again without ceasing to run, looking backward over his shoulder at the glare as he got up, running on among the invisible trees, panting, sobbing, "Father! Father!"

At midnight he was sitting on the crest of a hill. He did not know it was midnight and he did not know how far he had come. But there was no glare behind him now and he sat now, his back toward what he had called home for four days anyhow, his face toward the dark woods which he would enter when breath was strong again, small, shaking steadily in the chill darkness, hugging himself into the remainder of his thin, rotten shirt, the grief and despair now no longer terror and fear but just grief and despair. *Father. My father,* he thought. "He was brave!" he cried suddenly, aloud but not loud, no more than a whisper. "He was! He was in the war! He was in Colonel Sartoris' cav'ry!" not knowing that his father had gone to that war a private in the fine old European sense, wearing no uniform, admitting the authority of and giving fidelity to no man or army or flag, going to war as Malbrouck* himself did: for booty—it meant nothing and less than nothing to him if it were enemy booty or his own.

The slow constellations wheeled on. It would be dawn and then sun-up after a while and he would be hungry. But that would be tomorrow and now he was only cold, and walking would cure that. His breathing was easier now and he decided to get up and go on, and then he found that he had been asleep because he knew it was almost dawn, the night almost over. He could tell that from the whippoorwills. They were everywhere now among the dark trees below him, constant and inflectioned and ceaseless, so that, as the instant for giving over to the day birds drew nearer and nearer, there was no interval at all between them. He got up. He was a little stiff, but walking would cure that too as it would the cold, and soon there would be the sun. He went on down the hill, toward the dark woods within which the liquid silver voices of the birds called unceasing—the rapid and urgent beating of the urgent and quiring heart of the late spring night. He did not look back.

Writing Assignments for "Barn Burning"

I. Brief Papers
   A. 1. What did Abner Snopes do during the Civil War?
      2. Explain why Sarty feels peace and joy when he first sees Major de Spain's house.
      3. Why does Sarty's mother beg Abner to let her clean Major de Spain's rug?
      4. Explain why Abner Snopes burns down barns.

   B. Choose one assertion below and develop or refute it:
      1. "Barn Burning" is a story in which justice triumphs.
      2. Abner Snopes is a sadist: he enjoys inflicting pain upon others.
      3. The story has an affirmative ending.
      4. The story repudiates the commandment to "honor thy father and mother."

   C. 1. Do you find Abner Snopes wholly despicable or do you see some admirable qualities in him?
      2. Who do you like best, Sarty or his unnamed older brother? Why?
      3. Are you glad that Sarty runs away? Why?

*Malbrouck: The French spelling for Marlborough; John Churchill, first Duke of Marlborough, was rewarded with an earldom for deserting King James II of England and joining the opposing forces of William of Orange, later King William III.

4. What do you think of Sarty's mother? How does your attitude toward her affect your interpretation of the story?

II. Longer Papers

A. A *developing* character changes in important ways during a story whereas a *static* character remains essentially unchanged. Things happen *to* a static character but things happen *within* a developing one. Is Sarty a static or developing character?

B. What does "Barn Burning" tell us about human freedom?

C. Compare Sarty to his brother and sisters in order to explain why it is he—and not they—who runs away.

D. Focusing on the story's last two paragraphs but using earlier hints as well, explain what you think the future holds for Sarty.

E. Ab tells Sarty, "You're getting to be a man. You got to learn." What is it, precisely, that Sarty learns during the story? Does it make him a man?

III. Comparative Papers

A. Develop or refute the assertion that both "Barn Burning" and "Four Summers" make clear that human freedom is an illusion: we have no choice except to become what our heredity and environment determine.

B. Explain why, given what she wants to say, Joyce Carol Oates chooses the first-person narrative point of view for "Four Summers" and why, given what he wants to say, Faulkner chooses the third-person point of view.

C. Compare the concluding paragraphs of "Barn Burning" and "Four Summers" in order to demonstrate differences in tone between the two stories.

D. Your high school principal has invited you to give a 10-minute talk on Career Day to juniors and seniors who want to work with children and teenagers. Keeping your audience in mind, prepare the script for a talk in which you share your insights from two or more stories about growing up: "Four Summers," "Barn Burning," "Araby," "I'm a Fool," "The Downward Path to Wisdom," and "Indian Camp."

CHARLOTTE PERKINS GILMAN
The Yellow Wall-Paper

Before Reading

Read the first five or six sentences of "The Yellow Wall-Paper." Then, in 10 minutes of free writing, explain what you expect from the rest of the story.

It is very seldom that mere ordinary people like John and myself secure ancestral halls for the summer.

A colonial mansion, a hereditary estate. I would say a haunted house, and reach the height of romantic felicity—but that would be asking too much of fate!

Still I will proudly declare that there is something queer about it.

Else, why should it be let so cheaply? And why have stood so long untenanted?

John laughs at me, of course, but one expects that in marriage.

John is practical in the extreme. He has no patience with faith, an intense horror of superstition, and he scoffs openly at any talk of things not to be felt and seen and put down in figures.

John is a physician, and *perhaps*—(I would not say it to a living soul, of course, but this is dead paper and a great relief to my mind—) *perhaps* that is one reason I do not get well faster.

You see he does not believe I am sick!

And what can one do?

If a physician of high standing, and one's own husband, assures friends and relatives that there is really nothing the matter with one but temporary nervous depression—a slight hysterical tendency—what is one to do?

My brother is also a physician, and also of high standing, and he says the same thing.

So I take phosphates or phosphites—whichever it is, and tonics, and journeys, and air, and exercise, and am absolutely forbidden to "work" until I am well again.

Personally, I disagree with their ideas.

Personally, I believe that congenial work, with excitement and change, would do me good.

But what is one to do?

I did write for a while in spite of them; but it *does* exhaust me a good deal—having to be so sly about it, or else meet with heavy opposition.

I sometimes fancy that in my condition if I had less opposition and more

THE YELLOW WALL-PAPER   First published in 1892. Charlotte Perkins (Stetson) Gilman (1860–1935) was born in Connecticut and lived in California and other locations. She was active in the struggle to secure voting rights for women and in other social and political movements.

society and stimulus—but John says the very worst thing I can do is to think about my condition, and I confess it always makes me feel bad.

So I will let it alone and talk about the house.

The most beautiful place! It is quite alone, standing well back from the road, quite three miles from the village. It makes me think of English places that you read about, for there are hedges and walls and gates that lock, and lots of separate little houses for the gardeners and people.

There is a *delicious* garden! I never saw such a garden—large and shady, full of box-bordered paths, and lined with long grape-covered arbors with seats under them.

There were greenhouses, too, but they are all broken now.

There was some legal trouble, I believe, something about the heirs and co-heirs; anyhow, the place has been empty for years.

That spoils my ghostliness, I am afraid, but I don't care—there is something strange about the house—I can feel it.

I even said so to John one moonlight evening, but he said what I felt was a *draught,* and shut the window.

I get unreasonably angry with John sometimes. I'm sure I never used to be so sensitive. I think it is due to this nervous condition.

But John says if I feel so, I shall neglect proper self-control; so I take pains to control myself—before him, at least, and that makes me very tired.

I don't like our room a bit. I wanted one downstairs that opened on the piazza and had roses all over the window, and such pretty old-fashioned chintz hangings! but John would not hear of it.

He said there was only one window and not room for two beds, and no near room for him if he took another.

He is very careful and loving, and hardly lets me stir without special direction.

I have a schedule prescription for each hour in the day; he takes all care from me, and so I feel basely ungrateful not to value it more.

He said we came here solely on my account, that I was to have perfect rest and all the air I could get. "Your exercise depends on your strength, my dear," said he, "and your food somewhat on your appetite; but air you can absorb all the time." So we took the nursery at the top of the house.

It is a big, airy room, the whole floor nearly, with windows that look all ways, and air and sunshine galore. It was nursery first and then playroom and gymnasium, I should judge; for the windows are barred for little children, and there are rings and things in the walls.

The paint and paper look as if a boys' school had used it. It is stripped off—the paper—in great patches all around the head of my bed, about as far as I can reach, and in a great place on the other side of the room low down. I never saw a worse paper in my life.

One of those sprawling flamboyant patterns committing every artistic sin.

It is dull enough to confuse the eye in following, pronounced enough to constantly irritate and provoke study, and when you follow the lame uncertain curves for a little distance they suddenly commit suicide—plunge off at outrageous angles, destroy themselves in unheard of contradictions.

The color is repellent, almost revolting; a smouldering unclean yellow, strangely faded by the slow-turning sunlight.

It is a dull yet lurid orange in some places, a sickly sulphur tint in others.

No wonder the children hated it! I should hate it myself if I had to live in this room long.

There comes John, and I must put this away,—he hates to have me write a word.

We have been here two weeks, and I haven't felt like writing before, since that first day.

I am sitting by the window now, up in this atrocious nursery, and there is nothing to hinder my writing as much as I please, save lack of strength.

John is away all day, and even some nights when his cases are serious.

I am glad my case is not serious!

But these nervous troubles are dreadfully depressing.

John does not know how much I really suffer. He knows there is no *reason* to suffer, and that satisfies him.

Of course it is only nervousness. It does weigh on me so not to do my duty in any way!

I meant to be such a help to John, such a real rest and comfort, and here I am a comparative burden already!

Nobody would believe what an effort it is to do what little I am able—to dress and entertain, and order things.

It is fortunate Mary is so good with the baby. Such a dear baby!

And yet I *cannot* be with him, it makes me so nervous.

I suppose John never was nervous in his life. He laughs at me so about this wall-paper!

At first he meant to repaper the room, but afterwards he said that I was letting it get the better of me, and that nothing was worse for a nervous patient than to give way to such fancies.

He said that after the wall-paper was changed it would be the heavy bedstead, and then the barred windows, and then that gate at the head of the stairs, and so on.

"You know the place is doing you good," he said, "and really, dear, I don't care to renovate the house just for a three months' rental."

"Then do let us go downstairs," I said, "there are such pretty rooms there."

Then he took me in his arms and called me a blessed little goose, and said he would go down cellar, if I wished, and have it whitewashed into the bargain.

But he is right enough about the beds and windows and things.

It is as airy and comfortable a room as any one need wish, and, of course, I would not be so silly as to make him uncomfortable just for a whim.

I'm really getting quite fond of the big room, all but that horrid paper.

Out of one window I can see the garden, those mysterious deep-shaded arbors, the riotous old-fashioned flowers, and bushes and gnarly trees.

Out of another I get a lovely view of the bay and a little private wharf belonging to the estate. There is a beautiful shaded lane that runs down there from the house. I always fancy I see people walking in these numerous paths and arbors, but John has cautioned me not to give way to fancy in the least. He says that with my imaginative power and habit of storymaking, a nervous weakness like mine is sure to lead to all manner of excited fancies, and that I ought to use my will and good sense to check the tendency. So I try.

I think sometimes that if I were only well enough to write a little it would relieve the press of ideas and rest me.

But I find I get pretty tired when I try.

It is so discouraging not to have any advice and companionship about my work. When I get really well, John says we will ask Cousin Henry and Julia down for a long visit; but he says he would as soon put fireworks in my pillow-case as to let me have those stimulating people about now.

I wish I could get well faster.

But I must not think about that. This paper looks to me as if it *knew* what a vicious influence it had!

There is a recurrent spot where the pattern lolls like a broken neck and two bulbous eyes stare at you upside down.

I get positively angry with the impertinence of it and the everlastingness. Up and down and sideways they crawl, and those absurd, unblinking eyes are everywhere. There is one place where two breadths didn't match, and the eyes go all up and down the line, one a little higher than the other.

I never saw so much expression in an inanimate thing before, and we all know how much expression they have! I used to lie awake as a child and get more entertainment and terror out of blank walls and plain furniture than most children could find in a toy-store.

I remember what a kindly wink the knobs of our big, old bureau used to have, and there was one chair that always seemed like a strong friend.

I used to feel that if any of the other things looked too fierce I could always hop into that chair and be safe.

The furniture in this room is no worse than inharmonious, however, for we had to bring it all from downstairs. I suppose when this was used as a playroom they had to take the nursery things out, and no wonder! I never saw such ravages as the children have made here.

The wall-paper, as I said before, is torn off in spots, and it sticketh closer than a brother—they must have had perseverance as well as hatred.

Then the floor is scratched and gouged and splintered, the plaster itself is dug out here and there, and this great heavy bed which is all we found in the room, looks as if it had been through the wars.

But I don't mind it a bit—only the paper.

There comes John's sister. Such a dear girl as she is, and so careful of me! I must not let her find me writing.

She is a perfect and enthusiastic housekeeper, and hopes for no better profession. I verily believe she thinks it is the writing which made me sick!

But I can write when she is out, and see her a long way off from these windows.

There is one that commands the road, a lovely shaded winding road, and one that just looks off over the country. A lovely country, too, full of great elms and velvet meadows.

This wall-paper has a kind of sub-pattern in a different shade, a particularly irritating one, for you can only see it in certain lights, and not clearly then.

But in the places where it isn't faded and where the sun is just so—I can see a strange, provoking, formless sort of figure, that seems to skulk about behind that silly and conspicuous front design.

There's sister on the stairs!

Well, the Fourth of July is over! The people are all gone and I am tired out. John thought it might do me good to see a little company, so we just had mother and Nellie and the children down for a week.

Of course I didn't do a thing. Jennie sees to everything now.

But it tired me all the same.

John says if I don't pick up faster he shall send me to Weir Mitchell* in the fall.

But I don't want to go there at all. I had a friend who was in his hands once, and she says he is just like John and my brother, only more so!

Besides, it is such an undertaking to go so far.

I don't feel as if it was worth while to turn my hand over for anything, and I'm getting dreadfully fretful and querulous.

I cry at nothing, and cry most of the time.

Of course I don't when John is here, or anybody else, but when I am alone.

And I am alone a good deal just now. John is kept in town very often by serious cases, and Jennie is good and lets me alone when I want her to.

So I walk a little in the garden or down that lovely lane, sit on the porch under the roses, and lie down up here a good deal.

I'm getting really fond of the room in spite of the wall-paper. Perhaps *because* of the wall-paper.

It dwells in my mind so!

I lie here on this great immovable bed—it is nailed down, I believe—and follow that pattern about by the hour. It is as good as gymnastics, I assure you. I start, we'll say, at the bottom, down in the corner over there where it has not been touched, and I determine for the thousandth time that I *will* follow that pointless pattern to some sort of a conclusion.

I know a little of the principle of design, and I know this thing was not arranged on any laws of radiation, or alternation, or repetition, or symmetry, or anything else that I ever heard of.

*Weir Mitchell: Silas Weir Mitchell (1829–1914), American physician and author best known for his psychological and historical writings.

It is repeated, of course, by the breadths, but not otherwise.

Looked at in one way each breadth stands alone, the bloated curves and flourishes—a kind of "debased Romanesque" with *delirium tremens* go waddling up and down in isolated columns of fatuity.

But, on the other hand, they connect diagonally, and the sprawling outlines run off in great slanting waves of optic horror, like a lot of wallowing seaweeds in full chase.

The whole thing goes horizontally, too, at least it seems so, and I exhaust myself in trying to distinguish the order of its going in that direction.

They have used a horizontal breadth for a frieze, and that adds wonderfully to the confusion.

There is one end of the room where it is almost intact, and there, when the crosslights fade and the low sun shines directly upon it, I can almost fancy radiation after all,—the interminable grotesques seem to form around a common centre and rush off in headlong plunges of equal distraction.

It makes me tired to follow it. I will take a nap I guess.

I don't know why I should write this.

I don't want to.

I don't feel able.

And I know John would think it absurd. But I *must* say what I feel and think in some way—it is such a relief!

But the effort is getting to be greater than the relief.

Half the time now I am awfully lazy, and lie down ever so much.

John says I mustn't lose my strength, and has me take cod liver oil and lots of tonics and things, to say nothing of ale and wine and rare meat.

Dear John! He loves me very dearly, and hates to have me sick. I tried to have a real earnest reasonable talk with him the other day, and tell him how I wish he would let me go and make a visit to Cousin Henry and Julia.

But he said I wasn't able to go, nor able to stand it after I got there; and I did not make out a very good case for myself, for I was crying before I had finished.

It is getting to be a great effort for me to think straight. Just this nervous weakness I suppose.

And dear John gathered me up in his arms, and just carried me upstairs and laid me on the bed, and sat by me and read to me till it tired my head.

He said I was his darling and his comfort and all he had, and that I must take care of myself for his sake, and keep well.

He says no one but myself can help me out of it, that I must use my will and self-control and not let any silly fancies run away with me.

There's one comfort, the baby is well and happy, and does not have to occupy this nursery with the horrid wall-paper.

If we had not used it, that blessed child would have! What a fortunate escape! Why, I wouldn't have a child of mine, an impressionable little thing, live in such a room for worlds.

I never thought of it before, but it is lucky that John kept me here after all, I can stand it so much easier than a baby, you see.

Of course I never mention it to them any more—I am too wise,—but I keep watch of it all the same.

There are things in that paper that nobody knows but me, or ever will.

Behind that outside pattern the dim shapes get clearer every day.

It is always the same shape, only very numerous.

And it is like a woman stooping down and creeping about behind that pattern. I don't like it a bit. I wonder—I begin to think—I wish John would take me away from here!

It is so hard to talk with John about my case, because he is so wise, and because he loves me so.

But I tried it last night.

It was moonlight. The moon shines in all around just as the sun does.

I hate to see it sometimes, it creeps so slowly, and always comes in by one window or another.

John was asleep and I hated to waken him, so I kept still and watched the moonlight on that undulating wall-paper till I felt creepy.

The faint figure behind seemed to shake the pattern, just as if she wanted to get out.

I got up softly and went to feel and see if the paper *did* move, and when I came back John was awake.

"What is it, little girl?" he said. "Don't go walking about like that—you'll get cold."

I thought it was a good time to talk, so I told him that I really was not gaining here, and that I wished he would take me away.

"Why, darling!" said he, "our lease will be up in three weeks, and I can't see how to leave before.

"The repairs are not done at home, and I cannot possibly leave town just now. Of course if you were in any danger, I could and would, but you really are better, dear, whether you can see it or not. I am a doctor, dear, and I know. You are gaining flesh and color, your appetite is better, I feel really much easier about you."

"I don't weigh a bit more," said I, "nor as much; and my appetite may be better in the evening when you are here, but it is worse in the morning when you are away!"

"Bless her little heart!" said he with a big hug, "she shall be as sick as she pleases! But now let's improve the shining hours by going to sleep, and talk about it in the morning!"

"And you won't go away?" I asked gloomily.

"Why, how can I, dear? It is only three weeks more and then we will take a nice little trip of a few days while Jennie is getting the house ready. Really dear you are better!"

"Better in body perhaps—" I began, and stopped short, for he sat up straight and looked at me with such a stern, reproachful look that I could not say another word.

"My darling," said he, "I beg of you, for my sake and for our child's sake, as well as for your own, that you will never for one instant let that idea enter your mind! There is nothing so dangerous, so fascinating, to a temperament like yours. It is a false and foolish fancy. Can you not trust me as a physician when I tell you so?"

So of course I said no more on that score, and we went to sleep before long. He thought I was asleep first, but I wasn't, and lay there for hours trying to decide whether that front pattern and the back pattern really did move together or separately.

On a pattern like this, by daylight, there is a lack of sequence, a defiance of law, that is a constant irritant to a normal mind.

The color is hideous enough, and unreliable enough, and infuriating enough, but the pattern is torturing.

You think you have mastered it, but just as you get well underway in following, it turns a back-somersault and there you are. It slaps you in the face, knocks you down, and tramples upon you. It is like a bad dream.

The outside pattern is a florid arabesque, reminding one of a fungus. If you can imagine a toadstool in joints, an interminable string of toadstools, budding and sprouting in endless convolutions—why, that is something like it.

That is, sometimes!

There is one marked peculiarity about this paper, a thing nobody seems to notice but myself, and that is that it changes as the light changes.

When the sun shoots in through the east window—I always watch for that first long, straight ray—it changes so quickly that I never can quite believe it.

That is why I watch it always.

By moonlight—the moon shines in all night when there is a moon—I wouldn't know it was the same paper.

At night in any kind of light, in twilight, candlelight, lamplight, and worst of all by moonlight, it becomes bars! The outside pattern I mean, and the woman behind it is as plain as can be.

I didn't realize for a long time what the thing was that showed behind, that dim sub-pattern, but now I am quite sure it is a woman.

By daylight she is subdued, quiet. I fancy it is the pattern that keeps her so still. It is so puzzling. It keeps me quiet by the hour.

I lie down ever so much now. John says it is good for me, and to sleep all I can.

Indeed he started the habit by making me lie down for an hour after each meal.

It is a very bad habit I am convinced, for you see I don't sleep.

And that cultivates deceit, for I don't tell them I'm awake—O no!

The fact is I am getting a little afraid of John.

He seems very queer sometimes, and even Jennie has an inexplicable look.

It strikes me occasionally, just as a scientific hypothesis,—that perhaps it is the paper!

I have watched John when he did not know I was looking, and come into the room suddenly on the most innocent excuses, and I've caught him several times *looking at the paper!* And Jennie too. I caught Jennie with her hand on it once.

She didn't know I was in the room, and when I asked her in a quiet, a very quiet voice, with the most restrained manner possible, what she was doing with the paper—she turned around as if she had been caught stealing, and looked quite angry—asked me why I should frighten her so!

Then she said that the paper stained everything it touched, that she had found yellow smooches on all my clothes and John's, and she wished we would be more careful!

Did not that sound innocent? But I know she was studying that pattern, and I am determined that nobody shall find it out but myself!

Life is very much more exciting now than it used to be. You see I have something more to expect, to look forward to, to watch. I really do eat better, and am more quiet than I was.

John is so pleased to see me improve! He laughed a little the other day, and said I seemed to be flourishing in spite of my wall-paper.

I turned it off with a laugh. I had no intention of telling him it was *because* of the wall-paper—he would make fun of me. He might even want to take me away.

I don't want to leave now until I have found it out. There is a week more, and I think that will be enough.

I'm feeling ever so much better! I don't sleep much at night, for it is so interesting to watch developments; but I sleep a good deal in the daytime.

In the daytime it is tiresome and perplexing.

There are always new shoots on the fungus, and new shades of yellow all over it. I cannot keep count of them, though I have tried conscientiously.

It is the strangest yellow, that wall-paper! It makes me think of all the yellow things I ever saw—not beautiful ones like buttercups, but old foul, bad yellow things.

But there is something else about that paper—the smell! I noticed it the moment we came into the room, but with so much air and sun it was not bad. Now we have had a week of fog and rain, and whether the windows are open or not, the smell is here.

It creeps all over the house.

I find it hovering in the dining-room, skulking in the parlor, hiding in the hall, lying in wait for me on the stairs.

It gets into my hair.

Even when I go to ride, if I turn my head suddenly and surprise it—there is that smell!

Such a peculiar odor, too! I have spent hours in trying to analyze it, to find what it smelled like.

It is not bad—at first, and very gentle, but quite the subtlest, most enduring odor I ever met.

In this damp weather it is awful. I wake up in the night and find it hanging over me.

It used to disturb me at first. I thought seriously of burning the house—to reach the smell.

But now I am used to it. The only thing I can think of that it is like is the *color* of the paper! A yellow smell.

There is a very funny mark on this wall, low down, near the mopboard. A streak that runs round the room. It goes behind every piece of furniture, except the bed, a long, straight, even *smooch,* as if it had been rubbed over and over.

I wonder how it was done and who did it, and what they did it for. Round and round and round—round and round and round!—it makes me dizzy!

I really have discovered something at last.

Through watching so much at night, when it changes so, I have finally found out.

The front pattern *does* move—and no wonder! The woman behind shakes it!

Sometimes I think there are a great many women behind, and sometimes only one, and she crawls around fast, and her crawling shakes it all over.

Then in the very bright spots she keeps still, and in the very shady spots she just takes hold of the bars and shakes them hard.

And she is all the time trying to climb through. But nobody could climb through that pattern—it strangles so; I think that is why it has so many heads.

They get through, and then the pattern strangles them off and turns them upside down, and makes their eyes white!

If those heads were covered or taken off it would not be half so bad.

I think that woman gets out in the daytime!

And I'll tell you why—privately—I've seen her!

I can see her out of every one of my windows!

It is the same woman, I know, for she is always creeping, and most women do not creep by daylight.

I see her in that long shaded lane, creeping up and down. I see her in those dark grape arbors, creeping all around the garden.

I see her on that long road under the trees, creeping along, and when a carriage comes she hides under the blackberry vines.

I don't blame her a bit. It must be very humiliating to be caught creeping by daylight!

I always lock the door when I creep by daylight. I can't do it at night, for I know John would suspect something at once.

And John is so queer now, that I don't want to irritate him. I wish he would take another room! Besides, I don't want anybody to get that woman out at night but myself.

I often wonder if I could see her out of all the windows at once.

But, turn as fast as I can, I can only see out of one at one time.

And though I always see her, she *may* be able to creep faster than I can turn!

I have watched her sometimes away off in the open country, creeping as fast as a cloud shadow in a high wind.

If only that top pattern could be gotten off from the under one! I mean to try it, little by little.

I have found out another funny thing, but I shan't tell it this time! It does not do to trust people too much.

There are only two more days to get this paper off, and I believe John is beginning to notice. I don't like the look in his eyes.

And I heard him ask Jennie a lot of professional questions about me. She had a very good report to give.

She said I slept a good deal in the daytime.

John knows I don't sleep very well at night, for all I'm so quiet!

He asked me all sorts of questions, too, and pretended to be very loving and kind.

As if I couldn't see through him!

Still, I don't wonder he acts so, sleeping under this paper for three months.

It only interests me, but I feel sure John and Jennie are secretly affected by it.

Hurrah! This is the last day, but it is enough. John is to stay in town over night, and won't be out until this evening.

Jennie wanted to sleep with me—the sly thing! but I told her I should undoubtedly rest better for a night all alone.

That was clever, for really I wasn't alone a bit! As soon as it was moonlight and that poor thing began to crawl and shake the pattern, I got up and ran to help her.

I pulled and she shook, I shook and she pulled, and before morning we had peeled off yards of that paper.

A strip about as high as my head and half around the room.

And then when the sun came and that awful pattern began to laugh at me, I declared I would finish it to-day!

We go away to-morrow, and they are moving all my furniture down again to leave things as they were before.

Jennie looked at the wall in amazement, but I told her merrily that I did it out of pure spite at the vicious thing.

She laughed and said she wouldn't mind doing it herself, but I must not get tired.

How she betrayed herself that time!

But I am here, and no person touches this paper but me,—not *alive!*

She tried to get me out of the room—it was too patent! But I said it was so quiet and empty and clean now that I believed I would lie down again and sleep all I could; and not to wake me even for dinner—I would call when I woke.

So now she is gone, and the servants are gone, and the things are gone, and there is nothing left but that great bedstead nailed down, with the canvas mattress we found on it.

We shall sleep downstairs to-night, and take the boat home to-morrow.

I quite enjoy the room, now it is bare again.

How those children did tear about here!

This bedstead is fairly gnawed!

But I must get to work.

I have locked the door and thrown the key down into the front path.

I don't want to go out, and I don't want to have anybody come in, till John comes.

I want to astonish him.

I've got a rope up here that even Jennie did not find. If that woman does get out, and tries to get away, I can tie her!

But I forgot I could not reach far without anything to stand on!

This bed will *not* move!

I tried to lift and push it until I was lame, and then I got so angry I bit off a little piece at one corner—but it hurt my teeth.

Then I peeled off all the paper I could reach standing on the floor. It sticks horribly and the pattern just enjoys it! All those strangled heads and bulbous eyes and waddling fungus growths just shriek with derision!

I am getting angry enough to do something desperate. To jump out of the window would be admirable exercise, but the bars are too strong even to try.

Besides I wouldn't do it. Of course not. I know well enough that a step like that is improper and might be misconstrued.

I don't like to *look* out of the windows even—there are so many of those creeping women, and they creep so fast.

I wonder if they all come out of that wall-paper as I did?

But I am securely fastened now by my well-hidden rope—you don't get *me* out in the road there!

I suppose I shall have to get back behind the pattern when it comes night, and that is hard!

It is so pleasant to be out in this great room and creep around as I please!

I don't want to go outside. I won't, even if Jennie asks me to.

For outside you have to creep on the ground, and everything is green instead of yellow.

But here I can creep smoothly on the floor, and my shoulder just fits in that long smooch around the wall, so I cannot lose my way.

Why there's John at the door!

It is no use, young man, you can't open it!

How he does call and pound!

Now he's crying for an axe.

It would be a shame to break down that beautiful door!

"John dear!" said I in the gentlest voice, "the key is down by the front steps, under a plantain leaf!"

That silenced him for a few moments.

Then he said—very quietly indeed, "Open the door, my darling!"

"I can't," said I. "The key is down by the front door under a plantain leaf!"

And then I said it again, several times, very gently and slowly, and said it so often that he had to go and see, and he got it of course, and came in. He stopped short by the door.

"What is the matter?" he cried. "For God's sake, what are you doing!"

I kept on creeping just the same, but I looked at him over my shoulder.

"I've got out at last," said I, "in spite of you and Jane. And I've pulled off most of the paper, so you can't put me back!"

Now why should that man have fainted? But he did, and right across my path by the wall, so that I had to creep over him every time!

Writing Assignments for "The Yellow Wall-Paper"

I. Brief Papers

A. 1. Explain the setting of the story. (Is the narrator right in thinking that the building used to be a boy's school?)
   2. Summarize John's attitude toward his wife.
   3. Why does John insist that his wife stay in the upstairs room?
   4. Explain John's attitude toward his wife's writing.
   5. Why does John faint at the end of the story?

B. Argue for or against one of the assertions below:
   1. The narrator is right in saying that "It is so hard to talk with John about my case . . ." (p. 117).
   2. John does more to prevent his wife's recovery than to help it.
   3. John is deliberately trying to drive his wife mad.
   4. Sexist attitudes contribute significantly to—and may actually be the cause of—the narrator's problems.

C. 1. Is there anything that could have been done, at the beginning of the summer, to help the narrator?
   2. John says that he loves his wife. Do you believe him?
   3. Do you find the story plausible? Why or why not?

II. Longer Papers

A. John, the narrator's husband, "has no patience with faith, an intense horror of superstition, and he scoffs openly at any talk of things not to be felt and seen and put down in figures" (p. 111). Does the story as a whole endorse or challenge his position?

B. Trace the progress of the narrator's "temporary nervous depression" (p. 111).

C. A parable is an illustrative story that answers a question, teaches a lesson, or draws a moral. Show that "The Yellow Wall-Paper" can be read as a parable of women's plight in a man's world.

D. What kinds of patterns can you find in "The Yellow Wall-Paper"? What does the story as a whole say about patterns?

E. Explore some of the connections between the style of the story—the way it is presented—and its content and meaning.

III. Dramatic Irony in "The Yellow Wall-Paper"

Using the sentences below as a starting point, construct a short essay that defines *dramatic irony* and illustrates its use in "The Yellow Wall-Paper."

1. There are many instances of dramatic irony in "The Yellow Wall-Paper."
2. "The Yellow Wall-Paper" is a short story.
3. "The Yellow Wall-Paper" is written by Charlotte Perkins Gilman.
4. These are instances of a character saying or believing one thing when the opposite is in fact true.

5. Here is an example of dramatic irony.
6. It occurs in the opening line of the story.
7. The narrator describes herself as an "ordinary" person.

8. This description is ironic.
9. The narrator is anything but ordinary.
10. That is something we gradually learn.

11. This is another example of dramatic irony.
12. The narrator writes, "I am glad my case is not serious!" (p. 113).

13. This is actually the truth.
14. Her case is serious.
15. It is so serious that within three months she becomes totally unable to distinguish what is real from what is imaginary.

16. But irony is also directed at the narrator's husband.
17. It is almost as much irony as is directed at the narrator herself.
18. The narrator's husband is a doctor.

19. This is ironic.
20. The doctor should know better.
21. The doctor believes that his wife is in no real danger.

22. The doctor even thinks this.
23. His thinking this is ironic.
24. His wife is improving.

25. "John is so pleased to see me improve!" (p. 119).
26. In fact, his wife is getting progressively worse.

27. This is one of the story's most ironic statements.
28. The narrator says that her husband is "so wise" (p. 117).

29. This is really the case.
30. The husband turns out to be wrong in just about every conceivable way.
31. The many instances of dramatic irony in "The Yellow Wall-Paper" all underline this.
32. There is a human tendency to confuse truth and error.

CONRAD AIKEN
Silent Snow, Secret Snow

Before Reading

Free write for 10 minutes about a time when you retreated—at least temporarily—from the real everyday world into a world of your own. What were the attractions of your own world?

I

Just why it should have happened, or why it should have happened just when it did, he could not, of course, possibly have said; nor perhaps would it even have occurred to him to ask. The thing was above all a secret, something to be preciously concealed from Mother and Father; and to that very fact it owed an enormous part of its deliciousness. It was like a peculiarly beautiful trinket to be carried unmentioned in one's trouser pocket—a rare stamp, an old coin, a few tiny gold links found trodden out of shape on the path in the park, a pebble of carnelian, a seashell distinguishable from all others by an unusual spot or stripe—and, as if it were any one of these, he carried around with him everywhere a warm and persistent and increasingly beautiful sense of possession. Nor was it only a sense of possession—it was also a sense of protection. It was as if, in some delightful way, his secret gave him a fortress, a wall behind which he could retreat into heavenly seclusion. This was almost the first thing he had noticed about it—apart from the oddness of the thing itself—and it was this that now again, for the fiftieth time, occurred to him, as he sat in the little schoolroom. It was the half-hour for geography. Miss Buell was revolving with one finger, slowly, a huge terrestrial globe which had been placed on her desk. The green and yellow continents passed and repassed, questions were asked and

SILENT SNOW, SECRET SNOW   First published in 1932. Conrad Aiken (1889–1973) was born in Savannah, Georgia, and grew up in Massachusetts.

answered, and now the little girl in front of him, Deirdre, who had a funny little constellation of freckles on the back of her neck, exactly like the Big Dipper, was standing up and telling Miss Buell that the equator was the line that ran round the middle.

Miss Buell's face, which was old and grayish and kindly, with gray stiff curls beside the cheeks, and eyes that swam very brightly, like little minnows, behind thick glasses, wrinkled itself into a complication of amusements.

"Ah! I see. The earth is wearing a belt, or a sash. Or someone drew a line round it!"

"Oh no—not that—I mean—"

In the general laughter, he did not share, or only a very little. He was thinking about the Arctic and Antarctic regions, which of course, on the globe, were white. Miss Buell was now telling them about the tropics, the jungles, the steamy heat of equatorial swamps, where the birds and butterflies, and even the snakes, were like living jewels. As he listened to these things, he was already, with a pleasant sense of half-effort, putting his secret between himself and the words. Was it really an effort at all? For effort implied something voluntary, and perhaps even something one did not especially want; whereas this was distinctly pleasant, and came almost of its own accord. All he needed to do was to think of that morning, the first one, and then of all the others—

But it was all so absurdly simple! It had amounted to so little. It was nothing, just an idea—and just why it should have become so wonderful, so permanent, was a mystery—a very pleasant one, to be sure, but also, in an amusing way, foolish. However, without ceasing to listen to Miss Buell, who had now moved up to the north temperate zones, he deliberately invited his memory of the first morning. It was only a moment or two after he had waked up—or perhaps the moment itself. But was there, to be exact, an exact moment? Was one awake all at once? or was it gradual? Anyway, it was after he had stretched a lazy hand up toward the headrail, and yawned, and then relaxed again among his warm covers, all the more grateful on a December morning, that the thing had happened. Suddenly, for no reason, he had thought of the postman, he remembered the postman. Perhaps there was nothing so odd in that. After all, he heard the postman almost every morning in his life—his heavy boots could be heard clumping round the corner at the top of the little cobbled hill-street, and then, progressively nearer, progressively louder, the double knock at each door, the crossings and re-crossings of the street, till finally the clumsy steps came stumbling across to the very door, and the tremendous knock came which shook the house itself.

(Miss Buell was saying, "Vast wheat-growing areas in North America and Siberia."

Deirdre had for the moment placed her left hand across the back of her neck.)

But on this particular morning, the first morning, as he lay there with his eyes closed, he had for some reason *waited* for the postman. He wanted to hear him come round the corner. And that was precisely the joke—he never did. He never came. He never had come—*round the corner*—again. For when at last the steps were heard, they had already, he was quite sure, come a little down the hill, to the first house; and even so, the steps were curiously different—they were softer, they had a new secrecy about them, they were muffled and indistinct; and while the rhythm of them was the same, it now said a new thing—it said peace, it said remoteness, it said cold, it said sleep. And he had understood the situation at once—nothing could have seemed simpler—there had been snow in the night, such as all winter he had been longing for; and it was this which had rendered the postman's first footsteps inaudible, and the later ones faint. Of course! How lovely! And even now it must be snowing—it was going to be a snowy day—the long white ragged lines were drifting and sifting across the street, across the faces of the old houses, whispering and hushing, making little triangles of white in the corners between cobblestones, seething a little when the wind blew them over the ground to a drifted corner; and so it would be all day, getting deeper and deeper and silenter and silenter.

(Miss Buell was saying, "Land of perpetual snow.")

All this time, of course (while he lay in bed), he had kept his eyes closed, listening to the nearer progress of the postman, the muffled footsteps thumping and slipping on the snow-sheathed cobbles; and all the other sounds—the double knocks, a frosty far-off voice or two, a bell ringing thinly and softly as if under a sheet of ice—had the same slightly abstracted quality, as if removed by one degree from actuality—as if everything in the world had been insulated by snow. But when at last, pleased, he opened his eyes, and turned them toward the window, to see for himself this long-desired and now so clearly imagined miracle—what he saw instead was brilliant sunlight on a roof; and when, astonished, he jumped out of bed and stared down into the street, expecting to see the cobbles obliterated by the snow, he saw nothing but the bare bright cobbles themselves.

Queer, the effect this extraordinary surprise had had upon him—all the following morning he had kept with him a sense as of snow falling about him, a secret screen of new snow between himself and the world. If he had not dreamed such a thing—and how could he have dreamed it while awake?—how else could one explain it? In any case, the delusion had been so vivid as to affect his entire behavior. He could not now remember whether it was on the first or the second morning—or was it even the third?—that his mother had drawn attention to some oddness in his manner.

"But my darling"—she had said at the breakfast table—"what has come over you? You don't seem to be listening. . . ."

And how often that very thing had happened since!

(Miss Buell was now asking if anyone knew the difference between the North Pole and the Magnetic Pole. Deirdre was holding up her flickering brown hand, and he could see the four white dimples that marked the knuckles.)

Perhaps it hadn't been either the second or third morning—or even the fourth or fifth. How could he be sure? How could he be sure just when the delicious *progress* had become clear? Just when it had really *begun?* The intervals weren't very precise. . . . All he now knew was, that at some point or other— perhaps the second day, perhaps the sixth—he had noticed that the presence of the snow was a little more insistent, the sound of it clearer; and, conversely, the sound of the postman's footsteps more indistinct. Not only could he not hear the steps come round the corner, he could not even hear them at the first house. It was below the first house that he heard them; and then, a few days later, it was below the second house that he heard them; and a few days later again, below the third. Gradually, gradually, the snow was becoming heavier, the sound of its seething louder, the cobblestones more and more muffled. When he found, each morning, on going to the window, after the ritual of listening, that the roofs and cobbles were as bare as ever, it made no difference. This was, after all, only what he had expected. It was even what pleased him, what rewarded him: the thing was his own, belonged to no one else. No one else knew about it, not even his mother and father. There, outside, were the bare cobbles; and here, inside, was the snow. Snow growing heavier each day, muffling the world, hiding the ugly, and deadening increasingly—above all— the steps of the postman.

"But, my darling"—she had said at the luncheon table—"what has come over you? You don't seem to listen when people speak to you. That's the third time I've asked you to pass your plate. . . ."

How was one to explain this to Mother? or to Father? There was, of course, nothing to be done about it: nothing. All one could do was to laugh embarrassedly, pretend to be a little ashamed, apologize, and take a sudden and somewhat disingenuous interest in what was being done or said. The cat had stayed out all night. He had a curious swelling on his left cheek—perhaps somebody had kicked him, or a stone had struck him. Mrs. Kempton was or was not coming to tea. The house was going to be housecleaned, or "turned out," on Wednesday instead of Friday. A new lamp was provided for his evening work—perhaps it was eyestrain which accounted for this new and so peculiar vagueness of his—Mother was looking at him with amusement as she said this, but with something else as well. A new lamp? A new lamp. Yes, Mother, No, Mother, Yes, Mother. School is going very well. The geometry is very easy. The history is very dull. The geography is very interesting—particularly when it takes one to the North Pole. Why the North Pole? Oh, well, it would be fun to be an explorer. Another Peary or Scott or Shackleton.* And then abruptly he found his interest in the talk at an end, stared at the pudding on his plate, listened, waited, and began once more—ah, how heavenly, too, the first begin- nings—to hear or feel—for could he actually hear it?—the silent snow, the secret snow.

(Miss Buell was telling them about the search for the Northwest Passage, about Hendrik Hudson, the *Half Moon.*)†

---

*Peary or Scott or Shackleton: Robert Edwin Peary (1856–1920), American explorer and the first person to reach the North Pole (April 6, 1909); Robert Falcon Scott (1868–1912) and Sir Ernest Henry Shackleton (1874–1922) were both British explorers of the Antarctic.
†The Northwest Passage, Hendrik Hudson, the *Half Moon:* On his ship the *Half Moon,* explorer Hendrik Hudson (?–1611) searched for the Northwest Passage, a water route connecting the Atlantic and Pacific Oceans. He discovered the Hudson River in New York and Hudson Bay in Canada but not the Northwest Passage.

   This had been, indeed, the only distressing feature of the new experience; the fact that it so increasingly had brought him into a kind of mute misunderstanding, or even conflict, with his father and mother. It was as if he were trying to lead a double life. On the one hand, he had to be Paul Hasleman, and keep up the appearance of being that person—dress, wash, and answer intelligently when spoken to—; on the other, he had to explore this new world which had been opened to him. Nor could there be the slightest doubt—not the slightest—that the new world was the profounder and more wonderful of the two. It was irresistible. It was miraculous. Its beauty was simply beyond anything—beyond speech as beyond thought—utterly incommunicable. But how then, between the two worlds, of which he was thus constantly aware, was he to keep a balance? One must get up, one must go to breakfast, one must talk with Mother, go to school, do one's lessons—and, in all this, try not to appear too much of a fool. But if all the while one was also trying to extract the full deliciousness of another and quite separate existence, one which could not easily (if at all) be spoken of—how was one to manage? How was one to explain? Would it be safe to explain? Would it be absurd? Would it merely mean that he would get into some obscure kind of trouble?

   These thoughts came and went, came and went, as softly and secretly as the snow; they were not precisely a disturbance, perhaps they were even a pleasure; he liked to have them; their presence was something almost palpable, something he could stroke with his hand, without closing his eyes, and without ceasing to see Miss Buell and the schoolroom and the globe and the freckles on Deirdre's neck; nevertheless he did in a sense cease to see, or to see the obvious external world, and substituted for this vision the vision of snow, the sound of snow, and the slow, almost soundless, approach of the postman. Yesterday, it had been only at the sixth house that the postman had become audible; the snow was much deeper now, it was falling more swiftly and heavily, the sound of its seething was more distinct, more soothing, more persistent. And this morning, it had been—as nearly as he could figure—just above the seventh house—perhaps only a step or two above; at most, he had heard two or three footsteps before the knock had sounded. . . . And with each such narrowing of the sphere, each nearer approach of the limit at which the postman was first audible, it was odd how sharply was increased the amount of illusion which had to be carried into the ordinary business of daily life. Each day, it was harder to get out of bed, to go to the window, to look out at the—as always—perfectly empty and snowless street. Each day it was more difficult to go through the perfunctory motions of greeting Mother and Father at breakfast, to reply to their questions, to put his books together and go to school. And at school, how extraordinarily hard to conduct with success simultaneously the public life and the life that was secret! There were times when he longed—positively ached—to tell everyone about it—to burst out with it—only to be checked almost at once by a far-off feeling as of some faint absurdity which was inherent in it—but *was* it absurd?—and more importantly by a sense of mysterious power in his very secrecy. Yes; it must be kept secret. That, more and more, became clear. At whatever cost to himself, whatever pain to others—

(Miss Buell looked straight at him, smiling, and said, "Perhaps we'll ask Paul. I'm sure Paul will come out of his daydream long enough to be able to tell us. Won't you, Paul?" He rose slowly from his chair, resting one hand on the brightly varnished desk, and deliberately stared through the snow toward the blackboard. It was an effort, but it was amusing to make it. "Yes," he said slowly, "it was what we now call the Hudson River. This he thought to be the Northwest Passage. He was disappointed." He sat down again, and as he did so Deirdre half turned in her chair and gave him a shy smile, of approval and admiration.)

At whatever pain to others.

This part of it was very puzzling, very puzzling. Mother was very nice, and so was Father. Yes, that was all true enough. He wanted to be nice to them, to tell them everything—and yet, was it really wrong of him to want to have a secret place of his own?

At bed-time, the night before, Mother had said, "If this goes on, my lad, we'll have to see a doctor, we will! We can't have our boy—" But what was it she had said? "Live in another world"? "Live so far away"? The word "far" had been in it, he was sure, and then Mother had taken up a magazine again and laughed a little, but with an expression which wasn't mirthful. He had felt sorry for her. . . .

The bell rang for dismissal. The sound came to him through long curved parallels of falling snow. He saw Deirdre rise, and had himself risen almost as soon—but not quite as soon—as she.

II

On the walk homeward, which was timeless, it pleased him to see through the accompaniment, or counterpoint, of snow, the items of mere externality on his way. There were many kinds of brick in the sidewalks, and laid in many kinds of pattern. The garden walls, too, were various, some of wooden palings, some of plaster, some of stone. Twigs of bushes leaned over the walls: the little hard green winter-buds of lilac, on gray stems, sheathed and fat; other branches very thin and fine and black and desiccated. Dirty sparrows huddled in the bushes, as dull in color as dead fruit left in leafless trees. A single starling creaked on a weather vane. In the gutter, beside a drain, was a scrap of torn and dirty newspaper, caught in a little delta of filth; the word ECZEMA appeared in large capitals, and below it was a letter from Mrs. Amelia D. Cravath, 2100 Pine Street, Fort Worth, Texas, to the effect that after being a sufferer for years she had been cured by Caley's Ointment. In the little delta, beside the fan-shaped and deeply runneled continent of brown mud, were lost twigs, descended from their parent trees, dead matches, a rusty horse-chestnut burr, a small concentration of eggshell, a streak of yellow sawdust which had been wet and now was dry and congealed, a brown pebble, and a broken feather. Farther on was a cement sidewalk, ruled into geometrical parallelograms, with a brass inlay at one end commemorating the contractors who had laid it, and, halfway across, an irregular and random series of dog-tracks, immortalized in synthetic stone. He knew these well, and always stepped on them; to cover the little hollows with his own foot had always been a queer pleasure; today he did it once more, but perfunctorily and detachedly, all the while thinking of something else. That was a dog, a long time ago, who had made a mistake and walked on the cement while it was still wet. He had probably wagged his tail, but that hadn't been recorded. Now, Paul Hasleman, aged twelve, on his way home from school, crossed the same river, which in the meantime had frozen into rock. Homeward through the snow, the snow falling in bright sunshine. Homeward?

Then came the gateway with the two posts surmounted by egg-shaped stones which had been cunningly balanced on their ends, as if by Columbus,* and mortared in the very act of balance; a source of perpetual wonder. On the brick wall just beyond, the letter H had been stenciled, presumably for some purpose.

H? H.

The green hydrant, with a little green-painted chain attached to the brass screw-cap.

The elm tree, with the great gray wound in the bark, kidney-shaped, into which he always put his hand—to feel the cold but living wood. The injury, he had been sure, was due to the gnawings of a tethered horse. But now it deserved only a passing palm, a merely tolerant eye. There were more important things. Miracles. Beyond the thoughts of trees, mere elms. Beyond the thoughts of sidewalks, mere stone, mere brick, mere cement. Beyond the thoughts even of his own shoes, which trod these sidewalks obediently, bearing a burden—far above—of elaborate mystery. He watched them. They were not very well polished; he had neglected them, for a very good reason: they were one of the many parts of the increasing difficulty of the daily return to daily life, the morning struggle. To get up, having at last opened one's eyes, to go to the window, and discover no snow, to wash, to dress, to descend the curving stairs to breakfast—

At whatever pain to others, nevertheless, one must persevere in severance, since the incommunicability of the experience demanded it. It was desirable, of course, to be kind to Mother and Father, especially as they seemed to be worried, but it was also desirable to be resolute. If they should decide—as appeared likely—to consult the doctor, Doctor Howells, and have Paul inspected, his heart listened to through a kind of dictaphone, his lungs, his stomach—well, that was all right. He would go through with it. He would give them answer for question, too—perhaps such answers as they hadn't expected? No. That would never do. For the secret world must, at all costs, be preserved.

The bird-house in the apple tree was empty—it was the wrong time of year for wrens. The little round black door had lost its pleasure. The wrens were enjoying other houses, other nests, remoter trees. But this too was a notion which he only vaguely and grazingly entertained—as if, for the moment, he

---

*by Columbus: At a banquet in Spain following his discovery of the new world, Columbus was asked by an envious courtier whether others wouldn't have eventually accomplished exactly what he did. In response, Columbus challenged everyone present to try to balance an egg on its end. No one could. Columbus then smashed an egg down on the table and left it standing—to demonstrate that only after he himself had shown the way could others think about duplicating his feats.

merely touched an edge of it; there was something further on, which was already assuming a sharper importance; something which already teased at the corners of his eyes, teasing also at the corner of his mind. It was funny to think that he so wanted this, so awaited it—and yet found himself enjoying this momentary dalliance with the bird-house, as if for a quite deliberate postponement and enhancement of the approaching pleasure. He was aware of his delay, of his smiling and detached and now almost uncomprehending gaze at the little bird-house; he knew what he was going to look at next: it was his own little cobbled hill-street, his own house, the little river at the bottom of the hill, the grocer's shop with the cardboard man in the window—and now, thinking of all this, he turned his head, still smiling, and looking quickly right and left through the snow-laden sunlight.

And the mist of snow, as he had foreseen, was still on it—a ghost of snow falling in the bright sunlight, softly and steadily floating and turning and pausing, soundlessly meeting the snow that covered, as with a transparent mirage, the bare bright cobbles. He loved it—he stood still and loved it. Its beauty was paralyzing—beyond all words, all experience, all dream. No fairy story he had ever read could be compared with it—none had ever given him this extraordinary combination of ethereal loveliness with a something else, unnameable, which was just faintly and deliciously terrifying. What was this thing? As he thought of it, he looked upward toward his own bedroom window, which was open—and it was as if he looked straight into the room and saw himself lying half awake in his bed. There he was—at this very instant he was still perhaps actually there—more truly there than standing here at the edge of the cobbled hill-street, with one hand lifted to shade his eyes against the snow-sun. Had he indeed ever left his room in all this time? since that very first morning? Was the whole progress still being enacted there, was it still the same morning, and himself not yet wholly awake? And even now, had the postman not yet come round the corner? . . .

This idea amused him, and automatically, as he thought of it, he turned his head and looked toward the top of the hill. There was, of course, nothing there—nothing and no one. The street was empty and quiet. And all the more because of its emptiness it occurred to him to count the houses—a thing which, oddly enough, he hadn't before thought of doing. Of course, he had known there weren't many—many, that is, on his own side of the street, which were the ones that figured in the postman's progress—but nevertheless it came as something of a shock to find that there were precisely *six,* above his own house—his own house was the seventh.

Six!

Astonished, he looked at his own house—looked at the door, on which was the number thirteen—and then realized that the whole thing was exactly and logically and absurdly what he ought to have known. Just the same, the realization gave him abruptly, and even a little frighteningly, a sense of hurry. He was being hurried—he was being rushed. For—he knit his brow—he couldn't be mistaken—it was just above the *seventh* house, his *own* house, that the postman had first been audible this very morning. But in that case—in that case—did it mean that tomorrow he would hear nothing? The knock he had heard must have been the knock of their own door. Did it mean—and this was an idea which gave him a really extraordinary feeling of surprise—that he would never hear the postman again?—that tomorrow morning the postman would already have passed the house, in a snow so deep as to render his footsteps completely inaudible? That he would have made his approach down the snow-filled street so soundlessly, so secretly, that he, Paul Hasleman, there lying in bed, would not have waked in time, or waking, would have heard nothing?

But how could that be? Unless even the knocker should be muffled in the snow—frozen tight, perhaps? . . . But in that case—

A vague feeling of disappointment came over him; a vague sadness as if he felt himself deprived of something which he had long looked forward to, something much prized. After all this, all this beautiful progress, the slow delicious advance of the postman through the silent and secret snow, the knock creeping closer each day, and the footsteps nearer, the audible compass of the world thus daily narrowed, narrowed, narrowed, as the snow soothingly and beautifully encroached and deepened, after all this, was he to be defrauded of the one thing he had so wanted—to be able to count, as it were, the last two or three solemn footsteps, as they finally approached his own door? Was it all going to happen, at the end, so suddenly? or indeed, had it already happened? with no slow and subtle gradations of menace, in which he could luxuriate?

He gazed upward again, toward his own window which flashed in the sun; and this time almost with a feeling that it would be better if he *were* still in bed, in that room; for in that case this must still be the first morning, and there would be six more mornings to come—or, for that matter, seven or eight or nine—how could he be sure?—or even more.

III

After supper, the inquisition began. He stood before the doctor, under the lamp, and submitted silently to the usual thumpings and tappings.

"Now will you please say 'Ah!'?"

"Ah!"

"Now again, please, if you don't mind."

"Ah."

"Say it slowly, and hold it if you can—"

"Ah-h-h-h-h-h—"

"Good."

How silly all this was. As if it had anything to do with his throat! Or his heart, or lungs!

Relaxing his mouth, of which the corners, after all this absurd stretching, felt uncomfortable, he avoided the doctor's eyes, and stared toward the fire-place, past his mother's feet (in gray slippers) which projected from the green chair, and his father's feet (in brown slippers) which stood neatly side by side on the hearth rug.

"Hm. There is certainly nothing wrong there . . .."

He felt the doctor's eyes fixed upon him, and, as if merely to be polite, returned the look, but with a feeling of justifiable evasiveness.

"Now, young man, tell me—do you feel all right?"

"Yes, sir, quite all right."

"No headaches? no dizziness?"

"No, I don't think so."

"Let me see. Let's get a book, if you don't mind—yes, thank you, that will do splendidly—and now, Paul, if you'll just read it, holding it as you would normally hold it—"

He took the book and read:

"And another praise have I to tell for this the city our mother, the gift of a great god, a glory of the land most high; the might of horses, the might of young horses, the might of the sea. . . . For thou, son of Cronus, our lord Poseidon, hath throned herein this pride, since in these roads first thou didst show forth the curb that cures the rage of steeds. And the shapely oar, apt to men's hands, hath a wondrous speed on the brine, following the hundred-footed Nereids. . . . O land that art praised above all lands, now is it for thee to make those bright praises seen in deeds."*

He stopped, tentatively, and lowered the heavy book.

"No—as I thought—there is certainly no superficial sign of eyestrain."

Silence thronged the room, and he was aware of the focused scrutiny of the three people who confronted him. . . .

"We could have his eyes examined—but I believe it is something else."

"What could it be?" That was his father's voice.

"It's only this curious absent-mindedness—" This was his mother's voice.

In the presence of the doctor, they both seemed irritatingly apologetic.

"I believe it is something else. Now Paul—I would like very much to ask you a question or two. You will answer them, won't you—you know I'm an old, old friend of yours, eh? That's right! . . ."

His back was thumped twice by the doctor's fat fist—then the doctor was grinning at him with false amiability, while with one fingernail he was scratching the top button of his waistcoat. Beyond the doctor's shoulder was the fire, the fingers of flame making light prestidigitation against the sooty fireback, the soft sound of their random flutter the only sound.

"I would like to know—is there anything that worries you?"

The doctor was again smiling, his eyelids low against the little black pupils, in each of which was a tiny white bead of light. Why answer him? why answer him at all? "At whatever pain to others"—but it was all a nuisance, this necessity for resistance, this necessity for attention; it was as if one had been stood up on a brilliantly lighted stage, under a great round blaze of spotlight; as if one were

*"And another praise . . .": The passage Paul reads is from *Oedipus at Colonus* by the Greek dramatist Sophocles (495?–406 B.C.). In Greek mythology, Cronus was the ruler of the universe until overthrown by his son, Zeus. Poseidon was the Greek god of the sea and the builder of the walls of Troy. The Nereids were sea nymphs.

merely a trained seal, or a performing dog, or a fish, dipped out of an aquarium and held up by the tail. It would serve them right if he were merely to bark or growl. And meanwhile, to miss these last few precious hours, these hours of which each minute was more beautiful than the last, more menacing—! He still looked, as if from a great distance, at the beads of light in the doctor's eyes, at the fixed false smile, and then, beyond, once more at his mother's slippers, his father's slippers, the soft flutter of the fire. Even here, even amongst these hostile presences, and in this arranged light, he could see the snow, he could hear it—it was in the corners of the room, where the shadow was deepest, under the sofa, behind the half-opened door which led to the dining room. It was gentler here, softer, its seethe the quietest of whispers, as if, in deference to a drawing room, it had quite deliberately put on its "manners"; it kept itself out of sight, obliterated itself, but distinctly with an air of saying, "Ah, but just wait! Wait till we are alone together! Then I will begin to tell you something new! Something white! something cold! something sleepy! something of cease, and peace, and the long bright curve of space! Tell them to go away. Banish them. Refuse to speak. Leave them, go upstairs to your room, turn out the light and get into bed—I will go with you, I will be waiting for you, I will tell you a better story than Little Kay of the Skates, or The Snow Ghost—I will surround your bed, I will close the windows, pile a deep drift against the door, so that none will ever again be able to enter. Speak to them! . . . ." It seemed as if the little hissing voice came from a slow white spiral of falling flakes in the corner by the front window—but he could not be sure. He felt himself smiling, then, and said to the doctor, but without looking at him, looking beyond him still—

"Oh no, I think not—"

"But are you sure, my boy?"

His father's voice came softly and coldly then—the familiar voice of silken warning.

"You needn't answer at once, Paul—remember we're trying to help you—think it over and be quite sure, won't you?"

He felt himself smiling again, at the notion of being quite sure. What a joke! As if he weren't so sure that reassurance was no longer necessary, and all this cross-examination a ridiculous farce, a grotesque parody! What could they know about it? these gross intelligences, these humdrum minds so bound to the usual, the ordinary? Impossible to tell them about it! Why, even now, even now, with the proof so abundant, so formidable, so imminent, so appallingly present here in this very room, could they believe it?—could even his mother believe it? No—it was only too plain that if anything were said about it, the merest hint given, they would be incredulous—they would laugh—they would say "Absurd!"—think things about him which weren't true. . . .

"Why no, I'm not worried—why should I be?"

He looked then straight at the doctor's low-lidded eyes, looked from one of them to the other, from one bead of light to the other, and gave a little laugh.

The doctor seemed to be disconcerted by this. He drew back in his chair, resting a fat white hand on either knee. The smile faded slowly from his face.

"Well, Paul!" he said, and paused gravely, "I'm afraid you don't take this quite seriously enough. I think you perhaps don't quite realize—don't quite realize—" He took a deep quick breath and turned, as if helplessly, at a loss for words, to the others. But Mother and Father were both silent—no help was forthcoming.

"You must surely know, be aware, that you have not been quite yourself, of late? Don't you know that? . . ."

It was amusing to watch the doctor's renewed attempt at a smile, a queer disorganized look, as of confidential embarrassment.

"I feel all right, sir," he said, and again gave the little laugh.

"And we're trying to help you." The doctor's tone sharpened.

"Yes, sir, I know. But why? I'm all right. I'm just *thinking,* that's all."

His mother made a quick movement forward, resting a hand on the back of the doctor's chair.

"Thinking?" she said. "But my dear, about what?"

This was a direct challenge—and would have to be directly met. But before he met it, he looked again into the corner by the door, as if for reassurance. He smiled again at what he saw, at what he heard. The little spiral was still there, still softly whirling, like the ghost of a white kitten chasing the ghost of a white tail, and making as it did so the faintest of whispers. It was all right! If only he could remain firm, everything was going to be all right.

"Oh, about anything, about nothing—*you* know the way you do!"

"You mean—daydreaming?"

"Oh, no—thinking!"

"But thinking about *what?*"

"Anything."

He laughed a third time—but this time, happening to glance upward toward his mother's face, he was appalled at the effect his laughter seemed to have upon her. Her mouth had opened in an expression of horror. . . . This was too bad! Unfortunate! He had known it would cause pain, of course—but he hadn't expected it to be quite so bad as this. Perhaps—perhaps if he just gave them a tiny gleaming hint—?

"About the snow," he said.

"What on earth?" This was his father's voice. The brown slippers came a step nearer on the hearth-rug.

"But my dear, what do you mean?" This was his mother's voice.

The doctor merely stared.

"Just *snow,* that's all. I like to think about it."

"Tell us about it, my boy."

"But that's all it is. There's nothing to tell. *You* know what snow is?"

This he said almost angrily, for he felt that they were trying to corner him. He turned sideways so as no longer to face the doctor, and the better to see the inch of blackness between the window-sill and the lowered curtain—the cold inch of beckoning and delicious night. At once he felt better, more assured.

"Mother—can I go to bed, now, please? I've got a headache."

"But I thought you said—"

"It's just come. It's all these questions—! Can I, mother?"

"You can go as soon as the doctor has finished."

"Don't you think this thing ought to be gone into thoroughly, and *now?*" This was Father's voice. The brown slippers again came a step nearer, the voice was the well-known "punishment" voice, resonant and cruel.

"Oh, what's the use, Norman—"

Quite suddenly, everyone was silent. And without precisely facing them, nevertheless he was aware that all three of them were watching him with an extraordinary intensity—staring hard at him—as if he had done something monstrous, or was himself some kind of monster. He could hear the soft irregular flutter of the flames; the cluck-click-cluck-click of the clock; far and faint, two sudden spurts of laughter from the kitchen, as quickly cut off as begun; a murmur of water in the pipes; and then, the silence seemed to deepen, to spread out, to become world-long and world-wide, to become timeless and shapeless, and to center inevitably and rightly, with a slow and sleepy but enormous concentration of all power, on the beginning of a new sound. What this new sound was going to be, he knew perfectly well. It might begin with a hiss, but it would end with a roar—there was no time to lose—he must escape. It mustn't happen here—

Without another word, he turned and ran up the stairs.

IV

Not a moment too soon. The darkness was coming in long white waves. A prolonged sibilance filled the night—a great seamless seethe of wild influence went abruptly across it—a cold low humming shook the windows. He shut the door and flung off his clothes in the dark. The bare black floor was like a little raft tossed in waves of snow, almost overwhelmed, washed under whitely, up again, smothered in curled billows of feather. The snow was laughing; it spoke from all sides at once; it pressed closer to him as he ran and jumped exulting into his bed.

"Listen to us!" it said. "Listen! We have come to tell you the story we told you about. You remember? Lie down. Shut your eyes, now—you will no longer see much—in this white darkness who could see, or want to see? We will take the place of everything. . . . Listen—"

A beautiful varying dance of snow began at the front of the room, came forward and then retreated, flattened out toward the floor, then rose fountain-like to the ceiling, swayed, recruited itself from a new stream of flakes which poured laughing in through the humming window, advanced again, lifted long white arms. It said peace, it said remoteness, it said cold—it said—

But then a gash of horrible light fell brutally across the room from the opening door—the snow drew back hissing—something alien had come into the room—something hostile. This thing rushed at him, clutched at him, shook him—and he was not merely horrified, he was filled with such a loathing as he had never known. What was this? this cruel disturbance? this act of anger and hate? It was as if he had to reach up a hand toward another world for any understanding of it—an effort of which he was only barely capable. But of that other world he still remembered just enough to know the exorcising words. They tore themselves from his other life suddenly—

   "Mother! Mother! Go away! I hate you!"

And with that effort, everything was solved, everything became all right: the seamless hiss advanced once more, the long white wavering lines rose and fell like enormous whispering sea-waves, the whisper becoming louder, the laughter more numerous.

   "Listen!" it said. "We'll tell you the last, the most beautiful and secret story—shut your eyes—it is a very small story—a story that gets smaller and smaller—it comes inward instead of opening like a flower—it is a flower becoming a seed—a little cold seed—do you hear? we are leaning closer to you—"

   The hiss was now becoming a roar—the whole world was a vast moving screen of snow—but even now it said peace, it said remoteness, it said cold, it said sleep.

Writing Assignments for "Silent Snow, Secret Snow"

I. Brief Papers
   A. 1. What happens to Paul at the end of the story?
      2. Why does Paul's saying "Mother! Mother! Go away. I hate you!" (p. 138) mean that "everything was solved, everything became all right . . ."?
      3. Explain why Paul prefers his secret world to the real world.
      4. How convincing and how well written is the following student response to the previous question?

         > Paul prefers his secret world because he finds the real world ugly and disturbing. The snow is "muffling the world, hiding the ugly." When Paul is walking home from school, the world around him is described as sordid. Eczema ointment advertisements, "caught in a little delta of filth" in the gutter, and dirty dead-colored sparrows are mentioned. By contrast, the snow, described as "a peculiarly beautiful trinket," soothes him. He escapes from his depressing environment into the marvelous fantasy in his mind.

      5. Explain why Paul's final secret is the story of "a flower becoming a seed."

   B. Argue for or against one of the assertions below:
      1. Paul—like Hudson, Scott, and Peary—is an explorer.
      2. Paul creates a world of his own in part because he is mistreated and unloved by his parents.
      3. Paul is the model or prototype of the artist or poet, and so the story might well have been titled "A Portrait of the Artist as a Young Man."

C. 1. Do you think Paul is mad? Why or why not?
   2. What would you have done had you been Paul's mother or father? Be as specific as you can.
   3. Do you find the story plausible? Why or why not?
   4. Are you tempted by Paul's world? Why or why not?

II. Longer Papers

A. Explain how the classroom geography lesson relates to the story as a whole.
B. Support or refute the argument that the story implies that Paul is right to reject the ugly, sordid world of reality for the more beautiful world of his own creation.
C. Explain how Paul's motto—"At whatever cost to himself, whatever pain to others" (p. 129)—works itself out in the story.
D. Explain how the sounds, words, and sentences of "Silent Snow, Secret Snow" help us to experience Paul's world.

III. Comparative Papers

A. Argue for or against the assertion that both "Silent Snow, Secret Snow" and "The Yellow Wall-Paper" illustrate that mental disorder cannot be treated in any way: it is beyond human control.
B. Explain why in both "Silent Snow, Secret Snow" and "The Yellow Wall-Paper" the fantasy world is made not only plausible but perhaps even attractive.
C. What do "Silent Snow, Secret Snow" and "The Yellow Wall-Paper" suggest about the connection between madness and artistic creativity?
D. Develop or refute the assertion that both "Silent Snow, Secret Snow" and "The Yellow Wall-Paper" imply that madness is a form of suicide.
E. You have been invited to make a brief, informal talk to the Psychology Club on the general topic "What the Short Story Can Teach Us about Psychology." Keeping in mind that you are expected to narrow and focus that topic, write the script for your talk. Draw your examples and supporting material from both "The Yellow Wall-Paper" and "Silent Snow, Secret Snow" (and, if you choose, other stories as well).

RAY BRADBURY

There Will Come Soft Rains

Before Reading

How do you think the world and human existence will be different 40 or 50 years from now? Free write on this question for 5 or 10 minutes.

In the living room the voice-clock sang, *Tick-tock, seven o'clock, time to get up, time to get up, seven o'clock!* as if it were afraid that nobody would. The morning house lay empty. The clock ticked on, repeating and repeating its sounds into the emptiness. *Seven-nine, breakfast time, seven-nine!*

In the kitchen the breakfast stove gave a hissing sigh and ejected from its warm interior eight pieces of perfectly browned toast, eight eggs sunnyside up, sixteen slices of bacon, two coffees, and two cool glasses of milk.

"Today is August 4, 2026," said a second voice from the kitchen ceiling, "in the city of Allendale, California." It repeated the date three times for memory's sake. "Today is Mr. Featherstone's birthday. Today is the anniversary of Tilita's marriage. Insurance is payable, as are the water, gas, and light bills."

Somewhere in the walls, relays clicked, memory tapes glided under electric eyes.

Eight-one, tick-tock, eight-one o'clock, off to school, off to work, run, run, eight-one! But no doors slammed, no carpets took the soft tread of rubber heels. It was raining outside. The weather box on the front door sang quietly: "Rain, rain, go away; rubbers, raincoats for today . . ." And the rain tapped on the empty house, echoing.

Outside, the garage chimed and lifted its door to reveal the waiting car. After a long wait the door swung down again.

At eight-thirty the eggs were shriveled and the toast was like stone. An aluminum wedge scraped them into the sink, where hot water whirled them down a metal throat which digested and flushed them away to the distant sea. The dirty dishes were dropped into a hot washer and emerged twinkling dry.

Nine-fifteen, sang the clock, *time to clean.*

Out of warrens in the wall, tiny robot mice darted. The rooms were acrawl with the small cleaning animals, all rubber and metal. They thudded against chairs, whirling their mustached runners, kneading the rug nap, sucking gently at hidden dust. Then, like mysterious invaders, they popped into their burrows. Their pink electric eyes faded. The house was clean.

Ten o'clock. The sun came out from behind the rain. The house stood alone

THERE WILL COME SOFT RAINS   First published in 1948. Ray Bradbury (1920–   ) is an American writer of fantasy and science fiction whose best known books are *The Martian Chronicles* and *Fahrenheit 451.*

in a city of rubble and ashes. This was the one house left standing. At night the ruined city gave off a radioactive glow which could be seen for miles.

Ten-fifteen. The garden sprinklers whirled up in golden founts, filling the soft morning air with scatterings of brightness. The water pelted windowpanes, running down the charred west side where the house had been burned evenly free of its white paint. The entire west face of the house was black, save for five places. Here the silhouette in paint of a man mowing a lawn. Here, as in a photograph, a woman bent to pick flowers. Still farther over, their images burned on wood in one titanic instant, a small boy, hands flung into the air; higher up, the image of a thrown ball, and opposite him a girl, hands raised to catch a ball which never came down.

The five spots of paint—the man, the woman, the children, the ball—remained. The rest was a thin charcoaled layer.

The gentle sprinkler rain filled the garden with falling light.

Until this day, how well the house had kept its peace. How carefully it had inquired, "Who goes there? What's the password?" and, getting no answer from lonely foxes and whining cats, it had shut up its windows and drawn shades in an old-maidenly preoccupation with self-protection which bordered on a mechanical paranoia.

It quivered at each sound, the house did. If a sparrow brushed a window, the shade snapped up. The bird, startled, flew off! No, not even a bird must touch the house!

The house was an altar with ten thousand attendants, big, small, servicing, attending, in choirs. But the gods had gone away, and the ritual of the religion continued senselessly, uselessly.

Twelve noon.

A dog whined, shivering, on the front porch.

The front door recognized the dog voice and opened. The dog, once huge and fleshy, but now gone to bone and covered with sores, moved in and through the house, tracking mud. Behind it whirred angry mice, angry at having to pick up mud, angry at inconvenience.

For not a leaf fragment blew under the door but what the wall panels flipped open and the copper scrap rats flashed swiftly out. The offending dust, hair, or paper, seized in miniature steel jaws, was raced back to the burrows. There, down tubes which fed into the cellar, it was dropped into the sighing vent of an incinerator which sat like evil Baal* in a dark corner.

The dog ran upstairs, hysterically yelping to each door, at last realizing, as the house realized, that only silence was here.

It sniffed the air and scratched the kitchen door. Behind the door, the stove was making pancakes which filled the house with a rich baked odor and the scent of maple syrup.

The dog frothed at the mouth, lying at the door, sniffing, its eyes turned to fire. It ran wildly in circles, biting at its tail, spun in a frenzy, and died. It lay in the parlor for an hour.

*Baal: A false god or idol, also known as Beelzebub.

Two o'clock, sang a voice.

Delicately sensing decay at last, the regiments of mice hummed out as softly as blown gray leaves in an electrical wind.

Two-fifteen.

The dog was gone.

In the cellar, the incinerator glowed suddenly and a whirl of sparks leaped up the chimney.

Two thirty-five.

Bridge tables sprouted from patio walls. Playing cards fluttered onto pads in a shower of pips. Martinis manifested on an oaken bench with egg-salad sandwiches. Music played.

But the tables were silent and the cards untouched.

At four o'clock the tables folded like great butterflies back through the paneled walls.

Four-thirty.

The nursery walls glowed.

Animals took shape: yellow giraffes, blue lions, pink antelopes, lilac panthers cavorting in crystal substance. The walls were glass. They looked out upon color and fantasy. Hidden films clocked through well-oiled sprockets, and the walls lived. The nursery floor was woven to resemble a crisp, cereal meadow. Over this ran aluminum roaches and iron crickets, and in the hot still air butterflies of delicate red tissue wavered among the sharp aroma of animal spoors! There was the sound like a great matted yellow hive of bees within a dark bellows, the lazy bumble of a purring lion. And there was the patter of okapi feet and the murmur of a fresh jungle rain, like other hoofs, falling upon the summer-starched grass. Now the walls dissolved into distances of parched weed, mile on mile, and warm endless sky. The animals drew away into thorn brakes and water holes.

It was the children's hour.

Five o'clock. The bath filled with clear hot water.

Six, seven, eight o'clock. The dinner dishes manipulated like magic tricks, and in the study a *click.* In the metal stand opposite the hearth where a fire now blazed up warmly, a cigar popped out, half an inch of soft gray ash on it, smoking, waiting.

Nine o'clock. The beds warmed their hidden circuits, for nights were cool here.

Nine-five. A voice spoke from the study ceiling:

"Mrs. McClellan, which poem would you like this evening?"

The house was silent.

The voice said at last, "Since you express no preference, I shall select a poem at random." Quiet music rose to back the voice. "Sara Teasdale. As I recall, your favorite. . . .

"There will come soft rains and the smell of the ground,
And swallows circling with their shimmering sound;

And frogs in the pools singing at night,
And wild plum-trees in tremulous white;

Robins will wear their feathery fire
Whistling their whims on a low fence-wire;

And not one will know of the war, not one
Will care at last when it is done.

Not one would mind, either bird nor tree
If mankind perished utterly;

And Spring herself, when she woke at dawn,
Would scarcely know that we were gone."*

The fire burned on the stone hearth and the cigar fell away into a mound of quiet ash on its tray. The empty chairs faced each other between the silent walls, and the music played.

At ten o'clock the house began to die.

The wind blew. A falling tree bough crashed through the kitchen window. Cleaning solvent, bottled, shattered over the stove. The room was ablaze in an instant!

"Fire!" screamed a voice. The house lights flashed, water pumps shot water from the ceilings. But the solvent spread on the linoleum, licking, eating under the kitchen door, while the voices took it up in chorus: "Fire, fire, fire!"

The house tried to save itself. Doors sprang tightly shut, but the windows were broken by the heat and the wind blew and sucked upon the fire.

The house gave ground as the fire in ten billion angry sparks moved with flaming ease from room to room and then up the stairs. While scurrying water rats squeaked from the walls, pistoled their water, and ran for more. And the wall sprays let down showers of mechanical rain.

But too late. Somewhere, sighing, a pump shrugged to a stop. The quenching rain ceased. The reserve water supply which had filled baths and washed dishes for many quiet days was gone.

The fire crackled up the stairs. It fed upon Picassos and Matisses† in the upper halls, like delicacies, baking off the oily flesh, tenderly crisping the canvases into black shavings.

Now the fire lay in beds, stood in windows, changed the colors of drapes!

And then, reinforcements.

*Sara Teasdale: U.S. poet (1884–1933); her poem "There Will Come Soft Rains" was published in 1920, two years after the end of World War I, at that time the most destructive war in history.
†Picassos and Matisses: Paintings by Pablo Picasso (1881–1973) and Henri Matisse (1869–1954), two of the twentieth-century's most renowned artists.

From attic trapdoors, blind robot faces peered down with faucet mouths gushing green chemical.

The fire backed off, as even an elephant must at the sight of a dead snake. Now there were twenty snakes whipping over the floor, killing the fire with a clear cold venom of green froth.

But the fire was clever. It had sent flame outside the house, up through the attic to the pumps there. An explosion! The attic brain which directed the pumps was shattered into bronze shrapnel on the beams.

The fire rushed back into every closet and felt of the clothes hung there.

The house shuddered, oak bone on bone, its bared skeleton cringing from the heat, its wire, its nerves revealed as if a surgeon had torn the skin off to let the red veins and capillaries quiver in the scalded air. Help, help! Fire! Run, run! Heat snapped mirrors like the first brittle winter ice. And the voices wailed Fire, fire, run, run, like a tragic nursery rhyme, a dozen voices, high, low, like children dying in a forest, alone, alone. And the voices fading as the wires popped their sheathings like hot chestnuts. One, two, three, four, five voices died.

In the nursery the jungle burned. Blue lions roared, purple giraffes bounded off. The panthers ran in circles, changing color, and ten million animals, running before the fire, vanished off toward a distant steaming river.
. . .

Ten more voices died. In the last instant under the fire avalanche, other choruses, oblivious, could be heard announcing the time, playing music, cutting the lawn by remote-control mower, or setting an umbrella frantically out and in the slamming and opening front door, a thousand things happening, like a clock shop when each clock strikes the hour insanely before or after the other, a scene of maniac confusion, yet unity; singing, screaming, a few last cleaning mice darting bravely out to carry the horrid ashes away! And one voice, with sublime disregard for the situation, read poetry aloud in the fiery study, until all the film spools burned, until all the wires withered and the circuits cracked.

The fire burst the house and let it slam flat down, puffing out skirts of spark and smoke.

In the kitchen, an instant before the rain of fire and timber, the stove could be seen making breakfasts at a psychopathic rate, ten dozen eggs, six loaves of toast, twenty dozen bacon strips, which, eaten by fire, started the stove working again, hysterically hissing!

The crash. The attic smashing into kitchen and parlor. The parlor into cellar, cellar into sub-cellar. Deep freeze, armchair, film tapes, circuits, beds, and all like skeletons thrown in a cluttered mound deep under.

Smoke and silence. A great quantity of smoke.

Dawn showed faintly in the east. Among the ruins, one wall stood alone. Within the wall, a last voice said, over and over again and again, even as the sun rose to shine upon the heaped rubble and steam:

"Today is August 5, 2026, today is August 5, 2026, today is . . . ."

Writing Assignments for "There Will Come Soft Rains"

I. Brief Papers
  A. 1. In reading the story, how soon did you sense that something was wrong? What made you think so?
     2. What can we learn about life in 2026 through the description of breakfast: "In the kitchen the breakfast stove gave a hissing sigh and ejected from its warm interior eight pieces of perfectly browned toast, eight eggs sunnyside up, sixteen slices of bacon, two coffees, and two cool glasses of milk?"
     3. Why does the "voice-clock" speak in rhymes?
     4. Why is the house called an "altar" and its activities described as "the ritual of the religion" (p. 141)?
     5. Explain how Bradbury sustains reader interest in a story in which there is not a single human being.
     6. Point out several instances of personification—the attribution of human qualities and characteristics to nonhuman things—and explain how personification functions in the story.

  B. Argue for or against the assertion that the story predicts that the world will be destroyed by thermonuclear war.

  C. 1. Does the story's depiction of human existence in the year 2026 strike you as plausible? As probable? Why or why not?
     2. Aside from the destruction, does human existence in 2026 strike you as more pleasurable and fulfilling than it is right now? Why or why not?

II. Longer Papers
  A. Expand one of your brief papers into a full-length essay.
  B. It is ironic that the story ends with dawn showing in the east and the sun rising. Identify other instances of irony in the story and then explain how the overall use of irony contributes to the story's meanings and implications.
  C. How does the form and content of the Sara Teasdale poem "There Will Come Soft Rains" relate to the story as a whole?
  D. The story's longest paragraph describes a scene on the nursery walls. In what sense is the description of the animals and their behavior a commentary on what happens in the story?
  E. Eleven paragraphs of the story focus on the family dog. How do they contribute to the story's meanings and impact?
  F. Argue for or against the assertion that the story strongly implies a causal connection between the quality of daily life in 2026 and the fact that life has now been destroyed.

URSULA K. LE GUIN
Nine Lives

Before Reading

Would you like to have a clone of yourself or an absolutely identical twin, someone who would look exactly like you as well as think and feel precisely as you do? Why or why not? Free write on this question for 5 or 10 minutes.

She was alive inside but dead outside, her face a black and dun net of wrinkles, tumors, cracks. She was bald and blind. The tremors that crossed Libra's face were mere quiverings of corruption. Underneath, in the black corridors, the halls beneath the skin, there were crepitations in darkness, ferments, chemical nightmares that went on for centuries. "O the damned flatulent planet," Pugh murmured as the dome shook and a boil burst a kilometer to the southwest, spraying silver pus across the sunset. The sun had been setting for the last two days. "I'll be glad to see a human face."

"Thanks," said Martin.

"Yours is human to be sure," said Pugh, "but I've seen it so long I can't see it."

Radvid signals cluttered the communicator which Martin was operating, faded, returned as face and voice. The face filled the screen, the nose of an Assyrian king, the eyes of a samurai, skin bronze, eyes the color of iron: young, magnificent. "Is that what human beings look like?" said Pugh with awe. "I'd forgotten."

"Shut up, Owen, we're on."

"Libra Exploratory Mission Base, come in please, this is *Passerine* launch."

"Libra here. Beam fixed. Come on down, launch."

"Expulsion in seven E-seconds. Hold on." The screen blanked and sparkled.

"Do they all look like that? Martin, you and I are uglier men than I thought."

"Shut up, Owen. . . ."

For twenty-two minutes Martin followed the landing craft down by signal and then through the cleared dome they saw it, small star in the blood-colored east, sinking. It came down neat and quiet, Libra's thin atmosphere carrying little sound. Pugh and Martin closed the headpieces of their imsuits, zipped out of the dome airlocks, and ran with soaring strides, Nijinsky and Nureyev*,

*Nijinski and Nureyev: Noted Russian ballet dancers.

NINE LIVES First published in 1968. Ursula K. Le Guin (1929–) was born in California and educated at Radcliffe College and Columbia University. She says that in her science fiction she is describing "certain aspects of psychological reality . . . by inventing elaborately circumstantial lies."

toward the boat. Three equipment modules came floating down at four-minute intervals from each other and hundred-meter intervals east of the boat. "Come on out," Martin said on his suit radio, "we're waiting at the door."

"Come on in, the methane's fine," said Pugh.

The hatch opened. The young man they had seen on the screen came out with one athletic twist and leaped down onto the shaky dust and clinkers of Libra. Martin shook his hand, but Pugh was staring at the hatch, from which another young man emerged with the same neat twist and jump, followed by a young woman who emerged with the same neat twist, ornamented by a wriggle, and the jump. They were all tall, with bronze skin, black hair, high-bridged noses, epicanthic fold, the same face. They all had the same face. The fourth was emerging from the hatch with a neat twist and jump. "Martin bach," said Pugh, "we've got a clone."

"Right," said one of them, "we're a tenclone. John Chow's the name. You're Lieutenant Martin?"

"I'm Owen Pugh."

"Alvaro Guillen Martin," said Martin, formal, bowing slightly. Another girl was out, the same beautiful face; Martin stared at her and his eye rolled like a nervous pony's. Evidently he had never given any thought to cloning and was suffering technological shock. "Steady," Pugh said in the Argentine dialect, "it's only excess twins." He stood close by Martin's elbow. He was glad himself of the contact.

It is hard to meet a stranger. Even the greatest extravert meeting even the meekest stranger knows a certain dread, though he may not know he knows it. Will he make a fool of me wreck my image of myself invade me destroy me change me? Will he be different from me? Yes, that he will. There's the terrible thing: the strangeness of the stranger.

After two years on a dead planet, and the last half year isolated as a team of two, oneself and one other, after that it's even harder to meet a stranger, however welcome he may be. You're out of the habit of difference, you've lost the touch; and so the fear revives, the primitive anxiety, the old dread.

The clone, five males and five females, had got done in a couple of minutes what a man might have got done in twenty: greeted Pugh and Martin, had a glance at Libra, unloaded the boat, made ready to go. They went, and the dome filled with them, a hive of golden bees. They hummed and buzzed quietly, filled up all silences, all spaces with a honey-brown swarm of human presence. Martin looked bewildered at the long-limbed girls, and they smiled at him, three at once. Their smile was gentler than that of the boys, but no less radiantly self-possessed.

"Self-possessed," Owen Pugh murmured to his friend, "that's it. Think of it, to be oneself ten times over. Nine seconds for every motion, nine ayes on every vote. It would be glorious." But Martin was asleep. And the John Chows had all gone to sleep at once. The dome was filled with their quiet breathing. They were young, they didn't snore. Martin sighed and snored, his Hershey-bar-colored face relaxed in the dim afterglow of Libra's primary, set at last. Pugh had cleared the dome and stars looked in, Sol among them, a great company of lights, a clone of splendors. Pugh slept and dreamed of a one-eyed giant who chased him through the shaking halls of Hell.

From his sleeping bag Pugh watched the clone's awakening. They all got up within one minute except for one pair, a boy and a girl, who lay snugly tangled and still sleeping in one bag. As Pugh saw this there was a shock like one of Libra's earthquakes inside him, a very deep tremor. He was not aware of this and in fact thought he was pleased at the sight; there was no other such comfort on this dead hollow world. More power to them, who made love. One of the others stepped on the pair. They woke and the girl sat up flushed and sleepy, with bare golden breasts. One of her sisters murmured something to her; she shot a glance at Pugh and disappeared in the sleeping bag; from another direction came a fierce stare, from still another direction a voice: "Christ, we're used to having a room to ourselves. Hope you don't mind, Captain Pugh."

"It's a pleasure," Pugh said half truthfully. He had to stand up then wearing only the shorts he slept in, and he felt like a plucked rooster, all white scrawn and pimples. He had seldom envied Martin's compact brownness so much. The United Kingdom had come through the Great Famines well, losing less than half its population: a record achieved by rigorous food control. Black marketeers and hoarders had been executed. Crumbs had been shared. Where in richer lands most had died and a few had thrived, in Britain fewer died and none throve. They all got lean. Their sons were lean, their grandsons lean, small, brittle-boned, easily infected. When civilization became a matter of standing in lines, the British had kept queue, and so had replaced the survival of the fittest with the survival of the fair-minded. Owen Pugh was a scrawny little man. All the same, he was there.

At the moment he wished he wasn't.

At breakfast a John said, "Now if you'll brief us, Captain Pugh—"

"Owen, then."

"Owen, we can work out our schedule. Anything new on the mine since your last report to your Mission? We saw your reports when *Passerine* was orbiting Planet V, where they are now."

Martin did not answer, though the mine was his discovery and project, and Pugh had to do his best. It was hard to talk to them. The same faces, each with the same expression of intelligent interest, all leaned toward him across the table at almost the same angle. They all nodded together.

Over the Exploitation Corps insigne on their tunics each had a nameband, first name John and last name Chow of course, but the middle names different. The men were Aleph, Kaph, Yod, Gimel, and Samedh; the women Sadhe, Daleth, Zayin, Beth, and Resh. Pugh tried to use the names but gave it up at once; he could not even tell sometimes which one had spoken, for all the voices were alike.

Martin buttered and chewed his toast, and finally interrupted: "You're a team. Is that it?"

"Right," said two Johns.

"God, what a team! I hadn't seen the point. How much do you each know what the others are thinking?"

"Not at all, properly speaking," replied one of the girls, Zayin. The others watched her with the proprietary, approving look they had. "No ESP, nothing fancy. But we think alike. We have exactly the same equipment. Given the same stimulus, the same problem, we're likely to be coming up with the same reactions and solutions at the same time. Explanations are easy—don't even have to make them, usually. We seldom misunderstand each other. It does facilitate our working as a team."

"Christ yes," said Martin. "Pugh and I have spent seven hours out of ten for six months misunderstanding each other. Like most people. What about emergencies, are you as good at meeting the unexpected problem as a nor . . . an unrelated team?"

"Statistics so far indicate that we are," Zayin answered readily. Clones must be trained, Pugh thought, to meet questions, to reassure and reason. All they said had the slightly bland and stilted quality of answers furnished to the Public. "We can't brainstorm as singletons can, we as a team don't profit from the interplay of varied minds; but we have a compensatory advantage. Clones are drawn from the best human material, individuals of IIQ ninety-ninth percentile, Genetic Constitution alpha double A, and so on. We have more to draw on than most individuals do."

"And it's multiplied by a factor of ten. Who is—who was John Chow?"

"A genius surely," Pugh said politely. His interest in cloning was not so new and avid as Martin's.

"Leonardo Complex type," said Yod. "Biomath, also a cellist and an undersea hunter, and interested in structural engineering problems and so on. Died before he'd worked out his major theories."

"Then you each represent a different facet of his mind, his talents?"

"No," said Zayin, shaking her head in time with several others. "We share the basic equipment and tendencies, of course, but we're all engineers in Planetary Exploitation. A later clone can be trained to develop other aspects of the basic equipment. It's all training; the genetic substance is identical. We *are* John Chow. But we are differently trained."

Martin looked shell-shocked. "How old are you?"

"Twenty-three."

"You say he died young—had they taken germ cells from him beforehand or something?"

Gimel took over: "He died at twenty-four in an air car crash. They couldn't save the brain, so they took some intestinal cells and cultured them for cloning. Reproductive cells aren't used for cloning, since they have only half the chromosomes. Intestinal cells happen to be easy to despecialize and reprogram for total growth."

"All chips off the old block," Martin said valiantly. "But how can . . . some of you be women . . . ?"

Beth took over: "It's easy to program half the clonal mass back to the female. Just delete the male gene from half the cells and they revert to the basic, that is, the female. It's trickier to go the other way, have to hook in artificial Y chromosomes. So they mostly clone from males, since clones function best bisexually."

Gimel again: "They've worked these matters of technique and function out carefully. The taxpayer wants the best for his money, and of course clones are expensive. With the cell manipulations, and the incubation in Ngama Placentae, and the maintenance and training of the foster-parent groups, we end up costing about three million apiece."

"For your next generation," Martin said, still struggling, "I suppose you . . . you breed?"

"We females are sterile," said Beth with perfect equanimity. "You remember that the Y chromosome was deleted from our original cell. The males can interbreed with approved singletons, if they want to. But to get John Chow again as often as they want, they just reclone a cell from this clone."

Martin gave up the struggle. He nodded and chewed cold toast. "Well," said one of the Johns, and all changed mood, like a flock of starlings that change course in one wingflick, following a leader so fast that no eye can see which leads. They were ready to go. "How about a look at the mine? Then we'll unload the equipment. Some nice new models in the roboats; you'll want to see them. Right?" Had Pugh or Martin not agreed they might have found it hard to say so. The Johns were polite but unanimous; their decisions carried. Pugh, Commander of Libra Base 2, felt a qualm. Could he boss around this superman/woman-entity-of-ten? and a genius at that? He stuck close to Martin as they suited for outside. Neither said anything.

Four apiece in the three large airjets, they slipped off north from the dome, over Libra's dun rugose skin, in starlight.

"Desolate," one said.

It was a boy and girl with Pugh and Martin. Pugh wondered if these were the two that had shared a sleeping bag last night. No doubt they wouldn't mind if he asked them. Sex must be as handy as breathing to them. Did you two breathe last night?

"Yes," he said, "it is desolate."

"This is our first time off, except training on Luna." The girl's voice was definitely a bit higher and softer.

"How did you take the big hop?"

"They doped us. I wanted to experience it." That was the boy; he sounded wistful. They seemed to have more personality, only two at a time. Did repetition of the individual negate individuality?

"Don't worry," said Martin, steering the sled, "you can't experience no-time because it isn't there."

"I'd just like to once," one of them said. "So we'd know."

The Mountains of Merioneth showed leprotic in starlight to the east, a plume of freezing gas trailed silvery from a vent-hole to the west, and the sled tilted groundward. The twins braced for the stop at one moment, each with a slight protective gesture to the other. Your skin is my skin, Pugh thought, but literally, no metaphor. What would it be like, then, to have someone as close to you as that? Always to be answered when you spoke; never to be in pain alone. Love your neighbor as you love yourself. . . . That hard old problem was solved. The neighbor was the self: the love was perfect.

And here was Hellmouth, the mine.

Pugh was the Exploratory Mission's E.T. geologist, and Martin his technician and cartographer; but when in the course of a local survey Martin had discovered the U-mine, Pugh had given him full credit, as well as the onus of prospecting the lode and planning the Exploitation Team's job. These kids had been sent out from Earth years before Martin's reports got there and had not known what their job would be until they got here. The Exploitation Corps simply sent out teams regularly and blindly as a dandelion sends out its seed, knowing there would be a job for them on Libra or the next planet out or one they hadn't even heard about yet. The government wanted uranium too urgently to wait while reports drifted home across the lightyears. The stuff was like gold, old-fashioned but essential, worth mining extraterrestrially and shipping interstellar. Worth its weight in people, Pugh thought sourly, watching the tall young men and women go one by one, glimmering in starlight, into the black hole Martin had named Hellmouth.

As they went in their homeostatic forehead-lamps brightened. Twelve nodding gleams ran along the moist, wrinkled walls. Pugh heard Martin's radiation counter peeping twenty to the dozen up ahead. "Here's the drop-off," said Martin's voice in the suit intercom, drowning out the peeping and the dead silence that was around them. "We're in a side-fissure, this is the main vertical vent in front of us." The black void gaped, its far side not visible in the headlamp beams. "Last vulcanism seems to have been a couple of thousand years ago. Nearest fault is twenty-eight kilos east, in the Trench. This area seems to be as safe seismically as anything in the area. The big basalt-flow overhead stabilizes all these substructures, so long as it remains stable itself. Your central lode is thirty-six meters down and runs in a series of five bubble caverns northeast. It is a lode, a pipe of very high-grade ore. You saw the percentage figures, right? Extraction's going to be no problem. All you've got to do is get the bubbles topside."

"Take off the lid and let 'em float up." A chuckle. Voices began to talk, but they were all the same voice and the suit radio gave them no location in space. "Open the thing right up.—Safer that way.—But it's a solid basalt roof, how thick, ten meters here?—Three to twenty, the report said.—Blow good ore all over the lot.—Use this access we're in, straighten it a bit and run slider rails for the robos.—Import burros.—Have we got enough propping material?— What's your estimate of total payload mass, Martin?"

"Say over five million kilos and under eight."

"Transport will be here in ten E-months.—It'll have to go pure.—No, they'll have the mass problem in NAFAL shipping licked by now, remember it's been sixteen years since we left Earth last Tuesday.—Right, they'll send the whole lot back and purify it in Earth orbit.—Shall we go down, Martin?"

"Go on. I've been down."

The first one—Aleph? (Heb., the ox, the leader)—swung onto the ladder and down; the rest followed. Pugh and Martin stood at the chasm's edge. Pugh set his intercom to exchange only with Martin's suit, and noticed Martin doing the same. It was a bit wearing, this listening to one person think aloud in ten voices, or was it one voice speaking the thoughts of ten minds?

"A great gut," Pugh said, looking down into the black pit, its veined and warted walls catching stray gleams of headlamps far below. "A cow's bowel. A bloody great constipated intestine."

Martin's counter peeped like a lost chicken. They stood inside the dead but epileptic planet, breathing oxygen from tanks, wearing suits impermeable to corrosives and harmful radiations, resistant to a 200-degree range of temperatures, tear-proof, and as shock-resistant as possible given the soft vulnerable stuff inside.

"Next hop," Martin said, "I'd like to find a planet that has nothing whatever to exploit."

"You found this."

"Keep me home next time."

Pugh was pleased. He had hoped Martin would want to go on working with him, but neither of them was used to talking much about their feelings, and he had hesitated to ask. "I'll try that," he said.

"I hate this place. I like caves, you know. It's why I came in here. Just spelunking. But this one's a bitch. Mean. You can't ever let down in here. I guess this lot can handle it, though. They know their stuff."

"Wave of the future, whatever," said Pugh.

The wave of the future came swarming up the ladder, swept Martin to the entrance, gabbled at and around him: "Have we got enough material for supports? —If we convert one of the extractor servos to anneal, yes. —Sufficient if we miniblast? —Kaph can calculate stress." Pugh had switched his intercom back to receive them; he looked at them, so many thoughts jabbering in an eager mind, and at Martin standing silent among them, and at Hellmouth and the wrinkled plain. "Settled! How does that strike you as a preliminary schedule, Martin?"

"It's your baby," Martin said.

Within five E-days the Johns had all their material and equipment unloaded and operating and were starting to open up the mine. They worked with total efficiency. Pugh was fascinated and frightened by their effectiveness, their confidence, their independence. He was no use to them at all. A clone, he thought, might indeed be the first truly stable, self-reliant human being. Once adult it would need nobody's help. It would be sufficient to itself physically, sexually, emotionally, intellectually. Whatever he did, any member of it would always receive the support and approval of his peers, his other selves. Nobody else was needed.

Two of the clone stayed in the dome doing calculations and paperwork, with frequent sled trips to the mine for measurements and tests. They were the mathematicians of the clone, Zayin and Kaph. That is, as Zayin explained, all ten had had thorough mathematical training from age three to twenty-one, but from twenty-one to twenty-three she and Kaph had gone on with math while the others intensified study in other specialties, geology, mining, engineering, electronic engineering, equipment robotics, applied atomics, and so on. "Kaph and I feel," she said, "that we're the element of the clone closest to what John Chow was in his singleton lifetime. But of course he was principally in biomath, and they didn't take us far in that."

"They needed us most in this field," Kaph said, with the patriotic priggishness they sometimes evinced.

Pugh and Martin soon could distinguish this pair from the others, Zayin by gestalt, Kaph only by a discolored left fourth fingernail, got from an ill-aimed hammer at the age of six. No doubt there were many such differences, physical and psychological, among them; nature might be identical, nurture could not be. But the differences were hard to find. And part of the difficulty was that they never really talked to Pugh and Martin. They joked with them, were polite, got along fine. They gave nothing. It was nothing one could complain about; they were very pleasant, they had the standardized American friendliness. "Do you come from Ireland, Owen?"

"Nobody comes from Ireland, Zayin."

"There are lots of Irish-Americans."

"To be sure, but no more Irish. A couple of thousand in all the island, the last I knew. They didn't go in for birth control, you know, so the food ran out. By the Third Famine there were no Irish left at all but the priesthood, and they all celibate, or nearly all."

Zayin and Kaph smiled stiffly. They had no experience of either bigotry or irony. "What are you then, ethnically?" Kaph asked, and Pugh replied, "A Welshman."

"Is it Welsh that you and Martin speak together?"

None of your business, Pugh thought, but said, "No, it's his dialect, not mine: Argentinean. A descendant of Spanish."

"You learned it for private communication?"

"Whom had we here to be private from? It's just that sometimes a man likes to speak his native language."

"Ours is English," Kaph said unsympathetically. Why should they have sympathy? That's one of the things you give because you need it back.

"Is Wells quaint?" asked Zayin.

"Wells? Oh, Wales, it's called. Yes, Wales is quaint." Pugh switched on his rock-cutter, which prevented further conversation by a synapse-destroying whine, and while it whined he turned his back and said a profane word in Welsh.

That night he used the Argentine dialect for private communication. "Do they pair off in the same couples or change every night?"

Martin looked surprised. A prudish expression, unsuited to his features, appeared for a moment. It faded. He too was curious. "I think it's random."

"Don't whisper, man, it sounds dirty. I think they rotate."

"On a schedule?"

"So nobody gets omitted."

Martin gave a vulgar laugh and smothered it. "What about us? Aren't we omitted?"

"That doesn't occur to them."

"What if I proposition one of the girls?"

"She'd tell the others and they'd decide as a group."

"I am not a bull," Martin said, his dark, heavy face heating up. "I will not be judged—"

"Down, down, *machismo*," said Pugh. "Do you mean to proposition one?"

Martin shrugged, sullen. "Let 'em have their incest."

"Incest is it, or masturbation?"

"I don't care, if they'd do it out of earshot!"

The clone's early attempts at modesty had soon worn off, unmotivated by any deep defensiveness of self or awareness of others. Pugh and Martin were daily deeper swamped under the intimacies of its constant emotional-sexual-mental interchange: swamped yet excluded.

"Two months to go," Martin said one evening.

"To what?" snapped Pugh. He was edgy lately, and Martin's sullenness got on his nerves.

"To relief."

In sixty days the full crew of their Exploratory Mission were due back from their survey of the other planets of the system. Pugh was aware of this.

"Crossing off the days on your calendar?" he jeered.

"Pull yourself together, Owen."

"What do you mean?"

"What I say."

They parted in contempt and resentment.

Pugh came in after a day alone on the Pampas, a vast lava plain the nearest edge of which was two hours south by jet. He was tired but refreshed by solitude. They were not supposed to take long trips alone but lately had often done so. Martin stooped under bright lights, drawing one of his elegant masterly charts. This one was of the whole face of Libra, the cancerous face. The dome was otherwise empty, seeming dim and large as it had before the clone came. "Where's the golden horde?"

Martin grunted ignorance, cross-hatching. He straightened his back to glance round at the sun, which squatted feebly like a great red toad on the eastern plain, and at the clock, which said 18:45. "Some big quakes today," he said, returning to his map. "Feel them down there? Lots of crates were falling around. Take a look at the seismo."

The needle jigged and wavered on the roll. It never stopped dancing here. The roll had recorded five quakes of major intensity back in midafternoon; twice the needle had hopped off the roll. The attached computer had been activated to emit a slip reading, "Epicenter 61' N by 42'4" E."

"Not in the Trench this time."

"I thought it felt a bit different from usual. Sharper."

"In Base One I used to lie awake all night feeling the ground jump. Queer how you get used to things."

"Go spla if you didn't. What's for dinner?"

"I thought you'd have cooked it."

"Waiting for the clone."

Feeling put upon, Pugh got out a dozen dinnerboxes, stuck two in the Instobake, pulled them out. "All right, here's dinner."

"Been thinking," Martin said, coming to table. "What if some clone cloned itself? Illegally. Made a thousand duplicates—ten thousand. Whole army. They could make a tidy power grab, couldn't they?"

"But how many millions did this lot cost to rear? Artificial placentate and all that. It would be hard to keep secret, unless they had a planet to themselves. . . . Back before the Famines when Earth had national governments, they talked about that: clone your best soldiers, have whole regiments of them. But the food ran out before they could play that game."

They talked amicably, as they used to do.

"Funny," Martin said, chewing. "They left early this morning, didn't they?"

"All but Kaph and Zayin. They thought they'd get the first payload above ground today. What's up?"

"They weren't back for lunch."

"They won't starve, to be sure."

"They left at seven."

"So they did." Then Pugh saw it. The air tanks held eight hours' supply.

"Kaph and Zayin carried out spare cans when they left. Or they've got a heap out there."

"They did, but they brought the whole lot in to recharge." Martin stood up, pointing to one of the stacks of stuff that cut the dome into rooms and alleys.

"There's an alarm signal on every imsuit."

"It's not automatic."

Pugh was tired and still hungry. "Sit down and eat, man. That lot can look after themselves."

Martin sat down but did not eat. "There was a big quake, Owen. The first one. Big enough it scared me."

After a pause Pugh sighed and said, "All right."

Unenthusiastically, they got out the two-man sled that was always left for them and headed it north. The long sunrise covered everything in poisonous red jello. The horizontal light and shadow made it hard to see, raised walls of fake iron ahead of them which they slid through, turned the convex plain beyond Hellmouth into a great dimple full of bloody water. Around the tunnel entrance a wilderness of machinery stood, cranes and cables and servos and wheels and diggers and robocarts and sliders and control huts, all slanting and bulking incoherently in the red light. Martin jumped from the sled, ran into the mine. He came out again, to Pugh. "Oh God, Owen, it's down," he said. Pugh went in and saw, five meters from the entrance, the shiny moist, black wall that ended the tunnel. Newly exposed to air, it looked organic, like visceral tissue. The tunnel entrance, enlarged by blasting and double-tracked for robocarts, seemed unchanged until he noticed thousands of tiny spiderweb cracks in the walls. The floor was wet with some sluggish fluid.

"They were inside," Martin said.

"They may be still. They surely had extra air cans—"

"Look, Owen, look at the basalt flow, at the roof, don't you see what the quake did, look at it."

The low hump of land that roofed the caves still had the unreal look of an optical illusion. It had reversed itself, sunk down, leaving a vast dimple or pit. When Pugh walked on it he saw that it too was cracked with many tiny fissures. From some a whitish gas was seeping, so that the sunlight on the surface of the gas pool was shafted as if by the waters of a dim red lake.

"The mine's not on the fault. There's no fault here!"

Pugh came back to him quickly. "No, there's no fault, Martin—Look, they surely weren't all inside together."

Martin followed him and searched among the wrecked machines dully, then actively. He spotted the airsled. It had come down heading south, and stuck at an angle in a pothole of colloidal dust. It had carried two riders. One was half sunk in the dust, but his suit meters registered normal functioning; the other hung strapped onto the tilted sled. Her imsuit had burst open on the broken legs, and the body was frozen hard as any rock. That was all they found. As both regulation and custom demanded, they cremated the dead at once with the laser guns they carried by regulation and had never used before. Pugh, knowing he was going to be sick, wrestled the survivor onto the two-man sled and sent Martin off to the dome with him. Then he vomited and flushed the waste out of his suit, and finding one four-man sled undamaged, followed after Martin, shaking as if the cold of Libra had got through to him.

The survivor was Kaph. He was in deep shock. They found a swelling on the occiput that might mean concussion, but no fracture was visible.

Pugh brought two glasses of food concentrate and two chasers of aquavit. "Come on," he said. Martin obeyed, drinking off the tonic. They sat down on crates near the cot and sipped the aquavit.

Kaph lay immobile, face like beeswax, hair bright black to the shoulders, lips stiffly parted for faintly gasping breaths.

"It must have been the first shock, the big one," Martin said. "It must have slid the whole structure sideways. Till it fell in on itself. There must be gas layers in the lateral rocks, like those formations in the Thirty-first Quadrant. But there wasn't any sign—" As he spoke the world slid out from under them. Things leaped and clattered, hopped and jigged, shouted Ha! Ha! Ha! "It was like this at fourteen hours," said Reason shakily in Martin's voice, amidst the unfastening and ruin of the world. But Unreason sat up, as the tumult lessened and things ceased dancing, and screamed aloud.

Pugh leaped across his spilt aquavit and held Kaph down. The muscular body flailed him off. Martin pinned the shoulders down. Kaph screamed, struggled, choked; his face blackened. "Oxy," Pugh said, and his hand found the right needle in the medical kit as if by homing instinct; while Martin held the mask he struck the needle home to the vagus nerve, restoring Kaph to life.

"Didn't know you knew that stunt," Martin said, breathing hard.

"The Lazarus Jab, my father was a doctor. It doesn't often work," Pugh said. "I want that drink I spilled. Is the quake over? I can't tell."

"Aftershocks. It's not just you shivering."

"Why did he suffocate?"

"I don't know, Owen. Look in the book."

Kaph was breathing normally and his color was restored; only the lips were still darkened. They poured a new shot of courage and sat down by him again with their medical guide. "Nothing about cyanosis or asphyxiation under 'Shock' or 'Concussion.' He can't have breathed in anything with his suit on. I don't know. We'd get as much good out of *Mother Mog's Home Herbalist.* . . . 'Anal Hemorrhoids,' fy!" Pugh pitched the book to a crate table. It fell short, because either Pugh or the table was still unsteady.

"Why didn't he signal?"

"Sorry?"

"The eight inside the mine never had time. But he and the girl must have been outside. Maybe she was in the entrance and got hit by the first slide. He must have been outside, in the control hut maybe. He ran in, pulled her out, strapped her onto the sled, started for the dome. And all that time never pushed the panic button in his imsuit. Why not?"

"Well, he'd had that whack on his head. I doubt he ever realized the girl was dead. He wasn't in his senses. But if he had been I don't know if he'd have thought to signal us. They looked to one another for help."

Martin's face was like an Indian mask, grooves at the mouth corners, eyes of dull coal. "That's so. What must he have felt, then, when the quake came and he was outside, alone—"

In answer Kaph screamed.

He came off the cot in the heaving convulsions of one suffocating, knocked Pugh right down with his flailing arm, staggered into a stack of crates and fell to the floor, lips blue, eyes white. Martin dragged him back onto the cot and gave him a whiff of oxygen, then knelt by Pugh, who was sitting up, and wiped at his cut cheekbone. "Owen, are you all right, are you going to be all right, Owen?"

"I think I am," Pugh said. "Why are you rubbing that on my face?"

It was a short length of computer tape, now spotted with Pugh's blood. Martin dropped it. "Thought it was a towel. You clipped your cheek on that box there."

"Is he out of it?"

"Seems to be."

They stared down at Kaph lying stiff, his teeth a white line inside dark parted lips.

"Like epilepsy. Brain damage maybe?"

"What about shooting him full of meprobamate?"

Pugh shook his head. "I don't know what's in that shot I already gave him for shock. Don't want to overdose him."

"Maybe he'll sleep it off now."

"I'd like to myself. Between him and the earthquake I can't seem to keep on my feet."

"You got a nasty crack there. Go on, I'll sit up a while."

Pugh cleaned his cut cheek and pulled off his shirt, then paused.

"Is there anything we ought to have done—have tried to do—"

"They're all dead," Martin said heavily, gently.

Pugh lay down on top of his sleeping bag and one instant later was wakened by a hideous, sucking, struggling noise. He staggered up, found the needle, tried three times to jab it in correctly and failed, began to massage over Kaph's heart. "Mouth-to-mouth," he said, and Martin obeyed. Presently Kaph drew a harsh breath, his heartbeat steadied, his rigid muscles began to relax.

"How long did I sleep?"

"Half an hour."

They stood up sweating. The ground shuddered, the fabric of the dome sagged and swayed. Libra was dancing her awful polka again, her *Totentanz.* * The sun, though rising, seemed to have grown larger and redder; gas and dust must have been stirred up in the feeble atmosphere.

"What's wrong with him, Owen?"

"I think he's dying with them."

"Them— But they're all dead, I tell you."

"Nine of them. They're all dead, they were crushed or suffocated. They were all him, he is all of them. They died, and now he's dying their deaths one by one."

"Oh, pity of God," said Martin.

The next time was much the same. The fifth time was worse, for Kaph fought and raved, trying to speak but getting no words out, as if his mouth were stopped with rocks or clay. After that the attacks grew weaker, but so did he. The eighth seizure came at about four-thirty; Pugh and Martin worked till five-thirty doing all they could to keep life in the body that slid without protest into death. They kept him, but Martin said, "The next will finish him." And it did; but Pugh breathed his own breath into the inert lungs, until he himself passed out.

He woke. The dome was opaqued and no light on. He listened and heard the breathing of two sleeping men. He slept, and nothing woke him till hunger did.

The sun was well up over the dark plains, and the planet had stopped dancing. Kaph lay asleep. Pugh and Martin drank tea and looked at him with proprietary triumph.

When he woke Martin went to him: "How do you feel, old man?" There was no answer. Pugh took Martin's place and looked into the brown, dull eyes

Totentanz: A German word meaning either dance of death or dance of the dead.

that gazed toward but not into his own. Like Martin he quickly turned away. He heated food concentrate and brought it to Kaph. "Come on, drink."

He could see the muscles in Kaph's throat tighten. "Let me die," the young man said.

"You're not dying."

Kaph spoke with clarity and precision: "I am nine-tenths dead. There is not enough of me left alive."

That precision convinced Pugh, and he fought the conviction. "No," he said, peremptory. "They are dead. The others. Your brothers and sisters. You're not them, you're alive. You are John Chow. Your life is in your own hands."

The young man lay still, looking into a darkness that was not there.

Martin and Pugh took turns taking the Exploitation hauler and a spare set of robos over to Hellmouth to salvage equipment and protect it from Libra's sinister atmosphere, for the value of the stuff was, literally, astronomical. It was slow work for one man at a time, but they were unwilling to leave Kaph by himself. The one left in the dome did paperwork, while Kaph sat or lay and stared into his darkness and never spoke. The days went by, silent.

The radio spat and spoke: the Mission calling from the ship. "We'll be down on Libra in five weeks, Owen. Thirty-four E-days nine hours I make it as of now. How's tricks in the old dome?"

"Not good, chief. The Exploit team were killed, all but one of them, in the mine. Earthquake. Six days ago."

The radio crackled and sang starsong. Sixteen seconds' lag each way; the ship was out around Planet II now. "Killed, all but one? You and Martin were unhurt?"

"We're all right, chief."

Thirty-two seconds.

"Passerine left an Exploit team out here with us. I may put them on the Hellmouth project then, instead of the Quadrant Seven project. We'll settle that when we come down. In any case you and Martin will be relieved at Dome Two. Hold tight. Anything else?"

"Nothing else."

Thirty-two seconds.

"Right then. So long, Owen."

Kaph had heard all this, and later on Pugh said to him, "The chief may ask you to stay here with the other Exploit team. You know the ropes here." Knowing the exigencies of Far Out life, he wanted to warn the young man. Kaph made no answer. Since he had said, "There is not enough of me left alive," he had not spoken a word.

"Owen," Martin said on suit intercom, "he's spla. Insane. Psycho."

"He's doing very well for a man who's died nine times."

"Well? Like a turned-off android is well? The only emotion he has left is hate. Look at his eyes."

"That's not hate, Martin. Listen, it's true that he has, in a sense, been dead.

I cannot imagine what he feels. But it's not hatred. He can't even see us. It's too dark."

"Throats have been cut in the dark. He hates us because we're not Aleph and Yod and Zayin."

"Maybe. But I think he's alone. He doesn't see us or hear us, that's the truth. He never had to see anyone else before. he never was alone before. He had himself to see, talk with, live with, nine other selves all his life. He doesn't know how you go it alone. He must learn. Give him time."

Martin shook his heavy head. "Spla," he said. "Just remember when you're alone with him that he could break your neck one-handed."

"He could do that," said Pugh, a short, soft-voiced man with a scarred cheekbone; he smiled. They were just outside the dome airlock, programming one of the servos to repair a damaged hauler. They could see Kaph sitting inside the great half-egg of the dome like a fly in amber.

"Hand me the insert pack there. What makes you think he'll get any better?"

"He has a strong personality, to be sure."

"Strong? Crippled. Nine-tenths dead, as he put it."

"But he's not dead. He's a live man: John Kaph Chow. He had a jolly queer upbringing, but after all every boy has got to break free of his family. He will do it."

"I can't see it."

"Think a bit, Martin bach. What's this cloning for? To repair the human race. We're in a bad way. Look at me. My IIQ and GC are half this John Chow's. Yet they wanted me so badly for the Far Out Service that when I volunteered they took me and fitted me out with an artificial lung and corrected my myopia. Now if there were enough good sound lads about would they be taking one-lunged short-sighted Welshmen?"

"Didn't know you had an artificial lung."

"I do then. Not tin, you know. Human, grown in a tank from a bit of somebody; cloned, if you like. That's how they make replacement organs, the same general idea as cloning, but bits and pieces instead of whole people. It's my own lung now, whatever. But what I am saying is this, there are too many like me these days and not enough like John Chow. They're trying to raise the level of the human genetic pool, which is a mucky little puddle since the population crash. So then if a man is cloned, he's a strong and clever man. It's only logic, to be sure."

Martin grunted; the servo began to hum.

Kaph had been eating little; he had trouble swallowing his food, choking on it, so that he would give up trying after a few bites. He had lost eight or ten kilos. After three weeks or so, however, his appetite began to pick up, and one day he began to look through the clone's possessions, the sleeping bags, kits, papers which Pugh had stacked neatly in a far angle of a packing-crate alley. He sorted, destroyed a heap of papers and oddments, made a small packet of what remained, then relapsed into his walking coma.

Two days later he spoke. Pugh was trying to correct a flutter in the tape-player and failing; Martin had the jet out, checking their maps of the Pampas. "Hell and damnation!" Pugh said, and Kaph said in a toneless voice, "Do you want me to do that?"

Pugh jumped, controlled himself, and gave the machine to Kaph. The young man took it apart, put it back together, and left it on the table.

"Put on a tape," Pugh said with careful casualness, busy at another table.

Kaph put on the topmost tape, a chorale. He lay down on his cot. The sound of a hundred human voices singing together filled the dome. He lay still, his face blank.

In the next days he took over several routine jobs, unasked. He undertook nothing that wanted initiative, and if asked to do anything he made no response at all.

"He's doing well," Pugh said in the dialect of Argentina.

"He's not. He's turning himself into a machine. Does what he's programmed to do, no reaction to anything else. He's worse off than when he didn't function at all. He's not human any more."

Pugh sighed. "Well, good night," he said in English. "Good night, Kaph."

"Good night," Martin said; Kaph did not.

Next morning at breakfast Kaph reached across Martin's plate for the toast. "Why don't you ask for it?" Martin said with the geniality of repressed exasperation. "I can pass it."

"I can reach it," Kaph said in his flat voice.

"Yes, but look. Asking to pass things, saying good night or hello, they're not important, but all the same when somebody says something a person ought to answer. . . ."

The young man looked indifferently in Martin's direction; his eyes still did not seem to see clear through to the person he looked toward. "Why should I answer?"

"Because somebody has said something to you."

"Why?"

Martin shrugged and laughed. Pugh jumped up and turned on the rock-cutter.

Later on he said, "Lay off that, please, Martin."

"Manners are essential in small isolated crews, some kind of manners, whatever you work out together. He's been taught that, everybody in Far Out knows it. Why does he deliberately flout it?"

"Do you tell yourself good night?"

"So?"

"Don't you see Kaph's never known anyone but himself?"

Martin brooded and then broke out. "Then by God this cloning business is all wrong. It won't do. What are a lot of duplicate geniuses going to do for us when they don't even know we exist?"

Pugh nodded. "It might be wiser to separate the clones and bring them up with others. But they make such a grand team this way."

"Do they? I don't know. If this lot had been ten average inefficient E.T.

engineers, would they all have got killed? What if, when the quake came and things started caving in, what if all those kids ran the same way, farther into the mine, maybe, to save the one who was farthest in? Even Kaph was outside and went in. . . . It's hypothetical. But I keep thinking, out of ten ordinary confused guys, more might have got out."

"I don't know. It's true that identical twins tend to die at about the same time, even when they have never seen each other. Identity and death, it is very strange. . . ."

The days went on, the red sun crawled across the dark sky, Kaph did not speak when spoken to, Pugh and Martin snapped at each other more frequently each day. Pugh complained of Martin's snoring. Offended, Martin moved his cot clear across the dome and also ceased speaking to Pugh for some while. Pugh whistled Welsh dirges until Martin complained, and then Pugh stopped speaking for a while.

The day before the Mission ship was due, Martin announced he was going over to Merioneth.

"I thought at least you'd be giving me a hand with the computer to finish the rock analyses," Pugh said, aggrieved.

"Kaph can do that. I want one more look at the Trench. Have fun," Martin added in dialect, and laughed, and left.

"What is that language?"

"Argentinean. I told you that once, didn't I?"

"I don't know." After a while the young man added, "I have forgotten a lot of things, I think."

"It wasn't important, to be sure," Pugh said gently, realizing all at once how important this conversation was. "Will you give me a hand running the computer, Kaph?"

He nodded.

Pugh had left a lot of loose ends, and the job took them all day. Kaph was a good co-worker, quick and systematic, much more so than Pugh himself. His flat voice, now that he was talking again, got on the nerves; but it didn't matter, there was only this one day left to get through and then the ship would come, the old crew, comrades and friends.

During tea break Kaph said, "What will happen if the Explore ship crashes?"

"They'd be killed."

"To you, I mean."

"To us? We'd radio SOS signals and live on half rations till the rescue cruiser from Area Three Base came. Four and a half E-years away it is. We have life support here for three men for, let's see, maybe between four and five years. A bit tight, it would be."

"Would they send a cruiser for three men?"

"They would."

Kaph said no more.

"Enough cheerful speculations," Pugh said cheerfully, rising to get back to work. He slipped sideways and the chair avoided his hand; he did a sort of half-pirouette and fetched up hard against the dome hide. "My goodness," he said, reverting to his native idiom, "what is it?"

"Quake," said Kaph.

The teacups bounced on the table with a plastic cackle, a litter of papers slid off a box, the skin of the dome swelled and sagged. Underfoot there was a huge noise, half sound, half shaking, a subsonic boom.

Kaph sat unmoved. An earthquake does not frighten a man who died in an earthquake.

Pugh, white-faced, wiry black hair sticking out, a frightened man, said, "Martin is in the Trench."

"What trench?"

"The big fault line. The epicenter for the local quakes. Look at the seismograph." Pugh struggled with the stuck door of a still-jittering locker.

"Where are you going?"

"After him."

"Martin took the jet. Sleds aren't safe to use during quakes. They go out of control."

"For God's sake man, shut up."

Kaph stood up, speaking in a flat voice as usual. "It's unnecessary to go out after him now. It's taking an unnecessary risk."

"If his alarm goes off, radio me," Pugh said, shut the head-piece of his suit, and ran to the lock. As he went out Libra picked up her ragged skirts and danced a belly dance from under his feet clear to the red horizon.

Inside the dome, Kaph saw the sled go up, tremble like a meteor in the dull red daylight, and vanish to the northeast. The hide of the dome quivered, the earth coughed. A vent south of the dome belched up a slow-flowing bile of black gas.

A bell shrilled and a red light flashed on the central control board. The sign under the light read Suit 2 and scribbled under that, A. G. M. Kaph did not turn the signal off. He tried to radio Martin, then Pugh, but got no reply from either.

When the aftershocks decreased he went back to work and finished up Pugh's job. It took him about two hours. Every half hour he tried to contact Suit 1 and got no reply, then Suit 2 and got no reply. The red light had stopped flashing after an hour.

It was dinnertime. Kaph cooked dinner for one and ate it. He lay down on his cot.

The aftershocks had ceased except for faint rolling tremors at long intervals. The sun hung in the west, oblate, pale red, immense. It did not sink visibly. There was no sound at all.

Kaph got up and began to walk about the messy, half-packed-up, overcrowded, empty dome. The silence continued. He went to the player and put on the first tape that came to hand. It was pure music, electronic, without harmonies, without voices. It ended. The silence continued.

Pugh's uniform tunic, one button missing, hung over a stack of rock samples. Kaph stared at it a while.

The silence continued.

The child's dream: There is no one else alive in the world but me. In all the world.

Low, north of the dome, a meteor flickered.

Kaph's mouth opened as if he were trying to say something, but no sound came. He went hastily to the north wall and peered out into the gelatinous red light.

The little star came in and sank. Two figures blurred the airlock. Kaph stood close beside the lock as they came in. Martin's imsuit was covered with some kind of dust so that he looked raddled and warty like the surface of Libra. Pugh had him by the arm.

"Is he hurt?"

Pugh shucked his suit, helped Martin peel off his. "Shaken up," he said, curt.

"A piece of cliff fell onto the jet," Martin said, sitting down at the table and waving his arms. "Not while I was in it though. I was parked, see, and poking about that carbon-dust area when I felt things humping. So I went out onto a nice bit of early igneous I'd noticed from above, good footing and out from under the cliffs. Then I saw this bit of the planet fall off onto the flyer, quite a sight it was, and after a while it occurred to me the spare aircans were in the flyer, so I leaned on the panic button. But I didn't get any radio reception, that's always happening here during quakes, so I didn't know if the signal was getting through either. And things went on jumping around and pieces of the cliff coming off. Little rocks flying around, and so dusty you couldn't see a meter ahead. I was really beginning to wonder what I'd do for breathing in the small hours, you know, when I saw old Owen buzzing up the Trench in all that dust and junk like a big ugly bat—"

"Want to eat?" said Pugh.

"Of course I want to eat. How'd you come through the quake here, Kaph? No damage? It wasn't a big one actually, was it, what's the seismo say? My trouble was I was in the middle of it. Old Epicenter Alvaro. Felt like Richter fifteen there—total destruction of planet—"

"Sit down," Pugh said. "Eat."

After Martin had eaten a little his spate of talk ran dry. He very soon went off to his cot, still in the remote angle where he had removed it when Pugh complained of his snoring. "Good night, you one-lunged Welshman," he said across the dome.

"Good night."

There was no more out of Martin. Pugh opaqued the dome, turned the lamp down to a yellow glow less than a candle's light, and sat doing nothing, saying nothing, withdrawn.

The silence continued.

"I finished the computations."

Pugh nodded thanks.

"The signal from Martin came through, but I couldn't contact you or him."

Pugh said with effort, "I should not have gone. He had two hours of air left even with only one can. He might have been heading home when I left. This way we were all out of touch with one another. I was scared."

The silence came back, punctuated now by Martin's long, soft snores.

"Do you love Martin?"

Pugh looked up with angry eyes: "Martin is my friend. We've worked together, he's a good man." He stopped. After a while he said, "Yes, I love him. Why did you ask that?"

Kaph said nothing, but he looked at the other man. His face was changed, as if he were glimpsing something he had not seen before; his voice too was changed. "How can you . . . How do you . . . ."

But Pugh could not tell him. "I don't know," he said, "it's practice, partly. I don't know. We're each of us alone, to be sure. What can you do but hold your hand out in the dark?"

Kaph's strange gaze dropped, burned out by its own intensity.

"I'm tired," Pugh said. "That was ugly, looking for him in all that black dust and muck, and mouths opening and shutting in the ground. . . . I'm going to bed. The ship will be transmitting to us by six or so." He stood up and stretched.

"It's a clone," Kaph said. "The other Exploit Team they're bringing with them."

"Is it then?"

"A twelveclone. They came out with us on the *Passerine.*"

Kaph sat in the small yellow aura of the lamp seeming to look past it at what he feared: the new clone, the multiple self of which he was not part. A lost piece of a broken set, a fragment, inexpert at solitude, not knowing even how you go about giving love to another individual, now he must face the absolute, closed self-sufficiency of the clone of twelve; that was a lot to ask of the poor fellow, to be sure. Pugh put a hand on his shoulder in passing. "The chief won't ask you to stay here with a clone. You can go home. Or since you're Far Out maybe you'll come on farther out with us. We could use you. No hurry deciding. You'll make out all right."

Pugh's quiet voice trailed off. He stood unbuttoning his coat, stopped a little with fatigue. Kaph looked at him and saw the thing he had never seen before, saw him: Owen Pugh, the other, the stranger who held his hand out in the dark.

"Good night," Pugh mumbled, crawling into his sleeping bag and half asleep already, so that he did not hear Kaph reply after a pause, repeating, across darkness, benediction.

Writing Assignments for "Nine Lives"

I. Brief Papers
   A. 1. Describe the setting of the story: when and where does it take place?
      2. According to the story, what has happened to the world since the twentieth century?

3. Are Pugh and Martin characterized as individuals or is one a clone of the other?
4. Why do Kaph and Zayin not radio to Pugh and Martin for help as soon as they realize that the mine has been hit by a quake?
5. Why does Kaph, a clone himself, fear the arrival of the twelveclone?
6. Explain what is meant by the statement that it is "the strangeness of the stranger" that is "the terrible thing" (p. 147).
7. What does the story have to say about human loneliness and human isolation?

B. Argue for or against one of the assertions below:
1. The story itself does not take a stand for or against the practice of cloning.
2. If 10 average people, instead of 10 clones, had been assigned to work in the mine, they would not all have been killed by the earthquake.
3. The story as a whole endorses Pugh's comment that it would be "glorious" to be a clone.
4. The story presents human love as frightening, uncertain, and difficult.

C. 1. Do you think it is accurate to say that the clones love each other? Why or why not?
2. How would you describe the sexual behavior of the clones? As incest? as masturbation? as something else?
3. When Kaph asks Pugh if he loves Martin, Pugh says, "Yes. I love him." Do you think he really does?
4. Pugh wonders, "What would it be like, then, to have someone as close to you as that? Always to be answered when you spoke; never to be in pain alone. Love your neighbor as you love yourself. . . . That hard old problem was solved. The neighbor was self: the love was perfect" (p. 151). Do you agree that what Pugh describes is perfect love?
5. "A clone . . . might indeed be the first truly stable, self-reliant human being" (p. 152). Do you agree?
6. Do you agree that sympathy is "one of the things you give because you need it back"?

II. Longer Papers
A. How does the story define and characterize love?
B. "I'll be glad to see a human face," Owen Pugh says in the opening paragraph. How does the story define "human?" Include in your paper a response to the question, "Are the clones human?"
C. "Identity and death, it is very strange," Pugh says at one point (p. 162). According to the story, how are identity and death related?
D. In what ways is the last line of the story both a summation and a conclusion of what has come before?
E. What does the story say about the origin and persistence of bigotry and prejudice?
F. In an introductory note she wrote for "Nine Lives," Ursula K. Le Guin said that she uses the scientific element in this story "not as an end in itself, but as a

metaphor or symbol, a means of saying something not otherwise expressible." Explain in what ways science fiction works in "Nine Lives" as "a metaphor or symbol."

G. According to the story, what are the most distinctively human qualities and characteristics?

III. Comparative Papers

A. What, taken together, do "Nine Lives" and "There Will Come Soft Rains" say about sameness and repetition in human experience?

B. In what ways does Le Guin's vision of the future in "Nine Lives" differ from Bradbury's in "There Will Come Soft Rains?"

C. Argue for or against the assertion that "Nine Lives" is a more affirmative story than "There Will Come Soft Rains."

PHILIP ROTH
Defender of the Faith

Before Reading

Free write for 5 to 10 minutes on either what the phrase "defender of the faith" means to you or what you think a story titled "Defender of the Faith" will be about.

In May of 1945, only a few weeks after the fighting had ended in Europe,* I was rotated back to the States, where I spent the remainder of the war with a training company at Camp Crowder, Missouri. Along with the rest of the Ninth Army, I had been racing across Germany so swiftly during the late winter and spring that when I boarded the plane, I couldn't believe its destination lay to the west. My mind might inform me otherwise, but there was an inertia of the spirit that told me we were flying to a new front, where we would disembark and continue our push eastward—eastward until we'd circled the globe, marching through villages along whose twisting, cobbled streets crowds of the enemy would watch us take possession of what, up till then, they'd considered their own. I had changed enough in two years not to mind the trembling of old people, the crying of the very young, the uncertainty and fear in the eyes of the once arrogant. I had been fortunate enough to develop an infantryman's heart, which, like his feet, at first aches and swells but finally grows horny enough for him to travel the weirdest paths without feeling a thing.

Captain Paul Barrett was my C.O. in Camp Crowder. The day I reported for duty, he came out of his office to shake my hand. He was short, gruff, and fiery, and—indoors or out—he wore his polished helmet liner pulled down to his little eyes. In Europe, he had received a battlefield commission and a serious chest wound, and he'd been returned to the States only a few months before. He spoke easily to me, and at the evening formation he introduced me to the troops. "Gentlemen," he said. "Sergeant Thurston, as you know, is no longer with this company. Your new first sergeant is Sergeant Nathan Marx, here. He is a veteran of the European theater, and consequently will expect to find a company of soldiers here, and not a company of *boys.*"

I sat up late in the orderly room that evening, trying half-heartedly to solve the riddle of duty rosters, personnel forms, and morning reports. The Charge of Quarters slept with his mouth open on a mattress on the floor. A trainee stood reading the next day's duty roster, which was posted on the bulletin board just inside the screen door. It was a warm evening, and I could hear radios playing dance music over in the barracks. The trainee, who had

---

*in Europe: Although Germany surrendered to the Allies on May 7, 1945, World War II did not end until Japan surrendered four months later.

DEFENDER OF THE FAITH   First published in 1959. Philip Roth, born in 1933 in Newark, New Jersey, often writes in his short stories and novels of Jewish middle-class life.

been staring at me whenever he thought I wouldn't notice, finally took a step in my direction.

"Hey, Sarge—we having a G.I. party tomorrow night?" he asked. A G.I. party is a barracks cleaning.

"You usually have them on Friday nights?" I asked him.

"Yes," he said, and then he added, mysteriously, "that's the whole thing."

"Then you'll have a G.I. party."

He turned away, and I heard him mumbling. His shoulders were moving and I wondered if he was crying.

"What's your name, soldier?" I asked.

He turned, not crying at all. Instead, his green-speckled eyes, long and narrow, flashed like fish in the sun. He walked over to me and sat on the edge of my desk. He reached out a hand. "Sheldon," he said.

"Stand on your feet, Sheldon."

Getting off the desk, he said, "Sheldon Grossbart." He smiled at the familiarity into which he'd led me.

"You against cleaning the barracks Friday night, Grossbart?" I said. "Maybe we shouldn't have G.I. parties. Maybe we should get a maid." My tone startled me. I felt I sounded like every top sergeant I had ever known.

"No, Sergeant." He grew serious, but with a seriousness that seemed to be only the stifling of a smile. "It's just—G.I. parties on Friday night, of all nights."

He slipped up onto the corner of the desk again—not quite sitting, but not quite standing, either. He looked at me with those speckled eyes flashing, and then made a gesture with his hand. It was very slight—no more than a movement back and forth of the wrist—and yet it managed to exclude from our affairs everything else in the orderly room, to make the two of us the center of the world. It seemed, in fact, to exclude everything even about the two of us except our hearts.

"Sergeant Thurston was one thing," he whispered, glancing at the sleeping C.Q., "but we thought that with you here things might be a little different."

"We?"

"The Jewish personnel."

"Why?" I asked, harshly. "What's on your mind?" Whether I was still angry at the "Sheldon" business, or now at something else, I hadn't time to tell, but clearly I was angry.

"We thought you—Marx, you know, like Karl Marx. The Marx Brothers. Those guys are all—M-a-r-x. Isn't that how *you* spell it, Sergeant?"

"M-a-r-x."

"Fishbein said—" He stopped. "What I mean to say, Sergeant—" His face and neck were red, and his mouth moved but no words came out. In a moment, he raised himself to attention, gazing down at me. It was as though he had suddenly decided he could expect no more sympathy from me than from Thurston, the reason being that I was of Thurston's faith, and not his. The young man had managed to confuse himself as to what my faith really was, but I felt no desire to straighten him out. Very simply, I didn't like him.

When I did nothing but return his gaze, he spoke, in an altered tone. "You see, Sergeant," he explained to me, "Friday nights, Jews are supposed to go to services."

"Did Sergeant Thurston tell you you couldn't go to them when there was a G.I. party?"

"No."

"Did he say you had to stay and scrub the floors?"

"No, Sergeant."

"Did the Captain say you had to stay and scrub the floors?"

"That isn't it, Sergeant. It's the other guys in the barracks." He leaned toward me. "They think we're goofing off. But we're not. That's when Jews go to services, Friday night. We have to."

"Then go."

"But the other guys make accusations. They have no right."

"That's not the Army's problem, Grossbart. It's a personal problem you'll have to work out yourself."

"But it's un*fair.*"

I got up to leave. "There's nothing I can do about it," I said.

Grossbart stiffened and stood in front of me. "But this is a matter of *religion,* sir."

"Sergeant," I said.

"I mean 'Sergeant,' " he said, almost snarling.

"Look, go see the chaplain. You want to see Captain Barrett, I'll arrange an appointment."

"No, no. I don't want to make trouble, Sergeant. That's the first thing they throw up to you. I just want my rights!"

"Damn it, Grossbart, stop whining. You have your rights. You can stay and scrub floors or you can go to shul—"*

The smile swam in again. Spittle gleamed at the corners of his mouth. "You mean church, Sergeant."

"I mean shul, Grossbart!"

I walked past him and went outside. Near me, I heard the scrunching of the guard's boots on gravel. Beyond the lighted windows of the barracks, young men in T shirts and fatigue pants were sitting on their bunks, polishing their rifles. Suddenly there was a light rustling behind me. I turned and saw Grossbart's dark frame fleeing back to the barracks, racing to tell his Jewish friends that they were right—that, like Karl and Harpo, I was one of them.

The next morning, while chatting with Captain Barrett, I recounted the incident of the previous evening. Somehow, in the telling, it must have seemed to the Captain that I was not so much explaining Grossbart's position as defending it. "Marx, I'd fight side by side with a nigger if the fella proved to me he was a man. I pride myself," he said, looking out the window, "that I've got an open mind. Consequently, Sergeant, nobody gets special treatment here, for the

*shul: Synagogue.

good *or* the bad. All a man's got to do is prove himself. A man fires well on the range, I give him a weekend pass. He scores high in P.T., he gets a weekend pass. He *earns* it." He turned from the window and pointed a finger at me. "You're a Jewish fella, am I right, Marx?"

"Yes, sir."

"And I admire you. I admire you because of the ribbons on your chest. I judge a man by what he shows me on the field of battle, Sergeant. It's what he's got *here,*" he said, and then, though I expected he would point to his chest, he jerked a thumb toward the buttons straining to hold his blouse across his belly. "Guts," he said.

"O.K., sir. I only wanted to pass on to you how the men felt."

"Mr. Marx, you're going to be old before your time if you worry about how the men feel. Leave that stuff to the chaplain—that's his business, not yours. Let's us train these fellas to shoot straight. If the Jewish personnel feels the other men are accusing them of goldbricking—well, I just don't know. Seems awful funny that suddenly the Lord is calling so loud in Private Grossman's ear he's just got to run to church."

"Synagogue," I said.

"Synagogue is right, Sergeant. I'll write that down for handy reference. Thank you for stopping by."

That evening, a few minutes before the company gathered outside the orderly room for the chow formation, I called the C.Q., Corporal Robert LaHill, in to see me. LaHill was a dark, burly fellow whose hair curled out of his clothes wherever it could. He had a glaze in his eyes that made one think of caves and dinosaurs. "LaHill," I said, "when you take the formation, remind the men that they're free to attend church services *whenever* they are held, provided they report to the orderly room before they leave the area."

LaHill scratched his wrist, but gave no indication that he'd heard or understood.

"LaHill," I said, "*church.* You remember? Church, priest, Mass, confession."

He curled one lip into a kind of smile; I took it for a signal that for a second he had flickered back up into the human race.

"Jewish personnel who want to attend services this evening are to fall out in front of the orderly room at 1900," I said. Then, as an afterthought, I added, "By order of Captain Barrett."

A little while later, as the day's last light—softer than any I had seen that year—began to drop over Camp Crowder, I heard LaHill's thick, inflectionless voice outside my window: "Give me your ears, troopers. Toppie says for me to tell you that at 1900 hours all Jewish personnel is to fall out in front, here, if they want to attend the Jewish Mass."

At seven o'clock, I looked out the orderly-room window and saw three soldiers in starched khakis standing on the dusty quadrangle. They looked at their watches and fidgeted while they whispered back and forth. It was getting dimmer, and, alone on the otherwise deserted field, they looked tiny. When I opened the door, I heard the noises of the G.I. party coming from the surrounding barracks—bunks being pushed to the walls, faucets pounding water into buckets, brooms whisking at the wooden floors, cleaning the dirt away for Saturday's inspection. Big puffs of cloth moved round and round on the windowpanes. I walked outside, and the moment my foot hit the ground I thought I heard Grossbart call to the others "Ten-*hut!*" Or maybe, when they all three jumped to attention, I imagined I heard the command.

Grossbart stepped forward, "Thank you, sir," he said.

" 'Sergeant,' Grossbart," I reminded him. "You call officers 'sir.' I'm not an officer. You've been in the Army three weeks—you know that."

He turned his palms out at his sides to indicate that, in truth, he and I lived beyond convention. "Thank you anyway," he said.

"Yes," a tall boy behind him said. "Thanks a lot."

And the third boy whispered, "Thank you," but his mouth barely fluttered, so that he did not alter by more than a lip's movement his posture of attention.

"For what?" I asked.

Grossbart snorted happily. "For the announcement. The Corporal's announcement. It helped. It made it—"

"Fancier." The tall boy finished Grossbart's sentence.

Grossbart smiled. "He means formal, sir. Public," he said to me. "Now it won't seem as though we're just taking off—goldbricking because the work has begun."

"It was by order of Captain Barrett," I said.

"Aaah, but you pull a little weight," Grossbart said. "So we thank you." Then he turned to his companions. "Sergeant Marx, I want you to meet Larry Fishbein."

The tall boy stepped forward and extended his hand. I shook it. "You from New York?" he asked.

"Yes."

"Me, too." He had a cadaverous face that collapsed inward from his cheekbone to his jaw, and when he smiled—as he did at the news of our communal attachment—revealed a mouthful of bad teeth. He was blinking his eyes a good deal, as though he were fighting back tears. "What borough?" he asked.

I turned to Grossbart. "It's five after seven. What time are services?"

"Shul," he said, smiling, "is in ten minutes. I want you to meet Mickey Halpern. This is Nathan Marx, our sergeant."

The third boy hopped forward. "Private Michael Halpern." He saluted.

"Salute officers, Halpern," I said. The boy dropped his hand, and, on its way down, in his nervousness, checked to see if his shirt pockets were buttoned.

"Shall I march them over, sir?" Grossbart asked. "Or are you coming along?"

From behind Grossbart, Fishbein piped up. "Afterward, they're having refreshments. A ladies auxiliary from St. Louis, the rabbi told us last week."

"The chaplain," Halpern whispered.

"You're welcome to come along," Grossbart said.

To avoid his plea, I looked away, and saw, in the windows of the barracks, a cloud of faces staring out at the four of us. "Hurry along, Grossbart," I said.

"O.K., then," he said. He turned to the others. "Double time, *march!*"

They started off, but ten feet away Grossbart spun around and, running backward, called to me "Good *shabbus,* * sir!" And then the three of them were swallowed into the alien Missouri dusk.

Even after they had disappeared over the parade ground, whose green was now a deep blue, I could hear Grossbart singing the double-time cadence, and as it grew dimmer and dimmer, it suddenly touched a deep memory—as did the slant of the light—and I was remembering the shrill sounds of a Bronx playground where, years ago, beside the Grand Concourse,† I had played on long spring evenings such as this. It was a pleasant memory for a young man so far from peace and home, and it brought so many recollections with it that I began to grow exceedingly tender about myself. In fact, I indulged myself in a reverie so strong that I felt as though a hand were reaching down inside me. It had to reach so very far to touch me! It had to reach past those days in the forests of Belgium, and past the dying I'd refused to weep over; past the nights in German farmhouses whose books we'd burned to warm us; past endless stretches when I had shut off all softness I might feel for my fellows, and had managed even to deny myself the posture of a conqueror—the swagger that I, as a Jew, might well have worn as my boots whacked against the rubble of Wesel, Münster, and Braunschweig.‡

But now one night noise, one rumor of home and time past, and memory plunged down through all I had anesthetized, and came to what I suddenly remembered was myself. So it was not altogether curious that, in search of more of me, I found myself following Grossbart's tracks to Chapel No. 3, where the Jewish services were being held.

I took a seat in the last row, which was empty. Two rows in front of me sat Grossbart, Fishbein, and Halpern, holding little white Dixie cups. Each row of seats was raised higher than the one in front of it, and I could see clearly what was going on. Fishbein was pouring the contents of his cup into Grossbart's, and Grossbart looked mirthful as the liquid made a purple arc between Fishbein's hand and his. In the glaring yellow light, I saw the chaplain standing on the platform at the front; he was chanting the first line of the responsive reading. Grossbart's prayer book remained closed on his lap; he was swishing the cup around. Only Halpern responded to the chant by praying. The fingers of his right hand were spread wide across the cover of his open book. His cap was pulled down low onto his brow, which made it round, like a yarmulke.§ From time to time, Grossbart wet his lips at the cup's edge; Fishbein, his long yellow face a dying light bulb, looked from here to there, craning forward to catch sight of the faces down the row, then of those in front of him, then behind. He saw

shabbus: Yiddish, Sabbath.

†Grand Concourse: An expressway in the Bronx, New York City.

‡Wesel, Münster, Braunschweig: German cities virtually destroyed by Allied shelling during World War II.

§yarmulke: Skullcap worn by observing Jewish males as a sign of respect for God.

me, and his eyelids beat a tattoo. His elbow slid into Grossbart's side, his neck inclined toward his friend, he whispered something, and then, when the congregation next responded to the chant, Grossbart's voice was among the others. Fishbein looked into his book now, too; his lips, however, didn't move.

Finally, it was time to drink the wine. The chaplain smiled down at them as Grossbart swigged his in one long gulp, Halpern sipped, meditating, and Fishbein faked devotion with an empty cup. "As I look down amongst the congregation"—the chaplain grinned at the word—"this night, I see many new faces, and I want to welcome you to Friday-night services here at Camp Crowder. I am Major Leo Ben Ezra, your chaplain." Though an American, the chaplain spoke deliberately—syllable by syllable, almost—as though to communicate, above all, with the lip readers in his audience. "I have only a few words to say before we adjourn to the refreshment room, where the kind ladies of the Temple Sinai, St. Louis, Missouri, have a nice setting for you."

Applause and whistling broke out. After another momentary grin, the chaplain raised his hands, palms out, his eyes flicking upward a moment, as if to remind the troops where they were and Who Else might be in attendance. In the sudden silence that followed, I thought I heard Grossbart cackle, "Let the goyim* clean the floors!" Were those the words? I wasn't sure, but Fishbein, grinning, nudged Halpern. Halpern looked dumbly at him, then went back to his prayer book, which had been occupying him all through the rabbi's talk. One hand tugged at the black kinky hair that stuck out under his cap. His lips moved.

The rabbi continued. "It is about the food that I want to speak to you for a moment. I know, I know, I know," he intoned, wearily, "how in the mouths of most of you the *trafe*† food tastes like ashes. I know how you gag, some of you, and how your parents suffer to think of their children eating foods unclean and offensive to the palate. What can I tell you? I can only say, close your eyes and swallow as best you can. Eat what you must to live, and throw away the rest. I wish I could help more. For those of you who find this impossible, may I ask that you try and try, but then come to see me in private. If your revulsion is so great, we will have to seek aid from those higher up."

A round of chatter rose and subsided. Then everyone sang "Ain Kelohainu"‡; after all those years, I discovered I still knew the words. Then, suddenly, the service over, Grossbart was upon me. "Higher up? He means the General?"

"Hey, Shelly," Fishbein said, "he means God." He smacked his face and looked at Halpern. "How high can you go!"

"Sh-h-h!" Grossbart said. "What do you think, Sergeant?"

"I don't know," I said. "You better ask the chaplain."

"I'm going to. I'm making an appointment to see him in private. So is Mickey."

---

*goyim: Gentiles, not Jews.
†*trafe:* Nonkosher food and therefore unfit to eat.
‡"Ain Kelohainu": "There is no God like our God."

Halpern shook his head. "No, no, Sheldon—"

"You have rights, Mickey," Grossbart said. "They can't push us around."

"It's O.K.," said Halpern. "It bothers my mother, not me."

Grossbart looked at me. "Yesterday he threw up. From the hash. It was all ham and God knows what else."

"I have a cold—that was why," Halpern said. He pushed his yarmulke back into a cap.

"What about you, Fishbein?" I asked. "You kosher, too?"

He flushed. "A little. But I'll let it ride. I have a very strong stomach, and I don't eat a lot anyway." I continued to look at him, and he held up his wrist to reinforce what he'd just said; his watch strap was tightened to the last hole, and he pointed that out to me.

"But services are important to you?" I asked him.

He looked at Grossbart. "Sure, sir."

" 'Sergeant.' "

"Not so much at home," said Grossbart, stepping between us, "but away from home it gives one a sense of his Jewishness."

"We have to stick together," Fishbein said.

I started to walk toward the door; Halpern stepped back to make way for me.

"That's what happened in Germany," Grossbart was saying, loud enough for me to hear. "They didn't stick together. They let themselves get pushed around."

I turned. "Look, Grossbart. This is the Army, not summer camp."

He smiled. "So?"

Halpern tried to sneak off, but Grossbart held his arm.

"Grossbart, how old are you?" I asked.

"Nineteen."

"And you?" I said to Fishbein.

"The same. The same month, even."

"And what about him?" I pointed to Halpern, who had by now made it safely to the door.

"Eighteen," Grossbart whispered. "But like he can't tie his shoes or brush his teeth himself. I feel sorry for him."

"I feel sorry for all of us, Grossbart," I said, "but just act like a man. Just don't overdo it?"

"Overdo what, sir?"

"The 'sir' business, for one thing. Don't overdo that," I said.

I left him standing there. I passed by Halpern, but he did not look at me. Then I was outside, but, behind, I heard Grossbart call, "Hey, Mickey, my *leben,** come on back. Refreshments!"

"*Leben!*" My grandmother's word for me!

*   *   *   *   *

---

*leben: Darling.

One morning a week later, while I was working at my desk, Captain Barrett shouted for me to come into his office. When I entered, he had his helmet liner squashed down so far on his head that I couldn't even see his eyes. He was on the phone, and when he spoke to me, he cupped one hand over the mouthpiece. "Who the hell is Grossbart?"

"Third platoon, Captain," I said. "A trainee."

"What's all this stink about food? His mother called a goddam congressman about the food." He uncovered the mouthpiece and slid his helmet up until I could see his bottom eyelashes. "Yes, sir," he said into the phone. "Yes, sir. I'm still here, sir. I'm asking Marx, here, right now—"

He covered the mouthpiece again and turned his head back toward me. "Lightfoot Harry's on the phone," he said, between his teeth. "This congressman calls General Lyman, who calls Colonel Sousa, who calls the Major, who calls me. They're just dying to stick this thing on me. Whatsa matter?" He shook the phone at me. "I don't feed the troops? What is this?"

"Sir, Grossbart is strange—" Barrett greeted that with a mockingly indulgent smile. I altered my approach. "Captain, he's a very orthodox Jew, and so he's only allowed to eat certain foods."

"He throws up, the congressman said. Every time he eats something, his mother says, he throws up!"

"He's accustomed to observing the dietary laws, Captain."

"So why's his old lady have to call the White House?"

"Jewish parents, sir—they're apt to be more protective than you expect. I mean, Jews have a very close family life. A boy goes away from home, sometimes the mother is liable to get very upset. Probably the boy mentioned something in a letter, and his mother misinterpreted."

"I'd like to punch him one right in the mouth," the Captain said. "There's a war on, and he wants a silver platter!"

"I don't think the boy's to blame, sir. I'm sure we can straighten it out by just asking him. Jewish parents worry—"

"*All* parents worry, for Christ's sake. But they don't get on their high horse and start pulling strings—"

I interrupted, my voice higher, tighter than before. "The home life, Captain, is very important—but you're right, it may sometimes get out of hand. It's a very wonderful thing, Captain, but because it's so close, this kind of thing . . ."

He didn't listen any longer to my attempt to present both myself and Lightfoot Harry with an explanation for the letter. He turned back to the phone. "Sir?" he said. "Sir—Marx, here, tells me Jews have a tendency to be pushy. He says he thinks we can settle it right here in the company. . . . Yes, sir . . . I *will* call back, sir, soon as I can." He hung up. "Where are the men, Sergeant?"

"On the range."

With a whack on the top of his helmet, he crushed it down over his eyes again, and charged out of his chair. "We're going for a ride," he said.

The Captain drove, and I sat beside him. It was a hot spring day, and under my newly starched fatigues I felt as though my armpits were melting down into my sides and chest. The roads were dry, and by the time we reached the firing range, my teeth felt gritty with dust, though my mouth had been shut the whole trip. The Captain slammed the brakes on and told me to get the hell out and find Grossbart.

I found him on his belly, firing wildly at the five-hundred-feet target. Waiting their turns behind him were Halpern and Fishbein. Fishbein, wearing a pair of steel-rimmed G.I. glasses I hadn't seen on him before, had the appearance of an old peddler who would gladly have sold you his rifle and the cartridges that were slung all over him. I stood back by the ammo boxes, waiting for Grossbart to finish spraying the distant target. Fishbein straggled back to stand near me.

"Hello, Sergeant Marx," he said.

"How are you?" I mumbled.

"Fine, thank you. Sheldon's really a good shot."

"I didn't notice."

"I'm not so good, but I think I'm getting the hang of it now. Sergeant, I don't mean to, you know, ask what I shouldn't—" The boy stopped. He was trying to speak intimately, but the noise of the shooting forced him to shout at me.

"What is it?" I asked. Down the range, I saw Captain Barrett standing up in the jeep, scanning the line for me and Grossbart.

"My parents keep asking and asking where we're going," Fishbein said. "Everybody says the Pacific. I don't care, but my parents—If I could relieve their minds, I think I could concentrate more on my shooting."

"I don't know where, Fishbein. Try to concentrate anyway."

"Sheldon says you might be able to find out."

"I don't know a thing, Fishbein. You just take it easy, and don't let Sheldon—"

"*I'm* taking it easy, Sergeant. It's at home—"

Grossbart had finished on the line, and was dusting his fatigues with one hand. I called to him. "Grossbart, the Captain wants to see you."

He came toward us. His eyes blazed and twinkled. "Hi!"

"Don't point that rifle!" I said.

"I wouldn't shoot you, Sarge." He gave me a smile as wide as a pumpkin, and turned the barrel aside.

"Damn you, Grossbart, this is no joke! Follow me."

I walked ahead of him, and had the awful suspicion that, behind me, Grossbart was *marching,* his rifle on his shoulder as though he were a one-man detachment. At the jeep, he gave the Captain a rifle salute. "Private Sheldon Grossbart, sir."

"At ease, Grossman." The Captain sat down, slid over into the empty seat, and, crooking a finger, invited Grossbart closer.

"Bart, sir. Sheldon Gross*bart.* It's a common error." Grossbart nodded at me; *I* understood, he indicated. I looked away just as the mess truck pulled up to the range, disgorging a half-dozen K.P.s with rolled-up sleeves. The mess sergeant screamed at them while they set up the chow line equipment.

"Grossbart, your mama wrote some congressman that we don't feed you right. Do you know that?" the Captain said.

"It was my father, sir. He wrote to Representative Franconi that my religion forbids me to eat certain foods."

"What religion is that, Grossbart?"

"Jewish."

" 'Jewish, *sir,*' " I said to Grossbart.

"Excuse me, sir, Jewish, sir."

"What have you been living on?" the Captain asked. "You've been in the Army a month already. You don't look to me like you're falling to pieces."

"I eat because I have to, sir. But Sergeant Marx will testify to the fact that I don't eat one mouthful more than I need to in order to survive."

"Is that so, Marx?" Barrett asked.

"I've never seen Grossbart eat, sir," I said.

"But you heard the rabbi," Grossbart said. "He told us what to do, and I listened."

The Captain looked at me. "Well, Marx?"

"I still don't know what he eats and doesn't eat, sir."

Grossbart raised his arms to plead with me, and it looked for a moment as though he were going to hand me his weapon to hold. "But, Sergeant—"

"Look, Grossbart, just answer the Captain's questions," I said sharply.

Barrett smiled at me, and I resented it. "All right, Grossbart," he said. "What is it you want? The little piece of paper? You want out?"

"No, sir. Only to be allowed to live as a Jew. And for the others, too."

"What others?"

"Fishbein, sir, and Halpern."

"They don't like the way we serve, either?"

"Halpern throws up, sir. I've seen it."

"I thought *you* throw up."

"Just once, sir. I didn't know the sausage was sausage."

"We'll give menus, Grossbart. We'll show training films about the food, so you can identify when we're trying to poison you."

Grossbart did not answer. The men had been organized into two long chow lines. At the tail end of one, I spotted Fishbein—or, rather, his glasses spotted me. They winked sunlight back at me. Halpern stood next to him, patting the inside of his collar with a khaki handkerchief. They moved with the line as it began to edge up toward the food. The mess sergeant was still screaming at the K.P.s. For a moment, I was actually terrified by the thought that somehow the mess sergeant was going to become involved in Grossbart's problem.

"Marx," the Captain said, "you're a Jewish fella—am I right?"

I played straight man. "Yes, sir."

"How long you been in the Army? Tell this boy."

"Three years and two months."

"A year in combat, Grossbart. Twelve goddam months in combat all through Europe. I admire this man." The Captain snapped a wrist against my chest. "Do you hear him peeping about the food? Do you? I want an answer, Grossbart. Yes or no."

"No, sir."

"And why not? He's a Jewish fella."

"Some things are more important to some Jews than other things to other Jews."

Barrett blew up. "Look, Grossbart. Marx, here, is a good man—a goddam hero. When you were in high school, Sergeant Marx was killing Germans. Who does more for the Jews—you, by throwing up over a lousy piece of sausage, a piece of first-cut meat, or Marx, by killing those Nazi bastards? If I was a Jew, Grossbart, I'd kiss this man's feet. He's a goddam hero, and *he* eats what we give him. Why do you have to cause trouble is what I want to know! What is it you're buckin' for—a discharge?"

"No, sir."

"I'm talking to a wall! Sergeant, get him out of my way." Barrett swung himself back into the driver's seat. "I'm going to see the chaplain." The engine roared, the jeep spun around in a whirl of dust, and the Captain was headed back to camp.

For a moment, Grossbart and I stood side by side, watching the jeep. Then he looked at me and said, "I don't want to start trouble. That's the first thing they toss up to us."

When he spoke, I saw that his teeth were white and straight, and the sight of them suddenly made me understand that Grossbart actually did have parents—that once upon a time someone had taken little Sheldon to the dentist. He was their son. Despite all the talk about his parents, it was hard to believe in Grossbart as a child, an heir—as related by blood to anyone, mother, father, or, above all, to me. This realization led me to another.

"What does your father do, Grossbart?" I asked as we started to walk back toward the chow line.

"He's a tailor."

"An American?"

"Now, yes. A son in the Army," he said, jokingly.

"And your mother?" I asked.

He winked. "A *ballabusta*.* She practically sleeps with a dustcloth in her hand."

"She's also an immigrant?"

"All she talks is Yiddish, still."

"And your father, too?"

"A little English. 'Clean,' 'Press,' 'Take the pants in.' That's the extent of it. But they're good to me."

"Then, Grossbart—" I reached out and stopped him. He turned toward

ballabusta: Good housekeeper

me, and when our eyes met, his seemed to jump back, to shiver in their sockets. "Grossbart—you were the one who wrote that letter, weren't you?"

It took only a second or two for his eyes to flash happy again. "Yes." He walked on, and I kept pace. "It's what my father *would* have written if he had known how. It was his name, though. *He* signed it. He even mailed it. I sent it home. For the New York postmark."

I was astonished, and he saw it. With complete seriousness, he thrust his right arm in front of me. "Blood is blood, Sergeant," he said, pinching the blue vein in his wrist.

"What the hell *are* you trying to do, Grossbart?" I asked. "I've seen you eat. Do you know that? I told the Captain I don't know what you eat, but I've seen you eat like a hound at chow."

"We work hard, Sergeant. We're in training. For a furnace to work, you've got to feed it coal."

"Why did you say in the letter that you threw up all the time?"

"I was really talking about Mickey there. I was talking *for* him. He would never write, Sergeant, though I pleaded with him. He'll waste away to nothing if I don't help. Sergeant, I used my name—my father's name—but it's Mickey, and Fishbein, too, I'm watching out for."

"You're a regular Messiah, aren't you?"

We were at the chow line now.

"That's a good one, Sergeant," he said, smiling. "But who knows? Who can tell? Maybe you're the Messiah—a little bit. What Mickey says is the Messiah is a collective idea. He went to Yeshiva,* Mickey, for a while. He says *together* we're the Messiah. Me a little bit, you a little bit. You should hear that kid talk, Sergeant, when he gets going."

"Me a little bit, you a little bit," I said. "You'd like to believe that, wouldn't you, Grossbart? That would make everything so clean for you."

"It doesn't seem too bad a thing to believe, Sergeant. It only means we should all *give* a little, is all."

I walked off to eat my rations with the other noncoms.

Two days later, a letter addressed to Captain Barrett passed over my desk. It had come through the chain of command—from the office of Congressman Franconi, where it had been received, to General Lyman, to Colonel Sousa, to Major Lamont, now to Captain Barrett. I read it over twice. It was dated May 14, the day Barrett had spoken with Grossbart on the rifle range.

Dear Congressman:
First let me thank you for your interest in behalf of my son, Private Sheldon Grossbart. Fortunately, I was able to speak with Sheldon on the phone the other night, and I think I've been able to solve our problem. He is, as I mentioned in my last letter, a very religious boy, and it was only with the greatest difficulty that I could persuade him that the religious

*Yeshiva: Jewish seminary where Talmud, law, and ritual are major subjects.

thing to do—what God Himself would want Sheldon to do—would be to suffer the pangs of religious remorse for the good of his country and all mankind. It took some doing, Congressman, but finally he saw the light. In fact, what he said (and I wrote down the words on a scratch pad so as never to forget), what he said was "I guess you're right, Dad. So many millions of my fellow-Jews gave up their lives to the enemy, the least I can do is live for a while minus a bit of my heritage so as to help end this struggle and regain for all the children of God dignity and humanity." That, Congressman, would make any father proud.

By the way, Sheldon wanted me to know—and to pass on to you—the name of a soldier who helped him reach this decision: SERGEANT NATHAN MARX. Sergeant Marx is a combat veteran who is Sheldon's first sergeant. This man has helped Sheldon over some of the first hurdles he's had to face in the Army, and is in part responsible for Sheldon's changing his mind about the dietary laws. I know Sheldon would appreciate any recognition Marx could receive.

Thank you and good luck. I look forward to seeing your name on the next election ballot.

Respectfully,
Samuel E. Grossbart

Attached to the Grossbart communiqué was another, addressed to General Marshall Lyman, the post commander, and signed by Representative Charles E. Franconi, of the House of Representatives. The communiqué informed General Lyman that Sergeant Nathan Marx was a credit to the U.S. Army and the Jewish people.

What was Grossbart's motive in recanting? Did he feel he'd gone too far? Was the letter a strategic retreat—a crafty attempt to strengthen what he considered our alliance? Or had he actually changed his mind, via an imaginary dialogue beteween Grossbart *père* and Grossbart *fils*?* I was puzzled, but only for a few days—that is, only until I realized that, whatever his reasons, he had actually decided to disappear from my life; he was going to allow himself to become just another trainee. I saw him at inspection, but he never winked; at chow formations, but he never flashed me a sign. On Sunday, with the other trainees, he would sit around watching the noncoms' softball team, for which I pitched, but not once did he speak an unnecessary word to me. Fishbein and Halpern retreated, too—at Grossbart's command, I was sure. Apparently he had seen that wisdom lay in turning back before he plunged over into the ugliness of privilege undeserved. Our separation allowed me to forgive him our past encounters, and finally, to admire him for his good sense.

Meanwhile, free of Grossbart, I grew used to my job and my administrative tasks. I stepped on a scale one day, and discovered I had truly become a noncombatant; I had gained seven pounds. I found patience to get past the first three pages of a book. I thought about the future more and more, and wrote letters to girls I'd known before the war. I even got a few answers. I sent away to Columbia for a Law School catalogue. I continued to follow the war in the Pacific, but it was not my war. I thought I could see the end, and sometimes,

*père and fils: French, Father and son.

at night, I dreamed that I was walking on the streets of Manhattan—Broadway, Third Avenue, 116th Street, where I had lived the three years I attended Columbia. I curled myself around these dreams and I began to be happy.

And then, one Sunday, when everybody was away and I was alone in the orderly room reading a month-old copy of the *Sporting News,* Grossbart reappeared.

"You a baseball fan, Sergeant?"

I looked up. "How are you?"

"Fine," Grossbart said. "They're making a soldier out of me."

"How are Fishbein and Halpern?"

"Coming along," he said. "We've got no training this afternoon. They're at the movies."

"How come you're not with them?"

"I wanted to come over and say hello."

He smiled—a shy, regular-guy smile, as though he and I well knew that our friendship drew its sustenance from unexpected visits, remembered birthdays, and borrowed lawnmowers. At first it offended me, and then the feeling was swallowed by the general uneasiness I felt at the thought that everyone on the post was locked away in a dark movie theater and I was here alone with Grossbart. I folded up my paper.

"Sergeant," he said, "I'd like to ask a favor. It is a favor, and I'm making no bones about it."

He stopped, allowing me to refuse him a hearing—which, of course, forced me into a courtesy I did not intend. "Go ahead."

"Well, actually, it's two favors."

I said nothing.

"The first one's about these rumors. Everybody says we're going to the Pacific."

"As I told your friend Fishbein, I don't know," I said. "You'll just have to wait to find out. Like everybody else."

"You think there's a chance of any of us going East?"

"Germany?" I said. "Maybe."

"I meant New York."

"I don't think so, Grossbart. Offhand."

"Thanks for the information, Sergeant," he said.

"It's not information, Grossbart. Just what I surmise."

"It certainly would be good to be near home. My parents—you know." He took a step toward the door and then turned back. "Oh, the other thing. May I ask the other?"

"What is it?"

"The other thing is—I've got relatives in St. Louis, and they say they'll give me a whole Passover dinner if I can get down there. God, Sergeant, that'd mean an awful lot to me."

I stood up. "No passes during basic, Grossbart."

"But we're off from now till Monday morning, Sergeant. I could leave the post and no one would even know."

"I'd know. You'd know."

"But that's all. Just the two of us. Last night, I called my aunt, and you should have heard her. 'Come—come,' she said. 'I got gefilte fish, *chrain**—the works!' Just a day, Sergeant. I'd take the blame if anything happened."

"The Captain isn't here to sign a pass."

"You could sign."

"Look, Grossbart—"

"Sergeant, for two months, practically, I've been eating *trafe* till I want to die."

"I thought you'd made up your mind to live with it. To be minus a little bit of heritage."

He pointed a finger at me. "You!" he said. "That wasn't for you to read."

"I read it. So what?"

"The letter was addressed to a congressman."

"Grossbart, don't feed me any baloney. You *wanted* me to read it."

"Why are you persecuting me, Sergeant?"

"Are you kidding!"

"I've run into this before," he said, "but never from my own!"

"Get out of here, Grossbart! Get the hell out of my sight!"

He did not move. "Ashamed, that's what you are," he said. "So you take it out on the rest of us. They say Hitler himself was half a Jew. Hearing you, I wouldn't doubt it."

"What are you trying to do with me, Grossbart?" I asked him. "What are you after? You want me to give you special privileges, to change the food, to find out about your orders, to give you weekend passes."

"You even talk like a goy!" Grossbart shook his fist. "Is this just a weekend pass I'm asking for? Is a Seder† sacred, or not?"

Seder! It suddenly occurred to me that Passover had been celebrated weeks before. I said so.

"That's right," he replied. "Who says no? A month ago—and I was in the field eating hash! And now all I ask is a simple favor. A Jewish boy I thought would understand. My aunt's willing to go out of her way—to make a Seder a month later . . ." He turned to go, mumbling.

"Come back here!" I called. He stopped and looked at me. "Grossbart, why can't you be like the rest? Why do you have to stick out like a sore thumb?"

"Because I'm a Jew, Sergeant. I *am* different. Better, maybe not. But different."

"This is a war, Grossbart. For the time being *be* the same."

"I refuse."

"What?"

"I refuse. I can't stop being me, that's all there is to it." Tears came to his eyes. "It's a hard thing to be a Jew. But now I understand what Mickey says—it's a harder thing to stay one." He raised a hand sadly toward me. "Look at *you*."

---

*gefilte fish, *chrain:* Seasoned chopped fish and horseradish.
†Seder: Ceremonial dinner on the first evening of Passover.

"Stop crying!"

"Stop this, stop that, stop the other thing! *You* stop, Sergeant. Stop closing your heart to your own!" And, wiping his face with his sleeve, he ran out the door. "The least we can do for one another—the least . . ."

An hour later, looking out of the window, I saw Grossbart headed across the field. He wore a pair of starched khakis and carried a little leather ditty bag. I went out into the heat of the day. It was quiet; not a soul was in sight except, over by the mess hall, four K.P.s sitting around a pan, sloped forward from their waists, gabbing and peeling potatoes in the sun.

"Grossbart!" I called.

He looked toward me and continued walking.

"Grossbart, get over here!"

He turned and came across the field. Finally, he stood before me.

"Where are you going?" I asked.

"St. Louis. I don't care."

"You'll get caught without a pass."

"So I'll get caught without a pass."

"You'll go to the stockade."

"I'm *in* the stockade." He made an about-face and headed off.

I let him go only a step or two. "Come back here," I said, and he followed me into the office, where I typed out a pass and signed the Captain's name, and my own initials after it.

He took the pass and then, a moment later, reached out and grabbed my hand. "Sergeant, you don't know how much this means to me."

"O.K.," I said. "Don't get in any trouble."

"I wish I could show you how much this means to me."

"Don't do me any favors. Don't write any more congressmen for citations."

He smiled. "You're right. I won't. But let me do something."

"Bring me a piece of that gefilte fish. Just get out of here."

"I will!" he said. "With a slice of carrot and a little horseradish. I won't forget."

"All right. Just show your pass at the gate. And don't tell *anybody.*"

"I won't. It's a month late, but a good Yom Tov* to you."

"Good Yom Tov, Grossbart," I said.

"You're a good Jew, Sergeant. You like to think you have a hard heart, but underneath you're a fine, decent man. I mean that."

Those last three words touched me more than any words from Grossbart's mouth had the right to. "All right, Grossbart," I said. "Now call me 'sir,' and get the hell out of here."

He ran out the door and was gone. I felt very pleased with myself; it was a great relief to stop fighting Grossbart, and it had cost me nothing. Barrett would never find out, and if he did, I could manage to invent some excuse. For a while, I sat at my desk, comfortable in my decision. Then the screen door flew

*Yom Tov: Holiday (literally, praise the day).

back and Grossbart burst in again. "Sergeant!" he said. Behind him I saw Fishbein and Halpern, both in starched khakis, both carrying ditty bags like Grossbart's.

"Sergeant, I caught Mickey and Larry coming out of the movies. I almost missed them."

"Grossbart—did I say to tell no one?" I said.

"But my aunt said I could bring friends. That I should, in fact."

"*I'm* the Sergeant, Grossbart—not your aunt!"

Grossbart looked at me in disbelief. He pulled Halpern up by his sleeve. "Mickey, tell the Sergeant what this would mean to you."

Halpern looked at me and, shrugging, said, "A lot."

Fishbein stepped forward without prompting. "This would mean a great deal to me and my parents, Sergeant Marx."

"No!" I shouted.

Grossbart was shaking his head. "Sergeant, I could see you denying me, but how can you deny Mickey, a Yeshiva boy—that's beyond me."

"I'm not denying Mickey anything," I said. "You just pushed a little too hard, Grossbart. *You* denied him."

"I'll give him my pass, then," Grossbart said. "I'll give him my aunt's address and a little note. At least let him go."

In a second, he had crammed the pass into Halpern's pants pocket. Halpern looked at me, and so did Fishbein. Grossbart was at the door, pushing it open. "Mickey, bring me a piece of gefilte fish, at least," he said, and then he was outside again.

The three of us looked at one another, and then I said, "Halpern, hand that pass over."

He took it from his pocket and gave it to me. Fishbein had now moved to the doorway, where he lingered. He stood there for a moment with his mouth slightly open, and then he pointed to himself. "And me?" he asked.

His utter ridiculousness exhausted me. I slumped down in my seat and felt pulses knocking at the back of my eyes. "Fishbein," I said, "you understand I'm not trying to deny you anything, don't you? If it was my Army, I'd serve gefilte fish in the mess hall. I'd sell *kugel** in the PX, honest to God."

Halpern smiled.

"You understand, don't you, Halpern?"

"Yes, Sergeant."

"And you, Fishbein? I don't want enemies. I'm just like you—I want to serve my time and go home. I miss the same things you miss."

"Then, Sergeant," Fishbein said, "why don't you come, too?"

"Where?"

"To St. Louis. To Shelly's aunt. We'll have a regular Seder. Play hide-the-matzoh."† He gave me a broad, black-toothed smile.

**kugel:* Baked pudding, usually potato or noodle.
†matzoh: Unleavened bread eaten at Passover to commemorate the hurried departure of the Israelites from Egypt.

I saw Grossbart again, on the other side of the screen.

"Psst!" He waved a piece of paper. "Mickey, here's the address. Tell her I couldn't get away."

Halpern did not move. He looked at me, and I saw the shrug moving up his arms into his shoulders again. I took the cover off my typewriter and made out passes for him and Fishbein. "Go," I said. "The three of you."

I thought Halpern was going to kiss my hand.

That afternoon, in a bar in Joplin, I drank beer and listened with half an ear to the Cardinal game. I tried to look squarely at what I'd become involved in, and began to wonder if perhaps the struggle with Grossbart wasn't as much my fault as his. What was I that I had to *muster* generous feeling? Who was I to have been feeling so grudging, so tight-hearted? After all, I wasn't being asked to move the world. Had I a right, then, or a reason, to clamp down on Grossbart, when that meant clamping down on Halpern, too? And Fishbein—that ugly, agreeable soul? Out of the many recollections of my childhood that had tumbled over me these past few days I heard my grandmother's voice: "What are you making a *tsimmes?*"* It was what she would ask my mother when, say, I had cut myself while doing something I shouldn't have done, and her daughter was busy bawling me out. I needed a hug and a kiss, and my mother would moralize. But my grandmother knew—mercy overrides justice. I should have known it, too. Who was Nathan Marx to be such a penny pincher with kindness? Surely, I thought, the Messiah himself—if He should ever come—won't niggle over nickels and dimes. God willing, he'll hug and kiss.

The next day, while I was playing softball over on the parade ground, I decided to ask Bob Wright, who was noncom in charge of Classification and Assignment, where he thought our trainees would be sent when their cycle ended, in two weeks. I asked casually, between innings, and he said, "They're pushing them all into the Pacific. Shulman cut the orders on your boys the other day."

The news shocked me, as though I were the father of Halpern, Fishbein, and Grossbart.

That night, I was just sliding into sleep when someone tapped on my door. "Who is it?" I asked.

"Sheldon."

He opened the door and came in. For a moment, I felt his presence without being able to see him. "How was it?" I asked.

He popped into sight in the near-darkness before me. "Great, Sergeant." Then he was sitting on the edge of the bed. I sat up.

"How about you?" he asked. "Have a nice weekend?"

"Yes."

"The others went to sleep." He took a deep, paternal breath. We sat silent

*tsimmes: Fuss, commotion, big deal.

for a while, and a homey feeling invaded my ugly little cubicle; the door was locked, the cat was out, the children were safely in bed.

"Sergeant, can I tell you something? Personal?"

I did not answer, and he seemed to know why. "Not about me. About Mickey. Sergeant, I never felt for anybody like I feel for him. Last night I heard Mickey in the bed next to me. He was crying so, it could have broken your heart. Real sobs."

"I'm sorry to hear that."

"I had to talk to him to stop him. He held my hand, Sergeant—he wouldn't let it go. He was almost hysterical. He kept saying if he only knew where we were going. Even if he knew it *was* the Pacific, that would be better than nothing. Just to know."

Long ago, someone had taught Grossbart the sad rule that only lies can get the truth. Not that I couldn't believe in the fact of Halpern's crying; his eyes *always* seemed red-rimmed. But, fact or not, it became a lie when Grossbart uttered it. He was entirely strategic. But then—it came with the force of indictment—so was I! There are strategies of aggression, but there are strategies of retreat as well. And so, recognizing that I myself had not been without craft and guile, I told him what I knew. "It is the Pacific."

He let out a small gasp, which was not a lie. "I'll tell him. I wish it was otherwise."

"So do I."

He jumped on my words. "You mean you think you could do something? A change, maybe?"

"No, I couldn't do a thing."

"Don't you know anybody over at C. and A.?"

"Grossbart, there's nothing I can do," I said. "If your orders are for the Pacific, then it's the Pacific."

"But Mickey—"

"Mickey, you, me—everybody, Grossbart. There's nothing to be done. Maybe the war'll end before you go. Pray for a miracle."

"But—"

"Good night, Grossbart." I settled back, and was relieved to feel the springs unbend as Grossbart rose to leave. I could see him clearly now; his jaw had dropped, and he looked like a dazed prizefighter. I noticed for the first time a little paper bag in his hand.

"Grossbart." I smiled. "My gift?"

"Oh, yes, Sergeant. Here—from all of us." He handed me the bag. "It's egg roll."

"Egg roll?" I accepted the bag and felt a damp grease spot on the bottom. I opened it, sure that Grossbart was joking.

"We thought you'd probably like it. You know—Chinese egg roll. We thought you'd probably have a taste for—"

"Your aunt served egg roll?"

"She wasn't home."

"Grossbart, she invited you. You told me she invited you and your friends."

"I know," he said. "I just reread the letter. *Next* week."

I got out of bed and walked to the window. "Grossbart," I said. But I was not calling to him.

"What?"

"What are you, Grossbart? Honest to God, what are you?"

I think it was the first time I'd asked him a question for which he didn't have an immediate answer.

"How can you do this to people?" I went on.

"Sergeant, the day away did us all a world of good. Fishbein, you should see him, he *loves* Chinese food."

"But the Seder," I said.

"We took second best, Sergeant."

Rage came charging at me. I didn't sidestep. "Grossbart, you're a liar!" I said. "You're a schemer and a crook. You've got no respect for anything. Nothing at all. Not for me, the truth—not even for poor Halpern! You use us all—"

"Sergeant, Sergeant, I feel for Mickey. Honest to God, I do. I *love* Mickey. I try—"

"You try! You feel!" I lurched toward him and grabbed his shirt front. I shook him furiously. "Grossbart, get out! Get out and stay the hell away from me. Because if I see you, I'll make your life miserable. *You understand that?*"

"Yes."

I let him free, and when he walked from the room, I wanted to spit on the floor where he had stood. I couldn't stop the fury. It engulfed me, owned me, till it seemed I could only rid myself of it with tears or an act of violence. I snatched from the bed the bag Grossbart had given me and, with all my strength, threw it out the window. And the next morning, as the men policed the area around the barracks, I heard a great cry go up from one of the trainees, who had been anticipating only his morning handful of cigarette butts and candy wrappers. "Egg roll!" he shouted. "Holy Christ, Chinese goddam egg roll!"

A week later, when I read the orders that had come down from C. and A., I couldn't believe my eyes. Every single trainee was to be shipped to Camp Stoneman, California, and from there to the Pacific—every trainee but one. Private Sheldon Grossbart. He was to be sent to Fort Monmouth, New Jersey. I read the mimeographed sheet several times. Dee, Farrell, Fishbein, Fuselli, Fylypowycz, Glinicki, Gromke, Gucwa, Halpern, Hardy, Helebrandt, right down to Anton Zygadlo—all were to be headed West before the month was out. All except Grossbart. He had pulled a string, and I wasn't it.

I lifted the phone and called C. and A.

The voice on the other end said smartly, "Corporal Shulman, sir."

"Let me speak to Sergeant Wright."

"Who is this calling, sir?"

"Sergeant Marx."

And, to my surprise, the voice said, *"Oh!"* Then, "Just a minute, Sergeant."

Shulman's *"Oh!"* stayed with me while I waited for Wright to come to the phone. Why *"Oh!"*? Who was Shulman? And then, so simply, I knew I'd discovered the string that Grossbart had pulled. In fact, I could hear Grossbart the day he'd discovered Shulman in the PX, or in the bowling alley, or maybe even at services. "Glad to meet you. Where you from? Bronx? Me, too. Do you know So-and-So? And So-and-So? Me, too! You work at C. and A.? Really? Hey, how's chances of getting East? Could you do something? Change something? Swindle, cheat, lie? We gotta help each other, you know. If the Jews in Germany . . ."

Bob Wright answered the phone. "How are you, Nate? How's the pitching arm?"

"Good. Bob, I wonder if you could do me a favor." I heard clearly my own words, and they so reminded me of Grossbart that I dropped more easily than I could have imagined into what I had planned. "This may sound crazy, Bob, but I got a kid here on orders to Monmouth who wants them changed. He had a brother killed in Europe, and he's hot to go to the Pacific. Says he'd feel like a coward if he wound up Stateside. I don't know, Bob—can anything be done? Put somebody else in the Monmouth slot?"

"Who?" he asked cagily.

"Anybody. First guy in the alphabet. I don't care. The kid just asked if something could be done."

"What's his name?"

"Grossbart, Sheldon."

Wright didn't answer.

"Yeah," I said. "He's a Jewish kid, so he thought I could help him out. You know."

"I guess I can do something," he finally said. "The Major hasn't been around for weeks. Temporary duty to the golf course. I'll try, Nate, that's all I can say."

"I'd appreciate it, Bob. See you Sunday." And I hung up, perspiring.

The following day, the corrected orders appeared: Fishbein, Fuselli, Fylypowycz, Glinicki, Gromke, Grossbart, Gucwa, Halpern, Hardy . . . Lucky Private Harley Alton was to go to Fort Monmouth, New Jersey, where, for some reason or other, they wanted an enlisted man with infantry training.

After chow that night, I stopped back at the orderly room to straighten out the guard-duty roster. Grossbart was waiting for me. He spoke first.

"You son of a bitch!"

I sat down at my desk, and while he glared at me, I began to make the necessary alterations in the duty roster.

"What do you have against me?" he cried. "Against my family? Would it kill you for me to be near my father, God knows how many months he has left to him?"

"Why so?"

"His heart," Grossbart said. "He hasn't had enough troubles in a lifetime, you've got to add to them. I curse the day I ever met you, Marx! Shulman told me what happened over there. There's no limit to your anti-Semitism, is there? The damage you've done here isn't enough. You have to make a special phone call! You really want me dead!"

I made the last notations in the duty roster and got up to leave. "Good night, Grossbart."

"You owe me an explanation!" He stood in my path.

"Sheldon, you're the one who owes explanations."

He scowled. "To *you?*"

"To me, I think so—yes. Mostly to Fishbein and Halpern."

"That's right, twist things around. I owe nobody nothing. I've done all I could for them. Now I think I've got the right to watch out for myself."

"For each other we have to learn to watch out, Sheldon. You told me yourself."

"You call this watching out for me—what you did?"

"No. For all of us."

I pushed him aside and started for the door. I heard his furious breathing behind me, and it sounded like steam rushing from an engine of terrible strength.

"You'll be all right," I said from the door. And, I thought, so would Fishbein and Halpern be all right, even in the Pacific, if only Grossbart continued to see—in the obsequiousness of the one, the soft spirituality of the other—some profit for himself.

I stood outside the orderly room, and I heard Grossbart weeping behind me. Over in the barracks, in the lighted windows, I could see the boys in their T shirts sitting on their bunks talking about their orders, as they'd been doing for the past two days. With a kind of quiet nervousness, they polished shoes, shined belt buckles, squared away underwear, trying as best they could to accept their fate. Behind me, Grossbart swallowed hard, accepting his. And then, resisting with all my will an impulse to turn and seek pardon for my vindictiveness, I accepted my own.

Writing Assignments for "Defender of the Faith"

I. Brief Papers

   A. 1. How has Sergeant Marx been changed by his World War II experiences?
      2. What does Marx mean when he tells Grossbart not to overdo "the 'sir' business" (p. 175)?
      3. How does their conduct at *shul* illustrate differences among Grossbart, Fishbein, and Halpern?
      4. Marx asks at one point, "What are you, Grossbart?" (p. 188). How would you characterize Grossbart?
      5. How informative and how effectively written is the following student response to the previous question?

In Philip Roth's "Defender of the Faith," when Sergeant Marx asks, "What are you, Grossbart?", I would answer by saying he was conniving and only out to better himself. When Grossbart finds out that Sergeant Marx was a Jew like himself he takes advantage of him in almost any way that he can. First, Grossbart gets out of cleaning out the barracks every Friday night to go to church. After being allowed to go to church he did not talk to the sergeant for about two weeks, but when he wanted a pass to see his Aunt for the weekend he went and begged him and told the Sergeant, "They say Hitler himself was half a Jew. Hearing you, I wouldn't doubt it." After Grossbart begged and ridiculed him for so long he ultimately let Grossbart go. Finally, when Grossbart finds out that Shulman, who was Jewish, worked at the C. and A., he used the same tactics that he used on Marx to get Shulman to change his order and send him to New Jersey instead of the Pacific. Grossbart, who constantly said that he was only looking out for his two Jewish friends, in the end got what he deserved by being sent to the Pacific.

6. Why are there so many references to Captain Barrett's eyes?
7. Marx says that he himself has been guilty of "craft and guile" (p. 187). Has he?
8. What does Marx mean when he says that by changing Grossbart's orders, he is watching out "for all of us" (p. 190)?

B. Argue for or against one of the assertions below:
   1. Grossbart genuinely cares about Fishbein and Halpern.
   2. Grossbart is right in charging that Marx, although a Jew himself, is nevertheless anti-Semitic.
   3. Although Captain Barrett prides himself on his open mind, he is in fact a bigot.
   4. Marx changes Grossbart's orders primarily to reform Grossbart.

C. 1. Do you think Marx was right to have Grossbart's orders changed?
   2. Do you agree with Grossbart that Marx is a "fine, decent man" (p. 184)?
   3. Do you believe, like Grossbart, in "the sad law that only lies can get you the truth" (p. 187)? How does your answer affect your attitude toward Grossbart and your interpretation of the story?

II. Longer Papers
A. Support, modify, or refute the assertion that by the end of the story Sergeant Marx has proven himself to be a true "defender of the faith."
B. Argue for or against the assertion that Marx is a *developing* rather than a *static* character—that he changes in important ways.
C. Classify and analyze the different strategies Grossbart uses to manipulate people, and explain why they usually succeed.
D. What does the story say about our ability to learn and change and grow from our experiences?
E. Develop, modify, or refute the assertion that "Defender of the Faith" is a story in which "mercy overrides justice" (p. 186).

III. Characterization in "Defender of the Faith"

From the sentences below construct a short essay that lists the most common methods of *characterization* and then illustrate the use of one such method in "Defender of the Faith."

1. This occurs whenever you tell a joke or story.
2. You are likely to use several different methods.
3. The methods are to present your fictional characters.

4. This is usually the case.
5. You will tell what a character says.
6. You will tell what a character does.
7. This is often the case.
8. You will describe what a character looks like.

9. This depends on the narrative point of view you have chosen.
10. You may comment directly on a character.
11. "The detective was stupid" is a direct comment on a character.
12. You may report what a character is thinking.
13. "The doctor thought that she had stopped the bleeding" is an example of what a character is thinking.

14. Here is still another method of characterization.
15. This method involves the use of one character.
16. That character is sometimes called a *foil*.
17. That character clarifies the qualities of another character.
18. Or that character underscores the qualities of another character.

19. This is true in "Defender of the Faith."
20. Philip Roth characterizes Captain Paul Barrett in certain ways.
21. The ways help us to better understand Sergeant Nathan Marx.
22. The ways help us to better appreciate Sergeant Nathan Marx.

23. Captain Barrett is a *foil* in this way.
24. His limitations call attention by contrast to the more admirable qualities of Sergeant Marx.

25. Here is an example.
26. Barrett is intolerant of blacks.
27. Barrett calls blacks "niggers."
28. Barrett is intolerant of Jews.
29. Barrett calls Jews "pushy."
30. Barrett makes Marx's open-mindedness all the more evident.

31. Here is another example.
32. Barrett has a one-sided approach to life.

33. Barrett cares not at all about the heart or feelings.
34. Barrett makes Marx's efforts to balance opposites more attractive.
35. Marx tries to balance opposites like the head and the heart.
36. Marx tries to balance opposites like mercy and justice.

37. This is in conclusion.
38. Captain Barrett is intolerant.
39. Captain Barrett is narrow-minded.
40. Captain Barrett emphasizes the complex humanity of Sergeant Marx.
41. Captain Barrett enhances the complex humanity of Sergeant Marx.

LIONEL TRILLING
Of This Time, Of That Place

Before Reading

Do you think that reading literature—stories, poems, and plays—helps you to understand yourself and others better? Free write for 5 to 10 minutes on this question.

I

It was a fine September day. By noon it would be summer again but now it was true autumn with a touch of chill in the air. As Joseph Howe stood on the porch of the house in which he lodged, ready to leave for his first class of the year, he thought with pleasure of the long indoor days that were coming. It was a moment when he could feel glad of his profession.

On the lawn the peach tree was still in fruit and young Hilda Aiken was taking a picture of it. She held the camera tight against her chest. She wanted the sun behind her but she did not want her own long morning shadow in the foreground. She raised the camera but that did not help, and she lowered it but that made things worse. She twisted her body to the left, then to the right. In the end she had to step out of the direct line of the sun. At last she snapped the shutter and wound the film with intense care.

Howe, watching her from the porch, waited for her to finish and called good morning. She turned, startled, and almost sullenly lowered her glance. In the year Howe had lived at the Aikens', Hilda had accepted him as one of her family, but since his absence of the summer she had grown shy. Then suddenly she lifted her head and smiled at him, and the humorous smile confirmed his pleasure in the day. She picked up her bookbag and set off for school.

The handsome houses on the streets to the college were not yet fully

OF THIS TIME, OF THAT PLACE   First published in 1943. Lionel Trilling (1905–1975) was born in New York City and spent most of his life there as a teacher of English and American literature at Columbia University.

awake but they looked very friendly. Howe went by the Bradby house where he would be a guest this evening at the first dinner-party of the year. When he had gone the length of the picket fence, the whitest in town, he turned back. Along the path there was a fine row of asters and he went through the gate and picked one for his buttonhole. The Bradbys would be pleased if they happened to see him invading their lawn and the knowledge of this made him even more comfortable.

He reached the campus as the hour was striking. The students were hurrying to their classes. He himself was in no hurry. He stopped at his dim cubicle of an office and lit a cigarette. The prospect of facing his class had suddenly presented itself to him and his hands were cold, the lawful seizure of power he was about to make seemed momentous. Waiting did not help. He put out his cigarette, picked up a pad of theme paper and went to his classroom.

As he entered, the rattle of voices ceased and the twenty-odd freshmen settled themselves and looked at him appraisingly. Their faces seemed gross, his heart sank at their massed impassivity, but he spoke briskly.

"My name is Howe," he said and turned and wrote it on the blackboard. The carelessness of the scrawl confirmed his authority. He went on, "My office is 412 Slemp Hall and my office hours are Monday, Wednesday, and Friday from eleven-thirty to twelve-thirty."

He wrote, "M., W., F., 11:30–12:30." He said, "I'll be very glad to see any of you at that time. Or if you can't come then, you can arrange with me for some other time."

He turned again to the blackboard and spoke over his shoulder. "The text for the course is Jarman's *Modern Plays,* revised edition. The Co-op has it in stock." He wrote the name, underlined "revised edition" and waited for it to be taken down in the new notebooks.

When the bent heads were raised again he began his speech of prospectus. "It is hard to explain—," he said, and paused as they composed themselves. "It is hard to explain what a course like this is intended to do. We are going to try to learn something about modern literature and something about prose composition."

As he spoke, his hands warmed and he was able to look directly at the class. Last year on the first day the faces had seemed just as cloddish, but as the term wore on they became gradually alive and quite likable. It did not seem possible that the same thing could happen again.

"I shall not lecture in this course," he continued. "Our work will be carried on by discussion and we will try to learn by an exchange of opinion. But you will soon recognize that my opinion is worth more than anyone else's here."

He remained grave as he said it, but two boys understood and laughed. The rest took permission from them and laughed too. All Howe's private ironies protested the vulgarity of the joke but the laughter made him feel benign and powerful.

When the little speech was finished, Howe picked up the pad of paper he had brought. He announced that they would write an extemporaneous theme.

Its subject was traditional, "Who I am and why I came to Dwight College." By now the class was more at ease and it gave a ritualistic groan of protest. Then there was a stir as fountain-pens were brought out and the writing arms of the chairs were cleared and the paper was passed about. At last all the heads bent to work and the room became still.

Howe sat idly at his desk. The sun shone through the tall clumsy windows. The cool of the morning was already passing. There was a scent of autumn and of varnish, and the stillness of the room was deep and oddly touching. Now and then a student's head was raised and scratched in the old elaborate students' pantomime that calls the teacher to witness honest intellectual effort.

Suddenly a tall boy stood within the frame of the open door. "Is this," he said, and thrust a large nose into a college catalogue, "is this the meeting place of English 1A? The section instructed by Dr. Joseph Howe?"

He stood on the very sill of the door, as if refusing to enter until he was perfectly sure of all his rights. The class looked up from work, found him absurd and gave a low mocking cheer.

The teacher and the new student, with equal pointedness, ignored the disturbance. Howe nodded to the boy, who pushed his head forward and then jerked it back in a wide elaborate arc to clear his brow of a heavy lock of hair. He advanced into the room and halted before Howe, almost at attention. In a loud clear voice he announced, "I am Tertan, Ferdinand R., reporting at the direction of Head of Department Vincent."

The heraldic formality of this statement brought forth another cheer. Howe looked at the class with a sternness he could not really feel, for there was indeed something ridiculous about this boy. Under his displeased regard the rows of heads dropped to work again. Then he touched Tertan's elbow, led him up to the desk and stood so as to shield their conversation from the class.

"We are writing an extemporaneous theme," he said. "The subject is, 'Who I am and why I came to Dwight College.'"

He stripped a few sheets from the pad and offered them to the boy. Tertan hesitated and then took the paper but he held it only tentatively. As if with the effort of making something clear, he gulped, and a slow smile fixed itself on his face. It was at once knowing and shy.

"Professor," he said, "to be perfectly fair to my classmates"—he made a large gesture over the room—"and to you"—he inclined his head to Howe—"this would not be for me an extemporaneous subject."

Howe tried to understand. "You mean you've already thought about it—you've heard we always give the same subject? That doesn't matter."

Again the boy ducked his head and gulped. It was the gesture of one who wishes to make a difficult explanation with perfect candor. "Sir," he said, and made the distinction with great care, "the topic I did not expect but I have given much ratiocination to the subject."

Howe smiled and said, "I don't think that's an unfair advantage. Just go ahead and write."

Tertan narrowed his eyes and glanced sidewise at Howe. His strange mouth smiled. Then in quizzical acceptance, he ducked his head, threw back the heavy dank lock, dropped into a seat with a great loose noise and began to write rapidly.

The room fell silent again and Howe resumed his idleness. When the bell rang, the students who had groaned when the task had been set now groaned again because they had not finished. Howe took up the papers and held the class while he made the first assignment. When he dismissed it, Tertan bore down on him, his slack mouth held ready for speech.

"Some professors," he said, "are pedants. They are Dryasdusts. However, some professors are free souls and creative spirits. Kant, Hegel, and Nietzsche* were all professors." With this pronouncement he paused. "It is my opinion," he continued, "that you occupy the second category."

Howe looked at the boy in surprise and said with good-natured irony, "With Kant, Hegel, and Nietzsche?"

Not only Tertan's hand and head but his whole awkward body waved away the stupidity. "It is the kind and not the quantity of the kind," he said sternly.

Rebuked, Howe said as simply and seriously as he could, "It would be nice to think so." He added, "Of course I am not a professor."

This was clearly a disappointment but Tertan met it. "In the French sense," he said with composure. "Generically, a teacher."

Suddenly he bowed. It was such a bow, Howe fancied, as a stage-director might teach an actor playing a medieval student who takes leave of Abelard† —stiff, solemn, with elbows close to the body and feet together. Then, quite as suddenly, he turned and left.

A queer fish, and as soon as Howe reached his office he sifted through the batch of themes and drew out Tertan's. The boy had filled many sheets with his unformed headlong scrawl. "Who am I?" he had begun. "Here, in a mundane, not to say commercialized academe, is asked the question which from time long immemorably out of mind has accreted doubts and thoughts in the psyche of man to pester him as a nuisance. Whether in St. Augustine (or Austin as sometimes called) or Miss Bashkirtsieff or Frederic Amiel or Empedocles,‡ or in less lights of the intellect than these, this posed question has been ineluctable."

Howe took out his pencil. He circled "academe" and wrote "vocab," in the margin. He underlined "time long immemorably out of mind" and wrote

---

*Kant, Hegel, and Nietzsche: Influential German philosophers and teachers.

†Abelard: Peter Abelard (1079–1142), French philosopher, theologian, and teacher. Abelard's romance with his student, the beautiful and learned Heloise, led to his being castrated and temporarily imprisoned. He later built a monastery called the Paraclete and gave it to Heloise, who became abbess of a sisterhood there.

‡St. Augustine, Miss Bashkirtsieff, Frederick Amiel, Empedocles: St. Augustine (354–430), an early Christian church father and theologian; Maria Constantinowna Bashkirtsieff (1860–1884), a minor Russian writer; Frederic Amiel (1821–1881), Swiss poet, philosopher, and scholar; and Empedocles (495?–435 B.C.), Greek poet and philosopher who taught that the four indestructible elements were earth, water, air, and fire.

"Diction!" But this seemed inadequate for what was wrong. He put down his pencil and read ahead to discover the principle of error in the theme. "Today as ever, in spite of gloomy prophets of the dismal science (economics) the question is uninvalidated. Out of the starry depths of heaven hurtles this spear of query demanding to be caught on the shield of the mind ere it pierces the skull and the limbs be unstrung."

Baffled but quite caught, Howe read on. "Materialism, by which is meant the philosophic concept and not the moral idea, provides no aegis against the question which lies beyond the tangible (metaphysics). Existence without alloy is the question presented. Environment and heredity relegated aside, the rags and old clothes of practical life discarded, the name and the instrumentality of livelihood do not, as the prophets of the dismal science insist on in this connection, give solution to the interrogation which not from the professor merely but veritably from the cosmos is given. I think, therefore I am (cogito etc.) but who am I? Tertan I am, but what is Tertan? Of this time, of that place, of some parentage, what does it matter?"

Existence without alloy: the phrase established itself. Howe put aside Tertan's paper and at random picked up another. "I am Arthur J. Casebeer Jr." he read. "My father is Arthur J. Casebeer and my grandfather was Arthur J. Casebeer before him. My mother is Nina Wimble Casebeer. Both of them are college graduates and my father is in insurance. I was born in St. Louis eighteen years ago and we still make our residence there."

Arthur J. Casebeer, who knew who he was, was less interesting than Tertan, but more coherent. Howe picked up Tertan's paper again. It was clear that none of the routine marginal comments, no "sent. str." or "punct." or "vocab." could cope with this torrential rhetoric. He read ahead, contenting himself with underscoring the errors against the time when he should have the necessary "conference" with Tertan.

It was a busy and official day of cards and sheets, arrangements and small decisions, and it gave Howe pleasure. Even when it was time to attend the first of the weekly Convocations he felt the charm of the beginning of things when intention is still innocent and uncorrupted by effort. He sat among the young instructors on the platform and joined in their humorous complaints at having to assist at the ceremony, but actually he got a clear satisfaction from the ritual of prayer and prosy speech and even from wearing his academic gown. And when the Convocation was over the pleasure continued as he crossed the campus, exchanging greetings with men he had not seen since the spring. They were people who did not yet, and perhaps never would, mean much to him, but in a year they had grown amiably to be part of his life. They were his fellow townsmen.

The day had cooled again at sunset and there was a bright chill in the September twilight. Howe carried his voluminous gown over his arm, he swung his doctoral hood by its purple neckpiece and on his head he wore his mortarboard with its heavy gold tassel bobbing just over his eye. These were the weighty and absurd symbols of his new profession and they pleased him. At twenty-six Joseph Howe had discovered that he was neither so well off nor so bohemian as he had once thought. A small income, adequate when supplemented by a sizable cash legacy, was genteel poverty when the cash was all spent. And the literary life—the room at the Lafayette or the small apartment without a lease, the long summers on the Cape, the long afternoons and the social evenings—began to weary him. His writing filled his mornings and should perhaps have filled his life, yet it did not. To the amusement of his friends and with a certain sense that he was betraying his own freedom, he had used the last of his legacy for a year at Harvard. The small but respectable reputation of his two volumes of verse had proved useful—he continued at Harvard on a fellowship and when he emerged as Dr. Howe he received an excellent appointment, with prospects, at Dwight.

He had his moments of fear when all that had ever been said of the dangers of the academic life had occurred to him. But after a year in which he had tested every possibility of corruption and seduction he was ready to rest easy. His third volume of verse, most of it written in his first year of teaching, was not only ampler but, he thought, better than its predecessors.

There was a clear hour before the Bradby dinner-party and Howe looked forward to it. But he was not to enjoy it, for lying with his mail on the hall table was a copy of this quarter's issue of *Life and Letters,* to which his landlord subscribed. Its severe cover announced that its editor, Frederic Woolley, had this month contributed an essay called "Two Poets," and Howe, picking it up, curious to see who the two poets might be, felt his own name start out at him with cabalistic power—Joseph Howe. As he continued to turn the pages his hand trembled.

Standing in the dark hall, holding the neat little magazine, Howe knew that his literary contempt for Frederic Woolley meant nothing, for he suddenly understood how he respected Woolley in the way of the world. He knew this by the trembling of his hand. And of the little world as well as the great, for although the literary groups of New York might dismiss Woolley, his name carried high authority in the academic world. At Dwight it was even a revered name, for it had been here at the college that Frederic Woolley had made the distinguished scholarly career from which he had gone on to literary journalism. In middle life he had been induced to take the editorship of *Life and Letters,* a literary monthly not widely read but heavily endowed and in its pages he had carried on the defense of what he sometimes called the older values. He was not without wit, he had great knowledge and considerable taste and even in the full movement of the "new" literature he had won a certain respect for his refusal to accept it. In France, even in England, he would have been connected with a more robust tradition of conservatism, but America gave him an audience not much better than genteel. It was known in the college that to the subsidy of *Life and Letters* the Bradbys contributed a great part.

As Howe read, he saw that he was involved in nothing less than an event. When the Fifth Series of *Studies in Order and Value* came to be collected, this latest of Frederic Woolley's essays would not be merely another step in the old direction. Clearly and unmistakably, it was a turning point. All his literary life Woolley had been concerned with the relation of literature to morality, religion, and the private and delicate pieties, and he had been unalterably opposed to all that he had called "inhuman humanitarianism." But here, suddenly, dramatically late, he had made an about-face, turning to the public life and to the humanitarian politics he had so long despised. This was the kind of incident the histories of literature make much of. Frederic Woolley was opening for himself a new career and winning a kind of new youth. He contrasted the two poets, Thomas Wormser who was admirable, Joseph Howe who was almost dangerous. He spoke of the "precious subjectivism" of Howe's verse. "In times like ours," he wrote, "with millions facing penury and want, one feels that the qualities of the *tour d'ivoire* are well-nigh inhuman, nearly insulting. The *tour d'ivoire* becomes the *tour d'ivresse** and it is not self-intoxicated poets that our people need." The essay said more: "The problem is one of meaning. I am not ignorant that the creed of the esoteric poets declares that a poem does not and should not *mean* anything, that it *is* something. But poetry is what the poet makes it, and if he is a true poet he makes what his society needs. And what is needed now is the tradition in which Mr. Wormser writes, the true tradition of poetry. The Howes do no harm, but they do no good when positive good is demanded of all responsible men. Or do the Howes indeed do no harm? Perhaps Plato would have said they do, that in some ways theirs is the Phrygian music that turns men's minds from the struggle. Certainly it is true that Thomas Wormser writes in the lucid Dorian† mode which sends men into battle with evil."

It was easy to understand why Woolley had chosen to praise Thomas Wormser. The long, lilting lines of *Corn Under Willows* hymned, as Woolley put it, the struggle for wheat in the Iowa fields and expressed the real lives of real people. But why out of the dozen more notable examples he had chosen Howe's little volume as the example of "precious subjectivism" was hard to guess. In a way it was funny, this multiplication of himself into "the Howes." And yet this becoming the multiform political symbol by whose creation Frederic Woolley gave the sign of a sudden new life, this use of him as a sacrifice whose blood was necessary for the rites of rejuvenation, made him feel oddly unclean.

Nor could Howe get rid of a certain practical resentment. As a poet he had a special and respectable place in the college life. But it might be another thing to be marked as the poet of a willful and selfish obscurity.

As he walked to the Bradby's Howe was a little tense and defensive. It seemed to him that all the world knew of the "attack" and agreed with it. And indeed the Bradbys had read the essay but Professor Bradby, a kind and pretentious man, said, "I see my old friend knocked you about a bit, my boy," and his wife Eugenia looked at Howe with her childlike blue eyes and said, "I shall *scold* Frederic for the untrue things he wrote about you. You aren't the least obscure." They beamed at him. In their genial snobbery they seemed to feel

**tour d'ivoire* and *tour d'ivresse:* French, *tour d'ivoire* is an ivory tower, a place of mental withdrawal from reality and action, a symbol of escapism; *tour d'ivresse* is a tower of drunkenness or intoxication.
†Phrygian, Dorian: Phrygian is an ancient Greek mode in music characterized by its boldness and assertiveness; by contrast, Dorian is an ancient Greek mode in music characterized by its clarity and simplicity.

that he had distinguished himself. He was the leader of Howeism. He enjoyed the dinner-party as much as he had thought he would.

And in the following days, as he was more preoccupied with his duties, the incident was forgotten. His classes had ceased to be mere groups. Student after student detached himself from the mass and required or claimed a place in Howe's awareness. Of them all it was Tertan who first and most violently signaled his separate existence. A week after classes had begun Howe saw his silhouette on the frosted glass of his office door. It was motionless for a long time, perhaps stopped by the problem of whether or not to knock before entering. Howe called, "Come in!" and Tertan entered with his shambling stride.

He stood beside the desk, silent and at attention. When Howe asked him to sit down, he responded with a gesture of head and hand as if to say that such amenities were beside the point. Nevertheless he did take the chair. He put his ragged crammed briefcase between his legs. His face, which Howe now observed fully for the first time, was confusing, for it was made up of florid curves, the nose arched in the bone and voluted in the nostril, the mouth loose and soft and rather moist. Yet the face was so thin and narrow as to seem the very type of asceticism. Lashes of unusual length veiled the eyes and, indeed, it seemed as if there were a veil over the whole countenance. Before the words actually came, the face screwed itself into an attitude of preparation for them.

"You can confer with me now?" Tertan said.

"Yes, I'd be glad to. There are several things in your two themes I want to talk to you about." Howe reached for the packet of themes on his desk and sought for Tertan's. But the boy was waving them away.

"These are done perforce," he said. "Under the pressure of your requirement. They are not significant, mere duties." Again his great hand flapped vaguely to dismiss his themes. He leaned forward and gazed at his teacher.

"You are," he said, "a man of letters? You are a poet?" It was more declaration than question.

"I should like to think so," Howe said.

At first Tertan accepted the answer with a show of appreciation, as though the understatement made a secret between himself and Howe. Then he chose to misunderstand. With his shrewd and disconcerting control of expression, he presented to Howe a puzzled grimace. "What does that mean?" he said.

Howe retracted the irony. "Yes. I am a poet." It sounded strange to say.

"That," Tertan said, "is a wonder." He corrected himself with his ducking head. "I mean that is wonderful."

Suddenly he dived at the miserable briefcase between his legs, put it on his knees and began to fumble with the catch, all intent on the difficulty it presented. Howe noted that his suit was worn thin, his shirt almost unclean. He became aware, even, of a vague and musty odor of garments worn too long in unaired rooms. Tertan conquered the lock and began to concentrate upon a search into the interior. At last he held in his hand what he was after, a torn and crumpled copy of *Life and Letters*.

"I learned it from here," he said, holding it out.

Howe looked at him sharply, his hackles a little up. But the boy's face was not only perfectly innocent, it even shone with a conscious admiration. Apparently nothing of the import of the essay had touched him except the wonderful fact that his teacher was a "man of letters." Yet this seemed too stupid and Howe, to test it, said, "The man who wrote that doesn't think it's wonderful."

Tertan made a moist hissing sound as he cleared his mouth of saliva. His head, oddly loose on his neck, wove a pattern of contempt in the air. "A critic," he said, "who admits *prima facie* that he does not understand." Then he said grandly, "It is the inevitable fate."

It was absurd, yet Howe was not only aware of the absurdity but of a tension suddenly and wonderfully relaxed. Now that the "attack" was on the table between himself and this strange boy and subject to the boy's funny and absolutely certain contempt, the hidden force of his feeling was revealed to him in the very moment that it vanished. All unsuspected, there had been a film over the world, a transparent but discoloring haze of danger. But he had no time to stop over the brightened aspect of things. Tertan was going on. "I also am a man of letters. Putative."

"You have written a good deal?" Howe meant to be no more than polite and he was surprised at the tenderness he heard in his words.

Solemnly the boy nodded, threw back the dank lock and sucked in a deep anticipatory breath. "First, a work of homiletics, which is a defense of the principles of religious optimism against the pessimism of Schopenhauer and the humanism of Nietzsche."

"Humanism? Why do you call it humanism?"

"It is my nomenclature for making a deity of man," Tertan replied negligently. "Then three fictional works, novels. And numerous essays in science, combating materialism. Is it your duty to read these if I bring them to you?"

Howe answered simply, "No, it isn't exactly my duty, but I shall be happy to read them."

Tertan stood up and remained silent. He rested his bag on the chair. With a certain compunction—for it did not seem entirely proper that, of two men of letters, one should have the right to blue-pencil the other, to grade him or to question the quality of his "sentence structure"—Howe reached for Tertan's papers. But before he could take them up, the boy suddenly made his bow-to-Abelard, the stiff inclination of the body with the hands seeming to emerge from the scholar's gown. Then he was gone.

But after his departure something was still left of him. The timbre of his curious sentences, the downright finality of so quaint a phrase as "It is the inevitable fate" still rang in the air. Howe gave the warmth of his feeling to the new visitor who stood at the door announcing himself with a genteel clearing of the throat.

"Dr. Howe, I believe?" the student said. A large hand advanced into the room and grasped Howe's hand. "Blackburn, sir, Theodore Blackburn, vice-president of the Student Council. A great pleasure, sir."

Out of a pair of ruddy cheeks a pair of small eyes twinkled good-naturedly. The large face, the large body were not so much fat as beefy and suggested something "typical," monk, politician, or innkeeper.

Blackburn took the seat beside Howe's desk. "I may have seemed to introduce myself in my public capacity, sir," he said. "But it is really as an individual that I came to see you. That is to say, as one of your students to be."

He spoke with an "English" intonation and he went on, "I was once an English major, sir."

For a moment Howe was startled, for the roast-beef look of the boy and the manner of his speech gave a second's credibility to one sense of his statement. Then the collegiate meaning of the phrase asserted itself, but some perversity made Howe say what was not really in good taste even with so forward a student, "Indeed? What regiment?"

Blackburn stared and then gave a little pouf-pouf of laughter. He waved the misapprehension away. *"Very* good, sir. It certainly is an ambiguous term." He chuckled in appreciation of Howe's joke, then cleared his throat to put it aside. "I look forward to taking your course in the romantic poets, sir," he said earnestly. "To me the romantic poets are the very crown of English literature."

Howe made a dry sound, and the boy, catching some meaning in it, said, "Little as I know them, of course. But even Shakespeare who is so dear to us of the Anglo-Saxon tradition is in a sense but the preparation for Shelley, Keats and Byron. And Wadsworth."

Almost sorry for him, Howe dropped his eyes. With some embarrassment, for the boy was not actually his student, he said softly, "Wordsworth."

"Sir?"

"Wordsworth, not Wadsworth. You said Wadsworth."

"Did I, sir?" Gravely he shook his head to rebuke himself for the error. "Wordsworth, of course—slip of the tongue." Then, quite in command again, he went on. "I have a favor to ask of you, Dr. Howe. You see, I began my college course as an English major,"—he smiled—"as I said."

"Yes?"

"But after my first year I shifted. I shifted to the social sciences. Sociology and government—I find them stimulating and very *real."* He paused, out of respect for reality. "But now I find that perhaps I have neglected the other side."

"The other side?" Howe said.

"Imagination, fancy, culture. A well-rounded man." He trailed off as if there were perfect understanding between them. "And so, sir, I have decided to end my senior year with your course in the romantic poets."

His voice was filled with an indulgence which Howe ignored as he said flatly and gravely, "But that course isn't given until the spring term."

"Yes, sir, and that is where the favor comes in. Would you let me take your romantic prose course? I can't take it for credit, sir, my program is full, but just for background it seems to me that I ought to take it. I do hope," he concluded in a manly way, "that you will consent."

"Well, it's no great favor, Mr. Blackburn. You can come if you wish, though there's not much point in it if you don't do the reading."

The bell rang for the hour and Howe got up.

"May I begin with this class, sir?" Blackburn's smile was candid and boyish.

Howe nodded carelessly and together, silently, they walked to the class-room down the hall. When they reached the door Howe stood back to let his student enter, but Blackburn moved adroitly behind him and grasped him by the arm to urge him over the threshold. They entered together with Blackburn's hand firmly on Howe's bicep, the student inducting the teacher into his own room. Howe felt a surge of temper rise in him and almost violently he disengaged his arm and walked to the desk, while Blackburn found a seat in the front row and smiled at him.

II

The question was, At whose door must the tragedy be laid?*

All night the snow had fallen heavily and only now was abating in sparse little flurries. The windows were valanced high with white. It was very quiet, something of the quiet of the world had reached the class and Howe found that everyone was glad to talk or listen. In the room there was a comfortable sense of pleasure in being human.

Casebeer believed that the blame for the tragedy rested with heredity. Picking up the book he read, "The sins of the fathers are visited on their children." This opinion was received with general favor. Nevertheless Johnson ventured to say that the fault was all Pastor Manders' because the Pastor had made Mrs. Alving go back to her husband and was always hiding the truth. To this Hibbard objected with logic enough, "Well then, it was really all her husband's fault. He *did* all the bad things." De Witt, his face bright with an impatient idea, said that the fault was all society's. "By society I don't mean upper-crust society," he said. He looked around a little defiantly, taking in any members of the class who might be members of upper-crust society. "Not in that sense. I mean the social unit."

Howe nodded and said, "Yes, of course."

"If the society of the time had progressed far enough in science," De Witt went on, "then there would be no problem for Mr. Ibsen to write about. Captain Alving plays around a little, gives way to perfectly natural biological urges, and he gets a social disease, a venereal disease. If the disease is cured, no problem. Invent salvarsan and the disease is cured. The problem of heredity disappears and li'l Oswald just doesn't get paresis. No paresis, no problem—no problem, no play."

This was carrying the ark into battle and the class looked at De Witt with respectful curiosity. It was his usual way and on the whole they were sympathetic

---

*the tragedy: The play discussed in Howe's class is *Ghosts* by the Norwegian dramatist Henrik Ibsen (1828–1906).

with his struggle to prove to Howe that science was better than literature. Still, there was something in his reckless manner that alienated them a little.

"Or take birth control, for instance," De Witt went on. "If Mrs. Alving had had some knowledge of contraception, she wouldn't have had to have li'l Oswald at all. No li'l Oswald, no play."

The class was suddenly quieter. In the back row Stettenhover swung his great football shoulders in a righteous sulking gesture, first to the right, then to the left. He puckered his mouth ostentatiously. Intellect was always ending up by talking dirty.

Tertan's hand went up and Howe said, "Mr. Tertan." The boy shambled to his feet and began his long characteristic gulp. Howe made a motion with his fingers, as small as possible, and Tertan ducked his head and smiled in apology. He sat down. The class laughed. With more than half the term gone, Tertan had not been able to remember that one did not rise to speak. He seemed unable to carry on the life of the intellect without this mark of respect for it. To Howe the boy's habit of rising seemed to accord with the formal shabbiness of his dress. He never wore the casual sweaters and jackets of his classmates. Into the free and comfortable air of the college classroom he brought the stuffy sordid strictness of some crowded metropolitan high school.

"Speaking from one sense," Tertan began slowly, "there is no blame ascribable. From the sense of determinism, who can say where the blame lies? The preordained is the preordained and it cannot be said without rebellion against the universe, a palpable absurdity."

In the back row Stettenhover slumped suddenly in his seat, his heels held out before him, making a loud dry disgusted sound. His body sank until his neck rested on the back of his chair. He folded his hands across his belly and looked significantly out of the window, exasperated not only with Tertan but with Howe, with the class, with the whole system designed to encourage this kind of thing. There was a certain insolence in the movement and Howe flushed. As Tertan continued to speak, Howe walked casually toward the window and placed himself in the line of Stettenhover's vision. He stared at the great fellow, who pretended not to see him. There was so much power in the big body, so much contempt in the Greek-athlete face under the crisp Greek-athlete curls, that Howe felt almost physical fear. But at last Stettenhover admitted him to focus and under his disapproving gaze sat up with slow indifference. His eyebrows raised high in resignation, he began to examine his hands. Howe relaxed and turned his attention back to Tertan.

"Flux of existence," Tertan was saying, "produces all things, so that judgment wavers. Beyond the phenomena, what? But phenomena are adumbrated and to them we are limited."

Howe saw it for a moment as perhaps it existed in the boy's mind—the world of shadows which are cast by a great light upon a hidden reality as in the old myth of the Cave. But the little brush with Stettenhover had tired him and he said irritably, "But come to the point, Mr. Tertan."

He said it so sharply that some of the class looked at him curiously. For three months he had gently carried Tertan through his verbosities, to the vaguely respectful surprise of the other students, who seemed to conceive that there existed between this strange classmate and their teacher some special understanding from which they were content to be excluded. Tertan looked at him mildly and at once came brilliantly to the point. "This is the summation of the play," he said and took up his book and read, " 'Your poor father never found any outlet for the overmastering joy of life that was in him. And I brought no holiday into his home, either. Everything seemed to turn upon duty and I am afraid I made your poor father's home unbearable to him, Oswald.' Spoken by Mrs. Alving."

Yes, that was surely the "summation" of the play and Tertan had hit it, as he hit, deviously and eventually, the literary point of almost everything. But now, as always, he was wrapping it away from sight. "For most mortals," he said, "there are only joys of biological urgings, gross and crass, such as the sensuous Captain Alving. For certain few there are the transmutations beyond these to a contemplation of the utter whole."

Oh, the boy was mad. And suddenly the word, used in hyperbole, intended almost for the expression of exasperated admiration, became literal. Now that the word was used, it became simply apparent to Howe that Tertan was mad.

It was a monstrous word and stood like a bestial thing in the room. Yet it so completely comprehended everything that had puzzled Howe, it so arranged and explained what for three months had been perplexing him that almost at once its horror became domesticated. With this word Howe was able to understand why he had never been able to communicate to Tertan the value of a single criticism or correction of his wild, verbose themes. Their conferences had been frequent and long but had done nothing to reduce to order the splendid confusion of the boy's ideas. Yet, impossible though its expression was, Tertan's incandescent mind could always strike for a moment into some dark corner of thought.

And now it was suddenly apparent that it was not a faulty rhetoric that Howe had to contend with. With his new knowledge he looked at Tertan's face and wondered how he could have so long deceived himself. Tertan was still talking and the class had lapsed into a kind of patient unconsciousness, a coma of respect for words which, for all that most of them knew, might be profound. Almost with a suffusion of shame, Howe believed that in some dim way the class had long ago had some intimation of Tertan's madness. He reached out as decisively as he could to seize the thread of Tertan's discourse before it should be entangled further.

"Mr. Tertan says that the blame must be put upon whoever kills the joy of living in another. We have been assuming that Captain Alving was a wholly bad man, but what if we assume that he became bad only because Mrs. Alving, when they were first married, acted toward him in the prudish way she says she did?"

It was a ticklish idea to advance to freshmen and perhaps not profitable. Not all of them were following.

"That would put the blame on Mrs. Alving herself, whom most of you admire. And she herself seems to think so." He glanced at his watch. The hour was nearly over. "What do you think, Mr. De Witt?"

De Witt rose to the idea, wanted to know if society couldn't be blamed for educating Mrs. Alving's temperament in the wrong way. Casebeer was puzzled, Stettenhover continued to look at his hands until the bell rang.

Tertan, his brows louring in thought, was making as always for a private word. Howe gathered his books and papers to leave quickly. At this moment of his discovery and with the knowledge still raw, he could not engage himself with Tertan. Tertan sucked in his breath to prepare for speech and Howe made ready for the pain and confusion. But at that moment Casebeer detached himself from the group with which he had been conferring and which he seemed to represent. His constituency remained at a tactful distance. The mission involved the time of an assigned essay. Casebeer's presentation of the plea—it was based on the freshmen's heavy duties at the fraternities during Carnival Week—cut across Tertan's preparations for speech. "And so some of us fellows thought," Casebeer concluded with heavy solemnity, "that we could do a better job, give our minds to it more, if we had more time."

Tertan regarded Casebeer with mingled curiosity and revulsion. Howe not only said that he would postpone the assignment but went on to talk about the Carnival and even drew the waiting constituency into the conversation. He was conscious of Tertan's stern and astonished stare, then of his sudden departure.

Now that the fact was clear, Howe knew that he must act on it. His course was simple enough. He must lay the case before the Dean. Yet he hesitated. His feeling for Tertan must now, certainly, be in some way invalidated. Yet could he, because of a word, hurry to assign to official and reasonable solicitude what had been, until this moment, so various and warm? He could at least delay and, by moving slowly, lend a poor grace to the necessary, ugly act of making his report.

It was with some notion of keeping the matter in his own hands that he went to the Dean's office to look up Tertan's records. In the outer office the Dean's secretary greeted him brightly and at his request brought him the manila folder with the small identifying photograph pasted in the corner. She laughed. "He was looking for the birdie in the wrong place," she said.

Howe leaned over her shoulder to look at the picture. It was as bad as all the Dean's-office photographs were, but it differed from all that Howe had ever seen. Tertan, instead of looking into the camera, as no doubt he had been bidden, had, at the moment of exposure, turned his eyes upward. His mouth, as though conscious of the trick played on the photographer, had the sly superior look that Howe knew.

The secretary was fascinated by the picture. "What a funny boy," she said. "He looks like Tartuffe!"*

*Tartuffe: Hypocritical central character in the comedy *Tartuffe, or the Imposter,* by the French dramatist Molière (1622–1673).

And so he did, with the absurd piety of the eyes and the conscious slyness of the mouth and the whole face bloated by the bad lens.

"Is he *like* that?" the secretary said.

"Like Tartuffe? No."

From the photograph there was little enough comfort to be had. The records themselves gave no clue to madness, though they suggested sadness enough. Howe read of a father, Stanislaus Tertan, born in Budapest and trained in engineering in Berlin, once employed by the Hercules Chemical Corporation—this was one of the factories that dominated the south end of the town—but now without employment. He read of a mother Erminie (Youngfellow) Tertan, born in Manchester, educated at a Normal School at Leeds, now housewife by profession. The family lived on Greenbriar Street, which Howe knew as a row of once elegant homes near what was now the factory district. The old mansions had long ago been divided into small and primitive apartments. Of Ferdinand himself there was little to learn. He lived with his parents, had attended a Detroit high school and had transferred to the local school in his last year. His rating for intelligence, as expressed in numbers, was high, his scholastic record was remarkable, he held a college scholarship for his tuition.

Howe laid the folder on the secretary's desk. "Did you find what you wanted to know?" she asked.

The phrases from Tertan's momentous first theme came back to him. "Tertan I am, but what is Tertan? Of this time, of that place, of some parentage, what does it matter?"

"No, I didn't find it," he said.

Now that he had consulted the sad half-meaningless record he knew all the more firmly that he must not give the matter out of his own hands. He must not release Tertan to authority. Not that he anticipated from the Dean anything but the greatest kindness for Tertan. The Dean would have the experience and skill which he himself could not have. One way or another the Dean could answer the question, "What is Tertan?" Yet this was precisely what he feared. He alone could keep alive—not forever but for a somehow important time—the question, "What is Tertan?" He alone could keep it still a question. Some sure instinct told him that he must not surrender the question to a clean official desk in a clear official light to be dealt with, settled and closed.

He heard himself saying, "Is the Dean busy at the moment? I'd like to see him."

His request came thus unbidden, even forbidden, and it was one of the surprising and startling incidents of his life. Later, when he reviewed the events, so disconnected in themselves or so merely odd, of the story that unfolded for him that year, it was over this moment, on its face the least notable, that he paused longest. It was frequently to be with fear and never without a certainty of its meaning in his own knowledge of himself that he would recall this simple, routine request and the feeling of shame and freedom it gave him as he sent everything down the official chute. In the end, of course, no matter what he did to "protect" Tertan, he would have had to make the same request and lay the matter on the Dean's clean desk. But it would always be a landmark of his life that, at the very moment when he was rejecting the official way, he had been, without will or intention, so gladly drawn to it.

After the storm's last delicate flurry, the sun had come out. Reflected by the new snow, it filled the office with a golden light which was almost musical in the way it made all the commonplace objects of efficiency shine with a sudden sad and noble significance. And the light, now that he noticed it, made the utterance of his perverse and unwanted request even more momentous.

The secretary consulted the engagement pad. "He'll be free any minute. Don't you want to wait in the parlor?"

She threw open the door of the large and pleasant room in which the Dean held his Committee meetings and in which his visitors waited. It was designed with a homely elegance on the masculine side of the eighteenth-century manner. There was a small coal fire in the grate and the handsome mahogany table was strewn with books and magazines. The large windows gave on the snowy lawn and there was such a fine width of window that the white casements and walls seemed at this moment but a continuation of the snow, the snow but an extension of casement and walls. The outdoors seemed taken in and made safe, the indoors seemed luxuriously freshened and expanded.

Howe sat down by the fire and lighted a cigarette. The room had its intended effect upon him. He felt comfortable and relaxed, yet nicely organized, some young diplomatic agent of the eighteenth century, the newly fledged Swift carrying out Sir William Temple's business.* The rawness of Tertan's case quite vanished. He crossed his legs and reached for a magazine.

It was that famous issue of *Life and Letters* that his idle hand had found and his blood raced as he sifted through it and the shape of his own name, Joseph Howe, sprang out at him, still cabalistic in its power. He tossed the magazine back on the table as the door of the Dean's office opened and the Dean ushered out Theodore Blackburn.

"Ah, Joseph!" the Dean said.

Blackburn said, "Good morning, Doctor." Howe winced at the title and caught the flicker of amusement over the Dean's face. The Dean stood with his hand high on the doorjamb and Blackburn, still in the doorway, remained standing almost under his long arm.

Howe nodded briefly to Blackburn, snubbing his eager deference. "Can you give me a few minutes?" he said to the Dean.

"All the time you want. Come in." Before the two men could enter the office, Blackburn claimed their attention with a long full "Er." As they turned to him, Blackburn said, "Can *you* give *me* a few minutes, Dr. Howe?" His eyes sparkled at the little audacity he had committed, the slightly impudent play with hierarchy. Of the three of them Blackburn kept himself the lowest, but he reminded Howe of his subaltern relation to the Dean.

*Swift, Sir William Temple: Jonathan Swift (1667–1745), English satirist and author of *Gulliver's Travels*, served early in his career as secretary to Sir William Temple (1628–1699), a diplomat and writer.

"I mean, of course," Blackburn went on easily, "when you've finished with the Dean."

"I'll be in my office shortly," Howe said, turned his back on the ready "Thank you, sir," and followed the Dean into the inner room.

"Energetic boy," said the Dean. "A bit beyond himself but very energetic. Sit down."

The Dean lighted a cigarette, leaned back in his chair, sat easy and silent for a moment, giving Howe no signal to go ahead with business. He was a young Dean, not much beyond forty, a tall handsome man with sad, ambitious eyes. He had been a Rhodes scholar. His friends looked for great things from him and it was generally said that he had notions of education which he was not yet ready to try to put into practice.

His relaxed silence was meant as a compliment to Howe. He smiled and said, "What's the business, Joseph?"

"Do you know Tertan—Ferdinand Tertan, a freshman?"

The Dean's cigarette was in his mouth and his hands were clasped behind his head. He did not seem to search his memory for the name. He said, "What about him?"

Clearly the Dean knew something and he was waiting for Howe to tell him more. Howe moved only tentatively. Now that he was doing what he resolved not to do, he felt more guilty at having been so long deceived by Tertan and more need to be loyal to his error.

"He's a strange fellow," he ventured. He said stubbornly, "In a strange way he's very brilliant." He concluded, "But very strange."

The springs of the Dean's swivel chair creaked as he came out of his sprawl and leaned forward to Howe. "Do you mean he's so strange that it's something you could give a name to?"

Howe looked at him stupidly. "What do you mean?" he said.

"What's his trouble?" the Dean said more neutrally.

"He's very brilliant, in a way. I looked him up and he has a top intelligence rating. But somehow, and it's hard to explain just how, what he says is always on the edge of sense and doesn't quite make it."

The Dean looked at him and Howe flushed up. The Dean had surely read Woolley on the subject of "the Howes" and the *tour d'ivresse.* Was that quick glance ironical?

The Dean picked up some papers from his desk and Howe could see that they were in Tertan's impatient scrawl. Perhaps the little gleam in the Dean's glance had come only from putting facts together.

"He sent me this yesterday," the Dean said. "After an interview I had with him. I haven't been able to do more than glance at it. When you said what you did, I realized there was something wrong."

Twisting his mouth, the Dean looked over the letter. "You seem to be involved," he said without looking up. "By the way, what did you give him at midterm?"

Flushing, setting his shoulders, Howe said firmly, "I gave him A-minus."

The Dean chuckled. "Might be a good idea if some of our boys went crazy—just a little." He said, "Well," to conclude the matter and handed the papers to Howe. "See if this is the same thing you've been finding. Then we can go into the matter again."

Before the fire in the parlor, in the chair that Howe had been occupying, sat Blackburn. He sprang to his feet as Howe entered.

"I said my office, Mr. Blackburn." Howe's voice was sharp. Then he was almost sorry for the rebuke, so clearly and naively did Blackburn seem to relish his stay in the parlor, close to authority.

"I'm in a bit of a hurry, sir," he said, "and I did want to be sure to speak to you, sir."

He was really absurd, yet fifteen years from now he would have grown up to himself, to the assurance and mature beefiness. In banks, in consular offices, in brokerage firms, on the bench, more seriously affable, a little sterner, he would make use of his ability to be administered by his job. It was almost reassuring. Now he was exercising his too-great skill on Howe. "I owe you an apology, sir," he said.

Howe knew that he did but he showed surprise.

"I mean, Doctor, after your having been so kind about letting me attend your class, I stopped coming." He smiled in deprecation. "Extra-curricular activities take up so much of my time. I'm afraid I undertook more than I could perform."

Howe had noticed the absence and had been a little irritated by it after Blackburn's elaborate plea. It was an absence that might be interpreted as a comment on the teacher. But there was only one way for him to answer. "You've no need to apologize," he said. "It's wholly your affair."

Blackburn beamed. "I'm so glad you feel that way about it, sir. I was worried you might think I had stayed away because I was influenced by—" He stopped and lowered his eyes.

Astonished, Howe said, "Influenced by what?"

"Well, by—" Blackburn hesitated and for answer pointed to the table on which lay the copy of *Life and Letters.* Without looking at it, he knew where to direct his hand. "By the unfavorable publicity, sir." He hurried on. "And that brings me to another point, sir. I am secretary of Quill and Scroll, sir, the student literary society, and I wonder if you would address us. You could read your own poetry, sir, and defend your own point of view. It would be very interesting."

It was truly amazing. Howe looked long and cruelly into Blackburn's face, trying to catch the secret of the mind that could have conceived this way of manipulating him, this way so daring and inept—but not entirely inept—with its malice so without malignity. The face did not yield its secret. Howe smiled broadly and said, "Of course I don't think you were influenced by the unfavorable publicity."

"I'm still going to take—regularly, for credit—your romantic poets course next term," Blackburn said.

"Don't worry, my dear fellow, don't worry about it."

Howe started to leave and Blackburn stopped him with, "But about Quill, sir?"

"Suppose we wait until next term? I'll be less busy then."

And Blackburn said, "Very good, sir, and thank you."

In his office the little encounter seemed less funny to Howe, was even in some indeterminate way disturbing. He made an effort to put it from his mind by turning to what was sure to disturb him more, the Tertan letter read in the new interpretation. He found what he had always found, the same florid leaps beyond fact and meaning, the same headlong certainty. But as his eye passed over the familiar scrawl it caught his own name and for the second time that hour he felt the race of his blood.

"The Paraclete," Tertan had written to the Dean, "from a Greek word meaning to stand in place of, but going beyond the primitive idea to mean traditionally the helper, the one who comforts and assists, cannot without fundamental loss be jettisoned. Even if taken no longer in the supernatural case, the concept remains deeply in the human consciousness inevitably. Humanitarianism is no reply, for not every man stands in the place of every other man for this other's comrade comfort. But certain are chosen out of the human race to be the consoler of some other. Of these, for example, is Joseph Barker Howe, Ph.D. Of intellects not the first yet of true intellect and lambent instructions, given to that which is intuitive and irrational, not to what is logical in the strict word, what is judged by him is of the heart and not the head. Here is one chosen, in that he chooses himself to stand in the place of another for comfort and consolation. To him more than another I give my gratitude, with all respect to our Dean who reads this, a noble man, but merely dedicated, not consecrated. But not in the aspect of the Paraclete only is Dr. Joseph Barker Howe established, for he must be the Paraclete to another aspect of himself, that which is driven and persecuted by the lack of understanding in the world at large, so that he in himself embodies the full history of man's tribulations and, overflowing upon others, notably the present writer, is the ultimate end."

This was love. There was no escape from it. Try as Howe might to remember that Tertan was mad and all his emotions invalidated, he could not destroy the effect upon him of his student's stern, affectionate regard. He had betrayed not only a power of mind but a power of love. And however firmly he held before his attention the fact of Tertan's madness, he could do nothing to banish the physical sensation of gratitude he felt. He had never thought of himself as "driven and persecuted" and he did not now. But still he could not make meaningless his sensation of gratitude. The pitiable Tertan sternly pitied him, and comfort came from Tertan's never-to-be comforted mind.

III

In an academic community, even an efficient one, official matters move slowly. The term drew to a close with no action in the case of Tertan, and Joseph Howe had to confront a curious problem. How should he grade his strange student, Tertan?

Tertan's final examination had been no different from all his other writing, and what did one "give" such a student? De Witt must have his A, that was clear. Johnson would get a B. With Casebeer it was a question of a B-minus or

a C-plus, and Stettenhover, who had been crammed by the team tutor to fill half
a blue-book with his thin feminine scrawl, would have his C-minus which he
would accept with mingled indifference and resentment. But with Tertan it was
not so easy.

The boy was still in the college process and his name could not be omitted
from the grade sheet. Yet what should a mind under suspicion of madness be
graded? Until the medical verdict was given, it was for Howe to continue as
Tertan's teacher and to keep his judgment pedagogical. Impossible to give him
an F: he had not failed. B was for Johnson's stolid mediocrity. He could not be
put on the edge of passing with Stettenhover, for he exactly did not pass. In
energy and richness of intellect he was perhaps even De Witt's superior, and
Howe toyed grimly with the notion of giving him an A, but that would lower
the value of the A De Witt had won with his beautiful and clear, if still arrogant,
mind. There was a notation which the Registrar recognized—Inc. for Incom-
plete and in the horrible comedy of the situation, Howe considered that. But
really only a mark of M for Mad would serve.

In his perplexity, Howe sought the Dean, but the Dean was out of town.
In the end, he decided to maintain the A-minus he had given Tertan at midterm.
After all, there had been no falling away from that quality. He entered it on
the grade sheet with something like bravado.

Academic time moves quickly. A college year is not really a year, lacking
as it does three months. And it is endlessly divided into units which, at their
beginning, appear larger than they are—terms, half-terms, months, weeks. And
the ultimate unit, the hour, is not really an hour, lacking as it does ten minutes.
And so the new term advanced rapidly and one day the fields about the town
were all brown, cleared of even the few thin patches of snow which had lingered
so long.

Howe, as he lectured on the romantic poets, became conscious of Blackburn emanating wrath. Blackburn did it well, did it with enormous dignity. He
did not stir in his seat, he kept his eyes fixed on Howe in perfect attention, but
he abstained from using his notebook, there was no mistaking what he proposed
to himself as an attitude. His elbow on the writing-wing of the chair, his chin
on the curled fingers of his hand, he was the embodiment of intellectual indignation. He was thinking his own thoughts, would give no public offense, yet
would claim his due, was not to be intimidated. Howe knew that he would
present himself at the end of the hour.

Blackburn entered the office without invitation. He did not smile, there
was no cajolery about him. Without invitation he sat down beside Howe's desk.
He did not speak until he had taken the blue-book from his pocket. He said,
"What does this mean, sir?"

It was a sound and conservative student tactic. Said in the usual way it
meant, "How could you have so misunderstood me?" or "What does this mean
for my future in the course?" But there were none of the humbler tones in
Blackburn's way of saying it.

Howe made the established reply, "I think that's for you to tell me."

Blackburn continued icy. "I'm sure I can't, sir."

There was a silence between them. Both dropped their eyes to the blue-book on the desk. On its cover Howe had penciled: "F. This is very poor work."

Howe picked up the blue-book. There was always the possibility of injustice. The teacher may be bored by the mass of papers and not wholly attentive. A phrase, even the student's handwriting, may irritate him unreasonably. "Well," said Howe, "let's go through it."

He opened the first page. "Now here: you write, 'In *The Ancient Mariner,* Coleridge lives in and transports us to a honey-sweet world where all is rich and strange, a world of charm to which we can escape from the humdrum existence of our daily lives, the world of romance. Here, in this warm and honey-sweet land of charming dreams we can relax and enjoy ourselves.' "

Howe lowered the paper and waited with a neutral look for Blackburn to speak. Blackburn returned the look boldly, did not speak, sat stolid and lofty. At last Howe said, speaking gently, "Did you mean that, or were you just at a loss for something to say?"

"You imply that I was just 'bluffing'?" The quotation marks hung palpable in the air about the word.

"I'd like to know. I'd prefer believing that you were bluffing to believing that you really thought this."

Blackburn's eyebrows went up. From the height of a great and firm-based idea he looked at his teacher. He clasped the crags for a moment and then pounced, craftily, suavely. "Do you mean, Dr. Howe, that there aren't two opinions possible?"

It was superbly done in its air of putting all of Howe's intellectual life into the balance. Howe remained patient and simple. "Yes, many opinions are possible, but not this one. Whatever anyone believes of *The Ancient Mariner,* no one can in reason believe that it represents a—a honey-sweet world in which we can relax."

"But that is what I *feel,* sir."

This was well done too. Howe said, "Look, Mr. Blackburn. Do you really relax with hunger and thirst, the heat and the sea-serpents, the dead men with staring eyes, Life in Death and the skeletons? Come now, Mr. Blackburn."

Blackburn made no answer and Howe pressed forward. "Now you say of Wordsworth, 'Of peasant stock himself, he turned from the effete life of the salons and found in the peasant the hope of a flaming revolution which would sweep away all the old ideas. This is the subject of his best poems.' "

Beaming at his teacher with youthful eagerness, Blackburn said, "Yes, sir, a rebel, a bringer of light to suffering mankind. I see him as a kind of Prothemeus."

"A kind of what?"

"Prothemeus, sir."

"Think, Mr. Blackburn. We were talking about him only today and I mentioned his name a dozen times. You don't mean Prothemeus. You mean—" Howe waited but there was no response.

"You mean Prometheus."

Blackburn gave no assent and Howe took the reins. "You've done a bad job here, Mr. Blackburn, about as bad as could be done." He saw Blackburn stiffen and his genial face harden again. "It shows either a lack of preparation or a complete lack of understanding." He saw Blackburn's face begin to go to pieces and he stopped.

"Oh, sir," Blackburn burst out, "I've never had a mark like this before, never anything below a B, never. A thing like this has never happened to me before."

It must be true, it was a statement too easily verified. Could it be that other instructors accepted such flaunting nonsense? Howe wanted to end the interview. "I'll set it down to lack of preparation," he said. "I know you're busy. That's not an excuse but it's an explanation. Now suppose you really prepare and then take another quiz in two weeks. We'll forget this one and count the other."

Blackburn squirmed with pleasure and gratitude. "Thank you, sir. You're really very kind, very kind."

Howe rose to conclude the visit. "All right then—in two weeks."

It was that day that the Dean imparted to Howe the conclusion of the case of Tertan. It was simple and a little anticlimactic. A physician had been called in, and had said the word, given the name.

"A classic case, he called it," the Dean said. "Not a doubt in the world," he said. His eyes were full of miserable pity and he clutched at a word. "A classic case, a classic case." To his aid and to Howe's there came the Parthenon* and the form of the Greek drama, the Aristotelian logic,† Racine‡ and the Well-Tempered Clavichord,§ the blueness of the Aegean# and its clear sky. Classic— that is to say, without a doubt, perfect in its way, a veritable model, and, as the Dean had been told, sure to take a perfectly predictable and inevitable course to a foreknown conclusion.

It was not only pity that stood in the Dean's eyes. For a moment there was fear too. "Terrible," he said, "it is simply terrible."

Then he went on briskly. "Naturally we've told the boy nothing. And naturally we won't. His tuition's paid by his scholarship and we'll continue him on the rolls until the end of the year. That will be kindest. After that the matter will be out of our control. We'll see, of course, that he gets into the proper hands. I'm told there will be no change, he'll go on like this, be as good as this, for four to six months. And so we'll just go along as usual."

So Tertan continued to sit in Section 5 of English 1A, to his classmates still

---

*Parthenon: Most famous Greek temple, built 447–438 B.C. on the Acropolis in Athens and often considered the height of classical achievement.

†Aristotelian logic: The formal system of deductive reasoning developed and taught by the classical Greek philosopher Aristotle (384–322 B.C.).

‡Racine: Jean Racine (1639–1699), French neoclassical poet and dramatist whose tragedies are noted for their dignity, elegance, and control.

§the Well-Tempered Clavichord: Forty-eight sets of preludes and fugues in all keys, by the neoclassical German composer Johann Sebastian Bach (1685–1750).

#Aegean: The Aegean Sea, an arm of the Mediterranean Sea that borders Greece and that was important to the development of classical Greek civilization.

a figure of curiously dignified fun, symbol to most of them of the respectable but absurd intellectual life. But to his teacher he was now very different. He had not changed—he was still the greyhound casting for the scent of ideas and Howe could see that he was still the same Tertan, but he could not feel it. What he felt as he looked at the boy sitting in his accustomed place was the hard blank of a fact. The fact itself was formidable and depressing. But what Howe was chiefly aware of was that he had permitted the metamorphosis of Tertan from person to fact.

As much as possible he avoided seeing Tertan's upraised hand and eager eye. But the fact did not know of its mere factuality, it continued its existence as if it were Tertan, hand up and eye questioning, and one day it appeared in Howe's office with a document.

"Even the spirit who lives egregiously, above the herd, must have its relations with the fellowman," Tertan declared. He laid the document on Howe's desk. It was headed "Quill and Scroll Society of Dwight College. Application for Membership."

"In most ways these are crass minds," Tertan said, touching the paper. "Yet as a whole, bound together in their common love of letters, they transcend their intellectual lacks, since it is not a paradox that the whole is greater than the sum of its parts."

"When are the elections?" Howe asked.

"They take place tomorrow."

"I certainly hope you will be successful."

"Thank you. Would you wish to implement that hope?" A rather dirty finger pointed to the bottom of the sheet. "A faculty recommender is necessary," Tertan said stiffly, and waited.

"And you wish me to recommend you?"

"It would be an honor."

"You may use my name."

Tertan's finger pointed again. "It must be a written sponsorship, signed by the sponsor." There was a large blank space on the form under the heading, "Opinion of Faculty Sponsor."

This was almost another thing and Howe hesitated. Yet there was nothing else to do and he took out his fountain pen. He wrote, "Mr. Ferdinand Tertan is marked by his intense devotion to letters and by his exceptional love of all things of the mind." To this he signed his name which looked bold and assertive on the white page. It disturbed him, the strange affirming power of a name. With a businesslike air, Tertan whipped up the paper, folded it with decision and put it into his pocket. He bowed and took his departure, leaving Howe with the sense of having done something oddly momentous.

And so much now seemed odd and momentous to Howe that should not have seemed so. It was odd and momentous, he felt, when he sat with Blackburn's second quiz before him and wrote in an excessively firm hand the grade of C-minus. The paper was a clear, an indisputable failure. He was carefully and consciously committing a cowardice. Blackburn had told the truth when he had pleaded his past record. Howe had consulted it in the Dean's office. It showed no grade lower than a B-minus. A canvass of some of Blackburn's previous instructors had brought vague attestations to the adequate powers of a student imperfectly remembered and sometimes surprise that his abilities could be questioned at all.

As he wrote the grade, Howe told himself that this cowardice sprang from an unwillingness to have more dealings with a student he disliked. He knew it was simpler than that. He knew he feared Blackburn: that was the absurd truth. And cowardice did not solve the matter after all. Blackburn, flushed with a first success, attacked at once. The minimal passing grade had not assuaged his feelings and he sat at Howe's desk and again the blue-book lay between them. Blackburn said nothing. With an enormous impudence, he was waiting for Howe to speak and explain himself.

At last Howe said sharply and rudely, "Well?" His throat was tense and the blood was hammering in his head. His mouth was tight with anger at himself for his disturbance.

Blackburn's glance was almost baleful. "This is impossible, sir."

"But there it is," Howe answered.

"Sir?" Blackburn had not caught the meaning but his tone was still haughty.

Impatiently Howe said, "There it is, plain as day. Are you here to complain again?"

"Indeed I am, sir." There was surprise in Blackburn's voice that Howe should ask the question.

"I shouldn't complain if I were you. You did a thoroughly bad job on your first quiz. This one is a little, only a very little, better." This was not true. If anything, it was worse.

"That might be a matter of opinion, sir."

"It is a matter of opinion. Of my opinion."

"Another opinion might be different, sir."

"You really believe that?" Howe said.

"Yes." The omission of the "sir" was monumental.

"Whose, for example?"

"The Dean's, for example." Then the fleshy jaw came forward a little. "Or a certain literary critic's, for example."

It was colossal and almost too much for Blackburn himself to handle. The solidity of his face almost crumpled under it. But he withstood his own audacity and went on. "And the Dean's opinion might be guided by the knowledge that the person who gave me this mark is the man whom a famous critic, the most eminent judge of literature in this country, called a drunken man. The Dean might think twice about whether such a man is fit to teach Dwight students."

Howe said in quiet admonition, "Blackburn, you're mad," meaning no more than to check the boy's extravagance.

But Blackburn paid no heed. He had another shot in the locker. "And the Dean might be guided by the information, of which I have evidence, documentary evidence,"—he slapped his breast pocket twice—"that this same person personally recommended to the college literary society, the oldest in the country, that he personally recommended a student who is crazy, who threw the meeting into an uproar, a psychiatric case. The Dean might take that into account.''

Howe was never to learn the details of that "uproar." He had always to content himself with the dim but passionate picture which at that moment sprang into his mind, of Tertan standing on some abstract height and madly denouncing the multitude of Quill and Scroll who howled him down.

He sat quiet a moment and looked at Blackburn. The ferocity had entirely gone from the student's face. He sat regarding his teacher almost benevolently. He had played a good card and now, scarcely at all unfriendly, he was waiting to see the effect. Howe took up the blue-book and negligently sifted through it. He read a page, closed the book, struck out the C-minus and wrote an F.

"Now you may take the paper to the Dean," he said. "You may tell him that after reconsidering it, I lowered the grade."

The gasp was audible. "Oh sir!" Blackburn cried. "Please!" His face was agonized. "It means my graduation, my livelihood, my future. Don't do this to me."

"It's done already."

Blackburn stood up. "I spoke rashly, sir, hastily. I had no intention, no real intention, of seeing the Dean. It rests with you—entirely, entirely. I *hope* you will restore the first mark."

"Take the matter to the Dean or not, just as you choose. The grade is what you deserve and it stands."

Blackburn's head dropped. "And will I be failed at midterm, sir?"

"Of course."

From deep out of Blackburn's great chest rose a cry of anguish. "Oh sir, if you want me to go down on my knees to you, I will, I will."

Howe looked at him in amazement.

"I will, I will. On my knees, sir. This mustn't, mustn't happen."

He spoke so literally, meaning so very truly that his knees and exactly his knees were involved and seeming to think that he was offering something of tangible value to his teacher, that Howe, whose head had become icy clear in the nonsensical drama, thought, "The boy is mad," and began to speculate fantastically whether something in himself attracted or developed aberration. He could see himself standing absurdly before the Dean and saying, "I've found another. This time it's the vice-president of the Council, the manager of the debating team, and secretary of Quill and Scroll."

One more such discovery, he thought, and he himself would be discovered! And there, suddenly, Blackburn was on his knees with a thump, his huge thighs straining his trousers, his hands outstretched in a great gesture of supplication.

With a cry, Howe shoved back his swivel chair and it rolled away on its casters half across the little room. Blackburn knelt for a moment to nothing at all, then got to his feet.

Howe rose abruptly. He said, "Blackburn, you will stop acting like an idiot. Dust your knees off, take your paper and get out. You've behaved like a fool and a malicious person. You have half a term to do a decent job. Keep your silly mouth shut and try to do it. Now get out."

Blackburn's head was low. He raised it and there was a pious light in his eyes. "Will you shake hands, sir?" he said. He thrust out his hand.

"I will not," Howe said.

Head and hand sank together. Blackburn picked up his blue-book and walked to the door. He turned and said, "Thank you, sir." His back, as he departed, was heavy with tragedy and stateliness.

IV

After years of bad luck with the weather, the College had a perfect day for Commencement. It was wonderfully bright, the air so transparent, the wind so brisk that no one could resist talking about it.

As Howe set out for the campus he heard Hilda calling from the back yard. She called, "Professor, professor," and came running to him.

Howe said, "What's this 'professor' business?"

"Mother told me," Hilda said. "You've been promoted. And I want to take your picture."

"Next year," said Howe. "I won't be a professor until next year. And you know better than to call anybody 'professor.' "

"It was just in fun," Hilda said. She seemed disappointed.

"But you can take my picture if you want. I won't look much different next year." Still, it was frightening. It might mean that he was to stay in this town all his life.

Hilda brightened. "Can I take it in this?" she said, and touched the gown he carried over his arm.

Howe laughed. "Yes, you can take it in this."

"I'll get my things and meet you in front of Otis," Hilda said. "I have the background all picked out."

On the campus the Commencement crowd was already large. It stood about in eager, nervous little family groups. As he crossed, Howe was greeted by a student, capped and gowned, glad of the chance to make an event for his parents by introducing one of his teachers. It was while Howe stood there chatting that he saw Tertan.

He had never seen anyone quite so alone, as though a circle had been woven about him to separate him from the gay crowd on the campus. Not that Tertan was not gay, he was the gayest of all. Three weeks had passed since Howe had last seen him, the weeks of examination, the lazy week before Commencement, and this was now a different Tertan. On his head he wore a panama hat, broadbrimmed and fine, of the shape associated with South American planters. He wore a suit of raw silk, luxurious but yellowed with age and much too tight, and he sported a whangee cane. He walked sedately, the hat tilted at a devastating angle, the stick coming up and down in time to his measured tread. He had, Howe guessed, outfitted himself to greet the day in the clothes of that ruined father whose existence was on record in the Dean's office. Gravely and arrogantly he surveyed the scene—in it, his whole bearing seemed to say, but not of it. With his haughty step, with his flashing eye, Tertan was coming nearer. Howe did not wish to be seen. He shifted his position slightly. When he looked again, Tertan was not in sight.

The chapel clock struck the quarter hour. Howe detached himself from his chat and hurried to Otis Hall at the far end of the campus. Hilda had not yet come. He went up into the high portico and, using the glass of the door for a mirror, put on his gown, adjusted the hood on his shoulders and set the mortarboard on his head. When he came down the steps Hilda had arrived.

Nothing could have told him more forcibly that a year had passed than the development of Hilda's photographic possessions from the box camera of the previous fall. By a strap about her neck was hung a leather case, so thick and strong, so carefully stitched and so molded to its contents that it could only hold a costly camera. The appearance was deceptive, Howe knew, for he had been present at the Aikens' pre-Christmas conference about its purchase. It was only a fairly good domestic camera. Still, it looked very impressive. Hilda carried another leather case from which she drew a collapsible tripod. Decisively she extended each of its gleaming legs and set it up on the path. She removed the camera from its case and fixed it to the tripod. In its compact efficiency the camera almost had a life of its own, but Hilda treated it with easy familiarity, looked into its eye, glanced casually at its gauges. Then from a pocket she took still another leather case and drew from it a small instrument through which she looked first at Howe, who began to feel inanimate and lost, and then at the sky. She made some adjustment on the instrument, then some adjustment on the camera. She swept the scene with her eye, found a spot and pointed the camera in its direction. She walked to the spot, stood on it and beckoned to Howe. With each new leather case, with each new instrument and with each new adjustment she had grown in ease and now she said, "Joe, will you stand here?"

Obediently Howe stood where he was bidden. She had yet another instrument. She took out a tape-measure on a mechanical spool. Kneeling down before Howe, she put the little metal ring of the tape under the tip of his shoe. At her request, Howe pressed it with his toe. When she had measured her distance, she nodded to Howe who released the tape. At a touch, it sprang back into the spool. "You have to be careful if you're going to get what you want," Hilda said. "I don't believe in all this snap-snap-snapping," she remarked loftily. Howe nodded in agreement, although he was beginning to think Hilda's care excessive.

Now at last the moment had come. Hilda squinted into the camera, moved the tripod slightly. She stood to the side, holding the plunger of the shutter-cable. "Ready," she said. "Will you relax, Joseph, please?" Howe realized that he was standing frozen. Hilda stood poised and precise as a setter, one hand holding the little cable, the other extended with curled dainty fingers like a dancer's as if expressing to her subject the precarious delicacy of the moment. She pressed the plunger and there was the click. At once she stirred to action, got behind the camera, turned a new exposure. "Thank you," she said. "Would you stand under that tree and let me do a character study with light and shade?"

The childish absurdity of the remark restored Howe's ease. He went to the little tree. The pattern the leaves made on his gown was what Hilda was after. He had just taken a satisfactory position when he heard in the unmistakable voice, "Ah, Doctor! Having your picture taken?"

Howe gave up the pose and turned to Blackburn who stood on the walk, his hands behind his back, a little too large for his bachelor's gown. Annoyed that Blackburn should see him posing for a character study in light and shade, Howe said irritably, "Yes, having my picture taken."

Blackburn beamed at Hilda. "And the little photographer," he said. Hilda fixed her eyes on the ground and stood closer to her brilliant and aggressive camera. Blackburn, teetering on his heels, his hands behind his back, wholly prelatical and benignly patient, was not abashed at the silence. At last Howe said, "If you'll excuse us, Mr. Blackburn, we'll go on with the picture."

"Go right ahead, sir. I'm running along." But he only came closer. "Dr. Howe," he said fervently, "I want to tell you how glad I am that I was able to satisfy your standards at last."

Howe was surprised at the hard insulting brightness of his own voice and even Hilda looked up curiously as he said, "Nothing you have ever done has satisfied me and nothing you could ever do would satisfy me, Blackburn."

With a glance at Hilda, Blackburn made a gesture as if to hush Howe—as though all his former bold malice had taken for granted a kind of understanding between himself and his teacher, a secret which must not be betrayed to a third person. "I only meant, sir," he said, "that I was able to pass your course after all."

Howe said, "You didn't pass my course. I passed you out of my course. I passed you without even reading your paper. I wanted to be sure the college would be rid of you. And when all the grades were in and I did read your paper, I saw I was right not to have read it first."

Blackburn presented a stricken face. "It was very bad, sir?"

But Howe had turned away. The paper had been fantastic. The paper had been, if he wished to see it so, mad. It was at this moment that the Dean came up behind Howe and caught his arm. "Hello, Joseph," he said. "We'd better be getting along, it's almost late."

He was not a familiar man, but when he saw Blackburn, who approached to greet him, he took Blackburn's arm, too. "Hello, Theodore," he said. Leaning forward on Howe's arm and on Blackburn's, he said, "Hello, Hilda dear." Hilda replied quietly, "Hello, Uncle George."

Still clinging to their arms, still linking Howe and Blackburn, the Dean said, "Another year gone, Joe, and we've turned out another crop. After you've been here a few years, you'll find it reasonably upsetting—you wonder how there can be so many graduating classes while you stay the same. But of course you don't stay the same." Then he said, "Well," sharply, to dismiss the thought. He pulled Blackburn's arm and swung him around to Howe. "Have you heard about Teddy Blackburn?" he asked. "He has a job already, before graduation, the first man of his class to be placed." Expectant of congratulations, Blackburn beamed at Howe. Howe remained silent.

"Isn't that good?" the Dean said. Still Howe did not answer and the Dean, puzzled and put out, turned to Hilda. "That's a very fine-looking camera, Hilda." She touched it with affectionate pride.

"Instruments of precision," said a voice. "Instruments of precision." Of the three with joined arms, Howe was the nearest to Tertan, whose gaze took in all the scene except the smile and the nod which Howe gave him. The boy leaned on his cane. The broad-brimmed hat, canting jauntily over his eye, confused the image of his face that Howe had established, suppressed the rigid lines of the ascetic and brought out the baroque curves. It made an effect of perverse majesty.

"Instruments of precision," said Tertan for the last time, addressing no one, making a casual comment to the universe. And it occurred to Howe that Tertan might not be referring to Hilda's equipment. The sense of the thrice-woven circle of the boy's loneliness smote him fiercely. Tertan stood in majestic jauntiness, superior to all the scene, but his isolation made Howe ache with a pity of which Tertan was more the cause than the object, so general and indiscriminate was it.

Whether in his sorrow he made some unintended movement toward Tertan which the Dean checked or whether the suddenly tightened grip on his arm was the Dean's own sorrow and fear, he did not know. Tertan watched them in the incurious way people watch a photograph being taken and suddenly the thought that, to the boy, it must seem that the three were posing for a picture together made Howe detach himself almost rudely from the Dean's grasp.

"I promised Hilda another picture," he announced—needlessly, for Tertan was no longer there, he had vanished in the last sudden flux of visitors who, now that the band had struck up, were rushing nervously to find seats.

"You'd better hurry," the Dean said. "I'll go along, it's getting late for me." He departed and Blackburn walked stately by his side.

Howe again took his position under the little tree which cast its shadow over his face and gown. "Just hurry, Hilda, won't you?" he said. Hilda held the cable at arm's length, her other arm crooked and her fingers crisped. She rose on her toes and said "Ready," and pressed the release. "Thank you," she said gravely and began to dismantle her camera as he hurried off to join the procession.

Writing Assignments for "Of This Time, Of That Place"

I. Brief Papers
  A. 1. Why does Joseph Howe like being a college professor?
     2. Why is it appropriate that the story ends with Howe hurrying off to join the graduation procession?
     3. Explain the significance of Blackburn's being the first in his class to get a job.
     4. When Tertan says "Instruments of precision" (p. 221), what might he be referring to other than Hilda's instruments?

5. Why, after telling himself that "he must not release Tertan to authority" (p. 207), does Howe then report Tertan to the Dean?

6. Explain how the two camera scenes—at beginning and end—relate to the story.

B. Argue for or against one of the assertions below:
1. It is necessary for Howe to report Tertan to the Dean.
2. Joseph Howe is likely to live in the same college town for the rest of his life.
3. Frederic Woolley's comment—"The Howes do no harm, but they do no good when positive good is demanded of all responsible men" (p. 199)—describes Joseph Howe the person as well as Joseph Howe the poet.
4. Tertan is right in calling Howe a "paraclete" (p. 211).

C. 1. Do you believe that Tertan is mad? Why or why not?
2. How informative and effectively written is the following response to the previous question?

> Tertan is not any more mad than any other character in Lionel Trilling's "Of This Time, Of That Place." Howe believes Tertan is mad and tries "to reduce to order the splendid confusion of the boy's ideas" (p. 205). Yet, at the same time, Wooley accuses Howe of being "the poet of a willful and selfish obscurity" (p. 199). Howe seems to be associating Tertan's unclear writing with his madness, while he himself is accused of the same type of writing. Howe also accuses Blackburn of being mad when he threatens to see the Dean about the grade he received on his second paper, it being a substantially lower grade than what he was used to. When Blackburn's threats become pleas, Howe's thoughts become "icy clear" (p. 217) and he is convinced of Blackburn's madness. When toying with the idea of reporting Blackburn to the Dean he decides not to because "one more such discovery, he thought, and he himself would be discovered!" (p. 217). At this point, Howe realizes that he too is mad, or, perhaps, that he is the only one of the three who is in fact mad.

3. Would you, in Howe's place, report Tertan to the Dean? Why or why not?
4. How would you have evaluated Tertan's first in-class paper?
5. Do you like Theodore Blackburn? Why or why not?
6. Would you, in Howe's place, give Blackburn a passing grade? Why or why not?

II. Longer Papers

A. Explain how the way you respond to one of the questions in part C above affects your overall response to and interpretation of the story.

B. How is the classroom discussion of the play (Henrik Ibsen's *Ghosts*) relevant to the story?

    C. Explain to what extent Woolsey's commentary on Joseph Howe and Thomas Wormser in *Life and Letters* is also a commentary on what takes place in the story itself.

    D. It may not be coincidental that the magazine has the title of *Life and Letters.* What does the story as a whole say about the connection between letters (or literature) and life?

    E. Tertan tells Howe that some professors are "pedants" but that others are "free souls and creative spirits" (p. 196). In which category does Howe belong?

    F. Tertan writes to the Dean that Howe "embodies the full history of man's tribulations" (p. 211). Is Tertan right or wrong?

    G. How accurately do the Dean's words—"You stay the same. But of course you don't stay the same" (p. 220)—explain what has happened to Howe during the previous year?

    H. Read the Samuel Taylor Coleridge poem called "Kubla Khan" on p. 679 of this book and then, keeping the poem in mind, reread "Of This Time, Of That Place." Now explain how "Kubla Khan" helps you understand the story more fully and experience it more deeply.

III. *Comparative Papers*

    A. Argue that either Sergeant Marx of "Defender of the Faith" or Professor Howe of "Of This Time, Of That Place" is the truer defender of the faith.

    B. Compare Howe's decision to report Tertan to the Dean with Marx's decision to change Grossbart's orders in order to decide which of the two decisions is more admirable.

    C. Taking your examples from the conduct of both Sheldon Grossbart in "Defender of the Faith" and Theodore Blackburn of "Of This Time, Of That Place," explain the most important psychological strategies for using and manipulating others.

    D. Drawing upon stories like "Of This Time, Of That Place," "A Jury of Her Peers," "Forcing the End," "The Yellow Wall-Paper," "Silent Snow, Secret Snow," "Dream Children," and "The Cask of Amontillado," construct a definition of madness.

F. SCOTT FITZGERALD
Winter Dreams

Before Reading

Are you a person who expects a lot out of life and who goes after it intensely? Or are you a person who doesn't expect much from life and who pretty much settles for whatever you can get? Free write on one or both of these questions for 5 to 10 minutes.

I

Some of the caddies were poor as sin and lived in one-room houses with a neurasthenic cow in the front yard, but Dexter Green's father owned the second best grocery-store in Black Bear—the best one was "The Hub," patronized by the wealthy people from Sherry Island—and Dexter caddied only for pocket-money.

In the fall when the days became crisp and gray, and the long Minnesota winter shut down like the white lid of a box, Dexter's skis moved over the snow that hid the fairways of the golf course. At these times the country gave him a feeling of profound melancholy—it offended him that the links should lie in enforced fallowness, haunted by ragged sparrows for the long season. It was dreary, too, that on the tees where the gay colors fluttered in summer there were now only the desolate sand-boxes knee-deep in crusted ice. When he crossed the hills the wind blew cold as misery, and if the sun was out he tramped with his eyes squinted up against the hard dimensionless glare.

In April the winter ceased abruptly. The snow ran down into Black Bear Lake scarcely tarrying for the early golfers to brave the season with red and black balls. Without elation, without an interval of moist glory, the cold was gone.

Dexter knew that there was something dismal about this Northern spring, just as he knew there was something gorgeous about the fall. Fall made him clinch his hands and tremble and repeat idiotic sentences to himself, and make brisk abrupt gestures of command to imaginary audiences and armies. October filled him with hope which November raised to a sort of ecstatic triumph, and in this mood the fleeting brilliant impressions of the summer at Sherry Island were ready grist to his mill. He became a golf champion and defeated Mr. T. A. Hedrick in a marvellous match played a hundred times over the fairways of his imagination, a match each detail of which he changed about untiringly— sometimes he won with almost laughable ease, sometimes he came up magnificently from behind. Again, stepping from a Pierce-Arrow automobile, like Mr.

WINTER DREAMS   First published in 1926 in a collection of Fitzgerald short stories titled *All the Sad Young Men*. Like Dexter Green of "Winter Dreams" (and like Nick Carraway of *The Great Gatsby*), F. Scott Fitzgerald (1896–1940) was born in the upper Midwest and educated in the East at an Ivy League school. He lived in New York City, on Long Island, in Paris, and in Hollywood.

Mortimer Jones, he strolled frigidly into the lounge of the Sherry Island Golf Club—or perhaps, surrounded by an admiring crowd, he gave an exhibition of fancy diving from the spring-board of the club raft. . . . Among those who watched him in open-mouthed wonder was Mr. Mortimer Jones.

And one day it came to pass that Mr. Jones—himself and not his ghost— came up to Dexter with tears in his eyes and said that Dexter was the —— best caddy in the club, and wouldn't he decide not to quit if Mr. Jones made it worth his while, because every other —— caddy in the club lost one ball a hole for him—regularly——

"No, sir," said Dexter decisively, "I don't want to caddy any more." Then, after a pause: "I'm too old."

"You're not more than fourteen. Why the devil did you decide just this morning that you wanted to quit? You promised that next week you'd go over to the state tournament with me."

"I decided I was too old."

Dexter handed in his "A Class" badge, collected what money was due him from the caddy master, and walked home to Black Bear Village.

"The best —— caddy I ever saw," shouted Mr. Mortimer Jones over a drink that afternoon. "Never lost a ball! Willing! Intelligent! Quiet! Honest! Grateful!"

The little girl who had done this was eleven—beautifully ugly as little girls are apt to be who are destined after a few years to be inexpressibly lovely and bring no end of misery to a great number of men. The spark, however, was perceptible. There was a general ungodliness in the way her lips twisted down at the corners when she smiled, and in the—Heaven help us!—in the almost passionate quality of her eyes. Vitality is born early in such women. It was utterly in evidence now, shining through her thin frame in a sort of glow.

She had come eagerly out on to the course at nine o'clock with a white linen nurse and five small new golf-clubs in a white canvas bag which the nurse was carrying. When Dexter first saw her she was standing by the caddy house, rather ill at ease and trying to conceal the fact by engaging her nurse in an obviously unnatural conversation graced by startling and irrelevant grimaces from herself.

"Well, it's certainly a nice day, Hilda," Dexter heard her say. She drew down the corners of her mouth, smiled, and glanced furtively around, her eyes in transit falling for an instant on Dexter.

Then to the nurse:

"Well, I guess there aren't very many people out here this morning, are there?"

The smile again—radiant, blatantly artificial—convincing.

"I don't know what we're supposed to do now," said the nurse, looking nowhere in particular.

"Oh, that's all right. I'll fix it up."

Dexter stood perfectly still, his mouth slightly ajar. He knew that if he moved forward a step his stare would be in her line of vision—if he moved backward he would lose his full view of her face. For a moment he had not realized how young she was. Now he remembered having seen her several times the year before—in bloomers.

Suddenly, involuntarily, he laughed, a short abrupt laugh—then, startled by himself, he turned and began to walk quickly away.

"Boy!"

Dexter stopped.

"Boy——"

Beyond question he was addressed. Not only that, but he was treated to that absurd smile, that preposterous smile—the memory of which at least a dozen men were to carry into middle age.

"Boy, do you know where the golf teacher is?"

"He's giving a lesson."

"Well, do you know where the caddy-master is?"

"He isn't here yet this morning."

"Oh." For a moment this baffled her. She stood alternately on her right and left foot.

"We'd like to get a caddy," said the nurse. "Mrs. Mortimer Jones sent us out to play golf, and we don't know how without we get a caddy."

Here she was stopped by an ominous glance from Miss Jones, followed immediately by the smile.

"There aren't any caddies here except me," said Dexter to the nurse, "and I got to stay here in charge until the caddy-master gets here."

"Oh."

Miss Jones and her retinue now withdrew, and at a proper distance from Dexter became involved in a heated conversation, which was concluded by Miss Jones taking one of the clubs and hitting it on the ground with violence. For further emphasis she raised it again and was about to bring it down smartly upon the nurse's bosom, when the nurse seized the club and twisted it from her hands.

"You damn little mean old *thing!*" cried Miss Jones wildly.

Another argument ensued. Realizing that the elements of comedy were implied in the scene, Dexter several times began to laugh, but each time restrained the laugh before it reached audibility. He could not resist the monstrous conviction that the little girl was justified in beating the nurse.

The situation was resolved by the fortuitous appearance of the caddy-master, who was appealed to immediately by the nurse.

"Miss Jones is to have a little caddy, and this one says he can't go."

"Mr. McKenna said I was to wait here till you came," said Dexter quickly.

"Well, he's here now." Miss Jones smiled cheerfully at the caddy-master. Then she dropped her bag and set off at a haughty mince toward the first tee.

"Well?" The caddy-master turned to Dexter. "What you standing there like a dummy for? Go pick up the young lady's clubs."

"I don't think I'll go out to-day," said Dexter.

"You don't——"

"I think I'll quit."

The enormity of his decision frightened him. He was a favorite caddy, and the thirty dollars a month he earned through the summer were not to be made elsewhere around the lake. But he had received a strong emotional shock, and his perturbation required a violent and immediate outlet.

It is not so simple as that, either. As so frequently would be the case in the future, Dexter was unconsciously dictated to by his winter dreams.

II

Now, of course, the quality and the seasonability of these winter dreams varied, but the stuff of them remained. They persuaded Dexter several years later to pass up a business course at the State university—his father, prospering now, would have paid his way—for the precarious advantage of attending an older and more famous university in the East, where he was bothered by his scanty funds. But do not get the impression, because his winter dreams happened to be concerned at first with musings on the rich, that there was anything merely snobbish in the boy. He wanted not association with glittering things and glittering people—he wanted the glittering things themselves. Often he reached out for the best without knowing why he wanted it—and sometimes he ran up against the mysterious denials and prohibitions in which life indulges. It is with one of those denials and not with his career as a whole that this story deals.

He made money. It was rather amazing. After college he went to the city from which Black Bear Lake draws its wealthy patrons. When he was only twenty-three and had been there not quite two years, there were already people who liked to say: "Now *there's* a boy——" All about him rich men's sons were peddling bonds precariously, or investing patrimonies precariously, or plodding through the two dozen volumes of the "George Washington Commercial Course," but Dexter borrowed a thousand dollars on his college degree and his confident mouth, and bought a partnership in a laundry.

It was a small laundry when he went into it, but Dexter made a specialty of learning how the English washed fine woolen golf-stockings without shrinking them, and within a year he was catering to the trade that wore knickerbockers. Men were insisting that their Shetland hose and sweaters go to his laundry, just as they had insisted on a caddy who could find golf-balls. A little later he was doing their wives' lingerie as well—and running five branches in different parts of the city. Before he was twenty-seven he owned the largest string of laundries in his section of the country. It was then that he sold out and went to New York. But the part of his story that concerns us goes back to the days when he was making his first big success.

When he was twenty-three Mr. Hart—one of the gray-haired men who liked to say "Now there's a boy"—gave him a guest card to the Sherry Island Golf Club for a week-end. So he signed his name one day on the register, and that afternoon played golf in a foursome with Mr. Hart and Mr. Sandwood and Mr. T. A. Hedrick. He did not consider it necessary to remark that he had once carried Mr. Hart's bag over this same links, and that he knew every trap and gully with his eyes shut—but he found himself glancing at the four caddies who trailed them, trying to catch a gleam or gesture that would remind him of himself, that would lessen the gap which lay between his present and his past.

It was a curious day, slashed abruptly with fleeting, familiar impressions. One minute he had the sense of being a trespasser—in the next he was impressed by the tremendous superiority he felt toward Mr. T. A. Hedrick, who was a bore and not even a good golfer any more.

Then, because of a ball Mr. Hart lost near the fifteenth green, an enormous thing happened. While they were searching the stiff grasses of the rough there was a clear call of "Fore!" from behind a hill in their rear. And as they all turned abruptly from their search a bright new ball sliced abruptly over the hill and caught Mr. T. A. Hedrick in the abdomen.

"By Gad!" cried Mr. T. A. Hedrick, "they ought to put some of these crazy women off the course. It's getting to be outrageous."

A head and a voice came up together over the hill:

"Do you mind if we go through?"

"You hit me in the stomach!" declared Mr. Hedrick wildly.

"Did I?" The girl approached the group of men. "I'm sorry. I yelled 'Fore!' "

Her glance fell casually on each of the men—then scanned the fairway for her ball.

"Did I bounce into the rough?"

It was impossible to determine whether this question was ingenuous or malicious. In a moment, however, she left no doubt, for as her partner came up over the hill she called cheerfully:

"Here I am! I'd have gone on the green except that I hit something."

As she took her stance for a short mashie shot, Dexter looked at her closely. She wore a blue gingham dress, rimmed at throat and shoulders with a white edging that accentuated her tan. The quality of exaggeration, of thinness, which had made her passionate eyes and down-turning mouth absurd at eleven, was gone now. She was arrestingly beautiful. The color in her cheeks was centred like the color in a picture—it was not a "high" color, but a sort of fluctuating and feverish warmth, so shaded that it seemed at any moment it would recede and disappear. This color and the mobility of her mouth gave a continual impression of flux, of intense life, of passionate vitality—balanced only partially by the sad luxury of her eyes.

She swung her mashie impatiently and without interest, pitching the ball into a sand-pit on the other side of the green. With a quick, insincere smile and a careless "Thank you!" she went on after it.

"That Judy Jones!" remarked Mr. Hedrick on the next tee, as they waited—some moments—for her to play on ahead. "All she needs is to be turned up and spanked for six months and then to be married off to an old-fashioned cavalry captain."

"My God, she's good-looking!" said Mr. Sandwood, who was just over thirty.

"Good-looking!" cried Mr. Hedrick contemptuously, "she always looks as if she wanted to be kissed! Turning those big cow-eyes on every calf in town!"

It was doubtful if Mr. Hedrick intended a reference to the maternal instinct.

"She'd play pretty good golf if she'd try," said Mr. Sandwood.

"She has no form," said Mr. Hedrick solemnly.

"She has a nice figure," said Mr. Sandwood.

"Better thank the Lord she doesn't drive a swifter ball," said Mr. Hart, winking at Dexter.

Later in the afternoon the sun went down with a riotous swirl of gold and varying blues and scarlets, and left the dry, rustling night of Western summer. Dexter watched from the veranda of the Golf Club, watched the even overlap of the waters in the little wind, silver molasses under the harvest-moon. Then the moon held a finger to her lips and the lake became a clear pool, pale and quiet. Dexter put on his bathing-suit and swam out to the farthest raft, where he stretched dripping on the wet canvas of the springboard.

There was a fish jumping and a star shining and the lights around the lake were gleaming. Over on a dark peninsula a piano was playing the songs of last summer and of summers before that—songs from "Chin-Chin" and "The Count of Luxemburg" and "The Chocolate Soldier"—and because the sound of a piano over a stretch of water had always seemed beautiful to Dexter he lay perfectly quiet and listened.

The tune the piano was playing at that moment had been gay and new five years before when Dexter was a sophomore at college. They had played it at a prom once when he could not afford the luxury of proms, and he had stood outside the gymnasium and listened. The sound of the tune precipitated in him a sort of ecstasy and it was with that ecstasy he viewed what happened to him now. It was a mood of intense appreciation, a sense that, for once, he was magnificently attuned to life and that everything about him was radiating a brightness and a glamour he might never know again.

A low, pale oblong detached itself suddenly from the darkness of the Island, spitting forth the reverberated sound of a racing motor-boat. Two white streamers of cleft water rolled themselves out behind it and almost immediately the boat was beside him, drowning out the hot tinkle of the piano in the drone of its spray. Dexter raising himself on his arms was aware of a figure standing at the wheel, of two dark eyes regarding him over the lengthening space of water—then the boat had gone by and was sweeping in an immense and purposeless circle of spray round and round in the middle of the lake. With equal eccentricity one of the circles flattened out and headed back toward the raft.

"Who's that?" she called, shutting off her motor. She was so near now that Dexter could see her bathing-suit, which consisted apparently of pink rompers.

The nose of the boat bumped the raft, and as the latter tilted rakishly he was precipitated toward her. With different degrees of interest they recognized each other.

"Aren't you one of those men we played through this afternoon?" she demanded.

He was.

"Well, do you know how to drive a motor-boat? Because if you do I wish you'd drive this one so I can ride on the surf-board behind. My name is Judy Jones"—she favored him with an absurd smirk—rather, what tried to be a smirk, for, twist her mouth as she might, it was not grotesque, it was merely beautiful—"and I live in a house over there on the Island, and in that house there is a man waiting for me. When he drove up at the door I drove out of the dock because he says I'm his ideal."

There was a fish jumping and a star shining and the lights around the lake were gleaming. Dexter sat beside Judy Jones and she explained how her boat was driven. Then she was in the water, swimming to the floating surf-board with a sinuous crawl. Watching her was without effort to the eye, watching a branch waving or a sea-gull flying. Her arms, burned to butternut, moved sinuously among the dull platinum ripples, elbow appearing first, casting the forearm back with a cadence of falling water, then reaching out and down, stabbing a path ahead.

They moved out into the lake; turning, Dexter saw that she was kneeling on the low rear of the now uptilted surf-board.

"Go faster," she called, "fast as it'll go."

Obediently he jammed the lever forward and the white spray mounted at the bow. When he looked around again the girl was standing up on the rushing board, her arms spread wide, her eyes lifted toward the moon.

"It's awful cold," she shouted. "What's your name?"

He told her.

"Well, why don't you come to dinner to-morrow night?"

His heart turned over like the fly-wheel of the boat, and, for the second time, her casual whim gave a new direction to his life.

III

Next evening while he waited for her to come down-stairs, Dexter peopled the soft deep summer room and the sun-porch that opened from it with the men who had already loved Judy Jones. He knew the sort of men they were—the men who when he first went to college had entered from the great prep schools with graceful clothes and the deep tan of healthy summers. He had seen that, in one sense, he was better than these men. He was newer and stronger. Yet in acknowledging to himself that he wished his children to be like them he was admitting that he was but the rough, strong stuff from which they eternally sprang.

When the time had come for him to wear good clothes, he had known who were the best tailors in America, and the best tailors in America had made him the suit he wore this evening. He had acquired that particular reserve peculiar to his university, that set it off from other universities. He recognized the value to him of such a mannerism and he had adopted it; he knew that to be careless in dress and manner required more confidence than to be careful. But carelessness was for his children. His mother's name had been Krimslich. She was a Bohemian of the peasant class and she had talked broken English to the end of her days. Her son must keep to the set patterns.

At a little after seven Judy Jones came down-stairs. She wore a blue silk afternoon dress, and he was disappointed at first that she had not put on something more elaborate. This feeling was accentuated when, after a brief greeting, she went to the door of a butler's pantry and pushing it open called: "You can serve dinner, Martha." He had rather expected that a butler would announce dinner, that there would be a cocktail. Then he put these thoughts behind him as they sat down side by side on a lounge and looked at each other.

"Father and mother won't be here," she said thoughtfully.

He remembered the last time he had seen her father, and he was glad the parents were not to be here to-night—they might wonder who he was. He had been born in Keeble, a Minnesota village fifty miles farther north, and he always gave Keeble as his home instead of Black Bear Village. Country towns were well enough to come from if they weren't inconveniently in sight and used as footstools by fashionable lakes.

They talked of his university, which she had visited frequently during the past two years, and of the near-by city which supplied Sherry Island with its patrons, and whither Dexter would return next day to his prospering laundries.

During dinner she slipped into a moody depression which gave Dexter a feeling of uneasiness. Whatever petulance she uttered in her throaty voice worried him. Whatever she smiled at—at him, at a chicken liver, at nothing—it disturbed him that her smile could have no root in mirth, or even in amusement. When the scarlet corners of her lips curved down, it was less a smile than an invitation to a kiss.

Then, after dinner, she led him out on the dark sun-porch and deliberately changed the atmosphere.

"Do you mind if I weep a little?" she said.

"I'm afraid I'm boring you," he responded quickly.

"You're not. I like you. But I've just had a terrible afternoon. There was a man I cared about, and this afternoon he told me out of a clear sky that he was poor as a church-mouse. He'd never even hinted it before. Does this sound horribly mundane?"

"Perhaps he was afraid to tell you."

"Suppose he was," she answered. "He didn't start right. You see, if I'd thought of him as poor—well, I've been mad about loads of poor men, and fully intended to marry them all. But in this case, I hadn't thought of him that way, and my interest in him wasn't strong enough to survive the shock. As if a girl calmly informed her fiancé that she was a widow. He might not object to widows, but——

"Let's start right," she interrupted herself suddenly. "Who are you, any-how?"

For a moment Dexter hesitated. Then:

"I'm nobody," he announced. "My career is largely a matter of futures."

"Are you poor?"

"No," he said frankly, "I'm probably making more money than any man my age in the Northwest. I know that's an obnoxious remark, but you advised me to start right."

There was a pause. Then she smiled and the corners of her mouth drooped and an almost imperceptible sway brought her closer to him, looking up into his eyes. A lump rose in Dexter's throat, and he waited breathless for the experiment, facing the unpredictable compound that would form mysteriously from the elements of their lips. Then he saw—she communicated her excitement to him, lavishly, deeply, with kisses that were not a promise but a fulfilment. They aroused in him not hunger demanding renewal but surfeit that would demand more surfeit . . . kisses that were like charity, creating want by holding back nothing at all.

It did not take him many hours to decide that he had wanted Judy Jones ever since he was a proud, desirous little boy.

IV

It began like that—and continued, with varying shades of intensity, on such a note right up to the dénouement. Dexter surrendered a part of himself to the most direct and unprincipled personality with which he had ever come in contact. Whatever Judy wanted, she went after with the full pressure of her charm. There was no divergence of method, no jockeying for position or premeditation of effects—there was very little mental side to any of her affairs. She simply made men conscious to the highest degree of her physical loveliness. Dexter had no desire to change her. Her deficiencies were knit up with a passionate energy that transcended and justified them.

When, as Judy's head lay against his shoulder that first night, she whispered, "I don't know what's the matter with me. Last night I thought I was in love with a man and to-night I think I'm in love with you———"—it seemed to him a beautiful and romantic thing to say. It was the exquisite excitability that for the moment he controlled and owned. But a week later he was compelled to view this same quality in a different light. She took him in her roadster to a picnic supper, and after supper she disappeared, likewise in her roadster, with another man. Dexter became enormously upset and was scarcely able to be decently civil to the other people present. When she assured him that she had not kissed the other man, he knew she was lying—yet he was glad that she had taken the trouble to lie to him.

He was, as he found before the summer ended, one of a varying dozen who circulated about her. Each of them had at one time been favored above all others—about half of them still basked in the solace of occasional sentimental revivals. Whenever one showed signs of dropping out through long neglect, she granted him a brief honeyed hour, which encouraged him to tag along for a year or so longer. Judy made these forays upon the helpless and defeated without malice, indeed half unconscious that there was anything mischievous in what she did.

When a new man came to town every one dropped out—dates were automatically cancelled.

The helpless part of trying to do anything about it was that she did it all herself. She was not a girl who could be "won" in the kinetic sense—she was proof against cleverness, she was proof against charm; if any of these assailed her too strongly she would immediately resolve the affair to a physical basis, and under the magic of her physical splendor the strong as well as the brilliant played her game and not their own. She was entertained only by the gratification of her desires and by the direct exercise of her own charm. Perhaps from so much youthful love, so many youthful lovers, she had come, in self-defense, to nourish herself wholly from within.

Succeeding Dexter's first exhilaration came restlessness and dissatisfaction. The helpless ecstasy of losing himself in her was opiate rather than tonic. It was fortunate for his work during the winter that those moments of ecstasy came infrequently. Early in their acquaintance it had seemed for a while that there was a deep and spontaneous mutual attraction—that first August, for example—three days of long evenings on her dusky veranda, of strange wan kisses through the late afternoon, in shadowy alcoves or behind the protecting trellises of the garden arbors, of mornings when she was fresh as a dream and almost shy at meeting him in the clarity of the rising day. There was all the ecstasy of an engagement about it, sharpened by his realization that there was no engagement. It was during those three days that, for the first time, he had asked her to marry him. She said "maybe some day," she said "kiss me," she said "I'd like to marry you," she said "I love you"—she said—nothing.

The three days were interrupted by the arrival of a New York man who visited at her house for half September. To Dexter's agony, rumor engaged them. The man was the son of the president of a great trust company. But at the end of a month it was reported that Judy was yawning. At a dance one night she sat all evening in a motor-boat with a local beau, while the New Yorker searched the club for her frantically. She told the local beau that she was bored with her visitor, and two days later he left. She was seen with him at the station, and it was reported that he looked very mournful indeed.

On this note the summer ended. Dexter was twenty-four, and he found himself increasingly in a position to do as he wished. He joined two clubs in the city and lived at one of them. Though he was by no means an integral part of the stag-lines at these clubs, he managed to be on hand at dances where Judy Jones was likely to appear. He could have gone out socially as much as he liked—he was an eligible young man, now, and popular with down-town fathers. His confessed devotion to Judy Jones had rather solidified his position. But he had no social aspirations and rather despised the dancing men who were always on tap for the Thursday or Saturday parties and who filled in at dinners with the younger married set. Already he was playing with the idea of going East to New York. He wanted to take Judy Jones with him. No disillusion as to the world in which she had grown up could cure his illusion as to her desirability.

Remember that—for only in the light of it can what he did for her be understood.

Eighteen months after he first met Judy Jones he became engaged to another girl. Her name was Irene Scheerer, and her father was one of the men who had always believed in Dexter. Irene was light-haired and sweet and honorable, and a little stout, and she had two suitors whom she pleasantly relinquished when Dexter formally asked her to marry him.

Summer, fall, winter, spring, another summer, another fall—so much he had given of his active life to the incorrigible lips of Judy Jones. She had treated him with interest, with encouragement, with malice, with indifference, with contempt. She had inflicted on him the innumerable little slights and indignities possible in such a case—as if in revenge for having ever cared for him at all. She had beckoned him and yawned at him and beckoned him again and he had responded often with bitterness and narrowed eyes. She had brought him ecstatic happiness and intolerable agony of spirit. She had caused him untold inconvenience and not a little trouble. She had insulted him, and she had ridden over him, and she had played his interest in her against his interest in his work—for fun. She had done everything to him except to criticise him—this she had not done—it seemed to him only because it might have sullied the utter indifference she manifested and sincerely felt toward him.

When autumn had come and gone again it occurred to him that he could not have Judy Jones. He had to beat this into his mind but he convinced himself at last. He lay awake at night for a while and argued it over. He told himself the trouble and the pain she had caused him, he enumerated her glaring deficiencies as a wife. Then he said to himself that he loved her, and after a while he fell asleep. For a week, lest he imagined her husky voice over the telephone or her eyes opposite him at lunch, he worked hard and late, and at night he went to his office and plotted out his years.

At the end of a week he went to a dance and cut in on her once. For almost the first time since they had met he did not ask her to sit out with him or tell her that she was lovely. It hurt him that she did not miss these things—that was all. He was not jealous when he saw that there was a new man to-night. He had been hardened against jealousy long before.

He stayed late at the dance. He sat for an hour with Irene Scheerer and talked about books and about music. He knew very little about either. But he was beginning to be master of his own time now, and he had a rather priggish notion that he—the young and already fabulously successful Dexter Green—should know more about such things.

That was in October, when he was twenty-five. In January, Dexter and Irene became engaged. It was to be announced in June, and they were to be married three months later.

The Minnesota winter prolonged itself interminably, and it was almost May when the winds came soft and the snow ran down into Black Bear Lake at last. For the first time in over a year Dexter was enjoying a certain tranquillity of spirit. Judy Jones had been in Florida, and afterward in Hot Springs, and somewhere she had been engaged, and somewhere she had broken it off. At first, when Dexter had definitely given her up, it had made him sad that people still linked them together and asked for news of her, but when he began to be placed at dinner next to Irene Scheerer people didn't ask him about her any more—they told him about her. He ceased to be an authority on her.

May at last. Dexter walked the streets at night when the darkness was damp as rain, wondering that so soon, with so little done, so much of ecstasy had gone from him. May one year back had been marked by Judy's poignant, unforgivable, yet forgiven turbulence—it had been one of those rare times when he fancied she had grown to care for him. That old penny's worth of happiness he had spent for this bushel of content. He knew that Irene would be no more than a curtain spread behind him, a hand moving among gleaming teacups, a voice calling to children . . . fire and loveliness were gone, the magic of nights and the wonder of the varying hours and seasons . . . slender lips, down-turning, dropping to his lips and bearing him up into a heaven of eyes. . . . The thing was deep in him. He was too strong and alive for it to die lightly.

In the middle of May when the weather balanced for a few days on the thin bridge that led to deep summer he turned in one night at Irene's house. Their engagement was to be announced in a week now—no one would be surprised at it. And to-night they would sit together on the lounge at the University Club and look on for an hour at the dancers. It gave him a sense of solidity to go with her—she was so sturdily popular, so intensely "great."

He mounted the steps of the brownstone house and stepped inside.

"Irene," he called.

Mrs. Scheerer came out of the living-room to meet him.

"Dexter," she said, "Irene's gone up-stairs with a splitting headache. She wanted to go with you but I made her go to bed."

"Nothing serious, I——"

"Oh, no. She's going to play golf with you in the morning. You can spare her for just one night, can't you, Dexter?"

Her smile was kind. She and Dexter liked each other. In the living-room he talked for a moment before he said good-night.

Returning to the University Club, where he had rooms, he stood in the doorway for a moment and watched the dancers. He leaned against the door-post, nodded at a man or two—yawned.

"Hello, darling."

The familiar voice at his elbow startled him. Judy Jones had left a man and crossed the room to him—Judy Jones, a slender enamelled doll in cloth of gold: gold in a band at her head, gold in two slipper points at her dress's hem. The fragile glow of her face seemed to blossom as she smiled at him. A breeze of warmth and light blew through the room. His hands in the pockets of his dinner-jacket tightened spasmodically. He was filled with a sudden excitement.

"When did you get back?" he asked casually.

"Come here and I'll tell you about it."

She turned and he followed her. She had been away—he could have wept at the wonder of her return. She had passed through enchanted streets, doing things that were like provocative music. All mysterious happenings, all fresh and quickening hopes, had gone away with her, come back with her now.

She turned in the doorway.

"Have you a car here? If you haven't, I have."

"I have a coupé."

In then, with a rustle of golden cloth. He slammed the door. Into so many cars she had stepped—like this—like that—her back against the leather, so—her elbow resting on the door—waiting. She would have been soiled long since had there been anything to soil her—except herself—but this was her own self outpouring.

With an effort he forced himself to start the car and back into the street. This was nothing, he must remember. She had done this before, and he had put her behind him, as he would have crossed a bad account from his books.

He drove slowly down-town and, affecting abstraction, traversed the deserted streets of the business section, peopled here and there where a movie was giving out its crowd or where consumptive or pugilistic youth lounged in front of pool halls. The clink of glasses and the slap of hands on the bars issued from saloons, cloisters of glazed glass and dirty yellow light.

She was watching him closely and the silence was embarrassing, yet in this crisis he could find no casual word with which to profane the hour. At a convenient turning he began to zigzag back toward the University Club.

"Have you missed me?" she asked suddenly.

"Everybody missed you."

He wondered if she knew of Irene Scheerer. She had been back only a day—her absence had been almost contemporaneous with his engagement.

"What a remark!" Judy laughed sadly—without sadness. She looked at him searchingly. He became absorbed in the dashboard.

"You're handsomer than you used to be," she said thoughtfully. "Dexter, you have the most rememberable eyes."

He could have laughed at this, but he did not laugh. It was the sort of thing that was said to sophomores. Yet it stabbed at him.

"I'm awfully tired of everything, darling." She called every one darling, endowing the endearment with careless, individual comraderie. "I wish you'd marry me."

The directness of this confused him. He should have told her now that he was going to marry another girl, but he could not tell her. He could as easily have sworn that he had never loved her.

"I think we'd get along," she continued, on the same note, "unless probably you've forgotten me and fallen in love with another girl."

Her confidence was obviously enormous. She had said, in effect, that she found such a thing impossible to believe, that if it were true he had merely committed a childish indiscretion—and probably to show off. She would forgive him, because it was not a matter of any moment but rather something to be brushed aside lightly.

"Of course you could never love anybody but me," she continued, "I like the way you love me. Oh, Dexter, have you forgotten last year?"

"No, I haven't forgotten."

"Neither have I!"

Was she sincerely moved—or was she carried along by the wave of her own acting?

"I wish we could be like that again," she said, and he forced himself to answer:

"I don't think we can."

"I suppose not. . . . I hear you're giving Irene Scheerer a violent rush."

There was not the faintest emphasis on the name, yet Dexter was suddenly ashamed.

"Oh, take me home," cried Judy suddenly; "I don't want to go back to that idiotic dance—with those children."

Then, as he turned up the street that led to the residence district, Judy began to cry quietly to herself. He had never seen her cry before.

The dark street lightened, the dwellings of the rich loomed up around them, he stopped his coupé in front of the great white bulk of the Mortimer Joneses' house, somnolent, gorgeous, drenched with the splendor of the damp moonlight. Its solidity startled him. The strong walls, the steel of the girders, the breadth and beam and pomp of it were there only to bring out the contrast with the young beauty beside him. It was sturdy to accentuate her slightness—as if to show what a breeze could be generated by a butterfly's wing.

He sat perfectly quiet, his nerves in wild clamor, afraid that if he moved he would find her irresistibly in his arms. Two tears had rolled down her wet face and trembled on her upper lip.

"I'm more beautiful than anybody else," she said brokenly, "why can't I be happy?" Her moist eyes tore at his stability—her mouth turned slowly downward with an exquisite sadness: "I'd like to marry you if you'll have me, Dexter. I suppose you think I'm not worth having, but I'll be so beautiful for you, Dexter."

A million phrases of anger, pride, passion, hatred, tenderness fought on his lips. Then a perfect wave of emotion washed over him, carrying off with it a sediment of wisdom, of convention, of doubt, of honor. This was his girl who was speaking, his own, his beautiful, his pride.

"Won't you come in?" He heard her draw in her breath sharply.

Waiting.

"All right," his voice was trembling, "I'll come in."

V

It was strange that neither when it was over nor a long time afterward did he regret that night. Looking at it from the perspective of ten years, the fact that Judy's flare for him endured just one month seemed of little importance. Nor did it matter that by his yielding he subjected himself to a deeper agony in the end and gave serious hurt to Irene Scheerer and to Irene's parents, who had befriended him. There was nothing sufficiently pictorial about Irene's grief to stamp itself on his mind.

Dexter was at bottom hard-minded. The attitude of the city on his action was of no importance to him, not because he was going to leave the city, but because any outside attitude on the situation seemed superficial. He was completely indifferent to popular opinion. Nor, when he had seen that it was no use, that he did not possess in himself the power to move fundamentally or to hold Judy Jones, did he bear any malice toward her. He loved her, and he would love her until the day he was too old for loving—but he could not have her. So he tasted the deep pain that is reserved only for the strong, just as he had tasted for a little while the deep happiness.

Even the ultimate falsity of the grounds upon which Judy terminated the engagement that she did not want to "take him away" from Irene—Judy who had wanted nothing else—did not revolt him. He was beyond any revulsion or any amusement.

He went East in February with the intention of selling out his laundries and settling in New York—but the war came to America in March and changed his plans. He returned to the West, handed over the management of the business to his partner, and went into the first officers' training-camp in late April. He was one of those young thousands who greeted the war with a certain amount of relief, welcoming the liberation from webs of tangled emotion.

VI

This story is not his biography, remember, although things creep into it which have nothing to do with those dreams he had when he was young. We are almost done with them and with him now. There is only one more incident to be related here, and it happens seven years farther on.

It took place in New York, where he had done well—so well that there were no barriers too high for him. He was thirty-two years old, and, except for one flying trip immediately after the war, he had not been West in seven years. A man named Devlin from Detroit came into his office to see him in a business way, and then and there this incident occurred, and closed out, so to speak, this particular side of his life.

"So you're from the Middle West," said the man Devlin with careless curiosity. "That's funny—I thought men like you were probably born and raised on Wall Street. You know—wife of one of my best friends in Detroit came from your city. I was an usher at the wedding."

Dexter waited with no apprehension of what was coming.

"Judy Simms," said Devlin with no particular interest; "Judy Jones she was once."

"Yes, I knew her." A dull impatience spread over him. He had heard, of course, that she was married—perhaps deliberately he had heard no more.

"Awfully nice girl," brooded Devlin meaninglessly, "I'm sort of sorry for her."

"Why?" Something in Dexter was alert, receptive, at once.

"Oh, Lud Simms has gone to pieces in a way. I don't mean he ill-uses her, but he drinks and runs around——"

"Doesn't she run around?"

"No. Stays at home with her kids."

"Oh."

"She's a little too old for him," said Devlin.

"Too old!" cried Dexter. "Why, man, she's only twenty-seven."

He was possessed with a wild notion of rushing out into the streets and taking a train to Detroit. He rose to his feet spasmodically.

"I guess you're busy," Devlin apologized quickly. "I didn't realize——"

"No, I'm not busy," said Dexter, steadying his voice. "I'm not busy at all. Not busy at all. Did you say she was—twenty-seven? No, I said she was twenty-seven."

"Yes, you did," agreed Devlin dryly.

"Go on, then. Go on."

"What do you mean?"

"About Judy Jones."

Devlin looked at him helplessly.

"Well, that's—I told you all there is to it. He treats her like the devil. Oh, they're not going to get divorced or anything. When he's particularly outrageous she forgives him. In fact, I'm inclined to think she loves him. She was a pretty girl when she first came to Detroit."

A pretty girl! The phrase struck Dexter as ludicrous.

"Isn't she—a pretty girl, any more?"

"Oh, she's all right."

"Look here," said Dexter, sitting down suddenly. "I don't understand. You say she was a 'pretty girl' and now you say she's 'all right.' I don't understand what you mean—Judy Jones wasn't a pretty girl, at all. She was a great beauty. Why, I knew her, I knew her. She was——"

Devlin laughed pleasantly.

"I'm not trying to start a row," he said. "I think Judy's a nice girl and I like her. I can't understand how a man like Lud Simms could fall madly in love with her, but he did." Then he added: "Most of the women like her."

Dexter looked closely at Devlin, thinking wildly that there must be a reason for this, some insensitivity in the man or some private malice.

"Lots of women fade just like *that*," Devlin snapped his fingers. "You must have seen it happen. Perhaps I've forgotten how pretty she was at her wedding. I've seen her so much since then, you see. She has nice eyes."

A sort of dullness settled down upon Dexter. For the first time in his life he felt like getting very drunk. He knew that he was laughing loudly at something Devlin had said, but he did not know what it was or why it was funny. When, in a few minutes, Devlin went he lay down on his lounge and looked out the window at the New York sky-line into which the sun was sinking in dull lovely shades of pink and gold.

He had thought that having nothing else to lose he was invulnerable at last—but he knew that he had just lost something more, as surely as if he had married Judy Jones and seen her fade away before his eyes.

The dream was gone. Something had been taken from him. In a sort of panic he pushed the palms of his hands into his eyes and tried to bring up a picture of the waters lapping on Sherry Island and the moonlit veranda, and gingham on the golf-links and the dry sun and the gold color of her neck's soft down. And her mouth damp to his kisses and her eyes plaintive with melancholy and her freshness like new fine linen in the morning. Why, these things were no longer in the world! They had existed and they existed no longer.

For the first time in years the tears were streaming down his face. But they were for himself now. He did not care about mouth and eyes and moving hands. He wanted to care, and he could not care. For he had gone away and he could never go back any more. The gates were closed, the sun was gone down, and there was no beauty but the gray beauty of steel that withstands all time. Even the grief he could have borne was left behind in the country of illusion, of youth, of the richness of life, where his winter dreams had flourished.

"Long ago," he said, "long ago, there was something in me, but now that thing is gone. Now that thing is gone, that thing is gone. I cannot cry. I cannot care. That thing will come back no more."

Writing Assignments for "Winter Dreams"

I. Brief Papers

    A. 1. What do Dexter's three fantasies—becoming golf champion, strolling into the country club, and giving a diving exhibition—have in common?
      2. Explain why Dexter quits his job as caddy and in what sense his quitting is related to his winter dreams.
      3. Why does Dexter feel "offended" by the "enforced fallowness" of the golf course during winter?
      4. What can we learn about Judy Jones by watching her play golf?
      5. What does the story's narrator mean when he calls Judy Jones "unprincipled" (p. 232)?
      6. Compare and contrast Judy Jones and Irene Scheerer in order to identify what you consider to be their most important difference.

    B. Argue for or against one of the assertions below:
      1. Dexter is not genuinely in love with Judy Jones.
      2. Fitzgerald wants us to think less of Dexter because of his continuing attachment to Judy.
      3. If Dexter had married Irene, he would have experienced deep happiness.
      4. How convincing and well written is the following student response to the previous question?

> Had Dexter Green married Irene Scheerer he would have had to settle for a life of discontent. Dexter had lived his life always reaching for more. Even after he had built up the largest string of laundries in his part of the country and thus gained the respect of Mr. T. A. Hedrick and other prominent people of Sherry Island Dexter was still not satisfied. He gave up his laundries and moved to New York to what seemed to be bigger and better things. Contrastingly, by marrying Irene he would have been stuck with a woman who "would be no more than a curtain spread behind him, a hand moving among gleaming teacups, a voice calling to children" (p. 235). Furthermore, only one week before Dexter's planned engagement announcement to Irene the author describes Dexter and his feelings toward Judy by saying "the thing was deep in him. He was too strong and alive for it to die lightly." This shows that by marrying Irene Scheerer Dexter himself would end his hopes and chances of having Judy Jones, resulting in Dexter knowing little happiness.

5. What Devlin tells Dexter about Judy is so implausible that it must be a lie.
6. By marrying Lud Simms, Judy Jones got exactly what she deserved.

C. 1. If you were in Dexter's position, would you have married Irene Scheerer? Why or why not?
2. Do you agree with Mr. T. A. Hedrick that what Judy Jones needed was "to be turned up and spanked for six months and then to be married off to an old-fashioned cavalry captain" (p. 228)?
3. Why do you think Judy married Lud Simms?
4. Do you think women readers respond differently to Judy Jones than men? Why or why not?

II. Longer Papers
A. At one point Judy asks Dexter—and herself—"why can't I be happy?" (p. 237). What does the story have to say about happiness?
B. Explain why Dexter is more devastated by Devlin's story than by Judy's rejection.
C. There are many glowing descriptions—of shining stars, gleaming lights, and water like "silver molasses under the harvest moon." How do these descriptive passages affect your response to the story?
D. In what sense is the story a commentary on wealth and what it means to be wealthy?
E. Argue for or against the assertion that the story's moral is to go through life with your feet on the ground so as not to be swept away by romantic illusions or foolish dreams.
F. You just received a letter from a high school friend, a junior, who has been assigned an in-class report on "the major themes and meanings of 'Winter Dreams.'" The letter is a plea for your help. Write a letter to your friend that identifies and explains in detail the story's "major themes and meanings" but that does so in a way that will be clear to a high school junior who must re-explain what you say to other high school juniors.

III. Point of View in "Winter Dreams"
From the sentences below construct a short essay that defines *point of view* and illustrates its use in "Winter Dreams."

1. Whenever you tell a story you have choices.
2. The choices are for telling the story.

3. One important choice involves narrative point of view.
4. Narrative point of view is the perspective or vantage point from which you present the action of the story.
5. You present the action of the story to your listener.
6. Or you present the action of the story to your reader.

7. You may present the action as if you directly participated in it.
8. Instead, you may present the action as if you were an observer removed from it.

9. This is true if you are a participant.
10. You will probably use first-person pronouns.
11. "I," "me," and "my" are first-person pronouns.
12. This perspective is called *first-person point of view.*

13. This is true if you are an observer.
14. You are more likely to use third-person pronouns.
15. "She," "he," "her," "him," and "his" are third-person pronouns.
16. This approach is called *third-person point of view.*

17. This is true in "Winter Dreams."
18. F. Scott Fitzgerald has chosen the third-person point of view.

19. Fitzgerald's story is about Dexter Green.
20. But Fitzgerald's story is not told by Dexter Green.
21. Fitzgerald's story is told by an unidentified observer.

22. Suppose the story had been a first-person narrative.
23. Then its opening paragraph would not have read that "Dexter Green's father owned the second best grocery-store in Black Bear."
24. Then its opening paragraph would not have read "Dexter caddied only for pocket-money."
25. Its first paragraph would have read "My father owned the second best grocery-store in Black Bear."
26. And its first paragraph would have read "I caddied only for pocket-money."

27. Fitzgerald may have chosen the third-person point of view for this reason.
28. The third-person point of view enables him to make clear his admiration for Dexter.

29. This is because of the third-person perspective.
30. Fitzgerald can tell us directly that Dexter's attachment to Judy Jones continues not because of Dexter's weakness.
31. Fitzgerald can tell us directly that Dexter's attachment to Judy Jones continues because Dexter is "too strong and alive for it to die lightly" (p. 235).

32. Here is another sign of Fitzgerald's admiration for Dexter.
33. It occurs at the time of Judy's final rejection.
34. The narrator–observer tells us that Dexter "tasted the deep pain that is reserved for the strong, just as he had tasted for a little while the deep happiness" (p. 237).

35. Suppose Fitzgerald had allowed Dexter to tell his story in his own words.
36. Such statements would have made Dexter seem more boastful than admirable.

IRWIN SHAW
The Girls in Their Summer Dresses

Before Reading

Do you agree that "Jealousy is an inevitable—and perhaps even a healthy—part of any genuinely loving relationship?" Free write on this question for 5 or 10 minutes.

Fifth Avenue was shining in the sun when they left the Brevoort.* The sun was warm, even though it was February, and everything looked like Sunday morning—the buses and the well-dressed people walking slowly in couples and the quiet buildings with the windows closed.

Michael held Frances' arm tightly as they walked toward Washington Square in the sunlight. They walked lightly, almost smiling, because they had slept late and had a good breakfast and it was Sunday. Michael unbuttoned his coat and let it flap around him in the mild wind.

"Look out," Frances said as they crossed Eighth Street. "You'll break your neck." Michael laughed and Frances laughed with him.

"She's not so pretty," Frances said. "Anyway, not pretty enough to take a chance of breaking your neck."

Michael laughed again. "How did you know I was looking at her?"

Frances cocked her head to one side and smiled at her husband under the brim of her hat. "Mike, darling," she said.

"O.K.," he said. "Excuse me."

Frances patted his arm lightly and pulled him along a little faster toward Washington Square. "Let's not see anybody all day," she said. "Let's just hang around with each other. You and me. We're always up to our neck in people, drinking their Scotch or drinking our Scotch; we only see each other in bed. I want to go out with my husband all day long. I want him to talk only to me and listen only to me."

"What's to stop us?" Michael asked.

"The Stevensons. They want us to drop by around one o'clock and they'll drive us into the country."

"The cunning Stevensons," Mike said. "Transparent. They can whistle. They can go driving in the country by themselves."

"Is it a date?"

"It's a date."

*the Brevoort: Once a fashionable Fifth Avenue hotel in New York City.

THE GIRLS IN THEIR SUMMER DRESSES   First published in 1939. Irwin Shaw was born in Brooklyn in 1913 and educated at Brooklyn College. For Shaw, the writer fills "the need of humanity . . . for magic and distant worlds, for disguised moralizing that will set every day transactions into larger perspectives, for the compression of great matters into digestible portions, for the shaping of mysteries into sharply edged and comprehensible symbols."

Frances leaned over and kissed him on the tip of the ear.

"Darling," Michael said, "this is Fifth Avenue."

"Let me arrange a program," Frances said. "A planned Sunday in New York for a young couple with money to throw away."

"Go easy."

"First let's go to the Metropolitan Museum of Art," Frances suggested, because Michael had said during the week he wanted to go. "I haven't been there in three years and there're at least ten pictures I want to see again. Then we can take the bus down to Radio City and watch them skate. And later we'll go down to Cavanagh's and get a steak as big as a blacksmith's apron, with a bottle of wine, and after that there's a French picture at the Filmarte that everybody says—say, are you listening to me?"

"Sure," he said. He took his eyes off the hatless girl with the dark hair, cut dancer-style like a helmet, who was walking past him.

"That's the program for the day," Frances said flatly. "Or maybe you'd just rather walk up and down Fifth Avenue."

"No," Michael said. "Not at all."

"You always look at other women," Frances said. "Everywhere. Every damned place we go."

"No, darling," Michael said, "I look at everything. God gave me eyes and I look at women and men in subway excavations and moving pictures and the little flowers of the field. I casually inspect the universe."

"You ought to see the look in your eye," Frances said, "as you casually inspect the universe on Fifth Avenue."

"I'm a happily married man." Michael pressed her elbow tenderly. "Example for the whole twentieth century—Mr. and Mrs. Mike Loomis. Hey, let's have a drink," he said, stopping.

"We just had breakfast."

"Now listen, darling," Mike said, choosing his words with care, "it's a nice day and we both felt good and there's no reason why we have to break it up. Let's have a nice Sunday."

"All right. I don't know why I started this. Let's drop it. Let's have a good time."

They joined hands consciously and walked without talking among the baby carriages and the old Italian men in their Sunday clothes and the young women with Scotties in Washington Square Park.

"At least once a year everyone should go to the Metropolitan Museum of Art," Frances said after a while, her tone a good imitation of the tone she had used at breakfast and at the beginning of their walk. "And it's nice on Sunday. There're a lot of people looking at the pictures and you get the feeling maybe Art isn't on the decline in New York City, after all—"

"I want to tell you something," Michael said very seriously. "I have not touched another woman. Not once. In all the five years."

"All right," Frances said.

"You believe that, don't you?"

"All right."

They walked between the crowded benches, under the scrubby city-park trees.

"I try not to notice it," Frances said, "but I feel rotten inside, in my stomach, when we pass a woman and you look at her and I see that look in your eye and that's the way you looked at me the first time. In Alice Maxwell's house. Standing there in the living room, next to the radio, with a green hat on and all those people."

"I remember the hat," Michael said.

"The same look," Frances said. "And it makes me feel bad. It makes me feel terrible."

"Sh-h-h, please, darling, sh-h-h."

"I think I would like a drink now," Frances said.

They walked over to a bar on Eighth Street, not saying anything, Michael automatically helping her over curbstones and guiding her past automobiles. They sat near a window in the bar and the sun streamed in and there was a small, cheerful fire in the fireplace. A little Japanese waiter came over and put down some pretzels and smiled happily at them.

"What do you order after breakfast?" Michael asked.

"Brandy, I suppose," Frances said.

"Courvoisier," Michael told the waiter. "Two Courvoisiers."

The waiter came with the glasses and they sat drinking the brandy in the sunlight. Michael finished half his and drank a little water.

"I look at women," he said. "Correct. I don't say it's wrong or right. I look at them. If I pass them on the street and I don't look at them, I'm fooling you, I'm fooling myself."

"You look at them as though you want them," Frances said, playing with her brandy glass. "Every one of them."

"In a way," Michael said, speaking softly and not to his wife, "in a way that's true. I don't do anything about it, but it's true."

"I know it. That's why I feel bad."

"Another brandy," Michael called. "Waiter, two more brandies."

He sighed and closed his eyes and rubbed them gently with his fingertips. "I love the way women look. One of the things I like best about New York is the battalions of women. When I first came to New York from Ohio that was the first thing I noticed, the million wonderful women, all over the city. I walked around with my heart in my throat."

"A kid," Frances said. "That's a kid's feeling."

"Guess again," Michael said. "Guess again. I'm older now. I'm a man getting near middle age, putting on a little fat, and I still love to walk along Fifth Avenue at three o'clock on the east side of the street between Fiftieth and Fifty-seventh Streets. They're all out then, shopping, in their furs and their crazy hats, everything all concentrated from all over the world into seven blocks—the best furs, the best clothes, the handsomest women, out to spend money and feeling good about it."

The Japanese waiter put the two drinks down, smiling with great happiness.

"Everything is all right?" he asked.

"Everything is wonderful," Michael said.

"If it's just a couple of fur coats," Frances said, "and forty-five dollar hats—"

"It's not the fur coats. Or the hats. That's just the scenery for that particular kind of woman. Understand," he said, "you don't have to listen to this."

"I want to listen."

"I like the girls in the offices. Neat with their eyeglasses, smart, chipper, knowing what everything is about. I like the girls on Forty-fourth Street at lunchtime, the actresses, all dressed up on nothing a week. I like the salesgirls in the stores, paying attention to you first because you're a man, leaving the lady customers waiting. I got all this stuff accumulated in me because I've been thinking about it for ten years and now you've asked for it and here it is."

"Go ahead," Frances said.

"When I think of New York City, I think of all the girls on parade in the city. I don't know whether it's something special with me or whether every man in the city walks around with the same feeling inside him, but I feel as though I'm at a picnic in this city. I like to sit near the women in the theatres, the famous beauties who've taken six hours to get ready and look it. And the young girls at the football games, with the red cheeks, and when the warm weather comes, the girls in their summer dresses." He finished his drink. "That's the story."

Frances finished her drink and swallowed two or three times extra. "You say you love me?"

"I love you."

"I'm pretty, too," Frances said. "As pretty as any of them."

"You're beautiful," Michael said.

"I'm good for you," Frances said, pleading. "I've made a good wife, a good housekeeper, a good friend. I'd do any damn thing for you."

"I know," Michael said. He put his hand out and grasped hers.

"You'd like to be free to—" Frances said.

"Sh-h-h."

"Tell the truth." She took her hand away from under his.

Michael flicked the edge of his glass with his finger. "O.K.," he said gently. "Sometimes I feel I would like to be free."

"Well," Frances said, "any time you say."

"Don't be foolish." Michael swung his chair around to her side of the table and patted her thigh.

She began to cry silently into her handkerchief, bent over just enough so that nobody else in the bar would notice. "Someday," she said, crying, "you're going to make a move."

Michael didn't say anything. He sat watching the bartender slowly peel a lemon.

"Aren't you?" Frances asked harshly. "Come on, tell me. Talk. Aren't you?"

"Maybe," Michael said. He moved his chair back again. "How the hell do I know?"

"You know," Frances persisted. "Don't you know?"

"Yes," Michael said after a while, "I know."

Frances stopped crying then. Two or three snuffles into the handkerchief and she put it away and her face didn't tell anything to anybody. "At least do me one favor," she said.

"Sure."

"Stop talking about how pretty this woman is or that one. Nice eyes, nice breasts, a pretty figure, good voice." She mimicked his voice. "Keep it to yourself. I'm not interested."

Michael waved to the waiter. "I'll keep it to myself," he said.

Frances flicked the corners of her eyes. "Another brandy," she told the waiter.

"Two," Michael said.

"Yes, ma'am, yes, sir," said the waiter, backing away.

Frances regarded Michael coolly across the table. "Do you want me to call the Stevensons?" she asked. "It'll be nice in the country."

"Sure," Michael said. "Call them."

She got up from the table and walked across the room toward the telephone. Michael watched her walk, thinking what a pretty girl, what nice legs.

Writing Assignments for "The Girls in Their Summer Dresses"

I. Brief Papers

A. 1. Write a plot summary of the story: what happens and why?

2. How informative and well written is the following student response to the previous question?

> In the beginning of Irwin Shaw's "The Girls in Their Summer Dresses," Frances and Michael Loomis appear to be a happily married couple who are looking forward to spending a Sunday afternoon in the city. However, soon after they begin walking down Fifth Avenue, it becomes obvious that Michael's obsession with watching beautiful women upsets Frances and is a major problem in their relationship. Frances apparently gets very upset when Michael looks at other women, though she tries to hide it by distracting herself with making plans for their afternoon together. Michael knows that Frances is upset and tries to console her by assuring her that he hasn't touched another woman in the five years that they have been married. He knows that this is the real reason why Frances is upset, but since he hasn't actually cheated on her, she can only complain about the way he looks at women. When Frances asks him, Michael admits that he may someday cheat on her. She is understandably upset by this, but soon recovers and tries to act like everything is the same between them by deciding to go to the country

with their friends after all. The only thing she asks him to do is not talk about other women to her. She wants their relationship to continue as it always had been by trying to forget the whole conversation.

3. Summarize the social and economic situation of the Loomises.
4. Explain why Michael and Frances decide to go to the country with the Stephensons when they had earlier rejected that plan.
5. What are the major signs that the relationship between Frances and Michael has changed?

B. Argue for or against one of the assertions below:
  1. Frances is right in thinking that Michael's attitude toward women is immature and in calling it "a kid's feeling" (p. 245).
  2. Frances is a selfish and insensitive nag.
  3. Michael is more at fault than Frances for the deterioration of their relationship.
  4. Despite a minor disagreement, the story ends optimistically.

C. 1. Who do you find to be more sympathetically portrayed, Frances or Michael?
  2. Do you think there is something wrong with Frances for feeling "terrible" inside when Michael looks at other women?
  3. Construct a conversation between Frances and Michael after they have returned home following an afternoon with the Stephensons.
  4. Do you think that everything would have been fine if only Frances had pretended not to notice Michael's looking at other women?
  5. Michael says that he loves Frances. What do you think?

II. Longer Papers
A. Develop one of your brief papers into a more substantial one.
B. Is the story sexist? That is, does it endorse the domination and exploitation of women by men.
C. Argue for or against the assertion that the story makes clear that the most basic problem between Frances and Michael is their complete lack of spiritual and religious values.
D. If Michael is "a happily married man" and an "example for the whole twentieth century" (p. 244), what does the story say about marriage in the twentieth century?
E. Of his looking at women, Michael comments, "I don't say it's wrong or it's right" (p. 245). But does the story as a whole make any moral judgments? Does the story show actions to be either "right" or "wrong," or does it present conduct without passing moral judgment?

III. Comparative Papers
A. Compare and contrast the attitudes toward women of Dexter Green in "Winter Dreams" and Michael Loomis in "The Girls in Their Summer Dresses" in order to argue that one's views are more mature than the other's.

B. Argue for or against the assertion that Dexter Green and Michael Loomis get into trouble for the same reason: both are romantic dreamers.

C. Explain why you find either "Winter Dreams" or "The Girls in Their Summer Dresses" to be more powerful and moving than the other.

D. On the basis of "The Girls in Their Summer Dresses" and several other stories of your choice—perhaps "The Murder," "A Jury of Her Peers," "The Downward Path to Wisdom," "Four Summers," and "Winter Dreams"—explain what twentieth-century writers have to say about marriage.

IV. *Objective Point of View in*
   "The Girls in Their Summer Dresses"
   From the sentences below, construct a short essay that defines *objective point of view* and briefly illustrates its use in "The Girls in Their Summer Dresses."

1. Irwin Shaw tells "The Girls in Their Summer Dresses" from a narrative point of view.
2. The narrative point of view is known as *dramatic*.
3. The narrative point of view is also known as *objective*.

4. His point of view is called *dramatic* for this reason.
5. We are not given direct access to the thoughts of his characters.
6. This is also the case in most plays, movies, and other dramatic presentations.
7. We can usually infer what Frances and Michael are thinking and feeling.
8. We infer from what they say.
9. We infer from how they say it.
10. We infer from what they do.
11. But we are not allowed inside them.
12. This is with one major exception.

13. Here is an example.
14. Shaw does not tell us that Frances becomes angry.
15. This is when Michael continues to look longingly at other women.

16. Shaw allows us to infer Frances' anger.
17. We infer it from what she says.
18. We infer it from how she says it.
19. " 'You always look at other women,' Frances said. 'Everywhere. Every damned place we go' " (p. 244).

20. The sentences suggest anger.
21. The sentences are short.
22. The sentences are abrupt.
23. The repetition suggests anger.
24. Especially the profanity suggests anger.

25. The dramatic point of view is sometimes called *objective*.
26. Shaw chose the dramatic point of view for "The Girls in Their Summer Dresses."
27. It is called objective because the action seems to be presented objectively.
28. The action is presented without comment.
29. The action is presented without judgment.

30. It's as if this is the case.
31. Shaw followed Michael and Frances around New York City one Sunday morning.
32. Shaw had a sound camera.
33. Shaw photographed their every move.
34. Shaw recorded their every word.
35. Shaw does not interpret what he sees and hears.
36. Shaw does not judge what he sees and hears.

37. One advantage of the objective point of view is its realism and plausibility.

38. Shaw seems to be saying this to us:
39. "You don't have to accept my attitudes or values. Here is the way it happened. Judge for yourself."

40. Perhaps the major disadvantage of the objective point of view is its restrictiveness.
41. The objective point of view denies us the direct experience of thought and feeling.
42. The direct experience of thought and feeling is often a rich source of interest and meaning in fiction.
43. The objective point of view is difficult to handle over long stretches of narrative.

44. This is one reason why few short stories use the objective point of view exclusively.
45. This is one reason why hardly any novels use the objective point of view exclusively.

46. Even "The Girls in Their Summer Dresses" shifts away from the objective point of view.
47. It does so in its last sentence.

48. In the last sentence we are granted access to Michael's thoughts.
49. This occurs for the first time.
50. "She got up from the table and walked across the room toward the telephone. Michael watched her walk, thinking what a pretty girl, what nice legs" (p. 247).

NATHANIEL HAWTHORNE
Rappaccini's Daughter

Before Reading

What are you willing to give up for the man or woman you love? What are you not willing to give up? Free write on one or both of these questions for 5 to 10 minutes.

A young man, named Giovanni Guasconti, came, very long ago, from the more southern region of Italy, to pursue his studies at the University of Padua. Giovanni, who had but a scanty supply of gold ducats in his pocket, took lodgings in a high and gloomy chamber of an old edifice which looked not unworthy to have been the palace of a Paduan noble, and which, in fact, exhibited over its entrance the armorial bearings of a family long since extinct. The young stranger, who was not unstudied in the great poem of his country, recollected that one of the ancestors of this family, and perhaps an occupant of this very mansion, had been pictured by Dante as a partaker of the immortal agonies of his Inferno. These reminiscences and associations, together with the tendency to heartbreak natural to a young man for the first time out of his native sphere, caused Giovanni to sigh heavily as he looked around the desolate and ill-furnished apartment.

"Holy Virgin, signor!" cried old Dame Lisabetta, who, won by the youth's remarkable beauty of person, was kindly endeavoring to give the chamber a habitable air, "what a sigh was that to come out of a young man's heart! Do you find this old mansion gloomy? For the love of Heaven, then, put your head out of the window, and you will see as bright sunshine as you have left in Naples."

Guasconti mechanically did as the old woman advised, but could not quite agree with her that the Paduan sunshine was as cheerful as that of southern Italy. Such as it was, however, it fell upon a garden beneath the window and expended its fostering influences on a variety of plants, which seemed to have been cultivated with exceeding care.

"Does this garden belong to the house?" asked Giovanni.

"Heaven forbid, signor, unless it were fruitful of better pot herbs than any that grow there now," answered old Lisabetta. "No; that garden is cultivated by the own hands of Signor Giacomo Rappaccini, the famous doctor, who, I warrant him, has been heard of as far as Naples. It is said that he distils these plants into medicines that are as potent as a charm. Oftentimes you may see the signor doctor at work, and perchance the signora, his daughter, too, gathering the strange flowers that grow in the garden."

The old woman had now done what she could for the aspect of the

RAPPACCINI'S DAUGHTER   First published in 1844. Nathaniel Hawthorne (1804–1864) is the author of novels like *The Scarlet Letter* and of stories that he called "allegories of the heart."

chamber; and, commending the young man to the protection of the saints, took her departure.

Giovanni still found no better occupation than to look down into the garden beneath his window. From its appearance, he judged it to be one of those botanic gardens which were of earlier date in Padua than elsewhere in Italy or in the world. Or, not improbably, it might once have been the pleasure-place of an opulent family; for there was the ruin of a marble fountain in the centre, sculptured with rare art, but so woefully shattered that it was impossible to trace the original design from the chaos of remaining fragments. The water, however, continued to gush and sparkle into the sunbeams as cheerfully as ever. A little gurgling sound ascended to the young man's window and made him feel as if the fountain were an immortal spirit, that sung its song unceasingly and without heeding the vicissitudes around it, while one century imbodied it in marble and another scattered the perishable garniture on the soil. All about the pool into which the water subsided grew various plants, that seemed to require a plentiful supply of moisture for the nourishment of gigantic leaves, and, in some instances, flowers gorgeously magnificent. There was one shrub in particular, set in a marble vase in the midst of the pool, that bore a profusion of purple blossoms, each of which had the lustre and richness of a gem; and the whole together made a show so resplendent that it seemed enough to illuminate the garden, even had there been no sunshine. Every portion of the soil was peopled with plants and herbs, which, if less beautiful, still bore tokens of assiduous care, as if all had their individual virtues, known to the scientific mind that fostered them. Some were placed in urns, rich with old carving, and others in common garden pots; some crept serpent-like along the ground or climbed high, using whatever means of ascent was offered them. One plant had wreathed itself round a statue of Vertumnus,* which was thus quite veiled and shrouded in a drapery of hanging foliage, so happily arranged that it might have served a sculptor for a study.

While Giovanni stood at the window he heard a rustling behind a screen of leaves, and became aware that a person was at work in the garden. His figure soon emerged into view, and showed itself to be that of no common laborer, but a tall, emaciated, sallow, and sickly-looking man, dressed in a scholar's garb of black. He was beyond the middle term of life, with gray hair, a thin, gray beard, and a face singularly marked with intellect and cultivation, but which could never, even in his more youthful days, have expressed much warmth of heart.

Nothing could exceed the intentness with which this scientific gardener examined every shrub which grew in his path: it seemed as if he was looking into their inmost nature, making observations in regard to their creative essence, and discovering why one leaf grew in this shape and another in that, and wherefore such and such flowers differed among themselves in hue and perfume. Nevertheless, in spite of this deep intelligence on his part, there was no approach to intimacy between himself and these vegetable existences. On the

---

*Vertumnus: Roman god of the seasons.

contrary, he avoided their actual touch or the direct inhaling of their odors with a caution that impressed Giovanni most disagreebly; for the man's demeanor was that of one walking among malignant influences, such as savage beasts, or deadly snakes, or evil spirits, which, should he allow them one moment of license, would wreak upon him some terrible fatality. It was strangely frightful to the young man's imagination to see this air of insecurity in a person cultivating a garden, that most simple and innocent of human toils, and which had been alike the joy and labor of the unfallen parents of the race. Was this garden, then, the Eden of the present world? And this man, with such a perception of harm in what his own hands caused to grow,—was he the Adam?

The distrustful gardener, while plucking away the dead leaves or pruning the too luxuriant growth of the shrubs, defended his hands with a pair of thick gloves. Nor were these his only armor. When, in his walk through the garden, he came to the magnificent plant that hung its purple gems beside the marble fountain, he placed a kind of mask over his mouth and nostrils, as if all this beauty did but conceal a deadlier malice; but, finding his task still too dangerous, he drew back, removed the mask, and called loudly, but in the infirm voice of a person affected with inward disease,—

"Beatrice! Beatrice!"

"Here am I, my father. What would you?" cried a rich and youthful voice from the window of the opposite house—a voice as rich as a tropical sunset, and which made Giovanni, though he knew not why, think of deep hues of purple or crimson and of perfumes heavily delectable. "Are you in the garden?"

"Yes, Beatrice," answered the gardener; "and I need your help."

Soon there emerged from under a sculptured portal the figure of a young girl, arrayed with as much richness of taste as the most splendid of the flowers, beautiful as the day, and with a bloom so deep and vivid that one shade more would have been too much. She looked redundant with life, health, and energy; all of which attributes were bound down and compressed, as it were, and girdled tensely, in their luxuriance, by her virgin zone.* Yet Giovanni's fancy must have grown morbid while he looked down into the garden; for the impression which the fair stranger made upon him was as if there were another flower, the human sister of those vegetable ones, as beautiful as they, more beautiful than the richest of them, but still to be touched only with a glove, nor to be approached without a mask. As Beatrice came down the garden path, it was observable that she handled and inhaled the odor of several of the plants which her father had most sedulously avoided.

"Here, Beatrice," said the latter, "see how many needful offices require to be done to our chief treasure. Yet, shattered as I am, my life might pay the penalty of approaching it so closely as circumstances demand. Henceforth, I fear, this plant must be consigned to your sole charge."

"And gladly will I undertake it," cried again the rich tones of the young lady, as she bent towards the magnificent plant and opened her arms as if to embrace it. "Yes, my sister, my splendor, it shall be Beatrice's task to nurse and

---

*virgin zone: Girdlelike belt customarily worn by unmarried girls.

serve thee; and thou shalt reward her with thy kisses and perfumed breath, which to her is as the breath of life."

Then, with all the tenderness in her manner that was so strikingly expressed in her words, she busied herself with such attentions as the plant seemed to require; and Giovanni, at his lofty window, rubbed his eyes, and almost doubted whether it were a girl tending her favorite flower, or one sister performing the duties of affection to another. The scene soon terminated. Whether Dr. Rappaccini had finished his labors in the garden, or that his watchful eye had caught the stranger's face, he now took his daughter's arm and retired. Night was already closing in; oppressive exhalations seemed to proceed from the plants and steal upward past the open window; and Giovanni, closing the lattice, went to his couch and dreamed of a rich flower and beautiful girl. Flower and maiden were different, and yet the same, and fraught with some strange peril in either shape.

But there is an influence in the light of morning that tends to rectify whatever errors of fancy, or even of judgment, we may have incurred during the sun's decline, or among the shadows of the night, or in the less wholesome glow of moonshine. Giovanni's first movement, on starting from sleep, was to throw open the window and gaze down into the garden which his dreams had made so fertile of mysteries. He was surprised, and a little ashamed, to find how real and matter-of-fact an affair it proved to be, in the first rays of the sun which gilded the dewdrops that hung upon leaf and blossom, and, while giving a brighter beauty to each rare flower, brought every thing within the limits of ordinary experience. The young man rejoiced that, in the heart of the barren city, he had the privilege of overlooking this spot of lovely and luxuriant vegetation. It would serve, he said to himself, as a symbolic language to keep him in communication with Nature. Neither the sickly and thoughtworn Dr. Giacomo Rappaccini, it is true, nor his brilliant daughter, were now visible; so that Giovanni could not determine how much of the singularity which he attributed to both was due to their own qualities and how much to his wonder-working fancy; but he was inclined to take a most rational view of the whole matter.

In the course of the day he paid his respects to Signor Pietro Baglioni, professor of medicine in the university, a physician of eminent repute, to whom Giovanni had brought a letter of introduction. The professor was an elderly personage, apparently of genial nature and habits that might almost be called jovial. He kept the young man to dinner, and made himself very agreeable by the freedom and liveliness of his conversation, especially when warmed by a flask or two of Tuscan wine. Giovanni, conceiving that men of science, inhabitants of the same city, must needs be on familiar terms with one another, took an opportunity to mention the name of Dr. Rappaccini. But the professor did not respond with so much cordiality as he had anticipated.

"Ill would it become a teacher of the divine art of medicine," said Professor Pietro Baglioni, in answer to a question of Giovanni, "to withhold due and well-considered praise of a physician so eminently skilled as Rappaccini; but, on the other hand, I should answer it but scantily to my conscience were I to permit a worthy youth like yourself, Signor Giovanni, the son of an ancient friend, to imbibe erroneous ideas respecting a man who might hereafter chance to hold your life and death in his hands. The truth is, our worshipful Dr. Rappaccini has as much science as any member of the faculty—with perhaps one single exception—in Padua, or all Italy; but there are certain grave objections to his professional character."

"And what are they?" asked the young man.

"Has my friend Giovanni any disease of body or heart, that he is so inquisitive about physicians?" said the professor, with a smile. "But as for Rappaccini, it is said of him—and I, who know the man well, can answer for its truth—that he cares infinitely more for science than for mankind. His patients are interesting to him only as subjects for some new experiment. He would sacrifice human life, his own among the rest, or whatever else was dearest to him, for the sake of adding so much as a grain of mustard seed to the great heap of his accumulated knowledge."

"Methinks he is an awful man indeed," remarked Guasconti, mentally recalling the cold and purely intellectual aspect of Rappaccini. "And yet, worshipful professor, is it not a noble spirit? Are there many men capable of so spiritual a love of science?"

"God forbid," answered the professor, somewhat testily; "at least, unless they take sounder views of the healing art than those adopted by Rappaccini. It is his theory that all medicinal virtues are comprised within those substances which we term vegetable poisons. These he cultivates with his own hands, and is said even to have produced new varieties of poison more horribly deleterious than Nature, without the assistance of this learned person, would ever have plagued the world withal. That the signor doctor does less mischief than might be expected with such dangerous substances, is undeniable. Now and then, it must be owned, he has effected, or seemed to effect, a marvellous cure; but, to tell you my private mind, Signor Giovanni, he should receive little credit for such instances of success,—they being probably the work of chance,—but should be held strictly accountable for his failures, which may justly be considered his own work."

The youth might have taken Baglioni's opinions with many grains of allowance had he known that there was a professional warfare of long continuance between him and Dr. Rappaccini, in which the latter was generally thought to have gained the advantage. If the reader be inclined to judge for himself, we refer him to certain black-letter tracts* on both sides, preserved in the medical department of the University of Padua.

"I know not, most learned professor," returned Giovanni, after musing on what had been said of Rappaccini's exclusive zeal for science,—"I know not how dearly this physician may love his art; but surely there is one object more dear to him. He has a daughter."

"Aha!" cried the professor, with a laugh. "So now our friend Giovanni's secret is out. You have heard of this daughter, whom all the young men in

*black-letter tracts: Early printers used type with a heavy (black-letter) face.

Padua are wild about, though not half a dozen have ever had the good hap to
see her face. I know little of the Signora Beatrice save that Rappaccini is said
to have instructed her deeply in his science, and that, young and beautiful as
fame reports her, she is already qualified to fill a professor's chair. Perchance
her father destines her for mine! Other absurd rumors there be, not worth
talking about or listening to. So now, Signor Giovanni, drink off your glass of
lachryma."

Guasconti returned to his lodgings somewhat heated with the wine he had
quaffed, and which caused his brain to swim with strange fantasies in reference
to Dr. Rappaccini and the beautiful Beatrice. On his way, happening to pass by
a florist's, he bought a fresh bouquet of flowers.

Ascending to his chamber, he seated himself near the window, but within
the shadow thrown by the depth of the wall, so that he could look down into
the garden with little risk of being discovered. All beneath his eye was a
solitude. The strange plants were basking in the sunshine, and now and then
nodding gently to one another, as if in acknowledgment of sympathy and
kindred. In the midst, by the shattered fountain, grew the magnificent shrub,
with its purple gems clustering all over it; they glowed in the air, and gleamed
back again out of the depths of the pool, which thus seemed to overflow with
colored radiance from the rich reflection that was steeped in it. At first, as we
have said, the garden was a solitude. Soon, however,—as Giovanni had half
hoped, half feared, would be the case,—a figure appeared beneath the antique
sculptured portal, and came down between the rows of plants, inhaling their
various perfumes as if she were one of those beings of old classic fable that lived
upon sweet odors. On again beholding Beatrice, the young man was even
startled to perceive how much her beauty exceeded his recollection of it; so
brilliant, so vivid, was its character, that she glowed amid the sunlight, and, as
Giovanni whispered to himself, positively illuminated the more shadowy intervals of the garden path. Her face being now more revealed than on the former
occasion, he was struck by its expression of simplicity and sweetness—qualities
that had not entered into his idea of her character, and which made him ask
anew what manner of mortal she might be. Nor did he fail again to observe,
or imagine, an analogy between the beautiful girl and the gorgeous shrub that
hung its gemlike flowers over the fountain—a resemblance which Beatrice
seemed to have indulged a fantastic humor in heightening, both by the arrangement of her dress and the selection of its hues.

Approaching the shrub, she threw open her arms, as with a passionate
ardor, and drew its branches into an intimate embrace—so intimate that her
features were hidden in its leafy bosom and her glistening ringlets all intermin-
gled with the flowers.

"Give me thy breath, my sister," exclaimed Beatrice; "for I am faint with
common air. And give me this flower of thine, which I separate with gentlest
fingers from the stem and place it close beside my heart."

With these words the beautiful daughter of Rappaccini plucked one of the
richest blossoms of the shrub, and was about to fasten it in her bosom. But now,
unless Giovanni's draughts of wine had bewildered his senses, a singular inci-

dent occurred. A small orange-colored reptile, of the lizard or chameleon species, chanced to be creeping along the path, just at the feet of Beatrice. It appeared to Giovanni,—but, at the distance from which he gazed, he could scarcely have seen anything so minute,—it appeared to him, however, that a drop or two of moisture from the broken stem of the flower descended upon the lizard's head. For an instant the reptile contorted itself violently, and then lay motionless in the sunshine. Beatrice observed this remarkable phenomenon, and crossed herself, sadly, but without surprise; nor did she therefore hesitate to arrange the fatal flower in her bosom. There it blushed, and almost glimmered with the dazzling effect of a precious stone, adding to her dress and aspect the one appropriate charm which nothing else in the world could have supplied. But Giovanni, out of the shadow of his window, bent forward and shrank back, and murmured and trembled.

"Am I awake? Have I my senses?" said he to himself. "What is this being? Beautiful shall I call her, or inexpressibly terrible?"

Beatrice now strayed carelessly through the garden, approaching closer beneath Giovanni's window, so that he was compelled to thrust his head quite out of its concealment in order to gratify the intense and painful curiosity which she excited. At this moment there came a beautiful insect over the garden wall: it had, perhaps, wandered through the city, and found no flowers or verdure among those antique haunts of men until the heavy perfumes of Dr. Rappaccini's shrubs had lured it from afar. Without alighting on the flowers this winged brightness seemed to be attracted by Beatrice, and lingered in the air and fluttered about her head. Now, here it could not be but that Giovanni Guasconti's eyes deceived him. Be that as it might be, he fancied that, while Beatrice was gazing at the insect with childish delight, it grew faint and fell at her feet; its bright wings shivered; it was dead—from no cause that he could discern, unless it were the atmosphere of her breath. Again Beatrice crossed herself and sighed heavily as she bent over the dead insect.

An impulsive movement of Giovanni drew her eyes to the window. There she beheld the beautiful head of the young man—rather a Grecian than an Italian head, with fair, regular features, and a glistening of gold among his ringlets—gazing down upon her like a being that hovered in mid air. Scarcely knowing what he did, Giovanni threw down the bouquet which he had hitherto held in his hand.

"Signora," said he, "there are pure and healthful flowers. Wear them for the sake of Giovanni Guasconti."

"Thanks, signor," replied Beatrice, with her rich voice, that came forth as it were like a gush of music, and with a mirthful expression half childish and half womanlike. "I accept your gift, and would fain recompense it with this precious purple flower; but, if I toss it into the air, it will not reach you. So Signor Guasconti must even content himself with my thanks."

She lifted the bouquet from the ground, and then, as if inwardly ashamed at having stepped aside from her maidenly reserve to respond to a stranger's greeting, passed swiftly homeward through the garden. But, few as the moments were, it seemed to Giovanni, when she was on the point of vanishing beneath the sculptured portal, that his beautiful bouquet was already beginning to wither in her grasp. It was an idle thought; there could be no possibility of distinguishing a faded flower from a fresh one at so great a distance.

For many days after this incident the young man avoided the window that looked into Dr. Rappaccini's garden, as if something ugly and monstrous would have blasted his eyesight had he been betrayed into a glance. He felt conscious of having put himself, to a certain extent, within the influence of an unintelligible power by the communication which he had opened with Beatrice. The wisest course would have been, if his heart were in any real danger, to quit his lodgings and Padua itself at once; the next wiser, to have accustomed himself, as far as possible, to the familiar and daylight view of Beatrice—thus bringing her rigidly and systematically within the limits of ordinary experience. Least of all, while avoiding her sight, ought Giovanni to have remained so near this extraordinary being that the proximity and possibility even of intercourse should give a kind of substance and reality to the wild vagaries which his imagination ran riot continually in producing. Guasconti had not a deep heart—or, at all events, its depths were not sounded now; but he had a quick fancy, and an ardent southern temperament, which rose every instant to a higher fever pitch. Whether or no Beatrice possessed those terrible attributes, that fatal breath, the affinity with those so beautiful and deadly flowers which were indicated by what Giovanni had witnessed, she had at least instilled a fierce and subtle poison into his system. It was not love, although her rich beauty was a madness to him; nor horror, even while he fancied her spirit to be imbued with the same baneful essence that seemed to pervade her physical frame; but a wild offspring of both love and horror that had each parent in it, and burned like one and shivered like the other. Giovanni knew not what to dread; still less did he know what to hope; yet hope and dread kept a continual warfare in his breast; alternately vanquishing one another and starting up afresh to renew the contest. Blessed are all simple emotions, be they dark or bright! It is the lurid intermixture of the two that produces the illuminating blaze of the infernal regions.

Sometimes he endeavored to assuage the fever of his spirit by a rapid walk through the streets of Padua or beyond its gates: his footsteps kept time with the throbbing of his brain, so that the walk was apt to accelerate itself to a race. One day he found himself arrested; his arm was seized by a portly personage, who had turned back on recognizing the young man and expended much breath in overtaking him.

"Signor Giovanni! Stay, my young friend!" cried he. "Have you forgotten me? That might well be the case if I were as much altered as yourself."

It was Baglioni, whom Giovanni had avoided ever since their first meeting, from a doubt that the professor's sagacity would look too deeply into his secrets. Endeavoring to recover himself, he stared forth wildly from his inner world into the outer one and spoke like a man in a dream.

"Yes; I am Giovanni Guasconti. You are Professor Pietro Baglioni. Now let me pass!"

"Not yet, not yet, Signor Giovanni Guasconti," said the professor, smiling, but at the same time scrutinizing the youth with an earnest glance. "What!

did I grow up side by side with your father? and shall his son pass me like a stranger in these old streets of Padua? Stand still, Signor Giovanni; for we must have a word or two before we part."

"Speedily, then, most worshipful professor, speedily," said Giovanni, with feverish impatience. "Does not your worship see that I am in haste?"

Now, while he was speaking there came a man in black along the street, stooping and moving feebly like a person in inferior health. His face was all overspread with a most sickly and sallow hue, but yet so pervaded with an expression of piercing and active intellect that an observer might easily have overlooked the merely physical attributes and have seen only this wonderful energy. As he passed, this person exchanged a cold and distant salutation with Baglioni, but fixed his eyes upon Giovanni with an intentness that seemed to bring out whatever was within him worthy of notice. Nevertheless, there was a peculiar quietness in the look, as if taking merely a speculative, not a human, interest in the young man.

"It is Dr. Rappaccini!" whispered the professor when the stranger had passed. "Has he ever seen your face before?"

"Not that I know," answered Giovanni, starting at the name.

"He *has* seen you! he must have seen you!" said Baglioni, hastily. "For some purpose or other, this man of science is making a study of you. I know that look of his! It is the same that coldly illuminates his face as he bends over a bird, a mouse, or a butterfly; which, in pursuance of some experiment, he has killed by the perfume of a flower; a look as deep as Nature itself, but without Nature's warmth of love. Signor Giovanni, I will stake my life upon it, you are the subject of one of Rappaccini's experiments!"

"Will you make a fool of me?" cried Giovanni, passionately. *"That,* signor professor, were an untoward experiment."

"Patience! patience!" replied the imperturbable professor. "I tell thee, my poor Giovanni, that Rappaccini has a scientific interest in thee. Thou hast fallen into fearful hands! And the Signora Beatrice,—what part does she act in this mystery?"

But Guasconti, finding Baglioni's pertinacity intolerable, here broke away, and was gone before the professor could again seize his arm. He looked after the young man intently and shook his head.

"This must not be," said Baglioni to himself. "The youth is the son of my old friend, and shall not come to any harm from which the arcana of medical science can preserve him. Besides, it is too insufferable an impertinence in Rappaccini thus to snatch the lad out of my own hands, as I may say, and make use of him for his infernal experiments. This daughter of his! It shall be looked to. Perchance, most learned Rappaccini, I may foil you where you little dream of it!"

Meanwhile Giovanni had pursued a circuitous route, and at length found himself at the door of his lodgings. As he crossed the threshold he was met by old Lisabetta, who smirked and smiled, and was evidently desirous to attract his attention; vainly, however, as the ebullition of his feelings had momentarily subsided into a cold and dull vacuity. He turned his eyes full upon the withered face that was puckering itself into a smile, but seemed to behold it not. The old dame, therefore, laid her grasp upon his cloak.

"Signor! signor!" whispered she, still with a smile over the whole breadth of her visage, so that it looked not unlike a grotesque carving in wood, darkened by centuries. "Listen, signor! There is a private entrance into the garden!"

"What do you say?" exclaimed Giovanni, turning quickly about, as if an inanimate thing should start into feverish life. "A private entrance into Dr. Rappaccini's garden?"

"Hush! hush! not so loud!" whispered Lisabetta, putting her hand over his mouth. "Yes; into the worshipful doctor's garden, where you may see all his fine shrubbery. Many a young man in Padua would give gold to be admitted among those flowers."

Giovanni put a piece of gold into her hand.

"Show me the way," said he.

A surmise, probably excited by his conversation with Baglioni, crossed his mind, that this interposition of old Lisabetta might perchance be connected with the intrigue, whatever were its nature, in which the professor seemed to suppose that Dr. Rappaccini was involving him. But such a suspicion, though it disturbed Giovanni, was inadequate to restrain him. The instant that he was aware of the possibility of approaching Beatrice, it seemed an absolute necessity of his existence to do so. It mattered not whether she were angel or demon; he was irrevocably within her sphere, and must obey the law that whirled him onward, in ever-lessening circles, towards a result which he did not attempt to foreshadow; and yet, strange to say, there came across him a sudden doubt whether this intense interest on his part were not delusory; whether it were really of so deep and positive a nature as to justify him in now thrusting himself into an incalculable position; whether it were not merely the fantasy of a young man's brain, only slightly or not at all connected with his heart.

He paused, hesitated, turned half about, but again went on. His withered guide led him along several obscure passages, and finally undid a door, through which, as it was opened, there came the sight and sound of rustling leaves, with the broken sunshine glimmering among them. Giovanni stepped forth, and, forcing himself through the entanglement of a shrub that wreathed its tendrils over the hidden entrance, stood beneath his own window in the open area of Dr. Rappaccini's garden.

How often is it the case that, when impossibilities have come to pass and dreams have condensed their misty substance into tangible realities, we find ourselves calm, and even coldly self-possessed, amid circumstances which it would have been a delirium of joy or agony to anticipate! Fate delights to thwart us thus. Passion will choose his own time to rush upon the scene, and lingers sluggishly behind when an appropriate adjustment of events would seem to summon his appearance. So was it now with Giovanni. Day after day his pulses had throbbed with feverish blood at the improbable idea of an interview with Beatrice, and of standing with her, face to face, in this very garden, basking in the Oriental sunshine of her beauty, and snatching from her full gaze the mystery which he deemed the riddle of his own existence. But now there was a singular and untimely equanimity within his breast. He threw a glance around the garden to discover if Beatrice or her father were present, and, perceiving that he was alone, began a critical observation of the plants.

The aspect of one and all of them dissatisfied him; their gorgeousness seemed fierce, passionate, and even unnatural. There was hardly an individual shrub which a wanderer, straying by himself through a forest, would not have been startled to find growing wild, as if an unearthly face had glared at him out of the thicket. Several also would have shocked a delicate instinct by an appearance of artificialness indicating that there had been such commixture, and, as it were, adultery of various vegetable species, that the production was no longer of God's making, but the monstrous offspring of man's depraved fancy, glowing with only an evil mockery of beauty. They were probably the result of experiment, which in one or two cases had succeeded in mingling plants individually lovely into a compound possessing the questionable and ominous character that distinguished the whole growth of the garden. In fine, Giovanni recognized but two or three plants in the collection, and those of a kind that he well knew to be poisonous. While busy with these contemplations he heard the rustling of a silken garment, and, turning, beheld Beatrice emerging from beneath the sculptured portal.

Giovanni had not considered with himself what should be his deportment; whether he should apologize for his intrusion into the garden, or assume that he was there with the privity at least, if not by the desire, of Dr. Rappaccini or his daughter; but Beatrice's manner placed him at his ease, though leaving him still in doubt by what agency he had gained admittance. She came lightly along the path and met him near the broken fountain. There was surprise in her face, but brightened by a simple and kind expression of pleasure.

"You are a connoisseur in flowers, signor," said Beatrice, with a smile, alluding to the bouquet which he had flung her from the window. "It is no marvel, therefore, if the sight of my father's rare collection has tempted you to take a nearer view. If he were here, he could tell you many strange and interesting facts as to the nature and habits of these shrubs; for he has spent a lifetime in such studies, and this garden is his world."

"And yourself, lady," observed Giovanni, "if fame says true,—you likewise are deeply skilled in the virtues indicated by these rich blossoms and these spicy perfumes. Would you deign to be my instructress, I should prove an apter scholar than if taught by Signor Rappaccini himself."

"Are there such idle rumors?" asked Beatrice, with the music of a pleasant laugh. "Do people say that I am skilled in my father's science of plants? What a jest is there! No; though I have grown up among these flowers, I know no more of them than their hues and perfume; and sometimes methinks I would fain rid myself of even that small knowledge. There are many flowers here, and those not the least brilliant, that shock and offend me when they meet my eye. But pray, signor, do not believe these stories about my science. Believe nothing of me save what you see with your own eyes."

"And must I believe all that I have seen with my own eyes?" asked Giovanni, pointedly, while the recollection of former scenes made him shrink.

"No, signora; you demand too little of me. Bid me believe nothing save what comes from your own lips."

It would appear that Beatrice understood him. There came a deep flush to her cheek; but she looked full into Giovanni's eyes, and responded to his gaze of uneasy suspicion with a queenlike haughtiness.

"I do so bid you, signor," she replied. "Forget whatever you may have fancied in regard to me. If true to the outward senses, still it may be false in its essence; but the words of Beatrice Rappaccini's lips are true from the depths of the heart outward. Those you may believe."

A fervor glowed in her whole aspect and beamed upon Giovanni's consciousness like the light of truth itself; but while she spoke there was a fragrance in the atmosphere around her, rich and delightful, though evanescent, yet which the young man, from an indefinable reluctance, scarcely dared to draw into his lungs. It might be the odor of the flowers. Could it be Beatrice's breath which thus embalmed her words with a strange richness, as if by steeping them in her heart? A faintness passed like a shadow over Giovanni and flitted away; he seemed to gaze through the beautiful girl's eyes into her transparent soul, and felt no more doubt or fear.

The tinge of passion that had colored Beatrice's manner vanished; she became gay, and appeared to derive a pure delight from her communion with the youth not unlike what the maiden of a lonely island might have felt conversing with a voyager from the civilized world. Evidently her experience of life had been confined within the limits of that garden. She talked now about matters as simple as the daylight or summer clouds, and now asked questions in reference to the city, or Giovanni's distant home, his friends, his mother, and his sisters—questions indicating such seclusion, and suck lack of familiarity with modes and forms, that Giovanni responded as if to an infant. Her spirit gushed out before him like a fresh rill that was just catching its first glimpse of the sunlight and wondering at the reflections of earth and sky which were flung into its bosom. There came thoughts, too, from a deep source, and fantasies of a gemlike brilliancy, as if diamonds and rubies sparkled upward among the bubbles of the fountain. Ever and anon there gleamed across the young man's mind a sense of wonder that he should be walking side by side with the being who had so wrought upon his imagination, whom he had idealized in such hues of terror, in whom he had positively witnessed such manifestations of dreadful attributes—that he should be conversing with Beatrice like a brother, and should find her so human and so maidenlike. But such reflections were only momentary; the effect of her character was too real not to make itself familiar at once.

In this free intercourse they had strayed through the garden, and now, after many turns among its avenues, were come to the shattered fountain, beside which grew the magnificent shrub, with its treasury of glowing blossoms. A fragrance was diffused from it which Giovanni recognized as identical with that which he had attributed to Beatrice's breath, but incomparably more powerful. As her eyes fell upon it, Giovanni beheld her press her hand to her bosom as if her heart were throbbing suddenly and painfully.

"For the first time in my life," murmured she, addressing the shrub, "I had forgotten thee."

"I remember, signora," said Giovanni, "that you once promised to reward me with one of these living gems for the bouquet which I had the happy boldness to fling to your feet. Permit me now to pluck it as a memorial of this interview."

He made a step towards the shrub with extended hand; but Beatrice darted forward, uttering a shriek that went through his heart like a dagger. She caught his hand and drew it back with the whole force of her slender figure. Giovanni felt her touch thrilling through his fibres.

"Touch it not!" exclaimed she, in a voice of agony. "Not for thy life! It is fatal!"

Then, hiding her face, she fled from him and vanished beneath the sculptured portal. As Giovanni followed her with his eyes, he beheld the emaciated figure and pale intelligence of Dr. Rappaccini, who had been watching the scene, he knew not how long, within the shadow of the entrance.

No sooner was Guasconti alone in his chamber than the image of Beatrice came back to his passionate musings, invested with all the witchery that had been gathering around it ever since his first glimpse of her, and now likewise imbued with a tender warmth of girlish womanhood. She was human; her nature was endowed with all gentle and feminine qualities; she was worthiest to be worshipped; she was capable, surely, on her part, of the height and heroism of love. Those tokens which he had hitherto considered as proofs of a frightful peculiarity in her physical and moral system were now either forgotten or by the subtle sophistry of passion transmitted into a golden crown of enchantment, rendering Beatrice the more admirable by so much as she was the more unique. Whatever had looked ugly was now beautiful; or, if incapable of such a change, it stole away and hid itself among those shapeless half ideas which throng the dim region beyond the daylight of our perfect consciousness. Thus did he spend the night, nor fell asleep until the dawn had begun to awake the slumbering flowers in Dr. Rappaccini's garden, whither Giovanni's dreams doubtless led him. Up rose the sun in his due season, and, flinging his beams upon the young man's eyelids, awoke him to a sense of pain. When thoroughly aroused, he became sensible of a burning and tingling agony in his hand—in his right hand—the very hand which Beatrice had grasped in her own when he was on the point of plucking one of the gemlike flowers. On the back of that hand there was now a purple print like that of four small fingers, and the likeness of a slender thumb upon his wrist.

O, how stubbornly does love,—or even that cunning semblance of love which flourishes in the imagination, but strikes no depth of root into the heart,—how stubbornly does it hold its faith until the moment comes when it is doomed to vanish into thin mist! Giovanni wrapped a handkerchief about his hand and wondered what evil thing had stung him, and soon forgot his pain in a revery of Beatrice.

After the first interview, a second was in the inevitable course of what we call fate. A third; a fourth; and a meeting with Beatrice in the garden was no longer an incident in Giovanni's daily life, but the whole space in which he might be said to live; for the anticipation and memory of that ecstatic hour made up the remainder. Nor was it otherwise with the daughter of Rappaccini. She watched for the youth's appearance and flew to his side with confidence as unreserved as if they had been playmates from early infancy—as if they were such playmates still. If, by any unwonted chance, he failed to come at the appointed moment, she stood beneath the window and sent up the rich sweetness of her tones to float around him in his chamber and echo and reverberate throughout his heart: "Giovanni! Giovanni! Why tarriest thou? Come down!" And down he hastened into that Eden of poisonous flowers.

But, with all this intimate familiarity, there was still a reserve in Beatrice's demeanor, so rigidly and invariably sustained that the idea of infringing it scarcely occurred to his imagination. By all appreciable signs, they loved; they had looked love with eyes that conveyed the holy secret from the depths of one soul into the depths of the other, as if it were too sacred to be whispered by the way; they had even spoken love in those gushes of passion when their spirits darted forth in articulated breath like tongues of long hidden flame; and yet there had been no seal of lips, no clasp of hands, nor any slightest caress such as love claims and hallows. He had never touched one of the gleaming ringlets of her hair; her garment—so marked was the physical barrier between them—had never been waved against him by a breeze. On the few occasions when Giovanni had seemed tempted to overstep the limit, Beatrice grew so sad, so stern, and withal wore such a look of desolate separation, shuddering at itself, that not a spoken word was requisite to repel him. At such times he was startled at the horrible suspicions that rose, monster-like, out of the caverns of his heart and stared him in the face; his love grew thin and faint as the morning mist; his doubts alone had substance. But, when Beatrice's face brightened again after the momentary shadow, she was transformed at once from the mysterious, questionable being whom he had watched with so much awe and horror; she was now the beautiful and unsophisticated girl whom he felt that his spirit knew with a certainty beyond all other knowledge.

A considerable time had now passed since Giovanni's last meeting with Baglioni. One morning, however, he was disagreeably surprised by a visit from the professor, whom he had scarcely thought of for whole weeks, and would willingly have forgotten still longer. Given up as he had long been to a pervading excitement, he could tolerate no companions except upon condition of their perfect sympathy with his present state of feeling. Such sympathy was not to be expected from Professor Baglioni.

The visitor chatted carelessly for a few moments about the gossip of the city and the university, and then took up another topic.

"I have been reading an old classic author lately," said he, "and met with a story that strangely interested me. Possibly you may remember it. It is of an Indian prince, who sent a beautiful woman as a present to Alexander the Great. She was as lovely as the dawn and gorgeous as the sunset; but what especially distinguished her was a certain rich perfume in her breath—richer than a garden of Persian roses. Alexander, as was natural to a youthful conqueror, fell in love at first sight with this magnificent stranger; but a certain sage physician, happening to be present, discovered a terrible secret in regard to her."

"And what was that?" asked Giovanni, turning his eyes downward to avoid those of the professor.

"That this lovely woman," continued Baglioni, with emphasis, "had been nourished with poisons from her birth upward, until her whole nature was so imbued with them that she herself had become the deadliest poison in existence. Poison was her element of life. With that rich perfume of her breath she blasted the very air. Her love would have been poison—her embrace death. Is not this a marvellous tale?"

"A childish fable," answered Giovanni, nervously starting from his chair. "I marvel how your worship finds time to read such nonsense among your graver studies."

"By the by," said the professor, looking uneasily about him, "what singular fragrance is this in your apartment? Is it the perfume of your gloves? It is faint, but delicious; and yet, after all, by no means agreeable. Were I to breathe it long, methinks it would make me ill. It is like the breath of a flower; but I see no flowers in the chamber."

"Nor are there any," replied Giovanni, who had turned pale as the professor spoke; "nor, I think, is there any fragrance except in your worship's imagination. Odors, being a sort of element combined of the sensual and the spiritual, are apt to deceive us in this manner. The recollection of a perfume, the bare idea of it, may easily be mistaken for a present reality."

"Ay; but my sober imagination does not often play such tricks," said Baglioni; "and, were I to fancy any kind of odor, it would be that of some vile apothecary drug, wherewith my fingers are likely enough to be imbued. Our worshipful friend Rappaccini, as I have heard, tinctures his medicaments with odors richer than those of Araby. Doubtless, likewise, the fair and learned Signora Beatrice would minister to her patients with draughts as sweet as a maiden's breath; but woe to him that sips them!"

Giovanni's face evinced many contending emotions. The tone in which the professor alluded to the pure and lovely daughter of Rappaccini was a torture to his soul; and yet the intimation of a view of her character, opposite to his own, gave instantaneous distinctness to a thousand dim suspicions, which now grinned at him like so many demons. But he strove hard to quell them and to respond to Baglioni with a true lover's perfect faith.

"Signor professor," said he, "you were my father's friend; perchance, too, it is your purpose to act a friendly part towards his son. I would fain feel nothing towards you save respect and deference; but I pray you to observe, signor, that there is one subject on which we must not speak. You know not the Signora Beatrice. You cannot, therefore, estimate the wrong—the blasphemy, I may even say—that is offered to her character by a light or injurious word."

"Giovanni! my poor Giovanni!" answered the professor, with a calm expression of pity, "I know this wretched girl far better than yourself. You shall hear the truth in respect to the poisoner Rappaccini and his poisonous daughter; yes, poisonous as she is beautiful. Listen; for, even should you do violence to my gray hairs, it shall not silence me. That old fable of the Indian woman has become a truth by the deep and deadly science of Rappaccini and in the person of the lovely Beatrice."

Giovanni groaned and hid his face.

"Her father," continued Baglioni, "was not restrained by natural affection from offering up his child in this horrible manner as the victim of his insane zeal for science; for, let us do him justice, he is as true a man of science as ever distilled his own heart in an alembic. What, then, will be your fate? Beyond a doubt you are selected as the material of some new experiment. Perhaps the result is to be death; perhaps a fate more awful still. Rappaccini, with what he calls the interest of science before his eyes, will hesitate at nothing."

"It is a dream," muttered Giovanni to himself; "surely it is a dream."

"But," resumed the professor, "be of good cheer, son of my friend. It is not yet too late for the rescue. Possibly we may even succeed in bringing back this miserable child within the limits of ordinary nature, from which her father's madness has estranged her. Behold this little silver vase! It was wrought by the hands of the renowned Benvenuto Cellini,* and is well worthy to be a love gift to the fairest dame in Italy. But its contents are invaluable. One little sip of this antidote would have rendered the most virulent poisons of the Borgias† innocuous. Doubt not that it will be as efficacious against those of Rappaccini. Bestow the vase, and the precious liquid within it, on your Beatrice, and hopefully await the result."

Baglioni laid a small, exquisitely wrought silver vial on the table and withdrew, leaving what he had said to produce its effect upon the young man's mind.

"We will thwart Rappaccini yet," thought he, chuckling to himself, as he descended the stairs; "but, let us confess the truth of him, he is a wonderful man—a wonderful man indeed; a vile empiric, however, in his practice, and therefore not to be tolerated by those who respect the good old rules of the medical profession."

Throughout Giovanni's whole acquaintance with Beatrice, he had occasionally, as we have said, been haunted by dark surmises as to her character; yet so thoroughly had she made herself felt by him as a simple, natural, most affectionate, and guileless creature, that the image now held up by Professor Baglioni looked as strange and incredible as if it were not in accordance with his own original conception. True, there were ugly recollections connected with his first glimpses of the beautiful girl; he could not quite forget the bouquet that withered in her grasp, and the insect that perished amid the sunny air, by no ostensible agency save the fragrance of her breath. These incidents, however, dissolving in the pure light of her character, had no longer the efficacy of facts, but were acknowledged as mistaken fantasies, by whatever

*Benvenuto Cellini: Italian sculptor, metalsmith, and writer (1500–1571).
†Borgias: Powerful Italian family rumored to have poisoned several of their enemies.

testimony of the senses they might appear to be substantiated. There is something truer and more real than what we can see with the eyes and touch with the finger. On such better evidence had Giovanni founded his confidence in Beatrice, though rather by the necessary force of her high attributes than by any deep and generous faith on his part. But now his spirit was incapable of sustaining itself at the height to which the early enthusiasm of passion had exalted it; he fell down, grovelling among earthly doubts, and defiled therewith the pure whiteness of Beatrice's image. Not that he gave her up; he did but distrust. He resolved to institute some decisive test that should satisfy him, once for all, whether there were those dreadful peculiarities in her physical nature which could not be supposed to exist without some corresponding monstrosity of soul. His eyes, gazing down afar, might have deceived him as to the lizard, the insect, and the flowers; but if he could witness, at the distance of a few paces, the sudden blight of one fresh and beautiful flower in Beatrice's hand, there would be room for no further question. With this idea he hastened to the florist's and purchased a bouquet that was still gemmed with the morning dewdrops.

It was now the customary hour of his daily interview with Beatrice. Before descending into the garden, Giovanni failed not to look at his figure in the mirror—a vanity to be expected in a beautiful young man, yet, as displaying itself at that troubled and feverish moment, the token of a certain shallowness of feeling and insincerity of character. He did gaze, however, and said to himself that his features had never before possessed so rich a grace, nor his eyes such vivacity, nor his cheeks so warm a hue of superabundant life.

"At least," thought he, "her poison has not yet insinuated itself into my system. I am no flower to perish in her grasp."

With that thought he turned his eyes on the bouquet, which he had never once laid aside from his hand. A thrill of indefinable horror shot through his frame on perceiving that those dewy flowers were already beginning to droop; they wore the aspect of things that had been fresh and lovely yesterday. Giovanni grew white as marble, and stood motionless before the mirror, staring at his own reflection there as at the likeness of something frightful. He remembered Baglioni's remark about the fragrance that seemed to pervade the chamber. It must have been the poison in his breath! Then he shuddered—shuddered at himself. Recovering from his stupor, he began to watch with curious eye a spider that was busily at work hanging its web from the antique cornice of the apartment, crossing and recrossing the artful system of interwoven lines—as vigorous and active a spider as ever dangled from an old ceiling. Giovanni bent towards the insect, and emitted a deep, long breath. The spider suddenly ceased its toil; the web vibrated with a tremor originating in the body of the small artisan. Again Giovanni sent forth a breath, deeper, longer, and imbued with a venomous feeling out of his heart: he knew not whether he were wicked, or only desperate. The spider made a convulsive gripe with his limbs and hung dead across the window.

"Accursed! accursed!" muttered Giovanni, addressing himself. "Hast thou grown so poisonous that this deadly insect perishes by thy breath?"

At that moment a rich, sweet voice came floating up from the garden.

"Giovanni! Giovanni! It is past the hour! Why tarriest thou? Come down!"

"Yes," muttered Giovanni again. "She is the only being whom my breath may not slay! Would that it might!"

He rushed down, and in an instant was standing before the bright and loving eyes of Beatrice. A moment ago his wrath and despair had been so fierce that he could have desired nothing so much as to wither her by a glance; but with her actual presence there came influences which had too real an existence to be at once shaken off; recollections of the delicate and benign power of her feminine nature, which had so often enveloped him in a religious calm; recollections of many a holy and passionate outgush of her heart, when the pure fountain had been unsealed from its depths and made visible in its transparency to his mental eye; recollections which, had Giovanni known how to estimate them, would have assured him that all this ugly mystery was but an earthly illusion, and that, whatever mist of evil might seem to have gathered over her, the real Beatrice was a heavenly angel. Incapable as he was of such high faith, still her presence had not utterly lost its magic. Giovanni's rage was quelled into an aspect of sullen insensibility. Beatrice, with a quick spiritual sense, immediately felt that there was a gulf of blackness between them which neither he nor she could pass. They walked on together, sad and silent, and came thus to the marble fountain and to its pool of water on the ground, in the midst of which grew the shrub that bore gemlike blossoms. Giovanni was affrighted at the eager enjoyment—the appetite, as it were—with which he found himself inhaling the fragrance of the flowers.

"Beatrice," asked he, abruptly, "whence came this shrub?"

"My father created it," answered she, with simplicity.

"Created it! created it!" repeated Giovanni. "What mean you, Beatrice?"

"He is a man fearfully acquainted with the secrets of Nature," replied Beatrice; "and, at the hour when I first drew breath, this plant sprang from the soil, the offspring of his science, of his intellect, while I was but his earthly child. Approach it not!" continued she, observing with terror that Giovanni was drawing nearer to the shrub. "It has qualities that you little dream of. But I, dearest Giovanni,—I grew up and blossomed with the plant and was nourished with its breath. It was my sister, and I loved it with a human affection; for, alas!—hast thou not suspected it?—there was an awful doom."

Here Giovanni frowned so darkly upon her that Beatrice paused and trembled. But her faith in his tenderness reassured her, and made her blush that she had doubted for an instant.

"There was an awful doom," she continued, "the effect of my father's fatal love of science, which estranged me from all society of my kind. Until Heaven sent thee, dearest Giovanni, O, how lonely was thy poor Beatrice!"

"Was it a hard doom?" asked Giovanni, fixing his eyes upon her.

"Only of late have I known how hard it was," answered she, tenderly. "O, yes; but my heart was torpid, and therefore quiet."

Giovanni's rage broke forth from his sullen gloom like a lightning flash out of a dark cloud.

"Accursed one!" cried he, with venomous scorn and anger. "And, finding thy solitude wearisome, thou hast severed me likewise from all the warmth of life and enticed me into thy region of unspeakable horror!"

"Giovanni!" exclaimed Beatrice, turning her large bright eyes upon his face. The force of his words had not found its way into her mind; she was merely thunderstruck.

"Yes, poisonous thing!" repeated Giovanni, beside himself with passion. "Thou hast done it! Thou hast blasted me! Thou hast filled my veins with poison! Thou hast made me as hateful, as ugly, as loathsome and deadly a creature as thyself—a world's wonder of hideous monstrosity! Now, if our breath be happily as fatal to ourselves as to all others, let us join our lips in one kiss of unutterable hatred, and so die!"

"What hast befallen me?" murmured Beatrice, with a low moan out of her heart. "Holy Virgin, pity me, a poor heart-broken child!"

"Thou,—dost thou pray?" cried Giovanni, still with the same fiendish scorn. "Thy very prayers, as they come from thy lips, taint the atmosphere with death. Yes, yes; let us pray! Let us to church and dip our fingers in the holy water at the portal! They that come after us will perish as by a pestilence! Let us sign crosses in the air! It will be scattering curses abroad in the likeness of holy symbols!"

"Giovanni," said Beatrice calmly, for her grief was beyond passion, "why dost thou join thyself with me thus in those terrible words? I, it is true, am the horrible thing thou namest me. But thou,—what hast thou to do, save with one other shudder at my hideous misery to go forth out of the garden and mingle with thy race, and forget that there ever crawled on earth such a monster as poor Beatrice?"

"Dost thou pretend ignorance?" asked Giovanni, scowling upon her. "Behold! this power have I gained from the pure daughter of Rappaccini."

There was a swarm of summer insects flitting through the air in search of the food promised by the flower odors of the fatal garden. They circled round Giovanni's head, and were evidently attracted towards him by the same influence which had drawn them for an instant within the sphere of the shrubs. He sent forth a breath among them, and smiled bitterly at Beatrice as at least a score of the insects fell dead upon the ground.

"I see it! I see it!" shrieked Beatrice. "It is my father's fatal science! No, no, Giovanni; it was not I! Never! never! I dreamed only to love thee and be with thee a little time, and so to let thee pass away, leaving but thine image in mine heart; for, Giovanni, believe it, though my body be nourished with poison, my spirit is God's creature, and craves love as its daily food. But my father,—he has united us in this fearful sympathy. Yes; spurn me, tread upon me, kill me! O, what is death after such words as thine? But it was not I. Not for a world of bliss would I have done it."

Giovanni's passion had exhausted itself in its outburst from his lips. There now came across him a sense, mournful, and not without tenderness, of the intimate and peculiar relationship between Beatrice and himself. They stood, as it were, in an utter solitude, which would be made none the less solitary by the densest throng of human life. Ought not, then, the desert of humanity around them to press this insulated pair closer together? If they should be cruel to one another, who was there to be kind to them? Besides, thought Giovanni, might there not still be a hope of his returning within the limits of ordinary nature, and leading Beatrice, the redeemed Beatrice, by the hand? O, weak, and selfish, and unworthy spirit, that could dream of an earthly union and earthly happiness as possible, after such deep love had been so bitterly wronged as was Beatrice's love by Giovanni's blighting words! No, no; there could be no such hope. She must pass heavily, with that broken heart, across the borders of Time—she must bathe her hurts in some fount of paradise, and forget her grief in the light of immortality, and *there* be well.

But Giovanni did not know it.

"Dear Beatrice," said he, approaching her, while she shrank away as always at his approach, but now with a different impulse, "dearest Beatrice, our fate is not yet so desperate. Behold! there is a medicine, potent, as a wise physician has assured me, and almost divine in its efficacy. It is composed of ingredients the most opposite to those by which thy awful father has brought this calamity upon thee and me. It is distilled of blessed herbs. Shall we not quaff it together, and thus be purified from evil?"

"Give it to me!" said Beatrice, extending her hand to receive the little silver vial which Giovanni took from his bosom. She added, with a peculiar emphasis, "I will drink; but do thou await the result."

She put Baglioni's antidote to her lips; and, at the same moment, the figure of Rappaccini emerged from the portal and came slowly towards the marble fountain. As he drew near, the pale man of science seemed to gaze with a triumphant expression at the beautiful youth and maiden, as might an artist who should spend his life in achieving a picture or a group of statuary and finally be satisfied with his success. He paused; his bent form grew erect with conscious power; he spread out his hands over them in the attitude of a father imploring a blessing upon his children; but those were the same hands that had thrown poison into the stream of their lives. Giovanni trembled. Beatrice shuddered nervously, and pressed her hand upon her heart.

"My daughter," said Rappaccini, "thou art no longer lonely in the world. Pluck one of those precious gems from thy sister shrub and bid thy bridegroom wear it in his bosom. It will not harm him now. My science and the sympathy between thee and him have so wrought within his system that he now stands apart from common men, as thou dost, daughter of my pride and triumph, from ordinary women. Pass on, then, through the world, most dear to one another and dreadful to all besides!"

"My father," said Beatrice, feebly,—and still as she spoke she kept her hand upon her heart,—"wherefore didst thou inflict this miserable doom upon thy child?"

"Miserable!" exclaimed Rappaccini. "What mean you, foolish girl? Dost thou deem it misery to be endowed with marvellous gifts against which no power nor strength could avail an enemy—misery, to be able to quell the mightiest with a breath—misery, to be as terrible as thou art beautiful? Wouldst thou, then, have preferred the condition of a weak woman, exposed to all evil and capable of none?"

"I would fain have been loved, not feared," murmured Beatrice, sinking down upon the ground. "But now it matters not. I am going, father, where the evil which thou hast striven to mingle with my being will pass away like a dream—like the fragrance of these poisonous flowers, which will no longer taint my breath among the flowers of Eden. Farewell, Giovanni! Thy words of hatred are like lead within my heart; but they, too, will fall away as I ascend. O, was there not, from the first, more poison in thy nature than in mine?"

To Beatrice,—so radically had her earthly part been wrought upon by Rappaccini's skill,—as poison had been life, so the powerful antidote was death; and thus the poor victim of man's ingenuity and of thwarted nature, and of the fatality that attends all such efforts of perverted wisdom, perished there, at the feet of her father and Giovanni. Just at that moment Professor Pietro Baglioni looked forth from the window, and called loudly, in a tone of triumph mixed with horror, to the thunderstricken man of science,—

"Rappaccini! Rappaccini! and is *this* the upshot of your experiment?"

Writing Assignments for "Rappaccini's Daughter"

I. Brief Papers
  A. 1. How does Padua, the story's setting, differ from Naples, Giovanni's home city?
     2. Why is it significant that Giovanni lives in a house that may have been occupied by someone "pictured by Dante as a partaker of the immortal agonies of his Inferno" (p. 251)?
     3. Does the description of the marble fountain in Rappaccini's garden (p. 252) relate to anything else in the story?
     4. Characterize the relationship between Dr. Rappaccini and Professor Baglioni.
     5. Why does Dr. Rappaccini make his daughter poisonous?
     6. How would you describe Giovanni's condition at the end of the story?

  B. Argue for or against one of the assertions below:
     1. Giovanni is deeply in love with Beatrice.
     2. Beatrice is deeply in love with Giovanni.
     3. Rappaccini is completely evil: there is no good at all in him.
     4. Baglioni becomes involved only out of loyalty to Giovanni's father, an old friend.
     5. Beatrice deliberately deceives and lies to Giovanni throughout the story.
     6. Like most fairy tales, "Rappaccini's Daughter" presents reality as simple, clear, and easily understood.

C. 1. Do you like Professor Pietro Baglioni? Why or why not?

2. If you were Giovanni, what would you have done when Professor Baglioni suggested the use of an antidote for Beatrice?

3. Baglioni warns Giovanni that the result of his involvement with Rappaccini may be death or "perhaps a fate more awful still" (p. 266). What fate could be more awful than death?

4. Do you believe that the story is successful in showing that "There is something truer and more real than what we can see with the eyes and touch with the finger" (p. 267)?

5. Have you ever known anyone who was poisonous or have you ever been poisonous yourself?

II. Longer Papers

A. Beatrice's last words are a question to Giovanni: "Oh, was there not, from the first, more poison in thy nature than in mine?" How would you answer her question, and how does your answer help you understand the meanings of the story?

B. Explain how the story's references to Adam, Eve, and the Garden of Eden help us to better understand what happens in Rappaccini's garden.

C. Is there anything that Giovanni can do, once he arrives in Padua, to avert a catastrophe? Or is everything fated?

D. The final words are Baglioni's. In what sense do they both summarize and clarify his role in the story?

E. What does the story have to say about love and about faith and about the connection between the two?

F. Tell a story about your own encounter with either love or evil (or both) in such a way that it is a commentary on and a response to "Rappaccini's Daughter."

G. There are a group of fairy tales in which a young man—sometimes a prince—sets out to win the hand of the princess. Often the princess is in distress: she has been kidnapped or imprisoned or placed under a curse or spell. In order to win the maiden, the young man must pass a series of tests of his virtue, courage, and love. In some tales, the young man has the aid of an older and wiser counselor. The tests are difficult and risky—to fail them in some cases results in death—but the reward is great: to live happily ever after with the princess. How do the similarities and differences between "Rappaccini's Daughter" and these fairy tales help clarify the meanings and values of Hawthorne's story?

ANN BEATTIE
The Cinderella Waltz

Before Reading

Free write for 5 to 10 minutes on your idea and image of Prince Charming. How will you recognize him when he comes into your world?

Milo and Bradley are creatures of habit. For as long as I've known him, Milo has worn his moth-eaten blue scarf with the knot hanging so low on his chest that the scarf is useless. Bradley is addicted to coffee and carries a Thermos with him. Milo complains about the cold, and Bradley is always a little edgy. They come out from the city every Saturday—this is not habit but loyalty—to pick up Louise. Louise is even more unpredictable than most nine-year-olds; sometimes she waits for them on the front step, sometimes she hasn't even gotten out of bed when they arrive. One time she hid in a closet and wouldn't leave with them.

Today Louise has put together a shopping bag full of things she wants to take with her. She is taking my whisk and my blue pottery bowl, to make Sunday breakfast for Milo and Bradley; Beckett's *Happy Days,* which she has carried around for weeks, and which she looks through, smiling—but I'm not sure she's reading it; and a coleus growing out of a conch shell. Also, she has stuffed into one side of the bag the fancy Victorian-style nightgown her grandmother gave her for Christmas, and into the other she has tucked her octascope. Milo keeps a couple of dresses, a nightgown, a toothbrush, and extra sneakers and boots at his apartment for her. He got tired of rounding up her stuff to pack for her to take home, so he has brought some things for her that can be left. It annoys him that she still packs bags, because then he has to go around making sure that she has found everything before she goes home. She seems to know how to manipulate him, and after the weekend is over she calls tearfully to say that she has left this or that, which means that he must get his car out of the garage and drive all the way out to the house to bring it to her. One time, he refused to take the hour-long drive, because she had only left a copy of Tolkien's *The Two Towers.* The following weekend was the time she hid in the closet.

"I'll water your plant if you leave it here," I say now.

"I can take it," she says.

"I didn't say you couldn't take it. I just thought it might be easier to leave it, because if the shell tips over the plant might get ruined."

"O.K.," she says. "Don't water it today, though. Water it Sunday afternoon."

THE CINDERELLA WALTZ   First published in 1978. Ann Beattie (1947–   ) was born in Washington D.C., educated at American University and the University of Connecticut, and has taught at Harvard and the University of Virginia.

I reach for the shopping bag.

"I'll put it back on my window sill," she says. She lifts the plant out and carries it as if it's made of Steuben glass. Bradley bought it for her last month, driving back to the city, when they stopped at a lawn sale. She and Bradley are both very choosy, and he likes that. He drinks French-roast coffee; she will debate with herself almost endlessly over whether to buy a coleus that is primarily pink or lavender or striped.

"Has Milo made any plans for this weekend?" I ask.

"He's having a couple of people over tonight, and I'm going to help them make crêpes for dinner. If they buy more bottles of that wine with the yellow flowers on the label, Bradley is going to soak the labels off for me."

"That's nice of him," I say. "He never minds taking a lot of time with things."

"He doesn't like to cook, though. Milo and I are going to cook. Bradley sets the table and fixes flowers in a bowl. He thinks it's frustrating to cook."

"Well," I say, "with cooking you have to have a good sense of timing. You have to coordinate everything. Bradley likes to work carefully and not be rushed."

I wonder how much she knows. Last week she told me about a conversation she'd had with her friend Sarah. Sarah was trying to persuade Louise to stay around on the weekends, but Louise said she always went to her father's. Then Sarah tried to get her to take her along, and Louise said that she couldn't. "You could take her if you wanted to," I said later. "Check with Milo and see if that isn't right. I don't think he'd mind having a friend of yours occasionally."

She shrugged. "Bradley doesn't like a lot of people around," she said.

"Bradley likes you, and if she's your friend I don't think he'd mind."

She looked at me with an expression I didn't recognize; perhaps she thought I was a little dumb, or perhaps she was just curious to see if I would go on. I didn't know how to go on. Like an adult, she gave a little shrug and changed the subject.

At ten o'clock Milo pulls into the driveway and honks his horn, which makes a noise like a bleating sheep. He knows the noise the horn makes is funny, and he means to amuse us. There was a time just after the divorce when he and Bradley would come here and get out of the car and stand around silently, waiting for her. She knew that she had to watch for them, because Milo wouldn't come to the door. We were both bitter then, but I got over it. I still don't think Milo would have come into the house again, though, if Bradley hadn't thought it was a good idea. The third time Milo came to pick her up after he'd left home, I went out to invite them in, but Milo said nothing. He was standing there with his arms at his sides like a wooden soldier, and his eyes were as dead to me as if they'd been painted on. It was Bradley whom I reasoned with. "Louise is over at Sarah's right now, and it'll make her feel more comfortable if we're all together when she comes in," I said to him, and Bradley turned to Milo and said, "Hey, that's right. Why don't we go in for a quick cup of coffee?" I looked into the back seat of the car and saw his red Thermos there; Louise had told me about it. Bradley meant that they should come in and sit down. He was giving me even more than I'd asked for.

It would be an understatement to say that I disliked Bradley at first. I was actually afraid of him, afraid even after I saw him, though he was slender, and more nervous than I, and spoke quietly. The second time I saw him, I persuaded myself that he was just a stereotype, but someone who certainly seemed harmless enough. By the third time, I had enough courage to suggest that they come into the house. It was embarrassing for all of us, sitting around the table—the same table where Milo and I had eaten our meals for the years we were married. Before he left, Milo had shouted at me that the house was a farce, that my playing the happy suburban housewife was a farce, that it was unconscionable of me to let things drag on, that I would probably kiss him and say, "How was your day, sweetheart?" and that he should bring home flowers and the evening paper. "Maybe I would!" I screamed back. "Maybe it would be nice to do that, even if we were pretending, instead of you coming home drunk and not caring what had happened to me or to Louise all day." He was holding on to the edge of the kitchen table, the way you'd hold on to the horse's reins in a runaway carriage. "I care about Louise," he said finally. That was the most horrible moment. Until then, until he said it that way, I had thought that he was going through something horrible—certainly something was terribly wrong—but that, in his way, he loved me after all. *"You don't love me?"* I had whispered at once. It took us both aback. It was an innocent and pathetic question, and it made him come and put his arms around me in the last hug he ever gave me. "I'm sorry for you," he said, "and I'm sorry for marrying you and causing this, but you know who I love. I told you who I love." "But you were kidding," I said. "You didn't mean it. You were kidding."

When Bradley sat at the table that first day, I tried to be polite and not look at him much. I had gotten it through my head that Milo was crazy, and I guess I was expecting Bradley to be a horrible parody—Craig Russell doing Marilyn Monroe. Bradley did not spoon sugar into Milo's coffee. He did not even sit near him. In fact, he pulled his chair a little away from us, and in spite of his uneasiness he found more things to start conversations about than Milo and I did. He told me about the ad agency where he worked; he is a designer there. He asked if he could go out on the porch to see the brook—Milo had told him about the stream in the back of our place that was as thin as a pencil but still gave us our own watercress. He went out on the porch and stayed there for at least five minutes, giving us a chance to talk. We didn't say one word until he came back. Louise came home from Sarah's house just as Bradley sat down at the table again, and she gave him a hug as well as us. I could see that she really liked him. I was amazed that I liked him, too. Bradley had won and I had lost, but he was as gentle and low-key as if none of it mattered. Later in the week, I called him and asked him to tell me if any free-lance jobs opened in his advertising agency. (I do a little free-lance artwork, whenever I can arrange it.) The week after that, he called and told me about another agency, where they were looking for outside artists. Our calls to each other are always brief and for a purpose, but lately they're not just calls about business. Before Bradley left to scout some picture locations in Mexico, he called to say that Milo had told him that when the two of us were there years ago I had seen one of those big circular bronze Aztec calendars and I had always regretted not bringing it back. He wanted to know if I would like him to buy a calendar if he saw one like the one Milo had told him about.

Today, Milo is getting out of his car, his blue scarf flapping against his chest. Louise, looking out the window, asks the same thing I am wondering: "Where's Bradley?"

Milo comes in and shakes my hand, gives Louise a one-armed hug.

"Bradley thinks he's coming down with a cold," Milo says. "The dinner is still on, Louise. We'll do the dinner. We have to stop at Gristede's when we get back to town, unless your mother happens to have a tin of anchovies and two sticks of unsalted butter."

"Let's go to Gristede's," Louise says. "I like to go there."

"Let me look in the kitchen," I say. The butter is salted, but Milo says that will do, and he takes three sticks instead of two. I have a brainstorm and cut the cellophane on a leftover Christmas present from my aunt—a wicker plate that holds nuts and foil-wrapped triangles of cheese—and, sure enough: one tin of anchovies.

"We can go to the museum instead," Milo says to Louise. "Wonderful."

But then, going to the door, carrying her bag, he changes his mind. "We can go to America Hurrah, and if we see something beautiful we can buy it," he says.

They go off in high spirits. Louise comes up to his waist, almost, and I notice again that they have the same walk. Both of them stride forward with great purpose. Last week, Bradley told me that Milo had bought a weathervane in the shape of a horse, made around 1800, at America Hurrah, and stood it in the bedroom, and then was enraged when Bradley draped his socks over it to dry. Bradley is still learning what a perfectionist Milo is, and how little sense of humor he has. When we were first married, I used one of our pottery casserole dishes to put my jewelry in, and he nagged me until I took it out and put the dish back in the kitchen cabinet. I remember his saying that the dish looked silly on my dresser because it was obvious what it was and people would think we left our dishes lying around. It was one of the things that Milo wouldn't tolerate, because it was improper.

When Milo brings Louise back on Saturday night they are not in a good mood. The dinner was all right, Milo says, and Griffin and Amy and Mark were amazed at what a good hostess Louise had been, but Bradley hadn't been able to eat.

"Is he still coming down with a cold?" I ask. I was still a little shy about asking questions about Bradley.

Milo shrugs. "Louise made him take megadoses of vitamin C all weekend."

Louise says, "Bradley said that taking too much vitamin C was bad for your kidneys, though."

"It's a rotten climate," Milo says, sitting on the living-room sofa, scarf and coat still on. "The combination of cold and air pollution . . ."

Louise and I look at each other, and then back at Milo. For weeks now, he has been talking about moving to San Francisco, if he can find work there. (Milo is an architect.) This talk bores me, and it makes Louise nervous. I've asked him not to talk to her about it unless he's actually going to move, but he doesn't seem to be able to stop himself.

"O.K.," Milo says, looking at us both. "I'm not going to say anything about San Francisco."

"*California* is polluted," I say. I am unable to stop myself, either.

Milo heaves himself up from the sofa, ready for the drive back to New York. It is the same way he used to get off the sofa that last year he lived here. He would get up, dress for work, and not even go into the kitchen for breakfast—just sit, sometimes in his coat as he was sitting just now, and at the last minute he would push himself up and go out to the driveway, usually without a goodbye, and get in the car and drive off either very fast or very slowly. I liked it better when he made the tires spin in the gravel when he took off.

He stops at the doorway now, and turns to face me. "Did I take all your butter?" he says.

"No," I say. "There's another stick." I point into the kitchen.

"I could have guessed that's where it would be," he says, and smiles at me.

When Milo comes the next weekend, Bradley is still not with him. The night before, as I was putting Louise to bed, she said that she had a feeling he wouldn't be coming.

"I had that feeling a couple of days ago," I said. "Usually Bradley calls once during the week."

"He must still be sick," Louise said. She looked at me anxiously. "Do you think he is?"

"A cold isn't going to kill him," I said. "If he has a cold, he'll be O.K."

Her expression changed; she thought I was talking down to her. She lay back in bed. The last year Milo was with us, I used to tuck her in and tell her that everything was all right. What that meant was that there had not been a fight. Milo had sat listening to music on the phonograph, with a book or the newspaper in front of his face. He didn't pay very much attention to Louise, and he ignored me entirely. Instead of saying a prayer with her, the way I usually did, I would say to her that everything was all right. Then I would go downstairs and hope that Milo would say the same thing to me. What he finally did say one night was "You might as well find out from me as some other way."

"Hey, are you an old bag lady again this weekend?" Milo says now, stooping to kiss Louise's forehead.

"Because you take some things with you doesn't mean you're a bag lady," she says primly.

"Well," Milo says, "you start doing something innocently, and before you know it it can take you over."

He looks angry, and acts as though it's difficult for him to make conversation, even when the conversation is full of sarcasm and double-entendres.

"What do you say we get going?" he says to Louise.

In the shopping bag she is taking is her doll, which she has not played with for more than a year. I found it by accident when I went to tuck in a loaf of banana bread that I had baked. When I saw Baby Betsy, deep in the bag, I decided against putting the bread in.

"O.K.," Louise says to Milo. "Where's Bradley?"

"Sick," he says.

"Is he too sick to have me visit?"

"Good heavens, no. He'll be happier to see you than to see me."

"I'm rooting some of my coleus to give him," she says. "Maybe I'll give it to him like it is, in water, and he can plant it when it roots."

When she leaves the room, I go over to Milo. "Be nice to her," I say quietly.

"I'm nice to her," he says. "Why does everybody have to act like I'm going to grow fangs every time I turn around?"

"You were quite cutting when you came in."

"I was being self-deprecating." He sighs. "I don't really know why I come here and act this way," he says.

"What's the matter, Milo?"

But now he let me know he's bored with the conversation. He walks over to the table and picks up a *Newsweek* and flips through it. Louise comes back with the coleus in a water glass.

"You know what you could do," I say. "Wet a napkin and put it around that cutting and then wrap it in foil, and put it in water when you get there. That way, you wouldn't have to hold a glass of water all the way to New York."

She shrugs. "This is O.K.," she says.

"Why don't you take your mother's suggestion," Milo says. "The water will slosh out of the glass."

"Not if you don't drive fast."

"It doesn't have anything to do with my driving fast. If we go over a bump in the road, you're going to get all wet."

"Then I can put on one of my dresses at your apartment."

"Am I being unreasonable?" Milo says to me.

"I started it," I say. "Let her take it in the glass."

"Would you, as a favor, do what your mother says?" he says to Louise.

Louise looks at the coleus, and at me.

"Hold the glass over the seat instead of over your lap, and you won't get wet," I say.

"Your first idea was the best," Milo says.

Louise gives him an exasperated look and puts the glass down on the floor, pulls on her poncho, picks up the glass again and says a sullen goodbye to me, and goes out the front door.

"Why is this my fault?" Milo says. "Have I done anything terrible? I—"

"Do something to cheer yourself up," I say, patting him on the back.

He looks as exasperated with me as Louise was with him. He nods his head yes, and goes out the door.

"Was everything all right this weekend?" I ask Louise.

"Milo was in a bad mood, and Bradley wasn't even there on Saturday," Louise says. "He came back today and took us to the Village for breakfast."

"What did you have?"

"I had sausage wrapped in little pancakes and fruit salad and a rum bun."

"Where was Bradley on Saturday?"

She shrugs. "I didn't ask him."

She almost always surprises me by being more grownup than I give her credit for. Does she suspect, as I do, that Bradley has found another lover?

"Milo was in a bad mood when you two left here Saturday," I say.

"I told him if he didn't want me to come next weekend, just to tell me." She looks perturbed, and I suddenly realize that she can sound exactly like Milo sometimes.

"You shouldn't have said that to him, Louise," I say. "You know he wants you. He's just worried about Bradley."

"So?" she says. "I'm probably going to flunk math."

"No, you're not, honey. You got a C-plus on the last assignment."

"It still doesn't make my grade average out to a C."

"You'll get a C. It's all right to get a C."

She doesn't believe me.

"Don't be a perfectionist, like Milo," I tell her. "Even if you got a D, you wouldn't fail."

Louise is brushing her hair—thin, shoulder-length, auburn hair. She is already so pretty and so smart in everything except math that I wonder what will become of her. When I was her age, I was plain and serious and I wanted to be a tree surgeon. I went with my father to the park and held a stethoscope—a real one—to the trunks of trees, listening to their silence. Children seem older now.

"What do you think's the matter with Bradley?" Louise says. She sounds worried.

"Maybe the two of them are unhappy with each other right now."

She misses my point. "Bradley's sad, and Milo's sad that he's unhappy."

I drop Louise off at Sarah's house for supper. Sarah's mother, Martine Cooper, looks like Shelley Winters, and I have never seen her without a glass of Galliano on ice in her hand. She has a strong candy smell. Her husband has left her, and she professes not to care. She has emptied her living room of furniture and put up ballet bars on the walls, and dances in a purple leotard to records by Cher and Mac Davis. I prefer to have Sarah come to our house, but her mother is adamant that everything must be, as she puts it, "fifty-fifty." When Sarah visited us a week ago and loved the chocolate pie I had made, I sent two pieces home with her. Tonight, when I left Sarah's house, her mother gave me a bowl of Jell-O fruit salad.

The phone is ringing when I come in the door. It is Bradley.

"Bradley," I say at once, "whatever's wrong, at least you don't have a neighbor who just gave you a bowl of maraschino cherries in green Jell-O with a Reddi-Whip flower squirted on top."

"Jesus," he says. "You don't need me to depress you, do you?"

"What's wrong?" I say.

He sighs into the phone. "Guess what?" he says.

"What?"

"I've lost my job."

It wasn't at all what I was expecting to hear. I was ready to hear that he was leaving Milo, and I had even thought that that would serve Milo right. Part of me still wanted him punished for what he did. I was so out of my mind when Milo left me that I used to go over and drink Galliano with Martine Cooper. I even thought seriously about forming a ballet group with her. I would go to her house in the afternoon, and she would hold a tambourine in the air and I would hold my leg rigid and try to kick it.

"That's awful," I say to Bradley. "What happened?"

"They said it was nothing personal—they were laying off three people. Two other people are going to get the ax at the agency within the next six months. I was the first to go, and it was nothing personal. From twenty thousand bucks a year to nothing, and nothing personal, either."

"But your work is so good. Won't you be able to find something again?"

"Could I ask you a favor?" he says. "I'm calling from a phone booth. I'm not in the city. Could I come talk to you?"

"Sure," I say.

It seems perfectly logical that he should come alone to talk—perfectly logical until I actually see him coming up the walk. I can't entirely believe it. A year after my husband has left me, I am sitting with his lover—a man, a person I like quite well—and trying to cheer him up because he is out of work. ("Honey," my father would say, "listen to Daddy's heart with the stethoscope, or you can turn it toward you and listen to your own heart. You won't hear anything listening to a tree." Was my persistence willfulness, or belief in magic? Is it possible that I hugged Bradley at the door because I'm secretly glad he's down and out, the way I used to be? Or do I really want to make things better for him?)

He comes into the kitchen and thanks me for the coffee I am making, drapes his coat over the chair he always sits in.

"What am I going to do?" he asks.

"You shouldn't get so upset, Bradley," I say. "You know you're good. You won't have trouble finding another job."

"That's only half of it," he says. "Milo thinks I did this deliberately. He told me I was quitting on him. He's very angry at me. He fights with me, and then he gets mad that I don't enjoy eating dinner. My stomach's upset, and I can't eat anything."

"Maybe some juice would be better than coffee."

"If I didn't drink coffee, I'd collapse," he says.

I pour coffee into a mug for him, coffee into a mug for me.

"This is probably very awkward for you," he says. "That I come here and say all this about Milo."

"What does he mean about your quitting on him?"

"He said . . . he actually accused me of doing badly deliberately, so they'd fire me. I was so afraid to tell him the truth when I was fired that I pretended to be sick. Then I really *was* sick. He's never been angry at me this way. Is this always the way he acts? Does he get a notion in his head for no reason and then pick at a person because of it?"

I try to remember. "We didn't argue much," I say. "When he didn't want to live here, he made me look ridiculous for complaining when I knew something was wrong. He expects perfection, but what that means is that you do things his way."

"I *was*. I never wanted to sit around the apartment, the way he says I did. I even brought work home with me. He made me feel so bad all week that I went to a friend's apartment for the day on Saturday. Then he said I had walked out on the problem. He's a little paranoid. I was listening to the radio, and Carole King was singing 'It's Too Late,' and he came into the study and looked very upset, as though I had planned for the song to come on. I couldn't believe it."

"Whew," I say, shaking my head. "I don't envy you. You have to stand up to him. I didn't do that. I pretended the problem would go away."

"And now the problem sits across from you drinking coffee, and you're being nice to him."

"I know it. I was just thinking we look like two characters in some soap opera my friend Martine Cooper would watch."

He pushes his coffee cup away from him with a grimace.

"But anyway, I like you now," I say. "And you're exceptionally nice to Louise."

"I took her father," he says.

"Bradley—I hope you don't take offense, but it makes me nervous to talk about that."

"I don't take offense. But how can you be having coffee with me?"

"You invited yourself over so you could ask that?"

"Please," he says, holding up both hands. Then he runs his hands through his hair. "Don't make me feel illogical. He does that to me, you know. He doesn't understand it when everything doesn't fall right into line. If I like fixing up the place, keeping some flowers around, therefore I can't like being a working person, too, therefore I deliberately sabotage myself in my job." Bradley sips his coffee.

"I wish I could do something for him," he says in a different voice.

This is not what I expected, either. We have sounded like two wise adults, and then suddenly he has changed and sounds very tender. I realize the situation is still the same. It is two of them on one side and me on the other, even though Bradley is in my kitchen.

"Come and pick up Louise with me, Bradley," I say. "When you see Martine Cooper, you'll cheer up about your situation."

He looks up from his coffee. "You're forgetting what I'd look like to Martine Cooper," he says.

Milo is going to California. He has been offered a job with a new San Francisco architectural firm. I am not the first to know. His sister, Deanna, knows before I do, and mentions it when we're talking on the phone. "It's middle-age crisis," Deanna says sniffily. "Not that I need to tell you." Deanna would drop dead if she knew the way things are. She is scandalized every time a new display is put up in Bloomingdale's window. ("Those mannequins had eyes like an Egyptian princess, and *rags.* I swear to you, they had mops and brooms and ragged gauze dresses on, with whores' shoes—stiletto heels that prostitutes wear.")

I hang up from Deanna's call and tell Louise I'm going to drive to the gas station for cigarettes. I go there to call New York on their pay phone.

"Well, I only just knew," Milo says. "I found out for sure yesterday, and last night Deanna called and so I told her. It's not like I'm leaving tonight."

He sounds elated, in spite of being upset that I called. He's happy in the way he used to be on Christmas morning. I remember him once running into the living room in his underwear and tearing open the gifts we'd been sent by relatives. He was looking for the eight-slice toaster he was sure we'd get. We'd been given two-slice, four-slice, and six-slice toasters, but then we got no more. "Come out, my eight-slice beauty!" Milo crooned, and out came an electric clock, a blender, and an expensive electric pan.

"When are you leaving?" I ask him.

"I'm going out to look for a place to live next week."

"Are you going to tell Louise yourself this weekend?"

"Of course," he says.

"And what are you going to do about seeing Louise?"

"Why do you act as if I don't like Louise?" he says. "I will occasionally come back East, and I will arrange for her to fly to San Francisco on her vacations."

"It's going to break her heart."

"No it isn't. Why do you want to make me feel bad?"

"She's had so many things to adjust to. You don't have to go to San Francisco right now, Milo."

"It happens, if you care, that my own job is in jeopardy. This is a real chance for me, with a young firm. They really want me. But anyway, all we need in this happy group is to have you bringing in a couple of hundred dollars a month with your graphic work and me destitute and Bradley so devastated by being fired that of course he can't even look for work."

"I'll bet he is looking for a job," I say.

"Yes. He read the want ads today and then fixed a crab quiche."

"Maybe that's the way you like things, Milo, and people respond to you. You forbade me to work when we had a baby. Do you say anything encouraging to him about finding a job, or do you just take it out on him that he was fired?"

There is a pause, and then he almost seems to lose his mind with impatience.

"I can hardly *believe,* when I am trying to find a logical solution to all our problems, that I am being subjected, by telephone, to an unflattering psychological analysis by my ex-wife." He says this all in a rush.

"All right, Milo. But don't you think that if you're leaving so soon you ought to call her, instead of waiting until Saturday?"

Milo sighs very deeply. "I have more sense than to have important conversations on the telephone," he says.

Milo calls on Friday and asks Louise whether it wouldn't be nice if both of us came in and spent the night Saturday and if we all went to brunch together Sunday. Louise is excited. I never go into town with her.

Louise and I pack a suitcase and put it in the car Saturday morning. A cutting of ivy for Bradley has taken root, and she has put it in a little green plastic pot for him. It's heartbreaking, and I hope that Milo notices and has a tough time dealing with it. I am relieved I'm going to be there when he tells her, and sad that I have to hear it at all.

In the city, I give the car to the garage attendant, who does not remember me. Milo and I lived in the apartment when we were first married, and moved when Louise was two years old. When we moved, Milo kept the apartment and sublet it—a sign that things were not going well, if I had been one to heed such a warning. What he said was that if we were ever rich enough we could have the house in Connecticut *and* the apartment in New York. When Milo moved out of the house, he went right back to the apartment. This will be the first time I have visited there in years.

Louise strides in in front of me, throwing her coat over the brass coatrack in the entranceway—almost too casual about being there. She's the hostess at Milo's, the way I am at our house.

He has painted the walls white. There are floor-length white curtains in the living room, where my silly flowered curtains used to hang. The walls are bare, the floor has been sanded, a stereo as huge as a computer stands against one wall of the living room, and there are four speakers.

"Look around," Milo says. "Show your mother around, Louise."

I am trying to remember if I have ever told Louise that I used to live in this apartment. I must have told her, at some point, but I can't remember it.

"Hello," Bradley says, coming out of the bedroom.

"Hi, Bradley," I say. "Have you got a drink?"

Bradley looks sad. "He's got champagne," he says, and looks nervously at Milo.

"No one *has* to drink champagne," Milo says. "There's the usual assortment of liquor."

"Yes," Bradley says. "What would you like?"

"Some bourbon, please."

"Bourbon." Bradley turns to go into the kitchen. He looks different; his hair is different—more wavy—and he is dressed as though it were summer, in straight-legged white pants and black leather thongs.

"I want Perrier water with strawberry juice," Louise says, tagging along after Bradley. I have never heard her ask for such a thing before. At home, she drinks too many Cokes. I am always trying to get her to drink fruit juice.

Bradley comes back with two drinks and hands me one. "Did you want anything?" he says to Milo.

"I'm going to open the champagne in a moment," Milo says. "How have you been this week, sweetheart?"

"O.K.," Louise says. She is holding a pale-pink, bubbly drink. She sips it like a cocktail.

Bradley looks very bad. He has circles under his eyes, and he is ill at ease. A red light begins to blink on the phone-answering device next to where Bradley sits on the sofa, and Milo gets out of his chair to pick up the phone.

"Do you really want to talk on the phone right now?" Bradley asks Milo quietly.

Milo looks at him. "No, not particularly," he says, sitting down again. After a moment, the red light goes out.

"I'm going to mist your bowl garden," Louise says to Bradley, and slides off the sofa and goes to the bedroom. "Hey, a little toadstool is growing in here!" she calls back. "Did you put it there, Bradley?"

"It grew from the soil mixture, I guess," Bradley calls back. "I don't know how it got there."

"Have you heard anything about a job?" I ask Bradley.

"I haven't been looking, really," he says. "You know."

Milo frowns at him. "Your choice, Bradley," he says. "I didn't ask you to follow me to California. You can stay here."

"No," Bradley says. "You've hardly made me feel welcome."

"Should we have some champagne—all four of us—and you can get back to your bourbons later?" Milo says cheerfully.

We don't answer him, but he gets up anyway and goes to the kitchen. "Where have you hidden the tulip-shaped glasses, Bradley?" he calls out after a while.

"They should be in the cabinet on the far left," Bradley says.

"You're going with him?" I say to Bradley. "To San Francisco?"

He shrugs, and won't look at me. "I'm not quite sure I'm wanted," he says quietly.

The cork pops in the kitchen. I look at Bradley, but he won't look up. His new hairdo makes him look older. I remember that when Milo left me I went to the hairdresser the same week and had bangs cut. The next week, I went to a therapist who told me it was no good trying to hide from myself. The week after that, I did dance exercises with Martine Cooper, and the week after that the therapist told me not to dance if I wasn't interested in dancing.

"I'm not going to act like this is a funeral," Milo says, coming in with the glasses. "Louise, come in here and have champagne! We have something to have a toast about."

Louise comes into the living room suspiciously. She is so used to being refused even a sip of wine from my glass or her father's that she no longer even asks. "How come I'm in on this?" she asks.

"We're going to drink a toast to me," Milo says.

Three of the four glasses are clustered on the table in front of the sofa. Milo's glass is raised. Louise looks at me, to see what I'm going to say. Milo raises his glass even higher. Bradley reaches for a glass. Louise picks up a glass. I lean forward and take the last one.

"This is a toast to me," Milo says, "because I am going to be going to San Francisco."

It was not a very good or informative toast. Bradley and I sip from our glasses. Louise puts her glass down hard and bursts into tears, knocking the glass over. The champagne spills onto the cover of a big art book about the Unicorn Tapestries. She runs into the bedroom and slams the door.

Milo looks furious. "Everybody lets me know just what my insufficiencies are, don't they?" he says. "Nobody minds expressing himself. We have it all right out in the open."

"He's criticizing me," Bradley murmurs, his head still bowed. "It's because I was offered a job here in the city and I didn't automatically refuse it."

I turn to Milo. "Go say something to Louise, Milo," I say. "Do you think that's what somebody who isn't brokenhearted sounds like?"

He glares at me and stomps into the bedroom, and I can hear him talking to Louise reassuringly. "It doesn't mean you'll *never* see me," he says. "You can fly there, I'll come here. It's not going to be that different."

"You lied!" Louise screams. "You said we were going to brunch."

"We are. We are. I can't very well take us to brunch before Sunday, can I?"

"You didn't say you were going to San Francisco. What *is* San Francisco, anyway?"

"I just said so. I bought us a bottle of champagne. You can come out as soon as I get settled. You're going to like it there."

Louise is sobbing. She has told him the truth and she knows it's futile to go on.

By the next morning, Louise acts the way I acted—as if everything were just the same. She looks calm, but her face is small and pale. She looks very young. We walk into the restaurant and sit at the table Milo has reserved. Bradley pulls out a chair for me, and Milo pulls out a chair for Louise, locking his finger with hers for a second, raising her arm above her head, as if she were about to take a twirl.

She looks very nice, really. She has a ribbon in her hair. It is cold, and she should have worn a hat, but she wanted to wear the ribbon. Milo has good taste: the dress she is wearing, which he bought for her, is a hazy purple plaid, and it sets off her hair.

"Come with me. Don't be sad," Milo suddenly says to Louise, pulling her by the hand. "Come with me for a minute. Come across the street to the park for just a second, and we'll have some space to dance, and your mother and Bradley can have a nice quiet drink."

She gets up from the table and, looking long-suffering, backs into her coat, which he is holding for her, and the two of them go out. The waitress comes to the table, and Bradley orders three Bloody Marys and a Coke, and eggs Benedict for everyone. He asks the waitress to wait awhile before she brings the food. I have hardly slept at all, and having a drink is not going to clear my head. I have to think of things to say to Louise later, on the ride home.

"He takes so many *chances,*" I say. "He pushes things so far with people. I don't want her to turn against him."

"No," he says.

"Why are you going, Bradley? You've seen the way he acts. You know that when you get out there he'll pull something on you. Take the job and stay here."

Bradley is fiddling with the edge of his napkin. I study him. I don't know who his friends are, how old he is, where he grew up, whether he believes in God, or what he usually drinks. I'm shocked that I know so little, and I reach out and touch him. He looks up.

"Don't go," I say quietly.

The waitress puts the glasses down quickly and leaves, embarrassed because she thinks she's interrupted a tender moment. Bradley pats my hand on his arm. Then he says the thing that has always been between us, the thing too painful for me to envision or think about.

"I love him," Bradley whispers.

We sit quietly until Milo and Louise come into the restaurant, swinging hands. She is pretending to be a young child, almost a baby, and I wonder for an instant if Milo and Bradley and I haven't been playing house, too—pretending to be adults.

"Daddy's going to give me a first-class ticket," Louise says. "When I go to California we're going to ride in a glass elevator to the top of the Fairman Hotel."

"The Fairmont," Milo says, smiling at her.

Before Louise was born, Milo used to put his ear to my stomach and say that if the baby turned out to be a girl he would put her into glass slippers instead of bootees. Now he is the prince once again. I see them in a glass elevator, not long from now, going up and up, with the people below getting smaller and smaller, until they disappear.

Writing Assignments for "The Cinderella Waltz"

I. Brief Papers

    A. 1. Several times the narrator says that Milo is a perfectionist. What does she mean?

       2. Is the narrator herself a perfectionist?

       3. Why does Beattie include Sarah and Sarah's mother, Martine Cooper, in the story? What purpose do they serve?

       4. Why does the narrator tell Bradley not to go to San Francisco with Milo?

       5. "The Cinderella Waltz" appears in a collection of short stories by Ann Beattie

called *The Burning House.* Does this title shed any light on "The Cinderella Waltz" itself?
6. Do the many references to plants relate to anything else in the story?

B. Argue for or against one of the assertions below:
1. The narrator is right in saying that Milo lacks a sense of humor.
2. The narrator herself lacks a sense of humor.
3. Like most fairy tales, the story has a happy ending.
4. The narrator's marriage fails because she is a rotten wife.

C. 1. Bradley says that he loves Milo. What do you think?
2. The narrator wonders how much Louise knows about Milo and Bradley. What do you think?
3. The narrator tells us that she used to be bitter about the divorce but that she has gotten over it. Do you think she has?
4. If you were Bradley, would you go to San Francisco with Milo? Why or why not?
5. Milo tells Louise, "You start doing something innocently and before you know it it can take you over" (p. 277). Do you agree?

II. Longer Papers

A. Reread the fairy tale "Cinderella" and then explain whether or not you find "The Cinderella Waltz" an appropriate title.
B. How and why does the relationship between the narrator and Bradley change during the story? Are the changes plausible? What do they tell us about people and about relationships in general?
C. As fully as you can, characterize the story's narrator. What sort of a woman is she? What are her values, hopes, goals, and fears? Do you think that Beattie wants us to see her as representative of American women in the 1980s?
D. Explain as fully as you can the meanings and significance of the story's last paragraph. Does it both summarize what has come before and anticipate what will come later?
E. What does the story say about the chances for happiness?
F. The word "pretending" is mentioned several times. What does the story say about the ways in which we pretend and our reasons for pretending?
G. What attitude toward homosexuality emerges from the story?

III. Comparative Papers

A. In what ways are both "Rappaccini's Daughter" and "The Cinderella Waltz" like fairy tales? In what ways are they not?
B. Taken together, what do "Rappaccini's Daughter" and "The Cinderella Waltz" say about the situation of women in relationships with men?
C. Although both "Rappaccini's Daughter" and "The Cinderella Waltz" dramatize broken relationships, the stories contrast markedly in tone. Describe the contrasts in tone and explain how these contrasts contribute to differences between the two stories in meaning and in impact.

EDGAR ALLAN POE
The Cask of Amontillado

Before Reading

What kind of a person is capable of planning, perpetrating, and getting away with the perfect murder? Would you be able to do it? Free write on one or both of these questions for 5 or 10 minutes.

The thousand injuries of Fortunato I had borne as I best could, but when he ventured upon insult I vowed revenge. You, who so well know the nature of my soul, will not suppose, however, that I gave utterance to a threat. *At length* I would be avenged; this was a point definitely settled—but the very definitiveness with which it was resolved precluded the idea of risk. I must not only punish but punish with impunity. A wrong is unredressed when retribution overtakes its redresser. It is equally unredressed when the avenger fails to make himself felt as such to him who has done the wrong.

It must be understood that neither by word nor deed had I given Fortunato cause to doubt my good will. I continued, as was my wont, to smile in his face, and he did not perceive that my smile *now* was at the thought of his immolation.

He had a weak point—this Fortunato—although in other regards he was a man to be respected and even feared. He prided himself on his connoisseurship in wine. Few Italians have the true virtuoso spirit. For the most part their enthusiasm is adopted to suit the time and opportunity, to practice imposture upon the British and Austrian millionaires. In painting and gemmary, Fortunato, like his countrymen, was a quack, but in the matter of old wines he was sincere. In this respect I did not differ from him materially;—I was skilful in the Italian vintages myself, and bought largely whenever I could.

It was about dusk, one evening during the supreme madness of the carnival season, that I encountered my friend. He accosted me with excessive warmth, for he had been drinking much. The man wore motley.* He had on a tight-fitting parti-striped dress, and his head was surmounted by the conical cap and bells. I was so pleased to see him that I thought I should never have done wringing his hand.

I said to him—"My dear Fortunato, you are luckily met. How remarkably well you are looking to-day. But I have received a pipe of what passes for Amontillado,† and I have my doubts."

---

*motley: A garment of many colors worn by a fool or jester.
†Amontillado: A light Spanish sherry; a pipe is a large cask.

THE CASK OF AMONTILLADO   First published in 1846. Edgar Allan Poe (1809–1849) is the author of poems, stories, and criticism; he is usually considered the creator of the detective tale.

"How?" said he. "Amontillado? A pipe? Impossible! And in the middle of the carnival!"

"I have my doubts," I replied; "and I was silly enough to pay the full Amontillado price without consulting you in the matter. You were not to be found, and I was fearful of losing a bargain."

"Amontillado!"

"I have my doubts."

"Amontillado!"

"And I must satisfy them."

"Amontillado!"

"As you are engaged, I am on my way to Luchresi. If any one has a critical turn, it is he. He will tell me——"

"Luchresi cannot tell Amontillado from Sherry."

"And yet some fools will have it that his taste is a match for your own."

"Come, let us go."

"Whither?"

"To your vaults."

"My friend, no; I will not impose upon your good nature. I perceive you have an engagement. Luchresi——"

"I have no engagement;—come."

"My friend, no. It is not the engagement, but the severe cold with which I perceive you are afflicted. The vaults are insufferably damp. They are encrusted with niter."

"Let us go, nevertheless. The cold is merely nothing. Amontillado! You have been imposed upon. And as for Luchresi, he cannot distinguish Sherry from Amontillado."

Thus speaking, Fortunato possessed himself of my arm; and putting on a mask of black silk and drawing a *roquelaire** closely about my person, I suffered him to hurry me to my palazzo.

There were no attendants at home; they had absconded to make merry in honor of the time. I had told them that I should not return until the morning, and had given them explicit orders not to stir from the house. These orders were sufficient, I well knew, to insure their immediate disappearance, one and all, as soon as my back was turned.

I took from their sconces two flambeaux, and giving one to Fortunato, bowed him through several suites of rooms to the archway that led into the vaults. I passed down a long and winding staircase, requesting him to be cautious as he followed. We came at length to the foot of the descent, and stood together on the damp ground of the catacombs of the Montresors.

The gait of my friend was unsteady, and the bells upon his cap jingled as he strode.

"The pipe?" said he.

"It is farther on," said I; "but observe the white web-work which gleams from these cavern walls."

*roquelaire: French, a short cloak.

He turned towards me, and looked into my eyes with two filmy orbs that distilled the rheum of intoxication.

"Niter?" he asked at length.

"Niter," I replied. "How long have you had that cough?"

"Ugh! ugh! ugh!—ugh! ugh! ugh!—ugh! ugh! ugh! ugh! ugh! ugh!—ugh! ugh! ugh!"

My poor friend found it impossible to reply for many minutes.

"It is nothing," he said, at last.

"Come," I said, with decision, "we will go back; your health is precious. You are rich, respected, admired, beloved; you are happy, as once I was. You are a man to be missed. For me it is no matter. We will go back; you will be ill, and I cannot be responsible. Besides, there is Luchresi——"

"Enough," he said; "the cough is a mere nothing; it will not kill me. I shall not die of a cough."

"True—true," I replied; "and, indeed, I had no intention of alarming you unnecessarily—but you should use all proper caution. A draft of this Medoc* will defend us from the damps."

Here I knocked off the neck of a bottle which I drew from a long row of its fellows that lay upon the mold.

"Drink," I said, presenting him the wine.

He raised it to his lips with a leer. He paused and nodded to me familiarly, while his bells jingled.

"I drink," he said, "to the buried that repose around us."

"And I to your long life."

He again took my arm, and we proceeded.

"These vaults," he said, "are extensive."

"The Montresors," I replied, "were a great and numerous family."

"I forget your arms."

"A huge human foot d'or, in a field azure; the foot crushes a serpent rampant whose fangs are imbedded in the heel."

"And the motto?"

"Nemo me impune lacessit."†

"Good!" he said.

The wine sparkled in his eyes and the bells jingled. My own fancy grew warm with the Medoc. We had passed through long walls of piled skeletons, with casks and puncheons intermingling, into the inmost recesses of the catacombs. I paused again, and this time I made bold to seize Fortunato by an arm above the elbow.

"The niter!" I said; "see, it increases. It hangs like moss upon the vaults. We are below the river's bed. The drops of moisture trickle among the bones. Come, we will go back ere it is too late. Your cough——"

"It is nothing," he said; "let us go on. But first, another draft of the Medoc."

*Medoc: A French red wine.

†*Nemo me impune lacessit:* Latin, No one insults me with impunity.

I broke and reached him a flagon of De Grâve. He emptied it at a breath. His eyes flashed with a fierce light. He laughed and threw the bottle upward with a gesticulation I did not understand.

I looked at him in surprise. He repeated the movement—a grotesque one.

"You do not comprehend?" he said.

"Not I," I replied.

"Then you are not of the brotherhood."

"How?"

"You are not of the masons."*

"Yes, yes," I said; "yes, yes."

"You? Impossible! A mason?"

"A mason," I replied.

"A sign," he said, "a sign."

"It is this," I answered, producing from beneath the folds of my *roquelaire* a trowel.

"You jest," he exclaimed, recoiling a few paces. "But let us proceed to the Amontillado."

"Be it so," I said, replacing the tool beneath the cloak and again offering him my arm. He leaned upon it heavily. We continued our route in search of the Amontillado. We passed through a range of low arches, descended, passed on, and descending again, arrived at a deep crypt, in which the foulness of the air caused our flambeaux rather to glow than flame.

At the most remote end of the crypt there appeared another less spacious. Its walls had been lined with human remains, piled to the vault overhead, in the fashion of the great catacombs of Paris. Three sides of this interior crypt were still ornamented in this manner. From the fourth the bones had been thrown down, and lay promiscuously upon the earth, forming at one point a mound of some size. Within the wall thus exposed by the displacing of the bones, we perceived a still interior crypt or recess, in depth about four feet, in width three, in height six or seven. It seemed to have been constructed for no especial use within itself, but formed merely the interval between two of the colossal supports of the roof of the catacombs, and was backed by one of their circumscribing walls of solid granite.

It was in vain that Fortunato, uplifting his dull torch, endeavored to pry into the depth of the recess. Its termination the feeble light did not enable us to see.

"Proceed," I said; "herein is the Amontillado. As for Luchresi——"

"He is an ignoramus," interrupted my friend, as he stepped unsteadily forward, while I followed immediately at his heels. In an instant he had reached the extremity of the niche, and finding his progress arrested by the rock, stood stupidly bewildered. A moment more and I had fettered him to the granite. In its surface were two iron staples, distant from each other about two feet, horizontally. From one of these depended a short chain, from the other a padlock. Throwing the links about his waist, it was but the work of a few seconds to

*masons: The Freemasons, an international secret fraternal society.

secure it. He was too much astounded to resist. Withdrawing the key I stepped back from the recess.

"Pass your hand," I said, "over the wall; you cannot help feeling the niter. Indeed it is *very* damp. Once more let me *implore* you to return. No? Then I must positively leave you. But I must first render you all the little attentions in my power."

"The Amontillado!" ejaculated my friend, not yet recovered from his astonishment.

"True," I replied; "the Amontillado."

As I said these words I busied myself among the pile of bones of which I have before spoken. Throwing them aside, I soon uncovered a quantity of building stone and mortar. With these materials and with the aid of my trowel, I began vigorously to wall up the entrance of the niche.

I had scarcely laid the first tier of the masonry when I discovered that the intoxication of Fortunato had in a great measure worn off. The earliest indication I had of this was a low moaning cry from the depth of the recess. It was *not* the cry of a drunken man. There was then a long and obstinate silence. I laid the second tier, and the third, and the fourth; and then I heard the furious vibrations of the chain. The noise lasted for several minutes, during which, that I might hearken to it with the more satisfaction, I ceased my labors and sat down upon the bones. When at last the clanking subsided, I resumed the trowel, and finished without interruption the fifth, the sixth, and the seventh tier. The wall was now nearly upon a level with my breast. I again paused, and holding the flambeaux over the masonwork, threw a few feeble rays upon the figure within.

A succession of loud and shrill screams, bursting suddenly from the throat of the chained form, seemed to thrust me violently back. For a brief moment I hesitated, I trembled. Unsheathing my rapier, I began to grope with it about the recess; but the thought of an instant reassured me. I placed my hand upon the solid fabric of the catacombs, and felt satisfied. I reapproached the wall. I replied to the yells of him who clamored. I reechoed, I aided, I surpassed them in volume and in strength. I did this, and the clamorer grew still.

It was now midnight, and my task was drawing to a close. I had completed the eighth, the ninth and the tenth tier. I had finished a portion of the last and the eleventh; there remained but a single stone to be fitted and plastered in. I struggled with its weight; I placed it partially in its destined position. But now there came from out the niche a low laugh that erected the hairs upon my head. It was succeeded by a sad voice, which I had difficulty in recognizing as that of the noble Fortunato. The voice said—

"Ha! ha! ha!—he! he! he!—a very good joke, indeed—an excellent jest. We will have many a rich laugh about it at the palazzo—he! he! he!—over our wine—he! he! he!"

"The Amontillado!" I said.

"He! he! he!—hc! he! he!—yes, the Amontillado. But is it not getting late? Will not they be awaiting us at the palazzo, the Lady Fortunato and the rest? Let us be gone."

"Yes," I said, "let us be gone."

"For the love of God, Montresor!"

"Yes," I said, "for the love of God!"

But to these words I hearkened in vain for a reply. I grew impatient. I called aloud—

"Fortunato!"

No answer. I called again—

"Fortunato!"

No answer still. I thrust a torch through the remaining aperture and let it fall within. There came forth in return only a jingling of the bells. My heart grew sick; it was the dampness of the catacombs that made it so. I hastened to make an end of my labor. I forced the last stone into its position; I plastered it up. Against the new masonry I re-erected the old rampart of bones. For the half of a century no mortal has disturbed them. *In pace requiescat!**

Writing Assignments for "The Cask of Amontillado"

I. Brief Papers

A. 1. What is the evidence that Montresor has carefully planned the murder of Fortunato?

2. Why is it significant that the murder takes place during "the supreme madness of the carnival season" (p. 288)?

3. Explain the significance of one or more of the names in the story—Fortunato, Montresor, Luchresi.

4. Summarize in your own words Montresor's criteria for successful revenge and then explain whether they are met.

5. How does the Montresor family coat of arms relate to the events of the story?

6. Dramatic irony occurs when there is a discrepancy between what a character seems to be saying and what he or she actually means. For example, dramatic irony occurs when Montresor tells Fortunato that he is "luckily met" because Montresor knows that the meeting will be an unlucky one for Fortunato. Explain several other instances of dramatic irony in the story.

7. Explain the circumstances under which Montresor tells his story.

B. Argue for or against one of the assertions below:

1. Montresor is a sadist.

2. Montresor is a madman.

3. The "thousand injuries" and final "insult" are not the real reasons why Montresor vows revenge against Fortunato.

4. Montresor brilliantly manipulates Fortunato.

5. Montresor knows Fortunato well, but he knows himself even better.

C. 1. Explain your reaction to Montresor: do you find him more admirable than repulsive?

*In pace requiescat!: Latin, May he rest in peace!

2. Do you feel sorry for Fortunato? Why or why not?
3. Were you surprised to learn in the story's next-to-last sentence that the murder had taken place fifty years ago? Why or why not?

II. Longer Papers

A. Develop, modify, or refute the assertion that "The Cask of Amontillado" is the story of a perfect crime.
B. What does the story have to say about human nature?
C. Explain how the use of irony in "The Cask of Amontillado" helps to create the story's meanings.
D. According to the poet Richard Wilbur, Poe shows in all his stories that human beings suffer from self-division, from a split in personality, and that one part of the self is invariably at war with another part of the self. Argue for or against the assertion that Wilbur's statement applies to "The Cask of Amontillado."
E. Some readers of "The Cask of Amontillado" believe that Montresor is not fully aware of the significance of what he says, that he thinks he is telling one story but actually tells another. What do you think?
F. Poe has written several other stories in which the narrator thinks he has committed the perfect murder: "The Black Cat," "The Imp of the Perverse," and "The Tell-Tale Heart." Read and analyze one or more of these stories in order to explain how they help you better understand and appreciate "The Cask of Amontillado."

FLANNERY O'CONNOR
Good Country People

Before Reading

What does the phrase "good country people" mean to you? What is there about the "country" that presumably helps people living there to be "good"? Free write on one or both of these questions for 5 or 10 minutes.

Besides the neutral expression that she wore when she was alone, Mrs. Freeman had two others, forward and reverse, that she used for all her human dealings. Her forward expression was steady and driving like the advance of a heavy truck. Her eyes never swerved to left or right but turned as the story turned as if they followed a yellow line down the center of it. She seldom used the other expression because it was not often necessary for her to retract a statement, but when she did, her face came to a complete stop, there was an almost imperceptible movement of her black eyes, during which they seemed

GOOD COUNTRY PEOPLE   First published in 1955. Flannery O'Connor (1925–1964) was born in Savannah and spent most of her life in Milledgeville, Georgia. A Roman Catholic throughout her life, she once described her fiction as pervaded by a "sense of Mystery which cannot be accounted for by human formula."

to be receding, and then the observer would see that Mrs. Freeman, though she might stand there as real as several grain sacks thrown on top of each other, was no longer there in spirit. As for getting anything across to her when this was the case, Mrs. Hopewell had given it up. She might talk her head off. Mrs. Freeman could never be brought to admit herself wrong on any point. She would stand there and if she could be brought to say anything, it was something like, "Well, I wouldn't of said it was and I wouldn't of said it wasn't," or letting her gaze range over the top kitchen shelf where there was an assortment of dusty bottles, she might remark, "I see you ain't ate many of them figs you put up last summer."

They carried on their most important business in the kitchen at breakfast. Every morning Mrs. Hopewell got up at seven o'clock and lit her gas heater and Joy's. Joy was her daughter, a large blonde girl who had an artificial leg. Mrs. Hopewell thought of her as a child though she was thirty-two years old and highly educated. Joy would get up while her mother was eating and lumber into the bathroom and slam the door, and before long, Mrs. Freeman would arrive at the back door. Joy would hear her mother call, "Come on in," and then they would talk for a while in low voices that were indistinguishable in the bathroom. By the time Joy came in, they had usually finished the weather report and were on one or the other of Mrs. Freeman's daughters, Glynese or Carramae. Joy called them Glycerin and Caramel. Glynese, a redhead, was eighteen and had many admirers; Carramae, a blonde, was only fifteen but already married and pregnant. She could not keep anything on her stomach. Every morning Mrs. Freeman told Mrs. Hopewell how many times she had vomited since the last report.

Mrs. Hopewell liked to tell people that Glynese and Carramae were two of the finest girls she knew and that Mrs. Freeman was a *lady* and that she was never ashamed to take her anywhere or introduce her to anybody they might meet. Then she would tell how she had happened to hire the Freemans in the first place and how they were a godsend to her and how she had had them four years. The reason for her keeping them so long was that they were not trash. They were good country people. She had telephoned the man whose name they had given as a reference and he had told her that Mr. Freeman was a good farmer but that his wife was the nosiest woman ever to walk the earth. "She's got to be into everything," the man said. "If she don't get there before the dust settles, you can bet she's dead, that's all. She'll want to know all your business. I can stand him real good," he had said, "but me nor my wife neither could have stood that woman one more minute on this place." That had put Mrs. Hopewell off for a few days.

She had hired them in the end because there were no other applicants but she had made up her mind beforehand exactly how she would handle the woman. Since she was the type who had to be into everything, then, Mrs. Hopewell had decided, she would not only let her be into everything, she would *see to it* that she was into everything—she would give her the responsibility of everything, she would put her in charge. Mrs. Hopewell had no bad qualities of her own but she was able to use other people's in such a constructive

way that she never felt the lack. She had hired the Freemans and she had kept
them four years.

Nothing is perfect. This was one of Mrs. Hopewell's favorite sayings.
Another was: that is life! And still another, the most important, was: well,
other people have their opinions too. She would make these statements, usually at the table, in a tone of gentle insistence as if no one held them but her,
and the large hulking Joy, whose constant outrage had obliterated every expression from her face, would stare just a little to the side of her, her eyes icy
blue, with the look of someone who has achieved blindness by an act of will
and means to keep it.

When Mrs. Hopewell said to Mrs. Freeman that life was like that, Mrs.
Freeman would say, "I always said so myself." Nothing had been arrived at by
anyone that had not first been arrived at by her. She was quicker than Mr.
Freeman. When Mrs. Hopewell said to her after they had been on the place a
while, "You know, you're the wheel behind the wheel," and winked, Mrs.
Freeman had said, "I know it. I've always been quick. It's some that are quicker
than others."

"Everybody is different," Mrs. Hopewell said.

"Yes, most people is," Mrs. Freeman said.

"It takes all kinds to make the world."

"I always said it did myself."

The girl was used to this kind of dialogue for breakfast and more of it for
dinner; sometimes they had it for supper too. When they had no guest they ate
in the kitchen because that was easier. Mrs. Freeman always managed to arrive
at some point during the meal and to watch them finish it. She would stand in
the doorway if it were summer but in the winter she would stand with one elbow
on top of the refrigerator and look down on them, or she would stand by the
gas heater, lifting the back of her skirt slightly. Occasionally she would stand
against the wall and roll her head from side to side. At no time was she in any
hurry to leave. All this was very trying on Mrs. Hopewell but she was a woman
of great patience. She realized that nothing is perfect and that in the Freemans
she had good country people and that if, in this day and age, you get good
country people, you had better hang onto them.

She had had plenty of experience with trash. Before the Freemans she had
averaged one tenant family a year. The wives of these farmers were not the kind
you would want to be around you for very long. Mrs. Hopewell, who had
divorced her husband long ago, needed someone to walk over the fields with
her; and when Joy had to be impressed for these services, her remarks were
usually so ugly and her face so glum that Mrs. Hopewell would say, "If you can't
come pleasantly, I don't want you at all," to which the girl, standing square and
rigid-shouldered with her neck thrust slightly forward, would reply, "If you
want me, here I am—LIKE I AM."

Mrs. Hopewell excused this attitude because of the leg (which had been
shot off in a hunting accident when Joy was ten). It was hard for Mrs. Hopewell
to realize that her child was thirty-two now and that for more than twenty years
she had had only one leg. She thought of her still as a child because it tore her

heart to think instead of the poor stout girl in her thirties who had never danced a step or had any *normal* good times. Her name was really Joy but as soon as she was twenty-one and away from home, she had had it legally changed. Mrs. Hopewell was certain that she had thought and thought until she had hit upon the ugliest name in any language. Then she had gone and had the beautiful name, Joy, changed without telling her mother until after she had done it. Her legal name was Hulga.

When Mrs. Hopewell thought the name, Hulga, she thought of the broad blank hull of a battleship. She would not use it. She continued to call her Joy to which the girl responded but in a purely mechanical way.

Hulga had learned to tolerate Mrs. Freeman, who saved her from taking walks with her mother. Even Glynese and Carramae were useful when they occupied attention that might otherwise have been directed at her. At first she had thought she could not stand Mrs. Freeman for she had found that it was not possible to be rude to her. Mrs. Freeman would take on strange resentments and for days together she would be sullen but the source of her displeasure was always obscure; a direct attack, a positive leer, blatant ugliness to her face—these never touched her. And without warning one day, she began calling her Hulga.

She did not call her that in front of Mrs. Hopewell who would have been incensed but when she and the girl happened to be out of the house together, she would say something and add the name Hulga to the end of it, and the big spectacled Joy-Hulga would scowl and redden as if her privacy had been intruded upon. She considered the name her personal affair. She had arrived at it first purely on the basis of its ugly sound and then the full genius of its fitness had struck her. She had a vision of the name working like the ugly sweating Vulcan* who stayed in the furnace and to whom, presumably, the goddess had to come when called. She saw it as the name of her highest creative act. One of her major triumphs was that her mother had not been able to turn her dust into Joy, but the greater one was that she had been able to turn it herself into Hulga. However, Mrs. Freeman's relish for using the name only irritated her. It was as if Mrs. Freeman's beady steel-pointed eyes had penetrated far enough behind her face to reach some secret fact. Something about her seemed to fascinate Mrs. Freeman and then one day Hulga realized that it was the artificial leg. Mrs. Freeman had a special fondness for the details of secret infections, hidden deformities, assaults upon children. Of diseases, she preferred the lingering or incurable. Hulga had heard Mrs. Hopewell give her the details of the hunting accident, how the leg had been literally blasted off, how she had never lost consciousness. Mrs. Freeman could listen to it any time as if it had happened an hour ago.

When Hulga stumped into the kitchen in the morning (she could walk without making the awful noise but she made it—Mrs. Hopewell was certain—because it was ugly-sounding), she glanced at them and did not speak. Mrs.

*Vulcan: In Roman mythology, the god of fire and the forge, and the only god who was ugly and deformed. Vulcan was the husband of Venus, goddess of love and beauty.

Hopewell would be in her red kimono with her hair tied around her head in rags. She would be sitting at the table, finishing her breakfast and Mrs. Freeman would be hanging by her elbow outward from the refrigerator, looking down at the table. Hulga always put her eggs on the stove to boil and then stood over them with her arms folded, and Mrs. Hopewell would look at her—a kind of indirect gaze divided between her and Mrs. Freeman—and would think that if she would only keep herself up a little, she wouldn't be so bad looking. There was nothing wrong with her face that a pleasant expression wouldn't help. Mrs. Hopewell said that people who looked on the bright side of things would be beautiful even if they were not.

Whenever she looked at Joy this way, she could not help but feel that it would have been better if the child had not taken the Ph.D. It had certainly not brought her out any and now that she had it, there was no more excuse for her to go to school again. Mrs. Hopewell thought it was nice for girls to go to school to have a good time but Joy had "gone through." Anyhow, she would not have been strong enough to go again. The doctors had told Mrs. Hopewell that with the best of care, Joy might see forty-five. She had a weak heart. Joy had made it plain that if it had not been for this condition, she would be far from these red hills and good country people. She would be in a university lecturing to people who knew what she was talking about. And Mrs. Hopewell could very well picture her there, looking like a scarecrow and lecturing to more of the same. Here she went about all day in a six-year-old skirt and a yellow sweat shirt with a faded cowboy on a horse embossed on it. She thought this was funny; Mrs. Hopewell thought it was idiotic and showed simply that she was still a child. She was brilliant but she didn't have a grain of sense. It seemed to Mrs. Hopewell that every year she grew less like other people and more like herself—bloated, rude, and squint-eyed. And she said such strange things! To her own mother she had said—without warning, without excuse, standing up in the middle of a meal with her face purple and her mouth half full—"Woman! do you ever look inside? Do you ever look inside and see what you are *not?* God!" she had cried sinking down again and staring at her plate, "Malebranche* was right: we are not our own light. We are not our own light!" Mrs. Hopewell had no idea to this day what brought that on. She had only made the remark, hoping Joy would take it in, that a smile never hurt anyone.

The girl had taken the Ph.D. in philosophy and this left Mrs. Hopewell at a complete loss. You could say, "My daughter is a nurse," or "My daughter is a school teacher," or even, "My daughter is a chemical engineer." You could not say, "My daughter is a philosopher." That was something that had ended with the Greeks and Romans. All day Joy sat on her neck in a deep chair, reading. Sometimes she went for walks but she didn't like dogs or cats or birds or flowers or nature or nice young men. She looked at nice young men as if she could smell their stupidity.

*Malebranche: Nicholas Malebranche (1638–1715), French philosopher who argued that God is the only source of knowledge.

One day Mrs. Hopewell had picked up one of the books the girl had just put down and opening it at random, she read, "Science, on the other hand, has to assert its soberness and seriousness afresh and declare that it is concerned solely with what-is. Nothing—how can it be for science anything but a horror and a phantasm? If science is right, then one thing stands firm: science wishes to know nothing of nothing. Such is after all the strictly scientific approach to Nothing. We know it by wishing to know nothing of Nothing." These words had been underlined with a blue pencil and they worked on Mrs. Hopewell like some evil incantation in gibberish. She shut the book quickly and went out of the room as if she were having a chill.

This morning when the girl came in, Mrs. Freeman was on Carramae. "She thrown up four times after supper," she said, "and was up twict in the night after three o'clock. Yesterday she didn't do nothing but ramble in the bureau drawer. All she did. Stand up there and see what she could run up on."

"She's got to eat," Mrs. Hopewell muttered, sipping her coffee, while she watched Joy's back at the stove. She was wondering what the child had said to the Bible salesman. She could not imagine what kind of a conversation she could possibly have had with him.

He was a tall gaunt hatless youth who had called yesterday to sell them a Bible. He had appeared at the door, carrying a large black suitcase that weighted him so heavily on one side that he had to brace himself against the door facing. He seemed on the point of collapse but he said in a cheerful voice, "Good morning, Mrs. Cedars!" and set the suitcase down on the mat. He was not a bad-looking young man though he had on a bright blue suit and yellow socks that were not pulled up far enough. He had prominent face bones and a streak of sticky-looking brown hair falling across his forehead.

"I'm Mrs. Hopewell," she said.

"Oh!" he said, pretending to look puzzled but with his eyes sparkling, "I saw it said 'The Cedars,' on the mailbox so I thought you was Mrs. Cedars!" and he burst out in a pleasant laugh. He picked up the satchel and under cover of a pant, he fell forward into her hall. It was rather as if the suitcase had moved first, jerking him after it. "Mrs. Hopewell!" he said and grabbed her hand. "I hope you are well!" and he laughed again and then all at once his face sobered completely. He paused and gave her a straight earnest look and said, "Lady, I've come to speak of serious things."

"Well, come in," she muttered, none too pleased because her dinner was almost ready. He came into the parlor and sat down on the edge of a straight chair and put the suitcase between his feet and glanced around the room as if he were sizing her up by it. Her silver gleamed on the two sideboards; she decided he had never been in a room as elegant as this.

"Mrs. Hopewell," he began, using her name in a way that sounded almost intimate, "I know you believe in Christun service."

"Well yes," she murmured.

"I know," he said and paused, looking very wise with his head cocked on one side, "that you're a good woman. Friends have told me."

Mrs. Hopewell never liked to be taken for a fool. "What are you selling?" she asked.

"Bibles," the young man said and his eye raced around the room before he added, "I see you have no family Bible in your parlor, I see that is the one lack you got!"

Mrs. Hopewell could not say, "My daughter is an atheist and won't let me keep the Bible in the parlor." She said, stiffening slightly, "I keep my Bible by my bedside." This was not the truth. It was in the attic somewhere.

"Lady," he said, "the word of God ought to be in the parlor."

"Well, I think that's a matter of taste," she began. "I think . . ."

"Lady," he said, "for a Chrustian, the word of God ought to be in every room in the house besides in his heart. I know you're a Chrustian because I can see it in every line of your face."

She stood up and said, "Well, young man, I don't want to buy a Bible and I smell my dinner burning."

He didn't get up. He began to twist his hands and looking down at them, he said softly, "Well lady, I'll tell you the truth—not many people want to buy one nowadays and besides, I know I'm real simple. I don't know how to say a thing but to say it. I'm just a country boy." He glanced up into her unfriendly face. "People like you don't like to fool with country people like me!"

"Why!" she cried, "good country people are the salt of the earth! Besides, we all have different ways of doing, it takes all kinds to make the world go 'round. That's life!"

"You said a mouthful," he said.

"Why, I think there aren't enough good country people in the world!" she said, stirred. "I think that's what's wrong with it!"

His face had brightened. "I didn't inraduce myself," he said. "I'm Manley Pointer from out in the country around Willohobie, not even from a place, just from near a place."

"You wait a minute," she said. "I have to see about my dinner." She went out to the kitchen and found Joy standing near the door where she had been listening.

"Get rid of the salt of the earth," she said, "and let's eat."

Mrs. Hopewell gave her a pained look and turned the heat down under the vegetables. *"I can't be rude to anybody,"* she murmured and went back into the parlor.

He had opened the suitcase and was sitting with a Bible on each knee.

"You might as well put those up," she told him. "I don't want one."

"I appreciate your honesty," he said. "You don't see any more real honest people unless you go way out in the country."

"I know," she said, "real genuine folks!" Through the crack in the door she heard a groan.

"I guess a lot of boys come telling you they're working their way through college," he said, "but I'm not going to tell you that. Somehow," he said, "I don't want to go to college. I want to devote my life to Chrustian service. See," he said, lowering his voice, "I got this heart condition. I may not live long. When you know it's something wrong with you and you may not live long, well then, lady . . ." He paused, with his mouth open, and stared at her.

He and Joy had the same condition! She knew that her eyes were filling with tears but she collected herself quickly and murmured, "Won't you stay for dinner? We'd love to have you!" and was sorry the instant she heard herself say it.

"Yes mam," he said in an abashed voice, "I would sher love to do that!"

Joy had given him one look on being introduced to him and then throughout the meal had not glanced at him again. He had addressed several remarks to her, which she had pretended not to hear. Mrs. Hopewell could not understand deliberate rudeness, although she lived with it, and she felt she had always to overflow with hospitality to make up for Joy's lack of courtesy. She urged him to talk about himself and he did. He said he was the seventh child of twelve and that his father had been crushed under a tree when he himself was eight year old. He had been crushed very badly, in fact, almost cut in two and was practically not recognizable. His mother had got along the best she could by hard working and she had always seen that her children went to Sunday School and that they read the Bible every evening. He was now nineteen year old and he had been selling Bibles for four months. In that time he had sold seventy-seven Bibles and had the promise of two more sales. He wanted to become a missionary because he thought that was the way you could do most for people. "He who losest his life shall find it," he said simply and he was so sincere, so genuine and earnest that Mrs. Hopewell would not for the world have smiled. He prevented his peas from sliding onto the table by blocking them with a piece of bread which he later cleaned his plate with. She could see Joy observing sidewise how he handled his knife and fork and she saw too that every few minutes, the boy would dart a keen appraising glance at the girl as if he were trying to attract her attention.

After dinner Joy cleared the dishes off the table and disappeared and Mrs. Hopewell was left to talk with him. He told her again about his childhood and his father's accident and about various things that had happened to him. Every five minutes or so she would stifle a yawn. He sat for two hours until finally she told him she must go because she had an appointment in town. He packed his Bibles and thanked her and prepared to leave, but in the doorway he stopped and wrung her hand and said that not on any of his trips had he met a lady as nice as her and he asked if he could come again. She had said she would always be happy to see him.

Joy had been standing in the road, apparently looking at something in the distance, when he came down the steps toward her, bent to the side with his heavy valise. He stopped where she was standing and confronted her directly. Mrs. Hopewell could not hear what he said but she trembled to think what Joy would say to him. She could see that after a minute Joy said something and that then the boy began to speak again, making an excited gesture with his free hand. After a minute Joy said something else at which the boy began to speak once more. Then to her amazement, Mrs. Hopewell saw the two of them walk off together, toward the gate. Joy had walked all the way to the gate with him and Mrs. Hopewell could not imagine what they had said to each other, and she had not yet dared to ask.

Mrs. Freeman was insisting upon her attention. She had moved from the refrigerator to the heater so that Mrs. Hopewell had to turn and face her in order to seem to be listening. "Glynese gone out with Harvey Hill again last night," she said. "She had this sty."

"Hill," Mrs. Hopewell said absently, "is that the one who works in the garage?"

"Nome, he's the one that goes to chiropracter school," Mrs. Freeman said. "She had this sty. Been had it two days. So she says when he brought her in the other night he says, 'Lemme get rid of that sty for you,' and she says, 'How?' and he says, 'You just lay yourself down acrost the seat of that car and I'll show you.' So she done it and he popped her neck. Kept on a-popping it several times until she made him quit. This morning," Mrs. Freeman said, "she ain't got no sty. She ain't got no traces of a sty."

"I never heard of that before," Mrs. Hopewell said.

"He ast her to marry him before the Ordinary,"* Mrs. Freeman went on, "and she told him she wasn't going to be married in no *office.*"

"Well, Glynese is a fine girl," Mrs. Hopewell said. "Glynese and Carramae are both fine girls."

"Carramae said when her and Lyman was married Lyman said it sure felt sacred to him. She said he said he wouldn't take five hundred dollars for being married by a preacher."

"How much would he take?" the girl asked from the stove.

"He said he wouldn't take five hundred dollars," Mrs. Freeman repeated.

"Well we all have work to do," Mrs. Hopewell said.

"Lyman said it just felt more sacred to him," Mrs. Freeman said. "The doctor wants Carramae to eat prunes. Says instead of medicine. Says them cramps is coming from pressure. You know where I think it is?"

"She'll be better in a few weeks," Mrs. Hopewell said.

"In the tube," Mrs. Freeman said. "Else she wouldn't be as sick as she is."

Hulga had cracked her two eggs into a saucer and was bringing them to the table along with a cup of coffee that she had filled too full. She sat down carefully and began to eat, meaning to keep Mrs. Freeman there by questions if for any reason she showed an inclination to leave. She could perceive her mother's eye on her. The first roundabout question would be about the Bible salesman and she did not wish to bring it on. "How did he pop her neck?" she asked.

Mrs. Freeman went into a description of how he had popped her neck. She said he owned a '55 Mercury but that Glynese said she would rather marry a man with only a '36 Plymouth who would be married by a preacher. The girl

*Ordinary: A Justice of the Peace who performs the ceremony of marriage not in church but in chambers.

asked what if he had a '32 Plymouth and Mrs. Freeman said what Glynese had said was a '36 Plymouth.

Mrs. Hopewell said there were not many girls with Glynese's common sense. She said what she admired in those girls was their common sense. She said that reminded her that they had a nice visitor yesterday, a young man selling Bibles. "Lord," she said, "he bored me to death but he was so sincere and genuine I couldn't be rude to him. He was just good country people, you know," she said, "—just the salt of the earth."

"I seen him walk up," Mrs. Freeman said, "and then later—I seen him walk off," and Hulga could feel the slight shift in her voice, the slight insinuation, that he had not walked off alone, had he? Her face remained expressionless but the color rose into her neck and she seemed to swallow it down with the next spoonful of egg. Mrs. Freeman was looking at her as if they had a secret together.

"Well, it takes all kinds of people to make the world go 'round," Mrs. Hopewell said. "It's very good we aren't all alike."

"Some people are more alike than others," Mrs. Freeman said.

Hulga got up and stumped, with about twice the noise that was necessary, into her room and locked the door. She was to meet the Bible salesman at ten o'clock at the gate. She had thought about it half the night. She had started thinking of it as a great joke and then she had begun to see profound implications in it. She had lain in bed imagining dialogues for them that were insane on the surface but that reached below to depths that no Bible salesman would be aware of. Their conversation yesterday had been of this kind.

He had stopped in front of her and had simply stood there. His face was bony and sweaty and bright, with a little pointed nose in the center of it, and his look was different from what it had been at the dinner table. He was gazing at her with open curiosity, with fascination, like a child watching a new fantastic animal at the zoo, and he was breathing as if he had run a great distance to reach her. His gaze seemed somehow familiar but she could not think where she had been regarded with it before. For almost a minute he didn't say anything. Then on what seemed an insuck of breath, he whispered, "You ever ate a chicken that was two days old?"

The girl looked at him stonily. He might have just put this question up for consideration at the meeting of a philosophical association. "Yes," she presently replied as if she had considered it from all angles.

"It must have been mighty small!" he said triumphantly and shook all over with little nervous giggles, getting very red in the face, and subsiding finally into his gaze of complete admiration, while the girl's expression remained exactly the same.

"How old are you?" he asked softly.

She waited some time before she answered. Then in a flat voice she said, "Seventeen."

His smiles came in succession like waves breaking on the surface of a little lake. "I see you got a wooden leg," he said. "I think you're real brave. I think you're real sweet."

The girl stood blank and solid and silent.

"Walk to the gate with me," he said. "You're a brave sweet little thing and I liked you the minute I seen you walk in the door."

Hulga began to move forward.

"What's your name?" he asked, smiling down on the top of her head.

"Hulga," she said.

"Hulga," he murmured, "Hulga. Hulga. I never heard of anybody name Hulga before. You're shy, aren't you, Hulga?" he asked.

She nodded, watching his large red hand on the handle of the giant valise.

"I like girls that wear glasses," he said. "I think a lot. I'm not like these people that a serious thought don't ever enter their heads. It's because I may die."

"I may die too," she said suddenly and looked up at him. His eyes were very small and brown, glittering feverishly.

"Listen," he said, "don't you think some people was meant to meet on account of what all they got in common and all? Like they both think serious thoughts and all?" He shifted the valise to his other hand so that the hand nearest her was free. He caught hold of her elbow and shook it a little. "I don't work on Saturday," he said. "I like to walk in the woods and see what Mother Nature is wearing. O'er the hills and far away. Pic-nics and things. Couldn't we go on a pic-nic tomorrow? Say yes, Hulga," he said and gave her a dying look as if he felt his insides about to drop out of him. He had even seemed to sway slightly toward her.

During the night she had imagined that she seduced him. She imagined that the two of them walked on the place until they came to the storage barn beyond the two back fields and there, she imagined, that things came to such a pass that she very easily seduced him and that then, of course, she had to reckon with his remorse. True genius can get an idea across even to an inferior mind. She imagined that she took his remorse in hand and changed it into a deeper understanding of life. She took all his shame away and turned it into something useful.

She set off for the gate at exactly ten o'clock, escaping without drawing Mrs. Hopewell's attention. She didn't take anything to eat, forgetting that food is usually taken on a picnic. She wore a pair of slacks and a dirty white shirt, and as an afterthought, she had put some Vapex on the collar of it since she did not own any perfume. When she reached the gate no one was there.

She looked up and down the empty highway and had the furious feeling that she had been tricked, that he had only meant to make her walk to the gate after the idea of him. Then suddenly he stood up, very tall, from behind a bush on the opposite embankment. Smiling, he lifted his hat which was new and wide-brimmed. He had not worn it yesterday and she wondered if he had bought it for the occasion. It was toast-colored with a red and white band around it and was slightly too large for him. He stepped from behind the bush still carrying the black valise. He had on the same suit and the same yellow socks sucked down in his shoes from walking. He crossed the highway and said, "I knew you'd come!"

The girl wondered acidly how he had known this. She pointed to the valise and asked, "Why did you bring your Bibles?"

He took her elbow, smiling down on her as if he could not stop. "You can never tell when you'll need the word of God, Hulga," he said. She had a moment in which she doubted that this was actually happening and then they began to climb the embankment. They went down into the pasture toward the woods. The boy walked lightly by her side, bouncing on his toes. The valise did not seem to be heavy today; he even swung it. They crossed half the pasture without saying anything and then, putting his hand easily on the small of her back, he asked softly, "Where does your wooden leg join on?"

She turned an ugly red and glared at him and for an instant the boy looked abashed. "I didn't mean you no harm," he said. "I only meant you're so brave and all. I guess God takes care of you."

"No," she said, looking forward and walking fast, "I don't even believe in God."

At this he stopped and whistled. "No!" he exclaimed as if he were too astonished to say anything else.

She walked on and in a second he was bouncing at her side, fanning with his hat. "That's very unusual for a girl," he remarked, watching her out of the corner of his eye. When they reached the edge of the wood, he put his hand on her back again and drew her against him without a word and kissed her heavily.

The kiss, which had more pressure than feeling behind it, produced that extra surge of adrenalin in the girl that enables one to carry a packed trunk out of a burning house, but in her, the power went at once to the brain. Even before he released her, her mind, clear and detached and ironic anyway, was regarding him from a great distance, with amusement but with pity. She had never been kissed before and she was pleased to discover that it was an unexceptional experience and all a matter of the mind's control. Some people might enjoy drain water if they were told it was vodka. When the boy, looking expectant but uncertain, pushed her gently away, she turned and walked on, saying nothing as if such business, for her, were common enough.

He came along panting at her side, trying to help her when he saw a root that she might trip over. He caught and held back the long swaying blades of thorn vine until she had passed beyond them. She led the way and he came breathing heavily behind her. Then they came out on a sunlit hillside, sloping softly into another one a little smaller. Beyond, they could see the rusted top of the old barn where the extra hay was stored.

The hill was sprinkled with small pink weeds. "Then you ain't saved?" he asked suddenly, stopping.

The girl smiled. It was the first time she had smiled at him at all. "In my economy," she said, "I'm saved and you are damned but I told you I didn't believe in God."

Nothing seemed to destroy the boy's look of admiration. He gazed at her now as if the fantastic animal at the zoo had put its paw through the bars and given him a loving poke. She thought he looked as if he wanted to kiss her again and she walked on before he had the chance.

"Ain't there somewheres we can sit down sometime?" he murmured, his voice softening toward the end of the sentence.

"In that barn," she said.

They made for it rapidly as if it might slide away like a train. It was a large two-story barn, cool and dark inside. The boy pointed up the ladder that led into the loft and said, "It's too bad we can't go up there."

"Why can't we?" she asked.

"Yer leg," he said reverently.

The girl gave him a contemptuous look and putting both hands on the ladder, she climbed it while he stood below, apparently awestruck. She pulled herself expertly through the opening and then looked down at him and said, "Well, come on if you're coming," and he began to climb the ladder, awkwardly bringing the suitcase with him.

"We won't need the Bible," she observed.

"You never can tell," he said, panting. After he had got into the loft, he was a few seconds catching his breath. She had sat down in a pile of straw. A wide sheath of sunlight, filled with dust particles, slanted over her. She lay back against a bale, her face turned away, looking out the front opening of the barn where hay was thrown from a wagon into the loft. The two pink-speckled hillsides lay back against a dark ridge of woods. The sky was cloudless and cold blue. The boy dropped down by her side and put one arm under her and the other over her and began methodically kissing her face, making little noises like a fish. He did not remove his hat but it was pushed far enough back not to interfere. When her glasses got in his way, he took them off of her and slipped them into his pocket.

The girl at first did not return any of the kisses but presently she began to and after she had put several on his cheek, she reached his lips and remained there, kissing him again and again as if she were trying to draw all the breath out of him. His breath was clear and sweet like a child's and the kisses were sticky like a child's. He mumbled about loving her and about knowing when he first seen her that he loved her, but the mumbling was like the sleepy fretting of a child being put to sleep by his mother. Her mind, throughout this, never stopped or lost itself for a second to her feelings. "You ain't said you love me none," he whispered finally, pulling back from her. "You got to say that."

She looked away from him off into the hollow sky and then down at a black ridge and then down farther into what appeared to be two green swelling lakes. She didn't realize he had taken her glasses but this landscape could not seem exceptional to her for she seldom paid any close attention to her surroundings.

"You got to say it," he repeated. "You got to say you love me."

She was always careful how she committed herself. "In a sense," she began, "if you use the word loosely, you might say that. But it's not a word I use. I don't have illusions. I'm one of those people who see *through* to nothing."

The boy was frowning. "You got to say it. I said it and you got to say it," he said.

The girl looked at him almost tenderly. "You poor baby," she murmured. "It's just as well you don't understand," and she pulled him by the neck, facedown, against her. "We are all damned," she said, "but some of us have taken off our blindfolds and see that there's nothing to see. It's a kind of salvation."

The boy's astonished eyes looked blankly through the ends of her hair. "Okay," he almost whined, "but do you love me or don'tcher?"

"Yes," she said and added, "in a sense. But I must tell you something. There mustn't be anything dishonest between us." She lifted his head and looked him in the eye. "I am thirty years old," she said. "I have a number of degrees."

The boy's look was irritated but dogged. "I don't care," he said. "I don't care a thing about what all you done. I just want to know if you love me or don'tcher?" and he caught her to him and wildly planted her face with kisses until she said, "Yes, yes."

"Okay then," he said, letting her go. "Prove it."

She smiled, looking dreamily out on the shifty landscape. She had seduced him without even making up her mind to try. "How?" she asked, feeling that he should be delayed a little.

He leaned over and put his lips to her ear. "Show me where your wooden leg joins on," he whispered.

The girl uttered a sharp little cry and her face instantly drained of color. The obscenity of the suggestion was not what shocked her. As a child she had sometimes been subject to feelings of shame but education had removed the last traces of that as a good surgeon scrapes for cancer; she would no more have felt it over what he was asking than she would have believed in his Bible. But she was as sensitive about the artificial leg as a peacock about his tail. No one ever touched it but her. She took care of it as someone else would his soul, in private and almost with her own eyes turned away. "No," she said.

"I known it," he muttered, sitting up. "You're just playing me for a sucker."

"Oh no no!" she cried. "It joins on at the knee. Only at the knee. Why do you want to see it?"

The boy gave her a long penetrating look. "Because," he said, "it's what makes you different. You ain't like anybody else."

She sat staring at him. There was nothing about her face or her round freezing-blue eyes to indicate that this had moved her; but she felt as if her heart had stopped and left her mind to pump her blood. She decided that for the first time in her life she was face to face with real innocence. This boy, with an instinct that came from beyond wisdom, had touched the truth about her. When after a minute, she said in a hoarse high voice, "All right," it was like surrendering to him completely. It was like losing her own life and finding it again, miraculously, in his.

Very gently he began to roll the slack leg up. The artificial limb, in a white sock and brown flat shoe, was bound in a heavy material like canvas and ended in an ugly jointure where it was attached to the stump. The boy's face and his voice were entirely reverent as he uncovered it and said, "Now show me how to take it off and on."

She took it off for him and put it back on again and then he took it off himself, handling it as tenderly as if it were a real one. "See!" he said with a delighted child's face. "Now I can do it myself!"

"Put it back on," she said. She was thinking that she would run away with him and that every night he would take the leg off and every morning put it back on again. "Put it back on," she said.

"Not yet," he murmured, setting it on its foot out of her reach. "Leave it off for a while. You got me instead."

She gave a little cry of alarm but he pushed her down and began to kiss her again. Without the leg she felt entirely dependent on him. Her brain seemed to have stopped thinking altogether and to be about some other function that it was not very good at. Different expressions raced back and forth over her face. Every now and then the boy, his eyes like two steel spikes, would glance behind him where the leg stood. Finally she pushed him off and said, "Put it back on me now."

"Wait," he said. He leaned the other way and pulled the valise toward him and opened it. It had a pale blue spotted lining and there were only two Bibles in it. He took one of these out and opened the cover of it. It was hollow and contained a pocket flask of whiskey, a pack of cards, and a small blue box with printing on it. He laid these out in front of her one at a time in an evenly spaced row, like one presenting offerings at the shrine of a goddess. He put the blue box in her hand. THIS PRODUCT TO BE USED ONLY FOR THE PREVENTION OF DISEASE, she read, and dropped it. The boy was unscrewing the top of the flask. He stopped and pointed, with a smile, to the deck of cards. It was not an ordinary deck but one with an obscene picture on the back of each card. "Take a swig," he said, offering her the bottle first. He held it in front of her, but like one mesmerized, she did not move.

Her voice when she spoke had an almost pleading sound. "Aren't you," she murmured, "aren't you just good country people?"

The boy cocked his head. He looked as if he were just beginning to understand that she might be trying to insult him. "Yeah," he said, curling his lip slightly, "but it ain't held me back none. I'm as good as you any day in the week."

"Give me my leg," she said.

He pushed it farther away with his foot. "Come on now, let's begin to have us a good time," he said coaxingly. "We ain't got to know one another good yet."

"Give me my leg!" she screamed and tried to lunge for it but he pushed her down easily.

"What's the matter with you all of a sudden?" he asked, frowning as he screwed the top on the flask and put it quickly back inside the Bible. "You just a while ago said you didn't believe in nothing. I thought you was some girl!"

Her face was almost purple. "You're a Christian!" she hissed. "You're a fine Christian! You're just like them all—say one thing and do another. You're a perfect Christian, you're . . ."

The boy's mouth was set angrily. "I hope you don't think," he said in a lofty indignant tone, "that I believe in that crap! I may sell Bibles but I know which end is up and I wasn't born yesterday and I know where I'm going!"

"Give me my leg!" she screeched. He jumped up so quickly that she barely saw him sweep the cards and the blue box back into the Bible and throw the Bible into the valise. She saw him grab the leg and then she saw it for an instant slanted forlornly across the inside of the suitcase with a Bible at either side of its opposite ends. He slammed the lid shut and snatched up the valise and swung it down the hole and then stepped through himself.

When all of him had passed but his head, he turned and regarded her with a look that no longer had any admiration in it. "I've gotten a lot of interesting things," he said. "One time I got a woman's glass eye this way. And you needn't to think you'll catch me because Pointer ain't really my name. I use a different name at every house I call at and don't stay nowhere long. And I'll tell you another thing, Hulga," he said, using the name as if he didn't think much of it, "you ain't so smart. I been believing in nothing ever since I was born!" and then the toast-colored hat disappeared down the hole and the girl was left, sitting on the straw in the dusty sunlight. When she turned her churning face toward the opening, she saw his blue figure struggling successfully over the green speckled lake.

Mrs. Hopewell and Mrs. Freeman, who were in the back pasture, digging up onions, saw him emerge a little later from the woods and head across the meadow toward the highway. "Why, that looks like that nice dull young man that tried to sell me a Bible yesterday," Mrs. Hopewell said, squinting. "He must have been selling them to the Negroes back in there. He was so simple," she said, "but I guess the world would be better off if we were all that simple."

Mrs. Freeman's gaze drove forward and just touched him before he disappeared under the hill. Then she returned her attention to the evil-smelling onion shoot she was lifting from the ground. "Some can't be that simple," she said. "I know I never could."

Writing Assignments for "Good Country People"

I. Brief Papers
  A. 1. Make a list of the clichés or common sayings in the story and explain what they have in common.
  2. Explain the purpose of either the first or last paragraph.
  3. Explain the significance of one or more of the characters' names: Mrs. Freeman, Mrs. Hopewell, Joy-Hulga, Manley Pointer.
  4. Point out several early hints that Manley Pointer is not the simple and innocent fellow that he pretends to be.
  5. What view of higher education emerges from the story?

B. Argue for or against one of the assertions below:
   1. Manley Pointer is the devil in disguise.
   2. Manley Pointer is Jesus Christ in disguise.
   3. Joy-Hulga is deceiving herself when she claims to believe in nothing.
   4. Joy-Hulga's statement that "True genius can get an idea across even to an inferior mind" (p. 304) summarizes an important meaning of the story.
   5. The story endorses Mrs. Hopewell's view of life.

C. 1. What in the story made you laugh? Why?
   2. Do you think that Joy-Hulga's experience with Manley Pointer is likely to change her in any way?
   3. At what point in the story do you feel most sympathy for Joy-Hulga? Why?
   4. How do you react to the passage on "Nothing" that Mrs. Hopewell reads in Joy-Hulga's book (p. 299)?
   5. The poet Robert Lowell writes, "I find it hard to think of a funnier or more frightening writer" than Flannery O'Connor. Do you agree that "Good Country People" is both funny and frightening?

II. Longer Papers

A. Develop one of your paragraphs into a full-length paper.
B. There are many references in "Good Country People" to eyes and blindfolds and blindness. What does the story say about "seeing"?
C. Since the story focuses on an episode involving Joy-Hulga and Manley Pointer, try to explain the presence of Mrs. Hopewell and Mrs. Freeman. (One reader thinks the story would improve if its last two paragraphs were eliminated. What do you think?)
D. Characterize the tone of "Good Country People." Is it an optimistic and affirmative story? Depressing and pessimistic? A mixture? How does the story's humor contribute to its tone?
E. "Good Country People" appeared in a collection of Flannery O'Connor stories that O'Connor herself describes as "stories about original sin." Explain in what sense "Good Country People" is "about original sin."
F. One reader has written that "O'Connor's stories are all about the operation of supernatural grace in the lives of natural men and women." Argue for or against the assertion that this statement applies to "Good Country People."

III. Comparative Papers

A. Explain why you believe either "The Cask of Amontillado" or "Good Country People" to be more effective than the other in communicating a sense of the mysterious, the unpredictable, and perhaps even the inexplicable in human experience.
B. Argue for or against the assertion that, taken together, "Good Country People" and "The Cask of Amontillado" show that by nature human beings are evil.
C. Taken together, what do "Good Country People" and "The Cask of Amontillado" say about the human capacity for self-deception?

D. Compare the use of irony in "Good Country People" and in "The Cask of Amontillado" in order to explain whether or not irony functions in essentially the same or in different ways in the two stories.

E. At one point in "Good Country People" Joy-Hulga boasts, "I don't have illusions" (p. 306). On the basis of this story and several others of your choice, explain which illusions—according to the writers of fiction—people are most likely to hold.

F. That Joy-Hulga has two names may suggest that she also has two selves or two natures. On the basis of "Good Country People" and other stories of your choice, explain whether short story writers tend to depict human beings as inevitably and permanently divided into two hostile, warring, and thoroughly incompatible parts.

ERNEST J. GAINES
The Sky Is Gray

Before Reading

Do you think children of the poor need to be taught in different ways than children of the well-to-do? Free write on this question for 5 or 10 minutes.

I

Go'n be coming in a few minutes. Coming round that bend down there full speed. And I'm go'n get out my handkerchief and wave it down, and we go'n get on it and go.

I keep on looking for it, but Mama don't look that way no more. She's looking down the road where we just come from. It's a long old road, and far 's you can see you don't see nothing but gravel. You got dry weeds on both sides, and you got trees on both sides, and fences on both sides, too. And you got cows in the pastures and they standing close together. And when we was coming out here to catch the bus I seen the smoke coming out of the cows's noses.

I look at my mama and I know what she's thinking. I been with Mama so much, just me and her, I know what she's thinking all the time. Right now it's home—Auntie and them. She's thinking if they got enough wood—if she left enough there to keep them warm till we get back. She's thinking if it go'n rain and if any of them go'n have to go out in the rain. She's thinking 'bout the hog—if he go'n get out, and if Ty and Val be able to get him back in. She always worry like that when she leaves the house. She don't worry too much if she leave me there with the smaller ones, 'cause she know I'm go'n look after them and look after Auntie and everything else. I'm the oldest and she say I'm the man.

I look at my mama and I love my mama. She's wearing that black coat and that black hat and she's looking sad. I love my mama and I want put my arm round her and tell her. But I'm not supposed to do that. She say that's weakness and that's crybaby stuff, and she don't want no crybaby round her. She don't want you to be scared, either. 'Cause Ty's scared of ghosts and she's always whipping him. I'm scared of the dark, too, but I make 'tend I ain't. I make 'tend I ain't 'cause I'm the oldest, and I got to set a good sample for the rest. I can't ever be scared and I can't ever cry. And that's why I never said nothing 'bout my teeth. It's been hurting me and hurting me close to a month now, but I never said it. I didn't say it 'cause I didn't want act like a crybaby, and 'cause I know

THE SKY IS GRAY   First published in 1963. Ernest J. Gaines was born in 1933 in the bayou country of Louisiana, a complex region of white, black, Cajun, and Creole communities which Gaines has drawn on for the setting of all his writings.

we didn't have enough money to go have it pulled. But, Lord, it been hurting me. And look like it wouldn't start till at night when you was trying to get yourself little sleep. Then soon 's you shut your eyes—ummm-ummm, Lord, look like it go right down to your heartstring.

"Hurting, hanh?' Ty'd say.

I'd shake my head, but—I wouldn't open my mouth for nothing. You open your mouth and let that wind in, and it almost kill you.

I'd just lay there and listen to them snore. Ty there, right 'side me, and Auntie and Val over by the fireplace. Val younger than me and Ty, and he sleeps with Auntie. Mama sleeps round the other side with Louis and Walker.

I'd just lay there and listen to them, and listen to that wind out there, and listen to that fire in the fireplace. Sometimes it'd stop long enough to let me get little rest. Sometimes it just hurt, hurt, hurt. Lord, have mercy.

2

Auntie knowed it was hurting me. I didn't tell nobody but Ty, 'cause we buddies and he ain't go'n tell nobody. But some kind of way Auntie found out. When she asked me, I told her no, nothing was wrong. But she knowed it all the time. She told me to mash up a piece of aspirin and wrap it in some cotton and jugg it down in that hole. I did it, but it didn't do no good. It stopped for a little while, and started right back again. Auntie wanted to tell Mama, but I told her, "Uh-uh." 'Cause I knowed we didn't have any money, and it just was go'n make her mad again. So Auntie told Monsieur Bayonne, and Monsieur Bayonne came over to the house and told me to kneel down 'side him on the fireplace. He put his finger in his mouth and made the Sign of the Cross on my jaw. The tip of Monsieur Bayonne's finger is some hard, 'cause he's always playing on that guitar. If we sit outside at night we can always hear Monsieur Bayonne playing on his guitar. Sometimes we leave him out there playing on the guitar.

Monsieur Bayonne made the Sign of the Cross over and over on my jaw, but that didn't do no good. Even when he prayed and told me to pray some, too, that tooth still hurt me.

"How you feeling?" he say.

"Same," I say.

He kept on praying and making the Sign of the Cross and I kept on praying, too.

"Still hurting?" he say.

"Yes, sir."

Monsieur Bayonne mashed harder and harder on my jaw. He mashed so hard he almost pushed me over on Ty. But then he stopped.

"What kind of prayers you praying, boy?" he say.

"Baptist," I say.

"Well, I'll be—no wonder that tooth still killing him. I'm going one way and he pulling the other. Boy, don't you know any Catholic prayers?"

"I know 'Hail Mary,' " I say.

"Then you better start saying it."

"Yes, sir."

He started mashing on my jaw again, and I could hear him praying at the same time. And, sure enough, after while it stopped hurting me.

Me and Ty went outside where Monsieur Bayonne's two hounds was and we started playing with them. "Let's go hunting," Ty say. "All right," I say; and we went on back in the pasture. Soon the hounds got on a trail, and me and Ty followed them all 'cross the pasture and then back in the woods, too. And then they cornered this little old rabbit and killed him, and me and Ty made them get back, and we picked up the rabbit and started on back home. But my tooth had started hurting me again. It was hurting me plenty now, but I wouldn't tell Monsieur Bayonne. That night I didn't sleep a bit, and first thing in the morning Auntie told me to go back and let Monsieur Bayonne pray over me some more. Monsieur Bayonne was in his kitchen making coffee when I got there. Soon 's he seen me he knowed what was wrong.

"All right, kneel down there 'side that stove," he say. "And this time make sure you pray Catholic. I don't know nothing 'bout that Baptist, and I don't want know nothing 'bout him."

3

Last night Mama say, "Tomorrow we going to town."

"It ain't hurting me no more," I say. "I can eat anything on it."

"Tomorrow we going to town," she say.

And after she finished eating, she got up and went to bed. She always go to bed early now. 'Fore Daddy went in the Army, she used to stay up late. All of us sitting out on the gallery or round the fire. But now, look like soon 's she finish eating she go to bed.

This morning when I woke up, her and Auntie was standing 'fore the fireplace. She say: "Enough to get there and get back. Dollar and a half to have it pulled. Twenty-five for me to go, twenty-five for him. Twenty-five for me to come back, twenty-five for him. Fifty cents left. Guess I get little piece of salt meat with that."

"Sure can use it," Auntie say. "White beans and no salt meat ain't white beans."

"I do the best I can," Mama say.

They was quiet after that, and I made 'tend I was still asleep.

"James, hit the floor," Auntie say.

I still made 'tend I was asleep. I didn't want them to know I was listening.

"All right," Auntie say, shaking me by the shoulder. "Come on. Today's the day."

I pushed the cover down to get out, and Ty grabbed it and pulled it back.

"You, too, Ty," Auntie say.

"I ain't getting no teef pulled," Ty say.

"Don't mean it ain't time to get up," Auntie say. "Hit it, Ty."

Ty got up grumbling.

"James, you hurry up and get in your clothes and eat your food," Auntie say. "What time y'all coming back?" she say to Mama.

"That 'leven o'clock bus," Mama say. "Got to get back in that field this evening."

"Get a move on you, James," Auntie say.

I went in the kitchen and washed my face, then I ate my breakfast. I was having bread and syrup. The bread was warm and hard and tasted good. And I tried to make it last a long time.

Ty came back there grumbling and mad at me.

"Got to get up," he say. "I ain't having no teefes pulled. What I got to be getting up for?"

Ty poured some syrup in his pan and got a piece of bread. He didn't wash his hands, neither his face, and I could see that white stuff in his eyes.

"You the one getting your teef pulled," he say. "What I got to get up for. I bet if I was getting a teef pulled, you wouldn't be getting up. Shucks; syrup again. I'm getting tired of this old syrup. Syrup, syrup, syrup. I'm go'n take with the sugar diabetes. I want me some bacon sometime."

"Go out in the field and work and you can have your bacon," Auntie say. She stood in the middle door looking at Ty. "You better be glad you got syrup. Some people ain't got that—hard's time is."

"Shucks," Ty say. "How can I be strong."

"I don't know too much 'bout your strength," Auntie say; "but I know where you go'n be hot at, you keep that grumbling up. James, get a move on you; your mama waiting."

I ate my last piece of bread and went in the front room. Mama was standing 'fore the fireplace warming her hands. I put on my coat and my cap, and we left the house.

4

I look down there again, but it still ain't coming. I almost say, "It ain't coming yet," but I keep my mouth shut. 'Cause that's something else she don't like. She don't like for you to say something just for nothing. She can see it ain't coming, I can see it ain't coming, so why say it ain't coming. I don't say it, I turn and look at the river that's back of us. It's so cold the smoke's just raising up from the water. I see a bunch of pool-doos not too far out—just on the other side the lilies. I'm wondering if you can eat pool-doos. I ain't too sure, 'cause I ain't never ate none. But I done ate owls and blackbirds, and I done ate redbirds, too. I didn't want kill the redbirds, but she made me kill them. They had two of them back there. One in my trap, one in Ty's trap. Me and Ty was go'n play with them and let them go, but she made me kill them 'cause we needed the food.

"I can't," I say. "I can't."

"Here," she say. "Take it."

"I can't," I say. "I can't. I can't kill him, Mama, please."

"Here," she say. "Take this fork, James."

"Please, Mama, I can't kill him," I say.

I could tell she was go'n hit me. I jerked back, but I didn't jerk back soon enough.

"Take it," she say.

I took it and reached in for him, but he kept on hopping to the back.

"I can't, Mama," I say. The water just kept on running down my face. "I can't," I say.

"Get him out of there," she say.

I reached in for him and he kept on hopping to the back. Then I reached in farther, and he pecked me on the hand.

"I can't, Mama," I say.

She slapped me again.

I reached in again, but he kept on hopping out my way. Then he hopped to one side and I reached there. The fork got him on the leg and I heard his leg pop. I pulled my hand out 'cause I had hurt him.

"Give it here," she say, and jerked the fork out my hand.

She reached in and got the little bird right in the neck. I heard the fork go in his neck, and I heard it go in the ground. She brought him out and helt him right in front of me.

"That's one," she say. She shook him off and gived me the fork. "Get the other one."

"I can't, Mama," I say. "I'll do anything, but don't make me do that."

She went to the corner of the fence and broke the biggest switch over there she could find. I knelt 'side the trap, crying.

"Get him out of there," she say.

"I can't, Mama."

She started hitting me 'cross the back. I went down on the ground, crying.

"Get him," she say.

"Octavia?" Auntie say.

'Cause she had come out of the house and she was standing by the tree looking at us.

"Get him out of there," Mama say.

"Octavia," Auntie say, "explain to him. Explain to him. Just don't beat him. Explain to him."

But she hit me and hit me and hit me.

I'm still young—I ain't no more than eight; but I know now; I know why I had to do it. (They was so little, though. They was so little. I 'member how I picked the feathers off them and cleaned them and helt them over the fire. Then we all ate them. Ain't had but a little bitty piece each, but we all had a little bitty piece, and everybody just looked at me 'cause they was so proud.) Suppose she had to go away? That's why I had to do it. Suppose she had to go away like Daddy went away? Then who was go'n look after us? They had to be somebody left to carry on. I didn't know it then, but I know it now. Auntie and Monsieur Bayonne talked to me and made me see.

5

Time I see it I get out my handkerchief and start waving. It's still 'way down there, but I keep waving anyhow. Then it come up and stop and me and Mama get on. Mama tell me go sit in the back while she pay. I do like she say, and the people look at me. When I pass the little sign that say "White" and "Colored," I start looking for a seat. I just see one of them back there, but I don't take it, 'cause I want my mama to sit down herself. She comes in the back and sit down, and I lean on the seat. They got seats in the front, but I know I can't sit there, 'cause I have to sit back of the sign. Anyhow, I don't want sit there if my mama go'n sit back here.

They got a lady sitting 'side my mama and she looks at me and smiles little bit. I smile back, but I don't open my mouth, 'cause the wind'll get in and make that tooth ache. The lady take out a pack of gum and reach me a slice, but I shake my head. The lady just can't understand why a little boy'll turn down gum, and she reach me a slice again. This time I point to my jaw. The lady understands and smiles little bit, and I smile little bit, but I don't open my mouth, though.

They got a girl sitting 'cross from me. She got on a red overcoat and her hair's plaited in one big plait. First, I make 'tend I don't see her over there, but then I start looking at her little bit. She make 'tend she don't see me, either, but I catch her looking that way. She got a cold, and every now and then she h'ist that little handkerchief to her nose. She ought to blow it, but she don't. Must think she's too much a lady or something.

Every time she h'ist that little handkerchief, the lady 'side her say something in her ear. She shakes her head and lays her hands in her lap again. Then I catch her kind of looking where I'm at. I smile at her little bit. But think she'll smile back? Uh-uh. She just turn up her little old nose and turn her head. Well, I show her both of us can turn us head. I turn mine too and look out at the river.

The river is gray. The sky is gray. They have pool-doos on the water. The water is wavy, and the pool-doos go up and down. The bus go round a turn, and you got plenty trees hiding the river. Then the bus go round another turn, and I can see the river again.

I look toward the front where all the white people sitting. Then I look at that little old gal again. I don't look right at her, 'cause I don't want all them people to know I love her. I just look at her little bit, like I'm looking out that window over there. But she knows I'm looking that way, and she kind of look at me, too. The lady sitting 'side her catch her this time, and she leans over and says something in her ear.

"I don't love him nothing," that little old gal says out loud.

Everybody back there hear her mouth, and all of them look at us and laugh.

"I don't love you, either," I say. "So you don't have to turn up your nose, Miss."

"You the one looking," she say.

"I wasn't looking at you," I say. "I was looking out that window, there."

"Out that window, my foot," she say. "I seen you. Everytime I turned round you was looking at me."

"You must of been looking yourself if you seen me all them times," I say.

"Shucks," she say, "I got me all kind of boyfriends."

"I got girlfriends, too," I say.

"Well, I just don't want you getting your hopes up," she say.

I don't say no more to that little old gal 'cause I don't want have to bust her in the mouth. I lean on the seat where Mama sitting, and I don't even look that way no more. When we get to Bayonne, she jugg her little old tongue out at me. I make 'tend I'm go'n hit her, and she duck down 'side her mama. And all the people laugh at us again.

6

Me and Mama get off and start walking in town. Bayonne is a little bitty town. Baton Rouge is a hundred times bigger than Bayonne. I went to Baton Rouge once—me, Ty, Mama, and Daddy. But that was 'way back yonder, 'fore Daddy went in the Army. I wonder when we go'n see him again. I wonder when. Look like he ain't ever coming back home. . . . Even the pavement all cracked in Bayonne. Got grass shooting right out the sidewalk. Got weeds in the ditch, too; just like they got at home.

It's some cold in Bayonne. Look like it's colder than it is home. The wind blows in my face, and I feel that stuff running down my nose. I sniff. Mama says use that handkerchief. I blow my nose and put it back.

We pass a school and I see them white children playing in the yard. Big old red school, and them children just running and playing. Then we pass a café, and I see a bunch of people in there eating. I wish I was in there 'cause I'm cold. Mama tells me keep my eyes in front where they belong.

We pass stores that's got dummies, and we pass another café, and then we pass a shoe shop, and that bald-head man in there fixing on a shoe. I look at him and I butt into that white lady, and Mama jerks me in front and tells me stay there.

We come up to the courthouse, and I see the flag waving there. This flag ain't like the one we got at school. This one here ain't got but a handful of stars. One at school got a big pile of stars—one for every state. We pass it and we turn and there it is—the dentist office. Me and Mama go in, and they got people sitting everywhere you look. They even got a little boy in there younger than me.

Me and Mama sit on that bench, and a white lady come in there and ask me what my name is. Mama tells her and the white lady goes on back. Then I hear somebody hollering in there. Soon 's that little boy hear him hollering, he starts hollering, too. His mama pats him and pats him, trying to make him hush up, but he ain't thinking 'bout his mama.

The man that was hollering in there comes out holding his jaw. He is a big old man and he's wearing overalls and a jumper.

"Got it, hanh?" another man asks him.

The man shakes his head—don't want open his mouth.

"Man, I thought they was killing you in there," the other man says. "Hollering like a pig under a gate."

The man don't say nothing. He just heads for the door, and the other man follows him.

"John Lee," the white lady says. "John Lee Williams."

The little boy juggs his head down in his mama's lap and holler more now. His mama tells him go with the nurse, but he ain't thinking 'bout his mama. His mama tells him again, but he don't even hear her. His mama picks him up and takes him in there, and even when the white lady shuts the door I can still hear little old John Lee.

"I often wonder why the Lord let a child like that suffer," a lady says to my mama. The lady's sitting right in front of us on another bench. She's got on a white dress and a black sweater. She must be a nurse or something herself, I reckon.

"Not us to question," a man says.

"Sometimes I don't know if we shouldn't," the lady says.

"I know definitely we shouldn't," the man says. The man looks like a preacher. He's big and fat and he's got on a black suit. He's got a gold chain, too.

"Why?" the lady says.

"Why anything?" the preacher says.

"Yes," the lady says. "Why anything?"

"Not us to question," the preacher says.

The lady looks at the preacher a little while and looks at Mama again.

"And look like it's the poor who suffers the most," she says. "I don't understand it."

"Best not to even try," the preacher says. "He works in mysterious ways—wonders to perform."

Right then little John Lee bust out hollering, and everybody turn they head to listen.

"He's not a good dentist," the lady says. "Dr. Robillard is much better. But more expensive. That's why most of the colored people come here. The white people go to Dr. Robillard. Y'all from Bayonne?"

"Down the river," my mama says. And that's all she go'n say, 'cause she don't talk much. But the lady keeps on looking at her, and so she says, "Near Morgan."

"I see," the lady says.

7

"That's the trouble with the black people in this country today," somebody else says. This one here's sitting on the same side me and Mama's sitting, and he is kind of sitting in front of that preacher. He looks like a teacher or somebody that goes to college. He's got on a suit, and he's got a book that he's been reading. "We don't question is exactly our problem," he says. "We should question and question and question—question everything."

The preacher just looks at him a long time. He done put a toothpick or something in his mouth, and he just keeps on turning and turning it. You can see he don't like that boy with that book.

"Maybe you can explain what you mean," he says.

"I said what I meant," the boy says. "Question everything. Every stripe, every star, every word spoken. Everything."

"It 'pears to me that this young lady and I was talking 'bout God, young man," the preacher says.

"Question Him, too," the boy says.

"Wait," the preacher says. "Wait now."

"You heard me right," the boy says. "His existence as well as everything else. Everything."

The preacher just looks across the room at the boy. You can see he's getting madder and madder. But mad or no mad, the boy ain't thinking 'bout him. He looks at that preacher just 's hard 's the preacher looks at him.

"Is this what they coming to?" the preacher says. "Is this what we educating them for?"

"You're not educating me," the boy says. "I wash dishes at night so that I can go to school in the day. So even the words you spoke need questioning."

The preacher just looks at him and shakes his head.

"When I come in this room and seen you there with your book, I said to myself, 'There's an intelligent man.' How wrong a person can be."

"Show me one reason to believe in the existence of a God," the boys says.

"My heart tells me," the preacher says.

" 'My heart tells me,' " the boys says. " 'My heart tells me.' Sure, 'My heart tells me.' And as long as you listen to what your heart tells you, you will have only what the white man gives you and nothing more. Me, I don't listen to my heart. The purpose of the heart is to pump blood throughout the body, and nothing else."

"Who's your paw, boy?" the preacher says.

"Why?"

"Who is he?"

"He's dead."

"And your mom?"

"She's in Charity Hospital with pneumonia. Half killed herself, working for nothing."

"And 'cause he's dead and she's sick, you mad at the world?"

"I'm not mad at the world. I'm questioning the world. I'm questioning it with cold logic, sir. What do words like Freedom, Liberty, God, White, Colored mean? I want to know. That's why *you* are sending us to school, to read and to ask questions. And because we ask these questions, you call us mad. No sir, it is not us who are mad."

"You keep saying 'us'?"

" 'Us.' Yes—us. I'm not alone."

The preacher just shakes his head. Then he looks at everybody in the room—everybody. Some of the people look down at the floor, keep from looking at him. I kind of look 'way myself, but soon 's I know he done turn his head, I look that way again.

"I'm sorry for you," he says to the boy.

"Why?" the boy says. "Why not be sorry for yourself? Why are you so much better off than I am? Why aren't you sorry for these other people in here? Why not be sorry for the lady who had to drag her child into the dentist office? Why not be sorry for the lady sitting on that bench over there? Be sorry for them. Not for me. Some way or the other I'm going to make it."

"No, I'm sorry for you," the preacher says.

"Of course, of course," the boy says, nodding his head. "You're sorry for me because I rock that pillar you're leaning on."

"You can't ever rock the pillar I'm leaning on, young man. It's stronger than anything man can ever do."

"You believe in God because a man told you to believe in God," the boy says. "A white man told you to believe in God. And why? To keep you ignorant so he can keep his feet on your neck."

"So now we the ignorant?" the preacher says.

"Yes," the boy says. "Yes." And he opens his book again.

The preacher just looks at him sitting there. The boy done forgot all about him. Everybody else make 'tend they done forgot the squabble, too.

Then I see that preacher getting up real slow. Preacher's a great big old man and he got to brace himself to get up. He comes over where the boy is sitting. He just stands there a little while looking down at him, but the boy don't raise his head.

"Get up, boy," preacher says.

The boy looks up at him, then he shuts his book real slow and stands up. Preacher just hauls back and hit him in the face. The boy falls back 'gainst the wall, but he straightens himself up and looks right back at that preacher.

"You forgot the other cheek," he says.

The preacher hauls back and hit him again on the other side. But this time the boy braces himself and don't fall.

"That hasn't changed a thing," he says.

The preacher just looks at the boy. The preacher's breathing real hard like he just run up a big hill. The boy sits down and opens his book again.

"I feel sorry for you," the preacher says. "I never felt so sorry for a man before."

The boy makes 'tend he don't even hear that preacher. He keeps on reading his book. The preacher goes back and gets his hat off the chair.

"Excuse me," he says to us. "I'll come back some other time. Y'all, please excuse me."

And he looks at the boy and goes out the room. The boy h'ist his hand up to his mouth one time to wipe 'way some blood. All the rest of the time he keeps on reading. And nobody else in there say a word.

8

Little John Lee and his mama come out the dentist office, and the nurse calls somebody else in. Then little bit later they come out, and the nurse calls another name. But fast 's she calls somebody in there, somebody else comes in the place where we sitting, and the room stays full.

The people coming in now, all of them wearing big coats. One of them says something 'bout sleeting, another one says he hope not. Another one says he think it ain't nothing but rain. 'Cause, he says, rain can get awful cold this time of year.

All round the room they talking. Some of them talking to people right by them, some of them talking to people clear 'cross the room, some of them talking to anybody'll listen. It's a little bitty room, no bigger than us kitchen, and I can see everybody in there. The little old room's full of smoke, 'cause you got two old men smoking pipes over by that side door. I think I feel my tooth thumping me some, and I hold my breath and wait. I wait and wait, but it don't thump me no more. Thank God for that.

I feel like going to sleep, and I lean back 'gainst the wall. But I'm scared to go to sleep. Scared 'cause the nurse might call my name and I won't hear her. And Mama might go to sleep, too, and she'll be mad if neither one of us heard the nurse.

I look up at Mama. I love my mama. I love my mama. And when cotton come I'm go'n get her a new coat. And I ain't go'n get a black one, either. I think I'm go'n get her a red one.

"They got some books over there," I say. "Want read one of them?"

Mama looks at the books, but she don't answer me.

"You got yourself a little man there," the lady says.

Mama don't say nothing to the lady, but she must've smiled, 'cause I seen the lady smiling back. The lady looks at me a little while, like she's feeling sorry for me.

"You sure got that preacher out here in a hurry," she says to that boy.

The boy looks up at her and looks in his book again. When I grow up I want be just like him. I want clothes like that and I want keep a book with me, too.

"You really don't believe in God?" the lady says.

"No," he says.

"But why?" the lady says.

"Because the wind is pink," he says.

"What?" the lady says.

The boy don't answer her no more. He just reads in his book.

"Talking 'bout the wind is pink," that old lady says. She's sitting on the same bench with the boy and she's trying to look in his face. The boy makes 'tend the old lady ain't even there. He just keeps on reading. "Wind is pink," she says again. "Eh, Lord, what children go'n be saying next?"

The lady 'cross from us bust out laughing.

"That's a good one," she says. "The wind is pink. Yes sir, that's a good one."

"Don't you believe the wind is pink?" the boy says. He keeps his head down in the book.

"Course I believe it, honey," the lady says. "Course I do." She looks at us and winks her eye. "And what color is grass, honey?"

"Grass? Grass is black."

She bust out laughing again. The boy looks at her.

"Don't you believe grass is black?" he says.

The lady quits her laughing and looks at him. Everybody else looking at him, too. The place quiet, quiet.

"Grass is green, honey," the lady says. "It was green yesterday, it's green today, and it's go'n be green tomorrow."

"How do you know it's green?"

"I know because I know."

"You don't know it's green," the boy says. "You believe it's green because someone told you it was green. If someone had told you it was black you'd believe it was black."

"It's green," the lady says. "I know green when I see green."

"Prove it's green," the boy says.

"Sure, now," the lady says. "Don't tell me it's coming to that."

"It's coming to just that," the boy says. "Words mean nothing. One means no more than the other."

"That's what it all coming to?" that old lady says. That old lady got on a turban and she got on two sweaters. She got a green sweater under a black sweater. I can see the green sweater 'cause some of the buttons on the other sweater's missing.

"Yes ma'am," the boy says. "Words mean nothing. Action is the only thing. Doing. That's the only thing."

"Other words, you want the Lord to come down here and show Hisself to you?" she says.

"Exactly, ma'am," he says.

"You don't mean that, I'm sure?" she says.

"I do, ma'am," he says.

"Done, Jesus," the old lady says, shaking her head.

"I didn't go 'long with that preacher at first," the other lady says; "but now—I don't know. When a person say the grass is black, he's either a lunatic or something's wrong."

"Prove to me that it's green," the boy says.

"It's green because the people say it's green."

"Those same people say we're citizens of these United States," the boy says.

"I think I'm a citizen," the lady says.

"Citizens have certain rights," the boy says. "Name me one right that you have. One right, granted by the Constitution, that you can exercise in Bayonne."

The lady don't answer him. She just looks at him like she don't know what he's talking 'bout. I know I don't.

"Things changing," she says.

"Things are changing because some black men have begun to think with their brains and not their hearts," the boy says.

"You trying to say these people don't believe in God?"

"I'm sure some of them do. Maybe most of them do. But they don't believe that God is going to touch these white people's hearts and change things tomorrow. Things change through action. By no other way."

Everybody sit quiet and look at the boy. Nobody says a thing. Then the lady 'cross the room from me and Mama just shakes her head.

"Let's hope that not all your generation feel the same way you do," she says.

"Think what you please, it doesn't matter," the boy says. "But it will be men who listen to their heads and not their hearts who will see that your children have a better chance than you had."

"Let's hope they ain't all like you, though," the old lady says. "Done forgot the heart absolutely."

"Yes ma'am, I hope they aren't all like me," the boy says. "Unfortunately, I was born too late to believe in your God. Let's hope that the ones who come after will have your faith—if not in your God, then in something else, something definitely that they can lean on. I haven't anything. For me, the wind is pink, the grass is black."

9

The nurse comes in the room where we all sitting and waiting and says the doctor won't take no more patients till one o'clock this evening.* My mama jumps up off the bench and goes up to the white lady.

"Nurse, I have to go back in the field this evening," she says.

"The doctor is treating his last patient now," the nurse says. "One o'clock this evening."

"Can I at least speak to the doctor?" my mama asks.

"I'm his nurse," the lady says.

"My little boy's sick," my mama says. "Right now his tooth almost killing him."

The nurse looks at me. She's trying to make up her mind if to let me come in. I look at her real pitiful. The tooth ain't hurting me at all, but Mama say it is, so I make 'tend for her sake.

"This evening," the nurse says, and goes on back in the office.

"Don't feel 'jected, honey," the lady says to Mama. "I been round them a long time—they take you when they want to. If you was white, that's something else; but we the wrong color."

Mama don't say nothing to the lady, and me and her go outside and stand 'gainst the wall. It's cold out there. I can feel that wind going through my coat. Some of the other people come out of the room and go up the street. Me and Mama stand there a little while and we start walking. I don't know where we going. When we come to the other street we just stand there.

"You don't have to make water, do you?" Mama says.

"No, ma'am," I say.

---

*evening: In some parts of the South, especially the rural areas, the period from noon through sunset and twilight.

We go on up the street. Walking real slow. I can tell Mama don't know where she's going. When we come to a store we stand there and look at the dummies. I look at a little boy wearing a brown overcoat. He's got on brown shoes, too. I look at my old shoes and look at his'n again. You wait till summer, I say.

Me and Mama walk away. We come up to another store and we stop and look at them dummies, too. Then we go on again. We pass a café where the white people in there eating. Mama tells me keep my eyes in front where they belong, but I can't help from seeing them people eat. My stomach starts to growling 'cause I'm hungry. When I see people eating, I get hungry; when I see a coat, I get cold.

A man whistles at my mama when we go by a filling station. She makes 'tend she don't even see him. I look back and I feel like hitting him in the mouth. If I was bigger, I say; if I was bigger, you'd see.

We keep on going. I'm getting colder and colder, but I don't say nothing. I feel that stuff running down my nose and I sniff.

"That rag," Mama says.

I get it out and wipe my nose. I'm getting cold all over now—my face, my hands, my feet, everything. We pass another little café, but this'n for white people, too, and we can't go in there, either. So we just walk. I'm so cold now I'm 'bout ready to say it. If I knowed where we was going I wouldn't be so cold, but I don't know where we going. We go, we go, we go. We walk clean out of Bayonne. Then we cross the street and we come back. Same thing I seen when I got off the bus this morning. Same old trees, same old walk, same old weeds, same old cracked pave—same old everything.

I sniff again.

"That rag," Mama says.

I wipe my nose real fast and jugg that handkerchief back in my pocket 'fore my hand gets too cold. I raise my head and I can see David's hardware store. When we come up to it, we go in. I don't know why, but I'm glad.

It's warm in there. It's so warm in there you don't ever want to leave. I look for the heater, and I see it over by them barrels. Three white men standing round the heater talking in Creole. One of them comes over to see what my mama want.

"Got any axe handles?" she says.

Me, Mama and the white man start to the back, but Mama stops me when we come up to the heater. She and the white man go on. I hold my hands over the heater and look at them. They go all the way to the back, and I see the white man pointing to the axe handles 'gainst the wall. Mama takes one of them and shakes it like she's trying to figure how much it weighs. Then she rubs her hand over it from one end to the other end. She turns it over and looks at the other side, then she shakes it again, and shakes her head and puts it back. She gets another one and she does it just like she did the first one, then she shakes her head. Then she gets a brown one and do it that, too. But she don't like this one, either. Then she gets another one, but 'fore she shakes it or anything, she looks at me. Look like she's trying to say something to me, but I don't know what it is. All I know is I done got warm now and I'm feeling right smart better. Mama shakes this axe handle just like she did the others, and shakes her head and says something to the white man. The white man just looks at his pile of axe handles, and when Mama pass him to come to the front, the white man just scratch his head and follows her. She tells me come on and we go on out and start walking again.

We walk and walk, and no time at all I'm cold again. Look like I'm colder now 'cause I can still remember how good it was back there. My stomach growls and I suck it in to keep Mama from hearing it. She's walking right 'side me, and it growls so loud you can hear it a mile. But Mama don't say a word.

10

When we come up to the courthouse, I look at the clock. It's got quarter to twelve. Mean we got another hour and a quarter to be out here in the cold. We go and stand 'side a building. Something hits my cap and I look up at the sky. Sleet's falling.

I look at Mama standing there. I want stand close 'side her, but she don't like that. She say that's crybaby stuff. She say you got to stand for yourself, by yourself.

"Let's go back to that office," she says.

We cross the street. When we get to the dentist office I try to open the door, but I can't. I twist and twist, but I can't. Mama pushes me to the side and she twist the knob, but she can't open the door, either. She turns 'way from the door. I look at her, but I don't move and I don't say nothing. I done seen her like this before and I'm scared of her.

"You hungry?" she says. She says it like she's mad at me, like I'm the cause of everything.

"No, ma'am," I say.

"You want eat and walk back, or you rather don't eat and ride?"

"I ain't hungry," I say.

I ain't just hungry, but I'm cold, too. I'm so hungry and cold I want to cry. And look like I'm getting colder and colder. My feet done got numb. I try to work my toes, but I don't even feel them. Look like I'm go'n die. Look like I'm go'n stand right here and freeze to death. I think 'bout home. I think 'bout Val and Auntie and Ty and Louis and Walker. It's 'bout twelve o'clock and I know they eating dinner now. I can hear Ty making jokes. He done forgot 'bout getting up early this morning and right now he's probably making jokes. Always trying to make somebody laugh. I wish I was right there listening to him. Give anything in the world if I was home round the fire.

"Come on," Mama says.

We start walking again. My feet so numb I can't hardly feel them. We turn the corner and go on back up the street. The clock on the courthouse starts hitting for twelve.

The sleet's coming down plenty now. They hit the pave and bounce like rice. Oh, Lord; oh, Lord, I pray. Don't let me die, don't let me die, don't let me die, Lord.

11

Now I know where we going. We going back of town where the colored people eat. I don't care if I don't eat. I been hungry before. I can stand it. But I can't stand the cold.

I can see we go'n have a long walk. It's 'bout a mile down there. But I don't mind. I know when I get there I'm go'n warm myself. I think I can hold out. My hands numb in my pockets and my feet numb, too, but if I keep moving I can hold out. Just don't stop no more, that's all.

The sky's gray. The sleet keeps on falling. Falling like rain now—plenty, plenty. You can hear it hitting the pave. You can see it bouncing. Sometimes it bounces two times 'fore it settles.

We keep on going. We don't say nothing. We just keep on going, keep on going.

I wonder what Mama's thinking. I hope she ain't mad at me. When summer come I'm go'n pick plenty cotton and get her a coat. I'm go'n get her a red one.

I hope they'd make it summer all the time. I'd be glad if it was summer all the time—but it ain't. We got to have winter, too. Lord, I hate the winter. I guess everybody hate the winter.

I don't sniff this time. I get out my handkerchief and wipe my nose. My hands's so cold I can hardly hold the handkerchief.

I think we getting close, but we ain't there yet. I wonder where everybody is. Can't see a soul but us. Look like we the only two people moving round today. Must be too cold for the rest of the people to move round in.

I can hear my teeth. I hope they don't knock together too hard and make that bad one hurt. Lord, that's all I need, for that bad one to start off.

I hear a church bell somewhere. But today ain't Sunday. They must be ringing for a funeral or something.

I wonder what they doing at home. They must be eating. Monsieur Bayonne might be there with his guitar. One day Ty played with Monsieur Bayonne's guitar and broke one of the strings. Monsieur Bayonne was some mad with Ty. He say Ty wasn't go'n ever 'mount to nothing. Ty can go just like Monsieur Bayonne when he ain't there. Ty can make everybody laugh when he starts to mocking Monsieur Bayonne.

I used to like to be with Mama and Daddy. We used to be happy. But they took him in the Army. Now, nobody happy no more. . . . I be glad when Daddy comes home.

Monsieur Bayonne say it wasn't fair for them to take Daddy and give Mama nothing and give us nothing. Auntie say, "Shhh, Etienne. Don't let them hear you talk like that." Monsieur Bayonne say, "It's God truth. What they giving his children? They have to walk three and a half miles to school hot or cold. That's anything to give for a paw? She's got to work in the field rain or shine just to make ends meet. That's anything to give for a husband?" Auntie say, "Shhh, Etienne, shhh." "Yes, you right," Monsieur Bayonne say. "Best don't say it in front of them now. But one day they go'n find out. One day."

"Yes, I suppose so," Auntie say. "Then what, Rose Mary?" Monsieur Bayonne say. "I don't know, Etienne," Auntie say. "All we can do is us job, and leave everything else in His hand . . ."

We getting closer, now. We getting closer. I can even see the railroad tracks.

We cross the tracks, and now I see the café. Just to get in there, I say. Just to get in there. Already I'm starting to feel little better.

12

We go in. Ahh, it's good. I look for the heater; there 'gainst the wall. One of them little brown ones. I just stand there and hold my hands over it. I can't open my hands too wide 'cause they almost froze.

Mama's standing right 'side me. She done unbuttoned her coat. Smoke rises out of the coat, and the coat smells like a wet dog.

I move to the side so Mama can have more room. She opens out her hands and rubs them together. I rub mine together, too, 'cause this keep them from hurting. If you let them warm too fast, they hurt you sure. But if you let them warm just little bit at a time, and you keep rubbing them, they be all right every time.

They got just two more people in the café. A lady back of the counter, and a man on this side the counter. They been watching us ever since we come in.

Mama gets out the handkerchief and count up the money. Both of us know how much money she's got there. Three dollars. No, she ain't got three dollars, 'cause she had to pay us way up here. She ain't got but two dollars and a half left. Dollar and a half to get my tooth pulled, and fifty cents for us to go back on, and fifty cents worth of salt meat.

She stirs the money round with her finger. Most of the money is change 'cause I can hear it rubbing together. She stirs it and stirs it. Then she looks at the door. It's still sleeting. I can hear it hitting 'gainst the wall like rice.

"I ain't hungry, Mama," I say.

"Got to pay them something for they heat," she says.

She takes a quarter out the handkerchief and ties the handkerchief up again. She looks over her shoulder at the people, but she still don't move. I hope she don't spend the money. I don't want her spending it on me. I'm hungry, I'm almost starving I'm so hungry, but I don't want her spending the money on me.

She flips the quarter over like she's thinking. She's must be thinking 'bout us walking back home. Lord, I sure don't want walk home. If I thought it'd do any good to say something, I'd say it. But Mama makes up her own mind 'bout things.

She turns 'way from the heater right fast, like she better hurry up and spend the quarter 'fore she change her mind. I watch her go toward the counter. The man and the lady look at her, too. She tells the lady something and the lady walks away. The man keeps on looking at her. Her back's turned to the man, and she don't even know he's standing there.

The lady puts some cakes and a glass of milk on the counter. Then she pours up a cup of coffee and sets it 'side the other stuff. Mama pays her for the things and comes on back where I'm standing. She tells me sit down at the table 'gainst the wall.

The milk and the cakes's for me; the coffee's for Mama. I eat slow and I look at her. She's looking outside at the sleet. She's looking real sad. I say to myself, I'm go'n make all this up one day. You see, one day, I'm go'n make all this up. I want say it now; I want tell her how I feel right now; but Mama don't like for us to talk like that.

"I can't eat all this," I say.

They ain't got but just three little old cakes there. I'm so hungry right now, the Lord knows I can eat a hundred times three, but I want my mama to have one.

Mama don't even look my way. She knows I'm hungry, she knows I want it. I let it stay there a little while, then I get it and eat it. I eat just on my front teeth, though, 'cause if cake touch that back tooth I know what'll happen. Thank God it ain't hurt me at all today.

After I finish eating I see the man go to the juke box. He drops a nickel in it, then he just stand there a little while looking at the record. Mama tells me keep my eyes in front where they belong. I turn my head like she say, but then I hear the man coming toward us.

"Dance, pretty?" he says.

Mama gets up to dance with him. But 'fore you know it, she done grabbed the little man in the collar and done heaved him 'side the wall. He hit the wall so hard he stop the juke box from playing.

"Some pimp," the lady back of the counter says. "Some pimp."

The little man jumps up off the floor and starts toward my mama. 'Fore you know it, Mama done sprung open her knife and she's waiting for him.

"Come on," she says. "Come on. I'll gut you from your neighbo to your throat. Come on."

I go up to the little man to hit him, but Mama makes me come and stand 'side her. The little man looks at me and Mama and goes on back to the counter.

"Some pimp," the lady back of the counter says. "Some pimp." She starts laughing and pointing at the little man. "Yes sir, you a pimp, all right. Yes sir-ree."

13

"Fasten that coat, let's go," Mama says.

"You don't have to leave," the lady says.

Mama don't answer the lady, and we right out in the cold again. I'm warm right now—my hands, my ears, my feet—but I know this ain't go'n last too long. It done sleet so much now you got ice everywhere you look.

We cross the railroad tracks, and soon's we do, I get cold. That wind goes through this little old coat like it ain't even there. I got on a shirt and a sweater under the coat, but that wind don't pay them no mind. I look up and I can see we got a long way to go. I wonder if we go'n make it 'fore I get too cold.

We cross over to walk on the sidewalk. They got just one sidewalk back here, and it's over there.

After we go just a little piece, I smell bread cooking. I look, then I see a baker shop. When we get closer, I can smell it more better. I shut my eyes and make 'tend I'm eating. But I keep them shut too long and I butt up 'gainst a telephone post. Mama grabs me and see if I'm hurt. I ain't bleeding or nothing and she turns me loose.

I can feel I'm getting colder and colder, and I look up to see how far we still got to go. Uptown is 'way up yonder. A half mile more, I reckon. I try to think of something. They say think and you won't get cold. I think of that poem, "Annabel Lee."* I ain't been to school in so long—this bad weather—I reckon they done passed "Annabel Lee" by now. But passed it or not, I'm sure Miss Walker go'n make me recite it when I get there. That woman don't never forget nothing. I ain't never seen nobody like that in my life.

I'm still getting cold. "Annabel Lee" or no "Annabel Lee," I'm still getting cold. But I can see we getting closer. We getting there gradually.

Soon 's we turn the corner, I see a little old white lady up in front of us. She's the only lady on the street. She's all in black and she's got a long black rag over her head.

"Stop," she says.

Me and Mama stop and look at her. She must be crazy to be out in all this bad weather. Ain't got but a few other people out there, and all of them's men.

"Y'all done ate?" she says.

"Just finish," Mama says.

"Y'all must be cold then?" she says.

"We headed for the dentist," Mama says. "We'll warm up when we get there."

"What dentist?" the old lady says. "Mr. Bassett?"

"Yes, ma'am," Mama says.

"Come on in," the old lady says. "I'll telephone him and tell him y'all coming."

Me and Mama follow the old lady in the store. It's a little bitty store, and it don't have much in there. The old lady takes off her head rag and folds it up.

"Helena?" somebody calls from the back.

"Yes, Alnest?" the old lady says.

"Did you see them?"

"They're here. Standing beside me."

"Good. Now you can stay inside."

The old lady looks at Mama. Mama's waiting to hear what she brought us in here for. I'm waiting for that, too.

"I saw y'all each time you went by," she says. "I came out to catch you, but you were gone."

"We went back of town," Mama says.

---

*"Annabel Lee": Edgar Allan Poe's poem about the death of a beautiful and aristocratic maiden in a far-away land.

"Did you eat?"

"Yes, ma'am."

The old lady looks at Mama a long time, like she's thinking Mama might be just saying that. Mama looks right back at her. The old lady looks at me to see what I have to say. I don't say nothing. I sure ain't going 'gainst my mama.

"There's food in the kitchen," she says to Mama. "I've been keeping it warm."

Mama turns right around and starts for the door.

"Just a minute," the old lady says. Mama stops. "The boy'll have to work for it. It isn't free."

"We don't take no handout," Mama says.

"I'm not handing out anything," the old lady says. "I need my garbage moved to the front. Ernest has a bad cold and can't go out there."

"James'll move it for you," Mama says.

"Not unless you eat," the old lady says. "I'm old, but I have my pride, too, you know."

Mama can see she ain't go'n beat this old lady down, so she just shakes her head.

"All right," the old lady says. "Come into the kitchen."

She leads the way with that rag in her hand. The kitchen is a little bitty little old thing, too. The table and the stove just 'bout fill it up. They got a little room to the side. Somebody in there laying 'cross the bed—'cause I can see one of his feet. Must be the person she was talking to: Ernest or Alnest—something like that.

"Sit down," the old lady says to Mama. "Not you," she says to me. "You have to move the cans."

"Helena?" the man says in the other room.

"Yes, Alnest?" the old lady says.

"Are you going out there again?"

"I must show the boy where the garbage is, Alnest," the old lady says.

"Keep that shawl over your head," the old man says.

"You don't have to remind me, Alnest. Come, boy," the old lady says.

We go out in the yard. Little old back yard ain't no bigger than the store or the kitchen. But it can sleet here just like it can sleet in any big back yard. And 'fore you know it, I'm trembling.

"There," the old lady says, pointing to the cans. I pick up one of the cans and set it right back down. The can's so light, I'm go'n see what's inside of it.

"Here," the old lady says. "Leave that can alone."

I look back at her standing there in the door. She's got that black rag wrapped round her shoulders, and she's pointing one of her little old fingers at me.

"Pick it up and carry it to the front," she says. I go by her with the can, and she's looking at me all the time. I'm sure the can's empty. I'm sure she could've carried it herself—maybe both of them at the same time. "Set it on the sidewalk by the door and come back for the other one," she says.

I go and come back, and Mama looks at me when I pass her. I get the other can and take it to the front. It don't feel a bit heavier than that first one. I tell myself I ain't go'n be nobody's fool, and I'm go'n look inside this can to see just what I been hauling. First, I look up the street, then down the street. Nobody coming. Then I look over my shoulder toward the door. That little old lady done slipped up there quiet 's mouse, watching me again. Look like she knowed what I was go'n do.

"Ehh, Lord," she says. "Children, children. Come in here, boy, and go wash your hands."

I follow her in the kitchen. She points toward the bathroom, and I go in there and wash up. Little bitty old bathroom, but it's clean, clean. I don't use any of her towels; I wipe my hands on my pants legs.

When I come back in the kitchen, the old lady done dished up the food. Rice, gravy, meat—and she even got some lettuce and tomato in a saucer. She even got a glass of milk and a piece of cake there, too. It looks so good, I almost start eating 'fore I say my blessing.

"Helena?" the old man says.

"Yes, Alnest?"

"Are they eating?"

"Yes," she says.

"Good," he says. "Now you'll stay inside."

The old lady goes in there where he is and I can hear them talking. I look at Mama. She's eating slow like she's thinking. I wonder what's the matter now. I reckon she's thinking 'bout home.

The old lady comes back in the kitchen.

"I talked to Dr. Bassett's nurse," she says. "Dr. Bassett will take you as soon as you get there."

"Thank you, ma'am," Mama says.

"Perfectly all right," the old lady says. "Which one is it?"

Mama nods toward me. The old lady looks at me real sad. I look sad, too.

"You're not afraid, are you?" she says.

"No, ma'am," I say.

"That's a good boy," the old lady says. "Nothing to be afraid of. Dr. Bassett will not hurt you."

When me and Mama get through eating, we thank the old lady again.

"Helena, are they leaving?" the old man says.

"Yes, Alnest."

"Tell them I say good-bye."

"They can hear you, Alnest."

"Good-bye both mother and son," the old man says. "And may God be with you."

Me and Mama tell the old man good-bye, and we follow the old lady in the front room. Mama opens the door to go out, but she stops and comes back in the store.

"You sell salt meat?" she says.

"Yes."

"Give me two bits worth."

"That isn't very much salt meat," the old lady says.

"That's all I have," Mama says.

The old lady goes back of the counter and cuts a big piece off the chunk. Then she wraps it up and puts it in a paper bag.

"Two bits," she says.

"That looks like awful lot of meat for a quarter," Mama says.

"Two bits," the old lady says. "I've been selling salt meat behind this counter twenty-five years. I think I know what I'm doing."

"You got a scale there," Mama says.

"What?" the old lady says.

"Weigh it," Mama says.

"What?" the old lady says. "Are you telling me how to run my business?"

"Thanks very much for the food," Mama says.

"Just a minute," the old lady says.

"James," Mama says to me. I move toward the door.

"Just one minute, I said," the old lady says.

Me and Mama stop again and look at her. The old lady takes the meat out of the bag and unwraps it and cuts 'bout half of it off. Then she wraps it up again and juggs it back in the bag and gives the bag to Mama. Mama lays the quarter on the counter.

"Your kindness will never be forgotten," she says. "James," she says to me.

We go out, and the old lady comes to the door to look at us. After we go a little piece I look back, and she's still there watching us.

The sleet's coming down heavy, heavy now, and I turn up my coat collar to keep my neck warm. My mama tells me turn it right back down.

"You not a bum," she says. "You a man."

Writing Assignments for "The Sky Is Gray"

I. Brief Papers

  A. 1. When and where does the story take place?

  2. Why does James' mother insist that he kill the redbirds?

  3. Explain what James means by "crybaby stuff."

  4. Why does the preacher leave the dentist's office after he has twice hit the boy with the book?

  5. Explain the relevance of the scene on the bus between James and the girl his age.

  6. Why does the old lady ask James to move her garbage cans?

  7. How informative and well written is the following student response to the previous question?

    In the last section of the story "The Sky is Gray," the old woman lures James and his mother into her store by telling them that she will call the dentist to tell him to be expecting James. After getting them into the store, the old woman proceeds with the next step of her plan and invites them to come back into her kitchen and have something to eat. James' mother is quick to refuse the kind offer by walking toward the door. The old woman adds "the boy will have to work for it. It isn't free." ("it" meaning the meal; p. 331). Trying to persuade them to stay, the old woman convinces James and his mother that if James would take out the trash it would be doing both she and her husband a favor. Now, James' mother could justify taking a meal from the old woman. Having watched James and his mother walk by the store a couple of times, the old woman knew that they were cold and hungry. So she planned the whole scenario for James to move the empty cans; thus making James and his mother feel that they weren't just accepting handouts.

B. Argue for or against one of the assertions below.
   1. The story strongly suggests that James' Daddy will never return home.
   2. The story implies that the preacher is fully justified in striking the boy.
   3. As its title suggests, "The Sky is Gray" is a somber story without a trace of humor.
   4. Even for an eight-year-old, James is rather dull, slow, and dim-witted.

C. 1. What do you think the future holds for James?
   2. Do you think that James' mother is unnecessarily harsh—and sometimes even cruel—to him?
   3. Would you agree that, by the end of the story, James has become "a man?"
   4. Take any one scene in "The Sky is Gray" that you found moving or touching and explain in some detail why you responded emotionally to it.

II. Longer Papers
A. Expand one of your brief papers into a full-length essay.
B. Explain how your response to a moving or touching scene in "The Sky is Gray" (see question I.C.4) affects your understanding and interpretation of the story. Would the meaning of the story be different for you if that scene were missing?
C. James' mother says, "I do the best I can." Analyze her behavior throughout the story in order to assess the accuracy of her statement.
D. Argue for or against the assertion that the story as a whole strongly endorses the boy's statement that black people should listen to their head rather than their heart.
E. Develop, modify, or refute the assertion that the story as a whole strongly endorses the preacher's statement that we should not question God.
F. What does the story have to say about pride?
G. Your high school English teacher has written you to ask which short story, of those you have read this term, you think would be most appropriate for him to teach next year in a literature course for high school seniors. Choose "The Sky is Gray" (or another short story) and then explain in clear and convincing detail why you believe that this story is especially appropriate for high school seniors.

III. The Allusion to "Annabel Lee" in "The Sky is Gray"

From the sentences below, construct a short essay that explains how the *allusion* to "Annabel Lee" helps contribute to the meaning of "The Sky is Gray."

1. James walks back to the dentist's office during the cold and sleet.
2. He tries to think of something that will take his mind off the cold.

3. James remembers what he has been studying in school.
4. He has been studying "Annabel Lee."
5. "Annabel Lee" is a poem by Edgar Allan Poe.

6. James thinks of the poem.
7. But it does not help James feel any better.

8. James admits this.
9. " 'Annabel Lee' or no 'Annabel Lee,' I'm still getting cold" (p. 330).

10. But Gaines' allusion to "Annabel Lee" may help in this way.
11. We can better understand the implications of "The Sky Is Gray."
12. We can better understand especially if we remember the content of Poe's poem.

13. "Annabel Lee" is like the Gaines story in this respect.
14. It tells of a cold, chilling world.
15. It is a world that kills innocent maidens like Annabel Lee.
16. But there the similarity ends.

17. The narrator of "Annabel Lee" is unlike James and his mother in this respect.
18. The narrator of "Annabel Lee" can afford to spend most of his time dreaming and fantasizing.

19. The narrator of "Annabel Lee" uses dreams to escape from the unpleasant realities of his world.
20. The narrator of "Annabel Lee" uses dreams to re-experience the joy of being with Annabel Lee.
21. In fantasy he re-experiences the joy of being with Annabel Lee.

22. This is most important.
23. The narrator of "Annabel Lee" seems to have no worries over money.
24. The narrator of "Annabel Lee" seems to have no worries over toothaches.
25. The narrator of "Annabel Lee" seems to have no worries over raising a family.
26. The narrator of "Annabel Lee" seems to have no worries over buying food.

27. The world of "Annabel Lee" seems totally divorced from the world in which James lives.

28. "Annabel Lee" is the kind of material that James and his classmates are reading in school.
29. The allusion to "Annabel Lee" may suggest something about the education that James and others like him receive.
30. Their education has no real relation to their lives.

31. "The Sky Is Gray" implies this.
32. An irrelevant education is just one further burden.
33. The burden is borne by a people oppressed in so many other ways.

RICHARD WRIGHT
The Man Who Lived Underground

Before Reading

A racist assumes that psychocultural traits and capacities are determined by biological race and that races differ decisively from one another; a racist often believes in the inherent superiority of a particular race and its right to dominate other races. Do you consider American society to be racist? Free write about this question for 5 or 10 minutes.

I've got to hide, he told himself. His chest heaved as he waited, crouching in a dark corner of the vestibule. He was tired of running and dodging. Either he had to find a place to hide, or he had to surrender. A police car swished by through the rain, its siren rising sharply. They're looking for me all over . . . He crept to the door and squinted through the fogged plate glass. He stiffened as the siren rose and died in the distance. Yes, he had to hide, but where? He gritted his teeth. Then a sudden movement in the street caught his attention. A throng of tiny columns of water snaked into the air from the perforations of a manhole cover. The columns stopped abruptly, as though the perforations had become clogged; a gray spout of sewer water jutted up from underground and lifted the circular metal cover, juggled it for a moment, then let it fall with a clang.

He hatched a tentative plan: he would wait until the siren sounded far off, then he would go out. He smoked and waited, tense. At last the siren gave him his signal; it wailed, dying, going away from him. He stepped to the sidewalk, then paused and looked curiously at the open manhole, half expecting the cover to leap up again. He went to the center of the street and stooped and peered into the hole, but could see nothing. Water rustled in the black depths.

THE MAN WHO LIVED UNDERGROUND   First published in 1944. Richard Wright (1908–1960) was born on a plantation near Natchez, Mississippi, and lived in Memphis, Chicago, New York, and Europe. His best-known writings are his novel *Native Son* and his autobiography *Black Boy.*

He started with terror; the siren sounded so near that he had the idea that he had been dreaming and had awakened to find the car upon him. He dropped instinctively to his knees and his hands grasped the rim of the manhole. The siren seemed to hoot directly above him and with a wild gasp of exertion he snatched the cover far enough off to admit his body. He swung his legs over the opening and lowered himself into watery darkness. He hung for an eternal moment to the rim by his finger tips, then he felt rough metal prongs and at once, he knew that sewer workmen used these ridges to lower themselves into manholes. Fist over fist, he let his body sink until he could feel no more prongs. He swayed in dank space; the siren seemed to howl at the very rim of the manhole. He dropped and was washed violently into an ocean of warm, leaping water. His head was battered against a wall and he wondered if this were death. Frenziedly his fingers clawed and sank into a crevice. He steadied himself and measured the strength of the current with his own muscular tension. He stood slowly in water that dashed past his knees with fearful velocity.

He heard a prolonged scream of brakes and the siren broke off. Oh, God! They had found him! Looming above his head in the rain a white face hovered over the hole. "How did this damn thing get off?" he heard a policeman ask. He saw the steel cover move slowly until the hole looked like a quarter moon turned black. "Give me a hand here," someone called. The cover clanged into place, muffling the sights and sounds of the upper world. Knee-deep in the pulsing current, he breathed with aching chest, filling his lungs with the hot stench of yeasty rot.

From the perforations of the manhole cover, delicate lances of hazy violet sifted down and wove a mottled pattern upon the surface of the streaking current. His lips parted as a car swept past along the wet pavement overhead, its heavy rumble soon dying out, like the hum of a plane speeding through a dense cloud. He had never thought that cars could sound like that; everything seemed strange and unreal under here. He stood in darkness for a long time, knee-deep in rustling water, musing.

The odor of rot had become so general that he no longer smelled it. He got his cigarettes, but discovered that his matches were wet. He searched and found a dry folder in the pocket of his shirt and managed to strike one; it flared weirdly in the wet gloom, glowing greenishly, turning red, orange, then yellow. He lit a crumpled cigarette; then, by the flickering light of the match, he looked for support so that he would not have to keep his muscles flexed against the pouring water. His pupils narrowed and he saw to either side of him two steaming walls that rose and curved inward some six feet above his head to form a dripping, mouse-colored dome. The bottom of the sewer was a sloping V-trough. To the left, the sewer vanished in ashen fog. To the right was a steep down-curve into which water plunged.

He saw now that had he not regained his feet in time, he would have been swept to death, or had he entered any other manhole he would have probably drowned. Above the rush of the current he heard sharper juttings of water; tiny streams were spewing into the sewer from smaller conduits. The match died; he struck another and saw a mass of debris sweep past him and clog the throat of the down-curve. At once the water began rising rapidly. Could he climb out before he drowned? A long hiss sounded and the debris was sucked from sight; the current lowered. He understood now what had made the water toss the manhole cover; the down-curve had become temporarily obstructed and the perforations had become clogged.

He was in danger; he might slide into a down-curve; he might wander with a lighted match into a pocket of gas and blow himself up; or he might contract some horrible disease . . . Though he wanted to leave, an irrational impulse held him rooted. To the left, the convex ceiling swooped to a height of less than five feet. With cigarette slanting from pursed lips, he waded with taut muscles, his feet sloshing over the slimy bottom, his shoes sinking into spongy slop, the slate-colored water cracking in creamy foam against his knees. Pressing flat his left palm against the lowered ceiling, he struck another match and saw a metal pole nestling in a niche of the wall. Yes, some sewer workman had left it. He reached for it, then jerked his head away as a whisper of scurrying life whisked past and was still. He held the match close and saw a huge rat, wet with slime, blinking beady eyes and baring tiny fangs. The light blinded the rat and the frizzled head moved aimlessly. He grabbed the pole and let it fly against the rat's soft body; there was shrill piping and the grizzly body splashed into the dun-colored water and was snatched out of sight, spinning in the scuttling stream.

He swallowed and pushed on, following the curve of the misty cavern, sounding the water with the pole. By the faint light of another manhole cover he saw, amid loose wet brick, a hole with walls of damp earth leading into blackness. Gingerly he poked the pole into it; it was hollow and went beyond the length of the pole. He shoved the pole before him, hoisted himself upward, got to his hands and knees, and crawled. After a few yards he paused, struck to wonderment by the silence; it seemed that he had traveled a million miles away from the world. As he inched forward again he could sense the bottom of the dirt tunnel becoming dry and lowering slightly. Slowly he rose and to his astonishment he stood erect. He could not hear the rustling of the water now and he felt confoundingly alone, yet lured by the darkness and silence.

He crept a long way, then stopped, curious, afraid. He put his right foot forward and it dangled in space; he drew back in fear. He thrust the pole outward and it swung in emptiness. He trembled, imagining the earth crumbling and burying him alive. He scratched a match and saw that the dirt floor sheered away steeply and widened into a sort of cave some five feet below him. An old sewer, he muttered. He cocked his head, hearing a feathery cadence which he could not identify. The match ceased to burn.

Using the pole as a kind of ladder, he slid down and stood in darkness. The air was a little fresher and he could still hear vague noises. Where was he? He felt suddenly that someone was standing near him and he turned sharply, but there was only darkness. He poked cautiously and felt a brick wall; he followed it and the strange sounds grew louder. He ought to get out of here. This was crazy. He could not remain here for any length of time; there was no food and no place to sleep. But the faint sounds tantalized him; they were strange but familiar. Was it a motor? A baby crying? Music? A siren? He groped on, and the sounds came so clearly that he could feel the pitch and timbre of human voices. Yes, singing! That was it! He listened with open mouth. It was a church service. Enchanted, he groped toward the waves of melody.

Jesus, take me to your home above
And fold me in the bosom of Thy love . . .

The singing was on the other side of the brick wall. Excited, he wanted to watch the service without being seen. Whose church was it? He knew most of the churches in this area above ground, but the singing sounded too strange and detached for him to guess. He looked to the left, to the right, down to the black dirt, then upward and was startled to see a bright sliver of light slicing the darkness like the blade of a razor. He struck one of his two remaining matches and saw rusty pipes running along an old concrete ceiling. Photographically he located the exact position of the pipes in his mind. The match flame sank and he sprang upward; his hands clutched a pipe. He swung his legs and tossed his body onto the bed of pipes and they creaked, swaying up and down; he thought that the tier was about to crash, but nothing happened. He edged to the crevice and saw a segment of black men and women, dressed in white robes, singing, holding tattered songbooks in their black palms. His first impulse was to laugh, but he checked himself.

What was he doing? He was crushed with a sense of guilt. Would God strike him dead for that? The singing swept on and he shook his head, disagreeing in spite of himself. They oughtn't to do that, he thought. But he could think of no reason *why* they should not do it. Just singing with the air of the sewer blowing in on them . . . He felt that he was gazing upon something abysmally obscene, yet he could not bring himself to leave.

After a long time he grew numb and dropped to the dirt. Pain throbbed in his legs and a deeper pain, induced by the sight of those black people groveling and begging for something they could never get, churned in him. A vague conviction made him feel that those people should stand unrepentant and yield no quarter in singing and praying, yet *he* had run away from the police, had pleaded with them to believe in *his* innocence. He shook his head, bewildered.

How long had he been down here? He did not know. This was a new kind of living for him; the intensity of feelings he had experienced when looking at the church people sing made him certain that he had been down here a long time, but his mind told him that the time must have been short. In this darkness the only notion he had of time was when a match flared and measured time by its fleeting light. He groped back through the hole toward the sewer and the waves of song subsided and finally he could not hear them at all. He came to where the earth hole ended and he heard the noise of the current and time lived again for him, measuring the moments by the wash of the water.

The rain must have slackened, for the flow of water had lessened and came only to his ankles. Ought he to go up into the streets and take his chances on hiding somewhere else? But they would surely catch him. The mere thought of dodging and running again from the police made him tense. No, he would stay and plot how to elude them. But what could he do down here? He walked forward into the sewer and came to another manhole cover; he stood beneath it, debating. Fine pencils of gold spilled suddenly from the little circles in the manhole cover and trembled on the surface of the current. Yes, street lamps . . . It must be night . . .

He went forward for about a quarter of an hour, wading aimlessly, poking the pole carefully before him. Then he stopped, his eyes fixed and intent. What's that? A strangely familiar image attracted and repelled him. Lit by the yellow stems from another manhole cover was a tiny nude body of a baby snagged by debris and half-submerged in water. Thinking that the baby was alive, he moved impulsively to save it, but his roused feelings told him that it was dead, cold, nothing, the same nothingness he had felt while watching the men and women singing in the church. Water blossomed about the tiny legs, the tiny arms, the tiny head, and rushed onward. The eyes were closed, as though in sleep; the fists were clenched, as though in protest; and the mouth gaped black in a soundless cry.

He straightened and drew in his breath, feeling that he had been staring for all eternity at the ripples of veined water skimming impersonally over the shriveled limbs. He felt as condemned as when the policemen had accused him. Involuntarily he lifted his hand to brush the vision away, but his arm fell listlessly to his side. Then he acted; he closed his eyes and reached forward slowly with the soggy shoe of his right foot and shoved the dead baby from where it had been lodged. He kept his eyes closed, seeing the little body twisting in the current as it floated from sight. He opened his eyes, shivered, placed his knuckles in the sockets, hearing the water speed in the somber shadows.

He tramped on, sensing at times a sudden quickening in the current as he passed some conduit whose waters were swelling the stream that slid by his feet. A few minutes later he was standing under another manhole cover, listening to the faint rumble of noises above ground. Streetcars and trucks, he mused. He looked down and saw a stagnant pool of gray-green sludge; at intervals a balloon pocket rose from the scum, glistening a bluish-purple, and burst. Then another. He turned, shook his head, and tramped back to the dirt cave by the church, his lips quivering.

Back in the cave, he sat and leaned his back against a dirt wall. His body was trembling slightly. Finally his senses quieted and he slept. When he awakened he felt stiff and cold. He had to leave this foul place, but leaving meant facing those policemen who had wrongly accused him. No, he could not go back aboveground. He remembered the beating they had given him and how he had signed his name to a confession, a confession which he had not even read. He had been too tired when they had shouted at him, demanding that he sign his name; he had signed it to end his pain.

He stood and groped about in the darkness. The church singing had stopped. How long had he slept? He did not know. But he felt refreshed and hungry. He doubled his fist nervously, realizing that he could not make a decision. As he walked about he stumbled over an old rusty iron pipe. He picked it up and felt a jagged edge. Yes, there was a brick wall and he could dig into it. What would he find? Smiling, he groped to the brick wall, sat, and began digging idly into damp cement. I can't make any noise, he cautioned himself. As time passed he grew thirsty, but there was no water. He had to kill time or go aboveground. The cement came out of the wall easily; he extracted four bricks and felt a soft draft blowing into his face. He stopped, afraid. What was beyond? He waited a long time and nothing happened; then he began digging again, soundlessly, slowly; he enlarged the hole and crawled through into a dark room and collided with another wall. He felt his way to the right; the wall ended and his fingers toyed in space, like the antennae of an insect.

He fumbled on and his feet struck something hollow, like wood. What's this? He felt with his fingers. Steps . . . He stooped and pulled off his shoes and mounted the stairs and saw a yellow chink of light shining and heard a low voice speaking. He placed his eye to a keyhole and saw the nude waxen figure of a man stretched out upon a white table. The voice, low-pitched and vibrant, mumbled indistinguishable words, neither rising nor falling. He craned his neck and squinted to see the man who was talking, but he could not locate him. Above the naked figure was suspended a huge glass container filled with a blood-red liquid from which a white rubber tube dangled. He crouched closer to the door and saw the tip end of a black object lined with pink satin. A coffin, he breathed. This is an undertaker's establishment . . . A fine-spun lace of ice covered his body and he shuddered. A throaty chuckle sounded in the depths of the yellow room.

He turned to leave. Three steps down it occurred to him that a light switch should be nearby; he felt along the wall, found an electric button, pressed it, and a blinding glare smote his pupils so hard that he was sightless, defenseless. His pupils contracted and he wrinkled his nostrils at a peculiar odor. At once he knew that he had been dimly aware of this odor in the darkness, but the light had brought it sharply to his attention. Some kind of stuff they use to embalm, he thought. He went down the steps and saw piles of lumber, coffins, and a long workbench. In one corner was a tool chest. Yes, he could use tools, could tunnel through walls with them. He lifted the lid of the chest and saw nails, a hammer, a crowbar, a screwdriver, a light bulb, and a long length of electric wire. Good! He would lug these back to his cave.

He was about to hoist the chest to his shoulders when he discovered a door behind the furnace. Where did it lead? He tried to open it and found it securely bolted. Using the crowbar so as to make no sound, he pried the door open; it swung on creaking hinges, outward. Fresh air came to his face and he caught the faint roar of faraway sound. Easy now, he told himself. He widened the door and a lump of coal rattled toward him. A coalbin . . . Evidently the door led into another basement. The roaring noise was louder, but he could not identify it. Where was he? He groped slowly over the coal pile, then ranged in darkness over a gritty floor. The roaring noise seemed to come from above him, then below. His fingers followed a wall until he touched a wooden ridge. A door, he breathed.

The noise died to a low pitch; he felt his skin prickle. It seemed that he was playing a game with an unseen person whose intelligence outstripped his. He put his ear to the flat surface of the door. Yes, voices . . . Was this a prize fight stadium? The sound of the voices came near and sharp, but he could not tell if they were joyous or despairing. He twisted the knob until he heard a soft click and felt the springy weight of the door swinging toward him. He was afraid to open it, yet captured by curiosity and wonder. He jerked the door wide and saw on the far side of the basement a furnace glowing red. Ten feet away was still another door, half ajar. He crossed and peered through the door into an empty, high-ceilinged corridor that terminated in a dark complex of shadow. The belling voices rolled about him and his eagerness mounted. He stepped into the corridor and the voices swelled louder. He crept on and came to a narrow stairway leading circularly upward; there was no question but that he was going to ascend those stairs.

Mounting the spiraled staircase, he heard the voices roll in a steady wave, then leap to crescendo, only to die away, but always remaining audible. Ahead of him glowed red letters: E—X—I—T. At the top of the steps he paused in front of a black curtain that fluttered uncertainly. He parted the folds and looked into a convex depth that gleamed with clusters of shimmering lights. Sprawled below him was a stretch of human faces, tilted upward, chanting, whistling, screaming, laughing. Dangling before the faces, high upon a screen of silver, were jerking shadows. A movie, he said with slow laughter breaking from his lips.

He stood in a box in the reserved section of a movie house and the impulse he had had to tell the people in the church to stop their singing seized him. These people were laughing at their lives, he thought with amazement. They were shouting and yelling at the animated shadows of themselves. His compassion fired his imagination and he stepped out of the box, walked out upon thin air, walked on down to the audience; and, hovering in the air just above them, he stretched out his hand to touch them . . . His tension snapped and he found himself back in the box, looking down into the sea of faces. No; it could not be done; he could not awaken them. He sighed. Yes, these people were children, sleeping in their living, awake in their dying.

He turned away, parted the black curtain, and looked out. He saw no one. He started down the white stone steps and when he reached the bottom he saw a man in trim blue uniform coming toward him. So used had he become to being underground that he thought that he could walk past the man, as though he were a ghost. But the man stopped. And he stopped.

"Looking for the men's room, sir?" the man asked, and without waiting for an answer, he turned and pointed. "This way, sir. The first door to your right."

He watched the man turn and walk up the steps and go out of sight. Then he laughed. What a funny fellow! He went back to the basement and stood in the red darkness, watching the glowing embers in the furnace. He went to the sink and turned the faucet and the water flowed in a smooth silent stream that looked like a spout of blood. He brushed the mad image from his mind and began to wash his hands leisurely, looking about for the usual bar of soap. He found one and rubbed it in his palms until a rich lather bloomed in his cupped fingers, like a scarlet sponge. He scrubbed and rinsed his hands meticulously, then hunted for a towel; there was none. He shut off the water, pulled off his shirt, dried his hands on it; when he put it on again he was grateful for the cool dampness that came to his skin.

Yes, he was thirsty; he turned on the faucet again, bowled his fingers and when the water bubbled over the brim of his cupped palms, he drank in long, slow swallows. His bladder grew tight; he shut off the water, faced the wall, bent his head, and watched a red stream strike the floor. His nostrils wrinkled against acrid wisps of vapor; though he had tramped in the waters of the sewer, he stepped back from the wall so that his shoes, wet with sewer slime, would not touch his urine.

He heard footsteps and crawled quickly into the coalbin. Lumps rattled noisily. The footsteps came into the basement and stopped. Who was it? Had someone heard him and come down to investigate? He waited, crouching, sweating. For a long time there was silence, then he heard the clang of metal and a brighter glow lit the room. Somebody's tending the furnace, he thought. Footsteps came closer and he stiffened. Looming before him was a white face lined with coal dust, the face of an old man with watery blue eyes. Highlights spotted his gaunt cheekbones, and he held a huge shovel. There was a screechy scrape of metal against stone, and the old man lifted a shovelful of coal and went from sight.

The room dimmed momentarily, then a yellow glare came as coal flared at the furnace door. Six times the old man came to the bin and went to the furnace with shovels of coal, but not once did he lift his eyes. Finally he dropped the shovel, mopped his face with a dirty handkerchief, and sighed: "Wheeew!" He turned slowly and trudged out of the basement, his footsteps dying away.

He stood, and lumps of coal clattered down the pile. He stepped from the bin and was startled to see the shadowy outline of an electric bulb hanging above his head. Why had not the old man turned it on? Oh, yes . . . He understood. The old man had worked here for so long that he had no need for light; he had learned a way of seeing in his dark world, like those sightless worms that inch along underground by a sense of touch.

His eyes fell upon a lunch pail and he was afraid to hope that it was full. He picked it up; it was heavy. He opened it. *Sandwiches!* He looked guiltily around; he was alone. He searched farther and found a folder of matches and a half-empty tin of tobacco; he put them eagerly into his pocket and clicked off the light. With the lunch pail under his arm, he went through the door, groped over the pile of coal, and stood again in the lighted basement of the undertaking establishment. I've got to get those tools, he told himself. And turn off that light. He tiptoed back up the steps and switched off the light; the invisible voice still droned on behind the door. He crept down and, seeing with his fingers, opened the lunch pail and tore off a piece of paper bag and brought out the tin and spilled grains of tobacco into the makeshift concave. He rolled it and wet it with spittle, then inserted one end into his mouth and lit it: he sucked smoke that bit his lungs. The nicotine reached his brain, went out along his arms to his finger tips, down to his stomach, and over all the tired nerves of his body.

He carted the tools to the hole he had made in the wall. Would the noise of the falling chest betray him? But he would have to take a chance; he had to have those tools. He lifted the chest and shoved it; it hit the dirt on the other side of the wall with a loud clatter. He waited, listening; nothing happened. Head first, he slithered through and stood in the cave. He grinned, filled with a cunning idea. Yes, he would now go back into the basement of the undertaking establishment and crouch behind the coal pile and dig another hole. Sure! Fumbling, he opened the tool chest and extracted a crowbar, a screwdriver, and a hammer; he fastened them securely about his person.

With another lumpish cigarette in his flexed lips, he crawled back through the hole and over the coal pile and sat, facing the brick wall. He jabbed with the crowbar and the cement sheered away; quicker than he thought, a brick came loose. He worked an hour; the other bricks did not come easily. He sighed, weak from effort. I ought to rest a little, he thought. I'm hungry. He felt his way back to the cave and stumbled along the wall till he came to the tool chest. He sat upon it, opened the lunch pail, and took out two thick sandwiches. He smelled them. Pork chops . . . His mouth watered. He closed his eyes and devoured a sandwich, savoring the smooth rye bread and juicy meat. He ate rapidly, gulping down lumpy mouthfuls that made him long for water. He ate the other sandwich and found an apple and gobbled that up too, sucking the core till the last trace of flavor was drained from it. Then, like a dog, he ground the meat bones with his teeth, enjoying the salty, tangy marrow. He finished and stretched out full length on the ground and went to sleep. . . .

. . . His body was washed by cold water that gradually turned warm and he was buoyed upon a stream and swept out to sea where waves rolled gently and suddenly he found himself walking upon the water how strange and delightful to walk upon the water and he came upon a nude woman holding a nude baby in her arms and the woman was sinking into the water holding the baby above her head and screaming *help* and he ran over the water to the woman and he reached her just before she went down and he took the baby from her hands and stood watching the breaking bubbles where the woman sank and he called *lady* and still no answer yes dive down there and rescue that woman but he could not take this baby with him and he stopped and laid the baby tenderly upon the surface of the water expecting it to sink but it floated and he leaped into the water and held his breath and strained his eyes to see through the gloomy volume of water but there was no woman and he opened his mouth and called *lady* and the water bubbled and his chest ached and his arms were tired but he could not see the woman and he called again *lady lady* and his feet touched sand at the bottom of the sea and his chest felt as though it would burst and he bent his knees and propelled himself upward and water rushed past him and his head bobbed out and he breathed deeply and looked around where was the baby the baby was gone and he rushed over the water looking for the baby calling *where is it* and the empty sky and sea threw back his voice *where is it* and he began to doubt that he could stand upon the water and then he was sinking and as he struggled the water rushed him downward spinning dizzily and he opened his mouth to call for help and water surged into his lungs and he choked . . .

He groaned and leaped erect in the dark, his eyes wide. The images of terror that thronged his brain would not let him sleep. He rose, made sure that the tools were hitched to his belt, and groped his way to the coal pile and found the rectangular gap from which he had taken the bricks. He took out the crowbar and hacked. Then dread paralyzed him. How long had he slept? Was it day or night now? He had to be careful. Someone might hear him if it were day. He hewed softly for hours at the cement, working silently. Faintly quivering in the air above him was the dim sound of yelling voices. Crazy people, he muttered. They're still there in that movie . . .

Having rested, he found the digging much easier. He soon had a dozen bricks out. His spirits rose. He took out another brick and his fingers fluttered in space. Good! What lay ahead of him? Another basement? He made the hole larger, climbed through, walked over an uneven floor and felt a metal surface. He lighted a match and saw that he was standing behind a furnace in a basement; before him, on the far side of the room, was a door. He crossed and opened it; it was full of odds and ends. Daylight spilled from a window above his head.

Then he was aware of a soft, continuous tapping. What was it? A clock? No, it was louder than a clock and more irregular. He placed an old empty box beneath the window, stood upon it, and looked into an areaway. He eased the window up and crawled through; the sound of the tapping came clearly now. He glanced about; he was alone. Then he looked upward at a series of window ledges. The tapping identified itself. That's a typewriter, he said to himself. It seemed to be coming from just above. He grasped the ridges of a rain pipe and lifted himself upward; through a half-inch opening of window he saw a doorknob about three feet away. No, it was not a doorknob; it was a small circular disk made of stainless steel with many fine markings upon it. He held his breath; an eerie white hand, seemingly detached from its arm, touched the metal knob and whirled it, first to the left, then to the right. It's a safe! . . . Suddenly he could see the dial no more; a huge metal door swung slowly toward him and he was looking into a safe filled with green wads of paper money, rows of coins wrapped in brown paper, and glass jars and boxes of various sizes. His heart quickened. Good Lord! The white hand went in and out of the safe, taking wads of bills and cylinders of coins. The hand vanished and he heard the muffled click of the big door as it closed. Only the steel dial was visible now. The typewriter still tapped in his ears, but he could not see it. He blinked, wondering if what he had seen was real. There was more money in that safe than he had seen in all his life.

As he clung to the rain pipe, a daring idea came to him and he pulled the screwdriver from his belt. If the white hand twirled that dial again, he would be able to see how far to left and right it spun and he would have the combination! His blood tingled. I can scratch the numbers right here, he thought. Holding the pipe with one hand, he made the sharp edge of the screwdriver bite into the brick wall. Yes, he could do it. Now, he was set. Now, he had a reason for staying here in the underground. He waited for a long time, but the white hand did not return. Goddamn! Had he been more alert, he could have counted the twirls and he would have had the combination. He got down and stood in the areaway, sunk in reflection.

How could he get into that room? He climbed back into the basement and saw wooden steps leading upward. Was that the room where the safe stood? Fearing that the dial was now being twirled, he clambered through the window, hoisted himself up the rain pipe, and peered; he saw only the naked gleam of the steel dial. He got down and doubled his fists. Well, he would explore the basement. He returned to the basement room and mounted the steps to the door and squinted through the keyhole; all was dark, but the tapping was still somewhere near, still faint and directionless. He pushed the door in; along one wall of a room was a table piled with radios and electrical equipment. A radio shop, he muttered.

Well, he could rig up a radio in his cave. He found a sack, slid the radio into it, and slung it across his back. Closing the door, he went down the steps and stood again in the basement, disappointed. He had not solved the problem of the steel dial and he was irked. He set the radio on the floor and again hoisted himself through the window and up the rain pipe and squinted; the metal door was swinging shut. Goddamn! He's worked the combination again. If I had been patient, I'd have had it! How could he get into that room? He *had* to get into it. He could jimmy the window, but it would be much better if he could get in without any traces. To the right of him, he calculated, should be the basement of the building that held the safe; therefore, if he dug a hole right *here,* he ought to reach his goal.

He began a quiet scraping; it was hard work, for the bricks were not damp. He eventually got one out and lowered it softly to the floor. He had to be careful; perhaps people were beyond this wall. He extracted a second layer of brick and found still another. He gritted his teeth, ready to quit. I'll dig one more, he resolved. When the next brick came out he felt air blowing into his face. He waited to be challenged, but nothing happened.

He enlarged the hole and pulled himself through and stood in quiet darkness. He scratched a match to flame and saw steps; he mounted and peered through a keyhole; Darkness . . . He strained to hear the typewriter, but there was only silence. Maybe the office had closed? He twisted the knob and swung the door in; a frigid blast made him shiver. In the shadows before him were halves and quarters of hogs and lambs and steers hanging from metal hooks on the low ceiling, red meat encased in folds of cold white fat. Fronting him was frost-coated glass from behind which came indistinguishable sounds. The odor of fresh raw meat sickened him and he backed away. A meat market, he whispered.

He ducked his head, suddenly blinded by light. He narrowed his eyes; the red-white rows of meat were drenched in yellow glare. A man wearing a crimson spotted jacket came in and took down a bloody meat cleaver. He eased the door to, holding it ajar just enough to watch the man, hoping that the darkness in which he stood would keep him from being seen. The man took down a hunk of steer and placed it upon a bloody wooden block and bent forward and whacked with the cleaver. The man's face was hard, square, grim; a jet of mustache smudged his upper lip and a glistening cowlick of hair fell over his left eye. Each time he lifted the cleaver and brought it down upon the meat, he let out a short, deep-chested grunt. After he had cut the meat, he wiped blood off the wooden block with a sticky wad of gunny sack and hung the cleaver upon a hook. His face was proud as he placed the chunk of meat in the crook of his elbow and left.

The door slammed and the light went off; once more he stood in shadow. His tension ebbed. From behind the frosted glass he heard the man's voice: "Forty-eight cents a pound, ma'am." He shuddered, feeling that there was something he had to do. But what? He stared fixedly at the cleaver, then he sneezed and was terrified for fear that the man had heard him. But the door did not open. He took down the cleaver and examined the sharp edge smeared with cold blood. Behind the ice-coated glass a cash register rang with a vibrating, musical tinkle.

Absent-mindedly holding the meat cleaver, he rubbed the glass with his thumb and cleared a spot that enabled him to see into the front of the store. The shop was empty, save for the man who was now putting on his hat and coat. Beyond the front window a wan sun shone in the streets; people passed and now and then a fragment of laughter or the whir of a speeding auto came to him. He peered closer and saw on the right counter of the shop a mosquito netting covering pears, grapes, lemons, oranges, bananas, peaches, and plums. His stomach contracted.

The man clicked out the light and he gritted his teeth, muttering, Don't lock the icebox door . . . The man went through the door of the shop and locked it from the outside. Thank God! Now, he would eat some more! He waited, trembling. The sun died and its rays lingered on in the sky, turning the streets to dusk. He opened the door and stepped inside the shop. In reverse letters across the front window was: NICK'S FRUITS AND MEATS. He laughed, picked up a soft ripe yellow pear and bit into it; juice squirted; his mouth ached as his saliva glands reacted to the acid of the fruit. He ate three pears, gobbled six bananas, and made away with several oranges, taking a bite out of their tops and holding them to his lips and squeezing them as he hungrily sucked the juice.

He found a faucet, turned it on, laid the cleaver aside, pursed his lips under the stream until his stomach felt about to burst. He straightened and belched, feeling satisfied for the first time since he had been underground. He sat upon the floor, rolled and lit a cigarette, his bloodshot eyes squinting against the film of drifting smoke. He watched a patch of sky turn red, then purple; night fell and he lit another cigarette, brooding. Some part of him was trying to remember the world he had left, and another part of him did not want to remember it. Sprawling before him in his mind was his wife, Mrs. Wooten for whom he worked, the three policemen who had picked him up . . . He possessed them now more completely than he had ever possessed them when he had lived aboveground. How this had come about he could not say, but he had no desire to go back to them. He laughed, crushed the cigarette, and stood up.

He went to the front door and gazed out. Emotionally he hovered between the world aboveground and the world underground. He longed to go out, but sober judgment urged him to remain here. Then impulsively he pried the lock loose with one swift twist of the crowbar; the door swung outward. Through the twilight he saw a white man and a white woman coming toward him. He held himself tense, waiting for them to pass; but they came directly to the door and confronted him.

"I want to buy a pound of grapes," the woman said.

Terrified, he stepped back into the store. The white man stood to one side and the woman entered.

"Give me a pound of dark ones," the woman said.

The white man came slowly forward, blinking his eyes.

"Where's Nick?" the man asked.

"Were you just closing?" the woman asked.

"Yes, ma'am," he mumbled. For a second he did not breathe, then he mumbled again: "Yes, ma'am."

"I'm sorry," the woman said.

The street lamps came on, lighting the store somewhat. Ought he run? But that would raise an alarm. He moved slowly, dreamily, to a counter and lifted up a bunch of grapes and showed them to the woman.

"Fine," the woman said. "But isn't that more than a pound?"

He did not answer. The man was staring at him intently.

"Put them in a bag for me," the woman said, fumbling with her purse. "Yes, ma'am."

He saw a pile of paper bags under a narrow ledge; he opened one and put the grapes in.

"Thanks," the woman said, taking the bag and placing a dime in his dark palm.

"Where's Nick?" the man asked again. "At supper?"

"Sir? Yes, sir," he breathed.

They left the store and he stood trembling in the doorway. When they were out of sight, he burst out laughing and crying. A trolley car rolled noisily past and he controlled himself quickly. He flung the dime to the pavement with a gesture of contempt and stepped into the warm night air. A few shy stars trembled above him. The look of things was beautiful, yet he felt a lurking threat. He went to an unattended newsstand and looked at a stack of papers. He saw a headline: HUNT NEGRO FOR MURDER.

He felt that someone had slipped up on him from behind and was stripping off his clothes; he looked about wildly, went quickly back into the store, picked up the meat cleaver where he had left it near the sink, then made his way through the icebox to the basement. He stood for a long time, breathing heavily. They know I didn't do anything, he muttered. But how could he prove it? He had signed a confession. Though innocent, he felt guilty, condemned. He struck a match and held it near the steel blade, fascinated and repelled by the dried blotches of blood. Then his fingers gripped the handle of the cleaver with all the strength of his body, he wanted to fling the cleaver from him, but he could not. The match flame wavered and fled; he struggled through the hole and put the cleaver in the sack with the radio. He was determined to keep it, for what purpose he did not know.

He was about to leave when he remembered the safe. Where was it? He wanted to give up, but felt that he ought to make one more try. Opposite the last hole he had dug, he tunneled again, plying the crowbar. Once he was so exhausted that he lay on the concrete floor and panted. Finally he made another hole. He wriggled through and his nostrils filled with the fresh smell of coal. He struck a match; yes, the usual steps led upward. He tiptoed to a door and eased it open. A fair-haired white girl stood in front of a steel cabinet, her blue eyes wide upon him. She turned chalky and gave a high-pitched scream. He bounded down the steps and raced to his hole and clambered through, replacing the bricks with nervous haste. He paused, hearing loud voices.

"What's the matter, Alice?"

"A man . . ."

"What man? Where?"

"A man was at that door . . ."

"Oh, nonsense!"

"He was looking at me through the door!"

"Aw, you're dreaming."

"I *did* see a man!"

The girl was crying now.

"There's nobody here."

Another man's voice sounded.

"What is it, Bob?"

"Alice says she saw a man in here, in that door!"

"Let's take a look."

He waited, poised for flight. Footsteps descended the stairs.

"There's nobody down here."

"The window's locked."

"And there's no door."

"You ought to fire that dame."

"Oh, I don't know. Women are that way."

"She's too hysterical."

The men laughed. Footsteps sounded again on the stairs. A door slammed. He sighed, relieved that he had escaped. But he had not done what he had set out to do; his glimpse of the room had been too brief to determine if the safe was there. He had to know. Boldly he groped through the hole once more; he reached the steps and pulled off his shoes and tiptoed up and peered through the keyhole. His head accidentally touched the door and it swung silently in a fraction of an inch; he saw the girl bent over the cabinet, her back to him. Beyond her was the safe. He crept back down the steps, thinking exultingly: I found it!

Now he had to get the combination. Even if the window in the areaway was locked and bolted, he could gain entrance when the office closed. He scoured through the holes he had dug and stood again in the basement where he had left the radio and the cleaver. Again he crawled out of the window and lifted himself up the rain pipe and peered. The steel dial showed lonely and bright, reflecting the yellow glow of an unseen light. Resigned to a long wait, he sat and leaned against the wall. From far off came the faint sounds of life aboveground; once he looked with a baffled expression at the dark sky. Frequently he rose and climbed the pipe to see the white hand spin the dial, but nothing happened. He bit his lip with impatience. It was not the money that was luring him, but the mere fact that he could get it with impunity. Was the hand now twirling the dial? He rose and looked, but the white hand was not in sight.

Perhaps it would be better to watch continuously? Yes; he clung to the pipe and watched the dial until his eyes thickened with tears. Exhausted, he stood again in the areaway. He heard a door being shut and he clawed up the pipe and looked. He jerked tense as a vague figure passed in front of him. He stared unblinkingly, hugging the pipe with one hand and holding the screwdriver with the other, ready to etch the combination upon the wall. His ears caught: *Dong . . . Dong . . . Dong . . . Dong . . . Dong . . . Dong . . . Dong.* . . . Seven o'clock, he whispered. Maybe they were closing now? What kind of a store would be open as late as this? he wondered. Did anyone live in the rear? Was there a night watchman? Perhaps the safe was *already* locked for the night! Goddamn! While he had been eating in that shop, they had locked up everything . . . Then, just as he was about to give up, the white hand touched the dial and turned it once to the right and stopped at six. With quivering fingers, he etched 1—R—6 upon the brick wall with the tip of the screwdriver. The hand twisted the dial twice to the left and stopped at two, and he engraved 2—L—2 upon the wall. The dial was spun four times to the right and stopped at six again: he wrote 4—R—6. The dial rotated three times to the left and was centered straight up and down; he wrote 3—L—0. The door swung open and again he saw the piles of green money and the rows of wrapped coins. I got it, he said grimly.

Then he was stone still, astonished. There were two hands now. A right hand lifted a wad of green bills and deftly slipped it up the sleeve of the left arm. The hands trembled; again the right hand slipped a packet of bills up the left sleeve. He's stealing he said to himself. He grew indignant, as if the money belonged to him. Though *he* had planned to steal the money, he despised and pitied the man. He felt that his stealing the money and the man's stealing were two entirely different things. He wanted to steal the money merely for the sensation involved in getting it, and he had no intention whatever of spending a penny of it; but he knew that the man who was now stealing it was going to spend it, perhaps for pleasure. The huge steel door closed with a soft click.

Though angry, he was somewhat satisfied. The office would close soon. I'll clean the place out, he mused. He imagined the entire office staff cringing with fear; the police would question everyone for a crime they had not committed, just as they had questioned him. And they would have no idea of how the money had been stolen until they discovered the holes he had tunneled in the walls of the basements. He lowered himself and laughed mischievously, with the abandoned glee of an adolescent.

He flattened himself against the wall as the window above him closed with a rasping sound. He looked; somebody was bolting the window securely with a metal screen. That won't help you, he snickered to himself. He clung to the rain pipe until the yellow light in the office went out. He went back into the basement, picked up the sack containing the radio and cleaver, and crawled through the two holes he had dug and groped his way into the basement of the building that held the safe. He moved in slow motion, breathing softly. Be careful now, he told himself. There might be a night watchman . . . In his memory was the combination written in bold white characters as upon a blackboard. Eel-like he squeezed through the last hole and crept up the steps and put his hand on the knob and pushed the door in about three inches. Then his courage ebbed; his imagination wove dangers for him.

Perhaps the night watchman was waiting in there, ready to shoot. He dangled his cap on a forefinger and poked it past the jamb of the door. If anyone fired, they would hit his cap; but nothing happened. He widened the door, holding the crowbar high above his head, ready to beat off an assailant. He stood like that for five minutes; the rumble of a streetcar brought him to himself. He entered the room. Moonlight floated in from a side window. He confronted the safe, then checked himself. Better take a look around first . . . He stepped about and found a closed door. Was the night watchman in there? He opened it and saw a washbowl, a faucet, and a commode. To the left was still another door that opened into a huge dark room that seemed empty; on the far side of that room he made out the shadow of still another door. Nobody's here, he told himself.

He turned back to the safe and fingered the dial; it spun with ease. He laughed and twirled it just for fun. Get to work, he told himself. He turned the dial to the figures he saw on the blackboard of his memory; it was so easy that he felt that the safe had not been locked at all. The heavy door eased loose and he caught hold of the handle and pulled hard, but the door swung open with a slow momentum of its own. Breathless, he gaped at wads of green bills, rows of wrapped coins, curious glass jars full of white pellets, and many oblong green metal boxes. He glanced guiltily over his shoulder; it seemed impossible that someone should not call to him to stop.

They'll be surprised in the morning, he thought. He opened the top of the sack and lifted a wad of compactly tied bills; the money was crisp and new. He admired the smooth, cleancut edges. The fellows in Washington sure know how to make this stuff, he mused. He rubbed the money with his fingers, as though expecting it to reveal hidden qualities. He lifted the wad to his nose and smelled the fresh odor of ink. Just like any other paper, he mumbled. He dropped the wad into the sack and picked up another. Holding the bag, he thought and laughed.

There was in him no sense of possessiveness; he was intrigued with the form and color of the money, with the manifold reactions which he knew that men aboveground held toward it. The sack was one-third full when it occurred to him to examine the denominations of the bills; without realizing it, he had put many wads of one-dollar bills into the sack. Aw, nuts, he said in disgust. Take the big ones . . . He dumped the one-dollar bills onto the floor and swept all the hundred-dollar bills he could find into the sack, then he raked in rolls of coins with crooked fingers.

He walked to a desk upon which sat a typewriter, the same machine which the blond girl had used. He was fascinated by it; never in his life had he used one of them. It was a queer instrument of business, something beyond the rim of his life. Whenever he had been in an office where a girl was typing, he had almost always spoken in whispers. Remembering vaguely what he had seen others do, he inserted a sheet of paper into the machine; it went in lopsided and he did not know how to straighten it. Spelling in a soft diffident voice, he pecked out his name on the keys: *freddaniels.* He looked at it and laughed. He would learn to type correctly one of these days.

Yes, he would take the typewriter too. He lifted the machine and placed it atop the bulk of money in the sack. He did not feel that he was stealing, for the cleaver, the radio, the money, and the typewriter were all on the same level of value, all meant the same thing to him. They were the serious toys of the men who lived in the dead world of sunshine and rain he had left, the world that had condemned him, branded him guilty.

But what kind of a place is this? He wondered. What was in that dark room to his rear? He felt for his matches and found that he had only one left. He leaned the sack against the safe and groped forward into the room, encountering smooth, metallic objects that felt like machines. Baffled, he touched a wall and tried vainly to locate an electric switch. Well, he *had* to strike his last match. He knelt and struck it, cupping the flame near the floor with his palms. The place seemed to be a factory, with benches and tables. There were bulbs with green shades spaced about the tables; he turned on a light and twisted it low so that the glare was limited. He saw a half-filled packet of cigarettes and appropriated it. There were stools at the benches and he concluded that men worked here at some trade. He wandered and found a few half-used folders of matches. If only he could find more cigarettes! But there were none.

But what kind of a place was this? On a bench he saw a pad of paper captioned: PEER'S—MANUFACTURING JEWELERS. His lips formed an "Oh," then he snapped off the light and ran back to the safe and lifted one of the glass jars and stared at the tiny white pellets. Gingerly he picked up one and found that it was wrapped in tissue paper. He peeled the paper and saw a glittering stone that looked like glass, glinting white and blue sparks. Diamonds, he breathed.

Roughly he tore the paper from the pellets and soon his palm quivered with precious fire. Trembling, he took all four glass jars from the safe and put them into the sack. He grabbed one of the metal boxes, shook it, and heard a tinny rattle. He pried off the lid with the screwdriver. Rings! Hundreds of them . . . Were they worth anything? He scooped up a handful and jets of fire shot fitfully from the stones. These are diamonds too, he said. He pried open another box. Watches! A chorus of soft, metallic ticking filled his ears. For a moment he could not move, then he dumped all the boxes into the sack.

He shut the safe door, then stood looking around, anxious not to overlook anything. Oh! He had seen a door in the room where the machines were. What was in there? More valuables? He re-entered the room, crossed the floor, and stood undecided before the door. He finally caught hold of the knob and pushed the door in; the room beyond was dark. He advanced cautiously inside and ran his fingers along the wall for the usual switch, then he was stark still. *Something had moved in the room!* What was it? Ought he to creep out, taking the rings and diamonds and money? Why risk what he already had? He waited and the ensuing silence gave him confidence to explore further. Dare he strike a match? Would not a match flame make him a good target? He tensed again as he heard a faint sigh; he was now convinced that there was something alive near him, something that lived and breathed. On tiptoe he felt slowly along the wall, hoping that he would not collide with anything. Luck was with him; he found the light switch.

No; don't turn the light on . . . Then suddenly he realized that he did not know in what direction the door was. Goddamn! He had to turn the light on or strike a match. He fingered the switch for a long time, then thought of an idea. He knelt upon the floor, reached his arm up to the switch and flicked the button, hoping that if anyone shot, the bullet would go above his head. The moment the light came on he narrowed his eyes to see quickly. He sucked in his breath and his body gave a violent twitch and was still. In front of him, so close that it made him want to bound up and scream, was a human face.

He was afraid to move lest he touch the man. If the man had opened his eyes at that moment, there was no telling what he might have done. The man—long and rawboned—was stretched out on his back upon a little cot, sleeping in his clothes, his head cushioned by a dirty pillow; his face, clouded by a dark stubble of beard, looked straight up to the ceiling. The man sighed, and he grew tense to defend himself; the man mumbled and turned his face away from the light. I've got to turn off that light, he thought. Just as he was about to rise, he saw a gun and cartridge belt on the floor at the man's side. Yes, he would take the gun and cartridge belt, not to use them, but just to keep them, as one takes a memento from a country fair. He picked them up and was about to click off the light when his eyes fell upon a photograph perched upon a chair near the man's head; it was the picture of a woman, smiling, shown against a background of open fields; at the woman's side were two young children, a boy and a girl. He smiled indulgently; he could send a bullet into that man's brain and time would be over for him. . . .

He clicked off the light and crept silently back into the room where the safe stood; he fastened the cartridge belt about him and adjusted the holster at his right hip. He strutted about the room on tiptoe, lolling his head nonchalantly, then paused, abruptly pulled the gun, and pointed it with grim face toward an imaginary foe. "Boom!" he whispered fiercely. Then he bent forward with silent laughter. That's just like they do it in the movies, he said.

He contemplated his loot for a long time, then got a towel from the washroom and tied the sack securely. When he looked up he was momentarily frightened by his shadow looming on the wall before him. He lifted the sack, dragged it down the basement steps, lugged it across the basement, gasping for breath. After he had struggled through the hole, he clumsily replaced the bricks, then tussled with the sack until he got it to the cave. He stood in the dark, wet with sweat, brooding about the diamonds, the rings, the watches, the money; he remembered the singing in the church, the people yelling in the movie, the dead baby, the nude man stretched out upon the white table . . . He saw these items hovering before his eyes and felt that some dim meaning linked them together, that some magical relationship made them kin. He stared with vacant eyes, convinced that all of these images, with their tongueless reality, were striving to tell him something . . .

Later, seeing with his fingers, he untied the sack and set each item neatly upon the dirt floor. Exploring, he took the bulb, the socket, and the wire out of the tool chest; he was elated to find a double socket at one end of the wire. He crammed the stuff into his pockets and hoisted himself upon the rusty pipes and squinted into the church; it was dim and empty. Somewhere in this wall were live electric wires; but where? He lowered himself, groped and tapped the wall with the butt of the screwdriver, listening vainly for hollow sounds. I'll just take a chance and dig, he said.

For an hour he tried to dislodge a brick, and when he struck a match, he found that he had dug a depth of only an inch! No use in digging here, he sighed. By the flickering light of a match, he looked upward, then lowered his eyes, only to glance up again, startled. Directly above his head, beyond the pipes, was a wealth of electric wiring. I'll be damned, he snickered.

He got an old dull knife from the chest and, seeing again with his fingers, separated the two strands of wire and cut away the insulation. Twice he received a slight shock. He scraped the wiring clean and managed to join the two twin ends, then screwed in the bulb. The sudden illumination blinded him and he shut his lids to kill the pain in his eyeballs. I've got that much done, he thought jubilantly.

He placed the bulb on the dirt floor and the light cast a blatant glare on the bleak clay walls. Next he plugged one end of the wire that dangled from the radio into the light socket and bent down and switched on the button; almost at once there was the harsh sound of static, but no words or music. Why won't it work? he wondered. Had he damaged the mechanism in any way? Maybe it needed grounding? Yes . . . He rummaged in the tool chest and found another length of wire, fastened it to the ground of the radio, and then tied the opposite end to a pipe. Rising and growing distinct, a slow strain of music entranced him with its measured sound. He sat upon the chest, deliriously happy.

Later he searched again in the chest and found a half-gallon can of glue; he opened it and smelled a sharp odor. Then he recalled that he had not even looked at the money. He took a wad of green bills and weighed it in his palm, then broke the seal and held one of the bills up to the light and studied it closely. *The United States of America will pay to the bearer on demand one hundred dollars*, he read in slow speech; then: *This note is legal tender for all debts, public and private* . . . He broke into a musing laugh, feeling that he was reading of the doings of people who lived on some far-off planet. He turned the bill over and saw on the other side of it a delicately beautiful building gleaming with paint and set amidst green grass. He had no desire whatever to count the money; it was what it stood for—the various currents of life swirling aboveground—that captivated him. Next he opened the rolls of coins and let them slide from their paper wrappings to the ground; the bright, new gleaming pennies and nickels and dimes piled high at his feet, a glowing mound of shimmering copper and silver. He sifted them through his fingers, listening to their tinkle as they struck the conical heap.

Oh, yes! He had forgotten. He would now write his name on the typewriter. He inserted a piece of paper and poised his fingers to write. But what was his name? He stared, trying to remember. He stood and glared about the dirt cave, his name on the tip of his lips. But it would not come to him. Why was he here? Yes, he had been running away from the police. But why? His mind was blank. He bit his lips and sat again, feeling a vague terror. But why worry? He laughed, then pecked slowly: *itwasalonghotday.* He was determined to type the sentence without making any mistakes. How did one make capital letters? He experimented and luckily discovered how to lock the machine for capital letters and then shift it back to lower case. Next he discovered how to make spaces, then he wrote neatly and correctly: *It was a long hot day.* Just why he selected that sentence he did not know; it was merely the ritual of performing the thing that appealed to him. He took the sheet out of the machine and looked around with stiff neck and hard eyes and spoke to an imaginary person:

"Yes, I'll have the contracts ready tomorrow."

He laughed. That's just the way they talk, he said. He grew weary of the game and pushed the machine aside. His eyes fell upon the can of glue, and a mischievous idea bloomed in him, filling him with nervous eagerness. He leaped up and opened the can of glue, then broke the seals on all the wads of money. I'm going to have some wallpaper, he said with a luxurious, physical laugh that made him bend at the knees. He took the towel with which he had tied the sack and balled it into a swab and dipped it into the can of glue and dabbed glue onto the wall; then he pasted one green bill by the side of another. He stepped back and cocked his head. Jesus! That's funny . . . He slapped his thighs and guffawed. He had triumphed over the world aboveground! He was free! If only people could see this! He wanted to run from this cave and yell his discovery to the world.

He swabbed all the dirt walls of the cave and pasted them with green bills; when he had finished the walls blazed with a yellow-green fire. Yes, this room would be his hide-out; between him and the world that had branded him guilty would stand this mocking symbol. He had not stolen the money; he had simply picked it up, just as a man would pick up firewood in a forest. And that was how the world aboveground now seemed to him, a wild forest filled with death.

The walls of money finally palled on him and he looked about for new interests to feed his emotions. The cleaver! He drove a nail into the wall and hung the bloody cleaver upon it. Still another idea welled up. He pried open the metal boxes and lined them side by side on the dirt floor. He grinned at the gold and fire. From one box he lifted up a fistful of ticking gold watches and dangled them by their gleaming chains. He stared with an idle smile, then began to wind them up; he did not attempt to set them at any given hour, for there was no time for him now. He took a fistful of nails and drove them into the papered walls and hung the watches upon them, letting them swing down by their glittering chains, trembling and ticking busily against the backdrop of green with the lemon sheen of the electric light shining upon the metal watch casings, converting the golden disks into blobs of liquid yellow. Hardly had he hung up the last watch than the idea extended itself; he took more nails from the chest and drove them into the green paper and took the boxes of rings and went from nail to nail and hung up the golden bands. The blue and white sparks from the stones filled the cave with brittle laughter, as though enjoying his hilarious secret. People certainly can do some funny things, he said to himself.

He sat upon the tool chest, alternately laughing and shaking his head soberly. Hours later he became conscious of the gun sagging at his hip and he pulled it from the holster. He had seen men fire guns in movies, but somehow his life had never led him into contact with firearms. A desire to feel the sensation others felt in firing came over him. But someone might hear . . . Well, what if they did? They would not know where the shot had come from. Not in their wildest notions would they think that it had come from under the streets! He tightened his fingers on the trigger; there was a deafening report and it seemed that the entire underground had caved in upon his eardrums; and in the same instant there flashed an orange-blue spurt of flame that died quickly but lingered on as a vivid after-image. He smelled the acrid stench of burnt powder filling his lungs and he dropped the gun abruptly.

The intensity of his feelings died and he hung the gun and cartridge belt upon the wall. Next he lifted the jars of diamonds and turned them bottom upward, dumping the white pellets upon the ground. One by one he picked them up and peeled the tissue paper from them and piled them in a neat heap. He wiped his sweaty hands on his trousers, lit a cigarette, and commenced playing another game. He imagined that he was a rich man who lived above-ground in the obscene sunshine and he was strolling through a park of a summer morning, smiling, nodding to his neighbors, sucking an after-breakfast cigar. Many times he crossed the floor of the cave, avoiding the diamonds with his feet, yet subtly gauging his footsteps so that his shoes, wet with sewer slime, would strike the diamonds at some undetermined moment. After twenty minutes of sauntering, his right foot smashed into the heap and diamonds lay scattered in all directions, glinting with a million tiny chuckles of icy laughter. Oh, shucks, he mumbled in mock regret, intrigued by the damage he had wrought. He continued walking, ignoring the brittle fire. He felt that he had a glorious victory locked in his heart.

He stooped and flung the diamonds more evenly over the floor and they showered rich sparks, collaborating with him. He went over the floor and trampled the stones just deeply enough for them to be faintly visible, as though they were set deliberately in the prongs of a thousand rings. A ghostly light bathed the cave. He sat on the chest and frowned. Maybe *any*thing's right, he mumbled. Yes, if the world as men had made it was right, then anything else was right, any act a man took to satisfy himself, murder, theft, torture.

He straightened with a start. What was happening to him? He was drawn to these crazy thoughts, yet they made him feel vaguely guilty. He would stretch out upon the ground, then get up; he would want to crawl again through the holes he had dug, but would restrain himself; he would think of going up into the streets, but fear would hold him still. He stood in the middle of the cave, surrounded by green walls and a laughing floor, trembling. He was going to do something, but what? Yes, he was afraid of himself, afraid of doing some nameless thing.

To control himself, he turned on the radio. A melancholy piece of music rose. Brooding over the diamonds on the floor was like looking up into a sky full of restless stars; then the illusion turned into its opposite: he was high up in the air looking down at the twinkling lights of a sprawling city. The music ended and a man recited news events. In the same attitude in which he had contemplated the city, so now, as he heard the cultivated tone, he looked down upon land and sea as men fought, as cities were razed, as planes scattered death upon open towns, as long lines of trenches wavered and broke. He heard the names of generals and the names of mountains and the names of countries and the names and numbers of divisions that were in action on different battle fronts. He saw black smoke billowing from the stacks of warships as they neared each other over wastes of water and heard their huge thunder as red-hot shells screamed across the surface of night seas. He saw hundreds of planes wheeling and droning in the sky and heard the clatter of machine guns as they fought each other and he saw planes falling in plumes of smoke and blaze of fire. He saw steel tanks rumbling across fields of ripe wheat to meet other tanks and there was a loud clang of steel as numberless tanks collided. He saw troops with fixed bayonets charging in waves against other troops who held fixed bayonets and men groaned as steel ripped into their bodies and they went down to die . . . The voice of the radio faded and he was staring at the diamonds on the floor at his feet.

He shut off the radio, fighting an irrational compulsion to act. He walked aimlessly about the cave, touching the walls with his finger tips. Suddenly he stood still. *What was the matter with him?* Yes, he knew . . . It was these walls; these crazy walls were filling him with a wild urge to climb out into the dark sunshine aboveground. Quickly he doused the light to banish the shouting walls, then sat again upon the tool chest. Yes, he was trapped. His muscles were flexed taut and sweat ran down his face. He knew now that he could not stay here and he could not go out. He lit a cigarette with shaking fingers; the match flame revealed the green-papered walls with militant distinctness; the purple on the gun barrel glinted like a threat; the meat cleaver brooded with its eloquent splotches of blood; the mound of silver and copper smoldered angrily; the diamonds winked at him from the floor, and the gold watches ticked and trembled, crowning time the king of consciousness, defining the limits of living . . . The match blaze died and he bolted from where he stood and collided brutally with the nails upon the walls. The spell was broken. He shuddered, feeling that, in spite of his fear, sooner or later he would go up into that dead sunshine and somehow say something to somebody about all this.

He sat again upon the tool chest. Fatigue weighed upon his forehead and eyes. Minutes passed and he relaxed. He dozed, but his imagination was alert. He saw himself rising, wading again in the sweeping water of the sewer; he came to a manhole and climbed out and was amazed to discover that he hoisted himself into a room filled with armed policemen who were watching him intently. He jumped awake in the dark; he had not moved. He sighed, closed his eyes, and slept again; this time his imagination designed a scheme of protection for him. His dreaming made him feel that he was standing in a room watching over his own nude body lying stiff and cold upon a white table. At the far end of the room he saw a crowd of people huddled in a corner, afraid of his body. Though lying dead upon the table, he was standing in some mysterious way at his side, warding off the people, guarding his body, and laughing to himself as he observed the situation. They're scared of me, he thought.

He awakened with a start, leaped to his feet, and stood in the center of the black cave. It was a full minute before he moved again. He hovered between sleeping and waking, unprotected, a prey of wild fears. He could neither see nor hear. One part of him was asleep; his blood coursed slowly and his flesh was numb. On the other hand he was roused to a strange, high pitch of tension. He lifted his fingers to his face, as though about to weep. Gradually his hands lowered and he struck a match, looking about, expecting to see a door through which he could walk to safety; but there was no door, only the green walls and the moving floor. The match flame died and it was dark again.

Five minutes later he was still standing when the thought came to him that he had been asleep. Yes . . . But he was not yet fully awake; he was still queerly blind and deaf. How long had he slept? Where was he? Then suddenly he recalled the green-papered walls of the cave and in the same instant he heard loud singing coming from the church beyond the wall. Yes, they woke me up, he muttered. He hoisted himself and lay atop the bed of pipes and brought his face to the narrow slit. Men and women stood here and there between pews. A song ended and a young black girl tossed back her head and closed her eyes and broke plaintively into another hymn:

> *Glad, glad, glad, oh, so glad*
> *I got Jesus in my soul . . .*

Those few words were all she sang, but what her words did not say, her emotions said as she repeated the lines, varying the mood and tempo, making her tone express meanings which her conscious mind did not know. Another woman melted her voice with the girl's, and then an old man's voice merged with that of the two women. Soon the entire congregation was singing:

> *Glad, glad, glad, oh, so glad*
> *I got Jesus in my soul . . .*

They're wrong, he whispered in the lyric darkness. He felt that their search for a happiness they could never find made them feel that they had

committed some dreadful offense which they could not remember or understand. He was now in possession of the feeling that had gripped him when he
had first come into the underground. It came to him in a series of questions:
Why was this sense of guilt so seemingly innate, so easy to come by, to think,
to feel, so verily physical? It seemed that when one felt this guilt one was
retracing in one's feelings a faint pattern designed long before; it seemed that
one was always trying to remember a gigantic shock that had left a haunting
impression upon one's body which one could not forget or shake off, but which
had been forgotten by the conscious mind, creating in one's life a state of eternal
anxiety.

He had to tear himself away from this; he got down from the pipes. His
nerves were so taut that he seemed to feel his brain pushing through his skull.
He felt that he had to do something, but he could not figure out what it was.
Yet he knew that if he stood here until he made up his mind, he would never
move. He crawled through the hole he had made in the brick wall and the
exertion afforded him respite from tension. When he entered the basement of
the radio store, he stopped in fear, hearing loud voices.

"Come on, boy! Tell us what you did with the radio!"

"Mister, I didn't steal the radio! I swear!"

He heard a dull thumping sound and he imagined a boy being struck
violently.

"Please, mister!"

"Did you take it to a pawn shop?"

"No, sir! I didn't steal the radio! I got a radio at home," the boy's voice
pleaded hysterically. "Go to my home and look!"

There came to his ears the sound of another blow. It was so funny that
he had to clap his hand over his mouth to keep from laughing out loud. They're
beating some poor boy, he whispered to himself, shaking his head. He felt a
sort of distant pity for the boy and wondered if he ought to bring back the radio
and leave it in the basement. No. Perhaps it was a good thing that they were
beating the boy; perhaps the beating would bring to the boy's attention, for the
first time in his life, the secret of his existence, the guilt that he could never get
rid of.

Smiling, he scampered over a coal pile and stood again in the basement
of the building where he had stolen the money and jewelry. He lifted himself
into the areaway, climbed the rain pipe, and squinted through a two-inch
opening of window. The guilty familiarity of what he saw made his muscles
tighten. Framed before him in a bright tableau of daylight was the night
watchman sitting upon the edge of a chair, stripped to the waist, his head
sagging forward, his eyes red and puffy. The watchman's face and shoulders
were stippled with red and black welts. Back of the watchman stood the safe,
the steel door wide open showing the empty vault. Yes, they think he did it,
he mused.

Footsteps sounded in the room and a man in a blue suit passed in front
of him, then another, then still another. Policemen, he breathed. Yes, they were
trying to make the watchman confess, just as they had once made him confess

to a crime he had not done. He stared into the room, trying to recall something. Oh . . . Those were the same policemen who had beaten him, had made him sign that paper when he had been too tired and sick to care. Now, they were doing the same thing to the watchman. His heart pounded as he saw one of the policemen shake a finger into the watchman's face.

"Why don't you admit it's an inside job, Thompson?" the policeman said.

"I've told you all I know," the watchman mumbled through swollen lips.

"But nobody was here but you!" the policeman shouted.

"I was sleeping," the watchman said. "It was wrong, but I was sleeping all that night!"

"Stop telling us that lie!"

"It's the truth!"

"When did you get the combination?"

"I don't know how to open the safe," the watchman said.

He clung to the rain pipe, tense; he wanted to laugh, but he controlled himself. He felt a great sense of power; yes, he could go back to the cave, rip the money off the walls, pick up the diamonds and rings, and bring them here and write a note, telling them where to look for their foolish toys. No . . . What good would that do? It was not worth the effort. The watchman was guilty; although he was not guilty of the crime of which he had been accused, he was guilty, had always been guilty. The only thing that worried him was that the man who had been really stealing was not being accused. But he consoled himself: they'll catch him sometime during his life.

He saw one of the policemen slap the watchman across the mouth.

"Come clean, you bastard!"

"I've told you all I know," the watchman mumbled like a child.

One of the police went to the rear of the watchman's chair and jerked it from under him; the watchman pitched forward upon his face.

"Get up!" a policeman said.

Trembling, the watchman pulled himself up and sat limply again in the chair.

"Now, are you going to talk?"

"I've told you all I know," the watchman gasped.

"Where did you hide the stuff?"

"I didn't take it!"

"Thompson, your brains are in your feet," one of the policemen said. "We're going to string you up and get them back into your skull."

He watched the policemen clamp handcuffs on the watchman's wrists and ankles; then they lifted the watchman and swung him upside-down and hoisted his feet to the edge of a door. The watchman hung, head down, his eyes bulging. They're crazy, he whispered to himself as he clung to the ridges of the pipe.

"You going to talk?" a policeman shouted into the watchman's ear.

He heard the watchman groan.

"We'll let you hang there till you talk, see?"

He saw the watchman close his eyes.

"Let's take 'im down. He passed out," a policeman said.

He grinned as he watched them take the body down and dump it carelessly upon the floor. The policeman took off the handcuffs.

"Let 'im come to. Let's get a smoke," a policeman said.

The three policemen left the scope of his vision. A door slammed. He had an impulse to yell to the watchman that he could escape through the hole in the basement and live with him in the cave. But he wouldn't understand, he told himself. After a moment he saw the watchman rise and stand, swaying from weakness. He stumbled across the room to a desk, opened a drawer, and took out a gun. He's going to kill himself, he thought, intent, eager, detached, yearning to see the end of the man's actions. As the watchman stared vaguely about he lifted the gun to his temple; he stood like that for some minutes, biting his lips until a line of blood etched its way down a corner of his chin. No, he oughtn't do that, he said to himself in a mood of pity.

"Don't!" he half whispered and half yelled.

The watchman looked wildly about; he had heard him. But it did not help; there was a loud report and the watchman's head jerked violently and he fell like a log and lay prone, the gun clattering over the floor.

The three policemen came running into the room with drawn guns. One of the policemen knelt and rolled the watchman's body over and stared at a ragged, scarlet hole in the temple.

"Our hunch was right," the kneeling policeman said. "He was guilty, all right."

"Well, this ends the case," another policeman said.

"He knew he was licked," the third one said with grim satisfaction.

He eased down the rain pipe, crawled back through the holes he had made, and went back into his cave. A fever burned in his bones. He had to act, yet he was afraid. His eyes stared in the darkness as though propped open by invisible hands, as though they had become lidless. His muscles were rigid and he stood for what seemed to him a thousand years.

When he moved again his actions were informed with precision, his muscular system reinforced from a reservoir of energy. He crawled through the hole of earth, dropped into the gray sewer current, and sloshed ahead. When his right foot went forward at a street intersection, he fell backward and shot down into water. In a spasm of terror his right hand grabbed the concrete ledge of a down-curve and he felt the streaking water tugging violently at his body. The current reached his neck and for a moment he was still. He knew if he moved clumsily he would be sucked under. He held onto the ledge with both hands and slowly pulled himself up. He sighed, standing once more in the sweeping water, thankful that he had missed death.

He waded on through sludge, moving with care, until he came to a web of light sifting down from a manhole cover. He saw steel hooks running up the side of the sewer wall; he caught hold and lifted himself and put his shoulder to the cover and moved it an inch. A crash of sound came to him as he looked into a hot glare of sunshine through which blurred shapes moved. Fear scalded him and he dropped back into the pallid current and stood paralyzed in the shadows. A heavy car rumbled past overheard, jarring the pavement, warning him to stay in his world of dark light, knocking the cover back into place with an imperious clang.

He did not know how much fear he felt, for fear claimed him completely; yet it was not a fear of the police or of people, but a cold dread at the thought of the actions he knew he would perform if he went out into that cruel sunshine. His mind said no; his body said yes; and his mind could not understand his feelings. A low whine broke from him and he was in the act of uncoiling. He climbed upward and heard the faint honking of auto horns. Like a frantic cat clutching a rag, he clung to the steel prongs and heaved his shoulder against the cover and pushed it off halfway. For a split second his eyes were drowned in the terror of yellow light and he was in a deeper darkness than he had ever known in the underground.

Partly out of the hole, he blinked, regaining enough sight to make out meaningful forms. An odd thing was happening: No one was rushing forward to challenge him. He had imagined the moment of his emergence as a desperate tussle with men who wanted to cart him off to be killed; instead, life froze about him as the traffic stopped. He pushed the cover aside, stood, swaying in a world so fragile that he expected it to collapse and drop him into some deep void. But nobody seemed to pay him heed. The cars were now swerving to shun him and the gaping hole.

"Why in hell don't you put up a red light, dummy?" a raucous voice yelled.

He understood; they thought that he was a sewer workman. He walked toward the sidewalk, weaving unsteadily through the moving traffic.

"Look where you're going, nigger!"

"That's right! Stay there and get killed!"

"You blind, you bastard?"

"Go home and sleep your drunk off!"

A policeman stood at the curb, looking in the opposite direction. When he passed the policeman, he feared that he would be grabbed, but nothing happened. Where was he? Was this real? He wanted to look about to get his bearings, but felt that something awful would happen to him if he did. He wandered into a spacious doorway of a store that sold men's clothing and saw his reflection in a long mirror: his cheekbones protruded from a hairy black face; his greasy cap was perched askew upon his head and his eyes were red and glassy. His shirt and trousers were caked with mud and hung loosely. His hands were gummed with a black stickiness. He threw back his head and laughed so loudly that passers-by stopped and stared.

He ambled on down the sidewalk, not having the merest notion of where he was going. Yet, sleeping within him, was the drive to go somewhere and say something to somebody. Half an hour later his ears caught the sound of spirited singing.

The Lamb, the Lamb, the Lamb
I hear thy voice a-calling
The Lamb, the Lamb, the Lamb
I feel thy grace a-falling

A church! He exclaimed. He broke into a run and came to brick steps leading downward to a subbasement. This is it! The church into which he had peered. Yes, he was going in and tell them. What? He did not know; but, once face to face with them, he would think of what to say. Must be Sunday, he mused. He ran down the steps and jerked the door open; the church was crowded and a deluge of song swept over him.

The Lamb, the Lamb, the Lamb
Tell me again your story
The Lamb, the Lamb, the Lamb
Flood my soul with your glory

He stared at the singing faces with a trembling smile.
"Say!" he shouted.
Many turned to look at him, but the song rolled on. His arm was jerked violently.
"I'm sorry, Brother, but you can't do that in here," a man said.
"But, mister!"
"You can't act rowdy in God's house," the man said.
"He's filthy," another man said.
"But I want to tell 'em," he said loudly.
"He stinks," someone muttered.
The song had stopped, but at once another one began.

Oh, wondrous sight upon the cross
Vision sweet and divine
Oh, wondrous sight upon the cross
Full of such love sublime

He attempted to twist away, but other hands grabbed him and rushed him into the doorway.
"Let me alone!" he screamed, struggling.
"Get out!"
"He's drunk," somebody said. "He ought to be ashamed!"
"He acts crazy!"
He felt that he was failing and he grew frantic.
"But, mister, let me tell—"
"Get away from this door, or I'll call the police!"
He stared, his trembling smile fading in a sense of wonderment.
"The police," he repeated vacantly.

"Now, get!"

He was pushed toward the brick steps and the door banged shut. The waves of song came.

Oh, wondrous sight, wondrous sight
Lift my heavy heart above
Oh, wondrous sight, wondrous sight
Fill my weary soul with love

He was smiling again now. Yes, the police . . . That was it! Why had he not thought of it before? The idea had been deep down in him, and only now did it assume supreme importance. He looked up and saw a street sign: COURT STREET—HARTSDALE AVENUE. He turned and walked northward, his mind filled with the image of the police station. Yes, that was where they had beaten him, accused him, and had made him sign a confession of his guilt. He would go there and clear up everything, make a statement. What statement? He did not know. He was the statement, and since it was all so clear to him, surely he would be able to make it clear to others.

He came to the corner of Hartsdale Avenue and turned westward. Yeah, there's the station . . . A policeman came down the steps and walked past him without a glance. He mounted the stone steps and went through the door, paused; he was in a hallway where several policemen were standing, talking, smoking. One turned to him.

"What do you want, boy?"

He looked at the policeman and laughed.

"What in hell are you laughing about?" the policeman asked.

He stopped laughing and stared. His whole being was full of what he wanted to say to them, but he could not say it.

"Are you looking for the Desk Sergeant?"

"Yes, sir," he said quickly; then: "Oh, no, sir."

"Well, make up your mind, now."

Four policemen grouped themselves around him.

"I'm looking for the men," he said.

"What men?"

Peculiarly, at that moment he could not remember the names of the policemen; he recalled their beating him, the confession he had signed, and how he had run away from them. He saw the cave next to the church, the money on the walls, the gun, the rings, the cleaver, the watches, and the diamonds on the floor.

"They brought me here," he began.

"When?"

His mind flew back over the blur of the time lived in the underground blackness. He had no idea of how much time had elapsed, but the intensity of what had happened to him told him that it could not have transpired in a short space of time, yet his mind told him that time must have been brief.

"It was a long time ago." He spoke like a child relating a dimly remembered dream. "It was a long time," he repeated, following the promptings of his emotions. "They beat me . . . I was scared . . . I ran away."

A policeman raised a finger to his temple and made a derisive circle.

"Nuts," the policeman said.

"Do you know what place this is, boy?"

"Yes, sir. The police station," he answered sturdily, almost proudly.

"Well, who do you want to see?"

"The men," he said again, feeling that surely they knew the men. "You know the men," he said in a hurt tone.

"What's your name?"

He opened his lips to answer and no words came. He had forgotten. But what did it matter if he had? It was not important.

"Where do you live?"

Where did he live? It had been so long ago since he had lived up here in this strange world that he felt it was foolish even to try to remember. Then for a moment the old mood that had dominated him in the underground surged back. He leaned forward and spoke eagerly.

"They said I killed the woman."

"What woman?" a policeman asked.

"And I signed a paper that said I was guilty," he went on, ignoring their questions. "Then I ran off . . ."

"Did you run off from an institution?"

"No, sir," he said, blinking and shaking his head. "I came from under the ground. I pushed off the manhole cover and climbed out . . ."

"All right, now," a policeman said, placing an arm about his shoulder. "We'll send you to the psycho and you'll be taken care of."

"Maybe he's a Fifth Columnist!" a policeman shouted.

There was laughter and, despite his anxiety, he joined in. But the laughter lasted so long that it irked him.

"I got to find those men," he protested mildly.

"Say, boy, what have you been drinking?"

"Water," he said. "I got some water in a basement."

"Were the men you ran away from dressed in white, boy?"

"No, sir," he said brightly. "They were men like you."

An elderly policeman caught hold of his arm.

"Try and think hard. Where did they pick you up?"

He knotted his brows in an effort to remember, but he was blank inside. The policeman stood before him demanding logical answers and he could no longer think with his mind; he thought with his feelings and no words came.

"I was guilty," he said. "Oh, no, sir. I wasn't then, I mean, mister!"

"Aw, talk sense. Now, where did they pick you up?"

He felt challenged and his mind began reconstructing events in reverse; his feelings ranged back over the long hours and he saw the cave, the sewer, the bloody room where it was said that a woman had been killed.

"Oh, yes, sir," he said, smiling. "I was coming from Mrs. Wooten's."

"Who is she?"

"I work for her."

"Where does she live?"

"Next door to Mrs. Peabody, the woman who was killed."

The policemen were very quiet now, looking at him intently.

"What do you know about Mrs. Peabody's death, boy?"

"Nothing, sir. But they said I killed her. But it doesn't make any difference, I'm guilty!"

"What are you talking about, boy?"

His smile faded and he was possessed with memories of the underground; he saw the cave next to the church and his lips moved to speak. But how could he say it? The distance between what he felt and what these men meant was vast. Something told him, as he stood there looking into their faces, that he would never be able to tell them, that they would never believe him even if he told them.

"All the people I saw was guilty," he began slowly.

"Aw, nuts," a policeman muttered.

"Say," another policeman said, "that Peabody woman was killed over on Winewood. That's Number Ten's beat."

"Where's Number Ten?" a policeman asked.

"Upstairs in the swing room," someone answered.

"Take this boy up, Sam," a policeman ordered.

"O.K. Come along, boy."

An elderly policeman caught hold of his arm and led him up a flight of wooden stairs, down a long hall, and to a door.

"Squad Ten!" the policeman called through the door.

"What?" a gruff voice answered.

"Someone to see you!"

"About what?"

The old policeman pushed the door in and then shoved him into the room.

He stared, his lips open, his heart barely beating. Before him were the three policemen who had picked him up and had beaten him to extract the confession. They were seated about a small table, playing cards. The air was blue with smoke and sunshine poured through a high window, lighting up fantastic smoke shapes. He saw one of the policemen look up; the policeman's face was tired and a cigarette drooped limply from one corner of his mouth and both of his fat, puffy eyes were squinting and his hands gripped his cards.

"Lawson!" the man exclaimed.

The moment the man's name sounded he remembered the names of all of them: Lawson, Murphy, and Johnson. How simple it was. He waited, smiling, wondering how they would react when they knew that he had come back.

"Looking for me?" the man who had been called Lawson mumbled, sorting his cards. "For what?"

So far only Murphy, the red-headed one, had recognized him.

"Don't you-all remember me?" he blurted, running to the table.

All three of the policemen were looking at him now. Lawson, who seemed the leader, jumped to his feet.

"Where in hell have you been?"

"Do you know 'im, Lawson?" the old policeman asked.

"Huh?" Lawson frowned. "Oh, yes. I'll handle 'im." The old policeman left the room and Lawson crossed to the door and turned the key in the lock "Come here, boy," he ordered in a cold tone.

He did not move; he looked from face to face. Yes, he would tell them about his cave.

"He looks batty to me," Johnson said, the one who had not spoken before.

"Why in hell did you come back here?" Lawson said.

"I—I just didn't want to run away no more," he said. "I'm all right, now." He paused; the men's attitude puzzled him.

"You've been hiding, huh?" Lawson asked in a tone that denoted that he had not heard his previous words. "You told us you were sick, and when we left you in the room, you jumped out of the window and ran away."

Panic filled him. Yes, they were indifferent to what he would say! They were waiting for him to speak and they would laugh at him. He had to rescue himself from this bog; he had to force the reality of himself upon them.

"Mister, I took a sackful of money and pasted it on the walls . . ." he began.

"I'll be damned," Lawson said.

"Listen," said Murphy, "let me tell you something for your own good. We don't want you, see? You're free, free as air. Now go home and forget it. It was all a mistake. We caught the guy who did the Peabody job. He wasn't colored at all. He was an Eyetalian."

"Shut up!" Lawson yelled. "Have you no sense!"

"But I want to tell 'im," Murphy said.

"We can't let this crazy fool go," Lawson exploded. "He acts nuts, but this may be a stunt . . ."

"I was down in the basement," he began in a childlike tone, as though repeating a lesson learned by heart; "and I went into a movie . . ." His voice failed. He was getting ahead of his story. First, he ought to tell them about the singing in the church, but what words could he use? He looked at them appealingly. "I went into a shop and took a sackful of money and diamonds and watches and rings . . . I didn't steal 'em, I'll give 'em all back. I just took 'em to play with . . ." He paused, stunned by their disbelieving eyes.

Lawson lit a cigarette and looked at him coldly.

"What did you do with the money?" he asked in a quiet, waiting voice.

"I pasted the hundred-dollar bills on the walls."

"What walls?" Lawson asked.

"The walls of the dirt room," he said, smiling, "the room next to the church. I hung up the rings and the watches and I stamped the diamonds into the dirt . . ." He saw that they were not understanding what he was saying. He grew frantic to make them believe, his voice tumbled on eagerly. "I saw a dead baby and a dead man . . ."

"Aw, you're nuts," Lawson snarled, shoving him into a chair.

"But mister . . ."

"Johnson, where's the paper he signed?" Lawson asked.

"What paper?"

"The confession, fool!"

Johnson pulled out his billfold and extracted a crumpled piece of paper.

"Yes, sir, mister," he said, stretching forth his hand. "That's the paper I signed . . ."

Lawson slapped him and he would have toppled had his chair not struck a wall behind him. Lawson scratched a match and held the paper over the flame; the confession burned down to Lawson's finger-tips.

He stared, thunderstruck; the sun of the underground was fleeting and the terrible darkness of the day stood before him. They did not believe him, but he *had* to make them believe him!

"But mister . . ."

"It's going to be all right, boy," Lawson said with a quiet, soothing laugh. "I've burned your confession, see? You didn't sign anything." Lawson came close to him with the black ashes in his palm. "You don't remember a thing about this, do you?"

"Don't you-all be scared of me," he pleaded, sensing their uneasiness. "I'll sign another paper, if you want me to. I'll show you the cave."

"What's your game, boy?" Lawson asked suddenly.

"What are you trying to find out?" Johnson asked.

"Who sent you here?" Murphy demanded.

"Nobody sent me, mister," he said. "I just want to show you the room . . ."

"Aw, he's plumb bats," Murphy said. "Let's ship 'im to the psycho."

"No," Lawson said. "He's playing a game and I wish to God I knew what it was."

There flashed through his mind a definite way to make them believe him; he rose from the chair with nervous excitement.

"Mister, I saw the night watchman blow his brains out because you accused him of stealing," he told them. "But he didn't steal the money and diamonds. I took 'em."

Tigerishly Lawson grabbed his collar and lifted him bodily.

"Who told you about that?"

"Don't get excited, Lawson," Johnson said. "He read about it in the papers."

Lawson flung him away.

"He couldn't have," Lawson said, pulling papers from his pocket. "I haven't turned in the reports yet."

"Then how *did* he find out?" Murphy asked.

"Let's get out of here," Lawson said with quick resolution. "Listen, boy, we're going to take you to a nice, quiet place, see?"

"Yes, sir," he said. "And I'll show you the underground."

"Goddamn," Lawson muttered, fastening the gun at his hip. He narrowed his eyes at Johnson and Murphy. "Listen," he spoke just above a whisper, "say nothing about this, you hear?"

"O.K.," Johnson said.

"Sure," Murphy said.

Lawson unlocked the door and Johnson and Murphy led him down the stairs. The hallway was crowded with policemen.

"What have you got there, Lawson?"

"What did he do, Lawson?"

"He's psycho, ain't he, Lawson?"

Lawson did not answer; Johnson and Murphy led him to the car parked at the curb, pushed him into the back seat. Lawson got behind the steering wheel and the car rolled forward.

"What's up, Lawson?" Murphy asked.

"Listen," Lawson began slowly, "we tell the papers that he spilled about the Peabody job, then he escapes. The Wop is caught and we tell the papers that we steered them wrong to trap the real guy, see? Now this dope shows up and acts nuts. If we let him go, he'll squeal that we framed him, see?"

"I'm all right, mister," he said, feeling Murphy's and Johnson's arms locked rigidly into his. "I'm guilty . . . I'll show you everything in the underground. I laughed and laughed . . ."

"Shut that fool up!" Lawson ordered.

Johnson tapped him across the head with a blackjack and he fell back against the seat cushion, dazed.

"Yes, sir," he mumbled. "I'm all right."

The car sped along Hartsdale Avenue, then swung onto Pine Street and rolled to State Street, then turned south. It slowed to a stop, turned in the middle of a block, and headed north again.

"You're going around in circles, Lawson," Murphy said.

Lawson did not answer; he was hunched over the steering wheel. Finally he pulled the car to a stop at a curb.

"Say, boy, tell us the truth," Lawson asked quietly. "Where did you hide?"

"I didn't hide, mister."

The three policemen were staring at him now; he felt that for the first time they were willing to understand him.

"Then what happened?"

"Mister, when I looked through all of those holes and saw how people were living, I loved 'em . . ."

"Cut out that crazy talk!" Lawson snapped. "Who sent you back here?"

"Nobody, mister."

"Maybe he's talking straight," Johnson ventured.

"All right," Lawson said. "Nobody hid you. Now, tell us *where* you hid."

"I went underground . . ."

"What goddamn underground do you keep talking about?"

"I just went . . ." He paused and looked into the street, then pointed to a manhole cover. "I went down in there and stayed."

"In the *sewer?*"

"Yes, sir."

The policemen burst into a sudden laugh and ended quickly. Lawson swung the car around and drove to Woodside Avenue; he brought the car to a stop in front of a tall apartment building.

"What're we going to do, Lawson?" Murphy asked.

"I'm taking him up to my place," Lawson said. "We've got to wait until night. There's nothing we can do now."

They took him out of the car and led him into a vestibule.

"Take the steps," Lawson muttered.

They led him up four flights of stairs and into the living room of a small apartment. Johnson and Murphy let go of his arms and he stood uncertainly in the middle of the room.

"Now, listen, boy," Lawson began, "forget those wild lies you've been telling us. Where did you hide?"

"I just went underground, like I told you."

The room rocked with laughter. Lawson went to a cabinet and got a bottle of whiskey; he placed glasses for Johnson and Murphy. The three of them drank.

He felt that he could not explain himself to them. He tried to muster all the sprawling images that floated in him; the images stood out sharply in his mind, but he could not make them have the meaning for others that they had for him. He felt so helpless that he began to cry.

"He's nuts, all right," Johnson said. "All nuts cry like that."

Murphy crossed the room and slapped him.

"Stop that raving!"

A sense of excitement flooded him; he ran to Murphy and grabbed his arm.

"Let me show you the cave," he said. "Come on, and you'll see!"

Before he knew it a sharp blow had clipped him on the chin; darkness covered his eyes. He dimly felt himself being lifted and laid out on the sofa. He heard low voices and struggled to rise, but hard hands held him down. His brain was clearing now. He pulled to a sitting posture and stared with glazed eyes. It had grown dark. How long had he been out?

"Say, boy," Lawson said soothingly, "will you show us the underground?"

His eyes shone and his heart swelled with gratitude. Lawson believed him! He rose, glad; he grabbed Lawson's arm, making the policeman spill whiskey from the glass to his shirt.

"Take it easy, goddammit," Lawson said.

"Yes, sir."

"O.K. We'll take you down. But you'd better be telling us the truth, you hear?"

He clapped his hands in wild joy.

"I'll show you everything!"

He had triumphed at last! He would now do what he had felt was compelling him all along. At last he would be free of his burden.

"Take 'im down," Lawson ordered.

They led him down to the vestibule; when he reached the side-walk he saw that it was night and a fine rain was falling.

"It's just like when I went down," he told them.

"What?" Lawson asked.

"The rain," he said, sweeping his arm in a wide arc. "It was raining when I went down. The rain made the water rise and lift the cover off."

"Cut it out," Lawson snapped.

They did not believe him now, but they would. A mood of high selflessness throbbed in him. He could barely contain his rising spirits. They would see what he had seen; they would feel what he had felt. He would lead them through all the holes he had dug and . . . He wanted to make a hymn, prance about in physical ecstasy, throw his arm about the policemen in fellowship.

"Get into the car," Lawson ordered.

He climbed in and Johnson and Murphy sat at either side of him; Lawson slid behind the steering wheel and started the motor.

"Now, tell us where to go," Lawson said.

"It's right around the corner from where the lady was killed," he said.

The car rolled slowly and he closed his eyes, remembering the song he had heard in the church, the song that had wrought him to such a high pitch of terror and pity. He sang softly, lolling his head:

> Glad, glad, glad, oh, so glad
> I got Jesus in my soul . . .

"Mister," he said, stopping his song, "you ought to see how funny the rings look on the wall." He giggled. "I fired a pistol, too. Just once, to see how it felt."

"What do you suppose he's suffering from?" Johnson asked.

"Delusions of grandeur, maybe," Murphy said.

"Maybe it's because he lives in a white man's world," Lawson said.

"Say, boy, what did you eat down there?" Murphy asked, prodding Johnson anticipatorily with his elbow.

"Pears, oranges, bananas, and pork chops," he said.

The car filled with laughter.

"You didn't eat any watermelon?" Lawson asked, smiling.

"No, sir," he answered calmly. "I didn't see any."

The three policemen roared harder and louder.

"Boy, you're sure some case," Murphy said, shaking his head in wonder.

The car pulled to a curb.

"All right, boy," Lawson said. "Tell us where to go."

He peered through the rain and saw where he had gone down. The streets, save for a few dim lamps glowing softly through the rain, were dark and empty.

"Right there, mister," he said, pointing.

"Come on; let's take a look," Lawson said.

"Well, suppose he did hide down there," Johnson said, "what is that supposed to prove?"

"I don't believe he hid down there," Murphy said.

"It won't hurt to look," Lawson said. "Leave things to me."

Lawson got out of the car and looked up and down the street.

He was eager to show them the cave now. If he could show them what he had seen, then they would feel what he had felt and they in turn would show it to others and those others would feel as they had felt, and soon everybody would be governed by the same impulse of pity.

"Take 'im out," Lawson ordered.

Johnson and Murphy opened the door and pushed him out; he stood trembling in the rain, smiling. Again Lawson looked up and down the street; no one was in sight. The rain came down hard, slanting like black wires across the wind-swept air.

"All right," Lawson said. "Show us."

He walked to the center of the street, stopped and inserted a finger in one of the tiny holes of the cover and tugged, but he was too weak to budge it.

"Did you really go down in there, boy?" Lawson asked; there was a doubt in his voice.

"Yes, sir. Just a minute. I'll show you."

"Help 'im get that damn thing off," Lawson said.

Johnson stepped forward and lifted the cover; it clanged against the wet pavement. The hole gaped round and black.

"I went down in there," he announced with pride.

Lawson gazed at him for a long time without speaking, then he reached his right hand to his holster and drew his gun.

"Mister, I got a gun just like that down there," he said, laughing, and looking into Lawson's face. "I fired it once then hung it on the wall. I'll show you."

"Show us how you went down," Lawson said quietly.

"I'll go down first, mister, and then you-all can come after me, hear?" he spoke like a little boy playing a game.

"Sure, sure," Lawson said soothingly. "Go ahead. We'll come."

He looked brightly at the policemen; he was bursting with happiness. He bent down and placed his hands on the rim of the hole and sat on the edge, his feet dangling into watery darkness. He heard the familiar drone of the gray current. He lowered his body and hung for a moment by his fingers, then he went downward on the steel prongs, hand over hand, until he reached the last rung. He dropped and his feet hit the water and he felt the stiff current trying to suck him away. He balanced himself quickly and looked back upward at the policemen.

"Come on, you-all!" he yelled, casting his voice above the rustling at his feet.

The vague forms that towered above him in the rain did not move. He laughed, feeling that they doubted him. But, once they saw the things he had done, they would never doubt again.

"Come on! The cave isn't far!" he yelled. "But be careful when your feet hit the water, because the current's pretty rough down here!"

Lawson still held the gun. Murphy and Johnson looked at Lawson quizzically.

"What are we going to do, Lawson?" Murphy asked.

"We are not going to follow that crazy nigger down into that sewer, are we?" Johnson asked.

"Come on, you-all!" he begged in a shout.

He saw Lawson raise the gun and point it directly at him. Lawson's face twitched, as though he were hesitating.

Then there was a thunderous report and a streak of fire ripped through his chest. He was hurled into the water, flat on his back. He looked in amazement at the blurred white faces above him. They shot me, he said to himself. The water flowed past him, blossoming in foam about his arms, his legs, and his head. His jaw sagged and his mouth gaped soundless. A vast pain gripped his head and gradually squeezed out consciousness. As from a great distance he heard hollow voices.

"What did you shoot him for, Lawson?"

"I had to."

"Why?"

"You've got to shoot his kind. They'd wreck things."

As though in a deep dream, he heard a metallic clank; they had replaced the manhole cover, shutting out forever the sound of wind and rain. From overhead came the muffled roar of a powerful motor and the swish of a speeding car. He felt the strong tide pushing him slowly into the middle of the sewer, turning him about. For a split second there hovered before his eyes the glittering cave, the shouting walls, and the laughing floor . . . Then his mouth was full of thick, bitter water. The current spun him around. He sighed and closed his eyes, a whirling object rushing alone in the darkness, veering, tossing, lost in the heart of the earth.

Writing Assignments for "The Man Who Lived Underground"

I. Brief Papers
   A. 1. Why does the narrator eventually decide to come up from the underground?
      2. Explain why, after walking over the diamonds, the narrator feels he has won "a glorious victory" (p. 356).
      3. If you were not completely surprised by the ending of the story, explain how Wright uses foreshadowing, how he provides early clues and suggestions of what will happen later.
      4. Explain why the narrator interprets the scene of the men and women singing hymns as "something abysmally obscene" (p. 339).

   B. Argue for or against one of the assertions below:
      1. The story clearly implies that justice triumphs on earth.
      2. The narrator's stealing money and the other man's stealing money are, as the narrator says, "two entirely different things" (p. 350).
      3. It would make no difference to the story if the narrator were white instead of black.
      4. The story warns us against relying too completely on our heart and feelings.

C. 1. Describe your own feelings as you finished the story and learned that the police had shot and killed the narrator.
  2. How did you react to the scene in which Alice reports to two men that an intruder had been looking at her (p. 349)?
  3. What do you think the narrator means when he says that people are "sleeping in their living, awake in their dying"? Do these words relate in any way to your own experience?
  4. Free write for 5 to 10 minutes beginning with "I think 'The Man Who Lived Underground' is a religious story" or "I think 'The Man Who Lived Underground' is not a religious story."

II. Longer Papers

A. Write a paper on the topic generated by your free writing in C.4 above.
B. Argue for or against the assertion that Wright implies that the narrator of "The Man Who Lived Underground" is, in significant ways, like Jesus Christ.
C. The narrator thinks at one point, "Maybe anything's right. . . . Yes, if the world as men had made it was right, then anything else was right, any act a man took to satisfy himself, murder, theft, torture" (p. 356). Argue for or against the assertion that the story as a whole endorses this position.
D. Argue for or against the assertion that the story's narrator is a growing, maturing, developing character.
E. Several stanzas from hymns are sung in the story. Explain the relationship between the words of the hymns and the story as a whole.
F. Take any one important scene that occurs underground—the dead baby, the undertaker's establishment, the church, the movie house, the meat market, or any other—and explain how that scene contributes to the story as a whole.
G. What does the story say or imply about innocence and guilt?
H. Explain what the story has to say about seeing and blindness.

III. Comparative Papers

A. Explain what, taken together, "The Man Who Lived Underground" and "The Sky is Gray" present as the major hardships for a black person living in a world largely controlled by whites.
B. Argue for or against the assertion that "The Man Who Lived Underground" and "The Sky is Gray" are bleak, pessimistic stories in that each implies that the hostility between races is likely to last forever.
C. Defend, modify, or refute the contention that both "The Man Who Lived Underground" and "The Sky is Gray" make clear that there is no substantial basis for charges that blacks are discriminated against or mistreated by whites.
D. What do "The Man Who Lived Underground" and "The Sky is Gray" present as the most admirable human qualities and characteristics?
E. Argue for or against the assertion that both "The Man Who Lived Underground" and "The Sky is Gray" show that the most serious problem faced by black Americans is American capitalism and the so-called "free" enterprise system.

GAIL GODWIN
Dream Children

Before Reading

This story begins, *"The worst thing. Such a terrible thing to happen to a young woman."* What do you think is the worst thing that can happen to a young woman? Why? Free write on this question for 5 or 10 minutes.

The worst thing. Such a terrible thing to happen to a young woman. It's a wonder she didn't go mad.

As she went about her errands, a cheerful, neat young woman, a wife, wearing pants with permanent creases and safari jackets and high-necked sweaters that folded chastely just below the line of the small gold hoops she wore in her ears, she imagined people saying this, or thinking it to themselves. But nobody knew. Nobody knew anything, other than that she and her husband had moved here a year ago, as so many couples were moving farther away from the city, the husband commuting, or staying in town during the week—as hers did. There was nobody here, in this quaint, unspoiled village, nestled in the foothills of the mountains, who could have looked at her and guessed that anything out of the ordinary, predictable, auspicious spectrum of things that happen to bright, attractive young women had happened to her. She always returned her books to the local library on time; she bought liquor at the local liquor store only on Friday, before she went to meet her husband's bus from the city. He was something in television, a producer? So many ambitious young couples moving to this Dutch farming village, founded in 1690, to restore ruined fieldstone houses and plant herb gardens and keep their own horses and discover the relief of finding oneself insignificant in Nature for the first time!

A terrible thing. So freakish. If you read it in a story or saw it on TV, you'd say no, this sort of thing could never happen in an American hospital.

DePuy, who owned the old Patroon farm adjacent to her land, frequently glimpsed her racing her horse in the early morning, when the mists still lay on the fields, sometimes just before the sun came up and there was a frost on everything. "One woodchuck hole and she and that stallion will both have to be put out of their misery," he told his wife. "She's too reckless. I'll bet you her old man doesn't know she goes streaking to hell across the fields like that." Mrs. DePuy nodded, silent, and went about her business. She, too, watched that other woman ride, a woman not much younger than herself, but with an aura of romance—of tragedy, perhaps. The way she looked: like those heroines in English novels who ride off their bad tempers and unrequited love affairs,

DREAM CHILDREN First published in 1974. Gail Godwin (1937–) is a journalist, teacher, and writer of essays, short stories, and novels (*Glass People, The Odd Woman,* and *A Mother and Two Daughters*).

clenching their thighs against the flanks of spirited horses with murderous red eyes. Mrs. DePuy, who had ridden since the age of three, recognized something beyond recklessness in that elegant young woman, in her crisp checked shirts and her dove-gray jodhpurs. *She has nothing to fear anymore,* thought the farmer's wife, with sure feminine instinct; she both envied and pitied her. "What she needs is children," remarked DePuy.

"A Dry Sack, a Remy Martin, and . . . let's see, a half-gallon of the Chablis, and I think I'd better take a Scotch . . . and the Mouton-Cadet . . . and maybe a dry vermouth." Mrs. Frye, another farmer's wife, who runs the liquor store, asks if her husband is bringing company for the weekend. "He sure is; we couldn't drink all that by ourselves," and the young woman laughs, her lovely teeth exposed, her small gold earrings quivering in the light. "You know, I saw his name—on the television the other night," says Mrs. Frye. "It was at the beginning of that new comedy show, the one with the woman who used to be on another show with her husband and little girl, only they divorced, you know the one?" "Of course I do. It's one of my husband's shows. I'll tell him you watched it." Mrs. Frye puts the bottles in an empty box, carefully inserting wedges of cardboard between them. Through the window of her store she sees her customer's pert bottle-green car, some sort of little foreign car with the engine running, filled with groceries and weekend parcels, and that big silver-blue dog sitting up in the front seat just like a human being. "I think that kind of thing is so sad," says Mrs. Frye; "families breaking up, poor little children having to divide their loyalties." "I couldn't agree more," replies the young woman, nodding gravely. Such a personable, polite girl! "Are you sure you can carry that, dear? I can get Earl from the back. . . ." But the girl has it hoisted on her shoulder in a flash, is airily maneuvering between unopened cartons stacked in the aisle, in her pretty boots. Her perfume lingers in Mrs. Frye's store for a half-hour after she has driven away.

After dinner, her husband and his friends drank brandy. She lay in front of the fire, stroking the dog, and listening to Victoria Darrow, the news commentator, in person. A few minutes ago, they had all watched Victoria on TV. "That's right; thirty-nine!" Victoria now whispered to her. "What? That's kind of you. I'm photogenic, thank God, or I'd have been put out to pasture long before. . . . I look five, maybe seven years younger on the screen . . . but the point I'm getting at is, I went to this doctor and he said, 'If you want to do this thing, you'd better go home today and get started.' He told me—did you know this? Did you know that a woman is born with all the eggs she'll ever have, and when she gets to my age, the ones that are left have been rattling around so long they're a little shopworn; then every time you fly you get an extra dose of radioactivity, so those poor eggs. He told me when a woman over forty comes into his office pregnant, his heart sinks; that's why he quit practicing obstetrics, he said; he could still remember the screams of a woman whose baby he delivered . . . she was having natural childbirth and she kept saying, 'Why won't you let me see it, I insist on seeing it,' and so he had to, and he says he can still hear her screaming."

"Oh, what was—what was wrong with it?"

But she never got the answer. Her husband, white around the lips, was standing over Victoria ominously, offering the Remy Martin bottle. "Vicky, let me pour you some more," he said. And to his wife, "I think Blue Boy needs to go out."

"Yes, yes, of course. Please excuse me, Victoria. I'll just be . . ."

Her husband followed her to the kitchen, his hand on the back of her neck. "Are you okay? That stupid yammering bitch. She and her twenty-six-year-old lover! I wish I'd never brought them, but she's been hinting around the studio for weeks."

"But I like them, I like having them. I'm fine. Please go back. I'll take the dog out and come back. Please . . ."

"All right. If you're sure you're okay." He backed away, hands dangling at his sides. A handsome man, wearing a pink shirt with Guatemalan embroidery. Thick black hair and a face rather boyish, but cunning. Last weekend she had sat beside him, alone in this house, just the two of them, and watched him on television: a documentary, in several parts, in which TV "examines itself." There was his double, sitting in an armchair in his executive office, coolly replying to the questions of Victoria Darrow. *"Do you personally watch all the programs you produce, Mr. McNair?"* She watched the man on the screen, how he moved his lips when he spoke, but kept the rest of his face, his body perfectly still. Funny, she had never noticed this before. He managed to say that he did and did not watch all the programs he produced.

Now, in the kitchen, she looked at him backing away, a little like a renegade in one of his own shows—a desperate man, perhaps, who had just killed somebody and is backing away, hands dangling loosely at his sides, Mr. McNair, her husband. That man on the screen. Once a lover above her in bed. That friend who held her hand in the hospital. One hand in hers, the other holding the stopwatch. For a brief instant, all the images coalesce and she feels something again. But once outside, under the galaxies of autumn-sharp stars, the intelligent dog at her heels like some smart gray ghost, she is glad to be free of all that. She walks quickly over the damp grass to the barn, to look in on her horse. She understands something: her husband, Victoria Darrow lead double lives that seem perfectly normal to them. But if she told her husband that she, too, is in two lives, he would become alarmed; he would sell this house and make her move back to the city where he could keep an eye on her welfare.

She is discovering people like herself, down through the centuries, all over the world. She scours books with titles like *The Timeless Moment, The Sleeping Prophet, Between Two Worlds, Silent Union: A Record of Unwilled Communication;* collecting evidence, weaving a sort of underworld net of colleagues around her.

A rainy fall day. Too wet to ride. The silver dog asleep beside her in her special alcove, a padded window seat filled with pillows and books. She is looking down on the fields of dried lithrium, and the fir trees beyond, and the mountains gauzy with fog and rain, thinking, in a kind of terror and ecstasy, about all these connections. A book lies face down on her lap. She has just read the following:

> Theodore Dreiser* and his friend John Cowper Powys had been dining at Dreiser's place on West Fifty Seventh Street. As Powys made ready to leave and catch his train to the little town up the Hudson, where he was then living, he told Dreiser, "I'll appear before you here, later in the evening."
>   Dreiser laughed. "Are you going to turn yourself into a ghost, or have you a spare key?" he asked. Powys said he would return "in some form," he didn't know exactly what kind.

> After his friend left, Dreiser sat up and read for two hours. Then he looked up and saw Powys standing in the doorway to the living room. It was Powys' features, his tall stature, even the loose tweed garments which he wore. Dreiser rose at once and strode toward the figure, saying, "Well, John, you kept your word. Come on in and tell me how you did it." But the figure vanished when Dreiser came within three feet of it.
>   Dreiser then went to the telephone and called Powys' house in the country. Powys answered. Dreiser told him what had happened and Powys said, "I told you I'd be there and you oughtn't to be surprised." But he refused to discuss how he had done it, if, indeed, he knew how.

"But don't you get frightened, up here all by yourself, alone with all these creaky sounds?" asked Victoria, the next morning.

"No, I guess I'm used to them," she replied, breaking eggs into a bowl. "I know what each one means. The wood expanding and contracting . . . the wind getting caught between the shutter and the latch . . . Sometimes small animals get lost in the stone walls and scratch around till they find their way out . . . or die."

"Ugh. But don't you imagine things? I would, in a house like this. How old? That's almost three hundred years of lived lives, people suffering and shouting and making love and giving birth, under this roof. . . . You'd think there'd be a few ghosts around."

"I don't know," said her hostess blandly. "I haven't heard any. But of course, I have Blue Boy, so I don't get scared." She whisked the eggs, unable to face Victoria. She and her husband had lain awake last night, embarrassed at the sounds coming from the next room. No ghostly moans, those. "Why can't that bitch control herself, or at least lower her voice," he said angrily. He stroked his wife's arm, both of them pretending not to remember. She had bled for an entire year afterward, until the doctor said they would have to remove

*Theodore Dreiser: U.S. novelist (1871–1945).

everything. "I'm empty," she had said when her husband had tried again, after she was healed. "I'm sorry, I just don't feel anything." Now they lay tenderly together on these weekends, like childhood friends, like effigies on a lovers' tomb, their mutual sorrow like a sword between them. She assumed he had another life, or lives, in town. As she had here. Nobody is just one person, she had learned.

"I'm sure I would imagine things," said Victoria. "I would see things and hear things inside my head much worse than an ordinary murderer or rapist."

The wind caught in the shutter latch . . . a small animal dislodging pieces of fieldstone in its terror, sending them tumbling down the inner walls, from attic to cellar . . . a sound like a child rattling a jar full of marbles, or small stones . . .

"I have so little imagination," she said humbly, warming the butter in the omelet pan. She could feel Victoria Darrow's professional curiosity waning from her dull country life, focusing elsewhere.

Cunning!

As a child of nine, she had gone through a phase of walking in her sleep. One summer night, they found her bed empty, and after an hour's hysterical search they had found her in her nightgown, curled up on the flagstones beside the fishpond. She woke, baffled, in her father's tense clutch, the stars all over the sky, her mother repeating over and over again to the night at large, "Oh, my God, she could have drowned!" They took her to a child psychiatrist, a pretty Austrian woman who spoke to her with the same vocabulary she used on grownups, putting the child instantly at ease. "It is not at all uncommon what you did. I have known so many children who take little night journeys from their beds, and then they awaken and don't know what all the fuss is about! Usually these journeys are quite harmless, because children are surrounded by a magical reality that keeps them safe. Yes, the race of children possesses magically sagacious powers! But the grownups, they tend to forget how it once was for them. They worry, they are afraid of so many things. You do not want your mother and father, who love you so anxiously, to live in fear of you going to live with the fishes." She had giggled at the thought. The woman's steady gray-green eyes were trained on her carefully, suspending her in a kind of bubble. Then she had rejoined her parents, a dutiful "child" again, holding a hand up to each of them. The night journeys had stopped.

A thunderstorm one night last spring. Blue Boy whining in his insulated house below the garage. She had lain there, strangely elated by the nearness of the thunderclaps that tore at the sky, followed by instantaneous flashes of jagged light. Wondering shouldn't she go down and let the dog in; he hated storms. Then dozing off again . . .

She woke. The storm had stopped. The dark air was quiet. Something had changed, some small thing—what? She had to think hard before she found it: the hall light, which she kept burning during the week-nights when she was there alone, had gone out. She reached over and switched the button on her bedside lamp. Nothing. A tree must have fallen and hit a wire, causing the power to go off. This often happened here. No problem. The dog had stopped crying. She felt herself sinking into a delicious, deep reverie, the kind that sometimes came just before morning, as if her being broke slowly into tiny pieces and spread itself over the world. It was a feeling she had not known until she had lived by herself in this house: this weightless though conscious state in which she lay, as if in a warm bath, and yet was able to send her thoughts anywhere, as if her mind contained the entire world.

And as she floated in this silent world, transparent and buoyed upon the dream layers of the mind, she heard a small rattling sound, like pebbles being shaken in a jar. The sound came distinctly from the guest room, a room so chosen by her husband and herself because it was the farthest room from their bedroom on this floor. It lay above what had been the old side of the house, built seventy-five years before the new side, which was completed in 1753. There was a bed in it, and a chair, and some plants in the window. Sometimes on weekends when she could not sleep, she went and read there, or meditated, to keep from waking her husband. It was the room where Victoria Darrow and her young lover would not sleep the following fall, because she would say quietly to her husband, "No . . . not that room. I—I've made up the bed in the other room." "What?" he would want to know. "The one next to ours? Right under our noses?"

She did not lie long listening to this sound before she understood it was one she had never heard in the house before. It had a peculiar regularity to its rhythm; there was nothing accidental about it, nothing influenced by the wind, or the nerves of some lost animal. *K-chunk, k-chunk, k-chunk,* it went. At intervals of exactly a half-minute apart. She still remembered how to time such things, such intervals. She was as good as any stopwatch when it came to timing certain intervals.

K-chunk, k-chunk, k-chunk. That determined regularity. Something willed, something poignantly repeated, as though the repetition was a means of consoling someone in the dark. Her skin began to prickle. Often, lying in such states of weightless reverie, she had practiced the trick of sending herself abroad, into rooms of the house, out into the night to check on Blue Boy, over to the barn to look in on her horse, who slept standing up. Once she had heard a rather frightening noise, as if someone in the basement had turned on a faucet, and so she forced herself to "go down," floating down two sets of stairs into the darkness, only to discover what she had known all the time: the hookup system between the hot-water tank and the pump, which sounded like someone turning on the water.

Now she went through the palpable, prickly darkness, without lights, down the chilly hall in her sleeveless gown, into the guest room. Although there was no light, not even a moon shining through the window, she could make out the shape of the bed and then the chair, the spider plants on the window, and a small dark shape in one corner, on the floor, which she and her husband had painted a light yellow.

K-chunk, k-chunk, k-chunk. The shape moved with the noise.

Now she knew what they meant, that "someone's hair stood on end." It was true. As she forced herself across the borders of a place she had never been, she felt, distinctly, every single hair on her head raise itself a millimeter or so from her scalp.

She knelt down and discovered him. He was kneeling, a little cold and scared, shaking a small jar filled with some kind of pebbles. (She later found out, in a subsequent visit, that they were small colored shells, of a triangular shape, called coquinas: she found them in a picture in a child's nature book at the library.) He was wearing pajamas a little too big for him, obviously hand-me-downs, and he was exactly two years older than the only time she had ever held him in her arms.

The two of them knelt in the corner of the room, taking each other in. His large eyes were the same as before: dark and unblinking. He held the small jar close to him, watching her. He was not afraid, but she knew better than to move too close.

She knelt, the tears streaming down her cheeks, but she made no sound, her eyes fastened on that small form. And then the hall light came on silently, as well as the lamp beside her bed, and with wet cheeks and pounding heart she could not be sure whether or not she had actually been out of the room.

But what did it matter, on the level where they had met? He traveled so much farther than she to reach that room. (*"Yes, the race of children possesses magically sagacious powers!"*)

She and her husband sat together on the flowered chintz sofa, watching the last of the series in which TV purportedly examined itself. She said, "Did you ever think that the whole thing is really a miracle? I mean, here we sit, eighty miles away from your studios, and we turn on a little machine and there is Victoria, speaking to us as clearly as she did last weekend when she was in this very room. Why, it's magic, it's time travel and space travel right in front of our eyes, but because it's been 'discovered,' because the world understands that it's only little dots that transmit Victoria electrically to us, it's *all right.* We can bear it. Don't you sometimes wonder about all the miracles that haven't been officially approved yet? I mean, who knows, maybe in a hundred years everybody will take it for granted that they can send an image of themselves around in space by some perfectly natural means available to us now. I mean, when you think about it, what *is* space? What *is* time? Where do the so-called boundaries of each of us begin and end? Can anyone explain it?"

He was drinking Scotch and thinking how they had decided not to renew Victoria Darrow's contract. Somewhere on the edges of his mind hovered an anxious, growing certainty about his wife. At the local grocery store this morning, when he went to pick up a carton of milk and the paper, he had stopped to chat with DePuy. "I don't mean to interfere, but she doesn't know those fields," said the farmer. "Last year we had to shoot a mare, stumbled into one of those holes. . . . It's madness, the way she rides."

And look at her now, her face so pale and shining, speaking of miracles and space travel, almost on the verge of tears. . . .

And last night, his first night up from the city, he had wandered through the house, trying to drink himself into this slower weekend pace, and he had come across a pile of her books, stacked in the alcove where, it was obvious, she lay for hours, escaping into science fiction, and the occult.

Now his own face appeared on the screen. "I want to be fair," he was telling Victoria Darrow. "I want to be objective. . . . Violence has always been part of the human makeup. I don't like it anymore than you do, but there it is. I think it's more a question of whether we want to face things as they are or escape into fantasies of how we would like them to be."

Beside him, his wife uttered a sudden bell-like laugh.

("*. . . It's madness, the way she rides.*")

He did want to be fair, objective. She had told him again and again that she liked her life here. And he—well, he had to admit he liked his own present setup.

"I am a pragmatist," he was telling Virginia Darrow on the screen. He decided to speak to his wife about her riding and leave her alone about the books. She had the right to some escape, if anyone did. But the titles: *Marvelous Manifestations, The Mind Travellers, A Doctor Looks at Spiritualism, The Other Side* . . . Something revolted in him, he couldn't help it; he felt an actual physical revulsion at this kind of thinking. Still it was better than some other escapes. His friend Barnett, the actor, who said at night he went from room to room, after his wife was asleep, collecting empty glasses. ("Once I found one by the Water Pik, a second on the ledge beside the tub, a third on the back of the john, and a fourth on the floor beside the john. . . .")

He looked sideways at his wife, who was absorbed, it seemed, in watching him on the screen. Her face was tense, alert, animated. She did not look mad. She wore slim gray pants and a loose-knit pullover made of some silvery material, like a knight's chain mail. The lines of her profile were clear and silvery themselves, somehow sexless and pure, like a child's profile. He no longer felt lust when he looked at her, only a sad determination to protect her. He had a mistress in town, whom he loved, but he had explained, right from the beginning, that he considered himself married for the rest of his life. He told this woman the whole story. "And I am implicated in it. I could never leave her." An intelligent, sensitive woman, she had actually wept and said, "Of course not."

He always wore the same pajamas, a shade too big, but always clean. Obviously washed again and again in a machine that went through its cycles frequently. She imagined his "other mother," a harassed woman with several children, short on money, on time, on dreams—all the things she herself had too much of. The family lived, she believed, somewhere in Florida, probably on the west coast. She had worked that out from the little coquina shells: their bright colors, even in moonlight shining through a small window with spider plants in it. His face and arms had been suntanned early in the spring and late into the autumn. They never spoke or touched. She was not sure how much of this he understood. She tried and failed to remember where she herself had gone, in those little night journeys to the fishpond. Perhaps he never remembered afterward, when he woke up, clutching his jar, in a roomful of brothers and sisters. Or with a worried mother or father come to collect him, asleep by the sea. Once she had a very clear dream of the whole family, living in a trailer, with palm trees. But that was a dream; she recognized its difference in quality from those truly magic times when, through his own childish powers, he somehow found a will strong enough, or innocent enough, to project himself upon her still-floating consciousness, as clearly and as believably as her own husband's image on the screen.

There had been six of those times in six months. She dared to look forward to more. So unafraid he was. The last time was the day after Victoria Darrow and her young lover and her own good husband had returned to the city. She had gone farther with the child than ever before. On a starry-clear, cold September Monday, she had coaxed him down the stairs and out of the house with her. He held to the banisters, a child unused to stairs, and yet she knew there was no danger; he floated in his own dream with her. She took him to see Blue Boy. Who disappointed her by whining and backing away in fear. And then to the barn to see the horse. Who perked up his ears and looked interested. There was no touching, of course, no touching or speaking. Later she wondered if horses, then, were more magical than dogs. If dogs were more "realistic." She was glad the family was poor, the mother harassed. They could not afford any expensive child psychiatrist who would hypnotize him out of his night journeys.

He loved her. She knew that. Even if he never remembered her in his other life.

"At last I was beginning to understand what Teilhard de Chardin* meant when he said that man's true home is the mind. I understood that when the mystics tell us that the mind is a place, they *don't mean it as a metaphor.* I found these new powers developed with practice. I had to detach myself from my ordinary physical personality. The intelligent part of me had to remain wide awake, and move down into this world of thoughts, dreams and memories. After several such journeyings I understood something else: dream and reality aren't competitors, but reciprocal sources of consciousness." This she read in a "respectable book," by a "respectable man," a scientist, alive and living in England, only a few years older than herself. She looked down at the dog, sleeping on the rug. His lean silvery body actually ran as he slept! Suddenly his muzzle lifted, the savage teeth snapped. Where was he "really" now? Did the dream rabbit in his jaws know it was a dream? There was much to think about, between her trips to the nursery.

Would the boy grow, would she see his body slowly emerging from its child's shape, the arms and legs lengthening, the face thinning out into a man's—like a certain advertisement for bread she had seen on TV where a child grows up, in less than a half-minute of sponsor time, right before the viewer's eyes. Would he grow into a man, grow a beard . . . outgrow the nursery region of his mind where they had been able to meet?

*Teilhard de Chardin: French geologist and philosopher (1881–1955).

And yet, some daylight part of his mind must have retained an image of her from that single daylight time they had looked into each other's eyes.

The worst thing, such an awful thing to happen to a young woman . . . She was having this natural childbirth, you see, her husband in the delivery room with her, and the pains were coming a half-minute apart, and the doctor had just said, "This is going to be a breeze, Mrs. McNair," and they never knew exactly what went wrong, but all of a sudden the pains stopped and they had to go in after the baby without even time to give her a saddle block or any sort of anesthetic. . . . They must have practically had to tear it out of her . . . the husband fainted. The baby was born dead, and they gave her a heavy sedative to put her out all night.

When she woke the next morning, before she had time to remember what had happened, a nurse suddenly entered the room and laid a baby in her arms. "Here's your little boy," she said cheerfully, and the woman thought, with a profound, religious relief, *So that other nightmare was a dream,* and she had the child at her breast feeding him before the nurse realized her mistake and rushed back into the room, but they had to knock the poor woman out with more sedatives before she would let the child go. She was screaming and so was the little baby and they clung to each other till she passed out.

They would have let the nurse go, only it wasn't entirely her fault. The hospital was having a strike at the time; some of the nurses were outside picketing and this nurse had been working straight through for forty-eight hours, and when she was questioned afterward she said she had just mixed up the rooms, and yet, she said, when she had seen the woman and the baby clinging to each other like that, she had undergone a sort of revelation in her almost hallucinatory exhaustion: the nurse said she saw that all children and mothers were interchangeable, that nobody could own anybody or anything, anymore than you could own an idea that happened to be passing through the air and caught on your mind, or anymore than you owned the rosebush that grew in your back yard. There were only mothers and children, she realized; though, afterward, the realization faded.

It was the kind of freakish thing that happens once in a million times, and it's a wonder the poor woman kept her sanity.

In the intervals, longer than those measured by any stopwatch, she waited for him. In what the world accepted as "time," she shopped for groceries, for clothes; she read; she waved from her bottle-green car to Mrs. Frye, trimming the hedge in front of the liquor store, to Mrs. DePuy, hanging out her children's pajamas in the back yard of the old Patroon farm. She rode her horse through the fields of the waning season, letting him have his head; she rode like the wind, a happy, happy woman. She rode faster than fear because she was a woman in a dream, a woman anxiously awaiting her child's sleep. The stallion's hoofs pounded the earth. Oiling his tractor, DePuy resented the foolish woman and almost wished for a woodchuck hole to break that arrogant ride. Wished deep in a violent level of himself he never knew he had. For he was a kind, distracted father and husband, a practical, hard-working man who would never descend deeply into himself. Her body, skimming through time, felt weightless to the horse.

Was she a woman riding a horse and dreaming she was a mother who anxiously awaited her child's sleep; or was she a mother dreaming of herself as a free spirit who could ride her horse like the wind because she had nothing to fear?

I am a happy woman, that's all I know. Who can explain such things?

Writing Assignments for "Dream Children"

I. Brief Papers
   A. 1. What is the "terrible thing" that has happened to Mrs. McNair?
      2. Why aren't we told the "terrible thing" immediately and all at once?
      3. Why does Mrs. McNair race her horse so recklessly?
      4. How can it be explained that DePuy, a kind man, hopes that Mrs. McNair's horse will hit a woodchuck hole?
      5. Why does Gail Godwin include in her story the scene in the liquor store (p. 376)?
      6. Why is the story called "Dream Children" instead of "Dream Child"?
      7. Why is Victoria Darrow in the story?
      8. List as many references to time as you can, and then explain whether or not you can find a pattern of any kind there.

   B. Argue for or against one of the assertions below:
      1. Mrs. McNair is a madwoman.
      2. Mrs. McNair can't really be happy; she only thinks she's happy.
      3. It is cruel and immoral for Mr. McNair to have a mistress.
      4. Only someone who believes in time travel, ESP, and UFO's can take this story seriously.

   C. 1. Do you feel sorry for Mrs. McNair? Why or why not?
      2. Do you feel sorry for Mr. McNair? Why or why not?
      3. What do you think Mrs. DePuy means when she thinks, "She has nothing to fear anymore" (p. 376)?
      4. Do you find the story optimistic? Pessimistic? A mixture? How do you feel at the story's conclusion?

II. Longer Papers
   A. What does the story have to say about the relationship between dream and reality?

B. How does the story develop the idea that "Nobody is just one person"?
C. A number of readers find "Dream Children" to be one of the most touching and poignant stories they have ever read. If you agree, try to explain why the story moves you so deeply.
D. "Dream Children" is the story of events that, out of context, might seem improbable and even unbelievable. How has Gail Godwin told her story so as to make them credible?
E. According to the story, what is the relationship between childhood and adulthood? Does the story support the psychiatrist's statement that grownups "are afraid of so many things" (p. 379)?

DAVID QUAMMEN

Walking Out

Before Reading

Think back to a time when one or both of your parents made you do something that you really didn't want to do but that they thought you'd enjoy—camping or hunting or fishing; taking a trip to the shore or the mountains or the city; or going to a symphony or ballet or play or sporting event. Free write for 5 or 10 minutes about what happened.

As the train rocked dead at Livingston he saw the man, in a worn khaki shirt with button flaps buttoned, arms crossed. The boy's hand sprang up by reflex, and his face broke into a smile. The man smiled back gravely, and nodded. He did not otherwise move. The boy turned from the window and, with the awesome deliberateness of a fat child harboring reluctance, began struggling to pull down his bag. His father would wait on the platform. First sight of him had reminded the boy that nothing was simple enough now for hurrying.

They drove in the old open Willys toward the cabin beyond town. The windshield of the Willys was up, but the fine cold sharp rain came into their faces, and the boy could not raise his eyes to look at the road. He wore a rain parka his father had handed him at the station. The man, protected by only the khaki, held his lips strung in a firm silent line that seemed more grin than wince. Riding through town in the cold rain, open topped and jaunty, getting drenched as though by necessity, was—the boy understood vaguely—somehow in the spirit of this season.

"We have a moose tag," his father shouted.

The boy said nothing. He refused to care what it meant, that they had a moose tag.

WALKING OUT   First published in 1980. David Quammen (1948–   ) was born in Cincinnati and educated at Yale and Oxford University. He writes short stories, novels, and science books.

"I've got one picked out. A bull. I've stalked him for two weeks. Up in the Crazies. When we get to the cabin, we'll build a good roaring fire." With only the charade of a pause, he added, "Your mother." It was said like a question. The boy waited. "How is she?"

"All right, I guess." Over the jeep's howl, with the wind stealing his voice, the boy too had to shout.

"Are you friends with her?"

"I guess so."

"Is she still a beautiful lady?"

"I don't know. I guess so. I don't know that."

"You must know that. Is she starting to get wrinkled like me? Does she seem worried and sad? Or is she just still a fine beautiful lady? You must know that."

"She's still a beautiful lady, I guess."

"Did she tell you any messages for me?"

"She said . . . she said I should give you her love," the boy lied, impulsively and clumsily. He was at once embarrassed that he had done it.

"Oh," his father said. "Thank you, David."

They reached the cabin on a mile of dirt road winding through meadow to a spruce grove. Inside, the boy was enwrapped in the strong syncretic smell of all seasonal mountain cabins: pine resin and insect repellent and a mustiness suggesting damp bathing trunks stored in a drawer. There were yellow pine floors and ropework throw rugs and a bead curtain to the bedroom and a cast-iron cook stove with none of the lids or handles missing and a pump in the kitchen sink and old issues of *Field and Stream,* and on the mantel above where a fire now finally burned was a picture of the boy's grandfather, the railroad telegrapher, who had once owned the cabin. The boy's father cooked a dinner of fried ham, and though the boy did not like ham he had expected his father to cook canned stew or Spam, so he said nothing. His father asked him about school and the boy talked and his father seemed to be interested. Warm and dry, the boy began to feel safe from his own anguish. Then his father said:

"We'll leave tomorrow around ten."

Last year on the boy's visit they had hunted birds. They had lived in the cabin for six nights, and each day they had hunted pheasant in the wheat stubble, or blue grouse in the woods, or ducks along the irrigation slews. The boy had been wet and cold and miserable at times, but each evening they returned to the cabin and to the boy's suitcase of dry clothes. They had eaten hot food cooked on a stove, and had smelled the cabin smell, and had slept together in a bed. In six days of hunting, the boy had not managed to kill a single bird. Yet last year he had known that, at least once a day, he would be comfortable, if not happy. This year his father planned that he should not even be comfortable. He had said in his last letter to Evergreen Park, before the boy left Chicago but when it was too late for him not to leave, that he would take the boy camping in the mountains, after big game. He had pretended to believe that the boy would be glad.

The Willys was loaded and moving by ten minutes to ten. For three hours they drove, through Big Timber, and then north on the highway, and then back west again on a logging road that took them winding and bouncing higher into the mountains. Thick cottony streaks of white cloud hung in among the mountaintop trees, light and dense dollops against the bulking sharp dark olive, as though in a black-and-white photograph. They followed the gravel road for an hour, and the boy thought they would soon have a flat tire or break an axle. If they had a flat, the boy knew, his father would only change it and drive on until they had the second, farther from the highway. Finally they crossed a creek and his father plunged the Willys off into a bed of weeds.

His father said, "Here."

The boy said, "Where?"

"Up that little drainage. At the head of the creek."

"How far is it?"

"Two or three miles."

"Is that where you saw the moose?"

"No. That's where I saw the sheepman's hut. The moose is farther. On top."

"Are we going to sleep in a hut? I thought we were going to sleep in a tent."

"No. Why should we carry a tent up there when we have a perfectly good hut?"

The boy couldn't answer that question. He thought now that this might be the time when he would cry. He had known it was coming.

"I don't much want to sleep in a hut," he said, and his voice broke with the simple honesty of it, and his eyes glazed. He held his mouth tight against the trembling.

As though something had broken in him too, the boy's father laid his forehead down on the steering wheel, against his knuckles. For a moment he remained bowed, breathing exhaustedly. But he looked up again before speaking.

"Well, we don't have to, David."

The boy said nothing.

"It's an old sheepman's hut made of logs, and it's near where we're going to hunt, and we can fix it dry and good. I thought you might like that. I thought it might be more fun than a tent. But we don't have to do it. We can drive back to Big Timber and buy a tent, or we can drive back to the cabin and hunt birds, like last year. Whatever you want to do. You have to forgive me the kind of ideas I get. I hope you will. We don't have to do anything that you don't want to do."

"No," the boy said. "I want to."

"Are you sure?"

"No," the boy said. "But I just want to."

They bushwhacked along the creek, treading a thick soft mixture of moss and humus and needles, climbing upward through brush. Then the brush thinned and they were ascending an open creek bottom, thirty yards wide, darkened by fir and cedar. Farther, and they struck a trail, which led them upward along the creek. Farther still, and the trail received a branch, then another, then forked.

"Who made this trail? Did the sheepman?"

"No," his father said. "Deer and elk."

Gradually the creek's little canyon narrowed, steep wooded shoulders funneling closer on each side. For a while the game trails forked and converged like a maze, but soon again there were only two branches, and finally one, heavily worn. It dodged through alder and willow, skirting tangles of browned raspberry, so that the boy and his father could never see more than twenty feet ahead. When they stopped to rest, the boy's father unstrapped the .270 from his pack and loaded it.

"We have to be careful now," he explained. "We may surprise a bear."

Under the cedars, the creek bottom held a cool dampness that seemed to be stored from one winter to the next. The boy began at once to feel chilled. He put on his jacket, and they continued climbing. Soon he was sweating again in the cold.

On a small flat where the alder drew back from the creek, the hut was built into one bank of the canyon, with the sod of the hillside lapping out over its roof. The door was a low dark opening. Forty or fifty years ago, the boy's father explained, this hut had been built and used by a Basque* shepherd. At that time there had been many Basques in Montana, and they had run sheep all across this ridge of the Crazies. His father forgot to explain what a Basque was, and the boy didn't remind him.

They built a fire. His father had brought sirloin steaks and an onion for dinner, and the boy was happy with him about that. As they ate, it grew dark, but the boy and his father had stocked a large comforting pile of naked deadfall. In the darkness, by firelight, his father made chocolate pudding. The pudding had been his father's surprise. The boy sat on a piece of canvas and added logs to the fire while his father drank coffee. Sparks rose on the heat and the boy watched them climb toward the cedar limbs and the black pools of sky. The pudding did not set.

"Do you remember your grandfather, David?"

"Yes," the boy said, and wished it were true. He remembered a funeral when he was three.

"Your grandfather brought me up on this mountain when I was seventeen. That was the last year he hunted." The boy knew what sort of thoughts his father was having. But he knew also that his own home was in Evergreen Park, and that he was another man's boy now, with another man's name, though this indeed was his father. "Your grandfather was fifty years older than me."

The boy said nothing.

"And I'm thirty-four years older than you."

"And I'm only eleven," the boy cautioned him.

"Yes," said his father. "And someday you'll have a son and you'll be forty

*Basque: A person from the Western Pyrenees Mountains in southern Europe, between France and Spain.

years older than him, and you'll want so badly for him to know who you are that you could cry."

The boy was embarrassed.

"And that's called the cycle of life's infinite wisdom," his father said, and laughed at himself unpleasantly.

"What did he die of?" the boy asked, desperate to escape the focus of his father's rumination.

"He was eighty-seven then. Christ. He was tired." The boy's father went silent. Then he shook his head, and poured himself the remaining coffee.

Through that night the boy was never quite warm. He slept on his side with his knees drawn up, and this was uncomfortable but his body seemed to demand it for warmth. The hard cold mountain earth pressed upward through the mat of fir boughs his father had laid, and drew heat from the boy's body like a pallet of leeches. He clutched the bedroll around his neck and folded the empty part at the bottom back under his legs. Once he woke to a noise. Though his father was sleeping between him and the door of the hut, for a while the boy lay awake, listening worriedly, and then woke again on his back to realize time had passed. He heard droplets begin to hit the canvas his father had spread over the sod roof of the hut. But he remained dry.

He rose to the smell of a fire. The tarp was rigid with sleet and frost. The firewood and the knapsacks were frosted. It was that gray time of dawn before any blue and, through the branches above, the boy was unable to tell whether the sky was murky or clear. Delicate sheet ice hung on everything, but there was no wetness. The rain seemed to have been hushed by the cold.

"What time is it?"

"Early yet."

"How early?" The boy was thinking about the cold at home as he waited outside on 96th Street for his school bus. That was the cruelest moment of his day, but it seemed a benign and familiar part of him compared to this.

"Early. I don't have a watch. What difference does it make, David?"

"Not any."

After breakfast they began walking up the valley. His father had the .270, and the boy carried an old Winchester .30-30, with open sights. The walking was not hard, and with this gentle exercise in the cold morning the boy soon felt fresh and fine. Now I'm hunting for moose with my father, he told himself. That's just what I'm doing. Few boys in Evergreen Park had ever been moose hunting with their fathers in Montana, he knew. I'm doing it now, the boy told himself.

Reaching the lip of a high meadow, a mile above the shepherd's hut, they had not seen so much as a magpie.

Before them, across hundreds of yards, opened a smooth lake of tall lifeless grass, browned by September drought and killed by the frosts and beginning to rot with November's rain. The creek was here a deep quiet channel of smooth curves overhung by the grass, with a dark surface like heavy oil. When they had come fifty yards into the meadow, his father turned and pointed out to the boy a large ponderosa pine with a forked crown that marked the head of their creek valley. He showed the boy a small aspen grove midway across the meadow, toward which they were aligning themselves.

"Near the far woods is a beaver pond. The moose waters there. We can wait in the aspens and watch the whole meadow without being seen. If he doesn't come, we'll go up another canyon, and check again on the way back."

For an hour, and another, they waited. The boy sat with his hands in his jacket pockets, bunching the jacket tighter around him, and his buttocks drew cold moisture from the ground. His father squatted on his heels like a country man, rising periodically to inspect the meadow in all directions. Finally he stood up; he fixed his stare on the distant fringe of woods and, like a retriever, did not move. He said, "David."

The boy stood beside him. His father placed a hand on the boy's shoulder. The boy saw a large dark form rolling toward them like a great slug in the grass.

"Is it the moose?"

"No," said his father. "That is a grizzly bear, David. An old male grizzly."

The boy was impressed. He sensed an aura of power and terror and authority about the husky shape, even at two hundred yards.

"Are we going to shoot him?"

"No."

"Why not?"

"We don't have a permit," his father whispered. "And because we don't want to."

The bear plowed on toward the beaver pond for a while, then stopped. It froze in the grass and seemed to be listening. The boy's father added: "That's not hunting for the meat. That's hunting for the fear. I don't need the fear. I've got enough in my life already."

The bear turned and moiled off quickly through the grass. It disappeared back into the far woods.

"He heard us."

"Maybe," the boy's father said. "Let's go have a look at that beaver pond."

A sleek furred carcass lay low in the water, swollen grotesquely with putrescence and coated with glistening blowflies. Four days, the boy's father guessed. The moose had been shot at least eighteen times with a .22 pistol. One of its eyes had been shot out; it had been shot twice in the jaw; and both quarters on the side that lay upward were ruined with shots. Standing up to his knees in the sump, the boy's father took the trouble of counting the holes, and probing one of the slugs out with his knife. That only made him angrier. He flung the lead away.

For the next three hours, with his father withdrawn into a solitary and characteristic bitterness, the boy felt abandoned. He did not understand why a moose would be slaughtered with a light pistol and left to rot. His father did not bother to explain; like the bear, he seemed to understand it as well as he needed to. They walked on, but they did not really hunt.

They left the meadow for more pine, and now tamarack, naked tamarack, the yellow needles nearly all down and going ginger where they coated the trail.

The boy and his father hiked along a level path into another canyon, this one vast at the mouth and narrowing between high ridges of bare rock. They crossed and recrossed the shepherd's creek, which in this canyon was a tumbling free-stone brook. Following five yards behind his father, watching the cold, unapproachable rage that shaped the line of the man's shoulders, the boy was miserably uneasy because his father had grown so distant and quiet. They climbed over deadfalls blocking the trail, skirted one boulder large as a cabin, and blundered into a garden of nettles that stung them fiercely through their trousers. They saw fresh elk scat, and they saw bear, diarrhetic with late berries. The boy's father eventually grew bored with brooding, and showed the boy how to stalk. Before dusk that day they had shot an elk.

An open and gently sloped hillside, almost a meadow, ran for a quarter mile in quaking aspen, none over fifteen feet tall. The elk was above. The boy's father had the boy brace his gun in the notch of an aspen and take the first shot. The boy missed. The elk reeled and bolted down and his father killed it before it made cover. It was a five-point bull. They dressed the elk out and dragged it down to the cover of large pines, near the stream, where they would quarter it tomorrow, and then they returned under twilight to the hut.

That night even the fetal position could not keep the boy warm. He shivered wakefully for hours. He was glad that the following day, though full of walking and butchery and oppressive burdens, would be their last in the woods. He heard nothing. When he woke, through the door of the hut he saw whiteness like bone.

Six inches had fallen, and it was still snowing. The boy stood about in the campsite, amazed. When it snowed three inches in Evergreen Park, the boy would wake before dawn to the hiss of sand trucks and the ratchet of chains. Here there had been no warning. The boy was not much older than he had been yesterday, and the transformation of the woods seemed mysterious and benign and somehow comic. He thought of Christmas. Then his father barked at him.

His father's mood had also changed, but in a different way; he seemed serious and hurried. As he wiped the breakfast pots clean with snow, he gave the boy orders for other chores. They left camp with two empty pack frames, both rifles, and a handsaw and rope. The boy soon understood why his father felt pressure of time: it took them an hour to climb the mile to the meadow. The snow continued. They did not rest until they reached the aspens.

"I had half a mind at breakfast to let the bull lie and pack us straight down out of here," his father admitted. "Probably smarter and less trouble in the long run. I could have come back on snowshoes next week. But by then it might be three feet deep and starting to drift. We can get two quarters out today. That will make it easier for me later." The boy was surprised by two things: that his father would be so wary in the face of a gentle snowfall and that he himself would have felt disappointed to be taken out of the woods that morning. The air of the meadow teemed with white.

"If it stops soon, we're fine," said his father.

It continued.

The path up the far canyon was hard climbing in eight inches of snow. The boy fell once, filling his collar and sleeves, and the gun-sight put a small gouge in his chin. But he was not discouraged. That night they would be warm and dry at the cabin. A half mile on and he came up beside his father, who had stopped to stare down at dark splashes of blood.

Heavy tracks and a dragging belly mark led up to the scramble of deepening red, and away. The tracks were nine inches long and showed claws. The boy's father knelt. As the boy watched, one shining maroon splotch the size of a saucer sank slowly beyond sight into the snow. The blood was warm.

Inspecting the tracks carefully, his father said, "She's got a cub with her."

"What happened?"

"Just a kill. Seems to have been a bird. That's too much blood for a grouse, but I don't see signs of any four-footed creature. Maybe a turkey." He frowned thoughtfully. "A turkey without feathers. I don't know. What I dislike is coming up on her with a cub." He drove a round into the chamber of the .270.

Trailing red smears, the tracks preceded them. Within fifty feet they found the body. It was half-buried. The top of its head had been shorn away, and the cub's brains had been licked out.

His father said "Christ," and plunged off the trail. He snapped at the boy to follow closely.

They made a wide crescent through brush and struck back after a quarter mile. His father slogged ahead in the snow, stopping often to stand holding his gun ready and glancing around while the boy caught up and passed him. The boy was confused. He knew his father was worried, but he did not feel any danger himself. They met the trail again, and went on to the aspen hillside before his father allowed them to rest. The boy spat on the snow. His lungs ached badly.

"Why did she do that?"

"She didn't. Another bear got her cub. A male. Maybe the one we saw yesterday. Then she fought him for the body, and she won. We didn't miss them by much. She may even have been watching. Nothing could put her in a worse frame of mind."

He added: "If we so much as see her, I want you to pick the nearest big tree and start climbing. Don't stop till you're twenty feet off the ground. I'll stay down and decide whether we have to shoot her. Is your rifle cocked?"

"No."

"Cock it, and put on the safety. She may be a black bear and black bears can climb. If she comes up after you, lean down and stick your gun in her mouth and fire. You can't miss."

He cocked the Winchester, as his father had said.

They angled downhill to the stream, and on to the mound of their dead elk. Snow filtered down steadily in purposeful silence. The boy was thirsty. It could not be much below freezing, he was aware, because with the exercise his bare hands were comfortable, even sweating between the fingers.

"Can I get a drink?"

"Yes. Be careful you don't wet your feet. And don't wander anywhere. We're going to get this done quickly."

He walked the few yards, ducked through the brush at streamside, and knelt in the snow to drink. The water was painful to his sinuses and bitterly cold on his hands. Standing again, he noticed an animal body ahead near the stream bank. For a moment he felt sure it was another dead cub. During that moment his father called:

"David! Get up here right now!"

The boy meant to call back. First he stepped closer to turn the cub with his foot. The touch brought it alive. It rose suddenly with a high squealing growl and whirled its head like a snake and snapped. The boy shrieked. The cub had his right hand in its jaws. It would not release.

It thrashed senselessly, working its teeth deeper and tearing flesh with each movement. The boy felt no pain. He knew his hand was being damaged and that realization terrified him and he was desperate to get the hand back before it was ruined. But he was helpless. He sensed the same furious terror racking the cub that he felt in himself, and he screamed at the cub almost reasoningly to let him go. His screams scared the cub more. Its head snatched back and forth. The boy did not think to shout for his father. He did not see him or hear him coming.

His father moved at full stride in a slowed laboring run through the snow, saying nothing and holding the rifle he did not use, crossed the last six feet still gathering speed, and brought his right boot up into the cub's belly. That kick seemed to lift the cub clear of the snow. It opened its jaws to another shrill piggish squeal, and the boy felt dull relief on his hand, as though his father had pressed open the blades of a spring trap with his foot. The cub tumbled once and disappeared over the stream bank, then surfaced downstream, squalling and paddling. The boy looked at his hand and was horrified. He still had no pain, but the hand was unrecognizable. His fingers had been peeled down through the palm like flaps on a banana. Glands at the sides of his jaw threatened that he would vomit, and he might have stood stupidly watching the hand bleed if his father had not grabbed him.

He snatched the boy by the arm and dragged him toward a tree without even looking at the boy's hand. The boy jerked back in angry resistance as though he had been struck. He screamed at his father. He screamed that his hand was cut, believing his father did not know, and as he screamed he began to cry. He began to feel hot throbbing pain. He began to worry about the blood he was losing. He could imagine his blood melting red holes in the snow behind him and he did not want to look. He did not want to do anything until he had taken care of his hand. At that instant he hated his father. But his father was stronger. He all but carried the boy to a tree.

He lifted the boy. In a voice that was quiet and hurried and very unlike the harsh grip with which he had taken the boy's arm, he said:

"Grab hold and climb up a few branches as best you can. Sit on a limb and hold tight and clamp the hand under your other armpit, if you can do that. I'll be right back to you. Hold tight because you're going to get dizzy." The boy groped desperately for a branch. His father supported him from beneath, and waited. The boy clambered. His feet scraped at the trunk. Then he was in the tree. Bark flakes and resin were stuck to the raw naked meat of his right hand. His father said:

"Now here, take this. Hurry."

The boy never knew whether his father himself had been frightened enough to forget for that moment about the boy's hand, or whether his father was still thinking quite clearly. His father may have expected that much. By the merciless clarity of his own standards, he may have expected that the boy should be able to hold onto a tree, and a wound, and a rifle, all with one hand. He extended the stock of the Winchester toward the boy.

The boy wanted to say something, but his tears and his fright would not let him gather a breath. He shuddered, and could not speak. "David," his father urged. The boy reached for the stock and faltered and clutched at the trunk with his good arm. He was crying and gasping, and he wanted to speak. He was afraid he would fall out of the tree. He released his grip once again, and felt himself tip. His father extended the gun higher, holding the barrel. The boy swung out his injured hand, spraying his father's face with blood. He reached and he tried to close torn dangling fingers around the stock and he pulled the trigger.

The bullet entered low on his father's thigh and shattered the knee and traveled down the shin bone and into the ground through his father's heel.

His father fell, and the rifle fell with him. He lay in the snow without moving. The boy thought he was dead. Then the boy saw him grope for the rifle. He found it and rolled onto his stomach, taking aim at the sow grizzly. Forty feet up the hill, towering on hind legs, she canted her head to one side, indecisive. When the cub pulled itself up a snowbank from the stream, she coughed at it sternly. The cub trotted straight to her with its head low. She knocked it off its feet with a huge paw, and it yelped. Then she turned quickly. The cub followed.

The woods were silent. The gunshot still echoed awesomely back to the boy but it was an echo of memory, not sound. He felt nothing. He saw his father's body stretched on the snow and he did not really believe he was where he was. He did not want to move: he wanted to wake. He sat in the tree and waited. The snow fell as gracefully as before.

His father rolled onto his back. The boy saw him raise himself to a sitting position and look down at the leg and betray no expression, and then slump back. He blinked slowly and lifted his eyes to meet the boy's eyes. The boy waited. He expected his father to speak. He expected his father to say *Shinny down using your elbows and knees and get the first-aid kit and boil water and phone the doctor. The number is taped to the dial.* His father stared. The boy could see the flicker of thoughts behind his father's eyes. His father said nothing. He raised his arms slowly and crossed them over his face, as though to nap in the sun.

The boy jumped. He landed hard on his feet and fell onto his back. He stood over his father. His hand dripped quietly onto the snow. He was afraid that his father was deciding to die. He wanted to beg him to reconsider. The boy had never before seen his father hopeless. He was afraid.

But he was no longer afraid of his father.

Then his father uncovered his face and said, "Let me see it."

They bandaged the boy's hand with a sleeve cut from the other arm of his shirt. His father wrapped the hand firmly and split the sleeve end with his deer knife and tied it neatly in two places. The boy now felt searing pain in his torn palm, and his stomach lifted when he thought of the damage, but at least he did not have to look at it. Quickly the plaid flannel bandage began to soak through maroon. They cut a sleeve from his father's shirt to tie over the wound in his thigh. They raised the trouser leg to see the long swelling bruise down the calf where he was hemorrhaging into the bullet's tunnel. Only then did his father realize that he was bleeding also from the heel. The boy took off his father's boot and placed a half-clean handkerchief on the insole where the bullet had exited, as his father instructed him. Then his father laced the boot on again tightly. The boy helped his father to stand. His father tried a step, then collapsed in the snow with a blasphemous howl of pain. They had not known that the knee was shattered.

The boy watched his father's chest heave with the forced sighs of suffocating frustration, and heard the air wheeze through his nostrils. His father relaxed himself with the breathing, and seemed to be thinking. He said,

"You can find your way back to the hut."

The boy held his own breath and did not move.

"You can, can't you?"

"But I'm not. I'm not going alone. I'm only going with you."

"All right, David, listen carefully," his father said. "We don't have to worry about freezing. I'm not worried about either of us freezing to death. No one is going to freeze in the woods in November, if he looks after himself. Not even in Montana. It just isn't that cold. I have matches and I have a fresh elk. And I don't think this weather is going to get any worse. It may be raining again by morning. What I'm concerned about is the bleeding. If I spend too much time and effort trying to walk out of here, I could bleed to death.

"I think your hand is going to be all right. It's a bad wound, but the doctors will be able to fix it as good as new. I can see that. I promise you that. You'll be bleeding some too, but if you take care of that hand it won't bleed any more walking than if you were standing still. Then you'll be at the doctor's tonight. But if I try to walk out on this leg it's going to bleed and keep bleeding and I'll lose too much blood. So I'm staying here and bundling up warm and you're walking out to get help. I'm sorry about this. It's what we have to do.

"You can't possibly get lost. You'll just follow this trail straight down the canyon the way we came up, and then you'll come to the meadow. Point yourself toward the big pine tree with the forked crown. When you get to that tree you'll find the creek again. You may not be able to see it, but make yourself quiet and listen for it. You'll hear it. Follow that down off the mountain and past the hut till you get to the jeep."

He struggled a hand into his pocket. "You've never driven a car, have you?"

The boy's lips were pinched. Muscles in his cheeks ached from clenching his jaws. He shook his head.

"You can do it. It isn't difficult." His father held up a single key and began telling the boy how to start the jeep, how to work the clutch, how to find reverse and then first and then second. As his father described the positions on the floor shift the boy raised his swaddled right hand. His father stopped. He rubbed at his eye sockets, like a man waking.

"Of course," he said. "All right. You'll have to help me."

Using the saw with his left hand, the boy cut a small forked aspen. His father showed the boy where to trim it so that the fork would reach just to his armpit. Then they lifted him to his feet. But the crutch was useless on a steep hillside of deep grass and snow. His father leaned over the boy's shoulders and they fought the slope for an hour.

When the boy stepped in a hole and they fell, his father made no exclamation of pain. The boy wondered whether his father's knee hurt as badly as his own hand. He suspected it hurt worse. He said nothing about his hand, though several times in their climb it was twisted or crushed. They reached the trail. The snow had not stopped, and their tracks were veiled. His father said:

"We need one of the guns. I forgot. It's my fault. But you'll have to go back down and get it."

The boy could not find the tree against which his father said he had leaned the .270, so he went toward the stream and looked for blood. He saw none. The imprint of his father's body was already softened beneath an inch of fresh silence. He scooped his good hand through the snowy depression and was startled by cool slimy blood, smearing his fingers like phlegm. Nearby he found the Winchester.

"The lucky one," his father said. "That's all right. Here." He snapped open the breach and a shell flew and he caught it in the air. He glanced dourly at the casing, then cast it aside in the snow. He held the gun out for the boy to see, and with his thumb let the hammer down one notch.

"Remember?" he said. "The safety."

The boy knew he was supposed to feel great shame, but he felt little. His father could no longer hurt him as he once could, because the boy was coming to understand him. His father could not help himself. He did not want the boy to feel contemptible, but he needed him to, because of the loneliness and the bitterness and the boy's mother; and he could not help himself.

After another hour they had barely traversed the aspen hillside. Pushing the crutch away in angry frustration, his father sat in the snow. The boy did not know whether he was thinking carefully of how they might get him out, or still laboring with the choice against despair. The light had wilted to something more like moonlight than afternoon. The sweep of snow had gone gray, depthless, flat, and the sky warned sullenly of night. The boy grew restless. Then it was decided. His father hung himself piggyback over the boy's shoulders, holding the rifle. The boy supported him with elbows crooked under his father's knees. The boy was tall for eleven years old, and heavy. The boy's father weighed 164 pounds.

The boy walked.

He moved as slowly as drifting snow: a step, then time, then another step.

The burden at first seemed to him overwhelming. He did not think he would be able to carry his father far.

He took the first few paces expecting to fall. He did not fall, so he kept walking. His arms and shoulders were not exhausted as quickly as he had thought they would be, so he kept walking. Shuffling ahead in the deep powder was like carrying one end of an oak bureau up stairs. But for a surprisingly long time the burden did not grow any worse. He found balance. He found rhythm. He was moving.

Dark blurred the woods, but the snow was luminous. He could see the trail well. He walked.

"How are you, David? How are you holding up?"

"All right."

"We'll stop for a while and let you rest. You can set me down here." The boy kept walking. He moved so ponderously, it seemed after each step that he had stopped. But he kept walking.

"You can set me down. Don't you want to rest?"

The boy did not answer. He wished that his father would not make him talk. At the start he had gulped for air. Now he was breathing low and regularly. He was watching his thighs slice through the snow. He did not want to be disturbed. After a moment he said, "No."

He walked. He came to the cub, shrouded beneath new snow, and did not see it, and fell over it. His face was smashed deep into the snow by his father's weight. He could not move. But he could breathe. He rested. When he felt his father's thigh roll across his right hand, he remembered the wound. He was lucky his arms had been pinned to his sides, or the hand might have taken the force of their fall. As he waited for his father to roll himself clear, the boy noticed the change in temperature. His sweat chilled him quickly. He began shivering.

His father had again fallen in silence. The boy knew that he would not call out or even mention the pain in his leg. The boy realized that he did not want to mention his hand. The blood soaking the outside of his flannel bandage had grown sticky. He did not want to think of the alien tangle of flesh and tendons and bones wrapped inside. There was pain, but he kept the pain at a distance. It was not *his* hand any more. He was not counting on ever having it back. If he was resolved about that, then the pain was not his either. It was merely pain of which he was aware. His good hand was numb.

"We'll rest now."

"I'm not tired," the boy said. "I'm just getting cold."

"We'll rest," said his father. "I'm tired."

Under his father's knee, the boy noticed, was a cavity in the snow, already melted away by fresh blood. The dark flannel around his father's thigh did not appear sticky. It gleamed.

His father instructed the boy how to open the cub with the deer knife. His father stood on one leg against a deadfall, holding the Winchester ready, and glanced around on all sides as he spoke. The boy used his left hand and both his knees. He punctured the cub low in the belly, to a soft squirting sound, and

sliced upward easily. He did not gut the cub. He merely cut out a large square
of belly meat. He handed it to his father, in exchange for the rifle.

His father peeled off the hide and left the fat. He sawed the meat in half.
One piece he rolled up and put in his jacket pocket. The other he divided again.
He gave the boy a square thick with glistening raw fat.

"Eat it. The fat too. Especially the fat. We'll cook the rest farther on. I
don't want to build a fire here and taunt Momma."

The meat was chewy. The boy did not find it disgusting. He was hungry.

His father sat back on the ground and unlaced the boot from his good foot.
Before the boy understood what he was doing, he had relaced the boot. He was
holding a damp wool sock.

"Give me your left hand." The boy held out his good hand, and his father
pulled the sock down over it. "It's getting a lot colder. And we need that hand."

"What about yours? We need your hands too. I'll give you my—"

"No, you won't. We need your feet more than anything. It's all right. I'll
put mine inside your shirt."

He lifted his father, and the went on. The boy walked.

He moved steadily through cold darkness. Soon he was sweating again,
down his ribs and inside his boots. Only his hands and ears felt as though
crushed in a cold metal vise. But his father was shuddering. The boy stopped.

His father did not put down his legs. The boy stood on the trail and
waited. Slowly he released his wrist holds. His father's thighs slumped. The boy
was careful about the wounded leg. His father's grip over the boy's neck did
not loosen. His fingers were cold against the boy's bare skin.

"Are we at the hut?"

"No. We're not even to the meadow."

"Why did you stop?" his father asked.

"It's so cold. You're shivering. Can we build a fire?"

"Yes," his father said hazily. "We'll rest. What time is it?"

"We don't know," the boy said. "We don't have a watch."

The boy gathered small deadwood. His father used the Winchester stock
to scoop snow away from a boulder, and they placed the fire at the boulder's
base. His father broke up pine twigs and fumbled dry toilet paper from his
breast pocket and arranged the wood, but by then his fingers were shaking too
badly to strike a match. The boy lit the fire. The boy stamped down the snow,
as his father instructed, to make a small ovenlike recess before the fire boulder.
He cut fir boughs to floor the recess. He added more deadwood. Beyond the
invisible clouds there seemed to be part of a moon.

"It stopped snowing," the boy said.

"Why?"

The boy did not speak. His father's voice had sounded unnatural. After
a moment his father said:

"Yes, indeed. It stopped."

They roasted pieces of cub meat skewered on a green stick. Dripping fat
made the fire spatter and flare. The meat was scorched on the outside and raw
within. It tasted as good as any meat the boy had ever eaten. They burned their

palates on hot fat. The second stick smoldered through before they had noticed, and that batch of meat fell in the fire. The boy's father cursed once and reached into the flame for it and dropped it and clawed it out, and then put his hand in the snow. He did not look at the blistered fingers. They ate. The boy saw that both his father's hands had gone clumsy and almost useless.

The boy went for more wood. He found a bleached deadfall not far off the trail, but with one arm he could only break up and carry small loads. They lay down in the recess together like spoons, the boy nearer the fire. They pulled fir boughs into place above them, resting across the snow. They pressed close together. The boy's father was shivering spastically now, and he clenched the boy in a fierce hug. The boy put his father's hands back inside his own shirt. The boy slept. He woke when the fire faded and added more wood and slept. He woke again and tended the fire and changed places with his father and slept. He slept less soundly with his father between him and the fire. He woke again when his father began to vomit.

The boy was terrified. His father wrenched with sudden vomiting that brought up cub meat and yellow liquid and blood and sprayed them across the snow by the grayish-red glow of the fire and emptied his stomach dry and then would not release him. He heaved on pathetically. The boy pleaded to be told what was wrong. His father could not or would not answer. The spasms seized him at the stomach and twisted the rest of his body taut in ugly jerks. Between the attacks he breathed with a wet rumbling sound deep in his chest, and did not speak. When the vomiting subsided, his breathing stretched itself out into long bubbling sighs, then shallow gasps, then more liquidy sighs. His breath caught and froth rose in his throat and into his mouth and he gagged on it and began vomiting again. The boy thought his father would choke. He knelt beside him and held him and cried. He could not see his father's face well and he did not want to look closely while the sounds that were coming from inside his father's body seemed so unhuman. The boy had never been more frightened. He wept for himself, and for his father. He knew from the noises and move-ments that his father must die. He did not think his father could ever be human again.

When his father was quiet, he went for more wood. He broke limbs from the deadfall with fanatic persistence and brought them back in bundles and built the fire up bigger. He nestled his father close to it and held him from behind. He did not sleep, though he was not awake. He waited. Finally he opened his eyes on the beginnings of dawn. His father sat up and began to spit.

"One more load of wood and you keep me warm from behind and then we'll go."

The boy obeyed. He was surprised that his father could speak. He thought it strange now that his father was so concerned for himself and so little con-cerned for the boy. His father had not even asked how he was.

The boy lifted his father, and walked.

Sometime while dawn was completing itself, the snow had resumed. It did not filter down soundlessly. It came on a slight wind at the boy's back, blowing down the canyon. He felt as though he were tumbling forward with the snow into a long vertical shaft. He tumbled slowly. His father's body protected the boy's back from being chilled by the wind. They were both soaked through their clothes. His father was soon shuddering again.

The boy walked. Muscles down the back of his neck were sore from yesterday. His arms ached, and his shoulders and thighs, but his neck hurt him most. He bent his head forward against the weight and the pain, and he watched his legs surge through the snow. At his stomach he felt the dull ache of hunger, not as an appetite but as an affliction. He thought of the jeep. He walked.

He recognized the edge of the meadow but through the snow-laden wind he could not see the cluster of aspens. The snow became deeper where he left the wooded trail. The direction of the wind was now variable, sometimes driving snow into his face, sometimes whipping across him from the right. The grass and snow dragged at his thighs, and he moved by stumbling forward and then catching himself back. Twice he stepped into small overhung fingerlets of the stream, and fell violently, shocking the air from his lungs and once nearly spraining an ankle. Farther out into the meadow, he saw the aspens. They were a hundred yards off to his right. He did not turn directly toward them. He was afraid of crossing more hidden creeks on the intervening ground. He was not certain now whether the main channel was between him and the aspen grove or behind him to the left. He tried to project from the canyon trail to the aspens and on to the forked pine on the far side of the meadow, along what he remembered as almost a straight line. He pointed himself toward the far edge, where the pine should have been. He could not see a forked crown. He could not even see trees. He could see only a vague darker corona above the curve of white. He walked.

He passed the aspens and left them behind. He stopped several times with the wind rasping against him in the open meadow, and rested. He did not set his father down. His father was trembling uncontrollably. He had not spoken for a long time. The boy wanted badly to reach the far side of the meadow. His socks were soaked and his boots and cuffs were glazed with ice. The wind was chafing his face and making him dizzy. His thighs felt as if they had been bruised with a club. The boy wanted to give up and set his father down and whimper that this had gotten to be very unfair; and he wanted to reach the far trees. He did not doubt which he would do. He walked.

He saw trees. Raising his head painfully, he squinted against the rushing flakes. He did not see the forked crown. He went on, and stopped again, and craned his neck, and squinted. He scanned a wide angle of pines, back and forth. He did not see it. He turned his body and his burden to look back. The snow blew across the meadow and seemed, whichever way he turned, to be streaking into his face. He pinched his eyes tighter. He could still see the aspens. But he could not judge where the canyon trail met the meadow. He did not know from just where he had come. He looked again at the aspens, and then ahead to the pines. He considered the problem carefully. He was irritated that the forked ponderosa did not show itself yet, but not worried. He was forced to estimate. He estimated, and went on in that direction.

When he saw a forked pine it was far off to the left of his course. He turned and marched toward it gratefully. As he came nearer, he bent his head up to look. He stopped. The boy was not sure that this was the right tree. Nothing about it looked different, except the thick cakes of snow weighting its limbs, and nothing about it looked especially familiar. He had seen thousands of pine trees in the last few days. This was one like the others. It definitely had a forked crown. He entered the woods at its base.

He had vaguely expected to join a trail. There was no trail. After two hundred yards he was still picking his way among trees and deadfalls and brush. He remembered the shepherd's creek that fell off the lip of the meadow and led down the first canyon. He turned and retraced his tracks to the forked pine.

He looked for the creek. He did not see it anywhere near the tree. He made himself quiet, and listened. He heard nothing but wind, and his father's tremulous breathing.

"Where is the creek?"

His father did not respond. The boy bounced gently up and down, hoping to jar him alert.

"Where is the creek? I can't find it."

"What?"

"We crossed the meadow and I found the tree but I can't find the creek. I need you to help."

"The compass is in my pocket," his father said.

He lowered his father into the snow. He found the compass in his father's breast pocket, and opened the flap, and held it level. The boy noticed with a flinch that his right thigh was smeared with fresh blood. For an instant he thought he had a new wound. Then he realized that the blood was his father's. The compass needle quieted.

"What do I do?"

His father did not respond. The boy asked again. His father said nothing. He sat in the snow and shivered.

The boy left his father and made random arcs within sight of the forked tree until he found a creek. They followed it onward along the flat and then where it gradually began sloping away. The boy did not see what else he could do. He knew that this was the wrong creek. He hoped that it would flow into the shepherd's creek, or at least bring them out on the same road where they had left the jeep. He was very tired. He did not want to stop. He did not care any more about being warm. He wanted only to reach the jeep, and save his father's life.

He wondered whether his father would love him more generously for having done it. He wondered whether his father would ever forgive him for having done it.

If he failed, his father could never again make him feel shame, the boy thought naively. So he did not worry about failing. He did not worry about dying. His hand was not bleeding, and he felt strong. The creek swung off and down to the left. He followed it, knowing that he was lost. He did not want to reverse himself. He knew that turning back would make him feel confused and desperate and frightened. As long as he was following some pathway, walking, going down, he felt strong.

That afternoon he killed a grouse. He knocked it off a low branch with a heavy short stick that he threw like a boomerang. The grouse fell in the snow and floundered and the boy ran up and plunged on it. He felt it thrashing against his chest. He reached in and it nipped him and he caught it by the neck and squeezed and wrenched mercilessly until long after it stopped writhing. He cleaned it as he had seen his father clean grouse and built a small fire with matches from his father's breast pocket and seared the grouse on a stick. He fed his father. His father could not chew. The boy chewed mouthfuls of grouse, and took the chewed gobbets in his hand, and put them into his father's mouth. His father could swallow. His father could no longer speak.

The boy walked. He thought of his mother in Evergreen Park, and at once he felt queasy and weak. He thought of his mother's face and her voice as she was told that her son was lost in the woods in Montana with a damaged hand that would never be right, and with his father, who had been shot and was unconscious and dying. He pictured his mother receiving the news that her son might die himself, unless he could carry his father out of the woods and find his way to the jeep. He saw her face change. He heard her voice. The boy had to stop. He was crying. He could not control the shape of his mouth. He was not crying with true sorrow, as he had in the night when he held his father and thought his father would die; he was crying in sentimental self-pity. He sensed the difference. Still he cried.

He must not think of his mother, the boy realized. Thinking of her could only weaken him. If she knew where he was, what he had to do, she could only make it impossible for him to do it. He was lucky that she knew nothing, the boy thought.

No one knew what the boy was doing, or what he had yet to do. Even the boy's father no longer knew. The boy was lucky. No one was watching, no one knew, and he was free to be capable.

The boy imagined himself alone at his father's grave. The grave was open. His father's casket had already been lowered. The boy stood at the foot in his black Christmas suit, and his hands were crossed at his groin, and he was not crying. Men with shovels stood back from the grave, waiting for the boy's order for them to begin filling it. The boy felt a horrible swelling sense of joy. The men watched him, and he stared down into the hole. He knew it was a lie. If his father died, the boy's mother would rush out to Livingston and have him buried and stand at the grave in a black dress and veil squeezing the boy to her side like he was a child. There was nothing the boy could do about that. All the more reason he must keep walking.

Then she would tow the boy back with her to Evergreen Park. And he would be standing on 96th Street in the morning dark before his father's cold body had even begun to grow alien and decayed in the buried box. She would drag him back, and there would be nothing the boy could do. And he realized that if he returned with his mother after the burial, he would never again see

the cabin outside Livingston. He would have no more summers and no more
Novembers anywhere but in Evergreen Park.

The cabin now seemed to be at the center of the boy's life. It seemed to
stand halfway between this snowbound creek valley and the train station in
Chicago. It would be his cabin soon.

The boy knew nothing about his father's will, and he had never been told
that legal ownership of the cabin was destined for him. Legal ownership did not
matter. The cabin might be owned by his mother, or sold to pay his father's
debts, or taken away by the state, but it would still be the boy's cabin. It could
only forever belong to him. His father had been telling him *Here, this is yours.
Prepare to receive it.* The boy had sensed that much. But he had been threatened,
and unwilling. The boy realized now that he might be resting warm in the cabin
in a matter of hours, or he might never see it again. He could appreciate the
justice of that. He walked.

He thought of his father as though his father were far away from him. He
saw himself in the black suit at the grave, and he heard his father speak to him
from aside: *That's good. Now raise your eyes and tell them in a man's voice to begin
shoveling. Then turn away and walk slowly back down the hill. Be sure you don't cry.
That's good.* The boy stopped. He felt his glands quiver, full of new tears. He
knew that it was a lie. His father would never be there to congratulate him. His
father would never know how well the boy had done.

He took deep breaths. He settled himself. Yes, his father would know
somehow, the boy believed. His father had known all along. His father knew.

He built the recess just as they had the night before, except this time he
found flat space between a stone back and a large fallen cottonwood trunk. He
scooped out the snow, he laid boughs, and he made a fire against each reflector.
At first the bed was quite warm. Then the melt from the fires began to run down
and collect in the middle, forming a puddle of wet boughs under them. The boy
got up and carved runnels across the packed snow to drain the fires. He went
back to sleep and slept warm, holding his father. He rose again each half hour
to feed the fires.

The snow stopped in the night, and did not resume. The woods seemed
to grow quieter, settling, sighing beneath the new weight. What was going to
come had come.

The boy grew tired of breaking deadwood and began walking again
before dawn and walked for five more hours. He did not try to kill the grouse
that he saw because he did not want to spend time cleaning and cooking it. He
was hurrying now. He drank from the creek. At one point he found small black
insects like winged ants crawling in great numbers across the snow near the
creek. He stopped to pinch up and eat thirty or forty of them. They were
tasteless. He did not bother to feed any to his father. He felt he had come a
long way down the mountain. He thought he was reaching the level now where
there might be roads. He followed the creek, which had received other
branches and grown to a stream. The ground was flattening again and the
drainage was widening, opening to daylight. As he carried his father, his head

ached. He had stopped noticing most of his other pains. About noon of that day he came to the fence.

It startled him. He glanced around, his pulse drumming suddenly, preparing himself at once to see the long empty sweep of snow and broken fence posts and thinking of Basque shepherds fifty years gone. He saw the cabin and the smoke. He relaxed, trembling helplessly into laughter. He relaxed, and was unable to move. Then he cried, still laughing. He cried shamelessly with relief and dull joy and wonder, for as long as he wanted. He held his father, and cried. But he set his father down and washed his own face with snow before he went to the door.

He crossed the lot walking slowly, carrying his father. He did not now feel tired.

The young woman's face was drawn down in shock and revealed at first nothing of friendliness.

"We had a jeep parked somewhere, but I can't find it," the boy said. "This is my father."

They would not talk to him. They stripped him and put him before the fire wrapped in blankets and started tea and made him wait. He wanted to talk. He wished they would ask him a lot of questions. But they went about quickly and quietly, making things warm. His father was in the bedroom.

The man with the face full of dark beard had telephoned for a doctor. He went back into the bedroom with more blankets, and stayed. His wife went from room to room with hot tea. She rubbed the boy's naked shoulders through the blanket, and held a cup to his mouth, but she would not talk to him. He did not know what to say to her, and he could not move his lips very well. But he wished she would ask him some questions. He was restless, thawing in silence before the hearth.

He thought about going back to their own cabin soon. In his mind he gave the bearded man directions to take him and his father home. It wasn't far. It would not require much of the man's time. They would thank him, and give him an elk steak. Later he and his father would come back for the jeep. He could keep his father warm at the cabin as well as they were doing here, the boy knew.

While the woman was in the bedroom, the boy overheard the bearded man raise his voice:

"He what?"

"He carried him out," the woman whispered.

"What do you mean, carried him?"

"Carried him. On his back. I saw."

"Carried him from where?"

"Where it happened. Somewhere on Sheep Creek, maybe."

"Eight miles?"

"I know."

"*Eight miles?* How could he do that?"

"I don't know. I suppose he couldn't. But he did."

The doctor arrived in half an hour, as the boy was just starting to shiver.

The doctor went into the bedroom and stayed five minutes. The woman poured the boy more tea and knelt beside him and hugged him around the shoulders.

When the doctor came out, he examined the boy without speaking. The boy wished the doctor would ask him some questions, but he was afraid he might be shivering too hard to answer in a man's voice. While the doctor touched him and probed him and took his temperature, the boy looked the doctor directly in the eye, as though to show him he was really all right.

The doctor said:

"David, your father is dead. He has been dead for a long time. Probably since yesterday."

"I know that," the boy said.

Writing Assignments for "Walking Out"

I. Brief Papers
   A. 1. In what ways do the opening two paragraphs of the story prepare us for what is to come?
      2. Why does David lie to his father by telling him that his mother sends her love (p. 387)?
      3. Once David is inside his father's cabin, he begins "to feel safe from his own anguish" (p. 387). What is the source of David's anguish?
      4. What does David's father mean by "the cycle of life's infinite wisdom" (p. 390), and why does he laugh at himself unpleasantly when he refers to it?
      5. Why doesn't David's father want to shoot the old grizzly bear and what does this reaction reveal about him?
      6. Why, at the end of the story, does David wish the woman and doctor would ask him a lot of questions?

   B. Argue for or against one of the assertions below:
      1. No one would have been hurt if only David's father had been a more knowledgable and competent woodsman.
      2. David is right in thinking that his father wanted David "to feel contemptible" (p. 397).
      3. David's father knew he was likely to die on the trip home.
      4. At the end of the story David really didn't know the truth about his father's condition; he only said what he did to avoid embarrassment.

   C. 1. Do you think David's father genuinely cares for David? Why or why not?
      2. What do you think David's father means when he says, "I don't need the fear. I've got enough in my life already" (p. 391)?
      3. David's father becomes angry when he finds the body of the moose that had been shot with the .22 pistol. Did what happened make you angry, too? Why or why not?
      4. On the morning that it snowed, did you get the feeling that something serious would go wrong? Why? What did you think would happen?

5. Did you suspect the truth about what happened to David's father before you were told so in the story? If so, why?

6. Did you find the story believable? Why or why not?

II. Longer Papers

A. Explain how the references to animals in the story—especially to the bears and cubs—contribute to our understanding of human relationships.

B. Would you call "Walking Out" an initiation story? If so, into what is David initiated?

C. Some short stories are *didactic*—they try to influence our conduct by teaching us a lesson or by inculcating a moral truth. But other stories are not primarily concerned with lessons or morals. In which category does "Walking Out" belong? Why?

D. Argue for or against the assertion that David grows and matures as a result of his experience.

E. What is the purpose of the many references to David's home outside Chicago in Evergreen Park and to his life there?

III. Comparative Papers

A. "Walking Out," like Hemingway's "Indian Camp," is the story of a journey taken by a father and son away from civilization and into more primitive territory. Taken together, what do the two stories say about such journeys?

B. Compare "Walking Out" to another story that focuses on a young person— "Indian Camp," "The Downward Path to Wisdom," "I'm a Fool," "Araby," or "Barn Burning"—to explain which kinds of experiences are most likely to be learning experiences.

C. "Walking Out" is one of several stories in this book that focuses on the relationship between a child and parent; others include "Indian Camp," "The Downward Path to Wisdom," "Four Summers," "Barn Burning," "Silent Snow, Secret Snow," "Rappaccini's Daughter," "The Cinderella Waltz," "Good Country People," "The Sky is Gray," "Dream Children," and "The Sorrows of Gin." Select two or more of these stories, and then explain what they show to be the most serious obstacles to a good parent–child relationship.

RAYMOND CARVER

What We Talk About When We Talk About Love

Before Reading

Do you think it is possible to stop loving someone or to fall out of love? Or do you think anyone who has fallen out of love was never really in love in the first place? Free write on this question for 5 or 10 minutes.

My friend Mel McGinnis was talking. Mel McGinnis is a cardiologist, and sometimes that gives him the right.

The four of us were sitting around his kitchen table drinking gin. Sunlight filled the kitchen from the big window behind the sink. There were Mel and me and his second wife, Teresa—Terri, we called her—and my wife, Laura. We lived in Albuquerque then. But we were all from somewhere else.

There was an ice bucket on the table. The gin and the tonic water kept going around, and we somehow got on the subject of love. Mel thought real love was nothing less than spiritual love. He said he'd spent five years in a seminary before quitting to go to medical school. He said he still looked back on those years in the seminary as the most important years in his life.

Terri said the man she lived with before she lived with Mel loved her so much he tried to kill her. Then Terri said, "He beat me up one night. He dragged me around the living room by my ankles. He kept saying, 'I love you, I love you, you bitch.' He went on dragging me around the living room. My head kept knocking on things." Terri looked around the table. "What do you do with love like that?"

She was a bone-thin woman with a pretty face, dark eyes, and brown hair that hung down her back. She liked necklaces made of turquoise, and long pendant earrings.

"My God, don't be silly. That's not love, and you know it," Mel said. "I don't know what you'd call it, but I sure know you wouldn't call it love."

"Say what you want to, but I know it was," Terri said. "It may sound crazy to you, but it's true just the same. People are different, Mel. Sure, sometimes he may have acted crazy. Okay. But he loved me. In his own way maybe, but he loved me. There was love there, Mel. Don't say there wasn't."

Mel let out his breath. He held his glass and turned to Laura and me. "The man threatened to kill me," Mel said. He finished his drink and reached for the gin bottle. "Terri's a romantic. Terri's of the kick-me-so-I'll-know-you-love-me

WHAT WE TALK ABOUT WHEN WE TALK ABOUT LOVE   First published in 1978. Raymond Carver (1938–   ) was born and grew up in the Pacific Northwest, and has lived in California, Iowa, Texas, and, most recently, New York, where he teaches writing at Syracuse University.

school. Terri, hon, don't look that way." Mel reached across the table and touched Terri's cheek with his fingers. He grinned at her.

"Now he wants to make up," Terri said.

"Make up what?" Mel said. "What is there to make up? I know what I know. That's all."

"How'd we get started on this subject, anyway?" Terri said. She raised her glass and drank from it. "Mel always has love on his mind," she said. "Don't you, honey?" She smiled. And I thought that was the last of it.

"I just wouldn't call Ed's behavior love. That's all I'm saying, honey," Mel said. "What about you guys?" Mel said to Laura and me. "Does that sound like love to you?"

"I'm the wrong person to ask," I said. "I didn't even know the man. I've only heard his name mentioned in passing. I wouldn't know. You'd have to know the particulars. But I think what you're saying is that love is an absolute."

Mel said, "The kind of love I'm talking about is. The kind of love I'm talking about, you don't try to kill people."

Laura said, "I don't know anything about Ed, or anything about the situation. But who can judge anyone else's situation?"

I touched the back of Laura's hand. She gave me a quick smile. I picked up Laura's hand. It was warm, the nails polished, perfectly manicured. I encircled the broad wrist with my fingers, and I held her.

"When I left, he drank rat poison," Terri said. She clasped her arms with her hands. "They took him to the hospital in Santa Fe. That's where we lived then, about ten miles out. They saved his life. But his gums went crazy from it. I mean they pulled away from his teeth. After that, his teeth stood out like fangs. My God," Terri said. She waited a minute, then let go of her arms and picked up her glass.

"What people won't do!" Laura said.

"He's out of the action now," Mel said. "He's dead."

Mel handed me the saucer of limes. I took a section, squeezed it over my drink, and stirred the ice cubes with my finger.

"It gets worse," Terri said. "He shot himself in the mouth. But he bungled that too. Poor Ed," she said. Terri shook her head.

"Poor Ed nothing," Mel said. "He was dangerous."

Mel was forty-five years old. He was tall and rangy with curly soft hair. His face and arms were brown from the tennis he played. When he was sober, his gestures, all his movements, were precise, very careful.

"He did love me though, Mel. Grant me that," Terri said. "That's all I'm asking. He didn't love me the way you love me. I'm not saying that. But he loved me. You can grant me that, can't you?"

"What do you mean, he bungled it?" I said.

Laura leaned forward with her glass. She put her elbows on the table and held her glass in both hands. She glanced from Mel to Terri and waited with a look of bewilderment on her open face, as if amazed that such things happened to people you were friendly with.

"How'd he bungle it when he killed himself?" I said.

"I'll tell you what happened," Mel said. "He took this twenty-two pistol he'd bought to threaten Terri and me with. Oh, I'm serious, the man was always threatening. You should have seen the way we lived in those days. Like fugitives. I even bought a gun myself. Can you believe it? A guy like me? But I did. I bought one for self-defense and carried it in the glove compartment. Sometimes I'd have to leave the apartment in the middle of the night. To go to the hospital, you know? Terri and I weren't married then, and my first wife had the house and kids, the dog, everything, and Terri and I were living in this apartment here. Sometimes, as I say, I'd get a call in the middle of the night and have to go in to the hospital at two or three in the morning. It'd be dark out there in the parking lot, and I'd break into a sweat before I could even get to my car. I never knew if he was going to come up out of the shrubbery or from behind a car and start shooting. I mean, the man was crazy. He was capable of wiring a bomb, anything. He used to call my service at all hours and say he needed to talk to the doctor, and when I'd return the call, he'd say, 'Son of a bitch, your days are numbered.' Little things like that. It was scary, I'm telling you."

"I still feel sorry for him," Terri said.

"It sounds like a nightmare," Laura said. "But what exactly happened after he shot himself?"

Laura is a legal secretary. We'd met in a professional capacity. Before we knew it, it was a courtship. She's thirty-five, three years younger than I am. In addition to being in love, we like each other and enjoy one another's company. She's easy to be with.

"What happened?" Laura said.

Mel said. "He shot himself in the mouth in his room. Someone heard the shot and told the manager. They came in with a passkey, saw what had happened, and called an ambulance. I happened to be there when they brought him in, alive but past recall. The man lived for three days. His head swelled up to twice the size of a normal head. I'd never seen anything like it, and I hope I never do again. Terri wanted to go in and sit with him when she found out about it. We had a fight over it. I didn't think she should see him like that. I didn't think she should see him, and I still don't."

"Who won the fight?" Laura said.

"I was in the room with him when he died," Terri said. "He never came up out of it. But I sat with him. He didn't have anyone else."

"He was dangerous," Mel said. "If you call that love, you can have it."

"It was love," Terri said. "Sure, it's abnormal in most people's eyes. But he was willing to die for it. He did die for it."

"I sure as hell wouldn't call it love," Mel said. "I mean, no one knows what he did it for. I've seen a lot of suicides, and I couldn't say anyone ever knew what they did it for."

Mel put his hands behind his neck and tilted his chair back. "I'm not interested in that kind of love," he said. "If that's love, you can have it."

Terri said, "We were afraid. Mel even made a will out and wrote to his brother in California who used to be a Green Beret. Mel told him who to look for if something happened to him."

Terri drank from her glass. She said, "But Mel's right—we lived like fugitives. We were afraid. Mel was, weren't you, honey? I even called the police at one point, but they were no help. They said they couldn't do anything until Ed actually did something. Isn't that a laugh?" Terri said.

She poured the last of the gin into her glass and waggled the bottle. Mel got up from the table and went to the cupboard. He took down another bottle.

"Well, Nick and I know what love is," Laura said. "For us, I mean," Laura said. She bumped my knee with her knee. "You're supposed to say something now," Laura said, and turned her smile on me.

For an answer, I took Laura's hand and raised it to my lips. I made a big production out of kissing her hand. Everyone was amused.

"We're lucky," I said.

"You guys," Terri said. "Stop that now. You're making me sick. You're still on the honeymoon, for God's sake. You're still gaga, for crying out loud. Just wait. How long have you been together now? How long has it been? A year? Longer than a year?"

"Going on a year and a half," Laura said, flushed and smiling.

"Oh, now," Terri said. "Wait awhile."

She held her drink and gazed at Laura.

"I'm only kidding," Terri said.

Mel opened the gin and went around the table with the bottle.

"Here, you guys," he said. "Let's have a toast. I want to propose a toast. A toast to love. To true love," Mel said.

We touched glasses.

"To love," we said.

Outside in the backyard, one of the dogs began to bark. The leaves of the aspen that leaned past the window ticked against the glass. The afternoon sun was like a presence in this room, the spacious light of ease and generosity. We could have been anywhere, somewhere enchanted. We raised our glasses again and grinned at each other like children who had agreed on something forbidden.

"I'll tell you what real love is," Mel said. "I mean, I'll give you a good example. And then you can draw your own conclusions." He poured more gin into his glass. He added an ice cube and a sliver of lime. We waited and sipped our drinks. Laura and I touched knees again. I put a hand on her warm thigh and left it there.

"What do any of us really know about love?" Mel said. "It seems to me we're just beginners at love. We say we love each other and we do, I don't doubt it. I love Terri and Terri loves me, and you guys love each other too. You know the kind of love I'm talking about now. Physical love, that impulse that drives you to someone special, as well as love of the other person's being, his or her essence, as it were. Carnal love and, well, call it sentimental love, the day-to-day caring about the other person. But sometimes I have a hard time accounting for the fact that I must have loved my first wife too. But I did, I know I did. So I suppose I am like Terri in that regard. Terri and Ed." He thought about it and then he went on. "There was a time when I thought I loved my first wife more than life itself. But now I hate her guts. I do. How do you explain that? What happened to that love? What happened to it, is what I'd like to know. I wish someone could tell me. Then there's Ed. Okay, we're back to Ed. He loves Terri so much he tries to kill her and he winds up killing himself." Mel stopped talking and swallowed from his glass. "You guys have been together eighteen months and you love each other. It shows all over you. You glow with it. But you both loved other people before you met each other. You've both been married before, just like us. And you probably loved other people before that too, even. Terri and I have been together five years, been married for four. And the terrible thing, the terrible thing is, but the good thing too, the saving grace, you might say, is that if something happened to one of us—excuse me for saying this—but if something happened to one of us tomorrow, I think the other one, the other person, would grieve for a while, you know, but then the surviving party would go out and love again, have someone else soon enough. All this, all of this love we're talking about, it would just be a memory. Maybe not even a memory. Am I wrong? Am I way off base? Because I want you to set me straight if you think I'm wrong. I want to know. I mean, I don't know anything, and I'm the first one to admit it."

"Mel, for God's sake," Terri said. She reached out and took hold of his wrist. "Are you getting drunk? Honey? Are you drunk?"

"Honey, I'm just talking," Mel said. "All right? I don't have to be drunk to say what I think. I mean, we're all just talking, right?" Mel said. He fixed his eyes on her.

"Sweetie, I'm not criticizing," Terri said.

She picked up her glass.

"I'm not on call today," Mel said. "Let me remind you of that. I am not on call," he said.

"Mel, we love you," Laura said.

Mel looked at Laura. He looked at her as if he could not place her, as if she was not the woman she was.

"Love you too, Laura," Mel said. "And you, Nick, love you too. You know something?" Mel said. "You guys are our pals," Mel said.

He picked up his glass.

Mel said, "I was going to tell you about something. I mean, I was going to prove a point. You see, this happened a few months ago, but it's still going on right now, and it ought to make us feel ashamed when we talk like we know what we're talking about when we talk about love."

"Come on now," Terri said. "Don't talk like you're drunk if you're not drunk."

"Just shut up for once in your life," Mel said very quietly. "Will you do me a favor and do that for a minute? So as I was saying, there's this old couple who had this car wreck out on the interstate. A kid hit them and they were all torn to shit and nobody was giving them much chance to pull through."

Terri looked at us and then back at Mel. She seemed anxious, or maybe that's too strong a word.

Mel was handing the bottle around the table.

"I was on call that night," Mel said. "It was May or maybe it was June. Terri and I had just sat down to dinner when the hospital called. There'd been this thing out on the interstate. Drunk kid, teenager, plowed his dad's pickup into this camper with this old couple in it. They were up in their mid-seventies, that couple. The kid—eighteen, nineteen, something—he was DOA. Taken the steering wheel through his sternum. The old couple, they were alive, you understand. I mean, just barely. But they had everything. Multiple fractures, internal injuries, hemorrhaging, contusions, lacerations, the works, and they each of them had themselves concussions. They were in a bad way, believe me. And, of course, their age was two strikes against them. I'd say she was worse off than he was. Ruptured spleen along with everything else. Both kneecaps broken. But they'd been wearing their seatbelts and, God knows, that's what saved them for the time being."

"Folks, this is an advertisement for the National Safety Council," Terri said. "This is your spokesman, Dr. Melvin R. McGinnis, talking." Terri laughed. "Mel," she said, "sometimes you're just too much. But I love you, hon," she said.

"Honey, I love you," Mel said.

He leaned across the table. Terri met him halfway. They kissed.

"Terri's right," Mel said as he settled himself again. "Get those seatbelts on. But seriously, they were in some shape, those oldsters. By the time I got down there, the kid was dead, as I said. He was off in a corner, laid out on a gurney. I took one look at the old couple and told the ER nurse to get me a neurologist and an orthopedic man and a couple of surgeons down there right away."

He drank from his glass. "I'll try to keep this short," he said. "So we took the two of them up to the OR and worked like fuck on them most of the night. They had these incredible reserves, those two. You see that once in a while. So we did everything that could be done, and toward morning we're giving them a fifty-fifty chance, maybe less than that for her. So here they are, still alive the next morning. So, okay, we move them into the ICU, which is where they both kept plugging away at it for two weeks, hitting it better and better on all the scopes. So we transfer them out to their own room."

Mel stopped talking. "Here," he said, "let's drink this cheapo gin the hell up. Then we're going to dinner, right? Terri and I know a new place. That's where we'll go, to this new place we know about. But we're not going until we finish up this cut-rate, lousy gin."

Terri said, "We haven't actually eaten there yet. But it looks good. From the outside, you know."

"I like food," Mel said. "If I had it to do all over again, I'd be a chef, you know? Right, Terri?" Mel said.

He laughed. He fingered the ice in his glass.

"Terri knows," he said. "Terri can tell you. But let me say this. If I could come back again in a different life, a different time and all, you know what? I'd like to come back as a knight. You were pretty safe wearing all that armor. It was all right being a knight until gunpowder and muskets and pistols came along."

"Mel would like to ride a horse and carry a lance," Terri said.

"Carry a woman's scarf with you everywhere," Laura said.

"Or just a woman," Mel said.

"Shame on you," Laura said.

Terri said, "Suppose you came back as a serf. The serfs didn't have it so good in those days," Terri said.

"The serfs never had it good," Mel said. "But I guess even the knights were vessels to someone. Isn't that the way it worked? But then everyone is always a vessel to someone. Isn't that right? Terri? But what I liked about knights, besides their ladies, was that they had that suit of armor, you know, and they couldn't get hurt very easy. No cars in those days, you know? No drunk teenagers to tear into your ass."

"Vassals," Terri said.

"What?" Mel said.

"Vassals," Terri said. "They were called vassals, not vessels."

"Vassals, vessels," Mel said, "what the fuck's the difference? You knew what I meant anyway. All right," Mel said. "So I'm not educated. I learned my stuff. I'm a heart surgeon, sure, but I'm just a mechanic. I go in and I fuck around and I fix things. Shit," Mel said.

"Modesty doesn't become you," Terri said.

"He's just a humble sawbones," I said. "But sometimes they suffocated in all that armor, Mel. They'd even have heart attacks if it got too hot and they were too tired and worn out. I read somewhere that they'd fall off their horses and not be able to get up because they were too tired to stand with all that armor on them. They got trampled by their own horses sometimes."

"That's terrible," Mel said. "That's a terrible thing, Nicky. I guess they'd just lay there and wait until somebody came along and made a shish kebab out of them."

"Some other vessel," Terri said.

"That's right," Mel said. "Some vassal would come along and spear the bastard in the name of love. Or whatever the fuck it was they fought over in those days."

"Same things we fight over these days," Terri said.

Laura said, "Nothing's changed."

The color was still high in Laura's cheeks. Her eyes were bright. She brought her glass to her lips.

Mel poured himself another drink. He looked at the label closely as if studying a long row of numbers. Then he slowly put the bottle down on the table and slowly reached for the tonic water.

"What about the old couple?" Laura said. "You didn't finish that story you started."

Laura was having a hard time lighting her cigarette. Her matches kept going out.

The sunshine inside the room was different now, changing, getting thinner. But the leaves outside the window were still shimmering, and I stared at the pattern they made on the panes and on the Formica counter. They weren't the same patterns, of course.

"What about the old couple?" I said.

"Older but wiser," Terri said.

Mel stared at her.

Terri said, "Go on with your story, hon. I was only kidding. Then what happened?"

"Terri, sometimes," Mel said.

"Please, Mel," Terri said. "Don't always be so serious, sweetie. Can't you take a joke?"

"Where's the joke?" Mel said.

He held his glass and gazed steadily at his wife.

"What happened?" Laura said.

Mel fastened his eyes on Laura. He said, "Laura, if I didn't have Terri and if I didn't love her so much, and if Nick wasn't my best friend, I'd fall in love with you. I'd carry you off, honey," he said.

"Tell your story," Terri said. "Then we'll go to that new place, okay?"

"Okay," Mel said. "Where was I?" he said. He stared at the table and then he began again.

"I dropped in to see each of them every day, sometimes twice a day if I was up doing other calls anyway. Casts and bandages, head to foot, the both of them. You know, you've seen it in the movies. That's just the way they looked, just like in the movies. Little eye-holes and nose-holes and mouth-holes. And she had to have her legs slung up on top of it. Well, the husband was very depressed for the longest while. Even after he found out that his wife was going to pull through, he was still very depressed. Not about the accident, though. I mean, the accident was one thing, but it wasn't everything. I'd get up to his mouth-hole, you know, and he'd say no, it wasn't the accident exactly but it was because he couldn't see her through his eye-holes. He said that was what was making him feel so bad. Can you imagine? I'm telling you, the man's heart was breaking because he couldn't turn his goddamn head and *see* his goddamn wife."

Mel looked around the table and shook his head at what he was going to say.

"I mean, it was killing the old fart just because he couldn't *look* at the fucking woman."

We all looked at Mel.

"Do you see what I'm saying?" he said.

Maybe we were a little drunk by then. I know it was hard keeping things in focus. The light was draining out of the room, going back through the window where it had come from. Yet nobody made a move to get up from the table to turn on the overhead light.

"Listen," Mel said. "Let's finish this fucking gin. There's about enough left here for one shooter all around. Then let's go eat. Let's go to the new place."

"He's depressed," Terri said. "Mel, why don't you take a pill?"

Mel shook his head. "I've taken everything there is."

"We all need a pill now and then," I said.

"Some people are born needing them," Terri said.

She was using her finger to rub at something on the table. Then she stopped rubbing.

"I think I want to call my kids," Mel said. "Is that all right with everybody? I'll call my kids," he said.

Terri said, "What if Marjorie answers the phone? You guys, you've heard us on the subject of Marjorie? Honey, you know you don't want to talk to Marjorie. It'll make you feel even worse."

"I don't want to talk to Marjorie," Mel said. "But I want to talk to my kids."

"There isn't a day goes by that Mel doesn't say he wishes she'd get married again. Or else die," Terri said. "For one thing," Terri said, "she's bankrupting us. Mel says it's just to spite him that she won't get married again. She has a boyfriend who lives with her and the kids, so Mel is supporting the boyfriend too."

"She's allergic to bees," Mel said. "If I'm not praying she'll get married again, I'm praying she'll get herself stung to death by a swarm of fucking bees."

"Shame on you," Laura said.

"Bzzzzzzz," Mel said, turning his fingers into bees and buzzing them at Terri's throat. Then he let his hands drop all the way to his sides.

"She's vicious," Mel said. "Sometimes I think I'll go up there dressed like a beekeeper. You know, that hat that's like a helmet with the plate that comes down over your face, the big gloves, and the padded coat? I'll knock on the door and let loose a hive of bees in the house. But first I'd make sure the kids were out, of course."

He crossed one leg over the other. It seemed to take him a lot of time to do it. Then he put both feet on the floor and leaned forward, elbows on the table, his chin cupped in his hands.

"Maybe I won't call the kids, after all. Maybe it isn't such a hot idea. Maybe we'll just go eat. How does that sound?"

"Sounds fine to me," I said. "Eat or not eat. Or keep drinking. I could head right on out into the sunset."

"What does that mean, honey?" Laura said.

"It just means what I said," I said. "It means I could just keep going. That's all it means."

"I could eat something myself," Laura said. "I don't think I've ever been so hungry in my life. Is there something to nibble on?"

"I'll put out some cheese and crackers," Terri said.

But Terri just sat there. She did not get up to get anything.

Mel turned his glass over. He spilled it out on the table.

"Gin's gone," Mel said.

Terri said, "Now what?"

I could hear my heart beating. I could hear everyone's heart. I could hear the human noise we sat there making, not one of us moving, not even when the room went dark.

Writing Assignments for "What We Talk About When We Talk About Love"

I. Brief Papers

    A. 1. Analyze any one conversation or piece of dialogue in the story in order to show that more is going on than is at first apparent.

       2. Why is it significant that Mel is a cardiologist?

       3. "Do you see what I'm saying?" Mel asks, when he finishes his story about the old couple. What is he saying?

       4. Why does Mel have the impulse to call his children?

       5. Characterize Nick, the narrator of the story.

       6. Explain how the discussion of knights and vassals relates to the story as a whole.

       7. Why don't Mel, Terri, Nick, and Laura head for the "new place" at the end of the story?

    B. Argue for or against one of the assertions below:

       1. Mel is clearly right in asserting that Ed, the man Terri used to live with, never really loved her.

       2. We shouldn't take seriously what any of the characters say toward the end of the story because they've all been drinking so much that what they say has no relation to the real world.

       3. Mel's and Terri's marriage is in deep trouble.

       4. Nick's and Laura's marriage is in deep trouble.

    C. 1. Nick says that he and Laura are in love. Do you agree?

       2. Mel offers the old couple who are injured in the accident as an example of "true love." Do you agree with Mel?

       3. Mel and Terri say they love each other. Do you believe them?

II. Longer Papers
  A. Expand one of your brief papers into a full-length essay.
  B. One reader thinks that in Carver's stories "it is dangerous even to speak. Conversation completes the damage people have already done to one another in silence." How fully does this statement apply to "What We Talk About When We Talk About Love?"
  C. Mel says that he used to love his first wife "more than life itself." Now he wants to know "what happened to that love?" According to the story, what did happen?
  D. According to one reader of the story, "the couples are just waiting to be married to someone else." Support, modify, or refute this assertion.
  E. The final word in the story is "dark." In what ways does the story end in moral and emotional as well as physical darkness?
  F. How does the story as a whole define and characterize love?

TILLIE OLSEN
Tell Me a Riddle

Before Reading

What do you think are the major sources of pleasure in human experience? What are the major sources of pain? Free write on one or both of these questions for 5 or 10 minutes.

"These Things Shall Be"

1

For forty-seven years they had been married. How deep back the stubborn, gnarled roots of the quarrel reached, no one could say—but only now, when tending to the needs of others no longer shackled them together, the roots swelled up visible, split the earth between them, and the tearing shook even to the children, long since grown.

Why now, why now? wailed Hannah.
As if when we grew up weren't enough, said Paul.
Poor Ma. Poor Dad. It hurts so for both of them, said Vivi. They never had very much; at least in old age they should be happy.
Knock their heads together, insisted Sammy; tell 'em: you're too old for this kind of thing; no reason not to get along now.

TELL ME A RIDDLE   First published in 1956. Tillie Olsen was born in 1913 in Nebraska and has lived most of her life in San Francisco. As the mother of four children, she had little time for writing when young, and her first book—a collection of stories titled *Tell Me a Riddle*—was not published until 1962.

Lennie wrote to Clara: They've lived over so much together; what could possibly tear them apart?

Something tangible enough.

Arthritic hands, and such work as he got, occasional. Poverty all his life, and there was little breath left for running. He could not, could not turn away from this desire: to have the troubling of responsibility, the fretting with money, over and done with; to be free, to be *care*free where success was not measured by accumulation, and there was use for the vitality still in him.

There was a way. They could sell the house, and with the money join his lodge's Haven, cooperative for the aged. Happy communal life, and was he not already an official; had he not helped organize it, raise funds, served as a trustee?

But she—would not consider it.

"What do we need all this for?" he would ask loudly, for her hearing aid was turned down and the vacuum was shrilling. "Five rooms" (pushing the sofa so she could get into the corner) "furniture" (smoothing down the rug) "floors and surfaces to make work. Tell me, why do we need it?" And he was glad he could ask in a scream.

"Because I'm use't."

"Because you're use't. This is a reason, Mrs. Word Miser? Used to can get unused!"

"Enough unused I have to get used to already. . . . Not enough words?" turning off the vacuum a moment to hear herself answer. "Because soon enough we'll need only a little closet, no windows, no furniture, nothing to make work, but for worms. Because now I want room. . . . Screech and blow like you're doing, you'll need that closet even sooner. . . . Ha, again!" for the vacuum bag wailed, puffed half up, hung stubbornly limp. "This time fix it so it stays; quick before the phone rings and you get too important-busy."

But while he struggled with the motor, it seethed in him. Why fix it? Why have to bother? And if it can't be fixed, have to wring the mind with how to pay the repair? At the Haven they come in with their own machines to clean your room or your cottage; you fish, or play cards, or make jokes in the sun, not with knotty fingers fight to mend vacuums.

Over the dishes, coaxingly: "For once in your life, to be free, to have everything done for you, like a queen."

"I never liked queens."

"No dishes, no garbage, no towel to sop, no worry what to buy, what to eat."

"And what else would I do with my empty hands? Better to eat at my own table when I want, and to cook and eat how I want."

"In the cottages they buy what you ask, and cook it how you like. *You* are the one who always used to say: better mankind born without mouths and stomachs than always to worry for money to buy, to shop, to fix, to cook, to wash, to clean."

"How cleverly you hid that you heard. I said it then because eighteen hours a day I ran. And you never scraped a carrot or knew a dish towel sops.

Now—for you and me—who cares? A herring out of a jar is enough. But when *I* want, and nobody to bother." And she turned off her ear button, so she would not have to hear.

But as *he* had no peace, juggling and rejuggling the money to figure: how will I pay for this now?; prying out the storm windows (there they take care of this!; jolting in the streetcar on errands (there I would not have to ride to take care of this or that); fending the patronizing relatives just back from Florida (at the Haven it matters what one is, not what one can afford), he gave *her* no peace.

"Look! In their bulletin. A reading circle. Twice a week it meets."

"Haumm," her answer of not listening.

"A reading circle. Chekhov they read that you like, and Peretz. Cultured people at the Haven that you would enjoy."

"Enjoy!" She tasted the word. "Now, when it pleases you, you find a reading circle for me. And forty years ago when the children were morsels and there was a Circle, did you stay home with them once so I could go? Even once? You trained me well. I do not need others to enjoy. Others!" Her voice trembled. "Because *you* want to be there with others. Already it makes me sick to think of you always around others. Clown, grimacer, floormat, yesman, entertainer, whatever they want of you."

And now it was he who turned on the television loud so he need not hear.

Old scar tissue ruptured and the wounds festered anew. Chekhov indeed. She thought without softness of that young wife, who in the deep night hours while she nursed the current baby, and perhaps held another in her lap, would try to stay awake for the only time there was to read. She would feel again the weather of the outside on his cheek when, coming late from a meeting, he would find her so, and stimulated and ardent, sniffing her skin, coax: "I'll put the baby to bed, and you—put the book away, don't read, don't read."

That had been the most beguiling of all the "don't read, put your book away" her life had been. Chekhov indeed!

"Money?" She shrugged him off. "Could we get poorer than once we were? And in America, who starves?"

But as still he pressed:

"Let me alone about money. Was there ever enough? Seven little ones— for every penny I had to ask—and sometimes, remember, there was nothing. But always *I* had to manage. Now *you* manage. Rub your nose in it good."

But from those years she had had to manage, old humiliations and terrors rose up, lived again, and forced her to relive them. The children's needings; that grocer's face or this merchant's wife she had had to beg credit from when credit was a disgrace; the scenery of the long blocks walked around when she could not pay; school coming, and the desperate going over the old to see what could yet be remade; the soups of meat bones begged "for-the-dog" one winter. . . .

Enough. Now they had no children. Let *him* wrack his head for how they would live. She would not exchange her solitude for anything. *Never again to be forced to move to the rhythms of others.*

For in this solitude she had won to a reconciled peace.

Tranquillity from having the empty house no longer an enemy, for it stayed clean—not as in the days when it was her family, the life in it, that had seemed the enemy: tracking, smudging, littering, dirtying, engaging her in endless defeating battle—and on whom her endless defeat had been spewed.

The few old books, memorized from rereading; the pictures to ponder (the magnifying glass superimposed on her heavy eyeglasses). Or if she wishes, when he is gone, the phonograph, that if she turns up very loud and strains, she can hear: the ordered sounds and the struggling.

Out in the garden, growing things to nurture. Birds to be kept out of the pear tree, and when the pears are heavy and ripe, the old fury of work, for all must be canned, nothing wasted.

And her one social duty (for she will not go to luncheons or meetings) the boxes of old clothes left with her, as with a life-practised eye for finding what is still wearable within the worn (again the magnifying glass superimposed on the heavy glasses) she scans and sorts—this for rag or rummage, that for mending and cleaning, and this for sending away.

Being able at last to live within, and not move to the rhythms of others, as life had forced her to: denying; removing; isolating; taking the children one by one; then deafening, half-blinding—and at last, presenting her solitude.

And in it she had won to a reconciled peace.

Now he was violating it with his constant campaigning: *Sell the house and move to the Haven.* (You sit, you sit—there too you could sit like a stone.) He was making of her a battleground where old grievances tore. (Turn on your ear button—I am talking.) And stubbornly she resisted—so that from wheedling, reasoning, manipulation, it was bitterness he now started with.

And it came to where every happening lashed up a quarrel.

"I will sell the house anyway," he flung at her one night. "I am putting it up for sale. There will be a way to make you sign."

The television blared, as always it did on the evenings he stayed home, and as always it reached her only as noise. She did not know if the tumult was in her or outside. Snap! she turned the sound off. "Shadows," she whispered to him, pointing to the screen, "look, it is only shadows." And in a scream: "Did you say that you will sell the house? Look at me, not at that. I am no shadow. You cannot sell without me."

"Leave on the television. I am watching."

"Like Paulie, like Jenny, a four-year-old. Staring at shadows. *You cannot sell the house.*"

"I will. We are going to the Haven. There you would not hear the television when you do not want it. I could sit in the social room and watch. You could lock yourself up to smell your unpleasantness in a room by yourself—for who would want to come near you?"

"No, no selling." A whisper now.

"The television is shadows. Mrs. Enlightened! Mrs. Cultured! A world comes into your house—and it is shadows. People you would never meet in a thousand lifetimes. Wonders. When you were four years old, yes, like Paulie, like Jenny, did you know of Indian dances, alligators, how they use bamboo in

Malaya? No, you scratched in your dirt with the chickens and thought Olshana*
was the world. Yes, Mrs. Unpleasant, I will sell the house, for there better can
we be rid of each other than here."

She did not know if the tumult was outside, or in her. Always a ravening
inside, a pull to the bed, to lie down, to succumb.

"Have you thought maybe Ma should let a doctor have a look at her?"
asked their son Paul after Sunday dinner, regarding his mother crumpled on the
couch, instead of, as was her custom, busying herself in Nancy's kitchen.

"Why not the President too?"

"Seriously, Dad. This is the third Sunday she's lain down like that after
dinner. Is she that way at home?"

"A regular love affair with the bed. Every time I start to talk to her."

Good protective reaction, observed Nancy to herself. The workings of
hos-til-ity.

"Nancy could take her. I just don't like how she looks. Let's have Nancy
arrange an appointment."

"You think she'll go?" regarding his wife gloomily. "All right, we have
to have doctor bills, we have to have doctor bills." Loudly: "Something hurts
you?"

She startled, looked to his lips. He repeated: "Mrs. Take It Easy, something hurts?"

"Nothing. . . . Only you."

"A woman of honey. That's why you're lying down?"

"Soon I'll get up to do the dishes, Nancy."

"Leave them, Mother, I like it better this way."

"Mrs. Take It Easy, Paul says you should start ballet. You should go to
see a doctor and ask: how soon can you start ballet?"

"A doctor?" she begged. "Ballet?"

"We were talking, Ma," explained Paul, "you don't seem any too well.
It would be a good idea for you to see a doctor for a checkup."

"I get up now to do the kitchen. Doctors are bills and foolishness, my son.
I need no doctors."

"At the Haven," he could not resist pointing out, "a doctor is *not* bills.
He lives beside you. You start to sneeze, he is there before you open up a
Kleenex. You can be sick there for free, all you want."

"Diarrhea of the mouth, is there a doctor to make you dumb?"

"Ma. Promise me you'll go. Nancy will arrange it."

"It's all of a piece when you think of it," said Nancy, "the way she attacks
my kitchen, scrubbing under every cup hook, doing the inside of the oven so
I can't enjoy Sunday dinner, knowing that half-blind or not, she's going to find
every speck of dirt. . . ."

*Olshana: Ol'shany, a village in western Russia.

"Don't, Nancy, I've told you—it's the only way she knows to be useful. What did the *doctor* say?"

"A real fatherly lecture. Sixty-nine is young these days. Go out, enjoy life, find interests. Get a new hearing aid, this one is antiquated. Old age is sickness only if one makes it so. Geriatrics, Inc."

"So there was nothing physical."

"Of course there was. How can you live to yourself like she does without there being? Evidence of a kidney disorder, and her blood count is low. He gave her a diet, and she's to come back for follow-up and lab work. . . . But he was clear enough: Number One prescription—start living like a human being. . . . When I think of your dad, who could really play the invalid with that arthritis of his, as active as a teenager, and twice as much fun. . . ."

"You didn't tell me the doctor says your sickness is in you, how you live." He pushed his advantage. "Life and enjoyments you need better than medicine. And this diet, how can you keep it? To weigh each morsel and scrape away each bit of fat, to make this soup, that pudding. There, at the Haven, they have a dietician, they would do it for you."

She is silent.

"You would feel better there, I know it," he says gently. "There there is life and enjoyments all around."

"What is the matter, Mr. Importantbusy, you have no card game or meeting you can go to?"—turning her face to the pillow.

For a while he cut his meetings and going out, fussed over her diet, tried to wheedle her into leaving the house, brought in visitors:

"I should come to a fashion tea. I should sit and look at pretty babies in clothes I cannot buy. This is pleasure?"
"Always you are better than everyone else. The doctor said you should go out. Mrs. Brem comes to you with goodness and you turn her away."
"Because *you* asked her to, she asked me."

"They won't come back. People you need, the doctor said. Your own cousins I asked; they were willing to come and make peace as if nothing had happened. . . ."
"No more crushers of people, pushers, hypocrites, around me. No more in *my* house. You go to them if you like."

"Kind he is to visit. And you, like ice."
"A babbler. All my life around babblers. Enough!"

"She's even worse, Dad? Then let her stew a while," advised Nancy. "You can't let it destroy you; it's a psychological thing, maybe too far gone for any of us to help."

So he let her stew. More and more she lay silent in bed, and sometimes did not even get up to make the meals. No longer was the tongue-lashing inevitable if he left the coffee cup where it did not belong, or forgot to take out the garbage or mislaid the broom. The birds grew bold that summer and for once pocked the pears, undisturbed.

A bellyful of bitterness and every day the same quarrel in a new way and a different old grievance the quarrel forced her to enter and relive. And the new torment: I am not really sick, the doctor said it, then why do I feel so sick?

One night she asked him: "You have a meeting tonight? Do not go. Stay . . . with me."

He had planned to watch "This Is Your Life," but half sick himself from the heavy heat, and sickening therefore the more after the brooks and woods of the Haven, with satisfaction he grated:

"Hah, Mrs. Live Alone And Like It wants company all of a sudden. It doesn't seem so good the time of solitary when she was a girl exile in Siberia. 'Do not go. Stay with me.' A new song for Mrs. Free As A Bird. Yes, I am going out, and while I am gone chew this aloneness good, and think how you keep us both from where if you want people, you do not need to be alone."

"Go, go. All your life you have gone without me."

After him she sobbed curses he had not heard in years, old-country curses from their childhood: Grow, oh shall you grow like an onion, with your head in the ground. Like the hide of a drum shall you be, beaten in life, beaten in death. Oh shall you be like a chandelier, to hang, and to burn. . . .

She was not in their bed when he came back. She lay on the cot on the sun porch. All week she did not speak or come near him; nor did he try to make peace or care for her.

He slept badly, so used to her next to him. After all the years, old harmonies and dependencies deep in their bodies; she curled to him, or he coiled to her, each warmed, warming, turning as the other turned, the nights a long embrace.

It was not the empty bed or the storm that woke him, but a faint singing. *She* was singing. Shaking off the drops of rain, the lightning riving her lifted face, he saw her so; the cot covers on the floor.

"This is a private concert?" he asked. "Come in, you are wet."

"I can breathe now," she answered; "my lungs are rich." Though indeed the sound was hardly a breath.

"Come in, come in." Loosing the bamboo shades. "Look how wet you are." Half helping, half carrying her, still faint-breathing her song.

A Russian love song of fifty years ago.

He had found a buyer, but before he told her, he called together those children who were close enough to come. Paul, of course, Sammy from New Jersey, Hannah from Connecticut, Vivi from Ohio.

With a kindling of energy for her beloved visitors, she arrayed the house, cooked and baked. She was not prepared for the solemn after-dinner conclave, they too probing in and tearing. Her frightened eyes watched from mouth to mouth as each spoke.

His stories were eloquent and funny of her refusal to go back to the doctor; of the scorned invitations; of her stubborn silence or the bile "like a Niagara"; of her contrariness: "If I clean it's no good how I cleaned; if I don't clean, I'm still a master who thinks he has a slave."

(Vinegar he poured on me all his life; I am well marinated; how can I be honey now?)

Deftly he marched in the rightness for moving to the Haven; their money from social security free for visiting the children, not sucked into daily needs and into the house; the activities in the Haven for him; but mostly the Haven for *her:* her health, her need of care, distraction, amusement, friends who shared her interests.

"This does offer an outlet for Dad," said Paul; "he's always been an active person. And economic peace of mind isn't to be sneezed at, either. I could use a little of that myself."

But when they asked: "And you, Ma, how do you feel about it?" could only whisper:

"For him it is good. It is not for me. I can no longer live between people."

"You lived all your life *for* people," Vivi cried.

"Not with." Suffering doubly for the unhappiness on her children's faces.

"You have to find some compromise," Sammy insisted. "Maybe sell the house and buy a trailer. After forty-seven years there's surely some way you can find to live in peace."

"There is no help, my children. Different things we need."

"Then live alone!" He could control himself no longer. "I have a buyer for the house. Half the money for you, half for me. Either alone or with me to the Haven. You think I can live any longer as we are doing now?"

"Ma doesn't have to make a decision this minute, however you feel, Dad," Paul said quickly, "and you wouldn't want her to. Let's let it lay a few months, and then talk some more."

"I think I can work it out to take Mother home with me for a while," Hannah said. "You both look terrible, but especially you, Mother. I'm going to ask Phil to have a look at you."

"Sure," cracked Sammy. "What's the use of a doctor husband if you can't get free service out of him once in a while for the family? And absence might make the heart . . . you know."

"There was something after all," Paul told Nancy in a colorless voice. "That was Hannah's Phil calling. Her gall bladder. . . . Surgery."

"Her *gall* bladder. If that isn't classic. 'Bitter as gall'—talk of psychosom——"

He stepped closer, put his hand over her mouth, and said in the same colorless, plodding voice. "We have to get Dad. They operated at once. The cancer was everywhere, surrounding the liver, everywhere. They did what they could . . . at best she has a year. Dad . . . we have to tell him."

2

Honest in his weakness when they told him, and that she was not to know. "I'm not an actor. She'll know right away by how I am. Oh that poor woman. I am old too, it will break me into pieces. Oh that poor woman. She will spit on me: 'So my sickness was how I live.' Oh Paulie, how she will be, that poor woman. Only she should not suffer. . . . I can't stand sickness, Paulie, I can't go with you."

But went. And play-acted.

"A grand opening and you did not even wait for me. . . . A good thing Hannah took you with her."

"Fashion teas I needed. They cut out what tore in me; just in my throat something hurts yet. . . . Look! so many flowers, like a funeral. Vivi called, did Hannah tell you? And Lennie from San Francisco, and Clara; and Sammy is coming." Her gnome's face pressed happily into the flowers.

It is impossible to predict in these cases, but once over the immediate effects of the operation, she should have several months of comparative well-being.

The money, where will come the money?

Travel with her, Dad. Don't take her home to the old associations. The other children will want to see her.

The money, where will I wring the money?

Whatever happens, she is not to know. No, you can't ask her to sign papers to sell the house; nothing to upset her. Borrow instead, then after. . . .

I had wanted to leave you each a few dollars to make life easier, as other fathers do. There will be nothing left now. (Failure! you and your "business is exploitation." Why didn't you make it when it could be made?—Is that what you're thinking, Sammy?)

Sure she's unreasonable, Dad—but you have to stay with her; if there's to be any happiness in what's left of her life, it depends on you.

Prop me up, children, think of me, too. Shuffled, chained with her, bitter woman. No Haven, and the little money going. . . . How happy she looks, poor creature.

The look of excitement. The straining to hear everything (the new hearing aid turned full). Why are you so happy, dying woman?

How the petals are, fold on fold, and the gladioli color. The autumn air.

Stranger grandsons, tall above the little gnome grandmother, the little spry grandfather. Paul in a frenzy of picture-taking before going.

She, wandering the great house. Feeling the books; laughing at the maple shoemaker's bench of a hundred years ago used as a table. The ear turned to music.

"Let us go home. See how good I walk now." "One step from the hospital," he answers, "and she wants to fly. Wait till Doctor Phil says."

"Look—the birds too are flying home. Very good Phil is and will not show it, but he is sick of sickness by the time he comes home."

"Mrs. Telepathy, to read minds," he answers; "read mine what it says: when the trunks of medicines become a suitcase, then we will go."

The grandboys, they do not know what to say to us. . . . Hannah, she runs around here, there, when is there time for herself?

Let us go home. Let us go home.

Musing; gentleness—*but for the incidents of the rabbi in the hospital, and of the candles of benediction.*

Of the rabbi in the hospital:

Now tell me what happened, Mother.

From the sleep I awoke, Hannah's Phil, and he stands there like a devil in a dream and calls me by name. I cannot hear. I think he prays. Go away, please, I tell him, I am not a believer. Still he stands, while my heart knocks with fright.

You scared *him,* Mother. He thought you were delirious.

Who sent him? Why did he come to me?

It is a custom. The men of God come to visit those of their religion they might help. The hospital makes up the list for them—race, religion—and you are on the Jewish list.

Not for rabbis. At once go and make them change. Tell them to write: Race, human; Religion, none.

And of the candles of benediction:

Look how you have upset yourself, Mrs. Excited Over Nothing. Pleasant memories you should leave.

Go in, go back to Hannah and the lights. Two weeks I saw candles and said nothing. But she asked me.

So what was so terrible? She forgets you never did, she asks you to light the Friday candles and say the benediction like Phil's mother when she visits. If the candles give her pleasure, why shouldn't she have the pleasure?

Not for pleasure she does it. For emptiness. Because his family does. Because all around her do.

That is not a good reason too? But you did not hear her. For heritage, she told you. For the boys, from the past they should have tradition.

Superstition! From our ancestors, savages, afraid of the dark, of themselves: mumbo words and magic lights to scare away ghosts.

She told you: how it started does not take away the goodness. For centuries, peace in the house it means.

Swindler! does she look back on the dark centuries? Candles bought instead of bread and stuck into a potato for a candlestick? Religion that stifled and said: in Paradise, woman, you will be the footstool of your husband, and in life—poor chosen Jew—ground under, despised, trembling in cellars. And cremated. And cremated.

This is religion's fault? You think you are still an orator of the 1905 revolution? Where are the pills for quieting? Which are they?

Heritage. How have we come from our savage past, how no longer to be savages—this to teach. To look back and learn what humanizes—this to teach.

To smash all ghettos that divide us—not to go back, not to go back—this to teach. Learned books in the house, will humankind live or die, and she gives to her boys—superstition.

Hannah that is so good to you. Take your pill, Mrs. Excited For Nothing, swallow.

Heritage! But when did I have time to teach? Of Hannah I asked only hands to help.

Swallow.

Otherwise—musing; gentleness.

Not to travel. To go home.

The children want to see you. We have to show them you are as thorny a flower as ever.

Not to travel.

Vivi wants you should see her new baby. She sent the tickets—airplane tickets—a Mrs. Roosevelt* she wants to make of you. To Vivi's we have to go.

A new baby. How many warm, seductive babies. She holds him stiffly, *away* from her, so that he wails. And a long shudder begins, and the sweat beads on her forehead.

"Hush, shush," croons the grandfather, lifting him back. "You should forgive your grandmamma, little prince, she has never held a baby before, only seen them in glass cases. Hush, shush."

"You're tired, Ma," says Vivi. "The travel and the noisy dinner. I'll take you to lie down."

(A long travel from, to, what the feel of a baby evokes.)

In the airplane, cunningly designed to encase from motion (no wind, no feel of flight), she had sat severely and still, her face turned to the sky through which they cleaved and left no scar.

So this was how it looked, the determining, the crucial sky, and this was how man moved through it, remote above the dwindled earth, the concealed human life. Vulnerable life, that could scar.

There was a steerage ship of memory that shook across a great, circular sea: clustered, ill human beings; and through the thick-stained air, tiny fretting waters in a window round like the airplane's—sun round, moon round. (The round thatched roofs of Olshana.) Eye round—like the smaller window that framed distance the solitary year of exile when only her eyes could travel, and no voice spoke. And the polar winds hurled themselves across snows trackless and endless and white—like the clouds which had closed together below and hidden the earth.

*Mrs. Roosevelt: Eleanor Roosevelt logged thousands of air miles in service to her country and to her crippled husband, Franklin Delano Roosevelt, president of the United States from 1933 until his death in 1945.

Now they put a baby in her lap. Do not ask me, she would have liked to beg. Enough the worn face of Vivi, the remembered grandchildren. I cannot, cannot. . . .

Cannot what? Unnatural grandmother, not able to make herself embrace a baby.

She lay there in the bed of the two little girls, her new hearing aid turned full, listening to the sound of the children going to sleep, the baby's fretful crying and hushing, the clatter of dishes being washed and put away. They thought she slept. Still she rode on.

It was not that she had not loved her babies, her children. The love—the passion of tending—had risen with the need like a torrent; and like a torrent drowned and immolated all else. But when the need was done—oh the power that was lost in the painful damming back and drying up of what still surged, but had nowhere to go. Only the thin pulsing left that could not quiet, suffering over lives one felt, but could no longer hold nor help.

On that torrent she had borne them to their own lives, and the riverbed was desert long years now. Not there would she dwell, a memoried wraith. Surely that was not all, surely there was more. Still the springs, the springs were in her seeking. Somewhere an older power that beat for life. Somewhere coherence, transport, meaning. If they would but leave her in the air now stilled of clamor, in the reconciled solitude, to journey on.

And they put a baby in her lap. Immediacy to embrace, and the breath of *that* past: warm flesh like this that had claims and nuzzled away all else and with lovely mouths devoured; hot-living like an animal—intensely and now; the turning maze; the long drunkenness; the drowning into needing and being needed. Severely she looked back—and the shudder seized her again, and the sweat. Not that way. Not there, not now could she, not yet. . . .

And all that visit, she could not touch the baby.

"Daddy, is it the . . . sickness she's like that?" asked Vivi. "I was so glad to be having the baby—for her. I told Tim, it'll give her more happiness than anything, being around a baby again. And she hasn't played with him once."

He was not listening, "Aahh little seed of life, little charmer," he crooned, "Hollywood should see you. A heart of ice you would melt. Kick, kick. The future you'll have for a ball. In 2050 still kick. Kick for your grandaddy then."

Attentive with the older children; sat through their performances (command performance; we command you to be the audience); helped Ann sort autumn leaves to find the best for a school program; listened gravely to Richard tell about his rock collection, while her lips mutely formed the words to remember: *igneous, sedimentary, metamorphic;* looked for missing socks, books, and bus tickets; watched the children whoop after their grandfather who knew how to tickle, chuck, lift, toss, do tricks, tell secrets, make jokes, match riddle for riddle.

(Tell me a riddle, Grammy. I know no riddles, child.) Scrubbed sills and woodwork and furniture in every room; folded the laundry; straightened drawers; emptied the heaped baskets waiting for ironing (while he or Vivi or Tim nagged: You're supposed to rest here, you've been sick) but to none tended or gave food—and could not touch the baby.

After a week she said: "Let us go home. Today call about the tickets."

"You have important business, Mrs. Inahurry? The President waits to consult with you?" He shouted, for the fear of the future raced in him. "The clothes are still warm from the suitcase, your children cannot show enough how glad they are to see you, and you want home. There is plenty of time for home. We cannot be with the children at home."

"Blind to around you as always: the little ones sleep four in a room because we take their bed. We are two more people in a house with a new baby, and no help."

"Vivi is happy so. The children should have their grandparents a while, she told to me. I should have my mommy and daddy. . . ."

"Babbler and blind. Do you look at her so tired? How she starts to talk and she cries? I am not strong enough yet to help. Let us go home."

(To reconciled solitude.)

For it seemed to her the crowded noisy house was listening to her, listening for her. She could feel it like a great ear pressed under her heart. And everything knocked: quick constant raps: let me in, let me in.

How was it that soft reaching tendrils also became blows that knocked?

C'mon, Grandma, I want to show you. . . .

Tell me a riddle, Grandma. *(I know no riddles.)*

Look, Grammy, he's so dumb he can't even find his hands. (Dody and the baby on a blanket over the fermenting autumn mould.)

I made them—for you. (Ann) (Flat paper dolls with aprons that lifted on scalloped skirts that lifted on flowered pants; hair of yarn and great ringed questioning eyes.)

Watch me, Grandma. (Richard snaking up the tree, hanging exultant, free, with one hand at the top. Below Dody hunching over in pretend-cooking.) *(Climb too, Dody, climb and look.)*

Be my nap bed, Grammy. (The "No!" too late.)

Morty's abandoned heaviness, while his fingers ladder up and down her hearing-aid cord to his drowsy chant: eentsiebeentsiespider. *(Children trust.)*

It's to start off your own rock collection, Grandma.

That's a trilobite fossil, 200 million years old (millions of years on a boy's mouth) and that one's obsidian, black glass.

Knocked and knocked.

Mother, I *told* you the teacher said we had to bring it back all filled out this morning. Didn't you even ask Daddy? Then tell *me* which plan and I'll check it: evacuate or stay in the city or wait for you to come and take me away. (Seeing the look of straining to hear.) It's for Disaster, Grandma. *(Children trust.)*

Vivi in the maze of the long, the lovely drunkenness. The old old noises: baby sounds; screaming of a mother flayed to exasperation; children quarreling; children playing; singing; laughter.

And Vivi's tears and memories, spilling so fast, half the words not understood.

She had started remembering out loud deliberately, so her mother would know the past was cherished, still lived in her.

Nursing the baby: My friends marvel, and I tell them, oh it's easy to be such a cow. I remember how beautiful my mother seemed nursing my brother, and the milk just flows. . . . Was that Davy? It must have been Davy. . . .

Lowering a hem: How did you ever . . . when I think how you made everything we wore. . . . Time, just think, seven kids and Mommy sewed everything . . . do I remember you sang while you sewed? That white dress with the red apples on the skirt you fixed over for me, was it Hannah's or Clara's before it was mine?

Washing sweaters: Ma, I'll never forget, one of those days so nice you washed clothes outside; one of the first spring days it must have been. The bubbles just danced while you scrubbed, and we chased after, and you stopped to show us how to blow our own bubbles with green onion stalks . . . you always. . . .

"Strong onion, to still make you cry after so many years," her father said, to turn the tears into laughter.

While Richard bent over his homework: Where is it now, do we still have it, the Book of the Martyrs?* It always seemed so, well—exalted, when you'd put it on the round table and we'd all look at it together; there was even a halo from the lamp. The lamp with the beaded fringe you could move up and down; they're in style again, pulley lamps like that, but without the fringe. You know the book I'm talking about, Daddy, the Book of the Martyrs, the first picture was a bust of Spartacus† . . . Socrates?‡ I wish there was something like that for the children, Mommy, to give them what you. . . . (And the tears splashed again.)

(What I intended and did not? Stop it, daughter, stop it, leave that time. And he, the hypocrite, sitting there with tears in his eyes—it was nothing to you then, nothing.)

. . . The time you came to school and I almost died of shame because of your accent and because I knew you knew I was ashamed; how could I? . . . Sammy's harmonica and you danced to it once, yes you did, you and Davy squealing in your arms. . . . That time you bundled us up and walked us down to the railway station to stay the night 'cause it was heated and we didn't have

---

*the Book of the Martyrs: *The Book of Martyrs,* by the English clergyman John Foxe (1516–1587), told stories of the persecution of Protestant reformers, especially during the reign of Queen Mary I of England ("Bloody Mary"), 1553–1558.

†Spartacus: Leader of a slave revolt in Italy that threatened the Roman republic in the first century B.C.; after his death in battle, 6000 of his followers were crucified.

‡Socrates: Greek philosopher (469–399 B.C.) tried on charges of corrupting youth and of religious heresy; he was convicted and given poison hemlock to drink.

any coal, that winter of the strike, you didn't think I remembered that, did you, Mommy? . . . How you'd call us out to see the sunsets. . . .

Day after day, the spilling memories. Worse now, questions, too. Even the grandchildren: Grandma, in the olden days, when you were little. . . .

It was the afternoons that saved.

While they thought she napped, she would leave the mosaic on the wall (of children's drawings, maps, calendars, pictures, Ann's cardboard dolls with their great ringed questioning eyes) and hunch in the girls' closet on the low shelf where the shoes stood, and the girls' dresses covered.

For that while she would painfully sheathe against the listening house, the tendrils and noises that knocked, and Vivi's spilling memories. Sometimes it helped to braid and unbraid the sashes that dangled, or to trace the pattern on the hoop slips.

Today she had jacks and children under jet trails to forget. Last night, Ann and Dody silhouetted in the window against a sunset of flaming man-made clouds of jet trail, their jacks ball accenting the peaceful noise of dinner being made. Had she told them, yes she had told them of how they played jacks in her village though there was no ball, no jacks. Six stones, round and flat, toss them out, the seventh on the back of the hand, toss, catch and swoop up as many as possible, toss again. . . .

Of stones (repeating Richard) there are three kinds: earth's fire jetting; rock of layered centuries; crucibled new out of the old *(igneous, sedimentary, metamorphic)*. But there was that other—frozen to black glass, never to transform or hold the fossil memory . . . (let not my seed fall on stone). There was an ancient man* who fought to heights a great rock that crashed back down eternally—eternal labor, freedom, labor . . . (stone will perish, but the word remain). And you, David, who with a stone slew, screaming: Lord, take my heart of stone and give me flesh

Who was screaming? Why was she back in the common room of the prison, the sun motes dancing in the shafts of light, and the informer being brought in, a prisoner now, like themselves. And Lisa leaping, yes, Lisa, the gentle and tender, biting at the betrayer's jugular. Screaming and screaming.

No, it is the children screaming. Another of Paul and Sammy's terrible fights?

In Vivi's house. Severely: you are in Vivi's house.

Blows, screams, a call: "Grandma!" For her? Oh please not for her. Hide, hunch behind the dresses deeper. But a trembling little body hurls itself beside her—surprised, smothered laughter, arms surround her neck, tears rub dry on her cheek, and words too soft to understand whisper into her ear (Is this where you hide too, Grammy? It's my secret place, we have a secret now).

And the sweat beads, and the long shudder seizes.

*   *   *   *   *

*an ancient man: Sisyphus; in Greek mythology, Sisyphus was doomed forever in Hades to roll up a steep hill a heavy rock which always rolled down again.

It seemed the great ear pressed inside now, and the knocking. "We have to go home," she told him, "I grow ill here."

"It's your own fault, Mrs. Bodybusy, you do not rest, you do too much." He raged, but the fear was in his eyes. "It was a serious operation, they told you to take care. . . . All right, we will go to where you can rest."

But where? Not home to death, not yet. He had thought to Lennie's, to Clara's; beautiful visits with each of the children. She would have to rest first, be stronger. If they could but go to Florida—it glittered before him, the never-realized promise of Florida. California: of course. (The money, the money, dwindling!) Los Angeles first for sun and rest, then to Lennie's in San Francisco.

He told her the next day. "You saw what Nancy wrote: snow and wind back home, a terrible winter. And look at you—all bones and a swollen belly. I called Phil: he said: 'A prescription, Los Angeles sun and rest.' "

She watched the words on his lips. "You have sold the house," she cried, "that is why we do not go home. That is why you talk no more of the Haven, why there is money for travel. After the children you will drag me to the Haven."

"The Haven! Who thinks of the Haven any more? Tell her, Vivi, tell Mrs. Suspicious: a prescription, sun and rest, to make you healthy. . . . And how could I sell the house without *you*?"

At the place of farewells and greetings, of winds of coming and winds of going, they say their good-byes.

They look back at her with the eyes of others before them: Richard with her own blue blaze; Ann with the nordic eyes of Tim; Morty's dreaming brown of a great-grandmother he will never know; Dody with the laughing eyes of him who had been her springtide love (who stands beside her now); Vivi's, all tears.

The baby's eyes are closed in sleep.

Good-bye, my children.

3

It is to the back of the great city he brought her, to the dwelling places of the cast-off old. Bounded by two lines of amusement piers to the north and to the south, and between a long straight paving rimmed with black benches facing the sand—sands so wide the ocean is only a far fluting.

In the brief vacation season, some of the boarded stores fronting the sands open, and families, young people and children, may be seen. A little tasselled tram shuttles between the piers, and the lights of roller coasters prink and tweak over those who come to have sensation made in them.

The rest of the year it is abandoned to the old, all else boarded up and still; seemingly empty, except the occasional days and hours when the sun, like a tide, sucks them out of the low rooming houses, casts them onto the benches and sandy rim of the walk—and sweeps them into decaying enclosures once again.

A few newer apartments glint among the low bleached squares. It is in one of these Lennie's Jeannie has arranged their rooms. "Only a few miles north and south people pay hundreds of dollars a month for just this gorgeous air, Grandaddy, just this ocean closeness."

She had been ill on the plane, lay ill for days in the unfamiliar room. Several times the doctor came by—left medicine she would not take. Several times Jeannie drove in the twenty miles from work, still in her Visiting Nurse uniform, the lightness and brightness of her like a healing.

"Who can believe it is winter?" he asked one morning. "Beautiful it is outside like an ad. Come, Mrs. Invalid, come to taste it. You are well enough to sit in here, you are well enough to sit outside. The doctor said it too."

But the benches were encrusted with people, and the sands at the sidewalk's edge. Besides, she had seen the far ruffle of the sea: "there take me," and though she leaned against him, it was she who led.

Plodding and plodding, sitting often to rest, he grumbling. Patting the sand so warm. Once she scooped up a handful, cradling it close to her better eye; peered, and flung it back. And as they came almost to the brink and she could see the glistening wet, she sat down, pulled off her shoes and stockings, left him and began to run. "You'll catch cold," he screamed, but the sand in his shoes weighed him down—he who had always been the agile one—and already the white spray creamed her feet.

He pulled her back, took a handkerchief to wipe off the wet and the sand. "Oh no," she said, "the sun will dry," seized the square and smoothed it flat, dropped on it a mound of sand, knotted the kerchief corners and tied it to a bag—"to look at with the strong glass" (for the first time in years explaining an action of hers)—and lay down with the little bag against her cheek, looking toward the shore that nurtured life as it first crawled toward consciousness the millions of years ago.

He took her one Sunday in the evil-smelling bus, past flat miles of blister houses, to the home of relatives. Oh what is this? she cried as the light began to smoke and the houses to dim and recede. Smog, he said, everyone knows but you. . . . Outside he kept his arms about her, but she walked with hands pushing the heavy air as if to open it, whispered: who has done this? sat down suddenly to vomit at the curb and for a long while refused to rise.

One's age as seen on the altered face of those known in youth. Is this they he has come to visit? This Max and Rose, smooth and pleasant, introducing them to polite children, disinterested grandchildren, "the whole family, once a month on Sundays. And why not? We have the room, the help, the food."

Talk of cars, of houses, of success: this son that, that daughter this. And *your* children? Hastily skimped over, the intermarriages, the obscure work— "my doctor son-in-law, Phil"—all he has to offer. She silent in a corner. (Carsick like a baby, he explains.) Years since he has taken her to visit anyone but the children, and old apprehensions prickle: "no incidents," he silently begs, "no incidents." He itched to tell them. "A very sick woman," significantly, indicating her with his eyes, "a very sick woman." Their restricted faces did not react. "Have you thought maybe she'd do better at Palm Springs?" Rose asked. "Or at least a nicer section of the beach, nicer people, a pool." Not to have to say "money" he said instead: "would she have sand to look at through a magnifying glass?" and went on, detail after detail, the old habit betraying of parading the queerness of her for laughter.

After dinner—the others into the living room in men- or women-clusters, or into the den to watch TV—the four of them alone. She sat close to him, and did not speak. Jokes, stories, people they had known, beginning of reminiscence, Russia fifty-sixty years ago. Strange words across the Duncan Phyfe table: *hunger; secret meetings; human rights; spies; betrayals; prison; escape*—interrupted by one of the grandchildren: "Commercial's on; any Coke left? Gee, you're missing a real hair-raiser." And then a granddaughter (Max proudly: "look at her, an American queen") drove them home on her way back to U.C.L.A. No incident—except that there had been no incidents.

The first few mornings she had taken with her the magnifying glass, but he would sit only on the benches, so she rested at the foot, where slatted bench shadows fell, and unless she turned her hearing aid down, other voices invaded.

Now on the days when the sun shone and she felt well enough, he took her on the tram to where the benches ranged in oblongs, some with tables for checkers or cards. Again the blanket on the sand in the striped shadows, but she no longer brought the magnifying glass. He played cards, and she lay in the sun and looked towards the waters; or they walked—two blocks down to the scaling hotel, two blocks back—past chili-hamburger stands, open-doored bars, Next-to-New and perpetual rummage sale stores.

Once, out of the aimless walkers, slow and shuffling like themselves, someone ran unevenly towards them, embraced, kissed, wept: "dear friends, old friends." A friend of *hers,* not his: Mrs. Mays who had lived next door to them in Denver when the children were small.

Thirty years are compressed into a dozen sentences; and the present, not even in three. All is told: the children scattered; the husband dead; she lives in a room two blocks up from the sing hall—and points to the domed auditorium jutting before the pier. The leg? phlebitis; the heavy breathing? that, one does not ask. She, too, comes to the benches each day to sit. And tomorrow, tomorrow, are they going to the community sing? Of course he would have heard of it, everybody goes—the big doings they wait for all week. They have never been? She will come to them for dinner tomorrow and they will all go together.

So it is that she sits in the wind of the singing, among the thousand various faces of age.

She had turned off her hearing aid at once they came into the auditorium—as she would have wished to turn off sight.

One by one they streamed by and imprinted on her—and though the savage zest of their singing came voicelessly soft and distant, the faces still roared—the faces densened the air—chorded into

children-chants, mother-croons, singing of the chained love serenades, Beethoven storms, mad Lucia's scream,* drunken joy-songs, keens for the dead, work-
singing

> *while from floor to balcony to dome a bare-footed sore-covered little girl threaded the sound-
> thronged tumult, danced her ecstasy of grimace to flutes that scratched at a cross-roads village
> wedding*

Yes, faces became sound, and the sound became faces; and faces and sound
became weight—pushed, pressed

"Air"—her hands claw his.

"Whenever I enjoy myself. . . ." Then he saw the gray sweat on her face.
"Here. Up. Help me, Mrs. Mays," and they support her out to where she can
gulp the air in sob after sob.

"A doctor, we should get for her a doctor."

"Tch, it's nothing," says Ellen Mays, "I get it all the time. You've missed
the tram; come to my place. Fix your hearing aid, honey . . . close . . . tea. My
view. See, she *wants* to come. Steady now, that's how." Adding mysteriously:
"Remember your advice, easy to keep your head above water, empty things
float. Float."

The singing a fading march for them, tall woman with a swollen leg,
weaving little man, and the swollen thinness they help between.

The stench in the hall: mildew? decay? "We sit and rest then climb. My
gorgeous view. We help each other and here   we   are."

The stench along into the slab of room. A washstand for a sink, a box with
oilcloth tacked around for a cupboard, a three-burner gas plate. Artificial flowers, colorless with dust. Everywhere pictures foaming: wedding, baby, party,
vacation, graduation, family pictures. From the narrow couch under a slit of
window, sure enough the view: lurching rooftops and a scallop of ocean heaving, preening, twitching under the moon.

"While the water heats. Excuse me . . . down the hall." Ellen Mays has
gone.

"You'll live?" he asks mechanically, sat down to feel his fright; tried to
pull her alongside.

She pushed him away. "For air," she said; stood clinging to the dresser.
Then, in a terrible voice:

After a lifetime of room. Of many rooms.

Shhh.

You remember how she lived. Eight children. And now one room   like
a coffin.

She pays rent!

Shrinking the life of her   into one room   like a coffin   Rooms and
rooms like this   I lie on the quilt and hear them talk

---

*mad Lucia's scream: The "mad scene" from the opera *Lucia di Lammermoor* by Gaetano Donizetti
(1797–1848).

Please, Mrs. Orator-without-Breath.

Once you went for coffee I walked I saw A Balzac a Chekhov to write it Rummage Alone On scraps

Better old here than in the old country!

On scraps Yet they sang like like Wondrous! *Humankind one has to believe* So strong for what? To rot not grow?

Your poor lungs beg you. They sob between each word.

Singing. Unused the life in them. She in this poor room with her pictures Max You The children Everywhere unused the life And who has meaning? Century after century still all in us not to grow?

Coffins, rummage, plants: sick woman. Oh lay down. We will get for you the doctor.

"And when will it end. Oh, *the end.*" *That* nightmare thought, and this time she writhed, crumpled against him, seized his hand (for a moment again the weight, the soft distant roaring of humanity) and on the strangled-for breath, begged: "Man . . . we'll destroy ourselves?"

And looking for answer—in the helpless pity and fear for her (for *her*) that distorted his face—she understood the last months, and knew that she was dying.

4

"Let us go home," she said after several days.

"You are in training for a cross-country run? That is why you do not even walk across the room? Here, like a prescription Phil said, till you are stronger from the operation. You want to break doctor's orders?"

She saw the fiction was necessary to him, was silent; then: "At home I will get better. If the doctor here says?"

"And winter? And the visits to Lennie and to Clara? All right," for he saw the tears in her eyes, "I will write Phil, and talk to the doctor."

Days passed. He reported nothing. Jeannie came and took her out for air, past the boarded concessions, the hooded and tented amusement rides, to the end of the pier. They watched the spent waves feeding the new, the gulls in the clouded sky; even up where they sat, the wind-blown sand stung.

She did not ask to go down the crooked steps to the sea.

Back in her bed, while he was gone to the store, she said: "Jeannie, this doctor, he is not one I can ask questions. Ask him for me, can I go home?"

Jeannie looked at her, said quickly: "Of course, poor Granny. You want your own things around you, don't you? I'll call him tonight. . . . Look, I've something to show you," and from her purse unwrapped a large cookie, intricately shaped like a little girl. "Look at the curls—can you hear me well, Granny?—and the darling eyelashes. I just came from a house where they were baking them."

"The dimples, there in the knees," she marveled, holding it to the better light, turning, studying, "like art. Each singly they cut, or a mold?"

"Singly," said Jeannie, "and if it is a child only the mother can make them. Oh Granny, it's the likeness of a real little girl who died yesterday—Rosita. She was three years old. *Pan del Muerto,* the Bread of the Dead. It was the custom in the part of Mexico they came from."

Still she turned and inspected. "Look, the hollow in the throat, the little cross necklace. . . . I think for the mother it is a good thing to be busy with such bread. You know the family?"

Jeannie nodded. "On my rounds. I nursed. . . . Oh Granny, it is like a party; they play songs she liked to dance to. The coffin is lined with pink velvet and she wears a white dress. There are candles. . . ."

"In the house?" Surprised, "They keep her in the house?"

"Yes," said Jeannie, "and it is against the health law. The father said it will be sad to bury her in this country; in Oaxaca they have a feast night with candles each year; everyone picnics on the graves of those they loved until dawn."

"Yes, Jeannie, the living must comfort themselves." And closed her eyes.

"You want to sleep, Granny?"

"Yes, tired from the pleasure of you. I may keep the Rosita? There stand it, on the dresser, where I can see; something of my own around me."

In the kitchenette, helping her grandfather unpack the groceries, Jeannie said in her light voice:

"I'm resigning my job, Grandaddy."

"Ah, the lucky young man. Which one is he?"

"Too late. You're spoken for." She made a pyramid of cans, unstacked, and built again.

"Something is wrong with the job?"

"With me. I can't be"—she searched for the word—"What they call professional enough. I let myself feel things. And tomorrow I have to report a family. . . ." The cans clicked again. "It's not that, either. I just don't know what I want to do, maybe go back to school, maybe go to art school. I thought if you went to San Francisco I'd come along and talk it over with Momma and Daddy. But I don't see how you can go. She wants to go home. She asked me to ask the doctor."

The doctor told her himself. "Next week you may travel, when you are a little stronger." But next week there was the fever of an infection, and by the time that was over, she could not leave the bed—a rented hospital bed that stood beside the double bed he slept in alone now.

Outwardly the days repeated themselves. Every other afternoon and evening he went out to his newfound cronies, to talk and play cards. Twice a week, Mrs. Mays came. And the rest of the time, Jeannie was there.

By the sickbed stood Jeannie's FM radio. Often into the room the shapes of music came. She would lie curled on her side, her knees drawn up, intense in listening (Jeannie sketched her so, coiled, convoluted like an ear), then thresh her hand out and abruptly snap the radio mute—still to lie in her attitude of listening, concealing tears.

Once Jeannie brought in a young Marine to visit, a friend from high-school days she had found wandering near the empty pier. Because Jeannie asked him to, gravely, without self-consciousness, he sat himself cross-legged on the floor and performed for them a dance of his native Samoa.

Long after they left, a tiny thrumming sound could be heard where, in her bed, she strove to repeat the beckon, flight, surrender of his hands, the fluttering footbeats, and his low plaintive calls.

Hannah and Phil sent flowers. To deepen her pleasure, he placed one in her hair. "Like a girl," he said, and brought the hand mirror so she could see. She looked at the pulsing red flower, the yellow skull face; a desolate, excited laugh shuddered from her, and she pushed the mirror away—but let the flower burn.

The week Lennie and Helen came, the fever returned. With it the excited laugh, and incessant words. She, who in her life had spoken but seldom and then only when necessary (never having learned the easy, social uses of words), now in dying, spoke incessantly.

In a half-whisper: "Like Lisa she is, your Jeannie. Have I told you of Lisa who taught me to read? Of the highborn she was, but noble in herself. I was sixteen; they beat me; my father beat me so I would not go to her. It was forbidden, she was a Tolstoyan.* At night, past dogs that howled, terrible dogs, my son, in the snows of winter to the road, I to ride in her carriage like a lady, to books. To her, life was holy, knowledge was holy, and she taught me to read. They hung her. Everything that happens one must try to understand why. She killed one who betrayed many. Because of betrayal, betrayed all she lived and believed. In one minute she killed, before my eyes (there is so much blood in a human being, my son), in prison with me. All that happens, one must try to understand.

"The name?" Her lips would work. "The name that was their pole star; the doors of the death houses fixed to open on it; I read of it my year of penal servitude. Thuban!" very excited, "Thuban, in ancient Egypt the pole star. Can you see, look out to see it, Jeannie, if it swings around *our* pole star that seems to *us* not to move.

"Yes, Jeannie, at your age my mother and grandmother had already buried children . . . yes, Jeannie, it is more than oceans between Olshana and you . . . yes, Jeannie, they danced, and for all the bodies they had they might as well be chickens, and indeed, they scratched and flapped their arms and hopped.

"And Andrei Yefimitch, who for twenty years had never known of it and never wanted to know, said as if he wanted to cry: but why my dear friend this malicious laughter?" Telling to herself half-memorized phrases from her few books. "Pain I answer with tears and cries, baseness with indignation, meanness with repulsion . . . for life may be hated or wearied of, but never despised."

Delirious: "Tell me, my neighbor, Mrs. Mays, the pictures never lived, but what of the flowers? Tell them who ask: no rabbis, no ministers, no priests,

*Tolstoyan: Admirer of Leo Tolstoy (1828–1910), Russian writer *(War and Peace, Anna Karenina)*, social theorist, and pacifist.

no speeches, no ceremonies: ah, false—let the living comfort themselves. Tell Sammy's boy, he who flies, tell him to go to Stuttgart* and see where Davy has no grave. And what? . . . And what? where millions have no graves—save air."

In delirium or not, wanting the radio on; not seeming to listen, the words still jetting, wanting the music on. Once, silencing it abruptly as of old, she began to cry, unconcealed tears this time. "You have pain, Granny?" Jeannie asked.

"The music," she said, "still it is there and we do not hear; knocks, and our poor human ears too weak. What else, what else we do not hear?"

Once she knocked his hand aside as he gave her a pill, swept the bottles from her bedside table: "no pills, let me feel what I feel," and laughed as on his hands and knees he groped to pick them up.

Nighttimes her hand reached across the bed to hold his.

A constant retching began. Her breath was too faint for sustained speech now, but still the lips moved:

When no longer necessary   to injure others
Pick   pick pick   Blind chicken
As a human being   responsibility

"David!" imperious, "Basin!" and she would vomit, rinse her mouth, the wasted throat working to swallow, and begin the chant again.

She will be better off in the hospital now, the doctor said.

He sent the telegrams to the children, was packing her suitcase, when her hoarse voice startled. She had roused, was pulling herself to sitting.

"Where now?" she asked. "Where now do you drag me?"

"You do not even have to have a baby to go this time," he soothed, looking for the brush to pack. "Remember, after Davy you told me—worthy to have a baby for the pleasure of the ten-day rest in the hospital?"

"Where now? Not home yet?" her voice mourned. "Where *is* my home?"

He rose to ease her back. "The doctor, the hospital," he started to explain, but deftly, like a snake, she had slithered out of bed and stood swaying, propped behind the night table.

"Coward," she hissed, "runner."

"You stand," he said senselessly.

"To take me there and run. Afraid of a little vomit."

He reached her as she fell. She struggled against him, half slipped from his arms, pulled herself up again.

"Weakling," she taunted, "to leave me there and run. Betrayer. All your life you have run."

He sobbed, telling Jeannie. "A Marilyn Monroe to run for her virtue. Fifty-nine pounds she weighs, the doctor said, and she beats at me like a Dempsey. Betrayer, she cries, and I running like a dog when she calls; day and night, running to her, her vomit, the bedpan. . . ."

*Stuttgart: A city in southern West Germany that had been almost totally destroyed by Allied bombing during World War II.

"She needs you, Grandaddy," said Jeannie. "Isn't that what they call love? I'll see if she sleeps, and if she does, poor worn-out darling, we'll have a party, you and I: I brought us rum babas."

They did not move her. By her bed now stood the tall hooked pillar that held the solutions—blood and dextrose—to feed her veins. Jeannie moved down the hall to take over the sickroom, her face so radiant, her grandfather asked her once: "you are in love?" (shameful the joy, the pure overwhelming joy from being with her grandmother; the peace, the serenity that breathed.) "My darling escape," she answered incoherently, "my darling Granny"—as if that explained.

Now one by one the children came, those that were able. Hannah, Paul, Sammy. Too late to ask: and what did you learn with your living, Mother, and what do we need to know?

Clara, the eldest, clenched:

> Pay me back, Mother, pay me back for all you took from me. Those others you crowded into your heart. The hands I needed to be for you, the heaviness, the responsibility.
>
> Is this she? Noises the dying make, the crablike hands crawling over the covers. The ethereal singing.
>
> She hears that music, that singing from childhood; forgotten sound—not heard since, since. . . . And the hardness breaks like a cry: Where did we lose each other, first mother, singing mother?
>
> Annulled: the quarrels, the gibing, the harshness between; the fall into silence and the withdrawal.
>
> I do not know you, Mother. Mother, I never knew you.

Lennie, suffering not alone for her who was dying, but for that in her which never lived (for that which in him might never live). From him too, unspoken words: good-bye Mother who taught me to mother myself.

Not Vivi, who must stay with her children; not Davy, but he is already here, having to die again with her this time, for the living take their dead with them when they die.

Light she grew, like a bird, and, like a bird, sound bubbled in her throat while the body fluttered in agony. Night and day, asleep or awake (though indeed there was no difference now) the songs and the phrases leaping.

And he, who had once dreaded a long dying (from fear of himself, from horror of the dwindling money) now desired her quick death profoundly, for her sake. He no longer went out, except when Jeannie forced him; no longer laughed, except when, in the bright kitchenette, Jeannie coaxed his laughter (and she, who seemed to hear nothing else, would laugh too, conspiratorial wisps of laughter).

Light, like a bird, the fluttering body, the little claw hands, the beaked shadow on her face; and the throat, bubbling, straining.

He tried not to listen, as he tried not to look on the face in which only
the forehead remained familiar, but trapped with her the long nights in that little
room, the sounds worked themselves into his consciousness, with their punctuation of death swallows, whimpers, gurglings.

Even in reality (swallow) *life's lack of it*
Slaveships deathtrains clubs   eeenough
The bell   summon what enables

   78,000 in one minute (whisper of a scream) *78,000 human beings   we'll*
destroy ourselves?

"Aah, Mrs. Miserable," he said, as if she could hear, "all your life working, and now in bed you lie, servants to tend, you do not even need to call to
be tended, and still you work. Such hard work it is to die? Such hard work?"

The body threshed, her hand clung in his. A melody, ghost-thin, hovered
on her lips, and like a guilty ghost, the vision of her bent in listening to it,
silencing the record instantly he was near. Now, heedless of his presence, she
floated the melody on and on.

"Hid it from me," he complained, "how many times you listened to
remember it so?" And tried to think when she had first played it, or first begun
to silence her few records when he came near—but could reconstruct nothing.
There was only this room with its tall hooked pillar and its swarm of sounds.

No man one   except through others
Strong   with the not yet   in the now
Dogma dead   war dead   one country

"It helps, Mrs. Philosopher, words from books? It helps?" And it seemed
to him that for seventy years she had hidden a tape recorder, infinitely microscopic, within her, that it had coiled infinite mile on mile, trapping every song,
every melody, every word read, heard, and spoken—and that maliciously she
was playing back only what said nothing of him, of the children, of their intimate
life together.

"Left us indeed, Mrs. Babbler," he reproached, "you who called others
babbler and cunningly saved your words. A lifetime you tended and loved, and
now not a word of us, for us. Left us indeed? Left me."

And he took out his solitaire deck, shuffled the cards loudly, slapped them
down.

Lift high banner of reason (tatter of an orator's voice)
justice   freedom   light
Humankind   life worthy   capacities
Seeks (blur of shudder) *belong   human being*

"Words, words," he accused, "and what human beings did *you* seek
around you, Mrs. Live Alone, and what humankind think worthy?"

Though even as he spoke, he remembered she had not always been
isolated, had not always wanted to be alone (as he knew there had been a voice
before this gossamer one; before the hoarse voice that broke from silence to
lash, make incidents, shame him—a girl's voice of eloquence that spoke their
holiest dreams). But again he could reconstruct, image, nothing of what had
been before, or when, or how, it had changed.

Ace, queen, jack. The pillar shadow fell, so, in two tracks; in the mirror depths glistened a moonlike blob, the empty solution bottle. And it worked in him: *of reason and justice and freedom. . . . Dogma dead:* he remembered the full quotation, laughed bitterly. "Hah, good you do not know what you say; good Victor Hugo died and did not see it, his twentieth century."

Deuce, ten, five. Dauntlessly she began a song of their youth of belief:

These things shall be, a loftier race
than e'er the world hath known shall rise

with flame of freedom in their souls
and light of knowledge in their eyes

King, four, jack "In the twentieth century, hah!"

They shall be gentle, brave and strong
to spill no drop of blood, but dare
all . . .
    on earth and fire and sea and air

"To spill no drop of blood, hah! So, cadaver, and you too, cadaver Hugo, 'in the twentieth century ignorance will be dead, dogma will be dead, war will be dead, and for all mankind one country—of fulfillment?' Hah!"

And every life (long strangling cough) *shall*
    be a song

The cards fell from his fingers. Without warning, the bereavement and betrayal he had sheltered—compounded through the years—hidden even from himself—revealed itself,
    uncoiled,
    released,
    sprung

and with it the monstrous shapes of what had actually happened in the century.

A ravening hunger or thirst seized him. He groped into the kitchenette, switched on all three lights, piled a tray—"you have finished your night snack, Mrs. Cadaver, now I will have mine." And he was shocked at the tears that splashed on the tray.

"Salt tears. For free. I forgot to shake on salt?"

Whispered: "Lost, how much I lost."

Escaped to the grandchildren whose childhoods were childish, who had never hungered, who lived unravaged by disease in warm houses of many rooms, had all the school for which they cared, could walk on any street, stood a head taller than their grandparents, towered above—beautiful skins, straight backs, clear straightforward eyes. "Yes, you in Olshana," he said to the town of sixty years ago, "they would be nobility to you."

And was this not the dream then, come true in ways undreamed? he asked.

And are there no other children in the world? he answered, as if in her harsh voice.

And the flame of freedom, the light of knowledge?

And the drop, to spill no drop of blood?

And he thought that at six Jeannie would get up and it would be his turn to go to her room and sleep, that he could press the buzzer and she would come now; that in the afternoon Ellen Mays was coming, and this time they would play cards and he could marvel at how rouge can stand half an inch on the cheek; that in the evening the doctor would come, and he could beg him to be merciful, to stop the feeding solutions, to let her die.

To let her die, and with her their youth of belief out of which her bright, betrayed words foamed; stained words, that on her working lips came stainless.

Hours yet before Jeannie's turn. He could press the buzzer and wake her to come now; he could take a pill, and with it sleep; he could pour more brandy into his milk glass, though what he had poured was not yet touched.

Instead he went back, checked her pulse, gently tended with his knotty fingers as Jeannie had taught.

She was whimpering; her hand crawled across the covers for his. Compassionately he enfolded it, and with his free hand gathered up the cards again. Still was there thirst or hunger ravening in him.

That world of their youth—dark, ignorant, terrible with hate and disease—how was it that living in it, in the midst of corruption, filth, treachery, degradation, they had not mistrusted man nor themselves; had believed so beautifully, so . . . falsely?

"Aaah, children," he said out loud, "how we believed, how we belonged." And he yearned to package for each of the children, the grandchildren, for everyone, *that joyous certainty, that sense of mattering, of moving and being moved, of being one and indivisible with the great of the past, with all that freed, ennobled.* Package it, stand on corners, in front of stadiums and on crowded beaches, knock on doors, give it as a fabled gift.

"And why not in cereal boxes, in soap packages?" he mocked himself. "Aah. You have taken my senses, cadaver."

Words foamed, died unsounded. Her body writhed; she made kissing motions with her mouth. (Her lips moving as she read, poring over the Book of the Martyrs, the magnifying glass superimposed over the heavy eyeglasses.) *Still she believed?* "Eva!" he whispered. "Still you believed? You lived by it? These Things Shall Be?"

"One pound soup meat," she answered distinctly, "one soup bone."

"My ears heard you. Ellen Mays was witness: 'Humankind . . . one has to believe.'" Imploringly: "Eva!"

"Bread, day-old." She was mumbling. "Please, in a wooden box . . . for kindling. The thread, hah, the thread breaks. Cheap thread"—and a gurgling, enormously loud, began in her throat.

"I ask for stone; she gives me bread—day-old." He pulled his hand away, shouted: "Who wanted questions? Everything you have to wake?" Then dully, "Ah, let me help you turn, poor creature."

Words jumbled, cleared. In a voice of crowded terror:

"Paul, Sammy, don't fight.

"Hannah, have I ten hands?

"How can I give it, Clara, how can I give it if I don't have?"

"You lie," he said sturdily, "there was joy too." Bitterly: "Ah how cheap you speak of us at the last."

As if to rebuke him, as if her voice had no relationship with her flailing body, she sang clearly, beautifully, a school song the children had taught her when they were little; begged:

"Not look my hair where they cut. . . ."

(The crown of braids shorn.) And instantly he left the mute old woman poring over the Book of the Martyrs; went past the mother treading at the sewing machine, singing with the children; past the girl in her wrinkled prison dress, hiding her hair with scarred hands, lifting to him her awkward, shamed, imploring eyes of love; and took her in his arms, dear, personal, fleshed, in all the heavy passion he had loved to rouse from her.

"Eva!"

Her little claw hand beat the covers. How much, how much can a man stand? He took up the cards, put them down, circled the beds, walked to the dresser, opened, shut drawers, brushed his hair, moved his hand bit by bit over the mirror to see what of the reflection he could blot out with each move, and felt that at any moment he would die of what was unendurable. Went to press the buzzer to wake Jeannie, looked down, saw on Jeannie's sketch pad the hospital bed, with *her;* the double bed alongside, with him; the tall pillar feeding into her veins, and their hands, his and hers, clasped, feeding each other. And as if he had been instructed he went to his bed, lay down, holding the sketch (as if it could shield against the monstrous shapes of loss, of betrayal, of death) and with his free hand took hers back into his.

So Jeannie found them in the morning.

That last day the agony was perpetual. Time after time it lifted her almost off the bed, so they had to fight to hold her down. He could not endure and left the room; wept as if there never would be tears enough.

Jeannie came to comfort him. In her light voice she said: Grandaddy, Grandaddy don't cry. She is not there, she promised me. On the last day, she said she would go back to when she first heard music, a little girl on the road of the village where she was born. She promised me. It is a wedding and they dance, while the flutes so joyous and vibrant tremble in the air. Leave her there, Grandaddy, it is all right. She promised me. Come back, come back and help her poor body to die.

For two of that generation
Seevya and Genya
Infinite, dauntless, incorruptible

Death deepens the wonder

Writing Assignments for "Tell Me a Riddle"

I. Brief Papers

A. 1. What devices and strategies does David use to try to convince Eva to sell their house and move to the Haven?

2. Explain what Eva means when she tells David, "You trained me well. I do not need others to enjoy" (p. 420).

3. Write a biographical sketch of Eva's life.

4. What does Eva mean when she says that Hannah lights the candles of benediction "not for pleasure" but "for emptiness" (p. 427).

5. Point out several instances of humor in the story.

6. Explain why Eva reacts so intensely to the visit from the rabbi.

7. How does the title "Tell Me a Riddle" relate to the story as a whole?

8. How does the story define *freedom?*

B. Argue for or against one of the assertions below:

1. Eva is right in saying that "Vinegar [David] poured on me all his life" (p. 425).

2. Eva is wrong not to have gone to the Haven; she would have been happy there.

3. Eva's unwillingness to embrace her new grandchild shows that she never really cared for her own children.

4. "Tell Me a Riddle" is a feminist story, a story that is particularly sympathetic toward women.

C. 1. David once describes Eva as a thorny flower. Do you think his metaphor is an accurate and appropriate one?

2. At what point(s) in the story do you most strongly sympathize with David? Try to explain why your sympathies are strongest then.

3. What does the last phrase of the story—"Death deepens the wonder"—mean to you?

4. Eva tells David that our cultural heritage is important because we can learn from it "what humanizes." In what sense, if any, has reading and responding to "Tell Me a Riddle" been a humanizing experience for you?

II. Longer Papers

A. Explain the roots of the quarrel between Eva and David, what Eva calls "the old grievances."

B. Develop, modify, or refute the assertion that "Tell Me a Riddle" is guided by a pacifist philosophy: the story opposes war and any other use of physical force.

C. Eva says at one point during her disagreement with David, "Different things we need" (p. 425). Is she right?

D. David says that Eva is a "bitter woman." Do you agree?

E. Explain the difference, as Eva sees it, between "superstition" and heritage in order to make clear what she believes in and what she thinks children should be taught.

F. Argue for or against the assertion that "Tell Me a Riddle" is an affirmative story.

III. Comparative Papers

A. What, taken together, do "Tell Me a Riddle" and "What We Talk About When We Talk About Love" have to say about the place of pain and suffering in human experience?

B. Argue for or against the assertion that, taken together, "Tell Me a Riddle" and "What We Talk About When We Talk About Love" make clear that, whatever else it is, love is an emotion that cannot and does not last beyond a year or two; marriages may go on but love does not.

C. Defend, modify, or refute the assertion that both "What We Talk About When We Talk About Love" and "Tell Me a Riddle" present human beings as primarily selfish, weak, mean-spirited, and—therefore—despicable.

D. According to "What We Talk About When We Talk About Love" and "Tell Me a Riddle," what are the most valuable and worthwhile human experiences?

E. Compare "Tell Me a Riddle" to one or more stories involving the use of physical force and violence—"The Murder," "A Jury of Her Peers," "The Use of Force," "Forcing the End," "Indian Camp," "Barn Burning," "The Cask of Amontillado," "Good Country People," and "The Man Who Lived Underground"—in order to see if the respective writers agree on the consequences of force or on the place of violence in human experience.

IV. The Poetry of "Tell Me a Riddle"

Using the sentences below, construct a short essay that defines and illustrates the poetry in "Tell Me a Riddle."

1. Tillie Olsen has a short story.
2. The short story is called "Tell Me a Riddle."
3. "Tell Me a Riddle" is an example of fiction that resembles poetry.
4. That is, "Tell Me a Riddle" is an example of lyrical fiction.

5. "Tell Me a Riddle" is like a poem in this way.
6. "Tell Me a Riddle" makes imaginative use of language.
7. "Tell Me a Riddle" makes innovative use of language.

8. Here is an example.
9. The story speaks of "the children's *needings*" (p. 420).
10. It does not speak of the children's *needs*.
11. The children's *needs* is more prosaic than the children's *needings*.

12. The words of David have poetic and metaphorical qualities as well.
13. The words of Eva have poetic and metaphorical qualities as well.
14. David and Eva are the story's two central characters.

15. Here is an example of words with poetic and metaphorical qualities.
16. At one point Eva thinks this.
17. "Vinegar he poured on me all his life; I am well marinated; how can I be honey now?" (p. 425).

18. The story even looks like a poem at times.
19. Some of its lines are indented.
20. The line itself is often the major unit of meaning.
21. In these cases the sentence is not the major unit of meaning.

22. "Tell Me a Riddle" most obviously resembles a poem or song in this way.
23. "Tell Me a Riddle" makes consistent use of repetition.

24. "Tell Me a Riddle" repeats words.
25. "Tell Me a Riddle" repeats phrases.
26. "Tell Me a Riddle" repeats even whole sentences.

27. "Freedom" is a word that is repeated.
28. "Responsibility" is a word that is repeated.
29. "Spilling memories" is a phrase that is repeated.
30. "To spill no drop of blood" is a phrase that is repeated.
31. "She had won to a reconciled peace" is a sentence that is repeated.
32. "Children trust" is a sentence that is repeated.

33. This is often the case with "Tell Me a Riddle."
34. This is often the case with poetry.
35. Repetition occurs with variation.
36. First comes "Never again to be forced to move to the rhythms of others" (p. 420).
37. Then comes "Being able at last to live within, and not move to the rhythms of others" (p. 421).
38. First comes "Another of Paul and Sammy's terrible fights" (p. 432).
39. Then comes "Paul, Sammy, don't fight" (p. 444).

40. This is one of the most moving instances of repetition in the story.
41. It occurs toward the end of the story.
42. David repeats Eva's earlier words.
43. Eva's earlier words were, "Humankind . . . one has to believe." (p. 437).

44. "Tell Me a Riddle" has lyrical qualities.
45. They help give the story intensity.
46. They help give the story emotional impact.
47. Such intensity and emotional impact usually seem possible only through poetry.

JOHN CHEEVER
O Youth and Beauty!

Before Reading

Do you think that youth, the period from about 15 to 25, is the best time of life? Do you think that the older you get, the more dissatisfied and unhappy you'll become? Free write on one or both of these questions for 5 or 10 minutes.

At the tag end of nearly every long, large Saturday-night party in the suburb of Shady Hill, when almost everybody who was going to play golf or tennis in the morning had gone home hours ago and the ten or twelve people remaining seemed powerless to bring the evening to an end although the gin and whiskey were running low, and here and there a woman who was sitting out her husband would have begun to drink milk; when everybody had lost track of time, and the baby-sitters who were waiting at home for these diehards would have long since stretched out on the sofa and fallen into a deep sleep, to dream about cooking-contest prizes, ocean voyages, and romance; when the bellicose drunk, the crapshooter, the pianist, and the woman faced with the expiration of her hopes had all expressed themselves; when every proposal—to go to the Farquarsons' for breakfast, to go swimming, to go and wake up the Townsends, to go here and go there—died as soon as it was made, then Trace Bearden would begin to chide Cash Bentley about his age and thinning hair. The chiding was preliminary to moving the living-room furniture. Trace and Cash moved the tables and the chairs, the sofas and the fire screen, the woodbox and the footstool; and when they had finished, you wouldn't know the place. Then if the host had a revolver, he would be asked to produce it. Cash would take off his shoes and assume a starting crouch behind a sofa. Trace would fire the weapon out of an open window, and if you were new to the community and had not understood what the preparations were about, you would then realize that you were watching a hurdle race. Over the sofa went Cash, over the tables, over the fire screen and the woodbox. It was not exactly a race, since Cash ran it alone, but it was extraordinary to see this man of forty surmount so many obstacles so gracefully. There was not a piece of furniture in Shady Hill that Cash could not take in his stride. The race ended with cheers, and presently the party would break up.

Cash was, of course, an old track star, but he was never aggressive or tiresome about his brilliant past. The college where he had spent his youth had offered him a paying job on the alumni council, but he had refused it, realizing that that part of his life was ended. Cash and his wife, Louise, had two children,

O YOUTH AND BEAUTY! First published in 1954. John Cheever (1912–1982) was born in Quincy, Massachusetts, and spent all his life in New England and New York. Both his short stories and his novels focus on life in American suburbia.

and they lived in a medium-cost ranch house on Alewives Lane. They belonged to the country club, although they could not afford it, but in the case of the Bentleys nobody ever pointed this out, and Cash was one of the best-liked men in Shady Hill. He was still slender—he was careful about his weight—and he walked to the train in the morning with a light and vigorous step that marked him as an athlete. His hair was thin, and there were mornings when his eyes looked bloodshot, but this did not detract much from a charming quality of stubborn youthfulness.

In business Cash had suffered reverses and disappointments, and the Bentleys had many money worries. They were always late with their tax payments and their mortgage payments, and the drawer of the hall table was stuffed with unpaid bills; it was always touch and go with the Bentleys and the bank. Louise looked pretty enough on Saturday night, but her life was exacting and monotonous. In the pockets of her suits, coats, and dresses there were little wads and scraps of paper on which was written: "Oleomargarine, frozen spinach, Kleenex, dog biscuit; hamburger, pepper, lard . . ." When she was still half awake in the morning, she was putting on the water for coffee and diluting the frozen orange juice. Then she would be wanted by the children. She would crawl under the bureau on her hands and knees to find a sock for Toby. She would lie flat on her belly and wiggle under the bed (getting dust up her nose) to find a shoe for Rachel. Then there were the housework, the laundry, and the cooking, as well as the demands of the children. There always seemed to be shoes to put on and shoes to take off, snowsuits to be zipped and unzipped, bottoms to be wiped, tears to be dried, and when the sun went down (she saw it set from the kitchen window) there was the supper to be cooked, the baths, the bedtime story, and the Lord's Prayer. With the sonorous words of the Our Father in a darkened room the children's day was over, but the day was far from over for Louise Bentley. There were the darning, the mending, and some ironing to do, and after sixteen years of housework she did not seem able to escape her chores even while she slept. Snowsuits, shoes, baths, and groceries seemed to have permeated her subconscious. Now and then she would speak in her sleep—so loudly that she woke her husband. "I can't *afford* veal cutlets," she said one night. Then she sighed uneasily and was quiet again.

By the standards of Shady Hill, the Bentleys were a happily married couple, but they had their ups and downs. Cash could be very touchy at times. When he came home after a bad day at the office and found that Louise, for some good reason, had not started supper, he would be ugly. "Oh, for Christ sake!" he would say, and go into the kitchen and heat up some frozen food. He drank some whiskey to relax himself during this ordeal, but it never seemed to relax him, and he usually burned the bottom out of a pan, and when they sat down for supper the dining space would be full of smoke. It was only a question of time before they were plunged into a bitter quarrel. Louise would run upstairs, throw herself onto the bed and sob. Cash would grab the whiskey bottle and dose himself. These rows, in spite of the vigor with which Cash and Louise entered into them, were the source of a great deal of pain for both of them. Cash would sleep downstairs on the sofa, but sleep never repaired the damage, once the trouble had begun, and if they met in the morning, they would be at one another's throats in a second. Then Cash would leave for the train, and, as soon as the children had been taken to nursery school, Louise would put on her coat and cross the grass to the Beardens' house. She would cry into a cup of warmed-up coffee and tell Lucy Bearden her troubles. What was the meaning of marriage? What was the meaning of love? Lucy always suggested that Louise get a job. It would give her emotional and financial independence, and that, Lucy said, was what she needed.

The next night, things would get worse. Cash would not come home for dinner at all, but would stumble in at about eleven, and the whole sordid wrangle would be repeated, with Louise going to bed in tears upstairs and Cash again stretching out on the living-room sofa. After a few days and nights of this, Louise would decide that she was at the end of her rope. She would decide to go and stay with her married sister in Mamaroneck. She usually chose a Saturday, when Cash would be at home, for her departure. She would pack a suitcase and get her War Bonds from the desk. Then she would take a bath and put on her best slip. Cash, passing the bedroom door, would see her. Her slip was transparent, and suddenly he was all repentance, tenderness, charm, wisdom, and love. "Oh, my darling!" he would groan, and when they went downstairs to get a bite to eat about an hour later, they would be sighing and making cow eyes at one another; they would be the happiest married couple in the whole eastern United States. It was usually at about this time that Lucy Bearden turned up with the good news that she had found a job for Louise. Lucy would ring the doorbell, and Cash, wearing a bathrobe, would let her in. She would be brief with Cash, naturally, and hurry into the dining room to tell poor Louise the good news. "Well, that's very nice of you to have looked," Louise would say wanly, "but I don't think that I want a job any more. I don't think that Cash wants me to work, do you, sweetheart?" Then she would turn her big dark eyes on Cash, and you could practically smell smoke. Lucy would excuse herself hurriedly from this scene of depravity, but never left with any hard feelings, because she had been married for nineteen years herself and she knew that every union has its ups and downs. She didn't seem to leave any wiser, either; the next time the Bentleys quarreled, she would be just as intent as ever on getting Louise a job. But these quarrels and reunions, like the hurdle race, didn't seem to lose their interest through repetition.

On a Saturday night in the spring, the Farquarsons gave the Bentleys an anniversary party. It was their seventeenth anniversary. Saturday afternoon, Louise Bentley put herself through preparations nearly as arduous as the Monday wash. She rested for an hour, by the clock, with her feet high in the air, her chin in a sling, and her eyes bathed in some astringent solution. The clay packs, the too tight girdle, and the plucking and curling and painting that went on were all aimed at rejuvenation. Feeling in the end that she had not been entirely successful, she tied a piece of veiling over her eyes—but she was a lovely woman, and all the cosmetics that she had struggled with seemed, like her veil, to be drawn transparently over a face where mature beauty and a capacity for wit and passion were undisguisable. The Farquarsons' party was nifty, and the Bentleys had a wonderful time. The only person who drank too much was Trace Bearden. Late in the party, he began to chide Cash about his thinning hair and Cash good-naturedly began to move the furniture around. Harry Farquarson had a pistol, and Trace went out onto the terrace to fire it up at the sky. Over the sofa went Cash, over the end table, over the arms of the wing chair and the fire screen. It was a piece of carving on a chest that brought him down, and down he came like a ton of bricks.

Louise screamed and ran to where he lay. He had cut a gash in his forehead, and someone made a bandage to stop the flow of blood. When he tried to get up, he stumbled and fell again, and his face turned a terrible green. Harry telephoned Dr. Parminter, Dr. Hopewell, Dr. Altman, and Dr. Barnstable, but it was two in the morning and none of them answered. Finally, a Dr. Yerkes—a total stranger—agreed to come. Yerkes was a young man—he did not seem old enough to be a doctor—and he looked around at the disordered room and the anxious company as if there was something weird about the scene. He got off on the wrong foot with Cash. "What seems to be the matter, old-timer?" he asked.

Cash's leg was broken. The doctor put a splint on it, and Harry and Trace carried the injured man out to the doctor's car. Louise followed them in her own car to the hospital, where Cash was bedded down in a ward. The doctor gave Cash a sedative, and Louise kissed him and drove home in the dawn.

Cash was in the hospital for two weeks, and when he came home he walked with a crutch and his broken leg was in a heavy cast. It was another ten days before he could limp to the morning train. "I won't be able to run the hurdle race any more, sweetheart," he told Louise sadly. She said that it didn't matter, but while it didn't matter to her, it seemed to matter to Cash. He had lost weight in the hospital. His spirits were low. He seemed discontented. He did not himself understand what had happened. He, or everything around him, seemed subtly to have changed for the worse. Even his senses seemed to conspire to damage the ingenuous world that he had enjoyed for so many years. He went into the kitchen late one night to make himself a sandwich, and when he opened the icebox door he noticed a rank smell. He dumped the spoiled meat into the garbage, but the smell clung to his nostrils. A few days later he was in the attic, looking for his varsity sweater. There were no windows in the attic and his flashlight was dim. Kneeling on the floor to unlock a trunk, he broke a spider web with his lips. The frail web covered his mouth as if a hand had been put over it. He wiped it impatiently, but also with the feeling of having been gagged. A few nights later, he was walking down a New York side street in the rain and saw an old whore standing in a doorway. She was so sluttish and ugly that she looked like a cartoon of Death, but before he could appraise her—the instant his eyes took an impression of her crooked figure—his lips swelled, his breathing quickened, and he experienced all the other symptoms of erotic excitement. A few nights later, while he was reading *Time* in the living room, he noticed that the faded roses Louise had brought in from the garden smelled more of earth than of anything else. It was a putrid, compelling smell. He dropped the roses into a wastebasket, but not before they had reminded him of the spoiled meat, the whore, and the spider web.

He had started going to parties again, but without the hurdle race to run, the parties of his friends and neighbors seemed to him interminable and stale. He listened to their dirty jokes with an irritability that was hard for him to conceal. Even their countenances discouraged him, and, slumped in a chair, he would regard their skin and their teeth narrowly, as if he were himself a much younger man.

The brunt of his irritability fell on Louise, and it seemed to her that Cash, in losing the hurdle race, had lost the thing that had preserved his equilibrium. He was rude to his friends when they stopped in for a drink. He was rude and gloomy when he and Louise went out. When Louise asked him what was the matter, he only murmured, "Nothing, nothing, nothing," and poured himself some bourbon. May and June passed, and then the first part of July, without his showing any improvement.

Then it is a summer night, a wonderful summer night. The passengers on the eight-fifteen see Shady Hill—if they notice it at all—in a bath of placid golden light. The noise of the train is muffled in the heavy foliage, and the long car windows look like a string of lighted aquarium tanks before they flicker out of sight. Up on the hill, the ladies say to one another, "Smell the grass! Smell the trees!" The Farquarsons are giving another party, and Harry has hung a sign, WHISKEY GULCH, from the rose arbor, and is wearing a chef's white hat and an apron. His guests are still drinking, and the smoke from his meat fire rises, on this windless evening, straight up into the trees.

In the clubhouse on the hill, the first of the formal dances for the young people begins around nine. On Alewives Lane sprinklers continue to play after dark. You can smell the water. The air seems as fragrant as it is dark—it is a delicious element to walk through—and most of the windows on Alewives Lane are open to it. You can see Mr. and Mrs. Bearden, as you pass, looking at their television. Joe Lockwood, the young lawyer who lives on the corner, is practicing a speech to the jury before his wife. "I intend to show you," he says, "that a man of probity, a man whose reputation for honesty and reliability . . ." He waves his bare arms as he speaks. His wife goes on knitting. Mrs. Carver—Harry Farquarson's mother-in-law—glances up at the sky and asks, *"Where* did all the stars come from?" She is old and foolish, and yet she is right: Last night's stars seem to have drawn to themselves a new range of galaxies, and the night sky is not dark at all, except where there is a tear in the membrane of light. In the unsold house lots near the track a hermit thrush is singing.

The Bentleys are at home. Poor Cash has been so rude and gloomy that the Farquarsons have not asked him to their party. He sits on the sofa beside

Louise, who is sewing elastic into the children's underpants. Through the open window he can hear the pleasant sounds of the summer night. There is another party, in the Rogerses' garden, behind the Bentleys'. The music from the dance drifts down the hill. The band is sketchy—saxophone, drums, and piano—and all the selections are twenty years old. The band plays "Valencia," and Cash looks tenderly toward Louise, but Louise, tonight, is a discouraging figure. The lamp picks out the gray in her hair. Her apron is stained. Her face seems colorless and drawn. Suddenly, Cash begins frenziedly to beat his feet in time to the music. He sings some gibberish—Jabajabajabajaba—to the distant saxophone. He sighs and goes into the kitchen.

Here a faint, stale smell of cooking clings to the dark. From the kitchen window Cash can see the lights and figures of the Rogerses' party. It is a young people's party. The Rogers girl has asked some friends in for dinner before the dance, and now they seem to be leaving. Cars are driving away. "I'm covered with grass stains," a girl says. "I hope the old man remembered to buy gasoline," a boy says, and a girl laughs. There is nothing on their minds but the passing summer nights. Taxes and the elastic in underpants—all the unbeautiful facts of life that threaten to crush the breath out of Cash—have not touched a single figure in this garden. Then jealousy seizes him—such savage and bitter jealousy that he feels ill.

He does not understand what separates him from these children in the garden next door. He has been a young man. He has been a hero. He has been adored and happy and full of animal spirits, and now he stands in a dark kitchen, deprived of his athletic prowess, his impetuousness, his good looks—of everything that means anything to him. He feels as if the figures in the next yard are the specters from some party in that past where all his tastes and desires lie, and from which he has been cruelly removed. He feels like a ghost of the summer evening. He is sick with longing. Then he hears voices in the front of the house. Louise turns on the kitchen light. "Oh, here you are," she says. "The Beardens stopped in. I think they'd like a drink."

Cash went to the front of the house to greet the Beardens. They wanted to go up to the club, for one dance. They saw, at a glance, that Cash was at loose ends, and they urged the Bentleys to come. Louise got someone to stay with the children and then went upstairs to change.

When they got to the club, they found a few friends of their age hanging around the bar, but Cash did not stay in the bar. He seemed restless and perhaps drunk. He banged into a table on his way through the lounge to the ballroom. He cut in on a young girl. He seized her too vehemently and jigged her off in an ancient two-step. She signaled openly for help to a boy in the stag line, and Cash was cut out. He walked angrily off the dance floor onto the terrace. Some young couples there withdrew from one another's arms as he pushed open the screen door. He walked to the end of the terrace, where he hoped to be alone, but here he surprised another young couple, who got up from the lawn, where they seemed to have been lying, and walked off in the dark toward the pool.

Louise remained in the bar with the Beardens. "Poor Cash is tight," she said. And then, "He told me this afternoon that he was going to paint the storm windows," she said. "Well, he mixed the paint and washed the brushes and put on some old fatigues and went into the cellar. There was a telephone call for him at around five, and when I went down to tell him, do you know what he was doing? He was just sitting there in the dark with a cocktail shaker. He hadn't touched the storm windows. He was just sitting there in the dark, drinking Martinis."

"Poor Cash," Trace said.

"You ought to get a job," Lucy said. "That would give you emotional and financial independence." As she spoke, they all heard the noise of furniture being moved around in the lounge.

"Oh, my God!" Louise said. "He's going to run the race. Stop him, Trace, stop him! He'll hurt himself. He'll kill himself!"

They all went to the door of the lounge. Louise again asked Trace to interfere, but she could see by Cash's face that he was way beyond remonstrating with. A few couples left the dance floor and stood watching the preparations. Trace didn't try to stop Cash—he helped him. There was no pistol, so he slammed a couple of books together for the start.

Over the sofa went Cash, over the coffee table, the lamp table, the fire screen, and the hassock. All his grace and strength seemed to have returned to him. He cleared the big sofa at the end of the room and instead of stopping there, he turned and started back over the course. His face was strained. His mouth hung open. The tendons of his neck protruded hideously. He made the hassock, the fire screen, the lamp table, and the coffee table. People held their breath when he approached the final sofa, but he cleared it and landed on his feet. There was some applause. Then he groaned and fell. Louise ran to his side. His clothes were soaked with sweat and he gasped for breath. She knelt down beside him and took his head in her lap and stroked his thin hair.

Cash had a terrible hangover on Sunday, and Louise let him sleep until it was nearly time for church. The family went off to Christ Church together at eleven, as they always did. Cash sang, prayed, and got to his knees, but the most he ever felt in church was that he stood outside the realm of God's infinite mercy, and, to tell the truth, he no more believed in the Father, the Son, and the Holy Ghost than does my bull terrier. They returned home at one to eat the overcooked meat and stony potatoes that were their customary Sunday lunch. At around five, the Parminters called up and asked them over for a drink. Louise didn't want to go, so Cash went alone. (Oh, those suburban Sunday nights, those Sunday-night blues! Those departing weekend guests, those stale cocktails, those half-dead flowers, those trips to Harmon to catch the Century, those postmortems and pickup suppers!) It was sultry and overcast. The dog days were beginning. He drank gin with the Parminters for an hour or two and then went over to the Townsends' for a drink. The Farquarsons called up the Townsends and asked them to come over and bring Cash with them, and at the Farquarsons' they had some more drinks and ate the leftover party food. The

Farquarsons were glad to see that Cash seemed like himself again. It was half past ten or eleven when he got home. Louise was upstairs, cutting out of the current copy of *Life* those scenes of mayhem, disaster, and violent death that she felt might corrupt her children. She always did this. Cash came upstairs and spoke to her and then went down again. In a little while, she heard him moving the living-room furniture around. Then he called to her, and when she went down, he was standing at the foot of the stairs in his stocking feet, holding the pistol out to her. She had never fired it before, and the directions he gave her were not much help.

"Hurry up," he said, "I can't wait all night."

He had forgotten to tell her about the safety, and when she pulled the trigger nothing happened.

"It's that little lever," he said. "Press that little lever." Then, in his impatience, he hurdled the sofa anyhow.

The pistol went off and Louise got him in midair. She shot him dead.

Writing Assignments for "O Youth and Beauty!"

I. Brief Papers

A. 1. What does the hurdle race have in common with the quarrels and reunions of Cash and Louise?

2. How well written and informative is the student response below to the previous question?

> In the short story "O Youth and Beauty!," John Cheever makes it clear that the hurdle race and reunions occur over and over again. He describes both as though they follow a strict routine. In the case of the hurdle race, Trace Bearden would chide Cash "about his age and thinning hair," only "a preliminary to moving the living room furniture" (p. 449) for the race. After the course was set up, the host would be asked to produce a revolver and Trace would fire it out an open window to start the race. Whereas the hurdle race occurred "at the end of nearly every long, large Saturday-night party" (p. 449), the reunions usually followed a quarrel which began whenever Cash "came home after a bad day at the office and found that Louise, for some good reason, had not started supper" (p. 450). Cash would "heat up some frozen food, . . . usually (burning) the bottom out of a pan," and "it was only a question of time before they were plunged into a bitter quarrel (p. 450). These reunions and races "didn't seem to lose their interest through repetition" (p. 451). The hurdle race always "ended with cheers" (p. 449) and the reunions left the Bentleys "sighing and making cow eyes at one another" (p. 451).

3. Why is it significant that Cash runs the hurdle race alone and not against others?

4. What is the primary cause of Cash's restlessness and unease?

5. Explain the relationship in the story between youth and beauty.

6. What do Cash's reactions to the rank smell, the spider web, the whore, and the roses tell us about Cash himself?
7. What attitude toward attempts at rejuvenation emerges from the story?

B. Argue for or against one of the assertions below:
   1. Louise shoots Cash deliberately.
   2. Like Cash, Louise cannot accept the loss of youth and beauty.
   3. The story makes clear that the underlying cause of the Bentleys' problems is their lack of religious belief.

C. 1. Cheever writes, "By the standards of Shady Hill, the Bentleys were a happily married couple . . ." (p. 450). Are they a happily married couple by your standards?
   2. Lucy Bearden thinks that Louise Bentley's problems will be solved once Louise gets herself a job. Do you agree? How does your response affect the way you understand the story as a whole?
   3. Do you plan, like Louise Bentley, to shield your own children from potentially corrupting scenes in newspapers and magazines? How does your answer affect your attitude toward Louise and your interpretation of the story?
   4. Would you characterize the tone of the story as predominantly comic or tragic? Include in your answer a description of your response to the shooting of Cash: Were you deeply pained by it?

II. Longer Papers

A. Why do the hurdle races matter so much to Cash?
B. Explain the causes of "Sunday-night blues" and relate them to the story as a whole.
C. Argue for or against the assertion that there is really no way out of Cash's dilemma except through death: if Louise doesn't kill him, the hurdles will.
D. Does the story encourage us to reject the pursuit of youth and beauty as an illusory and harmful preoccupation?
E. Develop, modify, or refute the contention that the story illustrates the utter emptiness—the complete lack of substantial values—in middle-class America.
F. Pretend that you are a friend of Cash's and that Cash himself is now in the hospital recuperating from a broken leg. Write him a persuasive letter that will convince him to stop running the hurdles. In writing your letter, use what you have learned about Cash from the story.

JOHN CHEEVER

The Sorrows of Gin

Before Reading

When you were younger, you probably either ran away from home or thought about doing so—at least once. Free write for 5 or 10 minutes on the reasons kids want to run away.

It was a Sunday afternoon, and from her bedroom Amy could hear the Beardens coming in, followed a little while later by the Farquarsons and the Parminters. She went on reading *Black Beauty* until she felt in her bones that they might be eating something good. Then she closed her book and went down the stairs. The living-room door was shut, but through it she could hear the noise of loud talk and laughter. They must have been gossiping or worse, because they all stopped talking when she entered the room.

"Hi, Amy," Mr. Farquarson said.

"Mr. Farquarson spoke to you, Amy," her father said.

"Hello, Mr. Farquarson," she said. By standing outside the group for a minute, until they had resumed their conversation, and then by slipping past Mrs. Farquarson, she was able to swoop down on the nut dish and take a handful.

"Amy!" Mr. Lawton said.

"I'm sorry, Daddy," she said, retreating out of the circle, toward the piano.

"Put those nuts back," he said.

"I've handled them, Daddy," she said.

"Well, pass the nuts, dear," her mother said sweetly. "Perhaps someone else would like nuts."

Amy filled her mouth with the nuts she had taken, returned to the coffee table, and passed the nut dish.

"Thank you, Amy," they said, taking a peanut or two.

"How do you like your new school, Amy?" Mrs. Bearden asked.

"I like it," Amy said. "I like private schools better than public schools. It isn't so much like a factory."

"What grade are you in?" Mr. Bearden asked.

"Fourth," she said.

Her father took Mr. Parminter's glass and his own, and got up to go into the dining room and refill them. She fell into the chair he had left vacant.

"Don't sit in your father's chair, Amy," her mother said, not realizing that Amy's legs were worn out from riding a bicycle, while her father had done nothing but sit down all day.

THE SORROWS OF GIN First published in 1953.

As she walked toward the French doors, she heard her mother beginning to talk about the new cook. It was a good example of the interesting things they found to talk about.

"You'd better put your bicycle in the garage," her father said, returning with the fresh drinks. "It looks like rain."

Amy went out onto the terrace and looked at the sky, but it was not very cloudy, it wouldn't rain, and his advice, like all the advice he gave her, was superfluous. They were always at her. "Put your bicycle away." "Open the door for Grandmother, Amy." "Feed the cat." "Do your homework." "Pass the nuts." "Help Mrs. Bearden with her parcels." "Amy, please try and take more pains with your appearance."

They all stood, and her father came to the door and called her. "We're going over to the Parminters' for supper," he said. "Cook's here, so you won't be alone. Be sure and go to bed at eight like a good girl. And come and kiss me good night."

After their cars had driven off, Amy wandered through the kitchen to the cook's bedroom beyond it and knocked on the door. "Come in," a voice said, and when Amy entered, she found the cook, whose name was Rosemary, in her bathrobe, reading the Bible. Rosemary smiled at Amy. Her smile was sweet and her old eyes were blue. "Your parents have gone out *again?*" she asked. Amy said that they had, and the old woman invited her to sit down. "They do seem to enjoy themselves, don't they? During the four days I've been here, they've been out every night, or had people in." She put the Bible face down on her lap and smiled, but not at Amy. "Of course, the drinking that goes on here is all sociable, and what your parents do is none of my business, is it? I worry about drink more than most people, because of my poor sister. My poor sister drank too much. For ten years, I went to visit her on Sunday afternoons, and most of the time she was *non compos mentis.* * Sometimes I'd find her huddled up on the floor with one or two sherry bottles empty beside her. Sometimes she'd seem sober enough to a stranger, but I could tell in a second by the way she spoke her words that she'd drunk enough not to be herself any more. Now my poor sister is gone, I don't have anyone to visit at all."

"What happened to your sister?" Amy asked.

"She was a lovely person, with a peaches-and-cream complexion and fair hair," Rosemary said. "Gin makes some people gay—it makes them laugh and cry—but with my sister it only made her sullen and withdrawn. When she was drinking, she would retreat into herself. Drink made her contrary. If I'd say the weather was fine, she'd tell me I was wrong. If I'd say it was raining, she'd say it was clearing. She'd correct me about everything I said, however small it was. She died in Bellevue Hospital one summer when I was working in Maine. She was the only family I had."

The directness with which Rosemary spoke had the effect on Amy of making her feel grown, and for once politeness came to her easily. "You must miss your sister a great deal," she said.

non compos mentis: Latin, not in one's right mind.

"I was just sitting here now thinking about her. She was in service, like me, and it's lonely work. You're always surrounded by a family, and yet you're never a part of it. Your pride is often hurt. The Madams seem condescending and inconsiderate. I'm not blaming the ladies I've worked for. It's just in the nature of the relationship. They order chicken salad, and you get up before dawn to get ahead of yourself, and just as you've finished the chicken salad, they change their minds and want crab-meat soup."

"My mother changes her mind all the time," Amy said.

"Sometimes you're in a country place with nobody else in help. You're tired, but not too tired to feel lonely. You go out onto the servants' porch when the pots and pans are done, planning to enjoy God's creation, and although the front of the house may have a fine view of the lake or the mountains, the view from the back is never much. But there is the sky and the trees and the stars and the birds singing and the pleasure of resting your feet. But then you hear them in the front of the house, laughing and talking with their guests and their sons and daughters. If you're new and they whisper, you can be sure they're talking about you. That takes all the pleasure out of the evening."

"Oh," Amy said.

"I've worked in all kinds of places—places where there were eight or nine in help and places where I was expected to burn the rubbish myself, on winter nights, and shovel the snow. In a house where there's a lot of help, there's usually some devil among them—some old butler or parlormaid—who tries to make your life miserable from the beginning. 'The Madam doesn't like it this way,' and 'The Madam doesn't like it that way,' and 'I've been with the Madam for twenty years,' they tell you. It takes a diplomat to get along. Then there is the rooms they give you, and every one of them I've ever seen is cheerless. If you have a bottle in your suitcase, it's a terrible temptation in the beginning not to take a drink to raise your spirits. But I have a strong character. It was different with my poor sister. She used to complain about nervousness, but, sitting here thinking about her tonight, I wonder if she suffered from nervousness at all. I wonder if she didn't make it all up. I wonder if she just wasn't meant to be in service. Toward the end, the only work she could get was out in the country, where nobody else would go, and she never lasted much more than a week or two. She'd take a little gin for her nervousness, then a little for her tiredness, and when she'd drunk her own bottle and everything she could steal, they'd hear about it in the front part of the house. There was usually a scene, and my poor sister always liked to have the last word. Oh, if I had had my way, they'd be a law against it! It's not my business to advise you to take anything from your father, but I'd be proud of you if you'd empty his gin bottle into the sink now and then—the filthy stuff! But it's made me feel better to talk with you, sweetheart. It's made me not miss my poor sister so much. Now I'll read a little more in my Bible, and then I'll get you some supper."

The Lawtons had had a bad year with cooks—there had been five of them. The arrival of Rosemary had made Marcia Lawton think back to a vague theory of dispensations; she had suffered, and now she was being rewarded. Rosemary was clean, industrious, and cheerful, and her table—as the Lawtons said—was just like the Chambord.* On Wednesday night after dinner, she took the train to New York, promising to return on the evening train Thursday. Thursday morning, Marcia went into the cook's room. It was a distasteful but a habitual precaution. The absence of anything personal in the room—a package of cigarettes, a fountain pen, an alarm clock, a radio, or anything else that could tie the old woman to the place—gave her the uneasy feeling that she was being deceived, as she had so often been deceived by cooks in the past. She opened the closet door and saw a single uniform hanging there and, on the closet floor, Rosemary's old suitcase and the white shoes she wore in the kitchen. The suitcase was locked, but when Marcia lifted it, it seemed to be nearly empty.

Mr. Lawton and Amy drove to the station after dinner on Thursday to meet the eight-sixteen train. The top of the car was down, and the brisk air, the starlight, and the company of her father made the little girl feel kindly toward the world. The railroad station in Shady Hill resembled the railroad stations in old movies she had seen on television, where detectives and spies, bluebeards and their trusting victims, were met to be driven off to remote country estates. Amy liked the station, particularly toward dark. She imagined that the people who traveled on the locals were engaged on errands that were more urgent and sinister than commuting. Except when there was a heavy fog or a snowstorm, the club car that her father traveled on seemed to have the gloss and the monotony of the rest of his life. The locals that ran at odd hours belonged to a world of deeper contrasts, where she would like to live.

They were a few minutes early, and Amy got out of the car and stood on the platform. She wondered what the fringe of string that hung above the tracks at either end of the station was for, but she knew enough not to ask her father, because he wouldn't be able to tell her. She could hear the train before it came into view, and the noise excited her and made her happy. When the train drew in to the station and stopped, she looked in the lighted windows for Rosemary and didn't see her. Mr. Lawton got out of the car and joined Amy on the platform. They could see the conductor bending over someone in a seat, and finally the cook rose. She clung to the conductor as he led her out to the platform of the car, and she was crying. "Like peaches and cream," Amy heard her sob. "A lovely, lovely person." The conductor spoke to her kindly, put his arm around her shoulders, and eased her down the steps. Then the train pulled out, and she stood there drying her tears. "Don't say a word, Mr. Lawton," she said, "and I won't say anything." She held out a small paper bag. "Here's a present for you, little girl."

"Thank you, Rosemary," Amy said. She looked into the paper bag and saw that it contained several packets of Japanese water flowers.

Rosemary walked toward the car with the caution of someone who can hardly find the way in the dim light. A sour smell came from her. Her best coat was spotted with mud and ripped in the back. Mr. Lawton told Amy to get in

*Chambord: At the time of the story a chic and expensive restaurant on New York's fashionable East Side; now closed.

the back seat of the car, and made the cook sit in front, beside him. He slammed the car door shut after her angrily, and then went around to the driver's seat and drove home. Rosemary reached into her handbag and took out a Coca-Cola bottle with a cork stopper and took a drink. Amy could tell by the smell that the Coca-Cola bottle was filled with gin.

"Rosemary!" Mr. Lawton said.

"I'm lonely," the cook said. "I'm lonely, and I'm afraid, and it's all I've got."

He said nothing more until he had turned in to their drive and brought the car around to the back door. "Go and get your suitcase, Rosemary," he said. "I'll wait here in the car."

As soon as the cook had staggered into the house, he told Amy to go in by the front door. "Go upstairs to your room and get ready for bed."

Her mother called down the stairs when Amy came in, to ask if Rosemary had returned. Amy didn't answer. She went to the bar, took an open gin bottle, and emptied it into the pantry sink. She was nearly crying when she encountered her mother in the living room, and told her that her father was taking the cook back to the station.

When Amy came home from school the next day, she found a heavy, black-haired woman cleaning the living room. The car Mr. Lawton usually drove to the station was at the garage for a check-up, and Amy drove to the station with her mother to meet him. As he came across the station platform, she could tell, by the lack of color in his face, that he had had a hard day. He kissed her mother, touched Amy on the head, and got behind the wheel.

"You know," her mother said, "there's something terribly wrong with the guest-room shower."

"Damn it, Marcia," he said, "I wish you wouldn't always greet me with bad news!"

His grating voice oppressed Amy, and she began to fiddle with the button that raised and lowered the window.

"Stop that, Amy!" he said.

"Oh, well, the shower isn't important," her mother said. She laughed weakly.

"When I got back from San Francisco last week," he said, "you couldn't wait to tell me that we need a new oil burner."

"Well, I've got a part-time cook. That's good news."

"Is she a lush?" her father asked.

"Don't be disagreeable, dear. She'll get us some dinner and wash the dishes and take the bus home. We're going to the Farquarsons'."

"I'm really too tired to go anywhere," he said.

"Who's going to take care of me?" Amy asked.

"You always have a good time at the Farquarsons'," her mother said.

"Well, let's leave early," he said.

"Who's going to take care of me?" Amy asked.

"Mrs. Henlein," her mother said.

When they got home, Amy went over to the piano.

Her father washed his hands in the bathroom off the hall and then went to the bar. He came into the living room holding the empty gin bottle. "What's her name?" he asked.

"Ruby," her mother said.

"She's exceptional. She's drunk a quart of gin on her first day."

"Oh, dear!" her mother said. "Well, let's not make any trouble now."

"Everybody is drinking my liquor," her father shouted, "and I am God-damned sick and tired of it!"

"There's plenty of gin in the closet," her mother said. "Open another bottle."

"We paid that gardener three dollars an hour and all he did was sneak in here and drink up my Scotch. The sitter we had before we got Mrs. Henlein used to water my bourbon, and I don't have to remind you about Rosemary. The cook before Rosemary not only drank everything in my liquor cabinet but she drank all the rum, kirsch, sherry, and wine that we had in the kitchen for cooking. Then, there's that Polish woman we had last summer. Even the old laundress. *And* the painters. I think they must have put some kind of a mark on my door. I think the agency must have checked me off as an easy touch."

"Well, let's get through dinner, and then you can speak to her."

"The hell with that!" he said. "I'm not going to encourage people to rob me. *Ruby!*" He shouted her name several times but she didn't answer. Then she appeared in the dining-room doorway, wearing her hat and coat.

"I'm sick," she said. Amy could see that she was frightened.

"I should think you would be," her father said.

"I'm sick," the cook mumbled, "and I can't find anything around here, and I'm going home."

"Good," he said. "Good! I'm through with paying people to come in here and drink my liquor."

The cook started out the front way, and Marcia Lawton followed her into the front hall to pay her something. Amy had watched this scene from the piano bench, a position that was withdrawn but that still gave her a good view. She saw her father get a fresh bottle of gin and make a shaker of Martinis. He looked very unhappy.

"Well," her mother said when she came back into the room. "You know, she didn't look drunk."

"Please don't argue with me, Marcia," her father said. He poured two cocktails, said, "Cheers," and drank a little. "We can get some dinner at Orfeo's," he said.

"I suppose so," her mother said. "I'll rustle up something for Amy." She went into the kitchen, and Amy opened her music to "Reflets d'Automne." "COUNT," her music teacher had written. "COUNT and lightly, lightly . . ." Amy began to play. Whenever she made a mistake, she said "Darn it!" and started at the beginning again. In the middle of "Reflets d'Automne" it struck her that *she* was the one who had emptied the gin bottle. Her perplexity was so intense that she stopped playing, but her feelings did not go beyond perplexity, although she did not have the strength to continue playing the piano. Her mother relieved her. "Your supper's in the kitchen, dear," she said. "And you can take a popsicle out of the deep freeze for dessert. Just one."

Marcia Lawton held her empty glass toward her husband, who filled it from the shaker. Then she went upstairs. Mr. Lawton remained in the room, and, studying her father closely, Amy saw that his tense look had begun to soften. He did not seem so unhappy any more, and as she passed him on her way to the kitchen, he smiled at her tenderly and patted her on the top of the head.

When Amy had finished her supper, eaten her popsicle, and exploded the bag it came in, she returned to the piano and played "Chopsticks" for a while. Her father came downstairs in his evening clothes, put his drink on the mantelpiece, and went to the French doors to look at his terrace and his garden. Amy noticed that the transformation that had begun with a softening of his features was even more advanced. At last, he seemed happy. Amy wondered if he was drunk, although his walk was not unsteady. If anything it was more steady.

Her parents never achieved the kind of rolling, swinging gait that she saw impersonated by a tightrope walker in the circus each year while the band struck up "Show Me the Way to Go Home" and that she liked to imitate herself sometimes. She liked to turn round and round and round on the lawn, until, staggering and a little sick, she would whoop, "I'm drunk! I'm a drunken man!" and reel over the grass, righting herself as she was about to fall and finding herself not unhappy at having lost for a second her ability to see the world. But she had never seen her parents like that. She had never seen them hanging on to a lamppost and singing and reeling, but she had seen them fall down. They were never indecorous—they seemed to get more decorous and formal the more they drank—but sometimes her father would get up to fill everybody's glass and he would walk straight enough but his shoes would seem to stick to the carpet. And sometimes, when he got to the dining-room door, he would miss it by a foot or more. Once, she had seen him walk into the wall with such force that he collapsed onto the floor and broke most of the glasses he was carrying. One or two people laughed, but the laughter was not general or hearty, and most of them pretended that he had not fallen down at all. When her father got to his feet, he went right on to the bar as if nothing had happened. Amy had once seen Mrs. Farquarson miss the chair she was about to sit in, by a foot, and thump down onto the floor, but nobody laughed then, and they pretended that Mrs. Farquarson hadn't fallen down at all. They seemed like actors in a play. In the school play, when you knocked over a paper tree you were supposed to pick it up without showing what you were doing, so that you would not spoil the illusion of being in a deep forest, and that was the way *they* were when somebody fell down.

Now her father had that stiff, funny walk that was so different from the way he tramped up and down the station platform in the morning, and she could see that he was looking for something. He was looking for his drink. It was right on the mantelpiece, but he didn't look there. He looked on all the tables in the living room. Then he went out onto the terrace, and looked there, and then he came back into the living room and looked on all the tables again. Then he went back onto the terrace, and then back over the living-room tables, looking three times in the same place, although he was always telling her to look intelligently when she lost her sneakers or her raincoat. "Look for it, Amy," he was always saying. "Try and remember where you left it. I can't buy you a new raincoat every time it rains." Finally he gave up and poured himself a cocktail in another glass. "I'm going to get Mrs. Henlein," he told Amy, as if this were an important piece of information.

Amy's only feeling for Mrs. Henlein was indifference, and when her father returned with the sitter, Amy thought of the nights, stretching into weeks—the years, almost—when she had been cooped up with Mrs. Henlein. Mrs. Henlein was very polite and was always telling Amy what was ladylike and what was not. Mrs. Henlein also always wanted to know where Amy's parents were going and what kind of a party it was, although it was none of her business. She always sat down on the sofa as if she owned the place, and talked about people she had never even been introduced to, and asked Amy to bring her the newspaper, although she had no authority at all.

When Marcia Lawton came down, Mrs. Henlein wished her good evening. "Have a lovely party," she called after the Lawtons as they went out the door. Then she turned to Amy. "Where are your parents going, sweetheart?"

"I don't know," Amy said.

"But you must know, sweetheart. Put on your thinking cap and try and remember. Are they going to the club?"

"No," Amy said.

"I wonder if they could be going to the Trenchers'," Mrs. Henlein said. "The Trenchers' house was lighted up when we came by."

"They're not going to the Trenchers'," Amy said. "They hate the Trenchers."

"Well, where are they going, sweetheart?" Mrs. Henlein asked.

"They're going to the Farquarsons'," Amy said.

"Well, that's all I wanted to know, sweetheart," Mrs. Henlein said. "Now get me the newspaper and hand it to me politely. *Politely,*" she said, as Amy approached her with the paper. "It don't mean anything when you do things for your elders unless you do them politely." She put on her glasses and began to read the paper.

Amy went upstairs to her room. In a glass on her table were the Japanese flowers that Rosemary had brought her, blooming stalely in water that was colored pink from the dyes. Amy went down the back stairs and through the kitchen into the dining room. Her father's cocktail things were spread over the bar. She emptied the gin bottle into the pantry sink and then put it back where she found it. It was too late to ride her bicycle and too early to go to bed, and she knew that if she got anything interesting on the television, like a murder, Mrs. Henlein would make her turn it off. Then she remembered that her father had brought her home from his trip West a book about horses, and she ran cheerfully up the back stairs to read her new book.

It was after two when the Lawtons returned. Mrs. Henlein, asleep on the living-room sofa dreaming about a dusty attic, was awakened by their voices in the hall. Marcia Lawton paid her, and thanked her, and asked if anyone had called, and then went upstairs. Mr. Lawton was in the dining room, rattling the bottles around. Mrs. Henlein, anxious to get into her own bed and back to sleep, prayed that he wasn't going to pour himself another drink, as they so often did. She was driven home night after night by drunken gentlemen. He stood in the door of the dining room, holding an empty bottle in his hand. "You must be stinking, Mrs. Henlein," he said.

"Hmm," she said. She didn't understand.

"You drank a full quart of gin," he said.

The lackluster old woman—half between wakefulness and sleep—gathered together her bones and groped for her gray hair. It was in her nature to collect stray cats, pile the bathroom up to the ceiling with interesting and valuable newspapers, rouge, talk to herself, sleep in her underwear in case of fire, quarrel over the price of soup bones, and have it circulated around the neighborhood that when she finally died in her dusty junk heap, the mattress would be full of bankbooks and the pillow stuffed with hundred-dollar bills. She had resisted all these rich temptations in order to appear a lady and she was repaid by being called a common thief. She began to scream at him.

"You take that back, Mr. Lawton! You take back every one of those words you just said! I never stole anything in my whole life, and nobody in my family ever stole anything, and I don't have to stand here and be insulted by a drunk man. Why, as for drinking, I haven't drunk enough to fill an eyeglass for twenty-five years. Mr. Henlein took me to a place of refreshment twenty-five years ago, and I drank two Manhattan cocktails that made me so sick and dizzy that I've never liked the stuff ever since. How dare you speak to me like this! Calling me a thief and a drunken woman! Oh, you disgust me—you disgust me in your ignorance of all the trouble I've had. Do you know what I had for Christmas dinner last year? I had a bacon sandwich. Son of a bitch!" She began to weep. "I'm glad I said it!" she screamed. "It's the first time I've used a dirty word in my whole life and I'm glad I said it. Son of a bitch!" A sense of liberation, as if she stood at the bow of a great ship, came over her. "I lived in this neighborhood my whole life. I can remember when it was full of good farming people and there was fish in the rivers. My father had four acres of sweet meadowland and a name that was known far and wide, and on my mother's side I'm descended from patroons, Dutch nobility. My mother was the spit and image of Queen Wilhelmina. You think you can get away with insulting me, but you're very, very, very much mistaken." She went to the telephone and, picking up the receiver, screamed, "Police! Police! Police! This is Mrs. Henlein, and I'm over at the Lawtons'. He's drunk, and he's calling me insulting names, and I want you to come over here and arrest him!"

The voices woke Amy, and, lying in her bed, she perceived vaguely the pitiful corruption of the adult world; how crude and frail it was, like a piece of worn burlap, patched with stupidities and mistakes, useless and ugly, and yet they never saw its worthlessness, and when you pointed it out to them, they were indignant. But as the voices went on and she heard the cry "Police! Police!" she was frightened. She did not see how they could arrest her, although they could find her fingerprints on the empty bottle, but it was not her own danger that frightened her but the collapse, in the middle of the night, of her father's house. It was all her fault, and when she heard her father speaking into the extension telephone in the library, she felt sunk in guilt. Her father tried to be good and kind—oh, she knew he never meant to be anything else—and, remembering the expensive illustrated book about horses that he had brought her from the West, she had to set her teeth to keep from crying. She covered her head with a pillow and realized miserably that she would have to go away. She had plenty of friends from the time when they used to live in New York, or she could spend the night in the Park or hide in a museum. She would have to go away.

"Good morning," her father said at breakfast. "Ready for a good day!" Cheered by the swelling light in the sky, by the recollection of the manner in which he had handled Mrs. Henlein and kept the police from coming, refreshed by his sleep, and pleased at the thought of playing golf, Mr. Lawton spoke with feeling, but the words seemed to Amy offensive and fatuous; they took away her appetite, and she slumped over her cereal bowl, stirring it with a spoon. "Don't slump, Amy," he said. Then she remembered the night, the screaming, the resolve to go. His cheerfulness refreshed her memory. Her decision was settled. She had a ballet lesson at ten, and she was going to have lunch with Lillian Towele. Then she would leave.

Children prepare for a sea voyage with a toothbrush and a Teddy bear; they equip themselves for a trip around the world with a pair of odd socks, a conch shell, and a thermometer; books and stones and peacock feathers, candy bars, tennis balls, soiled handkerchiefs, and skeins of old string appear to them to be the necessities of travel, and Amy packed, that afternoon, with the impulsiveness of her kind. She was late coming home from lunch, and her getaway was delayed, but she didn't mind. She could catch one of the late-afternoon locals; one of the cooks' trains. Her father was playing golf and her mother was off somewhere. A part-time worker was cleaning the living room. When Amy had finished packing, she went into her parents' bathroom and flushed the toilet. While the water murmured, she took a twenty-dollar bill from her mother's desk. Then she went downstairs and left the house and walked around Blenhollow Circle and down Alewives Lane to the station. No regrets or good-bys formed in her mind. She went over the names of the friends she had in the city, in case she decided not to spend the night in a museum. When she opened the door of the waiting room, Mr. Flanagan, the stationmaster, was poking his coal fire.

"I want to buy a ticket to New York," Amy said.

"One-way or round-trip?"

"One-way, please."

Mr. Flanagan went through the door into the ticket office and raised the glass window. "I'm afraid I haven't got a half-fare ticket for you, Amy," he said. "I'll have to write one."

"That's all right," she said. She put the twenty-dollar bill on the counter.

"And in order to change that," he said, "I'll have to go over to the other side. Here's the four-thirty-two coming in now, but you'll be able to get the five-ten." She didn't protest, and went and sat beside her cardboard suitcase, which was printed with European hotel and place names. When the local had come and gone, Mr. Flanagan shut his glass window and walked over the footbridge to the north-bound platform and called the Lawtons'. Mr. Lawton had just come in from his game and was mixing himself a cocktail. "I think your daughter's planning to take some kind of a trip," Mr. Flanagan said.

It was dark by the time Mr. Lawton got down to the station. He saw his daughter through the station window. The girl sitting on the bench, the rich names on her paper suitcase, touched him as it was in her power to touch him only when she seemed helpless or when she was very sick. Someone had walked over his grave! He shivered with longing, he felt his skin coarsen as when, driving home late and alone, a shower of leaves on the wind crossed the beam of his headlights, liberating him for a second at the most from the literal symbols of his life—the buttonless shirts, the vouchers and bank statements, the order blanks, and the empty glasses. He seemed to listen—God knows for what. Commands, drums, the crackle of signal fires, the music of the glockenspiel—how sweet it sounds on the Alpine air—singing from a tavern in the pass, the honking of wild swans; he seemed to smell the salt air in the churches of Venice. Then, as it was with the leaves, the power of her figure to trouble him was ended; his gooseflesh vanished. He was himself. Oh, why should she want to run away? Travel—and who knew better than a man who spent three days of every fortnight on the road—was a world of overheated plane cabins and repetitious magazines, where even the coffee, even the champagne, tasted of plastics. How could he teach her that home sweet home was the best place of all?

Writing Assignments for "The Sorrows of Gin"

I. Brief Papers
  A. 1. Amy thinks her parents are "always at her." Is she right?
     2. How does drinking affect Mr. Lawton?
     3. Explain why Amy is more polite to Rosemary than to her parents.
     4. Describe and characterize the Lawtons' marriage.
     5. Why does Amy like Rosemary more than Mrs. Henlein?
     6. Explain why Amy thinks that she has to run away.
     7. What does the story's opening conversation tell us about the relationship between children and adults?

  B. Argue for or against one of the assertions below:
     1. Rosemary's coming home drunk is an implausible and unbelievable event since Rosemary had just spoken with Amy about "filthy" gin.
     2. The story as a whole endorses Amy's perception of the adult world as "crude and frail . . ., patched with stupidities and mistakes, useless and ugly . . ." (p. 466).

3. The life of the Lawtons and their friends is depicted as, above all, boring and monotonous.

C. 1. If all the advice Amy receives from her father is "superfluous" (p. 459), why do you think he gives it?
2. Why do you think the Lawtons spend so much time either going out or entertaining at home?
3. Do you feel greater sympathy for Amy or her parents? How does your response to this question affect your interpretation of the story?
4. Complete the sentence "What is missing from the lives of the Lawtons and their friends is . . ." by free writing for 5 minutes. Now look back over what you've written and select the most promising idea for a longer paper. Then explain to yourself in a paragraph why the idea is a promising one.

II. Longer Papers

A. Develop into a longer paper either the idea you generated in your free writing (I.C.4) or one of your other brief papers.
B. Argue for or against the assertion that the story, as its title suggests, is primarily a warning against excessive drinking.
C. Develop, modify, or refute the contention that, despite its title, the story ends on a positive, affirmative note.
D. Explain in detail how the final paragraph appropriately concludes the story.
E. What can we learn about the Lawtons and their values from the way they treat their daughter and their cooks?
F. The story contrasts a child's view of reality with an adult view. Which view, if either, does the story approve?

JOHN CHEEVER

The Country Husband

Before Reading

Have you ever wanted to do something that seemed exciting and adventurous but perhaps risky—like hitch-hiking across the country or climbing the Alps or becoming involved with an older man or woman—and then decided not to? Free write for 5 or 10 minutes on the reasons why you didn't go ahead and do it.

To begin at the beginning, the airplane from Minneapolis in which Francis Weed was traveling East ran into heavy weather. The sky had been a hazy blue, with the clouds below the plane lying so close together that nothing could be seen of the earth. Then mist began to form outside the windows, and they flew

THE COUNTRY HUSBAND   First published in 1954.

into a white cloud of such density that it reflected the exhaust fires. The color of the cloud darkened to gray, and the plane began to rock. Francis had been in heavy weather before, but he had never been shaken up so much. The man in the seat beside him pulled a flask out of his pocket and took a drink. Francis smiled at his neighbor, but the man looked away; he wasn't sharing his painkiller with anyone. The plane had begun to drop and flounder wildly. A child was crying. The air in the cabin was overheated and stale, and Francis' left foot went to sleep. He read a little from a paper book that he had bought at the airport, but the violence of the storm divided his attention. It was black outside the ports. The exhaust fires blazed and shed sparks in the dark, and, inside, the shaded lights, the stuffiness, and the window curtains gave the cabin an atmosphere of intense and misplaced domesticity. Then the lights flickered and went out. "You know what I've always wanted to do?" the man beside Francis said suddenly. "I've always wanted to buy a farm in New Hampshire and raise beef cattle." The stewardess announced that they were going to make an emergency landing. All but the child saw in their minds the spreading wings of the Angel of Death. The pilot could be heard singing faintly, "I've got sixpence, jolly, jolly sixpence. I've got sixpence to last me all my life . . ."* There was no other sound.

The loud groaning of the hydraulic valves swallowed up the pilot's song, and there was a shrieking high in the air, like automobile brakes, and the plane hit flat on its belly in a cornfield and shook them so violently that an old man up forward howled, "Me kidneys! Me kidneys!" The stewardess flung open the door, and someone opened an emergency door at the back, letting in the sweet noise of their continuing mortality—the idle splash and smell of a heavy rain. Anxious for their lives, they filed out of the doors and scattered over the cornfield in all directions, praying that the thread would hold. It did. Nothing happened. When it was clear that the plane would not burn or explode, the crew and the stewardess gathered the passengers together and led them to the shelter of a barn. They were not far from Philadelphia, and in a little while a string of taxis took them into the city. "It's just like the Marne,"† someone said, but there was surprisingly little relaxation of that suspiciousness with which many Americans regard their fellow-travelers.

In Philadelphia, Francis Weed got a train to New York. At the end of that journey, he crossed the city and caught, just as it was about to pull out, the commuting train that he took five nights a week to his home in Shady Hill.

He sat with Trace Bearden. "You know, I was in that plane that just crashed outside Philadelphia," he said. "We came down in a field . . ." He had traveled faster than the newspapers or the rain, and the weather in New York was sunny and mild. It was a day in late September, as fragrant and shapely as an apple. Trace listened to the story, but how could he get excited? Francis had

*"I've got sixpence . . .": A popular song in the 1940s, especially with Allied troops in World War II.

†the Marne: In 1914, the first year of World War I, the French government requisitioned hundreds of Paris taxicabs to transport troops to the Marne River in northern France to halt the advancing German army.

no powers that would let him re-create a brush with death—particularly in the atmosphere of a commuting train, journeying through a sunny countryside where already, in the slum gardens, there were signs of harvest. Trace picked up his newspaper, and Francis was left alone with his thoughts. He said good night to Trace on the platform at Shady Hill and drove in his secondhand Volkswagen up to the Blenhollow neighborhood, where he lived.

The Weeds' Dutch Colonial house was larger than it appeared to be from the driveway. The living room was spacious and divided like Gaul into three parts.* Around an ell to the left as one entered from the vestibule was the long table, laid for six, with candles and a bowl of fruit in the center. The sounds and smells that came from the open kitchen door were appetizing, for Julia Weed was a good cook. The largest part of the living room centered around a fireplace. On the right were some bookshelves and a piano. The room was polished and tranquil, and from the windows that opened to the west there was some late-summer sunlight, brilliant and as clear as water. Nothing here was neglected; nothing had not been burnished. It was not the kind of household where, after prying open a stuck cigarette box, you would find an old shirt button and a tarnished nickel. The hearth was swept, the roses on the piano were reflected in the polish of the broad top, and there was an album of Schubert waltzes on the rack. Louisa Weed, a pretty girl of nine, was looking out the western windows. Her younger brother Henry was standing beside her. Her still younger brother, Toby, was studying the figures of some tonsured monks drinking beer on the polished brass of the wood box. Francis, taking off his hat and putting down his paper, was not consciously pleased with the scene; he was not that reflective. It was his element, his creation, and he returned to it with that sense of lightness and strength with which any creature returns to its home. "Hi, everybody," he said. "The plane from Minneapolis . . ."

Nine times out of ten, Francis would be greeted with affection, but tonight the children are absorbed in their own antagonisms. Francis has not finished his sentence about the plane crash before Henry plants a kick in Louisa's behind. Louisa swings around, saying, *"Damn* you!" Francis makes the mistake of scolding Louisa for bad language before he punishes Henry. Now Louisa turns on her father and accuses him of favoritism. Henry is always right; she is persecuted and lonely; her lot is hopeless. Francis turns to his son, but the boy has justification for the kick—she hit him first; she hit him on the ear, which is dangerous. Louisa agrees with this passionately. She hit him on the ear, and she *meant* to hit him on the ear, because he messed up her china collection. Henry says that this is a lie. Little Toby turns away from the wood box to throw in some evidence for Louisa. Henry claps his hand over little Toby's mouth. Francis separates the two boys but accidentally pushes Toby into the wood box. Toby begins to cry. Louisa is already crying. Just then, Julia Weed comes into that part of the room where the table is laid. She is a pretty, intelligent woman, and the white in her

*divided like Gaul into three parts: Gaul, the name for ancient France, was divided into the three provinces of Aquitania, Belgica, and Lugdunensis.

hair is premature. She does not seem to notice the fracas. "Hello, darling," she says serenely to Francis. "Wash your hands, everyone. Dinner is ready." She strikes a match and lights the six candles in this vale of tears.

This simple announcement, like the war cries of the Scottish chieftains, only refreshes the ferocity of the combatants. Louisa gives Henry a blow on the shoulder. Henry, although he seldom cries, has pitched nine innings and is tired. He bursts into tears. Little Toby discovers a splinter in his hand and begins to howl. Francis says loudly that he has been in a plane crash and that he is tired. Julia appears again, from the kitchen, and, still ignoring the chaos, asks Francis to go upstairs and tell Helen that everything is ready. Francis is happy to go; it is like getting back to headquarters company.* He is planning to tell his oldest daughter about the airplane crash, but Helen is lying on her bed reading a *True Romance* magazine, and the first thing Francis does is to take the magazine from her hand and remind Helen that he has forbidden her to buy it. She did not buy it, Helen replies. It was given to her by her best friend, Bessie Black. Everybody reads *True Romance.* Bessie Black's father reads *True Romance.* There isn't a girl in Helen's class who doesn't read *True Romance.* Francis expresses his detestation of the magazine and then tells her that dinner is ready—although from the sounds downstairs it doesn't seem so. Helen follows him down the stairs. Julia has seated herself in the candlelight and spread a napkin over her lap. Neither Louisa nor Henry has come to the table. Little Toby is still howling, lying face down on the floor. Francis speaks to him gently: "Daddy was in a plane crash this afternoon, Toby. Don't you want to hear about it?" Toby goes on crying. "If you don't come to the table now, Toby," Francis says, "I'll have to send you to bed without any supper." The little boy rises, gives him a cutting look, flies up the stairs to his bedroom, and slams the door. "Oh dear," Julia says, and starts to go after him. Francis says that she will spoil him. Julia says that Toby is ten pounds underweight and has to be encouraged to eat. Winter is coming, and he will spend the cold months in bed unless he has his dinner. Julia goes upstairs. Francis sits down at the table with Helen. Helen is suffering from the dismal feeling of having read too intently on a fine day, and she gives her father and the room a jaded look. She doesn't understand about the plane crash, because there wasn't a drop of rain in Shady Hill.

Julia returns with Toby, and they all sit down and are served. "Do I have to look at that big, fat slob?" Henry says, of Louisa. Everybody but Toby enters into this skirmish, and it rages up and down the table for five minutes. Toward the end, Henry puts his napkin over his head and, trying to eat that way, spills spinach all over his shirt. Francis asks Julia if the children couldn't have their dinner earlier. Julia's guns are loaded for this. She can't cook two dinners and lay two tables. She paints with lightning strokes that panorama of drudgery in which her youth, her beauty, and her wit have been lost. Francis says that he must be understood; he was nearly killed in an airplane crash, and he doesn't like to come home every night to a battlefield. Now Julia is deeply committed.

*like getting back to headquarters company: Like returning to relative safety after having been in combat.

Her voice trembles. He doesn't come home every night to a battlefield. The accusation is stupid and mean. Everything was tranquil until he arrived. She stops speaking, puts down her knife and fork, and looks into her plate as if it is a gulf. She begins to cry. "Poor Mummy!" Toby says, and when Julia gets up from the table, drying her tears with a napkin, Toby goes to her side. "Poor Mummy," he says. "Poor Mummy!" And they climb the stairs together. The other children drift away from the battlefield, and Francis goes into the back garden for a cigarette and some air.

It was a pleasant garden, with walks and flower beds and places to sit. The sunset had nearly burned out, but there was still plenty of light. Put into a thoughtful mood by the crash and the battle, Francis listened to the evening sounds of Shady Hill. "Varmints! Rascals!" old Mr. Nixon shouted to the squirrels in his bird-feeding station. "Avaunt and quit my sight!" A door slammed. Someone was playing tennis on the Babcocks' court; someone was cutting grass. Then Donald Goslin, who lived at the corner, began to play the "Moonlight Sonata."* He did this nearly every night. He threw the tempo out the window and played it *rubato*† from beginning to end, like an outpouring of tearful petulance, lonesomeness, and self-pity—of everything it was Beethoven's greatness not to know. The music rang up and down the street beneath the trees like an appeal for love, for tenderness, aimed at some lonely housemaid—some fresh-faced, homesick girl from Galway,‡ looking at old snapshots in her third-floor room. "Here, Jupiter, here, Jupiter," Francis called to the Mercers' retriever. Jupiter crashed through the tomato vines with the remains of a felt hat in his mouth.

Jupiter was an anomaly. His retrieving instincts and his high spirits were out of place in Shady Hill. He was as black as coal, with a long, alert, intelligent, rakehell face. His eyes gleamed with mischief, and he held his head high. It was the fierce, heavily collared dog's head that appears in heraldry, in tapestry, and that used to appear on umbrella handles and walking sticks. Jupiter went where he pleased, ransacking wastebaskets, clotheslines, garbage pails, and shoe bags. He broke up garden parties and tennis matches, and got mixed up in the processional at Christ Church on Sunday, barking at the men in red dresses. He crashed through old Mr. Nixon's rose garden two or three times a day, cutting a wide swath through the Condesa de Sastagos,§ and as soon as Donald Goslin lighted his barbecue fire on Thursday nights, Jupiter would get the scent. Nothing the Goslins did could drive him away. Sticks and stones and rude commands only moved him to the edge of the terrace, where he remained, with his gallant and heraldic muzzle, waiting for Donald Goslin to turn his back and reach for the salt. Then he would spring onto the terrace, lift the steak lightly off the fire, and run away with the Goslins' dinner. Jupiter's days were num-

*"Moonlight Sonata": A well-known and often sentimentalized piano piece by the German composer Ludwig van Beethoven (1770–1827).
†*rubato:* Played with intentional deviations from a strict tempo.
‡Galway: A city and county in Ireland.
§Condesa de Sastagos: Roses that are difficult to grow and relatively rare.

bered. The Wrightsons' German gardener or the Farquarsons' cook would soon poison him. Even old Mr. Nixon might put some arsenic in the garbage that Jupiter loved. "Here, Jupiter, Jupiter!" Francis called, but the dog pranced off, shaking the hat in his white teeth. Looking in at the windows of his house, Francis saw that Julia had come down and was blowing out the candles.

Julia and Francis Weed went out a great deal. Julia was well liked and gregarious, and her love of parties sprang from a most natural dread of chaos and loneliness. She went through her morning mail with real anxiety, looking for invitations, and she usually found some, but she was insatiable, and if she had gone out seven nights a week, it would not have cured her of a reflective look—the look of someone who hears distant music—for she would always suppose that there was a more brilliant party somewhere else. Francis limited her to two week-night parties, putting a flexible interpretation on Friday, and rode through the weekend like a dory in a gale. The day after the airplane crash, the Weeds were to have dinner with the Farquarsons.

Francis got home late from town, and Julia got the sitter while he dressed, and then hurried him out of the house. The party was small and pleasant, and Francis settled down to enjoy himself. A new maid passed the drinks. Her hair was dark, and her face was round and pale and seemed familiar to Francis. He had not developed his memory as a sentimental faculty. Wood smoke, lilac, and other such perfumes did not stir him, and his memory was something like his appendix—a vestigial repository. It was not his limitation at all to be unable to escape the past; it was perhaps his limitation that he had escaped it so successfully. He might have seen the maid at other parties, he might have seen her taking a walk on Sunday afternoons, but in either case he would not be searching his memory now. Her face was, in a wonderful way, a moon face—Norman or Irish—but it was not beautiful enough to account for his feeling that he had seen her before, in circumstances that he ought to be able to remember. He asked Nellie Farquarson who she was. Nellie said that the maid had come through an agency, and that her home was Trénon, in Normandy*—a small place with a church and a restaurant that Nellie had once visited. While Nellie talked on about her travels abroad, Francis realized where he had seen the woman before. It had been at the end of the war. He had left a replacement depot with some other men and taken a three-day pass in Trénon. On their second day, they had walked out to a crossroads to see the public chastisement of a young woman who had lived with the German commandant during the Occupation.†

It was a cool morning in the fall. The sky was overcast, and poured down onto the dirt crossroads a very discouraging light. They were on high land and could see how like one another the shapes of the clouds and the hills were as they stretched off toward the sea. The prisoner arrived sitting on a three-legged stool in a farm cart. She stood by the cart while the mayor read the accusation

---

*Normandy: A region in northwest France on the English Channel and the major location of the Allied invasion of German-occupied Western Europe in World War II (D-Day).
†the Occupation: The German occupation and control of France and the low countries, 1940–1944.

and the sentence. Her head was bent and her face was set in that empty half smile behind which the whipped soul is suspended. When the mayor was finished, she undid her hair and let it fall across her back. A little man with a gray mustache cut off her hair with shears and dropped it on the ground. Then, with a bowl of soapy water and a straight razor, he shaved her skull clean. A woman approached and began to undo the fastenings of her clothes, but the prisoner pushed her aside and undressed herself. When she pulled her chemise over her head and threw it on the ground, she was naked. The women jeered; the men were still. There was no change in the falseness or the plaintiveness of the prisoner's smile. The cold wind made her white skin rough and hardened the nipples of her breasts. The jeering ended gradually, put down by the recognition of their common humanity. One woman spat on her, but some inviolable grandeur in her nakedness lasted through the ordeal. When the crowd was quiet, she turned—she had begun to cry—and, with nothing on but a pair of worn black shoes and stockings, walked down the dirt road alone away from the village. The round white face had aged a little, but there was no question but that the maid who passed his cocktails and later served Francis his dinner was the woman who had been punished at the crossroads.

The war seemed now so distant and that world where the cost of partisanship had been death or torture so long ago. Francis had lost track of the men who had been with him in Vésey. He could not count on Julia's discretion. He could not tell anyone. And if he had told the story now, at the dinner table, it would have been a social as well as a human error. The people in the Farquarsons' living room seemed united in their tacit claim that there had been no past, no war—that there was no danger or trouble in the world. In the recorded history of human arrangements, this extraordinary meeting would have fallen into place, but the atmosphere of Shady Hill made the memory unseemly and impolite. The prisoner withdrew after passing the coffee, but the encounter left Francis feeling languid; it had opened his memory and his senses, and left them dilated. He and Julia drove home when the party ended, and Julia went into the house. Francis stayed in the car to take the sitter home.

Expecting to see Mrs. Henlein, the old lady who usually stayed with the children, he was surprised when a young girl opened the door and came out onto the lighted stoop. She stayed in the light to count her textbooks. She was frowning and beautiful. Now, the world is full of beautiful young girls, but Francis saw here the difference between beauty and perfection. All those endearing flaws, moles, birthmarks, and healed wounds were missing, and he experienced in his consciousness that moment when music breaks glass, and felt a pang of recognition as strange, deep, and wonderful as anything in his life. It hung from her frown, from an impalpable darkness in her face—a look that impressed him as a direct appeal for love. When she had counted her books, she came down the steps and opened the car door. In the light, he saw that her cheeks were wet. She got in and shut the door.

"You're new," Francis said.

"Yes. Mrs. Henlein is sick. I'm Anne Murchison."

"Did the children give you any trouble?"

"Oh, no, no." She turned and smiled at him unhappily in the dim dashboard light. Her light hair caught on the collar of her jacket, and she shook her head to set it loose.

"You've been crying."

"Yes."

"I hope it was nothing that happened in our house."

"No, no, it was nothing that happened in your house." Her voice was bleak. "It's no secret. Everybody in the village knows. Daddy's an alcoholic, and he just called me from some saloon and gave me a piece of his mind. He thinks I'm immoral. He called just before Mrs. Weed came back."

"I'm sorry."

"Oh, *Lord!*" She gasped and began to cry. She turned toward Francis, and he took her in his arms and let her cry on his shoulder. She shook in his embrace, and this movement accentuated his sense of the fineness of her flesh and bone. The layers of their clothing felt thin, and when her shuddering began to diminish, it was so much like a paroxysm of love that Francis lost his head and pulled her roughly against him. She drew away. "I live on Belleview Avenue," she said. "You go down Lansing Street to the railroad bridge."

"All right." He started the car.

"You turn left at that traffic light. . . . Now you turn right here and go straight on toward the tracks."

The road Francis took brought him out of his own neighborhood, across the tracks, and toward the river, to a street where the near-poor lived, in houses whose peaked gables and trimmings of wooden lace conveyed the purest feelings of pride and romance, although the houses themselves could not have offered much privacy or comfort, they were all so small. The street was dark, and, stirred by the grace and beauty of the troubled girl, he seemed, in turning in to it, to have come into the deepest part of some submerged memory. In the distance, he saw a porch light burning. It was the only one, and she said that the house with the light was where she lived. When he stopped the car, he could see beyond the porch light into a dimly lighted hallway with an old-fashioned clothes tree. "Well, here we are," he said, conscious that a young man would have said something different.

She did not move her hands from the books, where they were folded, and she turned and faced him. There were tears of lust in his eyes. Determinedly—not sadly—he opened the door on his side and walked around to open hers. He took her free hand, letting his fingers in between hers, climbed at her side the two concrete steps, and went up a narrow walk through a front garden where dahlias, marigolds, and roses—things that had withstood the light frosts—still bloomed, and made a bittersweet smell in the night air. At the steps, she freed her hand and then turned and kissed him swiftly. Then she crossed the porch and shut the door. The porch light went out, then the light in the hall. A second later, a light went on upstairs at the side of the house, shining into a tree that was still covered with leaves. It took her only a few minutes to undress and get into bed, and then the house was dark.

Julia was asleep when Francis got home. He opened a second window and got into bed to shut his eyes on that night, but as soon as they were shut—as soon as he had dropped off to sleep—the girl entered his mind, moving with perfect freedom through its shut doors and filling chamber after chamber with her light, her perfume, and the music of her voice. He was crossing the Atlantic with her on the old *Mauretania** and, later, living with her in Paris. When he woke from his dream, he got up and smoked a cigarette at the open window. Getting back into bed, he cast around in his mind for something he desired to do that would injure no one, and he thought of skiing. Up through the dimness in his mind rose the image of a mountain deep in snow. It was late in the day. Wherever his eyes looked, he saw broad and heartening things. Over his shoulder, there was a snow-filled valley, rising into wooded hills where the trees dimmed the whiteness like a sparse coat of hair. The cold deadened all sound but the loud, iron clanking of the lift machinery. The light on the trails was blue, and it was harder than it had been a minute or two earlier to pick the turns, harder to judge—now that the snow was all deep blue—the crust, the ice, the bare spots, and the deep piles of dry powder. Down the mountain he swung, matching his speed against the contours of a slope that had been formed in the first ice age, seeking with ardor some simplicity of feeling and circumstance. Night fell then, and he drank a Martini with some old friend in a dirty country bar.

In the morning, Francis' snow-covered mountain was gone and he was left with his vivid memories of Paris and the *Mauretania*. He had been bitten gravely. He washed his body, shaved his jaws, drank his coffee, and missed the seven-thirty-one. The train pulled out just as he brought his car to the station, and the longing he felt for the coaches as they drew stubbornly away from him reminded him of the humors of love. He waited for the eight-two, on what was now an empty platform. It was a clear morning; the morning seemed thrown like a gleaming bridge of light over his mixed affairs. His spirits were feverish and high. The image of the girl seemed to put him into a relationship to the world that was mysterious and enthralling. Cars were beginning to fill up the parking lot, and he noticed that those that had driven down from the high land above Shady Hill were white with hoarfrost. This first clear sign of autumn thrilled him. An express train—a night train from Buffalo or Albany—came down the tracks between the platforms, and he saw that the roofs of the foremost cars were covered with a skin of ice. Struck by the miraculous physicalness of everything, he smiled at the passengers in the dining car, who could be seen eating eggs and wiping their mouths with napkins as they traveled. The sleeping-car compartments, with their soiled bed linen, trailed through the fresh morning like a string of rooming-house windows. Then he saw an extraordinary thing; at one of the bedroom windows sat an unclothed woman of exceptional beauty, combing her golden hair. She passed like an apparition through Shady Hill, combing and combing her hair, and Francis followed her with his eyes

---

Mauretania: British steamship, the fastest and most famous ocean liner of its day (1907–1935); its sister ship, the *Lusitania,* was torpedoed and sunk by a German submarine off Ireland in 1915.

until she was out of sight. Then old Mrs. Wrightson joined him on the platform and began to talk.

"Well, I guess you must be surprised to see me here the third morning in a row," she said, "but because of my window curtains I'm becoming a regular commuter. The curtains I bought on Monday I returned on Tuesday, and the curtains I bought Tuesday I'm returning today. On Monday, I got exactly what I wanted—it's a wool tapestry with roses and birds—but when I got them home, I found they were the wrong length. Well, I exchanged them yesterday, and when I got them home, I found they were still the wrong length. Now I'm praying to high Heaven that the decorator will have them in the right length, because you know my house, you *know* my living-room windows, and you can imagine what a problem they present. I don't know what to do with them."

"I know what to do with them," Francis said.

"What?"

"Paint them black on the inside, and shut up."

There was a gasp from Mrs. Wrightson, and Francis looked down at her to be sure that she knew he meant to be rude. She turned and walked away from him, so damaged in spirit that she limped. A wonderful feeling enveloped him, as if light were being shaken about him, and he thought again of Venus combing and combing her hair as she drifted through the Bronx. The realization of how many years had passed since he had enjoyed being deliberately impolite sobered him. Among his friends and neighbors, there were brilliant and gifted people— he saw that—but many of them, also, were bores and fools, and he had made the mistake of listening to them all with equal attention. He had confused a lack of discrimination with Christian love, and the confusion seemed general and destructive. He was grateful to the girl for this bracing sensation of independence. Birds were singing—cardinals and the last of the robins. The sky shone like enamel. Even the smell of ink from his morning paper honed his appetite for life, and the world that was spread out around him was plainly a paradise.

If Francis had believed in some hierarchy of love—in spirits armed with hunting bows, in the capriciousness of Venus and Eros*—or even in magical potions, philters, and stews, in scapulae and quarters of the moon, it might have explained his susceptibility and his feverish high spirits. The autumnal loves of middle age are well publicized, and he guessed that he was face to face with one of these, but there was not a trace of autumn in what he felt. He wanted to sport in the green woods, scratch where he itched, and drink from the same cup.

His secretary, Miss Rainey, was late that morning—she went to a psychiatrist three mornings a week—and when she came in, Francis wondered what advice a psychiatrist would have for him. But the girl promised to bring back into his life something like the sound of music. The realization that this music might lead him straight to a trial for statutory rape at the county courthouse collapsed his happiness. The photograph of his four children laughing into the camera on the beach at Gay Head† reproached him. On the letterhead of his

---

*Eros: Cupid, the son of Venus (Aphrodite), the goddess of love.

†Gay Head: A village on Martha's Vineyard, an island off the Massachusetts coast.

firm there was a drawing of the Laocoön* and the figure of the priest and his sons in the coils of the snake appeared to him to have the deepest meaning.

He had lunch with Pinky Trabert. At a conversational level, the mores of his friends were robust and elastic, but he knew that the moral card house would come down on them all—on Julia and the children as well—if he got caught taking advantage of a babysitter. Looking back over the recent history of Shady Hill for some precedent, he found there was none. There was no turpitude; there had not been a divorce since he lived there; there had not even been a breath of scandal. Things seemed arranged with more propriety even than in the Kingdom of Heaven. After leaving Pinky, Francis went to a jeweler's and bought the girl a bracelet. How happy this clandestine purchase made him, how stuffy and comical the jeweler's clerks seemed, how sweet the women who passed at his back smelled! On Fifth Avenue, passing Atlas with his shoulders bent under the weight of the world, Francis thought of the strenuousness of containing his physicalness within the patterns he had chosen.

He did not know when he would see the girl next. He had the bracelet in his inside pocket when he got home. Opening the door of his house, he found her in the hall. Her back was to him, and she turned when she heard the door close. Her smile was open and loving. Her perfection stunned him like a fine day—a day after a thunderstorm. He seized her and covered her lips with his, and she struggled but she did not have to struggle for long, because just then little Gertrude Flannery appeared from somewhere and said, "Oh, Mr. Weed . . ."

Gertrude was a stray. She had been born with a taste for exploration, and she did not have it in her to center her life with her affectionate parents. People who did not know the Flannerys concluded from Gertrude's behavior that she was the child of a bitterly divided family, where drunken quarrels were the rule. This was not true. The fact that little Gertrude's clothing was ragged and thin was her own triumph over her mother's struggle to dress her warmly and neatly. Garrulous, skinny, and unwashed, she drifted from house to house around the Blenhollow neighborhood, forming and breaking alliances based on an attachment to babies, animals, children her own age, adolescents, and sometimes adults. Opening your front door in the morning, you would find Gertrude sitting on your stoop. Going into the bathroom to shave, you would find Gertrude using the toilet. Looking into your son's crib, you would find it empty, and, looking further, you would find that Gertrude had pushed him in his baby carriage into the next village. She was helpful, pervasive, honest, hungry, and loyal. She never went home of her own choice. When the time to go arrived, she was indifferent to all its signs: "Go home, Gertrude," people could be heard saying in one house or another, night after night. "Go home, Gertrude. It's time for you to go home now, Gertrude." "You had better go home and get your supper, Gertrude." "I told you to go home twenty minutes ago, Gertrude."

*Laocoön: A famous Greek statue depicting the priest Laocoön and his two sons being crushed to death by two enormous sea serpents after he had warned the Trojans against letting the wooden horse into Troy.

"Your mother will be worrying about you, Gertrude." "Go home, Gertrude, go home."

There are times when the lines around the human eye seem like shelves of eroded stone and when the staring eye itself strikes us with such a wilderness of animal feeling that we are at a loss. The look Francis gave the little girl was ugly and queer, and it frightened her. He reached into his pocket—his hands were shaking—and took out a quarter. "Go home, Gertrude, go home, and don't tell anyone, Gertrude. Don't—" He choked and ran into the living room as Julia called down to him from upstairs to hurry and dress.

The thought that he would drive Anne Murchison home later that night ran like a golden thread through the events of the party that Francis and Julia went to, and he laughed uproariously at dull jokes, dried a tear when Mabel Mercer told him about the death of her kitten, and stretched, yawned, sighed, and grunted like any other man with a rendezvous at the back of his mind. The bracelet was in his pocket. As he sat talking, the smell of grass was in his nose, and he was wondering where he would park the car. Nobody lived in the old Parker mansion, and the driveway was used as a lovers' lane. Townsend Street was a dead end, and he could park there, beyond the last house. The old lane that used to connect Elm Street to the riverbanks was overgrown, but he had walked there with his children, and he could drive his car deep enough into the brushwoods to be concealed.

The Weeds were the last to leave the party, and their host and hostess spoke of their own married happiness while they all four stood in the hallway saying good night. "She's my girl," their host said, squeezing his wife. "She's my blue sky. After sixteen years, I still bite her shoulders. She makes me feel like Hannibal crossing the Alps."*

The Weeds drove home in silence. Francis brought the car up the drive-way and sat still, with the motor running. "You can put the car in the garage," Julia said as she got out. "I told the Murchison girl she could leave at eleven. Someone drove her home." She shut the door, and Francis sat in the dark. He would be spared nothing then, it seemed, that a fool was not spared: ravening lewdness, jealousy, this hurt to his feelings that put tears in his eyes, even scorn—for he could see clearly the image he now presented, his arms spread over the steering wheel and his head buried in them for love.

Francis had been a dedicated Boy Scout when he was young, and, remembering the precepts of his youth, he left his office early the next afternoon and played some round-robin squash, but, with his body toned up by exercise and a shower, he realized that he might better have stayed at his desk. It was a frosty night when he got home. The air smelled sharply of change. When he stepped into the house, he sensed an unusual stir. The children were in their best clothes, and when Julia came down, she was wearing a lavender dress and her diamond sunburst. She explained the stir: Mr. Hubber was coming at seven to take their

*Hannibal crossing the Alps: Hannibal, general of Carthage, used elephants to cross the Alps, previously thought uncrossable, and to attack Italy and Rome in 218 B.C.

photograph for the Christmas card. She had put out Francis' blue suit and a tie with some color in it, because the picture was going to be in color this year. Julia was lighthearted at the thought of being photographed for Christmas. It was the kind of ceremony she enjoyed.

Francis went upstairs to change his clothes. He was tired from the day's work and tired with longing, and sitting on the edge of the bed had the effect of deepening his weariness. He thought of Anne Murchison, and the physical need to express himself, instead of being restrained by the pink lamps on Julia's dressing table, engulfed him. He went to Julia's desk, took a piece of writing paper, and began to write on it. "Dear Anne, I love you, I love you, I love you . . ." No one would see the letter, and he used no restraint. He used phrases like "heavenly bliss," and "love nest." He salivated, sighed, and trembled. When Julia called him to come down, the abyss between his fantasy and the practical world opened so wide that he felt it affect the muscles of his heart.

Julia and the children were on the stoop, and the photographer and his assistant had set up a double battery of floodlights to show the family and the architectural beauty of the entrance to their house. People who had come home on a late train slowed their cars to see the Weeds being photographed for their Christmas card. A few waved and called to the family. It took half an hour of smiling and wetting their lips before Mr. Hubber was satisfied. The heat of the lights made an unfresh smell in the frosty air, and when they were turned off, they lingered on the retina of Francis' eyes.

Later that night, while Francis and Julia were drinking their coffee in the living room, the doorbell rang. Julia answered the door and let in Clayton Thomas. He had come to pay her for some theater tickets that she had given his mother some time ago, and that Helen Thomas had scrupulously insisted on paying for, though Julia had asked her not to. Julia invited him in to have a cup of coffee. "I won't have any coffee," Clayton said, "but I will come in for a minute." He followed her into the living room, said good evening to Francis, and sat awkwardly in a chair.

Clayton's father had been killed in the war, and the young man's father-lessness surrounded him like an element. This may have been conspicuous in Shady Hill because the Thomases were the only family that lacked a piece; all the other marriages were intact and productive. Clayton was in his second or third year of college, and he and his mother lived alone in a large house, which she hoped to sell. Clayton had once made some trouble. Years ago, he had stolen some money and run away; he had got to California before they caught up with him. He was tall and homely, wore horn-rimmed glasses, and spoke in a deep voice.

"When do you go back to college, Clayton?" Francis asked.

"I'm not going back," Clayton said. "Mother doesn't have the money, and there's no sense in all this pretense. I'm going to get a job, and if we sell the house, we'll take an apartment in New York."

"Won't you miss Shady Hill?" Julia asked.

"No," Clayton said. "I don't like it."

"Why not?" Francis asked.

"Well, there's a lot here I don't approve of," Clayton said gravely. "Things like the club dances. Last Saturday night, I looked in toward the end and saw Mr. Granner trying to put Mrs. Minot into the trophy case. They were both drunk. I disapprove of so much drinking."

"It was Saturday night," Francis said.

"And all the dovecotes are phony," Clayton said. "And the way people clutter up their lives. I've thought about it a lot, and what seems to me to be really wrong with Shady Hill is that it doesn't have any future. So much energy is spent in perpetuating the place—in keeping out undesirables, and so forth—that the only idea of the future anyone has is just more and more commuting trains and more parties. I don't think that's healthy. I think people ought to be able to dream big dreams about the future. I think people ought to be able to dream great dreams."

"It's too bad you couldn't continue with college," Julia said.

"I wanted to go to divinity school," Clayton said.

"What's your church?" Francis asked.

"Unitarian, Theosophist, Transcendentalist, Humanist,"* Clayton said.

"Wasn't Emerson a transcendentalist?" Julia asked.

"I mean the English transcendentalists," Clayton said. "All the American transcendentalists were goops."

"What kind of a job do you expect to get?" Francis asked.

"Well, I'd like to work for a publisher," Clayton said, "but everyone tells me there's nothing doing. But it's the kind of thing I'm interested in. I'm writing a long verse play about good and evil. Uncle Charlie might get me into a bank, and that would be good for me. I need the discipline. I have a long way to go in forming my character. I have some terrible habits. I talk too much. I think I ought to take vows of silence. I ought to try not to speak for a week, and discipline myself. I've thought of making a retreat at one of the Episcopalian monasteries, but I don't like the Trinitarianism."

"Do you have any girl friends?" Francis asked.

"I'm engaged to be married," Clayton said. "Of course, I'm not old enough or rich enough to have my engagement observed or respected or anything, but I bought a simulated emerald for Anne Murchison with the money I made cutting lawns this summer. We're going to be married as soon as she finishes school."

Francis recoiled at the mention of the girl's name. Then a dingy light seemed to emanate from his spirit, showing everything—Julia, the boy, the chairs—in their true colorlessness. It was like a bitter turn of the weather.

"We're going to have a large family," Clayton said. "Her father's a terrible rummy, and I've had my hard times, and we want to have lots of children. Oh, she's wonderful, Mr. and Mrs. Weed, and we have so much in

---

*Unitarian, Theosophist, Transcendentalist, Humanist: Religious philosophies that tend to emphasize the importance of humanity and of this world rather than the next. Clayton's naming four different philosophies may indicate his own exuberance and confusion.

common. We like all the same things. We sent out the same Christmas card last year without planning it, and we both have an allergy to tomatoes, and our eyebrows grow together in the middle. Well, good night."

Julia went to the door with him. When she returned, Francis said that Clayton was lazy, irresponsible, affected, and smelly. Julia said that Francis seemed to be getting intolerant; the Thomas boy was young and should be given a chance. Julia had noticed other cases where Francis had been short-tempered. "Mrs. Wrightson has asked everyone in Shady Hill to her anniversary party but us," she said.

"I'm sorry, Julia."

"Do you know why they didn't ask us?"

"Why?"

"Because you insulted Mrs. Wrightson."

"Then you know about it?"

"June Masterson told me. She was standing behind you."

Julia walked in front of the sofa with a small step that expressed, Francis knew, a feeling of anger.

"I did insult Mrs. Wrightson, Julia, and I meant to. I've never liked her parties, and I'm glad she's dropped us."

"What about Helen?"

"How does Helen come into this?"

"Mrs. Wrightson's the one who decides who goes to the assemblies."

"You mean she can keep Helen from going to the dances?"

"Yes."

"I hadn't thought of that."

"Oh, I knew you hadn't thought of it," Julia cried, thrusting hilt-deep into this chink of his armor. "And it makes me furious to see this kind of stupid thoughtlessness wreck everyone's happiness."

"I don't think I've wrecked anyone's happiness."

"Mrs. Wrightson runs Shady Hill and has run it for the last forty years. I don't know what makes you think that in a community like this you can indulge every impulse you have to be insulting, vulgar, and offensive."

"I have very good manners," Francis said, trying to give the evening a turn toward the light.

"Damn you, Francis Weed!" Julia cried, and the spit of her words struck him in the face. "I've worked hard for the social position we enjoy in this place, and I won't stand by and see you wreck it. You must have understood when you settled here that you couldn't expect to live like a bear in a cave."

"I've got to express my likes and dislikes."

"You can conceal your dislikes. You don't have to meet everything head-on, like a child. Unless you're anxious to be a social leper. It's no accident that we get asked out a great deal. It's no accident that Helen has so many friends. How would you like to spend your Saturday nights at the movies? How would you like to spend your Sundays raking up dead leaves? How would you like it if your daughter spent the assembly nights sitting at her window, listening to the music from the club? How would you like it—" He did something then that was, after all, not so unaccountable, since her words seemed to raise up between them a wall so deadening that he gagged: He struck her full in the face. She staggered and then, a moment later, seemed composed. She went up the stairs to their room. She didn't slam the door. When Francis followed, a few minutes later, he found her packing a suitcase.

"Julia, I'm very sorry."

"It doesn't matter," she said. She was crying.

"Where do you think you're going?"

"I don't know. I just looked at a timetable. There's an eleven-sixteen into New York. I'll take that."

"You can't go, Julia."

"I can't stay. I know that."

"I'm sorry about Mrs. Wrightson, Julia, and I'm—"

"It doesn't matter about Mrs. Wrightson. That isn't the trouble."

"What is the trouble?"

"You don't love me."

"I do love you, Julia."

"No, you don't."

"Julia, I do love you, and I would like to be as we were—sweet and bawdy and dark—but now there are so many people."

"You hate me."

"I don't hate you, Julia."

"You have no idea of how much you hate me. I think it's subconscious. You don't realize the cruel things you've done."

"What cruel things, Julia?"

"The cruel acts your subconscious drives you to in order to express your hatred of me."

"What, Julia?"

"I've never complained."

"Tell me."

"You don't know what you're doing."

"Tell me."

"Your clothes."

"What do you mean?"

"I mean the way you leave your dirty clothes around in order to express your subconscious hatred of me."

"I don't understand."

"I mean your dirty socks and your dirty pajamas and your dirty underwear and your dirty shirts!" She rose from kneeling by the suitcase and faced him, her eyes blazing and her voice ringing with emotion. "I'm talking about the fact that you've never learned to hang up anything. You just leave your clothes all over the floor where they drop, in order to humiliate me. You do it on purpose!" She fell on the bed, sobbing.

"Julia, darling!" he said, but when she felt his hand on her shoulder she got up.

"Leave me alone," she said. "I have to go." She brushed past him to the closet and came back with a dress. "I'm not taking any of the things you've given me," she said. "I'm leaving my pearls and the fur jacket."

"Oh, Julia!" Her figure, so helpless in its self-deceptions, bent over the suitcase made him nearly sick with pity. She did not understand how desolate her life would be without him. She didn't understand the hours that working women have to keep. She didn't understand that most of her friendships existed within the framework of their marriage, and that without this she would find herself alone. She didn't understand about travel, about hotels, about money. "Julia, I can't let you go! What you don't understand, Julia, is that you've come to be dependent on me."

She tossed her head back and covered her face with her hands. "Did you say that *I* was dependent on *you?*" she asked. "Is that what you said? And who is it that tells you what time to get up in the morning and when to go to bed at night? Who is it that prepares your meals and picks up your dirty clothes and invites your friends to dinner? If it weren't for me, your neckties would be greasy and your clothing would be full of moth holes. You were alone when I met you, Francis Weed, and you'll be alone when I leave. When Mother asked you for a list to send out invitations to our wedding, how many names did you have to give her? Fourteen!"

"Cleveland wasn't my home, Julia."

"And how many of your friends came to the church? Two!"

"Cleveland wasn't my home, Julia."

"Since I'm not taking the fur jacket," she said quietly, "you'd better put it back into storage. There's an insurance policy on the pearls that comes due in January. The name of the laundry and the maid's telephone number—all those things are in my desk. I hope you won't drink too much, Francis. I hope that nothing bad will happen to you. If you do get into serious trouble, you can call me."

"Oh, my darling, I can't let you go!" Francis said. "I can't let you go, Julia!" He took her in his arms.

"I guess I'd better stay and take care of you for a little while longer," she said.

Riding to work in the morning, Francis saw the girl walk down the aisle of the coach. He was surprised; he hadn't realized that the school she went to was in the city, but she was carrying books, she seemed to be going to school. His surprise delayed his reaction, but then he got up clumsily and stepped into the aisle. Several people had come between them, but he could see her ahead of him, waiting for someone to open the car door, and then, as the train swerved, putting out her hand to support herself as she crossed the platform into the next car. He followed her through that car and halfway through another before calling her name—"Anne! Anne!"—but she didn't turn. He followed her into still another car, and she sat down in an aisle seat. Coming up to her, all his feelings warm and bent in her direction, he put his hand on the back of her seat—even this touch warmed him—and, leaning down to speak to her, he saw that it was not Anne. It was an older woman wearing glasses. He went on deliberately into another car, his face red with embarrassment and the much deeper feeling of having his good sense challenged; for if he couldn't tell one person from another, what evidence was there that his life with Julia and the children had as much reality as his dreams of iniquity in Paris or the litter, the grass smell, and the cave-shaped trees in Lovers' Lane.

Late that afternoon, Julia called to remind Francis that they were going out for dinner. A few minutes later, Trace Bearden called. "Look, fellar," Trace said. "I'm calling for Mrs. Thomas. You know? Clayton, that boy of hers, doesn't seem able to get a job, and I wondered if you could help. If you'd call Charlie Bell—I know he's indebted to you—and say a good word for the kid, I think Charlie would—"

"Trace, I hate to say this," Francis said, "but I don't feel that I can do anything for that boy. The kid's worthless. I know it's a harsh thing to say, but it's a fact. Any kindness done for him would backfire in everybody's face. He's just a worthless kid, Trace, and there's nothing to be done about it. Even if we got him a job, he wouldn't be able to keep it for a week. I know that to be a fact. It's an awful thing, Trace, and I know it is, but instead of recommending that kid, I'd feel obliged to warn people against him—people who knew his father and would naturally want to step in and do something. I'd feel obliged to warn them. He's a thief . . ."

The moment this conversation was finished. Miss Rainey came in and stood by his desk. "I'm not going to be able to work for you any more, Mr. Weed," she said. "I can stay until the seventeenth if you need me, but I've been offered a whirlwind of a job, and I'd like to leave as soon as possible."

She went out, leaving him to face alone the wickedness of what he had done to the Thomas boy. His children in their photograph laughed and laughed, glazed with all the bright colors of summer, and he remembered that they had met a bagpiper on the beach that day and he had paid the piper a dollar to play them a battle song of the Black Watch.* The girl would be at the house when he got home. He would spend another evening among his kind neighbors, picking and choosing dead-end streets, cart tracks, and the driveways of abandoned houses. There was nothing to mitigate his feeling—nothing that laughter or a game of softball with the children would change—and, thinking back over the plane crash, the Farquarsons' new maid, and Anne Murchison's difficulties with her drunken father, he wondered how he could have avoided arriving at just where he was. He was in trouble. He had been lost once in his life, coming back from a trout stream in the north woods, and he had now the same bleak realization that no amount of cheerfulness or hopefulness or valor or perseverance could help him find, in the gathering dark, the path that he'd lost. He smelled the forest. The feeling of bleakness was intolerable, and he saw clearly that he had reached the point where he would have to make a choice.

He could go to a psychiatrist, like Miss Rainey; he could go to church and confess his lusts; he could go to a Danish massage parlor† in the West Seventies that had been recommended by a salesman; he could rape the girl or trust that

*the Black Watch: A British Highland regiment that fought in World War II.
†Danish massage parlor: Sometimes a cover for a house of prostitution.

he would somehow be prevented from doing this; or he could get drunk. It was his life, his boat, and, like every other man, he was made to be the father of thousands, and what harm could there be in a tryst that would make them both feel more kindly toward the world? This was the wrong train of thought, and he came back to the first, the psychiatrist. He had the telephone number of Miss Rainey's doctor, and he called and asked for an immediate appointment. He was insistent with the doctor's secretary—it was his manner in business—and when she said that the doctor's schedule was full for the next few weeks, Francis demanded an appointment that day and was told to come at five.

The psychiatrist's office was in a building that was used mostly by doctors and dentists, and the hallways were filled with the candy smell of mouthwash and memories of pain. Francis' character had been formed upon a series of private resolves—resolves about cleanliness, about going off the high diving board or repeating any other feat that challenged his courage, about punctuality, honesty, and virtue. To abdicate the perfect loneliness in which he had made his most vital decisions shattered his concept of character and left him now in a condition that felt like shock. He was stupefied. The scene for his *miserere mei Deus** was, like the waiting room of so many doctors' offices, a crude token gesture toward the sweets of domestic bliss: a place arranged with antiques, coffee tables, potted plants, and etchings of snow-covered bridges and geese in flight, although there were no children, no marriage bed, no stove, even, in this travesty of a house, where no one had ever spent the night and where the curtained windows looked straight onto a dark air shaft. Francis gave his name and address to a secretary and then saw, at the side of the room, a policeman moving toward him. "Hold it, hold it," the policeman said. "Don't move. Keep your hands where they are."

"I think it's all right, officer," the secretary began. "I think it will be—"

"Let's make sure," the policeman said, and he began to slap Francis' clothes, looking for what—pistols, knives, an icepick? Finding nothing, he went off, and the secretary began a nervous apology: "When you called on the telephone, Mr. Weed, you seemed very excited, and one of the doctor's patients has been threatening his life, and we have to be careful. If you want to go in now?" Francis pushed open a door connected to an electrical chime, and in the doctor's lair sat down heavily, blew his nose into a handkerchief, searched in his pockets for cigarettes, for matches, for something, and said hoarsely, with tears in his eyes, "I'm in love, Dr. Herzog."

It is a week or ten days later in Shady Hill. The seven-fourteen has come and gone, and here and there dinner is finished and the dishes are in the dish-washing machine. The village hangs, morally and economically, from a thread; but it hangs by its thread in the evening light. Donald Goslin has begun to worry the "Moonlight Sonata" again. *Marcato ma sempre pianissimo!*† He seems to be wringing out a wet bath towel, but the housemaid does not heed

*his *miserere mei Deus:* His confession; literally, the words mean "Have mercy upon me, O Lord."
†*Marcato ma sempre pianissimo!:* Latin, Emphatically but very softly.

him. She is writing a letter to Arthur Godfrey.* In the cellar of his house, Francis Weed is building a coffee table. Dr. Herzog recommended woodwork as a therapy, and Francis finds some true consolation in the simple arithmetic involved and in the holy smell of new wood. Francis is happy. Upstairs, little Toby is crying, because he is tired. He puts off his cowboy hat, gloves, and fringed jacket, unbuckles the belt studded with gold and rubies, the silver bullets and holsters, slips off his suspenders, his checked shirt, and Levis, and sits on the edge of his bed to pull off his high boots. Leaving this equipment in a heap, he goes to the closet and takes his space suit off a nail. It is a struggle for him to get into the long tights, but he succeeds. He loops the magic cape over his shoulders and, climbing onto the footboard of his bed, he spreads his arms and flies the short distance to the floor, landing with a thump that is audible to everyone in the house but himself.

"Go home, Gertrude, go home," Mrs. Masterson says. "I told you to go home an hour ago, Gertrude. It's way past your suppertime, and your mother will be worried. Go home!" A door on the Babcocks' terrace flies open, and out comes Mrs. Babcock without any clothes on, pursued by her naked husband. (Their children are away at boarding school, and their terrace is screened by a hedge.) Over the terrace they go and in at the kitchen door, as passionate and handsome a nymph and satyr† as you will find on any wall in Venice. Cutting the last of the roses in her garden, Julia hears old Mr. Nixon shouting at the squirrels in his bird-feeding station. "Rapscallions! Varmints! Avaunt and quit my sight!" A miserable cat wanders into the garden, sunk in spiritual and physical discomfort. Tied to its head is a small straw hat—a doll's hat—and it is securely buttoned into a doll's dress, from the skirts of which protrudes its long, hairy tail. As it walks, it shakes its feet, as if it had fallen into water.

"Here, pussy, pussy, pussy!" Julia calls.

"Here, pussy, here, poor pussy!" But the cat gives her a skeptical look and stumbles away in its skirts. The last to come is Jupiter. He prances through the tomato vines, holding in his generous mouth the remains of an evening slipper. Then it is dark; it is a night where kings in golden suits ride elephants over the mountains.

Writing Assignments for "The Country Husband"

I. Brief Papers

    A. 1. Why does no one in Shady Hill want to hear about Francis' brush with death?

       2. What is the connection between Francis' brush with death and his feelings for Anne Murchison?

       3. Why is Francis deliberately rude to Mrs. Wrightson?

       4. Explain why Jupiter is "out of place" in Shady Hill.

*Arthur Godfrey: Popular radio and television personality during the 1940s and 1950s.
†nymph and satyr: In Greek and Roman mythology, a nymph is a minor nature goddess and a satyr is a minor woodland god, half man and half goat; today the terms suggest a beautiful young woman and a lecherous man.

5. Why does the atmosphere of Shady Hill make Francis' wartime story of the naked woman appear "unseemly and impolite"?

6. Explain what the narrator means when he says that it may be Francis' limitation that he has so successfully escaped from his past (p. 474).

B. Argue for or against one of the assertions below:
1. Francis Weed's affection for Anne Murchison is a sign of his immaturity.
2. Francis doesn't really love Anne.
3. Julia is right in saying that, subconsciously, Francis hates her.
4. Francis is a sympathetically portrayed character.

C. 1. Why do you think Francis has forbidden Helen to read *True Romance?*
2. If you were Julia, would you have left Francis after he hit you? Why or why not?
3. Why do you think Julia changes her mind and decides not to leave?
4. Why do you think Julia wants to go to a party every night? Does your explanation lead you to sympathize with Julia? How does your judgment of Julia affect your interpretation of the story?

II. Longer Papers

A. Do you think that Shady Hill gets in the way—as Clayton Thomas claims it does—of dreaming "great dreams" (p. 482)?

B. Explain why it is appropriate that the story end with mention of both the "miserable cat" and Jupiter the dog.

C. What does the story say about the relationship between actualities and dreams?

D. Develop, modify, or refute the assertion that the story strongly implies that marriages are likely to become dull and unexciting.

E. Pretend that you are Dr. Herzog, the psychiatrist that Francis Weed consults. If you have advice for him other than to take up a hobby like woodworking, write him a letter with your diagnosis and recommendations.

III. Point of View in "The Country Husband"

Using the sentences below, construct a short essay that defines *limited omniscient point of view* and illustrates its use in "The Country Husband."

1. John Cheever chose a narrative point of view.
2. The point of view is known as *third-person limited omniscient.*
3. He chose it to tell his short story "The Country Husband."

4. The story's point of view is third person for this reason.
5. All the characters in the story are called by the third-person pronouns "he" and "she."

6. Suppose the story had been told from a first-person point of view.
7. Then one of the characters would have been the storyteller.
8. One of the characters would have been an "I."

9. Suppose the story's opening line were told from the first-person point of view.
10. Then the story's opening line might have read, "the airplane from Minneapolis in which I was traveling East ran into heavy weather."
11. Then the story's opening line would not read as it does in the actual text.
12. In the actual text it reads, "the airplane from Minneapolis in which Francis Weed was traveling . . . ."

13. The story is told from a limited omniscient point of view for this reason.
14. The reader is given direct access to the thoughts and feelings of only a single character.
15. That character is Francis Weed.

16. We are never permitted to know exactly what Julia Weed is thinking or feeling.
17. We are never permitted to know exactly what Anne Murchison is thinking or feeling.
18. We are never permitted to know exactly what any other characters are thinking or feeling.
19. However, we can sometimes infer their thoughts and feelings.
20. We make these inferences from what they say.
21. We make these inferences from what they do.

22. But we do get into Francis' heart and mind.
23. There, we discover, for example, his memories of wartime Normandy.
24. There, we discover, for example, his impulse to confess his lust in church.
25. There, we discover, for example, his trying to think of a pleasurable activity that will injure no one.

26. This happens in stories told from the third-person limited omniscient point of view.
27. We perceive a fictional world largely through the mind and senses of a single person.
28. For this reason that person is sometimes called the story's *point-of-view character.*

29. In "The Country Husband," the point-of-view character is Francis Weed.

30. It is often easy for a reader to identify with the point-of-view character.
31. It is often easy for a reader to sympathize with the point-of-view character.
32. It is often easy for a reader to accept the values of the point-of-view character.

33. One of the central questions about "The Country Husband" is this.
34. To what extent does the story encourage the reader to adopt the attitudes and values of Francis Weed?

JOHN CHEEVER
The Swimmer

Before Reading

Have you ever felt so superior to or so contemptuous of another person or group of people that you didn't want to associate with them or that you didn't want to look at them or touch them or have them near you? If so, free write for 5 or 10 minutes on what made you feel that way. If not, write an explanation of why you think others sometimes feel this way.

It was one of those midsummer Sundays when everyone sits around saying: "I *drank* too much last night." You might have heard it whispered by the parishioners leaving church, heard it from the lips of the priest himself, struggling with his cassock in the *vestiarium,* heard it from the golf links and the tennis courts, heard it from the wildlife preserve where the leader of the Audubon group was suffering from a terrible hangover. "I *drank* too much," said Donald Westerhazy. "We all *drank* too much," said Lucinda Merrill. "It must have been the wine," said Helen Westerhazy. "I *drank* too much of that claret."

This was at the edge of the Westerhazys' pool. The pool, fed by an artesian well with a high iron content, was a pale shade of green. It was a fine day. In the west there was a massive stand of cumulus cloud so like a city seen from a distance—from the bow of an approaching ship—that it might have had a name. Lisbon. Hackensack. The sun was hot. Neddy Merrill sat by the green water, one hand in it, one around a glass of gin. He was a slender man—he seemed to have the especial slenderness of youth—and while he was far from young he had slid down his banister that morning and given the bronze backside of Aphrodite on the hall table a smack, as he jogged toward the smell of coffee in his dining room. He might have been compared to a summer's day, particularly the last hours of one, and while he lacked a tennis racket or a sail bag the impression was definitely one of youth, sport, and clement weather. He had been swimming and now he was breathing deeply, stertorously as if he could gulp into his lungs the components of that moment, the heat of the sun, the intenseness of his pleasure. It all seemed to flow into his chest. His own house stood in Bullet Park, eight miles to the south, where his four beautiful daughters would have had their lunch and might be playing tennis. Then it occurred to him that by taking a dogleg to the southwest he could reach his home by water.

His life was not confining and the delight he took in this observation could not be explained by its suggestion of escape. He seemed to see, with a cartographer's eye, that string of swimming pools, that quasi-subterranean stream that curved across the county. He had made a discovery, a contribution to modern geography; he would name the stream Lucinda after his wife. He was not a

THE SWIMMER   First published in 1964.

practical joker nor was he a fool but he was determinedly original and had a vague and modest idea of himself as a legendary figure. The day was beautiful and it seemed to him that a long swim might enlarge and celebrate its beauty.

He took off a sweater that was hung over his shoulders and dove in. He had an inexplicable contempt for men who did not hurl themselves into pools. He swam a choppy crawl, breathing either with every stroke or every fourth stroke and counting somewhere well in the back of his mind the one-two one-two of a flutter kick. It was not a serviceable stroke for long distances but the domestication of swimming had saddled the sport with some customs and in his part of the world a crawl was customary. To be embraced and sustained by the light green water was less a pleasure, it seemed, than the resumption of a natural condition, and he would have liked to swim without trunks, but this was not possible, considering his project. He hoisted himself up on the far curb—he never used the ladder—and started across the lawn. When Lucinda asked where he was going he said he was going to swim home.

The only maps and charts he had to go by were remembered or imaginary but these were clear enough. First there were the Grahams, the Hammers, the Lears, the Howlands, and the Crosscups. He would cross Ditmar Street to the Bunkers and come, after a short portage, to the Levys, the Welchers, and the public pool in Lancaster. Then there were the Hallorans, the Sachses, the Biswangers, Shirley Adams, the Gilmartins, and the Clydes. The day was lovely, and that he lived in a world so generously supplied with water seemed like a clemency, a beneficence. His heart was high and he ran across the grass. Making his way home by an uncommon route gave him the feeling that he was a pilgrim, an explorer, a man with a destiny, and he knew that he would find friends all along the way; friends would line the banks of the Lucinda River.

He went through a hedge that separated the Westerhazys' land from the Grahams', walked under some flowering apple trees, passed the shed that housed their pump and filter, and came out at the Grahams' pool. "Why, Neddy," Mrs. Graham said, "what a marvelous surprise. I've been trying to get you on the phone all morning. Here, let me get you a drink." He saw then, like any explorer, that the hospitable customs and traditions of the natives would have to be handled with diplomacy if he was ever going to reach his destination. He did not want to mystify or seem rude to the Grahams nor did he have the time to linger there. He swam the length of their pool and joined them in the sun and was rescued, a few minutes later, by the arrival of two carloads of friends from Connecticut. During the uproarious reunions he was able to slip away. He went down by the front of the Grahams' house, stepped over a thorny hedge, and crossed a vacant lot to the Hammers'. Mrs. Hammer, looking up from her roses, saw him swim by although she wasn't quite sure who it was. The Lears heard him splashing past the open windows of their living room. The Howlands and the Crosscups were away. After leaving the Howlands' he crossed Ditmar Street and started for the Bunkers', where he could hear, even at that distance, the noise of a party.

The water refracted the sound of voices and laughter and seemed to suspend it in midair. The Bunkers' pool was on a rise and he climbed some stairs to a terrace where twenty-five or thirty men and women were drinking. The only person in the water was Rusty Towers, who floated there on a rubber raft. Oh how bonny and lush were the banks of the Lucinda River! Prosperous men and women gathered by the sapphire-colored waters while caterer's men in white coats passed them cold gin. Overhead a red de Haviland trainer was circling around and around and around in the sky with something like the glee of a child in a swing. Ned felt a passing affection for the scene, a tenderness for the gathering, as if it was something he might touch. In the distance he heard thunder. As soon as Enid Bunker saw him she began to scream: "Oh look who's here! What a marvelous surprise! When Lucinda said that you couldn't come I thought I'd *die.*" She made her way to him through the crowd, and when they had finished kissing she led him to the bar, a progress that was slowed by the fact that he stopped to kiss eight or ten other women and shake the hands of as many men. A smiling bartender he had seen at a hundred parties gave him a gin and tonic and he stood by the bar for a moment, anxious not to get stuck in any conversation that would delay his voyage. When he seemed about to be surrounded he dove in and swam close to the side to avoid colliding with Rusty's raft. At the far end of the pool he bypassed the Tomlinsons with a broad smile and jogged up the garden path. The gravel cut his feet but this was the only unpleasantness. The party was confined to the pool, and as he went toward the house he heard the brilliant, watery sound of voices fade, heard the noise of a radio from the Bunkers' kitchen, where someone was listening to a ballgame. Sunday afternoon. He made his way through the parked cars and down the grassy border of their driveway to Alewives Lane. He did not want to be seen on the road in his bathing trunks but there was no traffic and he made the short distance to the Levys' driveway, marked with a private property sign and a green tube for the *New York Times.* All the doors and windows of the big house were open but there were no signs of life; not even a dog barked. He went around the side of the house to the pool and saw that the Levys had only recently left. Glasses and bottles and dishes of nuts were on a table at the deep end, where there was a bathhouse or gazebo, hung with Japanese lanterns. After swimming the pool he got himself a glass and poured a drink. It was his fourth or fifth drink and he had swum nearly half the length of the Lucinda River. He felt tired, clean, and pleased at that moment to be alone; pleased with everything.

It would storm. The stand of cumulus cloud—that city—had risen and darkened, and while he sat there he heard the percussiveness of thunder again. The de Haviland trainer was still circling overhead and it seemed to Ned that he could almost hear the pilot laugh with pleasure in the afternoon; but when there was another peal of thunder he took off for home. A train whistle blew and he wondered what time it had gotten to be. Four? Five? He thought of the provincial station at that hour, where a waiter, his tuxedo concealed by a raincoat, a dwarf with some flowers wrapped in newspaper, and a woman who had been crying would be waiting for the local. It was suddenly growing dark; it was that moment when the pin-headed birds seem to organize their song into some acute and knowledgeable recognition of the storm's approach. Then there was a fine noise of rushing water from the crown of an oak at his back, as if a spigot there had been turned. Then the noise of fountains came from the crowns of all the tall trees. Why did he love storms, what was the meaning of his excitement when the door sprang open and the rain wind fled rudely up the stairs, why had the simple task of shutting the windows of an old house seemed fitting and urgent, why did the first watery notes of a storm wind have for him the unmistakable sound of good news, cheer, glad tidings? Then there was an explosion, a smell of cordite, and rain lashed the Japanese lanterns that Mrs. Levy had bought in Kyoto the year before last, or was it the year before that?

He stayed in the Levys' gazebo until the storm had passed. The rain had cooled the air and he shivered. The force of the wind had stripped a maple of its red and yellow leaves and scattered them over the grass and the water. Since it was midsummer the tree must be blighted, and yet he felt a peculiar sadness at this sign of autumn. He braced his shoulders, emptied his glass, and started for the Welchers' pool. This meant crossing the Lindleys' riding ring and he was surprised to find it overgrown with grass and all the jumps dismantled. He wondered if the Lindleys had sold their horses or gone away for the summer and put them out to board. He seemed to remember having heard something about the Lindleys and their horses but the memory was unclear. On he went, barefoot through the wet grass, to the Welchers', where he found their pool was dry.

This breach in his chain of water disappointed him absurdly, and he felt like some explorer who seeks a torrential headwater and finds a dead stream. He was disappointed and mystified. It was common enough to go away for the summer but no one ever drained his pool. The Welchers had definitely gone away. The pool furniture was folded, stacked, and covered with a tarpaulin. The bathhouse was locked. All the windows of the house were shut, and when he went around to the driveway in front he saw a for-sale sign nailed to a tree. When had he last heard from the Welchers—when, that is, had he and Lucinda last regretted an invitation to dine with them. It seemed only a week or so ago. Was his memory failing or had he so disciplined it in the repression of unpleasant facts that he had damaged his sense of the truth? Then in the distance he heard the sound of a tennis game. This cheered him, cleared away all his apprehensions and let him regard the overcast sky and the cold air with indifference. This was the day that Neddy Merrill swam across the county. That was the day! He started off then for his most difficult portage.

Had you gone for a Sunday afternoon ride that day you might have seen him, close to naked, standing on the shoulders of route 424, waiting for a chance to cross. You might have wondered if he was the victim of foul play, had his car broken down, or was he merely a fool. Standing barefoot in the deposits of the highway—beer cans, rags, and blowout patches—exposed to all kinds of ridicule, he seemed pitiful. He had known when he started that this was a part of his journey—it had been on his maps—but confronted with the lines of traffic, worming through the summery light, he found himself unprepared. He was laughed at, jeered at, a beer can was thrown at him, and he had no dignity or humor to bring to the situation. He could have gone back, back to the Westerhazys', where Lucinda would still be sitting in the sun. He had signed nothing, vowed nothing, pledged nothing not even to himself. Why, believing as he did, that all human obduracy was susceptible to common sense, was he unable to turn back? Why was he determined to complete his journey even if it meant putting his life in danger? At what point had this prank, this joke, this piece of horseplay become serious? He could not go back, he could not even recall with any clearness the green water at the Westerhazys', the sense of inhaling the day's components, the friendly and relaxed voices saying that they had *drunk* too much. In the space of an hour, more or less, he covered a distance that made his return impossible.

An old man, tooling down the highway at fifteen miles an hour, let him get to the middle of the road, where there was a grass divider. Here he was exposed to the ridicule of the northbound traffic, but after ten or fifteen minutes he was able to cross. From here he had only a short walk to the Recreation Center at the edge of the Village of Lancaster, where there were some handball courts and a public pool.

The effect of the water on voices, the illusion of brilliance and suspense, was the same here as it had been at the Bunkers' but the sounds here were louder, harsher, and more shrill, and as soon as he entered the crowded enclosure he was confronted with regimentation. "ALL SWIMMERS MUST TAKE A SHOWER BEFORE USING THE POOL. ALL SWIMMERS MUST USE THE FOOTBATH. ALL SWIMMERS MUST WEAR THEIR IDENTIFICATION DISKS." He took a shower, washed his feet in a cloudy and bitter solution and made his way to the edge of the water. It stank of chlorine and looked to him like a sink. A pair of lifeguards in a pair of towers blew police whistles at what seemed to be regular intervals and abused the swimmers through a public address system. Neddy remembered the sapphire water at the Bunkers' with longing and thought that he might contaminate himself—damage his own prosperousness and charm—by swimming in this murk, but he reminded himself that he was an explorer, a pilgrim, and that this was merely a stagnant bend in the Lucinda River. He dove, scowling with distaste, into the chlorine and had to swim with his head above water to avoid collisions, but even so he was bumped into, splashed and jostled. When he got to the shallow end both lifeguards were shouting at him: "Hey, you, you without the identification disk, get outa the water." He did, but they had no way of pursuing him and he went through the reek of suntan oil and chlorine out through the hurricane fence and passed the handball courts. By crossing the road he entered the wooded part of the Halloran estate. The woods were not cleared and the footing was treacherous and difficult until he reached the lawn and the clipped beech hedge that encircled their pool.

The Hallorans were friends, an elderly couple of enormous wealth who seemed to bask in the suspicion that they might be Communists. They were zealous reformers but they were not Communists, and yet when they were accused, as they sometimes were, of subversion, it seemed to gratify and excite them. Their beech hedge was yellow and he guessed this had been blighted like the Levys' maple. He called hullo, hullo, to warn the Hallorans of his approach, to palliate his invasion of their privacy. The Hallorans, for reasons that had never been explained to him, did not wear bathing suits. No explanations were in order, really. Their nakedness was a detail in their uncompromising zeal for reform and he stepped politely out of his trunks before he went through the opening in the hedge.

Mrs. Halloran, a stout woman with white hair and a serene face, was reading the *Times*. Mr. Halloran was taking beech leaves out of the water with a scoop. They seemed not surprised or displeased to see him. Their pool was perhaps the oldest in the county, a fieldstone rectangle, fed by a brook. It had no filter or pump and its waters were the opaque gold of the stream.

"I'm swimming across the county," Ned said.

"Why, I didn't know one could," exclaimed Mrs. Halloran.

"Well, I've made it from the Westerhazys'," Ned said. "That must be about four miles."

He left his trunks at the deep end, walked to the shallow end, and swam this stretch. As he was pulling himself out of the water he heard Mrs. Halloran say: "We've been *terribly* sorry to hear about all your misfortunes, Neddy."

"My misfortunes?" Ned asked. "I don't know what you mean."

"Why we heard that you'd sold the house and that your poor children . . ."

"I don't recall having sold the house," Ned said, "and the girls are at home."

"Yes," Mrs. Halloran sighed. "Yes . . ." Her voice filled the air with an unseasonable melancholy and Ned spoke briskly. "Thank you for the swim."

"Well, have a nice trip," said Mrs. Halloran.

Beyond the hedge he pulled on his trunks and fastened them. They were loose and he wondered if, during the space of an afternoon, he could have lost some weight. He was cold and he was tired and the naked Hallorans and their dark water had depressed him. The swim was too much for his strength but how could he have guessed this, sliding down the banister that morning and sitting in the Westerhazys' sun? His arms were lame. His legs felt rubbery and ached at the joints. The worst of it was the cold in his bones and the feeling that he might never be warm again. Leaves were falling down around him and he smelled woodsmoke on the wind. Who would be burning wood at this time of year?

He needed a drink. Whiskey would warm him, pick him up, carry him through the last of his journey, refresh his feeling that it was original and valorous to swim across the county. Channel swimmers took brandy. He needed a stimulant. He crossed the lawn in front of the Hallorans' house and went down a little path to where they had built a house for their only daughter Helen and her husband Eric Sachs. The Sachses' pool was small and he found Helen and her husband there.

"Oh, *Neddy*," Helen said. "Did you lunch at Mother's?"

"Not *really*," Ned said. "I *did* stop to see your parents." This seemed to be explanation enough. "I'm terribly sorry to break in on you like this but I've taken a chill and I wonder if you'd give me a drink."

"Why, I'd *love* to," Helen said, "but there hasn't been anything in this house to drink since Eric's operation. That was three years ago."

Was he losing his memory, had his gift for concealing painful facts let him forget that he had sold his house, that his children were in trouble, and that his friend had been ill? His eyes slipped from Eric's face to his abdomen, where he saw three pale, sutured scars, two of them at least a foot long. Gone was his navel, and what, Neddy thought, would the roving hand, bed-checking one's gifts at 3 A.M., make of a belly with no navel, no link to birth, this breach in the succession?

"I'm sure you can get a drink at the Biswangers'," Helen said. "They're having an enormous do. You can hear it from here. Listen!"

She raised her head and from across the road, the lawns, the gardens, the woods, the fields, he heard again the brilliant noise of voices over water. "Well, I'll get wet," he said, still feeling that he had no freedom of choice about his means of travel. He dove into the Sachses' cold water and, gasping, close to drowning, made his way from one end of the pool to the other. "Lucinda and I want *terribly* to see you," he said over his shoulder, his face set toward the Biswangers'. "We're sorry it's been so long and we'll call you *very* soon."

He crossed some fields to the Biswangers' and the sounds of revelry there. They would be honored to give him a drink, they would be happy to give him a drink, they would in fact be lucky to give him a drink. The Biswangers invited him and Lucinda for dinner four times a year, six weeks in advance. They were always rebuffed and yet they continued to send out their invitations, unwilling to comprehend the rigid and undemocratic realities of their society. They were the sort of people who discussed the price of things at cocktails, exchanged market tips during dinner, and after dinner told dirty stories to mixed company. They did not belong to Neddy's set—they were not even on Lucinda's Christmas card list. He went toward their pool with feelings of indifference, charity, and some unease, since it seemed to be getting dark and these were the longest days of the year. The party when he joined it was noisy and large. Grace Biswanger was the kind of hostess who asked the optometrist, the veterinarian, the real-estate dealer, and the dentist. No one was swimming and the twilight, reflected on the water of the pool, had a wintry gleam. There was a bar and he started for this. When Grace Biswanger saw him she came toward him, not affectionately as he had every right to expect, but bellicosely.

"Why, this party has everything," she said loudly, "including a gate crasher."

She could not deal him a social blow—there was no question about this and he did not flinch. "As a gate crasher," he asked politely, "do I rate a drink?"

"Suit yourself," she said. "You don't seem to pay much attention to invitations."

She turned her back on him and joined some guests, and he went to the bar and ordered a whiskey. The bartender served him but he served him rudely. His was a world in which the caterer's men kept the social score, and to be rebuffed by a part-time barkeep meant that he had suffered some loss of social esteem. Or perhaps the man was new and uninformed. Then he heard Grace at his back say: "They went for broke overnight—nothing but income—and he showed up drunk one Sunday and asked us to loan him five thousand dollars. . . ." She was always talking about money. It was worse than eating your peas off a knife. He dove into the pool, swam its length and went away.

The next pool on his list, the last but two, belonged to his old mistress, Shirley Adams. If he had suffered any injuries at the Biswangers' they would be cured here. Love—sexual roughhouse in fact—was the supreme elixir, the painkiller, the brightly colored pill that would put the spring back into his step, the joy of life in his heart. They had had an affair last week, last month, last year. He couldn't remember. It was he who had broken it off, his was the upper hand, and he stepped through the gate of the wall that surrounded her pool with nothing so considered as self-confidence. It seemed in a way to be his pool as the lover, particularly the illicit lover, enjoys the possessions of his mistress with an authority unknown to holy matrimony. She was there, her hair the color of brass, but her figure, at the edge of the lighted, cerulean water, excited in him no profound memories. It had been, he thought, a lighthearted affair, although she had wept when he broke it off. She seemed confused to see him and he wondered if she was still wounded. Would she, God forbid, weep again?

"What do you want?" she asked.

"I'm swimming across the county."

"Good Christ. Will you ever grow up?"

"What's the matter?"

"If you've come here for money," she said, "I won't give you another cent."

"You could give me a drink."

"I could but I won't. I'm not alone."

"Well, I'm on my way."

He dove in and swam the pool, but when he tried to haul himself up onto the curb he found that the strength in his arms and shoulders had gone, and he paddled to the ladder and climbed out. Looking over his shoulder he saw, in the lighted bathhouse, a young man. Going out onto the dark lawn he smelled chrysanthemums or marigolds—some stubborn autumnal fragrance—on the night air, strong as gas. Looking overhead he saw that the stars had come out, but why should he seem to see Andromeda, Cepheus, and Cassiopeia? What had become of the constellations of midsummer? He began to cry.

It was probably the first time in his adult life that he had ever cried, certainly the first time in his life that he had ever felt so miserable, cold, tired, and bewildered. He could not understand the rudeness of the caterer's barkeep or the rudeness of a mistress who had come to him on her knees and showered his trousers with tears. He had swum too long, he had been immersed too long, and his nose and his throat were sore from the water. What he needed then was a drink, some company, and some clean dry clothes, and while he could have cut directly across the road to his home he went on to the Gilmartins' pool. Here, for the first time in his life, he did not dive but went down the steps into the icy water and swam a hobbled side stroke that he might have learned as a youth. He staggered with fatigue on his way to the Clydes' and paddled the length of their pool, stopping again and again with his hand on the curb to rest. He climbed up the ladder and wondered if he had the strength to get home. He had done what he wanted, he had swum the county, but he was so stupefied with exhaustion that his triumph seemed vague. Stooped, holding onto the gateposts for support, he turned up the driveway of his own house.

The place was dark. Was it so late that they had all gone to bed? Had Lucinda stayed at the Westerhazys' for supper? Had the girls joined her there or gone someplace else? Hadn't they agreed, as they usually did on Sunday, to regret all their invitations and stay at home? He tried the garage doors to see what cars were in but the doors were locked and rust came off the handles onto his hands. Going toward the house, he saw that the force of the thunderstorm had knocked one of the rain gutters loose. It hung down over the front door like an umbrella rib, but it could be fixed in the morning. The house was locked, and he thought that the stupid cook or the stupid maid must have locked the place up until he remembered that it had been some time since they had employed a maid or a cook. He shouted, pounded on the door, tried to force it with his shoulder, and then, looking in at the windows, saw that the place was empty.

Writing Assignments for "The Swimmer"

I. Brief Papers

    A. 1. What physical changes happen to Ned during his swim home?
        2. Account for the opening scene at the Westerhazy pool: is it a memory? a reality? an hallucination?
        3. What are some of the signs that it may not be midsummer after all?
        4. What are the indications that either Ned's memory is failing or that he has learned to repress unpleasant facts?
        5. Identify some of the "rigid and undemocratic realities" (p. 497) of Ned's society.

    B. Argue for or against one of the assertions below:
        1. Ned Merrill has lost his mind.
        2. Ned's being so coldly and rudely treated at the Biswangers after being so warmly received at the Bunkers makes the entire story implausible.
        3. The story is constructed in such a way as to prevent us from sympathizing with Ned Merrill.

    C. 1. What do you think has happened to the Merrill daughters?
        2. Do you think Ned Merrill gets what he deserves?
        3. Do you think that Ned's relationship with Shirley Adams had been what he calls a "light-hearted affair"? How does your response to this question affect your attitude toward Ned and your interpretation of the story?

II. Longer Papers

    A. Explain why Ned Merrill wants to swim home.

    B. Argue for or against the assertion that "The Swimmer" is a story of total and unrelieved pessimism.

    C. Explain how the ending of the story is prepared for.

    D. Develop, modify, or refute the assertion that the story has a clear moral: too much drinking and too much partying lead to ruin.

    E. For a classmate who is convinced that the story is about swimming—nothing more—write a persuasive essay showing that there are deeper levels of meaning.

    F. Explain why the scenes are presented in the order they are. Could the party scenes at the Bunkers and Biswangers be reversed? Could the scene with Shirley Adams come toward the story's beginning or the scene with the Grahams toward the end?

III. Comparative Papers

    A. Develop one of your brief papers on a single Cheever story into a full-length paper on several Cheever stories.

    B. In "The Country Husband," Clayton Thomas says that what's "really wrong with Shady Hill is that it doesn't have any future" (p. 482). After explaining what Clayton means, argue for or against the accuracy of his assertion.

    C. Defend, modify, or refute the assertion that the world of Cheever's stories is a man's world in which women allow themselves to be subordinate to men.

    D. What are the positive values in Cheever's stories? That is, what personal qualities and attitudes and actions are shown to be the most admirable?

    E. Write a letter to friends of yours about to move into Shady Hill (or Bullet Park) advising them what to do and what not to do in order to get along with their new neighbors.

    F. Close friends of yours are considering moving to Shady Hill (or Bullet Park). Write them a personal letter persuading them not to do it.

    G. Explain what the style and tone of Cheever's short stories indicate about his attitude toward the people and communities he writes about.

    H. Select the Cheever story that, for you, is the most meaningful and most moving, and then explain either (1) why you find the story a powerful one or (2) why you find the story more powerful than another Cheever story.

    I. Each month the local Friends of the Library Association chooses a twentieth-century writer to feature in a book exhibit. For next month it is considering John Cheever, but a member recently wrote the Association charging Cheever with "a cynical view of humanity" and asserting that Cheever's fiction characteristically "holds men and women up to ridicule." On the basis of your having read several representative Cheever short stories, write a letter to the Association that either supports or refutes the charge.

PART TWO

WRITING ASSIGNMENTS FOR SELECTED NOVELS

JANE AUSTEN
Pride and Prejudice

Writing Assignments

I. VOLUME I

A. *Brief Papers*
1. a. Citing evidence from Chapter I, show that Mr. Bennet is a man of "sarcastic humour."
   b. How are Elizabeth and Jane contrasted in Chapter IV?
   c. How are Bingley and Darcy contrasted in Chapter IV?
   d. How are Elizabeth and Mary contrasted in Chapter VI?
   e. Look up the definition of "entail" in the *Oxford English Dictionary* and then write a paragraph explaining how and why the Bennets' estate is entailed.
   f. We are told that Mary rates Mr. Collins much higher than he is rated by the other Bennet daughters. Write a paragraph explaining why Mary gives Collins a higher rating than he receives from Elizabeth and Lydia.

2. Argue for or against one of these assertions:
   a. Elizabeth's walk to Netherfield (Chapter VII) is a reckless and unnecessary violation of good manners and rational conduct.
   b. Elizabeth acts selfishly in rejecting Mr. Collins because, if she accepts him, the Longbourn estate will remain in the family and her mother and sisters will not become homeless when Mr. Bennet dies.

3. a. How does the fact that Mr. Collins is a clergyman affect your response to his character? Would he be equally interesting if he were in some other profession?
   b. Elizabeth, Mr. Bennet, and most readers agree that Collins does not write like a "sensible man." Assume that you are a sensible person in Collins' position; write to Mr. Bennet, introducing yourself and explaining your intention to pay a visit.
   c. How does the fact that Elizabeth prefers reading to playing cards affect your response to her character?

B. *Ironic Dialogue in "Pride and Prejudice"*
Combine the following elements into a coherent paragraph that illustrates the use of *ironic dialogue* in *Pride and Prejudice*.

1. There is much humor in *Pride and Prejudice.*
2. The humor depends on the readers' ability.
3. The readers are able to pick up ironic implications in the dialogue.

4. Nearly everything Mr. Collins says is ironic.
5. He thinks this.
6. His words are a reflection.
7. They reflect his intelligence and good manners.
8. They actually reflect his ignorance and bad taste.

9. Here is an example.
10. Mr. Collins boasts.
11. He is skillful in making compliments.
12. He compliments Lady Catherine.
13. He seems to think that flattery is something to be proud of.

14. He also says this.
15. He calls his compliments "delicate."
16. The compliments are to Lady Catherine.
17. Most readers will have this opinion.
18. The compliments will seem crude and obvious.

19. Readers are likely to discover this.
20. There is a similar irony in the speech of Mary Bennet.
21. Mary is like Collins.
22. She thinks she has a deep moral intelligence.
23. She is poorly educated and pretentious.

24. Here is an example.
25. Mary speaks about Lydia's elopement in this way.
26. "This is a most unfortunate affair; and will probably be much talked of. But we must stem the tide of malice, and pour into the wounded bosoms of each other, the balm of sisterly consolation."

27. Mary strings together so many clichés.
28. Can a sensible reader take Mary seriously?
29. It hardly seems possible.

30. Mr. Bennet is not like Mary and Mr. Collins.
31. Mr. Bennet speaks.
32. Mr. Bennet does not expose his own folly.
33. He does this instead.
34. He reveals the folly of others.

35. Here is an example.
36. Mr. Collins says he feels obligated to flatter Lady Catherine.

37. Mr. Bennet replies, "You judge very properly and it is happy for you that you possess the talent of flattering with delicacy."

38. Most readers will think this.
39. Mr. Bennet is being ironic.
40. Mr. Bennet means the opposite of what he says.

41. Mr. Bennet really thinks this.
42. Mr. Collins judges very improperly.
43. This is usual.
44. Mr. Collins' "talent for flattering" does not make him admirable.
45. It makes him ridiculous.

C. *Longer Papers*
1. After hearing Mr. Collins' letter (Chapter XIII), Elizabeth says, "there is something very pompous in his style." Write a paper that explains and illustrates Elizabeth's meaning.
2. Mr. Collins' proposal to Elizabeth (Chapter XIX) is often cited as an instance of comic irony—ironic in that it creates an impression the opposite of that intended, comic in that it makes a self-important man look ridiculous. Choose three or four passages from the proposal and show how they contribute to the comic irony.
3. With particular reference to the three dance episodes (the Meryton ball, the dance at Sir William Lucas', and the Netherfield ball), explain the changing relationship between Darcy and Elizabeth.
4. Mr. Collins' engagement to Charlotte Lucas is a profound disappointment to both Mrs. Bennet and Elizabeth, but for very different reasons. Explain these reasons and show how they help us understand the problem that marriage poses for women in this novel.
5. Argue for or against one of these assertions:
   a. The first twelve chapters of the novel suggest that Jane, not Elizabeth, is the heroine.
   b. Darcy's attitude toward dancing (as revealed in Chapters III, VI, and XVIII) is consistent with good manners and good judgment.
   c. Many readers share Elizabeth's surprise and disappointment that Charlotte agrees to marry a pompous fool like Collins. Others say that if Elizabeth had a proper understanding of Charlotte's situation and character she would be neither shocked nor disappointed. Which argument do you favor?

II. VOLUME 2

A. *Brief Papers*
1. a. Explain the comic irony in any one of the following passages. That is, show that the narrator does not really expect us to approve the views of the townspeople (1) or the behavior of Lady Catherine (2)

but to see these views and behavior in a comic light. Or show that the speeches of Mrs. Bennet (3) or Mr. Collins (4) do not encourage us to take their opinions seriously but rather to see the folly of the speaker.

(1) "They saw him [Wickham] often, and to his other recommendations was now added that of general unreserve. The whole of what Elizabeth has already heard, his claims on Mr. Darcy, and all that he had suffered from him, was now openly acknowledged and publicly canvassed; and everybody was pleased to think how much they had always disliked Mr. Darcy before they had known anything of the matter" (Chapter I).

(2) "Whenever any of the cottagers were disposed to be quarrelsome, discontented or too poor, she [Lady Catherine] sallied forth into the village to settle their differences, silence their complaints, and scold them into harmony and plenty" (Chapter VIII).

(3) "The Lucases are very artful people indeed, sister. They are all for what they can get. I am sorry to say it of them, but so it is. It makes me very nervous and poorly. . . . However, your coming just at this time is the greatest of comforts, and I am very glad to hear what you tell us, of long sleeves" (Chapter II).

(4) "Lady Catherine is far from requiring the elegance of dress in us, which becomes herself and her daughter. I would advise you merely to put on whatever of your clothes is superior to the rest, there is no occasion for any thing more. Lady Catherine will not think any the worse of you for being simply dressed. She likes to have the distinction of rank preserved" (Chapter VI).

  b. How do you account for the fact that Elizabeth, after having met Miss de Brough, can still believe that Darcy will marry her?

  c. Explain the function of Colonel Fitzwilliam in the Hunsford episode. How does he contribute to our perception of Darcy and Elizabeth?

2. Argue for or against one of these assertions:
  a. In her natural inclinations and temperament, Elizabeth is more like Lydia than any of her other sisters.
  b. Elizabeth is justified in trying to prevent Lydia's vacation in Brighton.

3. a. In Chapter VIII, Darcy tells Elizabeth that he cannot readily mix with strangers. "I certainly have not the talent which some people possess of conversing easily with those I have never seen before. I cannot catch their tone of conversation, or appear interested in their concerns, as I often see done." How does this reply affect your view of Darcy?

      b. One sign of Elizabeth's intelligence and good sense is her ability to have a good time in limited circumstances, as in her visit to Hunsford. How does this quality in Elizabeth affect your response to her?

B. *Ironic Perspective in "Pride and Prejudice"*
Combine the following elements into a coherent paragraph on *ironic perspective* in *Pride and Prejudice.*

  1. *Pride and Prejudice* has a comic perspective.
  2. This perspective is consistently developed through irony.

  3. There is a central irony in the plot.
  4. The irony is located in two key discoveries.
  5. Elizabeth makes the discoveries.
  6. The first comes at midpoint in the novel.
  7. Darcy proposes marriage.
  8. Darcy despised Elizabeth.
  9. This is what Elizabeth thought.

 10. The second discovery comes at the end of the novel.
 11. Elizabeth realizes this.
 12. She loves Darcy.
 13. This is her better understanding.
 14. Darcy is a man she thought she despised.

 15. The narrator develops this irony.
 16. One way to develop irony is through dialogue.

 17. Elizabeth does not know Darcy's real feelings.
 18. Darcy tries to conceal his real feelings.
 19. This is because of his pride.
 20. Much of their dialogue is ironic.

 21. Darcy asks Elizabeth to dance with him.
 22. They are at the Lucas' party.
 23. Elizabeth refuses.
 24. She says, "Mr. Darcy is all politeness."

 25. Elizabeth's remark is ironic.
 26. It reminds us first of all of the Meryton ball.
 27. Darcy was rude to Elizabeth.
 28. He refused to dance with her.

 29. Elizabeth's remark refers to the present occasion.
 30. Elizabeth's remark is ironic.

31. She does not mean to compliment Darcy's manners.
32. She thinks this.
33. Darcy does not really want to dance with her.
34. He is merely being polite.

35. The reader knows this.
36. Darcy wants to dance with Elizabeth.
37. His "grim propriety" is partly due to his reserve.
38. It is partly due to his pride.

39. This ironic dialogue is amusing.
40. It is suspenseful.
41. It causes us to wonder.
42. Will this couple ever come to a better understanding?

C. *Longer Papers*
   1. After the arrival of Miss Bingley's letter from London, it is generally agreed that the affair with Jane and Bingley is over. How do Jane and Elizabeth differ in explaining the cause of Bingley's departure and how do we know, or strongly suspect, that Elizabeth's explanation is correct?
   2. Going beyond Elizabeth's stated reasons, explain why she deplores Charlotte's marriage to Collins, but at the same time approves Wickham's plan to marry Miss King.
   3. With particular reference to the Hunsford episode, show that Sir William Lucas is a snob developed along the same lines as Mr. Collins.
   4. Some say that the Hunsford episode shows that, all things considered, Charlotte has a satisfactory marriage and that Elizabeth was wrong to condemn her; others say that Charlotte's situation at Hunsford is oppressive and humiliating, just as bad as Elizabeth had foreseen. Write an argument supporting one of these positions.
   5. Argue for or against one of these assertions:
      a. Darcy is justified in trying to prevent Bingley from marrying Jane.
      b. The disclosure of Wickham's bad conduct surprises the reader as much as it surprises Elizabeth.

III. VOLUME 3

A. *Brief Papers*
   1. a. Explain how the grounds at Pemberly affect Elizabeth's view of Darcy's character and not simply her appreciation of his wealth.
      b. Why is Mrs. Reynolds especially important in changing Elizabeth's view of Darcy?
      c. Explain the comic irony in Mr. Collins' letter of condolence to Mr. Bennet (Chapter VI).

2. Argue for or against one of these assertions:
   a. Wickham's affair with Lydia is improbable and unexpected.
   b. Elizabeth is wrong to see the marriage of Jane and Bingley as the "happiest, wisest, and most reasonable end."

3. At first Darcy attempts to persuade Lydia to leave Wickham and return to her family. Only when she refuses does he arrange a marriage. Do you agree that, for Lydia, returning home would be a better solution than getting married? Explain.

B. *The Comic Point of View in "Pride and Prejudice"*
Combine the following elements into a coherent paragraph that explains the narrative's *comic point of view* in *Pride and Prejudice.*

1. *Pride and Prejudice* has a point of view.
2. The point of view is comic.
3. The point of view dwells on the folly of some characters.
4. It dwells on the wit of other characters.
5. It also reveals a rational and moral order.
6. The order is in society.
7. The order makes this possible.
8. Sensible characters can live happy and responsible lives.
9. Sensible characters may even get married.
10. They can still live happy and responsible lives.

11. The comic point of view encourages this.
12. We can see the cause of unhappiness.
13. It is mostly caused by errors.
14. These errors can be avoided.
15. Sensible people can avoid them.
16. The unhappiness is not caused by fate.
17. It is not caused by some inherent human perversity.

18. Charlotte Lucas makes a marriage.
19. It is merely a prudent marriage.
20. She has no feeling for her husband.
21. She has no respect for her husband.
22. This is likely.
23. She will be unhappy.
24. She may even deserve to be unhappy.

25. Lydia Bennet sacrifices prudence.
26. She even behaves immorally.
27. She does this for a passionate attachment.

28. This is likely.
29. She will make an unfortunate marriage.
30. She deserves an unfortunate marriage.

31. The comic view suggests this.
32. Darcy and Elizabeth are likely to have a fortunate marriage.
33. They are likely to have a "happy ending."
34. They overcame their pride and prejudice.
35. They struck a balance between prudence and passion.

36. In this novel there is a comic view.
37. It shows us a society.
38. The society may be foolish, hypocritical, and materialistic.
39. The society offers some people a fair chance.
40. They have a chance at "rational happiness" providing they do this.
41. They improve their dispositions.
42. Their desires are moderated.
43. Their faults are corrected.

C. *Longer Papers*

1. In the first chapter of the novel, Mr. Bennet says that he prefers Elizabeth to his other daughters because she has "something more of quickness than her sisters." Later, in Chapter VI, Volume I, the narrator says that Elizabeth has "more quickness and observation" than Jane, and finally, near the end of the novel, Darcy says that the origin of his love for Elizabeth was "the liveliness of your mind." It would seem, then, that Elizabeth's success as a fictive character will depend in great part on the reader's appreciation of her "quickness of observation." Go through the novel, writing down what you feel to be the best and most representative examples of Elizabeth's "quickness." Then write a paper showing how these passages reveal Elizabeth's character or what she calls "my philosophy."

2. Even after Lydia's marriage has been arranged, Elizabeth foresees that her sister will find "neither rational happiness nor worldly prosperity" (Chapter VII, Volume III). Presumably, "rational happiness" is what Elizabeth eventually achieves in her marriage and, according to some critics, it is what the novel mainly "teaches." Choose one of the following to write about.

   a. Write an extended definition of "rational happiness," showing who in the novel have achieved this happiness and who have not, and how it is attained.

   b. Some say that in *Pride and Prejudice* "rational happiness" in marriage is not happiness at all for a woman because it requires that she accept a subordinate and often demeaning role in a male-dominated society. From this point of view the novel does not

teach "rational happiness" but rather it satirizes a society that
equates reason with conformity. Argue for or against this assertion.

3. Show that in making what promises to be a happy marriage, Elizabeth
has achieved a good balance between the two extremes of thought
and feeling that are embodied in Charlotte on the one hand and Lydia
on the other.

4. The unity of a novel often depends on our recognition of correspond-
ences between certain events. Show how the following relationships
reflect on one another and help us better understand the character of
Wickham, the role of women, and Elizabeth's growing understanding
of herself and her situation.
   a. Wickham and Georgiana Darcy
   b. Wickham and Mary King
   c. Wickham and Lydia Bennet
   Note: This is the order in which these relationships occur in the life
   of Wickham, not the order in which they are disclosed in the narra-
   tion. In developing your paper, you may wish to consider how this
   inversion of events affects our response.

5. Mr. Collins writes three important letters in the novel—in Chapter XIII,
Volume I; Chapter VI, Volume III; and Chapter XVI, Volume III. Write
a paper showing how these letters not only characterize Mr. Collins
but also satirize the society represented in the novel.

6. Like all realistic novelists, Jane Austen is concerned with making her
characters' conduct seem probable, and so at a key point in the novel
the narrator pauses, as it were, to explain Elizabeth's surprising
"change of sentiment" about Darcy:

> If gratitude and esteem are good foundations of affection, Eliza-
> beth's change of sentiment will be neither improbable nor
> faulty. But if otherwise, if the regard springing from such sources
> is unreasonable and unnatural, in comparison of what is so often
> described as arising on a first interview with its object, and even
> before two words have been exchanged, nothing can be said in
> her defence, except that she had given somewhat of a trial to
> the latter method, in her partiality for Wickham, and that its
> ill-success might perhaps authorize her to seek the other less
> interesting mode of attachment. (Chapter IV, Volume III)

It is fairly common for readers, after finishing only the first third of the
novel, to say that they favor Wickham and hope that Elizabeth will
fall in love with him. Such readers seem to believe that a spontaneous
mutual attraction, like that between Wickham and Elizabeth, is the
most "interesting mode of attachment." Since the narrative is to
develop in another direction, it is the author's problem, as she ironically implies in the above passage, to reverse the readers' romantic

expectations and show that Elizabeth's story is just as interesting, even more interesting, than those that begin with "love at first sight." Do you think the author is successful in this respect? Write a paper explaining why you think *Pride and Prejudice* is more or less interesting than stories based on a more romantic and passionate "mode of attachment."

KATE CHOPIN

The Awakening

Writing Assignments

I. CHAPTERS I TO XVI

A. *Brief Papers*
  1. a. Explain what the opening chapter of *The Awakening* tells us about the relationship between Mr. and Mrs. Pontellier.
     b. Analyze the following passage in order to characterize its tone: "The mother-women seemed to prevail that summer at Grand Isle. It was easy to know them, fluttering about with extended, protecting wings when any harm, real or imaginary, threatened their precious brood. They were women who idolized their children, worshipped their husbands, and esteemed it a holy privilege to efface themselves as individuals and grow wings as ministering angels" (Chapter IV).
     c. Explain why Madame Ratignolle persists in making her pregnancy the subject of conversation (Chapter IV).
     d. Explain what the narrator means by "the dual life—that outward existence which conforms, the inward life which questions" (Chapter VII).
     e. Explain the implications of Robert's answering "Of course not" to Mariequita's asking him if the two lovers are married (Chapter XII).

  2. Argue for or against one of the following assertions:
     a. Edna has never loved her husband.
     b. Madame Ratignolle is right in telling Robert that Edna "is not one of us; she is not like us" (Chapter VIII).
     c. Chopin depicts Mademoiselle Reisz not as a true artist but as a phony and fraud.
     d. In the first sixteen chapters of the novel, the narrator openly and completely sympathizes with Edna.

  3. a. Do you sympathize more with Mr. Pontellier or Mrs. Pontellier during their quarrel in Chapter III? How does your response affect the way you interpret the novel?
     b. Do you agree with the ladies who declare that Mr. Pontellier is "the best husband in the world" (Chapter III)? How does your response affect the way you interpret the novel?

c. How do you react to Madame Ratignolle's spell of faintness (Chapter V)? How does your reaction affect your attitude toward Madame Ratignolle and toward Edna?

d. Complete one of the following sentences by free writing for 10 minutes:
   - "I think Edna changes in positive ways during her summer at Grand Isle because . . ."
   - "I think Edna changes in negative ways during her summer at Grand Isle because . . ."

Since the goal of free writing is to generate ideas quickly, do not worry about spelling, punctuation, grammar, or sentence structure. Just keep writing down whatever comes into your head about Edna's change. Don't stop writing for any reason. If you can't think of anything to say, just write "I can't think of anything to say" until something comes to mind. After 10 minutes, look back over your free writing and select from it the most promising idea for a full-length paper on the first sixteen chapters of *The Awakening*. Then, in a brief paragraph, explain why the idea is a promising one.

B. *Images of Confinement in the Opening Chapter of "The Awakening"*

Combine the sentences below into a short essay that defines *images of confinement* and briefly illustrates their function in the first chapter of the novel. Consider using your essay as the basis for a full-length paper on freedom and restriction in *The Awakening*.

1. Kate Chopin has a novel.
2. It is called *The Awakening*.
3. *The Awakening* explores questions about personal freedom.
4. Therefore, this is appropriate.
5. *The Awakening* begins with an image of freedom's opposite.
6. An image is a concrete representation.
7. Freedom's opposite is confinement.
8. Freedom's opposite is restriction.

9. "A green and yellow parrot, which hung in a cage outside the door, kept repeating over and over: 'Allez vous-en! Allez vous-en! Sapristi! That's all right!' "

10. Chopin's image of a caged parrot communicates more than a sense of confinement.

11. The bird in the cage repeats the same words over and over.
12. Therefore, Chopin's image implies this.
13. There is a connection between confinement and repetition.

14. The image as a whole seems to suggest this.
15. Repetition is in itself a kind of prison.
16. Sameness in itself is a kind of prison.

17. There is a relationship between confinement and repetition.
18. This relationship is reinforced by the second major image in the novel.
19. The second major image in the novel is a description of a mocking-bird.
20. The mocking-bird is also in a cage.
21. The mocking-bird whistles a tune.
22. The mocking-bird whistles "with maddening persistence."

23. The opening chapter of the novel begins with images of restriction.
24. The opening chapter of the novel ends with an image of freedom.
25. At least for Mr. Pontellier it ends with an image of freedom.

26. This happens at the end of the chapter.
27. Mr. Pontellier is on his way to Klein's Hotel.
28. He is going to play a game of billiards.
29. He is asked by his wife if he will be back for dinner.

30. Mr. Pontellier indicates that he may be back for dinner.
31. Mr. Pontellier indicates that he may not be back for dinner.
32. It all depends on who is at the hotel.
33. It all depends on the size of the billiards game.

34. This is obvious.
35. Mr. Pontellier is free to do as he pleases.

36. The Pontellier children want to follow their father.
37. The Pontellier children are not free to do so.

38. This seems to be the case.
39. Mrs. Pontellier is not free to follow him either.
40. Mrs. Pontellier is expected to look after the children.
41. Mrs. Pontellier is expected to prepare dinner.

C. *Longer Papers*
   1. Develop into a full-length paper the idea you generated in your free writing (III.D. above).
   2. Even before Edna returns to New Orleans from Grand Isle, she realizes that "she herself—her present self—was in some way different from the other self" (Chapter XIV). Identify the two selves of Edna and explain in detail the differences between them.

3. Adèle Ratignolle is a foil, a minor character who functions at least in part to clarify and emphasize—through contrast—the qualities and values of a more important character. Focusing on the first sixteen chapters of *The Awakening*, contrast Adèle Ratignolle with Edna Pontellier in order to define the central differences between the two women.

4. Explain in what ways the beginning of *The Awakening* is like *The Sleeping Beauty* and/or any other fairy tale.

II. CHAPTERS XVII TO XXVI

A. *Brief Papers*

1. a. Explain why Edna feels "depressed" by her visit to the Ratignolles (Chapter XVIII).

   b. Analyze the following passage in the context of *The Awakening* in order to explain whether it is the narrator, Edna, or both who perceive of Madame Ratignolle's existence as "colorless":

   > She was moved by a kind of commiseration for Madame Ratignolle,—a pity for that colorless existence which never uplifted its possessor beyond the region of blind contentment, in which no moment of anguish ever visited her soul, in which she would never have the taste of life's delirium (Chapter XVIII).

   c. Why does Dr. Mandelet "hope to heaven it isn't Alcée Arobin" (Chapter XXIII)?

   d. Compare and contrast Robert Lebrun with Alcée Arobin in order to identify what you take to be the central difference between them.

2. Argue for or against one of the following assertions:

   a. Mr. Pontellier is correct in thinking that his wife is "growing a little unbalanced mentally" (Chapter XIX).

   b. Dr. Mandelet deserves "his reputation for wisdom" (Chapter XXII).

   c. Robert loves Edna.

   d. Edna loves Robert.

3. a. Do you sympathize more with Mr. or Mrs. Pontellier during their quarrel about Edna's not keeping visiting hours (Chapter XVII)? How does your response affect your interpretation of the changes that are taking place within Edna?

   b. How do you respond to the advice that Edna's father, the colonel, gives to Edna's husband: "You are too lenient, too lenient by far,

Léonce. . . . Authority, coercion are what is needed. Put your foot down good and hard; the only way to manage a wife. Take my word for it." How does your response affect your interpretation of the novel?

c. How do you respond to "the animalism that stirred impatiently within" Edna (Chapter XXVI)? Should the animalism be encouraged? Or checked? How does your response affect your interpretation of the changes that are taking place within Edna?

d. How do you respond to Edna's answering Mademoiselle Reisz's question, "Why do you love him when you ought not to?" with these words: "Why? Because his hair is brown and grows away from his temples; because he opens and shuts his eyes, and his nose is a little out of drawing; because he has two lips and a square chin, and a little finger which he can't straighten from having played baseball too energetically in his youth. Because—" (Chapter XXVI). How does your response affect your attitude toward the relationship between Edna and Robert?

B. *The Characterization of Madame Ratignolle in "The Awakening"*

Read and analyze three or four of the passages below (or passages you have chosen yourself) in order to write a brief essay (about 250 words) in which you argue *either* (1) that Madame Ratignolle is characterized in *The Awakening* as an admirable and exemplary human being *or* (2) that Madame Ratignolle is characterized in *The Awakening* as a less than admirable and far from exemplary human being. Consider using your essay as the basis for a full-length paper on *The Awakening* in which you argue for or against the assertion that "The characterization of Madame Ratignolle in *The Awakening* has the effect of making Edna Pontellier more admirable and more sympathetic."

• Adèle Ratignolle "was the embodiment of every womanly charm and grace. If her husband did not adore her, he was a brute, deserving of death by slow torture" (Chapter IV).

• "About every two years she had a baby. At that time she had three babies, and was beginning to think of a fourth one. She was always talking about her 'condition.' Her 'condition' was in no way apparent, and no one would have known a thing about it but for her persistence in making it the subject of conversation" (Chapter IV).

• "Mrs. Pontellier liked to sit and gaze at her fair companion as she might look upon a faultless Madonna" (Chapter V).

• "Madame Ratignolle folded her sewing, placing thimble, scissors and thread all neatly together in the roll, which she pinned securely. She complained of faintness. Mrs. Pontellier flew for the cologne water and a fan. She bathed Madame Ratignolle's face with cologne, while Robert plied the fan with unnecessary vigor.

"The spell was soon over, and Mrs. Pontellier could not help wondering if there were not a little imagination responsible for its origin, for the rose tint had never faded from her friend's face" (Chapter V).

- "That summer at Grand Isle she began to loosen a little the mantle of reserve that had always enveloped her. There may have been—there must have been—influences, both subtle and apparent, working in their several ways to induce her to do this; but the most obvious was the influence of Adèle Ratignolle. The excessive physical charm of the Creole had first attracted her, for Edna had a sensuous susceptibility to beauty. Then the candor of the woman's whole existence, which every one might read, and which formed so striking a contrast to her own habitual reserve—this might have furnished a link. Who can tell what metals the gods use in forging the subtle bond which we call sympathy, which we might as well call love" (Chapter VII).
- Madame Ratignolle "played very well, keeping excellent waltz time and infusing an expression into the strains which was indeed inspiring. She was keeping up her music on account of the children, she said; because she and her husband both considered it a means of brightening the home and making it attractive" (Chapter IX).
- "Madame Ratignolle hoped that Robert would exercise extreme caution in dealing with the Mexicans, who, she considered, were a treacherous people, unscrupulous and revengeful. She trusted she did them no injustice in thus condemning them as a race. She had known personally but one Mexican, who made and sold excellent tamales, and whom she would have trusted implicitly, so soft-spoken was he. One day he was arrested for stabbing his wife. She never knew whether he had been hanged or not" (Chapter XV).
- Monsieur Ratignolle "spoke with an animation and earnestness that gave an exaggerated importance to every syllable he uttered. His wife was keenly interested in everything he said, laying down her fork the better to listen, chiming in, taking the words out of his mouth" (Chapter XVIII).
- "Monsieur and Madame Ratignolle made much of the Colonel, installing him as the guest of honor, and engaging him at once to dine with them the following Sunday, or any day which he might select. Madame coquetted with him in the most captivating and naive manner, with eyes, gestures, and a profusion of compliments, till the Colonel's old head felt thirty years younger on his padded shoulders. Edna marveled, not comprehending. She herself was almost devoid of coquetry" (Chapter XXIII).
- "Before leaving Madame Ratignolle said: 'In some way you seem to me like a child, Edna. You seem to act without a certain amount of reflection which is necessary in this life. That is the reason I want to say you mustn't mind if I advise you to be a little careful while you are living here alone. Why don't you have some one come and stay with you?' " (Chapter XXXIII).

- Edna "was still stunned and speechless with emotion when later she leaned over her friend to kiss her and softly say good-by. Adèle, pressing her cheek, whispered in an exhausted voice: 'Think of the children, Edna. Oh think of the children! Remember them!' " (Chapter XXXVII).

C. Longer Papers
1. Argue for or against the assertion that in the second third of *The Awakening* Edna becomes more and more selfish, immature, and irresponsible and therefore less admirable and even less likable.
2. Mademoiselle Reisz tells Edna that in order to succeed, "the artist must possess the courageous soul . . ., the brave soul. The soul that dares and defies" (Chapter XXI). Explain the connection between Mademoiselle Reisz's words and any character in *The Awakening*.
3. Edna asks Mademoiselle Reisz, "Do you suppose a woman knows why she loves? Does she select?" (Chapter XXVI). Compare this passage with the Emily Dickinson poem "The Soul Selects Her Own Society" (p. 751 of this book) in order to explain whether the position in the Dickinson poem is like, or unlike, Edna's position.

III. CHAPTER XXVII TO THE END

A. Brief Papers
1. a. Explain whether Edna is in any way described by Mademoiselle Reisz's statement "The bird that would soar above the level plain of tradition and prejudice must have strong wings. It is a sad spectacle to see the weaklings bruised, exhausted, fluttering back to earth" (Chapter XXVII).
   b. Explain why Edna moves to the "pigeon-house."
   c. Analyze the following passage in order to explain whether its tone is ironic, unironic, or a blend of the two: "The pigeon-house pleased her. It at once assumed the intimate character of a home, while she herself invested it with a charm which it reflected like a warm glow. There was with her a feeling of having descended in the social scale, with a corresponding sense of having risen in the spiritual. Every step which she took toward relieving herself from obligations added to her strength and expansion as an individual. She began to look with her own eyes; to see and to apprehend the deeper undercurrents of life. No longer was she content to 'feed upon opinion' when her soul had invited her" (Chapter XXXII).
   d. Explain the meaning of the sentence "she [Edna] had abandoned herself to Fate, and awaited the consequences with indifference" (Chapter XXXV).
   e. Interpret Robert's note to Edna: "I love you. Good-by—because I love you" (Chapter XXXVIII).

2. Argue for or against one of the following assertions:
   a. Edna and Alcée Arobin have had sexual intercourse.
   b. Edna's final act is an act of despair.
   c. The reviewer in 1899 who wrote that the novel illustrates "what an ugly, cruel, loathsome monster Passion can be" is absolutely correct.
   d. The more recent reader who wrote that "Quite frankly, the book is about sex" has utterly missed the point of the novel.

3. a. Does Léonce Pontellier's reaction to Edna's plan to move into the "pigeon-house" (Chapter XXXII) make you think more or less of him? How does your answer affect your interpretation of the conclusion of the novel?
   b. Madame Ratignolle tells Edna, "In some way you seem to me like a child . . ." (Chapter XXXIII). Do you think Edna is either childish or childlike? How does your response affect your interpretation of the conclusion of the novel?
   c. Does Edna's going to the aid of Madame Ratignolle (Chapters XXXVI to XXXVII) make you think more or less of her? How does your response affect your interpretation of the conclusion of the novel?
   d. Do you personally believe that it is "better to wake up after all, even to suffer, rather than to remain a dupe to illusions all one's life" (Chapter XXXVIII)? How does your answer affect your interpretation of the conclusion of the novel?

B. *Longer Papers*
   1. Develop one of your paragraphs on *The Awakening* into a full-length paper.
   2. To what extent, if any, is *The Awakening* written in such a way as to encourage its readers to sympathize and even identify with Edna?
   3. Explain how the other women in *The Awakening* help shape your reaction to Edna.
   4. One of the early reviewers of *The Awakening* questioned the appropriateness of the novel's title because Edna "can hardly be said to be fully awake." Her "awakening seems to have been confined entirely to the senses, while reason, judgment, and all the higher faculties and perceptions, whose office it is to weigh and criticise impulse and govern conduct, fell into slumber deep. . . ." Either develop or refute the reviewer's position.
   5. One reader has characterized *The Awakening* as "a novel exploring the consequences of personal—particularly sexual—freedom for the married woman." If you agree, explain what conclusions the novel reaches about the consequences of such freedom.
   6. Explain the purpose and significance of water in *The Awakening*.

7. Analyze the last paragraph of *The Awakening* in detail in order to argue for or against the assertion that Edna's suicide is a victory and a triumph for her.

8. What does *The Awakening* have to say about self-knowledge and self-deceit?

9. One of your former high school English teachers has been asked to appear before the Board of Education to answer questions about having taught *The Awakening* in senior English last term. One Board member, convinced that *The Awakening* is an immoral and dangerous book, is expected to make a motion that will prohibit its ever being taught again in the school district. But other members of the Board are inviting responses from the public, especially from anyone who has read the novel. Write the Board of Education a formal letter that takes a clear stand: either defend or condemn teaching *The Awakening* in a high school senior English course.

JAMES JOYCE

A Portrait of the Artist as a Young Man

Writing Assignments

I. CHAPTERS 1 AND 2

A. *Brief Papers*
1. a. Contrast Mrs. Dedalus and Dante (Mrs. Riordan).
   b. Charles Stewart Parnell was the leader of the Irish nationalist movement until the exposure of his long adulterous affair with Kitty O'Shea brought about his political defeat in 1890, partly because the Catholic bishops turned against him. Contrast the way Dante (Mrs. Riordan) and Mr. Dedalus see this event.
   c. Show that Eileen Vance is associated in Stephen's mind with the Virgin Mary.
   d. Compare Stephen's affair with Eileen in Chapter I to his affair with Emma in Chapter II.
   e. George Gordon, Lord Byron (1788–1824), was an English romantic poet who was much criticized for his immoral sexual conduct and for his attacks on orthodox Christianity. The poet Robert Southey said that Byron belonged to the "Satanic school" of poets. Compare Stephen's defense of Byron in Chapter II with his father's defense of Parnell in Chapter I.
   f. Contrast Stephen's fantasy of meeting Mercedes in the moonlit garden and his actual behavior with Emma on the train.
   g. Stephen's poem "To E_____C_____" is based on his tram ride with Emma. Explain the difference between the actual account and the poetic version.

2. Argue for or against one of these assertions:
   a. Mr. Casey is represented in an amusing and favorable way.
   b. Stephen is justified in being ashamed of his father's behavior in Cork.
   c. Father Dolan is meant to be a typical Catholic educator.
   d. Eileen and Emma are as responsible as the prostitute for drawing Stephen into sin.
   e. Stephen's surrender to the prostitute is an ugly and debasing experience.

3. a. Why do you think Stephen is supposed to apologize when his mother says, "O, Stephen will apologize"? What did Stephen do?

b. What is your response to the poem about eagles? Where do the eagles come from? Who orders them about? Why this particular punishment?

c. Do you agree with Dante that Parnell, or any political leader, should be dismissed from office for adultery or similar sexual misdeeds?

B. *Allusions in "A Portrait of the Artist as a Young Man"*
Combine the following elements into a coherent paper about *allusions* in *A Portrait of the Artist as a Young Man.*

1. Joyce enlarges our sense of his hero's experience.
2. Joyce makes many allusions or references to other poets and poetic works.

3. Stephen feels this.
4. Stephen's soul is drifting "like the barren shell of the moon" (Chapter II).
5. Stephen thinks of Shelley's poem about the pale moon.
6. The pale moon is "wandering companionless" through the sky.
7. The moon is an allusion.
8. The allusion reinforces Stephen's romantic sense of loneliness and exile.

9. Readers will perhaps remember this.
10. Readers are familiar with Shelley's life and work.
11. Shelley's greatest hero was Prometheus.
12. Prometheus was the Titan.
13. Prometheus defied Zeus.
14. Prometheus gave fire to humanity.

15. Prometheus refused to submit to authority based only on power.
16. Prometheus became a hero of certain romantic poets.
17. Prometheus is like Satan.

18. Some readers might see an indirect allusion to Prometheus.
19. Stephen is told this.
20. He must apologize.
21. If not, eagles will come and "pull out his eyes."
22. This punishment is similar to the one Zeus inflicted on Prometheus.

23. Stephen's religious rebellion is also expressed in allusions to Byron.
24. Byron is a nineteenth-century English romantic poet.
25. Byron is like Shelley.
26. Byron and Shelley are identified with the "Satanic school."

27. Stephen is beaten by the pious bully.
28. The bully is Heron.
29. Stephen defends his belief that Byron is the "greatest poet" (Chapter II).

30. This is not surprising.
31. Stephen is hostile to Dante.
32. Dante is a thirteenth-century poet.
33. Dante is best known for his justification of Hell.
34. Dante justifies Hell in *The Divine Comedy.*
35. Dante is best known for this belief.
36. Redemption and poetic inspiration come through chaste love.

37. Stephen is like the hero in Dante's poem in this way.
38. Stephen makes a symbolic journey through Hell.
39. Stephen is unlike the hero in Dante's poem.
40. Stephen does not accept the preacher's words.
41. Stephen rejects the church and defies damnation.

42. Stephen also makes fun of Dante's ideal of chaste love.
43. Stephen calls it a "spiritual-heroic refrigerating apparatus."

44. Stephen seeks inspiration in a more physical and erotic form of love.
45. This form of love is perhaps embodied in the birdgirl.
46. The birdgirl is an obvious contrast to the Christian ideal of love.
47. The Christian ideal is expressed in Dante's poem.

48. Readers recognize these allusions to Dante and other poets.
49. Readers will have a better understanding of Stephen's development as a poet.

C. *Longer Papers*
1. Show that in these chapters Stephen is represented as a child beset by fear, violence, and cruelty.
2. Show that in these chapters Stephen is especially sensitive to the ugliness of his physical environment.
3. Stephen tries, as he says, "to build a breakwater of order and elegance against the sordid tide of life without him." Show how Stephen tries to transform real ugliness into imaginary beauty and how he seeks to transform his own weak role into an heroic role.
4. For Stephen, The Tower of Ivory is a recurrent epithet or name for the Virgin Mary, but in this context, a novel about an artist, the name is likely also to suggest the ivory tower where certain types of artists and thinkers are said to dwell. What kind of artist lives in an ivory tower? Is there any similarity between living in an ivory tower and being devoted to the Virgin Mary? On the basis of these two chapters, do

you think Stephen is likely to become the kind of artist who will live in an ivory tower?

5. Some say that in these chapters Catholic education is represented as cruel and repressive. Others say that although some injustice does occur, the school is represented in a neutral if not a favorable way. Which view do you favor?

6. In reading fiction, an important problem is to discover how the narrator thinks and feels about the central character. Some say that in this novel the narrator's attitude toward Stephen is both sympathetic and mocking, but that the mocking or ironic tone is dominant. Others say that while the narrator does see Stephen as naive and priggish, the portrait is essentially approving and sympathetic. Using evidence from the first two chapters, argue for or against the assertion that the narrator is essentially sympathetic to Stephen.

7. In his encounter with Father Dolan, Stephen trembles with fear, suffers great physical pain, and sheds tears of shame. In his encounter with the prostitute, Stephen trembles with desire, swoons with pleasure, and weeps tears of joy. Argue for or against the assertion that in both cases Stephen should be seen as the helpless, and therefore innocent, victim of natural emotions.

II. CHAPTERS 3 AND 4

A. Brief Papers

1. a. Explain the role of the Virgin Mary in moving Stephen to repent and confess his sins.

    b. Show how, during his retreat, Stephen associates Emma with the Virgin Mary.

    c. Explain why Stephen decides not to become a priest.

    d. For the first time, Stephen identifies himself with Dedalus, or Daedalus, as it is usually spelled. Daedalus was a mythic Greek inventor and artist who, along with his son, Icarus, was imprisoned on the island of Crete by King Minos. Father and son escaped by flying away on wings which Daedalus made from feathers and beeswax. Daedalus warned his son not to fly too high or the heat of the sun would melt the wax in the wings. Icarus ignored the warning and fell to his death in the sea. Choose one of the following:
       • Show that during his sea walk, Stephen identifies with both Daedalus and Icarus, seeing them as a composite figure.
       • Show that the swimmers, the friends of Stephen, provide a counterpoint or warning to Stephen's dream of flight.

    e. Show that in this chapter Stephen rejects the Virgin Mary and takes the birdgirl as the object of his reverence and the source of his inspiration.

    f. Show that Stephen's vision of the birdgirl has its origin, in part, in his memory of Eileen and Emma.

2. Argue for or against one of these assertions:
   a. The Church is justified in condemning Stephen's relationship with whores.
   b. Stephen should not be made to feel guilty because he looks at "dirty" pictures, writes pornographic letters, and indulges in lustful dreams about Emma.
   c. Stephen sees the "man with the hat" as a type of artist and, in part, as an image of himself.
   d. The "hawklike man" in Stephen's vision is a representation of the anti-Christ, or Satan.

3. a. Which of the preacher's descriptions of suffering in Hell do you find the most effective? Explain.
   b. Some say that readers of this chapter are likely to be so repulsed by the God who designed Hell that they will side with Lucifer who said, "I will not serve." Is this your response? Explain.
   c. How do you respond to Stephen's belief that the way to wisdom is the way of sin and sensuality?
   d. What kind of writing would you expect from Stephen if the birdgirl continued to be the source of his inspiration?

B. *Symbol and Myth in "A Portrait of the Artist as a Young Man"*
   Combine the following elements into a coherent paper about *symbol and myth* in A Portrait of the Artist as a Young Man.

   1. There are repeated references to birds and the flight of birds.
   2. Joyce develops a symbolic and mythic structure.
   3. The structure enlarges the meaning of Stephen's story.

   4. This happens in the early part of the novel.
   5. Stephen feels helpless.
   6. Stephen sees himself as a victim of birds.
   7. Stephen is afraid of the eagles.
   8. The eagles "will pull out his eyes."
   9. Stephen is afraid of his cruel classmate.
   10. The classmate's name is Heron.

   11. Later, Stephen associates birds with his own desire.
   12. Stephen desires to be birdlike.
   13. Stephen desires to rise above his dull and sordid world.
   14. Stephen desires to rise on the wings of artistic inspiration and sexual ecstacy.

   15. These desires are embodied in the beautiful birdgirl.
   16. The birdgirl appears to Stephen.

17. The birdgirl is "a wild angel."
18. The birdgirl beckons him to "the gates of . . . error and glory."

19. Stephen identifies with Daedalus.
20. The symbolism of flight is given a mythic form.

21. Daedalus was a legendary Greek artist.
22. Daedalus' most famous achievement was to make wings of wax and feathers.
23. The wings enabled Daedalus and his son to escape from Crete.
24. Daedalus' son was Icarus.
25. Crete was their island prison.

26. Stephen wants to identify with Daedalus.
27. Daedalus is the heroic artist.
28. Daedalus is the "hawklike man flying sunward above the sea."
29. The myth also implies Stephen's kinship with Icarus.
30. Icarus had pride and daring.
31. Icarus flew too near the sun.
32. The heat melted his wings.
33. Icarus plunged into the sea.

34. The fall of Icarus introduces a fearful note into Stephen's final decision.
35. The fall of Icarus is traditionally associated with the fall of Satan.
36. Stephen decides to cut himself off from his family, his country, and his Catholic faith.

37. The myth of the birdman as artist is finally ambiguous.
38. The myth of the birdman as artist is like the story of Stephen Dedalus.

39. Will Stephen be like Daedalus?
40. Will Stephen fly to freedom and artistic fame?
41. Will Stephen be like Icarus?
42. Will Stephen soar beyond his limits?
43. Will Stephen fall into oblivion?

44. Stephen's fate is undetermined.
45. The symbolism of flight and the myth of the birdman may simply indicate the dangers of freedom and creativity.
46. This danger is faced by every artist and every human being.

C. *Longer Papers*
    1. Point out and explain the details which link Stephen's reception of Holy Communion at the end of Chapter III with his visit to the whore

at the end of Chapter II, and then explain why you think the reader is encouraged to compare these two events.

2. Compare the first two paragraphs in Chapter III with the final paragraphs of that chapter, from "He sat by the fire . . ." to "The ciborium had come to him." (The ciborium is the cup or bowl which holds the communion bread.) How does the descriptive detail at the end of the chapter indicate that Stephen has changed?

3. At the end of Chapters II and III, Stephen feels that he has wakened from a dream, that he has entered a new life, and that he is stronger and freer than he was before. Show how the experience recorded in Chapter III destroys the dream of freedom achieved in Chapter II and how the experience in Chapter IV destroys the dream of freedom achieved in Chapter III.

4. Some say that the preacher for Stephen's retreat is a reliable spokesman of those who believe in the Christian doctrine of Heaven and Hell and that the preacher's behavior is meant to discredit that doctrine. Others say that the preacher is an unreliable spokesman and that his sermon is meant to be recognized as a perversion or parody of that doctrine. Which view do you prefer?

5. Argue for or against the assertion that Stephen's rebirth at the end of Chapter IV, "his soul . . . swooning into some new world," is essentially the same as his rebirth, his "swoon of sin," at the end of Chapter II.

6. What is your response to the style of the last pages of Chapter IV, especially the vision of the birdgirl?

7. Although Hell is not preached as much today as in the past, the doctrine of eternal damnation is still central to Christian thought. How did reading this chapter affect your views on this doctrine?

III. CHAPTER 5

A. *Brief Papers*

1. a. Show why, according to Stephen's definitions, the death of the girl pierced in the heart by a piece of glass is not tragic.

b. How does the mad nun fit into Stephen's story?

c. How does Stephen's encounter with a flower seller fit into his story?

d. Explain the difference between Stephen's and Cranly's views of Rosie O'Grady.

2. Argue for or against one of these assertions:

a. Stephen's scorn for the dean of studies is justified.

b. Cranly is right in urging Stephen to make his Easter duty (go to Confession and receive Holy Communion) in order to please his mother.

3. a. How did you feel about Davin's refusal to stay with the peasant woman?
   b. How do you respond to the diary entries at the end of the novel?
   c. Do you agree with Davin that Stephen is a "born sneerer"? Explain.

B. *Longer Papers*

1. Trace the references to birds throughout the novel and show how the meanings and emotions they arouse help us understand Stephen's growing awareness of himself and his goal.
2. Argue for or against the assertion that Stephen's relationship with women indicates a favorable growth in his feeling and understanding.
3. Some say that readers of this novel are expected to see Stephen as admirable and heroic in his rebellion against the Irish Catholic Church and in his quest for artistic freedom. Others say that readers are expected to see Stephen in an ironic light, as one who may deserve our pity but who is lost, deluded, and even, according to some, doomed. Which view do you favor?
4. When Stephen tells Cranly that he will not consent to his mother's wish that he make his Easter duty (go to confession and receive Holy Communion), Cranly asks, "Why not?" to which Stephen replies, "I will not serve." Cranly says, "That remark was made before" (that is, by Satan who preferred to burn in Hell rather than serve in Heaven). Cite other instances in which Stephen is associated with Satan or with pagan figures who are implicitly the enemies of Christianity. Then write a paper explaining how these associations affect your response to Stephen's experience.
5. The epigraph to the novel refers to Daedalus "applying his mind to obscure [unfamiliar, strange] arts." Look up the story of Daedalus in Ovid's *Metamorphoses* or in *The Oxford Classical Dictionary*. How does this story affect your view of Daedalus as an artist and your understanding of Stephen's final prayer, "Old Father"?
6. The novel could have ended, seems to end, with Stephen's vision of the birdgirl at the end of Chapter IV. In what way is our view of Stephen's experience changed or modified by the last chapter?
7. Compare and contrast Stephen's vision of the birdgirl with his poem to the temptress in Chapter V. Do you think the temptress has replaced the birdgirl as Stephen's muse? If so, what difference will it make in his development as an artist? If not, what is Stephen's view of the temptress?
8. Both Davin's story and Stephen's poem are about a temptress. Compare and contrast these two literary pieces. Is the peasant woman also a muse? Does she stand in opposition to the temptress in Stephen's poem or are they complementary? Which do think is the better literary work, the poem or the story?

F. SCOTT FITZGERALD

The Great Gatsby

Writing Assignments

I. CHAPTERS I TO III

A. *Brief Papers*
1. a. Nick Carraway says that Tom Buchanan is beginning "to nibble at the edge of stale ideas" (Chapter I). Explain some of the "stale ideas" that have begun to interest Tom.
   b. Explain what Daisy's saying that the best thing a girl can be in this world is a "beautiful little fool" reveals about Daisy herself.
   c. Explain how Myrtle Wilson differs from Daisy so as to account for Tom's attraction to Myrtle.
   d. On a table in Tom and Myrtle's New York apartment are copies of *Town Tattle*, scandal magazines, and a book *Simon Called Peter* (Chapter II). In a letter to his editor Maxwell Perkins, F. Scott Fitzgerald asked if Perkins considered this juxtaposition "raw." "Let me know," Fitzgerald continued. "I think it's pretty necessary." Explain what might be considered "raw" here and then why Fitzgerald might find the material necessary.
   e. Explain the purpose of either the scene in Gatsby's library or the accident scene at the end of Gatsby's party (Chapter III).

2. Argue for or against one of the following assertions:
   a. Tom's hitting Myrtle after she keeps repeating Daisy's name (Chapter II) is a sign that Tom really loves Daisy.
   b. Nick's description of Gatsby as a romantic with an "extraordinary gift for hope" applies equally well to Nick himself—at least in the first three chapters of the novel.
   c. Nick contradicts himself when, in the same paragraph, he says that Gatsby represented everything for which he has unaffected scorn and yet that Gatsby turned out all right in the end.

3. a. What do you think Nick means in the novel's third paragraph by the "fundamental decencies"?
   b. How do you respond to Tom Buchanan on the basis of the first two chapters of *The Great Gatsby*? How does your response to Tom affect the way you feel about Jay Gatsby?
   c. What is your first reaction to Gatsby when he appears alone on his lawn at the end of Chapter I?

       d. How do you react to Nick's saying that "Dishonesty in a woman is a thing you never blame deeply . . ." (Chapter III)? How does your reaction affect your attitude toward Nick?

       e. Complete either of the following sentences by free writing for 10 minutes:
- "From what I know of Nick Carraway, I believe him when he says he is an honest person because . . ."
- "From what I know of Nick Carraway, I do *not* believe him when he says he is an honest person because . . ."

Since the goal of free writing is to generate ideas quickly, do not worry about spelling, punctuation, grammar, or sentence structure. Just keep writing down whatever comes into your head about Nick's honesty. Don't stop writing for any reason. If you can't think of anything to say, just write "I can't think of anything to say" until something comes to mind. After 10 minutes, look back over your free writing and select from it the most promising idea for a full-length paper on the opening chapters of *The Great Gatsby*. Then, in a brief paragraph, explain why the idea is a promising one.

B. *Longer Papers*
1. Develop into a full-length paper the idea you generated in your free writing (3.e. above).
2. Since Chapter II of *The Great Gatsby* contains only a brief mention of Jay Gatsby, explain the purpose of the chapter in the novel.
3. Nick Carraway describes himself in the opening of *The Great Gatsby* as a person who is inclined to reserve all judgments. Is that an accurate description of the Nick Carraway who appears in the first three chapters of the novel?
4. Compare and contrast Nick Carraway and Tom Buchanan in order to define the central differences in attitudes and values between the two men.

II. CHAPTERS IV TO VI

A. *Brief Papers*
1. a. Explain what Nick means by his earlier statement that there is something "gorgeous" about Jay Gatsby, "some heightened sensitivity to the promises of life."
    b. Explain why Nick tells us, at the beginning of Chapter IV, the names of the people who attend Gatsby's parties.
    c. Explain Daisy's reaction to Gatsby's party in Chapter VI. Which parts of the party does she enjoy and which parts displease her?

2. Argue for or against one of the following assertions:
    a. What Gatsby tells Nick on their ride to New York proves that Gatsby is an accomplished and habitual liar.

      b. Fitzgerald clearly shows that Nick's arranging for Gatsby to meet Daisy, a married woman, is an immoral act.

   3. a. What is your initial reaction to Meyer Wolfsheim? Does your reaction to Wolfsheim in any way change your feelings about Jay Gatsby?

      b. Does the story Jordan tells Nick in Chapter IV about Daisy's past— her relationship with Gatsby and her marriage to Tom Buchanan —in any way change your attitude toward either Tom or Daisy?

      c. How does the scene at Gatsby's house in Chapter VI involving Tom, a man named Sloane, and an unnamed woman affect your feelings toward Gatsby?

  B. *Longer Papers*
   1. Compare the trip Nick takes to New York with Gatsby (Chapter IV) with his earlier trip to New York with Tom Buchanan (Chapter II) in order to identify what you consider to be the most important differences between Tom and Gatsby.

   2. Explain where your sympathies lie in Chapter V of *The Great Gatsby.* That is, are you hoping for a reuniting of Daisy and Gatsby? How does your response to this question affect your interpretation of the novel?

   3. Rank the major characters of the first six chapters of *The Great Gatsby*—Nick, Tom, Daisy, Jordan, Myrtle, and Gatsby—in terms of what Nick calls the "fundamental decencies" (Chapter I). Who is the most decent and who is the least?

   4. Rank the major characters of the first six chapters of *The Great Gatsby*—from least sensitive to most sensitive—in terms of what Nick calls their "sensitivity to the promises of life," their "gift for hope," their "romantic readiness" (Chapter I).

III. CHAPTERS VII TO IX

  A. *Brief Papers*
   1. a. Explain who is responsible for Gatsby's death.

      b. Explain whether Nick, unlike Tom and Daisy, tries to clean up the mess.

      c. Explain the significance of the schedule and general resolves that young Jimmy Gatz had written on the back cover of his *Hopalong Cassidy* book.

      d. Explain why it is appropriate that Nick last sees Tom going into a jewelry store—perhaps to buy a pearl necklace or a pair of cuff buttons.

      e. Explain the significance of either (1) Nick's returning to the Midwest or (2) his selling his car before leaving.

2. Argue for or against one of the following assertions:
   a. None of Tom's accusations against Gatsby—for example, that Gatsby is a gambler and bootlegger with underworld connections—have any truth to them whatsoever.
   b. The eyes of Doctor T. J. Eckleburg clearly imply that, in the wasteland of twentieth-century America, God has disappeared.
   c. As the novel progresses, Nick understands Jay Gatsby better and better.

3. a. Do you think more or less of Jordan because she is "too wise to carry well-forgotten dreams from age to age" (Chapter VII)?
   b. Tom Buchanan believes that all his actions were "entirely justified." Do you agree? How does your response affect your interpretation of the end of the novel?
   c. How would you characterize the tone of the concluding three or four paragraphs of the novel? As hopeful? Despairing? Cynical? Exhausted? Indifferent?

4. Using the sentences below, construct an argument paragraph of approximately 150 words that supports one of the following two assertions and refutes the other:
   a. By the end of *The Great Gatsby* it has become clear that Tom and Daisy Buchanan are essentially alike.
   b. By the end of *The Great Gatsby* it has become clear that Tom and Daisy Buchanan differ substantially from each other.
   Whichever assertion you choose to support, feel free to add or change facts and details. You will probably want to add an introduction, a concluding sentence or two, and several transitions. You will certainly have to do some reorganizing.
   1. Both Tom and Daisy cause an automobile accident.
   2. Daisy has a sense of humor which Tom lacks.
   3. At one point Nick takes Daisy's smirk as asserting "her membership in a rather distinguished secret society to which she and Tom belonged" (Chapter I).
   4. Unlike Tom, Daisy does not seem to play around: she has "an absolutely perfect reputation" (Chapter IV).
   5. Tom says, "I've gotten to be a terrible pessimist about things" and Daisy says, "I'm pretty cynical about everything" (Chapter I).
   6. At one point Nick says that Daisy's "eyes flashed around her in a defiant way, rather like Tom's" (Chapter I).
   7. Whereas Tom has a hard, cruel body Daisy does not.
   8. Nick says that both Tom and Daisy are "careless people" who "smashed up things and creatures" (Chapter IX).
   9. Neither Tom nor Daisy clean up the messes they make.
   10. In contrast to Tom's dominating and manipulating others, Daisy is essentially passive.

11. After the fatal accident, Nick looks at Tom and Daisy and says, "Anybody would have said that they were conspiring together" (Chapter VII).
12. Tom's voice lacks the low, thrilling quality of Daisy's.

B. *The Symbolism of Automobile Driving in "The Great Gatsby"*

Using whatever information below you find most useful, construct an essay of 250 to 300 words in which you explain that, in *The Great Gatsby*, driving a car has *symbolic value*; that is, the way a person handles an automobile is a clear sign of the way he or she treats other people. To develop this position, feel free to add material of your own to the information below. You will need to create a brief introduction and conclusion and you will want to use transitions to connect the parts of your essay. Consider expanding and reworking this essay into a full-length paper on *The Great Gatsby*.

1. Two months after he married Daisy, Tom Buchanan got into an automobile accident in Santa Barbara. He ran into a wagon and tore off his car's front wheel. Tom was apparently unhurt but the girl who was with him—a chambermaid from the Santa Barbara Hotel—broke her arm (Chapter IV).
2. Jordan Baker once drove so close to a workman that the fender of her car flicked off one of his coat buttons. Nick called her a "rotten driver" and told her she should either drive more carefully or give up driving (Chapter III).
3. Nick sold his car to the grocer before heading back to the middle West (Chapter IX).
4. Daisy is driving the car that hits and kills Myrtle Wilson. She first turned away from Myrtle in the direction of a car coming the other direction, but she lost her nerve and turned back (Chapter VII).
5. Nick Carraway describes himself as someone who thinks slowly and who acts according to a set of internal rules that serve as "brakes" on his desires (Chapter III).
6. On the morning Jay Gatsby and Nick Carraway drive to New York together, Gatsby drives so fast that he is pulled over by a motorcycle policeman. But when Gatsby pulls out a white card from his wallet and shows it to the policeman, he receives an apology rather than a speeding ticket (Chapter IV).
7. At the end of one of Gatsby's parties, a drunken man drives his new car into a ditch, violently shearing off one of its wheels (Chapter III).
8. After the car she is driving strikes Myrtle, Daisy does not stop. Instead, she steps on the accelerator and speeds ahead until Gatsby makes her stop by pulling on the emergency brake (Chapter VII).
9. Jordan Baker once borrowed a convertible and left it out in the rain with its top down—and then lied about it (Chapter III).

10. After first denying and then acknowledging that she is a careless driver, Jordan tells Nick that she hates careless people and that's why she likes him (Chapter III).
11. Tom Buchanan has told Wilson that he will sell him a car, but Tom apparently has no such intention at all (Chapter II).

C. *Longer Papers*
1. Argue for or against the following statement: The title *The Great Gatsby* is obviously ironic because, by the end of the novel, we realize that there is nothing "great" about Jay Gatsby. He is a phony, a liar, and a gangster who gets exactly what he deserves. Finally, Gatsby is no better and no worse than Tom, Daisy, and the rest of their "rotten" crowd.
2. Argue for or against the following statement: The world of *The Great Gatsby* is a world without God. Fitzgerald makes clear throughout the novel either that God does not exist or that we in the twentieth century are no longer able to believe in his existence. *The Great Gatsby* shows humanity, for better or worse, alone in the universe.
3. Argue for or against the following statement: Nick Carraway is a growing, maturing, developing character who not only understands both himself and his world far better at the end than he had at the beginning (as especially the first two and last two pages of the novel make clear) but who himself becomes a different—and better—person as a result of his experience.
4. Argue for or against the following statement: The prevailing tone of *The Great Gatsby* is one of bleakness and despair. The despair is especially powerful at the end of the novel, when we come to realize that the most careless and irresponsible people have survived and prospered but that the most caring and responsible people have been defeated and destroyed. The novel concludes without a shred of hope.
5. Argue for or against the following statement: One of the major themes of *The Great Gatsby* is the foolishness of believing in and living by moral standards. Indeed, everything in the novel suggests that, in the twentieth century, it makes no sense to worry about right and wrong, good and bad, or ethical distinctions of any kind. But it makes perfect sense to do whatever is necessary in order to protect yourself and to survive. Nick himself accepts this amoral approach when he realizes, "There are only the pursued, the pursuing, the busy, and the tired" (Chapter IV).
6. Fitzgerald uses language creatively and innovatively in *The Great Gatsby*. He writes, for example, of a wrecked car that "crouches" in the garage, of a dog biscuit that decomposes "apathetically" in a saucer of milk, of the "ferocious indifference" of Gatsby's college, and of the "ecstatic cahoots" between Gatsby and Nick. Using these

or other examples, explain the connection between the wording and phrasing of *The Great Gatsby* and the view of life the novel communicates.

7. Explore in a full-length paper any important connection you find between *The Great Gatsby* and F. Scott Fitzgerald's short story "Winter Dreams," which is printed on pages 224–240 of this book. For example, is Fitzgerald's attitude toward the pursuit of a dream the same in both pieces? Do you think Dexter Green is like Jay Gatsby? Nick Carraway? Both? Neither? Are Judy Jones and Daisy Buchanan fundamentally alike? Does the short story end in essentially the same way as the novel?

8. Knowing that you have been studying *The Great Gatsby,* your high school English teacher has invited you to speak about the novel to his sophomore class. He has given you three statements from the novel that he has not been able to explain fully to his students. He would like you to pick *one* and—in a 10-minute talk—interpret its meaning and then explain how it relates to the novel as a whole. Here are the three statements:

   a. "The truth was that Jay Gatsby of West Egg, Long Island, sprang from his Platonic conception of himself" (Chapter VI).

   b. Gatsby "found that he had committed himself to the following of a grail" (Chapter VIII).

   c. "Gatsby believed in the green light, the orgiastic future that year by year recedes before us" (Chapter IX).

   Write the paper that you will later present to the class of high school sophomores.

ERNEST HEMINGWAY
The Sun Also Rises

Writing Assignments

I. BOOK I

A. Brief Papers
1. a. Explain Jake's injury, what he calls "the old grievance" (Chapter IV): what is it, how did it happen, and what are its consequences for Jake?
   b. Show that in Book I of *The Sun Also Rises* Jake Barnes often uses irony: he frequently says one thing but indicates through his tone that he means something else, sometimes even the opposite of what he seems to be saying.
   c. Explain why Jake thinks that W. H. Hudson's *The Purple Land* has become a "sinister" book for Robert Cohn (Chapter II).
   d. Explain why Jake wants to take a punch at the men who arrive with Brett at the dancing club (Chapter III).

2. Argue for or against one of the following assertions:
   a. Robert Cohn is a person who allows others to control his life.
   b. In Book I, Jake controls his own life except when it involves Brett Ashley.
   c. Book I of *The Sun Also Rises* presents "a parade of emotional cripples."
   d. It is ironic that Count Mippipopolous tells Jake "it is because I have lived very much that now I can enjoy everything so well" (Chapter VII) because the Count does not really know how to enjoy himself.

3. a. Aside from her looks, what is it that makes Brett so attractive to men?
   b. Do you think that the characters in *The Sun Also Rises* spend too much time drinking and partying? How does your response to this question affect your attitude toward the events of Part I of *The Sun Also Rises*?
   c. Complete either of the following sentences by free writing for 10 minutes:
      • "I admire Jake Barnes because . . . ."
      • "I do *not* admire Jake Barnes because . . . ."
      Since the goal of free writing is to generate ideas quickly, do not worry about spelling, punctuation, grammar, or sentence structure. Just keep writing down whatever comes into your head about

Jake Barnes. Don't stop writing for any reason. If you can't think of anything to say, just write "I can't think of anything to say" until something comes to mind. After ten minutes, look back over your free writing and select from it the most promising idea for a full-length paper on Book I of *The Sun Also Rises.* Then, in a brief paragraph, explain why the idea is a promising one.

B. *Longer Papers*
  1. Develop into a full-length paper the idea you generated in your free writing (3.c above).
  2. Jake says of his injury, "I try and play it along and just not make trouble for people" (Chapter IV). Expand paragraph 1.a. into a full-length paper that evaluates Jake's success in dealing with his injury.
  3. Expand paragraph 1.b. into a full-length paper that, focusing on Book I of *The Sun Also Rises,* explains why Jake Barnes uses irony and what his frequent use of irony tells us about the kind of person he is.
  4. Expand paragraph 1.c., 2.a., or 2.b. into a full-length paper which shows that, in contrast to Robert Cohn, Jake Barnes is depicted in the first half of *The Sun Also Rises* as someone who is usually able to control his own life.
  5. Argue for or against the assertion that, as Book I closes, Jake Barnes and Robert Cohn are in essentially the same position.
  6. Argue for or against the assertion that, as Book I closes, Jake Barnes and Count Mippipopolous are in essentially the same position.
  7. Compare and contrast Jake's ride with Georgette (Chapter III) to his ride with Brett (Chapters III and IV) in order to reach some conclusions about Jake's relationship with Brett.

II. BOOK II

A. *Brief Papers*
  1. a. Explain what can be learned about life in the United States—and why Jake Barnes lives in Europe instead—from the American family that Jake and Bill meet on the train (Chapter IX).
     b. Explain what we learn about Jake from the content of his prayer (Chapter X).
     c. What is the significance of the different ways in which Jake and Robert respond to the cathedral at Bayonne (Chapter X)?
     d. In what ways is the fiesta in general and the bullfight in particular like a war?
     e. Explain as clearly as you can what makes a bullfight aficionado. What is it that separates aficionados like Jake and Montoya from those who are not?
     f. Montoya tells Jake that most people don't know what a real bullfighter like Romero is worth. "They don't know what he means"

(Chapter XVI). Explain what Montoya means: what is the value of a bullfighter like Romero?

g. Why at the end of Book II has Jake gotten drunker than ever before?

2. Argue for or against one of the following assertions:
    a. Jake gets his money's worth of pleasure and enjoyment from his trip to Burguete and his stay there.
    b. Robert Cohn is accurate in calling Jake a "pimp" (Chapter XVII).
    c. Brett Ashley is not to blame for the trouble that Jake, Cohn, and Michael experience in Pamplona.
    d. When Jake and Brett are in Pamplona, it is Brett—and not Jake—who controls their relationship.

3. a. Do you think more or less of Brett Ashley because she becomes involved with Pedro Romero? How does your response to this question affect your understanding of the novel?
    b. Do you think more or less of Mike Campbell after learning of his reactions to Brett's involvement with Robert Cohn and Pedro Romero?
    c. Do you find Bill Gorton more or less admirable than Jake Barnes? Why?
    d. Do you think that Hemingway wants us to accept Jake's definition of immorality as "things that made you disgusted afterward" (Chapter XIV)?
    e. Has reading *The Sun Also Rises* changed in any way your attitude toward bullfighting? If so, explain how.

B. *The Escape to Burguete in "The Sun Also Rises"*
   Using the facts in the sentences below, write a coherent paragraph of approximately 150 words which develops the thesis that Jake's experiences at Burguete and the Irati River are a retreat from the conflicts of the real world. Use only those facts which help develop your thesis and exclude the rest. Feel free to change the wording and to add facts of your own. In any case, you will have to change the order of the facts below so as to coherently develop the idea that Jake's trip to Burguete is an escape from the harsh facts of reality.
   1. Brett is not in Burguete.
   2. Cohn and Mike are not in Burguete.
   3. Except for the woman innkeeper, there seem to be no women in Burguete.
   4. As Jake says, "There was no word from Robert Cohn nor from Brett and Mike" (Chapter XII).
   5. When Jake looks out the window of the inn, he sees an "old diligence" (Chapter XII).

6. A diligence is a stage coach.
7. According to Jake, the stage coach is left over from the days before buses.
8. Jake and Bill see cattle.
9. Jake and Bill do not see bulls.
10. Jake and Bill easily catch trout in the Irati River.
11. Jake catches his first trout soon after he puts his line in the water.
12. Jake catches six more trout soon after.
13. Paris is hot.
14. At Burguete, "there was always a breeze even in the heat of day" (Chapter XII).
15. Jake and Bill play "three-handed bridge" with an Englishman named Harris (Chapter XII).
16. Harris says, "Wonderful how one loses track of the days up here in the mountains" (Chapter XIII).
17. On the way to Burguete Jake and Bill see "the monastery of Roncesvalles" (Chapter XI).
18. Jake, Bill, and Harris later go through the monastery.
19. There are no side streets in Burguete.
20. The innkeeper at Burguete wears glasses.
21. Jake has no trouble sleeping in Burguete.
22. Jake has trouble sleeping in Paris.
23. The newspaper that Jake reads is one week old.

C. *Longer Papers*
1. Develop into a full-length paper any one of your earlier paragraphs on Book II of *The Sun Also Rises*.
2. Argue for or against the assertion that Book II of *The Sun Also Rises* makes clear that there is an important connection between bullfighting and human experience.
3. Argue for or against the assertion that Book I and Book II end in essentially the same way—with Jake's relationship to Brett the same as it has always been.
4. Explain why it is easier for Jake to get his money's worth of enjoyment and pleasure in Burguete than in Pamplona.
5. Using Jake's own definition of morality (Chapter XIV), evaluate the morality of his actions in Book II of *The Sun Also Rises*.
6. Jake says at one point that "The bill always came" (Chapter XIV). By the end of Book II, which characters in *The Sun Also Rises* have had to pay and in what form have they paid?

III. BOOK III

A. *Brief Papers*
1. a. In what ways is San Sebastian like Burguete?
   b. In what ways is San Sebastian different from Burguete?

  c. Explain why Jake describes his swimming and diving at San Sebastian in such detail and at such length.

  d. Explain why Jake purposely sleeps through the start of the bicycle race.

  e. Explain why Jake has been expecting a telegram or some other communication from Brett.

  f. The last line of *The Sun Also Rises* originally read, " 'Yes,' I said. 'It's nice as hell to think so.' " Explain the difference between the original and final versions.

2. Argue for or against one of the following assertions:

  a. Jake is right when he says, "I felt I was a fool to be going into Spain": His decision to return to Spain turns out to be a foolish one.

  b. In San Sebastian Jake once again gets his money's worth of life's pleasures and enjoyments.

  c. Brett dominates Jake in Madrid, just as she had in Paris and Pamplona.

  d. Jake's behavior in Book III demonstrates that he has learned nothing important from the bullfighting of Pedro Romero.

3. a. Would you have thought more or less of Jake if he had ignored Brett's telegram and not gone to Madrid? Explain.

  b. What do you think Brett implies about herself when she tells Jake that she is going back to Mike because "He's my sort of thing"?

  c. How do you think Brett will react to Jake's saying, "Yes, . . . Isn't it pretty to think so?"

B. *The Cab Rides in "The Sun Also Rises"*
  Combine the following sentences into an argument paragraph of approximately 150 words (and no longer than 200 words) that supports one of the following assertions and refutes the other:
  • The two cab rides of Brett and Jake in *The Sun Also Rises* are essentially alike.
  • The two cab rides of Brett and Jake in *The Sun Also Rises* are essentially different.
  Assume that your argument paragraph is part of a longer paper arguing either that (1) the relationship between Jake and Brett does not change in the course of the novel, or that (2) the relationship between Jake and Brett substantially changes during the course of the novel. If you think the relationship is unchanged, your paragraph should probably argue that the rides are alike; but if you think the relationship is changed, then you should argue that the rides are different. In either case, you may add and change facts or details, and you must construct a concluding sentence or two.

1. In *The Sun Also Rises* Jake takes two cab rides with Brett.
2. The first ride occurs in Book I.
3. It takes place in Paris.
4. The second ride occurs in Book III.
5. It takes place in Madrid.
6. The first ride takes place at night.
7. The second ride takes place during the day.
8. In each instance Jake sends a waiter to get the cab.
9. The first ride is suggested by Brett.
10. The second ride is initiated by Jake.
11. In both rides Jake and Brett are alone in the cab.
12. For the first ride, Jake asks Brett where they should go.
13. For the second ride, Jake selects the destination himself.
14. In both rides Jake puts his arm around Brett.
15. Jake stares at Brett during the first ride.
16. Jake does not stare at Brett during the second ride.
17. Jake is tense during the first ride.
18. Jake is not tense during the second ride; he is comfortable.
19. In both instances the cab ride jolts or presses Jake and Brett closer together.
20. The first ride ends with Jake's kissing Brett.
21. The second ride ends with Jake's saying, "Isn't it pretty to think so?"

C. *Longer Papers*
1. Develop any one or more of your earlier paragraphs or papers into a full-length paper that deals with the entire novel.
2. Argue for or against the following statement: By the end of *The Sun Also Rises,* Brett Ashley has emerged as an essentially admirable person. It is Brett who ends the affair with Romero, and she does so for the best of reasons—she does not want to corrupt him. But sending Romero away is but one reason why we so admire Brett. What makes Brett especially admirable is that she is almost always honest with herself and with others. It is largely because of her honesty that we find Brett at the end of the novel fully in control of herself and her life.
3. Argue for or against the following statement: *The Sun Also Rises* demonstrates, as Robert Cohn has suspected all along, that bullfighting is "an abnormal life." Indeed, Hemingway wants the reader to understand that bullfighting has no important relationship to human experience. Bullfighting represents nothing more than a temporary escape from the real conflicts of life, and the characters who involve themselves with bullfighting are not confronting life but retreating from it.
4. Argue for or against the following statement: *The Sun Also Rises* ends affirmatively because Jake Barnes has finally learned how to dominate Brett and thus to control his own life. Although Brett has dominated

Jake in Paris and Pamplona, it is Jake who controls their relationship in Madrid. And as Jake's eating a big meal at one of the world's finest restaurants suggests, his ability to control Brett means that he now knows how to get his money's worth of pleasure out of life.

5. Argue for or against the following statement: *The Sun Also Rises* presents motion which goes no place. At the end of the novel, Jake and Brett are right back where they started from because neither has really learned anything from their experiences. As the novel's epigraph from *Ecclesiastes* suggests, Jake and Brett go around in circles and get nowhere. Primarily for this reason, *The Sun Also Rises* is a novel of stasis, futility, and despair.

RALPH ELLISON

Invisible Man

Writing Assignments

I. PROLOGUE TO CHAPTER 6

A. *Brief Papers*
  1. a. During the battle royal, why is it significant that the narrator is knocked out just as he begins to consider adopting the strategy of humility and nonresistance?
     b. Explain why it is appropriate that the narrator describe his college campus as a "flower-studded wasteland" (Chapter 2).
     c. Explain why the whites seem to treat Jim Trueblood so well.
     d. Explain the significance of the name "The Golden Day."
     e. Explain why the narrator always feels uncomfortable when he is with the inmates from the mental asylum.
     f. Explain why it is significant that Homer Barbee is blind.
     g. Explain why it is appropriate that Homer Barbee's speech is delivered in the college chapel.
     h. Explain whether the names of characters—like Bledsoe, Trueblood, Norton, Supercargo, Homer Barbee—reveal anything about the characters themselves.

  2. Argue for or against one of the following assertions:
     a. Mr. Norton is right when he tells the narrator, "I know my life rather well" (Chapter 2).
     b. Mr. Norton feels weak and faint after hearing Trueblood's story because Norton himself has had incestuous desires for his own daughter.
     c. The narrator's attitude toward Jim Trueblood has changed profoundly since he first heard Trueblood's story.

  3. a. Do you find the men who attend the battle royal admirable? Why or why not? How does your response affect the way you react to the battle royal as a whole?
     b. Do you find Jim Trueblood admirable? Why or why not? How does your response affect the way you react to his story?
     c. Do you admire Dr. Bledsoe? Why or why not? How does your response affect the way you react to his actions toward the narrator?
     d. Complete the sentence "Reading the opening chapters of *Invisible Man* has made me see for the first time that . . ." by free writing for

10 minutes. Since the goal of free writing is to generate ideas quickly, do not worry about spelling, punctuation, grammar, or sentence structure. Just keep writing down whatever comes into your head on the topic. Don't stop writing for any reason. If you can't think of anything to say, just write "I can't think of anything to say" until something comes to mind. After 10 minutes, look back over your free writing and select from it the most promising idea for a full-length paper on the opening chapters of *Invisible Man*. Then, in a brief paragraph, explain why the idea is a promising one.

B. *The Symbolism of the Battle Royal in "Invisible Man"*
Use the sentences below as the basis for an essay that explains the *symbolism* of the battle royal in *Invisible Man*. For a later paper, consider writing about the symbolism of another chapter or episode in the novel.

1. The battle royal is in Chapter 1 of *Invisible Man*.
2. Ralph Ellison wrote *Invisible Man*.
3. The battle royal seems to be more than a literal description.
4. The description is of ten black boys.
5. The black boys are slugging it out with each other.
6. The slugging occurs in front of the town's most influential white citizens.

7. The battle royal is presented in a way.
8. The way makes the battle royal symbolic.
9. The battle royal is symbolic of the plight of the black person in white society.

10. Here is an early sign that the battle royal symbolizes blacks being oppressed by whites.
11. It is the white blindfold.
12. The white blindfold is placed over the eyes of each black fighter.

13. This detail suggests this.
14. The blacks have blinded themselves to this reality.
15. The reality is that whites are their real enemy.
16. The blacks have done this in exchange for a little money.

17. The blacks are unable to see the truth.
18. The blacks fight each other.
19. The blacks do not fight their true oppressor.

20. Here is the result of blacks fighting each other in the boxing ring.
21. Here is the result of blacks fighting each other in society at large.
22. The result is what the narrator describes as "complete anarchy."

23. The battle royal suggests this.
24. Blacks will be victimized so long as this happens.
25. Blacks continue to fight each other.
26. Blacks do not fight whites.
27. If so, the struggle between the narrator and Tatlock shows this.
28. The path of humility is the path of defeat.

29. The narrator is close to knocking out Tatlock.
30. Tatlock is larger than the narrator.
31. The narrator hears a white voice.
32. The white voice calls out, "I got my money on the big boy."
33. The narrator asks himself this.
34. Might this be a moment for humility?
35. Might this be a moment for nonresistance?

36. The narrator is considering nonresistance.
37. Just at this point he is hit by a vicious blow.
38. Just at this point he is knocked unconscious.

39. Ellison has a symbolic point.
40. The symbolic point seems clear.
41. Whites will take advantage of blacks.
42. These blacks practice humility.
43. These blacks practice nonresistance.
44. Whites will have these blacks beaten into full submission.

45. This is true of the battle royal as a whole.
46. It is a symbolic statement.
47. The statement is that blacks will be cruelly victimized.
48. The statement is that blacks will be painfully victimized.
49. The victimization will go on as long as blacks allow themselves to be blinded by white racists.
50. The victimization will go on as long as blacks allow themselves to be controlled by white racists.

C. *Longer Papers*
   1. Develop into a full-length paper the idea you generated in your free writing (3.d. above).
   2. In the "Prologue" to *Invisible Man,* the narrator says that the world does not move like an arrow but like a boomerang. Using two or three extended examples from the novel's first six chapters, explain in detail what he means.
   3. The narrator sometimes feels that he is carrying out his grandfather's advice without consciously trying to do so and without even fully

understanding what his grandfather meant. Explain one instance in which the narrator's deeds seem to be guided by his grandfather's words.

4. Explain how the narrator's dream at the end of Chapter 1 provides a commentary on and an interpretation of the battle royal.

5. Explain in what sense the narrator's graduation speech can be taken as "a triumph for our whole community" (Chapter 1).

6. Explain what the vet means when he tells Mr. Norton that it is appropriate that Norton and the narrator arrived at the Golden Day together.

7. After completing the exercise "The Symbolism of the Battle Royal," write a full-length interpretation of the symbolism of Jim Trueblood's story or of the events at the Golden Day or of any other chapter or episode in the opening quarter of *Invisible Man*.

II. CHAPTERS 7 TO 13

A. *Brief Papers*
1. a. Explain what the vet means when he tells the narrator to be his own father (Chapter 7).
   b. Explain why it is significant that the torch of the Statue of Liberty is almost lost in the fog (Chapter 8).
   c. Explain what Peter Wheatstraw means when he asks the narrator, "Why you trying to deny me?" (Chapter 9).
   d. Explain the significance of the blueprints in Peter Wheatstraw's cart.
   e. When the narrator reads the letter that Dr. Bledsoe had written to Mr. Emerson, he has the feeling that it all happened before. Explain in what sense it had.
   f. Look up the meaning of "whitewash" in a dictionary and then explain how its definition helps us to understand the episode at Liberty Paints.
   g. Explain why the narrator asks the doctor at the factory hospital if he knows Mr. Norton.
   h. Explain why the narrator occasionally feels resentful toward Mary Rambo.
   i. Explain what the narrator's dumping the spittoon on the man who looks like Bledsoe tells us about his changed attitudes and plans.
   j. Explain why the narrator feels "overcome by an intense feeling of freedom" (Chapter 12) while he is eating a yam in the street.

2. Argue for or against one of the following assertions:
   a. The vet the narrator meets on his bus ride north is just a malcontent and troublemaker: the narrator would be better off if he ignored everything the vet says.

b. When the narrator resists the temptation to order pork chops and grits at the drugstore restaurant, it is a sign of his growth and maturity.

c. The narrator's quarrel with Lucius Brockway makes it clear that the narrator himself is the cause of all his troubles: no one is to blame but the narrator alone.

3. a. When young Emerson is talking to the narrator, he mentions a session with his analyst. How would you diagnose Emerson's psychological problems? How does your diagnosis affect your interpretation of the meaning of the episode involving young Emerson and the narrator?

b. What is your attitude toward the doctors, nurses, and attendants at the factory hospital? How does your reaction to them affect the way you interpret the meaning of this episode?

c. What is your impression of the man who follows and talks with the narrator after his eviction speech? Do you, like the narrator, distrust him? Why or why not?

B. *Images of Death and Rebirth in "Invisible Man"*
Use the sentences below as the basis for an essay that illustrates how images of death and rebirth function in the novel.

1. Images of death and rebirth appear throughout *Invisible Man.*
2. Ralph Ellison wrote *Invisible Man.*
3. These images usually appear at certain points in the novel.
4. They are points when the narrator is about to change in a profound way.

5. These images begin with the novel's "Prologue."
6. In the novel's "Prologue" the narrator tells us this.
7. He lives in a hole.
8. His hole is less like a grave.
9. A grave is an image of death.
10. His hole is more like a womb.
11. A womb is an image of rebirth.

12. This happens later in the novel.
13. It happens at the factory hospital.
14. The narrator finds himself not in a grave.
15. The narrator finds himself in a container.
16. The container seems much like a coffin.
17. ". . . I discovered that I was not lying on an operating table but in a kind of glass and nickel box, the lid of which was propped open" (Chapter 11).

18. This happens soon afterward.
19. The narrator sees clouds.
20. The narrator sees blue space.
21. The narrator hears heavenly music.
22. The narrator hears a golden trumpet.
23. All these are signs of this.
24. The narrator has left this world for another.

25. These are images of death.
26. They are followed by equally clear images of rebirth.
27. The nurse clips through the cord.
28. The cord had been attached to the narrator's stomach.
29. It was as if the cord were an umbilical cord.
30. The narrator is pronounced "a new man."

31. This is as if to signal the narrator's rebirth.
32. The narrator soon finds a new mother.
33. The new mother is Mary Rambo.
34. The narrator soon finds a new home.
35. The new home is Mary's apartment.

36. This happens not long afterward.
37. This happens following the narrator's eviction speech.
38. Images of death and rebirth appear together again.

39. The narrator is running from the police.
40. The narrator cuts through a block.
41. On the block there are a dozen funeral parlors.

42. This is an image of death.
43. It is quickly followed by a concrete representation of rebirth.

44. This happens in the next block.
45. The narrator sees a car pull up to the curb.
46. The narrator sees a man leap out.
47. The man has a physician's bag.

48. From the stoop a voice calls.
49. The voice calls for the doctor to hurry.
50. Labor has already begun.

51. The narrator thinks this.
52. "What a hell of a time to be born."
53. The narrator himself is about to be reborn.

54. He will soon meet Brother Jack.
55. Brother Jack will give him a new address.
56. Brother Jack will give him a new identity.

57. This happens at the end of the novel.
58. Images of death and rebirth are still prominent.
59. The emphasis is on rebirth.

60. The narrator is still buried in his hole.
61. The narrator says this.
62. "I'm shaking off the old skin and I'll leave it here in the hole. I'm coming out. . . ."

C. *Longer Papers*
   1. Explain what the vet means when he tells the narrator to "Play the game, but don't believe in it—that much you owe yourself" (Chapter 7). How, for example, does the vet's advice compare to the grandfather's final words?
   2. What is the symbolic significance of the episode in which ingredients are mixed to produce Optic White paint at the Liberty Paint factory?
   3. In what ways do the narrator's experiences at the Liberty Paint factory typify or characterize the black person's position within American industry?
   4. Compare the narrator's eviction speech with his earlier graduation speech in order to argue for or against the assertion that the narrator has grown and matured since his high school days.
   5. At one point the narrator thinks, "When I discover who I am, I'll be free" (Chapter 12). Explain the relationship between freedom and self-knowledge in the first half of *Invisible Man*.

III. CHAPTERS 14 TO 21

A. *Brief Papers*
   1. a. Explain why the narrator feels so bad during his last morning at Mary's.
      b. Explain the meaning of the narrator's being unable to get rid of the package with the coins and broken iron.
      c. Explain the significance of the photograph of the former boxing champion that the narrator sees on the wall just before he gives his first speech for the Brotherhood.
      d. Explain the significance of the fact that, when giving his first speech for the Brotherhood, the narrator cannot see his audience.
      e. Explain the significance of the bullfighting scenes at the El Toro bar.

    f. Explain why the confrontation with Ras the Exhorter reminds the narrator of the battle royal.

    g. At one point the narrator looks at Brother Tarp and is reminded of his grandfather. Explain what the two men have in common.

    h. Explain why Tod Clifton left the Brotherhood, disappeared from Harlem, and began selling Sambo dolls.

    i. Explain why the narrator devotes so much of himself to organizing Tod Clifton's funeral.

2. Argue for or against one of the following assertions:

    a. One of the clear implications of the first three-fourths of *Invisible Man* is that you can't trust anybody.

    b. The tone of the first three-fourths of the novel is cynical, bitter, and overwhelmingly negative.

    c. The tone of the encounter between the narrator and the woman in Chapter 19 is essentially comic.

    d. The narrator is correct in calling the Sambo dolls "obscene" and in seeing Clifton's selling them as an act of betrayal.

3. a. After spending a night with the wife of an influential brother, the narrator has the feeling that he has been tested and has failed. Do you think he has?

    b. Do you think that Chapter 19, in which the narrator lectures on the "Woman Question," is sexist? Why or why not? How does your response affect your interpretation of this part of the novel?

    c. Evaluate the narrator's funeral oration for Tod Clifton. Do you find it effective? Why or why not?

    d. Some readers of *Invisible Man* believe that the Brotherhood is a thinly disguised characterization of the American Communist Party. What do you think? How does your response affect your interpretation of the novel?

B. *Longer Papers*

1. Develop into a full-length paper one of your shorter papers on *Invisible Man*.

2. Write an interpretation of the pipe banging in Chapter 15 as symbolic of the plight of black men and women in American society.

3. "How things were twisted around," the narrator thinks at one point. Can this statement serve as the motto of the narrator's life so far?

4. Compare the narrator's eviction speech with his first speech for the Brotherhood in order to argue that one is more effective than the other.

5. Explain what Tod Clifton means when he says that Ras the Exhorter is strong and dangerous "on the inside" (Chapter 18).

IV. CHAPTER XXII TO THE END

A. *Brief Papers*
  1. a. Explain what the narrator means when he asks Brother Jack if it wouldn't be better if everyone called him "Marse Jack" (Chapter 23).
     b. Explain what the narrator means when he says that some of him had died with Tod Clifton.
     c. Explain why it is that the narrator almost gets into a fight with Brother Maceo.
     d. As the narrator runs away from Ras' henchmen, why does he instinctively head in the direction of Mary's?
     e. Explain the significance of the narrator's meeting with Mr. Norton in the subway.

  2. Argue for or against one of the following assertions:
     a. Brother Jack's glass eye is a sign of his inability to see clearly.
     b. By the end of the novel, the narrator no longer believes his earlier statement that "politically, individuals were without meaning" (Chapter 21).
     c. Ras is right in accusing the narrator of being "a paid stooge of the white enslaver" (Chapter 23).
     d. With Sybil, the narrator tries to do what Rinehart would have done in similar circumstances, and his strategy fully succeeds.

  3. a. As the tenement building starts to burn, the narrator is seized with "a fierce sense of exaltation" (Chapter 25). Is this your reaction, too? How does your reaction affect your interpretation of the conclusion of the novel?
     b. The narrator comes to see Ras as a funny but dangerous man. Do you agree? How does your reaction affect your interpretation of the conclusion of the novel?
     c. Do you agree with the narrator that "humanity is won by continuing to play in face of certain defeat" (Epilogue)? How does your response affect your interpretation of the novel's conclusion?
     d. In the novel's last chapter the narrator tells us that he loves. Do you believe him? Why or why not? How does your response affect your understanding of the novel as a whole?

B. *Longer Papers*
  1. Explain the purpose and significance in *Invisible Man* of the many references to seeing and blindness.
  2. Explain what the narrator means by the "beautiful absurdity" (Chapter 25) of his American identity.
  3. When the narrator's briefcase is returned to him after being lost, the narrator feels as if he regained something "infinitely precious"

(Chapter 25). Explain why the briefcase and its contents are so valuable to the narrator.

4. Make a list of positive characters in *Invisible Man,* characters who the narrator finally wants to emulate in one way or another, and then make a list of negative characters, those whom the narrator finally does not want to follow. Then argue for or against the assertion that the narrator learns who he is not only from the good examples but from the poor examples as well.

5. Both in the first and next-to-last chapters of *Invisible Man,* the narrator says that the end was in the beginning. Explain what he means by that statement.

6. Argue for or against the assertion that the growth and maturity of the narrator can be measured by the differences in style and content of his four major speeches: the graduation speech, the eviction speech, the speech for the Brotherhood, and Tod Clifton's funeral oration.

7. During the Harlem race riot, the narrator wonders how it all got started. What, according to *Invisible Man,* is the answer?

8. Explain the purpose and significance in *Invisible Man* of the many references to sleeping, dreaming, and waking.

9. Argue for or against the assertion that *Invisible Man* is a sexist novel because it clearly implies that women are less important than men.

10. Early in the novel the narrator says that "I believe in nothing if not in action" (Prologue). Does the novel as a whole confirm or undermine his statement?

11. Toward the end of the novel the narrator describes himself as "knowing now who I was" (Chapter 25). Do you agree that the narrator has finally gained a clear sense of who he is?

12. Select from *Invisible Man* the chapter or episode that you found most powerful and moving. Then choose a chapter or episode that had little or no impact on you. Compare and contrast the two in order to explain why one affected you so much more deeply than the other.

13. Explain the contribution of music, including jazz, to the meaning and experience of *Invisible Man.*

14. Explain how reading *Invisible Man* helped you to see yourself or your world more clearly.

15. You have received an invitation from your school's International Club to present a paper to the club's membership on *Invisible Man.* More specifically, you have been asked to address the question, "Does *Invisible Man* contribute to racial understanding? That is, does the novel enable both blacks and whites to understand each other better?" You have been further requested to focus your paper on a single episode or on two or three related episodes. Write the paper that you will later present orally.

J. D. SALINGER

The Catcher in the Rye

Writing Assignments

I. CHAPTERS 1 TO 8

A. *Brief Papers*
  1. a. Describe Holden's attitude toward old Spencer.
     b. Why does Holden call his brother D.B. "a prostitute" (Chapter 1)?
     c. Why does Holden like his brother's story, "The Secret Goldfish"?
     d. What do Holden's references to his brother Allie tell us about Holden?
     e. Show that Holden likes to pretend that he is suffering and at times seems to provoke others to make him suffer.

  2. Argue for or against one of these assertions:
     a. Holden is just like Ackley. Both are outsiders who hate "Stradlater's guts and . . . *everybody's* guts, damn near" (Chapter 3).
     b. Holden is not justified in attacking Stradlater's seductive "technique" (Chapter 7). Stradlater plays the dating game the same way as most others his age.
     c. When Holden says that Jane Gallagher used to keep her kings "all lined up in the back row" when she played checkers, he means that she is not very bright (Chapter 4).
     d. Holden's reason for lying to Mrs. Morrow is the pleasure and power of skillful lying.

  3. a. Holden says, "I never yell 'Good luck!' at anybody. It sounds terrible, when you think about it" (Chapter 2). What does Holden mean? Do you agree with him?
     b. How do you respond to the lies Holden tells Mrs. Morrow?
     c. Why does Holden buy his red hunting cap and what does the cap tell us about him?
     d. Why does Holden think that Allie's baseball glove is a good subject for a paper? Do you agree?

B. *Longer Papers*
  1. Discuss the way Holden's use of the words "phony" and "corny" help define his values and frustrations.
  2. Discuss Ackley as a foil to Holden. That is, show that while they have similar roles at Pencey, they are different in significant ways.

3. Argue for or against one of these assertions:
   a. Holden himself is guilty of nearly all the faults he finds in others.
   b. Holden is completely out of line in questioning Stradlater about his date with Jane, and Stradlater is justified in telling him that it is a "professional secret" (Chapter 6).
   c. Old Spencer gives Holden good advice when he says, "Life *is* a game, boy. Life *is* a game one plays according to the rules" (Chapter 2).

II. CHAPTERS 9 TO 17

A. Brief Papers
   1. a. Show that Jane Gallagher had an unhappy home life.
      b. Why does Holden think Sally Hayes is a phony for wanting to go skating at Radio City?
      c. Why does Holden like the two nuns?
      d. Describe Holden's fantasy after he is beaten by Maurice, and explain why Holden blames the fantasy on the movies (Chapter 14).
      e. What does Holden think is the "best thing" about the Museum of Natural History (Chapter 16)?

   2. Argue for or against one of these assertions:
      a. Holden has good reason to suspect that Jane was sexually harassed by her stepfather.
      b. Holden hates Maurice for mostly the same reasons he hates Stradlater.
      c. Holden is really in love with Sally; he's just too mixed up to realize it.
      d. Holden's behavior with the three women from Seattle is sexist, snobbish, and generally phony.

   3. a. Do you agree with Holden that Jesus probably saved Judas?
      b. How do you interpret Holden's fantasy that he was shot by Maurice (Chapter 14)?
      c. From your own experience choose an instance of phony or corny behavior and describe it in Holden's tone and style.
      d. Holden says this about the way the past is preserved in the Museum of Natural History: "Certain things should stay the way they are. You ought to be able to stick them in one of those big glass cases and just leave them alone. I know it's impossible, but it's too bad anyway" (Chapter 16). How do you interpret this passage?

B. *Holden's Literary Heroes*

Combine the following elements into a coherent paper about Holden's literary heroes.

1. Holden reveals a good deal about himself.
2. Holden makes comments about literary figures.

3. Holden says this in the first sentence of the novel.
4. He is not going to give a history of his childhood.
5. He is not going to start with "all that David Copperfield kind of crap."
6. He implies that he does not like the classic schoolboy hero.

7. *David Copperfield* is the classic novel.
8. It is a novel about growing up.
9. It is a story about a poor boy.
10. He struggles against hardships and villainy.
11. He finally achieves success.

12. At first David is weak and passive.
13. He is afraid of the world.
14. He eventually asserts himself.
15. He overcomes his enemies.
16. He makes a mature marriage.
17. He becomes "the hero of my own life."
18. This is what he says.

19. Holden does not identify with this kind of hero.
20. This hero achieves a happy ending.
21. This hero adjusts to society.
22. Holden's heroes are different.
23. His heroes are outsiders.
24. His heroes remain outsiders.
25. They die in the end.
26. They cannot accept things as they are.

27. Holden likes Eustacia Vye.
28. She is passionate and rebellious.
29. She is a character in Thomas Hardy's *The Return of the Native.*

30. Eustacia rebels against her environment.
31. Her environment is gloomy and repressive.
32. She cannot escape her environment.
33. She cannot change her environment.
34. Eustacia commits suicide.

35. Holden also identifies with Hamlet.
36. Holden does not like the way Hamlet is played.
37. Hamlet is played by Laurence Olivier.
38. Olivier is a great British actor.

39. Olivier plays Hamlet as heroic.
40. He plays Hamlet as resolute.
41. He plays Hamlet "like a goddam general, instead of a sad, screwed-up type guy."

42. Holden is like Hamlet.
43. Holden is "a sad, screwed-up type guy."
44. Holden cannot act decisively.

C. *Longer Papers*
   1. How is Holden's treatment of the three women from Seattle and the crowd at Ernie's (especially Lillian Simmons) related to his views about popular art and entertainment?
   2. Analyze Holden's conduct on his date with Sally Hayes. Does he behave according to his own standards?
   3. Analyze Sally's conduct on her date with Holden. Do you agree with Holden that she is the "queen of the phonies"?
   4. What can we learn about Holden by comparing the episode when he is beaten by Maurice to the earlier episode when he was beaten by Stradlater?
   5. Argue for or against the assertion that Holden is in love with Jane Gallagher.
   6. Discuss Holden's concern for the ducks in Central Park. Do you think Holden is reassured by Howitz's faith in nature: "Mother Nature'd take care of *you,* wouldn't she?" (Chapter 12).

III. CHAPTERS 18 TO THE END

A. *Brief Papers*
   1. a. Describe Mr. Antolini's marriage.
      b. How do Holden and Mr. Antolini differ in their views on the use of digression in Oral Expression (Chapter 24)?
      c. Explain Holden's attitude toward unconventional sexual behavior.
      d. What does it mean to be a "catcher in the rye"?
      e. Explain the event that connects Mr. Antolini and James Castle.

   2. Argue for or against one of these assertions:
      a. James Castle is a projection of Holden's own fears and desires.
      b. Carl Luce gives Holden good advice, both by what he says and by the example of his relationship with the Chinese sculptress.

    c. Holden's dream of being a catcher in the rye is a sign that he has not learned anything; he still wants the impossible.

    d. Holden's dream of being a catcher in the rye fits with other signs that he wants to be a priest.

3. a. Do you agree with Holden that "old Jesus probably would've puked" if He saw the Christmas pageant at Radio City (Chapter 18)?

    b. When Phoebe asks Holden to name people he really likes, why doesn't he mention Jane Gallagher?

    c. How do you account for Holden's continuing interest in Egyptian mummies?

    d. How do you interpret the final scene when Holden watches Phoebe on the carousel?

    e. What does Holden mean by his last two lines: "Don't ever tell anybody anything. If you do, you start missing everybody"?

B. *Longer Papers*

1. Discuss Holden's relationship to either Jane or Phoebe and show how this relationship is related to the main action of the novel.

2. Discuss Holden's hatred of the movies and how this hatred is related to his views on life and art.

3. Discuss the character and function of Stradlater, Maurice, and Mr. Cudahy (Jane's stepfather).

4. Three older men who might have been able to help Holden are D. B., Carl Luce, and Mr. Antolini. Why is Holden unwilling or unable to learn from these men? Is he right or wrong in rejecting them?

5. Discuss Holden's relationship with Sally and Jane in order to illustrate his difficulty in coping with adult life.

6. Argue for or against one of these assertions:

    a. Stradlater and Sally Hayes are normal, well adjusted, and popular teenagers who do not deserve Holden's insults and abuse.

    b. What Holden calls phoniness is unavoidable in adult life. Holden himself is often phony by his own standards and he will never get well until he accepts this kind of behavior in himself and others.

    c. Those critics who want to ban this novel from high school classes and libraries are right: Holden's immoral and misguided rebellion against society is a dangerous and harmful example for teenagers.

    d. The only way Holden can become a catcher in the rye is to become a writer of stories.

PART THREE
POETRY

REG SANER

Green Feathers

Five minutes till dawn
and a moist breath of pine resin comes to me
as from across a lake. It smells of wet lumber, naked and fragrant,
whose sap is another nostalgia.

5   In the early air
we keep trying to catch sight of something lost up ahead,
a moment when the light seems to have seen us
exactly as we wish we were.

Like a heap of green feathers poised on the rim of a cliff?
10 Like a sure thing that hasn't quite happened?
Like a marvelous idea that won't work?

Routinely amazing—
how moss tufts, half mud, keep supposing
almost nothing is hopeless. How even the bluest potato
15 grew eyes on faith the light would be there
and it was.

1983

Writing Assignments for "Green Feathers"

I. Brief Papers
    A. 1. How do the references to moistness, wetness, water, and sap in the first stanza help you understand the rest of the poem?
        2. Explain the first line and how it relates to the rest of the poem.
        3. Explain the relationship of stanzas 2 and 3.
        4. Discuss the significance of the poet's choice of the color green, an uncommon color for feathers.
        5. What is the similarity between the moss tufts and the "bluest potato" in the last stanza?

B. Argue for or against either assertion below.
   1. The poem is as much about potential as it is about nature.
   2. The poem is as much about hope as it is about nature.

C. Do you find this poem primarily whimsical, humorous, or serious? Explain why
   you believe it affects you as it does.

II. Longer Papers
A. Expand any paragraph assignment into a full-length paper.
B. Discuss what the pine resin, moss tufts, and blue potato have in common and
   relate each to the central image of the poem—the green feathers.

III. Behind the Mask (The Persona in the Poem)
From the sentences below, construct a short essay revealing the complexity of the
persona in a poem.

1. Obviously, the most important character in many poems is the speaker.
2. The speaker is the *I* of the poem.
3. The speaker is the *persona* of the poem.

4. A hint to reading poetry well is hidden in the term *persona*.
5. *Persona* is Latin for mask.

6. Sometimes a poet writes about what happens to him or her, drawing heavily on
   autobiographical experience.
7. The poet might use *I* in the poem.
8. The poet is *not* the *I* in the poem.

9. The poet creates a speech about a situation.
10. Even though the situation has happened to the poet, the *I* is a character separate
    from the poet.

11. The poet is masked behind the *I.*
12. The *I*, the *persona,* is a character with life of his or her own.

13. Here is an example.
14. William Butler Yeats writes a poem about a visit to an estate named Coole.
15. The poem is entitled "The Wild Swans at Coole."

16. The poem has an autobiographical ring.
17. Readers shouldn't ask automatically what happens to Yeats at Coole.
18. Readers should ask first what happens to the persona next to the lake in the
    poem.

19. Here is another example.
20. In "Terence This Is Stupid Stuff," A. E. Housman creates several speakers, but Terence is the *I,* the *persona.*
21. Even though Terence offers advice about drinking and about writing poetry, readers shouldn't ask automatically what Housman thinks about drinking and about writing poetry.
22. Readers should ask instead what Terence says about drinking and about writing poetry.

23. One way to escape one trap of the novice reader is to do this.
24. At first, ask yourself, "Who is speaking in the poem?"

25. Always remember that it is *not* the poet; the poet is masked behind a veil.
26. The veil is the *persona.*

27. When you recognize the veil, you will be a more sophisticated reader.

ANNE SEXTON

The Twelve Dancing Princesses

Before Reading

Free write for 5 to 10 minutes about why some people, more than others, like to stay out all night dancing or partying.

> If you danced from midnight
> to six A.M. who would understand?
>
> The runaway boy
> who chucks it all
> 5   to live on the Boston Common*
> on speed and saltines,
> pissing in the duck pond,
> rapping with the street priest,
> trading talk like blows,
> 10   another missing person,
> would understand.
>
> The paralytic's wife
> who takes her love to town,
> sitting on the bar stool,

*Boston Common: Oldest public park in America, established in 1634.

15 downing stingers and peanuts,
    singing "That ole Ace down in the hole,"
    would understand.

    The passengers
    from Boston to Paris
20 watching the movie with dawn
    coming up like statues of honey,
    having partaken of champagne and steak
    while the world turned like a toy globe,
    those murderers of the nightgown
25 would understand.

    The amnesiac
    who tunes into a new neighborhood,
    having misplaced the past,
    having thrown out someone else's
30 credit cards and monogrammed watch,
    would understand.

    The drunken poet
    (a genius by daylight)
    who places long-distance calls
35 at three A.M. and then lets you sit
    holding the phone while he vomits
    (he calls it "The Night of the Long Knives")
    getting his kicks out of the death call,
    would understand.

40 The insomniac
    listening to his heart
    thumping like a June bug,
    listening on his transistor
    to Long John Nebel arguing from New York,
45 lying on his bed like a stone table,
    would understand.

    The night nurse
    with her eyes slit like Venetian blinds,
    she of the tubes and the plasma,
50 listening to the heart monitor,
    the death cricket bleeping,
    she who calls you "we"
    and keeps vigil like a ballistic missile,
    would understand.

55 Once
this king had twelve daughters,
each more beautiful than the other.
They slept together, bed by bed
in a kind of girls' dormitory.
60 At night the king locked and bolted the door.
How could they possibly escape?
Yet each morning their shoes
were danced to pieces.
Each was as worn as an old jockstrap.
65 The king sent out a proclamation
that anyone who could discover
where the princesses did their dancing
could take his pick of the litter.
However there was a catch.
70 If he failed, he would pay with his life.
Well, so it goes.

Many princes tried,
each sitting outside the dormitory,
the door ajar so he could observe
75 what enchantment came over the shoes.
But each time the twelve dancing princesses
gave the snoopy man a Mickey Finn*
and so he was beheaded.
Poof! Like a basketball.

80 It so happened that a poor soldier
heard about these strange goings on
and decided to give it a try.
On his way to the castle
he met an old old woman.
85 Age, for a change, was of some use.
She wasn't stuffed in a nursing home.
She told him not to drink a drop of wine
and gave him a cloak that would make
him invisible when the right time came.
90 And thus he sat outside the dorm.
The oldest princess brought him some wine
but he fastened a sponge beneath his chin,
looking the opposite of Andy Gump.†

*Mickey Finn: A sleeping pill or potion.
†Andy Gump: A cartoon character with a huge bulbous nose and no chin.

The sponge soaked up the wine,
95   and thus he stayed awake.
He feigned sleep however
and the princesses sprang out of their beds
and fussed around like a Miss America Contest.
Then the eldest went to her bed
100   and knocked upon it and it sank into the earth.
They descended down the opening
one after the other. The crafty soldier
put on his invisible cloak and followed.
Yikes, said the youngest daughter,
105   something just stepped on my dress.
But the oldest thought it just a nail.

Next stood an avenue of trees,
each leaf made of sterling silver.
The soldier took a leaf for proof.
110   The youngest heard the branch break
and said, Oof! Who goes there?
But the oldest said, Those are
the royal trumpets playing triumphantly.
The next trees were made of diamonds.
115   He took one that flickered like Tinkerbell
and the youngest said: Wait up! He is here!
But the oldest said: Trumpets, my dear.

Next they came to a lake where lay
twelve boats with twelve enchanted princes
120   waiting to row them to the underground castle.
The soldier sat in the youngest's boat
and the boat was as heavy as if an icebox
had been added but the prince did not suspect.

Next came the ball where the shoes did duty.
125   The princesses danced like taxi girls at Roseland
as if those tickets would run right out.
They were painted in kisses with their secret hair
and though the soldier drank from their cups
they drank down their youth with nary a thought.
130   Cruets of champagne and cups full of rubies.
They danced until morning and the sun came up
naked and angry and so they returned
by the same strange route. The soldier
went forward through the dormitory and into
135   his waiting chair to feign his druggy sleep.
That morning the soldier, his eyes fiery

like blood in a wound, his purpose brutal
as if facing a battle, hurried with his answer
as if to the Sphinx. The shoes! The shoes!
140 The soldier told. He brought forth
the silver leaf, the diamond the size of a plum.

He had won. The dancing shoes would dance
no more. The princesses were torn from
their night life like a baby from its pacifier.
145 Because he was old he picked the eldest.
At the wedding the princesses averted their eyes
and sagged like old sweatshirts.
Now the runaways would run no more and never
again would their hair be tangled into diamonds,
150 never again their shoes worn down to a laugh,
never the bed falling down into purgatory
to let them climb in after
with their Lucifer kicking.

1971

Writing Assignments for "The Twelve Dancing Princesses"

I. Brief Papers
    A. 1. Explain why one or more of the following would understand the need to dance from midnight to 6 A.M.: the paralytic's wife, the runaway, the amnesiac, the insomniac, the night nurse, the drunken poet.
       2. Sexton uses a number of comparisons between unlike objects or things, using *like* or *as* to link the two. Consider the following comparisons:

> • The princesses' shoes were as "worn as an old jockstrap" (line 64).
> • The princes were each beheaded "Poof! Like a basketball" (line 79).
> • The princesses "fussed around like a Miss America Contest" (line 98).

Find as many examples of these comparisons—called *similes*—as you can. Explain how Sexton uses them to establish tone or mood in the poem; or explain how Sexton uses them for different purposes.
       3. Explain why the princesses avert their eyes at their sister's wedding.

    B. Argue for or against either assertion below.
       1. Although the poem is humorous, it is really very sad.
       2. The poet believes the young princesses are better off before their nightly excursion is discovered.

    C. 1. Argue for or against the assertion that the more poetic and more imaginative you are, the more likely you will be to like this poem.
       2. Explain why you believe women might like this poem more than men would.

II. Longer Papers

    A. Some people believe that all fairy tales are about growing up. Show that this poem is about young women's transition from girlhood to womanhood.

    B. Explain why the poet begins and ends the fairy tale with allusions or references to a bed.

JOHN KEATS

Ode on a Grecian Urn

1

Thou still unravish'd bride of quietness,
   Thou foster-child of silence and slow time,
Sylvan* historian, who canst thus express
   A flowery tale more sweetly than our rhyme:
5 What leaf-fring'd legend haunts about thy shape
     Of deities or mortals, or of both,
       In Tempe or the dales of Arcady?†
    What men or gods are these? What maidens loth?
What mad pursuit? What struggle to escape?
10   What pipes and timbrels? What wild ecstasy?

2

Heard melodies are sweet, but those unheard
   Are sweeter; therefore, ye soft pipes, play on;
Not to the sensual ear, but, more endear'd,
   Pipe to the spirit ditties of no tone:
15 Fair youth, beneath the trees, thou canst not leave
     Thy song, nor ever can those trees be bare;
       Bold lover, never, never canst thou kiss,
Though winning near the goal—yet, do not grieve;
     She cannot fade, though thou hast not thy bliss,
20   For ever wilt thou love, and she be fair!

3

Ah, happy, happy boughs! that cannot shed
   Your leaves, nor ever bid the spring adieu;
And, happy melodist, unwearied,
   For ever piping songs for ever new;

---

*sylvan: Rustic: of woods or forests.
†Tempe or the dales of Arcady: Tempe, a valley in Thessaly, and Arcady, a state in ancient Greece, are both associated with pastoral ideals and natural, woodland settings.

25 More happy love! more happy, happy love!
        For ever warm and still to be enjoy'd,
            For ever panting, and for ever young;
        All breathing human passion far above,
            That leaves a heart high-sorrowful and cloy'd,
30   A burning forehead, and a parching tongue.

                4

        Who are these coming to the sacrifice?
            To what green altar, O mysterious priest,
        Lead'st thou that heifer lowing at the skies,
            And all her silken flanks with garlands drest?
35 What little town by river or sea shore,
            Or mountain-built with peaceful citadel,
                Is emptied of this folk, this pious morn?
        And, little town, thy streets forevermore
            Will silent be; and not a soul to tell
40   Why thou art desolate, can e'er return.

                5

        O Attic* shape! Fair attitude! with brede
            Of marble men and maidens overwrought,
        With forest branches and the trodden weed;
            Thou, silent form, dost tease us out of thought
45 As doth eternity: Cold Pastoral!
            When old age shall this generation waste,
                Thou shalt remain, in midst of other woe
        Than ours, a friend to man, to whom thou say'st,
        "Beauty is truth, truth beauty,"—that is all
50   Ye know on earth, and all ye need to know.

                                                        1820

Writing Assignments for "Ode on a Grecian Urn"

I. Brief Papers
    A. 1. In a dictionary find the following terms: *Sylvan, Tempe, Arcady,* and *Attic.*
       Explain what they show about the urn.
    2. Explain how *still* (line 1) can have two different meanings.
    3. Explain what the following pictures on the urn have in common: the "mad
       pursuit" of the young maidens (lines 8–10); the young piper beneath the trees
       (lines 14–15); the Bold Lover about to kiss his fair maid (lines 17–20); and the
       priest bringing the festooned heifer to sacrifice (lines 31–34).
    4. Why does Keats tell the Bold Lover not to grieve?

*Attic: Grecian, Greek.

B. Argue for or against the assertion that the speaker in the poem is not very realistic about life.

C. 1. Explain why you believe someone aged 18 will react quite differently to Keats' poem than someone aged 40.
   2. To the speaker the urn achieves an intense beauty. What do you believe could be "beautiful" about pictures on an ancient Greek urn?

II. Longer Papers
   A. Discuss why the poet finds the ancient urn beautiful. What do you believe comprises his definition of *beauty?* Do you agree with his definition?
   B. Develop any one of the paragraph topics into a full-length paper.
   C. Help settle a controversy. Because Keats neglected to use quotation marks, we do not know if the urn's message to the world is "Beauty is truth, truth beauty" (line 49) or if the urn's message is "Beauty is truth, truth beauty,—that is all / Ye know on earth, and all ye need to know" (lines 49–50). Which do you believe Keats intended and why?

JOHN KEATS

Ode to a Nightingale

1

My heart aches, and a drowsy numbness pains
  My sense, as though of hemlock* I had drunk,
Or emptied some dull opiate to the drains
  One minute past, and Lethe-wards† had sunk:
5 'Tis not through envy of thy happy lot,
    But being too happy in thine happiness,—
      That thou, light-winged Dryad‡ of the trees,
        In some melodious plot
    Of beechen green, and shadows numberless,
10   Singest of summer in full-throated ease.

2

O, for a draught of vintage! that hath been
  Cool'd a long age in the deep-delved earth,
Tasting of Flora§ and the country green,

*hemlock: A poisonous herb.
†Lethe-wards: Crossing the river Lethe in Hades causes forgetfulness.
‡Dryad: Spirit or nymph.
§Flora: Flowers, and the Roman goddess of flowers.

    Dance, and Provençal song,* and sunburnt mirth!
15 O for a beaker full of the warm South,
        Full of the true, the blushful Hippocrene,†
            With beaded bubbles winking at the brim,
                And purple-stained mouth;
        That I might drink, and leave the world unseen,
20   And with thee fade away into the forest dim:

        3
    Fade far away, dissolve, and quite forget
        What thou among the leaves hast never known,
    The weariness, the fever, and the fret
        Here, where men sit and hear each other groan;
25 Where palsy shakes a few, sad, last gray hairs,
        Where youth grows pale, and spectre-thin, and dies;
            Where but to think is to be full of sorrow
                And leaden-eyed despairs,
        Where Beauty cannot keep her lustrous eyes,
30   Or new Love pine at them beyond to-morrow.

        4
    Away! away! for I will fly to thee,
        Not charioted by Bacchus and his pards,‡
    But on the viewless wings of Poesy,
        Though the dull brain perplexes and retards:
35 Already with thee! tender is the night,
        And haply the Queen-Moon is on her throne,
            Cluster'd around by all her starry Fays;§
                But here there is no light,
        Save what from heaven is with the breezes blown
40   Through verdurous glooms and winding mossy ways.

        5
    I cannot see what flowers are at my feet,
        Nor what soft incense hangs upon the boughs,
    But, in embalmed darkness, guess each sweet
        Wherewith the seasonable month endows

*Provençal song: Provence, in southern France, was known in the late Middle Ages for its writers, singers, and lovers.
†Hippocrene: Fountain of the muses on Mt. Helicon, the supposed source of all poetic and creative inspiration.
‡Bacchus and his pards: Bacchus, god of wine and revelry, was often depicted in a chariot drawn by leopards.
§Fays: Fairies.

45   The grass, the thicket, and the fruit-tree wild;
     White hawthorn, and the pastoral eglantine;*
       Fast fading violets cover'd up in leaves;
         And mid-May's eldest child,
     The coming musk-rose, full of dewy wine,
50   The murmurous haunt of flies on summer eves.

6

Darkling I listen; and, for many a time
     I have been half in love with easeful Death,
Call'd him soft names in many a mused rhyme,
     To take into the air my quiet breath;
55   Now more than ever seems it rich to die,
     To cease upon the midnight with no pain,
       While thou art pouring forth thy soul abroad
         In such an ecstasy!
Still wouldst thou sing, and I have ears in vain—
60   To thy high requiem become a sod.

7

Thou wast not born for death, immortal Bird!
     No hungry generations tread thee down;
The voice I hear this passing night was heard
     In ancient days by emperor and clown:
65   Perhaps the self-same song that found a path
     Through the sad heart of Ruth,† when, sick for home,
       She stood in tears amid the alien corn;
         The same that oft-times hath
     Charm'd magic casements, opening on the foam
70   Of perilous seas, in faery lands forlorn.

8

Forlorn! the very word is like a bell
     To toll me back from thee to my sole self!
Adieu! the fancy cannot cheat so well
     As she is fam'd to do, deceiving elf.
75   Adieu! adieu! thy plaintive anthem fades
     Past the near meadows, over the still stream,
       Up the hill-side; and now 'tis buried deep
         In the next valley-glades:
     Was it a vision, or a waking dream?
80   Fled is that music:—Do I wake or sleep?

1819

*hawthorn and eglantine: Both are wild flowers; eglantine is honeysuckle.
†Ruth: From the biblical story of Ruth.

Writing Assignments for "Ode to a Nightingale"

I. Brief Papers

A. 1. Show that the nightingale's song inspires the persona's desire to escape earthly limitations.

2. Explain what the persona wishes to "quite forget" (line 21) that "thou among the leaves hast never known" (line 22).

3. Show that Keats appeals to all the senses—sight, sound, taste, touch, and kinesis (the sense of motion)—to capture the experience of the bird's flight.

4. What inspires the persona's realization that the nightingale "wast not born for death" (line 61)?

5. The word *forlorn* both concludes stanza seven and begins stanza eight. How do the word's various meanings enrich the poem?

6. Discuss the persona's confusion in the final stanza: "Was it a vision, or a waking dream? / Fled is that music:—Do I wake or sleep?" (lines 79–80).

B. Argue for or against either assertion below.

1. The escape the persona envisions is as dangerous as it is soothing.

2. The dream world and reality hold equal attractions for the persona throughout the poem.

C. 1. Do you believe someone melancholy or gloomy most of the time would like this poem more than other people would? Why or why not?

2. The year before he wrote this ode in 1819 was a tragic one for Keats. His brother Tom died of tuberculosis—a disease that earlier killed Keats' mother and which was to claim Keats two years later. His own failing health and poverty made his love for Fanny Brawne, his fiancee, more and more hopeless, their marriage out of the question. Discuss how these biographical facts affect your response to the poem.

II. Longer Papers

A. In a library project, spend time finding more information than given in the footnotes on the following: *Lethe, Dryad, Hippocrene, Bacchus* and *his pards* (leopards), and the biblical story of *Ruth.* Explain how allusions or stories enrich the poem.

B. Argue for or against the assertion that the speaker's state of mind in the final stanza is essentially unchanged from his state of mind in the first.

C. Compare this poem to Shelley's "To a Sky-Lark" (p. 574) or Hardy's "The Darkling Thrush" (p. 641). Which do you like better and why?

PERCY BYSSHE SHELLEY

To a Sky-Lark*

    Hail to thee, blithe Spirit!
       Bird thou never wert—
    That from Heaven, or near it,
       Pourest thy full heart
5   In profuse strains of unpremeditated art.

    Higher still and higher
       From the earth thou springest
    Like a cloud of fire;
       The blue deep thou wingest,
10 And singing still dost soar, and soaring ever singest.

    In the golden lightning
       Of the sunken Sun—
    O'er which clouds are brightning,
       Thou dost float and run;
15 Like an unbodied joy whose race is just begun.

    The pale purple even
       Melts around thy flight,
    Like a star of Heaven
       In the broad day-light
20 Thou art unseen—but yet I hear thy shrill delight.

    Keen as are the arrows
       Of that silver sphere,
    Whose intense lamp narrows
       In the white dawn clear
25 Until we hardly see—we feel that it is there.

    All the earth and air
       With thy voice is loud,
    As when Night is bare
       From one lonely cloud
30 The moon rains out her beams—and Heaven is overflowed.

    What thou art we know not;
       What is most like thee?

*Sky-Lark: The small songbird sings only in flight, usually when it is too high to be seen from the ground.

From rainbow clouds there flow not
  Drops so bright to see
35 As from thy presence showers a rain of melody.

  Like a Poet hidden
    In the light of thought,
  Singing hymns unbidden,
    Till the world is wrought
40 To sympathy with hopes and fears it heeded not:

  Like a high-born maiden
    In a palace-tower,
  Soothing her love-laden
    Soul in secret hour,
45 With music sweet as love—which overflows her bower:

  Like a glow-worm golden
    In a dell of dew,
  Scattering unbeholden
    Its aerial hue
50 Among the flowers and grass which screen it from the view:

  Like a rose embowered
    In its own green leaves—
  By warm winds deflowered—
    Till the scent it gives
55 Makes faint with too much sweet heavy-winged thieves:

  Sound of vernal showers
    On the twinkling grass,
  Rain-awakened flowers,
    All that ever was
60 Joyous, and clear and fresh, thy music doth surpass.

  Teach us, Sprite or Bird,
    What sweet thoughts are thine;
  I have never heard
    Praise of love or wine
65 That panted forth a flood of rapture so divine:

  Chorus Hymeneal*
    Or triumphal chaunt
  Matched with thine would be all

*Chorus Hymeneal: In celebration of marriage, after the Greek god of marriage, Hymen.

But an empty vaunt,
70 A thing wherein we feel there is some hidden want.

What objects are the fountains
    Of thy happy strain?
What fields or waves or mountains?
    What shapes of sky or plain?
75 What love of thine own kind? what ignorance of pain?

With thy clear keen joyance
    Languor cannot be—
Shadow of annoyance
    Never came near thee;
80 Thou lovest—but ne'er knew love's sad satiety.

Waking or asleep,
    Thou of death must deem
Things more true and deep
    Than we mortals dream,
85 Or how could thy notes flow in such a chrystal stream?

We look before and after,
    And pine for what is not—
Our sincerest laughter
    With some pain is fraught—
90 Our sweetest songs are those that tell of saddest thought.

Yet if we could scorn
    Hate and pride and fear;
If we were things born
    Not to shed a tear,
95 I know not how thy joy we ever should come near.

Better than all measures
    Of delightful sound—
Better than all treasures
    That in books are found—
100 Thy skill to poet were, thou Scorner of the ground!

Teach me half the gladness
    That thy brain must know,
Such harmonious madness
    From my lips would flow
105 The world should listen then—as I am listening now.

1820

Writing Assignments for "To a Sky-Lark"

I. Brief Papers

A. 1. Show that the poet believes the sky-lark possesses knowledge beyond human understanding.
   2. Explain how the poem is structured loosely around different questions the poet poses and addresses in stanzas 1–6, 7–12, and 13–22.
   3. Show one way in which the poet uses word choice, figurative language, repetition, or any other stylistic device to suggest the rapture and passion the bird inspires.

B. Argue for or against either assertion below.
   1. The poem shows us more about the persona than it does about the sky-lark.
   2. The speaker's excessive emotion might embarrass contemporary readers.

C. 1. "To a Sky-Lark" is usually omitted from textbooks written for classes like yours. Do you believe the poem is suitable or interesting? Why or why not?
   2. In stanza 18 (lines 86–90), the speaker claims that most people are unhappy because they want what they can't have. Do you agree with this description of the human condition? How does your agreement or disagreement affect your response to the poem?

II. Longer Papers

A. In his essay "A Defense of Poetry," Shelley claims that poets, more than any other people, understand human nature and the unchanging truths about people and the world. To what extent does he reveal such understanding in this poem?
B. Develop either B.1 or B.2 into a full-length paper.
C. Show how the stanzaic form—the length, rhythms, and punctuation of the stanzas—reinforces the poem's subject matter.

MARGARET ATWOOD

Against Still Life

Orange in the middle of a table:

It isn't enough
to walk around it
at a distance, saying
5   it's an orange:
nothing to do
with us, nothing
else: leave it alone

       I want to pick it up
10   in my hand
       I want to peel the
       skin off; I want
       more to be said to me
       than just Orange:
15   want to be told
       everything it has to say

       And you, sitting across
       the table, at a distance, with
       your smile contained, and like the orange
20   in the sun: silent:

       Your silence
       isn't enough for me
       now, no matter with what
       contentment you fold
25   your hands together; I want
       anything you can say
       in the sunlight:

       stories of your various
       childhoods, aimless journeyings,
30   your loves; your articulate
       skeleton; your posturings; your lies.

       These orange silences
       (sunlight and hidden smile)
       make me want to
35   wrench you into saying;
       now I'd crack your skull
       like a walnut, split it like a pumpkin
       to make you talk, or get
       a look inside

40   But quietly:
       if I take the orange
       with care enough and hold it
       gently

       I may find
45   an egg
       a sun
       an orange moon

perhaps a skull; center
of all energy
50 resting in my hand

can change it to
whatever I desire
it to be

and you, man, orange afternoon
55 lover, wherever
you sit across from me
(tables, trains, buses)

if I watch
quietly enough
60 and long enough

at last, you will say
(maybe without speaking)

(there are mountains
inside your skull
65 garden and chaos, ocean
and hurricane; certain
corners of rooms, portraits
of great-grandmothers, curtains
of a particular shade;
70 your deserts; your private
dinosaurs; the first
woman)

all I need to know:
tell me
75 everything
just as it was
from the beginning.

1966

Writing Assignments for "Against Still Life"

I. Brief Papers
  A. 1. How are the first two stanzas of the poem related to the second two?
      2. How are stanzas 5 and 6 related to the first four?

    3. What kind of relationship does the speaker want with the man in the poem?
    4. How does the poet use the colon (:) in the poem?
    5. What does the title mean in relation to the poem?

  B. Argue for or against either assertion below.
    1. The couple in the poem have a good relationship.
    2. The persona's attitude toward the man changes during the poem.

  C. 1. It is almost a cliché that women in our society are the more open, more communicative in relationships, while men are the more silent, the less willing to share. Do you believe this poem escapes such clichés? If so, how?
    2. Why do you believe the poet links an egg, a sun, a moon, and a skull in stanza 9?
    3. In stanzas 10 and 11, the persona hopes that if she watches "quietly" and "long enough," her lover "will say / (maybe without speaking)" what she wants to know. What do you think she means by that?

II. Longer Papers
  A. Compare this poem to Adrienne Rich's "Trying to Talk to a Man" (p. 742).
  B. Compare this poem to Irvin Shaw's short story "The Girls in Their Summer Dresses" (pp. 243–251).
  C. Show how punctuation is used appropriately and interestingly throughout the poem.

DYLAN THOMAS

Fern Hill

        Now as I was young and easy under the apple boughs
        About the lilting house and happy as the grass was green,
            The night above the dingle starry,
                Time let me hail and climb
5   Golden in the heydays of his eyes,
        And honored among wagons I was prince of the apple towns
        And once below a time I lordly had the trees and leaves
                Trail with daisies and barley
            Down the rivers of the windfall light.

10   And as I was green and carefree, famous among the barns
        About the happy yard and singing as the farm was home,
            In the sun that is young once only,
                Time let me play and be
            Golden in the mercy of his means,

15 And green and golden I was huntsman and herdsman, the calves
Sang to my horn, the foxes on the hills barked clear and cold,
    And the sabbath rang slowly
  In the pebbles of the holy streams.

  All the sun long it was running, it was lovely, the hay
20 Fields high as the house, the tunes from the chimneys, it was air
    And playing, lovely and watery
      And fire green as grass.
    And nightly under the simple stars
  As I rode to sleep the owls were bearing the farm away,
25 All the moon long I heard, blessed among stables, the nightjars
    Flying with the ricks, and the horses
      Flashing into the dark.

  And then to awake, and the farm, like a wanderer white
With the dew, come back, the cock on his shoulder: it was all
30   Shining, it was Adam and maiden,
    The sky gathered again
    And the sun grew round that very day.
So it must have been after the birth of the simple light
In the first, spinning place, the spellbound horses walking warm
35   Out of the whinnying green stable
    On to the fields of praise.

  And honored among foxes and pheasants by the gay house
Under the new made clouds and happy as the heart was long,
    In the sun born over and over,
40   I ran my heedless ways,
    My wishes raced through the house high hay
And nothing I cared, at my sky blue trades, that time allows
  In all his tuneful turning so few and such morning songs
    Before the children green and golden
45   Follow him out of grace.

  Nothing I cared, in the lamb white days, that time would take me
Up to the swallow thronged loft by the shadow of my hand,
    In the moon that is always rising,
    Nor that riding to sleep
50   I should hear him fly with the high fields
And wake to the farm forever fled from the childless land.
Oh as I was young and easy in the mercy of his means,
    Time held me green and dying
      Though I sang in my chains like the sea.

                           1938

Writing Assignments for "Fern Hill"

I. Brief Papers

A. 1. Find evidence in the poem that the speaker is less happy than he was in childhood.
   2. Throughout the poem, the poet suggests the power of time. He says, "Time *let me* hail and climb" (line 4); "Time *let me* play and be" (line 13); "time *allows* / In all his tuneful turning so few and such morning songs" (lines 42–43). Explain how time's power is central to the poem, relating these and other references to time to the last two lines in the final stanza.
   3. The following patterns of imagery appear a number of times in the poem. Choose one pattern and trace it throughout the poem. Explain how it helps you understand the poem:
      a. References to the color green.
      b. References to the color gold.
      c. References to the color white.
      d. References to heat and warmth.
      e. References to flight and upward movement.
      f. References to music.
      g. References to the sun and the moon.
      h. References to the running and racing.
   4. How does the biblical story in Genesis—of Adam and Eve's fall from grace—relate to the speaker's attitude toward childhood?

B. Argue for or against either assertion below.
   1. "Fern Hill" is a depressing poem.
   2. The poem prepares us for its somber conclusion well before the conclusion of stanza 5.

II. Longer Papers

A. Develop any one of the paragraph assignments into a full-length paper.
B. Some people evaluate a poem's power by measuring how its use of strikingly original language conveys universal truths or evokes intense emotional response. Clarifying and expanding on that criterion to suit your own tastes, evaluate this poem's power.
C. Discuss one or more of the central tensions within the poem: joy and despair, youth and age, life and death, innocence and experience, conscious and unconscious behavior, or imagination and reality.
D. "Fern Hill" and Walt Whitman's "Out of the Cradle Endlessly Rocking" (p. 583) both treat childhood experience recalled in maturity. Compare the speakers' experiences and their emotional reactions to those experiences.

WALT WHITMAN

Out of the Cradle Endlessly Rocking

Out of the cradle endlessly rocking,
Out of the mocking-bird's throat, the musical shuttle,
Out of the Ninth-month midnight,
Over the sterile sands and the fields beyond where the child
    leaving his bed wandered alone, bareheaded, barefoot,

5   Down from the showered halo,
Up from the mystic play of shadows twining and twisting as if
    they were alive,
Out from the patches of briers and blackberries,
From the memories of the bird that chanted to me,
From your memories sad brother, from the fitful risings and
    fallings I heard,
10 From under that yellow half-moon late-risen and swollen as if
    with tears,
From those beginning notes of yearning and love there in the
    mist,
From the thousand responses of my heart never to cease,
From the myriad thence aroused words,
From the word stronger and more delicious than any,
15 From such as now they start the scene revisiting,
As a flock, twittering, rising, or overhead passing,
Borne hither, ere all eludes me, hurriedly,
A man, yet by these tears a little boy again,
Throwing myself on the sand, confronting the waves,
20 I, chanter of pains and joys, uniter of here and hereafter,
Taking all hints to use them, but swiftly leaping beyond them,
A reminiscence sing.

Once Paumanok,*
When the lilac-scent was in the air and Fifth-month grass was
    growing,
25 Up this seashore in some briers,
Two feathered guests from Alabama, two together,
And their nest, and four light-green eggs spotted with brown,
And every day the he-bird to and fro near at hand,

*Paumanok: Long Island. Whitman was born near Huntington, Long Island, in 1819.

And every day the she-bird crouched on her nest, silent, with
    bright eyes,
30   And every day I, a curious boy, never too close, never disturbing
    them,
Cautiously peering, absorbing, translating.

Shine! shine! shine!
Pour down your warmth, great sun!
While we bask, we two together,

35   *Two together!*
Winds blow south, or winds blow north,
Day come white, or night come black,
Home, or rivers and mountains from home,
Singing all time, minding no time,
40   *While we two keep together.*

Till of a sudden,
May-be killed, unknown to her mate,
One forenoon the she-bird crouched not on the nest,
Nor returned that afternoon, nor the next,
45   Nor ever appeared again.

And thenceforward all summer in the sound of the sea,
And at night under the full of the moon in calmer weather,
Over the hoarse surging of the sea,
Or flitting from brier to brier by day,
50   I saw, I heard at intervals the remaining one, the he-bird,
The solitary guest from Alabama.

Blow! blow! blow!
Blow up sea-winds along Paumanok's shore;
I wait and I wait till you blow my mate to me.

55   Yes, when the stars glistened,
All night long on the prong of a moss-scalloped stake,
Down almost amid the slapping waves,
Sat the lone singer wonderful causing tears.

He called on his mate,
60   He poured forth the meanings which I of all men know.

Yes my brother I know,
The rest might not, but I have treasured every note,
For more than once dimly down to the beach gliding,

Silent, avoiding the moonbeams, blending myself with the
   shadows,
65   Recalling now the obscure shapes, the echoes, the sounds and
   sights after their sorts,
The white arms out in the breakers tirelessly tossing,
I, with bare feet, a child, the wind wafting my hair,
Listened long and long.

Listened to keep, to sing, now translating the notes,
70   Following you my brother.

Soothe! soothe! soothe!
Close on its wave soothes the wave behind,
And again another behind embracing and lapping, every one close,
But my love soothes not me, not me.
75   *Low hangs the moon, it rose late,*
It is lagging—O I think it is heavy with love, with love.

O madly the sea pushes upon the land,
With love, with love.

O night! do I not see my love fluttering out among the breakers?
80   *What is that little black thing I see there in the white?*

Loud! loud! loud!
Loud I call to you, my love!
High and clear I shoot my voice over the waves,
Surely you must know who is here, is here,
85   *You must know who I am, my love.*

Low-hanging moon!
What is that dusky spot in your brown yellow?
O it is the shape, the shape of my mate!
O moon do not keep her from me any longer.

90   *Land! land! O land!*
Whichever way I turn, O I think you could give me my mate back
*   again if you only would,*
For I am almost sure I see her dimly whichever way I look.

O rising stars!
Perhaps the one I want so much will rise, will rise with some of you.

95   *O throat! O trembling throat!*
Sound clearer through the atmosphere!

Pierce the woods, the earth,
Somewhere listening to catch you must be the one I want.

Shake out carols!
100 *Solitary here, the night's carols!*
Carols of lonesome love! death's carols!
Carols under that lagging, yellow, waning moon!
O under that moon where she droops almost down into the sea!
O reckless despairing carols.

105 *But soft! sink low!*
Soft, let me just murmur,
And do you wait a moment you husky-noised sea,
For somewhere I believe I heard my mate responding to me,
So faint, I must be still, be still to listen,
110 *But not altogether still, for then she might not come immediately to me.*

Hither my love!
Here I am! Here!
With this just-sustained note I announce myself to you,
This gentle call is for you my love, for you.

115 *Do not be decoyed elsewhere,*
That is the whistle of the wind, it is not my voice,
That is the fluttering, the fluttering of the spray,
Those are the shadows of leaves.

O darkness! O in vain!
120 *O I am very sick and sorrowful.*

O brown halo in the sky near the moon, drooping upon the sea!
O troubled reflection in the sea!
O throat! O throbbing heart!
And I singing uselessly, uselessly all the night.

125 *O past! O happy life! O songs of joy!*
In the air, in the woods, over fields,
Loved! loved! loved! loved! loved!
But my mate no more, no more with me!
We two together no more.

130 The aria sinking,
All else continuing, the stars shining,
The winds blowing, the notes of the bird continuous echoing,

With angry moans the fierce old mother incessantly moaning,
On the sands of Paumanok's shore gray and rustling,
135 The yellow half-moon enlarged, sagging down, drooping, the
    face of the sea almost touching,
The boy ecstatic, with his bare feet the waves, with his hair the
    atmosphere dallying,
The love in the heart long pent, now loose, now at last
    tumultuously bursting,
The aria's meaning, the ears, the soul, swiftly depositing,
The strange tears down the cheeks coursing,
140 The colloquy there, the trio, each uttering,
The undertone, the savage old mother incessantly crying,
To the boy's soul's questions sullenly timing, some drowned
    secret hissing,
To the outsetting bard.

Demon or bird! (said the boy's soul,)
145 Is it indeed toward your mate you sing? or is it really to me?
For I, that was a child, my tongue's use sleeping, now I have
    heard you,
Now in a moment I know what I am for, I awake,
And already a thousand singers, a thousand songs, clearer,
    louder and more sorrowful than yours,
A thousand warbling echoes have started to life within me,
    never to die.

150 O you singer solitary, singing by yourself, projecting me,
O solitary me listening, never more shall I cease perpetuating
    you,
Never more shall I escape, never more the reverberations,
Never more the cries of unsatisfied love be absent from me,
Never again leave me to be the peaceful child I was before
    what there in the night,
155 By the sea under the yellow and sagging moon,
The messenger there aroused, the fire, the sweet hell within,
The unknown want, the destiny of me.

O give me the clue! (it lurks in the night here somewhere,)
O if I am to have so much, let me have more!

160 A word then, (for I will conquer it,)
The word final, superior to all,
Subtle, sent up—what is it?—I listen;

Are you whispering it, and have been all the time, you
    sea-waves?
Is that it from your liquid rims and wet sands?

165   Whereto answering, the sea,
    Delaying not, hurrying not,
    Whispered me through the night, and very plainly before
        daybreak,
    Lisped to me the low and delicious word death,
    And again death, death, death, death,
170   Hissing melodious, neither like the bird nor like my
        aroused child's heart,
    But edging near as privately for me rustling at my feet,
    Creeping thence steadily up to my ears and laving me
        softly all over
    Death, death, death, death, death.

    Which I do not forget,
175   But fuse the song of my dusky demon and brother,

    That he sang to me in the moonlight on Paumanok's gray
        beach,
    With the thousand responsive songs at random,
    My own songs awaked from that hour,
    And with them the key, the word up from the waves,
180   The word of the sweetest song and all songs,
    That strong and delicious word which, creeping to my feet,
    (Or like some old crone rocking the cradle, swathed in sweet
        garments, bending aside,)
    The sea whispered me.

                                                  1881

Writing Assignments for
"Out of the Cradle Endlessly Rocking"

I. Brief Papers
    A. 1. Discuss several ways the poet links the boy and the bird.
        2. Show that the speaker's boyhood experience significantly changed his life.
        3. Discuss the kinds of birth—both literal and figurative—you find in the poem.
        4. Discuss the kinds of death—both literal and figurative—you find in the poem.
        5. In line 127, the bird sings, "Loved! loved! loved! loved! loved!" How does that
           relate to the speaker's repetition of the word "death" in line 173?

B. Argue for or against either assertion below.
1. The poet implies the bird's loss of its loved one has more lasting impact on the speaker's life than the bird's love itself.
2. Although significantly less exuberant, the last ten lines of the poem are no less optimistic than the first twenty-two lines.

C. 1. What do you believe the poet means when he writes that death is "The word of the sweetest song and all songs" (line 180)? How does your understanding of the line affect your response to the poem?
2. Which part of the poem affects you most intensely: (a) the speaker's recollection of his childhood experience; (b) the bird's lament for his lost love; (c) the young child's revelation after the bird's song; or (d) the speaker's mature revelation about death at the end of the poem? Why do you react as you do?

II. Longer Papers

A. After you have reread the poem at least twice, discuss how one of the following parts of the poem relates to the rest of the poem: the speaker's introduction (lines 1–22); the bird's lament for its lost love (lines 71–129); the young boy's reaction to the bird's song (lines 130–149); or the speaker's revelation about death at the end of the poem (lines 160–183).
B. "Out of the Cradle Endlessly Rocking" and Dylan Thomas' "Fern Hill" (p. 580) both treat childhood experience recalled in maturity. Compare the speakers' experiences and their emotional reactions to those experiences.

WILLIAM WORDSWORTH

Ode

INTIMATIONS OF IMMORTALITY FROM
RECOLLECTIONS OF EARLY CHILDHOOD

> The Child is father of the Man;
> And I could wish my days to be
> Bound each to each by natural piety.*

1

There was a time when meadow, grove, and stream,
The earth, and every common sight,
To me did seem
Appareled in celestial light,

---

*The Child . . . / . . . each to each by natural piety": The last lines of another Wordsworth poem, "My Heart Leaps Up."

5   The glory and the freshness of a dream.
    It is not now as it hath been of yore—
              Turn whereso'er I may,
                By night or day,
    The things which I have seen I now can see no more.

              2
10   The Rainbow comes and goes,
              And lovely is the Rose,
              The Moon doth with delight
    Look round her when the heavens are bare,
              Waters on a starry night
15   Are beautiful and fair;
        The sunshine is a glorious birth;
        But yet I know, where'er I go,
    That there hath passed away a glory from the earth.

              3
    Now while the birds thus sing a joyous song,
20   And while the young lambs bound
              As to the tabor's sound,
    To me alone there came a thought of grief:
    A timely utterance gave that thought relief,
              And I again am strong:
25 The cataracts blow their trumpets from the steep;
    No more shall grief of mine the season wrong;
    I hear the Echoes through the mountains throng,
    The Winds come to me from the fields of sleep,
              And all the earth is gay;
30   Land and sea
        Give themselves up to jollity,
              And with the heart of May
        Doth every Beast keep holiday—
              Thou Child of Joy,
35 Shout round me, let me hear thy shouts, thou
        happy Shepherd-boy!

              4
    Ye blessed Creatures, I have heard the call
        Ye to each other make; I see
    The heavens laugh with you in your jubilee;
        My heart is at your festival,
40   My head hath its coronal,
    The fullness of your bliss, I feel—I feel it all.
              Oh, evil day! if I were sullen
              While Earth herself is adorning,

This sweet May morning,
45   And the Children are culling
              On every side,
In a thousand valleys far and wide,
Fresh flowers; while the sun shines warm,
And the Babe leaps up on his Mother's arm—
50   I hear, I hear, with joy I hear!
         —But there's a Tree, of many, one,
A single Field which I have looked upon,
Both of them speak of something that is gone:
              The Pansy at my feet
55   Doth the same tale repeat:
Whither is fled the visionary gleam?
Where is it now, the glory and the dream?

                    5
Our birth is but a sleep and a forgetting:
The Soul that rises with us, our life's Star,*
60   Hath had elsewhere its setting,
              And cometh from afar:
         Not in entire forgetfulness,
         And not in utter nakedness,
But trailing clouds of glory do we come
65   From God, who is our home:
Heaven lies about us in our infancy!
Shades of the prison-house begin to close
              Upon the growing Boy
              But he
70 Beholds the light, and whence it flows,
              He sees it in his joy;
The Youth, who daily farther from the east
              Must travel, still is Nature's Priest,
              And by the vision splendid
75   Is on his way attended;
At length the Man perceives it die away,
And fade into the light of common day.

                    6
Earth fills her lap with pleasures of her own;
Yearnings she hath in her own natural kind,
80 And, even with something of a Mother's mind,
              And no unworthy aim,
              The homely Nurse doth all she can
To make her foster child, her Inmate Man,

*our life's Star: Our soul is our sun, our life-giving star.

Forget the glories he hath known,
85   And that imperial palace whence he came.

7

Behold the Child among his newborn blisses,
A six-years' Darling of a pygmy size!
See, where 'mid work of his own hand he lies,
Fretted by sallies of his mother's kisses,
90   With light upon him from his father's eyes!
See, at his feet, some little plan or chart,
Some fragment from his dream of human life,
Shaped by himself with newly-learned art;
A wedding or a festival,
95   A mourning or a funeral;
And this hath now his heart,
And unto this he frames his song;
Then will he fit his tongue
To dialogues of business, love, or strife;
100   But it will not be long
Ere this be thrown aside,
And with new joy and pride
The little Actor cons another part;
Filling from time to time his "humorous stage"
105   With all the Persons, down to palsied Age,
That Life brings with her in her equipage;
As if his whole vocation
Were endless imitation.

8

Thou, whose exterior semblance doth belie
110   Thy Soul's immensity;
Thou best Philosopher, who yet dost keep
Thy heritage, thou Eye among the blind,
That, deaf and silent, read'st the eternal deep,
Haunted forever by the eternal mind—
115   Mighty Prophet! Seer blest!
On whom those truths do rest,
Which we are toiling all our lives to find,
In darkness lost, the darkness of the grave;
Thou, over whom thy Immortality
120   Broods like the Day, a Master o'er a Slave,
A Presence which is not to be put by;
Thou little Child, yet glorious in the might
Of heaven-born freedom on thy being's height,

Why with such earnest pains dost thou provoke
125   The years to bring the inevitable yoke,
Thus blindly with thy blessedness at strife?
Full soon thy Soul shall have her earthly freight,
And custom lie upon thee with a weight,
Heavy as frost, and deep almost as life!

9

130   O joy! that in our embers
Is something that doth live,
That nature yet remembers
What was so fugitive!
The thought of our past years in me doth breed
135   Perpetual benediction: not indeed
For that which is most worthy to be blest;
Delight and liberty, the simple creed
Of Childhood, whether busy or at rest,
With new-fledged hope still fluttering in his breast—
140   Not for these I raise
The song of thanks and praise;
But for those obstinate questionings
Of sense and outward things,
Fallings from us, vanishings;
145   Blank misgivings of a Creature
Moving about in worlds not realized,
High instincts before which our mortal Nature
Did tremble like a guilty Thing surprised;
But for those first affections,
150   Those shadowy recollections,
Which, be they what they may,
Are yet the fountain light of all our day,
Are yet a master light of all our seeing;
Uphold us, cherish, and have power to make
155   Our noisy years seem moments in the being
Of the eternal Silence: truths that wake,
To perish never;
Which neither listlessness, nor mad endeavor,
Nor Man nor Boy,
160   Nor all that is at enmity with joy,
Can utterly abolish or destroy!
Hence in a season of calm weather
Though inland far we be,
Our Souls have sight of that immortal sea
165   Which brought us hither,

Can in a moment travel thither,
And see the Children sport upon the shore,
And hear the mighty waters rolling evermore.

10
Then sing, ye Birds, sing, sing a joyous song!
170   And let the young Lambs bound
             As to the tabor's sound!
We in thought will join your throng,
             Ye that pipe and ye that play,
             Ye that through your hearts today
175   Feel the gladness of the May!
What though the radiance which was once so bright
Be now forever taken from my sight,
             Though nothing can bring back the hour
Of splendor in the grass, of glory in the flower;
180   We will grieve not, rather find
             Strength in what remains behind;
             In the primal sympathy
             Which having been must ever be;
             In the soothing thoughts that spring
185   Out of human suffering;
             In the faith that looks through death,
In years that bring the philosophic mind.

11
And O, ye Fountains, Meadows, Hills, and Groves,
Forebode not any severing of our loves!
190   Yet in my heart of hearts I feel your might;
I only have relinquished one delight
To live beneath your more habitual sway.
I love the Brooks which down their channels fret,
Even more than when I tripped lightly as they;
195   The innocent brightness of a newborn Day
             Is lovely yet;
The clouds that gather round the setting sun
Do take a sober coloring from an eye
That hath kept watch o'er man's mortality;
200   Another race hath been, and other palms are won.
Thanks to the human heart by which we live,
Thanks to its tenderness, its joys, and fears,
To me the meanest flower that blows can give
Thoughts that do often lie too deep for tears.

1807

Writing Assignments for "Ode: Intimations of Immortality from Recollections of Early Childhood"

I. Brief Papers

A. 1. In stanzas 1–4 show that the speaker regrets that he cannot respond to nature as he once did.
   2. Read stanza 5 several times. Summarize as best you can the speaker's view of youth. Why does he believe a child's perceptions of nature are more intense and more immediate than an adult's?
   3. How are lines 59–65 in stanza 5 related to lines 149–151 in stanza nine?
   4. Reread stanzas 9 and 10 several times. Show that in those stanzas the speaker reconciles his feelings and comes to value his own perceptions of nature.
   5. Poems by nineteenth-century romantic poets such as Wordsworth, Coleridge, Keats, and Shelley are often marked by their intense emotion. Find one example of intense feeling in the poem and discuss how the language, the style, and/or the speaker's attitude reinforces the emotionalism of the passage.

B. Argue for or against either assertion below.
   1. Stanza 10 is the most important stanza in the poem.
   2. Although it is one of Wordsworth's most famous, this poem is not often included in textbooks for classes such as yours. Is it appropriate for your class?

C. 1. Do you believe you respond to nature differently now than you did as a child? How does your altered perspective affect your interpretation of Wordsworth's poem?
   2. Read the poem aloud to yourself once or twice. Write a paragraph about your reaction to that reading. Does it make you like the poem more? Less? Does its language move you? Embarrass you?

II. Longer Papers

A. Go through the poem and circle all the references to light. Discuss various meanings of light in the poem.
B. After rereading the poem several times (concentrating on the last two stanzas), discuss in what ways Wordsworth believes adults can appreciate nature more than children can. How does he believe their response alters over time?
C. Some people today find the intense emotions of poems from the romantic period to be excessive or even embarrassing. Find examples of language, style, or speaker's attitude that display intense emotions. Discuss why you like or why you are put off by the passages.
D. Discuss the relationship of the epigraph to the rest of the poem.

WILLIAM WORDSWORTH

*Lines**

COMPOSED A FEW MILES ABOVE TINTERN
ABBEY ON REVISITING THE BANKS OF THE
WYE DURING A TOUR, JULY 13, 1798

Five years have passed; five summers, with the length
Of five long winters! and again I hear
These waters, rolling from their mountain-springs
With a soft inland murmur. Once again
5   Do I behold these steep and lofty cliffs,
That on a wild secluded scene impress
Thoughts of more deep seclusion; and connect
The landscape with the quiet of the sky.
The day is come when I again repose
10   Here, under this dark sycamore, and view
These plots of cottage ground, these orchard tufts,
Which at this season, with their unripe fruits,
Are clad in one green hue, and lose themselves
'Mid groves and copses. Once again I see
15   These hedgerows, hardly hedgerows, little lines
Of sportive wood run wild; these pastoral farms,
Green to the very door; and wreaths of smoke
Sent up, in silence, from among the trees!
With some uncertain notice, as might seem
20   Of vagrant dwellers in the houseless woods,
Or of some Hermit's cave, where by his fire
The Hermit sits alone.
                  These beauteous forms,
Through a long absence, have not been to me
As is a landscape to a blind man's eye;
25   But oft, in lonely rooms, and 'mid the din
Of towns and cities, I have owed to them,
In hours of weariness, sensations sweet,
Felt in the blood, and felt along the heart;
And passing even into my purer mind,
30   With tranquil restoration—feelings too

---

*Lines: The poem was composed after Wordsworth had concluded a four-day walking tour with
his sister Dorothy through the Wye Valley in western England. He visited the ruins of Tintern
Abbey in Monmouthshire.

Of unremembered pleasure; such, perhaps,
As have no slight or trivial influence
On that best portion of a good man's life,
His little, nameless, unremembered, acts
35   Of kindness and of love. Nor less, I trust,
To them I may have owed another gift,
Of aspect more sublime; that blessed mood,
In which the burthen of the mystery,
In which the heavy and the weary weight
40   Of all this unintelligible world,
Is lightened—that serene and blessed mood,
In which the affections gently lead us on—
Until, the breath of this corporeal frame
And even the motion of our human blood
45   Almost suspended, we are laid asleep
In body, and become a living soul;
While with an eye made quiet by the power
Of harmony, and the deep power of joy,
We see into the life of things.

                                        If this
50   Be but a vain belief, yet, oh! how oft—
In darkness and amid the many shapes
Of joyless daylight; when the fretful stir
Unprofitable, and the fever of the world,
Have hung upon the beatings of my heart—
55   How oft, in spirit, have I turned to thee,
O sylvan Wye! thou wanderer through the woods,
How often has my spirit turned to thee!

     And now, with gleams of half-extinguished thought
With many recognitions dim and faint,
60   And somewhat of a sad perplexity,
The picture of the mind revives again;
While here I stand, not only with the sense
Of present pleasure, but with pleasing thoughts
That in this moment there is life and food
65   For future years. And so I dare to hope,
Though changed, no doubt, from what I was when first
I came among these hills; when like a roe
I bounded o'er the mountains, by the sides
Of the deep rivers, and the lonely streams,
70   Wherever nature led—more like a man

Flying from something that he dreads than one
Who sought the thing he loved. For nature then
(The coarser pleasures of my boyish days,
And their glad animal movements all gone by)
75   To me was all in all.—I cannot paint
What then I was. The sounding cataract
Haunted me like a passion; the tall rock,
The mountain, and the deep and gloomy wood,
Their colors and their forms, were then to me
80   An appetite; a feeling and a love,
That had no need of a remoter charm,
By thought supplied, nor any interest
Unborrowed from the eye.—That time is past,
And all its aching joys are now no more,
85   And all its dizzy raptures. Not for this
Faint I, nor mourn nor murmur; other gifts
Have followed; for such loss, I would believe,
Abundant recompense. For I have learned
To look on nature, not as in the hour
90   Of thoughtless youth; but hearing oftentimes
The still, sad music of humanity,
Nor harsh nor grating, though of ample power
To chasten and subdue. And I have felt
A presence that disturbs me with the joy
95   Of elevated thoughts; a sense sublime
Of something far more deeply interfused,
Whose dwelling is the light of setting suns,
And the round ocean and the living air,
And the blue sky, and in the mind of man:
100   A motion and a spirit, that impels
All thinking things, all objects of all thought,
And rolls through all things. Therefore am I still
A lover of the meadows and the woods,
And mountains; and of all that we behold
105   From this green earth; of all the mighty world
Of eye, and ear—both what they half create,
And what perceive; well pleased to recognize
In nature and the language of the sense
The anchor of my purest thoughts, the nurse,
110   The guide, the guardian of my heart, and soul
Of all my moral being.
                                    Nor perchance,
If I were not thus taught, should I the more
Suffer my genial spirits to decay:
For thou art with me here upon the banks
115   Of this fair river; thou my dearest Friend,

My dear, dear Friend; and in thy voice I catch
The language of my former heart, and read
My former pleasures in the shooting lights
Of thy wild eyes. Oh! yet a little while
120 May I behold in thee what I was once,
My dear, dear Sister! and this prayer I make,
Knowing that Nature never did betray
The heart that loved her; 'tis her privilege,
Through all the years of this our life, to lead
125 From joy to joy: for she can so inform
The mind that is within us, so impress
With quietness and beauty, and so feed
With lofty thoughts, that neither evil tongues,
Rash judgments, nor the sneers of selfish men,
130 Nor greetings where no kindness is, nor all
The dreary intercourse of daily life,
Shall e'er prevail against us, or disturb
Our cheerful faith, that all which we behold
Is full of blessings. Therefore let the moon
135 Shine on thee in thy solitary walk;
And let the misty mountain winds be free
To blow against thee: and, in after years,
When these wild ecstasies shall be matured
Into a sober pleasure; when thy mind
140 Shall be a mansion for all lovely forms,
Thy memory be as a dwelling place
For all sweet sounds and harmonies; oh! then,
If solitude, or fear, or pain, or grief
Should be thy portion, with what healing thoughts
145 Of tender joy wilt thou remember me,
And these my exhortations! Nor, perchance—
If I should be where I no more can hear
Thy voice, nor catch from thy wild eyes these gleams
Of past existence—wilt thou then forget
150 That on the banks of this delightful stream
We stood together; and that I, so long
A worshiper of Nature, hither came
Unwearied in that service; rather say
With warmer love—oh! with far deeper zeal
155 Of holier love. Nor wilt thou then forget,
That after many wanderings, many years
Of absence, these steep woods and lofty cliffs,
And this green pastoral landscape, were to me
More dear, both for themselves and for thy sake!

                                                    1798

Writing Assignments for "Lines: Composed a Few Miles above Tintern Abbey on Revisiting the Banks of the Wye during a Tour, July 13, 1798"

I. Brief Papers

    A. 1. Discuss images of solitude and stillness in lines 1–24.

        2. While the speaker has not committed to memory visual images of Tintern Abbey, the place has had an impact on him. Discuss how it has affected him in his absence (lines 25–49).

        3. In lines 65–82 the speaker describes his relationship with nature during his youth. How would you characterize it? What role did contemplation play in his feelings toward nature?

        4. Describe how the speaker's attitude toward nature has changed from his youth (lines 83–111). Why does the poet not mourn the loss of that time's "aching joys" (line 84) and "dizzy raptures" (line 85)?

        5. Look up *pantheism* in a dictionary. To what extent do you believe the poet's sentiments in lines 93–102 illustrate pantheism?

    B. 1. Which passages are you most likely to remember after you have forgotten the rest of the poem? Why do you find the passage(s) memorable?

        2. This is considered one of Wordsworth's most important poems, perhaps his *most* important poem. Do you believe the poem speaks directly to twentieth-century readers? Defend or attack its place in this course.

II. Longer Papers

    A. Explain how the poet blends the imagery, the moods, and the subject matter of the first two parts of the poem (lines 1–57 and lines 58–111) and in the final part (lines 111–159). Consider, if you like, how the speaker's "dear Sister" (line 121) helps rekindle the speaker's earlier attitude toward nature, how the speaker reaches a new realization of nature's evolving influence and impact on his life, or how the poet's use of language and imagery blends the earlier patterns of imagery (images of silence and sound, solitude and companionship, natural habitat and spiritual significance).

    B. In one of the most famous passages from the poem, Wordsworth describes nature as "The anchor of my purest thoughts, the nurse, / The guide, the guardian of my heart, and soul / Of all my moral being" (lines 109–111). What do you believe he means by the lines? Relate the lines to other parts of the poem, and discuss specifically if his impressions of nature have changed by the end of the poem.

WILLIAM WORDSWORTH

Composed upon Westminster Bridge*

Earth has not anything to show more fair:
Dull would he be of soul who could pass by
A sight so touching in its majesty;
This City now doth, like a garment, wear
5   The beauty of the morning; silent, bare,
Ships, towers, domes, theaters, and temples lie
Open unto the fields, and to the sky;
All bright and glittering in the smokeless air.
Never did sun more beautifully steep
10 In his first splendor, valley, rock, or hill;
Ne'er saw I, never felt, a calm so deep!
The river glideth at his own sweet will:
Dear God! the very houses seem asleep;
And all that mighty heart is lying still!

1807

Writing Assignments for "Composed upon Westminster Bridge"

I. Brief Papers
A. 1. The poet chooses to describe the city just at the break of day. How does that decision affect what he chooses to emphasize in the poem?
2. Show that the poet's language throughout the poem reinforces the references to sleep and stillness in the last two lines of the poem.
3. How does the poet's description of the city depart from readers' conventional expectations of a description of a city?

B. Read the poem aloud several times. How does the language of the poem and the repetition and rhythm affect your response to the poem and help establish the mood?

II. Longer Papers
A. Discuss how the poet uses references to nature to magnify the beauty of the city and to convey the effect of its beauty.
B. Compare "Composed upon Westminster Bridge" to Wendell Berry's "The Peace of Wild Things" (p. 635). How does each poet establish a predominant mood and central impression in each poem? Which poem do you prefer and why?

*Westminster Bridge: A bridge overlooking London and the Thames River, in view of Westminster Abbey.

GERARD MANLEY HOPKINS
Spring and Fall

To a young child

Márgarét, are you gríeving
Over Goldengrove unleaving?
Leáves, líke the things of man, you
With your fresh thoughts care for, can you?
5   Áh! ás the heart grows older
It will come to such sights colder
By and by, nor spare a sigh
Though worlds of wanwood leafmeal lie;
And yet you wíll weep and know why.
10   Now no matter, child, the name:
Sórrow's spríngs áre the same.
Nor mouth had, no nor mind, expressed
What heart heard of, ghost guessed:
It ís the blight man was born for,
15   It is Margaret you mourn for.

1918*

Writing Assignments for "Spring and Fall"

I. Brief Papers

A. 1. Paraphrase and summarize the first four lines of the poem, explaining how the second question (lines 3–4) helps you decipher the first question (lines 1–2).

2. Explain how the second four lines of the poem offer Margaret very little consolation.

3. Explain what the speaker means when he says, "Now no matter, child, the name: / Sorrow's springs are the same." Then discuss how these lines relate to the first two lines of the poem or the last two.

4. Hopkins often coins his own words to produce striking, original effects of sound and meaning. Discuss one example of such language play in the poem, deciding how the coined word or phrase affects the impact of the poem.

B. Argue for or against the assertion that the poem implies that the child's tears are inevitable.

*1918: Publication date. The poem was written in 1880.

C. If you have not already discussed the phrase in a previous paper, free write for 10 minutes about the following line: "Though worlds of wanwood leafmeal lie." Since the goal of free writing is to generate ideas quickly, do not worry about spelling, punctuation, grammar, or sentence structure. Just keep writing down whatever comes into your head about the line or about specific words in the line. If you can't think of anything to say, just write "I can't think of anything to say" until something comes into your mind. After 10 minutes, look back over your free writing and select from it the most promising idea for a paragraph on how the line affects your interpretation of the poem.

II. Longer Papers
A. Explain how the last six lines relate to the first nine, focusing especially on how the pain of children and adults is similar.
B. Read the story of Genesis in the Bible, paying close attention to Adam and Eve's fall from grace and their punishment. Explain how the story implies one way of understanding why "Sorrow's springs are the same" and how the title of the poem can have several meanings.
C. Explain to what extent you find the poem an unhappy or pessimistic one.

ADRIENNE RICH
Necessities of Life

Piece by piece I seem
to re-enter the world: I first began

a small, fixed dot, still see
that old myself, a dark-blue thumbtack

5   pushed into the scene,
a hard little head protruding

from the pointillist's* buzz and bloom.
After a time the dot

begins to ooze. Certain heats
10   melt it.
        Now I was hurriedly

*pointillism: Post-impressionist school of painting. The artists reduce color to its constituent shades and paint dots of the shades. The viewer's eye blends the dots into the shades.

blurring into ranges
of burnt red, burning green,

whole biographies swam up and
15 swallowed me like Jonah.*

Jonah! I was Wittgenstein,†
Mary Wollstonecraft, the soul

of Louis Jouvet, dead
in a blown-up photograph.

20 Till, wolfed almost to shreds,
I learned to make myself

unappetizing. Scaly as a dry bulb
thrown into a cellar

I used myself, let nothing use me.
25 Like being on a private dole,

sometimes more like kneading bricks in Egypt.‡
What life was there, was mine,

now and again to lay
one hand on a warm brick

30 and touch the sun's ghost
with economical joy,

now and again to name
over the bare necessities.

So much for those days. Soon
35 practice may make me middling-perfect, I'll

dare inhabit the world
trenchant in motion as an eel, solid

*Jonah: Prophet of the Old Testament. He was swallowed by a large fish but released after three days.
†Wittgenstein, Wollstonecraft, and Jouvet: Ludwig Wittgenstein (1889–1957), a philosopher; Mary Wollstonecraft (1759–1797), an English author and feminist; Louis Jouvet, a French director and actor. All three represent artists and intellectuals who have significantly influenced Rich's thinking.
‡kneading bricks in Egypt: The Pharaoh set the captive Israelites to making bricks to build Egyptian cities.

as a cabbage-head. I have invitations:
a curl of mist steams upward

40   from a field, visible as my breath,
houses along a road stand waiting

like old women knitting, breathless
to tell their tales.

1962

Writing Assignments for "Necessities of Life"

I. Brief Papers

A. 1. Find evidence in the poem that the speaker is undergoing a change in her life
and in her attitude toward her life.

2. The poem is a series of assertions, each terminated with a period. Go through
and circle all the periods in the poem, consider the relationship among the
assertions, and summarize in your own words how one of the passages reveals
a stage of the speaker's transformation.

3. Discuss the implications of the poet's use of the two colons in the poem
(stanzas 1 and 19).

4. Look up the word *trenchant* in any good dictionary. How do its various
meanings help you understand the poem and the speaker's new attitude toward herself?

B. When the poem first appeared in print it was entitled "Thirty-Three," Rich's age
when she wrote it. What is your reaction to the changed title? Which do you
prefer and why?

II. Longer Papers

A. Discuss in detail the speaker's reentry into the world and show how the poem's
structure—the stanzaic form, the series of assertions, and the punctuation—helps
reveal the progress of the transformation.

B. Adrienne Rich has written quite a bit about her "new beginning" at the midpoint
of her career. Discuss how the poem implies that it is, indeed, an autobiographical
account of a poet who reevaluates her life and her poetry. You may wish to
consider which images seem especially appropriate for an artist or writer to use.

C. Compare the Rich poem to any other Rich poem you have studied in this book,
focusing on the speaker's attitude toward herself, toward art and writing, or
toward human relationships. Pay attention to the date of publication for each
poem if you wish to show how Rich's poetry and thought have evolved.

ADRIENNE RICH

Diving into the Wreck

First having read the book of myths,
and loaded the camera,
and checked the edge of the knife-blade,
I put on
5   the body-armor of black rubber
the absurd flippers
the grave and awkward mask.
I am having to do this
not like Cousteau* with his
10   assiduous team
aboard the sun-flooded schooner
but here alone.

There is a ladder.
The ladder is always there
15   hanging innocently
close to the side of the schooner.
We know what it is for,
we who have used it.
Otherwise
20   it's a piece of maritime floss
some sundry equipment.

I go down.
Rung after rung and still
the oxygen immerses me
25   the blue light
the clear atoms
of our human air.
I go down.
My flippers cripple me,
30   I crawl like an insect down the ladder
and there is no one
to tell me when the ocean
will begin.

First the air is blue and then
35   it is bluer and then green and then
black I am blacking out and yet

*Cousteau: Jacques Yves Cousteau (1910–   ), French underwater explorer.

my mask is powerful
it pumps my blood with power
the sea is another story
40   the sea is not a question of power
I have to learn alone
to turn my body without force
in the deep element.

And now: it is easy to forget
45   what I came for
among so many who have always
lived here
swaying their crenellated* fans
between the reefs
50   and besides
you breathe differently down here.

I came to explore the wreck.
The words are purposes.
The words are maps.
55   I came to see the damage that was done
and the treasures that prevail.
I stroke the beam of my lamp
slowly along the flank
of something more permanent
60   than fish or weed

the thing I came for:
the wreck and not the story of the wreck
the thing itself and not the myth

the drowned face always staring
65   toward the sun
the evidence of damage
worn by salt and sway into this threadbare beauty
the ribs of the disaster
curving their assertion
70   among the tentative haunters.

This is the place.
And I am here, the mermaid whose dark hair
streams black, the merman in his armored body
We circle silently
75   about the wreck

*crenellated: Notched with projections, either rounded or scalloped.

we dive into the hold.
I am she: I am he

whose drowned face sleeps with open eyes
whose breasts still bear the stress
80   whose silver, copper, vermeil* cargo lies
obscurely inside barrels

half-wedged and left to rot
we are the half-destroyed instruments
that once held to a course
85   the water-eaten log
the fouled compass

We are, I am, you are
by cowardice or courage
the one who find our way
90   back to this scene
carrying a knife, a camera
a book of myths
in which
our names do not appear.

                                        1972

Writing Assignments for "Diving into the Wreck"

I. Brief Papers

    A. 1. Find as much evidence as you can that the poem is about self-exploration.

      2. Discuss the implications of one of the following as preparation for the dive: the "book of myths," the "loaded camera," or the "sharp-edged knife." To what extent does the item suggest why the diver makes her dive and what she expects to encounter.

      3. Go through the poem and trace the pronouns, noting where the poet uses references to *I, me,* and *my* and where she uses references to *he, she, we,* and *our.* Explain the pattern which emerges and relate it to the dive itself.

      4. Look up the term *androgyne* in the dictionary. How does the concept relate to the poem? Focus especially on the concluding three stanzas.

    B. Argue for or against the assertion that the poem implies in the last two stanzas that the woman may not have significantly improved her life by taking her dive.

*vermeil: Metal.

II. Longer Papers

A. To what extent has the diver changed by the end of the poem? How would you characterize the change? How does the language and the imagery of the poem reinforce the difference?

B. If you have studied other poems by Adrienne Rich in this book, compare this poem to one or more of them. Focus specifically on the speakers' state of mind or point of view, on the poems' subject matter and treatment of women's issues, on the similarities or differences in imagery, or on any element of the poems you find significant. Pay attention to the date of publication for each poem if you wish to show how Rich's poetry and thought have evolved.

C. Adrienne Rich is an avowed feminist. How does this information help you understand the poem and affect your response to it?

DANIELA GIOSEFFI

Some Slippery Afternoon

A silver watch you've worn for years
is suddenly gone
leaving a pale white stripe
blazing on your wrist.

5   A calendar marked with all
the appointments you meant to keep
disappears
leaving a faded spot on the wall
10   where it hung.
You search the house, yard, trash cans
for weeks
but never find it.

One night the glass in your windows
vanishes
15   leaving you sitting in a gust of wind.

You think how a leg is suddenly lost
beneath a subway train
or a taxi wheel
some slippery afternoon.

20   The child you've raised for years,
combing each lock,
tailoring each smile, each tear,

each valuable thought,
suddenly changes to a harlequin,
25   joins the circus passing in the street,
never to be seen again.

One morning you wash your face,
look into the mirror,
find the water has eroded your features,
30   worn them smooth as a rock in a brook.
A blank oval peers back at you
too mouthless to cry out.

1979

Writing Assignments for "Some Slippery Afternoon"

I. Brief Papers
   A. 1. Show that the poem is about the passing of time.
      2. What is the relationship of stanza 3 to the rest of the poem? How does the vanished glass and the "gust of wind" (line 15) relate to the other images of time's passing?
      3. Look up *harlequin* in the dictionary. Which of its various meanings help you understand the poem?
      4. Explain the significance of the title, "Some Slippery Afternoon."

   B. Argue for or against one of the assertions below.
      1. Women more than men can empathize with the speaker in the poem.
      2. The poem is primarily about growing old.
      3. The poem is primarily about anxiety, the loss of security, and/or the loss of self-confidence.

   C. 1. In stanza 3, the speaker says, "The child you've raised for years" (line 20) "suddenly changes to a harlequin" (line 24). What do you think the speaker means and how does that affect your understanding of the poem?
      2. Do you believe most people, no matter what their age, can sympathize with the speaker and the speaker's experience in the poem? Why or why not?

II. Longer Papers
   A. Develop any one of the paragraph topics into a full-length paper.
   B. Go through the poem and circle the images you consider particularly striking. Explain how those images reinforce the speaker's sense of loss and the poem's preoccupation with the passing of time.
   C. Explain the woman's self-revelation in the poem. What inspires it?

T. S. ELIOT
The Love Song of J. Alfred Prufrock

S'io credessi che mia risposta fosse
a persona che mai tornasse al mondo,
questa fiamma staria senza più scosse.
Ma per ciò che giammai di questo fondo
non tornò vivo alcun, s'i'odo il vero,
senza tema d'infamia it rispondo.*

Let us go then, you and I,
When the evening is spread out against the sky
Like a patient etherised upon a table;
Let us go, through certain half-deserted streets,
5   The muttering retreats
Of restless nights in one-night cheap hotels
And sawdust restaurants with oyster-shells:
Streets that follow like a tedious argument
Of insidious intent
10 To lead you to an overwhelming question . . .
Oh, do not ask, 'What is it?'
Let us go and make our visit.

In the room the women come and go
Talking of Michelangelo.†

15 The yellow fog that rubs its back upon the window-panes,
The yellow smoke that rubs its muzzle on the window-panes,
Licked its tongue into the corners of the evening,
Lingered upon the pools that stand in drains,
Let fall upon its back the soot that falls from chimneys,
20 Slipped by the terrace, made a sudden leap,
And seeing that it was a soft October night,
Curled once about the house, and fell asleep.

And indeed there will be time
For the yellow smoke that slides along the street
25 Rubbing its back upon the window-panes;

*S'io credessi che mia . . . it rispondo: The epigraph comes from Dante's *Inferno.* Count Guido da
Montefeltro's soul is enveloped in flame. His tongue, encased in the flame, moves or wavers when
he talks. Believing his hearer will not return to the world, Montefeltro offers to tell of his own sin.
The translation of the epigraph reads: "If I thought my reply were to someone who could ever
return to the world, this flame would waver no more. But since, I'm told, nobody ever escapes from
this pit, I'll tell you without fear of ill fame."
†Michelangelo: Italian sculptor and painter, 1475–1564.

There will be time, there will be time
To prepare a face to meet the faces that you meet;
There will be time to murder and create,
And time for all the works and days of hands
30   That lift and drop a question on your plate;
Time for you and time for me,
And time yet for a hundred indecisions,
And for a hundred visions and revisions,
Before the taking of a toast and tea.

35   In the room the women come and go
Talking of Michelangelo.

And indeed there will be time
To wonder, 'Do I dare?' and, 'Do I dare?'
Time to turn back and descend the stair,
40   With a bald spot in the middle of my hair—
(They will say: 'How his hair is growing thin!')
My morning coat, my collar mounting firmly to the chin,
My necktie rich and modest, but asserted by a simple pin—
They will say: 'But how his arms and legs are thin!')
45   Do I dare
Disturb the universe?
In a minute there is time
For decisions and revisions which a minute will reverse.

For I have known them all already, known them all—
50   Have known the evenings, mornings, afternoons,
I have measured out my life with coffee spoons;
I know the voices dying with a dying fall
Beneath the music from a farther room.
       So how should I presume?

55   And I have known the eyes already, known them all—
The eyes that fix you in a formulated phrase,
And when I am formulated, sprawling on a pin,
When I am pinned and wriggling on the wall,
Then how should I begin
60   To spit out all the butt-ends of my days and ways?
       And how should I presume?

And I have known the arms already, known them all—
Arms that are braceleted and white and bare
(But in the lamplight, downed with light brown hair!)
65   Is it perfume from a dress
That makes me so digress?

Arms that lie along a table, or wrap about a shawl.
   And should I then presume?
   And how should I begin?

70   Shall I say, I have gone at dusk through narrow streets
And watched the smoke that rises from the pipes
Of lonely men in shirt-sleeves, leaning out of windows? . . .

I should have been a pair of ragged claws
Scuttling across the floors of silent seas.

75   And the afternoon, the evening, sleeps so peacefully!
Smoothed by long fingers,
Asleep . . . tired . . . or it malingers,
Stretched on the floor, here beside you and me.
Should I, after tea and cakes and ices,
80   Have the strength to force the moment to its crisis?

But though I have wept and fasted, wept and prayed,
Though I have seen my head (grown slightly bald)
   brought in upon a platter,
I am no prophet—and here's no great matter;
I have seen the moment of my greatness flicker,
85   And I have seen the eternal Footman hold my coat, and
   snicker,
And in short, I was afraid.

And would it have been worth it, after all,
After the cups, the marmalade, the tea,
Among the porcelain, among some talk of you and me,
90   Would it have been worth while,
To have bitten off the matter with a smile,
To have squeezed the universe into a ball
To roll it towards some overwhelming question,
To say: 'I am Lazarus,* come from the dead,
95   Come back to tell you all, I shall tell you all'—
If one, settling a pillow by her head,
   Should say: 'That is not what I meant at all.
   That is not it, at all.'

And would it have been worth it, after all,
100   Would it have been worth while,
After the sunsets and the dooryards and the sprinkled
   streets,

*Lazarus: According to the biblical account in John 11, Jesus raises Lazarus from the dead.

After the novels, after the teacups, after the skirts that
    trail along the floor—
And this, and so much more?—
It is impossible to say just what I mean!
105   But as if a magic lantern threw the nerves in patterns
    on a screen:
Would it have been worth while
If one, settling a pillow or throwing off a shawl,
And turning toward the window, should say:
    'That is not it at all,
110   That is not what I meant, at all.'

            . . . . .

No! I am not Prince Hamlet,* nor was meant to be;
Am an attendant lord, one that will do
To swell a progress, start a scene or two,
Advise the prince; no doubt, an easy tool,
115   Deferential, glad to be of use,
Politic, cautious, and meticulous;
Full of high sentence, but a bit obtuse;
At times, indeed, almost ridiculous—
Almost, at times, the Fool.

120   I grow old . . . I grow old . . .
I shall wear the bottoms of my trousers rolled.

Shall I part my hair behind? Do I dare to eat a peach?
I shall wear white flannel trousers, and walk upon
    the beach.
I have heard the mermaids singing, each to each.

125   I do not think that they will sing to me.

I have seen them riding seaward on the waves
Combing the white hair of the waves blown back
When the wind blows the water white and black.

We have lingered in the chambers of the sea
130   By sea-girls wreathed with seaweed red and brown
Till human voices wake us, and we drown.

1917

*Prince Hamlet: Legendary Danish prince and hero of Shakespeare's play *Hamlet*.

Writing Assignments for "The Love Song of J. Alfred Prufrock"

I. Brief Papers

A. 1. Most people assume that the poem is a dramatic monologue in which Prufrock speaks only to himself. Find evidence in the poem to suggest that the speaker is, indeed, thinking or speaking only to himself.

2. Show that Prufrock worries about growing old and/or about his appearance.

3. Describe the kind of party Prufrock attends, discussing the social class of the people at the party, their topics of conversation, their attitude toward Prufrock, and/or Prufrock's attitude toward them.

4. Throughout the poem, Prufrock compares himself to a number of different characters or creatures. Select one or more from the references below and explain why the comparison is appropriate, what it tells us about Prufrock's personality, his state of mind, his anxieties, his attitude toward himself, or others' attitudes toward him:

   a. "I should have been a pair of ragged claws
      Scuttling across the floors of silent seas"
      (lines 73–74)

   b. "Though I have seen my head (grown slightly bald)
      brought in upon a platter,
      I am no prophet"
      (lines 82–83)

   c. "Would it have been worthwhile
      . . . .
      To say: 'I am Lazarus, come from the dead' "
      (lines 90, 94)

   d. "No! I am not Prince Hamlet, nor was meant to be
      Am an attendant lord . . .
      . . . .
      Almost, at times, the Fool"
      (lines 111–112, 119).

B. Argue for or against one of the assertions below.

1. Prufrock is normal—he suffers the same fears and the same insecurity that everyone today experiences.

2. Prufrock is unhappy because he is more sensitive than other people, more aware of how trivial and superficial his life is.

3. The description of the party and of the interest and personalities of the people who attend it are realistic.

C. Throughout the poem, Prufrock wishes for a life quite different from the one he has. What do you believe is wrong with Prufrock's life? What's missing? What, if anything, would make him happier?

D. In the following paragraph, the student discusses the partygoers in the poem. Read the paragraph, then respond to one of the questions following the paragraph:

> The women Prufrock describes are the snobs of the tearoom, seemingly displaying a small town pride in whatever cultural knowledge they possess, hence the repetition of their allusions to Michelangelo. Their knowledge of art is demeaned by the fact that they only seem to know one artist, and an extremely popular artist at that. The women are nasty and intimidating. They gossip, it appears, and Prufrock fears the things they will say about him behind his back. Lastly, the party-going women have no individuality. No one woman stands out. Through their snobbishness and insincerity, the women have beaten Prufrock down, made him weak and insecure, and he sees himself as foolish. Eliot portrays the inhumanity of man to man (in this case woman to man) and ends "Love Song" as pessimistically as possible.

1. In what ways could this writer better support her assertions? Rewrite the paragraph to include specific support from the text—actual quotes or more detailed analysis—to substantiate the writer's claims.
2. Write a brief paragraph defending or refuting the writer's claim that the women at the party have no individuality.

II. Longer Papers

A. Respond to one or more of the following questions which ask you to relate parts of the poem to the whole. In what ways are the last six lines an appropriate conclusion to the poem? How does the epigraph relate to the poem and to Prufrock specifically? How does the title relate to the rest of the poem?
B. Go through the poem and find as much evidence as possible that Prufrock feels insecure and out-of-place. Write a character sketch emphasizing his feelings of insecurity and inadequacy.
C. Write a paper about the difference in the dramatic setting at the beginning of the poem (lines 15–24 specifically) and at the end of the poem (lines 123–131). How does the former represent and reinforce the kind of life Prufrock has, the latter the kind of life he desires? Which images, sounds, or colors are particularly effective in each passage?
D. Eliot's style is notable for its vivid, yet seemingly unconnected or disjointed juxtaposition of images. Select images in the poem you find especially intense or especially remarkable. Write a paper discussing why the images are so vivid and appropriate, how they reveal something about Prufrock and the society which entraps him, or why they evoke such a strong personal response.

JAMES REISS

Pumas

A woman in a mauve dress mentions
her passion for pumas
I nod gravely and say
I saw a puma cross

5   outside my window once
years ago holed-up at a writers' colony
Out of the woods it stalked through the snow
pausing to lift each paw

Then topics shift
10   We move toward the bar and branch off
in separate directions

Later I wonder what she meant
If I who never saw a puma
or anything that winter but my bloated self
15   crouching in an outhouse mirror
was capable of such snowy untruth
what veils her words must also wear

1983

Writing Assignment for "Pumas"

I. Brief Papers
  A. 1. Show that the speaker and the woman are strangers.
     2. Compare the puma in the first two stanzas to the speaker's description of himself in the last stanza. How does the difference help you understand the poem?

  B. Argue for or against either assertion below.
     1. The speaker's interchange with the woman is typical of most casual social interchange.
     2. We like the speaker's response to the woman because it illustrates his imagination and his social ease.

  C. 1. To what extent do the only details you have about the woman—that she wears a mauve dress and has a "passion for pumas"—shape your response to her and to the speaker's reaction to her?

2. Would you react differently to the poem and to the speaker if he termed his story a "lie" and not a "snowy untruth"? How would that reaction affect your response to the poem?

II. Longer Papers

A. Discuss the different images in the poem, explaining why some are more attractive than others. How do the images relate to the poem's implications about how people reveal themselves to others?

B. Explain in detail how this poem communicates something about self-revelation and self-awareness.

JAMES DICKEY

Cherrylog Road

Off Highway 106
At Cherrylog Road I entered
The '34 Ford without wheels,
Smothered in kudzu,
5 With a seat pulled out to run
Corn whiskey down from the hills,

And then from the other side
Crept into an Essex
With a rumble seat of red leather
10 And then out again, aboard
A blue Chevrolet, releasing
The rust from its other color,

Reared up on three building blocks.
None had the same body heat;
15 I changed with them inward, toward
The weedy heart of the junkyard,
For I knew that Doris Holbrook
Would escape from her father at noon

And would come from the farm
20 To seek parts owned by the sun
Among the abandoned chassis,
Sitting in each in turn
As I did, leaning forward
As in a wild stock-car race

25 In the parking lot of the dead.
    Time after time, I climbed in
    And out the other side, like
    An envoy or movie star
    Met at the station by crickets.
30 A radiator cap raised its head,

    Become a real toad or a kingsnake
    As I neared the hub of the yard,
    Passing through many states,
    Many lives, to reach
35 Some grandmother's long Pierce-Arrow
    Sending platters of blindness forth

    From its nickel hubcaps
    And spilling its tender upholstery
    On sleepy roaches,
40 The glass panel in between
    Lady and colored driver
    Not all the way broken out,

    The back-seat phone
    Still on its hook.
45 I got in as though to exclaim,
    "Let us go to the orphan asylum,
    John; I have some old toys
    For children who say their prayers."

    I popped with sweat as I thought
50 I heard Doris Holbrook scrape
    Like a mouse in the southern-state sun
    That was eating the paint in blisters
    From a hundred car tops and hoods.
    She was tapping like code,

55 Loosening the screws,
    Carrying off headlights,
    Sparkplugs, bumpers,
    Cracked mirrors and gear-knobs,
    Getting ready, already,
60 To go back with something to show

    Other than her lips' new trembling
    I would hold to me soon, soon,

Where I sat in the ripped back seat
Talking over the interphone,
65   Praying for Doris Holbrook
To come from her father's farm

And to get back there
With no trace of me on her face
To be seen by her red-haired father
70   Who would change, in the squalling barn,
Her back's pale skin with a strop,
Then lay for me

In a bootlegger's roasting car
With a string-triggered 12-gauge shotgun
75   To blast the breath from the air.
Not cut by the jagged windshields,
Through the acres of wrecks she came
With a wrench in her hand,

Through dust where the blacksnake dies
80   Of boredom, and the beetle knows
The compost has no more life.
Someone outside would have seen
The oldest car's door inexplicably
Close from within:

85   I held her and held her and held her,
Convoyed at terrific speed
By the stalled, dreaming traffic around us,
So the blacksnake, stiff
With inaction, curved back
90   Into life, and hunted the mouse

With deadly overexcitement,
The beetles reclaimed their field
As we clung, glued together,
With the hooks of the seat springs
95   Working through to catch us red-handed
Amidst the gray breathless batting

That burst from the seat at our backs.
We left by separate doors
Into the changed, other bodies
100   Of cars, she down Cherrylog Road
And I to my motorcycle
Parked like the soul of the junkyard

                    Restored, a bicycle fleshed
                    With power, and tore off
        105   Up Highway 106, continually
                    Drunk on the wind in my mouth,
                    Wringing the handlebar for speed,
                    Wild to the wreckage forever.

                                                    1963

Writing Assignments for "Cherrylog Road"

I. Brief Papers

   A. 1. Explain the dramatic setting of the poem by discussing where the poem is set,
         who is involved in the action, and what is happening in the poem.
      2. Show that the couple in the poem—the speaker and Doris Holbrook—are both
         young and unsophisticated.
      3. How is stanza 9 related to stanzas 14 and 15? Why is Doris Holbrook identified
         with the mouse and the speaker with the blacksnake?
      4. Choose one of the following elements of the setting and discuss its appropriate-
         ness and its impact in the poem: the kudzu; any *one* of the cars—the '34 Ford,
         the Essex, the rusted Chevrolet, or the Pierce-Arrow; the "southern-state" in
         which the poem is set; or Cherrylog Road itself.
      5. How is stanza 4 related to the last stanza in the poem?

   B. Choose one assertion below, and develop or refute it:
      1. Some people might be offended by the poem because of its explicit sexuality.
         Do you think they should be? Why or why not?
      2. Some people might be offended by the sexual and racial stereotypes implied
         in stanzas 7 and 8. Do you think they should be? Why or why not?

   C. 1. How does the setting of the poem and/or the couple's economic and social
         class affect your response to the poem?
      2. Why do you think the poet has the speaker in the poem ride a motorcycle,
         not a car? How does that choice of vehicles affect your interpretation of the
         poem?

II. Longer Papers

   A. In stanza 5 the speaker refers to the "parking lot of the dead" (line 25). In stanzas
      17 and 18, he refers to his motorcycle as the "soul of the junkyard" (line 102)
      now "restored" (line 103). Discuss as fully as possible how the junkyard has been
      transformed.
   B. Argue for or against the assertion that the poet implies that sexual energy can
      vitalize and make attractive even the ugliest, most lifeless setting.
   C. Go through the poem and circle all the references to death, sleep, and passivity.
      How do those references prepare for the sexual encounter in lines 85–97?

D. Discuss the automobiles in the poem. You might consider ways in which the automobile is tied to the concept of male sexuality in our culture and how such associations help you understand this poem.
E. Discuss in what ways this is a typical love poem and in what ways it breaks many conventions or expectations of typical love poetry.

Comparative Papers from Chapter One: Youth and Self-Revelation

A. Compare several poems from this chapter which view youth differently. Explain how some poets treat youth more positively than others.
B. Argue for or against the assertion that only as people age do they gain any real understanding of life, of other people, and of themselves. Use evidence from several poems in this chapter to support your argument.
C. Argue for or against the assertion that youth is the best time of anyone's life. Support your argument with examples from several poems in this chapter.
D. In "The Love Song of J. Alfred Prufrock" (p. 611), T.S. Eliot writes: "There will be time, there will be time / To prepare a face to meet the faces that you meet" (lines 26–27). Discuss how this poem, plus other poems in this chapter, explores the use of masks. To what extent do all people create facades or "prepare faces" which hide them from others and from themselves?
E. Discuss several poems from this chapter that examine speakers who undergo transformations or have undergone transformations. What is the nature of the speakers' change? Do the speakers gain greater insights about themselves, about life, or about other people? To what extent is their change linked to natural aging processes? To what extent to other experiences? Evaluate, if you like, which poems are the most powerful or effective.
F. Find and discuss one poem in this chapter that depicts life in a way you hope you never experience it.
G. At the end of "Spring and Fall" (p. 602), Gerard Manley Hopkins writes: "It is Margaret you mourn for" (line 15), suggesting that all anguish, all despair, and all sadness relate to our aging and our sense of mortality. Write a paper about this poem or other poems from the text which tell you something about why people grieve.
H. Most of the poems in this chapter examine self-revelation, how people confront themselves, their existence, and their relationships. Choose a poem you especially like and then list stanza by stanza what occurs in the poem, what attitudes the speaker reveals, and what changing point of view the speaker adopts. Write a paper about how the structure of the poem helps us understand the speaker's growing self-awareness.
I. Select one poem from this book which changed your attitude toward something or someone. Discuss in a personal response paper how and why the poem changed you.

2 / Poems about Nature

————— ➤➤✕◀◀ —————

DAVID WAGONER

The Author of American Ornithology *Sketches a Bird, Now Extinct (Alexander Wilson, Wilmington, N.C., 1809)*

Before Reading

Free write for 5 or 10 minutes in response to the assertion: "Capturing animals for the sake of displaying them in zoos is justified."

> When he walked through town, the wing-shot bird he'd hidden
> Inside his coat began to cry like a baby,
> High and plaintive and loud as the calls he'd heard
> While hunting it in the woods, and goodwives stared
> 5 And scurried indoors to guard their own from harm.
>
> And the innkeeper and the goodmen in the tavern
> Asked him whether his child was sick, then laughed,
> Slapped knees, and laughed as he unswaddled his prize,
> His pride and burden: an ivory-billed woodpecker
> 10 As big as a crow, still wailing and squealing.
>
> Upstairs, when he let it go in his workroom,
> It fell silent at last. He told at dinner
> How devoted masters of birds drawn from the life
> Must gather their flocks around them with a rifle
> 15 And make them live forever inside books.
>
> Later, he found his bedspread covered with plaster
> And the bird clinging beside a hole in the wall
> Clear through to already-splintered weatherboards
> And the sky beyond. While he tied one of its legs
> 20 To a table-leg, it started wailing again
>
> And went on wailing as if toward cypress groves
> While the artist drew and tinted on fine vellum
> Its red cockade, gray claws, and sepia eyes
> From which a white wedge flowed to the lame wing
> 25 Like light flying and ended there in blackness.

He drew and studied for days, eating and dreaming
Fitfully through the dancing and loud drumming
Of an ivory bill that refused pecans and beetles,
Chestnuts and sweet-sour fruit of magnolias,
30   Riddling his table, slashing his fingers, wailing.

He watched it die, he said, with great regret.

1983

Writing Assignments for "The Author of *American Ornithology* Sketches a Bird, Now Extinct"

I. Brief Papers
   A. 1. Explain how the poet generates sympathy for the captured bird in stanzas 1 and 4.
      2. Show that the poet's attitude toward the ornithologist is most evident in stanza 3 and in the title of the poem.
      3. Explain how *one* of the following clusters is developed in the poem: images of imprisonment; images related to babies and children; images of light and dark; or images of life and death.

   B. Argue for or against either assertion below.
      1. The ornithologist feels regret.
      2. The poet believes the ornithologist is wrong.

   C. 1. Do you believe that making the bird "live forever inside books" (line 15) is worth the bird's life?
      2. In what ways does the bird's relentless struggle for freedom affect your response to the poem?

II. Longer Papers
   A. Choose any paragraph topic and develop it into a full-length paper.
   B. Most of David Wagoner's poems deal with gardens, animals, and birds. In fact, he has been dubbed by some critics as our contemporary Audubon. Consider the following poem by Wagoner and then write a paper showing that though the subjects—a woodpecker's death and a baby rhino's bath—are ostensibly quite different, the poet's style links the two. You may wish to consider one or more of the following topics, though you are not restricted to these:
      1. The poet's attitude toward the natural creatures.
      2. The poet's choice of objective point of view.
      3. The poet's use of concrete, specific imagery and dramatic experience.
      4. The poet's stanzaic form.

DAVID WAGONER
Washing a Young Rhinoceros

Inside its horse-high, bull-strong, hog-tight fence
It will stand beside you in a concrete garden,
Leaning your way
All thousand pounds of its half-grown body
5   To meet the water pouring out of your hose
The temperature of September.

And as slowly its patina (a gray compounded
Of peanut shells and marshmallows, straw and mud)
Begins to vanish
10 From the solid ribcage and the underbelly
Under your scrub-brush, you see, wrinkled and creased
As if in thought, its skin

From long underlip to fly-whisk gleam in the sun,
Erect ears turning backwards to learn how
15 You hum your pleasure,
And eyelashes above the jawbone hinges
Fluttering wetly as it waits transfixed
(The folds at the four leg-pits

Glistening pink now) for you never to finish
20 What feels more wonderful than opening
And closing its empty mouth
Around lettuce and grapes and fresh bouquets of carrots
And cabbage leaves, what feels as good to desire
As its fabulous horn.

1983

WILLIAM BLAKE

The Tyger

Tyger! Tyger! burning bright
In the forests of the night,
What immortal hand or eye
Could frame thy fearful symmetry?

5   In what distant deeps or skies
Burnt the fire of thine eyes?
On what wings dare he aspire?
What the hand, dare seize the fire?

And what shoulder, & what art,
10   Could twist the sinews of thy heart?
And when thy heart began to beat,
What dread hand? & what dread feet?

What the hammer? what the chain?
In what furnace was thy brain?
15   What the anvil? what dread grasp
Dare its deadly terrors clasp?

When the stars threw down their spears,
And water'd heaven with their tears,
Did he smile his work to see?
20   Did he who made the Lamb make thee?

Tyger! Tyger! burning bright
In the forests of the night,
What immortal hand or eye
Dare frame thy fearful symmetry?

1794

Writing Assignments for "The Tyger"

I. Brief Papers

   A. 1. Show that the tiger inspires in the poet both admiration and fear.
      2. Explain why the poem is structured as a series of questions.
      3. Explain why the poet changes *could* frame to *dare* frame from the first to the last stanza, the only difference in the two stanzas.

   B. Argue for or against the assertion that the poet is not interested in an answer to his questions, that, in fact, he implies his answer throughout the poem.

   C. 1. How does your reaction to the tiger's combined grace and predatory nature affect your response to the poem?
      2. Go through the poem and circle the words that invite your most intense response. Discuss what the words are and why they affect you as they do.

II. Longer Papers

   A. Develop any one of the paragraph assignments into a full-length paper.
   B. Write out the six stanzas of the poem side by side, so you can more easily study the structure. Consider how and where the poet uses repetition, where he repeats words from stanza to stanza and within stanzas. Consider the rhyme scheme. Note where the poet rhymes final words from line to line as well as within lines. Now, explain how the structure reinforces the notion of symmetry within the poem.

ALASTAIR REID

Curiosity

Before Reading

Free write for 5 or 10 minutes in response to the following question: "Do you believe anyone can ever have too much curiosity?"

may have killed the cat; more likely
the cat was just unlucky, or else curious
to see what death was like, having no cause
to go on licking paws, or fathering
5   litter on litter of kittens, predictably.

Nevertheless, to be curious
is dangerous enough. To distrust
what is always said, what seems,
to ask odd questions, interfere in dreams,
10 leave home, smell rats, have hunches,
cannot endear them to those doggy circles
where well-smelt baskets, suitable wives, good lunches
are the order of things, and where prevails
much wagging of incurious heads and tails.

15 Face it. Curiosity
will not cause him to die—
only lack of it will.
Never to want to see
the other side of the hill
20 or some improbable country
where living is an idyll
(although a probable hell)
would kill us all.
Only the curious
25 have, if they live, a tale
worth telling at all.

Dogs say cats love too much, are irresponsible,
are changeable, marry too many wives,
desert their children, chill all dinner tables
30 with tales of their nine lives.
Well, they are lucky. Let them be
nine-lived and contradictory,

curious enough to change, prepared to pay
the cat-price, which is to die
35   and die again and again,
each time with no less pain.
A cat minority of one
is all that can be counted on
to tell the truth. And what cats have to tell
40   on each return from hell
is this: that dying is what the living do,
that dying is what the loving do,
and that dead dogs are those who never know
that dying is what, to live, each has to do.

1959

Writing Assignments for "Curiosity"

I. Brief Papers
A. 1. Show that the dogs' lives and values are similar to many humans' lives and values.
   2. Why must cats "die" in order to live?
   3. According to the poet, "A cat minority of one / is all that can be counted on / to tell the truth" (lines 37–39). Explain.

B. 1. Argue for or against the assertion that people who are like the cats in the poem lead more fulfilled lives than people who are like the dogs.
   2. Argue for or against the assertion that the poem implies that it is only when you risk the most that you will experience the greatest satisfaction.

C. 1. What kinds of things must people risk or sacrifice in order to live like the cats in the poem?
   2. Pretend that you are coaching a theatre class and one student chooses "Curiosity" to read aloud as part of a stage presentation. Read the poem aloud several times, deciding the most effective delivery and write directions for your student, suggesting where her tone of voice needs to be more matter of fact or more impassioned, where she needs to read more slowly or more quickly, or giving her any other advice she needs to prepare a sensitive reading.

II. Longer Papers
A. Explain how the poet biases the reader in favor of the cat's life—through minimizing the dangers of such a life and through trivializing the dog's life. Use the language of the poem, the poet's attitude toward the subject, the details the poet selects to describe each life, or the structure of the poem itself to support your explanation.

B. Argue for or against the assertion that men are freer than women to live lives like the cats in the poem.

C. Explain how the poet's use of repetition reinforces our preference for the cat and our distaste for the dog.

D. Show that the poem suggests that many—maybe all—of our most difficult decisions force us to choose between the safe dog life and the more dangerous, yet more adventurous, cat life.

GALWAY KINNELL

The Bear

1

In late winter
I sometimes glimpse bits of steam
coming up from

some fault in the old snow
5   and bend close and see it is lung-colored
and put down my nose
and know
the chilly, enduring odor of bear.

2

I take a wolf's rib and whittle
10   it sharp at both ends
and coil it up
and freeze it in blubber and place it out
on the fairway of the bears.

And when it has vanished
15   I move out on the bear tracks,
roaming in circles
until I come to the first, tentative, dark
splash on the earth.

And I set out
20   running, following the splashes
of blood wandering over the world.
At the cut, gashed resting places
I stop and rest,
at the crawl-marks
25   where he lay out on his belly

to overpass some stretch of bauchy ice
I lie out
dragging myself forward with bear-knives in my fists.

3

On the third day I begin to starve,
30   at nightfall I bend down as I knew I would
at a turd sopped in blood,
and hesitate, and pick it up,
and thrust it in my mouth, and gnash it down,
and rise
35   and go on running.

4

On the seventh day,
living by now on bear blood alone,
I can see his upturned carcass far out ahead, a scraggled,
steamy hulk,
40   the heavy fur riffling in the wind.

I come up to him
and stare at the narrow-spaced, petty eyes,
the dismayed
face laid back on the shoulder, the nostrils
45   flared, catching
perhaps the first taint of me as he
died.

I hack
a ravine in his thigh, and eat and drink,
50   and tear him down his whole length
and open him and climb in
and close him up after me, against the wind,
and sleep.

5

And dream
55   of lumbering flatfooted
over the tundra,
stabbed twice from within,
splattering a trail behind me,
splattering it out no matter which way I lurch,
60   no matter which parabola of bear-transcendence,
which dance of solitude I attempt,
which gravity-clutched leap,
which trudge, which groan.

6

Until one day I totter and fall—
65   fall on this
    stomach that has tried so hard to keep up,
to digest the blood as it leaked in,
to break up
and digest the bone itself: and now the breeze
70   blows over me, blows off
the hideous belches of ill-digested bear blood
and rotted stomach
and the ordinary, wretched odor of bear,

blows across
75   my sore, lolled tongue a song
or screech, until I think I must rise up
and dance. And I lie still.

7

I awaken I think. Marshlights
reappear, geese
80   come trailing again up the flyway.
In her ravine under old snow the dam-bear
lies, licking
lumps of smeared fur
and drizzly eyes into shapes
85   with her tongue. And one
hairy-soled trudge stuck out before me,
the next groaned out,
the next,
the next,
90   the rest of my days I spend
wandering: wondering
what, anyway,
was that sticky infusion, that rank flavor of blood, that poetry,
    by which I lived?

1967

Writing Assignments for "The Bear"

I. Brief Papers

    A. 1. Show that even before stanza 4, the speaker of the poem begins to identify
        with the bear.
       2. Many contemporary poets seek to move away from ornamental or "pleasing"
        poetry. Explain in detail one way Kinnell achieves that goal in this poem.

3. Losing blood, splattering blood, consuming and drinking blood all figure in the poem. Why is blood so significant?
4. Explain why the poem begins in late winter and ends in early spring.

B. Argue for or against one of the assertions below.
1. The tension between life and death is the most important in the poem.
2. The tension between sleep and consciousness is the most important in the poem.
3. The tension between motion and passivity is the most important in the poem.

C. 1. Does your attitude toward the speaker in the poem change as the poem progresses?
2. If you were choosing poems about natural creatures to include in a high school anthology, would you select this one? Why or why not?
3. Do you find Kinnell's attempt to enter the experience of the wounded bear effective or offensive?

II. Longer Papers

A. Argue for or against the assertion that this poem could have as easily been included in a unit about poetry, art, and the artist's experience as in this unit about natural creatures.
B. Explain how stanza 4 is pivotal, in both form and content.
C. In stanza 5, the poet uses repetition of three participial phrases (lines 4–6) and then of five noun phrases (lines 7–10), all beginning with *which*. In both instances the repeated phrases vary in length—the participial phrases get progressively longer and the noun phrases get progressively shorter. Choose stanza five or any other stanza of the poem and analyze the poet's use of repetition. Read the stanza aloud several times. Note the length of the phrases and the repetition of certain constructions, of certain words, of varying sentence or phrase lengths. Write an essay showing how the use of repetition affects your response to the poem or how it reinforces the central impact or subject matter of the poem.
D. Show how your understanding of primitive sacrifice, religious rituals like Holy Communion, or spring festivals of rebirth and rejuvenation affects your response to the poem.

JAMES DICKEY

Encounter in the Cage Country

What I was would not work
For them all, for I had not caught
The lion's eye. I was walking down

The cellblock in green glasses   and came
5   At last to the place where someone was hiding
His spots in his black hide.

Unchangeably they were there,
Driven in as by eyes
Like mine, his darkness ablaze

10   In the stinking sun of the beast house.
Among the crowd, he found me
Out   and dropped his bloody snack

And came to the perilous edge
Of the cage, where the great bars tremble
15   Like wire. All Sunday ambling stopped,

The curved cells tightened around
Us all   as we saw he was watching only
Me. I knew the stage was set, and I began

To perform   first saunt'ring   then stalking
20   Back and forth like a sentry   faked
As if to run   and at one brilliant move

I made as though drawing a gun from my hip-
bone, the bite-sized children broke
Up   changing their concept of laughter,

25   But none of this changed his eyes, or changed
My green glasses. Alert, attentive,
He waited for what I could give him:

My moves   my throat   my wildest love,
The eyes behind my eyes. Instead, I left
30   Him, though he followed me right to the end

Of concrete. I wiped my face, and lifted off
My glasses. Light blasted the world of shade
Back under every park bush   the crowd

Quailed from me   I was inside and out
35 Of myself   and something was given a life-
mission to say to me hungrily over

And over and over   *your moves are exactly right*
For a few things in this world: we know you
When you come, Green Eyes, Green Eyes.

1961

Writing Assignments for "Encounter in the Cage Country"

I. Brief Papers
   A. 1. Show that the persona feels kinship with all the zoo animals.
      2. Explain how the sunglasses are an appropriate color and an appropriate link
         between the leopard and the persona.
      3. How does the poet's use of the cliché "the leopard can't change its spots"
         illuminate the speaker's character as well as the leopard's?
      4. Explain how the poet's *caesuras* (the breaks or the pauses between words in
         the lines of verse) contribute to the poem's effectiveness.

   B. Argue for or against the assertion that the poet invites you to admire the speaker
      in the poem.

   C. 1. How does the message from the wild creatures in the final stanza affect your
         response to the poem?
      2. What is your response to what the persona can share with the leopard: "My
         moves   my throat   my wildest love" (line 28)?

II. Longer Papers
   A. Some critics suggest that Dickey's poems brim with violence and brutality—even
      profound evil—while others believe that the poems suggest healthy energy and
      an honest acknowledgment of primal, passionate instincts. Discuss to what extent
      either or both of these critical stands enhance your appreciation or reading of this
      poem.
   B. Describe your encounter with the speaker as he encounters the leopard. Do you
      like him? How does your response to the speaker affect your understanding and
      appreciation of the poem?

WENDELL BERRY

The Peace of Wild Things

When despair for the world grows in me
and I wake in the night at the least sound
in fear of what my life and my children's lives may be,
I go and lie down where the wood drake
5   rests in his beauty on the water, and the great heron feeds.
I come into the peace of wild things
who do not tax their lives with forethought
of grief. I come into the presence of still water.
And I feel above me the day-blind stars
10   waiting with their light. For a time
I rest in the grace of the world, and am free.

1968

Writing Assignments for "The Peace of Wild Things"

I. Brief Papers

A. 1. What kind of fears plague the speaker in the poem?

   2. Look up *grief* in the dictionary. Which of its meanings seem(s) most appropriate in the poem? Discuss.

   3. Explain the relationship in the poem between "and I wake in the night at the least sound / in fear of what my life and my children's lives may be" (lines 2–3) and "I come into the peace of wild things / who do not tax their lives with forethought / of grief" (lines 6–8).

   4. Explain the paradox of the title of the poem by discussing how "wild" things are most peaceful.

B. Argue for or against either assertion below.

   1. From evidence stated and implied in the poem, it is obvious the speaker's peace will be short-lived.

   2. The speaker's solution—turning to the peace and the continuity of nature—is naive.

C. The poet writes, "I come into the presence of still water. / And I feel above me the day-blind stars / waiting with their light" (lines 8–10). Discuss your reaction to the images and language in those lines.

II. Longer Papers

A. Develop any one of the paragraph assignments into a full-length paper.

B. The poem is divided roughly into three sections: lines 1–3, lines 4–8, and lines 9–11. Discuss the relationship among the three parts of the poem.

WILLIAM STAFFORD

Traveling through the Dark

Traveling through the dark I found a deer
dead on the edge of the Wilson River road.
It is usually best to roll them into the canyon:
that road is narrow; to swerve might make more dead.

5   By glow of the tail-light I stumbled back of the car
and stood by the heap, a doe, a recent killing;
she had stiffened already, almost cold.
I dragged her off; she was large in the belly.

My fingers touching her side brought me the reason—
10   her side was warm; her fawn lay there waiting,
alive, still, never to be born.
Beside that mountain road I hesitated.

The car aimed ahead its lowered parking lights;
under the hood purred the steady engine.
15   I stood in the glare of the warm exhaust turning red;
around our group I could hear the wilderness listen.

I thought hard for us all—my only swerving—,
then pushed her over the edge into the river.

1960

Writing Assignments for "Traveling through the Dark"

I. Brief Papers
    A. 1. In stanza 1, the speaker says, "to swerve might make more dead" (line 4). Do
          you think the speaker refers to animals, to people, or to both? What evidence
          in the poem supports your view?
       2. Compare the use of *warm* in stanza 3 to its use in stanza 4.
       3. To whom does the speaker refer when, in the last stanza, he says, "I thought
          hard for us all" (line 17).
       4. Show that the speaker does not want to roll the doe into the river.

    B. Argue for or against either assertion below.
       1. The speaker chose the best alternative when he rolled the doe into the river.
       2. "Traveling through the Dark" is about morality.

C. What is your emotional reaction to the dramatic situation in the poem and to the speaker's reaction to it? Why do you feel as you do?

II. Longer Papers

A. To what extent is "Traveling through the Dark" an emotional poem? Discuss how it invites emotional reaction, explores and depicts an emotional situation, and/or illustrates the speaker's emotional reaction to that situation.

B. Stafford writes that language and poetry help people "to become more aware of what being alive means." In what ways does this poem make you more aware?

C. Discuss in detail why the poet entitles the poem "Traveling through the Dark."

GARY SNYDER

Hunting

THIS POEM IS FOR DEER*

"I dance on all the mountains
On five mountains, I have a dancing place
When they shoot at me I run
To my five mountains"

5   Missed a last shot
At the Buck, in twilight
So we came back sliding
On dry needles through cold pines.
Scared out a cottontail
10 Whipped up the winchester
Shot off its head.
The white body rolls and twitches
in the dark ravine
As we run down the hill to the car.
                  deer foot down scree
15 Picasso's fawn,† Issa's fawn,‡

Deer on the autumn mountain
Howling like a wise man

*This poem is for Deer: Section 8 of a long poem entitled "Hunting," which appears in its entirety in Snyder's book *Myths and Texts.*
†Picasso: A Spanish painter and sculptor (1881–1973) who lived and worked in France; noted for his experimental art forms.
‡Issa: Pen name of the Japanese poet Kobayashi (1763–1827), who lived in Shinona and Tokyo. His work in experimental forms of haiku, a short poem of seventeen syllables, like Picasso's art, was highly abstract.

Stiff springy jumps down the snowfields
20   Head held back, forefeet out,
Balls tight in a tough hair sack
Keeping the human soul from care
                  on the autumn mountain
Standing in late sun, ear-flick
25   Tail-flick, gold mist of flies
Whirling from nostril to eyes.

                 *   *   *

Home by night
             drunken eye
Still picks out Taurus*
30   Low, and growing high:
             four-point buck
Dancing in the headlights
             on the lonely road
A mile past the mill-pond,
35   With the car stopped, shot
That wild silly blinded creature down.

Pull out the hot guts
             with hard bare hands
While night-frost chills the tongue
40   and eye
The cold horn-bones.
The hunter's belt
             just below the sky
Warm blood in the car trunk.
45   Deer-smell,
             the limp tongue.

                 *   *   *

Deer don't want to die for me.
             I'll drink sea-water
Sleep on beach pebbles in the rain
50   Until the deer come down to die
             in pity for my pain.

                          1967

*Taurus: Star constellation between Aries and Orion; the symbol of Taurus is the bull.

Writing Assignments for "Hunting"

I. Brief Papers

A. 1. Show that the voice speaking in the first stanza of the poem is not the voice speaking in the last stanza.

 2. Show that the poem depends on a series of images or pictures—some associated with hunters, some associated with deer—to invite an emotional response from the reader.

 3. Compare the verbs associated with the hunters to those associated with the deer.

 4. Why does the persona wish to drink sea-water and sleep in the rain in the last stanza?

B. Argue for or against one of the assertions below.
 1. The poet finds the hunting distasteful and unnatural.
 2. This poem illustrates that—as some have claimed—Snyder is the poet of the common people.
 3. A deer hunter would not find the poem believable or enjoyable.

C. Does this poem parallel or contradict your experience with animals? Does it change your ideas about animals?

II. Longer Papers

A. In the poem, the hunters *slide* on dry pine needles (line 7), while the deer *scree* (an archaic term meaning "to slide") in the next section (line 15). The hunters run in *twilight* (line 6), the deer in *late sun* (line 24). Show that such comparisons between the hunter and deer illuminate their differences more than their similarities.

B. The contrasts in light and dark, death and life, dancing and falling, abound in the poem. Show how those contrasts influence your response to the poem.

C. How does the description of the deer, beginning with "Deer on the autumn mountain" (line 16) and ending with "Whirling from nostril to eyes" (line 26), affect your response to the poem?

CONSTANCE PIERCE

A Shift in Season

> All summer the cows
> Have grazed on the knoll,
> Lolled on the stream bank,
> Come tentative to the fence

5 For a sheaf of timothy,* a bouquet
   Of summer sentiment
   Treacherous as the jimson seed.†

   And they have clustered together
   And stared inscrutably
10 At all human motion.

   One, devastating
   In his perception,
   Has fastened me under his eye
   And asked the silent question.
15 In the night, he has
   Lowed into my dreams
   From across the gully,
   Thrust his soft meaty tongue
   Through the moonlight
20 And drawn the raphe‡ along my ear.

   Now in the first frost
   Of treachery's own season,
   His answer prickles
   In the air. The cows
25 Move back under the trees,
   A clump of comprehension—

   Staring,
   Peeing on their legs.
   There is no escape

30 From the clang and rumble
   Of their hooves on the truck bed.

   In the morning
   There is just the field.

                          1981

Writing Assignments for "A Shift in Season"

I. Brief Papers
    A. 1. Show that the speaker in the poem is troubled by the cows' fate.
       2. Show that the poet depicts the cows' behavior realistically.

*timothy: A perennial grass grown for hay.
†jimson seed: Jimson weed, grown from the seed, is poisonous.
‡raphe: The ridge of tissue where both sides of the tongue are joined.

3. Why is the "sheaf of timothy" (line 5) both sentimental and treacherous?

4. What silent question does the perceptive cow pose? How does it affect the speaker?

B. Argue for or against either assertion below.
1. The line "There is no escape" (line 29) has two meanings in the poem.
2. The speaker feels different toward the cows than most people would.

C. 1. Choose one of the following and explain how it affects your response to the poem: (1) the single cow's scrutiny of the speaker; (2) the "soft meaty tongue" (line 18) drawn along the speaker's ear; or (3) the "clang and rumble" (line 30) of the cows' hooves on the truckbed.
2. Do you believe most women would react differently to the poem than most men?

II. Longer Papers

A. Develop one of your brief papers into a full-length paper.

B. Explain how the poem evokes restrained emotion, not excessive sentimentality.

THOMAS HARDY

The Darkling Thrush

I leant upon a coppice* gate
    When Frost was specter-gray,
And Winter's dregs made desolate
    The weakening eye of day.
5 The tangled bine-stems† scored the sky
    Like strings of broken lyres,
And all mankind that haunted nigh
    Had sought their household fires.

The land's sharp features seemed to be
10   The Century's corpse outleant,
His crypt the cloudy canopy,
    The wind his death-lament.
The ancient pulse of germ and birth
    Was shrunken hard and dry,
15 And every spirit upon earth
    Seemed fervorless as I.

---

*coppice: A small wood or thicket.
†bine-stems: Shrubbery stems.

At once a voice arose among
    The bleak twigs overhead
In a full-hearted evensong
20   Of joy illimited;
An aged thrush, frail, gaunt, and small,
    In blast-beruffled plume,
Had chosen thus to fling his soul
    Upon the growing gloom.

25 So little cause for carolings
    Of such ecstatic sound
Was written on terrestrial things
    Afar or nigh around,
That I could think there trembled through
30   His happy good-night air
Some blessed Hope, whereof he knew
    And I was unaware.

1902*

Writing Assignments for "The Darkling Thrush"

I. Brief Papers
  A. 1. Show that the poet uses images or pictures associated with death.
     2. Show that the poet uses diction (words) associated with death.
     3. Show that the dramatic setting of the poem—the time of day, the time of year, and so on—reflects the persona's state of mind.
     4. Choose one stanza and explain how the poet gives human characteristics to inanimate objects, natural creatures, or abstractions.

  B. Argue for or against either assertion below.
     1. The poem is optimistic.
     2. The persona is likely to have a change of outlook on life because of the bird's song.

  C. 1. Some critics find Hardy's poems, while not poetically rich, examples of good common sense. Do you believe "The Darkling Thrush" is a poem of good common sense? Why or why not?
     2. Do you believe the kind of hope the bird's song might offer to those in the early twentieth century has changed any? Why or why not?

---

*1902: The poem was written on December 31, 1900, the end of the nineteenth century. Hardy alludes to the "Century's corpse" (line 10).

MARIANNE MOORE

Bird-Witted

With innocent wide penguin eyes, three
   large fledgling mockingbirds below
the pussy-willow tree,
   stand in a row
5 wings touching, feebly solemn,
   till they see
      their no longer larger
      mother bringing
something which will partially
10 feed one of them.

Toward the high-keyed intermittent squeak
   of broken carriage springs, made by
the three similar, meek-
   coated bird's-eye
15 freckled forms she comes; and when
   from the beak
      of one, the still living
      beetle has dropped
out, she picks it up and puts
20 it in again.

Standing in the shade till they have dressed
   their thickly filamented, pale
pussy-willow-surfaced
   coats, they spread tail
25 and wings, showing one by one,
   the modest

                   white stripe lengthwise on the
                   tail and crosswise
              underneath the wing, and the
   30   accordion

              is closed again. What delightful note
                   with rapid unexpected flute
              sounds leaping from the throat
                   of the astute
   35   grown bird, comes back to one from
              the remote
                        unenergetic sun-
                        lit air before
              the brood was here? How harsh
   40   the bird's voice has become.

              A piebald cat observing them,
                   is slowly creeping toward the trim
              trio on the tree stem.
                   Unused to him
   45   the three make room—uneasy
              new problem.
                        A dangling foot that missed
                        its grasp, is raised
              and finds the twig on which it
   50   planned to perch. The

              parent darting down, nerved by what chills
                   the blood, and by hope rewarded—
              of toil—since nothing fills
                   squeaking unfed
   55   mouths, wages deadly combat,
              and half kills
                        with bayonet beak and
                        cruel wings, the
              intellectual cautious-
   60   ly creeping cat.

                                                    1936

Writing Assignments for "Bird-Witted"

I. Brief Papers
   A. 1. Show that the poet invites sympathy for the mother mockingbird.
       2. Explain how the label "bird-witted" is disparaging when applied to the three
          fledgling mockingbirds.

3. Show that the label "bird-witted" is admiring when applied to the mother mockingbird.
4. Why does the poet label the cat "intellectual" in the last line of the poem?

B. Argue for or against either assertion below.
  1. "Bird-Witted" can best be appreciated when read silently, not aloud.
  2. The poem takes a grim view of creatures' natural instincts, the birds' as much as the cat's.

C. Do you react strongly to the poem? Why or why not?

II. Longer Papers

A. In the library, find a detailed account of the habits of mockingbirds—their mating customs, their care and feeding of their young, and their song. Discuss how the poet draws upon authentic details yet exercises poetic license as well in creating the poem.
B. Moore's poetry is praised most often for its nimble, hard wit and its intellectuality—not for its melody or its rich language. Judging from "Bird-Witted," do you agree or disagree with such an appraisal?
C. Explain how the poem treats the cat's and the birds' natural instincts. What perspective does it offer?

EDITH SITWELL

The Swans

In the green light of water, like the day
Under green boughs, the spray
And air-pale petals of the foam seem flowers—
Dark-leaved arbutus blooms with wax-pale bells
5   And their faint honey-smells,
The velvety syringa with smooth leaves,
Gloxinia with a green shade in the snow,
Jasmine and moon-clear orange-blossoms and green blooms
Of the wild strawberries from the shade of woods.
10 Their showers
Pelt the white women under the green trees,
Venusia, Cosmopolita, Pistillarine—
White solar statues, white rose-trees in snow
Flowering for ever, child-women, half stars
15 Half flowers, waves of the sea, born of a dream.

Their laughter flying through the trees like doves,
These angels come to watch their whiter ghosts

In the air-pale water, archipelagos
Of stars and young thin moons from great wings falling
20   As ripples widen.
These are their ghosts, their own white angels these!
O great wings spreading—
Your bones are made of amber, smooth and thin
Grown from the amber dust that was a rose
25   Or nymph in swan-smooth waters.
                                                  But Time's winter falls
With snows as soft, as soundless. . . . Then, who knows
Rose-footed swan from snow, or girl from rose?

                                                                      1942

Writing Assignments for "The Swans"

I. Brief Papers
   A. 1. Choose one or two lines from the poem and show how the poet mixes images
         or pictures—those of the swans, the women, the flowers, and the snow—to
         illustrate the essential similarity among them.
      2. Explain the final three lines of the poem. In what ways are the "Rose-footed
         swan" (line 27), the snow, a girl, and a rose indistinguishable?
      3. In the following phrases and lines from the poem, consider how the poet
         invites a response from two or more senses at the same time:

         • "a green shade in the snow" (line 7) mixes the sense of touch with color
         • "air-pale petals of the foam" (line 3) mixes the sense of touch with light and
           water

         When poets describe one kind of sensation in terms of another, they are using
         synaesthesia. Show how Sitwell employs synaesthesia throughout the poem.

   B. Argue for or against either assertion below.
      1. The poem would evoke a substantially different tone and mood if the poet had
         omitted the final three lines beginning with "But Time's winter falls . . ."
         (line 25).
      2. The overall mood of the poem is deathlike, sterile, and lifeless.

   C. 1. Read the poem aloud several times. Which phrases or lines seem to you most
         emotional? Write a paragraph explaining the associations you make to the
         sounds, the pictures, the language of the poem. (You may be surprised to find
         that the associations have nothing to do directly with swans, flowers, or
         moonlight.)
      2. Why do you believe swans are appropriate in a poem about beauty and
         mutability?

II. Longer Papers

A. Your friend at a neighboring college has just written you a letter. She must select a poem to present to her class, but her teacher wants her to focus on how the poem sounds, what images or pictures evoke the greatest response, or why readers respond to the language of the poem in certain ways. Write your friend a letter suggesting she select this poem and give her advice on preparing her presentation. You might begin by explaining that she can easily pick out phrases and lines which evoke intense response or pictures and images which inspire really sad or happy memories. Give your friend as much advice as possible in preparing her presentation.

B. Compare this poem with William Butler Yeats' poem, "The Wild Swans at Coole" (below). Which do you prefer and why?

WILLIAM BUTLER YEATS
*The Wild Swans at Coole**

The trees are in their autumn beauty,
The woodland paths are dry,
Under the October twilight the water
Mirrors a still sky;
5 Upon the brimming water among the stones
Are nine-and-fifty swans.

The nineteenth autumn has come upon me
Since I first made my count;
I saw, before I had well finished,
10 All suddenly mount
And scatter wheeling in great broken rings
Upon their clamorous wings.

I have looked upon those brilliant creatures,
And now my heart is sore.
15 All's changed since I, hearing at twilight,
The first time on this shore,
The bell-beat of their wings above my head,
Trod with a lighter tread.

Unwearied still, lover by lover,
20 They paddle in the cold
Companionable streams or climb the air;
Their hearts have not grown old;

*Coole: Coole Park, in Galway, Ireland, was the estate of Yeats's friend Lady Gregory, an Irish writer and supporter of Irish literature. Yeats spent several summers at Coole Park.

Passion or conquest, wander where they will,
Attend upon them still.

25 But now they drift on the still water,
Mysterious, beautiful;
Among what rushes will they build,
By what lake's edge or pool
Delight men's eyes when I awake some day
30 To find they have flown away?

1917

Writing Assignments for "The Wild Swans at Coole"

I. Brief Papers
  A. 1. Show that the speaker of the poem has changed even though the swans have not.
     2. Why does the speaker say "now my heart is sore" (line 14) when he witnesses the swans?
     3. What will have happened if, as he fears, the speaker awakens one day to find the swans have flown away?
     4. Explain how and why the motion of the swans and the water changes throughout the poem.

  B. Argue for or against one of the assertions below.
     1. It is significant that the swans are wild rather than tame creatures.
     2. The speaker's primary lament is that he is aging.
     3. The speaker's primary lament is his loss of "Passion or conquest" (line 23).

  C. 1. Do you sympathize with the speaker? Why or why not?
     2. Yeats wrote this poem when he was 51, and there is other evidence to link Yeats closely with the speaker of the poem. How does that information affect your response to the poem?
     3. In one myth, swans and singers or poets are associated because the swan supposedly sings sweetly just before its death. How does that idea affect your response to the poem?

II. Longer Papers
  A. Develop any one of the paragraph assignments into a full-length paper.
  B. Show that this poem or that both this poem and Edith Sitwell's poem "The Swans" (p. 645) rely for their effect on universal responses to the swan's almost magical beauty.
  C. Compare Shelley's "To a Sky-Lark" (p. 574) or Keats' "Ode to a Nightingale" (p. 570) to this poem. Which response to the problem of mortality do you prefer?
  D. Explain how the poet uses the word *still* throughout the poem.

ALFRED, LORD TENNYSON
The Eagle: A Fragment

He clasps the crag with crooked hands;
Close to the sun in lonely lands,
Ringed with the azure world, he stands.

The wrinkled sea beneath him crawls:
5   He watches from his mountain walls,
And like a thunderbolt he falls.

1851

Writing Assignments for "The Eagle"

I. Brief Papers

A. 1. Show that Tennyson depicts the eagle by comparing him to a human and next to a thunderbolt.

2. Explain in what ways the poet maintains the eagle's central importance throughout the poem, minimizing all else in the landscape.

3. Recast the poem in prose, using literal language, no figures of speech or comparisons. Your first sentence might read something like "The eagle is sitting on the side of a mountain, holding on with his talons." After you have written the prose form, explain why Tennyson's version is more appealing or more imaginative.

4. Show how the structure of the poem reinforces the subject matter.

B. Argue for or against the assertion that you can appreciate the poem only if you are already familiar with how eagles look and how they move.

II. Longer Papers

A. How does the setting of the poem—the mountain wall, the sun, the lonely land, the azure world—and the language describing it affect your responses to the poem?

B. What are the characteristics with which people conventionally endow eagles? Is it necessary to know these conventional associations in order to understand the poem?

GERARD MANLEY HOPKINS
*The Windhover**

To Christ Our Lord

I caught this morning morning's minion,† king-
   dom of daylight's dauphin,‡ dapple-dawn-drawn Falcon, in his
riding
   Of the rolling level underneath him steady air, and striding
High there, how he rung upon the rein of a wimpling wing
5 In his ecstasy! then off, off forth on swing,
   As a skate's heel sweeps smooth on a bow-bend: the hurl and
gliding
   Rebuffed the big wind. My heart in hiding
Stirred for a bird,—the achieve of, the mastery of the thing!

Brute beauty and valour and act, oh, air, pride, plume, here
10   Buckle! AND the fire that breaks from thee then, a billion
Times told lovelier, more dangerous, O my chevalier!§

   No wonder of it: shéer plód makes plough down sillion‖
Shine, and blue-bleak embers, ah my dear,
   Fall, gall themselves, and gash gold-vermilion.#

1918**

Writing Assignments for "The Windhover"

I. Brief Papers

  A. 1. Hopkins consistently points out that poetry should be read aloud and even
       suggests that his own poetry is meant wholly for recital, not for silent reading
       or study. Show one way "The Windhover" illustrates the principle.
     2. A windhover (a small falcon) can stop and hover in the air against the wind.
       Show how Hopkins captures such a feat.
     3. Compare the ways the speaker refers to the bird—"morning's minion" (line
       1), "daylight's dauphin" (line 2), and "dapple-dawn-drawn Falcon" (line 2)—

*Windhover: A kestral, a small falcon, which can hover in the air.
†minion: Darling.
‡dauphin: An heir.
§chevalier: A knight, a member of an order of gallantry.
‖sillion: Ridge between two furrows of a plowed field.
#vermilion: A bright scarlet red.
**1918: The publication date. The poem was written in 1877.

in the first ten lines to the way he addresses the bird in the last six lines—"my chevalier" (line 11) and "my dear" (line 13). Explain how the references in the last six lines could refer to more than the windhover itself.

4. Focusing especially on the lines "my heart in hiding / Stirred for a bird . . ." (lines 7–8), explain in what way the speaker is changed by witnessing the windhover.

5. Find one of the following words in the dictionary and explain how its various definitions enrich the poem: *minion, dauphin, wimpling,* or *vermillion.*

B. Argue for or against either assertion below.

1. The last six lines of the poem suggest God's terrible power as much as the bird's sublime loveliness.

2. "The Windhover" is primarily a religious meditation on the beauty and power of God, not a nature poem about a bird's flight.

C. 1. Does the fact that Hopkins was ordained a Jesuit priest the same year he wrote this poem affect your response to it? Why or why not?

2. Choose one line or one phrase you particularly enjoy reading aloud. Why do you enjoy it?

II. Longer Papers

A. The windhover in the poem sweeps in ecstasy, withstands and conquers incredibly overpowering force when rebuffed, and reacts with a fire more lovely and more dangerous when it dives. Using those examples and/or any other evidence you wish from the poem, discuss the poem's religious implications.

B. From his letters and journals, we know that Hopkins struggled with lifelong doubt about taking time from his work as a teacher and priest to write poetry. At times he went years without writing poetry, because he could not find it in his conscience to spend time on it. Still, he would be drawn back inevitably. Write a paper explaining why you believe writing poetry is or is not a waste of time for Hopkins as a priest.

C. Show how the poem's language—its word choice, its repetition of letters, of sounds, of words, or any element of its style—help depict the windhover's flight and the speaker's adoration.

ROBERT FROST

Design

Before Reading

Before Reading "Design" write for 5 to 10 minutes in response to the following question: "Do you think things occur in the world because of chance or because of design?"

I found a dimpled spider, fat and white,
On a white heal-all,* holding up a moth
Like a white piece of rigid satin cloth—
Assorted characters of death and blight
5   Mixed ready to begin the morning right,
Like the ingredients of a witches' broth—
A snow-drop spider, a flower like a froth,
And dead wings carried like a paper kite.

What had that flower to do with being white,
10   The wayside blue and innocent heal-all?
What brought the kindred spider to that height,
Then steered the white moth thither in the night?
What but design of darkness to appall?—
If design govern in a thing so small.

                                                          1936

Writing Assignments for "Design"

I. Brief Papers

    A. 1. Describe the dramatic scene in stanza one.

       2. Go through the poem and circle all the words describing the spider. How does the word choice affect your response to the poem?

       3. Summarize what questions the speaker poses in lines 9–12 and how he answers them in line 13.

       4. Explain the relationship between the first eight lines of the poem and the last six.

    B. Argue for or against the assertion that the final line of the poem is the most frightening in its implications, because the poet obviously implies that the situation is not based on chance.

II. Longer Papers

    A. The Argument from Design has been one of the traditional arguments used to prove the existence of God. Briefly, the Argument goes this way: if there is a clear and meaningful order in the created world, then there must be a creator or designer of that world. And, according to the Argument from Design, that creator is God. Discuss to what extent Frost relies on the Argument from Design in order to explain in his "Design" the relationship between the creation and its creator.

    B. Compare this poem to William Blake's "The Tyger" (p. 625). Discuss how both poems question the laws of nature and of God.

*white heal-all: Albino version of the common wild flower. Almost always purple or blue in color, the heal-all earned its name because it was once used widely as a folk-remedy or medicine.

EMILY DICKINSON
The Wind Took Up the Northern Things

The Wind took up the Northern Things
And piled them in the south—
Then gave the East unto the West
And opening his mouth

5   The four Divisions of the Earth
Did make as to devour
While everything to corners slunk
Behind the awful power—

The Wind—unto his Chambers went
10 And nature ventured out—
Her subjects scattered into place
Her systems ranged about

Again the smoke from Dwellings rose
The Day abroad was heard—
15 How intimate, a Tempest past
The Transport of the Bird—

1945*

Writing Assignments for "The Wind Took Up the Northern Things"

I. Brief Papers

   A. 1. Describe how Dickinson personifies the wind.

      2. Describe how Dickinson personifies nature.

   B. In "Apparently With No Surprise" (p. 654), Dickinson personifies frost as an "assassin." In "Because I Could Not Stop for Death" (p. 829), she depicts death as an insistent suitor; and, in "I Started Early—Took My Dog" (p. 655), she describes the sea as a powerful man whose "silver heel" grips the speaker's ankle. Argue for or against the assertion that the poet's personification of the wind in this poem is significantly different from the personification in her other poems.

*1945: The publication date, 59 years after Dickinson's death in 1886. The date conjectured for the earliest known manuscript of this poem is 1863.

II. Longer Papers

A. Discuss Dickinson's use of personification in this poem, or in this poem and several other Dickinson poems from this book. Explain how the personification affects your interpretation of the poem.

B. Some people believe Dickinson, who often depicts nature's savagery and mercilessness, creates in this poem a speaker who views nature quite differently from the poet herself. If that interpretation is a defensible one, then Dickinson has created a sustained parody or satire of views which trivialize or ignore nature's destructiveness and its power. Explain to what extent you believe the poet has, indeed, developed an ironic perspective in the poem.

EMILY DICKINSON

Apparently with No Surprise

> Apparently with no surprise
> To any happy Flower
> The Frost beheads it at its play—
> In accidental power—
> 5 The blonde Assassin passes on—
> The Sun proceeds unmoved
> To measure off another Day
> For an Approving God.

1890*

Writing Assignments for "Apparently with No Surprise"

I. Brief Papers

A. 1. How does the description of the "happy Flower," beheaded at "its play," imply the poet's attitude toward the subject matter of the poem and affect your response to it?

2. How does the first line of the poem prepare for the rest of the poem and help direct the reader's response to it?

3. What is the relationship between the first five lines of the poem and the last three?

B. Argue for or against the assertion that the poem is more whimsical than it is grim.

II. Longer Papers

A. How does the poet's choice of words and/or the structure of the poem direct the reader's response to the laws of nature she describes?

*1890: First publication date, four years after Dickinson's death in 1886. The date conjectured for the earliest known manuscript is 1884.

B. Compare this poem to "The Wind Took Up the Northern Things" (p. 653), "I Started Early—Took My Dog" (p. 655), or "Design" (p. 651). Discuss the poems' depictions of natural law and of God as well as their imagery, personification, or style.

EMILY DICKINSON

I Started Early—Took My Dog

I started Early—Took my Dog—
And visited the Sea—
The Mermaids in the Basement
Came out to look at me—

5   And Frigates—in the Upper Floor
Extended Hempen Hands—
Presuming Me to be a Mouse—
Aground—upon the Sands—

But no Man moved Me—till the Tide
10 Went past my simple Shoe—
And past my Apron—and my Belt
And past my Bodice—too—

And made as He would eat me up—
As wholly as a Dew
15 Upon a Dandelion's Sleeve—
And then—I started—too—

And He—He followed—close behind—
I felt His Silver Heel
Upon my Ankle—Then my Shoes
20 Would overflow with Pearl—

Until We met the Solid Town—
No One He seemed to know—
And bowing—with a Mighty look—
At me—The Sea withdrew—

1891*

*1891: The first publication date of the poem, five years after Dickinson's death in 1886. The date conjectured for the earliest known manuscript of the poem is 1862.

Writing Assignments for "I Started Early—Took My Dog"

I. Brief Papers
  A. 1. Describe the dramatic action of the poem, being as specific as possible about
        what actually occurs.
     2. In what ways does the poet personify the sea? Is it a friendly force? An ominous
        one? Something else?
     3. What is the mood and the speaker's attitude in the first two stanzas?
     4. How does the mood of the poem change in the third stanza?

  B. Argue for or against the assertion that the personification of the sea as a man
     emphasizes the power and the intimacy of the speaker's experience.

II. Longer Papers
  A. Discuss to what extent the speaker's experience in the poem is ordinary and to
     what extent it is extraordinary.
  B. Explain how the images throughout the poem establish the tone and mood of the
     poem, magnify the power of the sea, and minimize the strength and significance
     of the speaker.
  C. Discuss the relationship in tone, mood, and subject matter between the first two
     and the last four stanzas. How is stanza 3 a pivotal one?

The Use of Simile: When Deer Howl Like Wisemen and Laughter Flies Like Doves

Using the sentences below, write a short essay that defines and illustrates *simile,* one kind
of comparison or figurative language poets frequently create.

  1. When we see an eagle fly from a mountaintop to earth, we might say something.
  2. We might say "An eagle flew to the ground."
  3. We might say "An eagle swooped to earth."

  4. Tennyson sees an eagle fly to earth.
  5. He says something different.
  6. He says that *"like* a thunderbolt," the eagle falls.

  7. We hear deer baying one autumn afternoon.
  8. We might say we hear deer lowing on the hillside.
  9. Gary Snyder hears deer baying in the autumn.
 10. He says something different.
 11. Gary Snyder says the deer howl "like a wiseman."

12. Tennyson's and Snyder's comparisons are similes.
13. Similes are comparisons between two essentially different things.
14. Similes are signaled by the following words: *like, as, than, appears,* and *seems.*

15. David Wagoner says the bird continues wailing

> While the artist drew and tinted on fine vellum
> Its red cockade, gray claws, and sepia eyes
> From which a *white wedge flowed* to the lame wing
> *Like light flying* and ended there in blackness.

16. Wagoner uses a simile.
17. He compares the white wedge to light.
18. The poem is suddenly richer.
19. We see the bird more clearly.
20. We feel the bird's pain more acutely.
21. We sense the bird's encroaching death.

22. We do not need to know the term simile to appreciate how poets use them.

23. Jeffers says something that makes us feel sadder.
24. Jeffers says a hawk's wing trails "like a banner in defeat."

25. Sitwell says something that helps us sense beauty more deeply.
26. Sitwell says something that helps us enjoy language more intensely.
27. Sitwell says the "air-pale petals of foam *seem* flowers."
28. Sitwell says the women's laughter flies through the trees "like doves."

29. Through simile poets gain compactness and intensity.
30. Through simile poets invite fresh perspectives and evoke heightened emotional response.
31. Through simile poets achieve poetry.

Comparative Papers from Chapter Two: Nature

A. Discuss two or more poems from this chapter which present radically different views of nature.
B. Basing your argument on two or more poems from this chapter, argue for or against one of the following assertions:
  1. Several poems in the chapter imply that nature harbors malevolent intent against humans.
  2. Several poems in the chapter imply that, while nature's forces intend neither good nor evil, human beings tend to ascribe human characteristics to nature.

C. Discuss to what extent human beings feel compelled to personify nature and natural events, to describe them in human terms.

D. Compare William Wordsworth's imagery and word choice to Emily Dickinson's or Robert Frost's. How do their different styles reflect their different attitudes toward nature?

E. Find one poem in the chapter which states or implies an attitude toward nature different from your own. Complete the following sentence by free writing for 10 minutes: "I disagree with _____'s view of nature because . . . ." Since the goal of free writing is to generate ideas quickly, do not worry about spelling, punctuation, grammar, or sentence structure. Just keep writing down whatever comes into your head about why you disagree with the poem's depiction of nature. After 10 minutes, look back over your writing. As a way to test your ideas, set your clock and once again free write for 10 minutes, this time taking the opposite view you took previously. Discuss all the evidence you can find to support the view contrary to your own. Use your two free writings to help you expand your argument and to show your reader you have carefully considered all issues involved in interpreting the author's views fairly.

F. Compare one or two nature poems in the text which convey a clear message or moral to one or two which do not. Discuss how the poems differ in attitude, in imagery, in language, or in any other way you consider significant.

G. Choose one or more poems from this unit and show that poets often subordinate a creature's description, its habitat, its habits, and/or its nature in order to emphasize other matters.

H. We share, at times, an uneasy relationship with other creatures in our universe. We rely on animals for companionship and for food, yet we kill them for profit and for sport, hunting them often to extinction. We admire them for their "natural" ways, yet we fear their wildness, construing their natural predatory instincts as evil. Choose several poems from this unit and explain in detail how they illustrate our ambivalent, even schizophrenic, attitude toward the creatures.

I. In an essay entitled "The Damned Human Race," Samuel Clemens suggests that human beings are really at the bottom stage of development and should be considered the "lowest" animal. According to Clemens, we are the only animals who kill for pleasure, cruelty, or revenge; who wage war; or who feel shame. Using evidence from one or more poems in this unit, show that other poets would agree with Clemens' assessment.

J. Argue for or against the assertion that most poets admire natural creatures and believe humans would be happier if they were more like them.

K. Pretend you are starting a wildlife magazine devoted to the study and appreciation of natural creatures. For each edition you plan to print one poem that features animal life of some kind, completing the spread with commentary and photographs. Explain which poems from this unit you would select for the first few editions, choosing poems you believe your subscribers would enjoy. In your paper, be sure to explain how you expect your audience will respond to the poems you select.

3 / Poems about Students, Teachers, and Artists

TOM ROMANO

the teacher

Why do I forget question marks.
I am notorious for it.
My students scoff at me,
"How can you teach English when
5   you don't punctuate proper?"

I don't teach you anyway, I think,
just lead you like a scout master
and hope you'll dip your hand
into the brook—cold like no
10 tap water you've ever felt,
let you marvel, a little frightened,
at a snake, mouth agape,
before it darts between rocks,
an image you'll carry for years,
15 spur you to anger when I won't
stop to let you rest,
even hope you catch poison ivy,
and, as we race up the hill,
urge you on when
20 you leave me behind,
gasping,
a seeming spear
wedged between my ribs.

Of the absent question mark, I say,
25 "An innocent, harmless error,"
And those of you who aren't smug
point out that I should
extend to you
the same courteous understanding.
30 I uncap my canteen,
drop to the grass, and,
before I take a long swig,
say, "Why not."

1982

Writing Assignments for "The Teacher"

I. Brief Papers
   A. 1. What is the teacher's attitude toward his students? Try to find evidence not
         only in what he says but in other elements of the poem as well.
      2. Choose one of the following images or lines and discuss what the speaker
         really hopes will happen to his students:
         a. "and hope you'll dip your hand
            into the brook—cold like no
            tap water you've ever felt"
            (lines 8–10)
         b. "let you marvel . . . / at a snake . . . /
            an image you'll carry for years"
            (lines 11,12,14)
         c. "spur you to anger when I won't
            stop to let you rest,
            even hope you catch poison ivy"
            (lines 15–17)
      3. Go through the poem and circle all the punctuation marks. Explain why, in
         certain places, the poet observes conventions of punctuation and, in others,
         breaks them.

   B. Argue for or against the assertion that the speaker is wrong when he says, "I don't
      teach you" (line 6) to his students.

   C. 1. Does the teacher's admission that he forgets punctuation marks affect your
         response to him? Why or why not?
      2. Given evidence in the poem, write a short description of the speaker. What
         kind of teacher is he? Would you learn more from him than from other
         teachers? Less? Would you prefer him over other kinds?

II. Longer Papers
   A. This poem was not only published by the largest professional organization of
      English teachers in the nation but it was also distributed to all its members at an
      annual convention. Discuss in detail why you believe the organization chose to
      feature the poem. Why would English teachers find this poem significant or
      interesting?
   B. After examining the structure of the poem, explain as fully as possible how the
      three stanzas are related. How are the first and last stanzas related? Is there an
      extension or evolution of stanza 1? What is the connection between the second,
      long stanza and both stanzas 1 and 3?

STEPHEN SPENDER

An Elementary School Classroom in a Slum

Far far from gusty waves, these children's faces.
Like rootless weeds the torn hair round their paleness.
The tall girl with her weighed-down head. The paper-
seeming boy with rat's eyes. The stunted unlucky heir
5   Of twisted bones, reciting a father's gnarled disease,
His lesson from his desk. At back of the dim class
One unnoted, mild and young: his eyes live in a dream
Of squirrels' game, in tree room, other than this.

On sour cream walls, donations. Shakespeare's head
10   Cloudless at dawn, civilized dome riding all cities.
Belled, flowery, Tyrolese valley. Open-handed map
Awarding the world its world. And yet, for these
Children, these windows, not this world, are world,
Where all their future's painted with a fog,
15   A narrow street sealed in with a lead sky,
Far far from rivers, capes, and stars of words.

Surely Shakespeare is wicked, the map a bad example
With ships and sun and love tempting them to steal—
For lives that slyly turn in their cramped holes
20   From fog to endless night? On their slag heap, these children
Wear skins peeped through by bones, and spectacles of steel
With mended glass, like bottle bits in slag.
Tyrol is wicked; map's promising a fable:
All of their time and space are foggy slum,
So blot their maps with slums as big as doom.

25   Unless, governor, teacher, inspector, visitor,
This map becomes their window and these windows
That open on their lives like crouching tombs
Break, O break open, till they break the town
And show the children to the fields and all their world
30   Azure on their sands, to let their tongues
Run naked into books, the white and green leaves open
The history theirs whose language is the sun.

1942

Writing Assignments for "An Elementary School Classroom in a Slum"

I. Brief Papers

    A. 1. Describe the dramatic setting of the poem.

        2. Discuss how the slum imagery pervades all elements of the poem, not just the geographical setting.

        3. Explain the changing meaning of *world* in the following lines: ". . . Open-handed map / Awarding the world its world. And yet, for these / Children, these windows, not this world, are world."

        4. Go through the poem and circle all references to one of the following patterns of imagery: coldness and warmth; darkness and light; silence and sound; or captivity and freedom. Explain the imagery's appropriateness and impact in the poem.

    B. Argue for or against either assertion below.

        1. This is an optimistic poem.

        2. The poem is primarily a plea for action.

    C. Explain why you believe the poet wrote this poem. What might have inspired it?

II. Long Papers

    A. Explain how in the final stanza of the poem, the poet merges a number of different patterns of imagery he uses throughout the poem.

    B. Discuss map and window imagery throughout the poem. How are the two contrasted? How are they merged? Why are both appropriate in the poem?

    C. Explain to what extent you believe the poem can be read and appreciated apart from its social message and to what extent the message is crucial to its impact.

WALT WHITMAN

When I Heard the Learn'd Astronomer

> When I heard the learn'd astronomer,
> When the proofs, the figures, were ranged in columns before me,
> When I was shown the charts and diagrams, to add, divide, and
>   measure them,
>
> When I sitting heard the astronomer where he lectured with much
>   applause in the lecture-room,

5   How soon unaccountable I became tired and sick,
    Till rising and gliding out I wander'd off by myself,
    In the mystical moist night-air, and from time to time,
    Look'd up in perfect silence at the stars.

1865

Writing Assignments for "When I Heard the Learn'd Astronomer"

I. Brief Papers

A. 1. What inspires the speaker to leave the lecture room and wander off by himself? What are the results of his departure?
   2. Why are lines 2–4 the longest in the poem? In what other ways are the lines different from the rest of the poem? Why are they different?
   3. Look up *mystical* (line 7) in the dictionary. How do its various meanings help you understand and appreciate the poem?
   4. Go through the poem and circle all the verbs. Contrast the verbs in lines 1–4 with those in lines 6–8. How and why are they different?
   5. Explain the last line of the poem, focusing in part on its relationship to the first line.

B. Argue for or against the assertion that the speaker learns more *after* he leaves the hall than before.

C. 1. Why do you believe the astronomer affects the speaker as he does? Others apparently find his lecture stimulating.
   2. What is the difference between studying astronomy and studying the stars? Do you believe one is more important than the other? How does your belief affect your interpretation of the poem?

II. Longer Papers

A. Describe as fully as possible the speaker's personal philosophy of education. How does your understanding of his philosophy of education affect your interpretation of the poem?
B. Write a paper analyzing the structure of the poem. Concentrate on the length of the lines, the repetition of words or phrases, the number of contrasts in the poem, the verbs or other word choices, and/or any element of the poem's structure which you believe reinforces its meaning.

THEODORE ROETHKE

Dolor

I have known the inexorable sadness of pencils,
Neat in their boxes, dolor of pad and paper-weight,
All the misery of manilla folders and mucilage,
Desolation in immaculate public places,
5 Lonely reception room, lavatory, switchboard,
The unalterable pathos of basin and pitcher,
Ritual of multigraph, paper-clip, comma,
Endless duplication of lives and objects.
And I have seen dust from the walls of institutions,
10 Finer than flour, alive, more dangerous than silica,
Sift, almost invisible, through long afternoons of tedium,
Dropping a fine film on nails and delicate eyebrows,
Glazing the pale hair, the duplicate gray standard faces.

1948

Writing Assignments for "Dolor"

I. Brief Papers
  A. 1. In what way can this poem about an office also apply to a schoolroom?
     2. Discuss one way in which the first six lines of the poem are related.
     3. Go through the poem and circle all words or phrases related to sadness. Look up in a dictionary any unfamiliar words. Explain how the poet uses words related to sadness to convey both his message and his attitude toward his subject.
     4. Why do only three lines in the poem refer specifically to human beings? Discuss them.
     5. Roethke uses the poetic device known as *alliteration*—the repetition of initial consonants in close succession—in line 2: "dolor of *p*ad and *p*aper-weight." In the last three words of the poem he repeats vowel sounds—"gray standard faces"—in a more subtle poetic device called *assonance*. Both techniques affect a reader's response to a poem, because both manipulate the language and thus the emotional response to the language. Go through the poem and find examples of *alliteration* and/or *assonance*. Once you have found as many examples as you can, read the poem aloud several times, paying close attention to the effect of the alliteration and assonance. Do the devices slow down the line, speed it up, evoke special response? Write a paragraph explaining how one or both devices together with other strategies of sound and rhythm function in the poem.

6. Why is the "dust from the walls of the institutions" (line 9) both "alive" and "dangerous" (line 10)?

B. Argue for or against the assertion that the poet attacks the dehumanizing process inevitable in all institutions forced to deal with masses of people.

II. Longer Papers
Develop any brief paper into a full-length one.

THEODORE ROETHKE

Elegy for Jane

My student, thrown by a horse

I remember the neckcurls, limp and damp as tendrils;
And her quick look, a sidelong pickerel smile;
And how, once startled into talk, the light syllables leaped for her,
And she balanced in the delight of her thought,

5   A wren, happy, tail into the wind,
Her song trembling the twigs and small branches.
The shade sang with her;
The leaves, their whispers turned to kissing;
And the mold sang in the bleached valleys under the rose.

10   Oh, when she was sad, she cast herself down into such a pure
        depth,
Even a father could not find her:
Scraping her cheek against straw;
Stirring the clearest water.

My sparrow, you are not here,
15   Waiting like a fern, making a spiny shadow.
The sides of wet stones cannot console me,
Nor the moss, wound with the last light.

If only I could nudge you from this sleep,
My maimed darling, my skittery pigeon.
20   Over this damp grave I speak the words of my love:
I, with no rights in this matter,
Neither father nor lover.

1958

Writing Assignments for "Elegy for Jane"

I. Brief Papers

A. 1. Examine the direct and indirect comparisons between Jane and a bird. Why are the comparisons appropriate and how do they contribute to your understanding of the poem?

2. Show that the speaker's knowledge of Jane is the kind of information that only a teacher who is very observant could possess.

3. Choose one stanza from the poem and explain how all the nature imagery within the stanza conveys something about Jane and about the speaker's attitude toward her death.

4. Go through the poem and trace all references to water. How do the references change, how are they related, and how do they help you understand the poem or affect your response to it?

B. Argue for or against either assertion below.

1. The teacher's feelings for his student are appropriate, ones even her family would approve.

2. While the poem is sad, it is more optimistic than pessimistic.

C. 1. How does the epigraph, "My student, thrown by a horse," affect your response to the poem?

2. How do the final two lines of the poem affect your response to it? Why do they evoke those feelings?

II. Longer Papers

A. Explain in detail how the poet uses nature to describe Jane and to reveal his feelings about her death.

B. Go through the poem and circle all the verbs. Write a paper showing how the poet's choice of verbs evokes sympathy for Jane.

C. Often a poet relies on language—words, phrases, comparisons—to manipulate the reader's response very subtly. Go through the poem and consider any words, phrases, or comparisons that allude to blight or darkness, that allude—in essence—to death. Show that the poet manages to shape the reader's response through very subtle references or allusions to death throughout the poem.

DAVID WAGONER

The Truant Officer's Helper

> My only day in the black
> Old truant officer's truck,
> Grandfather and I
> Went lurching and jouncing

5   Over raw country roads
    To find boys playing hooky.
    Their mothers on sagging porches
    With steel-gray hair coming down
    The sides of their sad faces
10 Would say they didn't know
    What their boys were up to
    Or where in the world they were,
    But my grandfather knew.

    His voice as calm and soft
15 And sure as during grace,
    He told their mothers on them:
    They were fishing in Sippo Creek
    Or fighting in alleys
    Or playing with guinea pigs
20 In back of the hospital
    Or sniping butts in gutters
    Or swimming and taking leaks
    In the town's pure drinking water,
    Not listening to their teachers,
25 Not learning their three Rs.

    Bad boys stayed out of school
    With no excuse from doctors
    Or mothers, dentists or fathers.
    We hunted them everywhere:
30 In orchards and vacant lots,
    In carbarns and pool halls
    And down by the canal
    Where bums held their own classes,
    All those tempting places
35 I might have gone myself
    If I'd been old
    Or bad or brave enough.

    By afternoon we'd caught
    Only one guilty sinner
40 Red-handed with swiped berries,
    Red hair still wet,
    A trespassing skinny-dipper
    From out at the gravel pit,
    And we brought him back alive
45 To Henry Wadsworth Longfellow
    Junior High School, hanging
    His head. Grandfather told him

Never to yield to temptation,
Never to steal or tell stories,
50   To grow up good and smart
As a Presbyterian,
Then sent him to his Doom.

My mother knew where *I* was
And gave me a good excuse:
55   I was helping my grandfather
Find bad boys and refill
The shelves of a magic storehouse,
A cave of Ali Baba,
With jars of paste and notebooks
60   And chalk and bottles of ink
And rubber stamps and rulers.
Longfellow over the door
Told us the thoughts of youth
Were long, long thoughts, but mine
65   In that dim supply room
Were short as my light fingers.

That night in a shed loft
I flew with a featherbed
By lamplight, writing my first
70   Short story full of lies
About a secret country
And a boy who disobeyed
And ran away in a dream.
I tried hard to be good
75   And smart and made it up
Out of my own head
On that stolen paper,
My stolen pencil trembling.

                                            1983

Writing Assignments for "The Truant Officer's Helper"

I. Brief Papers
   A. 1. Discuss the age, the probable background, and the personality of the speaker.
      2. Show that the poem has humor.
      3. What does stanza 5 tell you about the speaker?

   B. Argue for or against either assertion below.
      1. The "bad boys" enjoy a healthy freedom that the speaker does not.
      2. This poem is dated in its subject and its appeal.

C. 1. Do you like the speaker? Why or why not?
  2. Do you sympathize with the "bad boys" sent to their "doom"? Why or why not?

II. Longer Papers
  A. Show how the humor and the narrative elements of the poem contribute to its success.
  B. Show the relationship between the last stanza and the rest of the poem.

DAVID WAGONER

The Best Slow Dancer

Under the sagging clotheslines of crepe paper
By the second string of teachers and wallflowers
In the school gym across the key through the glitter
Of mirrored light three-second rule forever
5   Suspended you danced with her the best slow dancer
Who stood on tiptoe who almost wasn't there
In your arms like music she knew just how to answer
The question mark of your spine your hand in hers
The other touching that place between her shoulders
10 Trembling your countless feet light-footed sure
To move as they wished wherever you might stagger
Without her she turned in time she knew where you were
In time she turned her body into yours
As you moved from thigh to secrets to breast yet never
15 Where you would be for all time never closer
Than your cheek against her temple her ear just under
Your lips that tried all evening long to tell her
You weren't the worst one not the boy whose mother
Had taught him to count to murmur over and over
20 One slide two slide three slide now no longer
The one in the hallway after class the scuffler
The double clubfoot gawker the mouth breather
With the wrong haircut who would never kiss her
But see her dancing off with someone or other
25 Older more clever smoother dreamier
Not waving a sister somebody else's partner
Lover while you went floating home through the air
To lie down lighter than air in a moonlit shimmer
Alone to whisper yourself to sleep remember.

Writing Assignments for "The Best Slow Dancer"

I. Brief Papers

A. 1. What is the relationship between the speaker and "the best slow dancer"? Do you think they know each other well?

2. Do you think the lack of punctuation in the poem is appropriate?

3. Who is the "you" referred to in line 27? Defend your answer.

B. Argue for or against the assertion that your parents' generation can identify better with the people and events in the poem than you can.

C. 1. Do you believe people who were popular in high school will react the same to this poem as those who were not?

2. Would you say this is a sad or happy poem?

II. Longer Papers

Describe how key images, punctuation, and unusual language contribute to the poem's nostalgic, bittersweet tone.

JOHN KEATS

*On First Looking into Chapman's Homer**

Much have I travell'd in the realms of gold,
And many goodly states and kingdoms seen;
Round many western islands have I been
Which bards in fealty to Apollo hold.
5   Oft of one wide expanse had I been told
That deep-brow'd Homer ruled as his demesne;†
Yet did I never breathe its pure serene
Till I heard Chapman speak out loud and bold:
Then felt I like some watcher of the skies
10   When a new planet swims into his ken;
Or like stout Cortez‡ when with eagle eyes
He star'd at the Pacific—and all his men
Look'd at each other with a wild surmise—
Silent, upon a peak in Darien.

1816

**Chapman's Homer: Chapman's translation of Homer's epic poems, *The Iliad* and *The Odyssey.*
†demesne: Realm, domain.
‡Cortez: Balboa, not Cortez, first sighted the Pacific from Darien, an isthmus between Columbia and Panama.

Writing Assignments for "On First Looking into Chapman's Homer"

I. Brief Papers

A. 1. In the first four lines of the poem, what does the speaker mean by traveling in "realms of gold" (line 1)? Explain why the comparison is apt.

   2. Choose one of the following comparisons or figures of speech and discuss its appropriateness in the poem:

      a. ". . . one wide expanse . . .
         That deep-browed Homer ruled . . ."
         (lines 5–6)

      b. ". . . did I never breathe its pure serene"
         (line 7)

      c. "Then felt I like some watcher of the skies
         When a new planet swims into his ken"
         (lines 9–10)

      d. ". . . like stout Cortez when with eagle eyes
         He star'd at the Pacific . . ."
         (lines 11–12)

   3. Find all the references to sight in the poem and discuss their appropriateness and their impact.

   4. Go through the poem and circle all the words with which you are not familiar, even those already footnoted. In a good dictionary, look up the words and study all the definitions. How do the words and their multiple meanings help you understand the poem better?

B. What is your reaction to the speaker's excitement about intellectual discovery? How does that affect your interpretation of the poem?

II. Longer Papers

A. This poem is an example of an Italian sonnet, a fourteen-line poem divided into two parts of eight lines (called an *octave*) and six lines (called a *sestet*). The Italian sonnet's rhyme scheme is predictable, and this poem illustrates it exactly. After looking through the following suggestions, write a paper about the poem's structure, using any of the points you discover as supporting evidence.

   1. Go through the poem and mark the rhyme scheme. Which lines rhyme in what pattern? (If you are not sure of a word's pronunciation, be sure to look it up.)

   2. What is the relationship of the first eight lines of the poem to the last six? Is there a time-sequence involved? How does punctuation mark the division as well as indicate the relationship? How does the rhyme scheme help mark the division?

   3. How are the first four lines of the poem related to the second four lines? How are lines 5–6 related to lines 7–8?

   4. How do certain lines prepare for other lines of the poem by moving from general to more specific imagery? By moving from proposition or assertion to elaboration? In other ways?

B. Discuss as fully as possible the poet's attitude toward his subject, specifically the attitude implied in the speaker's discovery of Chapman's Homer. What features of the poem best illustrate the attitude? (It might help you to consider what tone of voice the speaker would use if he were uttering his thoughts aloud.)

C. After reading the poem through once or twice, quickly react to it on paper. What do you like about the poem? How does it make you feel? What troubles or confuses you? Be as honest and as complete as you can. Once done, lay your notes aside and spend time with the following activities: look up all the words in the poem you do not understand (even those already footnoted); read all the topics included under I and II, answering quickly to yourself or on paper all the questions posed and considering how you would react to every topic (keep notes); pay close attention to the description of the sonnet structure outlined in II.A; finally, and most important, read the poem aloud three times, alternating each reading with a silent reading as well. Now, write as quickly as you can any new reactions you have to the poem, any new understanding you have gleaned. (Don't look back at your original notes until you have completed your second reaction.) Use your two responses as the basis for a paper on one of the following topics:

1. If you were a teacher responsible for teaching this poem to a class similar to yours, how would you approach the task? How would you introduce your students to the poem? What questions would you ask? What writing assignments would you make? What would be your reasons for assigning the poem? What do you want the students to gain from reading and writing about the poem?

2. Write a paper about how growing familiarity with a poem helps you not only understand it better but also like it more.

Feel free to use first person pronouns (I, me, my) in your paper and to refer specifically to your two responses.

PHILIP LARKIN

A Study of Reading Habits

When getting my nose in a book
Cured most things short of school,
It was worth ruining my eyes
To know I could still keep cool,
5   And deal out the old right hook
To dirty dogs twice my size.

Later, with inch-thick specs,
Evil was just my lark:
Me and my cloak and fangs
10   Had ripping times in the dark.

The women I clubbed with sex!
I broke them up like meringues.

Don't read much now: the dude
Who lets the girl down before
15 The hero arrives, the chap
Who's yellow and keeps the store,
Seem far too familiar. Get stewed:
Books are a load of crap.

1964

Writing Assignments for "A Study of Reading Habits"

I. Brief Papers
  A. 1. Explain one way in which the three stanzas of the poem are related.
     2. Choose one stanza of the poem and from the information in that stanza describe the speaker—his general age, his tastes in reading, his reasons for reading, and anything else you can glean from his reading habits.
     3. What does the speaker mean by the line "Get stewed: / Books are a load of crap" (lines 17–18)?
     4. The poem has a clear, consistent rhyme scheme. Go through the poem and mark the rhyme pattern. Read the poem aloud, paying close attention to the rhyme as well as the line length. How do both contribute to the poem's impact?

  B. Argue for or against either assertion below.
     1. The speaker's reading habits follow a predictable pattern.
     2. The reader should sympathize with the speaker in the poem.

  C. How do you respond to the speaker's advice in the last two lines of the poem? How does that affect your interpretation of the poem?

II. Longer Papers
  A. Argue for or against the assertion that the speaker's diction and his attitudes affect how readers will react to him and to his advice.
  B. Argue for or against the assertion that books *are* a waste of time.

ADRIENNE RICH

Aunt Jennifer's Tigers

Aunt Jennifer's tigers prance across a screen,
Bright topaz denizens of a world of green.
They do not fear the men beneath the tree;
They pace in sleek chivalric certainty.

5　Aunt Jennifer's fingers fluttering through her wool
Find even the ivory needle hard to pull.
The massive weight of Uncle's wedding band
Sits heavily upon Aunt Jennifer's hand.

When Aunt is dead, her terrified hands will lie
10　Still ringed with ordeals she was mastered by.
The tigers in the panel that she made
Will go on prancing, proud and unafraid.

1951

Writing Assignments for "Aunt Jennifer's Tigers"

I. Brief Papers
    A. 1. Draw a line down the center of your paper. On the left, quickly list all the
          words or phrases in the poem referring to Aunt Jennifer; on the right, list all
          the words or phrases pertaining to the tigers. Write a paragraph describing at
          least one difference between Aunt Jennifer and her tigers.
       2. Show that Rich has used the principle of contrast to organize her poem.

    B. Argue for or against the assertion that Aunt Jennifer has a happy, satisfied life.

    C. Do you think Aunt Jennifer should have responded as she did to the circumstances
       of her life? What would have been gained, or what lost, by a more open rebellion
       or a more complete acceptance?

II. Longer Papers
    A. Explain in detail how Aunt Jennifer differs from her tigers and what those differ-
       ences imply about Aunt Jennifer's life.
    B. In what way does Aunt Jennifer illustrate stereotypical views of the artist? In what
       way does she defy those stereotypes?

DYLAN THOMAS

In My Craft or Sullen Art

In my craft or sullen art
Exercised in the still night
When only the moon rages
And the lovers lie abed

5   With all their griefs in their arms,
     I labor by singing light
     Not for ambition or bread
     Or the strut and trade of charms
     On the ivory stages
10   But for the common wages
     Of their most secret heart.

     Not for the proud man apart
     From the raging moon I write
     On these spindrift pages
15   Nor for the towering dead
     With their nightingales and psalms
     But for the lovers, their arms
     Round the griefs of the ages,
     Who pay no praise or wages
20   Nor heed my craft or art.

                        1946

Writing Assignments for "In My Craft or Sullen Art"

I. Brief Papers
   A. 1. Show that the speaker is different from the lovers.
      2. Explain how the speaker is different from "the proud man apart" (line 12).
      3. Look up *sullen* in any good dictionary. Explain how its various meanings enrich the poem.
      4. What does the poet mean when he says the lovers' arms are around the "griefs of the ages" (line 18)?

   B. Argue for or against one of the assertions below.
      1. The speaker's craft satisfies him.
      2. The speaker channels his energy and his passion into his poetry although he would prefer to be one of the lovers.
      3. The speaker in the poem scorns the "proud man apart" (line 12).

   C. 1. How does the poet's use of the moonlight affect your response to the poem?
      2. Read the poem aloud several times, reading slowly, exaggerating and emphasizing different words each time. Write a paragraph describing the most effective tone of voice in which to read the poem. Should it be read angrily? Solemnly? Flippantly?

II. Longer Papers
  A. In what sense can each of the following be envied and/or pitied: the "proud man apart," the lovers, the speaker?
  B. Explain to what extent the speaker's poetry either is a compensation for a failure to love or is, in his eyes, superior to love.

A. E. HOUSMAN

Terence, This Is Stupid Stuff*

> "Terence, this is stupid stuff:
> You eat your victuals fast enough;
> There can't be much amiss, 'tis clear,
> To see the rate you drink your beer.
> 5 But oh, good Lord, the verse you make,
> It gives a chap the belly-ache.
> The cow, the old cow, she is dead;
> It sleeps well, the horned head:
> We poor lads, 'tis our turn now
> 10 To hear such tunes as killed the cow.
> Pretty friendship 'tis to rhyme
> Your friends to death before their time
> Moping melancholy mad:
> Come, pipe a tune to dance to, lad."
>
> 15 Why, if 'tis dancing you would be,
> There's brisker pipes than poetry.
> Say, for what were hop-yards meant,
> Or why was Burton built on Trent?†
> Oh many a peer of England brews
> 20 Livelier liquor than the Muse,
> And malt does more than Milton can
> To justify God's ways to man.‡
> Ale, man, ale's the stuff to drink

*Terence: Housman considered the title *The Poems of Terence Hearsay* for a volume of his own poetry, later entitled *The Shropshire Lad.* Many believe Housman chose Terence as a name for himself to defend his poetry from those who considered it too pessimistic. Terence was a Roman poet, author of satiric comedies.

†Burton built on Trent: Famous English brewing town, Burton was built on the Trent River in central England.

‡"And malt does more than Milton can / To justify God's ways to man": John Milton's stated purpose in *Paradise Lost* was "to justify the ways of God to men."

For fellows whom it hurts to think:
25   Look into the pewter pot
To see the world as the world's not.
And faith, 'tis pleasant till 'tis past:
The mischief is that 'twill not last.
Oh I have been to Ludlow fair*
30   And left my necktie God knows where,
And carried half-way home, or near,
Pints and quarts of Ludlow beer:
Then the world seemed none so bad,
And I myself a sterling lad;
35   And down in lovely muck I've lain,
Happy till I woke again.
Then I saw the morning sky:
Heigho, the tale was all a lie;
The world, it was the old world yet,
40   I was I, my things were wet,
And nothing now remained to do
But begin the game anew.

Therefore, since the world has still
Much good, but much less good than ill,
45   And while the sun and moon endure
Luck's a chance, but trouble's sure,
I'd face it as a wise man would,
And train for ill and not for good.
'Tis true, the stuff I bring for sale
50   Is not so brisk a brew as ale:
Out of a stem that scored the hand
I wrung it in a weary land.
But take it: if the smack is sour,
The better for the embittered hour;
55   It should do good to heart and head
When your soul is in my soul's stead;
And I will friend you, if I may,
In the dark and cloudy day.

There was a king reigned in the East:
60   There, when kings will sit to feast,
They get their fill before they think
With poisoned meat and poisoned drink.
He gathered all that springs to birth

*Ludlow fair: Market town in Shropshire, famous for its village meeting place and festival.

From the many-venomed earth;
65   First a little, thence to more,
He sampled all her killing store;
And easy, smiling, seasoned sound,
Sate the king when healths went round.
They put arsenic in his meat
70   And stared aghast to watch him eat;
They poured strychnine in his cup
And shook to see him drink it up:
They shook, they stared as white's their shirt:
Them it was their poison hurt.
75   —I tell the tale that I heard told.
Mithridates,* he died old.

1896

Writing Assignments for "Terence, This Is Stupid Stuff"

I. Brief Papers

A. 1. Assume one of the following roles and write a paragraph in your own words summarizing the attitudes expressed in the poem. Use the first person and make sure your statement shows you understand the poem.

a. Paraphrase the friends' complaints (lines 1–4).

b. Paraphrase Terence's response to his friends' complaints (lines 15–42).

2. Explain how the story of King Mithridates (lines 59–76) relates to the advice offered (lines 43–58) in the poem.

B. Study lines 43–58. Trying not to preach and trying to be as honest as you can, write a paragraph defending one of the following assertions.

1. The advice in lines 43–58 is still useful and appropriate.

2. The advice in lines 43–58 is impossible to follow.

3. No one who follows this advice could expect to enjoy life fully.

C. 1. Read the poem aloud with as much feeling and energy as you can muster. Then write a paragraph explaining if you believe the rhythm is appropriate or if it detracts from the poem.

2. Write a short letter to Terence describing something that has happened to you that supports his view of life.

II. Longer Papers

Argue that Terence, his friends, or neither win their argument.

---

*Mithridates: King of Pontus, who, according to tradition, took small doses of poison daily to help immunize himself.

SAMUEL TAYLOR COLERIDGE
*Kubla Khan**

In Xanadu did Kubla Khan
A stately pleasure dome decree:
Where Alph,† the sacred river, ran
Through caverns measureless to man
5   Down to a sunless sea.
So twice five miles of fertile ground
With walls and towers were girdled round:
And there were gardens bright with sinuous rills,
Where blossomed many an incense-bearing tree;
10 And here were forests ancient as the hills,
Enfolding sunny spots of greenery.

But oh! that deep romantic chasm which slanted
Down the green hill athwart a cedarn cover!
A savage place! as holy and enchanted
15 As e'er beneath a waning moon was haunted
By woman wailing for her demon lover!
And from this chasm, with ceaseless turmoil seething,
As if this earth in fast thick pants were breathing,
A mighty fountain momently was forced:
20 Amid whose swift half-intermitted burst
Huge fragments vaulted like rebounding hail,
Or chaffy grain beneath the thresher's flail:
And 'mid these dancing rocks at once and ever
It flung up momently the sacred river.
25 Five miles meandering with a mazy motion
Through wood and dale the sacred river ran,
Then reached the caverns measureless to man,
And sank in tumult to a lifeless ocean:
And 'mid this tumult Kubla heard from far
30 Ancestral voices prophesying war!
    The shadow of the dome of pleasure
    Floated midway on the waves;
    Where was heard the mingled measure
    From the fountain and the caves.

---

*"Kubla Khan": In a prose preface to his poem, Coleridge attributes his poem to a dream he had after reading from Samuel Purchas' *Purchas his Pilgrimage* (1613). Purchas's Cublai Can built a "stately Palace, . . . a sumptuous house of pleasure." The historical Kublai Khan was founder of the Mongol dynasty in China during the thirteenth century.
†Alph: Shortened form of Alpheus, a Greek river.

35 It was a miracle of rare device,
    A sunny pleasure dome with caves of ice!

    A damsel with a dulcimer
    In a vision once I saw:
    It was an Abyssinian maid,
40   And on her dulcimer she played,
    Singing of Mount Abora.
    Could I revive within me
    Her symphony and song,
    To such a deep delight 'twould win me,
45 That with music loud and long,
    I would build that dome in air,
    That sunny dome! those caves of ice!
    And all who heard should see them there,
    And all should cry, Beware! Beware!
50 His flashing eyes, his floating hair!
    Weave a circle around him thrice,
    And close your eyes with holy dread,
    For he on honeydew hath fed,
    And drunk the milk of Paradise.

                                        1816*

Writing Assignments for "Kubla Khan"

I. Brief Papers
   A. 1. Show that Kubla Khan's kingdom is full of contradictions.
      2. Show that Xanadu is sumptuously beautiful.
      3. Show that Xanadu is unnatural and/or insubstantial.

   B. Argue for or against either assertion below.
      1. The speaker in the poem would be lucky to revive his vision of the Abyssinian maid (line 43).
      2. The speaker would be in grave danger to return too often to Xanadu.

   C. How does the comparison in lines 13–14 affect your response to the poem?

II. Longer Papers
   A. Describe the poet's depiction of Xanadu. Relying on explicit and implicit evidence in the poem, discuss its appeal and its dangers.
   B. Argue that almost any image, picture, or detail in the poem can be explained as one facet of the poet's mind or imagination. (Use enough examples to support your claim.)

*1816: First publication date. Probably written in 1797.

C. Compare Coleridge's Xanadu to any other dreamlike Xanadu depicted in a film, a song, a story, or a poem.

Comparative Papers from Chapter Three: Students, Teachers, and Artists

A. Describe in detail several student–teacher relationships, using poems from this chapter to illustrate your description.

B. Several poems in this chapter are about teachers—their dreams, their goals, their feelings about students and about their profession. Examine and discuss depictions of teachers in several poems.

C. Several poems in this chapter are about students—their dreams, their goals, their feelings about teachers and about school. Examine and discuss depictions of students in several poems.

D. Referring to any poem or poems in this chapter and/or to any short story in this book, argue for or against the assertion that formal education does not prepare people to cope with day-to-day realities such as understanding and getting along with other people, weathering setbacks in personal ambitions and career goals, or surviving what may seem the whims of fate and chance.

E. The following passages are from Ralph Waldo Emerson's "The American Scholar," an essay some critics and scholars labeled America's "intellectual declaration of independence" when it was first presented in 1837:

1. "Books are the best of things well used; abused among the worst. What is the right use? What is the one end which all means go to effect? They are for nothing but to inspire."

2. "Books are for the scholar's idle times. When he can read God directly, the hour is too precious to be wasted in other men's transcripts of their readings."

3. "There goes in the world a notion, that the scholar should be a recluse, a valetudinarian,—as unfit for any handiwork or public labor as a penknife for an axe. The so-called 'practical men' sneer at speculative men, as if, because they speculate or *see,* they could do nothing. . . . Action is with the scholar subordinate, but it is essential. . . . [Action] is the raw material out of which the intellect moulds her splendid products."

4. "Life is our dictionary. Years are well spent in country labors; in town—in the insight into trades and manufactures; in frank intercourse with many men and women; in science; in art; to the one end of mastering in all their facts a language by which to illustrate and embody our perceptions. . . . Colleges and books only copy the language which the field and the work-yard made."

Read through the passages several times until you understand them and can paraphrase them. Once you feel you have a clear grasp of Emerson's assertions, write a paper examining any one or more of the quotes, referring to several poems in this chapter to support your explanation. Choose any one of the suggested topics below or fashion one of your own in consultation with your instructor.

1. To what extent do poets in this chapter imply that books are important and useful to students?

    2. Implied in Emerson's statements is the notion that experience—firsthand observation of the world and of nature in particular—is the best teacher. React to that assertion. To what extent do poets in this chapter imply similar notions?

F. Your best friend has just started student teaching in a college prep senior high school English class, and her supervising teacher has asked her to teach a unit of poems about teachers, students, and learning. Your friend, who has always been an excellent writer herself, is not as good as you are at reading and understanding poetry. Write your friend a letter, giving her as much help as possible. Suggest which three or four poems you would select, how you would teach them, ways to interest students in the poems, and what writing assignments would be appropriate.

G. Over a weekend break, you show your textbook to your neighbor, a high school principal, who must deal daily with the public's opinion of schools and teachers. Your neighbor is disturbed because some selections in this chapter imply that lectures are dull and uninforming, the institution of education is deadening and spiritless, books are a waste of time, and—even worse—that some teachers are lecherous. Write a paper—in letter form if you wish—addressing one or more of your neighbor's concerns.

H. Choose any poem in the chapter and write a detailed analysis of its structure, rhythm, language, and style. Explain as fully as possible why the poem is written as it is.

4 / Poems about Romantic Love and Passion

ANONYMOUS

Western Wind

Western wind, when will thou blow,
The small rain down can rain?
Christ, that my love were in my arms,
And I in my bed again!

14th century

Writing Assignments for "Western Wind"

I. Brief Papers

A. 1. Surmise as best you can the dramatic setting of the poem—who is involved, what is happening, where might the speaker be?
   2. Explain the connections between the first two and last two lines of the poem.
   3. Does the speaker use "Christ" as an oath, a prayer, or both? Explain.
   4. Write the last two lines of the poem in prose. Why is the poem's version more effective?

B. Argue for or against the assertion that the poem's brevity contributes to its eloquence and its impact.

C. 1. How does the brevity of the poem affect your interpretation of it? Would you have preferred to know more about the speaker, the lover, and the setting? Why or why not?
   2. Compare the following version of the poem to the correct version:

      Western Wind, when will thou blow,
      The small rain down can rain?
      Christ, that my love were in my arms,
      Then my soul might bloom again.

   Explain why you like the poem more or less with the different last line.

II. Longer Papers

A. To what extent can you empathize with the speaker and how does the poem's specificity—its references to the wind, rain, lover, and bed—affect your response to it? Discuss.

B. Compare the following poem, excerpted from Alfred, Lord Tennyson's "Maud;
A Monodrama" to "Western Wind":

> O that 't were possible
> After long grief and pain
> To find the arms of my true love
> Round me once again!

Which do you believe is a better poem? Why?

ANDREW MARVELL

To His Coy Mistress

      Had we but world enough, and time,
This coyness, Lady, were no crime.
We would sit down, and think which way
To walk, and pass our long love's day.
5 Thou by the Indian Ganges' side
Shouldst rubies find; I by the tide
Of Humber* would complain. I would
Love you ten years before the Flood,
And you should, if you please, refuse
10 Till the Conversion of the Jews.†
My vegetable love should grow
Vaster than empires and more slow;
An hundred years should go to praise
Thine eyes, and on thy forehead gaze;
15 Two hundred to adore each breast,
But thirty thousand to the rest;
An age at least to every part,
And the last age should show your heart.
For, Lady, you deserve this state,
20 Nor would I love at lower rate.
    But at my back I always hear
Time's wingèd chariot hurrying near;
And yonder all before us lie
Deserts of vast eternity.
25 Thy beauty shall no more be found,
Nor, in thy marble vault, shall sound
My echoing song; then worms shall try
That long-preserved virginity,

---

*Humber: Marvell's hometown—Hull—is located on this river in England. Both are well removed
from the Indian Ganges.
†Conversion of the Jews: Supposed to occur only at the end of the world.

And your quaint honour turn to dust,
30   And into ashes all my lust:
The grave's a fine and private place,
But none, I think, do there embrace.
   Now therefore, while the youthful hue
Sits on thy skin like morning dew,
35   And while thy willing soul transpires
At every pore with instant fires,
Now let us sport us while we may,
And now, like amorous birds of prey,
Rather at once our time devour
40   Than languish in his slow-chapt power.
Let us roll all our strength and all
Our sweetness up into one ball,
And tear our pleasures with rough strife
Thorough* the iron gates of life;
45   Thus, though we cannot make our sun
Stand still, yet we will make him run.

1681

Writing Assignments for "To His Coy Mistress"

I. Brief Papers
   A. 1. Look up the word *coy* in the dictionary. Explain how its various meanings help you understand the poem.
      2. Reread lines 1–20 several times until you can easily paraphrase most of the section. What is the relationship between the first two lines and the rest of the section (lines 3–20)?
      3. Go through lines 1–20 and circle all the words related to time. How do those references support the speaker's claims in lines 1–2 and 18–20?
      4. Go through lines 1–20 and circle all the words related to space and distance. How do those references support the speaker's claims in lines 1–2 and 18–20?
      5. Reread lines 21–32 several times until you can easily paraphrase most of the section. Explain one way the speaker alters his argument from the first section. For instance, discuss the change in references to time or space, the change in the speaker's attitude or tone, or any change from the first to second part of the poem you believe is important.
      6. Reread lines 33–46 until you can easily paraphrase most of the section. Explain one way the section grows out of the first two sections. For instance, discuss the references to time or space, the speaker's attitude or tone, or any change or extension from the first two sections you believe is important.
      7. Explain the last two lines of the poem. Why does the poet choose the *sun* as the key image in these lines?

*Thorough: Through.

B. Argue for or against one of the assertions below.
1. The speaker's reasoning is typical of the line or tactic men today might use to seduce shy or hesitant lovers.
2. Only the most naive of women would be swayed by the speaker's argument.
3. The speaker's argument is convincing because he appeals to everyone's fears of growing old and becoming undesirable.
4. The speaker's argument is not convincing because he defends an essentially immoral position.
5. The speaker's argument is convincing because he combines a realistic view of time with obvious passion for his lover.

C. 1. "To His Coy Mistress" continues to be one of the most often anthologized, most often taught poems in the English language. Do you think it deserves such popularity?
2. If you were the speaker's coy mistress, do you believe you would be convinced by his argument? What would sway your decision most?

II. Longer Papers

A. One way to evaluate the strength of an argument is to consider three criteria: how trustworthy the speaker is; how effectively the speaker appeals to reason and intellect; and how effectively the speaker appeals to emotions and feelings. Given those criteria, do you believe this poem embodies a convincing argument? To what extent can such criteria be applied fairly to a poem?

B. Line 34 offers an interesting textual question. The original edition ended the line with "glew" (glow); a later emendation of the text ended the line with "lew" (warmth); and another often-printed version ends the line with "dew." Use this textual alteration as a basis for a paper that argues one of the selections is most appropriate. Analyze the implications and the impact of each selection. Which is better for modern tastes? Should editors make an effort to preserve the original? (You might find it helpful to consult the *Oxford English Dictionary* in your library for the etymology of each word.)

C. Write a paper analyzing the structure of the poem, paying close attention to the relationship of the three sections. How does the poem's argument revolve around the three propositions, paraphrased roughly to begin "If we had enough time and space . . ." (lines 1–20); "But we don't have enough time, because . . ." (lines 21–32); and "So, therefore, let us . . ." (lines 33–46)? Are each of the propositions supportable and trustworthy?

D. In a paper different from II.C above, discuss the structure of the poem, noting the poem's divisions yet concentrating on structural questions other than the progression of the speaker's argument. For instance, consider the rhyme scheme and the pattern of punctuation in each section. Note the first and last couplet in each section of the poem and consider the relationship of these lines to the rest of the section. Go through the poem and note where the poet uses *I, you* or *thy,* and *we* or *us.* Or, consider how the speaker's tone or attitude toward his subject is related from section to section. Use any of that information to reveal how the poem's structure reinforces its subject matter and its impact.

E. "To His Coy Mistress" remains one of our most memorable poems largely because of its rich imagery and figurative language. Write a paper about one or more of its poetic devices, such as simile, metaphor, or imagery. You may choose to explore the beauty or appropriateness of single examples such as "My vegetable love should grow" (line 11) or "Time's winged chariot" (line 22). Or you may choose to examine one long comparison, such as the comparison of the lovers to birds of prey (lines 37–44) or the intricate comparison of youth, soul, and fire (lines 33–36).

III. The Use of Metaphor in "To His Coy Mistress"

Using the sentences below, construct a short essay that defines and illustrates *metaphor,* the most common kind of figurative language poets use.

1. A *metaphor* is a comparison between two things.
2. The comparison is implied.
3. The two things are essentially different.

4. A metaphor is not a direct comparison like a simile.
5. A metaphor does not rely on signal words such as *like, as, than, appears,* and *seems* to help form the comparison.
6. The comparison is made through substitution.

7. Here is an example.
8. Andrew Marvell writes, "But at my back I always hear / *Time's winged chariot* hurrying near."
9. Marvell does not say that time is *like* a winged chariot.

10. The metaphor implies that time is like a chariot with wings.
11. The metaphor reinforces the swiftness of time's flight.

12. Here is another example.
13. Marvell writes, "My *vegetable love* should grow / Vaster than empires and more slow."
14. The speaker compares the growth of love to the growth of vegetables.

15. The metaphor suggests this.
16. Such love is not fully human.

17. Here is another example.
18. Marvell compares death to sterile, dry deserts.
19. The speaker says, "before us lie / *Deserts of vast eternity.*"

20. Marvell's speaker may not sway his coy mistress.
21. Marvell does move his readers.
22. They experience his poem more completely.

23. The metaphor is a way of representing an experience.
24. The metaphor is perhaps the best way of representing an experience.
25. The experience is inexpressible by any other means.

26. That is why Aristotle praised metaphor.
27. Aristotle said metaphor is "the greatest thing by far" for poets.

ROBERT HERRICK

To the Virgins, To Make Much of Time

Gather ye rosebuds while ye may,
  Old time is still a-flying;
And this same flower that smiles today,
  Tomorrow will be dying.

5 The glorious lamp of heaven, the sun,
  The higher he's a-getting,
The sooner will his race be run,
  And nearer he's to setting.

That age is best which is the first,
10 When youth and blood are warmer,
But being spent, the worse, and worst
  Times still succeed the former.

Then be not coy, but use your time,
  And while ye may, go marry:
15 For having lost but once your prime,
  You may forever tarry.

1648

Writing Assignments for "To the Virgins, To Make Much of Time"

I. Brief Papers
  A. 1. Why does the poet choose rosebuds, not roses or other flowers?
     2. What is the relationship of the last two lines to the first two in each couplet? Do you notice a general pattern?
     3. *To marry* can mean to enter into a close or intimate relationship as well as to enter into wedlock. Explain why you believe the poet intends one meaning over another.

B. Argue for or against either assertion below.
  1. The poem's invitation to the young virgins to enjoy their youth and make much of their time could be offered only by a male writer.
  2. The poem is still contemporary in its subject matter and its advice.

C. 1. Do you agree with the advice the poem offers to the virgins? Why or why not?
  2. Do you agree that the "age is best which is the first, / When youth and blood are warmer" (lines 9–10)? Why or why not?

II. Longer Papers

A. Go through the poem and find all references to time. Explain how those examples relate to one another and how they are central to the poem's subject and message.
B. Robert Herrick, a rural clergyman for much of his life, was banished from London by the Puritans in 1647. His verse is still praised and enjoyed more for its pagan—not its religious—sensibilities, which include a celebration of life and pleasure, an awareness of the changing seasons and the cycles of time and life, and an exuberant treatment of physical love and passion. To what extent does "To the Virgins" illustrate these sensibilities?
C. This poem enjoyed great popularity as a song during the seventeenth century. Using examples from your favorite popular music, explain what characteristics or traits the poem has in common with music today.
D. "To the Virgins" is an example of a body of literature that has been called *carpe diem* literature, from the Latin phrase "to seize the day." One of the most famous embodiments of the *carpe diem* spirit, this poem entreats women to embrace love and passion while they are still young and lovely. More generally, the *carpe diem* spirit implies that each moment is to be seized, each experience lived fully and completely. Write a paper based on one of the following topics, referring to this poem and to other poems and stories in this book.
  1. Discuss to what extent the *carpe diem* impulse involves recklessness and even irresponsibility and to what extent it does offer a passionate, fulfilling life.
  2. Argue for or against the assertion that many writers suggest life's most intense joy and pleasure come to us only when we are brave or imaginative enough to "seize the day."

EDMUND WALLER

Go, Lovely Rose

Go, lovely rose!
Tell her that wastes her time and me
    That now she knows,
When I resemble her to thee,
5   How sweet and fair she seems to be.

Tell her that's young
And shuns to have her graces spied
  That hadst thou sprung
In deserts where no men abide,
10 Thou must have uncommended died.

Small is the worth
Of beauty from the light retired;
  Bid her come forth,
Suffer herself to be desired,
15 And not blush so to be admired.

Then die! that she
The common fate of all things rare
  May read in thee:
How small a part of time they share
20 That are so wondrous sweet and fair!

1645

Writing Assignments for "Go, Lovely Rose"

I. Brief Papers
A. 1. Summarize in your own words the message the speaker wishes the rose to convey to the young woman in stanzas 1–3.
   2. Why does the speaker choose to send a rose—not some other flower—to the young woman?
   3. Explain what you believe to be the speaker's attitude toward the young woman or the speaker's major motive in sending the rose.
   4. Explain the second line of the poem. Would the meaning be different if the speaker said, "Tell her that wastes her time and *mine*"? In what way?

B. Argue for or against either assertion below.
   1. The speaker presents a logical and reasonable argument when he says, "Small is the worth / Of beauty from the light retired" (lines 11–12).
   2. The speaker's primary motivation in sending the rose is sexual.

C. Do you believe that all things "sweet and fair" are more fleeting than anything else? How does your belief affect your interpretation of the poem?

II. Longer Papers
A. Develop any brief paper assignment into a full-length paper.
B. Turn to p. 689 in this book and read the description of *carpe diem* poetry, offered in II.D on that page. In what way is "Go, Lovely Rose" typical of the *carpe diem* impulse or spirit?

WILLIAM SHAKESPEARE

Sonnet 29 (When, in disgrace with Fortune and men's eyes)

When, in disgrace with Fortune and men's eyes,
I all alone beweep my outcast state,
And trouble deaf heaven with my bootless* cries,
And look upon myself and curse my fate,
5 Wishing me like to one more rich in hope,
Featured like him, like him with friends possessed,
Desiring this man's art and that man's scope,
With what I most enjoy contented least;
Yet in these thoughts myself almost despising
10 Haply I think on thee, and then my state,
Like to the lark at break of day arising
From sullen earth, sings hymns at heaven's gate:
    For thy sweet love remembered such wealth brings
    That then I scorn to change my state with kings.

1609

Writing Assignments for "Sonnet 29 (When, in disgrace with Fortune and men's eyes)"

I. Brief Papers
  A. 1. Look up the word *fortune* in the dictionary. Explain how its various meanings help you to understand the poem.
     2. Describe the speaker's state of mind, his attitude toward himself, and his behavior in the first four lines of the poem.
     3. Describe the men to whom the speaker compares himself in the second four lines of the poem. How are the men different from the speaker himself?
     4. Discuss the reference to the lark (lines 11–12), showing how the comparison between the lark and the speaker links the third quatrain (lines 9–12) with the first (lines 1–4) and appropriately develops the subject matter.

  B. Argue for or against the assertion that the speaker's attitude toward love is not very realistic, that sooner or later he will probably experience a reversal or a loss of love that will cast him deeper into despair than ever.

*bootless: Useless or futile.

C. Write a letter to your boyfriend or girlfriend, lover or spouse, in which you convey the same idea Shakespeare conveys in his poem. You don't need to refer directly to the poem, but show through your letter that you understand it.

II. Longer Papers

A. Trace the references to wealth throughout the poem. How do those references help structure the poem and reinforce the speaker's point of view?

B. Argue for or against the assertion that the kind of solace the speaker finds in love is not an enduring one.

C. One might argue that this sonnet's implication—that love can brighten an otherwise bleak existence and cheer us up when we most despair—is a relatively simple, unsophisticated notion. Write a paper reacting to one of the following topics:

1. The implications of this sonnet are more complex and more sophisticated than the paraphrase suggests.

2. Often the simplest sentiments can be the most profound; the value the sonnet places on love implies one of the few philosophies of life by which people may abide happily.

3. The language and style of the poem, not its implications or statements about love, are its most noteworthy features.

D. Trying to avoid easy generalizations, discuss whether people in their twenties are more likely to share the speaker's attitude toward love than people in their forties or fifties. How do your views affect your response to the poem?

WILLIAM SHAKESPEARE

Sonnet 18 (Shall I compare thee to a summer's day?)

Shall I compare thee to a summer's day?
Thou art more lovely and more temperate:
Rough winds do shake the darling buds of May,
And summer's lease hath all too short a date:
5   Sometime too hot the eye of heaven shines,
And often is his gold complexion dimmed,
And every fair from fair sometime declines,
By chance or nature's changing course untrimmed;
But thy eternal summer shall not fade
10 Nor lose possession of that fair thou owest,*

*Owest: Owns.

Nor shall Death brag thou wander'st in his shade,
When in eternal lines to time thou growest:
  So long as men can breathe or eyes can see,
  So long lives this, and this gives life to thee.

1609

Writing Assignments for "Sonnet 18 (Shall I compare thee to a summer's day?)"

I. Brief Papers

  A. 1. How is the summer's day flawed? Explain one or more of the flaws described in lines 3–8.
    2. Which lines in the poem refer directly to the speaker's lover? How much do you learn about her?
    3. Explain the comparison in one of the lines listed below, commenting on the effectiveness of the comparison, its appropriateness, its impact:
      a. "And summer's lease hath all too short a date"
      (line 4)
      b. "Sometime too hot the eye of heaven shines,
      And often is his gold complexion dimmed"
      (lines 5–6)
      c. "Nor shall death brag thou wander'st in his shade"
      (line 11)
    4. Show that the last six lines of the poem—particularly the last two lines—refer as much to poetry and this poem as they do to the speaker's lover.

  B. Argue for or against the assertion that this poem should not be considered a love poem so much as a poem about the nature of poetry.

  C. 1. Do you agree with the last two lines of the poem? Do you believe the lover is immortalized in this poem? Why or why not?
    2. Choose one or two lines which cause you difficulty. Reread the line(s) several times. Then, free write in response to the line(s), reacting to words or phrases evoking the strongest feelings, asking yourself questions you would like to pose for Shakespeare if you could talk with him; in short, writing any thoughts, ideas, or insights that come to you about the line(s). Don't worry about grammar, spelling, or anything except reacting to the poem. At the end of 10 minutes, look over the poem and what you have written. Does one insight strike you as more perceptive than others? Did something occur to you to help you better understand the line(s)? Try writing for 5 more minutes in response to that idea. Use the two free writings as a basis for a personal response paper on the difficult passage of the poem.

II. Longer Papers

A. In Sonnet 19, Shakespeare writes:

> "Yet do thy worst, old Time: despite thy wrong,
> My love shall in my verse ever live young"
> (lines 13–14)

In what ways does this final couplet compare to the final couplet in "Shall I compare thee to a summer's day?" How is the sentiment similar? Different? How are the tone and style different? Which is more effective?

B. Write a paper analyzing the structure of the poem. Consider how the first two and last two lines relate to the rest of the poem. How do the first eight lines relate to the last six? How do the quatrains of four lines each relate to one another? How does the poem's structure reinforce the subject matter and contribute to the poem's effectiveness?

C. In "Not Marble Nor the Gilded Monuments," Archibald Macleish claims that poets who praise women's beauty in their poems, boasting that "those they loved should be forever remembered" (line 3), are telling lies. After reading Macleish's poem (p. 697), write a paper comparing the two poets' views and offer your own opinion on the subject.

MICHAEL DRAYTON

Since There's No Help

Since there's no help, come let us kiss and part;
Nay, I have done, you get no more of me,
And I am glad, yea, glad with all my heart
That thus so cleanly I myself can free;
5   Shake hands for ever, cancel all our vows,
And when we meet at any time again,
Be it not seen in either of our brows
That we one jot of former love retain.
Now at the last gasp of Love's latest breath,
10   When, his pulse failing, Passion speechless lies,
When Faith is kneeling by his bed of death,
And Innocence is closing up his eyes,
    Now if thou wouldst, when all have given him over,
    From death to life thou mightst him yet recover.

1619

Writing Assignments for "Since There's No Help"

I. Brief Papers

A. 1. Discuss the dramatic setting of the poem by describing who is speaking to whom in the poem.
   2. Explain the speaker's unconventional use of *help* in the first line of the poem and suggest how it relates to the next eight lines.
   3. Are there any implications in the first eight lines that the speaker does not mean what he says in line 3: "And I am glad, yea, glad with all my heart"?
   4. Why is love depicted as a dying male in the last six lines?

B. Argue for or against the assertion that the speaker has ambivalent feelings about ending the relationship.

C. 1. Do you believe someone receiving this poem might experience a change of heart after reading it? How does your view of its effectiveness as a piece of persuasion affect your interpretation of the poem as a whole?
   2. This poem comes from a series of more than sixty sonnets Drayton wrote to one woman over a period of twenty years. Explain if that information affects your response to the poem and why it does or does not.

II. Longer Papers

A. During his lifetime, Drayton wrote copiously, producing sonnets, narrative poems, historical poems, songs, odes, and satires. "Since There's No Help," however, remains his most popular poem. In fact, it is the only poem most editors choose from his canon to publish. Explain why you believe the poem enjoys such popularity and has such enduring appeal.

B. Explain in detail the relationship of the first eight lines of the poem to the last six. Address one or more of the following topics in your paper: the speaker's attitude toward his lover; the lover's implied attitude toward the speaker; your attitude toward either or both. *Or,* if you wish, discuss how the shift from stated indifference to obvious desire is a predictable or a confusing one, one most lovers would or would not understand. *Or,* after going through the poem and circling the punctuation within each line and at the end of each line, write a paper analyzing the structural relationships within the poem.

WILLIAM BUTLER YEATS
When You Are Old

When you are old and grey and full of sleep,
And nodding by the fire, take down this book,
And slowly read, and dream of the soft look
Your eyes had once, and of their shadows deep;

5   How many loved your moments of glad grace,
And loved your beauty with love false or true,
But one man loved the pilgrim soul in you,
And loved the sorrows of your changing face;

And bending down beside the glowing bars,
10 Murmur, a little sadly, how Love fled
And paced upon the mountains overhead
And hid his face amid a crowd of stars.

1892

Writing Assignments for "When You Are Old"

I. Brief Papers
A. 1. How does the first line establish the dominant mood in the poem?
   2. Show that the speaker believes that other men's love for the woman is less significant and less enduring than his own love.
   3. In the last stanza, Yeats compares love to someone shy, someone who flees and hides his face. How does that image relate to the kind of love he describes in the second stanza?

B. Argue for or against either assertion below.
   1. This poem would disturb the woman to whom it is addressed.
   2. The older one is, the more he or she will appreciate and understand this poem.

C. Many people believe Yeats is one of the best modern poets, appealing to unsophisticated as well as sophisticated readers. Judging from this poem, why do you think he appeals to such a wide audience?

II. Longer Papers
A. Read the poem aloud several times or have the poem read aloud several times to you. After each reading, take notes on one or more of the following questions: what tone of voice is most appropriate? What kind of emotional reactions does this poem evoke when read aloud? To what extent does the language of the

poem—the figurative language or comparisons, the selection of words, and so on—affect your response to it? How does the rhyme scheme and the rhythm of the sentences affect your response? Write a paper explaining how the structure and tone of the poem reinforce its subject and impact.

B. Show that the poem magnifies the image of love in the final stanza in both size and elusiveness. Discuss how that enlarged image functions in the poem and how it affects your reactions to the speaker, the woman, and the poem itself.

C. Yeats wrote the following poem in his journal:

> Oh my beloved. How happy
> I was that day when you
> came here from the
> railway, and set your hair
> aright in my looking glass
> and then sat with me at
> my table, and lay resting
> in my big chair. I am
> like the children O my
> beloved and I play at
> marriage—I play with images of the life
> you will not give to me O
> my cruel one.

Although it treats a similar subject, Yeats chose to leave this poem unpublished, while he chose to publish "When You Are Old." In what ways are the poems similar? Different? Which is the more private or personal? Which is the more universal? Which do you believe makes a more enduring statement about love?

ARCHIBALD MACLEISH
"Not Marble nor the Gilded Monuments"*

The praisers of women in their proud and beautiful poems
Naming the grave mouth and the hair and the eyes
Boasted those they loved should be forever remembered
These were lies

5   The words sound but the face in the Istrian sun is forgotten
The poet speaks but to her dead ears no more

---

*"Not Marble Nor the Gilded Monuments": The first line of Shakespeare's "Sonnet 55." Shakespeare's first two lines read: "Not marble, nor the gilded monuments / Of princes, shall outlive this powerful rhyme." The poem is one of many such Renaissance poems which boast the immortality of verse or the permanence of poetry and thus the immortality of the one to whom the poem is addressed.

The sleek throat is gone—and the breast that was troubled to
    listen
Shadow from door

Therefore I will not praise your knees nor your fine walking
10 Telling you men shall remember your name as long
As lips move or breath is spent or the iron of English
Rings from a tongue

I shall say you were young and your arms straight and your
    mouth scarlet
I shall say you will die and none will remember you
15 Your arms change and none remember the swish of your
    garments
Nor the click of your shoe

Not with my hand's strength not with difficult labor
Springing the obstinate words to the bones of your breast
And the stubborn line to your young stride and the breath
    to your breathing
20 And the beat to your haste
Shall I prevail on the hearts of unborn men to remember

(What is a dead girl but a shadowy ghost
Or a dead man's voice but a distant and vain affirmation
Like dream words most)

25 Therefore I will not speak of the undying glory of women
I will say you were young and straight and your skin fair
And you stood in the door and the sun was a shadow of leaves
    on your shoulders
And a leaf on your hair

I will not speak of the famous beauty of dead women
30 I will say the shape of a leaf lay once on your hair
Till the world ends and the eyes are out and the mouths broken
Look! It is there!

                                      1930

Writing Assignments for " 'Not Marble nor the Gilded Monuments' "

I. Brief Papers
    A. 1. What does the speaker choose to praise about his lover and how is that
        different from the "lies" of other poets?

2. In stanza 5, how does the poet link his praise of his lover's youth and vitality to comments on writing poetry?

3. In stanza 8, the poet writes, "And you stood in the door and the sun was a shadow of leaves on your shoulders / And a leaf on your hair" (lines 27–28). In stanza 8, he alters the line to read, "I will say the shape of a leaf lay once on your hair" (line 30). What do you think the change in the line means and why is it important?

B. Argue for or against either assertion below.
   1. The poem is essentially no different—accomplishes no more—than the poems the speaker criticizes.
   2. The speaker's tribute would appeal to women more than the kind of poems the speaker criticizes.

C. 1. Read the poem aloud several times. Should the poem be read passionately? Sadly? Angrily? Discuss what tone of voice is most appropriate and explain why.
   2. Describe as fully as possible how the speaker feels about the woman he addresses in the poem. What evidence convinces you?

II. Longer Papers

A. This poem reacts to a number of love poems which claim to immortalize the beautiful women whom the poems praise. Discuss the kind of tribute the speaker claims he will make, how it differs from other poets' tributes, and to what extent it really is different.

B. Go through the poem and circle all the words related to death. Why does the poem use so many subtle and explicit references to death and how do the references reinforce the subject and the impact of the poem?

C. All except stanzas 5 and 6 follow a predictable pattern in rhyme and sentence length. How does the predictable pattern contribute to the poem's effectiveness and why does the poet alter the structure of stanzas five and six?

JOHN DONNE

Song

Before Reading

One rather old stereotypical view of women is that they are fickle, untrue, and not to be trusted in matters of love. Free write for 5 to 10 minutes about whether you believe the stereotype still exists today.

> Go and catch a falling star,
>   Get with child a mandrake root,*
> Tell me where all past years are,
>   Or who cleft the Devil's foot,
> 5   Teach me to hear mermaids singing,
>   Or to keep off envy's stinging,
>   And find
>   What wind
> Serves to advance an honest mind.
>
> 10 If thou beest born to strange sights,
>   Things invisible to see,
>   Ride ten thousand days and nights,
>   Till age snow white hairs on thee,
>   Thou, when thou return'st, wilt tell me
> 15 All strange wonders that befell thee,
>   And swear
>   No where
>   Lives a woman true, and fair.
>
>   If thou find'st one, let me know,
> 30 Such a pilgrimage were sweet;
>   Yet do not, I would not go,
>   Though at next door we might meet;
>   Though she were true when you met her,
>   And last till you write your letter,
> 25   Yet she
>   Will be
>   False, ere I come, to two, or three.

                                                    1633

Writing Assignments for "Song"

I. Brief Papers
   A. 1. In what way are all the tasks in stanza 1 similar?
      2. How are the tasks similar in stanzas 1 and 2? Why can those tasks be accomplished only by someone "born to strange sights, / Things invisible to see" (lines 10–11)?
      3. When one student was asked to show that the speaker in the poem is cynical, he wrote: "John Donne's poem entitled 'Song' is one that is heavy with cynicism. One can perhaps observe the speaker's cynical attitude by merely

*mandrake root: A plant with a forked or branched root, resembling a human body. Used in fertility and love potions.

looking at the words literally." Which words and images would best support this student's interpretation?

4. How do the final three lines in stanza 2 relate to the first two stanzas?

5. Look up *true* in the dictionary. Which meanings are most appropriate in the poem?

B. 1. What is your reaction to the poem? Do you find it realistic? Do you find it light and humorous? Do you find it offensive? Why do you feel as you do?

2. Write a short letter to your teacher, explaining how you believe the poem should be taught in your class. What elements of the poem should your teacher be certain to discuss? What questions of attitude and stereotype should your teacher raise?

3. The following is the entire paragraph from the student described in I.A.3:

> John Donne's poem entitled "Song" is one that is heavy with cynicism. One can perhaps observe the speaker's cynical attitude by merely looking at the words literally. In the very first stanza the speaker makes a list of tasks all of which are impossible. But he states them as if they were the easiest things in the world to do, "Go and catch a falling star, / Or who cleft the devil's foot" (lines 1 and 4). Here is where the cynicism shows itself the most. The speaker is drawing the parallel that it is about as easy to do these tasks as it is to find a "true woman." He then goes on to say that you can look the entire world over "And swear / No where / Lives a woman true and fair" (lines 16–18). In the third stanza the cynical attitude continues with the speaker explaining that, sure you might find what you think is a "true woman" "And last till you write your letter / Yet she / Will be / False . . ." (lines 25–27). It seems apparent that the speaker is speaking from experience of being hurt perhaps, and this can account for his cynical attitude.

Write a short letter to the student telling him why you believe this is or is not an effective, well-supported interpretation of cynicism in Donne's poem.

II. Longer Papers

A. Show how the poem is structured around the notion of impossibility, with each stanza assuming a more extreme, exaggerated stance.

B. What is the relationship of the last three lines in each stanza to the rest of the stanza? How do the lines comment upon or conclude each stanza?

C. Upon what stereotypes of women does the speaker base his claims? Do those stereotypes and generalizations still exist today in people's minds? To what extent do they prevail on this campus or among your friends? How do those stereotypes and your own beliefs affect your interpretation of the poem?

ROBERT BROWNING

Meeting at Night

1

The gray sea and the long black land;
And the yellow half-moon large and low;
And the startled little waves that leap
In fiery ringlets from their sleep,
5   As I gain the cove with pushing prow,
And quench its speed i' the slushy sand.

2

Then a mile of warm sea-scented beach;
Three fields to cross till a farm appears;
A tap at the pane, the quick sharp scratch
10   And blue spurt of a lighted match,
And a voice less loud, through its joys and fears,
Than the two hearts beating each to each!

1845

Writing Assignments for "Meeting at Night"

I. Brief Papers

   A. 1. Show how the poem appeals to the sense of sound or the sense of sight.
      2. Show how the poem appeals to senses other than the senses of sight and sound.
      3. Why is so much of the poem, a love poem, devoted to the speaker's journey? How does the description of the journey help convey the speaker's state of mind?

   B. Argue for or against either assertion below.
      1. If you didn't know the lover's destination, you would have no clue from the first ten lines of the poem.
      2. The poet could convey the speaker's feelings more intensely and more exactly if he paid more attention to the lovers' actual meeting.

   C. Do you believe a poem about a lover's journey away from his or her lover would emphasize different images? What might they be and how would they be treated differently?

II. Longer Papers

   A. Go through the poem and circle all the verbs. How do the verbs reinforce the intensity and immediacy of the lover's feelings?

B. Go through the poem and circle any words that suggest passion and love. Write a paper showing how the poet's choice of words helps convey the speaker's feelings, even though most of the poem describes the landscape.

C. After reading "Parting at Morning," printed below, respond to one of the following topics:

ROBERT BROWNING
Parting at Morning

> Round the cape of a sudden came the sea,
> And the sun looked over the mountain's rim:
> And straight was a path of gold for him,
> And the need of a world of men for me.

> 1845

a. Browning intended for the two poems to serve as companion pieces. In what ways does the setting in "Meeting at Night" compare to the setting in "Parting at Morning"? How do both settings convey the speaker's state of mind?

b. Why is the second poem shorter than the first and why is there significantly less description and detail?

c. The two poems—the second one particularly—are written from the male's perspective. Do you believe most women would prefer the first poem to the second? *Or,* do you believe most men would react differently to the two poems together than most women would react? Discuss either topic in detail.

d. Do you believe the philosophy of love implied in "Meeting at Night" is different from that implied in "Parting at Morning"? Explain.

MATTHEW ARNOLD
Dover Beach*

> The sea is calm tonight,
> The tide is full, the moon lies fair
> Upon the straits;—on the French coast the light
> Gleams and is gone; the cliffs of England stand,
> 5 Glimmering and vast, out in the tranquil bay.
> Come to the window, sweet is the night-air!
> Only, from the long line of spray
> Where the sea meets the moon-blanched land,
> Listen! you hear the grating roar

*Dover Beach: English coastline on the Strait of Dover which is located at the end of the English Channel between southeast England and northern France.

10   Of pebbles which the waves draw back, and fling.
At their return, up the high strand,
Begin, and cease, and then again begin,
With tremulous cadence slow, and bring
The eternal note of sadness in.

15   Sophocles* long ago
Heard it on the Aegean, and it brought
Into his mind the turbid ebb and flow
Of human misery; we
Find also in the sound a thought,
20   Hearing it by this distant northern sea.

The Sea of Faith
Was once, too, at the full, and round earth's shore
Lay like the folds of a bright girdle furled.
But now I only hear
25   Its melancholy, long, withdrawing roar,
Retreating, to the breath
Of the night-wind, down the vast edges drear
And naked shingles† of the world.

Ah, love, let us be true
30   To one another! for the world, which seems
To lie before us like a land of dreams,
So various, so beautiful, so new,
Hath really neither joy, nor love, nor light,
Nor certitude, nor peace, nor help for pain;
35   And we are here as on a darkling plain
Swept with confused alarms of struggle and flight,
Where ignorant armies clash by night.

1867

Writing Assignments for "Dover Beach"

I. Brief Papers

   A. 1. Show that the poet establishes a mood of tranquility in lines 1–6 in the poem.
      2. Show that the poet destroys the mood of tranquility in lines 7–14.
      3. How does the ebb and flow of the sea affect the speaker's mood?
      4. What is the dramatic setting of the poem? Where is the speaker and to whom does he speak?

*Sophocles: Greek playwright (see *Oedipus Rex,* pp. 847–895).
†naked shingles: Pebble-covered beaches.

5. What does the speaker mean when he says, "The Sea of Faith / Was once, too, at the full . . ." (lines 21–22)? In what has the speaker lost faith?
6. Discuss the meaning and the appropriateness of the comparison in the last three lines of the poem.

B. Argue for or against either assertion below.
  1. The "we" to whom the speaker refers (lines 35) includes more than the two lovers.
  2. The speaker's view of the world—deceptively beautiful, fresh, and promising but actually lacking joy, love, light, certainty, peace, or help from pain—is a realization each of us must accept sooner or later.

C. 1. Which part of the poem affects you most deeply—the speaker's plea for truth and fidelity (lines 29–30) or the speaker's certainty that there is nothing stable, lasting, or secure in the world? Why?
  2. What one line or image in the poem do you find most frightening? Discuss the implications of the line or image, explaining why you are so affected by it.

II. Longer Papers

A. Explain in detail the speaker's attitude toward his lover, toward the world, and toward the future.
B. How does the second stanza of the poem prepare for the third stanza? In which way is one more figurative than the other?
C. Write a paper explaining how the sound of the poem—the cadence, rhythm, and length of the lines—reinforces the subject matter and the mood of the poem.
D. Write a paper discussing how the poem's impact relies on cyclical patterns of the tides, the waves, the moon, youth and age, faith and despair, and/or struggle and passivity.

RICHARD WILBUR

A Late Aubade

You could be sitting now in a carrel
Turning some liver-spotted page,
Or rising in an elevator-cage
Toward Ladies' Apparel.

5   You could be planting a raucous bed
Of salvia, in rubber gloves,
Or lunching through a screed of someone's loves
With pitying head,

Or making some unhappy setter
10   Heel, or listening to a bleak
Lecture on Schoenberg's serial technique.
Isn't this better?

Think of all the time you are not
Wasting, and would not care to waste,
15   Such things, thank God, not being to your taste.
Think what a lot

Of time, by woman's reckoning,
You've saved, and so may spend on this,
You who had rather lie in bed and kiss
20   Than anything.

It's almost noon, you say? If so,
Time flies, and I need not rehearse
The rosebuds-theme of centuries of verse.
If you *must* go,

25   Wait for a while, then slip downstairs
And bring us up some chilled white wine,
And some blue cheese, and crackers, and some fine
Ruddy-skinned pears.

                                                        1948

Writing Assignments for "A Late Aubade"

I. Brief Papers
   A. 1. Show that the speaker describes everything his lover could be doing (lines
         1–11) as unappealing.
      2. What is the dramatic setting of the poem? Who is the speaker, to whom is he
         speaking, and about what?
      3. After reading "To the Virgins, To Make Much of Time" (p. 688), explain why
         the speaker of "A Late Aubade" does not need to "rehearse / The rosebuds-
         theme of centuries of verse" (lines 23–24).

   B. Choose one assertion below, and develop or refute it:
      1. The speaker wishes to persuade his lover as well as to praise her.
      2. After reading the description of *carpe diem* poetry, p. 689 in this book, show
         that this poem does or does not illustrate *carpe diem* poetry.

C. Describe either the speaker or his lover. What is important to each of them? What can you tell about each of their personalities from the poem?

II. Longer Papers

A. How do the last five lines of the poem relate to the rest of the poem in subject matter? In emotional and/or sensory impact?

B. Describe in detail the speaker, his attitude toward his lover, and her implied attitude toward him.

C. To what extent is this a typical *carpe diem* poem? To what extent does it differ from such poems?

ADRIENNE RICH

Living in Sin

She had thought the studio would keep itself;
no dust upon the furniture of love.
Half heresy, to wish the taps less vocal,
the panes relieved of grime. A plate of pears,
5   a piano with a Persian shawl, a cat
stalking the picturesque amusing mouse
had risen at his urging.
Not that at five each separate stair would writhe
under the milkman's tramp; that morning light
10   so coldly would delineate the scraps
of last night's cheese and three sepulchral bottles;
that on the kitchen shelf among the saucers
a pair of beetle-eyes would fix her own—
Envoy from some village in the moldings . . .
15   Meanwhile, he, with a yawn,
sounded a dozen notes upon the keyboard,
declared it out of tune, shrugged at the mirror,
rubbed at his beard, went out for cigarettes;
while she, jeered by the minor demons,
20   pulled back the sheets and made the bed and found
a towel to dust the table-top,
and let the coffee-pot boil over on the stove.
By evening she was back in love again,
though not so wholly but throughout the night
25   she woke sometimes to feel the daylight coming
like a relentless milkman up the stairs.

1955

Writing Assignments for "Living in Sin"

I. Brief Papers
A. 1. What kind of life, described in lines 3–7, does the young woman believe she will have with the artist?
   2. What kind of life, described in lines 8–14, does she actually have?
   3. Find one example of humor in the poem and explain why it is funny.
   4. Why does Rich entitle the poem "Living in Sin"?

B. Argue for or against either assertion below.
   1. The young woman feels only sexual attraction—not love—for the artist.
   2. The reader should sympathize with the young woman in the poem.

C. 1. How does the poet feel about the young woman in the poem? Do you believe she likes her? Pities her? Scorns her for her naiveté?
   2. Do you think most couples' notions of their love are as unrealistic as the young woman's? Why or why not?
   3. How does the description of the artist (lines 15–18) affect your response to the poem?

II. Longer Papers
A. Develop any of the preceding assignments into a full-length paper.
B. Discuss examples of humor in the poem. Is the poem most humorous in its details and examples, its comparisons and figurative language, its treatment of the young woman's naive expectations and the reality of her situation, or in a combination of all three?

HILDA DOOLITTLE

Fragment Thirty-Six

I know not what to do: my mind is divided.

Sappho*

I know not what to do,
my mind is reft:
is song's gift best?
is love's gift loveliest?
5   I know not what to do,

*Sappho: Greek poet who lived with her followers on the island Lesbos in about 600 B.C.

now sleep has pressed
weight on your eyelids.

Shall I break your rest,
devouring, eager?
10 is love's gift best?
nay, song's the loveliest:
yet were you lost,
what rapture
could I take from song?
15 what song were left?

I know not what to do:
to turn and slake
the rage that burns,
with my breath burn
20 and trouble your cool breath?
so shall I turn and take
snow in my arms?
(is love's gift best?)
yet flake on flake
25 of snow were comfortless,
did you lie wondering,
wakened yet unawake.

Shall I turn and take
comfortless snow within my arms?
30 press lips to lips
that answer not,
press lips to flesh
that shudders not nor breaks?

Is love's gift best?
35 shall I turn and slake
all the wild longing?
O I am eager for you!
as the Pleiads* shake
white light in whiter water
40 so shall I take you?

My mind is quite divided,
my minds hesitate,

*Pleiads: In Greek myth, the seven daughters of Atlas, who were metamorphosed into stars.

so perfect matched,
I know not what to do:
45   each strives with each
as two white wrestlers
standing for a match,
ready to turn and clutch
yet never shake muscle nor nerve nor tendon;
50   so my mind waits
to grapple with my mind,
yet I lie quiet,
I would seem at rest.

I know not what to do:
55   strain upon strain,
sound surging upon sound
makes my brain blind;
as a wave-line may wait to fall
yet (waiting for its falling)
60   still the wind may take
from off its crest,
white flake on flake of foam,
that rises,
seeming to dart and pulse
65   and rend the light,
so my mind hesitates
above the passion
quivering yet to break,
so my mind hesitates
70   above my mind,
listening to song's delight.

I know not what to do:
will the sound break,

rending the night
75   with rift on rift of rose
and scattered light?
will the sound break at last
as the wave hesitant,
or will the whole night pass
80   and I lie listening awake?

1924

Writing Assignments for "Fragment Thirty-Six"

I. Brief Papers

A. 1. Explain the dramatic setting of the poem by discussing where the speaker is, whom she is with, and what is happening. Give as much evidence as possible to support your conjecture.
   2. Show that the speaker feels intense passion for her lover.
   3. Go through the poem and circle all references to the speaker's lover. Explain how these references help you understand the lover's attitude toward the speaker.
   4. Go through the poem and circle all the references to song. How is the speaker's notion of "song's gift" (line 3) related to, yet different from, her desire for physical passion or "love's gift" (line 4)?

B. Argue for or against either assertion below.
   1. The speaker hesitates to awaken her lover because she fears she will be rebuffed.
   2. The speaker hesitates to awaken her lover because her fantasies are more satisfying.

C. 1. Ask someone you know who reads aloud very well to read the poem aloud to you several times. Free write in response to any words, ideas, or images the reading evokes. Write a brief paper based on one response.
   2. Do you believe that the speaker in the poem is clearly either male or female? Explain why you feel as you do.

II. Longer Papers

A. Explain why if you did not know this poem was published in 1924 you would still be able to guess that it was published in this century. What is modern about the subject matter, the speaker's voice, and/or the poet's style?

B. Hilda Doolittle has been praised for writing excellent erotic poetry. Do you believe this poem should be labeled erotic? Why or why not?

C. Go through the poem and trace one of the following references and explain how the pattern of references helps you understand the speaker's feelings, the lover's attitude toward the speaker, and/or any other important element of the poem: references to the color white; references to cold; references to heat; references to water; references to light. If you wish, combine any of the references—say, references to cold and to heat—into one category.

D. Write a paper about the structure of the poem and how it contributes to the speaker's conflict. Pay attention to the form of the stanzas, and the punctuation within and between stanzas.

E. Go through the poem and circle all the verbs. Explain how the selection of verbs reinforces the essential tension and conflict at the heart of the poem.

TESS GALLAGHER

Under Stars

The sleep of this night deepens
because I have walked coatless from the house
carrying the white envelope.
All night it will say one name
5   in its little tin house by the roadside.

I have raised the metal flag
so its shadow under the roadlamp
leaves an imprint on the rain-heavy bushes.
Now I will walk back
10 thinking of the few lights still on
in the town a mile away.

In the yellowed light of a kitchen
the millworker has finished his coffee,
his wife has laid out the white slices of bread
15 on the counter. Now while the bed they have left
is still warm, I will think of you, you
who are so far away
you have caused me to look up at the stars.

Tonight they have not moved
20 from childhood, those games played after dark.
Again I walk into the wet grass
toward the starry voices. Again, I
am the found one, intimate, returned
by all I touch on the way.

1978

Writing Assignments for "Under Stars"

I. Brief Papers
> A. 1. Explain the dramatic setting of the poem by discussing who is speaking, where
>   the speaker has been, and to whom the poem is addressed.
>   2. Show that the speaker's feelings for the recipient of the letter are implied in
>   the first stanza of the poem.
>   3. What is the relationship between the third stanza and the rest of the poem?
>   4. Trace all the references in the poem to light or all the references to darkness.
>   How do the references to one or to the other help you understand the
>   speaker's feelings for the recipient of the letter?

   B. Choose one assertion below, and develop or refute it:
     1. Although there is no direct evidence to support the supposition, the recipient of the letter probably returns the speaker's love.
     2. Although there is no direct evidence to support the supposition, the poem is a tender love poem.

   C. Why do you suppose the speaker chooses the nighttime to mail the letter?

II. Longer Papers
   A. Look for as many cause/effect relationships within the poem as you can find. In what way does the speaker attribute most of her actions to her lover and what does that imply about their relationship?
   B. Find as many direct or indirect references to the geometric form of the triangle as you can. How does the triangular shape reinforce the subject matter and the impact of the poem by linking the speaker, the stars, and the lover?
   C. Recall your own childhood games played "under stars." Why do the games, such as hide-and-go-seek and tag, come to the speaker's mind on this night? Explain in detail.

LINDA PASTAN
Prosody 101

When they taught me that what mattered most
was not the strict iambic line goose-stepping
over the page but the variations
in that line and the tension produced
5 on the ear by the surprise of difference,
I understood yet didn't understand
exactly, until just now, years later
in spring, with the trees already lacy
and camellias blowsy with middle age,
10 I looked out and saw what a cold front had done
to the garden, sweeping in like common language,
unexpected in the sensuous
extravagance of a Maryland spring.
There was a dark edge around each flower
15 as if it had been outlined in ink
instead of frost, and the tension I felt
between the expected and actual
was like that time I came to you, ready
to say goodbye for good, for you had been
20 a cold front yourself lately, and as I walked in

you laughed and lifted me up in your arms
as if I too were lacy with spring
instead of middle aged like the camellias,
and I thought: so this is Poetry!

1983

Writing Assignments for "Prosody 101"

I. Brief Papers

A. 1. Look up *prosody* in the dictionary. How do the various meanings help you understand the poem?
   2. Create a brief personality profile or description of the speaker. What is she like? How old is she? What matters most to her?
   3. How would you characterize the speaker's language? To what extent does it invite the reader to sympathize with her?
   4. Why is the poem titled "Prosody 101"?

B. Argue for or against one of the assertions below.
   1. This is a poem about poetry more than it is a poem about love.
   2. This is a poem about love more than it is a poem about poetry.
   3. This is a poem about expectation and reality more than it is a poem about poetry or about love.

C. Discuss why you think this is a great poem, a good poem, or a mediocre poem.

II. Longer Papers

A. This poem can be broken roughly into three parts (lines 1–5; lines 6–15; and lines 16–24). Read the poem carefully, noting the relationships among the three sections of the poem. Be sure to note repeated words from section to section, such as "tension" (line 4 and line 16) and "middle age" (line 9 and line 23). Discuss the relationships among the parts of the poem, showing how the last section grows naturally from parts one and two.

B. Explain as fully as possible the last line of the poem: "and I thought: so this is Poetry!" Be sure to consider why the poet capitalizes "poetry" and to what extent her definition is typical of most definitions of poetry.

C. Argue for or against the assertion that this poem *will* or *should* endure and be read hundreds of years from now.

EMILY DICKINSON
"I cannot live with You—"

I cannot live with You—
It would be Life—
And Life is over there—
Behind the Shelf

5   The Sexton keeps the Key to—
Putting up
Our Life—His Porcelain—
Like a Cup—

Discarded of the Housewife—
10   Quaint—or Broke—
A newer Sevres pleases—
Old Ones crack—

I could not die—with You—
For One must wait
15   To shut the Other's Gaze down—
You—could not—

And I—Could I stand by
And see You—freeze—
Without my Right of Frost—
20   Death's privilege?

Nor could I rise—with You—
Because Your Face
Would put out Jesus'—
That New Grace

25   Glow plain—and foreign
On my homesick Eye—
Except that You than He
Shone closer by—

They'd judge Us—How—
30   For You—served Heaven—You know,
Or sought to—
I could not—

Because You saturated Sight—
And I had no more Eyes
35 For sordid excellence
As Paradise

And were You lost, I would be—
Though My Name
Rang loudest
40 On the heavenly fame—

And were You—saved—
And I—condemned to be
Where You were not—
That self—were Hell to Me—

45 So We must meet apart—
You there—I—here—
With just the Door ajar
That Oceans are—and Prayer—
And that White Sustenance—
50 Despair—

1890

Writing Assignments for "I cannot live with You"

I. Brief Papers
    A. 1. Reread the poem two or three times, paying close attention to the speaker's attitude or tone. How would you describe it?
       2. Why is a broken or discarded cup appropriate in understanding the relationship described in the poem?
       3. In stanzas 4–7, the speaker describes why "I could not die—with You" (line 13). Paraphrase as carefully as you can what she says here.
       4. In stanzas 8–11, the speaker describes how heaven would have difficulty judging "Us." Paraphrase these stanzas and explain why such judgment would be difficult.
       5. Hell is traditionally defined as absence from God. How does the poem define hell, and how does this definition help us to understand the speaker's feelings?

    C. Some biographers and critics believe that Emily Dickinson was in love at one time with a married clergyman, who perhaps returned her love, but due to social and religious conventions would not act on his feelings. Does such knowledge change your reactions to the poem? Why or why not?

II. Longer Papers
   A. Trace the imagery of eyes and sight through the poem and show how they are appropriate.
   B. Explain how the poet uses religious imagery and doctrine throughout the poem to establish the seriousness and the hopelessness of her feelings.

Comparative Papers from Chapter Four:
Romantic Love and Passion

A. Thomas De Quincey, a British poet and essayist in the 1700s–1800s, distinguishes between a literature of knowledge and a literature of power. The purpose of literature of knowledge is *to teach,* while the purpose of the literature of power is *to move.* De Quincey favors the latter, claiming that the literature of power goes far beyond intellectual power to "the understanding of the heart." Obviously, the concept is a difficult one to understand, and it is not always easy to recognize the difference. Select poems from this chapter which you believe best illustrate the literature of power and discuss how they reflect or how they invite "the understanding of the heart."

B. Choose three or four poems from the chapter which you found particularly striking or effective. Determine to what extent the poems' subject matter, style, or impact influence your reaction to them. Write a paper examining the poems and their appeal. Discuss each poem separately, if you like; however, make sure a central controlling idea unifies your discussion.

C. According to R. D. Laing, "However lonely or sad one may be, one can exist alone." Which poets from this chapter would be most likely to agree or to disagree with Laing's statement? Defend your choices.

D. Spend some time viewing films or television programs popular with large segments of the population. How is love treated or depicted within such commercial entertainment? To what extent is it treated similarly or differently in the love poetry in this chapter?

E. In this chapter, there are selections from the 1600s to the present. What universal traits characterize good love poetry? What similar topics and attitudes endure from generation to generation with seemingly little change?

F. Your pen-pal in Australia has asked you to send her copies of several love poems that you like or that illustrate typical poems American college students study. Select the most appropriate poems from this unit, and write a letter to your friend explaining which poems you're sending and why.

G. In his *Autobiography,* Bertrand Russell says, "I have sought love, first because it brings ecstasy—ecstasy so great that I would often have sacrificed all the rest of my life for a few hours of joy. I have sought it next, because it relieves loneliness." Using this quotation as your point of departure and relying on poems from this chapter, write a paper responding to one of the following topics:
   1. The best, most moving love poems treat the ecstasy of love and passion, suggesting that no other experience is so fulfilling.

2. The best, most moving love poems deal less with love's passion than with love's ability to relieve loneliness and to provide companionship.

H. You have been asked to select three love poems from American or British poets to place in a time capsule along with a commentary explaining how each illustrates how human beings alive in the late 1900s feel about love and passion. You are free to select poems from any century so long as your commentary relates those poems to contemporary attitudes and feelings. Select three poems from this chapter and write the necessary commentary. (If you like, address your commentary to citizens of the future and use direct address.)

5 / Poems about Husbands, Wives, and Lovers

JOHN MILTON

Methought I Saw My Late Espoused Saint

Methought I saw my late espoused saint
   Brought to me like Alcestis* from the grave,
   Whom Jove's great son to her glad husband gave,
   Rescued from death by force though pale and faint.
5 Mine, as whom washed from spot of childbed taint,
   Purification in the old law did save,†
   And such, as yet once more I trust to have
   Full sight of her in Heaven without restraint,
   Came vested all in white, pure as her mind.
10 Her face was veiled, yet to my fancied sight,
   Love, sweetness, goodness, in her person shined
   So clear, as in no face with more delight.
   But O, as to embrace me she inclined,
   I waked, she fled, and day brought back my night.

1673

Writing Assignments for "Methought I Saw My Late Espoused Saint"

I. Brief Papers
  A. 1. Explain the dramatic situation of the poem. What is happening in the poem and
      what is likely to have led up to the experience?
    2. What specific language does the poet use to convey the ethereal, otherwordly
      nature of his dream vision? Explain.
    3. Explain the last line of the poem, focusing specifically on the phrase "and day
      brought back my night" (line 14).

*Alcestis: Hercules, "Jove's great son" (line 13), rescued Alcestis, wife of Admetus, from the underworld.
†"Mine, as whom washed . . . / . . . the old law did save": Leviticus XII describes a period of purification of women after childbirth. The line is particularly poignant because Milton's second wife died in childbirth in 1653.

B. 1. John Milton was blind at the time he wrote this poem. Read back through the poem with that knowledge, noting the references to sight and seeing. How does his blindness affect your interpretation of the poem?

2. John Milton's second wife died in childbirth twenty years before he wrote this poem. How does that affect your response to the poem, if at all?

II. Longer Papers

A. Go through the poem and circle all the words related to light and vision. Discuss their appropriateness and their implications in the poem.

B. Discuss in detail how the speaker's recollections of his wife are transformed through his dream. Explain how the language of the poem contributes to the depiction of the experience.

JOHN DONNE

A Valediction: Forbidding Mourning

As virtuous men pass mildly away,
    And whisper to their souls to go,
Whilst some of their sad friends do say
    The breath goes now, and some say, No;

5   So let us melt, and make no noise,
        No tear-floods, nor sigh-tempests move,
    'Twere profanation of our joys
        To tell the laity our love.

    Moving of th' earth* brings harms and fears,
10   Men reckon what it did and meant;
    But trepidation of the spheres,†
        Though greater far, is innocent.

    Dull sublunary‡ lovers' love
        (Whose soul is sense) cannot admit
15   Absence, because it doth remove
        Those things which elemented it.

*Moving of th' earth: Earthquakes.
†trepidation of the spheres: Some astronomers in Donne's day believed that the earth stood still and that the planets revolved around it in perfect circles. To explain abberations that contradicted the idea of circular planetary orbits, the astronomers argued that there were disturbances or "trepidation" in the movement of the planets.
‡sublunary: Earthly, ordinary.

But we by a love so much refined
   That our selves know not what it is,
Inter-assuréd of the mind,
20   Care less, eyes, lips, and hands to miss.

Our two souls therefore, which are one,
   Though I must go, endure not yet
A breach, but an expansion,
   Like gold to airy thinness beat.

25 If they be two, they are two so
   As stiff twin compasses are two;
Thy soul, the fixed foot, makes no show
   To move, but doth, if th' other do.

And though it in the center sit,
30   Yet when the other far doth roam,
It leans and hearkens after it,
   And grows erect, as that comes home.

Such wilt thou be to me, who must
   Like th' other foot, obliquely run;
35 Thy firmness makes my circle just,
   And makes me end where I begun.

                 1633

Writing Assignments for "A Valediction: Forbidding Mourning"

I. Brief Papers
  A. 1. Reread the first two stanzas several times. Explain why the speaker hopes he
      and the woman he loves can act with reserve when he leaves on his journey.
      Why would their love be diminished or profaned if they had a more tumultuous
      leave-taking?
    2. Explain why the speaker prefers their leave-taking to be more like "trepidation
      of the spheres" (line 11) than "moving of th' earth" (line 9). How are the
      effects of one less disruptive yet more profound than the other?
    3. Compare the sublunary (earthly) lovers—their relationship and their separa-
      tion—to the couple in the poem.
    4. Why is the couple's separation not so much a breach but an expansion? Why
      is the comparison to gold an appropriate one?
    5. Use a compass to draw a circle and a half-circle on a sheet of paper. Notice
      how the center of the compass anchors the leg holding the pencil. Notice also

the movement of the center leg, as it leans but stays fixed. Explain how the comparison of the couple to the compass is an appropriate one in the last three stanzas.

B. Argue for or against the assertion that this poem is reassuring and consoling.

C. 1. Do you believe the couple will miss one another more intensely than the other lovers described, even though they "Care less eyes, lips, and hands to miss" (line 20)? Why or why not?
   2. John Donne reportedly presented this poem to his wife as a gift before he left on a long journey. Explain how that affects your response to the poem.

II. Longer Papers

A. Describe the couple's attitude toward long separations, toward one another, toward other couples, and toward open displays of emotion. Assess how contemporary or how outdated their attitudes are.
B. Go through the poem and note all the comparisons the speaker uses. Discuss the appropriateness of the comparisons as well as how they suggest the gravity of the leave-taking and the depth of the couple's love.

WILLIAM SHAKESPEARE

Sonnet 116 (Let me not to the marriage of true minds admit impediments)

Let me not to the marriage of true minds
Admit impediments: Love is not love
Which alters when it alteration finds,
Or bends with the remover to remove:
5 Oh, no! it is an ever-fixéd mark,
That looks on tempests and is never shaken;
It is the star to every wandering bark,
Whose worth's unknown, although his height be taken.
Love's not Time's fool, though rosy lips and cheeks
10 Within his bending sickle's compass come;
Love alters not with his brief hours and weeks,
But bears it out even to the edge of doom.
   If this be error and upon me proved,
   I never writ, nor no man ever loved.

1609

Writing Assignments for "Sonnet 116 (Let me not to the marriage of true minds admit impediments)"

I. Brief Papers

A. 1. Look up *true* in the dictionary. How do its various meanings contribute to your understanding of the poem?
2. Explain what the poet means by marriage of minds.
3. Describe in your own words the poet's tests for true love.
4. Choose one of the following examples and explain how Shakespeare shows what love *is* by showing what love *is not:*
   a. "Love is not love / Which alters when it alteration finds" (lines 2–3)
   b. "Love's not Time's fool" (line 9)
   c. "Love alters not with his [time's] brief hours and weeks" (line 11)
5. Why is the "sickle's compass" an appropriate comparison or metaphor for time?

B. Argue for or against the assertion that the last line of the poem contradicts the line immediately preceding it.

C. This poem is more difficult to read and to understand than many others. Discuss why students in a class like yours should or should not be assigned this poem.

II. Longer Papers

A. One successful strategy to use in any argument is to raise and undermine opposing views. Show that Shakespeare is a successful strategist.
B. Greeting cards and popularized, sentimental verse are aflood with descriptions of love: "love is a warm puppy," "love is a spring walk," "love is holding hands," and so on. Explain why Shakespeare's poem is less sentimental and more enduring.
C. Discuss in what ways Shakespeare reveals the mystery or enigma of love, even while he is emphatically asserting its existence.
D. The following directions are intended to help you write a paper about the structure of the poem. Use any or all of the steps below in developing a paper which shows how the poem's form reinforces its meaning and its impact.
   1. "Let me not to the marriage of true minds" is a sonnet. A sonnet is a fourteen-line poem, following one of two conventional rhyme schemes—Italian or English (Shakespearean). This sonnet, like other Shakespearean sonnets, is divided into four parts—three quatrains (of four lines each) and a final couplet (two lines). Go through the poem and mark the three quatrains; it may be helpful to rephrase each in your own words. How are the quatrains both self-contained and related in meaning?

2. Rephrase the final couplet. What is its relationship to the rest of the poem? In what ways does it comment on the entire poem, allow insight into the poet's attitude toward his subject, or extend the poem?

3. Circle the final words in each line, noting particularly the rhyme scheme in each quatrain. Pay attention, also, to the punctuation at the end of each quatrain. How do the punctuation and the rhyme scheme allow each quatrain to function on its own as well as in the broader context of the poem?

4. Find other ways to discuss the structure of the poem. Pay attention, for instance, to repeated lines or patterns: for example, "Love is not love" (line 2) is repeated or echoed in "Love's not Time's fool" (line 9). *Or* consider the sandwich effect, the second quatrain forming a kind of filling for the first and third. If you are interested in studying the sonnet form further, see John Milton's "I Thought I Saw My Late Espoused Saint" (p. 719), George Meredith's "At Dinner She is Hostess, I am Host" (p. 732), Michael Drayton's "Since There's No Help" (p. 694), or other Shakespeare sonnets (pp. 691 and 692).

WILLIAM CARLOS WILLIAMS

This is Just to Say

I have eaten
the plums
that were in
the icebox

5   and which
you were probably
saving
for breakfast

Forgive me
10   they were delicious
so sweet
and so cold

1938

Writing Assignments for "This Is Just to Say"

I. Brief Papers

A. 1. Show that this poem appeals to the reader's senses.

2. Obviously the poem is a note the speaker leaves for someone. What can you infer about the speaker's personality from the poem?

B. Argue for or against either assertion below.
   1. The person for whom the note is written would probably not have been angry at the speaker for eating the plums.
   2. The note is more a love poem than an apology.

C. Judging from this brief poem, do you believe the couple in the poem have a good relationship? How would you describe it?

II. Longer Papers
   A. Explain in full what you can infer about the speaker in the poem, the person to whom he addresses his note, and the kind of relationship they have.
   B. An *image* in a poem is a word or cluster of words that refers to any kind of sensory experience. Show how this poem, as short as it is, appeals to a number of different senses and explain how that sensory appeal helps you understand the couple's relationship.

E. E. CUMMINGS

anyone lived in a pretty how town

anyone lived in a pretty how town
(with up so floating many bells down)
spring summer autumn winter
he sang his didn't he danced his did.

5   Women and men (both little and small)
cared for anyone not at all
they sowed their isn't they reaped their same
sun moon stars rain

children guessed (but only a few
10   and down they forgot as up they grew
autumn winter spring summer)
that noone loved him more by more

when by now and tree by leaf
she laughed his joy she cried his grief
15   bird by snow and stir by still
anyone's any was all to her

someones married their everyones
laughed their cryings and did their dance
(sleep wake hope and then) they
20   said their nevers they slept their dream

stars rain sun moon
(and only the snow can begin to explain
how children are apt to forget to remember
with up so floating many bells down)

25   one day anyone died i guess
(and noone stooped to kiss his face)
busy folk buried them side by side
little by little and was by was

all by all and deep by deep
30   and more by more they dream their sleep
noone and anyone earth by april
wish by spirit and if by yes.

Women and men (both dong and ding)
summer autumn winter spring
35   reaped their sowing and went their came
sun moon stars rain

                                    1940

Writing Assignments for "anyone lived in a pretty how town"

I. Brief Papers
   A. 1. Describe the kind of relationship "anyone" and "noone" have.
      2. Show that the townspeople are not as happy as "anyone" and "noone."
      3. Select one pair of lines from the following sets and explain how the difference
         in the two is important in the poem:

         • "he sang his didn't he danced his did" (line 4)
         • "they sowed their isn't they reaped their same" (line 7)

         • "she laughed his joy she cried his grief" (line 14)
         • "laughed their cryings and did their dance" (line 18)

         • ". . . they / said their nevers they slept their dream" (lines 19–20)
         • "and more by more they dream their sleep" (line 30)

      4. Why are children more likely than others to understand anyone and noone's
         love?

   B. Argue for or against one of the assertions below.
      1. This poem is optimistic about love.
      2. As their names imply, "anyone" and "noone" are very ordinary people.
      3. The poem is a defense of monogamy.

C. 1. Do you believe "anyone" and "noone" have a meaningful life even though people in the town take little notice of them?

   2. Find one or two lines in the poem that you have trouble understanding. Read them aloud several times. Take a moment and free write for 1 or 2 minutes about how the lines make you feel when you read them. Use that free writing as a basis for a brief paper on how the lines affect you or create a certain mood.

II. Longer Papers

A. Bertrand Russell once said, "Romantic love is the source of the most intense delights that life has to offer." To what extent does this poem illustrate the same attitude and to what extent do you agree with both the assertion and the poem's illustration of it?

B. Make a list of all the words, lines, and phrases describing the townspeople, their attitudes, their relationships, their lives. And then make a list of all the words, lines, and phrases describing "anyone" and "noone," their attitudes, their relationship, their life. Study the two lists and find what strikes you as a central or significant difference. Take a few minutes and write down as quickly as possible all your impressions, your reactions, and your feelings about the difference. Try that several times with different contrasts. Use those lists as the basis for a paper on one of the following topics:

   1. Show how the poem relies on contrasts—in the characters, in the language, in the stanza form, or in anything else you have discovered—for its major effect.

   2. Discuss how the poem evokes contrasting moods or feelings when comparing anyone and noone to the townspeople.

C. Argue for or against the assertion that, even though the poem's style is unorthodox, its subject matter and its implications are old-fashioned.

W. H. AUDEN

Lay Your Sleeping Head, My Love

Lay your sleeping head, my love,
Human on my faithless arm;
Time and fevers burn away
Individual beauty from
5 Thoughtful children, and the grave
Proves the child ephemeral:
But in my arms till break of day
Let the living creature lie,
Mortal, guilty, but to me
10 The entirely beautiful.

Soul and body have no bounds:
To lovers as they lie upon
Her tolerant enchanted slope
In their ordinary swoon.
15 Grave the vision Venus* sends
Of supernatural sympathy,
Universal love and hope;
While an abstract insight wakes
Among the glaciers and the rocks
20 The hermit's sensual ecstasy.

Certainty, fidelity
On the stroke of midnight pass
Like vibrations of a bell,
And fashionable madmen raise
25 Their pedantic boring cry:
Every farthing of the cost,
All the dreaded cards foretell,

Shall be paid, but from this night
Not a whisper, not a thought,
30 Not a kiss nor look be lost.

Beauty, midnight, vision dies:
Let the winds of dawn that blow
Softly round your dreaming head
Such a day of sweetness show
35 Eye and knocking heart may bless,
Find the mortal world enough;
Noons of dryness see you fed
By the involuntary powers,
Nights of insult let you pass
40 Watched by every human love.

1940

Writing Assignments for "Lay Your Sleeping Head, My Love"

I. Brief Papers
  A. 1. Show that the action in the poem progresses from night until morning.
      2. Show that the poet values passion and physical love above other kinds of beauty or knowledge.

*Venus: Aphrodite, the goddess of physical love and passion.

3. Look up *ephemeral* in the dictionary. Find other references to *ephemeral* existence in the poem and explain how they emphasize the urgency of the couple's passion.

4. How is the hermit's ecstasy (line 20) different from the lovers'? What inspires it? Why does one occur among glaciers and rocks, one on Venus' slope?

5. How are lines 36–40 related to lines 25–30?

B. Argue for or against the assertion that the couple's relationship is an illicit one.

C. Read the poem aloud several times. As soon as you finish reading, write down your immediate emotional reactions. Does the poem make you feel sad? Happy? Uneasy? Passionate? Lonely? Several conflicting emotions? Find and discuss the phrase or image in the poem that contributes to your emotional response.

II. Longer Papers

A. Develop any one of the topics for brief papers into a full-length paper.

B. In a book of children's songs and verse, find several lullabies, or recall lullabies from your youth. In what ways is this poem a typical lullaby? In what way is it different?

C. In stanza 1, the speaker describes his lover as "Mortal, guilty, but . . . / . . . entirely beautiful" (lines 9, 10). In the last stanza, he suggests that the lover may "Find the mortal world enough" (line 36). How do these and other references to guilt, sacrifice, and the soul contribute to your understanding of the poem?

D. Argue for or against the assertion that the poem implies that passion is superior to any other experience.

ROBERT BROWNING

My Last Duchess

Ferrara*

That's my last Duchess painted on the wall,
Looking as if she were alive. I call
That piece a wonder, now: Frà Pandolf's hands†
Worked busily a day, and there she stands.
5   Will't please you sit and look at her? I said
"Frà Pandolf" by design, for never read

---

*Ferrara: Based loosely on the life of Alfonso II, Duke of Ferrara in Italy. Browning has the Duke speak in the poem. Alfonso's first wife, Lucrezia, a young girl, died in 1561 after three years of marriage.

†Frà Pandolf's hands: Brother Pandolf is an imaginary painter.

Strangers like you that pictured countenance,
The depth and passion of its earnest glance,
But to myself they turned (since none puts by
10   The curtain I have drawn for you, but I)
And seemed as they would ask me, if they durst,
How such a glance came there; so, not the first
Are you to turn and ask thus. Sir, 'twas not
Her husband's presence only, called that spot
15   Of joy into the Duchess' cheek: perhaps
Frà Pandolf chanced to say "Her mantle laps
Over my lady's wrist too much," or "Paint
Must never hope to reproduce the faint
Half-flush that dies along her throat": such stuff
20   Was courtesy, she thought, and cause enough
For calling up that spot of joy. She had
A heart—how shall I say?—too soon made glad,
Too easily impressed; she liked whate'er
She looked on, and her looks went everywhere.
25   Sir, 'twas all one! My favor at her breast,
The dropping of the daylight in the West,
The bough of cherries some officious fool
Broke in the orchard for her, the white mule
She rode with round the terrace—all and each
30   Would draw from her alike the approving speech,
Or blush, at least. She thanked men—good! but thanked
Somehow—I know not how—as if she ranked
My gift of a nine-hundred-years-old name
With anybody's gift. Who'd stoop to blame
35   This sort of trifling? Even had you skill
In speech—(which I have not)—to make your will
Quite clear to such an one, and say, "Just this
Or that in you disgusts me; here you miss,
Or there exceed the mark"—and if she let
40   Herself be lessoned so, nor plainly set
Her wits to yours, forsooth, and made excuse
—E'en then would be some stooping; and I choose
Never to stoop. Oh sir, she smiled, no doubt,
Whene'er I passed her; but who passed without
45   Much the same smile? This grew; I gave commands;
Then all smiles stopped together. There she stands
As if alive. Will't please you rise? We'll meet
The company below, then. I repeat,
The Count your master's known munificence
50   Is ample warrant that no just pretense

Of mine for dowry will be disallowed;
Though his fair daughter's self, as I avowed
At starting, is my object. Nay, we'll go
Together down, sir. Notice Neptune,* though,
55   Taming a sea horse, thought a rarity,
Which Claus of Innsbruck† cast in bronze for me¹

1842

Writing Assignments for "My Last Duchess"

I. Brief Papers
  A. 1. Show that the Duke is aware of class distinctions, while his duchess was not.
     2. Show that the Duchess was not only beautiful but good-natured.
     3. Why does the Duke keep the picture of his last duchess behind a curtain which no one except him draws?
     4. What is the dramatic situation of the poem? That is, what is happening? What is the setting? What business is being transacted? (Pay close attention to lines 47–53.)
     5. What evidence is there in the poem, both stated and implied, that, as the duke says, "I choose / Never to stoop" (lines 42–43)?
     6. In the last lines, the duke points out a bronze statue of Neptune taming a sea horse. Why does the duke like the piece? Why is it appropriate in the poem?

  B. Argue for or against one of the assertions below.
     1. There is evidence in the poem to explain the last duchess's death.
     2. A marriage between the duke and the Count's daughter will take place.
     3. The duke felt something more than sexual jealousy toward his wife.

  C. 1. Do you believe the duke is insane? Why or why not?
     2. How do you believe people should react to the duke's monologue? How does that affect your interpretation of the poem?

II. Longer Papers
  A. Explain why the duke chooses to tell the count's emissary about the last duchess.
  B. A writer achieves *dramatic irony* when readers learn more about the characters— through their words and actions—than the characters themselves realize or when readers perceive characters differently than they perceive themselves. Show that we learn more about the duke than he himself understands.

*Neptune: God of the sea.
†Claus of Innsbruck: Like Brother Pandolf, Claus of Innsbruck is an imaginary sculptor.

C. Pretend you are the duke's guest. Write a letter to your master, the count, advising him on his plans to betroth his daughter to the duke.

GEORGE MEREDITH

Sonnet 17 (At dinner, she is hostess, I am host)

At dinner, she is hostess, I am host.
Went the feast ever cheerfuller? She keeps
The Topic over intellectual deeps
In buoyancy afloat. They see no ghost.
5   With sparkling surface-eyes we ply the ball:
It is in truth a most contagious game:
HIDING THE SKELETON, shall be its name.
Such play as this the devils might appall!
But here's the greater wonder: in that we,
10   Enamored of an acting naught can tire,
Each other, like true hypocrites, admire;
Warm-lighted looks, Love's ephemeridae,*
Shoot gayly o'er the dishes and the wine.
We waken envy of our happy lot.
15   Fast, sweet, and golden, shows the marriage knot.
Dear guests, you now have seen Love's corpse-light† shine.

1862

Writing Assignments for "Sonnet 17 (At dinner, she is hostess, I am host)"

I. Brief Papers
   A. 1. Explain the game "hiding the skeleton." What is the couple really hiding?
      2. Show that the couple is very skillful at their game.
      3. Find all the references related to death in the poem and discuss their appropriateness.
      4. What is especially ironic or surprising about the couplet: "We waken envy of our happy lot. / Fast, sweet, and golden shows the marriage knot"?

   B. Argue for or against the assertion that the couple's game is more painful than fun.

*ephemeridae: Insects which live for only one day.
†corpse-light: A slang expression at the time for swamp light caused by gas in the marshes.

II. Longer Papers
  A. This poem comes from a series of poems entitled *Modern Love.* To what extent
     is the poem a realistic depiction of modern love and relationships?
  B. Discuss the speaker's attitude toward his guests, his wife, and their charade.
  C. Do you believe couples your age or couples your parents' age are more likely to
     behave like the couple in the poem? Can you generalize? Discuss how your belief
     affects your interpretation of the poem.

ROBERT FROST
The Hill Wife

LONELINESS

HER WORD

One ought not to have to care
  So much as you and I
Care when the birds come round the house
  To seem to say good-by;

5 Or care so much when they come back
  With whatever it is they sing;
The truth being we are as much
  Too glad for the one thing

As we are too sad for the other here—
10   With birds that fill their breasts
But with each other and themselves
  And their built or driven nests.

HOUSE FEAR

Always—I tell you this they learned—
Always at night when they returned
15 To the lonely house from far away
To lamps unlighted and fire gone gray,
They learned to rattle the lock and key
To give whatever might chance to be
Warning and time to be off in flight:
20 And preferring the out- to the in-door night,
They learned to leave the house-door wide
Until they had lit the lamp inside.

THE SMILE

HER WORD

I didn't like the way he went away.
That smile! It never came of being gay.
25   Still he smiled—did you see him?—I was sure!
Perhaps because we gave him only bread
And the wretch knew from that that we were poor.
Perhaps because he let us give instead
Of seizing from us as he might have seized.
30   Perhaps he mocked at us for being wed,
Or being very young (and he was pleased
To have a vision of us old and dead).
I wonder how far down the road he's got.
He's watching from the woods as like as not.

THE OFT-REPEATED DREAM

35   She had no saying dark enough
     For the dark pine that kept
Forever trying the window-latch
     Of the room where they slept.

The tireless but ineffectual hands
40   That with every futile pass
Made the great tree seem as a little bird
     Before the mystery of glass!

It never had been inside the room,
     And only one of the two
45   Was afraid in an oft-repeated dream
     Of what the tree might do.

THE IMPULSE

It was too lonely for her there,
     And too wild,
And since there were but two of them,
50   And no child,

And work was little in the house,
     She was free,
And followed where he furrowed field,
     Or felled tree.

55   She rested on a log and tossed
       The fresh chips,
   With a song only to herself
       On her lips.

   And once she went to break a bough
60   Of black alder.
   She strayed so far she scarcely heard
       When he called her—

   And didn't answer—didn't speak—
       Or return.
65   She stood, and then she ran and hid
       In the fern.

   He never found her, though he looked
       Everywhere,
   And he asked at her mother's house
70   Was she there.

   Sudden and swift and light as that
       The ties gave,
   And he learned of finalities
       Besides the grave.

                           1916

Writing Assignments for "The Hill Wife"

I. Brief Papers
   A. 1. Find evidence in the first four parts of the poem that the wife's fear is more
       extreme than her husband's.
     2. Describe the couple's life-style and home life, focusing on those details most
       pertinent to the wife's flight at the end of the poem.
     3. Explain how the word *ties* in the last stanza of part four, "The Impulse," means
       more than the couple's ties to one another.

   B. Argue for or against one of the assertions below.
     1. The husband is insensitive to the wife's fear.
     2. It is loneliness that drives the woman to flight in the last part of the poem.
     3. By the last part of the poem the hill wife is insane.

   C. 1. Is there evidence that the hill wife would have been a different kind of
       woman—less frightened, more happy—if she had lived in a village or town?
       Discuss.
     2. Do you believe the husband could have prevented his wife's flight? How does
       your belief affect your interpretation of the poem?

II. Longer Papers

A. Trace in detail the woman's paranoia from section to section in the poem. How does each section reveal a deepening, progressive irrationality?

B. Explain in detail how the poem shifts in point of view and perspective from part to part.

C. Discuss how someone's personal fears could affect how he or she interprets the poem.

D. Compare this poem to the short stories "A Jury of Her Peers" (p. 13) or "The Yellow Wall-Paper" (p. 111).

ELLEN BRYANT VOIGT

Farm Wife

Dark as the spring river, the earth
opens each damp row as the farmer
swings the far side of the field.
The blackbirds flash their red
5 wing patches and wheel in his wake,
down to the black dirt; the windmill
grinds in its chain rig and tower.

In the kitchen, his wife is baking.
She stands in the door in her long white
10 gloves of flour. She cocks her head and
tries to remember, turns like the moon
toward the sea-black field. Her belly
is rising, her apron fills like a sail.
She is gliding now, the windmill churns
15 beneath her, she passes the farmer,
the fine map of the furrows.
The neighbors point to the bone-white
spot in the sky.
               Let her float
like a flat gull that swoops and circles,
20 before her husband comes in for supper,
before her children grow up and leave her,
before the pulley cranks her down
the dark shaft, and the church blesses
her stone bed, and the earth seals
its black mouth like a scar.

                                        1973

Writing Assignments for "Farm Wife"

I. Brief Papers

A. 1. Show that the poem is set in spring and discuss why that is an appropriate setting.
   2. The poem relies for effect on a series of particularly vivid images or pictures. Choose one of the following kinds of imagery and discuss its appropriateness.
      a. Light colors associated with the wife
      b. Dark colors associated with the farmer and the earth
      c. Flight imagery associated with the wife
      d. Plowing or earthbound imagery associated with the farmer
   3. Discuss ways in which the first and last stanza are related.

B. Argue for or against either assertion below.
   1. The farm wife's revery or flight is an escape from an unhappy life.
   2. The farmer is presented unfavorably, perhaps even associated with death.

C. 1. What kinds of things do you think the farm wife "tries to remember" (line 11) as she turns to the field where her husband is plowing?
   2. Obviously the farm wife leads a traditional domestic life. She is pictured in the kitchen baking, and one can infer from the last stanza that she is devoted to her children. How does the woman's domestic role affect your response to the poem?
   3. Why does the farm wife "fly"? How do you believe her husband, her children, and her neighbors might react if she told them about herself and her reveries?

II. Longer Papers

A. Some stereotypes depict farm wives as loving wives and mothers, cheerful, energetic, and particularly wise from living in close contact with the seasons and the earth. Other stereotypes, however, are more negative, depicting farm wives as lonely, subservient women, starved for companionship, for beauty, for laughter. To what extent is the farm wife in this poem stereotypical? In what ways is she not?

B. Argue for or against the assertion that every element of the poem—its imagery, its structure, its language, its content—invites you to like and sympathize with the farm wife.

C. Go through the poem stanza by stanza. Notice which character is emphasized in which stanza. Note which colors or movements dominate in each stanza. Pay close attention to any key image—sound, color, or motion—repeated from one stanza to the next or how ideas or phrases are altered from one stanza to the next. Discuss the structure of the poem and show how it enriches the poem's meaning and affects your response to it.

D. Compare the farm wife in this poem with any wife or wives depicted in other poems or stories in this book.

ANNE SEXTON
You All Know the Story of the Other Woman

Before Reading

In a society where 50 percent of husbands and wives have extramarital affairs, one would expect that there would be few stereotypes of "the other woman," yet some persist. Write for 5 to 10 minutes about one or more of these stereotypes.

It's a little Walden.*
She is private in her breathbed
as his body takes off and flies,
flies straight as an arrow.
5   But it's a bad translation.
Daylight is nobody's friend.
God comes in like a landlord
and flashes on his brassy lamp.
Now she is just so-so.
10   He puts his bones back on,
turning the clock back an hour.
She knows flesh, that skin balloon
the unbound limbs, the boards,
the roof, the removable roof.
15   She is his selection, part time.
You know the story too! Look,
when it is over he places her,
like a phone, back on the hook.

1967

Writing Assignments for "You All Know the Story of the Other Woman"

I. Brief Papers
   A. 1. Discuss the other woman's role in her lover's life.
       2. Explain the relationship between "It's a little Walden" (line 1) and "But it's a bad translation" (line 5).
       3. Show that the relationship means more to the woman than it does to the man.

*Walden: Henry David Thoreau spent two years at Walden Pond in relative seclusion in order to find meaning and purpose in his life. His book, *Walden, Or Life in the Woods* (1854), recounts his experiences there.

4. Why does the poet fuse the woman's knowledge of her lover's flesh with her knowledge of the room (lines 12–14)?

B. Argue for or against either assertion below.
   1. The poet feels sympathy for the other woman.
   2. The reader learns very little about the other woman's feelings or attitudes in the poem.

C. 1. Discuss why you do or do not feel sympathy for the other woman in the poem.
   2. One recent study found that over 50 percent of married men and women have had an extramarital affair before age 40 (*Psychology Today,* July 1983). How does that statistic affect your interpretation of the poem?

II. Longer Papers
   A. The poem obviously relies on a number of stereotypes. Do you believe Sexton's portrayal of the other woman is an accurate, realistic, or believable one? Why or why not?
   B. Discuss Sexton's attitude toward her subject matter. Is the prevailing mood in the poem one of bitterness? Anger? Humor? Explain how she conveys that attitude.
   C. Argue for or against the assertion that in the poem the other woman is victimized by her relationship with the man.
   D. Discuss the poet's use of simile and metaphor. How does figurative language contribute to the impact of the poem?

ANNE SEXTON

For My Lover, Returning to His Wife

Before Reading

Free write for 5 to 10 minutes in response to the following question: "Do you believe a man or woman with children is less likely than one without children to leave a spouse for a lover?"

> She is all there.
> She was melted carefully down for you
> and cast up from your childhood,
> cast up from your one hundred favorite aggies.
>
> 5   She has always been there, my darling.
> She is, in fact, exquisite.
> Fireworks in the dull middle of February
> and as real as a cast-iron pot.

Let's face it, I have been momentary.
10   A luxury. A bright red sloop in the harbor.
My hair rising like smoke from the car window.
Littleneck clams out of season.

She is more than that. She is your have to have,
has grown you your practical your tropical growth.
15   This is not an experiment. She is all harmony.
She sees to oars and oarlocks for the dinghy,

has placed wild flowers at the window at breakfast,
sat by the potter's wheel at midday,
set forth three children under the moon,
20   three cherubs drawn by Michelangelo,

done this with her legs spread out
in the terrible months in the chapel.
If you glance up, the children are there
like delicate balloons resting on the ceiling.

25   She has also carried each one down the hall
after supper, their heads privately bent,
two legs protesting, person to person,
her face flushed with a song and their little sleep.

I give you back your heart.
30   I give you permission—

for the fuse inside her, throbbing
angrily in the dirt, for the bitch in her
and the burying of her wound—
for the burying of her small red wound alive—

35   for the pale flickering flare under her ribs,
for the drunken sailor who waits in her left pulse,
for the mother's knee, for the stockings,
for the garter belt, for the call—

the curious call
40   when you will burrow in arms and breasts
and tug at the orange ribbon in her hair
and answer the call, the curious call.

She is so naked and singular.
She is the sum of yourself and your dream.

45 Climb her like a monument, step after step.
    She is solid.

    As for me, I am a watercolor.
    I wash off.

                                          1967

Writing Assignments for "For My Lover, Returning to His Wife"

I. Brief Papers
   A. 1. Choose one of the following comparisons and explain what it implies about
         the man's wife or his attitude toward her:
         a. "She was melted carefully down for you
            and cast up from your childhood,
            cast up from your one hundred favorite aggies" (lines 2–4)
         b. "[She is] Fireworks in the dull middle of February
            and as real as a cast-iron pot" (lines 7–8)
         c. "She is the sum of yourself and your dream.
            Climb her like a monument, step after step" (lines 44–45)
      2. Discuss the different implications of *there* in "She is all there" (line 1) and "She
         has always been there" (line 5).
      3. Why is the wife more like an artist, more like Michelangelo specifically, than
         the speaker, who claims, "I am a watercolor" (line 47)?
      4. How is the speaker's description of her lover's wife more negative in stanzas
         8 through 11 than in any other part of the poem?

   B. Argue for or against one of the assertions below.
      1. The speaker's description of the wife is more positive than negative.
      2. When the speaker gives her lover permission to make love to his wife, she is
         really admitting defeat, accepting the end of the affair.
      3. When the speaker gives her lover permission to make love to his wife, she
         hopes he will not accept.
      4. The speaker does not feel bitterness but some other emotion toward the wife.

   C. Do you feel sympathy for the speaker in the poem? Why or why not?

II. Longer Papers
   A. Using this poem or both this poem and "You All Know the Story of the Other
      Woman" (p. 738), discuss Sexton's depiction of extramarital affairs—why people
      have them, how people feel and behave during affairs, and what consequences
      the affairs have.
   B. In "You All Know the Story of the Other Woman" (p. 738) as well as in this poem,
      Sexton relies on a series of stereotypes—all suggesting the impermanence of an

extramarital love affair. Using examples from one or from both of these poems, discuss the negative stereotypes associated with such relationships. Try to assess to what extent the stereotypes reflect real relationships.

C. Discuss Sexton's use of simile and metaphor in this poem and in "You All Know the Story of the Other Woman." How does the figurative language contribute to the impact of the poem?

ADRIENNE RICH

Trying to Talk with a Man

Out in this desert we are testing bombs,

that's why we came here.

Sometimes I feel an underground river
forcing its way between deformed cliffs
5   an acute angle of understanding
moving itself like a locus of the sun
into this condemned scenery.

What we've had to give up to get here—
whole LP collections, films we starred in
10   playing in the neighborhoods, bakery windows
full of dry, chocolate-filled Jewish cookies,
the language of love-letters, of suicide notes,
afternoons on the riverbank
pretending to be children

15   Coming out to this desert
we meant to change the face of
driving among dull green succulents
walking at noon in the ghost town
surrounded by a silence

20   that sounds like the silence of the place
except that it came with us
and is familiar
and everything we were saying until now
was an effort to blot it out—

25   coming out here we are up against it
Out here I feel more helpless
with you than without you

You mention the danger
and list the equipment
30   we talk of people caring for each other
in emergencies—laceration, thirst—
but you look at me like an emergency

Your dry heat feels like power
your eyes are stars of a different magnitude
35   they reflect lights that spell out: EXIT
when you get up and pace the floor

talking of the danger
as if it were not ourselves
as if we were testing anything else.

1971

Writing Assignments for "Trying to Talk with a Man"

I. Brief Papers

A. 1. What is the dramatic setting of the poem? That is, where is it set, what is happening, and who is involved?

2. Show that the couple's relationship is in serious trouble.

3. From direct evidence in the poem and from what you can infer, describe the couple's past relationship. In what ways have they had "to give up" (line 8) that relationship to reach where they are?

4. In what way is the couple "testing bombs" (line 1)? Why is the comparison or metaphor appropriate?

5. Go through the poem and circle all the words and images related to dryness, aridity, thirst, or heat. Why are they appropriate in the poem?

B. Argue for or against either assertion below.

1. The man does not realize the significance of their trip or the gravity of their problems.

2. The reader feels greater sympathy for the speaker than for the man to whom she speaks.

C. Do you believe the couple's relationship is beyond repair, or do you believe they will or should reconcile their differences? Why or why not?

II. Longer Papers

A. Discuss as fully as possible how the poet sustains the comparison between testing bombs and the couple's efforts to communicate throughout the poem. Include, if you like, where bombs are tested, why they are tested, the immediate and long-range results of their testing, or whatever topic seems appropriate.

B. Find one other Rich poem in this book and compare it to this one, discussing one or more of the following topics: the speaker's or poet's attitude toward her topic; the role of women in the poems; the role of men in the poems; the images of heat, fire, dryness, or silence in the poems; or any other topic you deem appropriate.

ROBERT LOWELL

"To Speak of Woe That Is in Marriage"*

> "It is the future generation that presses into being by means of these exuberant feelings and supersensible soap bubbles of ours."
>
> Schopenhauer†

"The hot night makes us keep our bedroom windows open.
Our magnolia blossoms. Life begins to happen.
My hopped up husband drops his home disputes,
and hits the streets to cruise for prostitutes,
5   free-lancing out along the razor's edge.
This screwball might kill his wife, then take the pledge.
Oh the monotonous meanness of his lust. . . .
It's the injustice . . . he is so unjust—
whiskey-blind, swaggering home at five.
10   My only thought is how to keep alive.
What makes him tick? Each night now I tie
ten dollars and his car key to my thigh. . . .
Gored by the climacteric of his want,
he stalls above me like an elephant."

1958

Writing Assignments for " 'To Speak of Woe That Is in Marriage' "

I. Brief Papers

A. 1. Show that the wife has mixed feelings about her husband.
  2. Describe the couple's relationship. Upon what is it based? Why do they stay together?
  3. What is the relationship between the Schopenhauer epigraph and the poem? Upon what "exuberant feelings" is the poem based?

---

*"To Speak of Woe . . .": The title is a line taken from Chaucer's tale of the Wife of Bath. She speaks the line as she begins to chronicle her embattled relationships with five different husbands.
†Schopenhauer: German philosopher (1788–1860).

4. Find one humorous reference, line, or image in the poem and explain it.

5. Why is the poem set during hot summer nights?

B. Argue for or against either assertion below.

1. The woman in the poem is victimized by her husband.

2. The wife feels lust for her husband.

C. 1. Do you believe the speaker ties the ten dollars and the car key to her thigh to entice her husband, to appease his lust, to satisfy her own lust, or for other reasons? Discuss.

2. Passionate love is often akin in intensity to passionate hate. And sex itself can become an act of violence, domination, or brutality. Explain to what extent the couple in the poem display such a love/hate relationship.

3. Choose one or two lines from the poem you have particular trouble understanding. Set your clock or watch for 10 minutes. During that 10 minutes free write as much about that passage of the poem as possible. Do not worry about grammar, spelling, or even writing complete sentences. Just try to get as much on paper about the difficult line(s) as you can. Once you complete your free writing, look it over carefully. Did you discover something about the line or lines you had not noticed? Use the free writing as the basis for a personal response paper.

II. Longer Papers

A. You are a psychologist who has spoken recently with the wife in the poem. She has explained her feelings about her husband, his behavior and hers, and their relationship. Write a short case report for your files, summarizing the pertinent points and analyzing why they behave as they do. If you think it appropriate, prescribe whatever counseling or treatment either or both of them need.

B. Discuss to what extent this poem and/or other poems in this unit imply that marriage is as likely to cause woe as joy.

C. Read the poem aloud several times and go through the poem paying attention to the punctuation and the rhyme scheme. How does the poet use punctuation and rhyme to achieve a conversational quality and to establish a clear tone or voice in the poem?

D. Go to the library and find a translation of Chaucer's *Canterbury Tales*. Carefully read the Wife of Bath's description in the "Prologue" and "The Wife of Bath's Tale," paying attention to her attitude toward men and her philosophy of marriage. Discuss in detail how the poem and "The Wife of Bath's Tale" are related.

SYLVIA PLATH

The Applicant

Before Reading

Free write for 5 to 10 minutes about your ideal mate. What would he or she be like?

First, are you our sort of a person?
Do you wear
A glass eye, false teeth or a crutch,
A brace or a hook,
5   Rubber breasts or a rubber crotch,

Stitches to show something's missing? No, no? Then
How can we give you a thing?
Stop crying.
Open your hand.
10   Empty? Empty. Here is a hand

To fill it and willing
To bring teacups and roll away headaches
And do whatever you tell it.
Will you marry it?
15   It is guaranteed

To thumb shut your eyes at the end
And dissolve of sorrow.
We make new stock from the salt.
I notice you are stark naked.
20   How about this suit—

Black and stiff, but not a bad fit.
Will you marry it?
It is waterproof, shatterproof, proof
Against fire and bombs through the roof.
25   Believe me, they'll bury you in it.

Now your head, excuse me, is empty.
I have the ticket for that.
Come here, sweetie, out of the closet.
Well, what do you think of *that?*
30   *Naked as paper to start*

But in twenty-five years she'll be silver,
In fifty, gold.
A living doll, everywhere you look.
It can sew, it can cook,
35 *It can talk, talk, talk.*

It works, there is nothing wrong with it.
You have a hole, it's a poultice.
You have an eye, it's an image.
My boy, it's your last resort.
40 *Will you marry it, marry it, marry it.*

1962

Writing Assignments for "The Applicant"

I. Brief Papers

   A. 1. Show that the poem makes numerous allusions to traditional marriage customs.
      2. Spend 10 minutes free writing about the first seven lines of the poem. How do the lines relate to the subject of marriage?
      3. Take any part of the poem you find humorous and explain why.

   B. Argue for or against either assertion below.
      1. The poem is more insulting to men than to women.
      2. Most men, if they were honest, would find the wife described in the poem appealing.

   C. 1. How would you characterize the humor in the poem?
      2. In your opinion, how would a good spouse resemble the one in the poem? Differ?

II. Longer Papers

   A. The women's movement has been described by some as basically humorless. In what ways would this poem support or refute that claim?
   B. Characterize the nature of marital relationships described in this poem and in one or more of the following: Margaret Atwood's "Against Still Life" (p. 577); Robert Lowell's "To Speak of Woe That Is in Marriage" (p. 744); and/or George Meredith's "Sonnet 17 (At dinner she is hostess, I am host)" (p. 732).

JAMES DICKEY

Adultery

We have all been in rooms
We cannot die in, and they are odd places, and sad.
Often Indians are standing eagle-armed on hills

In the sunrise   open wide to the Great Spirit
5 Or gliding in canoes   or cattle are browsing on the walls
Far away   gazing down with the eyes of our children

Not far away   or there are men driving
The last railspike, which has turned
Gold in their hands. Gigantic forepleasure lives

10 Among such scenes, and we are alone with it
At last. There is always some weeping
Between us   and someone is always checking

A wrist watch by the bed to see how much
Longer we have left. Nothing can come
15 Of this   nothing can come

Of us: of me with my grim techniques
Or you who have sealed your womb
With a ring of convulsive rubber:

Although we come together,
20 Nothing will come of us. But we would not give
It up, for death is beaten

By praying Indians   by distant cows   historical
Hammers   by hazardous meetings that bridge
A continent. One could never die here

25 Never die   never die
While crying. My lover, my dear one
I will see you next week

When I'm in town. I will call you
If I can, Please get hold of   please don't
30 Oh God, Please don't any more I can't bear . . . Listen:

We have done it again   we are
Still living. Sit up and smile,
God bless you. Guilt is magical.

1961

Writing Assignments for "Adultery"

I. Brief Papers

A. 1. List all of the connotations you can think of for the word *adultery*. Which connotations agree with and which disagree with the connotations of *adultery* in the poem?

2. Describe how and why the pictures described in stanzas 1–3 are different in stanza 8.

3. How does the poet use *to die* both literally and figuratively in the poem?

4. In what ways is guilt magical?

B. Argue for or against one of the assertions below.

1. The poet believes adultery is wrong yet inescapably human.

2. The poet believes the couple's relationship in the poem is healthy.

3. The couple's affair is kept alive more by the risks they must take than by their love for each other.

C. If their marriage were feasible, do you believe the speaker would wish to marry his lover? Why or why not?

II. Longer Papers

A. Most couples who wed assume they will remain faithful to one another. Still, fairly large numbers become involved with others and have extramarital relationships. Using evidence from this poem, from other poems in the unit, and from your own observations, discuss why so many people are drawn to such relationships.

B. Do you believe your parents or someone your parents' age would react differently to this poem than you do? Why do you believe you share different or similar responses?

W. D. SNODGRASS

Leaving the Motel

Outside, the last kids holler
Near the pool: they'll stay the night.
Pick up the towels; fold your collar
Out of sight.

5   Check: is the second bed
     Unrumpled, as agreed?
     Landlords have to think ahead
     In case of need,

     Too. Keep things straight: don't take
10   The matches, the wrong keyrings—
     We've nowhere we could keep a keepsake—
     Ashtrays, combs, things

     That sooner or later others
     Would accidentally find.
15   Check: take nothing of one another's
     And leave behind

     Your license number only,
     Which they won't care to trace;
     We've paid. Still, should such things get lonely,
20   Leave in their vase

     An aspirin to preserve
     Our lilacs, the wayside flowers
     We've gathered and must leave to serve
     A few more hours;

25   That's all. We can't tell when
     We'll come back, can't press claims;
     We would no doubt have other rooms then,
     Or other names.

                                                        1968

Writing Assignments for "Leaving the Motel"

I. Brief Papers
   A. 1. What evidence is there that the couple leaving the motel are not married to
         each other?
      2. Explain how one of the following lines sheds light on the couple's relationship:
         a. "Landlords have to think ahead
            In case of need,
            Too."
            (lines 7–9)
         b. "That's all. We can't tell when
            We'll come back, can't press claims"
            (lines 24–25)
      3. Show that the couple in the poem care about other people's feelings.

B. Argue for or against either assertion below.
   1. While the poem appears to be a methodical list, it's a tender love poem.
   2. The poem depicts an adulterous affair favorably.

C. 1. What is your chief emotional reaction to the poem? Why do you feel as you do?
   2. If the poem had concluded with stanza 5, before the reference to the flowers, would your reaction to the poem be different? Why or why not?

II. Longer Papers

A. Discuss as fully as possible how the couple's actions and their ritual checklist show us a great deal about the kind of people they are and about their feelings for one another.
B. Go through the poem circling all punctuation and paying attention to the poem's structure. How do both show the couple's hesitancy, as well as their compulsion, to leave? How do both enhance the poem's meaning and your response to it?
C. Compare the poet's attitude toward adultery in this poem to James Dickey's attitude toward his subject in "Adultery" (p. 748).
D. Discuss the predominant mood of the poem. How does the poet achieve it?

EMILY DICKINSON

The Soul Selects Her Own Society

The Soul selects her own Society—
Then—shuts the Door—
To her divine Majority—
Present no more—

5 Unmoved—she notes the Chariots—pausing—
at her low Gate—
Unmoved—an Emperor be kneeling
Upon her Mat—

I've known her—from an ample nation—
10 Choose One—
Then—close the Valves of her attention—
Like Stone—

1890*

---

*1890: First publication date, four years after Dickinson's death in 1886. The date conjectured for the earliest known manuscript of the poem is 1862.

Writing Assignments for "The Soul Selects Her Own Society"

I. Brief Papers
A. 1. Paraphrase the poem in your own words. What is the poet saying?
   2. Trace the door imagery throughout the poem. How does it help unify the poem and why is it especially appropriate?
   3. In what ways is this a poem about love?
   4. Discuss how the speaker distinguishes herself from the soul. How does that distinction reinforce the poem's implications?

B. Argue for or against either assertion below.
   1. The compactness of the poem contributes to its intensity.
   2. The last stanza of the poem is more personal than the first two.

C. 1. Why do you think the poet says "The *Soul* selects her own Society," instead of "The *Heart* selects her own Society"? In what ways would the poem be different if the poet had chosen the latter? Would the poem be as effective?

II. Longer Papers
A. Explain how the images in the poem, as short as it is, are especially rich, striking, and appropriate.
B. Show how the length of the lines, the dashes, and the structure, especially in the last stanza, reinforce the finality of the soul's selection.
C. Discuss in detail how the poet implies our powerlessness over the soul's domination.

MONA VAN DUYN

Late Loving

> "What Christ was saying, what he meant [in the story of Mary and Martha] was that the pleasures of that hair, that ointment, must be taken. Because the accidents of death would deprive us soon enough. We must not deprive ourselves, our loved ones, of the luxury of our extravagant affections. We must not try to second-guess death by refusing to love the ones we loved. . . ."
>
> Mary Gordon, *Final Payments*

If in my mind I marry you every year
it is to calm an extravagance of love
with dousing custom, for it flames up fierce
and wild whenever I forget that we live

5   in double rooms whose temperature's controlled
by matrimony's turned-down thermostat.
I need the mnemonics, now that we are old,
of oath and law in re-memorizing that.
Our dogs are dead, our child never came true.
10 I might use up, in my weak-mindedness,
the whole human supply of warmth on you
before I could think of others and digress.
"Love" is finding the familiar dear.
"In love" is to be taken by surprise.
15 Over, in the shifty face you wear,
and over, in the assessments of your eyes,
you change, and with new sweet or barbed word
find out new entrances to my inmost nerve.
When you stand at the stove it's I who am most stirred.
20 When you finish work I rest without reserve.
Daytimes, sometimes, our three-legged race seems slow.
Squabbling onward, we chafe from being so near.
But all night long we lie like crescents of Velcro,
turning together till we re-adhere.
25 Since you, with longer stride and better vision,
more clearly see the finish line, I stoke
my hurrying self, to keep it in condition,
with light and life-renouncing meals of smoke.
As when a collector scoops two Monarchs in
30 at once, whose fresh flights to and from each other
are netted down, so in vows I re-imagine
I re-invoke what keeps us stale together.
What you try to give is more than I want to receive,
yet each month when you pick up scissors for our appointment
35 and my cut hair falls and covers your feet I believe
that the house is filled again with the odor of ointment.

Writing Assignments for "Late Loving"

I. Brief Papers
    A. 1. Show that the couple in the poem have been together a long time.
       2. Explain what the speaker means by " 'love' is finding the familiar dear. / 'In love' is to be taken by surprise" (lines 13–14).
       3. Show that at times the couple's relationship is very difficult.
       4. What is the relationship between the poem's epigraph and the first six lines of the poem?
       5. Trace images of fire, heat, and warmth throughout the poem, and discuss how any one of the images is particularly appropriate.

B. Argue for or against either assertion below.
   1. The woman in the poem denies herself a fully satisfying marriage when she calms "an extravagance of love / with dousing custom" (lines 2–3).
   2. The marriage depicted in the poem is probably happier than most.

C. 1. The speaker in the poem admits that she tries to "re-imagine" or "re-invoke what keeps us stale together" (lines 32–33). What do you think she means?
   2. Would you like a marriage such as the one described in the poem? Why or why not?

II. Longer Papers
A. A paradox is an assertion or idea that seems contradictory or opposed to common sense yet is perhaps true. Using that definition, explain how the speaker's love for her husband is paradoxical.
B. Compare this poem to any other poem in this unit, focusing on how the marriages are depicted, how the couple feel about one another, how relatively happy the relationships are, or on any aspect you think important.
C. Explain in detail how the epigraph relates to the body of the poem.
D. Show how the poet uses images of heat, fire, and warmth throughout the poem.

Comparative Papers from Chapter Five: Husbands, Wives, and Lovers

A. Many contemporary films imply that love is a destructive, even a subversive force, undermining the stability and the sanity of our lives. To what extent do poems in this unit support that notion? Contradict it?
B. Argue for or against the assertion that love and the desire to marry are inspired by emotions that remain universal and unchanging. Use evidence from one or more poems in this unit to support your claims.
C. Argue for or against the assertion that belief in monogamy is outdated, given contemporary mores and values, and that such belief may even contribute to unhealthy guilt and stagnant, unfulfilling relationships.
D. Write a paper showing how two or more poets from different centuries treat the same subject matter. Possible topics include intense passion and devotion, betrayal and adultery, companionship and friendship, or couples' attitudes toward one another and toward their relationship.
E. Explore the implications of one of the following quotes about love, marriage, and relationships. Use poems in this unit to illustrate and support your assertions:
   1. "Getting to know someone, entering that new world, is an ultimate, irretrievable leap into the unknown. The prospect is terrifying. The stakes are high. The emotions are overwhelming. In human experience, only the perennial themes can move us to such an extent. Death. Birth. The Grave. Love. Hate" (Eldridge Cleaver, "Prelude to Love—Three Letters," 1965).

2. "A friend is someone I can be myself with; with a lover, I'm all too often someone else, someone I'd rather be" (Susan Lee, "Friendship, Feminism, and Betrayal," 1975).

3. "Young men have strong passions, and tend to gratify them indiscriminately. Of the bodily desires, it is the sexual by which they are most swayed and in which they show absence of self-control. They are changeable and fickle in their desires, which are violent while they last, but quickly over . . ." (Aristotle, *Rhetoric*).

F. You have been invited to address a sociology class on how marital relationships are depicted in contemporary poetry. Use three or four poems from this unit to write your speech.

G. Choose the one poem in the unit that portrays love and/or marriage as you most wish it could be. Describe that ideal relationship, its depiction in the poem, and discuss to what extent one can realistically expect to experience such a love.

H. Discuss two or more poems in the unit which you believe are significant, enduring poems. What singles them out above others?

SAMUEL TAYLOR COLERIDGE

Frost at Midnight

The Frost performs its secret ministry,
Unhelped by any wind. The owlet's cry
Came loud—and hark, again! loud as before.
The inmates of my cottage, all at rest,
5 Have left me to that solitude, which suits
Abstruser musings: save that at my side
My cradled infant slumbers peacefully.
'Tis calm indeed! so calm, that it disturbs
And vexes meditation with its strange
10 And extreme silentness. Sea, hill, and wood,
This populous village! Sea, and hill, and wood,
With all the numberless goings-on of life,
Inaudible as dreams! the thin blue flame
Lies on my low-burnt fire, and quivers not;
15 Only that film, which fluttered on the grate,
Still flutters there, the sole unquiet thing.
Methinks its motion in this hush of nature
Gives it dim sympathies with me who live,
Making it a companionable form,
20 Whose puny flaps and freaks the idling Spirit
By its own moods interprets, everywhere
Echo or mirror seeking of itself,
And makes a toy of Thought.
                         But O! how oft,
How oft, at school, with most believing mind,
25 Presageful, have I gazed upon the bars,
To watch that fluttering *stranger!* and as oft
With unclosed lids, already had I dreamt
Of my sweet birthplace, and the old church tower,
Whose bells, the poor man's only music, rang
30 From morn to evening, all the hot fair-day,
So sweetly, that they stirred and haunted me
With a wild pleasure, falling on mine ear
Most like articulate sounds of things to come!
So gazed I, till the soothing things, I dreamt,

35   Lulled me to sleep, and sleep prolonged my dreams!
      And so I brooded all the following morn,
      Awed by the stern preceptor's face, mine eye
      Fixed with mock study on my swimming book:
      Save if the door half opened, and I snatched
40   A hasty glance, and still my heart leaped up,
      For still I hoped to see the *stranger's* face,
      Townsman, or aunt, or sister more beloved,
      My playmate when we both were clothed alike!

      Dear Babe, that sleepest cradled by my side,
45   Whose gentle breathings, heard in this deep calm,
      Fill up the interspersèd vacancies
      And momentary pauses of the thought!
      My babe so beautiful! it thrills my heart
      With tender gladness, thus to look at thee,
50   And think that thou shalt learn far other lore,
      And in far other scenes! For I was reared
      In the great city, pent 'mid cloisters dim,
      And saw nought lovely but the sky and stars.
      But *thou,* my babe! shalt wander like a breeze
55   By lakes and sandy shores, beneath the crags
      Of ancient mountain, and beneath the clouds,
      Which image in their bulk both lakes and shores
      And mountain crags: so shalt thou see and hear
      The lovely shapes and sounds intelligible
60   Of that eternal language, which thy God
      Utters, who from eternity doth teach
      Himself in all, and all things in himself.
      Great universal Teacher! he shall mold
      Thy spirit, and by giving make it ask.

65   Therefore all seasons shall be sweet to thee,
      Whether the summer clothe the general earth
      With greenness, or the redbreast sit and sing
      Betwixt the tufts of snow on the bare branch
      Of mossy apple tree, while the nigh thatch
70   Smokes in the sun-thaw; whether the eave-drops fall
      Heard only in the trances of the blast,
      Or if the secret ministry of frost
      Shall hang them up in silent icicles,
      Quietly shining to the quiet Moon.

1798

Writing Assignments for "Frost at Midnight"

I. Brief Papers
- A. 1. Describe the dramatic setting of the poem.
  2. After rereading the first seven lines of the poem, explain how the references to the frost, the owl, the solitude, and the sleeping baby contribute to the mood of the poem.
  3. Explain one way the speaker's recollections of his past (lines 24–42) are linked to his hopes for the baby's future (lines 44–64).
  4. Reread lines 54–64. Summarize in your own words the kind of relationship with nature and with the world the speaker hopes the baby will have.
  5. In lines 65–74, the speaker paints the kind of natural world in which he hopes the baby will grow. How does he romanticize the world, softening the harsher elements, making it an appealing place?

- B. Argue for or against either assertion below.
  1. The speaker's dreams for the baby are the same dreams most parents today have for their children.
  2. It is implied in the poem—through the speaker's attitude toward the child, through the description of nature—that the speaker has had an unhappy life.

- C. 1. Do you believe the speaker's hopes and plans for the baby are realistic? Why or why not? How does your reaction to those hopes affect your interpretation of the poem?
  2. Why do you believe the poem begins and ends with images of frost? How do those opening and closing passages affect your response to the poem?

II. Longer Papers
- A. Discuss how and why the description of nature at the end of the poem (lines 65–74) is different from the description of nature at the beginning.
- B. Go through the poem and find phrases, lines, or passages in which the language— the word choice, the repetition of sounds or letters, the rhythms, or the lengths of lines—reinforces the contemplative mood of the poem.
- C. Guided by the natural breaks in the text, discuss the structure of the poem.

WILLIAM BUTLER YEATS
*A Prayer for My Daughter**

Before Reading

Free write for 5 to 10 minutes in response to the following question: "If you had a baby daughter, what would you pray for her?"

> Once more the storm is howling, and half hid
> Under this cradle-hood and coverlid
> My child sleeps on. There is no obstacle
> But Gregory's wood and one bare hill
> 5 Whereby the haystack- and roof-levelling wind,
> Bred on the Atlantic, can be stayed;
> And for an hour I have walked and prayed
> Because of the great gloom that is in my mind.
>
> I have walked and prayed for this young child an hour
> 10 And heard the sea-wind scream upon the tower,
> And under the arches of the bridge, and scream
> In the elms above the flooded stream;
> Imagining in excited reverie
> That the future years had come,
> 15 Dancing to a frenzied drum,
> Out of the murderous innocence of the sea.
>
> May she be granted beauty and yet not
> Beauty to make a stranger's eye distraught,
> Or hers before a looking-glass, for such,
> 20 Being made beautiful overmuch,
> Consider beauty a sufficient end,
> Lose natural kindness and maybe
> The heart-revealing intimacy
> That chooses right, and never find a friend.
>
> 25 Helen† being chosen found life flat and dull
> And later had much trouble from a fool,‡
> While that great Queen,§ that rose out of the spray,

*Title: Yeats's daughter, Anne Butler, was born February 26, 1919.
†Helen: Helen of Troy whose beauty inspired Paris' love. When he stole her from her husband, the act triggered the Trojan War.
‡fool: Paris, Helen of Troy's lover.
§great Queen: Venus, goddess of love, is depicted by Botticelli, a fifteenth-century Italian painter, as rising from the sea.

Being fatherless could have her way
Yet chose a bandy-legged smith for man.*
30 It's certain that fine women eat
A crazy salad with their meat
Whereby the Horn of Plenty† is undone.

In courtesy I'd have her chiefly learned;
Hearts are not had as a gift but hearts are earned
35 By those that are not entirely beautiful;
Yet many, that have played the fool
For beauty's very self, has charm made wise,
And many a poor man that has roved,
Loved and thought himself beloved,
40 From a glad kindness cannot take his eyes.

May she become a flourishing hidden tree
That all her thoughts may like the linnet be,
And have no business but dispensing round
Their magnanimities of sound,
45 Nor but in merriment begin a chase,
Nor but in merriment a quarrel.
O may she live like some green laurel
Rooted in one dear perpetual place.

My mind, because the minds that I have loved,
50 The sort of beauty that I have approved,
Prosper but little, has dried up of late,
Yet knows that to be choked with hate
May well be of all evil chances chief.
If there's no hatred in a mind
55 Assault and battery of the wind
Can never tear the linnet from the leaf.

An intellectual hatred is the worst,
So let her think opinions are accursed.
Have I not seen the loveliest woman born
60 Out of the mouth of Plenty's horn,
Because of her opinionated mind
Barter that horn and every good
By quiet natures understood
For an old bellows full of angry wind?

*bandy-legged smith: Vulcan, god of fire, often depicted as squat and "bandy-legged." Husband of Venus.
†Horn of Plenty: The symbol of not only the good life but also the life of order, serenity, and custom. See lines 73–80.

65 Considering that, all hatred driven hence,
    The soul recovers radical innocence
    And learns at last that it is self-delighting,
    Self-appeasing, self-affrighting,
    And that its own sweet will is Heaven's will;
70 She can, though every face should scowl
    And every windy quarter howl
    Or every bellows burst, be happy still.

    And may her bridegroom bring her to a house
    Where all's accustomed, ceremonious;
75 For arrogance and hatred are the wares
    Peddled in the thoroughfares.
    How but in custom and in ceremony
    Are innocence and beauty born?
    Ceremony's a name for the rich horn,
80 And custom for the spreading laurel tree.

                                                    1919

Writing Assignments for "A Prayer for My Daughter"

I. Brief Papers
   A. 1. Describe the dramatic setting of the poem, concentrating on the description
         in the first two stanzas.
      2. Explain how the poet's diction—his choice of words—in the first two stanzas
         reinforces his state of mind.
      3. Basing your discussion primarily on stanzas 3 and 5, explain the kind of beauty
         the speaker wishes for his daughter.
      4. Explain why Yeats includes references to both Helen and Venus in stanzas 4.
         How do those references help link that stanza to the stanzas directly preced-
         ing and directly following it?

   B. Argue for or against either assertion below.
      1. The father's bitterness, especially evident in stanza 8, causes you to doubt the
         wisdom of his prayer.
      2. The father's hopes for his daughter are outdated.

   C. 1. Basing your discussion primarily on stanzas 7 and 8 (lines 49–64), discuss
         what inspires the speaker to believe that "opinions are accursed" (line 58) and
         explain how that belief colors your reaction to his prayer.
      2. To what extent do you agree with the father's prayer for his daughter? Do you
         believe he should wish for what he does?

II. Longer Papers

A. The speaker refers to three women in the poem—Helen (line 25), "that great Queen" (line 27), and "the loveliest woman born" (line 59). How do those references illustrate the father's attitude and how do they help you understand what he desires for his daughter?

B. Explain how the last two stanzas of the poem relate directly to the first two. You might discuss how the father's trust in custom and ceremony relates to the chaos he describes in the first two stanzas, how diction or word choice link the first two and last two stanzas, or how any elements of the poem are clearly linked in the beginning and ending stanzas.

C. Argue for or against the assertion that the father's prayer for his daughter is unrealistic, that the kind of beauty, intellectuality, and spirit he wishes for her are impossible to achieve.

D. After reading the exercises on rhyme and half-rhyme following this poem, write a paper discussing the use of half-rhyme in the poem, showing how it reinforces the father's attitude and how it enhances the impact of the poem.

III. Rhyme and Half-Rhyme

The purpose of this exercise is to introduce you to *rhyme*, one device poets use to create musical effect in their poetry. After reading "Rhyme and Half-Rhyme" below, write a paper which defines *rhyme*. Although you may wish to practice specific constructions you have learned throughout this book, you are free to form your essay in any way you like, so long as it is graceful and effective. (Note: All of the examples of rhyming words in this exercise come from William Butler Yeats' poem, "A Prayer for My Daughter," p. 759)

A. 1. *Come/drum, born/horn,* and *way/spray* are rhymes.
   2. The rhymes are sometimes called *true* rhymes or *perfect* rhymes.
B. 1. Rhymes are "true" or "perfect" if they meet three criteria:
   2. The initial consonant sounds are different.
   3. The final consonant sounds are the same.
   4. The vowel sounds within the words are the same.
C. 1. *Way/spray* and *be/tree* do not end in consonant sounds.
   2. The words are still true rhymes.
   3. They meet the other two criteria.
D. 1. *Slant rhyme* differs from true rhyme.
   2. The difference occurs when the vowel sounds within the words are different.
   3. Or, the difference occurs when the final consonant sounds are different.
E. 1. *Dull* and *fool* constitute a slant rhyme.
   2. The final consonant sounds are the same.
   3. The vowel sounds are different in the words.
F. 1. Yeats writes, "It's certain that fine women *eat* / A crazy salad with their *meat*" (lines 30–31).

2. The rhyme is a *true* rhyme.

3. The rhyme is an *end* rhyme.

G. 1. *End rhymes* occur in a place.

2. The place is at the end of lines of verse.

3. The place is the most common for all rhymes.

H. 1. Some rhymes are different from end rhymes.

2. The rhyming words occur within the same line.

3. Such rhymes are *internal rhymes.*

I. 1. Yeats might have said this.

2. "It's certain that fine women *eat* a crazy salad with their *meat.*"

3. He would place the rhyming *eat/meat* in one line.

4. He would illustrate internal rhyme.

J. 1. Most contemporary poets avoid internal rhymes.

2. The internal rhymes produce a sound.

3. The internal rhymes sound too jingly.

4. The internal rhymes sound too childish.

K. 1. Rhyme serves a function in poetry.

2. The function is to invite pleasure and gratification.

3. The pleasure is through the senses.

4. The gratification is through the senses.

L. 1. Poets create regular patterns of rhyme.

2. The patterns are harmonious.

3. The patterns establish the form of the stanza and poem.

M. 1. True rhyme reassures the reader.

2. The reassurance is through the harmonious pattern of rhyme.

3. The reassurance comes from the reader's reliance on predictable patterns.

N. 1. Slant rhyme affects readers differently from true rhyme.

2. It leaves readers more uneasy.

3. The uneasiness is due to the discordant sounds.

4. The uneasiness is due to the unpredictable sounds.

RICHARD WILBUR

The Writer

In her room at the prow of the house
Where light breaks, and the windows are tossed with
    linden,
My daughter is writing a story.

I pause in the stairwell, hearing
5   From her shut door a commotion of typewriter-keys
Like a chain hauled over a gunwale.

Young as she is, the stuff
Of her life is a great cargo, and some of it heavy:
I wish her a lucky passage.

10   But now it is she who pauses,
As if to reject my thought and its easy figure.
A stillness greatens, in which

The whole house seems to be thinking,
And then she is at it again with a bunched clamor
15   Of strokes, and again is silent.

I remember the dazed starling
Which was trapped in that very room, two years ago;
How we stole in, lifted a sash

And retreated, not to affright it;
20   And how for a helpless hour, through the crack of the
          door,
We watched the sleek, wild, dark

And iridescent creature
Batter against the brilliance, drop like a glove
To the hard floor, or the desk-top,

25   And wait then, humped and bloody,
For the wits to try it again; and how our spirits
Rose when, suddenly sure,

It lifted off from a chair-back,
Beating a smooth course for the right window
30   And clearing the sill of the world.

It is always a matter, my darling,
Of life or death, as I had forgotten. I wish
What I wished you before, but harder.

                                                    1967

Writing Assignments for "The Writer"

I. Brief Papers
  A. 1. Explain how the first stanza relates to the rest of the poem by establishing the
        mood and preparing for the subject matter.

2. In what ways does the young girl remind her father of the trapped starling?

3. What do you believe the speaker means when he says, "It is always a matter, my darling, / Of life or death, as I had forgotten. . . ." (lines 31–32)?

4. Choose one stanza you particularly like because of its language—its selection of words, its use of figurative language, or its particularly vivid imagery. Explain why the language is appropriate and effective.

B. Choose one assertion below and develop or refute it:
   1. Why do you believe the poet chooses to have the young girl writing, not engaging in some other activity?
   2. Write a short personality sketch of the speaker. What are his hopes for his daughter?

II. Longer Papers

A. In stanza 3, the speaker says, "I wish her a lucky passage" (line 9). In the last stanza, he says, ". . . I wish / What I wished you before, but harder" (lines 32–33). Explain what he means by the change and how the recollection of the starling inspires it.

B. How does the language of the poem—its word choice, its figurative language, and/or its imagery—reinforce its subject matter and intensify its impact?

C. Richard Wilbur's poetry has often been praised because it rejects the cynicism and pessimism typical in much contemporary poetry and because it embraces joy and optimism. To what extent does this poem illustrate that tendency?

ERICA JONG

On the First Night

On the first night
of the full moon,
the primeval sack of ocean
broke,
5 & I gave birth to you
little woman,
little carrot top,
little turned-up nose,
pushing you out of myself
10 as my mother
pushed
me out of herself,
as her mother did,
& her mother's mother before her,

15   all of us born
      of woman.

      I am the second daughter
      of a second daughter
      of a second daughter,
20   but you shall be the first.
      You shall see the phrase
      "second sex"
      only in puzzlement,
      wondering how anyone,
25   except a madman,
      could call you "second"
      when you are so splendidly
      first,
      conferring even on your mother
30   firstness, vastness, fullness
      as the moon at its fullest
      lights up the sky.

      Now the moon is full again
      & you are four weeks old.
35   Little lion, lioness,
      yowling for my breasts,
      growling at the moon,
      how I love your lustiness,
      your red face demanding,
40   your hungry mouth howling,
      your screams, your cries
      which all spell life
      in large letters
      the color of blood.

45   You are born a woman
      for the sheer glory of it,
      little redhead, beautiful screamer.
      You are no second sex,
      but the first of the first;
50   & when the moon's phases
      fill out the cycle
      of your life,
      you will crow
      for the joy
55   of being a woman,
      telling the pallid moon
      to go drown herself

in the blue ocean,
& glorying, glorying, glorying
60   in the rosy wonder
of your sunshining wondrous
self.

1983

Writing Assignments for "On the First Night"

I. Brief Papers
   A. 1. Discuss the relationship between stanza 1 and stanza 2 of the poem.
      2. Simone de Beauvoir's *The Second Sex,* the book which supplied a term Jong
         uses in her poem, has been called a "classic manifesto of the liberated
         women." In what ways does "On the First Night" reflect a feminist point of
         view?
      3. This poem comes from a collection, *Ordinary Miracles,* about the joys of
         motherhood. Show that the poem celebrates aspects of childbirth and infant
         care that are not usually treated joyfully and discuss why they are appropriate
         in the poem.

   B. Argue for or against the assertion that this poem would appeal more to women
      than to men.

   C. Some might claim that this poem is superficial, nothing more than the embarrass-
      ingly excessive adoration of a mother for her newborn. Explain why you agree
      or disagree with such a view.

II. Longer Papers
   Compare the mother–daughter relationship of this poem to that in Gwendolyn
   Brooks' "The Mother" (p. 773), or Lucille Clifton's "the thirty eighth year of my life"
   (p. 780). How are the speakers' attitudes toward their subjects similar or different,
   and how do you account for such differences?

MARK DEFOE

Daughters with Toad

Unblinking thing, as absolute as clay.
Fumed from the dank by my mower's snarl, he muses.
My daughters find him, and their squeals propel,
bounce him from his mope, ringing him with glee.

5   With sly, leery touch they probe his apathy
    unearthed—half-thrown, with a bloated thump
    he falls. They toy and stroke, forgive his piss,
    his pebbled hide, coo to his bulbous stare.

    Squat in their palms, he thrills with his pulse.
10 They lean near, enraptured by his ugliness,
    wild hair burnished down round him in bright waves.
    And they whisper, foreheads almost touching.

    Then each brings her lips to meet that grim crack
    of torpid mouth. They return him to the grass
15 to await the kisses' transformation.
    Nothing. The pale throat only swells the air

    and flutters, emits one pathetic croak.
    They laugh, and to the toad, their teeth so fine
    must gleam like the teeth of little foxes.
20 Uneaten, he ponders on, abandoned.

    My daughters are not sad. The day will be
    husband enough, obedient to whim—
    a royal ball. They waltz toward lunchtime,
    assuring me he spoke to them in prince.

                                              1983

Writing Assignments for "Daughters with Toad"

I. Brief Papers
  A. 1. The poem is based to some extent on a fairy tale. In the story, a princess
        transforms a toad into a handsome prince with her kiss. In what ways does the
        poem rely directly or indirectly on the fairy tale?
     2. Discuss how the father's perspective and attitude toward the toad is different
        from his daughters'.
     3. Find and discuss words in the poem which combine sound and meaning.

  B. Choose one assertion below, and develop or refute it:
     1. Write a short personality sketch of the speaker, relying on his description of
        the toad, his humorous account of the incident, and his implied attitude toward
        his daughters to provide information to support your generalizations.
     2. Do you believe the father's attitude toward the incident is strictly humorous?
        Wistful? Or something more?

II. *Longer Papers*

A. Choose any one of the paper assignments above and expand your response to
a full-length paper.

B. Many fairy tales are about growing up, and many psychologists believe that most
are about sexual initiation. Discuss the sexual references or implications of the
young girls' encounter with the toad and their father's reaction to it.

JOHN LOGAN

Lines to His Son on Reaching Adolescence

Before Reading

Free write for 5 to 10 minutes in response to the following question: "Do you believe
fathers must experience inevitable pain and sadness as they watch their sons grow up?"

> I've always thought Polonius* a dry
> And senile fop, fool to those he didn't love
> Though he had given life to them as father—
> To his beautiful young boy and beautiful
> 5   Young daughter; and loathed Augustine's†
> Lecherous old man who noticed that his son
> Naked at his bath, was growing up
> And told his wife a dirty joke. But
> I have given my own life to you my son
> 10   Remembering my fear, my joy and unbelief
> (And my disgust) when I saw you monkey
> Blue and blooded, shrouded with the light down
> Of the new born, the cord of flesh
> That held you to my wife cut free from her
> 15   And from my own remote body,
> And I could fill you up with epithets
> Like Ophelia's father, full of warnings,
> For I have learned what we must avoid
> And what must choose and how to be of use.
> 20   My father never taught me anything
> I needed for myself. It's no excuse,

*Polonius: The father of Ophelia and Laertes in Shakespeare's *Hamlet*. He is a long-winded
moralizer.

†Augustine: Christian philosopher and theologian (354–430 A.D.). He offers the example in his
treatise *City of God*.

For what he might have said I think
I would refuse, and besides (is it despair
I reach?) I feel we learn too late to teach.
25   And like Augustine's dad I have watched you bathe
Have seen as my own hair begins to fall
The fair gold beard upon your genital
That soon will flow with seed
And swell with love and pain (I almost add
30   Again). I cannot say to you whether
In a voice steady or unsteady, ah Christ
Please wait your father isn't ready.
You cannot wait, as he could not.
But for both our sakes I ask you, wrestle
35   Manfully against the ancient curse of snakes,
The bitter mystery of love, and learn to bear
The burden of the tenderness
That is hid in us. Oh you cannot
Spare yourself the sadness of Hippolytus*
40   Whom the thought of Phaedra
Turned from his beloved horse and bow,
My son, the arrow of my quiver,
The apple of my eye, but you can save your father
The awful agony of Laocoön†
45   Who could not stop the ruin of his son.
And as I can I will help you with my love.
Last I warn you, as Polonius,
Yet not as him, from now on I will not plead
As I have always done, for sons
50   Against their fathers who have wronged them.
I plead instead for us
Against the sons we hoped we would not hurt.

1963

Writing Assignments for "Lines to His Son on Reaching Adolescence"

I. Brief Papers

A. 1. Show that the speaker is a better, more sensitive father than the speaker's
father.

*Hippolytus and Phaedra: In Greek mythology, Hippolytus fled from the amorous advances of his
stepmother Phaedra and was killed when his chariot smashed into the rocks along the sea. Phaedra
hanged herself in despair after his death.
†Laocoön: Priest of Apollo who, along with his two sons, was crushed to death by a huge serpent
for opposing the admission of the wooden horse into Troy.

2. Go through the poem and circle any words and phrases which suggest that the father is aware he has limited power to help his son through his approaching manhood. Explain those words and phrases and how they help you understand the poem.
3. Explain what you believe the speaker means when he directs his son to "wrestle / Manfully against the ancient curse of snakes, / The bitter mystery of love" (lines 34–36).
4. Show how one of the three literary or mythical allusions—to Polonius, Augustine, or Laocoön—relates to the father's attitude toward his son. How is the speaker unlike the father alluded to?

B. In the poem the father laments that he cannot spare his son the pain associated with growing to manhood, but he can, he says, "help you with my love" (line 46). What kind of help does the poem imply the father can offer?

II. Longer Papers

A. At the end of the poem, the father says:

> . . . from now on I will not plead
> As I have always done, for sons
> Against their fathers who have wronged them.
> I plead instead for us
> Against the sons we hoped we would not hurt.
> (lines 48–52)

Explain the father's plea, relating it to the rest of the poem. Consider why his plea is different now that his son is reaching adolescence.

B. John Logan's poetry has been praised for its natural, almost conversational style. Write a paper exploring the conversational features of this poem, focusing on the digressions and parenthetical comments, on the organization of the father's thoughts, and on any element of the poem that strikes you as particularly conversational.

C. Explore to what extent this is an optimistic poem—one affirming the joy and mystery of life—and to what extent it is the opposite—an expression of despair because of the inevitable sadness and pain associated with growing up and growing old.

D. Show that throughout the poem the father links himself and his own experiences to his son's. Deal with the father's past experiences and with those he anticipates for his son.

DONALD HALL

My Son, My Executioner

My son, my executioner,
   I take you in my arms,
Quiet and small and just astir,
   And whom my body warms.

5 Sweet death, small son, our instrument
   Of immortality,
Your cries and hungers document
   Our bodily decay.

We twenty-five and twenty-two,
10   Who seemed to live forever,
Observe enduring life in you
   And start to die together.

1954

Writing Assignments for "My Son, My Executioner"

I. Brief Papers

  A. 1. Show that this poem is as much about the father's state of mind as it is about his child.

     2. In the first line of the poem, the speaker refers to his son as an "executioner." What other words and images reinforce the execution imagery?

     3. Why is the speaker's son both "sweet death" and the "instrument of immortality" to his parents?

     4. In an earlier version of the poem, the poet calls the child a "mortal paradox." After looking up *paradox* in the dictionary and studying its various meanings, explain how the last stanza of the poem implies that the child is, indeed, a mortal paradox.

  B. 1. Is the tone of the poem poignant? Bittersweet? Something else? Discuss the tone and how the poet achieves it in the poem.

     2. Describe your emotional reactions to the first line of the poem and discuss to what extent the poem helps resolve your conflicting emotional responses.

II. Longer Papers

  A. Discuss how the poem encourages you to respond both intellectually and emotionally. If you have written a paper in response to any of the topics under I.A or I.B, you may wish to incorporate that material into your paper.

B. One measure of excellence in poetry is the extent to which a poem melds its content and its language. Another measure is the extent to which it conveys some universal truth in a powerful way. Using one or both measures, evaluate "My Son, My Executioner."

GWENDOLYN BROOKS
The Mother

Before Reading

Write for 5 to 10 minutes about associations motherhood holds for you.

Abortions will not let you forget.
You remember the children you got that you did not get,
The damp small pulps with a little or with no hair,
The singers and workers that never handled the air.
5   You will never neglect or beat
Them, or silence or buy with a sweet.
You will never wind up the sucking-thumb
Or scuttle off ghosts that come.
You will never leave them, controlling your luscious sigh,
10   Return for a snack of them, with gobbling mother-eye.

I have heard in the voices of the wind the voices of my dim
    killed children.
I have contracted. I have eased
My dim dears at the breasts they could never suck.
I have said, Sweets, if I sinned, if I seized
15   Your luck
And your lives from your unfinished reach,
If I stole your births and your names,
Your straight baby tears and your games,
Your stilted or lovely loves, your tumults, your marriages, aches,
    and your deaths,
20   If I poisoned the beginnings of your breaths,
Believe that even in my deliberateness I was not deliberate.
Though why should I whine,
Whine that the crime was other than mine?—
Since anyhow you are dead.
25   Or rather, or instead,
You were never made.
But that too, I am afraid,
Is faulty: oh, what shall I say, how is the truth to be said?

You were born, you had body, you died.
30   It is just that you never giggled or planned or cried.

Believe me, I loved you all.
Believe me, I knew you, though faintly, and I loved, I loved you
All.

Writing Assignments for "The Mother"

I. Brief Papers

   A. 1. How does the speaker's descriptions of her aborted children evoke sympathy
         for them?
      2. How does the speaker's descriptions of her aborted children evoke sympathy
         for her?
      3. Consider the word choice in "I have contracted. I have eased" (line 12). Why
         is it appropriate?
      4. What does the speaker mean when she says, "If I poisoned the beginnings of
         your breaths, / Believe that even in my deliberateness I was not deliberate"
         (lines 20–21)?

   B. 1. There may be no more controversial issue than abortion. Explain how your
         attitude toward abortion affects your reaction to the poem.
      2. How do the lines "You will never neglect or beat / Them" (lines 5–6) affect
         your reactions to the mother and her plight?

II. Longer Papers

   A. How do the language and imagery of the poem evoke sympathy for both the
      aborted children and, at the same time, the mother?
   B. Compare this poem to Erica Jong's "On the First Night" (p. 765). Argue for or
      against the assertion that, while their circumstances differ radically, the mothers'
      attitudes are strikingly similar in the poems.
   C. Compare this poem to Erica Jong's "On the First Night" (p. 765) and Lucille
      Clifton's "the thirty eighth year of my life" (p. 780). In a personal response paper,
      examine why you believe one or two of the poems are better than the others. As
      your criteria for judgment, use the poem's language, imagery, subject matter, or
      any other aspect you think appropriate.

ALICE WALKER
Women

They were women then
My mama's generation
Husky of voice—Stout of
Step
5   With fists as well as
Hands
How they battered down
Doors
And ironed
10   Starched white
Shirts
How they led
Armies
Headragged Generals
15   Across mined
Fields
Booby-trapped
Ditches
To discover books
20   Desks
A place for us
How they knew what we
Must know
Without knowing a page
25   Of it
Themselves.

1973

Writing Assignments for "Women"

I. Brief Papers
  A. 1. Summarize in your own words the kind of women Walker praises in the poem. What are their values, their goals, or their motivations?
   2. Go through the poem and circle the verbs. How does the choice of verbs in the poem reinforce the tribute to the women?
   3. What do you believe the poet means when she writes: "How they led / Armies / Headragged Generals / Across mined / Fields / Booby-trapped / Ditches" (lines 12–18)? Why does she elect to use military imagery and language?

B. Argue for or against the assertion that this poem could apply, to some extent, to all mothers, not only to the black women of Walker's mother's generation.

C. Walker praises the women of the poem because "they knew what we / Must know / Without knowing a page / Of it / Themselves" (lines 22–26). According to the poem, what kinds of things have the mothers known that their children *must* know? To what extent is that knowledge still crucial today?

II. Longer Papers

A. Discuss as fully as possible the women the poem celebrates. Who are they? What is important to them? What do they seek to accomplish? How do they go about it? To what extent is the description still applicable today—more than ten years after the poem was published?

B. Discuss how the diction, structure, or any other element of the poem's style reinforces the poet's tribute to the women in the poem and how the language reveals the speaker's attitude toward them.

C. Compare this poem to Alice Walker's "For My Sister Molly Who in the Fifties" (p. 776) and Lucille Clifton's "the thirty eighth year of my life" (p. 780). Discuss how the poems illustrate similar or different kinds of women and mothers, how they share similar perceptions of women, or how they have moved you to a new or altered view of black women in our culture.

ALICE WALKER

For My Sister Molly Who in the Fifties

Once made a fairy rooster from
Mashed potatoes
Whose eyes I forget
But green onions were his tail
5 And his two legs were carrot sticks
A tomato slice his crown.
Who came home on vacation
When the sun was hot
and cooked
10 and cleaned
And minded least of all
The children's questions
A million or more
Pouring in on her
15 Who had been to school
And knew (and told us too) that certain
Words were no longer good

And taught me not to say us for we
No matter what "Sonny said" up the
20   road.

FOR MY SISTER MOLLY WHO IN THE FIFTIES
Knew Hamlet well and read into the night
And coached me in my songs of Africa
A continent I never knew
25   But learned to love
Because "they" she said could carry
A tune
And spoke in accents never heard
In Eatonton.
30   Who read from *Prose and Poetry*
And loved to read "Sam McGee from Tennessee"
On nights the fire was burning low
And Christmas wrapped in angel hair
And I for one prayed for snow.

35   WHO IN THE FIFTIES
Knew all the written things that made
Us laugh and stories by
The hour   Waking up the story buds
Like fruit. Who walked among the flowers
40   And brought them inside the house
And smelled as good as they
And looked as bright.
Who made dresses, braided
Hair. Moved chairs about
45   Hung things from walls
Ordered baths
Frowned on wasp bites
And seemed to know the endings
Of all the tales
50   I had forgot.

WHO OFF INTO THE UNIVERSITY
Went exploring   To London and
To Rotterdam
Prague and to Liberia
55   Bringing back the news to us
Who knew none of it
But followed
crops and weather
funerals and

60 Methodist Homecoming;
easter speeches,
groaning church.

WHO FOUND ANOTHER WORLD
Another life   With gentlefolk
65 Far less trusting
And moved and moved and changed
Her name
And sounded precise
When she spoke   And frowned away
70 Our sloppishness.

WHO SAW US SILENT
Cursed with fear   A love burning
Inexpressible
And sent me money not for me
75 But for "College."
Who saw me grow through letters
The words misspelled   But not
The longing   Stretching
Growth
80 The tied and twisting
Tongue
Feet no longer bare
Skin no longer burnt against
The cotton.

85 WHO BECAME SOMEONE OVERHEAD
A light   A thousand watts
Bright and also blinding
And saw my brothers cloddish
And me destined to be
90 Wayward
My mother remote   My father
A wearisome farmer
With heartbreaking
Nails.

95 FOR MY SISTER MOLLY WHO IN THE FIFTIES
Found much
Unbearable
Who walked where few had
Understood   And sensed our
100 Groping after light

And saw some extinguished
And no doubt mourned.

FOR MY SISTER MOLLY WHO IN THE FIFTIES
Left us.

1973

Writing Assignments for "For My Sister Molly Who in the Fifties"

I. Brief Papers

A. 1. Describe Molly before she goes to the university (lines 1–49).
   2. Describe Molly (lines 50–93) after she goes to the university, emphasizing the significant changes.
   3. Describe the dramatic setting, and explain how it plays an important role in your reaction to both Molly and the speaker in the poem.
   4. Why is it significant that Molly sees the speaker's misspelled words "but not / The longing   Stretching / Growth" (lines 76–78)?

B. Argue for or against either assertion below.
   1. Molly's life improves significantly after she goes to the university.
   2. When the speaker says in the last line that Molly "left us," she means more than a physical separation.

C. 1. To what extent do you believe the speaker comes to share the same values as her sister Molly?
   2. To what extent is it a compliment to Molly when the speaker says she "Became someone overhead / A light   A thousand watts" (lines 84–85)?

II. Longer Papers

A. There is a clear division between the first half of the poem (stanzas 1–3) and the second half (stanzas 4–9). Discuss the relationship between the two parts of the poem, emphasizing Molly's personality development, the speaker's growth and changing attitude, and/or any element of the poem you think important.
B. Discuss to what extent this poem reveres a college education and to what extent it condemns one.
C. Alice Walker is a noted black novelist, poet, and critic, and her poem treats two black women's growth, change, and attitudes. Discuss to what extent it is important to our response to the poem that the women are black.
D. Compare this poem to "Women" by Alice Walker (p. 775). How is Molly like the women Walker celebrates in her poem? How is she different?

LUCILLE CLIFTON

the thirty eighth year of my life

the thirty eighth year
of my life,
plain as bread
round as a cake
5   an ordinary woman.

an ordinary woman.

i had expected to be
smaller than this,
more beautiful,
10   wiser in Afrikan ways,
more confident,
i had expected
more than this.

i will be forty soon.
15   my mother once was forty.

my mother died at forty four,
a woman of sad countenance
leaving behind a girl
awkward as a stork.
20   my mother was thick,
her hair was a jungle and
she was very wise
and beautiful
and sad.

25   i have dreamed dreams
for you mama
more than once.
i have wrapped me
in your skin
30   and made you live again
more than once.
i have taken the bones you hardened
and built daughters

and they blossom and promise fruit
35   like Afrikan trees.
i am a woman now.
an ordinary woman.

in the thirty eighth
year of my life,
40   surrounded by life,
a perfect picture of
blackness blessed,
i had not expected this
loneliness.

45   if it is western,
if it is the final
Europe in my mind,
if in the middle of my life
i am turning the final turn
50   into the shining dark
let me come to it whole
and holy
not afraid
not lonely
55   out of my mother's life
into my own.
into my own.

i had expected more than this.
i had not expected to be
60   an ordinary woman.

1974

Writing Assignments for "the thirty eighth year of my life"

I. Brief Papers

    A. 1. Summarize what the speaker has expected from her life.
       2. Summarize how the speaker has failed to live up to her own expectations.
       3. To what extent do the speaker's memories of her mother shape her attitude toward herself?

    B. Argue for or against the assertion that the speaker's attitude toward her mother triggers her own feelings of inadequacy as well as her feelings of loneliness.

C. Describe what you believe to be the speaker's definition of an ordinary woman. How is her definition based on something other than what she accomplishes in her life?

II. Longer Papers

A. Go through the poem stanza by stanza, noting which stanzas focus primarily on the speaker, which primarily on her mother, and which on the two of them. Pay attention to any links—stated or implied—between the women's lives, attitudes, dreams. Write a paper showing how the speaker links herself to her mother throughout the poem—emphasizing the structure and development within the poem as well as its subject matter.

B. In this chapter you will find several other poems by black women poets about family relationships. Compare this poem to one of them: Walker's "Women" (p. 775) or "For My Sister Molly Who in the Fifties" (p. 776). Emphasize the speakers' attitudes toward older women or toward their mothers, their attitudes toward themselves, their values and goals in life, or any other elements of the poems you believe important. If you wish, evaluate which of the poems is the more powerful or moving.

W. S. MERWIN

The Salt Pond

Mid-September my dead father's birthday
again by the low shore I watch gulls fly inland
white gulls riding a knowledge older than they are

by now you are eighty-eight and need nothing old friend
5   twelve years in the white sky out of the wind

once more at the end of summer the first map of the coast
looks out from the wall
a shadow imperceptibly darkening
the names dissolve across it
10   white clouds race over the marshes

the gulls have gone with their age
I know the wind

1985

Writing Assignments for "The Salt Pond"

I. Brief Papers

    A. 1. Find and list as many references in the poem to natural forces as you can. Choose one force which seems particularly significant and explain why it's appropriate in this poem.

       2. How does the last line in the poem "I know the wind" relate to lines 4–5?

    B. Argue for or against the assertion that this poem is more about the persona's sense of human mortality than about his grief for his father.

    C. 1. What can you infer about the speaker in the poem, his father, and their relationship?

       2. Why do you believe the poet entitled his poem "The Salt Pond"?

II. Longer Papers

How does the poet use references to natural forces to establish meaning and tone in his poem?

Comparative Papers from Chapter Six: Family Relationships

A. Choose the poem from this chapter you liked the best because you found it the most honest, the most moving, or the most unusual. Complete the sentence, "I liked _____ best because . . ." by free writing for 10 minutes. Since the goal of free writing is to generate ideas quickly, do not worry about spelling, punctuation, grammar, or sentence structure. Just keep writing down whatever comes into your head about why the poem appeals to you and why it reveals something to you about your relationship with a family member. Don't stop writing for any reason. If you can't think of anything to say, just write "I can't think of anything to say" until something comes to mind. After 10 minutes look back over your free writing and select from it the most promising ideas and write a full-length paper.

B. Choose two or more poems from this unit which portray family relationships as you wish your own could be. Discuss in detail how the poems illustrate what, for you, is the ideal relationship.

C. Some psychologists believe many women feel unnecessary anxiety, guilt, and frustration because they accept overidealized notions of motherhood. One such notion is that a mother's love is unquestioning, unstinting, and unambivalent. Another is that motherhood is the most fulfilling experience of a woman's life. Explain how one or more poems from this chapter rely upon or react against such notions.

D. Argue for or against the assertion that, judging from several poems in this chapter, fathers are more likely to view their children's futures with fear than with any other emotion.

E. Choose and discuss one or more poems from this chapter which suggest how parents' desires for their children's futures are tied to their own lives and—most particularly—to their pasts.

F. In this chapter, Alice Walker, Lucille Clifton, and Adrienne Rich explore relationships among mothers, daughters, and sisters. Are such relationships usually depicted in positive or negative ways?

G. Poems involving family members will likely reveal more emotion than other poems because our feelings for family members involve our most intense love, guilt, fear, and—sometimes—hate. Select two or more poems from this chapter and explain how the word choice, the imagery, and subject matter of the poetry reveal intense feeling.

H. Select two or more poems which you believe display unrealistic attitudes toward family relationships and explain why they seem unrealistic.

7 / Poems about Adventure and the Supernatural

LORRAINE KARAFEL

Heroines

MEDEA:*

It is a familiar story:
she did it for love, she did it
to live with her husband

and her sons, blameless.
She must be blameless.
Perhaps it was something in her blood:

what else could we expect
from the niece of a sorceress:
the murder of a child,

her brother, her very blood, left
not as a way back but as a wall
separating her from home.

She knew about endless youth,
this killer, this goddess, and we
hope to learn her secrets,

her descendants, her followers
who worship her, who would do
anything for love—like her.

JUDITH:†

I would have to read that story again
to know why she pulled her knife so calmly
across the throat of Holofernes.

*Medea: Greek heroine who was exiled after betraying her father and killing her brother to help
Jason steal the Golden Fleece.
†Judith: Old testament heroine who saved her tribe by killing her lover Holofernes.

One moment she seemed to caress his hair
as a mother might, smoothing the curls,
arranging the loose strands.

And then she drew out her long knife:
it always has a jeweled handle, that knife,
but it is the blade that glints so brightly

in the slant of light from an unseen source.
On her lap, comforted, Holofernes
enjoys the scent of her velvet skirt.

He listens to the murmur of her pearls
as she bends so lovingly over him.
He feels perhaps the cold at his throat,

or perhaps only the heat of pain.
Does he accuse her in the last seconds,
or is it so sudden there is no thought?

And Judith—does she think about the blood
staining her dress, or is it just the knife
she thinks about, admiring how it gleams?

He stretches out his arms, then he stops.
Her maid waits in the shadowy background
holding a clean white cloth.

1986

Writing Assignments for "Heroines"

I. Brief Papers
   A. 1. Look up the word *heroine* in the dictionary. Choose any one of the definitions
         which seems appropriate and explain why Medea or Judith is a heroine.
      2. What does the writer mean by "She must be blameless" (line 5)?
      3. Show that Medea's story and Judith's story are told in very different ways.

   B. Argue for or against either assertion below.
      1. The writer admires Medea's followers, those "who would do / anything for
         love" (lines 17–18).
      2. Despite the title, neither of these women is portrayed as heroic.

   C. 1. Do you believe the two women, as they are portrayed, are heroines?
      2. Do you believe the poem could be classified as violent? Why or why not?

II. Longer Papers

A. Read short accounts of Medea in a mythology handbook and Judith in an encyclo-pedia of religion. Discuss how such information influences your reaction to the poem.
B. Discuss in detail why you believe the poem is entitled "Heroines."

ALFRED, LORD TENNYSON

Ulysses*

It little profits that an idle king,
By this still hearth, among these barren crags,
Matched with an aged wife, I mete and dole
Unequal laws unto a savage race,
5   That hoard, and sleep, and feed, and know not me.
I cannot rest from travel; I will drink
Life to the lees. All times I have enjoyed
Greatly, have suffered greatly, both with those
That loved me, and alone; on shore, and when
10   Through scudding drifts the rainy Hyades†
Vexed the dim sea. I am become a name;
For always roaming with a hungry heart
Much have I seen and known—cities of men
And manners, climates, councils, governments,
15   Myself not least, but honored of them all—
And drunk delight of battle with my peers,
Far on the ringing plains of windy Troy.
I am a part of all that I have met;
Yet all experience is an arch wherethrough
20   Gleams that untraveled world whose margin fades
Forever and forever when I move.
How dull it is to pause, to make an end,
To rust unburnished, not to shine in use!
As though to breathe were life! Life piled on life
25   Were all too little, and of one to me
Little remains; but every hour is saved
From that eternal silence, something more,
A bringer of new things; and vile it were
For some three suns to store and hoard myself,
30   And this grey spirit yearning in desire

*Ulysses: Odysseus, whose adventures are detailed in Homer's *Odyssey*. Tennyson depicts Ulysses, now aged, once again home in Ithaca, Greece.
†Hyades: Group of stars, sometimes called Pleiads, whose early morning rising signals rain.

To follow knowledge like a sinking star,
Beyond the utmost bound of human thought.
   This is my son, mine own Telemachus,
To whom I leave the scepter and the isle—
35 Well-loved of me, discerning to fulfill
This labor, by slow prudence to make mild
A rugged people, and through soft degrees
Subdue them to the useful and the good.
Most blameless is he, centered in the sphere
40 Of common duties, decent not to fail
In offices of tenderness, and pay
Meet adoration to my household gods,
When I am gone. He works his work, I mine.
   There lies the port; the vessel puffs her sail;
45 There gloom the dark, broad seas. My mariners,
Souls that have toiled, and wrought, and thought with me—
That ever with a frolic welcome took
The thunder and the sunshine, and opposed
Free hearts, free foreheads—you and I are old;
50 Old age hath yet his honor and his toil.
Death closes all; but something ere the end,
Some work of noble note, may yet be done,
Not unbecoming men that strove with Gods.
The lights begin to twinkle from the rocks;
55 The long day wanes; the slow moon climbs; the deep
Moans round with many voices. Come, my friends,
'Tis not too late to seek a newer world.
Push off, and sitting well in order smite
The sounding furrows; for my purpose holds
60 To sail beyond the sunset, and the baths
Of all the western stars, until I die.
It may be that the gulfs will wash us down;
It may be we shall touch the Happy Isles,*
And see the great Achilles, whom we knew.
65 Though much is taken, much abides; and though
We are not now that strength which in old days
Moved earth and heaven, that which we are, we are—
One equal temper of heroic hearts,
Made weak by time and fate, but strong in will
70 To strive, to seek, to find, and not to yield.

1842

---

*Happy Isles: Elysium, thought to be in the far-western oceans, was the resting place of heroes and
adventurers, such as Achilles.

Writing Assignments for "Ulysses"

I. Brief Papers
  A. 1. Describe the kind of life Ulysses yearns for.
     2. Why does Ulysses want to leave home once again?
     3. Describe Telemachus. How is he better suited than Ulysses to rule the people of Ithaca?
     4. Go through the poem and circle all references to the elements—to wind, rain, and the sea. How does the description of the elements reinforce Ulysses' desires?

  B. Argue for or against the assertion that Ulysses is realistic about himself, his abilities, and his crew when he says, "Come, my friends, / 'Tis not too late to seek a newer world" (lines 56–57).

  C. Some people believe Ulysses is courageous and heroic. Others believe he is an irresponsible ruler, ready to shirk his duty to his people and leave home when there is no political or military reason. Others believe he is silly or pathetic, an old man yearning after earlier adventure and glory. How do you react to his desires, his thirst for adventure?

II. Longer Papers
  A. Discuss in detail the last five lines of the poem, relating them to the rest of the piece, deciding if Ulysses' quest for adventure is a realistic or heroic one and deciding to what extent his decision is inevitable, one explained by Ulysses' statement to his men, "that which we are, we are" (line 67).
  B. To what extent are most people like Ulysses? To what extent are most people like Ulysses' subjects who "hoard, and sleep, and feed, and know not me" (line 5)? Draw specific evidence from the poem to support your assertions.
  C. Compare this poem to Alastair Reid's "Curiosity" (p. 627), discussing to what extent the poems treat similar subject matter and adopt similar perspectives.

W. H. AUDEN
The Wanderer

> Doom is dark and deeper than any sea-dingle.*
> Upon what man it fall
> In spring, day-wishing flowers appearing,
> Avalanche sliding, white snow from rock-face,

*sea-dingle: A dingle is a deep hollow or abyss.

5   That he should leave his house,
    No cloud-soft hand can hold him, restraint by women;
    But ever that man goes
    Through place-keepers, through forest trees,
    A stranger to strangers over undried sea,
10 Houses for fishes, suffocating water,
    Or lonely on fell* as chat,†
    By pot-holed becks‡
    A bird stone-haunting, an unquiet bird.

    There head falls forward, fatigued at evening,
15 And dreams of home,
    Waving from window, spread of welcome,
    Kissing of wife under single sheet;
    But waking sees
    Bird-flocks nameless to him, through doorway voices
20 Of new men making another love.

    Save him from hostile capture,
    From sudden tiger's spring at corner;
    Protect his house,
    His anxious house where days are counted
25 From thunderbolt protect,
    From gradual ruin spreading like a stain;
    Converting number from vague to certain,
    Bring joy, bring day of his returning,
    Lucky with day approaching, with leaning dawn.

                                                    1934

Writing Assignments for "The Wanderer"

I. Brief Papers

A. 1. Discuss the relationship of the first line to the rest of the poem. How does its
      language, its sounds, its mystery, and its subject matter establish the mood and
      the pattern for the rest of the piece?
   2. Choose one of the images or one of the short, fragmented descriptive passages
      of the first stanza and explain what it directly states and what it implies about
      the wanderer, his compulsion to wander, and the result of the wandering.
   3. Show that the wanderer experiences danger—mental as much as physical.
   4. Show that the poem contains elements of prayer.

*fell: A hill or mountain.
†chat: A small bird or any bird that "chats."
‡becks: Brooks or streams with rocky bottoms.

B. Argue for or against the assertion that the wanderer described in the poem has no choice, that he is compelled to wander.

C. Why do you believe the reason for the wanderer's leaving home is left unclear? Why is it given as an almost inevitable assumption that he will wander in the lines, "No cloud-soft hand can hold him, restraint by women; / But ever that man goes."

II. Longer Papers

A. Explain in what ways the poem captures the loneliness and the anxiety the wanderer feels.
B. The poem's impact rests as much on its language—its sounds and its images—as on its subject matter. Discuss how the language of the poem reinforces the subject.
C. Compare this poem to Alfred, Lord Tennyson's "Ulysses" (p. 787). Consider to what extent each poem deals with compulsive wanderlust.

PERCY BYSSHE SHELLEY

*Ozymandias**

I met a traveller from an antique land
Who said: Two vast and trunkless legs of stone
Stand in the desert . . . Near them, on the sand,
Half sunk, a shattered visage lies, whose frown,
5 And wrinkled lip, and sneer of cold command,
Tell that its sculptor well those passions read
Which yet survive, stamped on these lifeless things,
The hand that mocked them, and the heart that fed:
And on the pedestal these words appear:
10 'My name is Ozymandias, king of kings:
Look on my works, ye Mighty, and despair!'
Nothing beside remains. Round the decay
Of that colossal wreck, boundless and bare
The lone and level sands stretch far away.

1818

*Ozymandias: Greek name for King Ramses II of Egypt in the thirteenth century B.C. Diodorus Siculus, a Greek historian, stated that the largest statue in Greece had the inscription: "I am Ozymandias, king of kings; if anyone wishes to know what I am and where I lie—let him surpass me in some of my exploits."

Writing Assignments for "Ozymandias"

I. Brief Papers

    A. 1. Describe the statue of Ozymandias as it once was and as it was when the traveller in the poem saw it.

       2. What were the sculptor's perceptions of Ozymandias and how did he convey them?

       3. Explain the congruity or the irony of the words on the pedestal and the fate of the statue.

    B. Argue for or against either assertion below.

       1. The poem is primarily about human arrogance and its inevitable results.

       2. The poem is primarily about mutability and the inevitable decay of all things human.

    C. Why does the poet have the story of Ozymandias told by a speaker who relates it as it was told to him? Does the device reinforce Ozymandias' image of power? Or does it reinforce the deterioration of Ozymandias' power? How does it affect your response to Ozymandias and the fate of his statue?

II. Longer Papers

    A. Explain how the poem is based on irony or incongruities. You might discuss the relationship between Ozymandias' arrogance and the decline of his power. Or you might discuss the various perceptions of the speaker, the traveller, the sculptor, and Ozymandias. Explore any central irony or incongruity you find in the poem.

    B. Explain the last three lines of the poem, discussing in detail their relationship in content and in structure to the rest of the poem.

EMILY DICKINSON

One Need Not Be a Chamber—To Be Haunted

> One need not be a Chamber—to be Haunted—
> One need not be a House—
> The Brain has Corridors—surpassing
> Material Place—
>
> 5 Far safer, of a Midnight Meeting
> External Ghost
> Than its interior Confronting—
> That Cooler Host.

Far safer, through an Abbey gallop,
10   The Stones a'chase—
      Than Unarmed, one's a'self encounter—
      In lonesome Place—

      Ourself behind ourself, concealed—
      Should startle most—
15   Assassin hid in our Apartment
      Be Horror's least.

      The Body—borrows a Revolver—
      He bolts the Door—
      O'erlooking a superior spectre—
20   Or More—

1891*

Writing Assignments for "One Need Not Be a Chamber—To Be Haunted"

I. Brief Papers

    A. 1. Describe the conventional imagery of ghosts and haunted houses the poet uses in the poem.
       2. Summarize in your own words what the speaker finds more frightening than ghosts and haunted houses.
       3. Explain what the poet means when she writes: "Ourself behind ourself, concealed— / Should startle most—" (lines 13–14). How does your understanding of these lines affect your interpretation of the poem?

    B. Argue for or against the assertion that, although it was written in 1863, the poem adopts a contemporary attitude toward horror and fear.

    C. Psychological horror stems in part from our sense that everyone has a submerged self capable of monstrous thoughts, impulses, and acts. How does your own attitude toward psychological horror affect your interpretation of the poem?

II. Longer Papers

    A. Explain the threatening implications of the final stanza of the poem. How do the content, imagery, and language of the stanza relate to the rest of the poem?
    B. Show that the poet implies that psychological horror is more devastating and more inescapable than other kinds of fear and discuss to what extent your own attitude toward such horror affects your interpretation of the poem.

*1891: The publication date, five years after Dickinson's death in 1886. The date conjectured for the earliest known manuscript of the poem is 1863.

EDGAR ALLAN POE

Annabel Lee

It was many and many a year ago,
  In a kingdom by the sea,
That a maiden there lived whom you may know
  By the name of ANNABEL LEE,
5 And this maiden she lived with no other thought
  Than to love and be loved by me.

I was a child and *she* was a child,
  In this kingdom by the sea;
But we loved with a love that was more than love—
10 I and my ANNABEL LEE—
With a love that the wingèd seraphs of heaven
  Coveted her and me.

And this was the reason that, long ago,
  In this kingdom by the sea,
15 A wind blew out of a cloud, chilling
  My beautiful ANNABEL LEE;
So that her highborn kinsmen came
  And bore her away from me,
To shut her up in a sepulchre
20 In this kingdom by the sea.

The angels, not half so happy in heaven,
  Went envying her and me—
Yes!—that was the reason (as all men know,
  In this kingdom by the sea)
25 That the wind came out of the cloud by night,
  Chilling and killing my ANNABEL LEE.

But our love it was stronger by far than the love
  Of those who were older than we—
  Of many far wiser than we—
30 And neither the angels in heaven above,
  Nor the demons down under the sea,
Can ever dissever my soul from the soul
  Of the beautiful ANNABEL LEE:

For the moon never beams, without bringing me dreams
35 Of the beautiful ANNABEL LEE;

And the stars never rise, but I feel the bright eyes
    Of the beautiful ANNABEL LEE:
And so, all the night tide, I lie down by the side
Of my darling—my darling—my life and my bride,
40   In her sepulchre there by the sea—
    In her tomb by the sounding sea.

1847

Writing Assignments for "Annabel Lee"

I. Brief Papers
  A. 1. How did Annabel Lee die? How does the speaker of the poem believe she died?
     2. Show that the speaker of the poem spends much of his time—not just his nights—in dreams and fantasies.
     3. Describe the dramatic setting of the poem and explain how it affects your reaction to the speaker of the poem.

  B. Argue for or against the assertion that the speaker suffers from extreme paranoia, an irrational sense of persecution.

  C. Read the poem aloud several times. Or, if possible, have someone read the poem aloud to you several times. After each reading, quickly write down your response to the poem, noting any reaction you have to the poem's rhythm and language, to the speaker, to the subject matter, or to the emotional impact. Use your notes as the basis for a paragraph about the oral and aural quality of the poem.

II. Longer Papers
  A. Some people believe the speaker exhibits extreme, yet inevitable, grief. Others believe he exhibits extreme paranoia, obsessive behavior, and even insanity. Discuss your assessment of his psychological condition, referring to specific evidence in the text.
  B. Some contemporary readers find Poe's poetry too simple—even juvenile—because of its marked, insistent rhythm and its exotic, supernatural subject matter. Do you agree with the assertion that "Annabel Lee" is a juvenile poem? Why or why not?
  C. How do the lengths of the lines, the rhyme and the meter, the repetition and slightly altered repetition of the lines contribute to and reinforce the setting, the subject matter, and the speaker's state of mind in the poem?

JOHN KEATS

La Belle Dame Sans Merci*

O what can ail thee, knight-at-arms,
   Alone and palely loitering?
The sedge has withered from the lake,
   And no birds sing.

5 O what can ail thee, knight-at-arms,
   So haggard and so woe-begone?
The squirrel's granary is full,
   And the harvest's done.

I see a lily on thy brow
10   With anguish moist and fever dew,
And on thy cheek a fading rose
   Fast withereth too.

"I met a lady in the meads,
   Full beautiful—a faery's child;
15 Her hair was long, her foot was light,
   And her eyes were wild.

"I made a garland for her head,
   And bracelets too, and fragrant zone;
She looked at me as she did love,
20   And made sweet moan.

"I set her on my pacing steed,
   And nothing else saw all day long,
For sidelong would she bend, and sing
   A faery's song.

25 "She found me roots of relish sweet,
   And honey wild, and manna dew,
And sure in language strange she said—
   'I love thee true!'

"She took me to her elfin grot,
30   And there she wept and sighed full sore,

*"La Belle Dame . . .": "The Lovely Lady without Pity" or "The Lovely Merciless Beauty," a title
Keats takes directly from a medieval French poem.

And there I shut her wild wild eyes
    With kisses four.

"And there she lulled me asleep,
    And there I dreamed—ah! woe betide!
35 The latest dream I ever dreamed
    On the cold hill's side.

"I saw pale kings and princes too,
    Pale warriors, death-pale were they all;
They cried—'La Belle Dame sans Merci
40   Hath thee in thrall!'

"I saw their starved lips in the gloam,
    With horrid warning gaped wide,
And I awoke and found me here,
    On the cold hill's side.

45 "And this is why I sojourn here,
    Alone and palely loitering,
Though the sedge is withered from the lake
    And no birds sing."

                1820

Writing Assignments for "La Belle Dame Sans Merci"

I. Brief Papers
  A. 1. Describe the knight's appearance and his state of mind in the first three stanzas. Why are the lily and the fading rose appropriate flowers to describe the knight's appearance?
      2. How does the setting in the first three stanzas and the last stanza reinforce the knight's state of mind?
      3. Show that there is evidence that the lady in the meads is a temptress, a "femme fatale."
      4. Show that there is evidence that the lady in the meads has supernatural powers.
      5. Explain why the knight continues to loiter along the withered lake's shore.

  B. Argue for or against the assertion that the poem implies that passionate love is as likely to be a destructive force as a positive one.

  C. 1. Do you believe that most men think of women as temptresses and sirens who entice and destroy simultaneously? How does your belief affect your response to the poem?

2. Do you believe it is appropriate to describe love and passion in terms of bewitchment? Why or why not? How does your belief affect your response to the poem?

II. Longer Papers

A. Develop any brief paper into a full-length one.

B. Find all references to eyes and sight in the poem and explain their significance.

C. Describe the knight's dream (lines 35–40) and explain how the dream relates to the knight's experiences with the lady in the meads.

D. Discuss in detail the relationship between the first three stanzas (lines 1–12) and the last nine (lines 13–48).

E. Spend some time analyzing the four-line quatrains. How does the stanzaic form—especially the abbreviated final line in each stanza—affect the impact of the poem?

JOHN KEATS

*The Eve of St. Agnes**

1

St. Agnes' Eve—Ah, bitter chill it was!
The owl, for all his feathers, was a-cold;
The hare limp'd trembling through the frozen grass,
And silent was the flock in woolly fold:
5   Numb were the Beadsman's† fingers, while he told
His rosary, and while his frosted breath,
Like pious incense from a censer old,
Seem'd taking flight for heaven, without a death,
Past the sweet Virgin's picture, while his prayer he saith.

2

10   His prayer he saith, this patient, holy man;
Then he takes his lamp, and riseth from his knees,
And back returneth, meagre, barefoot, wan,
Along the chapel aisle by slow degrees:
The sculptur'd dead, on each side, seem to freeze,
15   Emprison'd in black, purgatorial rails:
Knights, ladies, praying in dumb orat'ries,

*The Eve of St. Agnes: St. Agnes, patron saint of virgins, was martyred in 303 A.D. Her feast day, January 21, is associated with a number of legends. According to one, virgins will dream of their future husbands if they perform appropriate rituals.
†Beadsman: A beadsman, paid to pray for his benefactor, "tells" the rosary by holding the string of rosary beads in his hand, counting his way around, saying one prayer per bead.

He passeth by; and his weak spirit fails
To think how they may ache in icy hoods and mails.

3

Northward he turneth through a little door,
20   And scarce three steps, ere Music's golden tongue
Flatter'd to tears this aged man and poor;
But no—already had his deathbell rung;
The joys of all his life were said and sung:
His was harsh penance on St. Agnes' Eve:
25   Another way he went, and soon among
Rough ashes sat he for his soul's reprieve,
And all night kept awake, for sinners' sake to grieve.

4

That ancient Beadsman heard the prelude soft;
And so it chanc'd, for many a door was wide,
30   From hurry to and fro. Soon, up aloft,
The silver, snarling trumpets 'gan to chide:
The level chambers, ready with their pride,
Were glowing to receive a thousand guests:
The carved angels, ever eager-eyed,
35   Star'd, where upon their heads the cornice rests,
With hair blown back, and wings put cross-wise on their breasts.

5

At length burst in the argent revelry,
With plume, tiara, and all rich array,
Numerous as shadows haunting fairily
40   The brain, new stuff'd, in youth, with triumphs gay
Of old romance. These let us wish away,
And turn, sole-thoughted, to one Lady there,
Whose heart had brooded, all that wintry day,
On love, and wing'd St. Agnes' saintly care,
45   As she had heard old dames full many times declare.

6

They told her how, upon St. Agnes' Eve,
Young virgins might have visions of delight,
And soft adorings from their loves receive
Upon the honey'd middle of the night,
50   If ceremonies due they did aright;
As, supperless to bed they must retire,
And couch supine their beauties, lily white;
Nor look behind, nor sideways, but require
Of heaven with upward eyes for all that they desire.

7

55   Full of this whim was thoughtful Madeline:
     The music, yearning like a god in pain,
     She scarcely heard: her maiden eyes divine,
     Fix'd on the floor, saw many a sweeping train
     Pass by—she heeded not at all: in vain
60   Came many a tiptoe, amorous cavalier,
     And back retir'd, not cool'd by high disdain;
     But she saw not: her heart was otherwhere:
     She sigh'd for Agnes' dreams, the sweetest of the year.

8

     She danc'd along with vague, regardless eyes,
65   Anxious her lips, her breathing quick and short:
     The hallow'd hour was near at hand: she sighs
     Amid the timbrels, and the throng'd resort
     Of whisperers in anger, or in sport;
     'Mid looks of love, defiance, hate, and scorn,
70   Hoodwink'd with faery fancy; all amort,
     Save to St. Agnes and her lambs unshorn,
     And all the bliss to be before to-morrow morn.

9

     So, purposing each moment to retire,
     She linger'd still. Meantime, across the moors,
75   Had come young Porphyro, with heart on fire
     For Madeline. Beside the portal doors,
     Buttress'd from moonlight, stands he, and implores
     All saints to give him sight of Madeline,
     But for one moment in the tedious hours,
80   That he might gaze and worship all unseen;
     Perchance speak, kneel, touch, kiss—in sooth such things
     have been.

10

     He ventures in: let no buzz'd whisper tell:
     All eyes be muffled, or a hundred swords
     Will storm his heart, Love's fev'rous citadel:
85   For him, those chambers held barbarian hordes,
     Hyena foemen, and hot-blooded lords,
     Whose very dogs would execrations howl
     Against his lineage: not one breast affords
     Him any mercy, in that mansion foul,
90   Save one old beldame, weak in body and in soul.

11

Ah, happy chance! the aged creature came,
Shuffling along with ivory-headed wand,
To where he stood, hid from the torch's flame,
Behind a broad hall-pillar, far beyond
95   The sound of merriment and chorus bland:
He startled her; but soon she knew his face,
And grasp'd his fingers in her palsied hand,
Saying, "Mercy, Porphyro! hie thee from this place;
They are all here to-night, the whole blood-thirsty race!

12

100   "Get hence! get hence! there's dwarfish Hildebrand;
He had a fever late, and in the fit
He cursed thee and thine, both house and land:
Then there's that old Lord Maurice, not a whit
More tame for his gray hairs—Alas me! flit!
105   Flit like a ghost away."—"Ah, Gossip dear,
We're safe enough; here in this arm-chair sit,
And tell me how"—"Good Saints! not here, not here;
Follow me, child, or else these stones will be thy bier."

13

He follow'd through a lowly arched way,
110   Brushing the cobwebs with his lofty plume,
And as she mutter'd "Well-a—well-a-day!"
He found him in a little moonlight room,
Pale, lattic'd, chill, and silent as a tomb.
"Now tell me where is Madeline," said he,
115   "O tell me, Angela, by the holy loom
Which none but secret sisterhood may see,
When they St. Agnes' wool are weaving piously."

14

"St. Agnes! Ah! it is St. Agnes' Eve—
Yet men will murder upon holy days:
120   Thou must hold water in a witch's sieve,
And be liege-lord of all the Elves and Fays,
To venture so: it fills me with amaze
To see thee, Porphyro!—St. Agnes' Eve!
God's help! my lady fair the conjuror plays
125   This very night: good angels her deceive!
But let me laugh awhile, I've mickle time to grieve."

15

Feebly she laugheth in the languid moon,
While Porphyro upon her face doth look,
Like puzzled urchin on an aged crone
130 Who keepeth clos'd a wond'rous riddle-book,
As spectacled she sits in chimney nook.
But soon his eyes grew brilliant, when she told
His lady's purpose; and he scarce could brook
Tears, at the thought of those enchantments cold,
135 And Madeline asleep in lap of legends old.

16

Sudden a thought came like a full-blown rose,
Flushing his brow, and in his pained heart
Made purple riot: then doth he propose
A stratagem, that makes the beldame start:
140 "A cruel man and impious thou art:
Sweet lady, let her pray, and sleep, and dream
Alone with her good angels, far apart
From wicked men like thee. Go, go!—I deem
Thou canst not surely be the same that thou didst
    seem."

17

145 "I will not harm her, by all saints I swear,"
Quoth Porphyro: "O may I ne'er find grace
When my weak voice shall whisper its last prayer,
If one of her soft ringlets I displace,
Or look with ruffian passion in her face:
150 Good Angela, believe me by these tears;
Or I will, even in a moment's space,
Awake, with horrid shout, my foemen's ears,
And beard them, though they be more fang'd than wolves and
    bears."

18

"Ah! why wilt thou affright a feeble soul?
155 A poor, weak, palsy-stricken, churchyard thing,
Whose passing-bell may ere the midnight toll;
Whose prayers for thee, each morn and evening,
Were never miss'd."—Thus plaining, doth she bring
A gentler speech from burning Porphyro;
160 So woful, and of such deep sorrowing,
That Angela gives promise she will do
Whatever he shall wish, betide her weal or woe.

19

Which was, to lead him, in close secrecy,
Even to Madeline's chamber, and there hide
165   Him in a closet, of such privacy
That he might see her beauty unespied,
And win perhaps that night a peerless bride,
While legion'd fairies pac'd the coverlet,
And pale enchantment held her sleepy-eyed.
170   Never on such a night have lovers met,
Since Merlin* paid his Demon all the monstrous debt.

20

"It shall be as thou wishest," said the Dame:
"All cates and dainties shall be stored there
Quickly on this feast-night: by the tambour frame
175   Her own lute thou wilt see: no time to spare,
For I am slow and feeble, and scarce dare
On such a catering trust my dizzy head.
Wait here, my child, with patience; kneel in prayer
The while: Ah! thou must needs the lady wed,
180   Or may I never leave my grave among the dead."

21

So saying, she hobbled off with busy fear.
The lover's endless minutes slowly pass'd;
The dame return'd, and whisper'd in his ear
To follow her; with aged eyes aghast
185   From fright of dim espial.† Safe at last,
Through many a dusky gallery, they gain
The maiden's chamber, silken, hush'd, and chaste;
Where Porphyro took covert, pleas'd amain.
His poor guide hurried back with agues in her brain.

22

190   Her falt'ring hand upon the balustrade,
Old Angela was feeling for the stair,
When Madeline, St. Agnes' charmed maid,
Rose, like a mission'd spirit, unaware:
With silver taper's light, and pious care,
195   She turn'd, and down the aged gossip led
To a safe level matting. Now prepare,
Young Porphyro, for gazing on that bed;
She comes, she comes again, like ring-dove fray'd and fled.

*Merlin: Magician in Arthurian legend.
†espial: Spying or the act of spying.

23

Out went the taper as she hurried in;
200   Its little smoke, in pallid moonshine, died:
She clos'd the door, she panted, all akin
To spirits of the air, and visions wide:
No uttered syllable, or, woe betide!
But to her heart, her heart was voluble,
205   Paining with eloquence her balmy side;
As though a tongueless nightingale should swell
Her throat in vain, and die, heart-stifled, in her dell.

24

A casement high and triple-arch'd there was,
All garlanded with carven imag'ries
210   Of fruits, and flowers, and bunches of knot-grass,
And diamonded with panes of quaint device,
Innumerable of stains and splendid dyes,
As are the tiger-moth's deep-damask'd wings;
And in the midst, 'mong thousand heraldries,
215   And twilight saints, and dim emblazonings,
A shielded scutcheon* blush'd with blood of queens and
kings.

25

Full on this casement shone the wintry moon,
And threw warm gules† on Madeline's fair breast,
As down she knelt for heaven's grace and boon;
220   Rose-bloom fell on her hands, together prest,
And on her silver cross soft amethyst,
And on her hair a glory, like a saint:
She seem'd a splendid angel, newly drest,
Save wings, for heaven:—Porphyro grew faint:
225   She knelt, so pure a thing, so free from mortal taint.

26

Anon his heart revives: her vespers done,
Of all its wreathed pearls her hair she frees;
Unclasps her warmed jewels one by one;
Loosens her fragrant boddice; by degrees
230   Her rich attire creeps rustling to her knees:
Half-hidden, like a mermaid in sea-weed,
Pensive awhile she dreams awake, and sees,

*scutcheon: A shield or emblem bearing a coat of arms.
†gules: A hue of red.

In fancy, fair St. Agnes in her bed,
But dares not look behind, or all the charm is fled.

27

235 Soon, trembling in her soft and chilly nest,
In sort of wakeful swoon, perplex'd she lay,
Until the poppied warmth of sleep oppress'd
Her soothed limbs, and soul fatigued away;
Flown, like a thought, until the morrow-day;
240 Blissfully haven'd both from joy and pain;
Clasp'd like a missal where swart Paynims pray;*
Blinded alike from sunshine and from rain,
As though a rose should shut, and be a bud again.

28

Stol'n to this paradise, and so entranced,
245 Porphyro gazed upon her empty dress,
And listen'd to her breathing, if it chanced
To wake into a slumberous tenderness;
Which when he heard, that minute did he bless,
And breath'd himself: then from the closet crept,
250 Noiseless as fear in a wide wilderness,
And over the hush'd carpet, silent, stept,
And 'tween the curtains peep'd, where, lo!—how fast she slept.

29

Then by the bed-side, where the faded moon
Made a dim, silver twilight, soft he set
255 A table, and, half anguish'd, threw thereon
A cloth of woven crimson, gold, and jet:—
O for some drowsy Morphean amulet!†
The boisterous, midnight, festive clarion,
The kettle-drum, and far-heard clarionet,
260 Affray his ears, though but in dying tone:—
The hall door shuts again, and all the noise is gone.

30

And still she slept an azure-lidded sleep,
In blanched linen, smooth, and lavender'd,
While he from forth the closet brought a heap
265 Of candied apple, quince, and plum, and gourd;

*"Clasped like a missal where swart Paynims pray": Clasped like a prayer book where dark pagans pray.
†Morphean amulet: A sleep-producing charm.

With jellies soother than the creamy curd,
And lucent syrops, tinct with cinnamon;
Manna and dates, in argosy transferr'd
From Fez; and spiced dainties, every one,
270   From silken Samarcand to cedar'd Lebanon.

          31
These delicates he heap'd with glowing hand
On golden dishes and in baskets bright
Of wreathed silver: sumptuous they stand
In the retired quiet of the night,
275   Filling the chilly room with perfume light.—
"And now, my love, my seraph fair, awake!
Thou art my heaven, and I thine eremite:*
Open thine eyes, for meek St. Agnes' sake,
Or I shall drowse beside thee, so my soul doth ache."

          32
280   Thus whispering, his warm, unnerved arm
Sank in her pillow. Shaded was her dream
By the dusk curtains:—'twas a midnight charm
Impossible to melt as iced stream:
The lustrous salvers in the moonlight gleam;
285   Broad golden fringe upon the carpet lies:
It seem'd he never, never could redeem
From such a steadfast spell his lady's eyes;
So mus'd awhile, entoil'd in woofed phantasies.

          33
Awakening up, he took her hollow lute,—
290   Tumultuous,—and, in chords that tenderest be,
He play'd an ancient ditty, long since mute,
In Provence call'd, "La belle dame sans merci":†
Close to her ear touching the melody;—
Wherewith disturb'd, she utter'd a soft moan:
295   He ceased—she panted quick—and suddenly
Her blue affrayed eyes wide open shone:
Upon his knees he sank, pale as smooth-sculptured stone.

          34
Her eyes were open, but she still beheld,
Now wide awake, the vision of her sleep:

*eremite: A religious hermit.
†"La belle dame sans merci": "The lovely merciless beauty" or "The lovely lady without pity,"
a poem by Alain Chartier, a medieval French poet. See Keats' poem by the same title, p. 796.

300 There was a painful change, that nigh expell'd
The blisses of her dream so pure and deep:
At which fair Madeline began to weep,
And moan forth witless words with many a sigh;
While still her gaze on Porphyro would keep;
305 Who knelt, with joined hands and piteous eye,
Fearing to move or speak, she look'd so dreamingly.

35

"Ah, Porphyro!" said she, "but even now
Thy voice was at sweet tremble in mine ear,
Made tuneable with every sweetest vow;
310 And those sad eyes were spiritual and clear:
How chang'd thou art! how pallid, chill, and drear!
Give me that voice again, my Porphyro,
Those looks immortal, those complainings dear!
Oh leave me not in this eternal woe,
315 For if thou diest, my love, I know not where to go."

36

Beyond a mortal man impassion'd far
At these voluptuous accents, he arose,
Ethereal, flush'd, and like a throbbing star
Seen mid the sapphire heaven's deep repose;
320 Into her dream he melted, as the rose
Blendeth its odour with the violet,—
Solution sweet: meantime the frost-wind blows
Like Love's alarum pattering the sharp sleet
Against the window-panes; St. Agnes' moon hath set.

37

325 'Tis dark: quick pattereth the flaw-blown sleet:
"This is no dream, my bride, my Madeline!"
'Tis dark: the iced gusts still rave and beat:
"No dream, alas! alas! and woe is mine!
Porphyro will leave me here to fade and pine.—
330 Cruel! what traitor could thee hither bring?
I curse not, for my heart is lost in thine,
Though thou forsakest a deceived thing;—
A dove forlorn and lost with sick unpruned wing."

38

"My Madeline! sweet dreamer! lovely bride!
335 Say, may I be for aye thy vassal blest?

Thy beauty's shield, heart-shap'd and vermeil* dyed?
Ah, silver shrine, here will I take my rest
After so many hours of toil and quest,
A famish'd pilgrim,—saved by miracle.
340   Though I have found, I will not rob thy nest
Saving of thy sweet self; if thou think'st well
To trust, fair Madeline, to no rude infidel.

39

"Hark! 'tis an elfin-storm from faery land,
Of haggard seeming, but a boon indeed:
345   Arise—arise! the morning is at hand;—
The bloated wassaillers will never heed:—
Let us away, my love, with happy speed;
There are no ears to hear, or eyes to see,—
Drown'd all in Rhenish† and the sleepy mead:
350   Awake! arise! my love, and fearless be,
For o'er the southern moors I have a home for thee."

40

She hurried at his words, beset with fears,
For there were sleeping dragons all around,
At glaring watch, perhaps, with ready spears—
355   Down the wide stairs a darkling way they found.—
In all the house was heard no human sound.
A chain-droop'd lamp was flickering by each door;
The arras, rich with horseman, hawk, and hound,
Flutter'd in the besieging wind's uproar;
360   And the long carpets rose along the gusty floor.

41

They glide, like phantoms, into the wide hall;
Like phantoms, to the iron porch, they glide;
Where lay the Porter, in uneasy sprawl,
With a huge empty flaggon by his side:
365   The wakeful bloodhound rose, and shook his hide,
But his sagacious eye an inmate owns:
By one, and one, the bolts full easy slide:—
The chains lie silent on the footworn stones;—
The key turns, and the door upon its hinges groans.

42

370   And they are gone: ay, ages long ago
These lovers fled away into the storm.

*vermeil dyed: Vermilion, bright red.
†Rhenish: Rhine wine.

That night the Baron dreamt of many a woe,
And all his warrior-guests, with shade and form
Of witch, and demon, and large coffin-worm,
375   Were long be-nightmar'd. Angela the old
Died palsy-twitch'd, with meagre face deform;
The Beadsman, after thousand aves told,
For aye unsought for slept among his ashes cold.

1820

Writing Assignments for "The Eve of St. Agnes"

I. Brief Papers
   A. 1. Write a concise summary of the plot of the poem.
      2. Show that images of coldness dominate stanza 1.
      3. "The Eve of St. Agnes" has been praised as Keats's best narrative poem (one which tells or presents a story). Consider the qualities or elements of a good story and choose one which functions in making "St. Agnes" a good story. Discuss that quality, offering examples from the poem.
      4. Describe the superstitions surrounding St. Agnes' Eve detailed in stanza 6. How do the superstitions blend the sexual with the spiritual?
      5. From the list below, select one of the patterns of imagery in the poem and go through the poem circling examples of the image wherever you find it. Explain how the image changes or remains the same throughout the poem.
         a. Images of youth.
         b. Images of old age.
         c. Images of warmth and heat.
         d. Images of coldness.
         e. Images of death.
         f. Images of vitality and life.
         g. Images of isolation and solitude.
         h. Images of revelry and merriment.
         i. Images of sexuality and sensuousness.
         j. Images of virginity and chastity.
         k. Images of dreaminess and sleep.
         l. Images of alertness.

   B. If this poem were staged as a play, do you believe it would appeal to contemporary audiences? Which features would be most appealing? Least appealing?

II. Longer Papers
   A. Stanzas 30 and 31, which describe the feast Porphyro spreads next to Madeline's bed, contain some of Keats' most lush (and most famous) lines. How does the language of the passage, the description of the feast, sustain the dreamlike and the fairy imagery of the poem as well as the sensual and the sexual appeals?

B. Show how the poem relies on a series of contrasts, and discuss how the contrasts intensify the experience and the impact of the poem.

C. Keats' poetry appeals to the senses. Select one of the following topics and write a paper explaining how the sensory appeal contributes to the poem's impact:

1. Select one stanza of the poem and explore the number of senses affected through the diction and through the images.

2. Go through the poem and find examples of how the language, the diction, or the images appeal to one sense—sight, sound, touch, taste, or feeling. Choose the most vivid examples as the basis for a paper on the poem's sensory appeal.

D. Argue for or against the assertion that "The Eve of St. Agnes" depicts in story form our most intense ambivalence about love—our desire to revel in the physical and sensual joys of love but our equally intense desire to exalt and spiritualize our feelings.

THOMAS LOVELL BEDDOES

The Phantom Wooer

A ghost, that loved a lady fair,
Ever in the starry air,
   Of midnight at her pillow stood;
And, with a sweetness skies above
5 The luring words of human love,
   Her soul the phantom wooed.
Sweet and sweet is their poisoned note,
The little snakes of silver throat,
In mossy skulls that nest and lie,
10 Ever singing, "Die, oh! die."

Young soul put off your flesh, and come
With me into the quiet tomb,
   Our bed is lovely, dark, and sweet;
The earth will swing us, as she goes,
15 Beneath our coverlid of snows,
   And the warm leaden sheet.
Dear and dear is their poisoned note,
The little snakes of silver throat,
In mossy skulls that nest and lie,
20 Ever singing, "Die, oh! die."

1849–1850

Writing Assignments for "The Phantom Wooer"

I. Brief Papers
- A. 1. The phantom uses "luring words of human love" (line 5) to woo his "lady fair" (line 1). Explain in what ways his appeal to the woman is couched in conventional and traditional love language.
  2. Show that the poem's impact rests in part on particularly grisly, bleak images of death.
  3. How do the last four lines in each stanza blend images both grim and beautiful to imply death's appeal?

- B. After several unsuccessful attempts, Beddoes committed suicide by taking poison. To what extent (if any at all) does that affect your response to the poem? Use specific passages from the poem or refer to actual lines and stanzas while discussing any added immediacy or intensity the biographical information invites.

II. Longer Papers
- A. Discuss to what extent the imagery and the language of the poem are likely to horrify contemporary audiences.
- B. Discuss the relationship within each stanza between the first six and the last four lines. How does the refrain in each stanza reinforce the subject matter of the first six lines while altering its mood and impact? What is the emotional impact of the last line in each stanza?

Comparative Papers from Chapter Seven: Adventure and the Supernatural

- A. Compare one of the poems in this chapter with a poem by the same author elsewhere in the book. Explain how the subject matter of each of the poems helps direct the poet's decisions about point of view, style, structure, word choice, and/or language. If you wish, discuss which poem you believe is more successful or more effective.
- B. Explain how several poems treat wanderlust and adventure. To what extent are they desirable or dangerous?
- C. Select the poem in this chapter you find most frightening and explain the sources of its terror.
- D. Choose several poems in this chapter which employ similar imagery or word choice. Explain how the poets use the same images or the same language to achieve different effects in their poems or different reactions from their readers.
- E. The Theatre Department on campus is seeking proposals which outline a dramatic presentation of any good poem about adventure or the supernatural. The proposal will be used in beginning theatre classes, where students must follow the proposal and actually stage the poem. Write a proposal explaining in detail how the class could

make an effective presentation of Tennyson's "Ulysses" (p. 787), Shelley's "Ozymandias" (p. 791), Poe's "Annabel Lee" (p. 794), or Keats' "La Belle Dame Sans Merci" (p. 796). Consider in your proposal what kind of set the class members should construct, what kind of music and lighting they should use, what kind of introduction and commentary should accompany the presentation, and what kind of presentation itself the students should develop. Address your proposal to the director of the undergraduate theatre classes.

RANDALL JARRELL

Next Day

Moving from Cheer to Joy, from Joy to All,
I take a box
And add it to my wild rice, my Cornish game hens.
The slacked or shorted, basketed, identical
5   Food-gathering flocks
Are selves I overlook. Wisdom, said William James,

Is learning what to overlook. And I am wise
If that is wisdom.
Yet somehow, as I buy All from these shelves
10   And the boy takes it to my station wagon,
What I've become
Troubles me even if I shut my eyes.

When I was young and miserable and pretty
And poor, I'd wish
15   What all girls wish: to have a husband,
A house and children. Now that I'm old, my wish
Is womanish:
That the boy putting groceries in my car

See me. It bewilders me he doesn't see me.
20   For so many years
I was good enough to eat: the world looked at me
And its mouth watered. How often they have undressed me,
The eyes of strangers!
And, holding their flesh within my flesh, their vile

25   Imaginings within my imagining,
I too have taken
The chance of life. Now the boy pats my dog
And we start home. Now I am good.
The last mistaken,
30   Ecstatic, accidental bliss, the blind

Happiness that, bursting, leaves upon the palm
Some soap and water—
It was so long ago, back in some Gay
Twenties, Nineties, I don't know. . . . Today I miss
35   My lovely daughter
Away at school, my sons away at school,

My husband away at work—I wish for them.
The dog, the maid,
And I go through the sure unvarying days
40   At home in them. As I look at my life,
I am afraid
Only that it will change, as I am changing:

I am afraid, this morning, of my face.
It looks at me
45   From the rear-view mirror, with the eyes I hate,
The smile I hate. Its plain, lined look
Of gray discovery
Repeats to me: "You're old." That's all, I'm old.

And yet I'm afraid, as I was at the funeral
50   I went to yesterday.
My friend's cold made-up face, granite among its flowers,
Her undressed, operated-on, dressed body
Were my face and body.
As I think of her I hear her telling me

55   How young I seem; I *am* exceptional;
I think of all I have.
But really no one is exceptional,
No one has anything, I'm anybody,
I stand beside my grave
60   Confused with my life, that is commonplace and solitary.

                                                        1965

Writing Assignments for "Next Day"

I. Brief Papers
    A. 1. Describe the speaker's life, discussing what she once was like and what she's
          like now. Use direct and implied evidence from the poem to support your
          description.
       2. Show that *Cheer, Joy,* and *All* can have more than one meaning in the poem.
          Why is their order in the first line important?

3. Show evidence throughout the poem that suggests the woman's confusion about her life.

4. Explain what the speaker means when she says, "I too have taken / The chance of life" (lines 26–27).

B. Argue for or against the assertion that the woman in the poem is unhappy primarily because she fears death.

C. 1. Even though "Next Day" was written by a man, do you believe the woman's attitude is a realistic one? Why or why not?

2. Which of the woman's desires as a girl and as a woman (stanza 3) are typical of most girls' and women's desires? Which are different?

II. Longer Papers

A. Pretend you are a psychologist who has been treating the speaker for acute depression. Write a case study of your patient, describing her life, her values, her fears, and her growing confusion. If you wish, suggest appropriate therapy or treatment.

B. Discuss how the structure of the poem and/or its language and style reinforce the subject matter and the woman's confusion.

C. The last line of the poem reveals the woman's growing confusion with a life that is both "commonplace and solitary" (line 60). From the evidence in the poem, discuss the kind of life she has had and how her friend's death influences her attitude toward her life.

THOMAS CAREW

The Second Rapture

No, worldling, no, 'tis not thy gold
Which thou dost use but to behold,
Nor fortune, honor, nor long life,
Children, or friends, nor a good wife
5   That makes thee happy; these things be
But shadows of felicity.
Give me a wench about thirteen,
Already voted to the queen*
Of lust and lovers, whose soft hair,
10 Fanned with the breath of gentle air,
O'erspreads her shoulders like a tent,
And is her veil and ornament:
Whose tender touch will make the blood
Wild in the aged and the good;

*voted to the queen: Devoted to Venus.

15 Whose kisses fastened to the mouth
   Of threescore years' and longer sloth
   Renew the age, and whose bright eye
   Obscures those lesser lights of sky;
   Whose snowy breasts (if we may call
20 That snow, that never melts at all)
   Makes Jove* invent a new disguise
   In spite of Juno's jealousies;
   Whose every part doth re-invite
   The old decayed appetite;
25 And in whose sweet embraces I
   May melt myself to lust, and die.
      This is true bliss, and I confess
      There is no other happiness.

                                                          1640

Writing Assignments for "The Second Rapture"

I. Brief Papers

A. 1. What conventional comparisons and descriptions does the poet use to describe the young girl's beauty (lines 7–20)?
   2. How is this poem unlike most love poetry?
   3. Why does the speaker use the word *confess* in the next to the last line?
   4. Look up the term *lechery* in the dictionary. To what extent is lechery the main subject of this poem?

B. 1. Some people might object to the poem's subject matter—an older man's passion for sexually active young girls. Do you find the poem offensive? Why or why not?
   2. Look up the word *wench* in a good dictionary. How do its various meanings affect your response to the poem?
   3. How do references to age (the girl is 13 and the male is 60 or older) affect your response to the poem?

II. Longer Papers

A. Which pictures or images in the poem evoke your most intense emotional response?
B. Why is the poem entitled "The Second Rapture"? Explain in detail.
C. Relationships between old men and young girls or women were common in fifteenth- and sixteenth-century literature. To what extent are they common today in novels, films, or television programs? Are those relationships treated seriously? Comically? As taboo?

*Jove: The father of the gods, Jove assumed various disguises to elude his wife Juno's jealousy and enjoy his amorous pursuits.

D. Some argue that, though brutally frank, the speaker's claim has merit. They believe
that sexual union reaffirms life, that union with one young and beautiful is finally
what makes one feel completely alive. Others claim that such a stance is lecherous
or even disgusting. They believe that a stable home, marriage, and children
provide dignity and "true bliss" (line 27). To what extent do you agree or disagree
with either stand as it is conveyed in the poem?

BEN JONSON

On My First Daughter

Here lies, to each her parents' ruth,*
Mary, the daughter of their youth;
Yet all heaven's gifts being heaven's due,
It makes the father less to rue.
5   At six months' end she parted hence
With safety of her innocence;
Whose soul heaven's queen, whose name she bears,
In comfort of her mother's tears,
Hath placed amongst her virgin-train:
10   Where, while that severed doth remain,
This grave partakes the fleshly birth;
Which cover lightly, gentle earth!

1616

Writing Assignments for "On My First Daughter"

I. Brief Papers
A. 1. Show that the father finds some consolation that his daughter died at a very
early age.
2. What does the poet mean when he says, "Yet all heaven's gifts being heaven's
due, / It makes the father less to rue" (lines 3–4)?
3. Show that the mother finds consolation similar to the father's.
4. Describe as best you can the father's attitude toward his daughter's death.

B. Argue for or against the assertion that the last two lines of the poem inspire you
to feel significantly greater sympathy for the speaker.

C. 1. How does the fact that the poem is based on the poet's personal experience
affect your response to it?

*ruth: Grief.

2. Write a description of the speaker—his beliefs, his feelings, his values—based on what is stated and what is implied in the poem.

II. Longer Papers
A. Develop any one of your brief papers into a full-length one.
B. Some people believe Jonson's elegies are powerful because of their restraint. Others believe Jonson's elegies are too intellectual, almost impersonal, and too severe. To what extent do you agree with one or both of these stances?

BEN JONSON

On My First Son

Farewell, thou child of my right hand and joy;
   My sin was too much hope of thee, loved boy.
Seven years thou were lent to me, and I thee pay,
   Exacted by thy fate, on the just day.
5 O, could I lose all father now! For why
   Will man lament the state he should envy?
To have so soon 'scaped world's and flesh's rage,
   And, if no other misery, yet age?
Rest in soft peace, and asked, say here doth lie
10   Ben Jonson, his best piece of poetry:
For whose sake, henceforth, all his vows be such,
   As what he loves may never like too much.

1616

Writing Assignments for "On My First Son"

I. Brief Papers
A. 1. The poem is divided roughly into three parts. Write a paragraph explaining in your own words what the poet says and means in one of the following parts of the poem:
   a. The poet's farewell to his son (lines 1–4).
   b. The poet's questioning of his own anguish and despair (lines 5–8).
   c. The poet's admonition to his son (lines 9–12).
  2. Show that the poet, no matter what he wishes he *could* feel, feels intense pain at the loss of his son.
  3. What does the speaker mean when he says his son was "his best piece of poetry"?

B. Argue for or against the assertion that only someone very religious could be consoled by the father's reasoning in lines 5–8.

C. How does the fact that the poem is based on the poet's personal experience affect your response to it?

II. Longer Papers
   A. To what extent does the poet balance emotion and restraint in the poem? Discuss.
   B. Write a paper comparing this poem to "On My First Daughter" (p. 817). Address one or more of the following questions. Which of the two elegies is the more emotional and why? To what extent is the difference in the elegies caused by the children's different ages and their different sexes? In which of the two elegies do you feel greater sympathy for the speaker? How is the father's grief displayed in each? What consolation does the father find in each?

DYLAN THOMAS

Do Not Go Gentle into That Good Night

Do not go gentle into that good night,
Old age should burn and rave at close of day;
Rage, rage against the dying of the light.

Though wise men at their end know dark is right,
5 Because their words had forked no lightning they
Do not go gentle into that good night.

Good men, the last wave by, crying how bright
Their frail deeds might have danced in a green bay,
Rage, rage against the dying of the light.

10 Wild men who caught and sang the sun in flight,
And learn, too late, they grieved it on its way,
Do not go gentle into that good night.

Grave men, near death, who see with blinding sight
Blind eyes could blaze like meteors and be gay,
15 Rage, rage against the dying of the light.

And you, my father, there on the sad height,
Curse, bless, me now with your fierce tears, I pray.
Do not go gentle into that good night.
Rage, rage against the dying of the light.

1951

Writing Assignments for "Do Not Go Gentle into That Good Night"

I. Brief Papers

A. 1. Summarize in your own words the speaker's attitude toward aging and death.
   2. Why does the speaker want his father to "Curse, bless, me now with your fierce tears" (line 17)?
   3. What do the wise men, good men, wild men, and grave men all share? Discuss one thing they have in common.
   4. Find two lines in the poem you have problems understanding. Spend 10 minutes free writing about the lines, reacting to any strong emotion or mental picture the lines evoke. Since the goal of free writing is to generate ideas quickly, do not worry about spelling, punctuation, grammar, or sentence structure. Just keep writing down whatever comes into your head. Don't stop writing for any reason. If you can't think of anything to say, just write "I can't think of anything to say" until something comes to mind. After 10 minutes, look back over your writing and find one idea to explore further. Write once again, this time for 5 minutes, about the idea. Use your free writings as a basis for a brief paper about the two lines.

B. Argue for or against the assertion that the speaker's attitude toward death differs from the beliefs of almost everyone in our society.

C. 1. Write about someone you know who "raged" against the dying of the light or who did not. How does that experience affect your interpretation of the poem?
   2. All the men described in the poem realize, only as they near death, that they have not lived as happily or as fully as they might have. Do you believe most people experience such a realization? How does your belief affect your interpretation of the poem?

II. Longer Papers

A. Thomas' poetry has been praised for being both violent and tender at the same time. How does this poem illustrate that paradox?
B. "Do Not Go Gentle into That Good Night" evokes such strong emotional response that one may overlook its carefully crafted organization and artistry. Consider one or more of the questions below and analyze the poet's style and language. Then write an essay about how the style and structure reinforce the subject matter.
   1. In what ways does the poet link stanzas 2 and 4? Stanzas 3 and 5?
   2. What is the relationship between the first and second line of each stanza in stanzas 2–5? How does the second line of each stanza justify the speaker's convictions?
   3. Find as many examples as possible of the poet's use of repetition—repeated lines, repeated words, and repeated letters and sounds. How does that repetition reinforce the speaker's entreaties and affect your response to the poem?

C. Have someone read the poem aloud to you several times. After each reading quickly jot down your reactions. Which words, mental pictures or images, or sounds impress you the most? After considering your reactions, discuss the central impression(s) the poem conveys. Does it convey grief? Anger? Passion? Despair? How does the poet achieve the impression(s)?

THOMAS GRAY

Elegy Written in a Country Churchyard

The curfew tolls the knell of parting day;
The lowing herd wind slowly o'er the lea;
The plowman homeward plods his weary way,
And leaves the world to darkness and to me.

5   Now fades the glimmering landscape on the sight,
And all the air a solemn stillness holds,
Save where the beetle wheels his droning flight,
And drowsy tinklings lull the distant folds;

Save that from yonder ivy-mantled tow'r,
10   The moping owl does to the moon complain
Of such as, wand'ring near her secret bow'r,
Molest her ancient solitary reign.

Beneath those rugged elms, that yew tree's shade,
Where heaves the turf in many a mold'ring heap,
15   Each in his narrow cell for ever laid,
The rude forefathers of the hamlet sleep.

The breezy call of incense-breathing Morn,
The swallow twitt'ring from the straw-built shed,
The cock's shrill clarion, or the echoing horn,
20   No more shall rouse them from their lowly bed.

For them no more the blazing hearth shall burn,
Or busy housewife ply her evening care;
No children run to lisp their sire's return,
Or climb his knees the envied kiss to share.

25   Oft did the harvest to their sickle yield;
Their furrow oft the stubborn glebe has broke;

How jocund did they drive their team afield!
How bowed the woods beneath their sturdy stroke!

Let not Ambition mock their useful toil,
30   Their homely joys, and destiny obscure;
Nor Grandeur hear with a disdainful smile,
The short and simple annals of the poor.

The boast of heraldry, the pomp of pow'r,
And all that beauty, all that wealth, e'er gave
35   Awaits alike th' inevitable hour.
The paths of glory lead but to the grave.

Nor you, ye proud, impute to these the fault
If Mem'ry o'er their tomb no trophies raise,
Where, through the long-drawn aisle and fretted vault,
40   The pealing anthem swells the note of praise.

Can storied urn or animated bust
Back to its mansion call the fleeting breath?
Can Honor's voice provoke the silent dust,
Or Flattery soothe the dull cold ear of Death?

45   Perhaps in this neglected spot is laid
Some heart once pregnant with celestial fire;
Hands that the rod of empire might have swayed,
Or waked to ecstasy the living lyre.

But Knowledge to their eyes her ample page,
50   Rich with the spoils of time, did ne'er unroll;
Chill Penury repressed their noble rage,
And froze the genial current of the soul.

Full many a gem of purest ray serene
The dark unfathomed caves of ocean bear;
55   Full many a flower is born to blush unseen,
And waste its sweetness on the desert air.

Some village Hampden,* that with dauntless breast
The little tyrant of his fields withstood;
Some mute inglorious Milton here may rest,
60   Some Cromwell guiltless of his country's blood.

*Hampden: John Hampden led the opposition to the rule of Charles I, who ruled Great Britain
from 1625 to 1649.

Th' applause of list'ning senates to command,
The threats of pain and ruin to despise,
To scatter plenty o'er a smiling land,
And read their hist'ry in a nation's eyes,

65   Their lot forbade: nor circumscribed alone
Their growing virtues, but their crimes confined;
Forbade to wade through slaughter to a throne
And shut the gates of mercy on mankind,

The struggling pangs of conscious truth to hide,
70   To quench the blushes of ingenuous shame,
Or heap the shrine of Luxury and Pride
With incense kindled at the Muse's flame.

Far from the madding crowd's ignoble strife,
Their sober wishes never learned to stray;
75   Along the cool sequestered vale of life
They kept the noiseless tenor of their way.

Yet ev'n these bones from insult to protect,
Some frail memorial still erected nigh,
With uncouth rimes and shapeless sculpture decked,
80   Implores the passing tribute of a sigh.

Their name, their years, spelt by th' unlettered Muse,
The place of fame and elegy supply;
And many a holy text around she strews,
That teach the rustic moralist to die.

85   For who, to dumb Forgetfulness a prey,
This pleasing anxious being e'er resigned,
Left the warm precincts of the cheerful day,
Nor cast one longing ling'ring look behind?

On some fond breast the parting soul relies,
90   Some pious drops the closing eye requires;
Ev'n from the tomb the voice of Nature cries,
Ev'n in our ashes live their wonted fires.

For thee who, mindful of th' unhonored dead,
Dost in these lines their artless tale relate,
95   If chance, by lonely contemplation led,
Some kindred spirit shall inquire thy fate,

Haply some hoary-headed swain may say,
"Oft have we seen him at the peep of dawn
Brushing with hasty steps the dews away
100   To meet the sun upon the upland lawn.

"There at the foot of yonder nodding beech
That wreathes its old fantastic roots so high,
His listless length at noontide would he stretch,
And pore upon the brook that babbles by.

105   "Hard by yon wood, now smiling as in scorn,
Mutt'ring his wayward fancies he would rove,
Now drooping, woeful wan, like one forlorn,
Or crazed with care, or crossed in hopeless love.

"One morn I missed him on the customed hill,
110   Along the heath and near his fav'rite tree;
Another came; nor yet beside the rill,
Nor up the lawn, nor at the wood was he;

"The next, with dirges due in sad array
Slow through the church-way path we saw him borne.
115   Approach and read (for thou canst read) the lay,
Graved on the stone beneath yon aged thorn."

THE EPITAPH

Here rests his head upon the lap of Earth
A youth to fortune and to fame unknown.
Fair Science frowned not on his humble birth,
120   And Melancholy marked him for her own.

Large was his bounty, and his soul sincere,
Heav'n did a recompense as largely send:
He gave to Misery all he had, a tear;
He gained from heav'n ('twas all he wished) a friend.

125   No farther seek his merits to disclose,
Or draw his frailties from their dread abode
(There they alike in trembling hope repose),
The bosom of his Father and his God.

1751

Writing Assignments for "Elegy Written in a Country Churchyard"

I. Brief Papers

  A. 1. Describe the dramatic setting of the poem, established most clearly in lines 1–16.

      2. In lines 1–44, the speaker reflects on death. Discuss one or more of the speaker's statements or implications.

      3. In lines 45–76, the speaker praises and defends humble, rural life. Show that the speaker believes such a life is dignified, even noble.

      4. Lines 77–128, which conclude the poem, are devoted to the young poet who lived in the village, frequented the graveyard, and wrote epitaphs for the village people. Respond to one of the following questions:

         a. What is the speaker's attitude toward the young poet in lines 77–92?

         b. How does the young poet's verse, the epitaphs and "uncouth rimes" (line 79) he scrawls, "teach the rustic moralist to die" (line 84)?

         c. How does the "hoary-headed swain" describe the young poet in lines 98–116?

         d. Based on his epitaph (lines 117–128), describe the young poet. What was important to him? What kind of person was he?

      5. The language in the poem is especially rich. Find one or two particularly striking lines, and explain how the language—the words, images, or comparisons—reinforces the subject matter of the poem.

  B. Lines 49–52 argue that the townspeople's poverty and lack of education destined them to live limited lives, just as "Full many a flower is born to blush unseen, / And waste its sweetness on the desert air" (lines 55–56). Argue for or against the assertion that the townspeople led unfulfilled lives by current standards.

  C. 1. After rereading lines 96–128, describe your own reactions to the young poet, his preoccupation with death and the graveyard, the villagers' clear liking for him, and his muttered "wayward fancies" (line 106).

      2. Do you believe it is a handicap to be raised in the country? How does your belief affect your interpretation of the poem?

II. Longer Papers

  A. Explain in detail why the speaker in the poem defends the unpretentious lifestyle of the villagers, and discuss how appropriate or valid his defense would be today for people with similar backgrounds.

  B. The poem is divided roughly into three parts: the speaker's reflection on death (lines 1–44); the dignity and quality of a simple, unpretentious lifestyle (lines 45–76); and the tribute to the young poet (lines 77–128). Using this rough division as a point of departure, respond to one of the following topics:

1. Discuss how the three parts of the poem overlap and relate to each other.
2. Discuss how the speaker's attitude changes or remains the same from one section to the next.
3. Discuss how the last part of the poem, the description of the young poet, evolves naturally from the first two parts, how the young poet embodies ideals expressed earlier in the poem.

C. Discuss to what extent this poem is outdated in its attitudes and subject matter and to what extent it reflects contemporary values and beliefs.

A. E. HOUSMAN

To an Athlete Dying Young

The time you won your town the race
We chaired you through the market place;
Man and boy stood cheering by,
And home we brought you shoulder-high.

5   Today, the road all runners come,
Shoulder-high we bring you home,
And set you at your threshold down,
Townsman of a stiller town.

Smart lad, to slip betimes away
10   From fields where glory does not stay
And early though the laurel grows
It withers quicker than the rose.

Eyes the shady night has shut
Cannot see the record cut,
15   And silence sounds no worse than cheers
After earth has stopped the ears:

Now you will not swell the rout
Of lads that wore their honors out,
Runners whom renown outran
20   And the name died before the man.

So set, before its echoes fade,
The fleet foot on the sill of shade,
And hold to the low lintel up
The still defended challenge cup.

25   And round that early laureled head
      Will flock to gaze the strengthless dead
      And find unwithered on its curls
      The garland briefer than a girl's.

                                                    1896

Writing Assignments for "To an Athlete Dying Young"

I. Brief Papers
  A. 1. Based on the first two stanzas, explain the dramatic setting of the poem,
        discussing who is speaking, on what occasion, and about whom.
     2. Look up *laurel* in the dictionary. Explain which meanings help you understand
        "And early though the laurel grows / It withers quicker than the rose."
     3. Look up *shade* in the dictionary. Show that the poet intended more than one
        meaning for *shady* (line 13) and *shade* (line 22).
     4. Relying on the last two stanzas, show that the athlete's death is a victory.

  B. Argue for or against either assertion below.
     1. The speaker's attitude toward the young athlete's death would be different if
        the young man had lost the race.
     2. The poem implies most people would live happier, more fulfilled lives if they
        died soon after their most successful, most exhilarating experience.

  C. Write a letter to the speaker in the poem, drawing on your own experience and
     observations. Agree or disagree with the speaker's attitude toward the young
     athlete's death.

II. Longer Papers
  A. Show that the poet sustains athletic imagery throughout the poem.
  B. Show that this poem is as much about growing old as it is about dying young.
  C. Explain why the subject matter—the death of a young *athlete,* not just a young
     man or woman—is appropriate. How does the subject matter affect your re-
     sponse to the poem?

EDWIN ARLINGTON ROBINSON

Richard Cory

Whenever Richard Cory went down town,
We people on the pavement looked at him:
He was a gentleman from sole to crown,
Clean favored, and imperially slim.

5   And he was always quietly arrayed,
    And he was always human when he talked;
    But still he fluttered pulses when he said,
    "Good-morning," and he glittered when he walked.

    And he was rich—yes, richer than a king—
10 And admirably schooled in every grace:
    In fine, we thought that he was everything
    To make us wish that we were in his place.

    So on we worked, and waited for the light,
    And went without the meat, and cursed the bread;
15 And Richard Cory, one calm summer night,
    Went home and put a bullet through his head.

                                              1897

Writing Assignments for "Richard Cory"

I. Brief Papers
   A. 1. Write a short character sketch of Richard Cory.
      2. Write a short character sketch of the speaker in the poem.
      3. Show that Richard Cory was respected for more than his wealth.
      4. Go through the poem and circle all the words or phrases connecting Richard
         Cory to wealth or to royalty. How do these words shape your response to
         Richard Cory and to the poem?

   B. Argue for or against either assertion below.
      1. "Richard Cory" is at best a mediocre poem, relying on the shock effect of a
         surprise ending and giving readers little reason to return and reread it.
      2. The presuicide Richard Cory represents the kind of person all of us wish we
         could be.

   C. Why do you believe Richard Cory committed suicide?

II. Longer Papers
   A. Develop any one of the paragraph assignments into a full-length paper.
   B. Discuss to what extent Richard Cory epitomizes the kind of person most people
      wish they could be and to what degree his suicide is a believable act. Focus your
      discussion on Cory's personality, his wealth and background, the speaker's atti-
      tude toward him, the likelihood he could have led a fulfilled, happy life, or any
      other element of the poem you wish.

EMILY DICKINSON

Because I Could Not Stop for Death

    Because I could not stop for Death—
    He kindly stopped for me—
    The Carriage held but just Ourselves—
    And Immortality.

5   We slowly drove—He knew no haste
    And I had put away
    My labor and my leisure too,
    For His Civility—

    We passed the School, where Children strove
10   At Recess—in the Ring—
    We passed the Fields of Gazing Grain—
    We passed the Setting Sun—

    Or rather—He passed Us—
    The Dews drew quivering and chill—
15   For only Gossamer, my Gown—
    My Tippet—only Tulle—

    We paused before a House that seemed
    A Swelling of the Ground—
    The Roof was scarcely visible—
20   The Cornice—in the Ground—

    Since then—'tis Centuries—and yet
    Feels shorter than the Day
    I first surmised the Horses' Heads
    Were toward Eternity—

                       1890*

Writing Assignments for "Because I Could Not Stop for Death"

I. Brief Papers

    A. 1. One common embodiment of death is that of a dark, enrobed figure. How
         does this poem embody death? Which of his qualities are most striking?

*1890: Publication date, four years after Dickinson's death in 1886. The date conjectured for the earliest known manuscript of the poem is 1862.

2. Show that the speaker is completely passive throughout the poem.
3. Look up *gossamer, tippet,* and *tulle* in a dictionary. Which meanings are most appropriate in the poem and how does the poet's choice of words affect your response to the poem?
4. Go through the poem and note the poet's use of punctuation, especially the dash. How does the punctuation reinforce the subject matter and the impact of the poem?

B. Argue for or against either assertion below.
1. While the speaker's attitude toward her death seems matter-of-fact, the impact of the poem is grim and frightening.
2. Most of our common assumptions about death resemble the speaker's.

C. 1. What do you find most frightening about the poet's depiction of death?
2. What do you find most reassuring about the poet's depiction of death?

II. Longer Papers
A. Discuss to what extent the writer balances emotion and restraint in the poem.
B. How does the speaker's embodiment of death differ from current stereotypical embodiments of death, popular in movies or on television? Is Dickinson's treatment of death more or less frightening than those stereotypes?
C. Go through the poem carefully, noting the progression of the action. Discuss the structure of the poem, dwelling specifically on the relationship of the final stanza to the rest of the poem.

EMILY DICKINSON

It's Easy to Invent a Life

It's easy to invent a Life—
God does it—every Day—
Creation—but the Gambol
Of His Authority—

5 It's easy to efface it—
The thrifty Deity
Could scarce afford Eternity
To Spontaneity—

The Perished Patterns murmur—
10 But His Perturbless Plan

Proceed—inserting Here—a Sun—
There—leaving out a Man—

1929*

Writing Assignments for "It's Easy to Invent a Life"

I. Brief Papers
 A. 1. Look up the word *gambol* in the dictionary. How do its various meanings help you understand the poem?
   2. To what extent is death important to the deity the speaker describes in the poem?
   3. Explain as fully as possible the relationship between stanza 1 and stanza 2, focusing on the subject matter, the structure, the language, the speaker's attitude, and/or any other element you find important.

 B. Argue for or against one of the assertions below.
   1. The speaker is angered by God's seeming indifference to death.
   2. The speaker is sarcastic when she says, "The thrifty Deity / Could scarce afford Eternity / To Spontaneity—" (lines 6–8).
   3. The deity described in the poem is callous and indifferent to human suffering.

 C. 1. What is your personal response to the deity described in the poem? What most affects your response?
   2. You are in charge of staging a reading of this poem for your oral interpretation class. Write a short paper explaining how someone should read the poem, what tone of voice she should use, where and how often she should pause, and what words or phrases she should stress. If you wish, give explicit instructions concerning appropriate attire for the speaker, the most effective set or background for the reading, or any other instructions which would enhance the presentation of the poem.

II. Longer Papers
 A. Go through the poem and circle words which clearly imply the speaker's attitude toward the deity she describes. Even if you know the meaning of the words, look them up in a good dictionary and consider all of their various meanings. Then, discuss the speaker's attitude toward God in the poem and how the poem's language reveals that attitude and shapes the reader's response.
 B. After reading "Because I Could Not Stop for Death" (p. 829), discuss how Dickinson treats death in both poems. Focus on the subject matter, the structure, the language, the speakers' attitudes, the readers' response, and/or any other element of the poems you believe important.

*1929: Publication date, 43 years after Dickinson's death in 1886. The date conjectured for the earliest known manuscript of the poem is 1863.

ROBERT FROST

Home Burial

He saw her from the bottom of the stairs
Before she saw him. She was starting down,
Looking back over her shoulder at some fear.
She took a doubtful step and then undid it
5   To raise herself and look again. He spoke
Advancing toward her: 'What is it you see
From up there always—for I want to know.'
She turned and sank upon her skirts at that,
And her face changed from terrified to dull.
10 He said to gain time: 'What is it you see.'

Mounting until she cowered under him.
'I will find out now—you must tell me, dear.'
She, in her place, refused him any help
With the least stiffening of her neck and silence.
15 She let him look, sure that he wouldn't see,
Blind creature; and awhile he didn't see.
But at last he murmured, 'Oh,' and again, 'Oh.'

'What is it—what?' she said.

                          'Just that I see.'

'You don't,' she challenged. 'Tell me what it is.'

20 'The wonder is I didn't see at once.
I never noticed it from here before.
I must be wonted to it—that's the reason.
The little graveyard where my people are!
So small the window frames the whole of it.
25 Not so much larger than a bedroom, it is?
There are three stones of slate and one of marble,
Broad-shouldered little slabs there in the sunlight
On the sidehill. We haven't to mind *those.*
But I understand: it is not the stones,
30 But the child's mound—'

                          'Don't, don't, don't, don't,' she cried.

She withdrew shrinking from beneath his arm
That rested on the bannister, and slid downstairs;

And turned on him with such a daunting look,
He said twice over before he knew himself:
35 'Can't a man speak of his own child he's lost?'

'Not you! Oh, where's my hat? Oh, I don't need it!
I must get out of here. I must get air.
I don't know rightly whether any man can.'

'Amy! Don't go to someone else this time.
40 Listen to me. I won't come down the stairs.'
He sat and fixed his chin between his fists.
'There's something I should like to ask you, dear,'

'You don't know how to ask it.'

                              'Help me, then.'

Her fingers moved the latch for all reply.

45 'My words are nearly always an offense.
I don't know how to speak of anything
So as to please you. But I might be taught
I should suppose. I can't say I see how.
A man must partly give up being a man
50 With women-folk. We could have some arrangement
By which I'd bind myself to keep hands off
Anything special you're a-mind to name.
Though I don't like such things 'twixt those that love.
Two that don't love can't live together without them.
55 But two that do can't live together with them.'
She moved the latch a little. 'Don't—don't go.
Don't carry it to someone else this time.
Tell me about it if it's something human.
Let me into your grief. I'm not so much
60 Unlike other folks as your standing there
Apart would make me out. Give me my chance.
I do think, though, you overdo it a little.
What was it brought you up to think it the thing
To take your mother-loss of a first child
65 So inconsolably—in the face of love.
You'd think his memory might be satisfied—'

'There you go sneering now!'

                              'I'm not, I'm not!
You make me angry. I'll come down to you.

God, what a woman! And it's come to this,
70   A man can't speak of his own child that's dead.'

'You can't because you don't know how to speak.
If you had any feelings, you that dug
With your own hand—how could you?—his little grave;
I saw you from that very window there,
75   Making the gravel leap and leap in air,
Leap up, like that, like that, and land so lightly
And roll back down the mound beside the hole.
I thought, Who is that man? I didn't know you.
And I crept down the stairs and up the stairs
80   To look again, and still your spade kept lifting.
Then you came in. I heard your rumbling voice
Out in the kitchen, and I don't know why,
But I went near to see with my own eyes.
You could sit there with the stains on your shoes
85   Of the fresh earth from your own baby's grave
And talk about your everyday concerns.
You had stood the spade up against the wall
Outside there in the entry, for I saw it.'

'I shall laugh the worst laugh I ever laughed.
90   I'm cursed. God, if I don't believe I'm cursed.'

'I can repeat the very words you were saying.
"Three foggy mornings and one rainy day
Will rot the best birch fence a man can build."
Think of it, talk like that at such a time!
95   What had how long it takes a birch to rot
To do with what was in the darkened parlor.
You *couldn't* care! The nearest friends can go
With anyone to death, comes so far short
They might as well not try to go at all.
100   No, from the time when one is sick to death,
One is alone, and he dies more alone.
Friends make pretense of following to the grave,
But before one is in it, their minds are turned
And making the best of their way back to life
105   And living people, and things they understand.
But the world's evil. I won't have grief so
If I can change it. Oh, I won't, I won't!'

'There, you have said it all and you feel better.
You won't go now. You're crying. Close the door.

110 The heart's gone out of it: why keep it up.
Amy! There's someone coming down the road!'

'*You*—oh, you think the talk is all. I must go—
Somewhere out of this house. How can I make you—'
'If—you—do!' She was opening the door wider.
115 'Where do you mean to go? First tell me that.
I'll follow and bring you back by force. I *will!*—'

1914

Writing Assignments for "Home Burial"

I. Brief Papers

A. 1. Explain in detail one example from the poem that illustrates the couple's inability to communicate.
2. Show evidence in the poem that implies the couple's relationship has eroded over a period of time.
3. Explain the dramatic situation of the poem, discussing in detail what leads to the couple's confrontation on the stairs.
4. Explain what the man means when he says, "A man must partly give up being a man / With women-folk" (lines 49–50).
5. Lines 53–55 are, perhaps, the most difficult in the poem. Read them through several times until you are confident that you understand them. Explain the husband's attitude toward love and communication within marriage and discuss how that attitude affects your response to the husband.

B. Argue for or against one of the assertions below.
1. The man feels the loss of their child less than does the woman.
2. The couple's relationship is unchanged at the end of the poem.
3. The poem is about the inability of men and women to understand one another's point of view more than it is a poem about death.

C. 1. The woman thinks her husband's words (lines 92–93) have nothing to do with the dead child. Do you agree?
2. Do you believe there is a solution to the couple's problem?
3. Pretend you are a writing teacher who receives the following brief paper from a conscientious student writer who pays close attention to your comments about her writing. Write a paragraph responding to the paper. Discuss the writer's strengths as a reader and as a writer, and suggest how she might expand or revise her comments.

> The basic conflict in the poem "Home Burial" centers on the different ways a husband and a wife deal with the death of their infant son. Amy, the wife, resents the perceived ease with which her husband figuratively

and literally buried the child. "You could sit there with the stain on your shoes / Of the fresh earth from your baby's grave / And talk about your everyday concerns."

The husband feels that Amy is oversensitive; "I do feel though, you overdo it a little," and that his is in a no-win situation. He never knows what he can and cannot mention to his wife: "We could have some arrangement / By which I'd bind myself to keep hands off / Anything special you're a mind to name." They seem incapable of settling their differences because Amy feels that "the world's evil" and that no one, not even her husband, cares about the death of her baby. The husband seems willing to try to help his wife. "Let me into your grief," but Amy interprets his willingness as the callousness which she so deeply resents. By the end of the poem, they have not reached a resolution. Both have stated their feelings but Amy leaves, refusing to go any farther toward an understanding.

II. Longer Papers

   A. In the poem, the husband says, "My words are nearly always an offense" (line 45). The woman says, "you don't know how to speak" (line 71). Discussing the subject matter, the dialogue, the structure of the poem, and/or the language, show that the couple has reached a complete inability to communicate.

   B. Study the woman's assessment of most people's reaction to death (lines 100–104). She concludes such a reaction is evil. To what extent do you think her assessment is accurate?

   C. One college freshman wrote the following introduction to an essay after reading "Home Burial." Read the paragraph and decide if you agree or disagree with his assertions. Write a paper supporting or refuting his claims.

   > Although the woman in Robert Frost's "Home Burial" implicitly accuses her husband of not caring about the death of their child, she is wrong; he probably feels just as much sorrow as she, but is simply not able to express it. Like most men of his time, the husband has probably been taught not to reveal his feelings to others. Therefore, he does not show his grief as his wife does, and she misunderstands the ways in which he attempts to alleviate his sorrows.

ALICE WALKER

Burial

I

They have fenced in the dirt road
that once led to Wards Chapel
A.M.E. church,
and cows graze

5   among the stones that
mark my family's graves.
The massive oak is gone
from out the church yard,
but the giant space is left
10   unfilled;
despite the two-lane blacktop
that slides across
the old, unalterable
roots.

II

15   Today I bring my own child here;
to this place where my father's
grandmother rests undisturbed
beneath the Georgia sun,
above her the neatstepping hooves
20   of cattle.
Here the graves soon grow back into the land.
Have been known to sink. To drop open without
warning. To cover themselves with wild ivy,
blackberries. Bittersweet and sage.
25   No one knows why. No one asks.
When Burning Off Day comes, as it does
some years,
the graves are haphazardly cleared and snakes
hacked to death and burned sizzling
30   in the brush. . . . The odor of smoke, oak
leaves, honeysuckle.
Forgetful of geographic resolutions as birds,
the farflung young fly South to bury
the old dead.

III

35   The old women move quietly up
and touch Sis Rachel's face.
"Tell Jesus I'm coming," they say.
"Tell Him I ain't goin' to *be*
long."

40   My grandfather turns his creaking head
away from the lavender box.
He does not cry. But looks afraid.
For years he called her "Woman";
shortened over the decades to
45   "'Oman."

On the cut stone for "'Oman's" grave
he did not notice
they had misspelled her name.

(The stone reads *Racher Walker*—not "Rachel"—
50 *Loving Wife, Devoted Mother.*)

          IV

As a young woman, who had known her? Tripping
eagerly, "loving wife," to my grandfather's
bed. Not pretty, but serviceable. A hard
worker, with rough, moist hands. Her own two
55 babies dead before she came.
Came to seven children.
To aprons and sweat.
Came to quiltmaking.
Came to canning and vegetable gardens
60 *big as fields.*
Came to fields to plow.
Cotton to chop.
Potatoes to dig.
Came to multiple measles, chickenpox,
65 *and croup.*
Came to water from springs.
Came to leaning houses one story high.
Came to rivalries. Saturday night battles.
Came to straightened hair, Noxzema, and
70 *feet washing at the Hardshell Baptist church.*
Came to zinnias around the woodpile.
Came to grandchildren not of her blood
whom she taught to dip snuff without
sneezing.

75 *Came to death blank, forgetful of it all.*

When he called her "'Oman" she no longer
listened. Or heard, or knew, or felt.

          V

It is not until I see my first-grade teacher
review her body that I cry.
80 Not for the dead, but for the gray in my
first-grade teacher's hair. For memories
of before I was born, when teacher and
grandmother loved each other; and later
above the ducks made of soap and the orange-

85   legged chicks Miss Reynolds drew over
     my own small hand
     on paper with wide blue lines.

          VI
     Not for the dead, but for memories. None of
     them sad. But seen from the angle of her
90   death.

                                                                    1972

Writing Assignments for "Burial"

I. Brief Papers

   A. 1. Show that Rachel Walker, the speaker's grandmother, had a hard life.
      2. Describe the speaker's attitude toward her grandmother.
      3. Describe the speaker's attitude toward her grandfather.
      4. Show that the poem is not structured chronologically.
      5. Explain how either Part I or Part VI relates to the rest of the poem.

   B. Argue for or against one of the assertions below.
      1. Rachel Walker's life would have been better if she had not married the
         speaker's grandfather.
      2. The poem treats men unsympathetically.
      3. The title "Burial" has more than one meaning.

   C. 1. How does the description of the grandfather in Part III and Part IV affect your
         response to the poem? What details or information influence you the most?
      2. What is your attitude toward the speaker in the poem?

II. Longer Papers

   A. Explain how your attitude toward the speaker, her grandmother, and her grandfa-
      ther influences your understanding and your appreciation of the poem.
   B. Some of Alice Walker's most memorable poems deal with compassion, love, and
      trust—lost and gained. To what extent does this poem deal with one or more of
      these subjects?
   C. Parts III and IV of the poem describe Rachel Walker's life and her funeral. Choose
      any other part of the poem—Part I, II, V, or VI—and explain in detail how that
      part relates to the rest of the poem and to Rachel Walker's life specifically.

ADRIENNE RICH

*Phantasia for Elvira Shatayev**

The cold felt cold until our blood
grew colder   then the wind
died down and we slept

If in this sleep I speak
5   it's with a voice no longer personal
(I want to say   *with voices*)
When the wind tore   our breath from us at last
we had no need of words
For months   for years   each one of us
10   had felt her own *yes*   growing in her
slowly forming   as she stood at windows   waited

for trains   mended her rucksack   combed her hair
What we were to learn   was simply   what we had
up here   as out of all words   that *yes*   gathered
15   its forces   fused itself   and only just in time
to meet a *No* of no degrees
the black hole   sucking the world in

I feel you climbing toward me
your cleated bootsoles leaving   their geometric bite
20   colossally embossed   on microscopic crystals
as when I trailed you in the Caucasus
Now I am further
ahead   than either of us dreamed   anyone would be
I have become

25   the white snow packed like asphalt by the wind
the women I love   lightly flung   against the mountain
that blue sky
our frozen eyes unribboned   through the storm
we could have stitched that blueness   together   like a quilt

30   You come (I know this)   with your love   your loss
strapped to your body   with your tape-recorder   camera
ice-pick   against advisement

*Elvira Shatayev: Shatayev was the leader of a women's climbing team. In August 1974, on Lenin Peak in the USSR, Shatayev and all the members of the team died in a storm. Shatayev's husband found and buried all the bodies.

to give us burial in the snow   and in your mind
While my body lies out here
35   flashing like a prism   into your eyes
how could you sleep   You climbed here for yourself
we climbed for ourselves

When you have buried us   told your story
ours does not end   we stream
40   into the unfinished   the unbegun
the possible
Every cell's core of heat   pulsed out of us
into the thin air   of the universe
the armature of rock beneath these snows
45   this mountain   which has taken   the imprint of our minds
through changes elemental and minute
as those we underwent
to bring each other here

choosing ourselves   each other   and this life
50   whose every breath   and grasp   and further foothold
is somewhere   still enacted   and continuing

In the diary I wrote: *Now we are ready*
and each of us knows it   I have never loved
like this   I have never seen
55   *my own forces so taken up and shared*
and given back
After the long training   the early sieges
we are moving almost effortlessly in our love

In the diary as the wind   began to tear
60   at the tents over us   I wrote:
We know now we have always been in danger
down in our separateness
and now up here together   but till now
we had not touched our strength

65   In the diary torn from my fingers I had written:
What does love mean
what does it mean   "to survive"
A cable of blue fire ropes our bodies
burning together in the snow   We will not live
70   *to settle for less   We have dreamed of this*
all of our lives

1975

Writing Assignments for "Phantasia for Elvira Shatayev"

I. Brief Papers
  A. 1. Look up the word *phantasia* (often listed under *fantasia*) in the dictionary. Discuss how its various meanings help you to understand the poem and affect your response to it.
     2. Show that the first eleven lines of the poem establish a mood and attitude toward the women's death prevalent throughout the rest of the poem.
     3. Explain one of the following lines in the poem, discussing its use of language, its subject, its implications about the speaker or the poet, or its effect on the reader:
        a. For months   for years   each one of us
           had felt her own *yes*   growing in her
           (lines 9–10)
        b. . . . You climbed here for yourself
           we climbed for ourselves
           (lines 36–37)
        c. *After the long training   the early sieges*
           we are moving almost effortlessly in our love
           (lines 57–58)
        d. . . . *We will not live*
           to settle for less   We have dreamed of this
           all of our lives
           (lines 69–71)
     4. Circle all references in the poem to heat, warmth, and fire. Show that fire is a positive force in the poem.
     5. Explain how the quest of the "you" addressed in stanzas 4, 6, and 7 is different from the quest of the women who die together.

  B. Argue for or against the assertion that, though it is about the death of many women, the poem is affirmative and optimistic.

  C. 1. How does the fact that the poem is based on a real incident affect your interpretation of the poem and your response to it?
     2. Write a letter to Adrienne Rich explaining why you find her poem particularly moving or particularly disturbing.

II. Longer Papers
  A. Discuss how the poet minimizes the grim aspects of the women's death and romanticizes the death itself. How does she make death attractive and even desirable? Focus on the language, the diction, the speaker's attitude, the imagery, or on any element of the poem you believe significant.
  B. Explain why feminists find Shatayev's death poignant and inspiring and why it might appeal to them both literally and figuratively. For instance, you might consider the implications in the women's dying together or in their dying while mountain climbing. Use examples from the poem to support your assertions.

Comparative Papers from Chapter Eight:
Age and Death

A. In a poem entitled "The Old Men Admiring Themselves in the Water," William Butler Yeats writes, "I heard the old, old men say, 'All that's beautiful drifts away / Like the waters.' " Using illustrations from one or more poems in this unit, explain how other poems treat old age and death. Is it a time when all beauty dies?
B. Sometimes in the face of death, people confront their lives and values, evaluating themselves as they have never done before. Relying on examples from one or more poems in this chapter, explain how confronting death inspires self-scrutiny and, if you like, how it brings about change.
C. Some people believe the ideal death occurs only at the end of a full, rich life. Others believe people who die in youth or at the height of fortune and success experience greater happiness in life than others who must suffer the disillusionment, the infirmity, or the pain of aging. Using examples from one or more poems in this chapter, discuss to what extent poets tend to agree with one of these views of death.
D. The following passage about death comes from a modern-day ghost story, *The Green Man,* a novel by British novelist Kingsley Amis. The dialogue occurs between Maurice Allington, whose father has died the night before, and Maurice's wife Joyce:

> Joyce said, "Isn't it incredible to think that last night Gramps was just as much alive as any of us?" She was never one to be put off a disturbing remark merely by its obviousness.
> "I suppose it is," I said. "But it's not the sort of thing anybody spends much time trying to take in, even in a situation like this, where you'd imagine none of us would be able to get our minds off it. That's what's really incredible. And I honestly can't see why everybody who isn't a child, everybody who's theoretically old enough to have understood what death means, doesn't spend all his time thinking about it. It's a pretty arresting thought, not being anywhere, and yet the world still being here. Simply having everything stopping forever, not just for millions of years. And getting to the point where that's all there in front of you. I can imagine anyone finding themselves thoroughly wrapped up in that prospect, especially since it's where we're going to get to sooner or later, and perhaps sooner. . . . With reasonable care and a hell of a lot of luck you might last another ten years, or five years, or two years, or six months, but then of course again on the other hand as I'm sure you'll appreciate trying to be completely objective about the matter you might not. So in the future, if there is any, every birthday is going to have a lot of things about it that make it feel like your last one. . . ."

Taking this quote as a point of departure and referring to one or more poems in this chapter, write a paper on one of the following topics:
1. How do poets in this chapter show how people avoid the knowledge of death and their own mortality?
2. How do poets in this chapter show how people in various age brackets behave differently when confronted with the death of close friends and loved ones or when faced with their own mortality?

E. Using examples from one or more of the poems in this chapter, argue for or against one of the following assertions:
   1. People should look forward to old age, because it is the only time in life when they are objective, rational, and free from excessive emotions and passions.
   2. Aging brings wisdom, self-acceptance, tolerance, and—ultimately—peace.
F. Consider the following poem entitled "Old Women":

BABETTE DEUTSCH
Old Women

> Old women sit, stiffly, mosaics of pain,
> Framed in drab doorways looking on the dark.
> Rarely they rouse to gossip or complain
> As dozing bitches break their dream to bark.
>
> 5 And then once more they fold their creaking bones
> In silence, pulled about them like a shawl.
> Their memories: a heap of tumbling stones,
> Once builded stronger than a city wall.
> Sometimes they mend the gaps with twitching hand,—
>
> 10 Because they see a woman big with child,
> Because a wet wind smells of grave-pocked land,
> Because a train wailed, because troops defiled.
> Sometimes old women limp through altered streets
> Whose hostile houses beat them down to earth;
>
> 15 Now in their beds they fumble at the sheets
> That once were spread for bridal, once for birth,
> And now are laid for women who are cold
> With difficult plodding or with sitting still.
> Old women, pitying all that age can kill,
>
> 20 Lie quiet, wondering that they are old.

After studying the poem, write a paper responding to one of the following topics:
1. Compare the poem's depiction of aging and impending death with one or more poems from this chapter. Discuss the poems' different subject matter, the poets' attitudes toward the subject matter, the poems' different imagery or language, and/or the readers' response to each poem.
2. Create a dialogue among three or more of the poets in this chapter in which they react to Deutsch's poem. You can create the poets' varying responses to the subject matter, the depiction of the old women's pain and bewilderment, the treatment of aging, the style and language of the poem, or any other element of the poem you think important. Be as inventive as you like in creating the dialogue, yet try to remain faithful to the poets' attitudes, based on your understanding of their own poems in this chapter.
3. Compare "Old Women" to one other poem from the chapter which you find significantly more sophisticated, more memorable, or simply better.

PART FOUR
DRAMA

SOPHOCLES

Oedipus Rex

Before Reading

Free write for 10 minutes on one of the following questions:

1. Many people believe that in this life good conduct is usually rewarded and wicked conduct is usually punished. Do you agree?
2. Some people believe that with forethought, prudence, and good conduct they will have a fair chance at happiness. Others think that forethought, prudence, and good conduct have very little effect on one's future, for no one can predict the outcome of any action, and happiness is largely a matter of luck. Which of these views do you favor?

CHARACTERS

Oedipus   Messenger
A Priest   Shepherd of Laïos
Creon   Second Messenger
Teiresias   Chorus of Theban Elders
Iocaste

THE SCENE   *Before the palace of Oedipus, King of Thebes. A central door and two lateral doors open onto a platform which runs the length of the façade. On the platform, right and left, are altars; and three steps lead down into the "orchestra," or chorus-ground. At the beginning of the action these steps are crowded by suppliants who have brought branches and chaplets of olive leaves and who lie in various attitudes of despair.* OEDIPUS *enters.*

PROLOGUE

OEDIPUS: My children, generations of the living
            In the line of Kadmos,* nursed at his ancient hearth:
            Why have you strewn yourselves before these altars
            In supplication, with your boughs and garlands?
            The breath of incense rises from the city
            With a sound of prayer and lamentation.
                                                Children,
            I would not have you speak through messengers,

chaplets: Wreaths of olive branches worn on the head.
*Kadmos: Legendary founder of Thebes.
OEDIPUS REX by Sophocles (496?–406 B.C.). The play was first performed in Athens in about 430 B.C. This English translation is by Dudley Fitts and Robert Fitzgerald.

And therefore I have come myself to hear you—
I, Oedipus, who bear the famous name.

(To a PRIEST:*)*

You, there, since you are eldest in the company,
Speak for them all, tell me what preys upon you,
Whether you come in dread, or crave some blessing:
Tell me, and never doubt that I will help you
In every way I can; I should be heartless
Were I not moved to find you suppliant here.
PRIEST: Great Oedipus, O powerful King of Thebes!
You see how all the ages of our people
Cling to your altar steps: here are boys
Who can barely stand alone, and here are priests
By weight of age, as I am a priest of God,*
And young men chosen from those yet unmarried;
As for the others, all that multitude,
They wait with olive chaplets in the squares,
At the two shrines of Pallas,† and where Apollo‡
Speaks in the glowing embers.
                                     Your own eyes
Must tell you: Thebes is tossed on a murdering sea
And can not lift her head from the death surge.
A rust consumes the buds and fruits of the earth;
The herds are sick; children die unborn,
And labor is vain. The god of plague and pyre
Raids like detestable lightning through the city,
And all the house of Kadmos is laid waste,
All emptied, and all darkened: Death alone
Battens upon the misery of Thebes.

You are not one of the immortal gods, we know;
Yet we have come to you to make our prayer
As to the man surest in mortal ways
And wisest in the ways of God. You saved us
From the Sphinx,§ that flinty singer, and the tribute‖

*God: Zeus, the father of the gods, principal deity of the Olympian religion.
†Pallas: Goddess of wisdom, protectress of Athens.
‡Apollo: God of the sun and of prophecy. At his shrine fortunes are told from the embers of burnt animals. Apollo is the chief protector of Thebes.
§Sphinx: Winged monster with the head of a woman and the body of a lion. She had once terrorized Thebes, destroying all who failed to answer her riddle: "What walks on four legs in the morning, two at noon, and three in the evening?" When Oedipus answered correctly, "Man," the Sphinx killed herself, ending a plague. Afterwards, Creon, acting as ruler of Thebes after the death of Laïos, offered Oedipus the throne and also the hand of Iocaste, the widow of Laïos.
‖Tribute: The Theban men killed by the Sphinx.

We paid to her so long; yet you were never
Better informed than we, nor could we teach you:
It was some god breathed in you to set us free.

Therefore, O mighty King, we turn to you:
Find us our safety, find us a remedy,
Whether by counsel of the gods or men.
A king of wisdom tested in the past
Can act in a time of troubles, and act well.
Noblest of men, restore
Life to your city! Think how all men call you
Liberator for your triumph long ago;
Ah, when your years of kingship are remembered,
Let them not say *We rose, but later fell*—
Keep the State from going down in the storm!
Once, years ago, with happy augury,
You brought us fortune; be the same again!
No man questions your power to rule the land:
But rule over men, not over a dead city!
Ships are only hulls, citadels are nothing,
When no life moves in the empty passageways.

OEDIPUS: Poor children! You may be sure I know
All that you longed for in your coming here.
I know that you are deathly sick; and yet,
Sick as you are, not one is as sick as I.
Each of you suffers in himself alone
His anguish, not another's; but my spirit
Groans for the city, for myself, for you.

I was not sleeping, you are not waking me.
No, I have been in tears for a long while
And in my restless thought walked many ways.
In all my search, I found one helpful course,
And that I have taken: I have sent Creon,
Son of Menoikeus, brother of the Queen,
To Delphi, Apollo's place of revelation,
To learn there, if he can,
What act or pledge of mine may save the city.
I have counted the days, and now, this very day,
I am troubled, for he has overstayed his time.
What is he doing? He has been gone too long.
Yet whenever he comes back, I should do ill
To scant whatever duty God reveals.

PRIEST: It is a timely promise. At this instant
They tell me Creon is here.

OEDIPUS: O Lord Apollo!

May his news be fair as his face is radiant!

PRIEST: It could not be otherwise: he is crowned with bay,
The chaplet is thick with berries.

OEDIPUS: We shall soon know;
He is near enough to hear us now.

(Enter CREON.*)*

O Prince:

Brother: son of Menoikeus:
What answer do you bring us from the god?

CREON: A strong one. I can tell you, great afflictions
Will turn out well, if they are taken well.

OEDIPUS: What was the oracle? These vague words
Leave me still hanging between hope and fear.

CREON: Is it your pleasure to hear me with all these
Gathered around us? I am prepared to speak,
But should we not go in?

OEDIPUS: Let them all hear it.
It is for them I suffer, more than for myself.

CREON: Then I will tell you what I heard at Delphi.

In plain words
The god commands us to expel from the land of Thebes
An old defilement we are sheltering.
It is a deathly thing, beyond cure;
We must not let it feed upon us longer.

OEDIPUS: What defilement? How shall we rid ourselves of it?

CREON: By exile or death, blood for blood. It was
Murder that brought the plague-wind on the city.

OEDIPUS: Murder of whom? Surely the god has named him?

CREON: My lord: long ago Laïos was our king,
Before you came to govern us.

OEDIPUS: I know;
I learned of him from others; I never saw him.

CREON: He was murdered; and Apollo commands us now
To take revenge upon whoever killed him.

OEDIPUS: Upon whom? Where are they? Where shall we find a clue
To solve that crime, after so many years?

CREON: Here in this land, he said.
                                   If we make enquiry,
We may touch things that otherwise escape us.

OEDIPUS: Tell me: Was Laïos murdered in his house,
Or in the fields, or in some foreign country?

CREON: He said he planned to make a pilgrimage.

He did not come home again.

OEDIPUS: And was there no one,
No witness, no companion, to tell what happened?

CREON: They were all killed but one, and he got away
So frightened that he could remember one thing only.

OEDIPUS: What was that one thing? One may be the key
To everything, if we resolve to use it.

CREON: He said that a band of highwaymen attacked them,
Outnumbered them, and overwhelmed the King.

OEDIPUS: Strange, that a highwayman should be so daring—
Unless some faction here bribed him to do it.

CREON: We thought of that. But after Laïos' death
New troubles arose and we had no avenger.

OEDIPUS: What troubles could prevent your hunting down the killers?

CREON: The riddling Sphinx's song
Made us deaf to all mysteries but her own.

OEDIPUS: Then once more I must bring what is dark to light.
It is most fitting that Apollo shows,
As you do, this compunction for the dead.
You shall see how I stand by you, as I should,
To avenge the city and the city's god,
And not as though it were for some distant friend,
But for my own sake, to be rid of evil.
Whoever killed King Laïos might—who knows?—
Decide at any moment to kill me as well.
By avenging the murdered king I protect myself.

Come, then, my children: leave the altar steps,
Lift up your olive boughs!
                                    One of you go
And summon the people of Kadmos to gather here.
I will do all that I can; you may tell them that.

(Exit a PAGE.*)*

So, with the help of God,
We shall be saved—or else indeed we are lost.

PRIEST: Let us rise, children. It was for this we came,
And now the King has promised it himself.
Phoibos* has sent us an oracle; may he descend
Himself to save us and drive out the plague.

(Exeunt OEDIPUS *and* CREON *into the palace by the central door. The* PRIEST
and the SUPPLIANTS *disperse R and L. After a short pause the* CHORUS *enters
the orchestra.)*

*Phoibos: Apollo.

PARODOS*

(STROPHE† 1)

CHORUS: What is God singing in his profound
      Delphi of gold and shadow?
      What oracle for Thebes, the sunwhipped city?

Fear unjoints me, the roots of my heart tremble.

Now I remember, O Healer,‡ your power, and wonder:
Will you send doom like a sudden cloud, or weave it
Like nightfall of the past?

Speak, speak to us, issue of holy sound:
Dearest to our expectancy: be tender!

(ANTISTROPHE§ 1)

Let me pray to Athene,|| the immortal daughter of Zeus,
And to Artemis# her sister
Who keeps her famous throne in the market ring,
And to Apollo, bowman** at the far butts of heaven—

O gods, descend! Like three streams leap against
The fires of our grief, the fires of darkness;
Be swift to bring us rest!

As in the old time from the brilliant house
Of air you stepped to save us, come again!

(STROPHE 2)

Now our afflictions have no end,
Now all our stricken host lies down
And no man fights off death with his mind;

The noble plowland bears no grain,
And groaning mothers can not bear—

---

*Parados: Formal song or ode, delivered by the chorus as it entered the theater, moving down the
aisles toward the playing area. In this play, the chorus represents the elders of Thebes.
†Strophe: Song chanted by the chorus as it danced from right to left.
‡Healer: Apollo, also the god of healing.
§Antistrophe: Song chanted by the chorus as it danced back from left to right.
||Athene: Pallas Athene, goddess of wisdom, patroness of Athens.
#Artemis: Goddess of the moon and the hunt.
**bowman: Apollo was also god of archery.

See, how our lives like birds take wing,
Like sparks that fly when a fire soars,
To the shore of the god of evening.*

(ANTISTROPHE 2)

The plague burns on, it is pitiless,
Though pallid children laden with death
Lie unwept in the stony ways,

And old gray women by every path
Flock to the strand about the altars

There to strike their breasts and cry
Worship of Phoibos in wailing prayers:
Be kind, God's golden child!

(STROPHE 3)

There are no swords in this attack by fire,
No shields, but we are ringed with cries.
Send the besieger plunging from our homes
Into the vast sea-room of the Atlantic
Or into the waves that foam eastward of Thrace—

For the day ravages what the night spares—

Destroy our enemy, lord of the thunder!
Let him be riven by lightning from heaven!

(ANTISTROPHE 3)

Phoibos Apollo, stretch the sun's bowstring,
That golden cord, until it sing for us,
Flashing arrows in heaven!
                              Artemis, Huntress,
Race with flaring lights upon our mountains!

O scarlet god, O golden-banded brow,
O Theban Bacchos† in a storm of Maenads,‡

(Enter OEDIPUS.*)*

Whirl upon Death, that all the Undying hate!
Come with blinding torches, come in joy!

*god of evening: Hades, the god of death.
†Bacchos: Also called Dionysos, the god of wine— hence scarlet-faced.
‡Maenads: Bacchos' attendant female revelers or worshipers.

SCENE I

OEDIPUS: Is this your prayer? It may be answered. Come,
    Listen to me, act as the crisis demands,
    And you shall have relief from all these evils.

    Until now I was a stranger to this tale,
    As I had been a stranger to the crime.
    Could I track down the murderer without a clue?
    But now, friends,
    As one who became a citizen after the murder,
    I make this proclamation to all Thebans:
    If any man knows by whose hand Laïos, son of Labdakos,
    Met his death, I direct that man to tell me everything,
    No matter what he fears for having so long withheld it.
    Let it stand as promised that no further trouble
    Will come to him, but he may leave the land in safety.

    Moreover: If anyone knows the murderer to be foreign,
    Let him not keep silent: he shall have his reward from me.
    However, if he does conceal it; if any man
    Fearing for his friend or for himself disobeys this edict,
    Hear what I propose to do:

    I solemnly forbid the people of this country,
    Where power and throne are mine, ever to receive that man
    Or speak to him, no matter who he is, or let him
    Join in sacrifice, lustration,* or in prayer.
    I decree that he be driven from every house,
    Being, as he is, corruption itself to us: the Delphic
    Voice of Zeus† has pronounced this revelation.
    Thus I associate myself with the oracle
    And take the side of the murdered king.

    As for the criminal, I pray to God—
    Whether it be a lurking thief, or one of a number—
    I pray that that man's life be consumed in evil and wretchedness.
    And as for me, this curse applies no less
    If it should turn out that the culprit is my guest here,
    Sharing my hearth.
               You have heard the penalty.
    I lay it on you now to attend to this
    For my sake, for Apollo's, for the sick

---

*lustration: Purification ceremonies.
†Voice of Zeus: Although the oracles at Delphi are inspired by Apollo, the ultimate source of all
knowledge and power is Zeus.

Sterile city that heaven has abandoned.
Suppose the oracle had given you no command:
Should this defilement go uncleansed for ever?
You should have found the murderer: your king,
A noble king, had been destroyed!
                                    Now I,
Having the power that he held before me,
Having his bed, begetting children there
Upon his wife, as he would have, had he lived—
Their son would have been my children's brother,
If Laïos had had luck in fatherhood!
(But surely ill luck rushed upon his reign)—
I say I take the son's part, just as though
I were his son, to press the fight for him
And see it won! I'll find the hand that brought
Death to Labdakos' and Polydoros' child,
Heir of Kadmos' and Agenor's line.*
And as for those who fail me,
May the gods deny them the fruit of the earth,
Fruit of the womb, and may they rot utterly!
Let them be wretched as we are wretched, and worse!

For you, for loyal Thebans, and for all
Who find my actions right, I pray the favor
Of justice, and of all the immortal gods.
CHORAGOS†:   Since I am under oath, my lord, I swear
    I did not do the murder, I can not name
    The murderer. Might not the oracle
    That has ordained the search tell where to find him?
OEDIPUS: An honest question. But no man in the world
    Can make the gods do more than the gods will.
CHORAGOS: There is one last expedient—
OEDIPUS: Tell me what it is.
    Though it seem slight, you must not hold it back.
CHORAGOS: A lord clairvoyant to the lord Apollo,
    As we all know, is the skilled Teiresias.
    One might learn much about this from him, Oedipus.
OEDIPUS: I am not wasting time:
    Creon spoke of this, and I have sent for him—
    Twice, in fact; it is strange that he is not here.
CHORAGOS: The other matter—that old report—seems useless.
OEDIPUS: Tell me. I am interested in all reports.

*Agenor's line: The royal line of Thebes descends from Agenor to Polydoros to Kadmus to
Labdakos to Laïos.
†Choragos: Leader or spokesman for the chorus.

CHORAGOS: The King was said to have been killed by highwaymen.
OEDIPUS: I know. But we have no witnesses to that.
CHORAGOS: If the killer can feel a particle of dread,
     Your curse will bring him out of hiding!
OEDIPUS: No.
     The man who dared that act will fear no curse.

(Enter the blind seer TEIRESIAS, *led by a* PAGE.)

CHORAGOS: But there is one man who may detect the criminal.
     This is Teiresias, this is the holy prophet
     In whom, alone of all men, truth was born.
OEDIPUS: Teiresias: seer: student of mysteries,
     Of all that's taught and all that no man tells,
     Secrets of Heaven and secrets of the earth:
     Blind though you are, you know the city lies
     Sick with plague; and from this plague, my lord,
     We find that you alone can guard or save us.

     Possibly you did not hear the messengers?
     Apollo, when we sent to him,
     Sent us back word that this great pestilence
     Would lift, but only if we established clearly
     The identity of those who murdered Laïos.
     They must be killed or exiled.
                                        Can you use
     Birdflight* or any art of divination
     To purify yourself, and Thebes, and me
     From this contagion? We are in your hands.
     There is no fairer duty
     Than that of helping others in distress.
TEIRESIAS: How dreadful knowledge of the truth can be
     When there's no help in truth! I knew this well,
     But made myself forget. I should not have come.
OEDIPUS: What is troubling you? Why are your eyes so cold?
TEIRESIAS: Let me go home. Bear your own fate, and I'll
     Bear mine. It is better so: trust what I say.
OEDIPUS: What you say is ungracious and unhelpful
     To your native country. Do not refuse to speak.
TEIRESIAS: When it comes to speech, your own is neither temperate
     Nor opportune. I wish to be more prudent.
OEDIPUS: In God's name, we all beg you—
TEIRESIAS: You are all ignorant.
     No; I will never tell you what I know.
     Now it is my misery; then, it would be yours.

*Birdflight: Prophets predicted the future by observing the flight of birds.

OEDIPUS: What! You do know something, and will not tell us?
You would betray us all and wreck the State?
TEIRESIAS: I do not intend to torture myself, or you.
Why persist in asking? You will not persuade me.
OEDIPUS: What a wicked old man you are! You'd try a stone's
Patience! Out with it! Have you no feeling at all?
TEIRESIAS: You call me unfeeling. If you could only see
The nature of your own feelings . . .
OEDIPUS: Why,
Who would not feel as I do? Who could endure
Your arrogance toward the city?
TEIRESIAS: What does it matter!
Whether I speak or not, it is bound to come.
OEDIPUS: Then, if "it" is bound to come, you are bound to tell me.
TEIRESIAS: No, I will not go on. Rage as you please.
OEDIPUS: Rage? Why not!
                                    And I'll tell you what I think:
You planned it, you had it done, you all but
Killed him with your own hands: if you had eyes,
I'd say the crime was yours, and yours alone.
TEIRESIAS: So? I charge you, then,
Abide by the proclamation you have made:
From this day forth
Never speak again to these men or to me;
You yourself are the pollution of this country.
OEDIPUS: You dare say that! Can you possibly think you have
Some way of going free, after such insolence?
TEIRESIAS: I have gone free. It is the truth sustains me.
OEDIPUS: Who taught you shamelessness? It was not your craft.
TEIRESIAS: You did. You made me speak. I did not want to.
OEDIPUS: Speak what? Let me hear it again more clearly.
TEIRESIAS: Was it not clear before? Are you tempting me?
OEDIPUS: I did not understand it. Say it again.
TEIRESIAS: I say that you are the murderer whom you seek.
OEDIPUS: Now twice you have spat out infamy. You'll pay for it!
TEIRESIAS: Would you care for more? Do you wish to be really angry?
OEDIPUS: Say what you will. Whatever you say is worthless,
TEIRESIAS: I say you live in hideous shame with those
Most dear to you. You can not see the evil.
OEDIPUS: It seems you can go on mouthing like this for ever.
TEIRESIAS: I can, if there is power in truth.
OEDIPUS: There is:
But not for you, not for you,
You sightless, witless, senseless, mad old man!
TEIRESIAS: You are the madman. There is no one here
Who will not curse you soon, as you curse me.

OEDIPUS: You child of endless night! You can not hurt me
    Or any other man who sees the sun.
TEIRESIAS: True: it is not from me your fate will come.
    That lies within Apollo's competence,
    As it is his concern.
OEDIPUS: Tell me:
    Are you speaking for Creon, or for yourself?
TEIRESIAS: Creon is no threat. You weave your own doom.
OEDIPUS: Wealth, power, craft of statesmanship!
    Kingly position, everywhere admired!
    What savage envy is stored up against these,
    If Creon, whom I trusted, Creon my friend,
    For this great office which the city once
    Put in my hands unsought—if for this power
    Creon desires in secret to destroy me!

    He has bought this decrepit fortune-teller, this
    Collector of dirty pennies, this prophet fraud—
    Why, he is no more clairvoyant than I am!
                              Tell us:
    Has your mystic mummery ever approached the truth?
    When that hellcat the Sphinx was performing here,
    What help were you to these people?
    Her magic was not for the first man who came along:
    It demanded a real exorcist. Your birds—
    What good were they? or the gods, for the matter of that?
    But I came by,
    Oedipus, the simple man, who knows nothing—
    I thought it out for myself, no birds helped me!
    And this is the man you think you can destroy,
    That you may be close to Creon when he's king!
    Well, you and your friend Creon, it seems to me,
    Will suffer most. If you were not an old man,
    You would have paid already for your plot.
CHORAGOS: We can not see that his words or yours
    Have been spoken except in anger, Oedipus,
    And of anger we have no need. How can God's will
    Be accomplished best? That is what most concerns us.
TEIRESIAS: You are a king. But where argument's concerned
    I am your man, as much a king as you.
    I am not your servant, but Apollo's.
    I have no need of Creon to speak for me.

    Listen to me. You mock my blindness, do you?
    But I say that you, with both your eyes, are blind:

You can not see the wretchedness of your life,
Nor in whose house you live, no, nor with whom.
Who are your father and mother? Can you tell me?
You do not even know the blind wrongs
That you have done them, on earth and in the world below.
But the double lash of your parents' curse will whip you
Out of this land some day, with only night
Upon your precious eyes.
Your cries then—where will they not be heard?
What fastness of Kithairon* will not echo them?
And that bridal-descant of yours—you'll know it then.
The song they sang when you came here to Thebes
And found your misguided berthing.
All this, and more, that you can not guess at now,
Will bring you to yourself among your children.

Be angry, then. Curse Creon. Curse my words.
I tell you, no man that walks upon the earth
Shall be rooted out more horribly than you.
OEDIPUS: Am I to bear this from him?—Damnation
Take you! Out of this place! Out of my sight!
TEIRESIAS: I would not have come at all if you had not asked me.
OEDIPUS: Could I have told that you'd talk nonsense, that
You'd come here to make a fool of yourself, and of me?
TEIRESIAS: A fool? Your parents thought me sane enough.
OEDIPUS: My parents again!—Wait: who were my parents?
THEIRESIAS: This day will give you a father, and break your heart.
OEDIPUS: Your infantile riddles! Your damned abracadabra!
TEIRESIAS: You were a great man once at solving riddles.
OEDIPUS: Mock me with that if you like; you will find it true.
TEIRESIAS: It was true enough. It brought about your ruin.
OEDIPUS: But if it saved this town?

(To the PAGE:*)*

TEIRESIAS: Boy, give me your hand.
OEDIPUS: Yes, boy; lead him away.
                              —While you are here
We can do nothing. Go; leave us in peace.
TEIRESIAS: I will go when I have said what I have to say.
How can you hurt me? And I tell you again:
The man you have been looking for all this time,
The damned man, the murderer of Laïos,
That man is in Thebes. To your mind he is foreign-born,

*Kithairon: Mountain range near Thebes where as an infant Oedipus was left to die.

But it will soon be shown that he is a Theban,
A revelation that will fail to please.
                                        A blind man,
Who has his eyes now; a penniless man, who is rich now;
And he will go tapping the strange earth with his staff.
To the children with whom he lives now he will be
Brother and father—the very same; to her
Who bore him, son and husband—the very same
Who came to his father's bed, wet with his father's blood.

Enough. Go think that over.
If later you find error in what I have said,
You may say that I have no skill in prophecy.

(Exit TEIRESIAS, *led by his* PAGE. OEDIPUS *goes into the palace.)*

ODE I

(STROPHE 1)

CHORUS: The Delphic stone* of prophecies
          Remembers ancient regicide
          And a still bloody hand.
          That killer's hour of flight has come.
          He must be stronger than riderless
          Coursers of untiring wind,
          For the son of Zeus† armed with his father's thunder
          Leaps in lightning after him;
          And the Furies‡ follow him, the sad Furies.

(ANTISTROPHE 1)

          Holy Parnassos's§ peak of snow
          Flashes and blinds that secret man,
          That all shall hunt him down:
          Though he may roam the forest shade
          Like a bull gone wild from pasture
          To rage through glooms of stone.
          Doom comes down on him; flight will not avail him;
          For the world's heart calls him desolate,
          And the immortal Furies follow, for ever follow.

---

*Delphic stone: Because Delphi was thought to be located at the Earth's center, the shrine contained a ceremonial stone called the Earth's Navel.
†Son of Zeus: Apollo, armed not only with his own weapon, the bow, but now his father's thunderbolts.
‡Furies: Underworld deities who avenged serious wrongs.
§Parnassos: Delphi is located on the slope of Parnassos, a mountain sacred to Apollo.

But now a wilder thing is heard
From the old man skilled at hearing Fate in the wingbeat of a bird.
Bewildered as a blown bird, my soul hovers and can not find
Foothold in this debate, or any reason or rest of mind.
But no man ever brought—none can bring
Proof of strife between Thebes' royal house,
Labdakos' line, and the son of Polybos*;
And never until now has any man brought word
Of Laïos' dark death staining Oedipus the King.

Divine Zeus and Apollo hold
Perfect intelligence alone of all tales ever told;
And well though this diviner† works, he works in his own night;
No man can judge that rough unknown or trust in second sight,
For wisdom changes hands among the wise.
Shall I believe my great lord criminal
At a raging word that a blind old man let fall?
I saw him, when the carrion woman‡ faced him of old,
Prove his heroic mind! These evil words are lies.

SCENE II

CREON: Men of Thebes:
        I am told that heavy accusations
        Have been brought against me by King Oedipus.

        I am not the kind of man to bear this tamely.

        If in these present difficulties
        He holds me accountable for any harm to him
        Through anything I have said or done—why, then,
        I do not value life in this dishonor.
        It is not as though this rumor touched upon
        Some private indiscretion. The matter is grave.
        The fact is that I am being called disloyal
        To the State, to my fellow citizens, to my friends.
CHORAGOS: He may have spoken in anger, not from his mind.
CREON: But did you not hear him say I was the one
        Who seduced the old prophet into lying?

*Son of Polybos: Polybos is the King of Corinth and at this point in the play both the Chorus and
Oedipus think that Polybos is Oedipus' father.
†diviner: Teiresias.
‡carrion woman: The Sphinx.

CHORAGOS: The thing was said; I do not know how seriously.
CREON: But you were watching him! Were his eyes steady?
　　Did he look like a man in his right mind?
CHORAGOS: I do not know.
　　I can not judge the behavior of great men.
　　But here is the King himself.

(Enter OEDIPUS.*)*

OEDIPUS: So you dared come back.
　　Why? How brazen of you to come to my house,
　　You murderer!
　　　　　　　　　Do you think I do not know
　　That you plotted to kill me, plotted to steal my throne?
　　Tell me, in God's name: am I coward, a fool,
　　That you should dream you could accomplish this?
　　A fool who could not see your slippery game?
　　A coward, not to fight back when I saw it?
　　You are the fool, Creon, are you not? hoping
　　Without support or friends to get a throne?
　　Thrones may be won or bought: you could do neither.
CREON: Now listen to me. You have talked; let me talk, too.
　　You can not judge unless you know the facts.
OEDIPUS: You speak well: there is one fact; but I find it hard
　　To learn from the deadliest enemy I have.
CREON: That above all I must dispute with you.
OEDIPUS: That above all I will not hear you deny.
CREON: If you think there is anything good in being stubborn
　　Against all reason, then I say you are wrong.
OEDIPUS: If you think a man can sin against his own kind
　　And not be punished for it, I say you are mad.
CREON: I agree. But tell me: what have I done to you?
OEDIPUS: You advised me to send for that wizard, did you not?
CREON: I did. I should do it again.
OEDIPUS: Very well. Now tell me:
　　How long has it been since Laïos—
CREON: What of Laïos?
OEDIPUS: Since he vanished in that onset by the road?
CREON: It was long ago, a long time.
OEDIPUS: And this prophet,
　　Was he practicing here then?
CREON: He was; and with honor, as now.
OEDIPUS: Did he speak of me at that time?
CREON: He never did;
　　At least, not when I was present.
OEDIPUS: But . . . the enquiry?
　　I suppose you held one?

CREON: We did, but we learned nothing.
OEDIPUS: Why did the prophet not speak against me then?
CREON: I do not know; and I am the kind of man
    Who holds his tongue when he has no facts to go on.
OEDIPUS: There's one fact that you know, and you could tell it.
CREON: What fact is that? If I know it, you shall have it.
OEDIPUS: If he were not involved with you, he could not say
    That it was I who murdered Laïos.
CREON: If he says that, you are the one that knows it!—
    But now it is my turn to question you.
OEDIPUS: Put your questions. I am no murderer.
CREON: First, then: You married my sister?
OEDIPUS: I married your sister.
CREON: And you rule the kingdom equally with her?
OEDIPUS: Everything that she wants she has from me.
CREON: And I am the third, equal to both of you?
OEDIPUS: That is why I call you a bad friend.
CREON: No. Reason it out, as I have done.
    Think of this first: Would any sane man prefer
    Power, with all a king's anxieties,
    To that same power and the grace of sleep?
    Certainly not I.
    I have never longed for the king's power—only his rights.
    Would any wise man differ from me in this?
    As matters stand, I have my way in everything
    With your consent, and no responsibilities.
    If I were king, I should be a slave to policy.

    How could I desire a scepter more
    Than what is now mine—untroubled influence?
    No, I have not gone mad; I need no honors,
    Except those with the perquisites I have now.
    I am welcome everywhere; every man salutes me,
    And those who want your favor seek my ear,
    Since I know how to manage what they ask.
    Should I exchange this ease for that anxiety?
    Besides, no sober mind is treasonable.
    I hate anarchy
    And never would deal with any man who likes it.

    Test what I have said. Go to the priestess
    At Delphi, ask if I quoted her correctly.
    And as for this other thing: if I am found
    Guilty of treason with Teiresias,
    Then sentence me to death! You have my word
    It is a sentence I should cast my vote for—

But not without evidence!
                              You do wrong
When you take good men for bad, bad men for good.
A true friend thrown aside—why, life itself
Is not more precious!
                              In time you will know this well:
For time, and time alone, will show the just man,
Though scoundrels are discovered in a day.

CHORAGOS: This is well said, and a prudent man would ponder it.
   Judgments too quickly formed are dangerous.

OEDIPUS: But is he not quick in his duplicity?
   And shall I not be quick to parry him?
   Would you have me stand still, hold my peace, and let
   This man win everything, through my inaction?

CREON: And you want—what is it, then? To banish me?

OEDIPUS: No, not exile. It is your death I want,
   So that all the world may see what treason means.

CREON: You will persist, then? You will not believe me?

OEDIPUS: How can I believe you?

CREON: Then you are a fool.

OEDIPUS: To save myself?

CREON: In justice, think of me.

OEDIPUS: You are evil incarnate.

CREON: But suppose that you are wrong?

OEDIPUS: Still I must rule.

CREON: But not if you rule badly.

OEDIPUS: O city, city!

CREON: It is my city, too!

CHORAGOS: Now, my lords, be still. I see the Queen,
   Iocaste, coming from her palace chambers;
   And it is time she came, for the sake of you both.
   This dreadful quarrel can be resolved through her.

                                        (Enter IOCASTE.*)*

IOCASTE: Poor foolish men, what wicked din is this?
   With Thebes sick to death, is it not shameful
   That you should rake some private quarrel up?

                                        (To OEDIPUS.*)*

Come into the house.

                  —And you, Creon, go now:
Let us have no more of this tumult over nothing.

CREON: Nothing? No, sister: what your husband plans for me
   Is one of two great evils: exile or death.

OEDIPUS: He is right.
                                    Why, woman I have caught him squarely
        Plotting against my life.
CREON: No! Let me die
        Accurst if ever I have wished you harm!
IOCASTE: Ah, believe it, Oedipus!
        In the name of the gods, respect this oath of his
        For my sake, for the sake of these people here!

(STROPHE 1)

CHORAGOS: Open your mind to her, my lord. Be ruled by her, I beg you!
OEDIPUS: What would you have me do?
CHORAGOS: Respect Creon's word. He has never spoken like a fool,
        And now he has sworn an oath.
OEDIPUS: You know what you ask?
CHORAGOS: I do.
OEDIPUS: Speak on, then.
CHORAGOS: A friend so sworn should not be baited so,
        In blind malice, and without final proof.
OEDIPUS: You are aware, I hope, that what you say
        Means death for me, or exile at the least.

(STROPHE 2)

CHORAGOS: No, I swear by Helios,* first in Heaven!
        May I die friendless and accurst,
    The worst of deaths, if ever I meant that!
            It is the withering fields
                That hurt my sick heart:
            Must we bear all these ills,
                And now your bad blood as well?
OEDIPUS: Then let him go. And let me die, if I must,
        Or be driven by him in shame from the land of Thebes.
        It is your unhappiness, and not his talk,
        That touches me.
                        As for him—
        Wherever he goes, hatred will follow him.
CREON: Ugly in yielding, as you were ugly in rage!
        Natures like yours chiefly torment themselves.
OEDIPUS: Can you not go? Can you not leave me?
CREON: I can.
        You do not know me; but the city knows me,
        And in its eyes I am just, if not in yours.

(Exit CREON.)

*Helios: The sun god.

(ANTISTROPHE 1)

CHORAGOS: Lady Iocaste, did you not ask the King to go to his chambers?
IOCASTE: First tell me what has happened.
CHORAGOS: There was suspicion without evidence; yet it rankled
    As even false charges will.
IOCASTE: On both sides?
CHORAGOS: On both.
IOCASTE: But what was said?
CHORAGOS: Oh let it rest, let it be done with!
    Have we not suffered enough?
OEDIPUS: You see to what your decency has brought you:
    You have made difficulties where my heart saw none.

(ANTISTROPHE 2)

CHORAGOS: Oedipus, it is not once only I have told you—
    You must know I should count myself unwise
    To the point of madness, should I now forsake you—
        You, under whose hand,
            In the storm of another time,
        Our dear land sailed out free.
        But now stand fast at the helm!
IOCASTE: In God's name, Oedipus, inform your wife as well:
    Why are you so set in this hard anger?
OEDIPUS: I will tell you, for none of these men deserves
    My confidence as you do. It is Creon's work,
    His treachery, his plotting against me.
IOCASTE: Go on, if you can make this clear to me.
OEDIPUS:
    He charges me with the murder of Laïos.
IOCASTE: Has he some knowledge? Or does he speak from hearsay?
OEDIPUS: He would not commit himself to such a charge,
    But he has brought in that damnable soothsayer
    To tell his story.
IOCASTE: Set your mind at rest.
    If it is a question of soothsayers, I tell you
    That you will find no man whose craft gives knowledge
    Of the unknowable.

                    Here is my proof:

                An oracle was reported to Laïos once
    (I will not say from Phoibos himself, but from
    His appointed ministers, at any rate)
    That his doom would be death at the hands of his own son—
    His son, born of his flesh and of mine!

Now, you remember the story: Laïos was killed
By marauding strangers where three highways meet;
But his child had not been three days in this world
Before the King had pierced the baby's ankles
And left him to die on a lonely mountainside.

Thus, Apollo never caused that child
To kill his father, and it was not Laïos' fate
To die at the hands of his son, as he had feared.
This is what prophets and prophecies are worth!
Have no dread of them.
                              It is God himself
Who can show us what he wills, in his own way.
OEDIPUS:
    How strange a shadowy memory crossed my mind,
    Just now while you were speaking; it chilled my heart.
IOCASTE: What do you mean? What memory do you speak of?
OEDIPUS: If I understand you, Laïos was killed
    At a place where three roads meet.
IOCASTE: So it was said;
    We have no later story.
OEDIPUS: Where did it happen?
IOCASTE: Phokis, it is called: at a place where the Theban Way
    Divides into the roads toward Delphi and Daulia.
OEDIPUS: When?
IOCASTE: We had the news not long before you came
    And proved the right to your succession here.
OEDIPUS: Ah, what net has God been weaving for me?
IOCASTE: Oedipus! Why does this trouble you?
OEDIPUS: Do not ask me yet.
    First, tell me how Laïos looked, and tell me
    How old he was.
IOCASTE: He was tall, his hair just touched
    With white; his form was not unlike your own.
OEDIPUS: I think that I myself may be accurst
    By my own ignorant edict.
IOCASTE: You speak strangely.
    It makes me tremble to look at you, my King.
OEDIPUS: I am not sure that the blind man can not see.
    But I should know better if you were to tell me—
IOCASTE: Anything—though I dread to hear you ask it.
OEDIPUS: Was the King lightly escorted, or did he ride
    With a large company, as a ruler should?
IOCASTE: There were five men with him in all: one was a herald,
    And a single chariot, which he was driving.
OEDIPUS: Alas, that makes it plain enough!

But who—
    Who told you how it happened?
IOCASTE: A household servant,
    The only one to escape.
OEDIPUS: And is he still
    A servant of ours?
IOCASTE: No; for when he came back at last
    And found you enthroned in the place of the dead king,
    He came to me, touched my hand with his, and begged
    That I would send him away to the frontier district
    Where only the shepherds go—
    As far away from the city as I could send him.
    I granted his prayer; for although the man was a slave,
    He had earned more than this favor at my hands.
OEDIPUS: Can he be called back quickly?
IOCASTE: Easily.
    But why?
OEDIPUS: I have taken too much upon myself
    Without enquiry; therefore I wish to consult him.
IOCASTE: Then he shall come.
                     But am I not one also
    To whom you might confide these fears of yours?
OEDIPUS: That is your right; it will not be denied you,
    Now least of all; for I have reached a pitch
    Of wild foreboding. Is there anyone
    To whom I should sooner speak?

    Polybos of Corinth is my father.
    My mother is a Dorian: Merope.
    I grew up chief among the men of Corinth
    Until a strange thing happened—
    Not worth my passion, it may be, but strange.

    At a feast, a drunken man maundering in his cups
    Cries out that I am not my father's son!

    I contained myself that night, though I felt anger
    And a sinking heart. The next day I visited
    My father and mother, and questioned them. They stormed,
    Calling it all the slanderous rant of a fool;
    And this relieved me. Yet the suspicion
    Remained always aching in my mind;
    I knew there was talk; I could not rest;
    And finally, saying nothing to my parents,
    I went to the shrine at Delphi.

The god dismissed my question without reply;
He spoke of other things.

                    Some were clear,
Full of wretchedness, dreadful, unbearable:
As, that I should lie with my own mother, breed
Children from whom all men would turn their eyes;
And that I should be my father's murderer.

I heard all this, and fled. And from that day
Corinth to me was only in the stars
Descending in that quarter of the sky,
As I wandered farther and farther on my way
To a land where I should never see the evil
Sung by the oracle. And I came to this country
Where, so you say, King Laïos was killed.

I will tell you all that happened there, my lady.

There were three highways
Coming together at a place I passed;
And there a herald came towards me, and a chariot
Drawn by horses, with a man such as you describe
Seated in it. The groom leading the horses
Forced me off the road at his lord's command;
But as this charioteer lurched over towards me
I struck him in my rage. The old man saw me
And brought his double goad down upon my head
As I came abreast.

                 He was paid back, and more!
Swinging my club in this right hand I knocked him
Out of his car, and he rolled on the ground.

                         I killed him.

I killed them all.
Now if that stranger and Laïos were—kin,
Where is a man more miserable than I?
More hated by the gods? Citizen and alien alike
Must never shelter me or speak to me—
I must be shunned by all.

                 And I myself
Pronounced this malediction upon myself!

Think of it: I have touched you with these hands,
These hands that killed your husband. What defilement!

Am I all evil, then? It must be so,
Since I must flee from Thebes, yet never again

See my own countrymen, my own country,
For fear of joining my mother in marriage
And killing Polybos, my father.
                                                   Ah,
If I was created so, born to this fate,
Who could deny the savagery of God?

O holy majesty of heavenly powers!
May I never see that day! Never!
Rather let me vanish from the race of men
Than know the abomination destined me!
CHORAGOS: We too, my lord, have felt dismay at this.
    But there is hope: you have yet to hear the shepherd.
OEDIPUS: Indeed, I fear no other hope is left me.
IOCASTE: What do you hope from him when he comes?
OEDIPUS: This much:
    If his account of the murder tallies with yours,
    Then I am cleared.
IOCASTE: What was it that I said
    Of such importance?
OEDIPUS: Why, "maurauders," you said,
    Killed the King, according to this man's story.
    If he maintains that still, if there were several,
    Clearly the guilt is not mine: I was alone.
    But if he says one man, singlehanded, did it,
    Then the evidence all points to me.
IOCASTE: You may be sure that he said there were several;
    And can he call back that story now? He cán not.
    The whole city heard it as plainly as I.
    But suppose he alters some detail of it:
    He can not ever show that Laïos' death
    Fulfilled the oracle: for Apollo said
    My child was doomed to kill him; and my child—
    Poor baby!—it was my child that died first.

    No. From now on, where oracles are concerned,
    I would not waste a second thought on any.
OEDIPUS: You may be right.
                                   But come: let someone go
    For the shepherd at once. This matter must be settled.
IOCASTE: I will send for him.
    I would not wish to cross you in anything,
    And surely not in this.—Let us go in.

(Exeunt into the palace.)

ODE II

CHORUS: Let me be reverent in the ways of right,
       Lowly the paths I journey on;
       Let all my words and actions keep
       The laws of the pure universe
       From highest Heaven handed down.
       For Heaven is their bright nurse,
       Those generations of the realms of light;
       Ah, never of mortal kind were they begot,
       Nor are they slaves of memory, lost in sleep:
       Their Father is greater than Time, and ages not.

       The tyrant is a child of Pride
       Who drinks from his great sickening cup
       Recklessness and vanity,
       Until from his high crest headlong
       He plummets to the dust of hope.
       That strong man is not strong.
       But let no fair ambition be denied;
       May God protect the wrestler for the State
       In government, in comely policy,
       Who will fear God, and on His ordinance wait.

       Haughtiness and the high hand of disdain
       Tempt and outrage God's holy law;
       And any mortal who dares hold
       No immortal Power in awe
       Will be caught up in a net of pain:
       The price for which his levity is sold.
       Let each man take due earnings, then,
       And keep his hands from holy things,
       And from blasphemy stand apart—
       Else the crackling blast of heaven
       Blows on his head, and on his desperate heart;
       Though fools will honor impious men,
       In their cities no tragic poet sings.

       Shall we lose faith in Delphi's obscurities,
       We who have heard the world's core
       Discredited, and the sacred wood

Of Zeus at Elis* praised no more?
The deeds and the strange prophecies
Must make a pattern yet to be understood.
Zeus, if indeed you are lord of all,
Throned in light over night and day,
Mirror this in your endless mind:
Our masters call the oracle
Words on the wind, and the Delphic vision blind!
Their hearts no longer know Apollo,
And reverence for the gods has died away.

SCENE III

(Enter IOCASTE.*)*

IOCASTE: Princes of Thebes, it has occurred to me
    To visit the altars of the gods, bearing
    These branches as a suppliant, and this incense.
    Our King is not himself: his noble soul
    Is overwrought with fantasies of dread,
    Else he would consider
    The new prophecies in the light of the old.
    He will listen to any voice that speaks disaster,
    And my advice goes for nothing.

(She approaches the altar.)

To you, then, Apollo,

    Lycean lord, since you are nearest, I turn in prayer.
    Receive these offerings, and grant us deliverance
    From defilement. Our hearts are heavy with fear
    When we see our leader distracted, as helpless sailors
    Are terrified by the confusion of their helmsman.

(Enter MESSENGER.*)*

MESSENGER: Friends, no doubt you can direct me:
    Where shall I find the house of Oedipus,
    Or, better still, where is the King himself?
CHORAGOS: It is this very place, stranger; he is inside.
    This is his wife and mother of his children.
MESSENGER: I wish her happiness in a happy house,
    Blest in all the fulfillment of her marriage.
IOCASTE: I wish as much for you: your courtesy
    Deserves a like good fortune. But now, tell me:

*Elis: The small country in which Olympia was located, the center of oracles of Zeus and Apollo.

Why have you come? What have you to say to us?
MESSENGER: Good news, my lady, for your house and your husband.
IOCASTE: What news? Who sent you here?
MESSENGER: I am from Corinth.
The news I bring ought to mean joy for you,
Though it may be you will find some grief in it.
IOCASTE: What is it? How can it touch us in both ways?
MESSENGER: The word is that the people of the Isthmus
Intend to call Oedipus to be their king.
IOCASTE: But old King Polybos—is he not reigning still?
MESSENGER: No. Death holds him in his sepulchre.
IOCASTE: What are you saying? Polybos is dead?
MESSENGER: If I am not telling the truth, may I die myself.

(To a MAIDSERVANT:*)*

IOCASTE: Go in, go quickly; tell this to your master.
O riddlers of God's will, where are you now!
This was the man whom Oedipus, long ago,
Feared so, fled so, in dread of destroying him—
But it was another fate by which he died.

(Enter OEDIPUS.*)*

OEDIPUS: Dearest Iocaste, why have you sent for me?
IOCASTE: Listen to what this man says, and then tell me
What has become of the solemn prophecies.
OEDIPUS: Who is this man? What is his news for me?
IOCASTE: He has come from Corinth to announce your father's death!
OEDIPUS: Is it true, stranger? Tell me in your own words.
MESSENGER: I can not say it more clearly: the King is dead.
OEDIPUS: Was it by treason? Or by an attack of illness?
MESSENGER: A little thing brings old men to their rest.
OEDIPUS: It was sickness, then?
MESSENGER: Yes, and his many years.
OEDIPUS: Ah!
Why should a man respect the Pythian hearth,* or
Give heed to the birds that jangle above his head?
They prophesied that I should kill Polybos,
Kill my own father; but he is dead and buried,
And I am here—I never touched him, never,
Unless he died of grief for my departure,
And thus, in a sense, through me. No. Polybos
Has packed the oracles off with him underground.
They are empty words.
IOCASTE: Had I not told you so?

*Pythian hearth: Delphi.

OEDIPUS: You had; it was my faint heart that betrayed me.
IOCASTE: From now on never think of those things again.
OEDIPUS: And yet—must I not fear my mother's bed?
IOCASTE: Why should anyone in this world be afraid,
        Since Fate rules us and nothing can be foreseen?
        A man should live only for the present day.
        Have no more fear of sleeping with your mother:
        How many men, in dreams, have lain with their mothers!
        No reasonable man is troubled by such things.
OEDIPUS: That is true; only—
        If only my mother were not still alive!
        But she is alive. I can not help my dread.
IOCASTE: Yet this news of your father's death is wonderful.
OEDIPUS: Wonderful. But I fear the living woman.
MESSENGER: Tell me, who is this woman that you fear?
OEDIPUS: It is Merope, man; the wife of King Polybos.
MESSENGER: Merope? Why should you be afraid of her?
OEDIPUS: An oracle of the gods, a dreadful saying.
MESSENGER: Can you tell me about it or are you sworn to silence?
OEDIPUS: I can tell you, and I will.
        Apollo said through his prophet that I was the man
        Who should marry his own mother, shed his father's blood
        With his own hands. And so, for all these years
        I have kept clear of Corinth, and no harm has come—
        Though it would have been sweet to see my parents again.
MESSENGER: And is this the fear that drove you out of Corinth?
OEDIPUS: Would you have me kill my father?
MESSENGER: As for that
        You must be reassured by the news I gave you.
OEDIPUS: If you could reassure me, I would reward you.
MESSENGER: I had that in mind, I will confess: I thought
        I could count on you when you returned to Corinth.
OEDIPUS: No: I will never go near my parents again.
MESSENGER: Ah, son, you still do not know what you are doing—
OEDIPUS: What do you mean? In the name of God tell me!
MESSENGER: —If these are your reasons for not going home.
OEDIPUS: I tell you, I fear the oracle may come true.
MESSENGER: And guilt may come upon you through your parents?
OEDIPUS: That is the dread that is always in my heart.
MESSENGER: Can you not see that all your fears are groundless?
OEDIPUS: How can you say that? They are my parents, surely?
MESSENGER: Polybos was not your father.
OEDIPUS: Not my father?
MESSENGER: No more your father than the man speaking to you.
OEDIPUS: But you are nothing to me!
MESSENGER: Neither was he.

OEDIPUS: Then why did he call me son?
MESSENGER: I will tell you:
     Long ago he had you from my hands, as a gift.
OEDIPUS: Then how could he love me so, if I was not his?
MESSENGER: He had no children, and his heart turned to you.
OEDIPUS: What of you? Did you buy me? Did you find me by chance?
MESSENGER: I came upon you in the crooked pass of Kithairon.
OEDIPUS: And what were you doing there?
MESSENGER: Tending my flocks.
OEDIPUS: A wandering shepherd?
MESSENGER: But your savior, son, that day.
OEDIPUS: From what did you save me?
MESSENGER: Your ankles should tell you that.
OEDIPUS: Ah, stranger, why do you speak of that childhood pain?
MESSENGER: I cut the bonds that tied your ankles together.
OEDIPUS: I have had the mark as long as I can remember.
MESSENGER: That was why you were given the name you bear.*
OEDIPUS: God! Was it my father or my mother who did it?
     Tell me!
MESSENGER: I do not know. The man who gave you to me
     Can tell you better than I.
OEDIPUS: It was not you that found me, but another?
MESSENGER: It was another shepherd gave you to me.
OEDIPUS: Who was he? Can you tell me who he was?
MESSENGER: I think he was said to be one of Laïos' people.
OEDIPUS: You mean the Laïos who was king here years ago?
MESSENGER: Yes; King Laïos; and the man was one of his herdsmen.
OEDIPUS: Is he still alive? Can I see him?
MESSENGER: These men here
     Know best about such things.
OEDIPUS: Does anyone here
     Know this shepherd that he is talking about?
     Have you seen him in the fields, or in the town?
     If you have, tell me. It is time things were made plain.
CHORAGOS: I think the man he means is that same shepherd
     You have already asked to see. Iocaste perhaps
     Could tell you something.
OEDIPUS: Do you know anything
     About him, Lady? Is he the man we have summoned?
     Is that the man this shepherd means?
IOCASTE: Why think of him?
     Forget this herdsman. Forget it all.
     This talk is a waste of time.
OEDIPUS: How can you say that,

*name you bear: Oedipus means "Swollen-foot."

When the clues to my true birth are in my hands?
IOCASTE: For God's love, let us have no more questioning!
    Is your life nothing to you?
    My own is pain enough for me to bear.
OEDIPUS: You need not worry. Suppose my mother a slave,
    And born of slaves: no baseness can touch you.
IOCASTE: Listen to me, I beg you: do not do this thing!
OEDIPUS: I will not listen; the truth must be made known.
IOCASTE: Everything that I say is for your own good!
OEDIPUS: My own good
    Snaps my patience, then; I want none of it.
IOCASTE: You are fatally wrong! May you never learn who you are!
OEDIPUS: Go, one of you, and bring the shepherd here.
    Let us leave this woman to brag of her royal name.
IOCASTE: Ah, miserable!
    That is the only word I have for you now.
    That is the only word I can ever have.

                                              (Exit into the palace.)

CHORAGOS: Why has she left us, Oedipus? Why has she gone
    In such a passion of sorrow? I fear this silence:
    Something dreadful may come of it.
OEDIPUS: Let it come!
    However base my birth, I must know about it.
    The Queen, like a woman, is perhaps ashamed
    To think of my low origin. But I
    Am a child of Luck; I can not be dishonored.
    Luck is my mother; the passing months, my brothers,
    Have seen me rich and poor.
                                    If this is so,
    How could I wish that I were someone else?
    How could I not be glad to know my birth?

ODE III

                                                        (STROPHE)

CHORUS: If ever the coming time were known
    To my heart's pondering,
    Kithairon, now by Heaven I see the torches
    At the festival of the next full moon,
    And see the dance, and hear the choir sing
    A grace to your gentle shade:
    Mountain where Oedipus was found,
    O mountain guard of a noble race!

May the god who heals us* lend his aid,
And let that glory come to pass
For our king's cradling-ground.

(ANTISTROPHE)

Of the nymphs† that flower beyond the years,
Who bore you, royal child,
To Pan‡ of the hills or the timberline Apollo,§
Cold in delight where the upland clears,
Or Hermes‖ for whom Kyllene's# heights are piled?
Or flushed as evening cloud,
Great Dionysos,** roamer of mountains,
He—was it he who found you there,
And caught you up in his own proud
Arms from the sweet god-ravisher††
Who laughed by the Muses' fountains?

SCENE IV

OEDIPUS: Sirs: though I do not know the man,
      I think I see him coming, this shepherd we want:
      He is old, like our friend here, and the men
      Bringing him seem to be servants of my house.
      But you can tell, if you have ever seen him.

(Enter SHEPHERD *escorted by servants.)*

CHORAGOS: I know him, he was Laïos' man. You can trust him.
OEDIPUS: Tell me first, you from Corinth: is this the shepherd
      We were discussing?
MESSENGER: This is the very man.

(To SHEPHERD*:)*

OEDIPUS: Come here. No, look at me. You must answer
      Everything I ask.—You belonged to Laïos?
SHEPHERD: Yes: born his slave, brought up in his house.
OEDIPUS: Tell me: what kind of work did you do for him?
SHEPHERD: I was a shepherd of his, most of my life.

*god who heals us: Apollo.
†nymphs: Immortal women of the woods and streams, often the lovers of gods and men. The chorus now believes that Oedipus is the child of a nymph and one of the gods.
‡Pan: God of flocks and wild life.
§timberline Apollo: Apollo was also associated with the care of flocks and herds.
‖Hermes: The messenger god.
#Kyllene: Mountain birthplace of Hermes.
**Dionysos: Bacchos, the god of revelry and wine.
††sweet god-ravisher: The nymph who is presumably Oedipus' mother.

OEDIPUS: Where mainly did you go for pasturage?
SHEPHERD: Sometimes Kithairon, sometimes the hills nearby.
OEDIPUS: Do you remember ever seeing this man out there?
SHEPHERD: What would he be doing there? This man?
OEDIPUS: This man standing here. Have you ever seen him before?
SHEPHERD: No. At least, not to my recollection.
MESSENGER: And that is not strange, my lord. But I'll refresh
    His memory: he must remember when we two
    Spent three whole seasons together, March to September,
    On Kithairon or thereabouts. He had two flocks;
    I had one. Each autumn I'd drive mine home
    And he would go back with his to Laïos' sheepfold.—
    Is this not true, just as I have described it?
SHEPHERD: True, yes; but it was all so long ago.
MESSENGER: Well, then: do you remember, back in those days,
    That you gave me a baby boy to bring up as my own?
SHEPHERD: What if I did? What are you trying to say?
MESSENGER: King Oedipus was once that little child.
SHEPHERD: Damn you, hold your tongue!
OEDIPUS: No more of that!
    It is your tongue needs watching, not this man's.
SHEPHERD: My King, my Master, what is it I have done wrong?
OEDIPUS: You have not answered his question about the boy.
SHEPHERD: He does not know . . . He is only making trouble . . .
OEDIPUS: Come, speak plainly, or it will go hard with you.
SHEPHERD: In God's name, do not torture an old man!
OEDIPUS: Come here, one of you; bind his arms behind him.
SHEPHERD: Unhappy king! What more do you wish to learn?
OEDIPUS: Did you give this man the child he speaks of?
SHEPHERD: I did.
    And I would to God I had died that very day.
OEDIPUS: You will die now unless you speak the truth.
SHEPHERD: Yet if I speak the truth, I am worse than dead.
OEDIPUS: Very well; since you insist upon delaying—
SHEPHERD: No! I have told you already that I gave him the boy.
OEDIPUS: Where did you get him? From your house? From somewhere else?
SHEPHERD: Not from mine, no. A man gave him to me.
OEDIPUS: Is that man here? Do you know whose slave he was?
SHEPHERD: For God's love, my King, do not ask me any more!
OEDIPUS: You are a dead man if I have to ask you again.
SHEPHERD: Then . . . Then the child was from the palace of Laïos.
OEDIPUS: A slave child? or a child of his own line?
SHEPHERD: Ah, I am on the brink of dreadful speech!
OEDIPUS: And I of dreadful hearing. Yet I must hear.
SHEPHERD: If you must be told, then . . .
                They said it was Laïos' child;

But it is your wife who can tell you about that.
OEDIPUS: My wife!—Did she give it to you?
SHEPHERD: My lord, she did.
OEDIPUS: Do you know why?
SHEPHERD: I was told to get rid of it.
OEDIPUS: An unspeakable mother!
SHEPHERD: There had been prophecies . . .
OEDIPUS: Tell me.
SHEPHERD: It was said that the boy would kill his own father.
OEDIPUS: Then why did you give him over to this old man?
SHEPHERD: I pitied the baby, my King,
        And I thought that this man would take him far away
        To his own country.
                          He saved him—but for what a fate!
        For if you are what this man says you are,
        No man living is more wretched than Oedipus.
OEDIPUS: Ah God!
        It was true!
                All the prophecies!
                              —Now,
        O Light, may I look on you for the last time!
        I, Oedipus,
        Oedipus, damned in his birth, in his marriage damned,
        Damned in the blood he shed with his own hand!

                                            (He rushes into the palace.)

ODE IV

                                                    (STROPHE 1)

CHORUS: Alas for the seed of men.

What measure shall I give these generations
That breathe on the void and are void
And exist and do not exist?

Who bears more weight of joy
Than mass of sunlight shifting in images,
Or who shall make his thought stay on
That down time drifts away?

Your splendor is all fallen.

O naked brow of wrath and tears,
O change of Oedipus!

I who saw your days call no man blest—
Your great days like ghosts gone.

(ANTISTROPHE 1)

That mind was a strong bow.

Deep, how deep you drew it then, hard archer,
At a dim fearful range,
And brought dear glory down!

You overcame the stranger—
The virgin with her hooking lion claws—
And though death sang, stood like a tower
To make pale Thebes take heart.

Fortress against our sorrow!

True king, giver of laws,
Majestic Oedipus!
No prince in Thebes had ever such renown,
No prince won such grace of power.

(STROPHE 2)

And now of all men ever known
Most pitiful is this man's story:
His fortunes are most changed, his state
Fallen to a low slave's
Ground under bitter fate.

O Oedipus, most royal one!
The great door* that expelled you to the light
Gave at night—ah, gave night to your glory:
As to the father, to the fathering son.

All understood too late.

How could that queen whom Laïos won,
The garden that he harrowed at his height,
Be silent when that act was done?

(ANTISTROPHE 2)

But all eyes fail before time's eye,
All actions come to justice there.
Though never willed, though far down the deep past,

*The great door: Reference to the womb of Iocaste.

Your bed, your dread sirings,
Are brought to book at last.
Child by Laïos doomed to die,
Then doomed to lose that fortunate little death,
Would God you never took breath in this air
That with my wailing lips I take to cry:

For I weep the world's outcast.

I was blind, and now I can tell why:
Asleep, for you had given ease of breath
To Thebes, while the false years went by.

EXODOS*

(Enter, from the palace, SECOND MESSENGER.)

SECOND MESSENGER: Elders of Thebes,† most honored in this land,
What horrors are yours to see and hear, what weight
Of sorrow to be endured, if, true to your birth,
You venerate the line of Labdakos!
I think neither Istros nor Phasis, those great rivers,
Could purify this place of the corruption
It shelters now, or soon must bring to light—
Evil not done unconsciously, but willed.

The greatest griefs are those we cause ourselves.
CHORAGOS: Surely, friend, we have grief enough already;
What new sorrow do you mean?
SECOND MESSENGER: The Queen is dead.
CHORAGOS: Iocaste? Dead? But at whose hand?
SECOND MESSENGER: Her own.
The full horror of what happened you can not know,
For you did not see it; but I, who did, will tell you
As clearly as I can how she met her death.

When she had left us,
In passionate silence, passing through the court,
She ran to her apartment in the house,
Her hair clutched by the fingers of both hands.
She closed the doors behind her; then, by that bed
Where long ago the fatal son was conceived—
That son who should bring about his father's death—
We heard her call upon Laïos, dead so many years,

*Exodos: The final scene of the play.
†Elders of Thebes: The Chorus.

And heard her wail for the double fruit of her marriage,
A husband by her husband, children by her child.

Exactly how she died I do not know:
For Oedipus burst in moaning and would not let us
Keep vigil to the end: it was by him
As he stormed about the room that our eyes were caught.
From one to another of us he went, begging a sword,
Cursing the wife who was not his wife, the mother
Whose womb had carried his own children and himself.
I do not know: it was none of us aided him,
But surely one of the gods was in control!
For with a dreadful cry
He hurled his weight, as though wrenched out of himself,
At the twin doors: the bolts gave, and he rushed in.
And there we saw her hanging, her body swaying
From the cruel cord she had noosed about her neck.
A great sob broke from him, heartbreaking to hear,
As he loosed the rope and lowered her to the ground.

I would blot out from my mind what happened next!
For the King ripped from her gown the golden brooches
That were her ornament, and raised them, and plunged them down
Straight into his own eyeballs, crying, "No more,
No more shall you look on the misery about me,
The horrors of my own doing! Too long you have known
The faces of those whom I should never have seen,
Too long been blind to those for whom I was searching!
From this hour, go in darkness!" And as he spoke,
He struck at his eyes—not once, but many times;
And the blood spattered his beard,
Bursting from his ruined sockets like red hail.

So from the unhappiness of two this evil has sprung,
A curse on the man and woman alike. The old
Happiness of the house of Labdakos
Was happiness enough: where is it today?
It is all wailing and ruin, disgrace, death—all
The misery of mankind that has a name—
And it is wholly and for ever theirs.
CHORAGOS: Is he in agony still? Is there no rest for him?
SECOND MESSENGER: He is calling for someone to lead him to the gates
So that all the children of Kadmos may look upon
His father's murderer, his mother's—no,
I can not say it!
                And then he will leave Thebes,

Self-exiled, in order that the curse
Which he himself pronounced may depart from the house.
He is weak, and there is none to lead him,
So terrible is his suffering.
                                        But you will see:
Look, the doors are opening; in a moment
You will see a thing that would crush a heart of stone.

(The central door is opened; OEDIPUS, *blinded, is led in.)*

CHORAGOS: Dreadful indeed for men to see.
    Never have my own eyes
    Looked on a sight so full of fear.

    Oedipus!
    What madness came upon you, what daemon
    Leaped on your life with heavier
    Punishment than a mortal man can bear?
    No: I can not even
    Look at you, poor ruined one.
    And I would speak, question, ponder,
    If I were able. No.
    You make me shudder.
OEDIPUS: God.   God.
    Is there a sorrow greater?
    Where shall I find harbor in this world?
    My voice is hurled far on a dark wind.
    What has God done to me?
CHORAGOS: Too terrible to think of, or to see.

                                                    (STROPHE 1)

OEDIPUS: O cloud of night,
    Never to be turned away: night coming on,
    I can not tell how: night like a shroud!

    My fair winds brought me here.
                                        O God. Again
    The pain of the spikes where I had sight,
    The flooding pain
    Of memory, never to be gouged out.
CHORAGOS: This is not strange.
    You suffer it all twice over, remorse in pain,
    Pain in remorse.

                                                (ANTISTROPHE 1)

OEDIPUS: Ah dear friend
    Are you faithful even yet, you alone?

Are you still standing near me, will you stay here,
Patient, to care for the blind?

                              The blind man!
Yet even blind I know who it is attends me,
By the voice's tone—
Though my new darkness hide the comforter.
CHORAGOS: Oh fearful act!
What god was it drove you to rake black
Night across your eyes?

                                                    (STROPHE 2)

OEDIPUS: Apollo. Apollo. Dear
Children, the god was Apollo.
He brought my sick, sick fate upon me.
But the blinding hand was my own!
How could I bear to see
When all my sight was horror everywhere?
CHORAGOS: Everywhere; that is true.
OEDIPUS: And now what is left?
Images? Love? A greeting even,
Sweet to the senses? Is there anything?
Ah, no, friends: lead me away.
Lead me away from Thebes.

                              Lead the great wreck
And hell of Oedipus, whom the gods hate.
CHORAGOS: Your fate is clear, you are not blind to that.
Would God you had never found it out!

                                                    (ANTISTROPHE 2)

OEDIPUS: Death take the man who unbound
My feet on that hillside
And delivered me from death to life! What life?
If only I had died,
This weight of monstrous doom
Could not have dragged me and my darlings down.
CHORAGOS: I would have wished the same.
OEDIPUS: Oh never to have come here
With my father's blood upon me! Never
To have been the man they call his mother's husband!
Oh accurst! Oh child of evil,
To have entered that wretched bed—

                              the selfsame one!
More primal than sin itself, this fell to me.
CHORAGOS: I do not know how I can answer you.
You were better dead than alive and blind.
OEDIPUS: Do not counsel me any more. This punishment

That I have laid upon myself is just.
If I had eyes,
I do not know how I could bear the sight
Of my father, when I came to the house of Death,
Or my mother: for I have sinned against them both
So vilely that I could not make my peace
By strangling my own life.
                              Or do you think my children,
Born as they were born, would be sweet to my eyes?
Ah never, never! Nor this town with its high walls,
Nor the holy images of the gods.
                              For I,
Thrice miserable!—Oedipus, noblest of all the line
Of Kadmos, have condemned myself to enjoy
These things no more, by my own malediction
Expelling that man whom the gods declared
To be a defilement in the house of Laïos.
After exposing the rankness of my own guilt,
How could I look men frankly in the eyes?
No, I swear it,
If I could have stifled my hearing at its source,
I would have done it and made all this body
A tight cell of misery, blank to light and sound:
So I should have been safe in a dark agony
Beyond all recollection.
                              Ah Kithairon!
Why did you shelter me? When I was cast upon you,
Why did I not die? Then I should never
Have shown the world my execrable birth.

Ah Polybos! Corinth, city that I believed
The ancient seat of my ancestors: how fair
I seemed, your child! And all the while this evil
Was cancerous within me!
                              For I am sick
In my daily life, sick in my origin.

O three roads, dark ravine, woodland and way
Where three roads met: you, drinking my father's blood,
My own blood, spilled by my own hand: can you remember
The unspeakable things I did there, and the things
I went on from there to do?
                              O marriage, marriage!
The act that engendered me, and again the act
Performed by the son in the same bed—
                              Ah, the net

Of incest, mingling fathers, brothers, sons,
With brides, wives, mothers: the last evil
That can be known by men: no tongue can say
How evil!
No. For the love of God, conceal me
Somewhere far from Thebes; or kill me; or hurl me
Into the sea, away from men's eyes for ever.

Come, lead me. You need not fear to touch me.
Of all men, I alone can bear this guilt.

(Enter CREON.*)*

CHORAGOS: We are not the ones to decide; but Creon here
      May fitly judge of what you ask. He only
      Is left to protect the city in your place.
OEDIPUS: Alas, how can I speak to him? What right have I
      To beg his courtesy whom I have deeply wronged?
CREON: I have not come to mock you, Oedipus,
      Or to reproach you, either.

(To ATTENDANTS:*)*

                  —You, standing there:
      If you have lost all respect for man's dignity,
      At least respect the flame of Lord Helios:
      Do not allow this pollution to show itself
      Openly here, an affront to the earth
      And Heaven's rain and the light of day. No, take him
      Into the house as quickly as you can.
      For it is proper
      That only the close kindred see his grief.
OEDIPUS: I pray you in God's name, since your courtesy
      Ignores my dark expectation, visiting
      With mercy this man of all men most execrable:
      Give me what I ask—for your good, not for mine.
CREON: And what is it that you would have me do?
OEDIPUS: Drive me out of this country as quickly as may be
      To a place where no human voice can ever greet me.
CREON: I should have done that before now—only,
      God's will had not been wholly revealed to me.
OEDIPUS: But his command is plain: the parricide
      Must be destroyed. I am that evil man.
CREON: That is the sense of it, yes; but as things are,
      We had best discover clearly what is to be done.
OEDIPUS: You would learn more about a man like me?
CREON: You are ready now to listen to the god.

OEDIPUS: I will listen. But it is to you
   That I must turn for help. I beg you, hear me.

   The woman in there—
   Give her whatever funeral you think proper:
   She is your sister.
                           —But let me go, Creon!
   Let me purge my father's Thebes of the pollution
   Of my living here, and go out to the wild hills,
   To Kithairon, that has won such fame with me,
   The tomb my mother and father appointed for me,
   And let me die there, as they willed I should.
   And yet I know
   Death will not ever come to me through sickness
   Or in any natural way: I have been preserved
   For some unthinkable fate. But let that be.

   As for my sons, you need not care for them.
   They are men, they will find some way to live.
   But my poor daughters, who have shared my table,
   Who never before have been parted from their father—
   Take care of them, Creon; do this for me.

   And will you let me touch them with my hands
   A last time, and let us weep together?
   Be kind, my lord,
   Great prince, be kind!
                           Could I but touch them,
   They would be mine again, as when I had my eyes.

   (Enter ANTIGONE *and* ISMENE, *attended.)*

   Ah, God!
   Is it my dearest children I hear weeping?
   Has Creon pitied me and sent my daughters?
CREON: Yes, Oedipus: I knew that they were dear to you
   In the old days, and know you must love them still.
OEDIPUS: May God bless you for this—and be a friendlier
   Guardian to you than he has been to me!

   Children, where are you?
   Come quickly to my hands: they are your brother's—
   Hands that have brought your father's once clear eyes
   To this way of seeing—
                           Ah dearest ones,
   I had neither sight nor knowledge then, your father

By the woman who was the source of his own life!
And I weep for you—having no strength to see you—,
I weep for you when I think of the bitterness
That men will visit upon you all your lives.
What homes, what festivals can you attend
Without being forced to depart again in tears?
And when you come to marriageable age,
Where is the man, my daughters, who would dare
Risk the bane that lies on all my children?
Is there any evil wanting? Your father killed
His father; sowed the womb of her who bore him;
Engendered you at the fount of his own existence!
That is what they will say of you.

                                        Then, whom
Can you ever marry? There are no bridegrooms for you,
And your lives must wither away in sterile dreaming.

O Creon, son of Menoikeus!
You are the only father my daughters have,
Since we, their parents, are both of us gone for ever.
They are your own blood: you will not let them
Fall into beggary and loneliness;
You will keep them from the miseries that are mine!
Take pity on them; see, they are only children,
Friendless except for you. Promise me this,
Great Prince, and give me your hand in token of it.

(CREON *clasps his right hand.*)

Children:
I could say much, if you could understand me,
But as it is, I have only this prayer for you:
Live where you can, be as happy as you can—
Happier, please God, than God has made your father!
CREON: Enough. You have wept enough. Now go within.
OEDIPUS: I must; but it is hard.
CREON: Time eases all things.
OEDIPUS: But you must promise—
CREON: .   Say what you desire.
OEDIPUS: Send me from Thebes!
CREON: God grant that I may!
OEDIPUS: But since God hates me . . .
CREON: No, he will grant your wish.
OEDIPUS: You promise?
CREON: I can not speak beyond my knowledge.
OEDIPUS: Then lead me in.
CREON: Come now, and leave your children.

OEDIPUS: No! Do not take them from me!
CREON: Think no longer
   That you are in command here, but rather think
   How, when you were, you served your own destruction.

(Exeunt into the house all but the CHORUS; *the* CHORAGOS *chants directly to the audience:)*

CHORAGOS: Men of Thebes: look upon Oedipus.

   This is the king who solved the famous riddle
   And towered up, most powerful of men.
   No mortal eyes but looked on him with envy,
   Yet in the end ruin swept over him.

   Let every man in mankind's frailty
   Consider his last day; and let none
   Presume on his good fortune until he find
   Life, at his death, a memory without pain.

Writing Assignments for "Oedipus Rex"

I. Brief Papers: Prologue and Parados

   A. 1. Although the Priest assumes that Oedipus has seen for himself the effects of
      the plague ("Your own eyes will tell you"), these effects cannot be seen by
      the audience except through the words of the actors, especially the Chorus
      in the Parados. Sometimes the Chorus employs simple images or word
      pictures—"pallid children / Lie unwept in the stony ways" (p. 853). But they
      also describe and explain the plague metaphorically, that is, by implicit or
      explicit comparisons. In the Parados the dominant metaphor for plague is
      fire. By explaining why fire is appropriate and how it is used, show how this
      metaphor helps us see and understand the plague.
      2. Explain the origin of Oedipus' fame and how the present crisis resembles the
      trouble in Thebes when Oedipus first came to that city.
      3. *Oedipus Rex* achieves much of its emotional impact through irony, espe-
      cially through the contrast between the meaning intended by the speaker and
      the meaning understood by the audience. When the chorus calls Oedipus
      "the man surest in mortal ways / and wisest in the ways of God" (p. 848),
      they are not being intentionally ironic; they really think that Oedipus is what
      he seems to be, a man successful in human affairs and favored by the gods.
      Choose one of the following:
         a. Explain the unintentional irony in this line by contrasting the chorus' view
         of Oedipus' situation with the understanding of the audience.
         b. Using the same method, explore the irony in Oedipus' declaration that
         he will find the killer of Laïos: "Then once more I must bring what is dark
         to light" (p. 851).

B. 1. The first lines of the Parados ("What is the God singing . . . what oracle for Thebes") make it clear that the chorus has not yet heard the news from Delphi. It might seem more natural if the playwright had begun with the description of the plague and the Chorus' desire to know its cause and then represented the arrival of Creon with the message. Write an argument for or against Sophocles' inversion of these two events.

2. The oracle says that the cause of the plague is the murder of the former king. Some critics argue, however, that the real cause of the plague is incest and that this "defilement," which is yet to be disclosed, is anticipated by the description of the plague. Argue for or against the assertion that the description of the plague points to incest rather than murder.

C. 1. Assume you are making a movie of *Oedipus Rex* and you want to open with a series of visual images that reveal the plague. Describe a few of these images and explain the particular effect you want to achieve.

2. Explain your response to the piety of the Chorus in the Parados, especially the belief that plague, or any natural disaster, is a sign of God's power, wonder, and justice.

II. Brief Papers: Scene I and Ode I

A. 1. Sophocles runs a great risk in having Teiresias solve the murder in the first scene. Why is it probable that Oedipus does not believe him?

2. Show how Teiresias and Oedipus are similar.

B. 1. "How could a wise ruler like Oedipus be foolish enough to accuse reputable men like Teiresias and Creon? This behavior is implausible and inconsistent with what we have been led to expect." Take issue with this assertion, arguing that Oedipus' accusation is plausible and consistent with his character.

2. Some say the Chorus fails to believe Teiresias because they are blinded by self-interest. Others say the Chorus has a sincere and disinterested confidence in Oedipus. Which view do you favor?

C. 1. How does the fact that Teiresias is old and blind affect your response to Scene I?

2. How do you respond to the Chorus' account of the murderer in the first two stanzas of Ode I?

III. Brief Papers: Scene II and Ode II

A. 1. Compare Creon's response to Oedipus' accusation with Oedipus' response to the accusation of Teiresias.

2. When Iocaste tells her story about Laïos and the old prophecy, she intends to be helpful and reassuring. Explain why her story is not reassuring to Oedipus.

3. Explain why, in Ode II, the Chorus' confidence in Oedipus is shaken.

B. 1. Argue for or against the assertion that Oedipus' suspicion of Teiresias and Creon reflects his fear and hatred of his own father.

   2. Argue for or against the assertion that in telling the story of the old prophecy, Iocaste unknowingly convicts herself of impiety.

C. 1. How do you respond to Creon's opinion that anyone would be foolish to exchange a life of privilege, honor, and safety for a life of power, responsibility, and danger?

   2. In Ode II the Chorus expresses its belief that the gods protect and reward those who are good and punish those who are evil. How does the action of the play affect your belief in such justice?

IV. Brief Papers: Scene III and Ode III

A. 1. Iocaste brings incense which burns before the altar of Apollo throughout the scene. Show how this stage device, along with the prayer to Apollo, reinforces the irony of the messenger's "good news."

   2. Explore the irony in Oedipus' explanation of Iocaste's sudden departure near the end of Scene III: "The Queen, like a woman, is perhaps ashamed / To think of my low origin. But I / am a child of Luck; I cannot be dishonored. Luck is my mother" (p. 876).

B. 1. Argue for or against the assertion that the arrival and motive of the Messenger from Corinth are natural and probable.

   2. Argue for or against the probability that the Chorus, on learning that Oedipus is not the son of King Polybus but a foundling, should become extravagantly optimistic.

C. 1. How does Ode III, especially the Chorus' expectation that Oedipus will discover he is the son of a god, affect your response to the play?

   2. How do you respond to Iocaste's scorn for prophecy and her conclusion that "A man should live only for the present day"?

V. Brief Papers: Scene IV, Ode IV, and Exodus

A. 1. Compare the arrival of the Shepherd with the arrival of Teiresias in Scene I.

   2. Compare Iocaste's account of how the child was sent to its death with the Shepherd's account of how he got the child.

B. 1. Argue for or against the assertion that the evidence in the play proves that Oedipus killed his father.

   2. Some say that it is wrong for Oedipus to blind himself; this act is yet another sign of his violent and rebellious temperament. Others say that it is right and noble for Oedipus to blind himself. Write an argument supporting one or the other of these assertions.

C. 1. When asked why he gave the child to the Corinthian shepherd, the Theban shepherd says, "I pitied the baby." How does the shepherd's good intention affect your response to this action?

2. How does the final reference to the Sphinx in Ode IV affect your response to the play?

VI. Foreshadowing in "Oedipus Rex"

Combine the following elements into a coherent paragraph that illustrates the use of *foreshadowing* in *Oedipus Rex*.

1. An event occurs in a play.
2. It occurs late in a play.
3. It resembles an earlier event.
4. This is sometimes said.
5. The earlier event foreshadows the later event.

6. *Foreshadowing* serves many purposes.
7. It unifies the action.
8. It increases suspense.
9. It illustrates a change in character.
10. It illustrates a change in fortune.

11. In *Oedipus Rex,* foreshadowing also helps.
12. It helps dramatize the playwright's views.
13. His views are about tragic heroism.
14. His views are about tragic suffering.

15. Here is an example.
16. We learn this early in the play.
17. Oedipus saves Thebes.
18. This happened many years ago.
19. Oedipus solved a riddle.
20. The riddle was made by the Sphinx.
21. This was an act of heroism.

22. It foreshadows the main plot.
23. Oedipus again saves Thebes.
24. This time he solves a murder.
25. King Laïos was murdered.

26. In both cases Thebes is saved.
27. It is saved by Oedipus.
28. For the hero there is a great difference.
29. The difference is in the outcome of the two adventures.

30. In the first adventure the hero plays a role.
31. He is a typical hero.
32. He saves the city.
33. He destroys a powerful enemy.
34. He marries a queen.
35. He is hailed as savior.
36. He is hailed as king.

37. In the second adventure he also saves the city.
38. He also destroys the enemy.
39. He is the enemy.
40. He destroys himself.
41. He destroys his queen.

42. The playwright uses this change of fortune.
43. The change helps us see Oedipus.
44. Oedipus is a type of tragic hero.
45. He makes noble efforts.
46. These efforts plunge him into guilt.
47. They plunge him into suffering.
48. They do not bring honor.
49. They do not bring happiness.

50. There is another foreshadowing event.
51. It helps reveal the play's tragic form.
52. The event is the departure of the prophet.
53. The prophet is blind.
54. His name is Teiresias.
55. He departs at the end of the first scene.

56. Teiresias was once honored by all of Thebes.
57. Teiresias is here dismissed from the city.
58. He is dismissed as a liar.
59. He is dismissed as a traitor.
60. This is a foreshadowing.
61. It foreshadows the final scene.

62. Oedipus is now also blind.
63. Oedipus is disgraced.
64. He is led into exile.

65. This is a use of foreshadowing.
66. It helps reveal a view of life.
67. It is a tragic view.
68. Only a few people are like Teiresias.

69. They are physically blind.
70. They see the truth.
71. Many are like Oedipus.
72. They think they see clearly.
73. They discover they are really blind.
74. It is too late.

VII. Longer Papers

A. There is some disagreement among critics about the prophecy to Laïos. Some say that Laïos begot the child in defiance of the oracle; others believe (as Iocastê implies) that the prophecy came after the child was born. Which view is most consistent with your reading of the play? In developing your argument, show why you think the opposing view is inadequate.

B. Some say that Oedipus' farewell to his daughters is meant to reinforce the theme of hereditary guilt and divine retribution; just as Oedipus inherited the guilt of Laïos, so the children of Oedipus will inherit his guilt. Others say that the primary intent of the farewell is to generate sympathy for Oedipus and to question the justice of his fall. Which view of the farewell is most consistent with your reading of the play? In developing your argument, show why you think the opposing view is inadequate.

C. Most critics agree with Aristotle at least in this—that good plotting depends on a necessary and probable sequence of discoveries which bring about a change in the hero's fortune. In popular thrillers, like the James Bond movies, the hero's fortune constantly changes but the general tendency is from bad to good: Bond destroys his enemies, saves civilization, preserves his good name, and wins the woman. In tragic plots these discoveries have the opposite tendency. Since discoveries in tragedy have results that are harmful to the hero, it will be better if they come about in a probable way. While we accept, and even expect, an improbable act which saves the hero, we do not want him to be ruined by mere chance. And it will be even more effective if the reversal comes about in an ironic way, as when new information is meant to be helpful but turns out to be otherwise. Using these criteria, analyze the major discoveries in *Oedipus Rex.*

D. *Oedipus Rex* is structured primarily around two stories. The first is the story of Oedipus' rise to fame even as he unwittingly fulfills the evil prophecy; the second, the plot itself, is the story of Oedipus' fall even as he heroically solves the mystery of the King's death. Beginning with the two oracles, show how the two stories mirror each other and explain how this mirroring influences your response to the play.

E. Through an analysis of the four odes and other statements by the Chorus, argue that, in spite of its continuing piety, the Chorus no longer really believes that good is rewarded and evil is punished.

F. A student interprets the tragedy of Oedipus in this way:

> Oedipus' fatal flaw is his excessive pride. He believes himself to be as good or better than the gods themselves; therefore, he has to be punished. Although there is nothing Oedipus can do to prevent the disgrace of killing

his father and marrying his mother, it is his fierce pride that will not let him accept this fate. Only when he loses his pride can he face the truth and receive retribution. This is his "fall." Although we pity Oedipus, we still admire him because he accepts the responsibility for his actions. He suffers for all humanity, and in this sacrifice, we feel atonement.

To what extent do you agree with this reading of the play?

WILLIAM SHAKESPEARE

Hamlet

Before Reading

In Hamlet's time, avenging a murder was considered wrong, as it is today, but then, as now, some people thought that revenge was in certain cases a necessary and even heroic way to achieve justice and restore order. Free write for 5 or 10 minutes about your opinion of revenge.

CHARACTERS

Claudius, King of Denmark

Hamlet, son of the former, and
   nephew to the present, King

Polonius, Lord Chamberlain

Horatio, friend of Hamlet

Laertes, son of Polonius

Voltemand

Cornelius

Rosencrantz } courtiers

Guildenstern

Osric

A Gentleman

A Priest

Lords, Ladies, Officers, Soldiers, Sailors, Messengers, and Attendants

Marcellus } officers

Bernardo

Francisco, a soldier

Reynaldo, servant to Polonius

Players

Two Clowns, gravediggers

Fortinbras, Prince of Norway

A Norwegian Captain

English Ambassadors

Gertrude, Queen of Denmark, and
   mother of Hamlet

Ophelia, daughter of Polonius

Ghost of Hamlet's Father

SCENE   *The action takes place in or near the royal castle of Denmark at Elsinore.*

ACT 1

SCENE 1   *A guard station atop the castle. Enter* BERNARDO *and* FRANCISCO, *two sentinels.*

BERNARDO: Who's there?

FRANCISCO: Nay, answer me. Stand and unfold yourself.

BERNARDO: Long live the king!

FRANCISCO: Bernardo?

BERNARDO: He.   5

FRANCISCO: You come most carefully upon your hour.

HAMLET by William Shakespeare (1564–1616) was produced before 1603 and fully published in 1604. It is arguably the greatest play written in English.

BERNARDO: 'Tis now struck twelve. Get thee to bed, Francisco.
FRANCISCO: For this relief much thanks. 'Tis bitter cold,
    And I am sick at heart.
BERNARDO: Have you had quiet guard?
FRANCISCO: Not a mouse stirring.   10
BERNARDO: Well, good night.
    If you do meet Horatio and Marcellus,
    The rivals° of my watch, bid them make haste.

(Enter HORATIO *and* MARCELLUS.*)*

FRANCISCO: I think I hear them. Stand, ho! Who is there?
HORATIO: Friends to this ground.
MARCELLUS: And liegemen to the Dane.°   15
FRANCISCO: Give you good night.
MARCELLUS: O, farewell, honest soldier!
    Who hath relieved you?
FRANCISCO: Bernardo hath my place.
    Give you good night.

(Exit FRANCISCO.*)*

MARCELLUS: Holla, Bernardo!
BERNARDO: Say—
    What, is Horatio there?
HORATIO: A piece of him.
BERNARDO: Welcome, Horatio. Welcome, good Marcellus.   20
HORATIO: What, has this thing appeared again tonight?
BERNARDO: I have seen nothing.
MARCELLUS: Horatio says 'tis but our fantasy,
    And will not let belief take hold of him
    Touching this dreaded sight twice seen of us.   25
    Therefore I have entreated him along
    With us to watch the minutes of this night,
    That if again this apparition come,
    He may approve° our eyes and speak to it.
HORATIO: Tush, tush, 'twill not appear.
BERNARDO: Sit down awhile,   30
    And let us once again assail your ears,
    That are so fortified against our story,
    What we have two nights seen.
HORATIO: Well, sit we down,
    And let us hear Bernardo speak of this.
BERNARDO: Last night of all,   35

13 companions   15 The "Dane" is the King of Denmark, who is also called "Denmark," as in
line 48 of this scene. In line 61 the same figure is used for the King of Norway.   29 confirm the
testimony of

When yond same star that's westward from the pole°
Had made his course t' illume that part of heaven
Where now it burns, Marcellus and myself,
The bell then beating one—

                                                        (Enter GHOST.*)*

MARCELLUS: Peace, break thee off. Look where it comes again.   40
BERNARDO: In the same figure like the king that's dead.
MARCELLUS: Thou art a scholar; speak to it, Horatio.
BERNARDO: Looks 'a° not like the king? Mark it, Horatio.
HORATIO: Most like. It harrows me with fear and wonder.
BERNARDO: It would be spoke to.
MARCELLUS: Speak to it, Horatio.   45
HORATIO: What art thou that usurp'st this time of night
   Together with that fair and warlike form
   In which the majesty of buried Denmark
   Did sometimes march? By heaven I charge thee, speak.
MARCELLUS: It is offended.
BERNARDO: See, it stalks away.   50
HORATIO: Stay. Speak, speak. I charge thee, speak.

                                                         (Exit GHOST.*)*

MARCELLUS: 'Tis gone and will not answer.
BERNARDO: How now, Horatio! You tremble and look pale.
   Is not this something more than fantasy?
   What think you on't?   55
HORATIO: Before my God, I might not this believe
   Without the sensible° and true avouch
   Of mine own eyes.
MARCELLUS: Is it not like the king?
HORATIO: As thou art to thyself.
   Such was the very armor he had on   60
   When he the ambitious Norway combated.
   So frowned he once when, in an angry parle,°
   He smote the sledded Polacks on the ice.
   'Tis strange.
MARCELLUS: Thus twice before, and jump° at this dead hour,   65
   With martial stalk hath he gone by our watch.
HORATIO: In what particular thought to work I know not,
   But in the gross and scope of mine opinion,
   This bodes some strange eruption to our state.
MARCELLUS: Good now, sit down, and tell me he that knows,   70
   Why this same strict and most observant watch
   So nightly toils the subject° of the land,

36 polestar   43 he   57 of the senses   62 parley   65 precisely   72 people

And why such daily cast of brazen cannon
And foreign mart for implements of war;
Why such impress of shipwrights, whose sore task   75
Does not divide the Sunday from the week.
What might be toward that this sweaty haste
Doth make the night joint-laborer with the day?
Who is't that can inform me?
HORATIO: That can I.
At least, the whisper goes so. Our last king,   80
Whose image even but now appeared to us,
Was as you know by Fortinbras of Norway,
Thereto pricked on by a most emulate pride,
Dared to the combat; in which our valiant Hamlet
(For so this side of our known world esteemed him)   85
Did slay this Fortinbras; who by a sealed compact
Well ratified by law and heraldry,
Did forfeit, with his life, all those his lands
Which he stood seized of,° to the conqueror;
Against the which a moiety competent°   90
Was gagéd° by our king; which had returned
To the inheritance of Fortinbras,
Had he been vanquisher; as, by the same covenant
And carriage of the article designed,
His fell to Hamlet. Now, sir, young Fortinbras,   95
Of unimprovéd mettle hot and full,
Hath in the skirts of Norway here and there
Sharked up a list of lawless resolutes
For food and diet to some enterprise
That hath a stomach in't; which is no other,   100
As it doth well appear unto our state,
But to recover of us by strong hand
And terms compulsatory, those foresaid lands
So by his father lost; and this, I take it,
Is the main motive of our preparations,   105
The source of this our watch, and the chief head
Of this post-haste and romage° in the land.
BERNARDO: I think it be no other but e'en so.
Well may it sort° that this portentous figure
Comes arméd through our watch so like the king   110
That was and is the question of these wars.
HORATIO: A mote° it is to trouble the mind's eye.
In the most high and palmy state of Rome,
A little ere the mightiest Julius fell,
The graves stood tenantless, and the sheeted dead   115

89 possessed   90 portion of similar value   91 pledged   107 stir   109 chance   112 speck of dust

Did squeak and gibber in the Roman streets;
As stars with trains of fire, and dews of blood,
Disasters in the sun; and the moist star,
Upon whose influence Neptune's empire stands,°
Was sick almost to doomsday with eclipse.   120
And even the like precurse° of feared events,
As harbingers preceding still the fates
And prologue to the omen coming on,
Have heaven and earth together demonstrated
Unto our climatures° and countrymen.   125

(Enter GHOST.*)*

But soft, behold, lo where it comes again!
I'll cross it° though it blast me.—Stay, illusion.

(It spreads [its] arms.)

If thou hast any sound or use of voice,
Speak to me.
If there be any good thing to be done,   130
That may to thee do ease, and grace to me,
Speak to me.
If thou art privy to thy country's fate,
Which happily foreknowing may avoid,
O, speak!   135
Or if thou hast uphoarded in thy life
Extorted treasure in the womb of earth,
For which, they say, you spirits oft walk in death,

(The cock crows.)

Speak of it. Stay, and speak. Stop it, Marcellus.
MARCELLUS: Shall I strike at it with my partisan°?   140
HORATIO: Do, if it will not stand.
BERNARDO: 'Tis here.
HORATIO: 'Tis here.
MARCELLUS: 'Tis gone.

(Exit GHOST.*)*

We do it wrong, being so majestical,
To offer it the show of violence;
For it is as the air, invulnerable,   145
And our vain blows malicious mockery.

---

119 Neptune was the Roman sea god; the "moist star" is the moon.   121 precursor   125 regions
127 Horatio means either that he will move across the Ghost's path in order to stop him or that
he will make the sign of the cross to gain power over him. The stage direction which follows is
somewhat ambiguous. "It" seems to refer to the Ghost, but the movement would be appropriate
to Horatio.   140 halberd

BERNARDO: It was about to speak when the cock crew.
HORATIO: And then it started like a guilty thing
    Upon a fearful summons. I have heard
    The cock, that is the trumpet to the morn,   150
    Doth with his lofty and shrill-sounding throat
    Awake the god of day, and at his warning,
    Whether in sea or fire, in earth or air,
    Th' extravagant and erring° spirit hies
    To his confine; and of the truth herein   155
    This present object made probation.°
MARCELLUS: It faded on the crowing of the cock.
    Some say that ever 'gainst that season comes
    Wherein our Savior's birth is celebrated,
    This bird of dawning singeth all night long,   160
    And then, they say, no spirit dare stir abroad,
    The nights are wholesome, then no planets strike,
    No fairy takes,° nor witch hath power to charm,
    So hallowed and so gracious is that time.
HORATIO: So have I heard and do in part believe it.   165
    But look, the morn in russet mantle clad
    Walks o'er the dew of yon high eastward hill.
    Break we our watch up, and by my advice
    Let us impart what we have seen tonight
    Unto young Hamlet, for upon my life   170
    This spirit, dumb to us, will speak to him.
    Do you consent we shall acquaint him with it,
    As needful in our loves, fitting our duty?
MARCELLUS: Let's do't, I pray, and I this morning know
    Where we shall find him most convenient.   175

(Exeunt.)

SCENE 2   *A chamber of state. Enter* KING CLAUDIUS, QUEEN GERTRUDE,
HAMLET, POLONIUS, LAERTES, OPHELIA, VOLTEMAND, CORNELIUS, *and
other members of the court.*

KING: Though yet of Hamlet our dear brother's death
    The memory be green, and that it us befitted
    To bear our hearts in grief, and our whole kingdom
    To be contracted in one brow of woe,
    Yet so far hath discretion fought with nature   5
    That we with wisest sorrow think on him,
    Together with remembrance of ourselves.
    Therefore our sometime sister, now our queen,

154 wandering out of bounds   156 proof   163 enchants

Th' imperial jointress° to this warlike state,
Have we, as 'twere with a defeated joy,   10
With an auspicious and a dropping eye,
With mirth in funeral, and with dirge in marriage,
In equal scale weighing delight and dole,
Taken to wife; nor have we herein barred
Your better wisdoms, which have freely gone   15
With this affair along. For all, our thanks.
Now follows that you know young Fortinbras,
Holding a weak supposal of our worth,
Or thinking by our late dear brother's death
Our state to be disjoint and out of frame,   20
Colleaguéd with this dream of his advantage,
He hath not failed to pester us with message
Importing the surrender of those lands
Lost by his father, with all bands of law,
To our most valiant brother. So much for him.   25
Now for ourself, and for this time of meeting,
Thus much the business is: we have here writ
To Norway, uncle of young Fortinbras—
Who, impotent and bedrid, scarcely hears
Of this his nephew's purpose—to suppress   30
His further gait° herein, in that the levies,
The lists, and full proportions are all made
Out of his subject; and we here dispatch
You, good Cornelius, and you, Voltemand,
For bearers of this greeting to old Norway,   35
Giving to you no further personal power
To business with the king, more than the scope
Of these dilated° articles allow.
Farewell, and let your haste commend your duty.

CORNELIUS
                In that, and all things will we show our duty.   40
VOLTEMAND

KING: We doubt it nothing, heartily farewell.

(Exeunt VOLTEMAND *and* CORNELIUS.*)*

And now, Laertes, what's the news with you?
You told us of some suit. What is't, Laertes?
You cannot speak of reason to the Dane
And lose your voice. What wouldst thou beg, Laertes,   45
That shall not be my offer, not thy asking?
The head is not more native to the heart,
The hand more instrumental° to the mouth,

9 A "jointress" is a widow who holds a *jointure* or life interest in the estate of her deceased husband.
31 progress 38 fully expressed 48 serviceable

Than is the throne of Denmark to thy father.
What wouldst thou have, Laertes?
LAERTES: My dread lord,   50
Your leave and favor to return to France,
From whence, though willingly, I came to Denmark
To show my duty in your coronation,
Yet now I must confess, that duty done,
My thoughts and wishes bend again toward France,   55
And bow them to your gracious leave and pardon.
KING: Have you your father's leave? What says Polonius?
POLONIUS: He hath, my lord, wrung from me my slow leave
By laborsome petition, and at last
Upon his will I sealed my hard consent.   60
I do beseech you give him leave to go.
KING: Take thy fair hour, Laertes. Time be thine,
And thy best graces spend it at thy will.
But now, my cousin° Hamlet, and my son—
HAMLET *(aside):*   A little more than kin, and less than kind.   65
KING: How is it that the clouds still hang on you?
HAMLET: Not so, my lord. I am too much in the sun.
QUEEN: Good Hamlet, cast thy nighted color off,
And let thine eye look like a friend on Denmark.
Do not for ever with thy vailéd lids°   70
Seek for thy noble father in the dust.
Thou know'st 'tis common—all that lives must die,
Passing through nature to eternity.
HAMLET: Ay, madam, it is common.
QUEEN: If it be,
Why seems it so particular with thee?   75
HAMLET: Seems, madam? Nay, it is. I know not "seems."
'Tis not alone my inky cloak, good mother,
Nor customary suits of solemn black,
Nor windy suspiration of forced breath,
No, nor the fruitful river in the eye,   80
Nor the dejected havior° of the visage,
Together with all forms, moods, shapes of grief,
That can denote me truly. These indeed seem,
For they are actions that a man might play,
But I have that within which passes show—   85
These but the trappings and the suits of woe.
KING: 'Tis sweet and commendable in your nature, Hamlet,
To give these mourning duties to your father,
But you must know your father lost a father,
That father lost, lost his, and the survivor bound   90

64 "Cousin" is used here as a general term of kinship.   70 lowered eyes   81 appearance

In filial obligation for some term
To do obsequious° sorrow. But to persever
In obstinate condolement is a course
Of impious stubbornness. 'Tis unmanly grief.
It shows a will most incorrect to° heaven,   95
A heart unfortified, a mind impatient,
An understanding simple and unschooled.
For what we know must be, and is as common
As any the most vulgar thing to sense,
Why should we in our peevish opposition   100
Take it to heart? Fie, 'tis a fault to heaven,
A fault against the dead, a fault to nature,
To reason most absurd, whose common theme
Is death of fathers, and who still hath cried,
From the first corse° till he that died today,   105
"This must be so." We pray you throw to earth
This unprevailing woe, and think of us
As of a father, for let the world take note
You are the most immediate° to our throne,
And with no less nobility of love   110
Than that which dearest father bears his son
Do I impart toward you. For your intent
In going back to school in Wittenberg,
It is most retrograde° to our desire,
And we beseech you, bend you to remain   115
Here in the cheer and comfort of our eye,
Our chiefest courtier, cousin, and our son.
QUEEN: Let not thy mother lose her prayers, Hamlet.
I pray thee stay with us, go not to Wittenberg.
HAMLET: I shall in all my best obey you, madam.   120
KING: Why, 'tis a loving and a fair reply.
Be as ourself in Denmark. Madam, come.
This gentle and unforced accord of Hamlet
Sits smiling to my heart, in grace whereof,
No jocund health that Denmark drinks today   125
But the great cannon to the clouds shall tell,
And the king's rouse° the heaven shall bruit° again,
Respeaking earthly thunder. Come away.

(Flourish. Exeunt all but HAMLET.*)*

HAMLET: O, that this too too solid flesh would melt,
Thaw, and resolve itself into a dew,   130
Or that the Everlasting had not fixed

92 suited for funeral obsequies   95 uncorrected toward   105 corpse   109 next in line
114 contrary   127 carousal   127 echo

His canon° 'gainst self-slaughter. O God, God,
How weary, stale, flat, and unprofitable
Seem to me all the uses of this world!
Fie on't, ah, fie, 'tis an unweeded garden   135
That grows to seed. Things rank and gross in nature
Possess it merely.° That it should come to this,
But two months dead, nay, not so much, not two.
So excellent a king, that was to this
Hyperion to a satyr,° so loving to my mother,   140
That he might not beteem° the winds of heaven
Visit her face too roughly. Heaven and earth,
Must I remember? Why, she would hang on him
As if increase of appetite had grown
By what it fed on, and yet, within a month—   145
Let me not think on't. Frailty, thy name is woman—
A little month, or ere those shoes were old
With which she followed my poor father's body
Like Niobe,° all tears, why she, even she—
O God, a beast that wants discourse of reason   150
Would have mourned longer—married with my uncle,
My father's brother, but no more like my father
Than I to Hercules.° Within a month,
Ere yet the salt of most unrighteous tears
Had left the flushing in her gallèd eyes,   155
She married. O, most wicked speed, to post
With such dexterity to incestuous sheets!
It is not, nor it cannot come to good.
But break my heart, for I must hold my tongue.

(Enter HORATIO, MARCELLUS, *and* BERNARDO.*)*

HORATIO: Hail to your lordship!
HAMLET: I am glad to see you well.   160
    Horatio—or I do forget myself.
HORATIO: The same, my lord, and your poor servant ever.
HAMLET: Sir, my good friend, I'll change° that name with you.
    And what make you from Wittenberg, Horatio?
    Marcellus?   165
MARCELLUS: My good lord!
HAMLET: I am very glad to see you. *(To* BERNARDO.*)* Good even, sir.—
    But what, in faith, make you from Wittenberg?

132 law   137 entirely   140 Hyperion, a sun god, stands here for beauty in contrast to the
monstrous satyr, a lecherous creature, half man and half goat.   141 permit   149 In Greek
mythology Niobe was turned to stone after a tremendous fit of weeping over the death of her
fourteen children, a misfortune brought about by her boasting over her fertility.   153 The demi-
god Hercules was noted for his strength and the series of spectacular labors which it allowed him
to accomplish.   163 exchange

HORATIO: A truant disposition, good my lord.
HAMLET: I would not hear your enemy say so,   170
    Nor shall you do my ear that violence
    To make it truster of your own report
    Against yourself. I know you are no truant.
    But what is your affair in Elsinore?
    We'll teach you to drink deep ere you depart.   175
HORATIO: My lord, I came to see your father's funeral.
HAMLET: I prithee do not mock me, fellow-student,
    I think it was to see my mother's wedding.
HORATIO: Indeed, my lord, it followed hard upon.
HAMLET: Thrift, thrift, Horatio. The funeral-baked meats   180
    Did coldly furnish forth the marriage tables.
    Would I had met my dearest° foe in heaven
    Or ever I had seen that day, Horatio!
    My father—methinks I see my father.
HORATIO: Where, my lord?
HAMLET: In my mind's eye, Horatio.   185
HORATIO: I saw him once, 'a was a goodly king.
HAMLET: 'A was a man, take him for all in all,
    I shall not look upon his like again.
HORATIO: My lord, I think I saw him yesternight.
HAMLET: Saw who?   190
HORATIO: My lord, the king your father.
HAMLET: The king my father?
HORATIO: Season° your admiration° for a while
    With an attent° ear till I may deliver°
    Upon the witness of these gentlemen
    This marvel to you.
HAMLET: For God's love, let me hear!   195
HORATIO: Two nights together had these gentlemen,
    Marcellus and Bernardo, on their watch
    In the dead waste and middle of the night
    Been thus encountered. A figure like your father,
    Armed at point exactly,° cap-a-pe,°   200
    Appears before them, and with solemn march
    Goes slow and stately by them. Thrice he walked
    By their oppressed and fear-surprisèd eyes
    Within his truncheon's° length, whilst they, distilled
    Almost to jelly with the act of fear,   205
    Stand dumb and speak not to him. This to me
    In dreadful secrecy impart they did,
    And I with them the third night kept the watch,

182 bitterest   192 moderate   192 wonder   193 attentive   193 relate   200 completely
200 from head to toe   204 baton of office

Where, as they had delivered, both in time,
Form of the thing, each word made true and good,   210
The apparition comes. I knew your father.
These hands are not more like.
HAMLET: But where was this?
MARCELLUS: My lord, upon the platform where we watch.
HAMLET: Did you not speak to it?
HORATIO: My lord, I did,
But answer made it none. Yet once methought   215
It lifted up its head and did address
Itself to motion, like as it would speak;
But even then the morning cock crew loud,
And at the sound it shrunk in haste away
And vanished from our sight.
HAMLET: 'Tis very strange.   220
HORATIO: As I do live, my honored lord, 'tis true,
And we did think it writ down in our duty
To let you know of it.
HAMLET: Indeed, sirs, but
This troubles me. Hold you the watch tonight?
ALL: We do, my lord.
HAMLET: Armed, say you?
ALL: Armed, my lord.   225
HAMLET: From top to toe?
ALL: My lord, from head to foot.
HAMLET: Then saw you not his face.
HORATIO: O yes, my lord, he wore his beaver° up.
HAMLET: What, looked he frowningly?
HORATIO: A countenance more in sorrow than in anger.   230
HAMLET: Pale or red?
HORATIO: Nay, very pale.
HAMLET: And fixed his eyes upon you?
HORATIO: Most constantly.
HAMLET: I would I had been there.
HORATIO: It would have much amazed you.
HAMLET: Very like.
Stayed it long?   235
HORATIO: While one with moderate haste might tell a hundred.
BOTH: Longer, longer.
HORATIO: Not when I saw't.
HAMLET: His beard was grizzled, no?
HORATIO: It was as I have seen it in his life,
A sable silvered.
HAMLET: I will watch tonight.   240

228 movable face protector

Perchance 'twill walk again.
HORATIO: I warr'nt it will.
HAMLET: If it assume my noble father's person,
　　　I'll speak to it though hell itself should gape°
　　　And bid me hold my peace. I pray you all,
　　　If you have hitherto concealed this sight,   245
　　　Let it be tenable° in your silence still,
　　　And whatsomever else shall hap tonight,
　　　Give it an understanding but no tongue.
　　　I will requite your loves. So fare you well.
　　　Upon the platform 'twixt eleven and twelve   250
　　　I'll visit you.
ALL: Our duty to your honor.
HAMLET: Your loves, as mine to you. Farewell.

                                                    (Exeunt all but HAMLET.*)*

My father's spirit in arms? All is not well.
I doubt° some foul play. Would the night were come!
Till then sit still, my soul. Foul deeds will rise,   255
Though all the earth o'erwhelm them, to men's eyes.

                                                                                    (Exit.)

SCENE 3   *The dwelling of* POLONIUS. *Enter* LAERTES *and* OPHELIA.

LAERTES: My necessaries are embarked. Farewell.
　　　And, sister, as the winds give benefit
　　　And convoy° is assistant,° do not sleep,
　　　But let me hear from you.
OPHELIA: Do you doubt that?
LAERTES: For Hamlet, and the trifling of his favor,   5
　　　Hold it a fashion and a toy in blood,
　　　A violet in the youth of primy° nature,
　　　Forward, not permanent, sweet, not lasting,
　　　The perfume and suppliance of a minute,
　　　No more.
OPHELIA: No more but so?
LAERTES: Think it no more.   10
　　　For nature crescent° does not grow alone
　　　In thews and bulk, but as this temple° waxes
　　　The inward service of the mind and soul
　　　Grows wide withal. Perhaps he loves you now,
　　　And now no soil nor cautel° doth besmirch   15
　　　The virtue of his will, but you must fear,

243 open (its mouth) wide   246 held   254 suspect   3 means of transport   3 available
7 of the spring   11 growing   12 body   15 deceit

His greatness weighed,° his will is not his own,
For he himself is subject to his birth.
He may not, as unvalued persons do,
Carve for himself, for on his choice depends   20
The safety and health of this whole state,
And therefore must his choice be circumscribed
Unto the voice° and yielding of that body
Whereof he is the head. Then if he says he loves you,
It fits your wisdom so far to believe it   25
As he in his particular act and place
May give his saying deed, which is no further
Than the main voice of Denmark goes withal.
Then weigh what loss your honor may sustain
If with too credent° ear you list° his songs,   30
Or lose your heart, or your chaste treasure open
To his unmastered importunity.
Fear it, Ophelia, fear it, my dear sister,
And keep you in the rear of your affection,
Out of the shot and danger of desire.   35
The chariest° maid is prodigal enough
If she unmask her beauty to the moon.
Virtue itself scapes not calumnious strokes.
The canker° galls the infants of the spring
Too oft before their buttons° be disclosed,   40
And in the morn and liquid dew of youth
Contagious blastments° are most imminent.
Be wary then; best safety lies in fear.
Youth to itself rebels, though none else near.
OPHELIA: I shall the effect of this good lesson keep   45
As watchman to my heart. But, good my brother,
Do not as some ungracious pastors do,
Show me the steep and thorny way to heaven,
Whiles like a puffed and reckless libertine
Himself the primrose path of dalliance treads   50
And recks° not his own rede.°
LAERTES: O, fear me not.

                                        (*Enter* POLONIUS.)

I stay too long. But here my father comes.
A double blessing is a double grace;
Occasion smiles upon a second leave.
POLONIUS: Yet here, Laertes? Aboard, aboard, for shame!   55
The wind sits in the shoulder of your sail,

17 rank considered   23 assent   30 credulous   30 listen to   36 most circumspect   39 rose
caterpillar   40 buds   42 blights   51 heeds   51 advice

And you are stayed for. There—my blessing with thee,
And these few precepts in thy memory
Look thou character.° Give thy thoughts no tongue,
Nor any unproportioned thought his act.   60
Be thou familiar, but by no means vulgar.
Those friends thou hast, and their adoption tried,
Grapple them unto thy soul with hoops of steel;
But do not dull° thy palm with entertainment
Of each new-hatched, unfledged comrade. Beware   65
Of entrance to a quarrel, but being in,
Bear't° that th' opposéd° may beware of thee.
Give every man thy ear, but few thy voice;°
Take each man's censure, but reserve thy judgment.
Costly thy habit as thy purse can buy,   70
But not expressed in fancy; rich not gaudy,
For the apparel oft proclaims the man,
And they in France of the best rank and station
Are of a most select and generous chief° in that.
Neither a borrower nor a lender be,   75
For loan oft loses both itself and friend,
And borrowing dulls th' edge of husbandry.
This above all, to thine own self be true,
And it must follow as the night the day
Thou canst not then be false to any man.   80
Farewell. My blessing season this in thee!
LAERTES: Most humbly do I take my leave, my lord.
POLONIUS: The time invites you. Go, your servants tend.°
LAERTES: Farewell, Ophelia, and remember well
What I have said to you.
OPHELIA: 'Tis in my memory locked,   85
And you yourself shall keep the key of it.
LAERTES: Farewell.

                                        (*Exit* LAERTES.)

POLONIUS: What is't, Ophelia, he hath said to you?
OPHELIA: So please you, something touching the Lord Hamlet.
POLONIUS: Marry, well bethought.   90
'Tis told me he hath very oft of late
Given private time to you, and you yourself
Have of your audience been most free and bounteous.
If it be so—as so 'tis put on me,
And that in way of caution—I must tell you,   95

59 write   64 make callous   67 conduct it   67 opponent   68 approval   74 eminence
83 await

You do not understand yourself so clearly
As it behooves my daughter and your honor.
What is between you? Give me up the truth.

OPHELIA: He hath, my lord, of late made many tenders
Of his affection to me.   100

POLONIUS: Affection? Pooh! You speak like a green girl,
Unsifted in such perilous circumstance.
Do you believe his tenders, as you call them?

OPHELIA: I do not know, my lord, what I should think.

POLONIUS: Marry, I will teach you. Think yourself a baby   105
That you have ta'en these tenders for true pay
Which are not sterling. Tender yourself more dearly,
Or (not to crack the wind of the poor phrase,
Running it thus) you'll tender me a fool.

OPHELIA: My lord, he hath importuned me with love   110
In honorable fashion.

POLONIUS: Ay, fashion you may call it. Go to, go to.

OPHELIA: And hath given countenance° to his speech, my lord,
With almost all the holy vows of heaven.

POLONIUS: Ay, springes° to catch woodcocks. I do know,   115
When the blood burns, how prodigal the soul
Lends the tongue vows. These blazes, daughter,
Giving more light than heat, extinct in both
Even in their promise, as it is a-making,
You must not take for fire. From this time   120
Be something scanter of your maiden presence.
Set your entreatments° at a higher rate
Than a command to parle. For Lord Hamlet,
Believe so much in him that he is young,
And with a larger tether may he walk   125
Than may be given you. In few, Ophelia,
Do not believe his vows, for they are brokers,°
Not of that dye which their investments° show,
But mere implorators° of unholy suits,
Breathing like sanctified and pious bawds,   130
The better to beguile. This is for all:
I would not, in plain terms, from this time forth
Have you so slander any moment leisure
As to give words or talk with the Lord Hamlet.
Look to't, I charge you. Come your ways.   135

OPHELIA: I shall obey, my lord.

(Exeunt.)

113 confirmation   115 snares   122 negotiations before a surrender   127 panders   128 garments
129 solicitors

SCENE 4 *The guard station. Enter* HAMLET, HORATIO *and* MARCELLUS.

HAMLET: The air bites shrewdly°; it is very cold.
HORATIO: It is a nipping and an eager° air.
HAMLET: What hour now?
HORATIO: I think it lacks of twelve.
MARCELLUS: No, it is struck.
HORATIO: Indeed? I heard it not. It then draws near the season   5
Wherein the spirit held his wont to walk.

(A flourish of trumpets, and two pieces go off.)

What does this mean, my lord?
HAMLET: The king doth wake tonight and takes his rouse,
Keeps wassail, and the swagg'ring up-spring° reels,
And as he drains his draughts of Rhenish down,   10
The kettledrum and trumpet thus bray out
The triumph of his pledge.
HORATIO: Is it a custom?
HAMLET: Ay, marry, is't,
But to my mind, though I am native here
And to the manner born, it is a custom   15
More honored in the breach than the observance.
This heavy-headed revel east and west
Makes us traduced and taxed of other nations.
They clepe° us drunkards, and with swinish phrase
Soil our addition,° and indeed it takes   20
From our achievements, though performed at height,
The pith and marrow of our attribute.°
So oft it chances in particular men,
That for some vicious mole of nature in them,
As in their birth, wherein they are not guilty   25
(Since nature cannot choose his origin),
By the o'ergrowth of some complexion,
Oft breaking down the pales° and forts of reason,
Or by some habit that too much o'er-leavens
The form of plausive° manners—that these men,   30
Carrying, I say, the stamp of one defect,
Being nature's livery or fortune's star,
His virtues else, be they as pure as grace,
As infinite as man may undergo,
Shall in the general censure take corruption   35
From that particular fault. The dram of evil

1 sharply   2 keen   9 a German dance   19 call   20 reputation   22 honor   28 barriers
30 pleasing

Doth all the noble substance often dout°
To his own scandal.

(Enter GHOST.)

HORATIO: Look, my lord, it comes.
HAMLET: Angels and ministers of grace defend us!
    Be thou a spirit of health or goblin damned,   40
    Bring with thee airs from heaven or blasts from hell,
    Be thy intents wicked or charitable,
    Thou com'st in such a questionable° shape
    That I will speak to thee. I'll call thee Hamlet,
    King, father, royal Dane. O, answer me!   45
    Let me not burst in ignorance, but tell
    Why thy canonized° bones, hearséd in death,
    Have burst their cerements°; why the sepulchre
    Wherein we saw thee quietly interred
    Hath oped his ponderous and marble jaws   50
    To cast thee up again. What may this mean
    That thou, dead corse, again in complete steel°
    Revisits thus the glimpses of the moon,
    Making night hideous, and we fools of nature
    So horridly to shake our disposition   55
    With thoughts beyond the reaches of our souls?
    Say, why is this? wherefore? what should we do?

(GHOST beckons.)

HORATIO: It beckons you to go away with it,
    As if it some impartment° did desire
    To you alone.
MARCELLUS: Look with what courteous action   60
    It waves° you to a more removéd° ground.
    But do not go with it.
HORATIO: No, by no means.
HAMLET: It will not speak; then I will follow it.
HORATIO: Do not, my lord.
HAMLET: Why, what should be the fear?
    I do not set my life at a pin's fee,°   65
    And for my soul, what can it do to that,
    Being a thing immortal as itself?
    It waves me forth again. I'll follow it.
HORATIO: What if it tempt you toward the flood, my lord,
    Or to the dreadful summit of the cliff   70

37 put out   43 prompting question   47 buried in accordance with church canons   48 gravecloths
52 armor   59 communication   61 beckons   61 distant   65 price

That beetles° o'er his base into the sea,
And there assume some other horrible form,
Which might deprive° your sovereignty of reason°
And draw you into madness? Think of it.
The very place puts toys of desperation,°   75
Without more motive, into every brain
That looks so many fathoms to the sea
And hears it roar beneath.

HAMLET: It waves me still.
Go on. I'll follow thee.

MARCELLUS: You shall not go, my lord.

HAMLET: Hold off your hands.   80

HORATIO: Be ruled. You shall not go.

HAMLET: My fate cries out
And makes each petty artery in this body
As hardy as the Nemean lion's nerve.°
Still am I called. Unhand me, gentlemen.
By heaven, I'll make a ghost of him that lets° me.   85
I say, away! Go on. I'll follow thee.

(Exeunt GHOST *and* HAMLET.*)*

HORATIO: He waxes desperate with imagination.

MARCELLUS: Let's follow. 'Tis not fit thus to obey him.

HORATIO: Have after. To what issue will this come?

MARCELLUS: Something is rotten in the state of Denmark.   90

HORATIO: Heaven will direct it.

MARCELLUS: Nay, let's follow him.

(Exeunt.)

SCENE 5   *Near the guard station. Enter* GHOST *and* HAMLET.

HAMLET: Whither wilt thou lead me? Speak. I'll go no further.

GHOST: Mark me.

HAMLET: I will.

GHOST: My hour is almost come,
When I to sulph'rous and tormenting flames
Must render up myself.

HAMLET: Alas, poor ghost!

GHOST: Pity me not, but lend thy serious hearing   5
To what I shall unfold.

HAMLET: Speak. I am bound to hear.

GHOST: So art thou to revenge, when thou shalt hear.

HAMLET: What?

---

71 juts out   73 take away   73 rational power   75 desperate fancies   83 The Nemean lion was
a mythological monster slain by Hercules as one of his twelve labors.   85 hinders

GHOST: I am thy father's spirit,
    Doomed for a certain term to walk the night,   10
    And for the day confined to fast in fires,
    Till the foul crimes done in my days of nature°
    Are burnt and purged away. But that I am forbid
    To tell the secrets of my prison house,
    I could a tale unfold whose lightest word   15
    Would harrow up thy soul, freeze thy young blood,
    Make thy two eyes like stars start from their spheres,
    Thy knotted and combinéd° locks to part,
    And each particular hair to stand an end,
    Like quills upon the fretful porpentine.°   20
    But this eternal blazon° must not be
    To ears of flesh and blood. List, list, O, list!
    If thou didst ever thy dear father love—
HAMLET: O God!
GHOST: Revenge his foul and most unnatural murder.   25
HAMLET: Murder!
GHOST: Murder most foul, as in the best it is,
    But this most foul, strange, and unnatural.
HAMLET: Haste me to know't, that I, with wings as swift
    As meditation or the thoughts of love,   30
    May sweep to my revenge.
GHOST: I find thee apt,
    And duller shouldst thou be than the fat weed
    That rots itself in ease on Lethe° wharf,—
    Wouldst thou not stir in this. Now, Hamlet, hear.
    'Tis given out that, sleeping in my orchard,   35
    A serpent stung me. So the whole ear of Denmark
    Is by a forgéd process° of my death
    Rankly abused. But know, thou noble youth,
    The serpent that did sting thy father's life
    Now wears his crown.
HAMLET: O my prophetic soul!   40
    My uncle!
GHOST: Ay, that incestuous, that adulterate beast,
    With witchcraft of his wits, with traitorous gifts—
    O wicked wit and gifts that have the power
    So to seduce!—won to his shameful lust   45
    The will of my most seeming virtuous queen.
    O Hamlet, what a falling off was there,
    From me, whose love was of that dignity

---

12 i.e., while I was alive   18 tangled   20 porcupine   21 description of eternity   33 The Lethe was one of the rivers of the classical underworld. Its specific importance was that its waters when drunk induced forgetfulness. The "fat weed" is the asphodel which grew there.   37 false report

That it went hand in hand even with the vow
I made to her in marriage, and to decline°   50
Upon a wretch whose natural gifts were poor
To those of mine!
But virtue, as it never will be moved,
Though lewdness court it in a shape of heaven,
So lust, though to a radiant angel linked,   55
Will sate itself in a celestial bed
And prey on garbage.
But soft, methinks I scent the morning air.
Brief let me be. Sleeping within my orchard,
My custom always of the afternoon,   60
Upon my secure hour thy uncle stole,
With juice of cursed hebona° in a vial,
And in the porches of my ears did pour
The leperous distilment, whose effect
Holds such an enmity with blood of man   65
That swift as quicksilver it courses through
The natural gates and alleys of the body,
And with a sudden vigor it doth posset°
And curd,° like eager° droppings into milk,
The thin and wholesome blood. So did it mine,   70
And a most instant tetter° barked about°
Most lazar-like° with vile and loathsome crust
All my smooth body.
Thus was I sleeping by a brother's hand
Of life, of crown, of queen at once dispatched,   75
Cut off even in the blossoms of my sin,
Unhouseled, disappointed, unaneled,°
No reck'ning made, but sent to my account
With all my imperfections on my head.
O, horrible! O, horrible! most horrible!   80
If thou hast nature in thee, bear it not.
Let not the royal bed of Denmark be
A couch for luxury° and damnéd incest.
But howsomever thou pursues this act,
Taint not thy mind, nor let thy soul contrive   85
Against thy mother aught. Leave her to heaven,
And to those thorns that in her bosom lodge
To prick and sting her. Fare thee well at once.
The glowworm shows the matin° to be near,

---

50 sink   62 a poison   68 coagulate   69 curdle   69 acid   71 a skin disease   71 covered like
bark   72 leper-like   77 The Ghost means that he died without the customary rites of the church,
that is, without receiving the sacrament, without confession, and without extreme unction.
83 lust   89 morning

And gins to pale his uneffectual fire.   90
Adieu, adieu, adieu. Remember me.

                                                                    (Exit.)

HAMLET: O all you host of heaven! O earth! What else?
        And shall I couple hell? O, fie! Hold, hold, my heart,
        And you, my sinews, grow not instant old,
        But bear me stiffly up. Remember thee?   95
        Ay, thou poor ghost, whiles memory holds a seat
        In this distracted globe.° Remember thee?
        Yea, from the table° of my memory
        I'll wipe away all trivial fond° records,
        All saws of books, all forms, all pressures past   100
        That youth and observation copied there,
        And thy commandment all alone shall live
        Within the book and volume of my brain,
        Unmixed with baser matter. Yes, by heaven!
        O most pernicious woman!   105
        O villain, villain, smiling, damnéd villain!
        My tables—meet it is I set it down
        That one may smile, and smile, and be a villain.
        At least I am sure it may be so in Denmark.
        So, uncle, there you are. Now to my word°:   110
        It is "Adieu, adieu. Remember me."
        I have sworn't.

        (Enter HORATIO *and* MARCELLUS.*)*

HORATIO: My lord, my lord!
MARCELLUS: Lord Hamlet!
HORATIO: Heavens secure him!
HAMLET: So be it!
MARCELLUS: Illo, ho, ho, my lord!   115
HAMLET: Hillo, ho, ho, boy!° Come, bird, come.
MARCELLUS: How is't, my noble lord?
HORATIO: What news, my lord?
HAMLET: O, wonderful!
HORATIO: Good my lord, tell it.
HAMLET: No, you will reveal it.
HORATIO: Not I, my lord, by heaven.
MARCELLUS: Nor I, my lord.   120
HAMLET: How say you then, would heart of man once think it?
        But you'll be secret?
BOTH: Ay, by heaven, my lord.
HAMLET: There's never a villain dwelling in all Denmark

97 skull   98 writing tablet   99 foolish   110 for my motto   116 a falconer's cry

But he's an arrant knave.

HORATIO: There needs no ghost, my lord, come from the grave   125
   To tell us this.

HAMLET: Why, right, you are in the right,
   And so without more circumstance at all
   I hold it fit that we shake hands and part,
   You, as your business and desire shall point you,
   For every man hath business and desire   130
   Such as it is, and for my own poor part,
   I will go pray.

HORATIO: These are but wild and whirling words, my lord.

HAMLET: I am sorry they offend you, heartily;
   Yes, faith, heartily.

HORATIO: There's no offence, my lord.   135

HAMLET: Yes, by Saint Patrick, but there is, Horatio,
   And much offence too. Touching this vision here,
   It is an honest ghost, that let me tell you.
   For your desire to know what is between us.
   O'ermaster't as you may. And now, good friends,   140
   As you are friends, scholars, and soldiers,
   Give me one poor request.

HORATIO: What is't, my lord? We will.

HAMLET: Never make known what you have seen tonight.

BOTH: My lord, we will not.

HAMLET: Nay, but swear't.

HORATIO: In faith,   145
   My lord, not I.

MARCELLUS: Nor I, my lord, in faith.

HAMLET: Upon my sword.

MARCELLUS: We have sworn, my lord, already.

HAMLET: Indeed, upon my sword, indeed.

(GHOST cries under the stage.)

GHOST: Swear.

HAMLET: Ha, ha, boy, say'st thou so? Art thou there, truepenny°?
   Come on. You hear this fellow in the cellarage.°   150
   Consent to swear.

HORATIO: Propose the oath, my lord.

HAMLET: Never to speak of this that you have seen,
   Swear by my sword.

GHOST *(beneath):*   Swear.

HAMLET: Hic et ubique?° Then we'll shift our ground.   155
   Come hither, gentlemen,
   And lay your hands again upon my sword.

149 old fellow   150 below   155 here and everywhere

Swear by my sword
Never to speak of this that you have heard.
GHOST *(beneath):*   Swear by his sword.   160
HAMLET: Well said, old mole! Canst work i' th' earth so fast?
A worthy pioneer!° Once more remove, good friends.
HORATIO: O day and night, but this is wondrous strange!
HAMLET: And therefore as a stranger give it welcome.
There are more things in heaven and earth, Horatio,   165
Than are dreamt of in your philosophy.
But come.
Here as before, never, so help you mercy,
How strange or odd some'er I bear myself
(As I perchance hereafter shall think meet   170
To put an antic° disposition on),
That you, at such times, seeing me, never shall,
With arms encumbered° thus, or this head-shake,
Or by pronouncing of some doubtful phrase,
As "Well, well, we know," or "We could, and if we would"   175
Or "If we list to speak," or "There be, and if they might"
Or such ambiguous giving out, to note
That you know aught of me—this do swear,
So grace and mercy at your most need help you.
GHOST *(beneath):*   Swear.   180

(They swear.)

HAMLET: Rest, rest, perturbéd spirit! So, gentlemen,
With all my love I do commend me to you,
And what so poor a man as Hamlet is
May do t'express his love and friending° to you,
God willing, shall not lack. Let us go in together,   185
And still your fingers on your lips, I pray.
The time is out of joint. O curséd spite
That ever I was born to set it right!
Nay, come, let's go together.

(Exeunt.)

ACT 2

SCENE 1   *The dwelling of* POLONIUS. *Enter* POLONIUS *and* REYNALDO.

POLONIUS: Give him this money and these notes, Reynaldo.
REYNALDO: I will, my lord.
POLONIUS: You shall do marvellous wisely, good Reynaldo,

162 soldier who digs trenches   171 mad   173 folded   184 friendship

Before you visit him, to make inquire°
Of his behavior.
REYNALDO: My lord, I did intend it.   5
POLONIUS: Marry, well said, very well said. Look you, sir.
Enquire me first what Danskers° are in Paris,
And how, and who, what means, and where they keep,°
What company, at what expense; and finding
By this encompassment° and drift of question   10
That they do know my son, come you more nearer
Than your particular demands° will touch it.
Take you as 'twere some distant knowledge of him,
As thus, "I know his father and his friends,
And in part him." Do you mark this, Reynaldo?   15
REYNALDO: Ay, very well, my lord.
POLONIUS: "And in part him, but," you may say, "not well,
But if't be he I mean, he's very wild,
Addicted so and so." And there put on him
What forgeries° you please; marry, none so rank°   20
As may dishonor him. Take heed of that.
But, sir, such wanton, wild, and usual slips
As are companions noted and most known
To youth and liberty.
REYNALDO: As gaming, my lord.
POLONIUS: Ay, or drinking, fencing, swearing, quarrelling, 25
Drabbing°—you may go so far.
REYNALDO: My lord, that would dishonor him.
POLONIUS: Faith, no, as you may season it in the charge.°
You must not put another scandal on him,
That he is open to incontinency.°   30
That's not my meaning. But breathe his faults so quaintly°
That they may seem the taints of liberty,°
The flash and outbreak of a fiery mind,
A savageness in unreclaiméd° blood,
Of general assault.°
REYNALDO: But, my good lord—   35
POLONIUS: Wherefore should you do this?
REYNALDO: Ay, my lord,
I would know that.
POLONIUS: Marry, sir, here's my drift,
And I believe it is a fetch of warrant.°
You laying these slight sullies on my son,
As 'twere a thing a little soiled i' th' working,   40

4 inquiry   7 Danes   8 live   10 indirect means   12 direct questions   20 lies   20 foul
26 whoring   28 soften the accusation   30 sexual excess   31 with delicacy   32 faults of freedom
34 untamed   35 touching everyone   38 permissible trick

Mark you,
Your party in converse,° him you would sound,
Having ever seen in the prenominate° crimes
The youth you breathe° of guilty, be assured
He closes with you in this consequence,   45
"Good sir," or so, or "friend," or "gentleman,"
According to the phrase or the addition
Of man and country.
REYNALDO: Very good, my lord.
POLONIUS: And then, sir, does 'a this—'a does—What was I about to
say?   50
By the mass, I was about to say something.
Where did I leave?
REYNALDO: At "closes in the consequence."
POLONIUS: At "closes in the consequence"—ay, marry,
He closes thus: "I know the gentleman.   55
I saw him yesterday, or th' other day,
Or then, or then, with such, or such, and as you say,
There was 'a gaming, there o'ertook in's rouse,
There falling out at tennis," or perchance
"I saw him enter such a house of sale,"   60
Videlicet,° a brothel, or so forth.
See you, now—
Your bait of falsehood takes this carp of truth,
And thus do we of wisdom and of reach,°
With windlasses and with assays of bias,°   65
By indirections find directions out;
So by my former lecture and advice
Shall you my son. You have me, have you not?
REYNALDO: My lord, I have.
POLONIUS: God b'wi' ye; fare ye well.
REYNALDO: Good my lord.   70
POLONIUS: Observe his inclination in yourself.
REYNALDO: I shall, my lord.
POLONIUS: And let him ply° his music.
REYNALDO: Well, my lord.
POLONIUS: Farewell.

(Exit REYNALDO.*)*

(Enter OPHELIA.*)*

How now, Ophelia, what's the matter?
OPHELIA: O my lord, my lord, I have been so affrighted!   75
POLONIUS: With what, i' th' name of God?

42 conversation   43 already named   44 speak   61 namely   64 ability   65 indirect tests
73 practice

OPHELIA: My lord, as I was sewing in my closet,°
    Lord Hamlet with his doublet° all unbraced,°
    No hat upon his head, his stockings fouled,
    Ungartered and down-gyvéd° to his ankle,   80
    Pale as his shirt, his knees knocking each other,
    And with a look so piteous in purport
    As if he had been looséd out of hell
    To speak of horrors—he comes before me.
POLONIUS: Mad for thy love?
OPHELIA: My lord, I do not know,   85
    But truly I do fear it.
POLONIUS: What said he?
OPHELIA: He took me by the wrist, and held me hard,
    Then goes he to the length of all his arm,
    And with his other hand thus o'er his brow,
    He falls to such perusal of my face   90
    As 'a would draw it. Long stayed he so.
    At last, a little shaking of mine arm,
    And thrice his head thus waving up and down,
    He raised a sigh so piteous and profound
    As it did seem to shatter all his bulk,°   95
    And end his being. That done, he lets me go,
    And with his head over his shoulder turned
    He seemed to find his way without his eyes,
    For out adoors he went without their help,
    And to the last bended° their light on me.   100
POLONIUS: Come, go with me. I will go seek the king.
    This is the very ecstasy of love,
    Whose violent property° fordoes° itself,
    And leads the will to desperate undertakings
    As oft as any passion under heaven   105
    That does afflict our natures. I am sorry.
    What, have you given him any hard words of late?
OPHELIA: No, my good lord, but as you did command
    I did repel° his letters, and denied
    His access to me.
POLONIUS: That hath made him mad.   110
    I am sorry that with better heed and judgment
    I had not quoted° him. I feared he did but trifle,
    And meant to wrack° thee; but beshrew my jealousy.
    By heaven, it is as proper to our age
    To cast beyond ourselves in our opinions   115
    As it is common for the younger sort

---

77 chamber   78 jacket   78 unlaced   80 fallen down like fetters   95 body   100 directed
103 character   103 destroys   109 refuse   112 observed   113 harm

To lack discretion. Come, go we to the king.
This must be known, which being kept close, might move
More grief to hide than hate to utter love.
Come.   120

                                                        (Exeunt.)

SCENE 2   *A public room. Enter* KING, QUEEN, ROSENCRANTZ *and* GUIL-
DENSTERN.

KING: Welcome, dear Rosencrantz and Guildenstern.
        Moreover that° we much did long to see you,
        The need we have to use you did provoke
        Our hasty sending. Something have you heard
        Of Hamlet's transformation—so call it,   5
        Sith° nor th' exterior nor the inward man
        Resembles that it was. What it should be,
        More than his father's death, that thus hath put him
        So much from th' understanding of himself,
        I cannot deem of. I entreat you both   10
        That, being of so young days° brought up with him,
        And sith so neighbored° to his youth and havior,
        That you vouchsafe your rest here in our court
        Some little time, so by your companies
        To draw him on to pleasures, and to gather   15
        So much as from occasion you may glean,
        Whether aught to us unknown afflicts him thus,
        That opened lies within our remedy.
QUEEN: Good gentlemen, he hath much talked of you,
        And sure I am two men there are not living   20
        To whom he more adheres. If it will please you
        To show us so much gentry° and good will
        As to expend your time with us awhile
        For the supply and profit of our hope,
        Your visitation shall receive such thanks   25
        As fits a king's remembrance.
ROSENCRANTZ: Both your majesties
        Might, by the sovereign power you have of us,
        Put your dread pleasures more into command
        Than to entreaty.
GUILDENSTERN: But we both obey,
        And here give up ourselves in the full bent°   30
        To lay our service freely at your feet,
        To be commanded.

2 in addition to the fact that   6 since   11 from childhood   12 closely allied   22 courtesy
30 completely

KING: Thanks, Rosencrantz and gentle Guildenstern.
QUEEN: Thanks, Guildenstern and gentle Rosencrantz.
  And I beseech you instantly to visit   35
  My too much changed son. Go, some of you,
  And bring these gentlemen where Hamlet is.
GUILDENSTERN: Heavens make our presence and our practices
  Pleasant and helpful to him!
QUEEN: Ay, amen!

(Exeunt ROSENCRANTZ *and* GUILDENSTERN.*)*

                                        (Enter POLONIUS.*)*

POLONIUS: Th' ambassadors from Norway, my good lord,   40
  Are joyfully returned.
KING: Thou still° hast been the father of good news.
POLONIUS: Have I, my lord? I assure you, my good liege,
  I hold my duty as I hold my soul,
  Both to my God and to my gracious king;   45
  And I do think—or else this brain of mine
  Hunts not the trail of policy° so sure
  As it hath used to do—that I have found
  The very cause of Hamlet's lunacy.
KING: O, speak of that, that do I long to hear.   50
POLONIUS: Give first admittance to th' ambassadors.
  My news shall be the fruit° to that great feast.
KING: Thyself do grace to them, and bring them in.

                                        (Exit POLONIUS.*)*

  He tells me, my dear Gertrude, he hath found
  The head and source of all your son's distemper.   55
QUEEN: I doubt it is no other but the main,
  His father's death and our o'erhasty marriage.
KING: Well, we shall sift° him.

(Enter Ambassadors [VOLTEMAND *and* CORNELIUS] *with*
POLONIUS.*)*

                          Welcome, my good friends,
  Say, Voltemand, what from our brother Norway?
VOLTEMAND: Most fair return of greetings and desires.   60
  Upon our first,° he sent out to suppress
  His nephew's levies, which to him appeared
  To be a preparation 'gainst the Polack,
  But better looked into, he truly found
  It was against your highness, whereat grieved,   65

42 ever   47 statecraft   52 dessert   58 examine   61 i.e., first appearance

That so his sickness, age, and impotence
Was falsely borne in hand,° sends out arrests°
On Fortinbras, which he in brief obeys,
Receives rebuke from Norway, and in fine,
Makes vow before his uncle never more 70
To give th' assay° of arms against your majesty.
Whereon old Norway, overcome with joy,
Gives him threescore thousand crowns in annual fee,
And his commission to employ those soldiers,
So levied as before, against the Polack, 75
With an entreaty, herein further shown,

(Gives CLAUDIUS *a paper.)*

That it might please you to give quiet pass°
Through your dominions for this enterprise,
On such regards of safety and allowance
As therein are set down.
KING: It likes° us well, 80
And at our more considered time° we'll read,
Answer, and think upon this business.
Meantime we thank you for your well-took° labor.
Go to your rest; at night we'll feast together.
Most welcome home!

(Exeunt AMBASSADORS.*)*

POLONIUS: This business is well ended. 85
My liege and madam, to expostulate°
What majesty should be, what duty is,
Why day is day, night night, and time is time,
Were nothing but to waste night, day, and time.
Therefore, since brevity is the soul of wit, 90
And tediousness the limbs and outward flourishes,°
I will be brief. Your noble son is mad.
Mad call I it, for to define true madness,
What is't but to be nothing else but mad?
But let that go.
QUEEN: More matter with less art. 95
POLONIUS: Madam, I swear I use no art at all.
That he is mad, 'tis true: 'tis true 'tis pity,
And pity 'tis 'tis true. A foolish figure,
But farewell it, for I will use no art.
Mad let us grant him, then, and now remains 100
That we find out the cause of this effect,

67 deceived   67 orders to stop   71 trial   77 safe conduct   80 pleases   81 time for more consideration   83 successful   86 discuss   91 adornments

Or rather say the cause of this defect,
For this effect defective comes by cause.
Thus it remains, and the remainder thus.
Perpend.°   105
I have a daughter—have while she is mine—
Who in her duty and obedience, mark,
Hath given me this. Now gather, and surmise.
    "To the celestial, and my soul's idol, the most beautified
Ophelia."—That's an ill phrase, a vile phrase, "beautified" is a   110
vile phrase. But you shall hear. Thus:
    "In her excellent white bosom, these, etc."
QUEEN: Came this from Hamlet to her?
POLONIUS: Good madam, stay awhile. I will be faithful.

        "Doubt thou the stars are fire,   115
            Doubt that the sun doth move;
        Doubt truth to be a liar;
            But never doubt I love.

        O dear Ophelia, I am ill at these numbers.°
I have not art to reckon my groans, but that I love thee best, O most 120
best, believe it. Adieu.
                    Thine evermore, most dear lady, whilst this
                    machine° is to him, HAMLET."
This in obedience hath my daughter shown me,
And more above, hath his solicitings,   125
As they fell out by time, by means, and place,
All given to mine ear.
KING: But how hath she
Received his love?
POLONIUS: What do you think of me?
KING: As of a man faithful and honorable.
POLONIUS: I would fain prove so. But what might you think,   130
When I had seen this hot love on the wing,
(As I perceived it, I must tell you that,
Before my daughter told me), what might you,
Or my dear majesty your queen here, think,
If I had played the desk or table-book,   135
Or given my heart a winking, mute and dumb,
Or looked upon this love with idle sight,°
What might you think? No, I went round° to work,

105 consider   119 verses   123 body   137 Polonius means that he would have been at fault if,
having seen Hamlet's attention to Ophelia, he had winked at it or not paid attention, an "idle sight,"
and if he had remained silent and kept the information to himself, as if it were written in a "desk"
or "table-book."   138 directly

And my young mistress thus I did bespeak:
"Lord Hamlet is a prince out of thy star.°   140
This must not be." And then I prescripts° gave her,
That she should lock herself from his resort,
Admit no messengers, receive no tokens.
Which done, she took° the fruits of my advice;
And he repelled, a short tale to make,   145
Fell into a sadness, then into a fast,
Thence to a watch, thence into a weakness,
Thence to a lightness, and by this declension,
Into the madness wherein now he raves,
And all we mourn for.
KING: Do you think 'tis this?   150
QUEEN: It may be, very like.
POLONIUS: Hath there been such a time—I would fain know that—
That I have positively said "Tis so,"
When it proved otherwise?
KING: Not that I know.
POLONIUS *(pointing to his head and shoulder):* Take this from this, if this
      be otherwise.   155
If circumstances lead me, I will find
Where truth is hid, though it were hid indeed
Within the centre.°
KING: How may we try it further?
POLONIUS: You know sometimes he walks four hours together
Here in the lobby.
QUEEN: So he does, indeed.   160
POLONIUS: At such a time I'll loose° my daughter to him.
Be you and I behind an arras° then.
Mark the encounter. If he love her not,
And be not from his reason fall'n thereon,
Let me be no assistant for a state,   165
But keep a farm and carters.
KING: We will try it.

(Enter HAMLET *reading a book.)*

QUEEN: But look where sadly the poor wretch comes reading.
POLONIUS: Away, I do beseech you both away
I'll board° him presently.

(Exeunt KING *and* QUEEN.*)*

                    O, give me leave.
How does my good Lord Hamlet?   170

---

140 beyond your sphere   141 orders   144 followed   158 of the earth   161 let loose
162 tapestry   169 accost

HAMLET: Well, God-a-mercy.

POLONIUS: Do you know me, my lord?

HAMLET: Excellent well, you are a fishmonger.

POLONIUS: Not I, my lord.

HAMLET: Then I would you were so honest a man.   175

POLONIUS: Honest, my lord?

HAMLET: Ay, sir, to be honest as this world goes, is to be one man picked
out of ten thousand.

POLONIUS: That's very true, my lord.

HAMLET: For if the sun breed maggots in a dead dog, being a god   180
kissing carrion°—Have you a daughter?

POLONIUS: I have, my lord.

HAMLET: Let her not walk i' th' sun. Conception is a blessing, but as your
daughter may conceive—friend, look to't.

POLONIUS: How say you by that? *(Aside.)* Still harping on my daughter.   185
Yet he knew me not at first. 'A said I was a fishmonger. 'A is far
gone. And truly in my youth I suffered much extremity for love.
Very near this. I'll speak to him again.—What do you read, my lord?

HAMLET: Words, words, words.

POLONIUS: What is the matter, my lord?   190

HAMLET: Between who?

POLONIUS: I mean the matter that you read, my lord.

HAMLET: Slanders, sir; for the satirical rogue says here that old men
have grey beards, that their faces are wrinkled, their eyes purging
thick amber and plum-tree gum, and that they have a plentiful lack   195
of wit, together with most weak hams°—all which, sir, though I most
powerfully and potently believe, yet I hold it not honesty to have it
thus set down, for yourself, sir, shall grow old as I am, if like a crab
you could go backward.

POLONIUS *(aside):*   Though this be madness, yet there is method in't.—   200
Will you walk out of the air, my lord?

HAMLET: Into my grave?

POLONIUS *(aside):*   Indeed, that's out of the air. How pregnant sometime
his replies are! a happiness that often madness hits on, which reason
and sanity could not so prosperously be delivered of. I will leave   205
him, and suddenly contrive the means of meeting between him and
my daughter.—My lord. I will take my leave of you.

HAMLET: You cannot take from me anything that I will more willingly
part withal—except my life, except my life, except my life.

(Enter GUILDENSTERN *and* ROSENCRANTZ.*)*

POLONIUS: Fare you well, my lord.   210

HAMLET: These tedious old fools!

---

181 A reference to the belief of the period that maggots were produced spontaneously by the action
of sunshine on carrion.   196 limbs

POLONIUS: You go to seek the Lord Hamlet. There he is.
ROSENCRANTZ *(to* POLONIUS*)*: God save you, sir!

(Exit POLONIUS.*)*

GUILDENSTERN: My honored lord!
ROSENCRANTZ: My most dear lord! 215
HAMLET: My excellent good friends! How dost thou, Guildenstern?
    Ah, Rosencrantz! Good lads, how do you both?
ROSENCRANTZ: As the indifferent° children of the earth.
GUILDENSTERN: Happy in that we are not over-happy;
    On Fortune's cap we are not the very button.° 220
HAMLET: Nor the soles of her shoe?
ROSENCRANTZ: Neither, my lord.
HAMLET: Then you live about her waist, or in the middle of her favors.
GUILDENSTERN: Faith, her privates we.
HAMLET: In the secret parts of Fortune? O, most true, she is a strumpet.° 225
    What news?
ROSENCRANTZ: None, my lord, but that the world's grown honest.
HAMLET: Then is doomsday near. But your news is not true. Let me
    question more in particular. What have you, my good friends, de-
    served at the hands of Fortune, that she sends you to prison hither? 230
GUILDENSTERN: Prison, my lord?
HAMLET: Denmark's a prison.
ROSENCRANTZ: Then is the world one.
HAMLET: A goodly one, in which there are many confines, wards,° and
    dungeons, Denmark being one o' th' worst. 235
ROSENCRANTZ: We think not so, my lord.
HAMLET: Why then 'tis none to you; for there is nothing either good
    or bad, but thinking makes it so. To me it is a prison.
ROSENCRANTZ: Why then your ambition makes it one. 'Tis too narrow
    for your mind. 240
HAMLET: O God, I could be bounded in a nutshell and count myself a
    king of infinite space, were it not that I have bad dreams.
GUILDENSTERN: Which dreams indeed are ambition; for the very sub-
    stance of the ambitious is merely the shadow of a dream.
HAMLET: A dream itself is but a shadow. 245
ROSENCRANTZ: Truly, and I hold ambition of so airy and light a quality
    that it is but a shadow's shadow.
HAMLET: Then are our beggars bodies, and our monarchs and out-
    stretched heroes the beggars' shadows. Shall we to th' court? for, by
    my fay,° I cannot reason. 250
BOTH: We'll wait upon you.

218 ordinary   220 i.e., on top   225 Hamlet is indulging in characteristic ribaldry. Guildenstern
means that they are "privates" = ordinary citizens, but Hamlet takes him to mean "privates" =
sexual organs and "middle of her favors" = waist = sexual organs.   234 cells   250 faith

HAMLET: No such matter. I will not sort° you with the rest of my servants; for to speak to you like an honest man, I am most dreadfully
attended. But in the beaten way of friendship, what make you at
Elsinore?   255

ROSENCRANTZ: To visit you, my lord; no other occasion.

HAMLET: Beggar that I am, I am even poor in thanks, but I thank you;
and sure, dear friends, my thanks are too dear a halfpenny.° Were
you not sent for? Is it your own inclining? Is it a free visitation?
Come, come, deal justly with me. Come, come, nay speak.   260

GUILDENSTERN: What should we say, my lord?

HAMLET: Why anything but to th' purpose. You were sent for, and there
is a kind of confession in your looks, which your modesties have not
craft enough to color. I know the good king and queen have sent
for you.   265

ROSENCRANTZ: To what end, my lord?

HAMLET: That you must teach me. But let me conjure you by the rights
of our fellowship, by the consonancy of our youth, by the obligation
of our ever-preserved love, and by what more dear a better proposer
can charge you withal, be even and direct° with me whether you   270
were sent for or no.

ROSENCRANTZ *(aside to* GUILDENSTERN*):*   What say you?

HAMLET *(aside):*   Nay, then, I have an eye of you.—If you love me, hold
not off.

GUILDENSTERN: My lord, we were sent for.   275

HAMLET: I will tell you why; so shall my anticipation prevent your
discovery,° and your secrecy to the king and queen moult no feather.
I have of late—but wherefore I know not—lost all my mirth, forgone
all custom of exercises; and indeed it goes so heavily with my disposition, that this goodly frame the earth seems to me a sterile promon-   280
tory, this most excellent canopy the air, look you, this brave o'er-
hanging firmament, this majestical roof fretted° with golden fire,
why it appeareth nothing to me but a foul and pestilent congregation
of vapors. What a piece of work is a man, how noble in reason, how
infinite in faculties, in form and moving, how express° and admirable   285
in action, how like an angel in apprehension, how like a god: the
beauty of the world, the paragon of animals. And yet to me, what
is this quintessence of dust? Man delights not me, nor woman neither, though by your smiling you seem to say so.

ROSENCRANTZ: My lord, there was no such stuff in my thoughts.   290

HAMLET: Why did ye laugh, then, when I said "Man delights not me"?

ROSENCRANTZ: To think, my lord, if you delight not in man, what
lenten° entertainment the players shall receive from you. We coted°
them on the way, and hither are they coming to offer you service.

252 include   258 not worth a halfpenny   270 straightforward   277 disclosure   282 ornamented
with fretwork   285 well built   293 scanty   293 passed

HAMLET: He that plays the king shall be welcome—his majesty shall   295
  have tribute on me; the adventurous knight shall use his foil and
  target°; the lover shall not sigh gratis; the humorous° man shall end
  his part in peace; the clown shall make those laugh whose lungs are
  tickle o' th' sere°; and the lady shall say her mind freely, or the blank
  verse shall halt for't. What players are they?   300
ROSENCRANTZ: Even those you were wont to take such delight in, the
  tragedians of the city.
HAMLET: How chances it they travel? Their residence, both in reputation and profit, was better both ways.
ROSENCRANTZ: I think their inhibition comes by the means of the late   305
  innovation.
HAMLET: Do they hold the same estimation they did when I was in the
  city? Are they so followed?
ROSENCRANTZ: No, indeed, are they not.
HAMLET: How comes it? Do they grow rusty?   310
ROSENCRANTZ: Nay, their endeavor keeps in the wonted pace; but
  there is, sir, an eyrie of children, little eyases,° that cry out on the
  top of question,° and are most tyrannically clapped for't. These are
  now the fashion, and so berattle the common stages (so they call
  them) that many wearing rapiers are afraid of goose quills° and dare   315
  scarce come thither.°
HAMLET: What, are they children? Who maintains 'em? How are they
  escoted°? Will they pursue the quality no longer than they can sing?
  Will they not say afterwards, if they should grow themselves to
  common players (as it is most like, if their means are no better), their   320
  writers do them wrong to make them exclaim against their own
  succession°?
ROSENCRANTZ: Faith, there has been much to do on both sides; and the
  nation holds it no sin to tarre° them to controversy. There was for
  a while no money bid for argument,° unless the poet and the player   325
  went to cuffs° in the question.
HAMLET: Is't possible?
GUILDENSTERN: O, there has been much throwing about of brains.
HAMLET: Do the boys carry it away?
ROSENCRANTZ: Ay, that they do, my lord, Hercules and his load too.°   330
HAMLET: It is not very strange, for my uncle is King of Denmark, and

297 sword and shield   297 eccentric   299 easily set off   312 little hawks   313 with a loud, high
delivery   315 pens of satirical writers   316 The passage refers to the emergence at the time of
the play of theatrical companies made up of children from London choir schools. Their performances became fashionable and hurt the business of the established companies. Hamlet says that
if they continue to act, "pursue the quality," when they are grown, they will find that they have
been damaging their own future careers.   318 supported   322 future careers   324 urge
325 paid for a play plot   326 blows   330 During one of his labors Hercules assumed for a time
the burden of the Titan Atlas, who supported the heavens on his shoulder. Also a reference to the
effect on business at Shakespeare's theater, the Globe.

those that would make mouths° at him while my father lived give
twenty, forty, fifty, a hundred ducats apiece for his picture in little.°
'Sblood, there is something in this more than natural, if philosophy
could find it out.   335

(A flourish.)

GUILDENSTERN: There are the players.
HAMLET: Gentlemen, you are welcome to Elsinore. Your hands. Come
then. Th' appurtenance of welcome is fashion and ceremony. Let me
comply with° you in this garb, lest my extent° to the players, which
I tell you must show fairly outwards, should more appear like enter- 340
tainment° than yours. You are welcome. But my uncle-father and
aunt-mother are deceived.
GUILDENSTERN: In what, my dear lord?
HAMLET: I am but mad north-north-west; when the wind is southerly I
know a hawk from a handsaw.°   345

(Enter POLONIUS.*)*

POLONIUS: Well be with you, gentlemen.
HAMLET: Hark you, Guildenstern—and you too—at each ear a hearer.
That great baby you see there is not yet out of his swaddling clouts.°
ROSENCRANTZ: Happily he is the second time come to them, for they
say an old man is twice a child.   350
HAMLET: I will prophesy he comes to tell me of the players. Mark
it.—You say right, sir, a Monday morning, 'twas then indeed.
POLONIUS: My lord, I have news to tell you.
HAMLET: My lord, I have news to tell you.
When Roscius was an actor in Rome—°   355
POLONIUS: The actors are come hither, my lord.
HAMLET: Buzz, buzz.
POLONIUS: Upon my honor—
HAMLET: Then came each actor on his ass—
POLONIUS: The best actors in the world, either for tragedy, comedy, 360
history, pastoral, pastoral-comical, historical-pastoral, tragical-histor-
ical, tragical-comical-historical-pastoral, scene individable, or poem
unlimited. Seneca cannot be too heavy nor Plautus too light. For the
law of writ and the liberty, these are the only men.°
HAMLET: O Jephtha, judge of Israel, what a treasure hadst thou!°   365

332 sneer   333 miniature   339 welcome   339 fashion   341 cordiality   345 A "hawk" is a
plasterer's tool; Hamlet may also be using "handsaw" = hernshaw = heron.   348 wrappings for
an infant   355 Roscius was the most famous actor of classical Rome.   364 Seneca and Plautus were
Roman writers of tragedy and comedy, respectively. The "law of writ" refers to plays written
according to such rules as the three unities; the "liberty" to those written otherwise.   365 To insure
victory, Jephtha promised to sacrifice the first creature to meet him on his return. Unfortunately,
his only daughter outstripped his dog and was the victim of his vow. The Biblical story is told in
Judges 11.

POLONIUS: What a treasure had he, my lord?
HAMLET: Why—

> "One fair daughter, and no more,
> The which he loved passing well."

POLONIUS *(aside):*   Still on my daughter.   370
HAMLET: Am I not i' th' right, old Jephtha?
POLONIUS: If you call me Jephtha, my lord, I have a daughter that I love
passing well.
HAMLET: Nay, that follows not.
POLONIUS: What follows then, my lord?   375
HAMLET: Why—

> "As by lot, God wot"

and then, you know,

> "It came to pass, as most like it was."

The first row° of the pious chanson° will show you more, for look   380
where my abridgement° comes.

(Enter the PLAYERS.*)*

You are welcome, masters; welcome, all.—I am glad to see thee
well.—Welcome, good friends.—O, old friend! Why thy face is
valanced° since I saw thee last. Com'st thou to beard me in Denmark?—What, my young lady and mistress? By'r lady, your ladyship   385
is nearer to heaven than when I saw you last by the altitude of a
chopine.° Pray God your voice, like a piece of uncurrent gold, be
not cracked within the ring.—Masters, you are all welcome. We'll
e'en to't like French falconers, fly at anything we see. We'll have a
speech straight. Come give us a taste of your quality,° come a passion-   390
ate speech.
FIRST PLAYER: What speech, my good lord?
HAMLET: I heard thee speak me a speech once, but it was never acted,
or if it was, not above once, for the play, I remember, pleased not
the million; 'twas caviary° to the general.° But it was—as I received   395
it, and others whose judgments in such matters cried in the top of°
mine—an excellent play, well digested° in the scenes, set down with

---

380 stanza   380 song   381 that which cuts short by interrupting   384 fringed (with a beard)
387 A reference to the contemporary theatrical practice of using boys to play women's parts. The
company's "lady" has grown in height by the size of a woman's thick-soled shoe, "chopine," since
Hamlet saw him last. The next sentence refers to the possibility, suggested by his growth, that the
young actor's voice may soon begin to change.   390 trade   395 caviar   395 masses
396 were weightier than   397 arranged

as much modesty as cunning. I remember one said there were no
sallets° in the lines to make the matter savory, nor no matter in the
phrase that might indict the author of affectation, but called it an   400
honest method, as wholesome as sweet, and by very much more
handsome than fine. One speech in't I chiefly loved. 'Twas Aeneas'
tale to Dido, and thereabout of it especially where he speaks of
Priam's slaughter.° If it live in your memory, begin at this line—let
me see, let me see: 405

          "The rugged Pyrrhus, like th' Hyrcanian beast"°—

'tis not so; it begins with Pyrrhus—

          "The rugged Pyrrhus, he whose sable arms,
          Black as his purpose, did the night resemble
          When he lay couchéd in th' ominous horse,°   410
          Hath now this dread and black complexion smeared
          With heraldry more dismal; head to foot
          Now is he total gules,° horridly tricked°
          With blood of fathers, mothers, daughters, sons,
          Baked and impasted° with the parching° streets,   415
          That lend a tyrannous and a damnéd light
          To their lord's murder. Roasted in wrath and fire,
          And thus o'er-sizéd° with coagulate° gore,
          With eyes like carbuncles, the hellish Pyrrhus
          Old grandsire Priam seeks."   420

So proceed you.

POLONIUS: Fore God, my lord, well spoken, with good accent and good
          discretion.
FIRST PLAYER: "Anon he° finds him°
          Striking too short at Greeks. His antique° sword,   425
          Rebellious° to his arm, lies where it falls,
          Repugnant to command. Unequal matched,
          Pyrrhus at Priam drives, in rage strikes wide.
          But with the whiff and wind of his fell sword
          Th' unnervéd father falls. Then senseless° Ilium,   430
          Seeming to feel this blow, with flaming top
          Stoops° to his base, and with a hideous crash

399 spicy passages   404 Aeneas, fleeing with his band from fallen Troy (Ilium), arrives in Carthage, where he tells Dido, the Queen of Carthage, of the fall of Troy. Here he is describing the
death of Priam, the aged king of Troy, at the hands of Pyrrhus, the son of the slain Achilles.
406 tiger   410 i.e., the Trojan horse   413 completely red   413 adorned   415 crusted
415 burning   418 glued over   418 clotted,   424 Pyrrhus   424 Priam   425 which he used when
young   426 refractory   430 without feeling   432 falls

Takes prisoner Pyrrhus' ear. For, lo! his sword,
Which was declining° on the milky head
Of reverend Priam, seemed i' th' air to stick.   435
So as a painted tyrant Pyrrhus stood,
And like a neutral to his will and matter,°
Did nothing.
But as we often see, against some storm,
A silence in the heavens, the rack° stand still,   440
The bold winds speechless, and the orb below
As hush as death, anon the dreadful thunder
Doth rend the region; so, after Pyrrhus' pause,
A rouséd vengeance sets him new awork,°
And never did the Cyclops' hammers fall   445
On Mars's armor, forged for proof eterne,°
With less remorse than Pyrrhus' bleeding sword
Now falls on Priam.
Out, out, thou strumpet, Fortune! All you gods,
In general synod take away her power,   450
Break all the spokes and fellies° from her wheel,
And bowl° the round nave° down the hill of heaven
As low as to the fiends."
POLONIUS: This is too long.
HAMLET: It shall to the barber's with your beard.—Prithee say on. He's   455
     for a jig,° or a tale of bawdry, or he sleeps. Say on; come to Hecuba.°
FIRST PLAYER: "But who, ah woe! had seen the mobled° queen—"
HAMLET: "The mobled queen"?
POLONIUS: That's good. "Mobled queen" is good.
FIRST PLAYER: "Run barefoot up and down, threat'ning the flames   460
     With bisson rheum,° a clout° upon that head
     Where late the diadem stood, and for a robe,
     About her lank and all o'er-teeméd loins,
     A blanket, in the alarm of fear caught up—
     Who this had seen, with tongue in venom steeped,   465
     'Gainst Fortune's state° would treason have pronounced.
     But if the gods themselves did see her then,
     When she saw Pyrrhus make malicious sport
     In mincing° with his sword her husband's limbs,
     The instant burst of clamor that she made,   470
     Unless things mortal move them not at all,

434 about to fall   437 between his will and the fulfillment of it   440 clouds   444 to work
446 Mars, as befits a Roman war god, had armor made for him by the blacksmith god Vulcan and
his assistants, the Cyclops. It was suitably impenetrable, of "proof eterne."   451 parts of the rim
452 roll   452 hub   456 a comic act   456 Hecuba was the wife of Priam and Queen of Troy.
Her "loins" are described below as "o'erteeméd" because of her unusual fertility. The number of
her children varies in different accounts, but twenty is a safe minimum.   457 muffled (in a hood)
461 blinding tears   461 cloth   466 government   469 cutting up

> Would have made milch° the burning eyes of heaven,
> And passion in the gods.''

POLONIUS: Look whe'r° he has not turned his color, and has tears in's
   eyes. Prithee no more.   475

HAMLET: 'Tis well. I'll have thee speak out the rest of this soon.—Good
   my lord, will you see the players well bestowed?° Do you hear, let
   them be well used, for they are the abstract° and brief chronicles of
   the time; after your death you were better have a bad epitaph than
   their ill report while you live.   480

POLONIUS: My lord, I will use them according to their desert.

HAMLET: God's bodkin, man, much better. Use every man after his
   desert, and who shall 'scape whipping? Use them after your own
   honor and dignity. The less they deserve, the more merit is in your
   bounty. Take them in.   485

POLONIUS: Come, sirs.

HAMLET: Follow him, friends. We'll hear a play tomorrow. (Aside to
   FIRST PLAYER:) Dost thou hear me, old friend, can you play ''The
   Murder of Gonzago''?

FIRST PLAYER: Ay, my lord.   490

HAMLET: We'll ha't tomorrow night. You could for a need study a
   speech of some dozen or sixteen lines which I would set down and
   insert in't, could you not?

FIRST PLAYER: Ay, my lord.

HAMLET: Very well. Follow that lord, and look you mock him not.   495

(Exeunt POLONIUS and PLAYERS.)

My good friends, I'll leave you till night. You are welcome to
Elsinore.

ROSENCRANTZ: Good my lord.

(Exeunt ROSENCRANTZ and GUILDENSTERN.)

HAMLET: Ay, so God b'wi'ye. Now I am alone.
   O, what a rogue and peasant slave am I!   500
   Is it not monstrous that this player here,
   But in a fiction, in a dream of passion,
   Could force his soul so to his own conceit°
   That from her working all his visage wanned;°
   Tears in his eyes, distraction in his aspect,°   505
   A broken voice, and his whole function suiting
   With forms to his conceit? And all for nothing,
   For Hecuba!
   What's Hecuba to him or he to Hecuba,

472 tearful (lit. milk-giving)   474 whether   477 provided for   478 summary   503 imagination
504 grew pale   505 face

That he should weep for her? What would he do   510
Had he the motive and the cue for passion
That I have? He would drown the stage with tears,
And cleave the general ear with horrid speech,
Make mad the guilty, and appal the free,
Confound the ignorant, and amaze indeed   515
The very faculties of eyes and ears.
Yet I,
A dull and muddy-mettled° rascal, peak°
Like John-a-dreams,° unpregnant° of my cause,
And can say nothing; no, not for a king   520
Upon whose property and most dear life
A damned defeat was made. Am I a coward?
Who calls me villain, breaks my pate across,
Plucks off my beard and blows it in my face,
Tweaks me by the nose, gives me the lie i' th' throat   525
As deep as to the lungs? Who does me this?
Ha, 'swounds, I should take it; for it cannot be
But I am pigeon-livered and lack gall°
To make oppression bitter, or ere this
I should 'a fatted all the region kites°   530
With this slave's offal. Bloody, bawdy villain!
Remorseless, treacherous, lecherous, kindless° villain!
Why, what an ass am I! This is most brave,
That I, the son of a dear father murdered,
Prompted to my revenge by heaven and hell,   535
Must like a whore unpack° my heart with words,
And fall a-cursing like a very drab,
A scullion!° Fie upon't! foh!
About, my brains. Hum—I have heard
That guilty creatures sitting at a play,   540
Have by the very cunning of the scene
Been struck so to the soul that presently
They have proclaimed° their malefactions;
For murder, though it have no tongue, will speak
With most miraculous organ. I'll have these players   545
Play something like the murder of my father
Before mine uncle. I'll observe his looks.
I'll tent° him to the quick. If 'a do blench,°
I know my course. The spirit that I have seen

518 dull-spirited   518 mope   519 a man dreaming   519 not quickened by   528 bitterness
530 birds of prey of the area   532 unnatural   536 relieve   538 In some versions of the play,
the word "stallion," a slang term for a prostitute, appears in place of "scullion."   543 admitted
548 try   548 turn pale

May be a devil, and the devil hath power   550
T' assume a pleasing shape, yea, and perhaps
Out of my weakness and my melancholy,
As he is very potent with such spirits,
Abuses me to damn me. I'll have grounds
More relative° than this. The play's the thing   555
Wherein I'll catch the conscience of the king.

(Exit.)

ACT 3

SCENE 1   *A room in the castle. Enter* KING, QUEEN, POLONIUS, OPHELIA,
ROSENCRANTZ, *and* GUILDENSTERN.

KING: And can you by no drift of conference°
    Get from him why he puts on this confusion,
    Grating so harshly all his days of quiet
    With turbulent° and dangerous lunacy?
ROSENCRANTZ: He does confess he feels himself distracted,   5
    But from what cause 'a will by no means speak.
GUILDENSTERN: Nor do we find him forward° to be sounded,°
    But with a crafty madness keeps aloof
    When we would bring him on to some confession
    Of his true state.
QUEEN: Did he receive you well?   10
ROSENCRANTZ: Most like a gentleman.
GUILDENSTERN: But with much forcing of his disposition.°
ROSENCRANTZ: Niggard of question, but of our demands°
    Most free in his reply.
QUEEN: Did you assay° him
    To any pastime?   15
ROSENCRANTZ: Madam, it so fell out that certain players
    We o'er-raught° on the way. Of these we told him,
    And there did seem in him a kind of joy
    To hear of it. They are here about the court,
    And as I think, they have already order   20
    This night to play before him.
POLONIUS: 'Tis most true,
    And he beseeched me to entreat your majesties
    To hear and see the matter.°
KING: With all my heart, and it doth much content me
    To hear him so inclined.   25

555 conclusive   1 line of conversation   4 disturbing   7 eager   7 questioned   12 conversation
13 to our questions   14 tempt   17 passed   23 performance

> Good gentlemen, give him a further edge,
> And drive his purpose° into these delights.

ROSENCRANTZ: We shall, my lord.

(Exeunt ROSENCRANTZ *and* GUILDENSTERN.*)*

KING: Sweet Gertrude, leave us too,
    For we have closely sent for Hamlet hither,
    That he, as 'twere by accident, may here   30
    Affront° Ophelia.
    Her father and myself (lawful espials°)
    Will so bestow ourselves that, seeing unseen,
    We may of their encounter frankly judge,
    And gather by him, as he is behaved,   35
    If't be th' affliction of his love or no
    That thus he suffers for.

QUEEN: I shall obey you.—
    And for your part, Ophelia, I do wish
    That your good beauties be the happy cause
    Of Hamlet's wildness. So shall I hope your virtues   40
    Will bring him to his wonted° way again,
    To both your honors.

OPHELIA: Madam, I wish it may.

(Exit QUEEN.*)*

POLONIUS: Ophelia, walk you here.—Gracious,° so please you,
    We will bestow ourselves.—*(To* OPHELIA:*)* Read on this book,
    That show of such an exercise° may color°   45
    Your loneliness.—We are oft to blame in this,
    'Tis too much proved, that with devotion's visage
    And pious action we do sugar o'er
    The devil himself.

KING *(aside):*   O, 'tis too true.
    How smart a lash that speech doth give my conscience!   50
    The harlot's cheek, beautied with plast'ring° art,
    Is not more ugly to the thing that helps it
    Than is my deed to my most painted word.
    O heavy burden!

POLONIUS: I hear him coming. Let's withdraw, my lord.   55

(Exeunt KING *and* POLONIUS.*)*

(Enter HAMLET.*)*

HAMLET: To be, or not to be, that is the question:
    Whether 'tis nobler in the mind to suffer

27 sharpen his intention   31 confront   32 justified spies   41 usual   43 Majesty   45 act of devotion   45 explain   51 thickly painted

The slings and arrows of outrageous fortune,
Or to take arms against a sea of troubles,
And by opposing end them. To die, to sleep—   60
No more; and by a sleep to say we end
The heartache, and the thousand natural shocks
That flesh is heir to. 'Tis a consummation
Devoutly to be wished—to die, to sleep—
To sleep, perchance to dream, ay there's the rub;   65
For in that sleep of death what dreams may come
When we have shuffled off this mortal coil°
Must give us pause—there's the respect°
That makes calamity of so long life.
For who would bear the whips and scorns of time,   70
Th' oppressor's wrong, the proud man's contumely,°
The pangs of despised love, the law's delay,
The insolence of office, and the spurns°
That patient merit of th' unworthy takes,
When he himself might his quietus° make   75
With a bare bodkin?° Who would fardels° bear,
To grunt and sweat under a weary life,
But that the dread of something after death,
The undiscovered country, from whose bourn°
No traveller returns, puzzles the will,   80
And makes us rather bear those ills we have
Than fly to others that we know not of?
Thus conscience does make cowards of us all;
And thus the native° hue of resolution
Is sicklied o'er with the pale cast of thought,   85
And enterprises of great pitch° and moment°
With this regard their currents turn awry
And lose the name of action.—Soft you now,
The fair Ophelia.—Nymph, in thy orisons°
Be all my sins remembered.
OPHELIA: Good my lord,   90
    How does your honor for this many a day?
HAMLET: I humbly thank you, well, well, well.
OPHELIA: My lord, I have remembrances of yours
    That I have longed long to re-deliver.
    I pray you now receive them.
HAMLET: No, not I,   95
    I never gave you aught.
OPHELIA: My honored lord, you know right well you did,

---

67 turmoil   68 consideration   71 insulting behavior   73 rejections   75 settlement   76 dagger
76 burdens   79 boundary   84 natural   86 height   86 importance   89 prayers

And with them words of so sweet breath composed
As made the things more rich. Their perfume lost,
Take these again, for to the noble mind   100
Rich gifts wax° poor when givers prove unkind.
There, my lord.

HAMLET: Ha, ha! are you honest?°

OPHELIA: My lord?

HAMLET: Are you fair?   105

OPHELIA: What means your lordship?

HAMLET: That if you be honest and fair, your honesty should admit no
discourse to your beauty.

OPHELIA: Could beauty, my lord, have better commerce° than with
honesty?   110

HAMLET: Ay, truly, for the power of beauty will sooner transform
honesty from what it is to a bawd than the force of honesty can
translate beauty into his likeness. This was sometime a paradox, but
now the time gives it proof. I did love you once.

OPHELIA: Indeed, my lord, you made me believe so.   115

HAMLET: You should not have believed me, for virtue cannot so inocu-
late° our old stock but we shall relish of it. I loved you not.

OPHELIA: I was the more deceived.

HAMLET: Get thee to a nunnery.° Why wouldst thou be a breeder of
sinners? I am myself indifferent° honest, but yet I could accuse me   120
of such things that it were better my mother had not borne me: I am
very proud, revengeful, ambitious, with more offences at my beck°
than I have thoughts to put them in, imagination to give them shape,
or time to act them in. What should such fellows as I do crawling
between earth and heaven? We are arrant° knaves all; believe none   125
of us. Go thy ways to a nunnery. Where's your father?

OPHELIA: At home, my lord.

HAMLET: Let the doors be shut upon him, that he may play the fool
nowhere but in's own house. Farewell.

OPHELIA: O, help him, you sweet heavens!   130

HAMLET: If thou dost marry, I'll give thee this plague for thy dowry: be
thou as chaste as ice, as pure as snow, thou shalt not escape calumny.
Get thee to a nunnery, farewell. Or if thou wilt needs marry, marry
a fool, for wise men know well enough what monsters° you make of
them. To a nunnery, go, and quickly too. Farewell.   135

OPHELIA: Heavenly powers, restore him!

HAMLET: I have heard of your paintings well enough. God hath given
you one face, and you make yourselves another. You jig, you amble,

101 become   103 chaste   109 intercourse   117 change by grafting   119 With typical ribaldry
Hamlet uses "nunnery" in two senses, the second as a slang term for brothel.   120 moderately
122 command   125 thorough   134 horned because cuckolded

and you lisp;° you nickname God's creatures, and make your wanton-
ness your ignorance.° Go to, I'll no more on't, it hath made me mad.   140
I say we will have no more marriages. Those that are married already, all but one, shall live. The rest shall keep as they are. To a
nunnery, go.

                                                                        (Exit.)

OPHELIA: O, what a noble mind is here o'erthrown!
          The courtier's, soldier's, scholar's, eye, tongue, sword,   145
          Th' expectancy° and rose° of the fair state,
          The glass° of fashion and the mould° of form,
          Th' observed of all observers, quite quite down!
          And I of ladies most deject and wretched,
          That sucked the honey of his music° vows,   150
          Now see that noble and most sovereign reason
          Like sweet bells jangled, out of time and harsh;
          That unmatched form and feature of blown° youth
          Blasted with ecstasy. O, woe is me
          T' have seen what I have seen, see what I see!   155

(Enter KING *and* POLONIUS.*)*

KING: Love! His affections do not that way tend,
          Nor what he spake, though it lacked form a little,
          Was not like madness. There's something in his soul
          O'er which his melancholy sits on brood,°
          And I do doubt° the hatch and the disclose°   160
          Will be some danger; which to prevent,
          I have in quick determination
          Thus set it down: he shall with speed to England
          For the demand of our neglected tribute.
          Haply the seas and countries different,   165
          With variable objects, shall expel
          This something-settled matter in his heart
          Whereon his brains still beating puts him thus
          From fashion of himself. What think you on't?
POLONIUS: It shall do well. But yet do I believe   170
          The origin and commencement of his grief
          Sprung from neglected love.—How now, Ophelia?
          You need not tell us what Lord Hamlet said,
          We heard it all.—My lord, do as you please,
          But if you hold it fit, after the play   175
          Let his queen-mother all alone entreat him

---

139 walk and talk affectedly   140 Hamlet means that women call things by pet names and then
blame the affectation on ignorance.   146 hope   146 ornament   147 mirror   147 model
150 musical   153 full-blown   159 i.e., like a hen   160 fear   160 result

To show his grief. Let her be round° with him,
And I'll be placed, so please you, in the ear°
Of all their conference. If she find him not,°
To England send him; or confine him where   180
Your wisdom best shall think.
KING: It shall be so.
Madness in great ones must not unwatched go.

(Exeunt.)

SCENE 2 *A public room in the castle. Enter* HAMLET *and three of the* PLAYERS.

HAMLET: Speak the speech, I pray you, as I pronounced it to you, trippingly on the tongue; but if you mouth it as many of our players do, I had as lief the town-crier spoke my lines. Nor do not saw the air too much with your hand thus, but use all gently, for in the very torrent, tempest, and as I may say, whirlwind of your passion, you   5
must acquire and beget a temperance that may give it smoothness. O, it offends me to the soul to hear a robustious° periwig-pated° fellow tear a passion to tatters, to very rags, to split the ears of the groundlings,° who for the most part are capable of° nothing but inexplicable dumb shows and noise. I would have such a fellow   10
whipped for o'erdoing Termagant. It out-herods Herod.° Pray you avoid it.
FIRST PLAYER: I warrant your honor.
HAMLET: Be not too tame neither, but let your own discretion be your tutor. Suit the action to the word, the word to the action, with this   15
special observance, that you o'erstep not the modesty of nature; for anything so o'erdone is from° the purpose of playing, whose end both at the first, and now, was and is, to hold as 'twere the mirror up to nature, to show virtue her own feature, scorn her own image, and the very age and body of the time his form and pressure.° Now   20
this overdone, or come tardy off, though it makes the unskilful° laugh, cannot but make the judicious grieve, the censure° of the which one must in your allowance o'erweigh a whole theatre of others. O, there be players that I have seen play—and heard others praise, and that highly—not to speak it profanely, that neither having   25
th' accent of Christians, nor the gait of Christian, pagan, nor man, have so strutted and bellowed that I have thought some of nature's journeymen° had made men, and not made them well, they imitated humanity so abominably.

FIRST PLAYER: I hope we have reformed that indifferently° with us.   30
HAMLET: O, reform it altogether. And let those that play your clowns
speak no more than is set down for them, for there be of them that
will themselves laugh, to set on some quantity of barren° spectators
to laugh too, though in the meantime some necessary question of the
play be then to be considered. That's villainous, and shows a most   35
pitiful ambition in the fool that uses it. Go, make you ready.

(Exeunt PLAYERS.*)*

(Enter POLONIUS, GUILDENSTERN, *and* ROSENCRANTZ.*)*

How now, my lord? Will the king hear this piece of work?
POLONIUS: And the queen too, and that presently.
HAMLET: Bid the players make haste.

(Exit POLONIUS.*)*

Will you two help to hasten them?   40
ROSENCRANTZ: Ay, my lord.

(Exeunt they two.)

HAMLET: What, ho, Horatio!

(Enter HORATIO.*)*

HORATIO: Here, sweet lord, at your service.
HAMLET: Horatio, thou art e'en as just a man
As e'er my conversation coped° withal.   45
HORATIO: O my dear lord!
HAMLET: Nay, do not think I flatter,
For what advancement may I hope from thee,
That no revenue hast but thy good spirits
To feed and clothe thee? Why should the poor be flattered?
No, let the candied tongue lick absurd pomp,   50
And crook the pregnant° hinges of the knee
Where thrift° may follow fawning. Dost thou hear?
Since my dear soul was mistress of her choice
And could of men distinguish her election,
S'hath sealed thee for herself, for thou hast been   55
As one in suff'ring all that suffers nothing,
A man that Fortune's buffets and rewards
Hast ta'en with equal thanks; and blest are those
Whose blood and judgment are so well commingled
That they are not a pipe° for Fortune's finger   60
To sound° what stop° she please. Give me that man
That is not passion's slave, and I will wear him

30 somewhat   33 dull-witted   45 encountered   51 quick to bend   52 profit   60 musical
instrument   61 play   61 note

In my heart's core, ay, in my heart of heart,
As I do thee. Something too much of this.
There is a play tonight before the king. 65
One scene of it comes near the circumstance
Which I have told thee of my father's death.
I prithee, when thou seest that act afoot,
Even with the very comment° of thy soul
Observe my uncle. If his occulted° guilt 70
Do not itself unkennel° in one speech,
It is a damnéd ghost that we have seen,
And my imaginations are as foul
As Vulcan's stithy.° Give him heedful note,°
For I mine eyes will rivet to his face, 75
And after we will both our judgments join
In censure of his seeming.°
HORATIO: Well, my lord.
If 'a steal aught the whilst this play is playing,
And 'scape detecting, I will pay° the theft.

(Enter Trumpets and Kettledrums, KING, QUEEN, POLONIUS, OPH-
ELIA, ROSENCRANTZ, GUILDENSTERN, *and other* LORDS *attendant.)*

HAMLET: They are coming to the play. I must be idle. 80
   Get you a place.
KING: How fares our cousin Hamlet?
HAMLET: Excellent, i' faith, of the chameleon's dish.° I eat the air, prom-
   ise-crammed. You cannot feed capons so.
KING: I have nothing with this answer, Hamlet. These words are not 85
   mine.
HAMLET: No, nor mine now. *(To* POLONIUS.*)* My lord, you played
   once i' th' university, you say?
POLONIUS: That did I, my lord, and was accounted a good actor.
HAMLET: What did you enact? 90
POLONIUS: I did enact Julius Cæsar. I was killed i' th' Capitol; Brutus
   killed me.°
HAMLET: It was a brute part of him to kill so capital a calf there. Be the
   players ready?
ROSENCRANTZ: Ay, my lord, they stay° upon your patience.° 95
QUEEN: Come hither, my dear Hamlet, sit by me.
HAMLET: No, good mother, here's metal more attractive.
POLONIUS *(to the* KING*):*   O, ho! do you mark that?
HAMLET: Lady, shall I lie in your lap?

69 keenest observation   70 hidden   71 break loose   74 smithy   74 careful attention
77 manner   79 repay   83 A reference to a popular belief that the chameleon subsisted on a diet
of air. Hamlet has deliberately misunderstood the King's question.   92 The assassination of Julius
Caesar by Brutus and others is the subject of another play by Shakespeare.   95 wait   95 leisure

(Lying down at OPHELIA*'s feet.)*

OPHELIA: No, my lord.   100
HAMLET: I mean, my head upon your lap?
OPHELIA: Ay, my lord.
HAMLET: Do you think I meant country matters?°
OPHELIA: I think nothing, my lord.
HAMLET: That's a fair thought to lie between maids' legs.   105
OPHELIA: What is, my lord?
HAMLET: Nothing.
OPHELIA: You are merry, my lord.
HAMLET: Who, I?
OPHELIA: Ay, my lord.   110
HAMLET: O God, your only jig-maker!° What should a man do but be
  merry? For look you how cheerfully my mother looks, and my father
  died within's two hours.
OPHELIA: Nay, 'tis twice two months, my lord.
HAMLET: So long? Nay then, let the devil wear black, for I'll have a suit   115
  of sables. O heavens! die two months ago, and not forgotten yet?
  Then there's hope a great man's memory may outlive his life half a
  year, but by'r lady 'a must build churches then, or else shall 'a suffer
  not thinking on, with the hobby-horse, whose epitaph is "For O, for
  O, the hobby-horse is forgot!"°   120

(The trumpets sound. Dumb Show follows. Enter a KING *and a* QUEEN
very lovingly; the QUEEN *embracing him and he her. She kneels, and makes
show of protestation unto him. He takes her up, and declines his head upon
her neck. He lies him down upon a bank of flowers; she, seeing him asleep,
leaves him. Anon come in another man, takes off his crown, kisses it, pours
poison in the sleeper's ears, and leaves him. The* QUEEN *returns, finds the*
KING *dead, makes passionate action. The* POISONER *with some three or
four come in again, seem to condole with her. The dead body is carried away.
The* POISONER *woos the* QUEEN *with gifts; she seems harsh awhile, but
in the end accepts love. Exeunt.)*

OPHELIA: What means this, my lord?
HAMLET: Marry, this is miching mallecho;° it means mischief.
OPHELIA: Belike this show imports° the argument° of the play.

                                                    (Enter PROLOGUE.*)*

HAMLET: We shall know by this fellow. The players cannot keep counsel; they'll tell all.   125

103 Presumably, rustic misbehavior, but here and elsewhere in this exchange Hamlet treats Ophelia
to some ribald double meanings.   111 writer of comic scenes   120 In traditional games and dances
one of the characters was a man represented as riding a horse. The horse was made of something
like cardboard and was worn about the "rider's" waist.   122 sneaking crime   123 explains
123 plot

OPHELIA: Will 'a tell us what this show meant?

HAMLET: Ay, or any show that you will show him. Be not you ashamed
   to show, he'll not shame to tell you what it means.

OPHELIA: You are naught,° you are naught. I'll mark° the play.

PROLOGUE: *For us, and for our tragedy,*   130
   Here stooping to your clemency,
   We beg your hearing patiently.

(Exit.)

HAMLET: Is this a prologue, or the posy° of a ring?

OPHELIA: 'Tis brief, my lord.

HAMLET: As woman's love.   135

   (Enter the PLAYER KING *and* QUEEN.*)*

PLAYER KING: *Full thirty times hath Phœbus' cart gone round*
   Neptune's salt wash and Tellus' orbèd ground,
   And thirty dozen moons with borrowed sheen°
   About the world have times twelve thirties been,
   Since love our hearts and Hymen did our hands   140
   Unite comutual° in most sacred bands.°

PLAYER QUEEN: *So many journeys may the sun and moon*
   Make us again count o'er ere love be done!
   But woe is me, you are so sick of late,
   So far from cheer and from your former state,   145
   That I distrust° you. Yet though I distrust,
   Discomfort you, my lord, it nothing must.
   For women's fear and love hold quantity,°
   In neither aught, or in extremity.°
   Now what my love is proof hath made you know,   150
   And as my love is sized,° my fear is so.
   Where love is great, the littlest doubts are fear;
   Where little fears grow great, great love grows there.

PLAYER KING: *Faith, I must leave thee, love, and shortly too;*
   My operant powers° their functions leave° to do.   155
   And thou shalt live in this fair world behind,
   Honored, beloved, and haply one as kind
   For husband shalt thou—

PLAYER QUEEN: *O, confound the rest!*
   Such love must needs be treason in my breast.

129 obscene   129 attend to   133 motto engraved inside   138 light   141 mutually
141 The speech contains several mythological references. "Phoebus" was a sun god, and his chariot
or "cart" the sun. The "salt wash" of Neptune is the ocean; "Tellus" was an earth goddess, and
her "orbed ground" is the earth, or globe. Hymen was the god of marriage.   146 fear for
148 agree in weight   149 The lady means without regard to too much or too little.   151 in size
155 active forces   155 cease

In second husband let me be accurst!   160
None wed the second but who killed the first.°
HAMLET: That's wormwood.
PLAYER QUEEN: *The instances° that second marriage move*
Are base respects° of thrift, but none of love.
A second time I kill my husband dead,   165
When second husband kisses me in bed.
PLAYER KING: *I do believe you think what now you speak,*
But what we do determine oft we break.
Purpose is but the slave to memory,
Of violent birth, but poor validity;   170
Which now, like fruit unripe, sticks on the tree,
But fall unshaken when they mellow be.
Most necessary 'tis that we forget
To pay ourselves what to ourselves is debt.
What to ourselves in passion we propose,   175
The passion ending, doth the purpose lose.
The violence of either grief or joy
Their own enactures° with themselves destroy.
Where joy most revels, grief doth most lament;
Grief joys, joy grieves, on slender accident.   180
This world is not for aye,° nor 'tis not strange
That even our loves should with our fortunes change;
For 'tis a question left us yet to prove,
Whether love lead fortune, or else fortune love.
The great man down, you mark his favorite flies;   185
The poor advanced makes friends of enemies;
And hitherto doth love on fortune tend,
For who not needs shall never lack a friend,
And who in want a hollow° friend doth try,
Directly seasons him° his enemy.   190
But orderly to end where I begun,
Our wills and fates do so contrary run
That our devices° still are overthrown;
Our thoughts are ours, their ends none of our own.
So think thou wilt no second husband wed,   195
But die thy thoughts when thy first lord is dead.
PLAYER QUEEN: *Nor earth to me give food, nor heaven light,*
Sport and repose lock from me day and night,
To desperation turn my trust and hope,
An anchor's cheer° in prison be my scope,   200

---

161 Though there is some ambiguity, she seems to mean that the only kind of woman who would
remarry is one who has killed or would kill her first husband.   163 causes   164 concerns
178 actions   181 eternal   189 false   190 ripens him into   193 plans   200 anchorite's food

Each opposite that blanks° the face of joy
Meet what I would have well, and it destroy,
Both here and hence° pursue me lasting strife,
If once a widow, ever I be wife!

HAMLET: If she should break it now!   205

PLAYER KING: *'Tis deeply sworn. Sweet, leave me here awhile.*
My spirits grow dull, and fain I would beguile
The tedious day with sleep.

(Sleeps.)

PLAYER QUEEN: *Sleep rock thy brain,*
And never come mischance between us twain!

(Exit.)

HAMLET: Madam, how like you this play?   210
QUEEN: The lady doth protest too much, methinks.
HAMLET: O, but she'll keep her word.
KING: Have you heard the argument? Is there no offence in't?
HAMLET: No, no, they do but jest, poison in jest; no offence i' th' world.
KING: What do you call the play?   215
HAMLET: "The Mouse-trap." Marry, how? Tropically.° This play is the
image of a murder done in Vienna. Gonzago is the duke's name; his
wife, Baptista. You shall see anon. 'Tis a knavish piece of work, but
what of that? Your majesty, and we that have free souls, it touches
us not. Let the galled jade wince, our withers are unwrung.°   220

(Enter LUCIANUS.*)*

This is one Lucianus, nephew to the king.
OPHELIA: You are as good as a chorus, my lord.
HAMLET: I could interpret between you and your love, if I could see the
puppets dallying.
OPHELIA: You are keen, my lord, you are keen.   225
HAMLET: It would cost you a groaning to take off mine edge.
OPHELIA: Still better, and worse.
HAMLET: So you mis-take your husbands.—Begin, murderer. Leave thy
damnable faces and begin. Come, the croaking raven doth bellow
for revenge.   230
LUCIANUS: *Thoughts black, hands apt, drugs fit, and time agreeing,*
Confederate season,° else no creature seeing,
Thou mixture rank, of midnight weeds collected,
With Hecate's ban thrice blasted, thrice infected,°

---

201 blanches   203 in the next world   216 figuratively   220 A "galled jade" is a horse, particularly one of poor quality, with a sore back. The "withers" are the ridge between a horse's shoulders;
"unwrung withers" are not chafed by the harness.   232 a helpful time for the crime   234 Hecate
was a classical goddess of witchcraft.

Thy natural magic° and dire property   235
On wholesome life usurps immediately.

(Pours the poison in his ears.)

HAMLET: 'A poisons him i' th' garden for his estate. His name's Gon-
zago. The story is extant, and written in very choice Italian. You
shall see anon how the murderer gets the love of Gonzago's wife.
OPHELIA: The king rises.   240
HAMLET: What, frighted with false fire?
QUEEN: How fares my lord?
POLONIUS: Give o'er the play.
KING: Give me some light. Away!
POLONIUS: Lights, lights, lights!   245

(Exeunt all but HAMLET *and* HORATIO.*)*

HAMLET: Why, let the strucken deer go weep,
                 The hart ungalléd° play.
             For some must watch while some must sleep;
                 Thus runs the world away.

Would not this, sir, and a forest of feathers°—if the rest of my 250
fortunes turn Turk with me—with two Provincial roses on my razed
shoes, get me a fellowship in a cry° of players?°
HORATIO: Half a share.
HAMLET: A whole one, I.

                 For thou dost know, O Damon dear,°   255
                     This realm dismantled was
                 Of Jove himself, and now reigns here
                     A very, very—peacock.

HORATIO: You might have rhymed.
HAMLET: O good Horatio, I'll take the ghost's word for a thousand 260
pound. Didst perceive?
HORATIO: Very well, my lord.
HAMLET: Upon the talk of the poisoning.
HORATIO: I did very well note° him.
HAMLET: Ah, ha! Come, some music. Come, the recorders.°   265
    For if the king like not the comedy,

235 native power   247 uninjured   250 plumes   252 company   252 Hamlet asks Horatio if
"this" recitation, accompanied with a player's costume, including plumes and rosettes on shoes
which have been slashed for decorative effect, might not entitle him to become a shareholder in
a theatrical company in the event that Fortune goes against him, "turn Turk."   255 Damon was
a common name for a young man or a shepherd in lyric, especially pastoral poetry. Jove was the
chief god of the Romans. The Reader may supply for himself the rhyme referred to by Horatio.
264 observe   265 wooden end-blown flutes

Why then, belike he likes it not, perdy.°
Come, some music.

(Enter ROSENCRANTZ *and* GUILDENSTERN.)

GUILDENSTERN: Good my lord, vouchsafe me a word with you.
HAMLET: Sir, a whole history.   270
GUILDENSTERN: The king, sir—
HAMLET: Ay, sir, what of him?
GUILDENSTERN: Is in his retirement° marvellous distempered.°
HAMLET: With drink, sir?
GUILDENSTERN: No, my lord, with choler.°   275
HAMLET: Your wisdom should show itself more richer to signify this to
    the doctor, for for me to put him to his purgation° would perhaps
    plunge him into more choler.
GUILDENSTERN: Good my lord, put your discourse° into some frame,°
    and start not so wildly from my affair.   280
HAMLET: I am tame, sir. Pronounce.
GUILDENSTERN: The queen your mother, in most great affliction of
    spirit, hath sent me to you.
HAMLET: You are welcome.
GUILDENSTERN: Nay, good my lord, this courtesy is not of the right   285
    breed. If it shall please you to make me a wholesome° answer, I will
    do your mother's commandment. If not, your pardon and my return°
    shall be the end of my business.
HAMLET: Sir, I cannot.
ROSENCRANTZ: What, my lord?   290
HAMLET: Make you a wholesome answer; my wit's diseased. But, sir,
    such answer as I can make, you shall command, or rather, as you say,
    my mother. Therefore no more, but to the matter. My mother, you
    say—
ROSENCRANTZ: Then thus she says: your behavior hath struck her into   295
    amazement and admiration.°
HAMLET: O wonderful son, that can so stonish a mother! But is there
    no sequel at the heels of this mother's admiration? Impart.°
ROSENCRANTZ: She desires to speak with you in her closet° ere you go
    to bed.   300
HAMLET: We shall obey, were she ten times our mother. Have you any
    further trade° with us?
ROSENCRANTZ: My lord, you once did love me.
HAMLET: And do still, by these pickers and stealers.°
ROSENCRANTZ: Good my lord, what is your cause of distemper? You   305

267 *par Dieu* (by God)   273 place to which he has retired   273 vexed   275 bile   277 treatment
with a laxative   279 speech   279 order   286 reasonable   287 i.e., to the Queen   296 wonder
298 tell me   299 bedroom   302 business   304 hands

do surely bar the door upon your own liberty, if you deny your griefs
to your friend.

HAMLET: Sir, I lack advancement.

ROSENCRANTZ: How can that be, when you have the voice of the king
himself for your succession in Denmark?   310

HAMLET: Ay, sir, but "while the grass grows"—the proverb° is something musty.

(Enter the PLAYERS *with recorders.)*

O, the recorders! Let me see one. To withdraw with you°—why do
you go about to recover the wind of me, as if you would drive me
into a toil?°   315

GUILDENSTERN: O my lord, if my duty be too bold, my love is too
unmannerly.

HAMLET: I do not well understand that. Will you play upon this pipe?°

GUILDENSTERN: My lord, I cannot.

HAMLET: I pray you.   320

GUILDENSTERN: Believe me, I cannot.

HAMLET: I do beseech you.

GUILDENSTERN: I know no touch of it,° my lord.

HAMLET: It is as easy as lying. Govern° these ventages° with your fingers
and thumb, give it breath with your mouth, and it will discourse   325
most eloquent music. Look you, these are the stops.°

GUILDENSTERN: But these cannot I command to any utt'rance of harmony. I have not the skill.

HAMLET: Why, look you now, how unworthy a thing you make of me!
You would play upon me, you would seem to know my stops, you   330
would pluck out the heart of my mystery, you would sound° me from
my lowest note to the top of my compass°; and there is much music,
excellent voice, in this little organ, yet cannot you make it speak.
'Sblood, do you think I am easier to be played on than a pipe? Call
me what instrument you will, though you can fret° me, you cannot   335
play upon me.

(Enter POLONIUS.*)*

God bless you, sir!

POLONIUS: My lord, the queen would speak with you, and presently.°

HAMLET: Do you see yonder cloud that's almost in shape of a camel?

POLONIUS: By th' mass, and 'tis like a camel indeed.   340

HAMLET: Methinks it is like a weasel.

POLONIUS: It is backed like a weasel.

---

311 The proverb ends "the horse starves."   313 let me step aside   315 The figure is from hunting.
"You will approach me with the wind blowing from me toward you in order to drive me into the
net."   318 recorder   323 have no ability   324 cover and uncover   324 holes   326 wind-holes
331 play   332 range   335 "Fret" is used in a double sense, to annoy and to play a guitar or similar
instrument using the "frets" or small bars on the neck.   338 at once

HAMLET: Or like a whale.
POLONIUS: Very like a whale.
HAMLET: Then I will come to my mother by and by. *(Aside.)* They fool   345
   me to the top of my bent.°—I will come by and by.
POLONIUS: I will say so.

(Exit POLONIUS.*)*

HAMLET: "By and by" is easily said. Leave me, friends.

(Exeunt all but HAMLET.*)*

'Tis now the very witching time of night,
When churchyards yawn, and hell itself breathes out   350
Contagion to this world. Now could I drink hot blood,
And do such bitter business as the day
Would quake to look on. Soft, now to my mother.
O heart, lose not thy nature; let not ever
The soul of Nero° enter this firm bosom.   355
Let me be cruel, not unnatural;
I will speak daggers to her, but use none.
My tongue and soul in this be hypocrites—
How in my words somever she be shent,°
To give them seals° never, my soul, consent!   360

(Exit.)

SCENE 3   *A room in the castle. Enter* KING, ROSENCRANTZ, *and* GUIL-
DENSTERN.

KING: I like him not,° nor stands it safe with us
   To let his madness range.° Therefore prepare you.
   I your commission will forthwith dispatch,
   And he to England shall along with you.
   The terms of our estate° may not endure   5
   Hazard so near's as doth hourly grow
   Out of his brows.
GUILDENSTERN: We will ourselves provide.°
   Most holy and religious fear it is
   To keep those many many bodies safe
   That live and feed upon your majesty.   10
ROSENCRANTZ: The single and peculiar° life is bound
   With all the strength and armor of the mind
   To keep itself from noyance,° but much more

---

346 treat me as an utter fool   355 The Emperor Nero, known for his excesses, was believed to
have been responsible for the death of his mother.   359 shamed   360 fulfillment in action
1 distrust him   2 roam freely   5 condition of the state   7 equip (for the journey)   11 individual
13 harm

That spirit upon whose weal° depends and rests
The lives of many. The cess° of majesty   15
Dies not alone, but like a gulf° doth draw
What's near it with it. It is a massy° wheel
Fixed on the summit of the highest mount,
To whose huge spokes ten thousand lesser things
Are mortised and adjoined,° which when it falls,   20
Each small annexment, petty consequence,
Attends° the boist'rous ruin. Never alone
Did the king sigh, but with a general groan.
KING: Arm you, I pray you, to this speedy voyage,
For we will fetters put about this fear,   25
Which now goes too free-footed.
ROSENCRANTZ: We will haste us.

    (Exeunt ROSENCRANTZ *and* GUILDENSTERN.*)*

                         (Enter POLONIUS.*)*

POLONIUS: My lord, he's going to his mother's closet.
Behind the arras I'll convey° myself
To hear the process.° I'll warrant she'll tax him home,°
And as you said, and wisely was it said,   30
'Tis meet that some more audience than a mother,
Since nature makes them partial, should o'erhear
The speech, of vantage.° Fare you well, my liege.
I'll call upon you ere you go to bed,
And tell you what I know.
KING: Thanks, dear my lord.   35

                         (Exit POLONIUS.*)*

O, my offence is rank, it smells to heaven;
It hath the primal eldest curse° upon't,
A brother's murder. Pray can I not,
Though inclination be as sharp as will.
My stronger guilt defeats my strong intent,   40
And like a man to double business° bound,
I stand in pause where I shall first begin,
And both neglect. What if this curséd hand
Were thicker than itself with brothers' blood,
Is there not rain enough in the sweet heavens   45
To wash it white as snow? Whereto serves mercy
But to confront the visage of offence?
And what's in prayer but this twofold force,

14 welfare 15 cessation 16 whirlpool 17 massive 20 attached 22 joins in 28 station
29 proceedings 29 sharply 33 from a position of vantage 37 i.e., of Cain 41 two mutually
opposed interests

To be forestalléd° ere we come to fall,
Or pardoned being down°? Then I'll look up.   50
My fault is past. But, O, what form of prayer
Can serve my turn? "Forgive me my foul murder"?
That cannot be, since I am still possessed
Of those effects° for which I did the murder—
My crown, mine own ambition, and my queen.   55
May one be pardoned and retain th' offence°?
In the corrupted currents of this world
Offence's gilded° hand may shove by justice,
And oft 'tis seen the wicked prize itself
Buys out the law. But 'tis not so above.   60
There is no shuffling; there the action° lies
In his true nature, and we ourselves compelled,
Even to the teeth and forehead of° our faults,
To give in evidence. What then? What rests°?
Try what repentance can. What can it not?   65
Yet what can it when one can not repent?
O wretched state! O bosom black as death!
O liméd° soul, that struggling to be free
Art more engaged! Help, angels! Make assay.
Bow, stubborn knees, and heart with strings of steel,   70
Be soft as sinews of the new-born babe.
All may be well.

(He kneels.)

(Enter HAMLET.*)*

HAMLET: Now might I do it pat,° now 'a is a-praying,
And now I'll do't—and so 'a goes to heaven,
And so am I revenged. That would be scanned.°   75
A villain kills my father, and for that,
I, his sole son, do this same villain send
To heaven.
Why, this is hire and salary, not revenge.
'A took my father grossly, full of bread,°   80
With all his crimes broad blown,° as flush° as May;
And how his audit stands who knows save heaven?
But in our circumstance and course of thought
'Tis heavy with him; and am I then revenged
To take him in the purging of his soul,   85
When he is fit and seasoned° for his passage?

---

49 prevented (from sin)   50 having sinned   54 gains   56 i.e., benefits of the offence
58 bearing gold as a bribe   61 case at law   63 face-to-face with   64 remains   68 caught as with
bird-lime   73 easily   75 deserves consideration   80 in a state of sin and without fasting
81 full-blown   81 vigorous   86 ready

No.
Up, sword, and know thou a more horrid hent.°
When he is drunk, asleep, or in his rage,
Or in th' incestuous pleasure of his bed,   90
At game a-swearing, or about some act
That has no relish° of salvation in't—
Then trip him, that his heels may kick at heaven,
And that his soul may be as damned and black
As hell, whereto it goes. My mother stays.   95
This physic° but prolongs thy sickly days.

                                                                      (Exit.)

KING *(rising):*   My words fly up, my thoughts remain below.
        Words without thoughts never to heaven go.

                                                                      (Exit.)

SCENE 4   *The Queen's chamber. Enter* QUEEN *and* POLONIUS.

POLONIUS: 'A will come straight. Look you lay home to° him.
        Tell him his pranks have been too broad° to bear with,
        And that your grace hath screen'd° and stood between
        Much heat and him. I'll silence me even here.
        Pray you be round.
QUEEN: I'll warrant you. Fear° me not.   5
        Withdraw, I hear him coming.

        *(*POLONIUS *goes behind the arras.)*

                                                              (Enter HAMLET.*)*

HAMLET: Now, mother, what's the matter?
QUEEN: Hamlet, thou hast thy father much offended.
HAMLET: Mother, you have my father much offended.
QUEEN: Come, come, you answer with an idle tongue.   10
HAMLET: Go, go, you question with a wicked tongue.
QUEEN: Why, how now, Hamlet?
HAMLET: What's the matter now?
QUEEN: Have you forgot me?
HAMLET: No, by the rood,° not so.
        You are the queen, your husband's brother's wife,
        And would it were not so, you are my mother.   15
QUEEN: Nay, then I'll set those to you that can speak.
HAMLET: Come, come, and sit you down. You shall not budge.
        You go not till I set you up a glass°

88 opportunity   92 flavor   96 medicine   1 be sharp with   2 outrageous   3 acted as a fire screen
5 doubt   13 cross   18 mirror

Where you may see the inmost part of you.
QUEEN: What wilt thou do? Thou wilt not murder me?   20
    Help, ho!
POLONIUS *(behind):*   What, ho! help!
HAMLET *(draws):*   How now, a rat?
    Dead for a ducat, dead!

(Kills POLONIUS *with a pass through the arras.)*

POLONIUS *(behind):*   O, I am slain!   25
QUEEN: O me, what hast thou done?
HAMLET: Nay, I know not.
    Is it the king?
QUEEN: O, what a rash and bloody deed is this!
HAMLET: A bloody deed!—almost as bad, good mother,
    As kill a king and marry with his brother.   30
QUEEN: As kill a king?
HAMLET: Ay, lady, it was my word.

                                           (Parting the arras.)

    Thou wretched, rash, intruding fool, farewell!
    I took thee for thy better. Take thy fortune.
    Thou find'st to be too busy° is some danger.—
    Leave wringing of your hands. Peace, sit you down   35
    And let me wring your heart, for so I shall
    If it be made of penetrable stuff,
    If damnéd custom have not brazed it° so
    That it be proof° and bulwark against sense.°
QUEEN: What have I done that thou dar'st wag thy tongue   40
    In noise so rude against me?
HAMLET: Such an act
    That blurs the grace and blush of modesty,
    Calls virtue hypocrite, takes off the rose
    From the fair forehead of an innocent love,
    And sets a blister° there, makes marriage-vows   45
    As false as dicers' oaths. O, such a deed
    As from the body of contraction° plucks
    The very soul, and sweet religion makes
    A rhapsody of words. Heaven's face does glow
    And this solidity and compound mass°   50
    With heated visage, as against the doom°—
    Is thought-sick at the act.
QUEEN: Ay me, what act.
    That roars so loud and thunders in the index°?

34 officious   38 plated it with brass   39 armor   39 feeling   45 brand   47 the marriage contract
50 meaningless mass (Earth)   51 Judgment Day   53 table of contents

HAMLET: Look here upon this picture° and on this,
    The counterfeit presentment of two brothers.   55
    See what a grace was seated on this brow:
    Hyperion's curls, the front° of Jove himself,
    An eye like Mars, to threaten and command,
    A station° like the herald Mercury°
    New lighted° on a heaven-kissing hill—   60
    A combination and a form indeed
    Where every god did seem to set his seal,°
    To give the world assurance of a man.
    This was your husband. Look you now what follows.
    Here is your husband, like a mildewed ear   65
    Blasting his wholesome brother. Have you eyes?
    Could you on this fair mountain leave to feed,
    And batten° on this moor? Ha! have you eyes?
    You cannot call it love, for at your age
    The heyday in the blood is tame, it's humble,   70
    And waits upon the judgment, and what judgment
    Would step from this to this? Sense sure you have,
    Else could you not have motion, but sure that sense
    Is apoplexed° for madness would not err,
    Nor sense to ecstasy was ne'er so thralled   75
    But it reserved some quantity° of choice
    To serve in such a difference. What devil was't
    That thus hath cozened° you at hoodman-blind°?
    Eyes without feeling, feeling without sight,
    Ears without hands or eyes, smelling sans° all,   80
    Or but a sickly part of one true sense
    Could not so mope.° O shame! where is thy blush?
    Rebellious hell,
    If thou canst mutine° in a matron's bones,
    To flaming youth let virtue be as wax   85
    And melt in her own fire. Proclaim no shame
    When the compulsive ardor gives the charge,°
    Since frost itself as actively doth burn,
    And reason panders° will.
QUEEN: O Hamlet, speak no more!
    Thou turn'st my eyes into my very soul;   90
    And there I see such black and grainéd° spots
    As will not leave their tinct.°
HAMLET: Nay, but to live

---

54 portrait   57 forehead   59 bearing   59 Mercury was a Roman god who served as the messenger of the gods.   60 newly alighted   62 mark of approval   68 feed greedily   74 paralyzed
76 power   78 cheated   78 blindman's buff   80 without   82 be stupid   84 commit mutiny
87 attacks   89 pimps for   91 ingrained   92 lose their color

In the rank sweat of an enseaméd° bed,
Stewed in corruption, honeying and making love
Over the nasty sty—
QUEEN: O, speak to me no more!   95
These words like daggers enter in my ears;
No more, sweet Hamlet.
HAMLET: A murderer and a villain,
A slave that is not twentieth part the tithe°
Of your precedent lord,° a vice of kings,°
A cutpurse° of the empire and the rule,   100
That from a shelf the precious diadem stole
And put it in his pocket—
QUEEN: No more.

                                        (Enter GHOST.)

HAMLET: A king of shreds and patches—
Save me and hover o'er me with your wings,   105
You heavenly guards! What would your gracious figure?
QUEEN: Alas, he's mad.
HAMLET: Do you not come your tardy° son to chide,
That lapsed in time and passion lets go by
Th' important acting of your dread command?   110
O, say!
GHOST: Do not forget. This visitation
Is but to whet thy almost blunted purpose.
But look, amazement on thy mother sits.
O, step between her and her fighting soul!   115
Conceit° in weakest bodies strongest works.
Speak to her, Hamlet.
HAMLET: How is it with you, lady?
QUEEN: Alas, how is't with you,
That you do bend° your eye on vacancy,
And with th' incorporal air do hold discourse?   120
Forth at your eyes your spirits wildly peep,
And as the sleeping soldiers in th' alarm,
Your bedded hairs like life in excrements°
Start up and stand an end. O gentle son,
Upon the heat and flame of thy distemper   125
Sprinkle cool patience. Whereon do you look?
HAMLET: On him, on him! Look you how pale he glares.
His form and cause conjoined,° preaching to stones,
Would make them capable.°—Do not look upon me,

93 greasy   98 one-tenth   99 first husband   99 The "Vice," a common figure in the popular
drama, was a clown or buffoon.   100 pickpocket   108 slow to act   116 imagination
119 turn   123 nails and hair   128 working together   129 of responding

Lest with piteous action you convert   130
My stern effects.° Then what I have to do
Will want true color—tears perchance for blood.
QUEEN: To whom do you speak this?
HAMLET: Do you see nothing there?
QUEEN: Nothing at all, yet all that is I see.   135
HAMLET: Nor did you nothing hear?
QUEEN: No, nothing but ourselves.
HAMLET: Why, look you there. Look how it steals away.
My father, in his habit° as he lived!
Look where he goes even now out at the portal.   140

(Exit GHOST.*)*

QUEEN: This is the very coinage° of your brain.
This bodiless creation ecstasy°
Is very cunning° in.
HAMLET: My pulse as yours doth temperately keep time,
And makes as healthful music. It is not madness   145
That I have uttered. Bring me to the test,
And I the matter will re-word, which madness
Would gambo° from. Mother, for love of grace,
Lay not that flattering unction° to your soul,
That not your trespass but my madness speaks.   150
It will but skin and film the ulcerous place
Whiles rank corruption, mining° all within,
Infects unseen. Confess yourself to heaven,
Repent what's past, avoid what is to come,
And do not spread the compost on the weeds,   155
To make them ranker. Forgive me this my virtue,
For in the fatness of these pursy° times
Virtue itself of vice must pardon beg,
Yea, curb° and woo for leave to do him good.
QUEEN: O Hamlet, thou hast cleft my heart in twain.   160
HAMLET: O, throw away the worser part of it,
And live the purer with the other half.
Good night—but go not to my uncle's bed.
Assume a virtue, if you have it not.
That monster custom° who all sense doth eat   165
Of habits evil, is angel yet in this,
That to the use of actions fair and good
He likewise gives a frock or livery
That aptly° is put on. Refrain tonight,
And that shall lend a kind of easiness   170

131 deeds   139 costume   141 invention   142 madness   143 skilled   148 shy away
149 ointment   152 undermining   157 bloated   159 bow   165 habit   169 easily

To the next abstinence; the next more easy;
For use almost can change the stamp of nature,
And either curb the devil, or throw him out
With wondrous potency. Once more, good night,
And when you are desirous to be blest,   175
I'll blessing beg of you. For this same lord
I do repent; but heaven hath pleased it so,
To punish me with this, and this with me,
That I must be their scourge and minister.
I will bestow° him and will answer well   180
The death I gave him. So, again, good night.
I must be cruel only to be kind.
Thus bad begins and worse remains behind.
One word more, good lady.
QUEEN: What shall I do?
HAMLET: Not this, by no means, that I bid you do: 185
Let the bloat° king tempt you again to bed,
Pinch wanton° on your cheek, call you his mouse,
And let him, for a pair of reechy° kisses,
Or paddling in your neck with his damned fingers,
Make you to ravel° all this matter out,   190
That I essentially am not in madness,
But mad in craft. 'Twere good you let him know,
For who that's but a queen, fair, sober, wise,
Would from a paddock,° from a bat, a gib,°
Such dear concernings hide? Who would so do?   195
No, in despite of sense and secrecy,
Unpeg the basket on the house's top,
Let the birds fly, and like the famous ape,
To try conclusions, in the basket creep
And break your own neck down.°   200
QUEEN: Be thou assured, if words be made of breath
And breath of life, I have no life to breathe
What thou hast said to me.
HAMLET: I must to England; you know that?
QUEEN: Alack,
I had forgot. 'Tis so concluded on.   205
HAMLET: There's letters sealed, and my two school-fellows,
Whom I will trust as I will adders fanged,
They bear the mandate°; they must sweep° my way
And marshal me to knavery. Let it work,

---

180 dispose of   186 bloated   187 lewdly   188 foul   190 reveal   194 toad   194 tomcat
200 Apparently a reference to a now lost fable in which an ape, finding a basket containing a cage
of birds on a housetop, opens the cage. The birds fly away. The ape, thinking that if he were in
the basket he too could fly, enters, jumps out, and breaks his neck.   208 command   208 prepare

For 'tis the sport to have the enginer°   210
Hoist with his own petar; and't shall go hard
But I will delve° one yard below their mines
And blow them at the moon. O, 'tis most sweet
When in one line two crafts directly meet.
This man shall set me packing.   215
I'll lug the guts into the neighbor room.
Mother, good night. Indeed, this counsellor
Is now most still, most secret, and most grave,
Who was in life a foolish prating knave.
Come sir, to draw toward an end with you.   220
Good night, mother.

(Exit the QUEEN. *Then exit* HAMLET *tugging* POLONIUS.*)*

ACT 4

SCENE 1   *A room in the castle. Enter* KING, QUEEN, ROSENCRANTZ *and*
GUILDENSTERN.

KING: There's matter in these sighs, these profound heaves,
You must translate°; 'tis fit we understand them.
Where is your son?
QUEEN: Bestow this place on us a little while.

(Exeunt ROSENCRANTZ *and* GUILDENSTERN.*)*

Ah, mine own lord, what have I seen tonight!   5
KING: What, Gertrude? How does Hamlet?
QUEEN: Mad as the sea and wind when both contend
Which is the mightier. In his lawless fit,
Behind the arras hearing something stir,
Whips out his rapier, cries "A rat, a rat!"   10
And in this brainish apprehension° kills
The unseen good old man.
KING: O heavy deed!
It had been so with us had we been there.
His liberty is full of threats to all—
To you yourself, to us, to every one.   15
Alas, how shall this bloody deed be answered?
It will be laid to us, whose providence°
Should have kept short, restrained, and out of haunt,°

210 The "enginer," or engineer, is a military man who is here described as being blown up by a
bomb of his own construction, "hoist with his own petar." The military figure continues in the
succeeding lines where Hamlet describes himself as digging a countermine or tunnel beneath the
one Claudius is digging to defeat Hamlet. In line 214 the two tunnels unexpectedly meet.
212 dig   2 explain   11 insane notion   17 prudence   18 away from court

This mad young man. But so much was our love,
We would not understand what was most fit;   20
But, like the owner of a foul disease,
To keep it from divulging, let it feed
Even on the pith of life. Where is he gone?
QUEEN: To draw apart the body he hath killed,
O'er whom his very madness, like some ore   25
Among a mineral of metals base,
Shows itself pure: 'a weeps for what is done.
KING: O Gertrude, come away!
The sun no sooner shall the mountains touch
But we will ship him hence, and this vile deed   30
We must with all our majesty and skill
Both countenance and excuse. Ho, Guildenstern!

(Enter ROSENCRANTZ *and* GUILDENSTERN.*)*

Friends both, go join you with some further aid.
Hamlet in madness hath Polonius slain,
And from his mother's closet hath he dragged him.   35
Go seek him out; speak fair, and bring the body
Into the chapel. I pray you haste in this.

(Exeunt ROSENCRANTZ *and* GUILDENSTERN.*)*

Come, Gertrude, we'll call up our wisest friends
And let them know both what we mean to do
And what's untimely done;   40
Whose whisper o'er the world's diameter,
As level° as the cannon to his blank,°
Transports his poisoned shot—may miss our name,
And hit the woundless air. O, come away!
My soul is full of discord and dismay.   45

(Exeunt.)

SCENE 2   *A passageway. Enter* HAMLET.

HAMLET: Safely stowed.—But soft, what noise? Who calls on Hamlet?
O, here they come.

(Enter ROSENCRANTZ, GUILDENSTERN, *and* OTHERS.*)*

ROSENCRANTZ: What have you done, my lord, with the dead body?
HAMLET: Compounded it with dust, whereto 'tis kin.
ROSENCRANTZ: Tell us where 'tis, that we may take it thence   5
And bear it to the chapel.

42 direct   42 mark

HAMLET: Do not believe it.

ROSENCRANTZ: Believe what?

HAMLET: That I can keep your counsel and not mine own. Besides, to
be demanded of° a sponge—what replication° should be made by the   10
son of a king?

ROSENCRANTZ: Take you me for a sponge, my lord?

HAMLET: Ay, sir, that soaks up the king's countenance,° his rewards, his
authorities. But such officers do the king best service in the end. He
keeps them like an apple in the corner of his jaw, first mouthed to   15
be last swallowed. When he needs what you have gleaned, it is but
squeezing you and, sponge, you shall be dry again.

ROSENCRANTZ: I understand you not, my lord.

HAMLET: I am glad of it. A knavish speech sleeps in a foolish ear.

ROSENCRANTZ: My lord, you must tell us where the body is, and go   20
with us to the king.

HAMLET: The body is with the king, but the king is not with the body.
The king is a thing—

GUILDENSTERN: A thing, my lord!

HAMLET: Of nothing. Bring me to him. Hide fox, and all after.°   25

                                                              (Exeunt.)

SCENE 3   *A room in the castle. Enter* KING.

KING: I have sent to seek him, and to find the body.
How dangerous is it that this man goes loose!
Yet must not we put the strong law on him.
He's loved of the distracted° multitude,
Who like not in their judgment but their eyes,   5
And where 'tis so, th' offender's scourge° is weighed,
But never the offence. To bear all smooth and even,
This sudden sending him away must seem
Deliberate pause.° Diseases desperate grown
By desperate appliance are relieved,   10
Or not at all.

(Enter ROSENCRANTZ, GUILDENSTERN, *and all the rest.)*

                      How now! what hath befall'n?

ROSENCRANTZ: Where the dead body is bestowed, my lord,
We cannot get from him.

KING: But where is he?

ROSENCRANTZ: Without,° my lord; guarded, to know° your pleasure.

KING: Bring him before us.

ROSENCRANTZ: Ho! bring in the lord.   15

---

10 questioned by   10 answer   13 favor   25 Apparently a reference to a children's game like
hide-and-seek.   4 confused   6 punishment   9 i.e., not an impulse   14 outside   14 await

(They enter with HAMLET.*)*

KING: Now, Hamlet, where's Polonius?

HAMLET: At supper.

KING: At supper? Where?

HAMLET: Not where he eats, but where 'a is eaten. A certain convoca-
  tion° of politic° worms are e'en at him. Your worm is your only   20
  emperor for diet. We fat all creatures else to fat us, and we fat
  ourselves for maggots. Your fat king and your lean beggar is but
  variable service—two dishes, but to one table. That's the end.

KING: Alas, alas!

HAMLET: A man may fish with the worm that hath eat of a king, and eat   25
  of the fish that hath fed of that worm.

KING: What dost thou mean by this?

HAMLET: Nothing but to show you how a king may go a progress
  through the guts of a beggar.

KING: Where is Polonius?   30

HAMLET: In heaven. Send thither to see. If your messenger find him not
  there, seek him i' th' other place yourself. But if, indeed, you find
  him not within this month, you shall nose° him as you go up the stairs
  into the lobby.

KING *(to* ATTENDANTS*):*   Go seek him there.   35

HAMLET: 'A will stay till you come.

(Exeunt ATTENDANTS.*)*

KING: Hamlet, this deed, for thine especial safety—
  Which we do tender,° as we dearly° grieve
  For that which thou hast done—must send thee hence
  With fiery quickness. Therefore prepare thyself.   40
  The bark is ready, and the wind at help,
  Th' associates tend, and everything is bent
  For England.

HAMLET: For England?

KING: Ay, Hamlet.

HAMLET: Good.

KING: So it is, if thou knew'st our purposes.

HAMLET: I see a cherub that sees them. But come, for England!   45
  Farewell, dear mother.

KING: Thy loving father, Hamlet.

HAMLET: My mother. Father and mother is man and wife, man and wife
  is one flesh. So, my mother. Come, for England.

(Exit.)

KING: Follow him at foot°; tempt him with speed aboard.   50
  Delay it not; I'll have him hence tonight.

20 gathering   20 statesmanlike   33 smell   38 consider   38 deeply   50 closely

Away! for everything is sealed and done
That else leans on th' affair. Pray you make haste.

(Exeunt all but the KING.*)*

And, England, if my love thou hold'st at aught—
As my great power thereof may give thee sense,°   55
Since yet thy cicatrice° looks raw and red
After the Danish sword, and thy free awe
Pays homage to us—thou mayst not coldly set°
Our sovereign process,° which imports at full
By letters congruing° to that effect   60
The present death of Hamlet. Do it, England,
For like the hectic° in my blood he rages,
And thou must cure me. Till I know 'tis done,
Howe'er my haps, my joys were ne'er begun.

(Exit.)

SCENE 4   *Near Elsinore. Enter* FORTINBRAS *with his army.*

FORTINBRAS: Go, captain, from me greet the Danish king.
Tell him that by his license Fortinbras
Craves the conveyance° of a promised march
Over his kingdom. You know the rendezvous.
If that his majesty would aught with us,   5
We shall express our duty in his eye,°
And let him know so.
CAPTAIN: I will do't, my lord.
FORTINBRAS: Go softly on.

(Exeunt all but the CAPTAIN.*)*

(Enter HAMLET, ROSENCRANTZ, GUILDENSTERN, *and* OTHERS.*)*

HAMLET: Good sir, whose powers are these?
CAPTAIN: They are of Norway, sir.   10
HAMLET: How purposed, sir, I pray you?
CAPTAIN: Against some part of Poland.
HAMLET: Who commands them, sir?
CAPTAIN: The nephew to old Norway, Fortinbras.
HAMLET: Goes it against the main° of Poland, sir,   15
Or for some frontier?
CAPTAIN: Truly to speak, and with no addition,°
We go to gain a little patch of ground

---

55 of its value   56 wound scar   58 set aside   59 mandate   60 agreeing   62 chronic fever
3 escort   6 presence   15 central part   17 exaggeration

That hath in it no profit but the name.
To pay five ducats,° five, I would not farm it;   20
Nor will it yield to Norway or the Pole
A ranker° rate should it be sold in fee.°
HAMLET: Why, then the Polack never will defend it.
CAPTAIN: Yes, it is already garrisoned.
HAMLET: Two thousand souls and twenty thousand ducats   25
Will not debate the question of this straw.
This is th' imposthume° of much wealth and peace,
That inward breaks, and shows no cause without
Why the man dies. I humbly thank you, sir.
CAPTAIN: God b'wi'ye, sir.

(Exit.)

ROSENCRANTZ: Will't please you go, my lord?   30
HAMLET: I'll be with you straight. Go a little before.

(Exeunt all but HAMLET.*)*

How all occasions do inform against me,
And spur my dull revenge! What is a man,
If his chief good and market° of his time
Be but to sleep and feed? A beast, no more.   35
Sure he that made us with such large discourse,°
Looking before and after, gave us not
That capability and godlike reason
To fust° in us unused. Now, whether it be
Bestial oblivion, or some craven scruple   40
Of thinking too precisely on th' event°—
A thought which, quartered, hath but one part wisdom
And ever three parts coward—I do not know
Why yet I live to say "This thing's to do,"
Sith° I have cause, and will, and strength, and means,   45
To do't. Examples gross as earth exhort me.
Witness this army of such mass and charge,°
Led by a delicate and tender prince,
Whose spirit, with divine ambition puffed,
Makes mouths at° the invisible event,   50
Exposing what is mortal and unsure
To all that fortune, death, and danger dare,
Even for an eggshell. Rightly to be great
Is not to stir without great argument,
But greatly to find quarrel in a straw   55

20 i.e., in rent   22 higher   22 outright   27 abscess   34 occupation   36 ample reasoning power
39 grow musty   41 outcome   45 since   47 expense   50 scorns

When honor's at the stake. How stand I then,
That have a father killed, a mother stained,
Excitements of my reason and my blood,
And let all sleep, while to my shame I see
The imminent death of twenty thousand men   60
That for a fantasy and trick of fame
Go to their graves like beds, fight for a plot
Whereon the numbers cannot try the cause,
Which is not tomb enough and continent
To hide the slain?° O, from this time forth,   65
My thoughts be bloody, or be nothing worth!

                                                   Exit.

SCENE 5   *A room in the castle. Enter* QUEEN, HORATIO *and a* GENTLE-
MAN.

QUEEN: I will not speak with her.
GENTLEMAN: She is importunate, indeed distract.
   Her mood will needs be pitied.
QUEEN: What would she have?
GENTLEMAN: She speaks much of her father, says she hears
   There's tricks i' th' world, and hems, and beats her heart,   5
   Spurns enviously at straws,° speaks things in doubt
   That carry but half sense. Her speech is nothing,
   Yet the unshaped use of it doth move
   The hearers to collection°; they yawn at it,
   And botch the words up fit to their own thoughts,   10
   Which, as her winks and nods and gestures yield them,
   Indeed would make one think there might be thought,
   Though nothing sure, yet much unhappily.
HORATIO: 'Twere good she were spoken with, for she may strew
   Dangerous conjectures in ill-breeding minds.   15
QUEEN: Let her come in.

                                      (Exit GENTLEMAN.*)*

(Aside.) To my sick soul, as sin's true nature is,
Each toy° seems prologue to some great amiss.°
So full of artless jealousy is guilt,
It spills itself in fearing to be spilt.   20

                                      (Enter OPHELIA *distracted.)*

65 The plot of ground involved is so small that it cannot contain the number of men involved in
fighting nor furnish burial space for the number of those who will die.   6 takes offense at trifles
9 an attempt to order   18 trifle   18 catastrophe

OPHELIA: Where is the beauteous majesty of Denmark?
QUEEN: How now, Ophelia!
OPHELIA: How should I your true love know

(She sings.)

From another one?
By his cockle hat and staff,°   25
And his sandal shoon.°
QUEEN: Alas, sweet lady, what imports this song?
OPHELIA: Say you? Nay, pray you mark.

He is dead and gone, lady,
He is dead and gone;   30
At his head a grass-green turf,
At his heels a stone.

O, ho!
QUEEN: Nay, but, Ophelia—
OPHELIA: Pray you mark.
White his shroud as the mountain snow—   35

(Enter KING.)

QUEEN: Alas, look here, my lord.
OPHELIA: Larded all with sweet flowers;
Which bewept to the grave did not go
With true-love showers.
KING: How do you, pretty lady?   40
OPHELIA: Well, God dild° you! They say the owl was a baker's daughter.
Lord, we know what we are, but know not what we may be. God
be at your table!
KING: Conceit° upon her father.
OPHELIA: Pray let's have no words of this, but when they ask you what 45
it means, say you this:

Tomorrow is Saint Valentine's day,
All in the morning betime,
And I a maid at your window,
To be your Valentine.   50
Then up he rose, and donn'd his clo'es,
And dupped° the chamber-door,
Let in the maid, that out a maid
Never departed more.

---

25 A "cockle hat," one decorated with a shell, indicated that the wearer had made a pilgrimage
to the shrine of St. James at Compostela in Spain. The staff also marked the carrier as a pilgrim.
26 shoes   41 yield   44 thought   52 opened

KING: Pretty Ophelia!   55
OPHELIA: Indeed, without an oath, I'll make an end on't.

> By Gis° and by Saint Charity,
> Alack, and fie for shame!
> Young men will do't, if they come to't;
> By Cock,° they are to blame.   60
> Quoth she "Before you tumbled me,
> You promised me to wed."

He answers:

> "So would I'a done, by yonder sun,
> An thou hadst not come to my bed."   65

KING: How long hath she been thus?
OPHELIA: I hope all will be well. We must be patient, but I cannot
choose but weep to think they would lay him i' th' cold ground. My
brother shall know of it, and so I thank you for your good counsel.
Come, my coach! Good night, ladies, good night. Sweet ladies, good   70
night, good night.

(Exit.)

KING: Follow her close; give her good watch, I pray you.

(Exeunt HORATIO *and* GENTLEMAN.*)*

O, this is the poison of deep grief; it springs
All from her father's death, and now behold!
O Gertrude, Gertrude!   75
When sorrows come, they come not single spies,
But in battalions: first, her father slain;
Next, your son gone, and he most violent author
Of his own just remove; the people muddied,°
Thick and unwholesome in their thoughts and whispers   80
For good Polonius' death; and we have done but greenly°
In hugger-mugger° to inter him; poor Ophelia
Divided from herself and her fair judgment,
Without the which we are pictures, or mere beasts;
Last, and as much containing as all these,   85
Her brother is in secret come from France,
Feeds on his wonder, keeps himself in clouds,
And wants not buzzers to infect his ear
With pestilent speeches of his father's death,
Wherein necessity, of matter beggared,°   90
Will nothing stick° our person to arraign°
In ear and ear.° O my dear Gertrude, this,

---

57 Jesus   60 God   79 disturbed   81 without judgment   82 haste   90 short on facts
91 hesitate   91 accuse   92 from both sides

Like to a murd'ring piece,° in many places
Gives me superfluous death. Attend,

(A noise within.)

(Enter a MESSENGER. *)*

Where are my Switzers°? Let them guard the door.   95
What is the matter?
MESSENGER: Save yourself, my lord.
   The ocean, overpeering of his list,°
   Eats not the flats with more impiteous° haste
   Than young Laertes, in a riotous head,°
   O'erbears your officers. The rabble call him lord,   100
   And as the world were now but to begin,
   Antiquity forgot, custom not known,
   The ratifiers and props of every word,
   They cry "Choose we, Laertes shall be king."
   Caps, hands, and tongues, applaud it to the clouds,   105
   "Laertes shall be king, Laertes king."
QUEEN: How cheerfully on the false trail they cry°!

(A noise within.)

   O, this is counter,° you false Danish dogs!
KING: The doors are broke.

   (Enter LAERTES, *with* OTHERS. *)*

LAERTES: Where is this king?—Sirs, stand you all without.   110
ALL: No, let's come in.
LAERTES: I pray you give me leave.
ALL: We will, we will.

(Exeunt his followers.)

LAERTES: I thank you. Keep° the door.—O thou vile king,
   Give me my father!
QUEEN: Calmly, good Laertes.
LAERTES: That drop of blood that's calm proclaims me bastard,   115
   Cries cuckold to my father, brands the harlot
   Even here between the chaste unsmirchéd brow
   Of my true mother.
KING: What is the cause, Laertes,
   That thy rebellion looks so giant-like?
   Let him go, Gertrude. Do not fear° our person.   120
   There's such divinity doth hedge a king
   That treason can but peep to° what it would,
   Acts little of his will. Tell me, Laertes,

---

93 a weapon designed to scatter its shot   95 Swiss guards   97 towering above its limits
98 pitiless   99 with an armed band   107 as if following the scent   108 backward   113 guard
120 fear for   122 look at over or through a barrier

Why thou art thus incensed. Let him go, Gertrude.
Speak, man.

LAERTES: Where is my father?
KING: Dead.   125
QUEEN: But not by him.
KING: Let him demand° his fill.
LAERTES: How came he dead? I'll not be juggled with.
    To hell allegiance, vows to the blackest devil,
    Conscience and grace to the profoundest pit!
    I dare damnation. To this point I stand,   130
    That both the worlds° I give to negligence,°
    Let come what comes, only I'll be revenged
    Most throughly for my father.
KING: Who shall stay you?
LAERTES: My will, not all the world's.
    And for my means, I'll husband° them so well   135
    They shall go far with little.
KING: Good Laertes,
    If you desire to know the certainty
    Of your dear father, is't writ in your revenge
    That, swoopstake,° you will draw both friend and foe,
    Winner and loser?
LAERTES: None but his enemies.   140
KING: Will you know them, then?
LAERTES: To his good friends thus wide I'll ope my arms,
    And like the kind life-rend'ring pelican,°
    Repast them with my blood.
KING: Why, now you speak
    Like a good child and a true gentleman.   145
    That I am guiltless of your father's death,
    And am most sensibly in grief for it,
    It shall as level° to your judgment 'pear
    As day does to your eye.

    (A noise within:) "Let her come in."

LAERTES: How now? What noise is that?   150

                                    (Enter OPHELIA.*)*

    O, heat dry up my brains! tears seven times salt
    Burn out the sense° and virtue° of mine eye!
    By heaven, thy madness shall be paid with weight
    Till our scale turn the beam. O rose of May,
    Dear maid, kind sister, sweet Ophelia!   155

126 question   131 i.e., this and the next   131 disregard   135 manage   139 sweeping the board
143 The pelican was believed to feed her young with her own blood.   148 plain   152 feeling
152 function

O heavens! is't possible a young maid's wits
Should be as mortal as an old man's life?
Nature is fine° in love, and where 'tis fine
It sends some precious instance of itself
After the thing it loves.°   160
OPHELIA: They bore him barefac'd on the bier;
                Hey non nonny, nonny, hey nonny;
                And in his grave rain'd many a tear—

Fare you well, my dove!
LAERTES: Hadst thou thy wits, and didst persuade revenge,   165
   It could not move thus.
OPHELIA: You must sing "A-down, a-down, and you call him a-down-
   a." O, how the wheel becomes it! It is the false steward, that stole
   his master's daughter.°
LAERTES: This nothing's more than matter.   170
OPHELIA: There's rosemary, that's for remembrance. Pray you, love,
   remember. And there is pansies, that's for thoughts.
LAERTES: A document° in madness, thoughts and remembrance fitted.
OPHELIA: There's fennel for you, and columbines. There's rue for you,
   and here's some for me. We may call it herb of grace a Sundays. O, 175
   you must wear your rue with a difference. There's a daisy. I would
   give you some violets, but they withered all when my father died.
   They say'a made a good end.
        (Sings.) For bonny sweet Robin is all my joy.
LAERTES: Thought and affliction, passion, hell itself,   180
   She turns to favor° and to prettiness.
OPHELIA: And will 'a not come again?
                And will 'a not come again?
                  No, no, he is dead,
                  Go to thy death-bed,   185
                He never will come again.

                His beard was as white as snow,
                All flaxen was his poll°;
                  He is gone, he is gone,
                  And we cast away moan: 190
                God-a-mercy on his soul!

And of all Christian souls, I pray God. God b'wi'you.

                                                    (Exit.)

158 refined   160 Laertes means that Ophelia, because of her love for her father, gave up her sanity as a token of grief at his death.   169 The "wheel" refers to the *burden* or refrain of a song, in this case "A-down, a-down, and you call him a-down-a." The ballad to which she refers was about a false steward. Others have suggested that the "wheel" is the Wheel of Fortune, a spinning wheel to whose rhythm such a song might have been sung or a kind of dance movement performed by Ophelia as she sings.   173 lesson   181 beauty   188 head

LAERTES: Do you see this, O God?
KING: Laertes, I must commune with your grief,
    Or you deny me right. Go but apart,   195
    Make choice of whom your wisest friends you will,
    And they shall hear and judge 'twixt you and me.
    If by direct or by collateral° hand
    They find us touched,° we will our kingdom give,
    Our crown, our life, and all that we call ours,   200
    To you in satisfaction; but if not,
    Be you content to lend your patience to us,
    And we shall jointly labor with your soul
    To give it due content.
LAERTES: Let this be so.
    His means of death, his obscure funeral—   205
    No trophy, sword, nor hatchment,° o'er his bones,
    No noble rite nor formal ostentation°—
    Cry to be heard, as 'twere from heaven to earth,
    That I must call't in question.
KING: So you shall;
    And where th' offence is, let the great axe fall.   210
    I pray you go with me.

                                           (Exeunt.)

SCENE 6 *Another room in the castle. Enter* HORATIO *and a* GENTLEMAN.

HORATIO: What are they that would speak with me?
GENTLEMAN: Sea-faring men, sir. They say they have letters for you.
HORATIO: Let them come in.

                             (Exit GENTLEMAN.*)*

    I do not know from what part of the world
    I should be greeted, if not from Lord Hamlet.   5

                             (Enter SAILORS.*)*

SAILOR: God bless you, sir.
HORATIO: Let him bless thee too.
SAILOR: 'A shall, sir, an't please him. There's a letter for you, sir—it
    came from th' ambassador that was bound for England—if your
    name be Horatio, as I am let to know° it is.   10
HORATIO *(reads):* "Horatio, when thou shalt have overlooked° this, give
    these fellows some means° to the king. They have letters for him. Ere
    we were two days old at sea, a pirate of very warlike appointment°

198 indirect   199 by guilt   206 coat of arms   207 pomp   10 informed   11 read through
12 access   13 equipment

gave us chase. Finding ourselves too slow of sail, we put on a compelled valor, and in the grapple I boarded them. On the instant they   15
got clear of our ship, so I alone became their prisoner. They have
dealt with me like thieves of mercy, but they knew what they did;
I am to do a good turn for them. Let the king have the letters I have
sent, and repair thou to me with as much speed as thou wouldest fly
death. I have words to speak in thine ear will make thee dumb; yet   20
are they much too light for the bore of the matter.° These good
fellows will bring thee where I am. Rosencrantz and Guildenstern
hold their course for England. Of them I have much to tell thee.
Farewell.

       He that thou knowest thine, Hamlet."
Come, I will give you way° for these your letters,   25
And do't the speedier that you may direct me
To him from whom you brought them.

                                (Exeunt.)

SCENE 7   *Another room in the castle. Enter* KING *and* LAERTES.

KING: Now must your conscience my acquittance seal,°
    And you must put me in your heart for friend,
    Sith you have heard, and with a knowing ear,
    That he which hath your noble father slain
    Pursued my life.
LAERTES: It well appears. But tell me   5
    Why you proceeded not against these feats,
    So criminal and so capital in nature,
    As by your safety, greatness, wisdom, all things else,
    You mainly were stirred up.
KING: O, for two special reasons,
    Which may to you, perhaps, seem much unsinewed,°   10
    But yet to me th' are strong. The queen his mother
    Lives almost by his looks, and for myself—
    My virtue or my plague, be it either which—
    She is so conjunctive° to my life and soul
    That, as the star moves not but in his sphere,°   15
    I could not but by her. The other motive,
    Why to a public count° I might not go,
    Is the great love the general gender° bear him,
    Who, dipping all his faults in their affection,

---

21 A figure from gunnery, referring to shot which is too small for the size of the weapon to be fired.
25 means of delivery 1 grant me innocent 10 weak 14 closely joined 15 A reference to the
Ptolemaic cosmology in which planets and stars were believed to revolve about the earth in
crystalline spheres concentric with the earth. 17 reckoning 18 common people

Work like the spring that turneth wood to stone,°   20
Convert his gyves° to graces; so that my arrows,
Too slightly timbered° for so loud a wind,
Would have reverted to my bow again,
But not where I have aimed them.

LAERTES: And so have I a noble father lost,   25
A sister driven into desp'rate terms,
Whose worth, if praises may go back again,
Stood challenger on mount of all the age
For her perfections. But my revenge will come.

KING: Break not your sleeps for that. You must not think   30
That we are made of stuff so flat and dull
That we can let our beard be shook with danger,
And think it pastime. You shortly shall hear more.
I loved your father, and we love our self,
And that, I hope, will teach you to imagine—   35

(Enter a MESSENGER *with letters.)*

MESSENGER: These to your majesty; this to the queen.
KING: From Hamlet! Who brought them?
MESSENGER: Sailors, my lord, they say. I saw them not.
They were given me by Claudio; he received them
Of him that brought them.
KING: Laertes, you shall hear them.—   40
Leave us.

(Exit MESSENGER*.)*

(Reads.) "High and mighty, you shall know I am set naked on your
kingdom. Tomorrow shall I beg leave to see your kingly eyes; when
I shall, first asking your pardon thereunto, recount the occasion of
my sudden and more strange return.   45
                                      Hamlet."
What should this mean? Are all the rest come back?
Or is it some abuse,° and no such thing?
LAERTES: Know you the hand?
KING: 'Tis Hamlet's character.° "Naked"!   50
And in a postscript here, he says "alone."
Can you devise° me?
LAERTES: I am lost in it, my lord. But let him come.
It warms the very sickness in my heart
That I shall live and tell him to his teeth   55
"Thus didest thou."

---

20 Certain English springs contain so much lime in the water that a lime covering will be deposited
on a log placed in one of them for a length of time.   21 fetters   22 shafted   48 trick
50 handwriting   52 explain it to

KING: If it be so, Laertes—
   As how should it be so, how otherwise?—
   Will you be ruled by me?
LAERTES: Ay, my lord,
   So you will not o'errule me to a peace.
KING: To thine own peace. If he be now returned,   60
   As checking at° his voyage, and that he means
   No more to undertake it, I will work him
   To an exploit now ripe in my device,
   Under the which he shall not choose but fall;
   And for his death no wind of blame shall breathe   65
   But even his mother shall uncharge° the practice
   And call it accident.
LAERTES: My lord, I will be ruled;
   The rather if you could devise it so
   That I might be the organ.°
KING: It falls right.
   You have been talked of since your travel much,   70
   And that in Hamlet's hearing, for a quality
   Wherein they say you shine. Your sum of parts
   Did not together pluck such envy from him
   As did that one, and that, in my regard,
   Of the unworthiest siege.°
LAERTES: What part is that, my lord?   75
KING: A very riband in the cap of youth,
   Yet needful too, for youth no less becomes
   The light and careless livery that it wears
   Than settled age his sables and his weeds,°
   Importing health and graveness. Two months since   80
   Here was a gentleman of Normandy.
   I have seen myself, and served against, the French,
   And they can° well on horseback, but this gallant
   Had witchcraft in't. He grew unto his seat,
   And to such wondrous doing brought his horse,   85
   As had he been incorpsed and demi-natured
   With the brave beast. So far he topped my thought
   That I, in forgery° of shapes and tricks,
   Come short of what he did.°
LAERTES: A Norman was't?
KING: A Norman.   90
LAERTES: Upon my life, Lamord.

---

61 turning aside from   66 not accuse   69 instrument   75 rank   79 dignified clothing
83 perform   88 imagination   89 The gentleman referred to was so skilled in horsemanship that
he seemed to share one body with the horse, "incorpsed." The King further extends the compliment by saying that he appeared like the mythical centaur, a creature who was man from the waist
up and horse from the waist down, therefore "demi-natured."

KING: The very same.
LAERTES: I know him well. He is the brooch indeed
     And gem of all the nation.
KING: He made confession° of you,
     And gave you such a masterly report   95
     For art and exercise in your defence,°
     And for your rapier most especial,
     That he cried out 'twould be a sight indeed
     If one could match you. The scrimers° of their nation
     He swore had neither motion, guard, nor eye,   100
     If you opposed them. Sir, this report of his
     Did Hamlet so envenom with his envy
     That he could nothing do but wish and beg
     Your sudden coming o'er, to play with you.
     Now out of this—
LAERTES: What out of this, my lord?   105
KING: Laertes, was your father dear to you?
     Or are you like the painting of a sorrow,
     A face without a heart?
LAERTES: Why ask you this?
KING: Not that I think you did not love your father,
     But that I know love is begun by time,   110
     And that I see in passages of proof,°
     Time qualifies the spark and fire of it.
     There lives within the very flame of love
     A kind of wick or snuff that will abate it,
     And nothing is at a like goodness still,   115
     For goodness, growing to a plurisy,°
     Dies in his own too much.° That we would do,
     We should do when we would; for this "would" changes,
     And hath abatements and delays as many
     As there are tongues, are hands, are accidents,   120
     And then this "should" is like a spendthrift's sigh
     That hurts by easing. But to the quick of th' ulcer—
     Hamlet comes back; what would you undertake
     To show yourself in deed your father's son
     More than in words?
LAERTES: To cut his throat i' th' church.   125
KING: No place indeed should murder sanctuarize°;
     Revenge should have no bounds. But, good Laertes,
     Will you do this? Keep close within your chamber.
     Hamlet returned shall know you are come home.

94 gave a report   96 skill in fencing   99 fencers   111 tests of experience   116 fullness
117 excess   126 provide sanctuary for murder

We'll put on those shall praise your excellence,   130
And set a double varnish° on the fame
The Frenchman gave you, bring you in fine° together,
And wager on your heads. He, being remiss,°
Most generous, and free from all contriving,
Will not peruse° the foils, so that with ease,   135
Or with a little shuffling, you may choose
A sword unbated,° and in a pass of practice
Requite him for your father.
LAERTES: I will do't,
And for that purpose I'll anoint my sword.
I bought an unction of a mountebank,   140
So mortal that but dip a knife in it,
Where it draws blood no cataplasm° so rare,
Collected from all simples° that have virtue
Under the moon, can save the thing from death
That is but scratched withal. I'll touch my point   145
With this contagion, that if I gall° him slightly,
It may be death.
KING: Let's further think of this,
Weigh what convenience both of time and means
May fit us to our shape. If this should fail,
And that our drift look° through our bad performance,   150
'Twere better not assayed. Therefore this project
Should have a back or second that might hold
If this did blast in proof.° Soft, let me see.
We'll make a solemn wager on your cunnings—
I ha't.   155
When in your motion you are hot and dry—
As make your bouts more violent to that end—
And that he calls for drink, I'll have preferred him
A chalice for the nonce, whereon but sipping,
If he by chance escape your venomed stuck,°   160
Our purpose may hold there.—But stay, what noise?

                                                    (Enter QUEEN.*)*

QUEEN: One woe doth tread upon another's heel,
    So fast they follow. Your sister's drowned, Laertes.
LAERTES: Drowned? O, where?
QUEEN: There is a willow grows aslant the brook   165
    That shows his hoar leaves in the glassy stream.
    Therewith fantastic garlands did she make

131 gloss   132 in short   133 careless   135 examine   137 not blunted   142 poultice
143 herbs   146 scratch   150 intent become obvious   153 fail when tried   160 thrust

Of crowflowers, nettles, daisies, and long purples
That liberal° shepherds give a grosser° name,
But our cold° maids do dead men's fingers call them.   170
There on the pendent boughs her coronet weeds
Clamb'ring to hang, an envious° sliver broke,
When down her weedy trophies and herself
Fell in the weeping brook. Her clothes spread wide,
And mermaid-like awhile they bore her up,   175
Which time she chanted snatches of old tunes,
As one incapable° of her own distress,
Or like a creature native and indued°
Unto that element. But long it could not be
Till that her garments, heavy with their drink,   180
Pulled the poor wretch from her melodious lay
To muddy death.
LAERTES: Alas, then she is drowned?
QUEEN: Drowned, drowned.
LAERTES: Too much of water hast thou, poor Ophelia,
And therefore I forbid my tears; but yet   185
It is our trick; nature her custom holds,
Let shame say what it will. When these are gone,
The woman will be out. Adieu, my lord.
I have a speech o' fire that fain would blaze
But that this folly drowns it.

                                                         (Exit.)

KING: Let's follow, Gertrude.   190
How much I had to do to calm his rage!
Now fear I this will give it start again;
Therefore let's follow.

                                                         (Exeunt.)

ACT 5

SCENE 1   *A churchyard. Enter two* CLOWNS.

CLOWN: Is she to be buried in Christian burial when she wilfully seeks
her own salvation?
OTHER: I tell thee she is. Therefore make her grave straight. The
crowner° hath sat on her,° and finds it Christian burial.

169 vulgar   169 coarser   170 chaste   172 malicious   177 unaware   178 habituated
4 coroner   4 held an inquest

CLOWN: How can that be, unless she drowned herself in her own de-   5
fence?

OTHER: Why, 'tis found so.

CLOWN: It must be "se offendendo'"°; it cannot be else. For here lies the
point: if I drown myself wittingly, it argues an act, and an act hath
three branches—it is to act, to do, to perform; argal,° she drowned   10
herself wittingly.

OTHER: Nay, but hear you, Goodman Delver.

CLOWN: Give me leave. Here lies the water; good. Here stands the man;
good. If the man go to this water and drown himself, it is, will he,
nill he, he goes—mark you that. But if the water come to him and   15
drown him, he drowns not himself. Argal, he that is not guilty of his
own death shortens not his own life.

OTHER: But is this law?

CLOWN: Ay, marry, is't; crowner's quest° law.

OTHER: Will you ha' the truth on't? If this had not been a gentlewoman,   20
she should have been buried out o' christian burial.

CLOWN: Why, there thou say'st. And the more pity that great folk
should have count'nance° in this world to drown or hang themselves
more than their even-Christen.° Come, my spade. There is no ancient
gentlemen but gard'ners, ditchers, and grave-makers. They hold up   25
Adam's profession.

OTHER: Was he a gentleman?

CLOWN: 'A was the first that ever bore arms.

OTHER: Why, he had none.

CLOWN: What, art a heathen? How dost thou understand the Scripture?   30
The Scripture says Adam digged. Could he dig without arms? I'll put
another question to thee. If thou answerest me not to the purpose,
confess thyself—

OTHER: Go to.

CLOWN: What is he that builds stronger than either the mason, the   35
shipwright, or the carpenter?

OTHER: The gallows-maker, for that frame outlives a thousand tenants.

CLOWN: I like thy wit well, in good faith. The gallows does well. But
how does it well? It does well to those that do ill. Now thou dost
ill to say the gallows is built stronger than the church. Argal, the   40
gallows may do well to thee. To't again,° come.

OTHER: Who builds stronger than a mason, a shipwright, or a carpenter?

CLOWN: Ay tell me that, and unyoke.°

OTHER: Marry, now I can tell.

CLOWN: To't.   45

___

8 an error for *se defendendo,* in self-defense   10 therefore   19 inquest   23 approval   24 fellow
Christians   41 guess again   43 finish the matter

OTHER: Mass, I cannot tell.

CLOWN: Cudgel thy brains no more about it, for your dull ass will not mend his pace with beating. And when you are asked this question next, say "a grave-maker." The houses he makes lasts till doomsday. Go, get thee in, and fetch me a stoup° of liquor.   50

(Exit OTHER CLOWN.)

(Enter HAMLET and HORATIO as CLOWN digs and sings.)

> In youth, when I did love, did love,
>   Methought it was very sweet,
> To contract° the time for-a my behove,°
>   O, methought there-a was nothing-a meet.°

HAMLET: Has this fellow no feeling of his business, that 'a sings in   55
grave-making?

HORATIO: Custom hath made it in him a property of easiness.

HAMLET: 'Tis e'en so. The hand of little employment hath the daintier sense.

CLOWN: But age, with his stealing steps,   60
                Hath clawed me in his clutch,
            And hath shipped me into the land,
                As if I had never been such.

(Throws up a skull.)

HAMLET: That skull had a tongue in it, and could sing once. How the knave jowls° it to the ground, as if 'twere Cain's jawbone, that did   65
the first murder! This might be the pate of a politician, which this ass now o'erreaches°; one that would circumvent God, might it not?

HORATIO: It might, my lord.

HAMLET: Or of a courtier, which could say "Good morrow, sweet lord! How dost thou, sweet lord?" This might be my Lord Such-a-one,   70
that praised my Lord Such-a-one's horse, when 'a meant to beg it, might it not?

HORATIO: Ay, my lord.

HAMLET: Why, e'en so, and now my Lady Worm's, chapless,° and knock'd abut the mazzard° with a sexton's spade. Here's fine revolu-   75
tion,° an we had the trick to see't. Did these bones cost no more the breeding but to play at loggets with them?° Mine ache to think on't.

CLOWN: A pick-axe and a spade, a spade,
                For and a shrouding sheet:
            O, a pit of clay for to be made   80
                For such a guest is meet.

(Throws up another skull.)

---

50 mug   53 shorten   53 advantage   54 The gravedigger's song is a free version of "The aged lover renounceth love" by Thomas, Lord Vaux, published in *Tottel's Miscellany,* 1557. 65 hurls   67 gets the better of   74 lacking a lower jaw   75 head   76 skull   77 "Loggets" were small pieces of wood thrown as part of a game.

HAMLET: There's another. Why may not that be the skull of a lawyer? Where be his quiddities now, his quillets, his cases, his tenures, and his tricks? Why does he suffer this mad knave now to knock him about the sconce° with a dirty shovel, and will not tell him of his 85 action of battery? Hum! This fellow might be in's time a great buyer of land, with his statutes, his recognizances, his fines, his double vouchers, his recoveries. Is this the fine° of his fines, and the recovery of his recoveries, to have his fine pate full of fine dirt? Will his vouchers vouch him no more of his purchases, and double ones too, 90 than the length and breadth of a pair of indentures°? The very conveyances of his lands will scarcely lie in this box, and must th' inheritor himself have no more, ha?°

HORATIO: Not a jot more, my lord.

HAMLET: Is not parchment made of sheepskins?   95

HORATIO: Ay, my lord, and of calves' skins too.

HAMLET: They are sheep and calves which seek out assurance in that. I will speak to this fellow. Whose grave's this, sirrah?

CLOWN: Mine, sir.
        (Sings.) O, a pit of clay for to be made—   100

HAMLET: I think it be thine indeed, for thou liest in't.

CLOWN: You lie out on't, sir, and therefore 'tis not yours. For my part, I do not lie in't, yet it is mine.

HAMLET: Thou dost lie in't, to be in't and say it is thine. 'Tis for the dead, not for the quick°; therefore thou liest.   105

CLOWN: 'Tis a quick lie, sir; 'twill away again from me to you.

HAMLET: What man dost thou dig it for?

CLOWN: For no man, sir.

HAMLET: What woman, then?

CLOWN: For none neither.   110

HAMLET: Who is to be buried in't?

CLOWN: One that was a woman, sir; but, rest her soul, she's dead.

HAMLET: How absolute° the knave is! We must speak by the card,° or equivocation will undo us. By the Lord, Horatio, this three years I have took note of it, the age is grown so picked° that the toe of the 115 peasant comes so near the heel of the courtier, he galls his kibe.° How long hast thou been a grave-maker?

CLOWN: Of all the days i' th' year, I came to't that day that our last King Hamlet overcame Fortinbras.

HAMLET: How long is that since?   120

CLOWN: Cannot you tell that? Every fool can tell that. It was that very day that young Hamlet was born—he that is mad, and sent into England.

---

85 head   88 end   91 contracts   93 In this speech Hamlet reels off a list of legal terms relating to property transactions.   105 living   113 precise   113 exactly   115 refined   116 rubs a blister on his heel

HAMLET: Ay, marry, why was he sent into England?

CLOWN: Why, because 'a was mad. 'A shall recover his wits there; or,   125
if 'a do not, 'tis no great matter there.

HAMLET: Why?

CLOWN: 'Twill not be seen in him there. There the men are as mad as
he.

HAMLET: How came he mad?   130

CLOWN: Very strangely, they say.

HAMLET: How strangely?

CLOWN: Faith, e'en with losing his wits.

HAMLET: Upon what ground?

CLOWN: Why, here in Denmark. I have been sexton here, man and boy,   135
thirty years.

HAMLET: How long will a man lie i' th' earth ere he rot?

CLOWN: Faith, if 'a be not rotten before 'a die—as we have many pocky°
corses now-a-days that will scarce hold the laying in—'a will last you
some eight year or nine year. A tanner will last you nine year.   140

HAMLET: Why he more than another?

CLOWN: Why, sir, his hide is so tanned with his trade that 'a will keep
out water a great while; and your water is a sore decayer of your
whoreson° dead body. Here's a skull now hath lien° you i' th' earth
three and twenty years.   145

HAMLET: Whose was it?

CLOWN: A whoreson mad fellow's it was. Whose do you think it was?

HAMLET: Nay, I know not.

CLOWN: A pestilence on him for a mad rogue! 'A poured a flagon of
Rhenish on my head once. This same skull, sir, was, sir, Yorick's   150
skull, the king's jester.

HAMLET *(takes the skull):*   This?

CLOWN: E'en that.

HAMLET: Alas, poor Yorick! I knew him, Horatio—a fellow of infinite
jest, of most excellent fancy. He hath bore me on his back a thousand   155
times, and now how abhorred in my imagination it is! My gorge°
rises at it. Here hung those lips that I have kissed I know not how
oft. Where be your gibes now, your gambols, your songs, your
flashes of merriment that were wont to set the table on a roar? Not
one now to mock your own grinning? Quite chap-fall'n°? Now get   160
you to my lady's chamber, and tell her, let her paint an inch thick,
to this favor° she must come. Make her laugh at that. Prithee,
Horatio, tell me one thing.

HORATIO: What's that, my lord?

HAMLET: Dost thou think Alexander looked o' this fashion i' th' earth?   165

138 corrupted by syphilis   144 bastard (not literally)   144 lain   156 throat   160 lacking a lower
jaw   162 appearance

HORATIO: E'en so.
HAMLET: And smelt so? Pah!

(Throws down the skull.)

HORATIO: E'en so, my lord.
HAMLET: To what base uses we may return, Horatio! Why may not
    imagination trace the noble dust of Alexander till 'a find it stopping   170
    a bung-hole?
HORATIO: 'Twere to consider too curiously° to consider so.
HAMLET: No, faith, not a jot, but to follow him thither with modesty°
    enough, and likelihood to lead it. Alexander died, Alexander was
    buried, Alexander returneth to dust; the dust is earth; of earth we   175
    make loam; and why of that loam whereto he was converted might
    they not stop a beer-barrel?

          Imperious Cæsar, dead and turned to clay,
          Might stop a hole to keep the wind away.
          O, that that earth which kept the world in awe   180
          Should patch a wall t'expel the winter's flaw!°

But soft, but soft awhile! Here comes the king,
The queen, the courtiers.

(Enter KING, QUEEN, LAERTES, *and the Corse with a* PRIEST *and*
LORDS *attendant.)*

              Who is this they follow?
And with such maiméd° rites? This doth betoken
The corse they follow did with desperate hand   185
Fordo° it own life. 'Twas of some estate.°
Couch° we awhile and mark.

(Retires with HORATIO.)

LAERTES: What ceremony else°?
HAMLET: That is Laertes, a very noble youth. Mark.
LAERTES: What ceremony else?   190
PRIEST: Her obsequies have been as far enlarged°
    As we have warranty. Her death was doubtful,
    And but that great command o'ersways the order,°
    She should in ground unsanctified been lodged
    Till the last trumpet. For charitable prayers,   195
    Shards, flints, and pebbles, should be thrown on her.
    Yet here she is allowed her virgin crants,°

172 precisely   173 moderation   181 gusty wind   184 cut short   186 destroy   186 rank
187 conceal ourselves   188 more   191 extended   193 usual rules   197 wreaths

Her maiden strewments,° and the bringing home
Of bell and burial.
LAERTES: Must there no more be done?
PRIEST: No more be done.   200
We should profane the service of the dead
To sing a requiem and such rest to her
As to peace-parted souls.
LAERTES: Lay her i' th' earth,
And from her fair and unpolluted flesh
May violets spring! I tell thee, churlish priest,   205
A minist'ring angel shall my sister be
When thou liest howling.°
HAMLET: What, the fair Ophelia!
QUEEN: Sweets to the sweet. Farewell!

                                        (Scatters flowers.)

I hoped thou shouldst have been my Hamlet's wife.
I thought thy bride-bed to have decked, sweet maid,   210
And not have strewed thy grave.
LAERTES: O, treble woe
Fall ten times treble on that curséd head
Whose wicked deed thy most ingenious sense°
Deprived thee of! Hold off the earth awhile,
Till I have caught her once more in mine arms.   215

                                        (Leaps into the grave.)

Now pile your dust upon the quick and dead,
Till of this flat a mountain you have made
T' o'er-top old Pelion or the skyish head
Of blue Olympus.°
HAMLET *(coming forward)*:   What is he whose grief   220
Bears such an emphasis, whose phrase of sorrow
Conjures° the wand'ring stars, and makes them stand
Like wonder-wounded hearers? This is I,
Hamlet the Dane.

(HAMLET leaps into the grave and they grapple.)

LAERTES: The devil take thy soul!
HAMLET: Thou pray'st not well.   225

198 flowers strewn on the grave   206 in Hell   213 lively mind   219 The rivalry between Laertes
and Hamlet in this scene extends even to their rhetoric. Pelion and Olympus, mentioned here by
Laertes, and Ossa, mentioned below by Hamlet, were Greek mountains noted in mythology for
their height. Olympus was the reputed home of the gods, and the other two were piled one on top
of the other by the Giants in an attempt to reach the top of Olympus and overthrow the gods.
222 casts a spell on

I prithee take thy fingers from my throat,
For though I am not splenitive° and rash,
Yet have I in me something dangerous,
Which let thy wisdom fear. Hold off thy hand.

KING: Pluck them asunder.   230

QUEEN: Hamlet! Hamlet!

ALL: Gentlemen!

HORATIO: Good my lord, be quiet.

(The ATTENDANTS *part them, and they come out of the grave.)*

HAMLET: Why, I will fight with him upon this theme
Until my eyelids will no longer wag.°   235

QUEEN: O my son, what theme?

HAMLET: I loved Ophelia. Forty thousand brothers
Could not with all their quantity of love
Make up my sum. What wilt thou do for her?

KING: O, he is mad, Laertes.   240

QUEEN: For love of God, forbear° him.

HAMLET: 'Swounds, show me what th'owt do.
Woo't° weep, woo't fight, woo't fast, woo't tear thyself,
Woo't drink up eisel,° eat a crocodile?
I'll do't. Dost come here to whine?   245
To outface° me with leaping in her grave?
Be buried quick with her, and so will I.
And if thou prate of mountains, let them throw
Millions of acres on us, till our ground,
Singeing his pate against the burning zone,°   250
Make Ossa like a wart! Nay, an thou'lt mouth,
I'll rant as well as thou.

QUEEN: This is mere madness;
And thus awhile the fit will work on him.
Anon, as patient as the female dove
When that her golden couplets° are disclosed,   255
His silence will sit drooping.

HAMLET: Hear you, sir.
What is the reason that you use me thus?
I loved you ever. But it is no matter.
Let Hercules himself do what he may,
The cat will mew, and dog will have his day.   260

KING: I pray thee, good Horatio, wait upon° him.

(Exeunt HAMLET *and* HORATIO.*)*

227 hot-tempered   235 move   241 bear with   243 will you   244 vinegar   246 get the best
of   250 sky in the torrid zone   255 pair of eggs   261 attend

(To LAERTES.*)* Strengthen your patience in our last night's speech.
We'll put the matter to the present push.°—
Good Gertrude, set some watch over your son.—
This grave shall have a living monument.   265
An hour of quiet shortly shall we see;
Till then in patience our proceeding be.

                                                              (Exeunt.)

SCENE 2   *A hall or public room. Enter* HAMLET *and* HORATIO.

HAMLET: So much for this, sir; now shall you see the other.
    You do remember all the circumstance?
HORATIO: Remember it, my lord!
HAMLET: Sir, in my heart there was a kind of fighting
    That would not let me sleep. Methought I lay   5
    Worse than the mutines° in the bilboes.° Rashly,
    And praised be rashness for it—let us know,
    Our indiscretion sometime serves us well,
    When our deep plots do pall; and that should learn° us
    There's a divinity that shapes our ends,   10
    Rough-hew them how we will—
HORATIO: That is most certain.
HAMLET: Up from my cabin,
    My sea-gown scarfed° about me, in the dark
    Groped I to find out them, had my desire,
    Fingered° their packet, and in fine° withdrew   15
    To mine own room again, making so bold,
    My fears forgetting manners, to unseal
    Their grand commission; where I found, Horatio—
    Ah, royal knavery!—an exact° command,
    Larded° with many several sorts of reasons,   20
    Importing Denmark's health, and England's too,
    With, ho! such bugs and goblins in my life,°
    That on the supervise,° no leisure bated,
    No, not to stay the grinding of the axe,
    My head should be struck off.
HORATIO: Is't possible?   25
HAMLET: Here's the commission; read it at more leisure.
    But wilt thou hear now how I did proceed?
HORATIO: I beseech you.
HAMLET: Being thus benetted° round with villainies,
    Or I could make a prologue to my brains,   30

---

263 immediate trial   6 mutineers   6 stocks   9 teach   13 wrapped   15 stole   15 quickly
19 precisely stated   20 garnished   22 such dangers if I remained alive   23 as soon as the
commission was read   29 caught in a net

They had begun the play. I sat me down,
Devised° a new commission, wrote it fair.°
I once did hold it, as our statists° do,
A baseness to write fair, and labored much
How to forget that learning; but sir, now   35
It did me yeoman's service. Wilt thou know
Th' effect° of what I wrote?
HORATIO: Ay, good my lord.
HAMLET: An earnest conjuration from the king,
    As England was his faithful tributary,°
    As love between them like the palm might flourish,   40
    As peace should still her wheaten garland wear
    And stand a comma 'tween their amities,°
    And many such like as's of great charge,°
    That on the view and knowing of these contents,
    Without debatement° further more or less,   45
    He should those bearers put to sudden death,
    Not shriving-time allowed.°
HORATIO: How was this sealed?
HAMLET: Why, even in that was heaven ordinant,°
    I had my father's signet in my purse,
    Which was the model of that Danish seal,   50
    Folded the writ up in the form of th' other,
    Subscribed it, gave't th' impression,° placed it safely,
    The changeling° never known. Now, the next day
    Was our sea-fight, and what to this was sequent°
    Thou knowest already.   55
HORATIO: So Guildenstern and Rosencrantz go to't.
HAMLET: Why, man, they did make love to this employment.
    They are not near° my conscience; their defeat°
    Does by their own insinuation grow.
    'Tis dangerous when the baser nature comes   60
    Between the pass° and fell° incenséd points
    Of mighty opposites.
HORATIO: Why, what a king is this!
HAMLET: Does it not, think thee, stand me now upon—
    He that hath killed my king and whored my mother,
    Popped in between th' election and my hopes,   65
    Thrown out his angle° for my proper life,
    And with such coz'nage°—is't not perfect conscience
    To quit° him with this arm? And is't not to be damned

32 made   32 legibly   33 politicians   37 contents   39 vassal   42 link friendships   43 import
45 consideration   47 without time for confession   48 operative   52 of the seal   53 alteration
54 followed   58 do not touch   58 death   61 thrust   61 cruel   66 fishhook   67 trickery
68 repay

To let this canker of our nature come
In further evil?   70
HORATIO: It must be shortly known to him from England
What is the issue° of the business there.
HAMLET: It will be short°; the interim is mine.
And a man's life's no more than to say "one."
But I am very sorry, good Horatio,   75
That to Laertes I forgot myself;
For by the image of my cause I see
The portraiture of his. I'll court his favors.
But sure the bravery° of his grief did put me
Into a tow'ring passion.
HORATIO: Peace; who comes here?   80

(Enter OSRIC.*)*

OSRIC: Your lordship is right welcome back to Denmark.
HAMLET: I humbly thank you, sir. *(Aside to* HORATIO.*)* Dost know this
water-fly?
HORATIO *(aside to* HAMLET*):*   No, my good lord.
HAMLET *(aside to* HORATIO*):*   Thy state is the more gracious, for 'tis a   85
vice to know him. He hath much land, and fertile. Let a beast be lord
of beasts, and his crib shall stand at the king's mess. 'Tis a chough,°
but as I say, spacious in the possession of dirt.
OSRIC: Sweet lord, if your lordship were at leisure, I should impart a
thing to you from his majesty.   90
HAMLET: I will receive it, sir, with all diligence of spirit. Put your
bonnet to his right use. 'Tis for the head.
OSRIC: I thank your lordship, it is very hot.
HAMLET: No, believe me, 'tis very cold; the wind is northerly.
OSRIC: It is indifferent° cold, my lord, indeed.   95
HAMLET: But yet methinks it is very sultry and hot for my complexion.°
OSRIC: Exceedingly, my lord; it is very sultry, as 'twere—I cannot tell
how. My lord, his majesty bade me signify to you that 'a has laid a
great wager on your head. Sir, this is the matter—
HAMLET: I beseech you, remember.   100

(HAMLET *moves him to put on his hat.)*

OSRIC: Nay, good my lord; for my ease, in good faith. Sir, here is newly
come to court Laertes; believe me, an absolute° gentleman, full of
most excellent differences,° of very soft society and great showing.°
Indeed, to speak feelingly of him, he is the card or calendar° of
gentry, for you shall find in him the continent° of what part a gentle-   105
man would see.

72 outcome   73 soon   79 exaggerated display   87 jackdaw   95 moderately   96 temperament
102 perfect   103 qualities   103 good manners   104 measure   105 sum total

HAMLET: Sir, his definement° suffers no perdition in you, though I know
    to divide him inventorially° would dozy° th' arithmetic of memory,
    and yet but yaw° neither in respect of his quick sail. But in the verity
    of extolment, I take him to be a soul of great article,° and his infusion°   110
    of such dearth and rareness as, to make true diction° of him, his
    semblage° is his mirror, and who else would trace° him, his um-
    brage,° nothing more.
OSRIC: Your lordship speaks most infallibly of him.
HAMLET: The concernancy,° sir? Why do we wrap the gentleman in our   115
    more rawer breath?°
OSRIC: Sir?
HORATIO: Is't not possible to understand in another tongue? You will
    to't, sir, really.
HAMLET: What imports the nomination° of this gentleman?   120
OSRIC: Of Laertes?
HORATIO *(aside):*   His purse is empty already. All's golden words are
    spent.
HAMLET: Of him, sir.
OSRIC: I know you are not ignorant—   125
HAMLET: I would you did, sir; yet, in faith, if you did, it would not much
    approve me. Well, sir.
OSRIC: You are not ignorant of what excellence Laertes is—
HAMLET: I dare not confess that, lest I should compare° with him in
    excellence; but to know a man well were to know himself.   130
OSRIC: I mean, sir, for his weapon; but in the imputation° laid on him
    by them, in his meed he's unfellowed.°
HAMLET: What's his weapon?
OSRIC: Rapier and dagger.
HAMLET: That's two of his weapons—but well.   135
OSRIC: The king, sir, hath wagered with him six Barbary horses, against
    the which he has impawned,° as I take it, six French rapiers and
    poniards, with their assigns,° as girdle, hangers, and so. Three of the
    carriages, in faith, are very dear to fancy,° very responsive to the
    hilts, most delicate° carriages, and of very liberal conceit.°   140
HAMLET: What call you the carriages?
HORATIO *(aside to* HAMLET*):*   I knew you must be edified by the mar-
    gent° ere you had done.
OSRIC: The carriages, sir, are the hangers.
HAMLET: The phrase would be more germane to the matter if we could   145
    carry a cannon by our sides. I would it might be hangers till then.
    But on! Six Barbary horses against six French swords, their assigns,

107 description   108 examine bit by bit   108 daze   109 steer wildly   110 scope   110 nature
111 telling   112 rival   112 keep pace with   113 shadow   115 meaning   116 cruder words
120 naming   129 i.e., compare myself   131 reputation   132 unequaled in his excellence
137 staked   138 appurtenances   139 finely designed   140 well adjusted   140 elegant design
143 marginal gloss

and three liberal conceited carriages; that's the French bet against
the Danish. Why is this all impawned, as you call it?

OSRIC: The king, sir, hath laid, sir, that in a dozen passes between your-   150
self and him he shall not exceed you three hits; he hath laid on twelve
for nine, and it would come to immediate trial if your lordship would
vouchsafe the answer.

HAMLET: How if I answer no?

OSRIC: I mean, my lord, the opposition of your person in trial.   155

HAMLET: Sir, I will walk here in the hall. If it please his majesty, it is
the breathing time° of day with me. Let the foils be brought, the
gentleman willing, and the king hold his purpose; I will win for him
an I can. If not, I will gain nothing but my shame and the odd hits.

OSRIC: Shall I deliver you so?   160

HAMLET: To this effect, sir, after what flourish your nature will.

OSRIC: I commend my duty to your lordship.

HAMLET: Yours, yours. *(Exit* OSRIC.*)* He does well to commend it
himself; there are no tongues else for's turn.

HORATIO: This lapwing runs away with the shell on his head.°   165

HAMLET: 'A did comply,° sir, with his dug° before 'a sucked it. Thus has
he, and many more of the same bevy that I know the drossy age dotes
on, only got the tune of the time; and out of an habit of encounter,
a kind of yesty° collection which carries them through and through
the most fanned and winnowed opinions; and do but blow them to   170
their trial, the bubbles are out.

(Enter a LORD.*)*

LORD: My lord, his majesty commended him to you by young Osric,
who brings back to him that you attend° him in the hall. He sends
to know if your pleasure hold to play with Laertes, or that you will
take longer time.   175

HAMLET: I am constant to my purposes; they follow the king's pleasure.
If his fitness speaks, mine is ready; now or whensoever, provided I
be so able as now.

LORD: The king and queen and all are coming down.

HAMLET: In happy time.   180

LORD: The queen desires you to use some gentle entertainment° to
Laertes before you fall to play.

HAMLET: She well instructs me.

(Exit LORD.*)*

HORATIO: You will lose this wager, my lord.

HAMLET: I do not think so. Since he went into France I have been in   185

---

157 time for exercise   165 The lapwing was thought to be so precocious that it could run
immediately after being hatched, even as here with bits of the shell still on its head.   166 deal
formally   166 mother's breast   169 yeasty   173 await   181 cordiality

continual practice. I shall win at the odds. But thou wouldst not think
how ill° all's here about my heart. But it is no matter.

HORATIO: Nay, good my lord—

HAMLET: It is but foolery, but it is such a kind of gaingiving° as would
perhaps trouble a woman.   190

HORATIO: If your mind dislike anything, obey it. I will forestall their
repair° hither, and say you are not fit.

HAMLET: Not a whit, we defy augury. There is special providence in the
fall of a sparrow. If it be now, 'tis not to come; if it be not to come,
it will be now; if it be not now, yet it will come. The readiness is all.   195
Since no man of aught he leaves knows, what is't to leave betimes?
Let be.

(A table prepared. Enter TRUMPETS, DRUMS, *and* OFFICERS *with cushions;* KING, QUEEN, OSRIC *and* ATTENDANTS *with foils, daggers, and*
LAERTES.*)*

KING: Come, Hamlet, come and take this hand from me.

(The KING *puts* LAERTES' *hand into* HAMLET'*s.)*

HAMLET: Give me your pardon, sir. I have done you wrong,
But pardon 't as you are a gentleman.   200
This presence° knows, and you must needs have heard,
How I am punished with a sore distraction.
What I have done
That might your nature, honor, and exception,°
Roughly awake, I here proclaim was madness.   205
Was 't Hamlet wronged Laertes? Never Hamlet.
If Hamlet from himself be ta'en away,
And when he's not himself does wrong Laertes,
Then Hamlet does it not, Hamlet denies it.
Who does it then? His madness. If't be so,   210
Hamlet is of the faction that is wronged;
His madness is poor Hamlet's enemy.
Sir, in this audience,
Let my disclaiming from° a purposed evil
Free° me so far in your most generous thoughts   215
That I have shot my arrow o'er the house
And hurt my brother.

LAERTES: I am satisfied in nature,
Whose motive in this case should stir me most
To my revenge. But in my terms of honor
I stand aloof, and will no reconcilement   220
Till by some elder masters of known honor

187 uneasy   189 misgiving   192 coming   201 company   204 resentment   214 denying of
215 absolve

I have a voice° and precedent of peace
To keep my name ungored.° But till that time
I do receive your offered love like love,
And will not wrong it.
HAMLET: I embrace it freely,   225
And will this brother's wager frankly° play.
Give us the foils.
LAERTES: Come, one for me.
HAMLET: I'll be your foil, Laertes. In mine ignorance
Your skill shall, like a star i' th' darkest night,
Stick fiery off° indeed.
LAERTES: You mock me, sir.   230
HAMLET: No, by this hand.
KING: Give them the foils, young Osric. Cousin Hamlet,
You know the wager?
HAMLET: Very well, my lord;
Your Grace has laid the odds o' th' weaker side.
KING: I do not fear it, I have seen you both;   235
But since he is bettered,° we have therefore odds.
LAERTES: This is too heavy; let me see another.
HAMLET: This likes° me well. These foils have all a° length?

(*They prepare to play.*)

OSRIC: Ay, my good lord.
KING: Set me the stoups of wine upon that table.   240
If Hamlet give the first or second hit,
Or quit in answer of° the third exchange,
Let all the battlements their ordnance fire.
The king shall drink to Hamlet's better breath,
And in the cup an union° shall he throw,   245
Richer than that which four successive kings
In Denmark's crown have worn. Give me the cups,
And let the kettle° to the trumpet speak,
The trumpet to the cannoneer without,
The cannons to the heavens, the heaven to earth,   250
"Now the king drinks to Hamlet." Come, begin—

(*Trumpets the while.*)

And you, the judges, bear a wary eye.
HAMLET: Come on, sir.
LAERTES: Come, my lord.

(*They play.*)

222 authority   223 unshamed   226 without rancor   230 shine brightly   236 reported better
238 suits   238 the same   242 repay   245 pearl   248 kettledrum

HAMLET: One.
LAERTES: No.
HAMLET: Judgment?
OSRIC: A hit, a very palpable hit.

(Drums, trumpets, and shot. Flourish; a piece goes off.)

LAERTES: Well, again.   255
KING: Stay, give me drink. Hamlet, this pearl is thine.
   Here's to thy health. Give him the cup.
HAMLET: I'll play this bout first; set it by awhile.
   Come.

                                      (They play.)

   Another hit; what say you?   260
LAERTES: I do confess't.
KING: Our son shall win.
QUEEN: He's fat,° and scant of breath.
   Here, Hamlet, take my napkin, rub thy brows.
   The queen carouses to thy fortune, Hamlet.
HAMLET: Good madam!   265
KING: Gertrude, do not drink.
QUEEN: I will, my lord; I pray you pardon me.
KING *(aside):*   It is the poisoned cup; it is too late.
HAMLET: I dare not drink yet, madam; by and by.
QUEEN: Come, let me wipe thy face.   270
LAERTES: My lord, I'll hit him now.
KING: I do not think't.
LAERTES *(aside):*   And yet it is almost against my conscience.
HAMLET: Come, for the third, Laertes. You do but dally.
   I pray you pass° with your best violence;
   I am afeard you make a wanton of me.°   275
LAERTES: Say you so? Come on.

                                      (They play.)

OSRIC: Nothing, neither way.
LAERTES: Have at you now!

   (LAERTES *wounds* HAMLET*: then, in scuffling, they change rapiers, and*
   HAMLET *wounds* LAERTES.*)*

KING: Part them. They are incensed.
HAMLET: Nay, come again.   280

                                  (The QUEEN *falls.)*

262 out of shape   274 attack   275 trifle with me

OSRIC: Look to the queen there, ho!

HORATIO: They bleed on both sides. How is it, my lord?

OSRIC: How is't, Laertes?

LAERTES: Why, as a woodcock to mine own springe,° Osric.
   I am justly killed with mine own treachery.   285

HAMLET: How does the queen?

KING: She swoons to see them bleed.

QUEEN: No, no, the drink, the drink! O my dear Hamlet!
   The drink, the drink! I am poisoned.

                                                                  (Dies.)

HAMLET: O, villainy! Ho! let the door be locked.
   Treachery! seek it out.   290

LAERTES: It is here, Hamlet. Hamlet, thou art slain;
   No med'cine in the world can do thee good.
   In thee there is not half an hour's life.
   The treacherous instrument is in thy hand,
   Unbated° and envenomed. The foul practice   295
   Hath turned itself on me. Lo, here I lie,
   Never to rise again. Thy mother's poisoned.
   I can no more. The king, the king's to blame.

HAMLET: The point envenomed too?
   Then, venom, to thy work.   300

                                        (Hurts the KING.)

ALL: Treason! treason!

KING: O, yet defend me, friends. I am but hurt.°

HAMLET: Here, thou incestuous, murd'rous, damnéd Dane,
   Drink off this potion. Is thy union here?
   Follow my mother.

                                       (The KING dies.)

LAERTES: He is justly served.   305
   It is a poison tempered° by himself.
   Exchange forgiveness with me, noble Hamlet.
   Mine and my father's death come not upon thee,
   Nor thine on me!

                                          (Dies.)

HAMLET: Heaven make thee free of° it! I follow thee.   310
   I am dead, Horatio. Wretched queen, adieu!°
   You that look pale and tremble at this chance,°
   That are but mutes or audience to this act,
   Had I but time, as this fell sergeant Death

284 snare   295 unblunted   302 wounded   306 mixed   310 forgive   312 circumstance

Is strict in his arrest,° O, I could tell you—   315
But let it be. Horatio, I am dead:
Thou livest; report me and my cause aright
To the unsatisfied.°
HORATIO: Never believe it.
I am more an antique Roman than a Dane.
Here's yet some liquor left.
HAMLET: As th'art a man,   320
Give me the cup. Let go. By heaven, I'll ha't.
O God, Horatio, what a wounded name,
Things standing thus unknown, shall live behind me!
If thou didst ever hold me in thy heart,
Absent thee from felicity awhile,   325
And in this harsh world draw thy breath in pain,
To tell my story.

(A march afar off.)

What warlike noise is this?
OSRIC: Young Fortinbras, with conquest come from Poland,
To th' ambassadors of England gives
This warlike volley.°
HAMLET: O, I die, Horatio!   330
The potent poison quite o'er-crows° my spirit.
I cannot live to hear the news from England,
But I do prophesy th' election lights
On Fortinbras. He has my dying voice.°
So tell him, with th' occurrents,° more and less,   335
Which have solicited°—the rest is silence.

(Dies.)

HORATIO: Now cracks a noble heart. Good night, sweet prince,
And flights of angels sing thee to thy rest!

(March within.)

Why does the drum come hither?

(Enter FORTINBRAS, *with the* AMBASSADORS *and with drum, colors,
and* ATTENDANTS.*)*

FORTINBRAS: Where is this sight?
HORATIO: What is it you would see?   340
If aught of woe or wonder, cease your search.

---

315 summons to court   318 uninformed   330 The staging presents some difficulties here. If Osric
is not clairvoyant, he must have left the stage at some point and returned. One possibility is that
he might have left to carry out Hamlet's order to lock the door (line 291) and returned when the
sound of the distant march is heard.   331 overcomes   334 support   335 circumstances
336 brought about this scene

FORTINBRAS: This quarry cries on havoc.° O proud death,
        What feast is toward° in thine eternal cell
        That thou so many princes at a shot
        So bloodily hast struck?
AMBASSADORS: The sight is dismal;   345
        And our affairs from England come too late.
        The ears are senseless° that should give us hearing
        To tell him his commandment is fulfilled,
        That Rosencrantz and Guildenstern are dead.
        Where should we have our thanks?
HORATIO: Not from his mouth,   350
        Had it th' ability of life to thank you.
        He never gave commandment for their death.
        But since, so jump° upon this bloody question,
        You from the Polack wars, and you from England,
        Are here arrived, give orders that these bodies   355
        High on a stage be placéd to the view,
        And let me speak to th' yet unknowing world
        How these things came about. So shall you hear
        Of carnal, bloody, and unnatural acts;
        Of accidental judgments, casual° slaughters;   360
        Of deaths put on by cunning and forced cause;
        And, in this upshot,° purposes mistook
        Fall'n on th' inventors' heads. All this can I
        Truly deliver.
FORTINBRAS: Let us haste to hear it,
        And call the noblest to the audience.°   365
        For me, with sorrow I embrace my fortune.
        I have some rights of memory° in this kingdom,
        Which now to claim my vantage° doth invite me.
HORATIO: Of that I shall have also cause to speak,
        And from his mouth whose voice will draw on more.   370
        But let this same be presently performed,
        Even while men's minds are wild, lest more mischance
        On plots and errors happen.
FORTINBRAS: Let four captains
        Bear Hamlet like a soldier to the stage,
        For he was likely, had he been put on,°   375
        To have proved most royal; and for his passage
        The soldier's music and the rite of war
        Speak loudly for him.

---

342 The game killed in the hunt proclaims a slaughter. 343 in preparation 347 without sense
of hearing 353 exactly 360 brought about by apparent accident 362 result 365 hearing
367 succession 368 position 375 elected king

Take up the bodies. Such a sight as this
Becomes the field, but here shows much amiss.   380
Go, bid the soldiers shoot.

(Exeunt marching. A peal of ordnance shot off.)

Writing Assignments for "Hamlet"

I. Brief Papers: Acts 1 and 2
  A. 1. How does the appearance of the ghost in the opening scene affect your impression of the next scene?
  2. Explain the difference in the way Hamlet speaks in soliloquy about his mother's marriage and the way, a few lines later, he speaks about the marriage to Horatio (Act 1, Scene 2, lines 137–159 and 176–181).
  3. Why is Denmark threatened by Norway and how is this trouble settled?
  4. Why do both Laertes and Polonius warn Ophelia against Hamlet?
  5. Show that most of Hamlet's "mad" speeches, while they confuse the other characters, make sense to the audience.
  6. In Act 2 the King schemes to discover the truth about Hamlet's madness while Hamlet schemes to discover the truth about Claudius' guilt. Explain these plans and what they have in common.
  7. Explain the difference in the way Hamlet talks to Horatio and the way he talks to Rosencrantz and Guildenstern.
  8. Show that by the end of Act 2 Claudius seems to hold a clear advantage in his conflict with Hamlet.

  B. Argue for or against one of these assertions:
  1. Hamlet's grief and bitterness are primarily caused by his mother's marriage, not his father's death.
  2. Polonius is a good father who desires what is best for his children.
  3. Polonius is justified both in having Reynaldo spy on Laertes and in having Ophelia spy on Hamlet.
  4. Rosencrantz and Guildenstern are not disloyal to Hamlet because they believe they are acting in his best interest.
  5. Ophelia is not disloyal to Hamlet because she believes she is acting in his best interest.
  6. If Hamlet had a stronger character, he would find a quick way to kill the King and bring good order to Denmark.

  C. 1. In your opinion, what was Gertrude's relationship with Claudius before her husband's death and what, if anything, does she know about the murder?
  2. How does the fact that Ophelia gives Hamlet's letters to her father affect your feeling about her?
  3. Near the end of Act 2, Hamlet asks himself, "Am I a coward?" Do you think he is a coward?

4. How do you respond to Hamlet's line, "Frailty, thy name is woman" (Act 1, Scene 2, line 146)?

5. Many people think Hamlet should act more quickly to restore order to Denmark. What do you think would be his best plan?

II. Brief Papers: Acts 3 and 4

A. 1. Explain Hamlet's meaning when he tells Guildenstern, "though you can fret me, you cannot play upon me" (Act 3, Scene 2, lines 335–336).

2. Explain how Ophelia and the King differ in interpreting Hamlet's outburst against marriage (Act 3, Scene 1, lines 144–161).

3. Summarize the action of the play that Hamlet presents at court.

4. Explain Hamlet's reasons for not killing the King when he is praying.

5. Why does Fortinbras' attack on Poland cause Hamlet to feel ashamed and to swear, "from this time forth, / My thoughts be bloody, or be nothing worth" (Act 4, Scene 4, lines 65–66)?

6. Contrast the effects of grief on Ophelia and Laertes.

7. Compare Claudius' plot to kill Hamlet in England with his plot to kill Hamlet when he comes home.

8. Discuss the difference between Ophelia's madness and Hamlet's.

B. Argue for or against one of these assertions:

1. Hamlet is a misogynist, a hater of women.

2. Hamlet's attempt to reform his mother ("let me wring your heart") is cruel and neurotic, the outbreak of repressed incestuous desire.

3. Hamlet is deluded in thinking his play is successful; his plan to trap the King fails in almost every way.

4. By the end of Act 3 Hamlet is more or less certain that he will have to kill Rosencrantz and Guildenstern.

5. Rosencrantz and Guildenstern know that Hamlet is to be killed in England.

6. The Queen is essentially accurate when she tells Claudius how Polonius was killed and how Hamlet felt afterwards.

7. Compared to Ophelia, Laertes is essentially successful in controlling his grief over the death of his father.

8. Laertes' rebellion is meant to show the audience how Hamlet should have acted when he first learned that *his* father was murdered.

9. Laertes is justified in plotting with the King to avenge his father's death.

C. 1. How do Hamlet's attacks on Ophelia, his mother, and women in general affect your response to the play?

2. How do you respond to Hamlet's playing hide-and-go-seek with the body of Polonius?

3. How do you respond to Hamlet's statement that "wise men know well enough what monsters you [women] make of them" (Act 3, Scene 1, line 134)?

4. Do you feel that Ophelia's madness is a sign of weakness?
5. How does Claudius' handling of Laertes' rebellion affect your estimate of the King's character?

III. Scenery in "Hamlet"
Combine the following elements into a coherent essay about *scenery* in *Hamlet*.

1. In Shakespeare's theater there were few props.
2. There were no stage lights.
3. There was little scenery.

4. The plays were performed in the afternoon.
5. They were performed in natural light.
6. They were performed without variations.
7. The variations are provided by stage lights.

8. There is a setting for each scene.
9. There are shifts from one scene to the next.
10. These scenes are represented mostly through dialogue.

11. There is an opening scene in *Hamlet*.
12. The scene is played on a bare stage.
13. The scene is played in broad daylight.
14. We know this.
15. It is a cold dark night.
16. The guards carry torches.
17. Francisco complains.
18. "'Tis bitter cold."

19. This happens later.
20. It happens in the same scene.
21. The sunrise is represented.
22. It is not represented by rising pink lights.
23. These lights are used in the modern theater.
24. Sunrise is represented by Horatio.
25. Horatio gives a poetic description.
26. "But look, the morn in russet mantle clad / Walks o'er the dew of yon eastward hill."

27. The castle has interior furnishings.
28. The furnishings are a few tables and chairs.
29. Servants can move the tables and chairs.
30. They can move them on and off the stage.
31. The flow of action is not interrupted.

32. Shakespeare's plays do not need blackouts or curtains.
33. The plays are like modern films.
34. There is this exception.
35. Scenic description is not provided by pictures.
36. Description is provided by words.

37. This happens at the end of Act 1, Scene 3.
38. The scene takes place in Polonius' apartment.
39. Ophelia and her father leave the stage.
40. Hamlet and Horatio walk on stage.
41. They begin Scene 4.

42. We know the setting has changed.
43. Hamlet says, "The air bites shrewdly; it is very cold."
44. This recalls Francisco's words in the first scene.

45. This midnight setting is reinforced.
46. The setting is atop the castle walls.
47. Horatio says, "it lacks of twelve."
48. Marcellus replies, "No, it is struck."

IV. *Brief Papers: Act 5*
   A. 1. Show how the graveyard scene makes fun of the belief that some people are better than others and so deserve better treatment.
      2. Describe Hamlet's feelings as he studies the skull of Yorick.
      3. What events on his voyage teach Hamlet that "There's a divinity that shapes our ends, / Rough-hew them how we will" (Scene 2, lines 10–11)?
      4. How does Hamlet arrange the death of Rosencrantz and Guildenstern?
      5. What does the "fall of a sparrow" have to do with Hamlet's agreeing to duel with Laertes (Scene 2, lines 193–197)?
      6. What goes wrong with the King's plan to murder Hamlet during the duel?

   B. Argue for or against one of these assertions:
      1. Rosencrantz and Guildenstern deserve exactly what they get.
      2. Hamlet leaps into Ophelia's grave not because he is deeply moved but because he is still pretending to be mad.
      3. Laertes' sudden confession and change of heart is improbable and sentimental; it would be better for the play if, like the King, he died unrepentent.
      4. It is impossible to agree with Fortinbras that Hamlet would have made a good king.

   C. 1. Do you agree with Hamlet's claim that he can now kill the King "in perfect conscience" (Scene 2, lines 67–68)?
      2. When the Queen dies, does Hamlet think that she will go to Heaven or does he think that, like the King, she too is damned?

3. Do you feel a sense of triumph or loss when you learn that Fortinbras will probably become King of Denmark?
4. When Horatio tells Hamlet's story, what do you think he will say about Hamlet's character?

V. Soliloquies in "Hamlet"

Combine the following elements into a coherent essay about the *soliloquies* in Hamlet.

1. The literal meaning of soliloquy is "to speak alone."
2. Soliloquy also means to speak to oneself.

3. In Shakespeare's theater the soliloquy is a stage convention.
4. The soliloquy enables characters to reveal their thoughts.
5. The audience needs to know these thoughts.
6. The audience could not discover these thoughts in other ways.

7. This happens in Act 3, Scene 2.
8. The King makes an abrupt departure.
9. He departs from the play-within-a-play.
10. This departure is not conclusive proof.
11. The departure does not prove the King's guilt.

12. Perhaps the King did not like the play.
13. Perhaps he suddenly became ill.
14. This is what the court seems to think.

15. In the next scene we are sure.
16. The King is really guilty.
17. The King confesses in a soliloquy.

18. Hamlet enters.
19. Hamlet sees his chance to kill the King.
20. Hamlet hesitates.
21. Hamlet reveals his inner conflict in a soliloquy.

22. Hamlet wants to kill Claudius.
23. Hamlet wants to send him to Hell.
24. He does not want to send him to Heaven.
25. Hamlet decides to wait.
26. He will catch the King in an evil act.
27. He will kill him then.

28. Hamlet leaves.
29. The King speaks again.

30. He speaks in a soliloquy.
31. He says his prayers are useless.
32. He says he cannot truly repent.

33. This is an unexpected disclosure.
34. The disclosure adds an ironic twist.
35. The irony is Hamlet's decision not to kill the King.

36. This concludes a famous episode in dramatic literature.
37. The episode would not be possible without soliloquies.

VI. Longer Papers

A. For all its philosophical and psychological complexity, *Hamlet* is essentially a thriller—a revenge plot in which an act of violence sets off a chain of plots and counterplots leading to a violent and exciting resolution. Discuss this chain of plots, showing how one causes the next.

B. Discuss *Hamlet,* not as simply a revenge play, but as an examination of the value of revenge. Does the play simply justify the idea of revenge, or does it distinguish between good and bad forms of revenge, or does it show that revenge is always the wrong way to restore social order.

C. Some say that Hamlet's hesitations are signs of weakness—a disease of the will—and that he could have (and should have) acted sooner. Others say that Hamlet is essentially justified in his doubts and delays. Which view do you favor?

D. The story of Hamlet's relationship with Ophelia is sketchy and uncertain. Did Hamlet really love and intend to marry Ophelia? Were they lovers? Why does Hamlet turn against her? Is Ophelia to blame for helping Polonius spy on Hamlet? Is Hamlet to blame for Ophelia's madness and death? Considering these and other questions raised in the play, how do you interpret this unhappy love affair?

E. Referring to the way he arranged the deaths of Rosencrantz and Guildenstern, Hamlet says:

> They are not near my conscience; their defeat
> Does by their own insinuation grow.
> 'Tis dangerous when the baser nature comes
> Between the pass and fell incenséd points
> Of mighty opposites.
> (Act 5, Scene 2, lines 58–62)

Hamlet means that Rosencrantz and Guildenstern deserve death because they sided with the King, Hamlet's "mighty opposite." To what extent do you agree with Hamlet's reasoning, not simply as it applies to Rosencrantz and Guildenstern but also to Polonius, Ophelia, Laertes, and the Queen? Should Hamlet be held morally responsible for any of these deaths?

F. What do you think will be Horatio's version of Hamlet's story and to what extent do you think it will agree with your version?

HENRIK IBSEN
Hedda Gabler

Before Reading

Free write for 5 or 10 minutes on one of the following topics:

1. In the late nineteenth century it was widely believed and expected that women should find the major source of their happiness and self-fulfillment in the roles of wife and mother. To what extent do you think this is still true today and to what extent do you think women should resist or reject these rôles?
2. According to many nineteenth-century dramatists the major cause of human suffering was not poverty, cruelty, or downright injustice but the boredom and repression imposed by conventional morality and social custom. To what extent do you think students are trapped in boring situations and obligations?

CHARACTERS

George Tesman

Hedda Tesman, his wife

Miss Juliana Tesman, his aunt

Mrs. Elvsted

Judge Brack

Eilert Lövborg

Berta, servant at the Tesmans

SCENE *The scene of the action is Tesman's house.*

ACT I

A spacious, handsome, and tastefully furnished drawing-room, decorated in dark colours. In the back, a wide doorway with curtains drawn back, leading into a smaller room decorated in the same style as the drawing-room. In the right-hand wall of the front room, a folding door leading out to the hall. In the opposite wall, on the left, a glass door, also with curtains drawn back. Through the panes can be seen part of a verandah outside, and trees covered with autumn foliage. An oval table, with a cover on it, and surrounded by chairs, stands well forward. In front, by the wall on the right, a wide stove of dark porcelain, a high-backed arm-chair, a cushioned foot-rest, and two footstools. A settee, with a small round table in front of it, fills the upper right-hand corner. In front, on the left, a little way from the wall, a sofa. Further back than the glass door, a piano. On either side of the doorway at the back a whatnot with terra-cotta and majolica ornaments.—Against the back wall of the inner room a sofa, with a table, and one or two chairs. Over the sofa hangs the portrait of a handsome elderly man in a General's uniform. Over the table a hanging lamp, with an opal glass shade.—A number of bouquets are

HEDDA GABLER by Henrik Ibsen (1828–1906) was published in 1890. Ibsen, a Norwegian playwright, was a powerful influence in modern theater. His other well-known plays in the realistic manner include *The Wild Duck, An Enemy of the People, A Doll's House,* and *Ghosts.*

arranged about the drawing-room, in vases and glasses. Others lie upon the tables. The floors in both rooms are covered with thick carpets.—Morning light. The sun shines in through the glass door.

     MISS JULIANA TESMAN, *with her bonnet on and carrying a parasol, comes in from the hall, followed by* BERTA, *who carries a bouquet wrapped in paper.* MISS TESMAN *is a comely and pleasant-looking lady of about sixty-five. She is nicely but simply dressed in a grey walking-costume.* BERTA *is a middle-aged woman of plain and rather countrified appearance.*

MISS TESMAN *(stops close to the door, listens, and says softly):* Upon my word, I don't believe they are stirring yet!

BERTA *(also softly):* I told you so, Miss. Remember how late the steamboat got in last night. And then, when they got home!—good Lord, what a lot the young mistress had to unpack before she could get to bed.

MISS TESMAN: Well, well—let them have their sleep out. But let us see that they get a good breath of the fresh morning air when they do appear. *(She goes to the glass door and throws it open.)*

BERTA *(beside the table, at a loss what to do with the bouquet in her hand):* I declare there isn't a bit of room left. I think I'll put it down here, Miss. *(She places it on the piano.)*

MISS TESMAN: So you've got a new mistress now, my dear Berta. Heaven knows it was a wrench to me to part with you.

BERTA *(on the point of weeping):* And do you think it wasn't hard for me too, Miss? After all the blessed years I've been with you and Miss Rina.

MISS TESMAN: We must make the best of it, Berta. There was nothing else to be done. George can't do without you, you see—he absolutely can't. He has had you to look after him ever since he was a little boy.

BERTA: Ah but, Miss Julia, I can't help thinking of Miss Rina lying helpless at home there, poor thing. And with only that new girl too! She'll never learn to take proper care of an invalid.

MISS TESMAN: Oh, I shall manage to train her. And of course, you know, I shall take most of it upon myself. You needn't be uneasy about my poor sister, my dear Berta.

BERTA: Well, but there's another thing, Miss. I'm so mortally afraid I shan't be able to suit the young mistress.

MISS TESMAN: Oh well—just at first there may be one or two things—

BERTA: Most like she'll be terrible grand in her ways.

MISS TESMAN: Well, you can't wonder at that—General Gabler's daughter! Think of the sort of life she was accustomed to in her father's time. Don't you remember how we used to see her riding down the road along with the General? In that long black habit—and with feathers in her hat?

BERTA: Yes, indeed—I remember well enough—! But good Lord, I should never have dreamt in those days that she and Master George would make a match of it.

MISS TESMAN: Nor I.—But, by-the-bye, Berta—while I think of it: in future you mustn't say Master George. You must say Dr. Tesman.

BERTA: Yes, the young mistress spoke of that too—last night—the moment they set foot in the house. Is it true then, Miss?

MISS TESMAN: Yes, indeed it is. Only think, Berta—some foreign university has made him a doctor—while he has been abroad, you understand. I hadn't heard a word about it, until he told me himself upon the pier.

BERTA: Well, well, he's clever enough for anything, he is. But I didn't think he'd have gone in for doctoring people too.

MISS TESMAN: No, no, it's not that sort of doctor he is. *(Nods significantly.)* But let me tell you, we may have to call him something still grander before long.

BERTA: You don't say so! What can that be, Miss?

MISS TESMAN *(smiling):* H'm—wouldn't you like to know! *(With emotion.)* Ah, dear, dear—if my poor brother could only look up from his grave now, and see what his little boy has grown into! *(Looks around.)* But bless me, Berta—why have you done this? Taken the chintz covers off all the furniture?

BERTA: The mistress told me to. She can't abide covers on the chairs, she says.

MISS TESMAN: Are they going to make this their everyday sitting-room then?

BERTA: Yes, that's what I understood—from the mistress. Master George—the doctor—he said nothing.

(GEORGE TESMAN comes from the right into the inner room, humming to himself, and carrying an unstrapped empty portmanteau. He is a middle-sized, young-looking man of thirty-three, rather stout, with a round, open, cheerful face, fair hair and beard. He wears spectacles, and is somewhat carelessly dressed in comfortable indoor clothes.)

MISS TESMAN: Good morning, good morning, George.

TESMAN *(in the doorway between the rooms):* Aunt Julia! Dear Aunt Julia! *(Goes up to her and shakes hands warmly.)* Come all this way—so early! Eh?

MISS TESMAN: Why, of course I had to come and see how you were getting on.

TESMAN: In spite of your having had no proper night's rest?

MISS TESMAN: Oh, that makes no difference to me.

TESMAN: Well, I suppose you got home all right from the pier? Eh?

MISS TESMAN: Yes, quite safely, thank goodness. Judge Brack was good enough to see me right to my door.

TESMAN: We were so sorry we couldn't give you a seat in the carriage. But you saw what a pile of boxes Hedda had to bring with her.

MISS TESMAN: Yes, she had certainly plenty of boxes.

BERTA *(to Tesman):* Shall I go in and see if there's anything I can do for the mistress?

TESMAN: No, thank you, Berta—you needn't. She said she would ring if she wanted anything.

BERTA *(going towards the right):* Very well.

TESMAN: But look here—take this portmanteau with you.

BERTA *(taking it):* I'll put it in the attic. *(She goes out by the hall door.)*

TESMAN: Fancy, Auntie—I had the whole of that portmanteau chock full of copies of documents. You wouldn't believe how much I have picked up from all the archives I have been examining—curious old details that no one has had any idea of——

MISS TESMAN: Yes, you don't seem to have wasted your time on your wedding trip, George.

TESMAN: No, that I haven't. But do take off your bonnet, Auntie. Look here! Let me untie the strings—eh?

MISS TESMAN (*while he does so*):   Well, well—this is just as if you were still at home with us.

TESMAN (*with the bonnet in his hand, looks at it from all sides*):   Why, what a gorgeous bonnet you've been investing in!

MISS TESMAN: I bought it on Hedda's account.

TESMAN: On Hedda's account? Eh?

MISS TESMAN: Yes, so that Hedda needn't be ashamed of me if we happened to go out together.

TESMAN (*patting her cheek*):   You always think of everything, Aunt Julia. (*Lays the bonnet on a chair beside the table.*) And now, look here—suppose we sit comfortably on the sofa and have a little chat, till Hedda comes. (*They seat themselves. She places her parasol in the corner of the sofa.*)

MISS TESMAN (*takes both his hands and looks at him*):   What a delight it is to have you again, as large as life, before my very eyes, George! My George—my poor brother's own boy!

TESMAN: And it's a delight for me, too, to see you again, Aunt Julia! You, who have been father and mother in one to me.

MISS TESMAN: Oh, yes, I know you will always keep a place in your heart for your old aunts.

TESMAN: And what about Aunt Rina? No improvement—eh?

MISS TESMAN: Oh, no—we can scarcely look for any improvement in her case, poor thing. There she lies, helpless, as she has lain for all these years. But heaven grant I may not lose her yet awhile! For if I did, I don't know what I should make of my life, George—especially now that I haven't you to look after any more.

TESMAN (*patting her back*):   There, there, there——!

MISS TESMAN (*suddenly changing her tone*):   And to think that here are you a married man, George!—And that you should be the one to carry off Hedda Gabler—the beautiful Hedda Gabler! Only think of it—she, that was so beset with admirers!

TESMAN (*hums a little and smiles complacently*):   Yes, I fancy I have several good friends about town who would like to stand in my shoes—eh?

MISS TESMAN: And then this fine long wedding-tour you have had! More than five—nearly six months—

TESMAN: Well, for me it has been a sort of tour of research as well. I have had to do so much grubbing among old records—and to read no end of books too, Auntie.

MISS TESMAN: Oh, yes, I suppose so. *(More confidentially, and lowering her voice a little.)* But listen now, George—have you nothing—nothing special to tell me?

TESMAN: As to our journey?

MISS TESMAN: Yes.

TESMAN: No, I don't know of anything except what I have told you in my letters. I had a doctor's degree conferred on me—but that I told you yesterday.

MISS TESMAN: Yes, yes, you did. But what I mean is—haven't you any—any—expectations——?

TESMAN: Expectations?

MISS TESMAN: Why, you know, George—I'm your old auntie!

TESMAN: Why, of course I have expectations.

MISS TESMAN: Ah!

TESMAN: I have every expectation of being a professor one of these days.

MISS TESMAN: Oh, yes, a professor——

TESMAN: Indeed, I may say I am certain of it. But my dear Auntie—you know all about that already!

MISS TESMAN *(laughing to herself):*   Yes, of course I do. You are quite right there. *(Changing the subject.)* But we were talking about your journey. It must have cost a great deal of money, George?

TESMAN: Well, you see—my handsome travelling-scholarship went a good way.

MISS TESMAN: But I can't understand how you can have made it go far enough for two.

TESMAN: No, that's not so easy to understand—eh?

MISS TESMAN: And especially travelling with a lady—they tell me that makes it ever so much more expensive.

TESMAN: Yes, of course—it makes it a little more expensive. But Hedda had to have this trip, Auntie! She really had to. Nothing else would have done.

MISS TESMAN: No, no, I suppose not. A wedding-tour seems to be quite indispensable nowadays.—But tell me now—have you gone thoroughly over the house yet?

TESMAN: Yes, you may be sure I have. I have been afoot ever since daylight.

MISS TESMAN: And what do you think of it all?

TESMAN: I'm delighted! Quite delighted! Only I can't think what we are to do with the two empty rooms between this inner parlour and Hedda's bedroom.

MISS TESMAN *(laughing):*   Oh, my dear George, I daresay you may find some use for them—in the course of time.

TESMAN: Why of course you are quite right, Aunt Julia! You mean as my library increases—eh?

MISS TESMAN: Yes, quite so, my dear boy. It was your library I was thinking of.

TESMAN: I am specially pleased on Hedda's account. Often and often, before we were engaged, she said that she would never care to live anywhere but in Secretary Falk's villa.

MISS TESMAN: Yes, it was lucky that this very house should come into the market, just after you had started.

TESMAN: Yes, Aunt Julia, the luck was on our side, wasn't it—eh?

MISS TESMAN: But the expense, my dear George! You will find it very expensive, all this.

TESMAN *(looks at her, a little cast down):*   Yes, I suppose I shall, Aunt!

MISS TESMAN: Oh, frightfully!

TESMAN: How much do you think? In round numbers?—Eh?

MISS TESMAN: Oh, I can't even guess until all the accounts come in.

TESMAN: Well, fortunately, Judge Brack has secured the most favourable terms for me,—so he said in a letter to Hedda.

MISS TESMAN: Yes, don't be uneasy, my dear boy.—Besides, I have given security for the furniture and all the carpets.

TESMAN: Security? You? My dear Aunt Julia—what sort of security could you give?

MISS TESMAN: I have given a mortgage on our annuity.

TESMAN *(jumps up):*   What! On your—and Aunt Rina's annuity!

MISS TESMAN: Yes, I knew of no other plan, you see.

TESMAN *(placing himself before her):*   Have you gone out of your senses, Auntie! Your annuity—it's all that you and Aunt Rina have to live upon.

MISS TESMAN: Well, well, don't get so excited about it. It's only a matter of form you know—Judge Brack assured me of that. It was he that was kind enough to arrange the whole affair for me. A mere matter of form, he said.

TESMAN: Yes, that may be all very well. But nevertheless——

MISS TESMAN: You will have your own salary to depend upon now. And, good heavens, even if we did have to pay up a little——! To eke things out a bit at the start——! Why, it would be nothing but a pleasure to us.

TESMAN: Oh, Auntie—will you never be tired of making sacrifices for me!

MISS TESMAN *(rises and lays her hands on his shoulders):*   Have I any other happiness in this world except to smooth your way for you, my dear boy? You, who have had neither father nor mother to depend on. And now we have reached the goal, George! Things have looked black enough for us, sometimes; but, thank heaven, now you have nothing to fear.

TESMAN: Yes, it is really marvellous how everything has turned out for the best.

MISS TESMAN: And the people who opposed you—who wanted to bar the way for you—now you have them at your feet. They have fallen, George. Your most dangerous rival—his fall was the worst.—And now he has to lie on the bed he has made for himself—poor misguided creature.

TESMAN: Have you heard anything of Eilert? Since I went away, I mean.

MISS TESMAN: Only that he is said to have published a new book.

TESMAN: What! Eilert Lövborg! Recently—eh?

MISS TESMAN: Yes, so they say. Heaven knows whether it can be worth anything! Ah, when your new book appears—that will be another story, George! What is it to be about?

TESMAN: It will deal with the domestic industries of Brabant* during the Middle Ages.

MISS TESMAN: Fancy—to be able to write on such a subject as that!

TESMAN: However, it may be some time before the book is ready. I have all these collections to arrange first, you see.

MISS TESMAN: Yes, collecting and arranging—no one can beat you at that. There you are my poor brother's own son.

TESMAN: I am looking forward eagerly to setting to work at it; especially now that I have my own delightful home to work in.

MISS TESMAN: And, most of all, now that you have got the wife of your heart, my dear George.

TESMAN *(embracing her):*   Oh, yes, yes, Aunt Julia. Hedda—she is the best part of it all! *(Looks towards the doorway.)* I believe I hear her coming—eh?

(HEDDA *enters from the left through the inner room. She is a woman of nine-and-twenty. Her face and figure show refinement and distinction. Her complexion is pale and opaque. Her steel-grey eyes express a cold, unruffled repose. Her hair is of an agreeable medium brown, but not particularly abundant. She is dressed in a tasteful, somewhat loose-fitting morning gown.)*

MISS TESMAN *(going to meet* HEDDA*):*   Good morning, my dear Hedda! Good morning, and a hearty welcome.

HEDDA *(holds out her hand):*   Good morning, dear Miss Tesman! So early a call! That is kind of you.

MISS TESMAN *(with some embarrassment):*   Well—has the bride slept well in her new home?

HEDDA: Oh yes, thanks. Passably.

TESMAN *(laughing):*   Passably! Come, that's good, Hedda! You were sleeping like a stone when I got up.

HEDDA: Fortunately. Of course one has always to accustom one's self to new surroundings, Miss Tesman—little by little. *(Looking towards the left.)* Oh—there the servant has gone and opened the verandah door, and let in a whole flood of sunshine.

MISS TESMAN *(going towards the door):*   Well, then, we will shut it.

HEDDA: No, no, not that! Tesman, please draw the curtains. That will give a softer light.

TESMAN *(at the door):*   All right—all right. There now, Hedda, now you have both shade and fresh air.

HEDDA: Yes, fresh air we certainly must have, with all these stacks of flow-ers——But—won't you sit down, Miss Tesman?

*Brabant: A duchy of Burgundy from 1190 to 1430, now a province in Belgium.

MISS TESMAN: No, thank you. Now that I have seen that everything is all right here—thank heaven!—I must be getting home again. My sister is lying longing for me, poor thing.

TESMAN: Give her my very best love, Auntie; and say I shall look in and see her later in the day.

MISS TESMAN: Yes, yes, I'll be sure to tell her. But by-the-bye, George— *(feeling in her dress pocket)*—I had almost forgotten—I have something for you here.

TESMAN: What is it, Auntie? Eh?

MISS TESMAN *(produces a flat parcel wrapped in newspaper and hands it to him)*: Look here, my dear boy.

TESMAN *(opening the parcel)*: Well, I declare!—Have you really saved them for me, Aunt Julia! Hedda! isn't this touching—eh?

HEDDA *(beside the whatnot on the right)*: Well, what is it?

TESMAN: My old morning-shoes! My slippers.

HEDDA: Indeed. I remember you often spoke of them while we were abroad.

TESMAN: Yes, I missed them terribly. *(Goes up to her.)* Now you shall see them, Hedda!

HEDDA *(going towards the stove)*: Thanks, I really don't care about it.

TESMAN *(following her)*: Only think—ill as she was, Aunt Rina embroidered these for me. Oh you can't think how many associations cling to them.

HEDDA *(at the table)*: Scarcely for me.

MISS TESMAN: Of course not for Hedda, George.

TESMAN: Well, but now that she belongs to the family, I thought——

HEDDA *(interrupting)*: We shall never get on with this servant, Tesman.

MISS TESMAN: Not get on with Berta?

TESMAN: Why, dear, what puts that in your head? Eh?

HEDDA *(pointing)*: Look there! She has left her old bonnet lying about on a chair.

TESMAN *(in consternation, drops the slippers on the floor)*: Why, Hedda—

HEDDA: Just fancy, if any one should come in and see it!

TESMAN: But Hedda—that's Aunt Julia's bonnet.

HEDDA: Is it!

MISS TESMAN *(taking up the bonnet)*: Yes, indeed it's mine. And, what's more, it's not old, Madam Hedda.

HEDDA: I really did not look closely at it, Miss Tesman.

MISS TESMAN *(trying on the bonnet)*: Let me tell you it's the first time I have worn it—the very first time.

TESMAN: And a very nice bonnet it is too—quite a beauty!

MISS TESMAN: Oh, it's no such great things, George. *(Looks around her.)* My parasol——? Ah, here. *(Takes it.)* For this is mine too—*(mutters)*—not Berta's.

TESMAN: A new bonnet and a new parasol! Only think, Hedda!

HEDDA: Very handsome indeed.

TESMAN: Yes, isn't it? Eh? But Auntie, take a good look at Hedda before you go! See how handsome she is!

MISS TESMAN: Oh, my dear boy, there's nothing new in that. Hedda was always lovely. *(She nods and goes towards the right.)*

TESMAN *(following):* Yes, but have you noticed what splendid condition she is in? How she has filled out on the journey?

HEDDA *(crossing the room):* Oh, do be quiet—!

MISS TESMAN *(who has stopped and turned):* Filled out?

TESMAN: Of course you don't notice it so much now that she has that dress on. But I, who can see—

HEDDA *(at the glass door, impatiently):* Oh, you can't see anything.

TESMAN: It must be the mountain air in the Tyrol—

HEDDA *(curtly, interrupting):* I am exactly as I was when I started.

TESMAN: So you insist; but I'm quite certain you are not. Don't you agree with me, Auntie?

MISS TESMAN *(who has been gazing at her with folded hands):* Hedda is lovely—lovely—lovely. *(Goes up to her, takes her head between both hands, draws it downwards, and kisses her hair.)* God bless and preserve Hedda Tesman—for George's sake.

HEDDA *(gently freeing herself):* Oh—! Let me go.

MISS TESMAN *(in quiet emotion):* I shall not let a day pass without coming to see you.

TESMAN: No you won't, will you, Auntie? Eh?

MISS TESMAN: Good-bye—good-bye!

(She goes out by the hall door. TESMAN accompanies her. The door remains half open. TESMAN can be heard repeating his message to Aunt Rina and his thanks for the slippers.)

(In the meantime, HEDDA walks about the room, raising her arms and clenching her hands as if in desperation. Then she flings back the curtains from the glass door, and stands there looking out.)

(Presently TESMAN returns and closes the door behind him.)

TESMAN *(picks up the slippers from the floor):* What are you looking at, Hedda?

HEDDA *(once more calm and mistress of herself):* I am only looking at the leaves. They are so yellow—so withered.

TESMAN *(wraps up the slippers and lays them on the table):* Well you see, we are well into September now.

HEDDA *(again restless):* Yes, to think of it!—Already in—in September.

TESMAN: Don't you think Aunt Julia's manner was strange, dear? Almost solemn? Can you imagine what was the matter with her? Eh?

HEDDA: I scarcely know her, you see. Is she not often like that?

TESMAN: No, not as she was today.

HEDDA *(leaving the glass door):* Do you think she was annoyed about the bonnet?

TESMAN: Oh, scarcely at all. Perhaps a little, just at the moment—

HEDDA: But what an idea, to pitch her bonnet about in the drawing-room! No one does that sort of thing.

TESMAN: Well you may be sure Aunt Julia won't do it again.

HEDDA: In any case, I shall manage to make my peace with her.

TESMAN: Yes, my dear, good Hedda, if you only would.

HEDDA: When you call this afternoon, you might invite her to spend the evening here.

TESMAN: Yes, that I will. And there's one thing more you could do that would delight her heart.

HEDDA: What is it?

TESMAN: If you could only prevail on yourself to say *du* * to her. For my sake, Hedda? Eh?

HEDDA: No, no, Tesman—you really mustn't ask that of me. I have told you so already. I shall try to call her "Aunt"; and you must be satisfied with that.

TESMAN: Well, well. Only I think now that you belong to the family, you—

HEDDA: H'm—I can't in the least see why—

(She goes up towards the middle doorway.)

TESMAN *(after a pause):*   Is there anything the matter with you, Hedda? Eh?

HEDDA: I'm only looking at my old piano. It doesn't go at all well with all the other things.

TESMAN: The first time I draw my salary, we'll see about exchanging it.

HEDDA: No, no—no exchanging. I don't want to part with it. Suppose we put it there in the inner room, and then get another here in its place. When it's convenient, I mean.

TESMAN *(a little taken aback):*   Yes—of course we could do that.

HEDDA *(takes up the bouquet from the piano):*   These flowers were not here last night when we arrived.

TESMAN: Aunt Julia must have brought them for you.

HEDDA *(examining the bouquet):*   A visiting-card. *(Takes it out and reads:)* "Shall return later in the day." Can you guess whose card it is?

TESMAN: No. Whose? Eh?

HEDDA: The name is "Mrs. Elvsted."

TESMAN: Is it really? Sheriff Elvsted's wife? Miss Rysing that was.

HEDDA: Exactly. The girl with the irritating hair, that she was always showing off. An old flame of yours I've been told.

TESMAN *(laughing):*   Oh, that didn't last long; and it was before I knew you, Hedda. But fancy her being in town!

HEDDA: It's odd that she should call upon us. I have scarcely seen her since we left school.

TESMAN: I haven't seen her either for—heaven knows how long. I wonder how she can endure to live in such an out-of-the-way hole—eh?

HEDDA *(after a moment's thought says suddenly):*   Tell me, Tesman—isn't it somewhere near there that he—that—Eilert Lövborg is living?

TESMAN: Yes, he is somewhere in that part of the country.

*du: Thou, a more friendly form of address.

(BERTA *enters by the hall door.*)

BERTA: That lady, ma'am, that brought some flowers a little while ago, is here
again. *(Pointing.)* The flowers you have in your hand, ma'am.

HEDDA: Ah, is she? Well, please show her in.

(BERTA *opens the door for* MRS. ELVSTED, *and goes out herself.—*MRS.
ELVSTED *is a woman of fragile figure, with pretty, soft features. Her eyes are light
blue, large, round, and somewhat prominent, with a startled, inquiring expression.
Her hair is remarkably light, almost flaxen, and unusually abundant and wavy.
She is a couple of years younger than* HEDDA. *She wears a dark visiting dress,
tasteful, but not quite in the latest fashion.*)

HEDDA *(receives her warmly):*   How do you do, my dear Mrs. Elvsted? It's
delightful to see you again.

MRS. ELVSTED *(nervously, struggling for self-control):*   Yes, it's a very long time
since we met.

TESMAN *(gives her his hand):*   And we too—eh?

HEDDA: Thanks for your lovely flowers—

MRS. ELVSTED: Oh, not at all—I would have come straight here yesterday
afternoon; but I heard that you were away—

TESMAN: Have you just come to town? Eh?

MRS. ELVSTED: I arrived yesterday, about midday. Oh, I was quite in despair
when I heard that you were not at home.

HEDDA: In despair! How so?

TESMAN: Why, my dear Mrs. Rysing—I mean Mrs. Elvsted—

HEDDA: I hope that you are not in any trouble?

MRS. ELVSTED: Yes, I am. And I don't know another living creature here that
I can turn to.

HEDDA *(laying the bouquet on the table):*   Come—let us sit here on the sofa—

MRS. ELVSTED: Oh, I am too restless to sit down.

HEDDA: Oh no, you're not. Come here. *(She draws* MRS. ELVSTED *down upon
the sofa and sits at her side.)*

TESMAN: Well? What is it, Mrs. Elvsted?

HEDDA: Has anything particular happened to you at home?

MRS. ELVSTED: Yes—and no. Oh—I am so anxious you should not misunderstand me—

HEDDA: Then your best plan is to tell us the whole story, Mrs. Elvsted.

TESMAN: I suppose that's what you have come for—eh?

MRS. ELVSTED: Yes, yes—of course it is. Well then, I must tell you—if you
don't already know—that Eilert Lövborg is in town, too.

HEDDA: Lövborg—!

TESMAN: What! Has Eilert Lövborg come back? Fancy that, Hedda!

HEDDA: Well, well—I hear it.

MRS. ELVSTED: He has been here a week already. Just fancy—a whole week!
In this terrible town, alone! With so many temptations on all sides.

HEDDA: But my dear Mrs. Elvsted—how does he concern you so much?

MRS. ELVSTED: *(Looks at her with a startled air, and says rapidly.)* He was the children's tutor.

HEDDA: Your children's?

MRS. ELVSTED: My husband's. I have none.

HEDDA: Your step-children's, then?

MRS. ELVSTED: Yes.

TESMAN *(somewhat hesitatingly):* Then was he—I don't know how to express it—was he—regular enough in his habits to be fit for the post? Eh?

MRS. ELVSTED: For the last two years his conduct has been irreproachable.

TESMAN: Has it indeed? Fancy that, Hedda!

HEDDA: I hear it.

MRS. ELVSTED: Perfectly irreproachable, I assure you! In every respect. But all the same—now that I know he is here—in this great town—and with a large sum of money in his hands—I can't help being in mortal fear for him.

TESMAN: Why did he not remain where he was? With you and your husband? Eh?

MRS. ELVSTED: After his book was published he was too restless and unsettled to remain with us.

TESMAN: Yes, by-the-bye, Aunt Julia told me he had published a new book.

MRS. ELVSTED: Yes, a big book, dealing with the march of civilisation—in broad outline, as it were. It came out about a fortnight ago. And since it has sold so well, and been so much read—and made such a sensation——

TESMAN: Has it indeed? It must be something he has had lying by since his better days.

MRS. ELVSTED: Long ago, you mean?

TESMAN: Yes.

MRS. ELVSTED: No, he has written it all since he has been with us—within the last year.

TESMAN: Isn't that good news, Hedda? Think of that.

MRS. ELVSTED: Ah, yes, if only it would last!

HEDDA: Have you seen him here in town?

MRS. ELVSTED: No, not yet. I have had the greatest difficulty in finding out his address. But this morning I discovered it at last.

HEDDA *(looks searchingly at her):* Do you know, it seems to me a little odd of your husband—h'm——

MRS. ELVSTED *(starting nervously):* Of my husband! What?

HEDDA: That he should send you to town on such an errand—that he does not come himself and look after his friend.

MRS. ELVSTED: Oh no, no—my husband has no time. And besides, I—I had some shopping to do.

HEDDA *(with a slight smile):* Ah, that is a different matter.

MRS. ELVSTED *(rising quickly and uneasily):* And now I beg and implore you, Mr. Tesman—receive Eilert Lövborg kindly if he comes to you! And that he is sure to do. You see you were such great friends in the old days. And then you are interested in the same studies—the same branch of science—so far as I can understand.

TESMAN: We used to be, at any rate.

MRS. ELVSTED: That is why I beg so earnestly that you—you too—will keep a sharp eye upon him. Oh, you will promise me that, Mr. Tesman—won't you?

TESMAN: With the greatest of pleasure, Mrs. Rysing——

HEDDA: Elvsted.

TESMAN: I assure you I shall do all I possibly can for Eilert. You may rely upon me.

MRS. ELVSTED: Oh, how very, very kind of you! *(Presses his hands.)* Thanks, thanks, thanks! *(Frightened.)* You see, my husband is so very fond of him!

HEDDA *(rising):* You ought to write to him, Tesman. Perhaps he may not care to come to you of his own accord.

TESMAN: Well, perhaps it would be the right thing to do, Hedda? Eh?

HEDDA: And the sooner the better. Why not at once?

MRS. ELVSTED *(imploringly):* Oh, if you only would!

TESMAN: I'll write this moment. Have you his address, Mrs.—Mrs. Elvsted.

MRS. ELVSTED: Yes. *(Takes a slip of paper from her pocket, and hands it to him.)* Here it is.

TESMAN: Good, good. Then I'll go in—— *(Looks about him.)* By-the-bye,—my slippers? Oh, here. *(Takes the packet, and is about to go.)*

HEDDA: Be sure you write him a cordial, friendly letter. And a good long one too.

TESMAN: Yes, I will.

MRS. ELVSTED: But please, please don't say a word to show that I have suggested it.

TESMAN: No, how could you think I would? Eh? *(He goes out to the right, through the inner room.)*

HEDDA *(goes up to MRS. ELVSTED, smiles, and says in a low voice):* There! We have killed two birds with one stone.

MRS. ELVSTED: What do you mean?

HEDDA: Could you not see that I wanted him to go?

MRS. ELVSTED: Yes, to write the letter——

HEDDA: And that I might speak to you alone.

MRS. ELVSTED *(confused):* About the same thing?

HEDDA: Precisely.

MRS. ELVSTED *(apprehensively):* But there is nothing more, Mrs. Tesman! Absolutely nothing!

HEDDA: Oh, yes, but there is. There is a great deal more—I can see that. Sit here—and we'll have a cosy, confidential chat. *(She forces MRS. ELVSTED to sit in the easy-chair beside the stove, and seats herself on one of the footstools.)*

MRS. ELVSTED *(anxiously, looking at her watch):* But, my dear Mrs. Tesman—I was really on the point of going.

HEDDA: Oh, you can't be in such a hurry.—Well? Now tell me something about your life at home.

MRS. ELVSTED: Oh, that is just what I care least to speak about.

HEDDA: But to me, dear——? Why, weren't we school-fellows?

MRS. ELVSTED: Yes, but you were in the class above me. Oh, how dreadfully afraid of you I was then!

HEDDA: Afraid of me?

MRS. ELVSTED: Yes, dreadfully. For when we met on the stairs you used always to pull my hair.

HEDDA: Did I, really?

MRS. ELVSTED: Yes, and once you said you would burn it off my head.

HEDDA: Oh, that was all nonsense, of course.

MRS. ELVSTED: Yes, but I was so silly in those days.—And since then, too—we have drifted so far—far apart from each other. Our circles have been so entirely different.

HEDDA: Well then, we must try to drift together again. Now listen! At school we said *du* to each other; and we called each other by our Christian names—

MRS. ELVSTED: No, I am sure you must be mistaken.

HEDDA: No, not at all! I can remember quite distinctly. So now we are going to renew our old friendship *(Draws the footstool closer to* MRS. ELVSTED.*)* There now! *(Kisses her cheek.)* You must say *du* to me and call me Hedda.

MRS. ELVSTED *(presses and pats her hands):*   Oh, how good and kind you are! I am not used to such kindness.

HEDDA: There, there, there! And I shall say *du* to you, as in the old days, and call you my dear Thora.

MRS. ELVSTEAD: My name is Thea.

HEDDA: Why, of course! I meant Thea. *(Looks at her compassionately.)* So you are not accustomed to goodness and kindness, Thea? Not in your own home?

MRS. ELVSTED: Oh, if I only had a home! But I haven't any; I have never had a home.

HEDDA *(looks at her for a moment):*   I almost suspected as much.

MRS. ELVSTED *(gazing helplessly before her):*   Yes—yes—yes.

HEDDA: I don't quite remember—was it not as housekeeper that you first went to Mr. Elvsted's?

MRS. ELVSTED: I really went as governess. But his wife—his late wife—was an invalid,—and rarely left her room. So I had to look after the housekeeping as well.

HEDDA: And then—at last—you became mistress of the house.

MRS. ELVSTED *(sadly):*   Yes, I did.

HEDDA: Let me see—about how long ago was that?

MRS. ELVSTED: My marriage?

HEDDA: Yes.

MRS. ELVSTED: Five years ago.

HEDDA: To be sure; it must be that.

MRS. ELVSTED: Oh, those five years——! Or at all events the last two or three of them! Oh, if you* could only imagine——

HEDDA *(giving her a little slap on the hand):* De? Fie, Thea!

MRS. ELVSTED: Yes, yes, I will try—— Well, if—you could only imagine and understand——

HEDDA *(lightly):* Eilert Lövborg has been in your neighbourhood about three years, hasn't he?

MRS. ELVSTED *(looks at her doubtfully):* Eilert Lövborg? Yes—he has.

HEDDA: Had you known him before, in town here?

MRS. ELVSTED: Scarcely at all. I mean—I knew him by name of course.

HEDDA: But you saw a good deal of him in the country?

MRS. ELVSTED: Yes, he came to us every day. You see, he gave the children lessons; for in the long run I couldn't manage it all myself.

HEDDA: No, that's clear.—And your husband——? I suppose he is often away from home?

MRS. ELVSTED: Yes. Being sheriff, you know, he has to travel about a good deal in his district.

HEDDA *(leaning against the arm of the chair):* Thea—my poor, sweet Thea— now you must tell me everything—exactly as it stands.

MRS. ELVSTED: Well then, you must question me.

HEDDA: What sort of man is your husband, Thea? I mean—you know—in everyday life. Is he kind to you?

MRS. ELVSTED *(evasively):* I am sure he means well in everything.

HEDDA: I should think he must be altogether too old for you. There is at least twenty years' difference between you, is there not?

MRS. ELVSTED *(irritably):* Yes, that is true, too. Everything about him is repellent to me! We have not a thought in common. We have no single point of sympathy—he and I.

HEDDA: But is he not fond of you all the same? In his own way?

MRS. ELVSTED: Oh, I really don't know. I think he regards me simply as a useful property. And then it doesn't cost much to keep me. I am not expensive.

HEDDA: That is stupid of you.

MRS. ELVSTED *(shakes her head):* It cannot be otherwise—not with him. I don't think he really cares for any one but himself—and perhaps a little for the children.

HEDDA: And for Eilert Lövborg, Thea.

MRS. ELVSTED *(looking at her):* For Eilert Lövborg? What puts that into your head?

---

*Mrs. Elvsted here uses the formal pronoun De, whereupon Hedda rebukes her. In her next speech Mrs. Elvsted says du.

HEDDA: Well, my dear—I should say, when he sends you after him all the way to town——*(Smiling almost imperceptibly.)* And besides, you said so yourself, to Tesman.

MRS. ELVSTED *(with a little nervous twitch):*   Did I? Yes, I suppose I did. *(Vehemently, but not loudly.)* No—I may just as well make a clean breast of it at once! For it must all come out in any case.

HEDDA: Why, my dear Thea——?

MRS. ELVSTED: Well, to make a long story short: My husband did not know that I was coming.

HEDDA: What! Your husband didn't know it!

MRS. ELVSTED: No, of course not. For that matter, he was away from home himself—he was travelling. Oh, I could bear it no longer, Hedda! I couldn't indeed—so utterly alone as I should have been in future.

HEDDA: Well? And then?

MRS. ELVSTED: So I put together some of my things—what I needed most—as quietly as possible. And then I left the house.

HEDDA: Without a word?

MRS. ELVSTED: Yes—and took the train straight to town.

HEDDA: Why, my dear, good Thea—to think of you daring to do it!

MRS. ELVSTED *(rises and moves about the room):*   What else could I possibly do?

HEDDA: But what do you think your husband will say when you go home again?

MRS. ELVSTED *(at the table, looks at her):*   Back to him?

HEDDA: Of course.

MRS. ELVSTED: I shall never go back to him again.

HEDDA *(rising and going towards her):*   Then you have left your home—for good and all?

MRS. ELVSTED: Yes. There was nothing else to be done.

HEDDA: But then—to take flight so openly.

MRS. ELVSTED: Oh, it's impossible to keep things of that sort secret.

HEDDA: But what do you think people will say of you, Thea?

MRS. ELVSTED: They may say what they like, for aught I care. *(Seats herself wearily and sadly on the sofa.)* I have done nothing but what I had to do.

HEDDA *(after a short silence):*   And what are your plans now? What do you think of doing?

MRS. ELVSTED: I don't know yet. I only know this, that I must live here, where Eilert Lövborg is—if I am to live at all.

HEDDA *(takes a chair from the table, seats herself beside her, and strokes her hands):*   My dear Thea—how did this—this friendship—between you and Eilert Lövborg come about?

MRS. ELVSTED: Oh, it grew up gradually. I gained a sort of influence over him.

HEDDA: Indeed?

MRS. ELVSTED: He gave up his old habits. Not because I asked him to, for I never dared do that. But of course he saw how repulsive they were to me; and so he dropped them.

HEDDA *(concealing an involuntary smile of scorn):* Then you have reclaimed him—as the saying goes—my little Thea.

MRS. ELVSTED: So he says himself, at any rate. And he, on his side, has made a real human being of me—taught me to think, and to understand so many things.

HEDDA: Did he give you lessons too, then?

MRS. ELVSTED: No, not exactly lessons. But he talked to me—talked about such an infinity of things. And then came the lovely, happy time when I began to share in his work—when he allowed me to help him!

HEDDA: Oh, he did, did he?

MRS. ELVSTED: Yes! He never wrote anything without my assistance.

HEDDA: You were two good comrades, in fact?

MRS. ELVSTED *(eagerly):* Comrades! Yes, fancy, Hedda—that is the very word he used!—Oh, I ought to feel perfectly happy; and yet I cannot; for I don't know how long it will last.

HEDDA: Are you no surer of him than that?

MRS. ELVSTED *(gloomily):* A woman's shadow stands between Eilert Lövborg and me.

HEDDA *(looks at her anxiously):* Who can that be?

MRS. ELVSTED: I don't know. Some one he knew in his—in his past. Some one he has never been able wholly to forget.

HEDDA: What has he told you—about this?

MRS. ELVSTED: He has only once—quite vaguely—alluded to it.

HEDDA: Well! And what did he say?

MRS. ELVSTED: He said that when they parted, she threatened to shoot him with a pistol.

HEDDA *(with cold composure):* Oh, nonsense! No one does that sort of thing here.

MRS. ELVSTED: No. And that is why I think it must have been that red-haired singing-woman whom he once—

HEDDA: Yes, very likely.

MRS. ELVSTED: For I remember they used to say of her that she carried loaded firearms.

HEDDA: Oh—then of course it must have been she.

MRS. ELVSTED *(wringing her hands):* And now just fancy, Hedda—I hear that this singing-woman—that she is in town again! Oh, I don't know what to do——

HEDDA *(glancing towards the inner room):* Hush! Here comes Tesman. *(Rises and whispers.)* Thea—all this must remain between you and me.

MRS. ELVSTED *(springing up):* Oh, yes, yes! for heaven's sake——!

(GEORGE TESMAN, with a letter in his hand, comes from the right through the inner room.)

TESMAN: There now—the epistle is finished.

HEDDA: That's right. And now Mrs. Elvsted is just going. Wait a moment—I'll go with you to the garden gate.

TESMAN: Do you think Berta could post the letter, Hedda dear?

HEDDA *(takes it):*   I will tell her to.

(BERTA *enters from the hall.*)

BERTA: Judge Brack wishes to know if Mrs. Tesman will receive him.

HEDDA: Yes, ask Judge Brack to come in. And look here—put this letter in the post.

BERTA *(taking the letter):*   Yes, ma'am. *(She opens the door for* JUDGE BRACK *and goes out herself.* BRACK *is a man of forty-five; thick-set, but well-built and elastic in his movements. His face is roundish with an aristocratic profile. His hair is short, still almost black, and carefully dressed. His eyes are lively and sparkling. His eyebrows thick. His moustaches are also thick, with short-cut ends. He wears a well-cut walking-suit, a little too youthful for his age. He uses an eye-glass, which he now and then lets drop.*

JUDGE BRACK *(with his hat in his hand, bowing):*   May one venture to call so early in the day?

HEDDA: Of course one may.

TESMAN *(presses his hand):*   You are welcome at any time. *(Introducing him.)* Judge Brack—Miss Rysing——

HEDDA: Oh——!

BRACK *(bowing):*   Ah—delighted——

HEDDA *(looks at him and laughs):*   It's nice to have a look at you by daylight, Judge!

BRACK: Do you find me—altered?

HEDDA: A little younger, I think.

BRACK: Thank you so much.

TESMAN: But what do you think of Hedda—eh? Doesn't she look flourishing? She has actually——

HEDDA: Oh, do leave me alone. You haven't thanked Judge Brack for all the trouble he has taken——

BRACK: Oh, nonsense—it was a pleasure to me——

HEDDA: Yes, you are a friend indeed. But here stands Thea all impatience to be off—so *au revoir* Judge. I shall be back again presently. *(Mutual salutations.* MRS. ELVSTED *and* HEDDA *go out by the hall door.)*

BRACK: Well,—is your wife tolerably satisfied——

TESMAN: Yes, we can't thank you sufficiently. Of course she talks of a little re-arrangement here and there; and one or two things are still wanting. We shall have to buy some additional trifles.

BRACK: Indeed!

TESMAN: But we won't trouble you about these things. Hedda says she herself will look after what is wanting.—Shan't we sit down? Eh?

BRACK: Thanks, for a moment. *(Seats himself beside the table.)* There is something I wanted to speak to you about, my dear Tesman.

TESMAN: Indeed? Ah, I understand! *(Seating himself.)* I suppose it's the serious part of the frolic that is coming now. Eh?

BRACK: Oh, the money question is not so very pressing; though, for that matter, I wish we had gone a little more economically to work.

TESMAN: But that would never have done, you know! Think of Hedda, my dear fellow! You, who know her so well——. I couldn't possibly ask her to put up with a shabby style of living!

BRACK: No, no—that is just the difficulty.

TESMAN: And then—fortunately—it can't be long before I receive my appointment.

BRACK: Well, you see—such things are often apt to hang fire for a time.

TESMAN: Have you heard anything definite? Eh?

BRACK: Nothing exactly definite——*(Interrupting himself.)* But, by-the-bye—I have one piece of news for you.

TESMAN: Well?

BRACK: Your old friend, Eilert Lövborg, has returned to town.

TESMAN: I know that already.

BRACK: Indeed! How did you learn it?

TESMAN: From that lady who went out with Hedda.

BRACK: Really? What was her name? I didn't quite catch it.

TESMAN: Mrs. Elvsted.

BRACK: Aha—Sheriff Elvsted's wife? Of course—he has been living up in their regions.

TESMAN: And fancy—I'm delighted to hear that he is quite a reformed character!

BRACK: So they say.

TESMAN: And then he has published a new book—eh?

BRACK: Yes, indeed he has.

TESMAN: And I hear it has made some sensation!

BRACK: Quite an unusual sensation.

TESMAN: Fancy—isn't that good news! A man of such extraordinary talents——I felt so grieved to think that he had gone irretrievably to ruin.

BRACK: That was what everybody thought.

TESMAN: But I cannot imagine what he will take to now! How in the world will he be able to make his living? Eh?

(During the last words, HEDDA *has entered by the hall door.)*

HEDDA *(to* BRACK, *laughing with a touch of scorn):*   Tesman is for ever worrying about how people are to make their living.

TESMAN: Well, you see, dear—we were talking about poor Eilert Lövborg.

HEDDA *(glancing at him rapidly):*   Oh, indeed? *(Seats herself in the arm-chair beside the stove and asks indifferently:)* What is the matter with him?

TESMAN: Well—no doubt he has run through all his property long ago; and he can scarcely write a new book every year—eh? So I really can't see what is to become of him.

BRACK: Perhaps I can give you some information on that point.

TESMAN: Indeed!

BRACK: You must remember that his relations have a good deal of influence.

TESMAN: Oh, his relations, unfortunately, have entirely washed their hands of him.

BRACK: At one time they called him the hope of the family.

TESMAN: At one time, yes! But he has put an end to all that.

HEDDA: Who knows? *(With a slight smile.)* I hear they have reclaimed him up at Sheriff Elvsted's——

BRACK: And then this book that he has published——

TESMAN: Well, well, I hope to goodness they may find something for him to do. I have just written to him. I asked him to come and see us this evening, Hedda dear.

BRACK: But, my dear fellow, you are booked for my bachelors' party this evening. You promised on the pier last night.

HEDDA: Had you forgotten, Tesman?

TESMAN: Yes, I had utterly forgotten.

BRACK: But it doesn't matter, for you may be sure he won't come.

TESMAN: What makes you think that? Eh?

BRACK *(with a little hesitation, rising and resting his hands on the back of his chair):* My dear Tesman—and you too, Mrs. Tesman—I think I ought not to keep you in the dark about something that—that——

TESMAN: That concerns Eilert——?

BRACK: Both you and him.

TESMAN: Well, my dear Judge, out with it.

BRACK: You must be prepared to find your appointment deferred longer than you desired or expected.

TESMAN *(jumping up uneasily):*   Is there some hitch about it? Eh?

BRACK: The nomination may perhaps be made conditional on the result of a competition——

TESMAN: Competition! Think of that, Hedda!

HEDDA *(leans farther back in the chair):*   Aha—aah!

TESMAN: But who can my competitor be? Surely not——?

BRACK: Yes, precisely—Eilert Lövborg.

TESMAN *(clasping his hands):*   No, no—it's quite inconceivable! Quite impossible! Eh?

BRACK: H'm—that is what it may come to, all the same.

TESMAN: Well but, Judge Brack—it would show the most incredible lack of consideration for me. *(Gesticulates with his arms.)* For—just think—I'm a married man! We have married on the strength of these prospects, Hedda and I; and run deep into debt; and borrowed money from Aunt Julia too. Good heavens, they had as good as promised me the appointment. Eh?

BRACK: Well, well, well—no doubt you will get it in the end; only after a contest.

HEDDA *(immovable in her arm-chair):*   Fancy, Tesman, there will be a sort of sporting interest in that.

TESMAN: Why, my dearest Hedda, how can you be so indifferent about it.

HEDDA *(as before):* I am not at all indifferent. I am most eager to see who wins.

BRACK: In any case, Mrs. Tesman, it is best that you should know how matters stand. I mean—before you set about the little purchases I hear you are threatening.

HEDDA: This can make no difference.

BRACK: Indeed! Then I have no more to say. Good-bye! *(To* TESMAN.*)* I shall look in on my way back from my afternoon walk, and take you home with me.

TESMAN: Oh yes, yes—your news has quite upset me.

HEDDA *(reclining, holds out her hand):* Good-bye, Judge; and be sure you call in the afternoon.

BRACK: Many thanks. Good-bye, good-bye!

TESMAN *(accompanying him to the door):* Good-bye, my dear Judge! You must really excuse me——

(JUDGE BRACK goes out by the hall door.)

TESMAN *(crosses the room):* Oh, Hedda—one should never rush into adventures. Eh?

HEDDA *(looks at him, smiling):* Do you do that?

TESMAN: Yes, dear—there is no denying—it was adventurous to go and marry and set up house upon mere expectations.

HEDDA: Perhaps you are right there.

TESMAN: Well—at all events, we have our delightful home, Hedda! Fancy, the home we both dreamed of—the home we were in love with, I may almost say. Eh?

HEDDA *(rising slowly and wearily):* It was part of our compact that we were to go into society—to keep open house.

TESMAN: Yes, if you only knew how I had been looking forward to it! Fancy—to see you as hostess—in a select circle! Eh? Well, well, well—for the present we shall have to get on without society, Hedda—only to invite Aunt Julia now and then.—Oh, I intended you to lead such an utterly different life, dear——!

HEDDA: Of course I cannot have my man in livery just yet.

TESMAN: Oh no, unfortunately. It would be out of the question for us to keep a footman, you know.

HEDDA: And the saddle-horse I was to have had——

TESMAN *(aghast):* The saddle-horse!

HEDDA: ——I suppose I must not think of that now.

TESMAN: Good heavens, no!—that's as clear as daylight.

HEDDA *(goes up the room):* Well, I shall have one thing at least to kill time with in the meanwhile.

TESMAN *(beaming):* Oh, thank heaven for that! What is it, Hedda? Eh?

HEDDA *(in the middle doorway, looks at him with covert scorn):* My pistols, George.

TESMAN *(in alarm):* Your pistols!

HEDDA *(with cold eyes):* General Gabler's pistols. *(She goes out through the inner room, to the left.)*

TESMAN *(rushes up to the middle doorway and calls after her):*   No, for heaven's sake, Hedda darling—don't touch those dangerous things! For my sake, Hedda! Eh?

ACT II

The room at the TESMANS' *as in the first Act, except that the piano has been removed, and an elegant little writing-table with book-shelves put in its place. A smaller table stands near the sofa on the left. Most of the bouquets have been taken away.* MRS. ELVSTED'S *bouquet is upon the large table in front.—It is afternoon.*

HEDDA, dressed to receive callers, is alone in the room. She stands by the open glass door, loading a revolver. The fellow to it lies in an open pistol-case on the writing-table.

HEDDA *(looks down the garden, and calls):*   So you are here again, Judge!
BRACK *(is heard calling from a distance):*   As you see, Mrs. Tesman!
HEDDA *(raises the pistol and points):*   Now I'll shoot you, Judge Brack!
BRACK *(calling unseen):*   No, no, no! Don't stand aiming at me!
HEDDA: This is what comes of sneaking in by the back way.*

(She fires.)

BRACK *(nearer):*   Are you out of your senses——!
HEDDA: Dear me—did I happen to hit you?
BRACK *(still outside):*   I wish you would let these pranks alone!
HEDDA   Come in then, Judge.

*(*JUDGE BRACK, *dressed as though for a men's party, enters by the glass door. He carries a light overcoat over his arm.)*

BRACK: What the deuce—haven't you tired of that sport, yet? What are you shooting at?
HEDDA: Oh, I am only firing in the air.
BRACK *(gently takes the pistol out of her hand):*   Allow me, madam! *(Looks at it.)* Ah—I know this pistol well! *(Looks around.)* Where is the case? Ah, here it is. *(Lays the pistol in it, and shuts it.)* Now we won't play at that game any more to-day.
HEDDA: Then what in heaven's name would you have me do with myself?
BRACK: Have you had no visitors?
HEDDA *(closing the glass door):*   Not one. I suppose all our set are still out of town.
BRACK: And is Tesman not at home either?
HEDDA *(at the writing-table, putting the pistol-case in a drawer which she shuts):*   No. He rushed off to his aunt's directly after lunch; he didn't expect you so early.

---

*"Bagveje": Means both "back ways" and "underhand courses."

BRACK: H'm—how stupid of me not to have thought of that!

HEDDA *(turning her head to look at him):* Why stupid?

BRACK: Because if I had thought of it I should have come a little—earlier.

HEDDA *(crossing the room):* Then you would have found no one to receive you; for I have been in my room changing my dress ever since lunch.

BRACK: And is there no sort of little chink that we could hold a parley through?

HEDDA: You have forgotten to arrange one.

BRACK: That was another piece of stupidity.

HEDDA: Well, we must just settle down here—and wait. Tesman is not likely to be back for some time yet.

BRACK: Never mind; I shall not be impatient.

(HEDDA seats herself in the corner of the sofa. BRACK lays his overcoat over the back of the nearest chair, and sits down, but keeps his hat in his hand. A short silence. They look at each other.)

HEDDA: Well?

BRACK *(in the same tone):* Well?

HEDDA: I spoke first.

BRACK *(bending a little forward):* Come, let us have a cosy little chat, Mrs. Hedda.

HEDDA *(leaning further back in the sofa):* Does it not seem like a whole eternity since our last talk? Of course I don't count those few words yesterday evening and this morning.

BRACK: You mean since our last confidential talk? Our last *tête-à-tête?*

HEDDA: Well, yes—since you put it so.

BRACK: Not a day has passed but I have wished that you were home again.

HEDDA: And I have done nothing but wish the same thing.

BRACK: You? Really, Mrs. Hedda? And I thought you had been enjoying your tour so much!

HEDDA: Oh, yes, you may be sure of that!

BRACK: But Tesman's letters spoke of nothing but happiness.

HEDDA: Oh, Tesman! You see, he thinks nothing so delightful as grubbing in libraries and making copies of old parchments, or whatever you call them.

BRACK *(with a spice of malice):* Well, that is his vocation in life—or part of it at any rate.

HEDDA: Yes, of course; and no doubt when it's your vocation——But *I!* Oh, my dear Mr. Brack, how mortally bored I have been.

BRACK *(sympathetically):* Do you really say so? In downright earnest?

HEDDA: Yes, you can surely understand it——! To go for six whole months without meeting a soul that knew anything of our circle, or could talk about the things we are interested in.

BRACK: Yes, yes—I too should feel that a deprivation.

HEDDA: And then, what I found most intolerable of all——

BRACK: Well?

HEDDA: ——was being everlastingly in the company of—one and the same
    person——

BRACK *(with a nod of assent):*   Morning, noon, and night, yes—at all possible
    times and seasons.

HEDDA: I said "everlastingly."

BRACK: Just so. But I should have thought, with our excellent Tesman, one
    could——

HEDDA: Tesman is—a specialist, my dear Judge.

BRACK: Undeniably.

HEDDA: And specialists are not at all amusing to travel with. Not in the long
    run at any rate.

BRACK: Not even—the specialist one happens to love?

HEDDA: Faugh—don't use that sickening word!

BRACK *(taken aback):*   What do you say, Mrs. Hedda?

HEDDA *(half laughing, half irritated):*   You should just try it! To hear of nothing
    but the history of civilisation, morning, noon, and night——

BRACK: Everlastingly.

HEDDA: Yes, yes, yes! And then all this about the domestic industry of the
    middle ages——! That's the most disgusting part of it!

BRACK *(looks searchingly at her):*   But tell me—in that case, how am I to under-
    stand your——? H'm——

HEDDA: My accepting George Tesman, you mean?

BRACK: Well, let us put it so.

HEDDA: Good heavens, do you see anything so wonderful in that?

BRACK: Yes and no—Mrs. Hedda.

HEDDA: I had positively danced myself tired, my dear Judge. My day was
    done—— *(With a slight shudder.)* Oh no—I won't say that; nor think it
    either!

BRACK: You have assuredly no reason to.

HEDDA: Oh, reasons——*(Watching him closely.)* And George Tesman—after
    all, you must admit that he is correctness itself.

BRACK: His correctness and respectability are beyond all question.

HEDDA: And I don't see anything absolutely ridiculous about him.—Do
    you?

BRACK: Ridiculous? N—no—I shouldn't exactly say so——

HEDDA: Well—and his powers of research, at all events, are untiring.—I see
    no reason why he should not one day come to the front, after all.

BRACK *(looks at her hesitatingly):*   I thought that you, like every one else, ex-
    pected him to attain the highest distinction.

HEDDA *(with an expression of fatigue):*   Yes, so I did.—And then, since he was
    bent, at all hazards, on being allowed to provide for me—I really don't
    know why I should not have accepted his offer?

BRACK: No—if you look at it in that light——

HEDDA: It was more than my other adorers were prepared to do for me, my
    dear Judge.

BRACK *(laughing):*   Well, I can't answer for all the rest; but as for myself, you know quite well that I have always entertained a—a certain respect for the marriage tie—for marriage as an institution, Mrs. Hedda.

HEDDA *(jestingly):*   Oh, I assure you I have never cherished any hopes with respect to you.

BRACK: All I require is a pleasant and intimate interior, where I can make myself useful in every way, and am free to come and go as—as a trusted friend——

HEDDA: Of the master of the house, do you mean?

BRACK *(bowing):*   Frankly—of the mistress first of all; but of course of the master, too, in the second place. Such a triangular friendship—if I may call it so—is really a great convenience for all parties, let me tell you.

HEDDA: Yes, I have many a time longed for some one to make a third on our travels. Oh—those railway-carriage *tête-à-têtes*——*!*

BRACK: Fortunately your wedding journey is over now.

HEDDA *(shaking her head):*   Not by a long—long way. I have only arrived at a station on the line.

BRACK: Well, then the passengers jump out and move about a little, Mrs. Hedda.

HEDDA: I never jump out.

BRACK: Really?

HEDDA: No—because there is always some one standing by to——

BRACK *(laughing):*   To look at your ankles, do you mean?

HEDDA: Precisely.

BRACK: Well but, dear me——

HEDDA *(with a gesture of repulsion):*   I won't have it. I would rather keep my seat where I happen to be—and continue the *tête-à-tête.*

BRACK: But suppose a third person were to jump in and join the couple.

HEDDA: Ah—that is quite another matter!

BRACK: A trusted, sympathetic friend——

HEDDA: ——with a fund of conversation on all sorts of lively topics——

BRACK: ——and not the least bit of a specialist!

HEDDA *(with an audible sigh):*   Yes, that would be a relief indeed.

BRACK *(hears the front door open, and glances in that direction):*   The triangle is completed.

HEDDA *(half aloud):*   And on goes the train.

(GEORGE TESMAN, *in a grey walking-suit, with a soft felt hat, enters from the hall. He has a number of unbound books under his arm and in his pockets.)*

TESMAN *(goes up to the table beside the corner settee):*   Ouf—what a load for a warm day—all these books. *(Lays them on the table.)* I'm positively perspiring, Hedda. Hallo—are you there already, my dear Judge? Eh? Berta didn't tell me.

BRACK *(rising):*   I came in through the garden.

HEDDA: What books have you got there?

TESMAN *(stands looking them through):*   Some new books on my special subjects—quite indispensable to me.

HEDDA: Your special subjects?

BRACK: Yes, books on his special subjects, Mrs. Tesman. *(*BRACK *and* HEDDA *exchange a confidential smile.)*

HEDDA: Do you need still more books on your special subjects?

TESMAN: Yes, my dear Hedda, one can never have too many of them. Of course one must keep up with all that is written and published.

HEDDA: Yes, I suppose one must.

TESMAN *(searching among his books):*   And look here—I have got hold of Eilert Lövborg's new book too. *(Offering it to her.)* Perhaps you would like to glance through it, Hedda? Eh?

HEDDA: No, thank you. Or rather—afterwards perhaps.

TESMAN: I looked into it a little on the way home.

BRACK: Well, what do you think of it—as a specialist?

TESMAN: I think it shows quite remarkable soundness of judgment. He never wrote like that before. *(Putting the books together.)* Now I shall take all these into my study. I'm longing to cut the leaves——! And then I must change my clothes. *(To* BRACK.*)* I suppose we needn't start just yet? Eh?

BRACK: Oh, dear no—there is not the slightest hurry.

TESMAN: Well then, I will take my time. *(Is going with his books, but stops in the doorway and turns.)* By-the-bye, Hedda—Aunt Julia is not coming this evening.

HEDDA: Not coming? Is it that affair of the bonnet that keeps her away?

TESMAN: Oh, not at all. How could you think such a thing of Aunt Julia? Just fancy——! The fact is, Aunt Rina is very ill.

HEDDA: She always is.

TESMAN: Yes, but to-day she is much worse than usual, poor dear.

HEDDA: Oh, then it's only natural that her sister should remain with her. I must bear my disappointment.

TESMAN: And you can't imagine, dear, how delighted Aunt Julia seemed to be—because you had come home looking so flourishing!

HEDDA *(half aloud, rising):*   Oh, those everlasting aunts!

TESMAN: What?

HEDDA *(going to the glass door):*   Nothing.

TESMAN: Oh, all right. *(He goes through the inner room, out to the right.)*

BRACK: What bonnet were you talking about?

HEDDA: Oh, it was a little episode with Miss Tesman this morning. She had laid down her bonnet on the chair there—*(looks at him and smiles)*—And I pretended to think it was the servant's.

BRACK *(shaking his head):*   Now my dear Mrs. Hedda, how could you do such a thing? To that excellent old lady, too!

HEDDA *(nervously crossing the room):*   Well, you see—these impulses come over me all of a sudden; and I cannot resist them. *(Throws herself down in the easy-chair by the stove.)* Oh, I don't know how to explain it.

BRACK *(behind the easy-chair)*:   You are not really happy—that is at the bottom of it.

HEDDA *(looking straight before her)*:   I know of no reason why I should be—happy. Perhaps you can give me one?

BRACK: Well—amongst other things, because you have got exactly the home you had set your heart on.

HEDDA *(looks up at him and laughs)*:   Do you too believe in that legend?

BRACK: Is there nothing in it, then?

HEDDA: Oh, yes, there is something in it.

BRACK: Well?

HEDDA: There is this in it, that I made use of Tesman to see me home from evening parties last summer—

BRACK: I, unfortunately, had to go quite a different way.

HEDDA: That's true. I know you were going a different way last summer.

BRACK *(laughing)*:   Oh fie, Mrs. Hedda! Well, then—you and Tesman——?

HEDDA: Well, we happened to pass here one evening; Tesman, poor fellow, was writhing in the agony of having to find conversation; so I took pity on the learned man——

BRACK *(smiles doubtfully)*:   You took pity? H'm——

HEDDA: Yes, I really did. And so—to help him out of his torment—I happened to say, in pure thoughtlessness, that I should like to live in this villa.

BRACK: No more than that?

HEDDA: Not that evening.

BRACK: But afterwards?

HEDDA: Yes, my thoughtlessness had consequences, my dear Judge.

BRACK: Unfortunately that too often happens, Mrs. Hedda.

HEDDA: Thanks! So you see it was this enthusiasm for Secretary's Falk's villa that first constituted a bond of sympathy between George Tesman and me. From that came our engagement and our marriage, and our wedding journey, and all the rest of it. Well, well, my dear Judge—as you make your bed so you must lie, I could almost say.

BRACK: This is exquisite! And you really cared not a rap about it all the time?

HEDDA: No, heaven knows I didn't.

BRACK: But now? Now that we have made it so homelike for you?

HEDDA: Uh—the rooms all seem to smell of lavender and dried rose-leaves.— But perhaps it's Aunt Julia that has brought that scent with her.

BRACK *(laughing)*:   No, I think it must be a legacy from the late Mrs. Secretary Falk.

HEDDA: Yes, there is an odour of mortality about it. It reminds me of a bouquet—the day after the ball. *(Clasps her hands behind her head, leans back in her chair and looks at him.)* Oh, my dear Judge—you cannot imagine how horribly I shall bore myself here.

BRACK: Why should not you, too, find some sort of vocation in life, Mrs. Hedda?

HEDDA: A vocation—that should attract me?

BRACK: If possible, of course.

HEDDA: Heaven knows what sort of vocation that could be. I often wonder whether——*(Breaking off.)* But that would never do either.

BRACK: Who can tell? Let me hear what it is.

HEDDA: Whether I might not get Tesman to go into politics, I mean.

BRACK *(laughing):*   Tesman? No, really now, political life is not the thing for him—not at all in his line.

HEDDA: No, I daresay not.—But if I could get him into it all the same?

BRACK: Why—what satisfaction could you find in that? If he is not fitted for that sort of thing, why should you want to drive him into it?

HEDDA: Because I am bored, I tell you! *(After a pause.)* So you think it quite out of the question that Tesman should ever get into the ministry?

BRACK: H'm—you see, my dear Mrs. Hedda—to get into the ministry, he would have to be a tolerably rich man.

HEDDA *(rising impatiently):*   Yes, there we have it! It is this genteel poverty I have managed to drop into——! *(Crosses the room.)* That is what makes life so pitiable! So utterly ludicrous!—For that's what it is.

BRACK: Now *I* should say the fault lay elsewhere.

HEDDA: Where, then?

BRACK: You have never gone through any really stimulating experience.

HEDDA: Anything serious, you mean?

BRACK: Yes, you may call it so. But now you may perhaps have one in store.

HEDDA *(tossing her head):*   Oh, you're thinking of the annoyances about this wretched professorship! But that must be Tesman's own affair. I assure you I shall not waste a thought upon it.

BRACK: No, no, I daresay not. But suppose now that what people call—in elegant language—a solemn responsibility were to come upon you? *(Smiling.)* A new responsibility, Mrs. Hedda?

HEDDA *(angrily):*   Be quiet! Nothing of that sort will ever happen!

BRACK *(warily):*   We will speak of this again a year hence—at the very outside.

HEDDA *(curtly):*   I have no turn for anything of the sort, Judge Brack. No responsibilities for me!

BRACK: Are you so unlike the generality of women as to have no turn for duties which——?

HEDDA *(beside the glass door):*   Oh, be quiet, I tell you!—I often think there is only one thing in the world I have any turn for.

BRACK *(drawing near to her):*   And what is that, if I may ask?

HEDDA *(stands looking out):*   Boring myself to death. Now you know it. *(Turns, looks towards the inner room, and laughs.)* Yes, as I thought! Here comes the Professor.

BRACK *(softly, in a tone of warning):*   Come, come, come, Mrs. Hedda!

(GEORGE TESMAN, dressed for the party, with his gloves and hat in his hand, enters from the right through the inner room.)

TESMAN: Hedda, has no message come from Eilert Lövborg? Eh?

HEDDA: No.

TESMAN: Then you'll see he'll be here presently.

BRACK: Do you really think he will come?

TESMAN: Yes, I am almost sure of it. For what you were telling us this morning must have been a mere floating rumour.

BRACK: You think so?

TESMAN: At any rate, Aunt Julia said she did not believe for a moment that he would ever stand in my way again. Fancy that!

BRACK: Well then, that's all right.

TESMAN *(placing his hat and gloves on a chair on the right):* Yes, but you must really let me wait for him as long as possible.

BRACK: We have plenty of time yet. None of my guests will arrive before seven or half-past.

TESMAN: Then meanwhile we can keep Hedda company, and see what happens. Eh?

HEDDA *(placing* BRACK'S *hat and overcoat upon the corner settee):* And at the worst Mr. Lövborg can remain here with me.

BRACK *(offering to take his things):* Oh, allow me, Mrs. Tesman!—What do you mean by "At the worst"?

HEDDA: If he won't go with you and Tesman.

TESMAN *(looks dubiously at her):* But, Hedda dear—do you think it would quite do for him to remain with you? Eh? Remember, Aunt Julia can't come.

HEDDA: No, but Mrs. Elvsted is coming. We three can have a cup of tea together.

TESMAN: Oh, yes, that will be all right.

BRACK *(smiling):* And that would perhaps be the safest plan for him.

HEDDA: Why so?

BRACK: Well, you know, Mrs. Tesman, how you used to gird at my little bachelor parties. You declared they were adapted only for men of the strictest principles.

HEDDA: But no doubt Mr. Lövborg's principles are strict enough now. A converted sinner—— *(*BERTA *appears at the hall door.)*

BERTA: There's a gentleman asking if you are at home, ma'am——

HEDDA: Well, show him in.

TESMAN *(softly).* I'm sure it is he! Fancy that!

*(*EILERT LÖVBORG *enters from the hall. He is slim and lean; of the same age as* TESMAN, *but looks older and somewhat worn-out. His hair and beard are of a blackish brown, his face long and pale, but with patches of colour on the cheekbones. He is dressed in a well-cut black visiting suit, quite new. He has dark gloves and a silk hat. He stops near the door, and makes a rapid bow, seeming somewhat embarrassed.)*

TESMAN *(goes up to him and shakes him warmly by the hand):* Well, my dear Eilert—so at last we meet again!

EILERT LÖVBORG *(speaks in a subdued voice):*   Thanks for your letter, Tesman. *(Approaching* HEDDA.*)* Will you too shake hands with me, Mrs. Tesman?

HEDDA *(taking his hand):*   I am glad to see you, Mr. Lövborg. *(With a motion of her hand.)* I don't know whether you two gentlemen———?

LÖVBORG *(bowing slightly):*   Judge Brack, I think.

BRACK *(doing likewise):*   Oh yes,—in the old days———

TESMAN *(to* LÖVBORG, *with his hands on his shoulders):*   And now you must make yourself entirely at home, Eilert! Mustn't he, Hedda?—For I hear you are going to settle in town again? Eh?

LÖVBORG: Yes, I am.

TESMAN: Quite right, quite right. Let me tell you, I have got hold of your new book; but I haven't had time to read it yet.

LÖVBORG: You may spare yourself the trouble.

TESMAN: Why so?

LÖVBORG: Because there is very little in it.

TESMAN: Just fancy—how can you say so?

BRACK: But it has been very much praised, I hear.

LÖVBORG: That was what I wanted; so I put nothing into the book but what every one would agree with.

BRACK: Very wise of you.

TESMAN: Well but, my dear Eilert———!

LÖVBORG: For now I mean to win myself a position again—to make a fresh start.

TESMAN *(a little embarrassed):*   Ah, that is what you wish to do? Eh?

LÖVBORG *(smiling, lays down his hat, and draws a packet, wrapped in paper, from his coat pocket):*   But when this one appears, George Tesman, you will have to read it. For this is the real book—the book I have put my true self into.

TESMAN: Indeed? And what is it?

LÖVBORG: It is the continuation.

TESMAN: The continuation? Of what?

LÖVBORG: Of the book.

TESMAN: Of the new book?

LÖVBORG: Of course.

TESMAN: Why, my dear Eilert—does it not come down to our own days?

LÖVBORG: Yes, it does; and this one deals with the future.

TESMAN: With the future! But, good heavens, we know nothing of the future!

LÖVBORG: No; but there is a thing or two to be said about it all the same. *(Opens the packet.)* Look here———

TESMAN: Why, that's not your handwriting.

LÖVBORG: I dictated it. *(Turning over the pages.)* It falls into two sections. The first deals with the civilising forces of the future. And here is the second— *(running through the pages towards the end)*—forecasting the probable line of development.

TESMAN: How odd now! I should never have thought of writing anything of that sort.

HEDDA *(at the glass door, drumming on the pane):* H'm—I daresay not.

LÖVBORG *(replacing the manuscript in its paper and laying the packet on the table):* I brought it, thinking I might read you a little of it this evening.

TESMAN: That was very good of you, Eilert. But this evening——? *(Looking at* BRACK.*)* I don't quite see how we can manage it——

LÖVBORG: Well then, some other time. There is no hurry.

BRACK: I must tell you, Mr. Lövborg—there is a little gathering at my house this evening—mainly in honour of Tesman, you know——

LÖVBORG *(looking for his hat):* Oh—then I won't detain you——

BRACK: No, but listen—will you not do me the favour of joining us?

LÖVBORG *(curtly and decidedly):* No, I can't—thank you very much.

BRACK: Oh, nonsense—do! We shall be quite a select little circle. And I assure you we shall have a "lively time," as Mrs. Hed—as Mrs. Tesman says.

LÖVBORG: I have no doubt of it. But nevertheless——

BRACK: And then you might bring your manuscript with you, and read it to Tesman at my house. I could give you a room to yourselves.

TESMAN: Yes, think of that, Eilert,—why shouldn't you? Eh?

HEDDA *(interposing):* But, Tesman, if Mr. Lövborg would really rather not! I am sure Mr. Lövborg is much more inclined to remain here and have supper with me.

LÖVBORG *(looking at her):* With you, Mrs. Tesman?

HEDDA: And with Mrs. Elvsted.

LÖVBORG: Ah—— *(Lightly.)* I saw her for a moment this morning.

HEDDA: Did you? Well, she is coming this evening. So you see you are almost bound to remain, Mr. Lövborg, or she will have no one to see her home.

LÖVBORG: That's true. Many thanks, Mrs. Tesman—in that case I will remain.

HEDDA: Then I have one or two orders to give the servant—— *(She goes to the hall door and rings.* BERTA *enters.* HEDDA *talks to her in a whisper, and points towards the inner room.* BERTA *nods and goes out again.)*

TESMAN *(at the same time, to* LÖVBORG*):* Tell me, Eilert—is it this new subject—the future—that you are going to lecture about?

LÖVBORG: Yes.

TESMAN: They told me at the bookseller's that you are going to deliver a course of lectures this autumn.

LÖVBORG: That is my intention. I hope you won't take it ill, Tesman.

TESMAN: Oh no, not in the least! But——?

LÖVBORG: I can quite understand that it must be disagreeable to you.

TESMAN *(cast down):* Oh, I can't expect you, out of consideration for me, to——

LÖVBORG: But I shall wait till you have received your appointment.

TESMAN: Will you wait? Yes, but—yes, but—are you not going to compete with me? Eh?

LÖVBORG: No; it is only the moral victory I care for.

TESMAN: Why, bless me—then Aunt Julia was right after all! Oh yes—I knew it! Hedda! Just fancy—Eilert Lövborg is not going to stand in our way!

HEDDA *(curtly):* Our way? Pray leave me out of the question. *(She goes up towards the inner room, where* BERTA *is placing a tray with decanters and glasses on the table.* HEDDA *nods approval, and comes forward again.* BERTA *goes out.*)

TESMAN *(at the same time):*   And you, Judge Brack—what do you say to this? Eh?

BRACK: Well, I say that a moral victory—h'm—may be all very fine——

TESMAN: Yes, certainly. But all the same——

HEDDA *(looking at* TESMAN *with a cold smile):*   You stand there looking as if you were thunderstruck——

TESMAN: Yes—so I am—I almost think——

BRACK: Don't you see, Mrs. Tesman, a thunderstorm has just passed over?

HEDDA *(pointing towards the inner room):*   Will you not take a glass of cold punch, gentlemen?

BRACK *(looking at his watch):*   A stirrup-cup? Yes, it wouldn't come amiss.

TESMAN: A capital idea, Hedda! Just the thing! Now that the weight has been taken off my mind——

HEDDA: Will you not join them, Mr. Lövborg?

LÖVBORG *(with a gesture of refusal):*   No, thank you. Nothing for me.

BRACK: Why, bless me—cold punch is surely not poison.

LÖVBORG: Perhaps not for every one.

HEDDA: I will keep Mr. Lövborg company in the meantime.

TESMAN: Yes, yes, Hedda dear, do. *(He and* BRACK *go into the inner room, seat themselves, drink punch, smoke cigarettes, and carry on a lively conversation during what follows.* EILERT LÖVBORG *remains standing beside the stove.* HEDDA *goes to the writing-table.)*

HEDDA *(raising her voice a little):*   Do you care to look at some photographs, Mr. Lövborg? You know Tesman and I made a tour in the Tyrol on our way home? *(She takes up an album, and places it on the table beside the sofa, in the further corner of which she seats herself.* EILERT LÖVBORG *approaches, stops, and looks at her. Then he takes a chair and seats himself to her left, with his back towards the inner room.)*

HEDDA *(opening the album):*   Do you see this range of mountains, Mr. Lövborg? It's the Ortler group. Tesman has written the name underneath. Here it is: "The Ortler group near Meran."

LÖVBORG *(who has never taken his eyes off her, says softly and slowly):*   Hedda— Gabler!

HEDDA *(glancing hastily at him):*   Ah! Hush!

LÖVBORG *(repeats softly):*   Hedda Gabler!

HEDDA *(looking at the album):*   That was my name in the old days—when we two knew each other.

LÖVBORG: And I must teach myself never to say Hedda Gabler again—never, as long as I live.

HEDDA *(still turning over the pages):*   Yes, you must. And I think you ought to practise in time. The sooner the better, I should say.

LÖVBORG *(in a tone of indignation):*   Hedda Gabler married? And married to —George Tesman!

HEDDA: Yes—so the world goes.

LÖVBORG: Oh, Hedda, Hedda—how could you throw yourself away!

HEDDA *(looks sharply at him):*   What? I can't allow this!

LÖVBORG: What do you mean? *(TESMAN comes into the room and goes towards the sofa.)*

HEDDA *(hears him coming and says in an indifferent tone):*   And this is a view from the Val d'Ampezzo, Mr. Lövborg. Just look at these peaks! *(Looks affectionately up at TESMAN.)* What's the name of these curious peaks, dear?

TESMAN: Let me see. Oh, those are the Dolomites.

HEDDA: Yes, that's it!—Those are the Dolomites, Mr. Lövborg.

TESMAN: Hedda dear,—I only wanted to ask whether I shouldn't bring you a little punch after all? For yourself at any rate—eh?

HEDDA: Yes, do, please; and perhaps a few biscuits.

TESMAN: No cigarettes?

HEDDA: No.

TESMAN: Very well. *(He goes into the inner room and out to the right.* BRACK *sits in the inner room, and keeps an eye from time to time on* HEDDA *and* LÖVBORG.*)*

LÖVBORG *(softly, as before):*   Answer me, Hedda—How could you go and do this?

HEDDA *(apparently absorbed in the album):*   If you continue to say *du* to me I won't talk to you.

LÖVBORG: May I not say *du* when we are alone?

HEDDA: No. You may think it; but you mustn't say it.

LÖVBORG: Ah, I understand. It is an offence against George Tesman, whom you—love.

HEDDA *(glances at him and smiles):*   Love? What an idea!

LÖVBORG: You don't love him then!

HEDDA: But I won't hear of any sort of unfaithfulness! Remember that.

LÖVBORG: Hedda—answer me one thing—

HEDDA: Hush! *(TESMAN enters with a small tray from the inner room.)*

TESMAN: Here you are! Isn't this tempting? *(He puts the tray on the table.)*

HEDDA: Why do you bring it yourself?

TESMAN *(filling the glasses):*   Because I think it's such fun to wait upon you, Hedda.

HEDDA: But you have poured out two glasses. Mr. Lövborg said he wouldn't have any—

TESMAN: No, but Mrs. Elvsted will soon be here, won't she?

HEDDA: Yes, by-the-bye—Mrs. Elvsted—

TESMAN: Had you forgotten her? Eh?

HEDDA: We were so absorbed in these photographs. *(Shows him a picture.)* Do you remember this little village?

TESMAN: Oh, it's that one just below the Brenner Pass. It was there we passed the night—

HEDDA: —and met that lively party of tourists.

TESMAN: Yes, that was the place. Fancy—if we could only have had you with us, Eilert! Eh? *(He returns to the inner room and sits beside BRACK.)*

LÖVBORG: Answer me this one thing, Hedda—

HEDDA: Well?

LÖVBORG: Was there no love in your friendship for me either? Not a spark—not a tinge of love in it?

HEDDA: I wonder if there was? To me it seems as though we were two good comrades—two thoroughly intimate friends. *(Smilingly.)* You especially were frankness itself.

LÖVBORG: It was you that made me so.

HEDDA: As I look back upon it all, I think there was really something beautiful, something fascinating—something daring—in—in that secret intimacy—that comradeship which no living creature so much as dreamed of.

LÖVBORG: Yes, yes, Hedda! Was there not?—When I used to come to your father's in the afternoon—and the General sat over at the window reading his papers—with his back towards us—

HEDDA: And we two on the corner sofa—

LÖVBORG: Always with the same illustrated paper before us—

HEDDA: For want of an album, yes.

LÖVBORG: Yes, Hedda, and when I made my confessions to you—told you about myself, things that at that time no one else knew! There I would sit and tell you of my escapades—my days and nights of devilment. Oh, Hedda—what was the power in you that forced me to confess these things?

HEDDA: Do you think it was any power in me?

LÖVBORG: How else can I explain it? And all those—those roundabout questions you used to put to me—

HEDDA: Which you understood so particularly well—

LÖVBORG: How could you sit and question me like that? Question me quite frankly—

HEDDA: In roundabout terms, please observe.

LÖVBORG: Yes, but frankly nevertheless. Cross-question me about—all that sort of thing?

HEDDA: And how could you answer, Mr. Lövborg?

LÖVBORG: Yes, that is just what I can't understand—in looking back upon it. But tell me now, Hedda—was there not love at the bottom of our friendship? On your side, did you not feel as though you might purge my stains away—if I made you my confessor? Was it not so?

HEDDA: No, not quite.

LÖVBORG: What was your motive, then?

HEDDA: Do you think it quite incomprehensible that a young girl—when it can be done—without any one knowing—

LÖVBORG: Well?

HEDDA: —should be glad to have a peep, now and then, into a world which—

LÖVBORG: Which—?

HEDDA: —which she is forbidden to know anything about?

LÖVBORG: So that was it?

HEDDA: Partly. Partly—I almost think.

LÖVBORG: Comradeship in the thirst for life. But why should not that, at any rate, have continued?

HEDDA: The fault was yours.

LÖVBORG: It was you that broke with me.

HEDDA: Yes, when our friendship threatened to develop into something more serious. Shame upon you, Eilert Lövborg! How could you think of wronging your—your frank comrade?

LÖVBORG *(clenching his hands):*   Oh, why did you not carry out your threat? Why did you not shoot me down?

HEDDA: Because I have such a dread of scandal.

LÖVBORG: Yes, Hedda, you are a coward at heart.

HEDDA: A terrible coward. *(Changing her tone.)* But it was a lucky thing for you. And now you have found ample consolation at the Elvsteds'.

LÖVBORG: I know what Thea has confided to you.

HEDDA: And perhaps you have confided to her some thing about us?

LÖVBORG: Not a word. She is too stupid to understand anything of that sort.

HEDDA: Stupid?

LÖVBORG: She is stupid about matters of that sort.

HEDDA: And I am cowardly. *(Bends over towards him, without looking him in the face, and says more softly:)* But now I will confide something to you.

LÖVBORG *(eagerly):*   Well?

HEDDA: The fact that I dared not shoot you down—

LÖVBORG: Yes!

HEDDA: —that was not my most arrant cowardice—that evening.

LÖVBORG *(looks at her a moment, understands, and whispers passionately):*   Oh, Hedda! Hedda Gabler! Now I begin to see a hidden reason beneath our comradeship! You and I——! After all, then, it was your craving for life—

HEDDA *(softly, with a sharp glance):*   Take care! Believe nothing of the sort!

(Twilight has begun to fall. The hall door is opened from without by BERTA.*)*

HEDDA. *(Closes the album with a bang and calls smilingly):*   Ah, at last! My darling Thea,—come along!

*(*MRS. ELVSTED *enters from the hall. She is in evening dress. The door is closed behind her.)*

HEDDA *(on the sofa, stretches out her arms towards her):*   My sweet Thea—you can't think how I have been longing for you!

*(*MRS. ELVSTED, *in passing, exchanges slight salutations with the gentlemen in the inner room, then goes up to the table and gives* HEDDA *her hand.* EILERT LÖVBORG *has risen. He and* MRS. ELVSTED *greet each other with a silent nod.)*

MRS. ELVSTED: Ought I to go in and talk to your husband for a moment?

HEDDA: Oh, not at all. Leave those two alone. They will soon be going.

MRS. ELVSTED: Are they going out?

HEDDA: Yes, to a supper-party.

MRS. ELVSTED *(quickly, to* LÖVBORG*)*:   Not you?

LÖVBORG: No.

HEDDA: Mr. Lövborg remains with us.

MRS. ELVSTED: *(Takes a chair and is about to seat herself at his side.)* Oh, how nice it is here!

HEDDA: No, thank you, my little Thea! Not there! You'll be good enough to come over here to me. I will sit between you.

MRS. ELVSTED: Yes, just as you please.

(She goes round the table and seats herself on the sofa on HEDDA'S *right.* LÖVBORG *re-seats himself on his chair.)*

LÖVBORG *(after a short pause, to* HEDDA*)*:   Is not she lovely to look at?

HEDDA *(lightly stroking her hair)*:   Only to look at?

LÖVBORG: Yes. For we two—she and I—we are two real comrades. We have absolute faith in each other; so we can sit and talk with perfect frankness—

HEDDA: Not round about, Mr. Lövborg?

LÖVBORG: Well——

MRS. ELVSTED *(softly clinging close to* HEDDA*)*:   Oh, how happy I am, Hedda; for, only think, he says I have inspired him too.

HEDDA: *(Looks at her with a smile.)* Ah! Does he say that, dear?

LÖVBORG: And then she is so brave, Mrs. Tesman!

MRS. ELVSTED: Good heavens—am I brave?

LÖVBORG: Exceedingly—where your comrade is concerned.

HEDDA: Ah yes—courage! If one only had that!

LÖVBORG: What then? What do you mean?

HEDDA: Then life would perhaps be liveable, after all. *(With a sudden change of tone.)* But now, my dearest Thea, you really must have a glass of cold punch.

MRS. ELVSTED: No, thanks—I never take anything of that kind.

HEDDA: Well then, you, Mr. Lövborg.

LÖVBORG: Nor I, thank you.

MRS. ELVSTED: No, he doesn't either.

HEDDA: *(Looks fixedly at him.)* But if I say you shall?

LÖVBORG: It would be no use.

HEDDA *(laughing)*:   Then I, poor creature, have no sort of power over you?

LÖVBORG: Not in that respect.

HEDDA: But seriously, I think you ought to—for your own sake.

MRS. ELVSTED: Why, Hedda——!

LÖVBORG: How so?

HEDDA: Or rather on account of other people.

LÖVBORG: Indeed?

HEDDA: Otherwise people might be apt to suspect that—in your heart of hearts—you did not feel quite secure—quite confident in yourself.

MRS. ELVSTED *(softly)*:   Oh please, Hedda—.

LÖVBORG: People may suspect what they like—for the present.

MRS. ELVSTED *(joyfully):*   Yes, let them!

HEDDA: I saw it plainly in Judge Brack's face a moment ago.

LÖVBORG: What did you see?

HEDDA: His contemptuous smile, when you dared not go with them into the inner room.

LÖVBORG: Dared not? Of course I preferred to stop here and talk to you.

MRS. ELVSTED: What could be more natural, Hedda?

HEDDA: But the Judge could not guess that. And I saw, too, the way he smiled and glanced at Tesman when you dared not accept his invitation to this wretched little supper-party of his.

LÖVBORG: Dared not! Do you say I dared not?

HEDDA: *I* don't say so. But that was how Judge Brack understood it.

LÖVBORG: Well, let him.

HEDDA: Then you are not going with them?

LÖVBORG: I will stay here with you and Thea.

MRS. ELVSTED: Yes, Hedda—how can you doubt that?

HEDDA *(smiles and nods approvingly to* LÖVBORG*):*   Firm as a rock! Faithful to your principles, now and for ever! Ah, that is how a man should be! *(Turns to* MRS. ELVSTED *and caresses her.)* Well now, what did I tell you, when you came to us this morning in such a state of distraction—

LÖVBORG *(surprised):*   Distraction!

MRS. ELVSTED *(terrified):*   Hedda—oh Hedda——!

HEDDA: You can see for yourself; you haven't the slightest reason to be in such mortal terror——*(Interrupting herself.)* There! Now we can all three enjoy ourselves!

LÖVBORG *(who has given a start):*   Ah—what is all this, Mrs. Tesman?

MRS. ELVSTED: Oh my God, Hedda! What are you saying? What are you doing?

HEDDA: Don't get excited! That horrid Judge Brack is sitting watching you.

LÖVBORG: So she was in mortal terror! On my account!

MRS. ELVSTED *(softly and piteously):*   Oh, Hedda—now you have ruined every-thing!

LÖVBORG: *(Looks fixedly at her for a moment. His face is distorted.)* So that was my comrade's frank confidence in me?

MRS. ELVSTED *(imploringly):*   Oh, my dearest friend—only let me tell you—

LÖVBORG: *(Takes one of the glasses of punch, raises it to his lips, and says in a low, husky voice.)* Your health, Thea!
(He empties the glass, puts it down, and takes the second.)

MRS. ELVSTED *(softly):*   Oh, Hedda, Hedda—how could you do this?

HEDDA: *I* do it? *I?* Are you crazy?

LÖVBORG: Here's to your health too, Mrs. Tesman. Thanks for the truth. Hurrah for the truth!
(He empties the glass and is about to re-fill it.)

HEDDA: *(lays her hand on his arm.)* Come, come—no more for the present. Remember you are going out to supper.

MRS. ELVSTED: No, no, no!

HEDDA: Hush! They are sitting watching you.

LÖVBORG *(putting down the glass):*   Now, Thea—tell me the truth—

MRS. ELVSTED: Yes.

LÖVBORG: Did your husband know that you had come after me?

MRS. ELVSTED *(wringing her hands):*   Oh, Hedda—do you hear what he is asking?

LÖVBORG: Was it arranged between you and him that you were to come to town and look after me? Perhaps it was the Sheriff himself that urged you to come? Aha, my dear—no doubt he wanted my help in his office! Or was it at the card-table that he missed me?

MRS. ELVSTED *(softly, in agony):*   Oh, Lövborg, Lövborg—!

LÖVBORG: *(seizes a glass and is on the point of filling it.)* Here's a glass for the old Sheriff too!

HEDDA *(preventing him):*   No more just now. Remember you have to read your manuscript to Tesman.

LÖVBORG *(calmly, putting down the glass):*   It was stupid of me all this, Thea—to take it in this way, I mean. Don't be angry with me, my dear, dear comrade. You shall see—both you and the others—that if I was fallen once—now I have risen again! Thanks to you, Thea.

MRS. ELVSTED *(radiant with joy):*   Oh, heaven be praised—!

(BRACK has in the meantime looked at his watch. He and TESMAN rise and come into the drawing-room.)

BRACK: *(takes his hat and overcoat.)* Well, Mrs. Tesman, our time has come.

HEDDA: I suppose it has.

LÖVBORG *(rising):*   Mine too, Judge Brack.

MRS. ELVSTED *(softly and imploringly):*   Oh, Lövborg, don't do it!

HEDDA *(pinching her arm):*   They can hear you!

MRS. ELVSTED *(with a suppressed shriek):*   Ow!

LÖVBORG *(to* BRACK*):*   You were good enough to invite me.

BRACK: Well, are you coming after all?

LÖVBORG: Yes, many thanks.

BRACK: I'm delighted—

LÖVBORG *(to* TESMAN, *putting the parcel of MS. in his pocket):*   I should like to show you one or two things before I send it to the printers.

TESMAN: Fancy—that will be delightful. But, Hedda dear, how is Mrs. Elvsted to get home? Eh?

HEDDA: Oh, that can be managed somehow.

LÖVBORG *(looking towards the ladies):*   Mrs. Elvsted? Of course, I'll come again and fetch her. *(Approaching.)* At ten or thereabouts, Mrs. Tesman? Will that do?

HEDDA: Certainly. That will do capitally.

TESMAN: Well, then, that's all right. But you must not expect me so early, Hedda.

HEDDA: —Oh, you may stop as long—as long as ever you please.

MRS. ELVSTED *(trying to conceal her anxiety):*   Well then, Mr. Lövborg—I shall remain here until you come.

LÖVBORG *(with his hat in his hand):*   Pray do, Mrs. Elvsted.

BRACK: And now off goes the excursion train, gentlemen! I hope we shall have a lively time, as a certain fair lady puts it.

HEDDA: Ah, if only the fair lady could be present unseen—!

BRACK: Why unseen?

HEDDA: In order to hear a little of your liveliness at first hand, Judge Brack.

BRACK *(laughing):*   I should not advise the fair lady to try it.

TESMAN *(also laughing):*   Come, you're a nice one, Hedda! Fancy that!

BRACK: Well, good-bye, good-bye, ladies.

LÖVBORG *(bowing):*   About ten o'clock, then.

(BRACK, LÖVBORG, and TESMAN go out by the hall door. At the same time, BERTA enters from the inner room with a lighted lamp, which she places on the dining-room table; she goes out by the way she came.)

MRS. ELVSTED *(who has risen and is wandering restlessly about the room):*   Hedda—Hedda—what will come of all this?

HEDDA: At ten o'clock—he will be here. I can see him already—with vine-leaves in his hair—flushed and fearless—

MRS. ELVSTED: Oh, I hope he may.

HEDDA: And then, you see—then he will have regained control over himself. Then he will be a free man for all his days.

MRS. ELVSTED: Oh God!—if he would only come as you see him now!

HEDDA: He will come as I see him—so, and not otherwise! *(Rises and approaches THEA.)* You may doubt him as long as you please; *I* believe in him. And now we will try—

MRS. ELVSTED: You have some hidden motive in this, Hedda!

HEDDA: Yes, I have. I want for once in my life to have power to mould a human destiny.

MRS. ELVSTED: Have you not the power?

HEDDA: I have not—and have never had it.

MRS. ELVSTED: Not your husband's?

HEDDA: Do you think that is worth the trouble? Oh, if you could only understand how poor I am. And fate has made you so rich! *(Clasps her passionately in her arms.)* I think I must burn your hair off, after all.

MRS. ELVSTED: Let me go! Let me go! I am afraid of you, Hedda!

BERTA *(in the middle doorway):*   Tea is laid in the dining-room, ma'am.

HEDDA: Very well. We are coming.

MRS. ELVSTED: No, no, no! I would rather go home alone! At once!

HEDDA: Nonsense! First you shall have a cup of tea, you little stupid. And then—at ten o'clock—Eilert Lövborg will be here—with vine-leaves in his hair.

(She drags MRS. ELVSTED almost by force towards the middle doorway.)

ACT III

The room at the TESMANS'. *The curtains are drawn over the middle doorway, and also over the glass door. The lamp, half turned down, and with a shade over it, is burning on the table. In the stove, the door of which stands open, there has been a fire, which is now nearly burnt out.*

MRS. ELVSTED, *wrapped in a large shawl, and with her feet upon a foot-rest, sits close to the stove, sunk back in the arm-chair.* HEDDA, *fully dressed, lies sleeping upon the sofa, with a sofa-blanket over her.*

MRS. ELVSTED *(after a pause, suddenly sits up in her chair, and listens eagerly. Then she sinks back again wearily, moaning to herself):*   Not yet!—Oh God—oh God—not yet!

*(*BERTA *slips cautiously in by the hall door. She has a letter in her hand.)*

MRS. ELVSTED: *(Turns and whispers eagerly.)*   Well—has any one come?
BERTA *(softly):*   Yes, a girl has brought this letter.
MRS. ELVSTED *(quickly, holding out her hand):*   A letter! Give it to me!
BERTA: No, it's for Dr. Tesman, ma'am.
MRS. ELVSTED: Oh, indeed.
BERTA: It was Miss Tesman's servant that brought it. I'll lay it here on the table.
MRS. ELVSTED: Yes, do.
BERTA *(laying down the letter):*   I think I had better put out the lamp. It's smoking.
MRS. ELVSTED: Yes, put it out. It must soon be daylight now.
BERTA *(putting out the lamp):*   It is daylight already, ma'am.
MRS. ELVSTED: Yes, broad day! And no one come back yet—!
BERTA: Lord bless you, ma'am—I guessed how it would be.
MRS. ELVSTED: You guessed?
BERTA: Yes, when I saw that a certain person had come back to town—and that he went off with them. For we've heard enough about that gentleman before now.
MRS. ELVSTED: Don't speak so loud. You will waken Mrs. Tesman.
BERTA *(looks towards the sofa and sighs):*   No, no—let her sleep, poor thing. Shan't I put some wood on the fire?
MRS. ELVSTED: Thanks, not for me.
BERTA: Oh, very well. *(She goes softly out by the hall door.)*
HEDDA *(is awakened by the shutting of the door, and looks up):*   What's that—?
MRS. ELVSTED: It was only the servant—
HEDDA *(looking about her):*   Oh, we're here—! Yes, now I remember. *(Sits erect upon the sofa, stretches herself, and rubs her eyes.)* What o'clock is it, Thea?
MRS. ELVSTED: *(looks at her watch.)*   It's past seven.
HEDDA: When did Tesman come home?
MRS. ELVSTED: He has not come.
HEDDA: Not come home yet?

MRS. ELVSTED *(rising):*   No one has come.

HEDDA: Think of our watching and waiting here till four in the morning—

MRS. ELVSTED *(wringing her hands):*   And how I watched and waited for him!

HEDDA: *(yawns, and says with her hand before her mouth.)*   Well well—we might have spared ourselves the trouble.

MRS. ELVSTED·   Did you get a little sleep?

HEDDA: Oh yes; I believe I have slept pretty well. Have you not?

MRS. ELVSTED: Not for a moment. I couldn't, Hedda!—not to save my life.

HEDDA: *(rises and goes towards her.)*   There there there! There's nothing to be so alarmed about. I understand quite well what has happened.

MRS. ELVSTED: Well, what do you think? Won't you tell me?

HEDDA: Why, of course it has been a very late affair at Judge Brack's—

MRS. ELVSTED: Yes, yes, that is clear enough. But all the same—

HEDDA: And then, you see, Tesman hasn't cared to come home and ring us up in the middle of the night. *(Laughing.)* Perhaps he wasn't inclined to show himself either—immediately after a jollification.

MRS. ELVSTED: But in that case—where can he have gone?

HEDDA: Of course he has gone to his aunts' and slept there. They have his old room ready for him.

MRS. ELVSTED: No, he can't be with them; for a letter has just come for him from Miss Tesman. There it lies.

HEDDA: Indeed? *(Looks at the address.)* Why yes, it's addressed in Aunt Julia's own hand. Well then, he has remained at Judge Brack's. And as for Eilert Lövborg—he is sitting, with vine leaves in his hair, reading his manuscript.

MRS. ELVSTED: Oh Hedda, you are just saying things you don't believe a bit.

HEDDA: You really are a little blockhead, Thea.

MRS. ELVSTED: Oh yes, I suppose I am.

HEDDA: And how mortally tired you look.

MRS. ELVSTED: Yes, I am mortally tired.

HEDDA: Well then, you must do as I tell you. You must go into my room and lie down for a little while.

MRS. ELVSTED: Oh no, no—I shouldn't be able to sleep.

HEDDA: I am sure you would.

MRS. ELVSTED: Well, but your husband is certain to come soon now; and then I want to know at once—

HEDDA: I shall take care to let you know when he comes.

MRS. ELVSTED: Do you promise me, Hedda?

HEDDA: Yes, rely upon me. Just you go in and have a sleep in the meantime.

MRS. ELVSTED: Thanks; then I'll try to. *(She goes off through the inner room.)*

(HEDDA goes up to the glass door and draws back the curtains. The broad daylight streams into the room. Then she takes a little hand-glass from the writing-table, looks at herself in it, and arranges her hair. Next she goes to the hall door and presses the bell-button.)

(BERTA presently appears at the hall door.)

BERTA: Did you want anything, ma'am?

HEDDA: Yes; you must put some more wood in the stove. I am shivering.

BERTA: Bless me—I'll make up the fire at once. *(She rakes the embers together and lays a piece of wood upon them; then stops and listens.)* That was a ring at the front door, ma'am.

HEDDA: Then go to the door. I will look after the fire.

BERTA: It'll soon burn up. *(She goes out by the hall door.)*

> *(HEDDA kneels on the foot-rest and lays some more pieces of wood in the stove.)* *(After a short pause, GEORGE TESMAN enters from the hall. He looks tired and rather serious. He steals on tiptoe towards the middle doorway and is about to slip through the curtains.)*

HEDDA: *(at the stove, without looking up.)* Good morning.

TESMAN: *(turns.)* Hedda! *(approaching her.)* Good heavens—are you up so early? Eh?

HEDDA: Yes, I am up very early this morning.

TESMAN: And I never doubted you were still sound asleep! Fancy that, Hedda!

HEDDA: Don't speak so loud. Mrs. Elvsted is resting in my room.

TESMAN: Has Mrs. Elvsted been here all night?

HEDDA: Yes, since no one came to fetch her.

TESMAN: Ah, to be sure.

HEDDA: *(closes the door of the stove and rises.)* Well, did you enjoy yourselves at Judge Brack's?

TESMAN: Have you been anxious about me? Eh?

HEDDA: No, I should never think of being anxious. But I asked if you had enjoyed yourself.

TESMAN: Oh yes,—for once in a way. Especially the beginning of the evening; for then Eilert read me part of his book. We arrived more than an hour too early—fancy that! And Brack had all sorts of arrangements to make—so Eilert read to me.

HEDDA *(seating herself by the table on the right):* Well? Tell me, then—

TESMAN *(sitting on a footstool near the stove):* Oh Hedda, you can't conceive what a book that is going to be! I believe it is one of the most remarkable things that have ever been written. Fancy that!

HEDDA: Yes, yes; I don't care about that——

TESMAN: I must make a confession to you, Hedda. When he had finished reading—a horrid feeling came over me.

HEDDA: A horrid feeling?

TESMAN: I felt jealous of Eilert for having had it in him to write such a book. Only think, Hedda!

HEDDA: Yes, yes, I am thinking!

TESMAN: And then how pitiful to think that he—with all his gifts—should be irreclaimable, after all.

HEDDA: I suppose you mean that he has more courage than the rest?

TESMAN: No, not at all—I mean that he is incapable of taking his pleasures in moderation.

HEDDA: And what came of it all—in the end?

TESMAN: Well, to tell the truth, I think it might best be described as an orgie, Hedda.

HEDDA: Had he vine-leaves in his hair?

TESMAN: Vine-leaves? No, I saw nothing of the sort. But he made a long, rambling speech in honour of the woman who had inspired him in his work—that was the phrase he used.

HEDDA: Did he name her?

TESMAN: No, he didn't; but I can't help thinking he meant Mrs. Elvsted. You may be sure he did.

HEDDA: Well—where did you part from him?

TESMAN: On the way to town. We broke up—the last of us at any rate—all together; and Brack came with us to get a breath of fresh air. And then, you see, we agreed to take Eilert home; for he had had far more than was good for him.

HEDDA: I daresay.

TESMAN: But now comes the strange part of it, Hedda; or, I should rather say, the melancholy part of it. I declare I am almost ashamed—on Eilert's account—to tell you—

HEDDA: Oh, go on—

TESMAN: Well, as we were getting near town, you see, I happened to drop a little behind the others. Only for a minute or two—fancy that!

HEDDA: Yes, yes, yes, but——?

TESMAN: And then, as I hurried after them—what do you think I found by the wayside? Eh?

HEDDA: Oh, how should I know!

TESMAN: You mustn't speak of it to a soul, Hedda! Do you hear! Promise me, for Eilert's sake. (Draws a parcel, wrapped in paper, from his coat pocket.) Fancy, dear—I found this.

HEDDA: Is not that the parcel he had with him yesterday?

TESMAN: Yes, it is the whole of his precious, irreplaceable manuscript! And he had gone and lost it, and knew nothing about it. Only fancy, Hedda! So deplorably—

HEDDA: But why did you not give him back the parcel at once?

TESMAN: I didn't dare to—in the state he was then in—

HEDDA: Did you not tell any of the others that you had found it?

TESMAN: Oh, far from it! You can surely understand that, for Eilert's sake, I wouldn't do that.

HEDDA: So no one knows that Eilert Lövborg's manuscript is in your possession?

TESMAN: No. And no one must know it.

HEDDA: Then what did you say to him afterwards?

TESMAN: I didn't talk to him again at all; for when we got in among the streets, he and two or three of the others gave us the slip and disappeared. Fancy that!

HEDDA: Indeed! They must have taken him home then.

TESMAN: Yes, so it would appear. And Brack, too, left us.

HEDDA: And what have you been doing with yourself since?

TESMAN: Well, I and some of the others went home with one of the party, a jolly fellow, and took our morning coffee with him; or perhaps I should rather call it our night coffee—eh? But now, when I have rested a little, and given Eilert, poor fellow, time to have his sleep out, I must take this back to him.

HEDDA: *(holds out her hand for the packet.)* No—don't give it to him! Not in such a hurry, I mean. Let me read it first.

TESMAN: No, my dearest Hedda, I mustn't, I really mustn't.

HEDDA: You must not?

TESMAN: No—for you can imagine what a state of despair he will be in when he awakens and misses the manuscript. He has no copy of it, you must know! He told me so.

HEDDA *(looking searchingly at him):* Can such a thing not be reproduced? Written over again?

TESMAN: No, I don't think that would be possible. For the inspiration, you see—

HEDDA: Yes, yes—I suppose it depends on that. *(Lightly.)* But, by-the-bye—here is a letter for you.

TESMAN: Fancy——!

HEDDA *(handing it to him):* It came early this morning.

TESMAN: It's from Aunt Julia! What can it be? *(He lays the packet on the other footstool, opens the letter, runs his eye through it, and jumps up.)* Oh, Hedda—she says that poor Aunt Rina is dying!

HEDDA: Well, we were prepared for that.

TESMAN: And that if I want to see her again, I must make haste. I'll run in to them at once.

HEDDA *(suppressing a smile):* Will you run?

TESMAN: Oh, dearest Hedda—if you could only make up your mind to come with me! Just think!

HEDDA: *(rises and says wearily, repelling the idea.)* No, no, don't ask me. I will not look upon sickness and death. I loathe all sorts of ugliness.

TESMAN: Well, well, then—! *(Bustling around.)* My hat—My overcoat—? Oh, in the hall—I do hope I mayn't come too late, Hedda! Eh?

HEDDA: Oh, if you run—

(BERTA appears at the hall door.)

BERTA: Judge Brack is at the door, and wishes to know if he may come in.

TESMAN: At this time! No, I can't possibly see him.

HEDDA: But I can. *(To BERTA.)* Ask Judge Brack to come in. *(BERTA goes out.)*

HEDDA *(quickly, whispering):* The parcel, Tesman! *(She snatches it up from the stool.)*

TESMAN: Yes, give it to me!

HEDDA: No, no, I will keep it till you come back.

(She goes to the writing-table and places it in the bookcase. TESMAN *stands in a flurry of haste, and cannot get his gloves on.)*
*(*JUDGE BRACK *enters from the hall.)*

HEDDA *(nodding to him):* You are an early bird, I must say.

BRACK: Yes, don't you think so? *(To* TESMAN.*)* Are you on the move, too?

TESMAN: Yes, I must rush off to my aunts'. Fancy—the invalid one is lying at death's door, poor creature.

BRACK: Dear me, is she indeed? Then on no account let me detain you. At such a critical moment—

TESMAN: Yes, I must really rush—Good-bye! Good-bye! *(He hastens out by the hall door.)*

HEDDA *(approaching):* You seem to have made a particularly lively night of it at your rooms, Judge Brack.

BRACK: I assure you I have not had my clothes off, Mrs. Hedda.

HEDDA: Not you, either?

BRACK: No, as you may see. But what has Tesman been telling you of the night's adventures?

HEDDA: Oh, some tiresome story. Only that they went and had coffee somewhere or other.

BRACK: I have heard about that coffee-party already. Eilert Lövborg was not with them, I fancy?

HEDDA: No, they had taken him home before that.

BRACK: Tesman too?

HEDDA: No, but some of the others, he said.

BRACK *(smiling):* George Tesman is really an ingenuous creature, Mrs. Hedda.

HEDDA: Yes, heaven knows he is. Then is there something behind all this?

BRACK: Yes, perhaps there may be.

HEDDA: Well then, sit down, my dear Judge, and tell your story in comfort.

(She seats herself to the left of the table. BRACK *sits near her, at the long side of the table.)*

HEDDA: Now then?

BRACK: I had special reasons for keeping track of my guests—or rather of some of my guests—last night.

HEDDA: Of Eilert Lövborg among the rest, perhaps?

BRACK: Frankly, yes.

HEDDA: Now you make me really curious—

BRACK: Do you know where he and one or two of the others finished the night, Mrs. Hedda?

HEDDA: If it is not quite unmentionable, tell me.

BRACK: Oh no, it's not at all unmentionable. Well, they put in an appearance at a particularly animated soirée.

HEDDA: Of the lively kind?

BRACK: Of the very liveliest—

HEDDA: Tell me more of this, Judge Brack—

BRACK: Lövborg, as well as the others, had been invited in advance. I knew all about it. But he had declined the invitation; for now, as you know, he has become a new man.

HEDDA: Up at the Elvsteds', yes. But he went after all, then?

BRACK: Well, you see, Mrs. Hedda—unhappily the spirit moved him at my rooms last evening—

HEDDA: Yes, I hear he found inspiration.

BRACK: Pretty violent inspiration. Well, I fancy that altered his purpose; for we men folk are unfortunately not always so firm in our principles as we ought to be.

HEDDA: Oh, I am sure you are an exception, Judge Brack. But as to Lövborg—?

BRACK: To make a long story short—he landed at last in Mademoiselle Diana's rooms.

HEDDA: Mademoiselle Diana's?

BRACK: It was Mademoiselle Diana that was giving the soirée, to a select circle of her admirers and her lady friends.

HEDDA: Is she a red-haired woman?

BRACK: Precisely.

HEDDA: A sort of a—singer?

BRACK: Oh yes—in her leisure moments. And moreover a mighty huntress—of men—Mrs. Hedda. You have no doubt heard of her. Eilert Lövborg was one of her most enthusiastic protectors—in the days of his glory.

HEDDA: And how did all this end?

BRACK: Far from amicably, it appears. After a most tender meeting, they seem to have come to blows—

HEDDA: Lövborg and she?

BRACK: Yes. He accused her or her friends of having robbed him. He declared that his pocket-book had disappeared—and other things as well. In short, he seems to have made a furious disturbance.

HEDDA: And what came of it all?

BRACK: It came to a general scrimmage, in which the ladies as well as the gentlemen took part. Fortunately the police at last appeared on the scene.

HEDDA: The police too?

BRACK: Yes. I fancy it will prove a costly frolic for Eilert Lövborg, crazy being that he is.

HEDDA: How so?

BRACK: He seems to have made a violent resistance—to have hit one of the constables on the head and torn the coat off his back. So they had to march him off to the police-station with the rest.

HEDDA: How have you learnt all this?

BRACK: From the police themselves.

HEDDA (*gazing straight before her*):   So that is what happened. Then he had no vine-leaves in his hair.

BRACK: Vine-leaves, Mrs. Hedda?

HEDDA (*changing her tone*):   But tell me now, Judge— what is your real reason for tracking out Eilert Lövborg's movements so carefully?

BRACK: In the first place, it could not be entirely indifferent to me if it should appear in the police-court that he came straight from my house.

HEDDA: Will the matter come into court then?

BRACK: Of course. However, I should scarcely have troubled so much about that. But I thought that, as a friend of the family, it was my duty to supply you and Tesman with a full account of his nocturnal exploits.

HEDDA: Why so, Judge Brack?

BRACK: Why, because I have a shrewd suspicion that he intends to use you as a sort of blind.

HEDDA: Oh, how can you think such a thing!

BRACK: Good heavens, Mrs. Hedda—we have eyes in our head. Mark my words! This Mrs. Elvsted will be in no hurry to leave town again.

HEDDA: Well, even if there should be anything between them, I suppose there are plenty of other places where they could meet.

BRACK: Not a single home. Henceforth, as before, every respectable house will be closed against Eilert Lövborg.

HEDDA: And so ought mine to be, you mean?

BRACK: Yes. I confess it would be more than painful to me if this personage were to be made free of your house. How superfluous, how intrusive, he would be, if he were to force his way into—

HEDDA: —into the triangle?

BRACK: Precisely. It would simply mean that I should find myself homeless.

HEDDA: (*looks at him with a smile.*)   So you want to be the one cock in the basket—that is your aim.

BRACK (*nods slowly and lowers his voice*):   Yes, that is my aim. And for that I will fight—with every weapon I can command.

HEDDA (*her smile vanishing*):   I see you are a dangerous person—when it comes to the point.

BRACK: Do you think so?

HEDDA: I am beginning to think so. And I am exceedingly glad to think—that you have no sort of hold over me.

BRACK (*laughing equivocally*):   Well, well, Mrs. Hedda—perhaps you are right there. If I had, who knows what I might be capable of?

HEDDA: Come, come now, Judge Brack! That sounds almost like a threat.

BRACK (*rising*):   Oh, not at all! The triangle, you know, ought, if possible, to be spontaneously constructed.

HEDDA: There I agree with you.

BRACK: Well, now I have said all I had to say; and I had better be getting back to town. Good-bye, Mrs. Hedda. (*He goes towards the glass door.*)

HEDDA (*rising*):   Are you going through the garden?

BRACK: Yes, it's a short cut for me.

HEDDA: And then it is a back way, too.

BRACK: Quite so. I have no objection to back ways. They may be piquant enough at times.

HEDDA: When there is ball practice going on, you mean?

BRACK *(in the doorway, laughing to her):*   Oh, people don't shoot their tame poultry, I fancy.

HEDDA *(also laughing):*   Oh no, when there is only one cock in the basket—

(They exchange laughing nods of farewell. He goes. She closes the door behind him.)
(HEDDA, who has become quite serious, stands for a moment looking out. Presently she goes and peeps through the curtain over the middle doorway. Then she goes to the writing-table, takes LÖVBORG'S packet out of the bookcase, and is on the point of looking through its contents. BERTA is heard speaking loudly in the hall. HEDDA turns and listens. Then she hastily locks up the packet in the drawer, and lays the key on the inkstand.)
(EILERT LÖVBORG, with his greatcoat on and his hat in his hand, tears open the hall door. He looks somewhat confused and irritated.)

LÖVBORG *(looking towards the hall):*   And I tell you I must and will come in! There!

(He closes the door, turns, sees HEDDA, at once regains his self-control, and bows.)

HEDDA *(at the writing-table):*   Well, Mr. Lövborg, this is rather a late hour to call for Thea.

LÖVBORG: You mean rather an early hour to call on you. Pray pardon me.

HEDDA: How do you know that she is still here?

LÖVBORG: They told me at her lodgings that she had been out all night.

HEDDA *(going to the oval table):*   Did you notice anything about the people of the house when they said that?

LÖVBORG: *(looks inquiringly at her).*   Notice anything about them?

HEDDA: I mean, did they seem to think it odd?

LÖVBORG *(suddenly understanding):*   Oh yes, of course! I am dragging her down with me! However, I didn't notice anything.—I suppose Tesman is not up yet?

HEDDA: No—I think not—

LÖVBORG: When did he come home?

HEDDA: Very late.

LÖVBORG: Did he tell you anything?

HEDDA: Yes, I gathered that you had had an exceedingly jolly evening at Judge Brack's.

LÖVBORG: Nothing more?

HEDDA: I don't think so. However, I was so dreadfully sleepy—

(MRS. ELVSTED enters through the curtains of the middle doorway.)

MRS. ELVSTED *(going towards him):*   Ah, Lövborg! At last——!

LÖVBORG: Yes, at last. And too late!

MRS. ELVSTED: *(looks anxiously at him).*   What is too late?

LÖVBORG: Everything is too late now. It is all over with me.

MRS. ELVSTED: Oh no, no—don't say that!

LÖVBORG: You will say the same when you hear—

MRS. ELVSTED: I won't hear anything!

HEDDA: Perhaps you would prefer to talk to her alone! If so, I will leave you.

LÖVBORG: No, stay—you too. I beg you to stay.

MRS. ELVSTED: Yes, but I won't hear anything, I tell you.

LÖVBORG: It is not last night's adventures that I want to talk about.

MRS. ELVSTED: What is it then—?

LÖVBORG: I want to say that now our ways must part.

MRS. ELVSTED: Part!

HEDDA *(involuntarily):*   I knew it!

LÖVBORG: You can be of no more service to me, Thea.

MRS. ELVSTED: How can you stand there and say that! No more service to you! Am I not to help you now, as before? Are we not to go on working together?

LÖVBORG: Henceforward I shall do no work.

MRS. ELVSTED *(despairingly):*   Then what am I to do with my life?

LÖVBORG: You must try to live your life as if you had never known me.

MRS. ELVSTED: But you know I cannot do that!

LÖVBORG: Try if you cannot, Thea. You must go home again—

MRS. ELVSTED *(in vehement protest):*   Never in this world! Where you are, there will I be also! I will not let myself be driven away like this! I will remain here! I will be with you when the book appears.

HEDDA *(half aloud, in suspense):*   Ah yes—the book!

LÖVBORG: *(looks at her.)*   My book and Thea's; for that is what it is.

MRS. ELVSTED: Yes, I feel that it is. And that is why I have a right to be with you when it appears! I will see with my own eyes how respect and honour pour in upon you afresh. And the happiness—the happiness—oh, I must share it with you!

LÖVBORG: Thea—our book will never appear.

HEDDA: Ah!

MRS. ELVSTED: Never appear!

LÖVBORG: Can never appear.

MRS. ELVSTED *(in agonised foreboding):*   Lövborg—what have you done with the manuscript?

HEDDA: *(looks anxiously at him).*   Yes, the manuscript—?

MRS. ELVSTED: Where is it?

LÖVBORG: Oh Thea—don't ask me about it!

MRS. ELVSTED: Yes, yes, I will know. I demand to be told at once.

LÖVBORG: The manuscript— Well then—I have torn the manuscript into a thousand pieces.

MRS. ELVSTED: *(shrieks).*   Oh no, no—!

HEDDA *(involuntarily):*   But that's not—

LÖVBORG: *(looks at her).*   Not true, you think?

HEDDA *(collecting herself):*   Oh well, of course—since you say so. But it sounded so improbable—

LÖVBORG: It is true, all the same.

MRS. ELVSTED *(wringing her hands):*   Oh God—oh God, Hedda—torn his own work to pieces!

LÖVBORG: I have torn my own life to pieces. So why should I not tear my life-work too—?

MRS. ELVSTED: And you did this last night?

LÖVBORG: Yes, I tell you! Tore it into a thousand pieces and scattered them on the fiord—far out. There there is cool sea-water at any rate—let them drift upon it—drift with the current and the wind. And then presently they will sink—deeper and deeper—as I shall, Thea.

MRS. ELVSTED: Do you know, Lövborg, that what you have done with the book—I shall think of it to my dying day as though you had killed a little child.

LÖVBORG: Yes, you are right. It is a sort of child-murder.

MRS. ELVSTED: How could you, then—! Did not the child belong to me too?

HEDDA *(almost inaudibly):*   Ah, the child—

MRS. ELVSTED *(breathing heavily):*   It is all over then. Well, well, now I will go, Hedda.

HEDDA: But you are not going away from town?

MRS. ELVSTED: Oh, I don't know what I shall do. I see nothing but darkness before me. *(She goes out by the hall door.)*

HEDDA: *(stands waiting for a moment).*   So you are not going to see her home, Mr. Lövborg?

LÖVBORG: I? Through the streets? Would you have people see her walking with me?

HEDDA: Of course I don't know what else may have happened last night. But is it so utterly irretrievable?

LÖVBORG: It will not end with last night—I know that perfectly well. And the thing is that now I have no taste for that sort of life either. I won't begin it anew. She has broken my courage and my power of braving life out.

HEDDA *(looking straight before her):*   So that pretty little fool has had her fingers in a man's destiny. *(Looks at him.)* But all the same, how could you treat her so heartlessly.

LÖVBORG: Oh, don't say that it was heartless!

HEDDA: To go and destroy what has filled her whole soul for months and years! You do not call that heartless!

LÖVBORG: To you I can tell the truth, Hedda.

HEDDA: The truth?

LÖVBORG: First promise me—give me your word—that what I now confide to you Thea shall never know.

HEDDA: I give you my word.

LÖVBORG: Good. Then let me tell you that what I said just now was untrue.

HEDDA: About the manuscript?

LÖVBORG: Yes. I have not torn it to pieces—nor thrown it into the fiord.

HEDDA: No, n— But—where is it then?

LÖVBORG: I have destroyed it none the less—utterly destroyed it, Hedda!

HEDDA: I don't understand.

LÖVBORG: Thea said that what I had done seemed to her like a child-murder.

HEDDA: Yes, so she said.

LÖVBORG: But to kill this child—that is not the worst thing a father can do to it.

HEDDA: Not the worst?

LÖVBORG: No. I wanted to spare Thea from hearing the worst?

HEDDA: Then what is the worst?

LÖVBORG: Suppose now, Hedda, that a man—in the small hours of the morning—came home to his child's mother after a night of riot and debauchery, and said: "Listen—I have been here and there—in this place and in that. And I have taken our child with me—to this place and to that. And I have lost the child—utterly lost it. The devil knows into what hands it may have fallen—who may have had their clutches on it."

HEDDA: Well—but when all is said and done, you know—this was only a book—

LÖVBORG: Thea's pure soul was in that book.

HEDDA: Yes, so I understand.

LÖVBORG: And you can understand, too, that for her and me together no future is possible.

HEDDA: What path do you mean to take then?

LÖVBORG: None. I will only try to make an end of it all—the sooner the better.

HEDDA *(a step nearer him)*: Eilert Lövborg—listen to me.—Will you not try to—to do it beautifully?

LÖVBORG: Beautifully? *(Smiling).* With vine-leaves in my hair, as you used to dream in the old days—?

HEDDA: No, no. I have lost my faith in the vine-leaves. But beautifully nevertheless! For once in a way!—Good-bye! You must go now—and do not come here any more.

LÖVBORG: Good-bye, Mrs. Tesman. And give George Tesman my love. *(He is on the point of going.)*

HEDDA: No, wait! I must give you a memento to take with you.

(She goes to the writing-table and opens the drawer and the pistol-case; then returns to LÖVBORG *with one of the pistols.)*

LÖVBORG *(looks at her)*: This? Is this the memento?

HEDDA *(nodding slowly)*: Do you recognise it? It was aimed at you once.

LÖVBORG: You should have used it then.

HEDDA: Take it—and do you use it now.

LÖVBORG *(puts the pistol in his breast pocket)*: Thanks!

HEDDA: And beautifully, Eilert Lövborg. Promise me that!

LÖVBORG: Good-bye, Hedda Gabler. *(He goes out by the hall door.)*

(HEDDA listens for a moment at the door. Then she goes up to the writing-table, takes out the packet of manuscript, peeps under the cover, draws a few of the sheets half out, and looks at them. Next she goes over and seats herself in the arm-chair beside the stove, with the packet in her lap. Presently she opens the stove door, and then the packet.)

HEDDA *(throws one of the quires into the fire and whispers to herself):*   Now I am burning your child, Thea!—Burning it, curly-locks! *(Throwing one or two more quires into the stove.)* Your child and Eilert Lövborg's. *(Throws the rest in.)* I am burning—I am burning your child.

ACT IV

The same rooms at the TESMANS'. *It is evening. The drawing-room is in darkness. The back room is lighted by the hanging lamp over the table. The curtains over the glass door are drawn close.*

    HEDDA, *dressed in black, walks to and fro in the dark room. Then she goes into the back room and disappears for a moment to the left. She is heard to strike a few chords on the piano. Presently she comes in sight again, and returns to the drawing-room.*

    BERTA *enters from the right, through the inner room, with a lighted lamp, which she places on the table in front of the corner settee in the drawing-room. Her eyes are red with weeping, and she has black ribbons in her cap. She goes quietly and circumspectly out to the right.*

    HEDDA *goes up to the glass door, lifts the curtain a little aside, and looks out into the darkness.*

    Shortly afterwards, MISS TESMAN, *in mourning, with a bonnet and veil on, comes in from the hall.* HEDDA *goes towards her and holds out her hand.*

MISS TESMAN: Yes, Hedda, here I am, in mourning and forlorn; for now my poor sister has at last found peace.

HEDDA: I have heard the news already, as you see. Tesman sent me a card.

MISS TESMAN: Yes, he promised me he would. But nevertheless I thought that to Hedda—here in the house of life—I ought myself to bring the tidings of death.

HEDDA: That was very kind of you.

MISS TESMAN: Ah, Rina ought not to have left us just now. This is not the time for Hedda's house to be a house of mourning.

HEDDA *(changing the subject):*   She died quite peacefully, did she not, Miss Tesman?

MISS TESMAN: Oh, her end was so calm, so beautiful. And then she had the unspeakable happiness of seeing George once more—and bidding him good-bye.—Has he come home yet?

HEDDA: No. He wrote that he might be detained. But won't you sit down?

MISS TESMAN: No thank you, my dear, dear Hedda. I should like to, but I have so much to do. I must prepare my dear one for her rest as well as I can. She shall go to her grave looking her best.

HEDDA: Can I not help you in any way?

MISS TESMAN: Oh, you must not think of it! Hedda Tesman must have no hand in such mournful work. Nor let her thoughts dwell on it either—not at this time.

HEDDA: One is not always mistress of one's thoughts——

MISS TESMAN *(continuing):*   Ah yes, it is the way of the world. At home we shall be sewing a shroud; and here there will soon be sewing too, I suppose— but of another sort, thank God!

(GEORGE TESMAN enters by the hall door.)

HEDDA: Ah, you have come at last!

TESMAN: You here, Aunt Julia? With Hedda? Fancy that!

MISS TESMAN: I was just going, my dear boy. Well, have you done all you promised?

TESMAN: No; I'm really afraid I have forgotten half of it. I must come to you again to-morrow. To-day my brain is all in a whirl. I can't keep my thoughts together.

MISS TESMAN: Why, my dear George, you mustn't take it in this way.

TESMAN: Mustn't——? How do you mean?

MISS TESMAN: Even in your sorrow you must rejoice, as I do—rejoice that she is at rest.

TESMAN: Oh yes, yes—you are thinking of Aunt Rina.

HEDDA: You will feel lonely now, Miss Tesman.

MISS TESMAN: Just at first, yes. But that will not last very long, I hope. I daresay I shall soon find an occupant for poor Rina's little room.

TESMAN: Indeed? Who do you think will take it? Eh?

MISS TESMAN: Oh, there's always some poor invalid or other in want of nursing, unfortunately.

HEDDA: Would you really take such a burden upon you again?

MISS TESMAN: A burden! Heaven forgive you, child—it has been no burden to me.

HEDDA: But suppose you had a total stranger on your hands——

MISS TESMAN: Oh, one soon makes friends with sick folk; and it's such an absolute necessity for me to have some one to live for. Well, heaven be praised, there may soon be something in this house, too, to keep an old aunt busy.

HEDDA: Oh, don't trouble about anything here.

TESMAN: Yes, just fancy what a nice time we three might have together, if——?

HEDDA: If——?

TESMAN *(uneasily):*   Oh, nothing. It will all come right. Let us hope so—eh?

MISS TESMAN: Well, well, I daresay you two want to talk to each other. *(Smiling.)* And perhaps Hedda may have something to tell you too,

George. Good-bye! I must go home to Rina. *(Turning at the door.)* How strange it is to think that now Rina is with me and with my poor brother as well!

TESMAN: Yes, fancy that, Aunt Julia! Eh? *(MISS TESMAN goes out by the hall door.)*

HEDDA *(follows TESMAN coldly and searchingly with her eyes):*   I almost believe your Aunt Rina's death affects you more than it does your Aunt Julia.

TESMAN: Oh, it's not that alone. It's Eilert I am so terribly uneasy about.

HEDDA *(quickly):*   Is there anything new about him?

TESMAN: I looked in at his rooms this afternoon, intending to tell him the manuscript was in safe keeping.

HEDDA: Well, did you not find him?

TESMAN: No. He wasn't at home. But afterwards I met Mrs. Elvsted, and she told me that he had been here early this morning.

HEDDA: Yes, directly after you had gone.

TESMAN: And he said that he had torn his manuscript to pieces—eh?

HEDDA: Yes, so he declared.

TESMAN: Why, good heavens, he must have been completely out of his mind! And I suppose you thought it best not to give it back to him, Hedda?

HEDDA: No, he did not get it.

TESMAN: But of course you told him that we had it?

HEDDA: No. *(Quickly.)* Did you tell Mrs. Elvsted?

TESMAN: No; I thought I had better not. But you ought to have told him. Fancy, if, in desperation, he should go and do himself some injury! Let me have the manuscript, Hedda! I will take it to him at once. Where is it?

HEDDA *(cold and immovable, leaning on the arm-chair):*   I have not got it.

TESMAN: Have not got it? What in the world do you mean?

HEDDA: I have burnt it—every line of it.

TESMAN *(with a violent movement of terror):*   Burnt! Burnt Eilert's manuscript!

HEDDA: Don't scream so. The servant might hear you.

TESMAN: Burnt! Why, good God——! No, no, no! It's impossible!

HEDDA: It is so, nevertheless.

TESMAN: Do you know what you have done, Hedda? It's unlawful appropriation of lost property. Fancy that! Just ask Judge Brack, and he'll tell you what it is.

HEDDA: I advise you not to speak of it—either to Judge Brack, or to any one else.

TESMAN: But how could you do anything so unheard-of? What put it into your head? What possessed you? Answer me that—eh?

HEDDA *(suppressing an almost imperceptible smile):*   I did it for your sake, George.

TESMAN: For my sake!

HEDDA: This morning, when you told me about what he had read to you——

TESMAN: Yes, yes—what then?

HEDDA: You acknowledged that you envied him his work.

TESMAN: Oh, of course I didn't mean that literally.

HEDDA: No matter—I could not bear the idea that any one should throw you into the shade.

TESMAN *(in an outburst of mingled doubt and joy):*   Hedda! Oh, is this true? But—but—I never knew you to show your love like that before. Fancy that!

HEDDA: Well, I may as well tell you that—just at this time——*(Impatiently, breaking off.)* No, no; you can ask Aunt Julia. She will tell you, fast enough.

TESMAN: Oh, I almost think I understand you, Hedda! *(Clasps his hands together.)* Great heavens! do you really mean it! Eh?

HEDDA: Don't shout so. The servant might hear.

TESMAN *(laughing in irrepressible glee):*   The servant! Why, how absurd you are, Hedda. It's only my old Berta! Why, I'll tell Berta myself.

HEDDA *(clenching her hands together in desperation):*   Oh, it is killing me,—it is killing me, all this!

TESMAN: What is, Hedda? Eh?

HEDDA *(coldly, controlling herself):*   All this—absurdity, George.

TESMAN: Absurdity! Do you see anything absurd in my being overjoyed at the news! But after all—perhaps I had better not say anything to Berta.

HEDDA: Oh—why not that too?

TESMAN: No, no, not yet! But I must certainly tell Aunt Julia. And then that you have begun to call me George too! Fancy that! Oh, Aunt Julia will be so happy—so happy!

HEDDA: When she hears that I have burnt Eilert Lövborg's manuscript—for your sake?

TESMAN: No, by-the-bye—that affair of the manuscript—of course nobody must know about that. But that you love me so much, Hedda—Aunt Julia must really share my joy in that! I wonder, now, whether this sort of thing is usual in young wives? Eh?

HEDDA: I think you had better ask Aunt Julia that question too.

TESMAN: I will indeed, some time or other. *(Looks uneasy and downcast again.)* And yet the manuscript—the manuscript! Good God! it is terrible to think what will become of poor Eilert now.

(MRS. ELVSTED, *dressed as in the first Act, with hat and cloak, enters by the hall door.)*

MRS. ELVSTED *(greets them hurriedly, and says in evident agitation):*   Oh, dear Hedda, forgive my coming again.

HEDDA: What is the matter with you, Thea?

TESMAN: Something about Eilert Lövborg again—eh?

MRS. ELVSTED: Yes! I am dreadfully afraid some misfortune has happened to him.

HEDDA *(seizes her arm):*   Ah,—do you think so?

TESMAN: Why, good Lord—what makes you think that, Mrs. Elvsted?

MRS. ELVSTED: I heard them talking of him at my boarding-house—just as I came in. Oh, the most incredible rumours are afloat about him to-day.

TESMAN: Yes, fancy, so I heard too! And I can bear witness that he went straight home to bed last night. Fancy that!

HEDDA: Well, what did they say at the boarding-house?

MRS. ELVSTED: Oh, I couldn't make out anything clearly. Either they knew nothing definite, or else——They stopped talking when they saw me; and I did not dare to ask.

TESMAN (moving about uneasily): We must hope—we must hope that you misunderstood them, Mrs. Elvsted.

MRS. ELVSTED: No, no; I am sure it was of him they were talking. And I heard something about the hospital or——

TESMAN: The hospital?

HEDDA: No—surely that cannot be!

MRS. ELVSTED: Oh, I was in such mortal terror! I went to his lodgings and asked for him there.

HEDDA: You could make up your mind to that, Thea!

MRS. ELVSTED: What else could I do? I really could bear the suspense no longer.

TESMAN: But you didn't find him either—eh?

MRS. ELVSTED: No. And the people knew nothing about him. He hadn't been home since yesterday afternoon, they said.

TESMAN: Yesterday! Fancy, how could they say that?

MRS. ELVSTED: Oh, I am sure something terrible must have happened to him.

TESMAN: Hedda dear—how would it be if I were to go and make inquiries—?

HEDDA: No, no—don't you mix yourself up in this affair.

(JUDGE BRACK, with his hat in his hand, enters by the hall door, which BERTA opens, and closes behind him. He looks grave and bows in silence.)

TESMAN: Oh, is that you, my dear Judge? Eh?

BRACK: Yes. It was imperative I should see you this evening.

TESMAN: I can see you have heard the news about Aunt Rina?

BRACK: Yes, that among other things.

TESMAN: Isn't it sad—eh?

BRACK: Well, my dear Tesman, that depends on how you look at it.

TESMAN (looks doubtfully at him): Has anything else happened?

BRACK: Yes.

HEDDA (in suspense): Anything sad, Judge Brack?

BRACK: That, too, depends on how you look at it, Mrs. Tesman.

MRS. ELVSTED (unable to restrain her anxiety): Oh! it is something about Eilert Lövborg!

BRACK (with a glance at her): What makes you think that, Madam? Perhaps you have already heard something——?

MRS. ELVSTED *(in confusion):*   No, nothing at all, but——

TESMAN: Oh, for heaven's sake, tell us!

BRACK *(shrugging his shoulders):*   Well, I regret to say Eilert Lövborg has been taken to the hospital. He is lying at the point of death.

MRS. ELVSTED *(shrieks):*   Oh God! Oh God——!

TESMAN: To the hospital! And at the point of death.

HEDDA *(involuntarily):*   So soon then——

MRS. ELVSTED *(wailing):*   And we parted in anger, Hedda!

HEDDA *(whispers):*   Thea—Thea—be careful!

MRS. ELVSTED *(not heeding her):*   I must go to him! I must see him alive!

BRACK: It is useless, Madam. No one will be admitted.

MRS. ELVSTED: Oh, at least tell me what has happened to him? What is it?

TESMAN: You don't mean to say that he has himself——Eh?

HEDDA: Yes, I am sure he has.

TESMAN: Hedda, how can you——?

BRACK *(keeping his eyes fixed upon her):*   Unfortunately you have guessed quite correctly, Mrs. Tesman.

MRS. ELVSTED: Oh, how horrible!

TESMAN: Himself, then! Fancy that!

HEDDA: Shot himself!

BRACK: Rightly guessed again, Mrs. Tesman.

MRS. ELVSTED *(with an effort at self-control):*   When did it happen, Mr. Brack?

BRACK: This afternoon—between three and four.

TESMAN: But, good Lord, where did he do it? Eh?

BRACK *(with some hesitation):*   Where? Well—I suppose at his lodgings.

MRS. ELVSTED: No, that cannot be; for I was there between six and seven.

BRACK: Well, then, somewhere else. I don't know exactly. I only know that he was found——. He had shot himself—in the breast.

MRS. ELVSTED: Oh, how terrible! That he should die like that!

HEDDA *(to Brack):*   Was it in the breast?

BRACK: Yes—as I told you.

HEDDA: Not in the temple?

BRACK: In the breast, Mrs. Tesman.

HEDDA: Well, well—the breast is a good place, too.

BRACK: How do you mean, Mrs. Tesman?

HEDDA *(evasively):*   Oh, nothing—nothing.

TESMAN: And the wound is dangerous, you say—eh?

BRACK: Absolutely mortal. The end has probably come by this time.

MRS. ELVSTED: Yes, yes, I feel it. The end! The end! Oh, Hedda——!

TESMAN: But tell me, how have you learnt all this?

BRACK *(curtly):*   Through one of the police. A man I had some business with.

HEDDA *(in a clear voice):*   At last a deed worth doing!

TESMAN *(terrified):*   Good heavens, Hedda! what are you saying?

HEDDA: I say there is beauty in this.

BRACK: H'm, Mrs. Tesman——

TESMAN: Beauty! Fancy that!

MRS. ELVSTED: Oh, Hedda, how can you talk of beauty in such an act!

HEDDA: Eilert Lövborg has himself made up his account with life. He has had the courage to do—the one right thing.

MRS. ELVSTED: No, you must never think that was how it happened! It must have been in delirium that he did it.

TESMAN: In despair!

HEDDA: That he did not. I am certain of that.

MRS. ELVSTED: Yes, yes! In delirium! Just as when he tore up our manuscript.

BRACK *(starting)*:   The manuscript? Has he torn that up?

MRS. ELVSTED: Yes, last night.

TESMAN *(whispers softly)*:   Oh, Hedda, we shall never get over this.

BRACK: H'm, very extraordinary.

TESMAN *(moving about the room)*:   To think of Eilert going out of the world in this way! And not leaving behind him the book that would have immortalised his name——

MRS. ELVSTED: Oh, if only it could be put together again!

TESMAN: Yes, if it only could! I don't know what I would not give——

MRS. ELVSTED: Perhaps it can, Mr. Tesman.

TESMAN: What do you mean?

MRS. ELVSTED *(searches in the pocket of her dress)*:   Look here. I have kept all the loose notes he used to dictate from.

HEDDA *(a step forward)*:   Ah——!

TESMAN: You have kept them, Mrs. Elvsted! Eh?

MRS. ELVSTED: Yes, I have them here. I put them in my pocket when I left home. Here they still are——

TESMAN: Oh, do let me see them!

MRS. ELVSTED *(hands him a bundle of papers)*:   But they are in such disorder—all mixed up.

TESMAN: Fancy, if we could make something out of them, after all! Perhaps if we two put our heads together——

MRS. ELVSTED: Oh, yes, at least let us try——

TESMAN: We will manage it! We must! I will dedicate my life to this task.

HEDDA: You, George? Your life?

TESMAN: Yes, or rather all the time I can spare. My own collections must wait in the meantime. Hedda—you understand, eh? I owe this to Eilert's memory.

HEDDA: Perhaps.

TESMAN: And so, my dear Mrs. Elvsted, we will give our whole minds to it. There is no use in brooding over what can't be undone—eh? We must try to control our grief as much as possible, and——

MRS. ELVSTED: Yes, yes, Mr. Tesman, I will do the best I can.

TESMAN: Well then, come here. I can't rest until we have looked through the notes. Where shall we sit? Here? No, in there, in the back room. Excuse me, my dear Judge. Come with me, Mrs. Elvsted.

MRS. ELVSTED: Oh, if only it were possible! *(TESMAN and* MRS. ELVSTED *go into the back room. She takes off her hat and cloak. They both sit at the table under the hanging lamp, and are soon deep in an eager examination of the papers.* HEDDA *crosses to the stove and sits in the arm-chair. Presently* BRACK *goes up to her.)*

HEDDA *(in a low voice):* Oh, what a sense of freedom it gives one, this act of Eilert Lövborg's.

BRACK: Freedom, Mrs. Hedda? Well, of course, it is a release for him——

HEDDA: I mean for me. It gives me a sense of freedom to know that a deed of deliberate courage is still possible in this world,—a deed of spontaneous beauty.

BRACK *(smiling):* H'm—my dear Mrs. Hedda——

HEDDA: Oh, I know what you are going to say. For you are a kind of specialist too, like—you know!

BRACK *(looking hard at her):* Eilert Lövborg was more to you than perhaps you are willing to admit to yourself. Am I wrong?

HEDDA: I don't answer such questions. I only know that Eilert Lövborg has had the courage to live his life after his own fashion. And then—the last great act, with its beauty! Ah! that he should have the will and the strength to turn away from the banquet of life—so early.

BRACK: I am sorry, Mrs. Hedda,—but I fear I must dispel an amiable illusion.

HEDDA: Illusion?

BRACK: Which could not have lasted long in any case.

HEDDA: What do you mean?

BRACK: Eilert Lövborg did not shoot himself—voluntarily.

HEDDA: Not voluntarily?

BRACK: No. The thing did not happen exactly as I told it.

HEDDA *(in suspense):* Have you concealed something? What is it?

BRACK: For poor Mrs. Elvsted's sake I idealised the facts a little.

HEDDA: What are the facts?

BRACK: First, that he is already dead.

HEDDA: At the hospital?

BRACK: Yes—without regaining consciousness.

HEDDA: What more have you concealed?

BRACK: This—the event did not happen at his lodgings.

HEDDA: Oh, that can make no difference.

BRACK: Perhaps it may. For I must tell you—Eilert Lövborg was found shot in—in Mademoiselle Diana's boudoir.

HEDDA *(makes a motion as if to rise, but sinks back again):* That is impossible, Judge Brack! He cannot have been there again to-day.

BRACK: He was there this afternoon. He went there, he said, to demand the return of something which they had taken from him. Talked wildly about a lost child——

HEDDA: Ah—so that was why——

BRACK: I thought probably he meant his manuscript; but now I hear he destroyed that himself. So I suppose it must have been his pocket-book.

HEDDA: Yes, no doubt. And there—there he was found?

BRACK: Yes, there. With a pistol in his breast-pocket, discharged. The ball had lodged in a vital part.

HEDDA: In the breast—yes.

BRACK: No—in the bowels.

HEDDA *(looks up at him with an expression of loathing):*   That too! Oh, what curse is it that makes everything I touch turn ludicrous and mean?

BRACK: There is one point more, Mrs. Hedda—another disagreeable feature in the affair.

HEDDA: And what is that?

BRACK: The pistol he carried——

HEDDA *(breathless):*   Well? What of it?

BRACK: He must have stolen it.

HEDDA *(leaps up):*   Stolen it! That is not true! He did not steal it!

BRACK: No other explanation is possible. He must have stolen it——Hush!

(TESMAN and MRS. ELVSTED have risen from the table in the back room, and come into the drawing room.)

TESMAN *(with the papers in both his hands):*   Hedda dear, it is almost impossible to see under that lamp. Think of that!

HEDDA: Yes, I am thinking.

TESMAN: Would you mind our sitting at your writing-table—eh?

HEDDA: If you like. *(Quickly.)* No, wait! Let me clear it first!

TESMAN: Oh, you needn't trouble, Hedda. There is plenty of room.

HEDDA: No, no, let me clear it, I say! I will take these things in and put them on the piano. There! *(She has drawn out an object, covered with sheet music, from under the bookcase, places several other pieces of music upon it, and carries the whole into the inner room, to the left.* TESMAN *lays the scraps of paper on the writing-table, and moves the lamp there from the corner table. He and* MRS. ELVSTED *sit down and proceed with their work.* HEDDA *returns.)*

HEDDA *(behind* MRS. ELVSTED's *chair, gently ruffling her hair):*   Well, my sweet Thea,—how goes it with Eilert Lövborg's monument?

MRS. ELVSTED *(looks dispiritedly up at her):*   Oh, it will be terribly hard to put in order.

TESMAN: We must manage it. I am determined. And arranging other people's papers is just the work for me.

(HEDDA goes over to the stove, and seats herself on one of the footstools. BRACK *stands over her, leaning on the arm-chair.)*

HEDDA *(whispers):*   What did you say about the pistol?

BRACK *(softly):*   That he must have stolen it.

HEDDA: Why stolen it?

BRACK: Because every other explanation ought to be impossible, Mrs. Hedda.

HEDDA: Indeed?

BRACK *(glances at her):*   Of course Eilert Lövborg was here this morning. Was he not?

HEDDA: Yes.

BRACK: Were you alone with him?

HEDDA: Part of the time.

BRACK: Did you not leave the room whilst he was here?

HEDDA: No.

BRACK: Try to recollect. Were you not out of the room a moment?

HEDDA: Yes, perhaps just a moment—out in the hall.

BRACK: And where was your pistol-case during that time?

HEDDA: I had it locked up in——

BRACK: Well, Mrs. Hedda?

HEDDA: The case stood there on the writing-table.

BRACK: Have you looked since, to see whether both the pistols are there?

HEDDA: No.

BRACK: Well, you need not. I saw the pistol found in Lövborg's pocket, and I knew it at once as the one I had seen yesterday—and before, too.

HEDDA: Have you it with you?

BRACK: No; the police have it.

HEDDA: What will the police do with it?

BRACK: Search till they find the owner.

HEDDA: Do you think they will succeed?

BRACK *(bends over her and whispers):*   No, Hedda Gabler—not so long as I say nothing.

HEDDA *(looks frightened at him):*   And if you do not say nothing,—what then?

BRACK *(shrugs his shoulders):*   There is always the possibility that the pistol was stolen.

HEDDA *(firmly):*   Death rather than that.

BRACK *(smiling):*   People say such things—but they don't do them.

HEDDA *(without replying):*   And supposing the pistol was not stolen, and the owner is discovered? What then?

BRACK: Well, Hedda—then comes the scandal.

HEDDA: The scandal!

BRACK: Yes, the scandal—of which you are mortally afraid. You will, of course, be brought before the court—both you and Mademoiselle Diana. She will have to explain how the thing happened—whether it was an accidental shot or murder. Did the pistol go off as he was trying to take it out of his pocket, to threaten her with? Or did she tear the pistol out of his hand, shoot him, and push it back into his pocket? That would be quite like her; for she is an able-bodied young person, this same Mademoiselle Diana.

HEDDA: But *I* have nothing to do with all this repulsive business.

BRACK: No. But you will have to answer the question: Why did you give Eilert Lövborg the pistol? And what conclusions will people draw from the fact that you did give it to him?

HEDDA *(lets her head sink):*   That is true. I did not think of that.

BRACK: Well, fortunately, there is no danger, so long as I say nothing.

HEDDA *(looks up at him):*   So I am in your power, Judge Brack. You have me at your beck and call, from this time forward.

BRACK *(whispers softly):*   Dearest Hedda—believe me—I shall not abuse my advantage.

HEDDA: I am in your power none the less. Subject to your will and your demands. A slave, a slave then! *(Rises impetuously.)* No, I cannot endure the thought of that! Never!

BRACK *(looks half-mockingly at her):* People generally get used to the inevitable.

HEDDA *(returns his look):*   Yes, perhaps. *(She crosses to the writing-table. Suppressing an involuntary smile, she imitates* TESMAN'*s intonations.)* Well? Are you getting on, George? Eh?

TESMAN: Heaven knows, dear. In any case it will be the work of months.

HEDDA *(as before):*   Fancy that! *(Passes her hands softly through* MRS. ELVSTED'*S hair.)* Doesn't it seem strange to you, Thea? Here are you sitting with Tesman—just as you used to sit with Eilert Lövborg?

MRS. ELVSTED: Ah, if I could only inspire your husband in the same way.

HEDDA: Oh, that will come too—in time.

TESMAN: Yes, do you know, Hedda—I really think I begin to feel something of the sort. But won't you go and sit with Brack again?

HEDDA: Is there nothing I can do to help you two?

TESMAN: No, nothing in the world. *(Turning his head.)* I trust to you to keep Hedda company, my dear Brack.

BRACK *(with a glance at* HEDDA*):*   With the very greatest of pleasure.

HEDDA: Thanks. But I am tired this evening. I will go in and lie down a little on the sofa.

TESMAN: Yes, do dear—eh? *(*HEDDA *goes into the back room and draws the curtains. A short pause. Suddenly she is heard playing a wild dance on the piano.)*

MRS. ELVSTED *(starts from her chair):*   Oh—what is that?

TESMAN *(runs to the doorway):*   Why, my dearest Hedda—don't play dance music to-night! Just think of Aunt Rina! And of Eilert too!

HEDDA *(puts her head out between the curtains):*   And of Aunt Julia. And of all the rest of them.—After this, I will be quiet. *(Closes the curtains again.)*

TESMAN *(at the writing-table):*   It's not good for her to see us at this distressing work. I'll tell you what, Mrs. Elvsted,—you shall take the empty room at Aunt Julia's, and then I will come over in the evenings, and we can sit and work there—eh?

HEDDA *(in the inner room):*   I hear what you are saying, Tesman. But how am *I* to get through the evenings out here?

TESMAN *(turning over the papers):*   Oh, I daresay Judge Brack will be so kind as to look in now and then, even though I am out.

BRACK *(in the arm-chair, calls out gaily):*   Every blessed evening, with all the pleasure in life, Mrs. Tesman! We shall get on capitally together, we two!

HEDDA *(speaking loud and clear):*   Yes, don't you flatter yourself we will, Judge Brack? Now that you are the one cock in the basket——*(A shot is heard within.* TESMAN, MRS. ELVSTED, *and* BRACK *leap to their feet.)*

TESMAN: Oh, now she is playing with those pistols again.

(He throws back the curtains and runs in, followed by MRS. ELVSTED. HEDDA *lies stretched on the sofa, lifeless. Confusion and cries.* BERTA *enters in alarm from the right.)*

TESMAN *(shrieks to* BRACK*):*   Shot herself! Shot herself in the temple! Fancy that!

BRACK *(half-fainting in the arm-chair):*   Good God!—people don't do such things.

Writing Assignments for "Hedda Gabler"

I. Brief Papers: Act I

  A. 1. Show that in the opening scene Berta and Miss Tesman lead us to believe that George and Hedda's situation is hopeful and that there is an expectation of more good fortune to come.

     2. Show that Berta and Miss Tesman's comments in the opening scene are not as hopeful as they seem. Be precise in explaining how particular statements point to possible trouble for the marriage.

     3. Contrast Hedda and Tesman by explaining their reaction to Miss Tesman's new bonnet.

     4. Contrast Hedda and Tesman by explaining their reactions to George's slippers.

     5. Contrast Hedda and Thea in physical appearance and manner. Go beyond Ibsen's description by adding details and suggesting how, if you were casting these roles, the women would differ as personality types.

  B. 1. When George tells his aunt that his book "will deal with the domestic industries of Brabant in the Middle Ages," Miss Tesman replies, "Fancy—to be able to write on such a subject" (p. 1011). Argue for or against the assertion that Miss Tesman is genuinely impressed with George's project.

     2. Argue for or against the assertion that Hedda is justifiably annoyed with Tesman.

     3. Assume that the actress who plays Miss Tesman believes she is a foolish and meddling old woman with whom Hedda is justifiably annoyed. The director, on the other hand, believes that Miss Tesman should be represented as kind and sympathetic. Argue in support of either the actress or the director.

  C. 1. Tesman thinks that it is inappropriate for his wife to take a "sporting interest" in the competition between himself and Lövborg. How do you feel about Hedda's "sporting interest"?

     2. How do you respond to Hedda's playing with pistols?

II. Exposition in Drama

Combine the following elements into a coherent paragraph about the use of *exposition* in drama.

1. The dramatist is not like the novelist.
2. The dramatist cannot narrate background information.
3. The audience needs this information.
4. The audience needs it in order to follow the plot.

5. This information is called *exposition.*
6. This information must be conveyed in the lines.
7. The actors speak the lines.
8. The lines are spoken in the play.

9. This has happened over the years.
10. Playwrights have found this.
11. Certain dramatic strategies or conventions are well suited to the aims of exposition.

12. This happens in Greek drama.
13. The chorus discusses public events.
14. The Trojan War is such an event.
15. The plague in Thebes is such an event.
16. The chorus provides the historical background.
17. The chorus provides a moral perspective.
18. The hero is judged from a moral perspective.

19. This happens in Shakespearean drama.
20. Exposition is often provided in the speeches of public officials.
21. Exposition is often provided in a soliloquy.
22. In a soliloquy a character reveals his past history and his plans.
23. The character is like Richard III.
24. He speaks directly to the audience.

25. These conventions are not suitable in modern realistic drama.
26. The conventions are choral odes, formal speeches, and soliloquies.
27. Modern playwrights have had to find different ways of giving background information.

28. A familiar convention is "the feather-duster scene."
29. Two or more servants dust furniture.
30. They gossip about the affairs of the house.

31. Ibsen uses a variation of this convention.
32. It happens in the opening scene of *Hedda Gabler.*
33. Miss Tesman and Berta air the room.
34. Miss Tesman and Berta arrange the flowers.
35. Miss Tesman and Berta discuss George's marriage.
36. He is married to General Gabler's daughter.
37. General Gabler's daughter is "terrible grand in her ways."

38. This exposition has a purpose.

39. It gives information about the principal characters.

40. It stimulates interest in the coming conflict.

III. Brief Papers: Act II

A. 1. Unlike Tesman, who speaks literally and means no more than what he says, Hedda and Judge Brack speak metaphorically.

    a. Distinguish between the literal and implied meaning of the italicized words. Hedda pretends to shoot Judge Brack because he comes in "the *back way.*" Brack asks Hedda, "is there no sort of *little chink* that we could hold a *parley* through?" (p. 1027).

    b. In developing the metaphor of marriage as a long coach ride, Hedda says that when she gets to a station, "I never jump out." And the Judge guesses that she doesn't jump out because "There is always someone standing by to . . . look at your ankles" (p. 1029). What are they really talking about?

2. Contrast the characters of Lövborg and Tesman in a way that stresses the correlation between their social behavior and the kinds of books they write.

3. What does Hedda mean when she says that her real cowardice was not "The fact that I dared not shoot you down" (p. 1039). What was her real cowardice?

4. When Hedda calls Tesman a "specialist," she means more than the denotative meaning one finds in the dictionary. Explain what Hedda means by a "specialist."

B. 1. In this play motherhood is not only the expected role for a married woman but what Judge Brack calls her "solemn responsibility." Argue for or against the assertion that Hedda should accept this role.

2. In Hedda's society, women were denied the sexual freedom that was permitted to men and the play was considered important because it showed the consequences of this repression. Argue for or against the assertion that *Hedda Gabler* is outdated at least in this sense—that women now have as much sexual freedom as men.

3. Argue for or against the assertion that Hedda made a mistake in not having had an affair with Lövborg.

C. 1. How do you respond to Hedda's apparent distaste for motherhood?

2. How do you respond to Hedda's desire that Lövborg return with "vine leaves in his hair"? How does this response affect your judgment of Hedda and your reading of the play so far?

IV. Brief Papers: Act III

A. 1. What does the opening scene of Act III reveal about sexual roles in the world of *Hedda Gabler?*

2. Contrast Tesman's and Brack's accounts of Lövborg's movements after the Judge's party.

     3. How does Lövborg's confession of "child-murder" influence Hedda's decision to burn the manuscript?

  B. Argue for or against one of these assertions:
     1. Judge Brack contrived to bring about the fall of Lövborg.
     2. Hedda is essentially sympathetic, and perhaps even right, in believing that Lövborg should kill himself.

  C. 1. How do you respond to Hedda's refusal to go to Aunt Rina's deathbed: "I will not look upon sickness and death. I loathe all sorts of ugliness" (p. 1048).
     2. Describe what you take to be a typical party at Mademoiselle Diana's and indicate through your language your opinion of it.
     3. Hedda sees Lövborg's drinking as a more or less admirable rebellion against a repressive society. Is that your response? Explain.

V. Thea as Foil to Hedda
Combine the following elements into a coherent paragraph that explains the role of Thea as a *foil character*.

    1. Thea Elvsted is an ironic foil to Hedda Gabler.
    2. Thea is a foil in this respect.
    3. She is a contrast to the heroine.
    4. Thea is ironic in this respect.
    5. She appears to be weaker and more timid than Hedda.
    6. She is stronger and more fulfilled.

    7. Hedda has a main weakness.
    8. Hedda admits this.
    9. She has a fear of scandal.
  10. Years ago this fear prevented her from having an affair with Lövborg.

  11. This happened more recently.
  12. Hedda has a fear.
  13. Hedda fears public opinion.
  14. Hedda's fear causes this.
  15. Hedda makes a marriage.
  16. Her marriage is respectable.
  17. Her marriage is suffocating.
  18. Her marriage is to George Tesman.

  19. Thea is also trapped.
  20. She is trapped in a conventional marriage.
  21. She falls in love with Lövborg.
  22. Lövborg helps her to see herself in a new way.

23. Thea is unlike Hedda.
24. Thea has courage.
25. Thea defies society.
26. Thea achieves freedom and personal growth.

27. Thea is a *foil character.*
28. She provides a contrast to Hedda.
29. Thea further dramatizes the desperate position of women in Victorian society.

30. Thea can achieve selfhood only in this way.
31. She leaves her husband and children.

32. This is debatable.
33. Hedda achieves selfhood by killing herself.
34. She does this in her own view.
35. She performs a free and unconventional act.
36. She dares to do what "people don't do."

37. In the end, Thea is comparatively happy.
38. She even seems conventional.
39. Hedda is now the true outsider.
40. Her death is the play's strongest protest against society.

VI. Brief Papers: Act IV

A. 1. When Miss Tesman says, "This is not the time for Hedda's house to be a house of mourning" (p. 1056), she is, as usual, out of touch with Hedda's feelings. Contrast Miss Tesman's meaning with Hedda's view of the approaching happy event.
   2. Contrast the way Hedda imagined that Lövborg would die with the actual report of his death.
   3. What does Hedda mean when she says, on hearing of Lövborg's wound, "Well, well—the breast is a good place, too" (p. 1061).
   4. Show how in the final scene Judge Brack's way of addressing Hedda is a clue to his motive.

B. Argue for or against one of these assertions:
   1. Hedda is right in calling Judge Brack "a kind of specialist" (p. 1063).
   2. Judge Brack is responsible for Hedda's suicide.
   3. Hedda's suicide is an act of courage.

C. 1. How does Hedda's praise of Lövborg's suicide (as she imagined it) affect your view of her character?
   2. How does the fact that Hedda "shot herself in the temple" affect your view of her death?
   3. How does Judge Brack's final line, "people don't do such things," affect your response to the final scene?

VII. Longer Papers

A. Here are a few summary statements about sexual roles in Hedda Gabler's world:

1. There is a significant difference in the social status of unmarried men and women. An "old maid" or "old auntie" is typically a subordinate and slightly ridiculous figure, like Miss Tesman. But men like Judge Brack may prefer to remain bachelors and suffer no loss of status.

2. It is expected and accepted that men have more social and sexual freedom than women. A man should have some sexual experience before marriage, but a woman should be chaste and more or less uninformed about sexual matters.

3. Motherhood is not only the "most solemn" but also the most stimulating role for a woman.

4. When men and women work together as "comrades," the woman's role is mostly moral, inspirational, and secretarial (like Thea's); the creative force is supplied by the man.

   Focusing on any or all of these statements and using Ibsen's play as evidence, write a paper that argues that, fortunately or unfortunately, in today's society, (1) there has been a significant change in sexual roles and attitudes, or (2) there has been no significant change.

B. Write a paper which narrates or analyzes how the play has affected your understanding of your own situation when you feel trapped and "bored to death" by social conventions and pressures.

C. Write a paper that disagrees with one of the following arguments:

1. Hedda is a believable and interesting character until the very end of the play when she shoots herself in the head. Her suicide seems contrived and improbable. Realistically, Hedda would have adjusted to what is hardly a desperate situation. Her immediate reason for killing herself is to escape the judge's hold on her, but what he wants is essentially the same triangle that he and Hedda sought to bring about in Act I. In any case Hedda has always preferred Brack's company to Tesman's. Hedda's situation and her character make it very improbable that she would kill herself.

2. Hedda fails as a character because she is what Henry James calls a "morbidly special case"—a thoroughly neurotic personality. As a young girl she was a tease who liked to talk about sex but became hysterical when Lövborg tried to touch her. It is not the dread of scandal that explains Hedda's behavior in the play, but her fear and loathing of the female role in reproduction. Early in Act IV she cries out that her baby—or the prospect of having it—"is killing me." Given her morbid temperament, Hedda's suicide is probable, but she is not a realistic character with whom we can identify.

D. An early Ibsen play concludes with this line, spoken by the heroine—"Your community is a community of bachelor souls; you do not see women." Is this a valid assessment of the community in *Hedda Gabler*? In what sense do Tesman, Brack, and Lövborg see women—or fail to see them?

E. Consider all instances in which General Gabler's pistols are mentioned or used and write a paper about their function in the play.

OSCAR WILDE

The Importance of Being Earnest

Before Reading

Write for 5 or 10 minutes on one of the following topics:

1. In what way do the young people of your generation indicate—in their language, music, dress, and social conduct—their refusal to take seriously the conventional standards and expectations of adult society?
2. "A rose by any other name would smell as sweet." Do you agree with this famous opinion of Shakespeare's Juliet? Or do names give a person a certain quality, sweet or otherwise? Discuss the importance of having one name or another.

CHARACTERS

John Worthing
Algernon Moncrieff
Rev. Canon Chasuble, D.D.
Merriman, butler
Lane, manservant

Lady Bracknell
Gwendolen Fairfax
Cecily Cardew
Miss Prism, governess

ACT I

SCENE   *Morning-room in* ALGERNON'*s flat in Half-Moon Street. The room is luxuriously and artistically furnished. The sound of a piano is heard in the adjoining room.*

(LANE *is arranging afternoon tea on the table and, after the music has ceased,* ALGERNON *enters.*)

ALGERNON: Did you hear what I was playing, Lane?

LANE: I didn't think it polite to listen, sir.

ALGERNON: I'm sorry for that, for your sake. I don't play accurately—anyone can play accurately—but I play with wonderful expression. As far as the piano is concerned, sentiment is my forte. I keep science for Life.

LANE: Yes, sir.

ALGERNON: And, speaking of the science of Life, have you got the cucumber sandwiches cut for Lady Bracknell?

LANE: Yes, sir. (*Hands them on a salver.*)

ALGERNON: (*Inspects them, takes two, and sits down on the sofa.*) Oh! . . . by the

THE IMPORTANCE OF BEING EARNEST by Oscar Wilde (1854–1900) was first produced in London in 1895. The play is generally considered Wilde's masterpiece and is still one of the most popular comedies on British and American stages.

way, Lane, I see from your book that on Thursday night, when Lord Shoreman and Mr Worthing were dining with me, eight bottles of champagne are entered as having been consumed.

LANE: Yes, sir; eight bottles and a pint.

ALGERNON: Why is it that at a bachelor's establishment the servants invariably drink the champagne? I ask merely for information.

LANE: I attribute it to the superior quality of the wine, sir. I have often observed that in married households the champagne is rarely of a first-rate brand.

ALGERNON: Good heavens! Is marriage so demoralizing as that?

LANE: I believe it *is* a very pleasant state, sir. I have had very little experience of it myself up to the present. I have only been married once. That was in consequence of a misunderstanding between myself and a young person.

ALGERNON: *(Languidly.)* I don't know that I am much interested in your family life, Lane.

LANE: No, sir; it is not a very interesting subject. I never think of it myself.

ALGERNON: Very natural, I am sure. That will do, Lane, thank you.

LANE: Thank you, sir.

(LANE goes out.)

ALGERNON: Lane's views on marriage seem somewhat lax. Really, if the lower orders don't set us a good example, what on earth is the use of them? They seem, as a class, to have absolutely no sense of moral responsibility.

(Enter LANE.*)*

LANE: Mr Ernest Worthing.

(Enter JACK. LANE *goes out.)*

ALGERNON: How are you, my dear Ernest? What brings you up to town?

JACK: Oh, pleasure, pleasure! What else should bring one anywhere? Eating as usual, I see, Algy!

ALGERNON: *(Stiffly.)* I believe it is customary in good society to take some slight refreshment at five o'clock. Where have you been since last Thursday?

JACK: *(Sitting down on the sofa.)* In the country.

ALGERNON: What on earth do you do there?

JACK: *(Pulling off his gloves.)* When one is in town one amuses oneself. When one is in the country one amuses other people. It is excessively boring.

ALGERNON: And who are the people you amuse?

JACK: *(Airily.)* Oh, neighbours, neighbours.

ALGERNON: Got nice neighbours in your part of Shropshire?*

---

*Shropshire: Jack actually lives in Hertfordshire, which is just north of London, a hundred miles closer than Shropshire.

JACK: Perfectly horrid! Never speak to one of them.

ALGERNON: How immensely you must amuse them! *(Goes over and takes a sandwich.)* By the way, Shropshire is your county, is it not?

JACK: Eh? Shropshire? Yes, of course. Hallo! Why all these cups? Why cucumber sandwiches? Why such reckless extravagance in one so young? Who is coming to tea?

ALGERNON: Oh! merely Aunt Augusta and Gwendolen.

JACK: How perfectly delightful!

ALGERNON: Yes, that is all very well; but I am afraid Aunt Augusta won't quite approve of your being here.

JACK: May I ask why?

ALGERNON: My dear fellow, the way you flirt with Gwendolen is perfectly disgraceful. It is almost as bad as the way Gwendolen flirts with you.

JACK: I am in love with Gwendolen. I have come up to town expressly to propose to her.

ALGERNON: I thought you had come up for pleasure? . . . I call that business.

JACK: How utterly unromantic you are!

ALGERNON: I really don't see anything romantic in proposing. It is very romantic to be in love. But there is nothing romantic about a definite proposal. Why, one may be accepted. One usually is, I believe. Then the excitement is all over. The very essence of romance is uncertainty. If ever I get married, I'll certainly try to forget the fact.

JACK: I have no doubt about that, dear Algy. The Divorce Court was specially invented for people whose memories are so curiously constituted.

ALGERNON: Oh, there is no use speculating on that subject. Divorces are made in Heaven—*(JACK puts out his hand to take a sandwich. ALGERNON at once interferes.)* Please don't touch the cucumber sandwiches. They are ordered specially for Aunt Augusta. *(Takes one and eats it.)*

JACK: Well, you have been eating them all the time.

ALGERNON: That is quite a different matter. She is my aunt. *(Takes plate from below.)* Have some bread and butter. The bread and butter is for Gwendolen. Gwendolen is devoted to bread and butter.

JACK: *(Advancing to table and helping himself.)* And very good bread and butter it is too.

ALGERNON: Well, my dear fellow, you need not eat as if you were going to eat it all. You behave as if you were married to her already. You are not married to her already, and I don't think you ever will be.

JACK: Why on earth do you say that?

ALGERNON: Well, in the first place, girls never marry the men they flirt with. Girls don't think it right.

JACK: Oh, that is nonsense!

ALGERNON: It isn't. It is a great truth. It accounts for the extraordinary number of bachelors that one sees all over the place. In the second place, I don't give my consent.

JACK: Your consent!

ALGERNON: My dear fellow, Gwendolen is my first cousin. And before I allow you to marry her, you will have to clear up the whole question of Cecily. *(Rings bell.)*

JACK: Cecily! What on earth do you mean? What do you mean, Algy, by Cecily! I don't know any one of the name of Cecily.

(Enter LANE.*)*

ALGERNON: Bring me that cigarette case Mr Worthing left in the smoking-room the last time he dined here.

LANE: Yes, sir.

*(*LANE *goes out.)*

JACK: Do you mean to say you have had my cigarette case all this time? I wish to goodness you had let me know. I have been writing frantic letters to Scotland Yard about it. I was very nearly offering a large reward.

ALGERNON: Well, I wish you would offer one. I happen to be more than usually hard up.

JACK: There is no good offering a large reward now that the thing is found.

(Enter LANE *with the cigarette case on a salver.* ALGERNON *takes it at once.* LANE *goes out.)*

ALGERNON: I think that is rather mean of you, Ernest, I must say. *(Opens case and examines it.)* However, it makes no matter, for, now that I look at the inscription inside, I find that the thing isn't yours after all.

JACK: Of course it's mine. *(Moving to him.)* You have seen me with it a hundred times, and you have no right whatsoever to read what is written inside. It is a very ungentlemanly thing to read a private cigarette case.

ALGERNON: Oh! it is absurd to have a hard and fast rule about what one should read and what one shouldn't. More than half of modern culture depends on what one shouldn't read.

JACK: I am quite aware of the fact, and I don't propose to discuss modern culture. It isn't the sort of thing one should talk of in private. I simply want my cigarette case back.

ALGERNON: Yes; but this isn't your cigarette case. This cigarette case is a present from someone of the name of Cecily, and you said you didn't know anyone of that name.

JACK: Well, if you want to know, Cecily happens to be my aunt.

ALGERNON: Your aunt!

JACK: Yes. Charming old lady she is, too. Lives at Tunbridge Wells. Just give it back to me, Algy.

ALGERNON: *(Retreating to back of sofa.)* But why does she call herself little Cecily if she is your aunt and lives at Tunbridge Wells? *(Reading.)* 'From little Cecily with her fondest love.'

JACK: *(Moving to sofa and kneeling upon it.)* My dear fellow, what on earth is there in that? Some aunts are tall, some aunts are not tall. That is a matter that surely an aunt may be allowed to decide for herself. You seem to think that every aunt should be exactly like your aunt! That is absurd. For

Heaven's sake give me back my cigarette case. *(Follows* ALGERNON *round the room.)*

ALGERNON: Yes. But why does your aunt call you her uncle? 'From little Cecily, with her fondest love to her dear Uncle Jack.' There is no objection, I admit, to an aunt being a small aunt, but why an aunt, no matter what her size may be, should call her own nephew her uncle, I can't quite make out. Besides, your name isn't Jack at all; it is Ernest.

JACK: It isn't Ernest; it's Jack.

ALGERNON: You have always told me it was Ernest. I have introduced you to every one as Ernest. You answer to the name of Ernest. You look as if your name was Ernest. You are the most earnest-looking person I ever saw in my life. It is perfectly absurd your saying that your name isn't Ernest. It's on your cards. Here is one of them. *(Taking it from case.)* 'Mr Ernest Worthing, B.4, The Albany.' I'll keep this as a proof that your name is Ernest if ever you attempt to deny it to me, or to Gwendolen, or to anyone else. *(Puts the card in his pocket.)*

JACK: Well, my name is Ernest in town and Jack in the country, and the cigarette case was given to me in the country.

ALGERNON: Yes, but that does not account for the fact that your small Aunt Cecily, who lives at Tunbridge Wells, calls you her dear uncle. Come, old boy, you had much better have the thing out at once.

JACK: My dear Algy, you talk exactly as if you were a dentist. It is very vulgar to talk like a dentist when one isn't a dentist. It produces a false impression.

ALGERNON: Well, that is exactly what dentists always do. Now, go on! Tell me the whole thing. I may mention that I have always suspected you of being a confirmed and secret Bunburyist; and I am quite sure of it now.

JACK: Bunburyist? What on earth do you mean by a Bunburyist?

ALGERNON: I'll reveal to you the meaning of that incomparable expression as soon as you are kind enough to inform me why you are Ernest in town and Jack in the country.

JACK: Well, produce my cigarette case first.

ALGERNON: Here it is. *(Hands cigarette case.)* Now produce your explanation, and pray make it improbable. *(Sits on sofa.)*

JACK: My dear fellow, there is nothing improbable about my explanation at all. In fact it's perfectly ordinary. Old Mr Thomas Cardew, who adopted me when I was a little boy, made me in his will guardian to his granddaughter, Miss Cecily Cardew. Cecily, who addresses me as her uncle from motives of respect that you could not possibly appreciate, lives at my place in the country under the charge of her admirable governess, Miss Prism.

ALGERNON: Where is that place in the country, by the way?

JACK: That is nothing to you, dear boy. You are not going to be invited. . . . I may tell you candidly that the place is not in Shropshire.

ALGERNON: I suspected that, my dear fellow! I have Bunburyed all over Shropshire on two separate occasions. Now, go on. Why are you Ernest in town and Jack in the country?

JACK: My dear Algy, I don't know whether you will be able to understand
my real motives. You are hardly serious enough. When one is placed in
the position of guardian, one has to adopt a very high moral tone on all
subjects. It's one's duty to do so. And as a high moral tone can hardly be
said to conduce very much to either one's health or one's happiness, in
order to get up to town I have always pretended to have a younger
brother of the name of Ernest, who lives in the Albany, and gets into the
most dreadful scrapes. That, my dear Algy, is the whole truth pure and
simple.

ALGERNON: The truth is rarely pure and never simple. Modern life would
be very tedious if it were either, and modern literature a complete impossibility!

JACK: That wouldn't be at all a bad thing.

ALGERNON: Literary criticism is not your forte, my dear fellow. Don't try it.
You should leave that to people who haven't been at a University. They
do it so well in the daily papers. What you really are is a Bunburyist. I was
quite right in saying you were a Bunburyist. You are one of the most
advanced Bunburyists I know.

JACK: What on earth do you mean?

ALGERNON: You have invented a very useful younger brother called Ernest,
in order that you may be able to come up to town as often as you like.
I have invented an invaluable permanent invalid called Bunbury, in order
that I may be able to go down into the country whenever I choose.
Bunbury is perfectly invaluable. If it wasn't for Bunbury's extraordinary
bad health, for instance, I wouldn't be able to dine with you at Willis's
to-night, for I have been really engaged to Aunt Augusta* for more than
a week.

JACK: I haven't asked you to dine with me anywhere to-night.

ALGERNON: I know. You are absurdly careless about sending out invitations.
It is very foolish of you. Nothing annoys people so much as not receiving
invitations.

JACK: You had much better dine with your Aunt Augusta.

ALGERNON: I haven't the smallest intention of doing anything of the kind. To
begin with, I dined there on Monday, and once a week is quite enough
to dine with one's own relations. In the second place, whenever I do dine
there I am always treated as a member of the family, and sent down† with
either no woman at all, or two. In the third place, I know perfectly well
whom she will place me next to, to-night. She will place me next Mary
Farquhar, who always flirts with her own husband across the dinner-table.
That is not very pleasant. Indeed, it is not even decent . . . and that sort
of thing is enormously on the increase. The amount of women in London
who flirt with their own husbands is perfectly scandalous. It looks so bad.
It is simply washing one's clean linen in public. Besides, now that I know

---

*engaged to Aunt Augusta: Algernon is engaged to be a guest at her dinner party.
†sent down: Required to escort.

you to be a confirmed Bunburyist I naturally want to talk to you about Bunburying. I want to tell you the rules.

JACK: I'm not a Bunburyist at all. If Gwendolen accepts me, I am going to kill my brother, indeed I think I'll kill him in any case. Cecily is a little too much interested in him. It is rather a bore. So I am going to get rid of Ernest. And I strongly advise you to do the same with Mr . . . with your invalid friend who has the absurd name.

ALGERNON: Nothing will induce me to part with Bunbury, and if you ever get married, which seems to me extremely problematic, you will be very glad to know Bunbury. A man who marries without knowing Bunbury has a very tedious time of it.

JACK: That is nonsense. If I marry a charming girl like Gwendolen, and she is the only girl I ever saw in my life that I would marry, I certainly won't want to know Bunbury.

ALGERNON: Then your wife will. You don't seem to realize, that in married life three is company and two is none.

JACK: *(Sententiously.)* That, my dear young friend, is the theory that the corrupt French Drama has been propounding for the last fifty years.

ALGERNON: Yes; and that the happy English home has proved in half the time.

JACK: For heaven's sake, don't try to be cynical. It's perfectly easy to be cynical.

ALGERNON: My dear fellow, it isn't easy to be anything nowadays. There's such a lot of beastly competition about. *(The sound of an electric bell is heard.)* Ah! that must be Aunt Augusta. Only relatives, or creditors, ever ring in that Wagnerian manner.* Now, if I get her out of the way for ten minutes, so that you can have an opportunity for proposing to Gwendolen, may I dine with you tonight at Willis's?

JACK: I suppose so, if you want to.

ALGERNON: Yes, but you must be serious about it. I hate people who are not serious about meals. It is so shallow of them.

(Enter LANE.*)*

LANE: Lady Bracknell and Miss Fairfax.

(ALGERNON *goes forward to meet them. Enter* LADY BRACKNELL *and* GWEN-DOLEN.*)*

LADY BRACKNELL: Good afternoon, dear Algernon, I hope you are behaving very well.

ALGERNON: I'm feeling very well, Aunt Augusta.

LADY BRACKNELL: That's not quite the same thing. In fact the two things rarely go together. *(Sees* JACK *and bows to him with icy coldness.)*

ALGERNON: *(To* GWENDOLEN.*)* Dear me, you are smart!†

*Wagnerian manner: Like Wagner's operas, loud and long.
†smart: Smartly dressed, stylish.

GWENDOLEN: I am always smart! Am I not, Mr Worthing?

JACK: You're quite perfect, Miss Fairfax.

GWENDOLEN: Oh! I hope I am not that. It would leave no room for developments, and I intend to develop in many directions. *(GWENDOLEN and*
JACK *sit down together in the corner.)*

LADY BRACKNELL: I'm sorry if we are a little late, Algernon, but I was obliged
to call on dear Lady Harbury. I hadn't been there since her poor husband's
death. I never saw a woman so altered; she looks quite twenty years
younger. And now I'll have a cup of tea, and one of those nice cucumber
sandwiches you promised me.

ALGERNON: Certainly, Aunt Augusta. *(Goes over to tea-table.)*

LADY BRACKNELL: Won't you come and sit here, Gwendolen?

GWENDOLEN: Thanks, mamma, I'm quite comfortable where I am.

ALGERNON: *(Picking up empty plate in horror.)* Good heavens! Lane! Why are
there no cucumber sandwiches? I ordered them specially.

LANE: *(Gravely.)* There were no cucumbers in the market this morning, sir.
I went down twice.

ALGERNON: No cucumbers!

LANE: No, sir. Not even for ready money.*

ALGERNON: That will do, Lane, thank you.

LANE: Thank you, sir. *(Goes out.)*

ALGERNON: I am greatly distressed, Aunt Augusta, about there being no
cucumbers, not even for ready money.

LADY BRACKNELL: It really makes no matter, Algernon. I had some crumpets
with Lady Harbury, who seems to me to be living entirely for pleasure
now.

ALGERNON: I hear her hair has turned quite gold from grief.

LADY BRACKNELL: It certainly has changed its colour. From what cause I, of
course, cannot say. *(ALGERNON crosses and hands tea.)* Thank you, I've
quite a treat for you to-night, Algernon. I am going to send you down with
Mary Farquhar. She is such a nice woman, and so attentive to her husband.
It's delightful to watch them.

ALGERNON: I am afraid, Aunt Augusta, I shall have to give up the pleasure
of dining with you tonight after all.

LADY BRACKNELL: *(Frowning.)* I hope not, Algernon. It would put my table
completely out. Your uncle would have to dine upstairs. Fortunately he
is accustomed to that.

ALGERNON: It is a great bore, and, I need hardly say, a terrible disappointment to me, but the fact is I have just had a telegram to say that my poor
friend Bunbury is very ill again. *(Exchanges glances with* JACK.) They seem
to think I should be with him.

LADY BRACKNELL: It is very strange. This Mr Bunbury seems to suffer from
curiously bad health.

ALGERNON: Yes; poor Bunbury is a dreadful invalid.

---

*ready money: Cash as opposed to credit.

LADY BRACKNELL: Well, I must say, Algernon, that I think it is high time that Mr Bunbury made up his mind whether he was going to live or to die. This shilly-shallying with the question is absurd. Nor do I in any way approve of the modern sympathy with invalids. I consider it morbid. Illness of any kind is hardly a thing to be encouraged in others. Health is the primary duty of life. I am always telling that to your poor uncle, but he never seems to take much notice . . . as far as any improvement in his ailment goes. I should be much obliged if you would ask Mr Bunbury, from me, to be kind enough not to have a relapse on Saturday, for I rely on you to arrange my music for me. It is my last reception, and one wants something that will encourage conversation, particularly at the end of the season when everyone has practically said whatever they had to say, which, in most cases, was probably not much.

ALGERNON: I'll speak to Bunbury, Aunt Augusta, if he is still conscious, and I think I can promise you he'll be all right by Saturday. Of course the music is a great difficulty. You see, if one plays good music, people don't listen, and if one plays bad music people don't talk. But I'll run over the programme I've drawn out, if you will kindly come into the next room for a moment.

LADY BRACKNELL: Thank you, Algernon. It is very thoughtful of you. (Rising, and following ALGERNON.) I'm sure the programme will be delightful, after a few expurgations. French songs I cannot possibly allow. People always seem to think that they are improper, and either look shocked, which is vulgar, or laugh, which is worse. But German sounds a thoroughly respectable language, and, indeed I believe is so. Gwendolen, you will accompany me.

GWENDOLEN: Certainly, mamma.

(LADY BRACKNELL and ALGERNON go into the music-room, GWENDOLEN remains behind.)

JACK: Charming day it has been, Miss Fairfax.

GWENDOLEN: Pray don't talk to me about the weather, Mr Worthing. Whenever people talk to me about the weather, I always feel quite certain that they mean something else. And that makes me so nervous.

JACK: I do mean something else.

GWENDOLEN: I thought so. In fact, I am never wrong.

JACK: And I would like to be allowed to take advantage of Lady Bracknell's temporary absence. . . .

GWENDOLEN: I would certainly advise you to do so. Mamma has a way of coming back suddenly into a room that I have often had to speak to her about.

JACK: (Nervously.) Miss Fairfax, ever since I met you I have admired you more than any girl . . . I have ever met since . . . I met you.

GWENDOLEN: Yes, I am quite well aware of the fact. And I often wish that in public, at any rate, you had been more demonstrative. For me you have always had an irresistible fascination. Even before I met you I was far from indifferent to you. (JACK *looks at her in amazement.*) We live, as I hope you know, Mr Worthing, in an age of ideals. The fact is constantly mentioned in the more expensive monthly magazines, and has reached the provincial pulpits, I am told; and my ideal has always been to love someone of the name of Ernest. There is something in that name that inspires absolute confidence. The moment Algernon first mentioned to me that he had a friend called Ernest, I knew I was destined to love you.

JACK: You really love me, Gwendolen?

GWENDOLEN: Passionately!

JACK: Darling! You don't know how happy you've made me.

GWENDOLEN: My own Ernest!

JACK: But you don't really mean to say that you couldn't love me if my name wasn't Ernest?

GWENDOLEN: But your name is Ernest.

JACK: Yes, I know it is. But supposing it was something else? Do you mean to say you couldn't love me then?

GWENDOLEN: *(Glibly.)* Ah! that is clearly a metaphysical speculation, and like most metaphysical speculations has very little reference at all to the actual facts of real life, as we know them.

JACK: Personally, darling, to speak quite candidly, I don't much care about the name of Ernest. . . . I don't think the name suits me at all.

GWENDOLEN: It suits you perfectly. It is a divine name. It has music of its own. It produces vibrations.

JACK: Well, really, Gwendolen, I must say that I think there are lots of other much nicer names. I think Jack, for instance, a charming name.

GWENDOLEN: Jack? . . . No, there is very little music in the name Jack, if any at all, indeed. It does not thrill. It produces absolutely no vibrations. . . . I have known several Jacks, and they all, without exception, were more than usually plain. Besides, Jack is a notorious domesticity for John! And I pity any woman who is married to a man called John. She would probably never be allowed to know the entrancing pleasure of a single moment's solitude. The only really safe name is Ernest.

JACK: Gwendolen, I must get christened at once—I mean we must get married at once. There is no time to be lost.

GWENDOLEN: Married, Mr Worthing?

JACK: *(Astounded.)* Well . . . surely. You know that I love you, and you led me to believe, Miss Fairfax, that you were not absolutely indifferent to me.

GWENDOLEN: I adore you. But you haven't proposed to me yet. Nothing has been said at all about marriage. The subject has not even been touched on.

JACK: Well . . . may I propose to you now?

GWENDOLEN: I think it would be an admirable opportunity. And to spare you any possible disappointment, Mr Worthing, I think it only fair to tell you quite frankly beforehand that I am fully determined to accept you.

JACK: Gwendolen!

GWENDOLEN: Yes, Mr Worthing, what have you got to say to me?

JACK: You know what I have got to say to you.

GWENDOLEN: Yes, but you don't say it.

JACK: Gwendolen, will you marry me? *(Goes on his knees.)*

GWENDOLEN: Of course I will, darling. How long you have been about it! I am afraid you have had very little experience in how to propose.

JACK: My own one, I have never loved any one in the world but you.

GWENDOLEN: Yes, but men often propose for practice. I know my brother Gerald does. All my girl-friends tell me so. What wonderfully blue eyes you have, Ernest! They are quite, quite blue. I hope you will always look at me just like that, especially when there are other people present.

(Enter LADY BRACKNELL.*)*

LADY BRACKNELL: Mr Worthing! Rise, sir, from this semirecumbent posture. It is most indecorous.

GWENDOLEN: Mamma! *(He tries to rise; she restrains him.)* I must beg you to retire. This is no place for you. Besides, Mr Worthing has not quite finished yet.

LADY BRACKNELL: Finished what, may I ask?

GWENDOLEN: I am engaged to Mr Worthing, mamma. *(They rise together.)*

LADY BRACKNELL: Pardon me, you are not engaged to any one. When you do become engaged to some one, I, or your father, should his health permit him, will inform you of the fact. An engagement should come on a young girl as a surprise, pleasant or unpleasant, as the case may be. It is hardly a matter that she could be allowed to arrange for herself. . . . And now I have a few questions to put to you, Mr Worthing. While I am making these inquiries, you, Gwendolen, will wait for me below in the carriage.

GWENDOLEN: *(Reproachfully.)* Mamma!

LADY BRACKNELL: In the carriage, Gwendolen! *(*GWENDOLEN *goes to the door. She and* JACK *blow kisses to each other behind* LADY BRACKNELL*'s back.* LADY BRACKNELL *looks vaguely about as if she could not understand what the noise was. Finally turns round.)* Gwendolen, the carriage!

GWENDOLEN: Yes, mamma. *(Goes out, looking back at* JACK.*)*

LADY BRACKNELL: *(Sitting down.)* You can take a seat, Mr Worthing. *(Looks in her pocket for note-book and pencil.)*

JACK: Thank you, Lady Bracknell, I prefer standing.

LADY BRACKNELL: *(Pencil and note-book in hand.)* I feel bound to tell you that you are not down on my list of eligible young men, although I have the same list as the dear Duchess of Bolton has. We work together, in fact. However, I am quite ready to enter your name, should your answers be what a really affectionate mother requires. Do you smoke?

JACK: Well, yes, I must admit I smoke.

LADY BRACKNELL: I am glad to hear it. A man should always have an occupation of some kind. There are far too many idle men in London as it is. How old are you?

JACK: Twenty-nine.

LADY BRACKNELL: A very good age to be married at. I have always been of opinion that a man who desires to get married should know either everything or nothing. Which do you know?

JACK: *(After some hesitation.)* I know nothing, Lady Bracknell.

LADY BRACKNELL: I am pleased to hear it. I do not approve of anything that tampers with natural ignorance. Ignorance is like a delicate exotic fruit; touch it and the bloom is gone. The whole theory of modern education is radically unsound. Fortunately in England, at any rate, education produces no effect whatsoever. If it did, it would prove a serious danger to the upper classes, and probably lead to acts of violence in Grosvenor Square.* What is your income?

JACK: Between seven and eight thousand a year.

LADY BRACKNELL: *(Makes a note in her book.)* In land, or in investments?

JACK: In investments, chiefly.

LADY BRACKNELL: That is satisfactory. What between the duties† expected of one during one's lifetime, and the duties exacted from one after one's death, land has ceased to be either a profit or a pleasure. It gives one position, and prevents one from keeping it up. That's all that can be said about land.

JACK: I have a country house with some land, of course, attached to it, about fifteen hundred acres, I believe; but I don't depend on that for my real income. In fact, as far as I can make out, the poachers are the only people who make anything out of it.

LADY BRACKNELL: A country house! How many bedrooms? Well, that point can be cleared up afterwards. You have a town house, I hope? A girl with a simple, unspoiled nature, like Gwendolen, could hardly be expected to reside in the country.

JACK: Well, I own a house in Belgrave Square, but it is let by the year to Lady Bloxham. Of course, I can get it back whenever I like, at six months' notice.

LADY BRACKNELL: Lady Bloxham? I don't know her.

JACK: Oh, she goes about very little. She is a lady considerably advanced in years.

LADY BRACKNELL: Ah, nowadays that is no guarantee of respectability of character. What number in Belgrave Square?

JACK: 149.

LADY BRACKNELL: *(Shaking her head.)* The unfashionable side. I thought there was something. However, that could easily be altered.

JACK: Do you mean the fashion, or the side?

LADY BRACKNELL: *(Sternly.)* Both, if necessary, I presume. What are your politics?

JACK: Well, I am afraid I really have none. I am a Liberal Unionist.

---

*Grosvenor Square: An elegant residential area in London.
†duties: Taxes.

LADY BRACKNELL: Oh, they count as Tories. They dine with us. Or come in the evening, at any rate. Now to minor matters. Are your parents living?

JACK: I have lost both my parents.

LADY BRACKNELL: To lose one parent, Mr Worthing, may be regarded as a misfortune; to lose both looks like carelessness. Who was your father? He was evidently a man of some wealth. Was he born in what the Radical papers call the purple of commerce, or did he rise from the ranks of the aristocracy?

JACK: I am afraid I really don't know. The fact is, Lady Bracknell, I said I had lost my parents. It would be nearer the truth to say that my parents seem to have lost me. . . . I don't actually know who I am by birth. I was . . . well, I was found.

LADY BRACKNELL: Found!

JACK: The late Mr Thomas Cardew, an old gentleman of a very charitable and kindly disposition, found me, and gave me the name of Worthing, because he happened to have a first-class ticket for Worthing in his pocket at the time. Worthing is a place in Sussex. It is a seaside resort.

LADY BRACKNELL: Where did the charitable gentleman who had a first-class ticket for this seaside resort find you?

JACK: *(Gravely.)* In a hand-bag.

LADY BRACKNELL: A hand-bag?

JACK: *(Very seriously.)* Yes, Lady Bracknell. I was in a hand-bag—a somewhat large, black leather hand-bag, with handles to it—an ordinary hand-bag in fact.

LADY BRACKNELL: In what locality did this Mr James, or Thomas, Cardew come across this ordinary hand-bag?

JACK: In the cloak-room at Victoria Station. It was given to him in mistake for his own.

LADY BRACKNELL: The cloak-room at Victoria Station?

JACK: Yes. The Brighton line.

LADY BRACKNELL: The line is immaterial. Mr Worthing, I confess I feel somewhat bewildered by what you have just told me. To be born, or at any rate bred, in a hand-bag, whether it had handles or not, seems to me to display a contempt for the ordinary decencies of family life that reminds one of the worst excesses of the French Revolution. And I presume you know what that unfortunate movement led to? As for the particular locality in which the hand-bag was found, a cloak-room at a railway station might serve to conceal a social indiscretion—has probably, indeed, been used for that purpose before now—but it could hardly be regarded as an assured basis for a recognized position in good society.

JACK: May I ask you then what you would advise me to do? I need hardly say I would do anything in the world to ensure Gwendolen's happiness.

LADY BRACKNELL: I would strongly advise you, Mr Worthing, to try and acquire some relations as soon as possible, and to make a definite effort to produce at any rate one parent, of either sex, before the season is quite over.

JACK: Well, I don't see how I could possibly manage to do that. I can produce the hand-bag at any moment. It is in my dressing-room at home. I really think that should satisfy you, Lady Bracknell.

LADY BRACKNELL: Me, sir! What has it to do with me? You can hardly imagine that I and Lord Bracknell would dream of allowing our only daughter—a girl brought up with the utmost care—to marry into a cloak-room, and form an alliance with a parcel. Good morning, Mr Worthing!

(LADY BRACKNELL sweeps out in majestic indignation.)

JACK: Good morning! *(ALGERNON, from the other room, strikes up the Wedding March. JACK looks perfectly furious, and goes to the door.)* For goodness' sake don't play that ghastly tune, Algy! How idiotic you are!

(The music stops and ALGERNON enters cheerily.)

ALGERNON: Didn't it go off all right, old boy? You don't mean to say Gwendolen refused you? I know it is a way she has. She is always refusing people. I think it is most ill-natured of her.

JACK: Oh, Gwendolen is as right as a trivet.* As far as she is concerned, we are engaged. Her mother is perfectly unbearable. Never met such a Gorgon.† . . . I don't really know what a Gorgon is like, but I am quite sure that Lady Bracknell is one. In any case, she is a monster, without being a myth, which is rather unfair. . . . I beg your pardon, Algy, I suppose I shouldn't talk about your own aunt in that way before you.

ALGERNON: My dear boy, I love hearing my relations abused. It is the only thing that makes me put up with them at all. Relations are simply a tedious pack of people, who haven't got the remotest knowledge of how to live, nor the smallest instinct about when to die.

JACK: Oh, that is nonsense!

ALGERNON: It isn't!

JACK: Well, I won't argue about the matter. You always want to argue about things.

ALGERNON: That is exactly what things were originally made for.

JACK: Upon my word, if I thought that, I'd shoot myself. . . . *(A pause.)* You don't think there is any chance of Gwendolen becoming like her mother in about a hundred and fifty years, do you, Algy?

ALGERNON: All women become like their mothers. That is their tragedy. No man does. That's his.

JACK: Is that clever?

ALGERNON: It is perfectly phrased! and quite as true as any observation in civilized life should be.

JACK: I am sick to death of cleverness. Everybody is clever nowadays. You can't go anywhere without meeting clever people. The thing has become an absolute public nuisance. I wish to goodness we had a few fools left.

*Right as a trivet: Steady as a tripod, dependable.
†Gorgon: A mythical woman of hideous appearance whose look turned one to stone.

ALGERNON: We have.

JACK: I should extremely like to meet them. What do they talk about?

ALGERNON: The fools? Oh! about the clever people, of course.

JACK: What fools.

ALGERNON: By the way, did you tell Gwendolen the truth about your being Ernest in town, and Jack in the country?

JACK: *(In a very patronizing manner.)* My dear fellow, the truth isn't quite the sort of thing one tells to a nice, sweet, refined girl. What extraordinary ideas you have about the way to behave to a woman!

ALGERNON: The only way to behave to a woman is to make love to her, if she is pretty, and to someone else, if she is plain.

JACK: Oh, that is nonsense.

ALGERNON: What about your brother? What about the profligate Ernest?

JACK: Oh, before the end of the week I shall have got rid of him. I'll say he died in Paris of apoplexy. Lots of people die of apoplexy, quite suddenly, don't they?

ALGERNON: Yes, but it's hereditary, my dear fellow. It's a sort of thing that runs in families. You had much better say a severe chill.

JACK: You are sure a severe chill isn't hereditary, or anything of that kind?

ALGERNON: Of course it isn't!

JACK: Very well, then. My poor brother Ernest is carried off suddenly, in Paris, by a severe chill. That gets rid of him.

ALGERNON: But I thought you said that . . . Miss Cardew was a little too much interested in your poor brother Ernest? Won't she feel his loss a good deal?

JACK: Oh, that is all right. Cecily is not a silly romantic girl, I am glad to say. She has got a capital appetite, goes long walks, and pays no attention at all to her lessons.

ALGERNON: I would rather like to see Cecily.

JACK: I will take very good care you never do. She is excessively pretty, and she is only just eighteen.

ALGERNON: Have you told Gwendolen yet that you have an excessively pretty ward who is only just eighteen?

JACK: Oh! one doesn't blurt these things out to people. Cecily and Gwendolen are perfectly certain to be extremely great friends. I'll bet you anything you like that half an hour after they have met, they will be calling each other sister.

ALGERNON: Women only do that when they have called each other a lot of other things first. Now, my dear boy, if we want to get a good table at Willis's, we really must go and dress. Do you know it is nearly seven?

JACK: *(Irritably.)* Oh! it always is nearly seven.

ALGERNON: I'm hungry.

JACK: I never knew you when you weren't. . . .

ALGERNON: What shall we do after dinner? Go to a theatre?

JACK: Oh, no! I loathe listening.

ALGERNON: Well, let us go to the Club?

JACK: Oh, no! I hate talking.

ALGERNON: Well, we might trot round to the Empire* at ten?

JACK: Oh, no! I can't bear looking at things. It is so silly.

ALGERNON: Well, what shall we do?

JACK: Nothing!

ALGERNON: It is awfully hard work doing nothing. However, I don't mind hard work where there is no definite object of any kind.

(Enter LANE.*)*

LANE: Miss Fairfax.

(Enter GWENDOLEN. LANE *goes out.)*

ALGERNON: Gwendolen, upon my word!

GWENDOLEN: Algy, kindly turn your back. I have something very particular to say to Mr Worthing.

ALGERNON: Really, Gwendolen, I don't think I can allow this at all.

GWENDOLEN: Algy, you always adopt a strictly immoral attitude towards life. You are not quite old enough to do that. *(*ALGERNON *retires to the fire-place.)*

JACK: My own darling!

GWENDOLEN: Ernest, we may never be married. From the expression on mamma's face I fear we never shall. Few parents nowadays pay any regard to what their children say to them. The old-fashioned respect for the young is fast dying out. Whatever influence I ever had over mamma, I lost at the age of three. But although she may prevent us from becoming man and wife, and I may marry someone else, and marry often, nothing that she can possibly do can alter my eternal devotion to you.

JACK: Dear Gwendolen!

GWENDOLEN: The story of your romantic origin, as related to me by mamma, with unpleasing comments, has naturally stirred the deeper fibres of my nature. Your Christian name has an irresistible fascination. The simplicity of your character makes you exquisitely incomprehensible to me. Your town address at the Albany I have. What is your address in the country?

JACK: The Manor House, Woolton, Hertfordshire.

*(*ALGERNON, *who has been carefully listening, smiles to himself, and writes the address on his shirtcuff. Then picks up the Railway Guide.)*

GWENDOLEN: There is a good postal service, I suppose? It may be necessary to do something desperate. That of course will require serious considera-tion. I will communicate with you daily.

JACK: My own one!

GWENDOLEN: How long do you remain in town?

JACK: Till Monday.

GWENDOLEN: Good! Algy, you may turn round now.

*Empire: A famous music hall.

ALGERNON: Thanks, I've turned round already.

GWENDOLEN: You may also ring the bell.

JACK: You will let me see you to your carriage, my own darling?

GWENDOLEN: Certainly.

JACK: *(To* LANE, *who now enters.)* I will see Miss Fairfax out.

LANE: Yes, sir. *(*JACK *and* GWENDOLEN *go off.)*

> *(*LANE *presents several letters on a salver, to* ALGERNON. *It is to be surmised that they are bills, as* ALGERNON, *after looking at the envelopes, tears them up.)*

ALGERNON: A glass of sherry, Lane.

LANE: Yes, sir.

ALGERNON: Tomorrow, Lane, I'm going Bunburying.

LANE: Yes, sir.

ALGERNON: I shall probably not be back till Monday. You can put up my dress clothes, my smoking jacket, and all the Bunbury suits . . .

LANE: Yes, sir. *(Handling sherry.)*

ALGERNON: I hope tomorrow will be a fine day, Lane.

LANE: It never is, sir.

ALGERNON: Lane, you're a perfect pessimist.

LANE: I do my best to give satisfaction, sir.

> *(Enter* JACK. LANE *goes off.)*

JACK: There's a sensible, intellectual girl! the only girl I ever cared for in my life. *(*ALGERNON *is laughing immoderately.)* What on earth are you so amused at?

ALGERNON: Oh, I'm a little anxious about poor Bunbury, that is all.

JACK: If you don't take care, your friend Bunbury will get you into a serious scrape some day.

ALGERNON: I love scrapes. They are the only things that are never serious.

JACK: Oh, that's nonsense, Algy. You never talk anything but nonsense.

ALGERNON: Nobody ever does.

> *(*JACK *looks indignantly at him, and leaves the room.* ALGERNON *lights a cigarette, reads his shirtcuff, and smiles.)*

ACT DROP

ACT II

> SCENE   *Garden at the Manor House. A flight of grey stone steps leads up to the house. The garden, an old-fashioned one, full of roses. Time of year, July. Basket chairs, and a table covered with books, are set under a large yew-tree.*

> *(*MISS PRISM *discovered seated at the table.* CECILY *is at the back, watering flowers.)*

MISS PRISM: *(Calling.)* Cecily, Cecily! Surely such a utilitarian occupation as the watering of flowers is rather Moulton's duty than yours? Especially at a moment when intellectual pleasures await you. Your German grammar is on the table. Pray open it at page fifteen. We will repeat yesterday's lesson.

CECILY: *(Coming over very slowly.)* But I don't like German. It isn't at all a becoming language. I know perfectly well that I look quite plain after my German lesson.

MISS PRISM: Child, you know how anxious your guardian is that you should improve yourself in every way. He laid particular stress on your German, as he was leaving for town yesterday. Indeed, he always lays stress on your German when he is leaving for town.

CECILY: Dear Uncle Jack is so very serious! Sometimes he is so serious that I think he cannot be quite well.

MISS PRISM: *(Drawing herself up.)* Your guardian enjoys the best of health, and his gravity of demeanour is especially to be commended in one so comparatively young as he is. I know no one who has a higher sense of duty and responsibility.

CECILY: I suppose that is why he often looks a little bored when we three are together.

MISS PRISM: Cecily! I am surprised at you. Mr Worthing has many troubles in his life. Idle merriment and triviality would be out of place in his conversation. You must remember his constant anxiety about that unfortunate young man, his brother.

CECILY: I wish Uncle Jack would allow that unfortunate young man, his brother, to come down here sometimes. We might have a good influence over him, Miss Prism. I am sure you certainly would. You know German, and geology, and things of that kind influence a man very much. *(CECILY begins to write in her diary.)*

MISS PRISM: *(Shaking her head.)* I do not think that even I could produce any effect on a character that according to his own brother's admission is irretrievably weak and vacillating. Indeed I am not sure that I would desire to reclaim him. I am not in favour of this modern mania for turning bad people into good people at a moment's notice. As a man sows so let him reap. You must put away your diary, Cecily. I really don't see why you should keep a diary at all.

CECILY: I keep a diary in order to enter the wonderful secrets of my life. If I didn't write them down, I should probably forget all about them.

MISS PRISM: Memory, my dear Cecily, is the diary that we all carry about with us.

CECILY: Yes, but it usually chronicles the things that have never happened, and couldn't possibly have happened. I believe that Memory is responsible for nearly all the three-volume novels that Mudie* sends us.

---

*Mudie: A circulating library. The three-volume novels were popular sentimental romances of the time.

MISS PRISM: Do not speak slightingly of the three-volume novel, Cecily. I wrote one myself in earlier days.

CECILY: Did you really, Miss Prism? How wonderfully clever you are! I hope it did not end happily? I don't like novels that end happily. They depress me so much.

MISS PRISM: The good ended happily, and the bad unhappily. That is what Fiction means.

CECILY: I suppose so. But it seems very unfair. And was your novel ever published?

MISS PRISM: Alas! no. The manuscript unfortunately was abandoned. *(CECILY starts.)* I used the word in the sense of lost or mislaid. To your work, child, these speculations are profitless.

CECILY: *(Smiling.)* But I see dear Dr Chasuble coming up through the garden.

MISS PRISM: *(Rising and advancing.)* Dr Chasuble! This is indeed a pleasure.

(Enter CANON CHASUBLE.*)*

CHASUBLE: And how are we this morning? Miss Prism, you are, I trust, well?

CECILY: Miss Prism has just been complaining of a slight headache. I think it would do her so much good to have a short stroll with you in the Park, Dr Chasuble.

MISS PRISM: Cecily, I have not mentioned anything about a headache.

CECILY: No, dear Miss Prism, I know that, but I felt instinctively that you had a headache. Indeed I was thinking about that, and not about my German lesson, when the Rector came in.

CHASUBLE: I hope, Cecily, you are not inattentive.

CECILY: Oh, I am afraid I am.

CHASUBLE: That is strange. Were I fortunate enough to be Miss Prism's pupil, I would hang upon her lips. *(* MISS PRISM *glares.)* I spoke metaphorically.— My metaphor was drawn from bees. Ahem! Mr Worthing, I suppose, has not returned from town yet?

MISS PRISM: We do not expect him till Monday afternoon.

CHASUBLE: Ah yes, he usually likes to spend his Sunday in London. He is not one of those whose sole aim is enjoyment, as, by all accounts, that unfortunate young man his brother seems to be. But I must not disturb Egeria* and her pupil any longer.

MISS PRISM: Egeria? My name is Laetitia, Doctor.

CHASUBLE: *(Bowing.)* A classical allusion merely, drawn from the Pagan authors. I shall see you both no doubt at Evensong?

MISS PRISM: I think, dear Doctor, I will have a stroll with you. I find I have a headache after all, and a walk might do it good.

CHASUBLE: With pleasure, Miss Prism, with pleasure. We might go as far as the schools and back.

MISS PRISM: That would be delightful. Cecily, you will read your Political

---

*Egeria: A nymph believed by the ancient Romans to be the source of good instruction in politics and religion.

Economy in my absence. The chapter on the Fall of the Rupee* you may omit. It is somewhat too sensational. Even these metallic problems have their melodramatic side.

(Goes down the garden with DR CHASUBLE.*)*

CECILY: *(Picks up books and throws them back on table.)* Horrid Political Economy! Horrid Geography! Horrid, horrid German!

(Enter MERRIMAN *with a card on a salver.)*

MERRIMAN: Mr Ernest Worthing has just driven over from the station. He has brought his luggage with him.

CECILY: *(Takes the card and reads it.)* 'Mr Ernest Worthing, B.4, The Albany, W.' Uncle Jack's brother! Did you tell him Mr Worthing was in town?

MERRIMAN: Yes, Miss. He seemed very much disappointed. I mentioned that you and Miss Prism were in the garden. He said he was anxious to speak to you privately for a moment.

CECILY: Ask Mr Ernest Worthing to come here. I suppose you had better talk to the housekeeper about a room for him.

MERRIMAN: Yes, Miss. *(*MERRIMAN *goes off.)*

CECILY: I have never met any really wicked person before. I feel rather frightened. I am so afraid he will look just like every one else.

(Enter ALGERNON, *very gay and debonair.)*

He does!

ALGERNON: *(Raising his hat.)* You are my little cousin Cecily, I'm sure.

CECILY: You are under some strange mistake. I am not little. In fact, I believe I am more than usually tall for my age. *(*ALGERNON *is rather taken aback.)* But I am your cousin Cecily. You, I see from your card, are Uncle Jack's brother, my cousin Ernest, my wicked cousin Ernest.

ALGERNON: Oh! I am not really wicked at all, Cousin Cecily. You mustn't think that I am wicked.

CECILY: If you are not, then you have certainly been deceiving us all in a very inexcusable manner. I hope you have not been leading a double life, pretending to be wicked and being really good all the time. That would be hypocrisy.

ALGERNON: *(Looks at her in amazement.)* Oh! Of course I have been rather reckless.

CECILY: I am glad to hear it.

ALGERNON: In fact, now you mention the subject, I have been very bad in my own small way.

CECILY: I don't think you should be so proud of that, though I am sure it must have been very pleasant.

ALGERNON: It is much pleasanter being here with you.

----

*Rupee: The currency of India, a British colony at this time.

CECILY: I can't understand how you are here at all. Uncle Jack won't be back till Monday afternoon.

ALGERNON: That is a great disappointment. I am obliged to go up by the first train on Monday morning. I have a business appointment that I am anxious . . . to miss!

CECILY: Couldn't you miss it anywhere but in London?

ALGERNON: No: the appointment is in London.

CECILY: Well, I know, of course, how important it is not to keep a business engagement, if one wants to retain any sense of the beauty of life, but still I think you had better wait till Uncle Jack arrives. I know he wants to speak to you about your emigrating.

ALGERNON: About my what?

CECILY: Your emigrating. He has gone up to buy your outfit.

ALGERNON: I certainly wouldn't let Jack buy my outfit. He has no taste in neckties at all.

CECILY: I don't think you will require neckties. Uncle Jack is sending you to Australia.

ALGERNON: Australia! I'd sooner die.

CECILY: Well, he said at dinner on Wednesday night, that you would have to choose between this world, the next world, and Australia.

ALGERNON: Oh, well! The accounts I have received of Australia and the next world are not particularly encouraging. This world is good enough for me, Cousin Cecily.

CECILY: Yes, but are you good enough for it?

ALGERNON: I'm afraid I'm not that. That is why I want you to reform me. You might make that your mission, if you don't mind, Cousin Cecily.

CECILY: I'm afraid I've no time, this afternoon.

ALGERNON: Well, would you mind my reforming myself this afternoon?

CECILY: It is rather Quixotic of you. But I think you should try.

ALGERNON: I will. I feel better already.

CECILY: You are looking a little worse.

ALGERNON: That is because I am hungry.

CECILY: How thoughtless of me. I should have remembered that when one is going to lead an entirely new life, one requires regular and wholesome meals. Won't you come in?

ALGERNON: Thank you. Might I have a buttonhole first? I have never any appetite unless I have a buttonhole first.

CECILY: A Maréchal Niel?* *(Picks up scissors.)*

ALGERNON: No, I'd sooner have a pink rose.

CECILY: Why? *(Cuts a flower.)*

ALGERNON: Because you are like a pink rose, Cousin Cecily.

CECILY: I don't think it can be right for you to talk to me like that. Miss Prism never says such things to me.

---

*Maréchal Niel: A yellow rose.

ALGERNON: Then Miss Prism is a short-sighted old lady. (CECILY *puts the rose in his buttonhole.*) You are the prettiest girl I ever saw.

CECILY: Miss Prism says that all good looks are a snare.

ALGERNON: They are a snare that every sensible man would like to be caught in.

CECILY: Oh, I don't think I would care to catch a sensible man. I shouldn't know what to talk to him about.

(They pass into the house. MISS PRISM *and* DR CHASUBLE *return.)*

MISS PRISM: You are too much alone, dear Dr Chasuble. You should get married. A misanthrope I can understand—a womanthrope, never!

CHASUBLE: *(With a scholar's shudder.)* Believe me, I do not deserve so neologistic a phrase. The precept as well as the practice of the Primitive Church was distinctly against matrimony.

MISS PRISM: *(Sententiously.)* That is obviously the reason why the Primitive Church has not lasted up to the present day. And you do not seem to realize, dear Doctor, that by persistently remaining single, a man converts himself into a permanent public temptation. Men should be more careful; this very celibacy leads weaker vessels astray.

CHASUBLE: But is a man not equally attractive when married?

MISS PRISM: No married man is ever attractive except to his wife.

CHASUBLE: And often, I've been told, not even to her.

MISS PRISM: That depends on the intellectual sympathies of the woman. Maturity can always be depended on. Ripeness can be trusted. Young women are green. (DR CHASUBLE *starts.*) I spoke horticulturally. My metaphor was drawn from fruits. But where is Cecily?

CHASUBLE: Perhaps she followed us to the schools.

(Enter JACK *slowly from the back of the garden. He is dressed in the deepest mourning, with crepe hatband and black gloves.)*

MISS PRISM: Mr Worthing!

CHASUBLE: Mr Worthing?

MISS PRISM: This is indeed a surprise. We did not look for you till Monday afternoon.

JACK: *(Shakes* MISS PRISM*'s hand in a tragic manner.)* I have returned sooner than I expected. Dr Chasuble, I hope you are well?

CHASUBLE: Dear Mr Worthing, I trust this garb of woe does not betoken some terrible calamity?

JACK: My brother.

MISS PRISM: More shameful debts and extravagance?

CHASUBLE: Still leading his life of pleasure?

JACK: *(Shaking his head.)* Dead!

CHASUBLE: Your brother Ernest dead?

JACK: Quite dead.

MISS PRISM: What a lesson for him! I trust he will profit by it.

CHASUBLE: Mr Worthing, I offer you my sincere condolence. You have at least the consolation of knowing that you were always the most generous and forgiving of brothers.

JACK: Poor Ernest! He had many faults, but it is a sad, sad blow.

CHASUBLE: Very sad indeed. Were you with him at the end?

JACK: No. He died abroad; in Paris, in fact. I had a telegram last night from the manager of the Grand Hotel.

CHASUBLE: Was the cause of death mentioned?

JACK: A severe chill, it seems.

MISS PRISM: As a man sows, so shall he reap.

CHASUBLE: *(Raising his hand.)* Charity, dear Miss Prism, charity! None of us are perfect. I myself am peculiarly susceptible to draughts. Will the interment take place here?

JACK: No. He seems to have expressed a desire to be buried in Paris.

CHASUBLE: In Paris! *(Shakes his head.)* I fear that hardly points to any very serious state of mind at the last. You would no doubt wish me to make some slight allusion to this tragic domestic affliction next Sunday. *(JACK presses his hand convulsively.)* My sermon on the meaning of the manna in the wilderness can be adapted to almost any occasion, joyful, or, as in the present case, distressing. *(All sigh.)* I have preached it at harvest celebrations, christenings, confirmations, on days of humiliation and festal days. The last time I delivered it was in the Cathedral, as a charity sermon on behalf of the Society for the Prevention of Discontent among the Upper Orders. The Bishop, who was present, was much struck by some of the analogies I drew.

JACK: Ah! that reminds me, you mentioned christenings I think, Dr Chasuble? I suppose you know how to christen all right? *(DR CHASUBLE looks astounded.)* I mean, of course, you are continually christening, aren't you?

MISS PRISM: It is, I regret to say, one of the Rector's most constant duties in this parish. I have often spoken to the poorer classes on the subject. But they don't seem to know what thrift is.

CHASUBLE: But is there any particular infant in whom you are interested, Mr Worthing? Your brother was, I believe, unmarried, was he not?

JACK: Oh yes.

MISS PRISM: *(Bitterly.)* People who live entirely for pleasure usually are.

JACK: But it is not for any child, dear Doctor. I am very fond of children. No! the fact is, I would like to be christened myself, this afternoon, if you have nothing better to do.

CHASUBLE: But surely, Mr Worthing, you have been christened already?

JACK: I don't remember anything about it.

CHASUBLE: But have you any grave doubts on the subject?

JACK: I certainly intend to have. Of course I don't know if the thing would bother you in any way, or if you think I am a little too old now.

CHASUBLE: Not at all. The sprinkling, and, indeed, the immersion of adults is a perfectly canonical practice.

JACK: Immersion!

CHASUBLE: You need have no apprehensions. Sprinkling is all that is necessary, or indeed I think advisable. Our weather is so changeable. At what hour would you wish the ceremony performed?

JACK: Oh, I might trot round about five if that would suit you.

CHASUBLE: Perfectly, perfectly! In fact I have two similar ceremonies to perform at that time. A case of twins that occurred recently in one of the outlying cottages on your own estate. Poor Jenkins the carter, a most hard-working man.

JACK: Oh! I don't see much fun in being christened along with other babies. It would be childish. Would half-past five do?

CHASUBLE: Admirably! Admirably! *(Takes out watch.)* And now, dear Mr Worthing, I will not intrude any longer into a house of sorrow. I would merely beg you not to be too much bowed down by grief. What seem to us bitter trials are often blessings in disguise.

MISS PRISM: This seems to me a blessing of an extremely obvious kind.

(Enter CECILY *from the house.)*

CECILY: Uncle Jack! Oh, I am pleased to see you back. But what horrid clothes you have got on. Do go and change them.

MISS PRISM: Cecily!

CHASUBLE: My child! my child. *(*CECILY *goes towards* JACK; *he kisses her brow in a melancholy manner.)*

CECILY: What is the matter, Uncle Jack? Do look happy! You look as if you had a toothache, and I have got such a surprise for you. Who do you think is in the dining-room? Your brother!

JACK: Who?

CECILY: Your brother Ernest. He arrived about half an hour ago.

JACK: What nonsense! I haven't got a brother.

CECILY: Oh, don't say that. However badly he may have behaved to you in the past he is still your brother. You couldn't be so heartless as to disown him. I'll tell him to come out. And you will shake hands with him, won't you, Uncle Jack? *(Runs back into the house.)*

CHASUBLE: These are very joyful tidings.

MISS PRISM: After we had all been resigned to his loss, his sudden return seems to me peculiarly distressing.

JACK: My brother is in the dining-room? I don't know what it all means. I think it is perfectly absurd.

(Enter ALGERNON *and* CECILY *hand in hand. They come slowly up to* JACK.)*

JACK: Good heavens! *(Motions* ALGERNON *away.)*

ALGERNON: Brother John, I have come down from town to tell you that I am very sorry for all the trouble I have given you, and that I intend to lead a better life in the future. *(*JACK *glares at him and does not take his hand.)*

CECILY: Uncle Jack, you are not going to refuse your own brother's hand?

JACK: Nothing will induce me to take his hand. I think his coming down here disgraceful. He knows perfectly well why.

CECILY: Uncle Jack, do be nice. There is some good in everyone. Ernest has just been telling me about his poor invalid friend Mr Bunbury whom he goes to visit so often. And surely there must be much good in one who is kind to an invalid, and leaves the pleasures of London to sit by a bed of pain.

JACK: Oh! he has been talking about Bunbury, has he?

CECILY: Yes, he has told me all about poor Mr Bunbury, and his terrible state of health.

JACK: Bunbury! Well, I won't have him talk to you about Bunbury or about anything else. It is enough to drive one perfectly frantic.

ALGERNON: Of course I admit that the faults were all on my side. But I must say that I think that Brother John's coldness to me is peculiarly painful. I expected a more enthusiastic welcome especially considering it is the first time I have come here.

CECILY: Uncle Jack, if you don't shake hands with Ernest, I will never forgive you.

JACK: Never forgive me?

CECILY: Never, never, never!

JACK: Well, this is the last time I shall ever do it. *(Shakes hands with* ALGERNON *and glares.)*

CHASUBLE: It's pleasant, is it not, to see so perfect a reconciliation? I think we might leave the two brothers together.

MISS PRISM: Cecily, you will come with us.

CECILY: Certainly, Miss Prism. My little task of reconciliation is over.

CHASUBLE: You have done a beautiful action today, dear child.

MISS PRISM: We must not be premature in our judgements.

CECILY: I feel very happy. *(They all go off except* JACK *and* ALGERNON.*)*

JACK: You young scoundrel, Algy, you must get out of this place as soon as possible. I don't allow any Bunburying here.

(Enter MERRIMAN.*)*

MERRIMAN: I have put Mr Ernest's things in the room next to yours, sir. I suppose that is all right?

JACK: What?

MERRIMAN: Mr Ernest's luggage, sir. I have unpacked it and put it in the room next to your own.

JACK: His luggage?

MERRIMAN: Yes, sir. Three portmanteaus, a dressing-case, two hatboxes, and a large luncheon-basket.

ALGERNON: I am afraid I can't stay more than a week this time.

JACK: Merriman, order the dog-cart* at once. Mr Ernest has been suddenly called back to town.

---

*dog-cart: So named because its original purpose was to carry sportsmen and their dogs to the site of the hunt. It was drawn by horses.

MERRIMAN: Yes, sir. *(Goes back into the house.)*

ALGERNON: What a fearful liar you are, Jack. I have not been called back to town at all.

JACK: Yes, you have.

ALGERNON: I haven't heard any one call me.

JACK: Your duty as a gentleman calls you back.

ALGERNON: My duty as a gentleman has never interfered with my pleasures in the smallest degree.

JACK: I can quite understand that.

ALGERNON: Well, Cecily is a darling.

JACK: You are not to talk of Miss Cardew like that. I don't like it.

ALGERNON: Well, I don't like your clothes. You look perfectly ridiculous in them. Why on earth don't you go up and change? It is perfectly childish to be in deep mourning for a man who is actually staying for a whole week with you in your house as a guest. I call it grotesque.

JACK: You are certainly not staying with me for a whole week as a guest or anything else. You have got to leave . . . by the four-five train.

ALGERNON: I certainly won't leave you so long as you are in mourning. It would be most unfriendly. If I were in mourning you would stay with me, I suppose. I should think it very unkind if you didn't.

JACK: Well, will you go if I change my clothes?

ALGERNON: Yes, if you are not too long. I never saw anybody take so long to dress, and with such little result.

JACK: Well, at any rate, that is better than being always over-dressed as you are.

ALGERNON: If I am occasionally a little over-dressed, I make up for it by being always immensely over-educated.

JACK: Your vanity is ridiculous, your conduct an outrage, and your presence in my garden utterly absurd. However, you have got to catch the four-five, and I hope you will have a pleasant journey back to town. This Bunburying, as you call it, has not been a great success for you.

(Goes into the house.)

ALGERNON: I think it has been a great success. I'm in love with Cecily, and that is everything.

(Enter CECILY at the back of the garden. She picks up the can and begins to water the flowers.)

But I must see her before I go, and make arrangements for another Bunbury. Ah, there she is.

CECILY: Oh, I merely came back to water the roses. I thought you were with Uncle Jack.

ALGERNON: He's gone to order the dog-cart for me.

CECILY: Oh, is he going to take you for a nice drive?

ALGERNON: He's going to send me away.

CECILY: Then have we got to part?

ALGERNON: I am afraid so. It's a very painful parting.

CECILY: It is always painful to part from people whom one has known for a very brief space of time. The absence of old friends one can endure with equanimity. But even a momentary separation from any one to whom one has just been introduced is almost unbearable.

ALGERNON: Thank you.

(Enter MERRIMAN.*)*

MERRIMAN: The dog-cart is at the door, sir.

(ALGERNON *looks appealingly at* CECILY.*)*

CECILY: It can wait, Merriman . . . for . . . five minutes.

MERRIMAN.   Yes, Miss.

(Exit MERRIMAN.*)*

ALGERNON: I hope, Cecily, I shall not offend you if I state quite frankly and openly that you seem to me to be in every way the visible personification of absolute perfection.

CECILY: I think your frankness does you great credit, Ernest. If you will allow me, I will copy your remarks into my diary. *(Goes over to table and begins writing in diary.)*

ALGERNON: Do you really keep a diary? I'd give anything to look at it. May I?

CECILY: Oh no. *(Puts her hand over it.)* You see, it is simply a very young girl's record of her own thoughts and impressions, and consequently meant for publication. When it appears in volume form I hope you will order a copy. But pray, Ernest, don't stop. I delight in taking down from dictation. I have reached "absolute perfection." You can go on. I am quite ready for more.

ALGERNON: *(Somewhat taken aback.)* Ahem! Ahem!

CECILY: Oh, don't cough, Ernest. When one is dictating one should speak fluently and not cough. Besides, I don't know how to spell a cough. *(Writes as* ALGERNON *speaks.)*

ALGERNON: *(Speaking very rapidly.)* Cecily, ever since I first looked upon your wonderful and incomparable beauty, I have dared to love you wildly, passionately, devotedly, hopelessly.

CECILY: I don't think that you should tell me that you love me wildly, passionately, devotedly, hopelessly. Hopelessly doesn't seem to make much sense, does it?

ALGERNON: Cecily.

(Enter MERRIMAN.*)*

MERRIMAN: The dog-cart is waiting, sir.

ALGERNON: Tell it to come round next week, at the same hour.

MERRIMAN: *(Looks at* CECILY, *who makes no sign.)* Yes, sir.

(MERRIMAN *retires.)*

CECILY: Uncle Jack would be very much annoyed if he knew you were staying on till next week, at the same hour.

ALGERNON: Oh, I don't care about Jack. I don't care for anybody in the whole world but you. I love you, Cecily. You will marry me, won't you?

CECILY: You silly boy! Of course. Why, we have been engaged for the last three months.

ALGERNON: For the last three months?

CECILY: Yes, it will be exactly three months on Thursday.

ALGERNON: But how did we become engaged?

CECILY: Well, ever since dear Uncle Jack first confessed to us that he had a younger brother who was very wicked and bad, you of course have formed the chief topic of conversation between myself and Miss Prism. And of course a man who is much talked about is always very attractive. One feels there must be something in him, after all. I daresay it was foolish of me, but I fell in love with you, Ernest.

ALGERNON: Darling. And when was the engagement actually settled?

CECILY: On the 14th of February last. Worn out by your entire ignorance of my existence, I determined to end the matter one way or the other, and after a long struggle with myself I accepted you under this dear old tree here. The next day I bought this little ring in your name, and this is the little bangle with the true lover's knot I promised you always to wear.

ALGERNON: Did I give you this? It's very pretty, isn't it?

CECILY: Yes, you've wonderfully good taste, Ernest. It's the excuse I've always given for your leading such a bad life. And this is the box in which I keep all your dear letters. *(Kneels at table, opens box, and produces letters tied up with blue ribbon.)*

ALGERNON: My letters! But, my own sweet Cecily, I have never written you any letters.

CECILY: You need hardly remind me of that, Ernest. I remember only too well that I was forced to write your letters for you. I wrote always three times a week, and sometimes oftener.

ALGERNON: Oh, do let me read them, Cecily?

CECILY: Oh, I couldn't possibly. They would make you far too conceited. *(Replaces box.)* The three you wrote me after I had broken off the engagement are so beautiful, and so badly spelled, that even now I can hardly read them without crying a little.

ALGERNON: But was our engagement ever broken off?

CECILY: Of course it was. On the 22nd of last March. You can see the entry if you like. *(Shows diary.)* "Today I broke off my engagement with Ernest. I feel it is better to do so. The weather still continues charming."

ALGERNON: But why on earth did you break it off? What had I done? I had done nothing at all. Cecily, I am very much hurt indeed to hear you broke it off. Particularly when the weather was so charming.

CECILY: It would hardly have been a really serious engagement if it hadn't been broken off at least once. But I forgave you before the week was out.

ALGERNON: *(Crossing to her, and kneeling.)* What a perfect angel you are, Cecily.

CECILY: You dear romantic boy. *(He kisses her, she puts her fingers through his hair.)* I hope your hair curls naturally, does it?

ALGERNON: Yes, darling, with a little help from others.

CECILY: I am so glad.

ALGERNON: You'll never break off our engagement again, Cecily?

CECILY: I don't think I could break it off now that I have actually met you. Besides, of course, there is the question of your name.

ALGERNON: Yes, of course. *(Nervously.)*

CECILY: You must not laugh at me, darling, but it had always been a girlish dream of mine to love some one whose name was Ernest. *(* ALGERNON *rises,* CECILY *also.)* There is something in that name that seems to inspire absolute confidence. I pity any poor married woman whose husband is not called Ernest.

ALGERNON: But, my dear child, do you mean to say you could not love me if I had some other name?

CECILY: But what name?

ALGERNON: Oh, any name you like—Algernon—for instance . . .

CECILY: But I don't like the name of Algernon.

ALGERNON: Well, my own dear, sweet, loving little darling, I really can't see why you should object to the name of Algernon. It is not at all a bad name. In fact, it is rather an aristocratic name. Half of the chaps who get into the Bankruptcy Court are called Algernon. But seriously, Cecily . . . *(Moving to her.)* if my name was Algy, couldn't you love me?

CECILY: *(Rising.)* I might respect you, Ernest, I might admire your character, but I fear that I should not be able to give you my undivided attention.

ALGERNON: Ahem! Cecily! *(Picking up hat.)* Your Rector here is, I suppose, thoroughly experienced in the practice of all the rites and ceremonials of the Church?

CECILY: Oh, yes. Dr Chasuble is a most learned man. He has never written a single book, so you can imagine how much he knows.

ALGERNON: I must see him at once on a most important christening—I mean on most important business.

CECILY: Oh!

ALGERNON: I shan't be away more than half an hour.

CECILY: Considering that we have been engaged since February the 14th, and that I only met you to-day for the first time, I think it is rather hard that you should leave me for so long a period as half an hour. Couldn't you make it twenty minutes?

ALGERNON: I'll be back in no time. *(Kisses her and rushes down the garden.)*

CECILY: What an impetuous boy he is! I like his hair so much. I must enter his proposal in my diary.

(Enter MERRIMAN.*)*

MERRIMAN: A Miss Fairfax has just called to see Mr Worthing. On very important business, Miss Fairfax states.
CECILY: Isn't Mr Worthing in his library?
MERRIMAN: Mr Worthing went over in the direction of the Rectory some time ago.
CECILY: Pray ask the lady to come out here; Mr Worthing is sure to be back soon. And you can bring tea.
MERRIMAN: Yes, Miss.

(Goes out.)

CECILY: Miss Fairfax! I suppose one of the many good elderly women who are associated with Uncle Jack in some of his philanthropic work in London. I don't quite like women who are interested in philanthropic work. I think it is so forward of them.

(Enter MERRIMAN.*)*

MERRIMAN: Miss Fairfax.

(Enter GWENDOLEN. *Exit* MERRIMAN.*)*

CECILY: *(Advancing to meet her.)* Pray let me introduce myself to you. My name is Cecily Cardew.
GWENDOLEN: Cecily Cardew? *(Moving to her and shaking hands.)* What a very sweet name! Something tells me that we are going to be great friends. I like you already more than I can say. My first impressions of people are never wrong.
CECILY: How nice of you to like me so much after we have known each other such a comparatively short time. Pray sit down.
GWENDOLEN: *(Still standing up.)* I may call you Cecily, may I not?
CECILY: With pleasure!
GWENDOLEN: And you will always call me Gwendolen, won't you?
CECILY: If you wish.
GWENDOLEN: Then that is all quite settled, is it not?
CECILY: I hope so. *(A pause. They both sit down together.)*
GWENDOLEN: Perhaps this might be a favourable opportunity for my mentioning who I am. My father is Lord Bracknell. You have never heard of papa, I suppose?
CECILY: I don't think so.
GWENDOLEN: Outside the family circle, papa, I am glad to say, is entirely unknown. I think that is quite as it should be. The home seems to me to be the proper sphere for the man. And certainly once a man begins to

neglect his domestic duties he becomes painfully effeminate, does he not? And I don't like that. It makes men so very attractive. Cecily, mamma, whose views on education are remarkably strict, has brought me up to be extremely short-sighted; it is part of her system; so do you mind my looking at you through my glasses?

CECILY: Oh! not at all, Gwendolen. I am very fond of being looked at.

GWENDOLEN: *(After examining* CECILY *carefully through a lorgnette.)* You are here on a short visit, I suppose.

CECILY: Oh no! I live here.

GWENDOLEN: *(Severely.)* Really? Your mother, no doubt, or some female relative of advanced years, resides here also?

CECILY: Oh no! I have no mother, nor, in fact, any relations.

GWENDOLEN: Indeed?

CECILY: My dear guardian, with the assistance of Miss Prism, has the arduous task of looking after me.

GWENDOLEN: Your guardian?

CECILY: Yes, I am Mr Worthing's ward.

GWENDOLEN: Oh! It is strange he never mentioned to me that he had a ward. How secretive of him! He grows more interesting hourly. I am not sure, however, that the news inspires me with feelings of unmixed delight. *(Rising and going to her.)* I am very fond of you, Cecily; I have liked you ever since I met you! But I am bound to state that now that I know that you are Mr Worthing's ward, I cannot help expressing a wish you were— well, just a little older than you seem to be—and not quite so very alluring in appearance. In fact, if I may speak candidly——

CECILY: Pray do! I think that whenever one has anything unpleasant to say, one should always be quite candid.

GWENDOLEN: Well, to speak with perfect candour, Cecily, I wish that you were fully forty-two, and more than usually plain for your age. Ernest has a strong upright nature. He is the very soul of truth and honour. Disloyalty would be as impossible to him as deception. But even men of the noblest possible moral character are extremely susceptible to the influence of the physical charms of others. Modern, no less than Ancient History, supplies us with many most painful examples of what I refer to. If it were not so, indeed, History would be quite unreadable.

CECILY: I beg your pardon, Gwendolen, did you say Ernest?

GWENDOLEN: Yes.

CECILY: Oh, but it is not Mr Ernest Worthing who is my guardian. It is his brother—his elder brother.

GWENDOLEN: *(Sitting down again.)* Ernest never mentioned to me that he had a brother.

CECILY: I am sorry to say they have not been on good terms for a long time.

GWENDOLEN: Ah! that accounts for it. And now that I think of it I have never heard any man mention his brother. The subject seems distasteful to most men. Cecily, you have lifted a load from my mind. I was growing almost anxious. It would have been terrible if any cloud had come across a friendship like ours, would it not? Of course you are quite, quite sure that it is not Mr Ernest Worthing who is your guardian?

CECILY: Quite sure. *(A pause.)* In fact, I am going to be his.

GWENDOLEN: *(Inquiringly.)* I beg your pardon?

CECILY: *(Rather shy and confidingly.)* Dearest Gwendolen, there is no reason why I should make a secret of it to you. Our little county newspaper is sure to chronicle the fact next week. Mr Ernest Worthing and I are engaged to be married.

GWENDOLEN: *(Quite politely, rising.)* My darling Cecily, I think there must be some slight error. Mr Ernest Worthing is engaged to me. The announcement will appear in the *Morning Post* on Saturday at the latest.

CECILY: *(Very politely, rising.)* I am afraid you must be under some misconception. Ernest proposed to me exactly ten minutes ago. *(Shows diary.)*

GWENDOLEN: *(Examines diary through her lorgnette carefully.)* It is very curious, for he asked me to be his wife yesterday afternoon at 5:30. If you would care to verify the incident, pray do so. *(Produces diary of her own.)* I never travel without my diary. One should always have something sensational to read in the train. I am so sorry, dear Cecily, if it is any disappointment to you, but I am afraid I have the prior claim.

CECILY: It would distress me more than I can tell you, dear Gwendolen, if it caused you any mental or physical anguish, but I feel bound to point out that since Ernest proposed to you he clearly has changed his mind.

GWENDOLEN: *(Meditatively.)* If the poor fellow has been entrapped into any foolish promise, I shall consider it my duty to rescue him at once, and with a firm hand.

CECILY: *(Thoughtfully and sadly.)* Whatever unfortunate entanglement my dear boy may have got into, I will never reproach him with it after we are married.

GWENDOLEN: Do you allude to me, Miss Cardew, as an entanglement? You are presumptuous. On an occasion of this kind it becomes more than a moral duty to speak one's mind. It becomes a pleasure.

CECILY: Do you suggest, Miss Fairfax, that I entrapped Ernest into an engagement? How dare you? This is no time for wearing the shallow mask of manners. When I see a spade I call it a spade.

GWENDOLEN: *(Satirically.)* I am glad to say that I have never seen a spade. It is obvious that our social spheres have been widely different.

(Enter MERRIMAN, followed by the footman. He carries a salver, table cloth, and plate stand. CECILY is about to retort. The presence of the servants exercises a restraining influence, under which both girls chafe.)

MERRIMAN: Shall I lay tea here as usual, Miss?

CECILY: *(Sternly, in a calm voice.)* Yes, as usual. *(MERRIMAN begins to clear table and lay cloth. A long pause. CECILY and GWENDOLEN glare at each other.)*

GWENDOLEN: Are there many interesting walks in the vicinity, Miss Cardew?

CECILY: Oh! yes! a great many. From the top of one of the hills quite close one can see five counties.

GWENDOLEN: Five counties! I don't think I should like that; I hate crowds.

CECILY: *(Sweetly.)* I suppose that is why you live in town? *(GWENDOLEN bites her lip, and beats her foot nervously with her parasol.)*

GWENDOLEN: *(Looking around.)* Quite a well-kept garden this is, Miss Cardew.

CECILY: So glad you like it, Miss Fairfax.

GWENDOLEN: I had no idea there were any flowers in the country.

CECILY: Oh, flowers are as common here, Miss Fairfax, as people are in London.

GWENDOLEN: Personally I cannot understand how anybody manages to exist in the country, if anybody who is anybody does. The country always bores me to death.

CECILY: Ah! This is what the newspapers call agricultural depression, is it not? I believe the aristocracy are suffering very much from it just at present. It is almost an epidemic amongst them, I have been told. May I offer you some tea, Miss Fairfax?

GWENDOLEN: *(With elaborate politeness.)* Thank you. *(Aside.)* Detestable girl! But I require tea!

CECILY: *(Sweetly.)* Sugar?

GWENDOLEN: *(Superciliously.)* No, thank you. Sugar is not fashionable any more. *(CECILY looks angrily at her, takes up the tongs and puts four lumps of sugar into the cup.)*

CECILY: *(Severely.)* Cake or bread and butter?

GWENDOLEN: *(In a bored manner.)* Bread and butter, please. Cake is rarely seen at the best houses nowadays.

CECILY: *(Cuts a very large slice of cake and puts it on the tray.)* Hand that to Miss Fairfax.

(MERRIMAN does so, and goes out with footman. GWENDOLEN drinks the tea and makes a grimace. Puts down cup at once, reaches out her hand to the bread and butter, looks at it, and finds it is cake. Rises in indignation.)

GWENDOLEN: You have filled my tea with lumps of sugar, and though I asked most distinctly for bread and butter, you have given me cake. I am known for the gentleness of my disposition, and the extraordinary sweetness of my nature, but I warn you, Miss Cardew, you may go too far.

CECILY: *(Rising.)* To save my poor, innocent, trusting boy from the machinations of any other girl there are no lengths to which I would not go.

GWENDOLEN: From the moment I saw you I distrusted you. I felt that you were false and deceitful. I am never deceived in such matters. My first impressions of people are invariably right.

CECILY: It seems to me, Miss Fairfax, that I am trespassing on your valuable time. No doubt you have many other calls of a similar character to make in the neighbourhood.

(Enter JACK.*)*

GWENDOLEN: *(Catching sight of him.)* Ernest! My own Ernest!

JACK: Gwendolen! Darling! *(Offers to kiss her.)*

GWENDOLEN: *(Drawing back.)* A moment! May I ask if you are engaged to be married to this young lady? *(Points to* CECILY.*)*

JACK: *(Laughing.)* To dear little Cecily! Of course not! What could have put such an idea into your pretty little head?

GWENDOLEN: Thank you. You may! *(Offers her cheek.)*

CECILY: *(Very sweetly.)* I knew there must be some misunderstanding, Miss Fairfax. The gentleman whose arm is at present round your waist is my guardian, Mr John Worthing.

GWENDOLEN: I beg your pardon?

CECILY: This is Uncle Jack.

GWENDOLEN: *(Receding.)* Jack! Oh!

(Enter ALGERNON.*)*

CECILY: Here is Ernest.

ALGERNON: *(Goes straight over to* CECILY *without noticing anyone else.)* My own love! *(Offers to kiss her.)*

CECILY: *(Drawing back.)* A moment, Ernest! May I ask you—are you engaged to be married to this young lady?

ALGERNON: *(Looking round.)* To what young lady? Good heavens! Gwendolen!

CECILY: Yes: to good heavens, Gwendolen, I mean to Gwendolen.

ALGERNON: *(Laughing.)* Of course not! What could have put such an idea into your pretty little head?

CECILY: Thank you. *(Presenting her cheek to be kissed.)* You may. *(*ALGERNON *kisses her.)*

GWENDOLEN: I felt there was some slight error, Miss Cardew. The gentleman who is now embracing you is my cousin, Mr Algernon Moncrieff.

CECILY: *(Breaking away from* ALGERNON.*)* Algernon Moncrieff! Oh! *(The two girls move towards each other and put their arms round each other's waists as if for protection.)*

CECILY: Are you called Algernon?

ALGERNON: I cannot deny it.

CECILY: Oh!

GWENDOLEN: Is your name really John?

JACK: *(Standing rather proudly.)* I could deny it if I liked. I could deny anything if I liked. But my name certainly is John. It has been John for years.

CECILY: *(To* GWENDOLEN.*)* A gross deception has been practised on both of us.

GWENDOLEN: My poor wounded Cecily!

CECILY: My sweet wronged Gwendolen!

GWENDOLEN: *(Slowly and seriously.)* You will call me sister, will you not? *(They embrace.* JACK *and* ALGERNON *groan and walk up and down.)*

CECILY: *(Rather brightly.)* There is just one question I would like to be allowed to ask my guardian.

GWENDOLEN: An admirable idea! Mr Worthing, there is just one question I would like to be permitted to put to you. Where is your brother Ernest? We are both engaged to be married to your brother Ernest, so it is a matter of some importance to us to know where your brother Ernest is at present.

JACK: *(Slowly and hesitatingly.)* Gwendolen—Cecily—it is very painful for me to be forced to speak the truth. It is the first time in my life that I have ever been reduced to such a painful position, and I am really quite inexperienced in doing anything of the kind. However, I will tell you quite frankly that I have no brother Ernest. I have no brother at all. I never had a brother in my life, and I certainly have not the smallest intention of ever having one in the future.

CECILY: *(Surprised.)* No brother at all?

JACK: *(Cheerily.)* None!

GWENDOLEN: *(Severely.)* Had you never a brother of any kind?

JACK: *(Pleasantly.)* Never. Not even of any kind.

GWENDOLEN: I am afraid it is quite clear, Cecily, that neither of us is engaged to be married to anyone.

CECILY: It is not a very pleasant position for a young girl suddenly to find herself in. Is it?

GWENDOLEN: Let us go into the house. They will hardly venture to come after us there.

CECILY: No, men are so cowardly, aren't they? *(They retire into the house with scornful looks.)*

JACK: This ghastly state of things is what you call Bunburying I suppose?

ALGERNON: Yes, and a perfectly wonderful Bunbury it is. The most wonderful Bunbury I have ever had in my life.

JACK: Well, you've no right whatsoever to Bunbury here.

ALGERNON: That is absurd. One has a right to Bunbury anywhere one chooses. Every serious Bunburyist knows that.

JACK: Serious Bunburyist? Good heavens!

ALGERNON: Well, one must be serious about something, if one wants to have any amusement in life. I happen to be serious about Bunburying. What on earth you are serious about I haven't got the remotest idea. About everything, I should fancy. You have such an absolutely trivial nature.

JACK: Well, the only small satisfaction I have in the whole of this wretched business is that your friend Bunbury is quite exploded. You won't be able to run down to the country quite so often as you used to do, dear Algy. And a very good thing too.

ALGERNON: Your brother is a little off colour, isn't he, dear Jack? You won't be able to disappear to London quite so frequently as your wicked custom was. And not a bad thing either.

JACK: As for your conduct towards Miss Cardew, I must say that your taking in a sweet, simple, innocent girl like that is quite inexcusable. To say nothing of the fact that she is my ward.

ALGERNON: I can see no possible defence at all for your deceiving a brilliant, clever, thoroughly experienced young lady like Miss Fairfax. To say nothing of the fact that she is my cousin.

JACK: I wanted to be engaged to Gwendolen, that is all, I love her.

ALGERNON: Well, I simply wanted to be engaged to Cecily. I adore her.

JACK: There is certainly no chance of your marrying Miss Cardew.

ALGERNON: I don't think there is much likelihood, Jack, of you and Miss Fairfax being united.

JACK: Well, that is no business of yours.

ALGERNON: If it was my business, I wouldn't talk about it. *(Begins to eat muffins.)* It is very vulgar to talk about one's business. Only people like stockbrokers do that, and then merely at dinner parties.

JACK: How you can sit there, calmly eating muffins when we are in this horrible trouble, I can't make out. You seem to me to be perfectly heartless.

ALGERNON: Well, I can't eat muffins in an agitated manner. The butter would probably get on my cuffs. One should always eat muffins quite calmly. It is the only way to eat them.

JACK: I say it's perfectly heartless your eating muffins at all, under the circumstances.

ALGERNON: When I am in trouble, eating is the only thing that consoles me. Indeed, when I am in really great trouble, as any one who knows me intimately will tell you, I refuse everything except food and drink. At the present moment I am eating muffins because I am unhappy. Besides, I am particularly fond of muffins. *(Rising.)*

JACK: *(Rising.)* Well, there is no reason why you should eat them all in that greedy way. *(Takes muffins from* ALGERNON.*)*

ALGERNON: *(Offering tea-cake.)* I wish you would have tea-cake instead. I don't like tea-cake.

JACK: Good heavens! I suppose a man may eat his own muffins in his own garden.

ALGERNON: But you have just said it was perfectly heartless to eat muffins.

JACK: I said it was perfectly heartless of you, under the circumstances. That is a very different thing.

ALGERNON: That may be. But the muffins are the same. *(He seizes the muffin-dish from* JACK.*)*

JACK: Algy, I wish to goodness you would go.

ALGERNON: You can't possibly ask me to go without having some dinner. It's absurd. I never go without my dinner. No one ever does, except vegetarians and people like that. Besides I have just made arrangements with Dr Chasuble to be christened at a quarter to six under the name of Ernest.

JACK: My dear fellow, the sooner you give up that nonsense the better. I made arrangements this morning with Dr Chasuble to be christened myself at 5:30, and I naturally will take the name of Ernest. Gwendolen would wish it. We can't both be christened Ernest. It's absurd. Besides, I have a perfect right to be christened if I like. There is no evidence at all that I have ever been christened by anybody. I should think it extremely probable I never was, and so does Dr Chasuble. It is entirely different in your case. You have been christened already.

ALGERNON: Yes, but I have not been christened for years.

JACK: Yes, but you have been christened. That is the important thing.

ALGERNON: Quite so. So I know my constitution can stand it. If you are not quite sure about your ever having been christened, I must say I think it rather dangerous your venturing on it now. It might make you very unwell. You can hardly have forgotten that someone very closely connected with you was very nearly carried off this week in Paris by a severe chill.

JACK: Yes, but you said yourself that a severe chill was not hereditary.

ALGERNON: It usen't to be, I know—but I daresay it is now. Science is always making wonderful improvements in things.

JACK: *(Picking up the muffin-dish.)* Oh, that is nonsense; you are always talking nonsense.

ALGERNON: Jack, you are at the muffins again! I wish you wouldn't. There are only two left. *(Takes them.)* I told you I was particularly fond of muffins.

JACK: But I hate tea-cake.

ALGERNON: Why on earth then do you allow tea-cake to be served up for your guests? What ideas you have of hospitality!

JACK: Algernon! I have already told you to go. I don't want you here. Why don't you go!

ALGERNON: I haven't quite finished my tea yet! and there is still one muffin left. *(JACK groans, and sinks into a chair. ALGERNON continues eating.)*

ACT DROP

ACT III

SCENE   *Drawing-room at the Manor House*

(GWENDOLEN and CECILY are at the window, looking out into the garden.)

GWENDOLEN: The fact that they did not follow us at once into the house, as anyone else would have done, seems to me to show that they have some sense of shame left.

CECILY: They have been eating muffins. That looks like repentance.

GWENDOLEN: *(After a pause.)* They don't seem to notice us at all. Couldn't you cough?

CECILY: But I haven't got a cough.

GWENDOLEN: They're looking at us. What effrontery!

CECILY: They're approaching. That's very forward of them.

GWENDOLEN: Let us preserve a dignified silence.

CECILY: Certainly. It's the only thing to do now.

(Enter JACK *followed by* ALGERNON. *They whistle some dreadful popular air from a British Opera.)*

GWENDOLEN: This dignified silence seems to produce an unpleasant effect.

CECILY: A most distasteful one.

GWENDOLEN: But we will not be the first to speak.

CECILY: Certainly not.

GWENDOLEN: Mr Worthing, I have something very particular to ask you. Much depends on your reply.

CECILY: Gwendolen, your common sense is invaluable. Mr Moncrieff, kindly answer me the following question. Why did you pretend to be my guardian's brother?

ALGERNON: In order that I might have an opportunity of meeting you.

CECILY: *(To* GWENDOLEN.*)* That certainly seems a satisfactory explanation, does it not?

GWENDOLEN: Yes, dear, if you can believe him.

CECILY: I don't. But that does not affect the wonderful beauty of his answer.

GWENDOLEN: True. In matters of grave importance, style, not sincerity, is the vital thing. Mr Worthing, what explanation can you offer to me for pretending to have a brother? Was it in order that you might have an opportunity of coming up to town to see me as often as possible?

JACK: Can you doubt it, Miss Fairfax?

GWENDOLEN: I have the gravest doubts upon the subject. But I intend to crush them. This is not the moment for German scepticism.* *(Moving to* CECILY.*)* Their explanations appear to be quite satisfactory, especially Mr Worthing's. That seems to me to have the stamp of truth upon it.

CECILY: I am more than content with what Mr Moncrieff said. His voice alone inspires one with absolute credulity.

GWENDOLEN: Then you think we should forgive them?

CECILY: Yes. I mean no.

GWENDOLEN: True! I had forgotten. There are principles at stake that one cannot surrender. Which of us should tell them? The task is not a pleasant one.

CECILY: Could we not both speak at the same time?

GWENDOLEN: An excellent idea! I nearly always speak at the same time as other people. Will you take the time from me?

CECILY: Certainly. (GWENDOLEN *beats time with uplifted finger.)*

GWENDOLEN and CECILY: *(Speaking together.)* Your Christian names are still an insuperable barrier. That is all!

JACK and ALGERNON: *(Speaking together.)* Our Christian names! Is that all? But we are going to be christened this afternoon.

GWENDOLEN: *(To* JACK.*)* For my sake you are prepared to do this terrible thing?

JACK: I am.

---

*German scepticism: A reference to nineteenth-century scholarship which raised doubts about the truth of the *Bible.*

CECILY: *(To* ALGERNON.*)* To please me you are ready to face this fearful ordeal?

ALGERNON: I am!

GWENDOLEN: How absurd to talk of the equality of the sexes! Where questions of self-sacrifice are concerned, men are infinitely beyond us.

JACK: We are. *(Clasps hands with* ALGERNON.*)*

CECILY: They have moments of physical courage of which we women know absolutely nothing.

GWENDOLEN: *(To* JACK.*)* Darling!

ALGERNON: *(To* CECILY.*)* Darling! *(They fall into each other's arms.)*

(Enter MERRIMAN. *When he enters he coughs loudly, seeing the situation.)*

MERRIMAN: Ahem! Ahem! Lady Bracknell.

JACK: Good heavens!

(Enter LADY BRACKNELL. *The couples separate in alarm. Exit* MERRIMAN.*)*

LADY BRACKNELL: Gwendolen! What does this mean?

GWENDOLEN: Merely that I am engaged to be married to Mr Worthing, mamma.

LADY BRACKNELL: Come here. Sit down. Sit down immediately. Hesitation of any kind is a sign of mental decay in the young, of physical weakness in the old. *(Turns to* JACK.*)* Apprised, sir, of my daughter's sudden flight by her trusty maid, whose confidence I purchased by means of a small coin, I followed her at once by a luggage train. Her unhappy father is, I am glad to say, under the impression that she is attending a more than usually lengthy lecture by the University Extension Scheme on the Influence of a Permanent Income on Thought. I do not propose to undeceive him. Indeed I have never undeceived him on any question. I would consider it wrong. But of course, you will clearly understand that all communication between yourself and my daughter must cease immediately from this moment. On this point, as indeed on all points, I am firm.

JACK: I am engaged to be married to Gwendolen, Lady Bracknell!

LADY BRACKNELL: You are nothing of the kind, sir. And now as regards Algernon! . . . Algernon!

ALGERNON: Yes, Aunt Augusta.

LADY BRACKNELL: May I ask if it is in this house that your invalid friend Mr Bunbury resides?

ALGERNON: *(Stammering.)* Oh! No! Bunbury doesn't live here. Bunbury is somewhere else at present. In fact, Bunbury is dead.

LADY BRACKNELL: Dead! When did Mr Bunbury die? His death must have been extremely sudden.

ALGERNON: *(Airily.)* Oh! I killed Bunbury this afternoon. I mean poor Bunbury died this afternoon.

LADY BRACKNELL: What did he die of?

ALGERNON: Bunbury? Oh, he was quite exploded.

LADY BRACKNELL: Exploded! Was he the victim of a revolutionary outrage?

I was not aware that Mr Bunbury was interested in social legislation. If so, he is well punished for his morbidity.

ALGERNON: My dear Aunt Augusta, I mean he was found out! The doctors found out that Bunbury could not live, that is what I mean—so Bunbury died.

LADY BRACKNELL: He seems to have had great confidence in the opinion of his physicians. I am glad, however, that he made up his mind at the last to some definite course of action, and acted under proper medical advice. And now that we have finally got rid of this Mr Bunbury, may I ask, Mr Worthing, who is that young person whose hand my nephew Algernon is now holding in what seems to me a peculiarly unnecessary manner?

JACK: That lady is Miss Cecily Cardew, my ward. *(LADY BRACKNELL bows coldly to CECILY.)*

ALGERNON: I am engaged to be married to Cecily, Aunt Augusta.

LADY BRACKNELL: I beg your pardon?

CECILY: Mr Moncrieff and I are engaged to be married, Lady Bracknell.

LADY BRACKNELL: *(With a shiver, crossing to the sofa and sitting down.)* I do not know whether there is anything peculiarly exciting in the air of this particular part of Hertfordshire, but the number of engagements that go on seems to me considerably above the proper average that statistics have laid down for our guidance. I think some preliminary inquiry on my part would not be out of place. Mr Worthing, is Miss Cardew at all connected with any of the larger railway stations in London? I merely desire information. Until yesterday I had no idea that there were any families or persons whose origin was a Terminus. *(JACK looks perfectly furious, but restrains himself.)*

JACK: *(In a cold, clear voice.)* Miss Cardew is the granddaughter of the late Mr Thomas Cardew of 149 Belgrave Square, S.W.; Gervase Park, Dorking, Surrey; and the Sporran, Fifeshire, N.B.

LADY BRACKNELL: That sounds not unsatisfactory. Three addresses always inspire confidence, even in tradesmen. But what proof have I of their authenticity?

JACK: I have carefully preserved the Court Guides* of the period. They are open to your inspection, Lady Bracknell.

LADY BRACKNELL: *(Grimly.)* I have known strange errors in that publication.

JACK: Miss Cardew's family solicitors are Messrs Markby, Markby, and Markby.

LADY BRACKNELL: Markby, Markby, and Markby? A firm of the very highest position in their profession. Indeed I am told that one of the Mr Markby's is occasionally to be seen at dinner parties. So far I am satisfied.

JACK: *(Very irritably.)* How extremely kind of you, Lady Bracknell! I have also in my possession, you will be pleased to hear, certificates of Miss Cardew's birth, baptism, whooping cough, registration, vaccination, confirmation, and the measles; both the German and the English variety.

---

*Court Guides: A list of those who have been received at court, a sign of social distinction.

LADY BRACKNELL: Ah! A life crowded with incident, I see; though perhaps somewhat too exciting for a young girl. I am not myself in favour of premature experiences. *(Rises, looks at her watch.)* Gwendolen! the time approaches for our departure. We have not a moment to lose. As a matter of form, Mr Worthing, I had better ask you if Miss Cardew has any little fortune?

JACK: Oh! about a hundred and thirty thousand pounds in the Funds.* That is all. Good-bye, Lady Bracknell. So pleased to have seen you.

LADY BRACKNELL: *(Sitting down again.)* A moment, Mr Worthing. A hundred and thirty thousand pounds! And in the Funds! Miss Cardew seems to me a most attractive young lady, now that I look at her. Few girls of the present day have any really solid qualities, any of the qualities that last, and improve with time. We live, I regret to say, in an age of surfaces. *(To* CECILY.*)* Come over here, dear. *(*CECILY *goes across.)* Pretty child! your dress is sadly simple, and your hair seems almost as Nature might have left it. But we can soon alter all that. A thoroughly experienced French maid produces a really marvellous result in a very brief space of time. I remember recommending one to young Lady Lancing, and after three months her own husband did not know her.

JACK: And after six months nobody knew her.

LADY BRACKNELL: *(Glares at* JACK *for a few moments. Then bends, with a practised smile, to* CECILY.*)* Kindly turn round, sweet child. *(*CECILY *turns completely round.)* No, the side view is what I want. *(*CECILY *presents her profile.)* Yes, quite as I expected. There are distinct social possibilities in your profile. The two weak points in our age are its want of principle and its want of profile. The chin a little higher, dear. Style largely depends on the way the chin is worn. They are worn very high, just at present, Algernon!

ALGERNON: Yes, Aunt Augusta!

LADY BRACKNELL: There are distinct social possibilities in Miss Cardew's profile.

ALGERNON: Cecily is the sweetest, dearest, prettiest girl in the whole world. And I don't care twopence about social possibilities.

LADY BRACKNELL: Never speak disrespectfully of Society, Algernon. Only people who can't get into it do that. *(To* CECILY.*)* Dear child, of course you know that Algernon has nothing but his debts to depend upon. But I do not approve of mercenary marriages. When I married Lord Bracknell I had no fortune of any kind. But I never dreamed for a moment of allowing that to stand in my way. Well, I suppose I must give my consent.

ALGERNON: Thank you, Aunt Augusta.

LADY BRACKNELL: Cecily, you may kiss me!

CECILY: *(Kisses her.)* Thank you, Lady Bracknell.

LADY BRACKNELL: You may also address me as Aunt Augusta for the future.

CECILY: Thank you, Aunt Augusta.

LADY BRACKNELL: The marriage, I think, had better take place quite soon.

---

*Funds: Government bonds.

ALGERNON: Thank you, Aunt Augusta.

CECILY: Thank you, Aunt Augusta.

LADY BRACKNELL: To speak frankly, I am not in favour of long engagements. They give people the opportunity of finding out each other's character before marriage, which I think is never advisable.

JACK: I beg your pardon for interrupting you, Lady Bracknell, but this engagement is quite out of the question. I am Miss Cardew's guardian, and she cannot marry without my consent until she comes of age. That consent I absolutely decline to give.

LADY BRACKNELL: Upon what grounds, may I ask? Algernon is an extremely, I may almost say an ostentatiously, eligible young man. He has nothing, but he looks everything. What more can one desire?

JACK: It pains me very much to have to speak frankly to you, Lady Bracknell, about your nephew, but the fact is that I do not approve at all of his moral character. I suspect him of being untruthful. (ALGERNON *and* CECILY *look at him in indignant amazement.*)

LADY BRACKNELL: Untruthful! My nephew Algernon? Impossible! He is an Oxonian.*

JACK: I fear there can be no possible doubt about the matter. This afternoon during my temporary absence in London on an important question of romance, he obtained admission to my house by means of the false pretence of being my brother. Under an assumed name he drank, I've just been informed by my butler, an entire pint bottle of my Perrier-Jouet, Brut, '89; wine I was specially reserving for myself. Continuing his disgraceful deception, he succeeded in the course of the afternoon in alienating the affections of my only ward. He subsequently stayed to tea, and devoured every single muffin. And what makes his conduct all the more heartless is, that he was perfectly well aware from the first that I have no brother, that I never had a brother, and that I don't intend to have a brother, not even of any kind. I distinctly told him so myself yesterday afternoon.

LADY BRACKNELL: Ahem! Mr Worthing, after careful consideration I have decided entirely to overlook my nephew's conduct to you.

JACK: That is very generous of you, Lady Bracknell. My own decision, however, is unalterable. I decline to give my consent.

LADY BRACKNELL: *(To* CECILY.*)* Come here, sweet child. (CECILY *goes over.*) How old are you, dear?

CECILY: Well, I am really only eighteen, but I always admit to twenty when I go to evening parties.

LADY BRACKNELL: You are perfectly right in making some slight alteration. Indeed, no woman should ever be quite accurate about her age. It looks so calculating. . . . *(In a meditative manner.)* Eighteen, but admitting to twenty at evening parties. Well, it will not be very long before you are

*Oxonion: A graduate of Oxford University.

of age and free from the restraints of tutelage. So I don't think your guardian's consent is, after all, a matter of any importance.

JACK: Pray excuse me, Lady Bracknell, for interrupting you again, but it is only fair to tell you that according to the terms of her grandfather's will Miss Cardew does not come legally of age till she is thirty-five.

LADY BRACKNELL: That does not seem to me to be a grave objection. Thirty-five is a very attractive age. London society is full of women of the very highest birth who have, of their own free choice, remained thirty-five for years. Lady Dumbleton is an instance in point. To my own knowledge she has been thirty-five ever since she arrived at the age of forty, which was many years ago now. I see no reason why our dear Cecily should not be even still more attractive at the age you mention than she is at present. There will be a large accumulation of property.

CECILY: Algy, could you wait for me till I was thirty-five?

ALGERNON: Of course I could, Cecily. You know I could.

CECILY: Yes, I felt it instinctively, but I couldn't wait all that time. I hate waiting even five minutes for anybody. It always makes me rather cross. I am not punctual myself, I know, but I do like punctuality in others, and waiting, even to be married, is quite out of the question.

ALGERNON: Then what is to be done, Cecily?

CECILY: I don't know, Mr Moncrieff.

LADY BRACKNELL: My dear Mr Worthing, as Miss Cardew states positively that she cannot wait till she is thirty-five—a remark which I am bound to say seems to me to show a somewhat impatient nature—I would beg of you to reconsider your decision.

JACK: But my dear Lady Bracknell, the matter is entirely in your own hands. The moment you consent to my marriage with Gwendolen, I will most gladly allow your nephew to form an alliance with my ward.

LADY BRACKNELL: *(Rising and drawing herself up.)* You must be quite aware that what you propose is out of the question.

JACK: Then a passionate celibacy is all that any of us can look forward to.

LADY BRACKNELL: That is not the destiny I propose for Gwendolen. Algernon, of course, can choose for himself. *(Pulls out her watch.)* Come, dear *(*GWENDOLEN *rises.)*, we have already missed five, if not six, trains. To miss any more might expose us to comment on the platform.

(Enter DR CHASUBLE.*)*

CHASUBLE: Everything is quite ready for the christenings.

LADY BRACKNELL: The christenings, sir! Is not that somewhat premature?

CHASUBLE: *(Looking rather puzzled, and pointing to* JACK *and* ALGERNON.*)* Both these gentlemen have expressed a desire for immediate baptism.

LADY BRACKNELL: At their age? The idea is grotesque and irreligious! Algernon, I forbid you to be baptized. I will not hear of such excesses. Lord Bracknell would be highly displeased if he learned that that was the way in which you wasted your time and money.

CHASUBLE: Am I to understand then that there are to be no christenings at all this afternoon?

JACK: I don't think that, as things are now, it would be of much practical value to either of us, Dr Chasuble.

CHASUBLE: I am grieved to hear such sentiments from you, Mr Worthing. They savour of the heretical views of the Anabaptists,* views that I have completely refuted in four of my unpublished sermons. However, as your present mood seems to be one peculiarly secular, I will return to the church at once. Indeed, I have just been informed by the pew-opener that for the last hour and a half Miss Prism has been waiting for me in the vestry.

LADY BRACKNELL: *(Starting.)* Miss Prism! Did I hear you mention a Miss Prism?

CHASUBLE: Yes, Lady Bracknell. I am on my way to join her.

LADY BRACKNELL: Pray allow me to detain you for a moment. This matter may prove to be one of vital importance to Lord Bracknell and myself. Is this Miss Prism a female of repellent aspect, remotely connected with education?

CHASUBLE: *(Somewhat indignantly.)* She is the most cultivated of ladies, and the very picture of respectability.

LADY BRACKNELL: It is obviously the same person. May I ask what position she holds in your household?

CHASUBLE: *(Severely.)* I am a celibate, madam.

JACK: *(Interposing.)* Miss Prism, Lady Bracknell, has been for the last three years Miss Cardew's esteemed governess and valued companion.

LADY BRACKNELL: In spite of what I hear of her, I must see her at once. Let her be sent for.

CHASUBLE: *(Looking off.)* She approaches; she is nigh.

(Enter MISS PRISM *hurriedly.)*

MISS PRISM: I was told you expected me in the vestry, dear Canon. I have been waiting for you there for an hour and three-quarters. *(Catches sight of* LADY BRACKNELL, *who has fixed her with a stony glare.* MISS PRISM *grows pale and quails. She looks anxiously round as if desirous to escape.)*

LADY BRACKNELL: *(In a severe, judicial voice.)* Prism! *(*MISS PRISM *bows her head in shame.)* Come here, Prism! *(*MISS PRISM *approaches in a humble manner.)* Prism! Where is that baby? *(General consternation. The Canon starts back in horror.* ALGERNON *and* JACK *pretend to be anxious to shield* CECILY *and* GWENDOLEN *from hearing the details of a terrible public scandal.)* Twenty-eight years ago, Prism, you left Lord Bracknell's house, Number 104, Upper Grosvenor Street, in charge of a perambulator that contained a baby of the male sex. You never returned. A few weeks later, through the elaborate investigations of the Metropolitan police, the perambulator was

---

*Anabaptists: A Protestant sect who opposed infant baptism and held that the ritual was useless unless the person baptized was a believer.

discovered at midnight standing by itself in a remote corner of Bayswater. It contained the manuscript of a three-volume novel of more than usually revolting sentimentality. *(MISS PRISM starts in involuntary indignation.)* But the baby was not there. *(Every one looks at MISS PRISM.)* Prism! Where is that baby? *(A pause.)*

MISS PRISM: Lady Bracknell, I admit with shame that I do not know. I only wish I did. The plain facts of the case are these. On the morning of the day you mention, a day that is for ever branded on my memory, I prepared as usual to take the baby out in its perambulator. I had also with me a somewhat old, but capacious hand-bag in which I had intended to place the manuscript of a work of fiction that I had written during my few unoccupied hours. In a moment of mental abstraction, for which I can never forgive myself, I deposited the manuscript in the bassinette and placed the baby in the hand-bag.

JACK: *(Who has been listening attentively.)* But where did you deposit the hand-bag?

MISS PRISM: Do not ask me, Mr Worthing.

JACK: Miss Prism, this is a matter of no small importance to me. I insist on knowing where you deposited the hand-bag that contained that infant.

MISS PRISM: I left it in the cloak-room of one of the larger railway stations in London.

JACK: What railway station?

MISS PRISM: *(Quite crushed.)* Victoria. The Brighton line. *(Sinks into a chair.)*

JACK: I must retire to my room for a moment. Gwendolen, wait here for me.

GWENDOLEN: If you are not too long, I will wait here for you all my life.

(Exit JACK in great excitement.)

CHASUBLE: What do you think this means, Lady Bracknell?

LADY BRACKNELL: I dare not even suspect, Dr Chasuble. I need hardly tell you that in families of high position strange coincidences are not supposed to occur. They are hardly considered the thing.

(Noises heard overhead as if some one was throwing trunks about. Every one looks up.)

CECILY: Uncle Jack seems strangely agitated.

CHASUBLE: Your guardian has a very emotional nature.

LADY BRACKNELL: This noise is extremely unpleasant. It sounds as if he was having an argument. I dislike arguments of any kind. They are always vulgar, and often convincing.

CHASUBLE: *(Looking up.)* It has stopped now. *(The noise is redoubled.)*

LADY BRACKNELL: I wish he would arrive at some conclusion.

GWENDOLEN: This suspense is terrible. I hope it will last.

(Enter JACK with a hand-bag of black leather in his hand.)

JACK: *(Rushing over to MISS PRISM.)* Is this the hand-bag, Miss Prism? Examine it carefully before you speak. The happiness of more than one life depends on your answer.

MISS PRISM: *(Calmly.)* It seems to be mine. Yes, here is the injury it received through the upsetting of a Gower Street omnibus in younger and happier days. Here is the stain on the lining caused by the explosion of a temperance beverage, an incident that occurred at Leamington. And here, on the lock, are my initials. I had forgotten that in an extravagant mood I had had them placed there. The bag is undoubtedly mine. I am delighted to have it so unexpectedly restored to me. It has been a great inconvenience being without it all these years.

JACK: *(In a pathetic voice.)* Miss Prism, more is restored to you than this handbag. I was the baby you placed in it.

MISS PRISM: *(Amazed.)* You?

JACK: *(Embracing her.)* Yes . . . mother!

MISS PRISM: *(Recoiling in indignant astonishment.)* Mr. Worthing. I am unmarried!

JACK: Unmarried! I do not deny that is a serious blow. But after all, who has the right to cast a stone against one who has suffered? Cannot repentance wipe out an act of folly? Why should there be one law for men, and another for women? Mother, I forgive you. *(Tries to embrace her again.)*

MISS PRISM: *(Still more indignant.)* Mr Worthing, there is some error. *(Pointing to* LADY BRACKNELL.*)* There is the lady who can tell you who you really are.

JACK: *(After a pause.)* Lady Bracknell, I hate to seem inquisitive, but would you kindly inform me who I am?

LADY BRACKNELL: I am afraid that the news I have to give you will not altogether please you. You are the son of my poor sister, Mrs Moncrieff, and consequently Algernon's elder brother.

JACK: Algy's elder brother! Then I have a brother after all. I knew I had a brother! I always said I had a brother! Cecily—how could you have ever doubted that I had a brother? *(Seizes hold of* ALGERNON.*)* Dr Chasuble, my unfortunate brother. Miss Prism, my unfortunate brother. Gwendolen, my unfortunate brother. Algy, you young scoundrel, you will have to treat me with more respect in the future. You have never behaved to me like a brother in all your life.

ALGERNON: Well, not till to-day, old boy, I admit. I did my best, however, though I was out of practice. *(Shakes hands.)*

GWENDOLEN: *(To* JACK.*)* My own! But what own are you? What is your Christian name, now that you have become some one else?

JACK: Good heavens! . . . I had quite forgotten that point. Your decision on the subject of my name is irrevocable, I suppose?

GWENDOLEN: I never change, except in my affections.

CECILY: What a noble nature you have, Gwendolen!

JACK: Then the question had better be cleared up at once. Aunt Augusta, a moment. At the time when Miss Prism left me in the hand-bag, had I been christened already?

LADY BRACKNELL: Every luxury that money could buy, including christening, had been lavished on you by your fond and doting parents.

JACK: Then I was christened! That is settled. Now, what name was I given? Let me know the worst.

LADY BRACKNELL: Being the eldest son you were naturally christened after your father.

JACK: *(Irritably.)* Yes, but what was my father's Christian name?

LADY BRACKNELL: *(Meditatively.)* I cannot at the present moment recall what the General's Christian name was. But I have no doubt he had one. He was eccentric, I admit. But only in later years. And that was the result of the Indian climate, and marriage, and indigestion, and other things of that kind.

JACK: Algy! Can't you recollect what our father's Christian name was?

ALGERNON: My dear boy, we were never even on speaking terms. He died before I was a year old.

JACK: His name would appear in the Army Lists of the period, I suppose, Aunt Augusta?

LADY BRACKNELL: The General was essentially a man of peace, except in his domestic life. But I have no doubt his name would appear in any military directory.

JACK: The Army Lists of the last forty years are here. These delightful records should have been my constant study. *(Rushes to bookcase and tears the books out.)* M. Generals . . . Mallam, Maxbohm, Magley—what ghastly names they have—Markby, Migsby, Mobbs, Moncrieff! Lieutenant 1840, Captain, Lieutenant-Colonel, Colonel, General 1869, Christian names, Ernest John. *(Puts book very quietly down and speaks quite calmly.)* I always told you, Gwendolen, my name was Ernest, didn't I? Well, it is Ernest after all. I mean it naturally is Ernest.

LADY BRACKNELL: Yes, I remember now that the General was called Ernest. I knew I had some particular reason for disliking the name.

GWENDOLEN: Ernest! My own Ernest! I felt from the first that you could have no other name!

JACK: Gwendolen, it is a terrible thing for a man to find out suddenly that all his life he has been speaking nothing but the truth. Can you forgive me?

GWENDOLEN: I can. For I feel that you are sure to change.

JACK: My own one!

CHASUBLE: *(To* MISS PRISM.*)* Laetitia! *(Embraces her.)*

MISS PRISM: *(Enthusiastically.)* Frederick! At last!

ALGERNON: Cecily! *(Embraces her.)* At last!

JACK: Gwendolen! *(Embraces her.)* At last!

LADY BRACKNELL: My nephew, you seem to be displaying signs of triviality.

JACK: On the contrary, Aunt Augusta, I've now realized for the first time in my life the vital Importance of Being Earnest.

TABLEAU

CURTAIN

Writing Assignments for "The Importance of Being Earnest"

I. Brief Papers: Act I

A. 1. Wilde's characters often create a witty line by turning familiar sayings and proverbs upside down. By making fun of society's pet beliefs, the characters indirectly attack society itself. For example, the upper classes traditionally believed it was their duty to set a good example for the lower classes, but Algernon, commenting on his servant's irregular marriage, says, "Really, if the lower orders don't set us a good example, what on earth is the use of them? They seem, as a class, to have absolutely no sense of moral responsibility" (p. 1074). The line is amusing not only because it inverts popular belief but because it suggests that Algernon is serious about morality when in fact he is not. Choose two or three of the following lines and show how they ridicule conventional moral beliefs.

   a. "Divorces are made in Heaven" (p. 1075).

   b. "Produce your explanation and pray make it improbable" (p. 1077).

   c. "The amount of women in London who flirt with their own husbands is perfectly scandalous. It looks so bad. It is simply washing one's clean linen in public" (p. 1078).

   d. "You don't seem to realize that in married life three is company and two is none" (p. 1079).

   e. "I hate people who are not serious about meals" (p. 1079).

   f. "I don't mind hard work where there is no definite object of any kind" (p. 1088).

   g. "Few parents nowadays pay any regard to what their children say to them. The old-fashioned respect for the young is fast dying out" (p. 1088).

   2. Compare the way Jack uses his brother, Ernest, with the way Algernon uses Bunbury.

   3. Why is Algernon so opposed to marriage? Support your answer by analyzing the way he makes fun of marriage.

   4. In the first act, an eligible young man, Jack, proposes marriage to an eligible young woman, Gwendolen, and she accepts. How is this commonplace event made funny?

   5. Explain Algernon's meaning when he says to Jack: "Nothing will induce me to part with Bunbury, and if you ever get married, which seems to me extremely problematic, you will be very glad to know Bunbury. A man who marries without knowing Bunbury has a very tedious time of it" (p. 1079).

B. 1. Argue for or against the assertion that, in spite of the play's title, the first act indicates that Algernon, not Jack, is the principal character.

   2. In Act I, Lady Bracknell becomes an obstacle to the marriage of Jack and Gwendolen unless one of three things occur: (1) Lady Bracknell changes her mind; (2) Jack and Gwendolen marry without her consent; (3) Jack discovers a respectable set of parents. Argue that Act I leads the audience to expect that all solutions are equally probable, *or* to expect that one solution is probable but not the others.

C. 1. Choose one line or piece of dialogue that you think is especially clever or funny and explore your reasons for liking it.

2. Here are two bits of dialogue that may or may not have the same appeal today that they had in 1895. Choose one of the lines and explain how changes in social attitudes have modified its meaning. Do you think, in spite of these changes, the line is still funny? Explain.

   a. JACK: What extraordinary ideas you have about the way to behave to a woman.

   ALGERNON: The only way to behave to a woman is to make love to her, if she is pretty, and to someone else, if she is plain (p. 1087).

   b. JACK: Well, yes, I must admit I smoke.

   LADY BRACKNELL: I am glad to hear it. A man should have an occupation of some kind (p. 1083).

3. How do you respond to Gwendolen's quick acceptance of Jack's proposal? Do you think the comic intent here is to make fun of Gwendolen or to make fun of those women who react to proposals in more conventional ways— modest surprise, coy confusion, thoughtful deliberation?

4. How do you respond to Gwendolen's wish that Jack show more affection "in public," that he look at her adoringly "especially when there are other people present"?

II. Blocking Characters in "The Importance of Being Earnest"

Combine the following elements into a coherent paragraph that explains the function of *blocking characters* in *The Importance of Being Earnest*.

1. The climax of many comedies is the marriage of young lovers.
2. A good plot requires this.
3. The marriage is delayed.

4. This delay or suspense is usually achieved by characters.
5. They are called *blocking characters*.

6. They consciously oppose the marriage.
7. Their folly somehow stands in the marriage's way.

8. Parents are most frequently blocking characters.
9. Parents represent practical, puritanical, and antiromantic forces in society.

10. The marriage is often blocked.
11. It is blocked by some folly or fault.
12. The fault or folly is in one or both of the lovers.

13. This happens in *The Importance of Being Earnest*.
14. This is the play's primary plot.
15. Jack's plan to marry Gwendolen is initially blocked by the girl's mother.
16. The mother is Lady Bracknell.

17. Lady Bracknell is concerned with Jack's family background.
18. She is more concerned with this than with her daughter's desire.

19. Gwendolen herself also threatens to be a block.
20. Gwendolen is in love with Jack and willing to marry him.

21. She can only love someone named Ernest.
22. This is what she says.
23. Jack uses the name Ernest when he is with her in London.

24. The audience believes this.
25. The hero's name is Jack.
26. Gwendolen's infatuation with the name of Ernest seems likely to become an obstacle.

27. This happens at the end of Act I.
28. The audience is led to expect this.
29. Jack will discover a respectable set of parents.
30. Jack will get a new name.
31. This will satisfy the aristocratic conditions of Lady Bracknell.
32. This will satisfy the romantic expectations of Gwendolen.

III. Brief Papers: Act II

A. 1. As examples of comic dialogue, compare Cecily's acceptance of Algernon's proposal with Gwendolen's acceptance of Jack's proposal.
   2. In the muffin-eating scene in Act II, Algernon more or less repeats the cucumber sandwich episode in Act I. Explain the comic function of these two scenes.
   3. What differences, if any, do you see in the style and wit of Gwendolen and Cecily? Cite specific evidence to support your opinion.

B. 1. When Algernon tells Cecily, "You mustn't think that I am wicked," she replies: "If you are not, then you have certainly been deceiving us all in a very inexcusable manner. I hope you have not been leading a double life, pretending to be wicked and being really good all the time. That would be hypocrisy" (p. 1092). Some say that Cecily is simply confused about the meaning of "double life" and "hypocrisy," and that, in effect, she doesn't know what she's saying. Others say that Cecily is really intelligent and witty, and that in this particular speech, she means what she says, and what she says makes sense. Which view do you favor?
   2. Some say that it is a flaw in the play for Algernon, the cheerfully amoral bachelor who makes fun of marriage all through Act I, to propose to Cecily in Act II. Others say that Algernon's proposal is prepared for in Act I and is consistent with his character. Which view do you favor?

C. 1. Choose one or two lines or bits of dialogue that you find especially funny or clever and explain your reason for liking them.

2. How does Miss Prism's relationship with Dr. Chasuble affect your response to Cecily's relationship to Algernon?

3. Both Cecily and Gwendolen attach a good deal of importance to names. Do you find this altogether ridiculous or do you think it is fairly typical of young men and women? Explain.

IV. Witless Characters in "The Importance of Being Earnest"
Combine the following elements into a coherent paragraph that explains the function of *witless characters* in *The Importance of Being Earnest*.

1. In *The Importance of Being Earnest* the humor is heightened by contrast.
2. The contrast is between the young couples and Miss Prism and Dr. Chasuble.

3. The young couples are witty and pleasure seeking.
4. Miss Prism and Dr. Chasuble are witless and puritanical.
5. Algernon turns proverbs upside down.
6. Algernon says, "Divorces are made in Heaven."
7. Miss Prism recites platitudes.
8. Miss Prism says, "As a man sows, so let him reap."

9. Dr. Chasuble is equally ridiculous.
10. Dr. Chasuble has a conventional belief.
11. Dr. Chasuble believes that a love of Paris is a sign of immorality.
12. Paris is the city of artists and lovers.

13. Miss Prism and Dr. Chasuble are witless in themselves.
14. Not only that, they also favor witless books.

15. Dr. Chasuble preaches only one sermon.
16. The sermon is for all occasions.
17. The occasions are funerals, weddings, christenings.

18. Miss Prism urges Cecily to read German grammar.
19. German grammar is surely a witless subject.
20. Miss Prism is herself the author of a three-volume novel.
21. In this novel, the "good ended happily and the bad unhappily."

22. These are witless literary productions.
23. The literary productions are the moralizing novel and the conventional sermon.
24. These literary productions provide a vivid contrast to Wilde's play.
25. The play is witty and amoral.

V. Brief Papers: Act III
A. 1. Explain why Jack thinks that Miss Prism is his mother.
2. Having said in Act I that he would never part with Bunbury, why does Algernon let Bunbury die in Act III?

B. 1. In response to a question about Lady Bracknell's approval of Cecily as a wife
    for Algernon, one student writes:

> When Lady Bracknell finds out that Cecily has a lot of money her
> unfavorable attitude toward her marriage to Algernon changes to a
> favorable one. She now finds Cecily a "most attractive young lady" and
> then she explains how "few girls of the present have any really solid
> qualities, any of the qualities that last and improve with time. We live,
> I regret to say, in an age of surfaces" (p. 1113). Lady Bracknell means
> that money is a solid quality because it lasts and even improves with
> time (perhaps because of interest). Lady Bracknell compares the lasting
> quality of money with the nonlasting quality of people, especially
> women. She implies that most women, when first entering into mar-
> riage, have only their looks. But looks do not last or improve with time
> as money does. Young women eventually become old, wrinkled, and
> gray; but money will remain the same. Living in an "age of surfaces"
> implies that the only qualities society sees are those on the outside such
> as looks and personality. Lady Bracknell is wise and realistic in realizing
> that money is one of the "solid qualities."

  Do you agree with this interpretation?

 2. Argue for or against the assertion that Jack's final line is to be taken seriously
    in both these ways: he has become Ernest since that is his real name, and he
    has also become an earnest and morally serious person.

C. In many stories, the hero does not know his true parents because, shortly after
   his birth, he was switched with another baby, usually a servant's child. How does
   the fact that Jack was switched with Miss Prism's novel affect your response to
   this play?

VI. Longer Papers

A. Write a paper explaining the comic role of Jack's brother, Ernest, and Algernon's
   friend, Bunbury. Consider, in particular, the comic effects that are achieved by
   the announcement of their deaths and the relevance of these deaths to the central
   action and meaning of the play.

B. As the play's title ironically suggests, the principal aim of *The Importance of
   Being Earnest* is to make fun of truth, sincerity, and earnestness. Show how this
   aim is achieved through comic dialogue and plot development.

C. Some say that the moral point of the play is that Jack, when he discovers his true
   identity, does, in fact, become earnest. Having sown his wild oats in the guise
   of the fictitious Ernest, Jack becomes the true Ernest and is now ready to accept
   marriage, social obligations, and moral responsibility. Others say that Jack remains consistently amoral and that the play's aim, from beginning to end, is to
   discourage anyone from taking a serious view of society and its institutions,
   especially marriage. Argue for or against one of these views. If you do not agree

with either view, then state and defend your own opinion about the play's moral aim.

D. Wilde says that the play's "philosophy" is this: "We should treat all the trivial things of life seriously, and all the serious things of life with sincere and studied triviality." Analyzing the scenes you think are most successful, explain how Wilde develops his "philosophy."

ARTHUR MILLER
Death of a Salesman

Before Reading

Free write for 5 or 10 minutes on one of the following questions:

1. In a capitalistic society, employers are usually free to dismiss workers who are no longer needed or who cannot make a positive contribution. Many people oppose this practice, arguing that those who are willing to work and who continue to make an honest effort should not be fired. Which position do you favor?
2. Do you think that the most popular students in high school will be the most successful in adult life?

CHARACTERS

Willy Loman	Howard Wagner
Linda	Jenny
Biff	Stanley
Happy	Miss Forsythe
Bernard	Letta
The Woman	Charley
Uncle Ben	

THE PLACE.   WILLY LOMAN's *house and yard and various places he visits in the New York and Boston of today.*

Throughout the play, in the stage directions, left and right mean stage left and stage right.

ACT I

A melody is heard, played upon a flute. It is small and fine, telling of grass and trees and the horizon. The curtain rises.

Before us is the Salesman's house. We are aware of towering, angular shapes behind it, surrounding it on all sides. Only the blue light of the sky falls upon the house and forestage; the surrounding area shows an angry glow of orange. As more light appears, we see a solid vault of apartment houses around the small, fragile-seeming home. An air of the dream clings to the place, a dream rising out of reality. The kitchen at center seems actual enough, for there is a kitchen table with three chairs, and a refrigerator. But no other fixtures are seen. At the back of the kitchen there is a draped entrance, which leads to the living-room. To the right of the

DEATH OF A SALESMAN by Arthur Miller (1915–   ) was first produced in New York in 1949, winning the Pulitzer Prize for that year. The play is probably the best-known serious drama in American theater.

kitchen, on a level raised two feet, is a bedroom furnished only with a brass bedstead and a straight chair. On a shelf over the bed a silver athletic trophy stands. A window opens onto the apartment house at the side.

Behind the kitchen, on a level raised six and a half feet, is the boys' bedroom, at present barely visible. Two beds are dimly seen, and at the back of the room a dormer window. (This bedroom is above the unseen living-room.) At the left a stairway curves up to it from the kitchen.

The entire setting is wholly, or, in some places, partially transparent. The roof-line of the house is one-dimensional; under and over it we see the apartment buildings. Before the house lies an apron, curving beyond the forestage into the orchestra. This forward area serves as the back yard as well as the locale of all WILLY*'s imaginings and of his city scenes. Whenever the action is in the present the actors observe the imaginary wall-lines, entering the house only through its door at the left. But in the scenes of the past these boundaries are broken, and characters enter or leave a room by stepping "through" a wall onto the forestage.*

From the right, WILLY LOMAN, *the Salesman, enters, carrying two large sample cases. The flute plays on. He hears but is not aware of it. He is past sixty years of age, dressed quietly. Even as he crosses the stage to the doorway of the house, his exhaustion is apparent. He unlocks the door, comes into the kitchen, and thankfully lets his burden down, feeling the soreness of his palms. A word-sigh escapes his lips—it might be "Oh, boy, oh, boy." He closes the door, then carries his cases out into the living-room, through the draped kitchen doorway.*

LINDA, *his wife, has stirred in her bed at the right. She gets out and puts on a robe, listening. Most often jovial, she has developed an iron repression of her exceptions to* WILLY*'s behavior—she more than loves him, she admires him, as though his mercurial nature, his temper, his massive dreams and little cruelties, served her only as sharp reminders of the turbulent longings within him, longings which she shares but lacks the temperament to utter and follow to their end.*

LINDA *(Hearing* WILLY *outside the bedroom, calls with some trepidation):*   Willy!
WILLY: It's all right. I came back.
LINDA: Why? What happened? *(Slight pause.)* Did something happen, Willy?
WILLY: No, nothing happened.
LINDA: You didn't smash the car, did you?
WILLY *(With casual irritation):*   I said nothing happened. Didn't you hear me?
LINDA: Don't you feel well?
WILLY: I'm tired to the death. *(The flute has faded away. He sits on the bed beside her, a little numb.)* I couldn't make it. I just couldn't make it, Linda.
LINDA *(Very carefully, delicately):*   Where were you all day? You look terrible.
WILLY: I got as far as a little above Yonkers. I stopped for a cup of coffee. Maybe it was the coffee.
LINDA: What?
WILLY *(After a pause):*   I suddenly couldn't drive any more. The car kept going off onto the shoulder, y'know?
LINDA *(Helpfully):*   Oh. Maybe it was the steering again. I don't think Angelo knows the Studebaker.

WILLY: No, it's me, it's me. Suddenly I realize I'm goin' sixty miles an hour and I don't remember the last five minutes. I'm—I can't seem to—keep my mind to it.

LINDA: Maybe it's your glasses. You never went for your new glasses.

WILLY: No, I see everything. I came back ten miles an hour. It took me nearly four hours from Yonkers.

LINDA *(Resigned):*   Well, you'll just have to take a rest, Willy, you can't continue this way.

WILLY: I just got back from Florida.

LINDA: But you didn't rest your mind. Your mind is overactive, and the mind is what counts, dear.

WILLY: I'll start out in the morning. Maybe I'll feel better in the morning. *(She is taking off his shoes.)* These goddam arch supports are killing me.

LINDA: Take an aspirin. Should I get you an aspirin? It'll soothe you.

WILLY *(With wonder):*   I was driving along, you understand? And I was fine. I was even observing the scenery. You can imagine, me looking at scenery, on the road every week of my life. But it's so beautiful up there, Linda, the trees are so thick, and the sun is warm. I opened the windshield and just let the warm air bathe over me. And then all of a sudden I'm goin' off the road! I'm tellin' ya, I absolutely forgot I was driving. If I'd've gone the other way over the white line I might've killed somebody. So I went on again—and five minutes later I'm dreamin' again, and I nearly—*(He presses two fingers against his eyes.)* I have such thoughts, I have such strange thoughts.

LINDA: Willy, dear. Talk to them again. There's no reason why you can't work in New York.

WILLY: They don't need me in New York. I'm the New England man. I'm vital in New England.

LINDA: But you're sixty years old. They can't expect you to keep traveling every week.

WILLY: I'll have to send a wire to Portland. I'm supposed to see Brown and Morrison tomorrow morning at ten o'clock to show the line. Goddammit, I could sell them! *(He starts putting on his jacket.)*

LINDA *(Taking the jacket from him):*   Why don't you go down to the place tomorrow and tell Howard you've simply got to work in New York? You're too accommodating, dear.

WILLY: If old man Wagner was alive I'd a been in charge of New York now! That man was a prince, he was a masterful man. But that boy of his, that Howard, he don't appreciate. When I went north the first time, the Wagner Company didn't know where New England was!

LINDA: Why don't you tell those things to Howard, dear?

WILLY *(Encouraged):*   I will, I definitely will. Is there any cheese?

LINDA: I'll make you a sandwich.

WILLY: No, go to sleep. I'll take some milk. I'll be up right away. The boys in?

LINDA: They're sleeping. Happy took Biff on a date tonight.

WILLY *(Interested):* That so?

LINDA: It was so nice to see them shaving together, one behind the other, in the bathroom. And going out together. You notice? The whole house smells of shaving lotion.

WILLY: Figure it out. Work a lifetime to pay off a house. You finally own it, and there's nobody to live in it.

LINDA: Well, dear, life is a casting off. It's always that way.

WILLY: No, no, some people—some people accomplish something. Did Biff say anything after I went this morning?

LINDA: You shouldn't have criticized him, Willy, especially after he just got off the train. You mustn't lose your temper with him.

WILLY: When the hell did I lose my temper? I simply asked him if he was making any money. Is that a criticism?

LINDA: But, dear, how could he make any money?

WILLY *(Worried and angered):* There's such an undercurrent in him. He became a moody man. Did he apologize when I left this morning?

LINDA: He was crestfallen, Willy. You know how he admires you. I think if he finds himself, then you'll both be happier and not fight any more.

WILLY: How can he find himself on a farm? Is that a life? A farmhand? In the beginning, when he was young, I thought, well, a young man, it's good for him to tramp around, take a lot of different jobs. But it's more than ten years now and he has yet to make thirty-five dollars a week!

LINDA: He's finding himself, Willy.

WILLY: Not finding yourself at the age of thirty-four is a disgrace!

LINDA: Shh!

WILLY: The trouble is he's lazy, goddammit!

LINDA: Willy, please!

WILLY: Biff is a lazy bum!

LINDA: They're sleeping. Get something to eat. Go on down.

WILLY: Why did he come home? I would like to know what brought him home.

LINDA: I don't know. I think he's still lost, Willy. I think he's very lost.

WILLY: Biff Loman is lost. In the greatest country in the world a young man with such—personal attractiveness, gets lost. And such a hard worker. There's one thing about Biff—he's not lazy.

LINDA: Never.

WILLY *(With pity and resolve):* I'll see him in the morning; I'll have a nice talk with him. I'll get him a job selling. He could be big in no time. My God! Remember how they used to follow him around in high school? When he smiled at one of them their faces lit up. When he walked down the street . . . *(He loses himself in reminiscences.)*

LINDA *(Trying to bring him out of it):* Willy, dear, I got a new kind of American-type cheese today. It's whipped.

WILLY: Why do you get American when I like Swiss?

LINDA: I just thought you'd like a change—

WILLY: I don't want a change! I want Swiss cheese. Why am I always being contradicted?

LINDA *(With a covering laugh):*   I thought it would be a surprise.

WILLY: Why don't you open a window in here, for God's sake?

LINDA *(With infinite patience):*   They're all open, dear.

WILLY: The way they boxed us in here. Bricks and windows, windows and bricks.

LINDA: We should've bought the land next door.

WILLY: The street is lined with cars. There's not a breath of fresh air in the neighborhood. The grass don't grow any more, you can't raise a carrot in the back yard. They should've had a law against apartment houses. Remember those two beautiful elm trees out there? When I and Biff hung the swing between them?

LINDA: Yeah, like being a million miles from the city.

WILLY: They should've arrested the builder for cutting those down. They massacred the neighborhood. *(Lost)* More and more I think of those days, Linda. This time of year it was lilac and wisteria. And then the peonies would come out, and the daffodils. What fragrance in this room!

LINDA: Well, after all, people had to move somewhere.

WILLY: No, there's more people now.

LINDA: I don't think there's more people. I think—

WILLY: There's more people! That's what's ruining this country! Population is getting out of control. The competition is maddening! Smell the stink from that apartment house! And another one on the other side . . . How can they whip cheese?

(On WILLY's *last line,* BIFF *and* HAPPY *raise themselves up in their beds, listening.)*

LINDA: Go down, try it. And be quiet.

WILLY *(Turning to* LINDA, *guiltily):*   You're not worried about me, are you, sweetheart?

BIFF: What's the matter?

HAPPY: Listen!

LINDA: You've got too much on the ball to worry about.

WILLY: You're my foundation and my support, Linda.

LINDA: Just try to relax, dear. You make mountains out of molehills.

WILLY: I won't fight with him any more. If he wants to go back to Texas, let him go.

LINDA: He'll find his way.

WILLY: Sure. Certain men just don't get started till later in life. Like Thomas Edison, I think. Or B. F. Goodrich. One of them was deaf. *(He starts for the bedroom doorway.)* I'll put my money on Biff.

LINDA: And Willy—if it's warm Sunday we'll drive in the country. And we'll open the windshield, and take lunch.

WILLY: No, the windshields don't open on the new cars.

LINDA: But you opened it today.

WILLY: Me? I didn't. *(He stops.)* Now isn't that peculiar! Isn't that a remarkable—*(He breaks off in amazement and fright as the flute is heard distantly.)*

LINDA: What, darling?

WILLY: That is the most remarkable thing.

LINDA: What, dear?

WILLY: I was thinking of the Chevvy. *(Slight pause)* Nineteen twenty-eight
. . . when I had that red Chevvy—*(Breaks off)* That funny? I coulda sworn
I was driving that Chevvy today.

LINDA: Well, that's nothing. Something must've reminded you.

WILLY: Remarkable. Ts. Remember those days? The way Biff used to simo-
nize that car? The dealer refused to believe there was eighty thousand
miles on it. *(He shakes his head.)* Heh! *(To* LINDA*)* Close your eyes, I'll
be right up. *(He walks out of the bedroom.)*

HAPPY *(To* BIFF*):*   Jesus, maybe he smashed up the car again!

LINDA *(Calling after* WILLY*):*   Be careful on the stairs, dear! The cheese is on
the middle shelf! *(She turns, goes over to the bed, takes his jacket, and goes out
of the bedroom.)*

(Light has risen on the boys' room. Unseen, WILLY *is heard talking to himself,
"Eighty thousand miles," and a little laugh.* BIFF *gets out of bed, comes downstage
a bit, and stands attentively.* BIFF *is two years older than his brother* HAPPY,
*well built, but in these days bears a worn air and seems less self-assured. He has
succeeded less, and his dreams are stronger and less acceptable than* HAPPY's.
HAPPY *is tall, powerfully made. Sexuality is like a visible color on him, or a scent
that many women have discovered. He, like his brother, is lost, but in a different
way, for he has never allowed himself to turn his face toward defeat and is thus
more confused and hard-skinned, although seemingly more content.)*

HAPPY *(Getting out of bed):*   He's going to get his license taken away if he keeps
that up. I'm getting nervous about him, y'know, Biff?

BIFF: His eyes are going.

HAPPY: No, I've driven with him. He sees all right. He just doesn't keep his
mind on it. I drove into the city with him last week. He stops at a green
light and then it turns red and he goes. *(He laughs.)*

BIFF: Maybe he's color-blind.

HAPPY: Pop? Why he's got the finest eye for color in the business. You know
that.

BIFF *(Sitting down on his bed):*   I'm going to sleep.

HAPPY: You're not still sour on Dad, are you, Biff?

BIFF: He's all right, I guess.

WILLY *(Underneath them, in the living-room):*   Yes, sir, eighty thousand miles—
eighty-two thousand!

BIFF: You smoking?

HAPPY *(Holding out a pack of cigarettes):*   Want one?

BIFF *(Taking a cigarette):*   I can never sleep when I smell it.

WILLY: What a simonizing job, heh!

HAPPY *(With deep sentiment):*   Funny, Biff, y'know? Us sleeping in here again? The old beds. *(He pats his bed affectionately.)* All the talk that went across those two beds, huh? Our whole lives.

BIFF: Yeah. Lotta dreams and plans.

HAPPY *(With a deep and masculine laugh):*   About five hundred women would like to know what was said in this room.

(They share a soft laugh.)

BIFF: Remember that big Betsy something—what the hell was her name—over on Bushwick Avenue?

HAPPY *(Combing his hair):*   With the collie dog!

BIFF: That's the one. I got you in there, remember?

HAPPY: Yeah, that was my first time—I think. Boy, there was a pig! *(They laugh, almost crudely.)* You taught me everything I know about women. Don't forget that.

BIFF: I bet you forgot how bashful you used to be. Especially with girls.

HAPPY: Oh, I still am, Biff.

BIFF: Oh, go on.

HAPPY: I just control it, that's all. I think I got less bashful and you got more so. What happened, Biff? Where's the old humor, the old confidence? *(He shakes* BIFF's *knee.* BIFF *gets up and moves restlessly about the room.)* What's the matter?

BIFF: Why does Dad mock me all the time?

HAPPY: He's not mocking you, he—

BIFF: Everything I say there's a twist of mockery on his face. I can't get near him.

HAPPY: He just wants you to make good, that's all. I wanted to talk to you about Dad for a long time, Biff. Something's—happening to him. He—talks to himself.

BIFF: I noticed that this morning. But he always mumbled.

HAPPY: But not so noticeable. It got so embarrassing I sent him to Florida. And you know something? Most of the time he's talking to you.

BIFF: What's he say about me?

HAPPY: I can't make it out.

BIFF: What's he say about me?

HAPPY: I think the fact that you're not settled, that you're still kind of up in the air . . .

BIFF: There's one or two other things depressing him, Happy.

HAPPY: What do you mean?

BIFF: Never mind. Just don't lay it all to me.

HAPPY: But I think if you just got started—I mean—is there any future for you out there?

BIFF: I tell ya, Hap, I don't know what the future is. I don't know—what I'm supposed to want.

HAPPY: What do you mean?

BIFF: Well, I spent six or seven years after high school trying to work myself up. Shipping clerk, salesman, business of one kind or another. And it's a measly manner of existence. To get on that subway on the hot mornings in summer. To devote your whole life to keeping stock, or making phone calls, or selling or buying. To suffer fifty weeks of the year for the sake of a two-week vacation, when all you really desire is to be outdoors, with your shirt off. And always to have to get ahead of the next fella. And still—that's how you build a future.

HAPPY: Well, you really enjoy it on a farm? Are you content out there?

BIFF *(With rising agitation):*   Hap, I've had twenty or thirty different kinds of jobs since I left home before the war, and it always turns out the same. I just realized it lately. In Nebraska when I herded cattle, and the Dakotas, and Arizona, and now in Texas. It's why I came home now, I guess, because I realized it. This farm I work on, it's spring there now, see? And they've got about fifteen new colts. There's nothing more inspiring or— beautiful than the sight of a mare and a new colt. And it's cool there now, see? Texas is cool now, and it's spring. And whenever spring comes to where I am, I suddenly get the feeling, my God, I'm not gettin' anywhere! What the hell am I doing, playing around with horses, twenty-eight dollars a week! I'm thirty-four years old, I oughta be makin' my future. That's when I come running home. And now, I get here, and I don't know what to do with myself. *(After a pause)* I've always made a point of not wasting my life, and everytime I come back here I know that all I've done is to waste my life.

HAPPY: You're a poet, you know that, Biff? You're a—you're an idealist!

BIFF: No, I'm mixed up very bad. Maybe I oughta get married. Maybe I oughta get stuck into something. Maybe that's my trouble. I'm like a boy. I'm not married, I'm not in business, I just—I'm like a boy. Are you content, Hap? You're a success, aren't you? Are you content?

HAPPY: Hell, no!

BIFF: Why? You're making money, aren't you?

HAPPY *(Moving about with energy, expressiveness):*   All I can do now is wait for the merchandise manager to die. And suppose I get to be merchandise manager? He's a good friend of mine, and he just built a terrific estate on Long Island. And he lived there about two months and sold it, and now he's building another one. He can't enjoy it once it's finished. And I know that's just what I would do. I don't know what the hell I'm workin' for. Sometimes I sit in my apartment—all alone. And I think of the rent I'm paying. And it's crazy. But then, it's what I always wanted. My own apartment, a car, and plenty of women. And still, goddammit, I'm lonely.

BIFF *(With enthusiasm):*   Listen, why don't you come out West with me?

HAPPY: You and I, heh?

BIFF: Sure, maybe we could buy a ranch. Raise cattle, use our muscles. Men built like we are should be working out in the open.

HAPPY *(Avidly):*   The Loman Brothers, heh?

BIFF *(With vast affection):*   Sure, we'd be known all over the counties!

HAPPY *(Enthralled):*   That's what I dream about, Biff. Sometimes I want to just
rip my clothes off in the middle of the store and outbox that goddam
merchandise manager. I mean I can outbox, outrun, and outlift anybody
in that store, and I have to take orders from those common, petty sons-of-
bitches till I can't stand it any more.

BIFF: I'm tellin' you, kid, if you were with me I'd be happy out there.

HAPPY *(Enthused):*   See, Biff, everybody around me is so false that I'm constantly lowering my ideals . . .

BIFF: Baby, together we'd stand up for one another, we'd have someone to
trust.

HAPPY: If I were around you—

BIFF: Hap, the trouble is we weren't brought up to grub for money. I don't
know how to do it.

HAPPY: Neither can I!

BIFF: Then let's go!

HAPPY: The only thing is—what can you make out there?

BIFF: But look at your friend. Builds an estate and then hasn't the peace of
mind to live in it.

HAPPY: Yeah, but when he walks into the store the waves part in front of him.
That's fifty-two thousand dollars a year coming through the revolving
door, and I got more in my pinky finger than he's got in his head.

BIFF: Yeah, but you just said—

HAPPY: I gotta show some of those pompous, self-important executives over
there that Hap Loman can make the grade. I want to walk into the store
the way he walks in. Then I'll go with you, Biff. We'll be together yet,
I swear. But take those two we had tonight. Now weren't they gorgeous
creatures?

BIFF: Yeah, yeah, most gorgeous I've had in years.

HAPPY: I get that any time I want, Biff. Whenever I feel disgusted. The only
trouble is, it gets like bowling or something. I just keep knockin' them
over and it doesn't mean anything. You still run around a lot?

BIFF: Naa. I'd like to find a girl—steady, somebody with substance.

HAPPY: That's what I long for.

BIFF: Go on! You'd never come home.

HAPPY: I would! Somebody with character, with resistance! Like Mom,
y'know? You're gonna call me a bastard when I tell you this. That girl
Charlotte I was with tonight is engaged to be married in five weeks. *(He
tries on his new hat.)*

BIFF: No kiddin'!

HAPPY: Sure, the guy's in line for the vice-presidency of the store. I don't
know what gets into me, maybe I just have an overdeveloped sense of
competition or something, but I went and ruined her, and furthermore I
can't get rid of her. And he's the third executive I've done that to. Isn't
that a crummy characteristic? And to top it all, I go to their weddings!

(Indignantly, but laughing) Like I'm not supposed to take bribes. Manufac-
turers offer me a hundred-dollar bill now and then to throw an order their
way. You know how honest I am, but it's like this girl, see. I hate myself
for it. Because I don't want the girl, and, still, I take it and—I love it!

BIFF: Let's go to sleep.

HAPPY: I guess we didn't settle anything, heh?

BIFF: I just got one idea that I think I'm going to try.

HAPPY: What's that?

BIFF: Remember Bill Oliver?

HAPPY: Sure, Oliver is very big now. You want to work for him again?

BIFF: No, but when I quit he said something to me. He put his arm on my
shoulder, and he said, "Biff, if you ever need anything, come to me."

HAPPY: I remember that. That sounds good.

BIFF: I think I'll go to see him. If I could get ten thousand or even seven or
eight thousand dollars I could buy a beautiful ranch.

HAPPY: I bet he'd back you. 'Cause he thought highly of you, Biff. I mean,
they all do. You're well liked, Biff. That's why I say to come back here,
and we both have the apartment. And I'm tellin' you, Biff, any babe you
want . . .

BIFF: No, with a ranch I could do the work I like and still be something. I just
wonder though. I wonder if Oliver still thinks I stole that carton of
basketballs.

HAPPY: Oh, he probably forgot that long ago. It's almost ten years. You're
too sensitive. Anyway, he didn't really fire you.

BIFF: Well, I think he was going to. I think that's why I quit. I was never sure
whether he knew or not. I know he thought the world of me, though. I
was the only one he'd let lock up the place.

WILLY *(Below):*   You gonna wash the engine, Biff?

HAPPY: Shh!

*(BIFF looks at HAPPY, who is gazing down, listening. WILLY is mumbling in
the parlor.)*

HAPPY: You hear that?

(They listen. WILLY laughs warmly.)

BIFF *(Growing angry):*   Doesn't he know Mom can hear that?

WILLY: Don't get your sweater dirty, Biff!

(A look of pain crosses BIFF's face.)

HAPPY: Isn't that terrible? Don't leave again, will you? You'll find a job here.
You gotta stick around. I don't know what to do about him, it's getting
embarrassing.

WILLY: What a simonizing job!

BIFF: Mom's hearing that!

WILLY: No kiddin', Biff, you got a date? Wonderful!

HAPPY: Go on to sleep. But talk to him in the morning, will you?

BIFF *(Reluctantly getting into bed):*   With her in the house. Brother!

HAPPY *(Getting into bed):* I wish you'd have a good talk with him.

(The light on their room begins to fade.)

BIFF *(To himself in bed):*   That selfish, stupid . . .

HAPPY: Sh . . . Sleep, Biff.

(Their light is out. Well before they have finished speaking, WILLY's *form is dimly seen below in the darkened kitchen. He opens the refrigerator, searches in there, and takes out a bottle of milk. The apartment houses are fading out, and the entire house and surroundings become covered with leaves. Music insinuates itself as the leaves appear.)*

WILLY: Just wanna be careful with those girls, Biff, that's all. Don't make any promises. No promises of any kind. Because a girl, y'know, they always believe what you tell 'em, and you're very young, Biff, you're too young to be talking seriously to girls.

(Light rises on the kitchen. WILLY, *talking, shuts the refrigerator door and comes downstage to the kitchen table. He pours milk into a glass. He is totally immersed in himself, smiling faintly.)*

WILLY: Too young entirely, Biff. You want to watch your schooling first. Then when you're all set, there'll be plenty of girls for a boy like you. *(He smiles broadly at a kitchen chair.)* That so? The girls pay for you? *(He laughs.)* Boy, you must really be makin' a hit.

*(*WILLY *is gradually addressing—physically—a point offstage, speaking through the wall of the kitchen, and his voice has been rising in volume to that of a normal conversation.)*

WILLY: I been wondering why you polish the car so careful. Ha! Don't leave the hubcaps, boys. Get the chamois to the hubcaps. Happy, use newspaper on the windows, it's the easiest thing. Show him how to do it, Biff! You see, Happy? Pad it up, use it like a pad. That's it, that's it, good work. You're doin' all right, Hap. *(He pauses, then nods in approbation for a few seconds, then looks upward.)* Biff, first thing we gotta do when we get time is clip that big branch over the house. Afraid it's gonna fall in a storm and hit the roof. Tell you what. We get a rope and sling her around, and then we climb up there with a couple of saws and take her down. Soon as you finish the car, boys, I wanna see ya. I got a surprise for you, boys.

BIFF *(Offstage):*   Whatta ya got, Dad?

WILLY: No, you finish first. Never leave a job till you're finished—remember that. *(Looking toward the "big trees")* Biff, up in Albany I saw a beautiful hammock. I think I'll buy it next trip, and we'll hang it right between those two elms. Wouldn't that be something? Just swingin' there under those branches. Boy, that would be . . .

(YOUNG BIFF and YOUNG HAPPY appear from the direction WILLY was addressing. HAPPY carries rags and a pail of water. BIFF, wearing a sweater with a block "S," carries a football.)

BIFF *(Pointing in the direction of the car offstage):*   How's that, Pop, professional?

WILLY: Terrific. Terrific job, boys. Good work, Biff.

HAPPY: Where's the surprise, Pop?

WILLY: In the back seat of the car.

HAPPY: Boy! *(He runs off.)*

BIFF: What is it, Dad? Tell me, what'd you buy?

WILLY *(Laughing, cuffs him):*   Never mind, something I want you to have.

BIFF *(Turns and starts off):*   What is it, Hap?

HAPPY *(Offstage):*   It's a punching bag!

BIFF: Oh, Pop!

WILLY: It's got Gene Tunney's* signature on it!

(HAPPY runs onstage with a punching bag.)

BIFF: Gee, how'd you know we wanted a punching bag?

WILLY: Well, it's the finest thing for the timing.

HAPPY *(Lies down on his back and pedals with his feet):*   I'm losing weight, you notice, Pop?

WILLY *(To HAPPY):*   Jumping rope is good too.

BIFF: Did you see the new football I got?

WILLY *(Examining the ball):*   Where'd you get a new ball?

BIFF: The coach told me to practice my passing.

WILLY: That so? And he gave you the ball, heh?

BIFF: Well, I borrowed it from the locker room. *(He laughs confidentially.)*

WILLY *(Laughing with him at the theft):*   I want you to return that.

HAPPY: I told you he wouldn't like it!

BIFF *(Angrily):*   Well, I'm bringing it back!

WILLY *(Stopping the incipient argument, to HAPPY):*   Sure, he's gotta practice with a regulation ball, doesn't he? *(To BIFF)* Coach'll probably congratulate you on your initiative!

BIFF: Oh, he keeps congratulating my initiative all the time, Pop.

WILLY: That's because he likes you. If somebody else took that ball there'd be an uproar. So what's the report, boys, what's the report?

BIFF: Where'd you go this time, Dad? Gee we were lonesome for you.

WILLY *(Pleased, puts an arm around each boy and they come down to the apron):*   Lonesome, heh?

BIFF: Missed you every minute.

WILLY: Don't say? Tell you a secret, boys. Don't breathe it to a soul. Someday I'll have my own business, and I'll never have to leave home any more.

HAPPY: Like Uncle Charley, heh?

WILLY: Bigger than Uncle Charley! Because Charley is not—liked. He's liked, but he's not—well liked.

*Gene Tunney: Heavyweight boxing champion.

BIFF: Where'd you go this time, Dad?

WILLY: Well, I got on the road, and I went north to Providence. Met the Mayor.

BIFF: The Mayor of Providence!

WILLY: He was sitting in the hotel lobby.

BIFF: What'd he say?

WILLY: He said, "Morning!" And I said, "You got a fine city here, Mayor." And then he had coffee with me. And then I went to Waterbury. Waterbury is a fine city. Big clock city, the famous Waterbury clock. Sold a nice bill there. And then Boston—Boston is the cradle of the Revolution. A fine city. And a couple of other towns in Mass., and on to Portland and Bangor and straight home!

BIFF: Gee, I'd love to go with you sometime, Dad.

WILLY: Soon as summer comes.

HAPPY: Promise?

WILLY: You and Hap and I, and I'll show you all the towns. America is full of beautiful towns and fine, upstanding people. And they know me, boys, they know me up and down New England. The finest people. And when I bring you fellas up, there'll be open sesame for all of us, 'cause one thing, boys: I have friends. I can park my car in any street in New England, and the cops protect it like their own. This summer, heh?

BIFF and HAPPY *(Together)*: Yeah! You bet!

WILLY: We'll take our bathing suits.

HAPPY: We'll carry your bags, Pop!

WILLY: Oh, won't that be something! Me comin' into the Boston stores with you boys carryin' my bags. What a sensation!

(BIFF is prancing around, practicing passing the ball.)

WILLY: You nervous, Biff, about the game?

BIFF: Not if you're gonna be there.

WILLY: What do they say about you in school, now that they made you captain?

HAPPY: There's a crowd of girls behind him everytime the classes change.

BIFF *(Taking WILLY's hand)*: This Saturday, Pop, this Saturday—just for you, I'm going to break through for a touchdown.

HAPPY: You're supposed to pass.

BIFF: I'm takin' one play for Pop. You watch me, Pop, and when I take off my helmet, that means I'm breakin' out. Then you watch me crash through that line!

WILLY *(Kisses BIFF)*: Oh, wait'll I tell this in Boston!

(BERNARD enters in knickers. He is younger than BIFF, earnest and loyal, a worried boy.)

BERNARD: Biff, where are you? You're supposed to study with me today.

WILLY: Hey, looka Bernard. What're you lookin' so anemic about, Bernard?

BERNARD: He's gotta study, Uncle Willy. He's got Regents next week.

HAPPY *(Tauntingly, spinning* BERNARD *around):* Let's box, Bernard!

BERNARD: Biff! *(He gets away from* HAPPY.) Listen, Biff, I heard Mr. Birnbaum say that if you don't start studyin' math he's gonna flunk you, and you won't graduate. I heard him!

WILLY: You better study with him, Biff. Go ahead now.

BERNARD: I heard him!

BIFF: Oh, Pop, you didn't see my sneakers! *(He holds up a foot for* WILLY *to look at.)*

WILLY: Hey, that's a beautiful job of printing!

BERNARD *(Wiping his glasses):* Just because he printed University of Virginia on his sneakers doesn't mean they've got to graduate him, Uncle Willy!

WILLY *(Angrily):* What're you talking about? With scholarships to three universities they're gonna flunk him?

BERNARD: But I heard Mr. Birnbaum say—

WILLY: Don't be a pest, Bernard! *(To his boys)* What an anemic!

BERNARD: Okay, I'm waiting for you in my house, Biff.

*(*BERNARD *goes off. The* LOMANS *laugh.)*

WILLY: Bernard is not well liked, is he?

BIFF: He's liked, but he's not well liked.

HAPPY: That's right, Pop.

WILLY: That's just what I mean. Bernard can get the best marks in school, y'understand, but when he gets out in the business world, y'understand, you are going to be five times ahead of him. That's why I thank Almighty God you're both built like Adonises. Because the man who makes an appearance in the business world, the man who creates personal interest, is the man who gets ahead. Be liked and you will never want. You take me, for instance. I never have to wait in line to see a buyer. "Willy Loman is here!" That's all they have to know, and I go right through.

BIFF: Did you knock them dead, Pop?

WILLY: Knocked 'em cold in Providence, slaughtered 'em in Boston.

HAPPY *(On his back, pedaling again):* I'm losing weight, you notice, Pop?

*(*LINDA *enters, as of old, a ribbon in her hair, carrying a basket of washing.)*

LINDA *(With youthful energy):* Hello, dear!

WILLY: Sweetheart!

LINDA: How'd the Chevvy run?

WILLY: Chevrolet, Linda, is the greatest car ever built. *(To the boys)* Since when do you let your mother carry wash up the stairs?

BIFF: Grab hold there, boy!

HAPPY: Where to, Mom?

LINDA: Hang them up on the line. And you better go down to your friends, Biff. The cellar is full of boys. They don't know what to do with themselves.

BIFF: Ah, when Pop comes home they can wait!

WILLY *(Laughs appreciatively)*: You better go down and tell them what to do, Biff.

BIFF: I think I'll have them sweep out the furnace room.

WILLY: Good work, Biff.

BIFF *(Goes through wall-line of kitchen to doorway at back and calls down)*: Fellas! Everybody sweep out the furnace room! I'll be right down!

VOICES: All right! Okay, Biff.

BIFF: George and Sam and Frank, come out back! We're hangin' up the wash! Come on, Hap, on the double! *(He and* HAPPY *carry out the basket.)*

LINDA: The way they obey him!

WILLY: Well, that's training, the training. I'm tellin' you, I was sellin' thousands and thousands, but I had to come home.

LINDA: Oh, the whole block'll be at that game. Did you sell anything?

WILLY: I did five hundred gross in Providence and seven hundred gross in Boston.

LINDA: No! Wait a minute, I've got a pencil. *(She pulls pencil and paper out of her apron pocket.)* That makes your commission . . . Two hundred—my God! Two hundred and twelve dollars!

WILLY: Well, I didn't figure it yet, but . . .

LINDA: How much did you do?

WILLY: Well, I—I did—about a hundred and eighty gross in Providence. Well, no—it came to—roughly two hundred gross on the whole trip.

LINDA *(Without hesitation)*: Two hundred gross. That's . . . *(She figures.)*

WILLY: The trouble was that three of the stores were half closed for inventory in Boston. Otherwise I woulda broke records.

LINDA: Well, it makes seventy dollars and some pennies. That's very good.

WILLY: What do we owe?

LINDA: Well, on the first there's sixteen dollars on the refrigerator—

WILLY: Why sixteen?

LINDA: Well, the fan belt broke, so it was a dollar eighty.

WILLY: But it's brand new.

LINDA: Well, the man said that's the way it is. Till they work themselves in, y'know.

(They move through the wall-line into the kitchen.)

WILLY: I hope we didn't get stuck on that machine.

LINDA: They got the biggest ads of any of them!

WILLY: I know, it's a fine machine. What else?

LINDA: Well, there's nine-sixty for the washing machine. And for the vacuum cleaner there's three and a half due on the fifteenth. Then the roof, you got twenty-one dollars remaining.

WILLY: It don't leak, does it?

LINDA: No, they did a wonderful job. Then you owe Frank for the carburetor.

WILLY: I'm not going to pay that man! That goddam Chevrolet, they ought to prohibit the manufacture of that car!

LINDA: Well, you owe him three and a half. And odds and ends, comes to around a hundred and twenty dollars by the fifteenth.

WILLY: A hundred and twenty dollars! My God, if business don't pick up I don't know what I'm gonna do!

LINDA: Well, next week you'll do better.

WILLY: Oh, I'll knock 'em dead next week. I'll go to Hartford. I'm very well liked in Hartford. You know, the trouble is, Linda, people don't seem to take to me.

(They move onto the forestage.)

LINDA: Oh, don't be foolish.

WILLY: I know it when I walk in. They seem to laugh at me.

LINDA: Why? Why would they laugh at you? Don't talk that way, Willy.

(WILLY moves to the edge of the stage. LINDA goes into the kitchen and starts to darn stockings.)

WILLY: I don't know the reason for it, but they just pass me by. I'm not noticed.

LINDA: But you're doing wonderful, dear. You're making seventy to a hundred dollars a week.

WILLY: But I gotta be at it ten, twelve hours a day. Other men—I don't know—they do it easier. I don't know why—I can't stop myself—I talk too much. A man oughta come in with a few words. One thing about Charley. He's a man of few words, and they respect him.

LINDA: You don't talk too much, you're just lively.

WILLY *(Smiling):* Well, I figure, what the hell, life is short, a couple of jokes. *(To himself)* I joke too much! *(The smile goes.)*

LINDA: Why? You're—

WILLY: I'm fat. I'm very—foolish to look at, Linda. I didn't tell you, but Christmas time I happened to be calling on F. H. Stewarts, and a salesman I know, as I was going in to see the buyer I heard him say something about—walrus. And I—I cracked him right across the face. I won't take that. I simply will not take that. But they do laugh at me. I know that.

LINDA: Darling . . .

WILLY: I gotta overcome it. I know I gotta overcome it. I'm not dressing to advantage, maybe.

LINDA: Willy, darling, you're the handsomest man in the world—

WILLY: Oh, no, Linda.

LINDA: To me you are. *(Slight pause.)* The handsomest.

(From the darkness is heard the laughter of a woman. Willy doesn't turn to it, but it continues through LINDA's lines.)

LINDA: And the boys, Willy. Few men are idolized by their children the way you are.

(Music is heard as behind a scrim, to the left of the house, THE WOMAN, *dimly seen, is dressing.)*

WILLY *(With great feeling):*   You're the best there is, Linda, you're a pal, you know that? On the road—on the road I want to grab you sometimes and just kiss the life outa you.

(The laughter is loud now, and he moves into a brightening area at the left, where THE WOMAN *has come from behind the scrim and is standing, putting on her hat, looking into a "mirror" and laughing.)*

WILLY: 'Cause I get so lonely—especially when business is bad and there's nobody to talk to. I get the feeling that I'll never sell anything again, that I won't make a living for you, or a business, a business for the boys. *(He talks through* THE WOMAN's *subsiding laughter;* THE WOMAN *primps at the "mirror.")* There's so much I want to make for—
THE WOMAN: Me? You didn't make me, Willy. I picked you.
WILLY *(Pleased):*   You picked me?
THE WOMAN *(Who is quite proper-looking, Willy's age):*   I did. I've been sitting at that desk watching all the salesmen go by, day in, day out. But you've got such a sense of humor, and we do have such a good time together, don't we?
WILLY: Sure, sure. *(He takes her in his arms.)* Why do you have to go now?
THE WOMAN: It's two o'clock . . .
WILLY: No, come on in! *(He pulls her.)*
THE WOMAN: . . . my sisters'll be scandalized. When'll you be back?
WILLY: Oh, two weeks about. Will you come up again?
THE WOMAN: Sure thing. You do make me laugh. It's good for me. *(She squeezes his arm, kisses him.)* And I think you're a wonderful man.
WILLY: You picked me, heh?
THE WOMAN: Sure. Because you're so sweet. And such a kidder.
WILLY: Well, I'll see you next time I'm in Boston.
THE WOMAN: I'll put you right through to the buyers.
WILLY *(Slapping her bottom):*   Right. Well, bottoms up!
THE WOMAN *(Slaps him gently and laughs):*   You just kill me, Willy. *(He suddenly grabs her and kisses her roughly.)* You kill me. And thanks for the stockings. I love a lot of stockings. Well, good night.
WILLY: Good night. And keep your pores open!
THE WOMAN: Oh, Willy!

*(*THE WOMAN *bursts out laughing, and* LINDA's *laughter blends in.* THE WOMAN *disappears into the dark. Now the area at the kitchen table brightens.* LINDA *is sitting where she was at the kitchen table, but now is mending a pair of her silk stockings.)*

LINDA: You are, Willy. The handsomest man. You've got no reason to feel that—

WILLY (*Coming out of* THE WOMAN*'s dimming area and going over to Linda*):   I'll make it all up to you, Linda, I'll—

LINDA: There's nothing to make up, dear. You're doing fine, better than—

WILLY (*Noticing her mending*):   What's that?

LINDA: Just mending my stockings. They're so expensive—

WILLY (*Angrily, taking them from her*):   I won't have you mending stockings in this house! Now throw them out!

(LINDA *puts the stockings in her pocket.*)

BERNARD (*Entering on the run*):   Where is he? If he doesn't study!

WILLY (*Moving to the forestage, with great agitation*):   You'll give him the answers!

BERNARD: I do, but I can't on a Regents! That's a state exam! They're liable to arrest me!

WILLY: Where is he? I'll whip him, I'll whip him!

LINDA: And he'd better give back that football, Willy, it's not nice.

WILLY: Biff! Where is he? Why is he taking everything?

LINDA: He's too rough with the girls, Willy. All the mothers are afraid of him!

WILLY: I'll whip him!

BERNARD: He's driving the car without a license!

(THE WOMAN*'s laugh is heard.*)

WILLY: Shut up!

LINDA: All the mothers—

WILLY: Shut up!

BERNARD (*Backing quietly away and out*):   Mr. Birnbaum says he's stuck up.

WILLY: Get outa here!

BERNARD: If he doesn't buckle down he'll flunk math! (*He goes off.*)

LINDA: He's right, Willy, you've gotta—

WILLY (*Exploding at her*):   There's nothing the matter with him! You want him to be a worm like Bernard? He's got spirit, personality . . .

(*As he speaks,* LINDA, *almost in tears, exits into the living-room.* WILLY *is alone in the kitchen, wilting and staring. The leaves are gone. It is night again, and the apartment houses look down from behind.*)

WILLY: Loaded with it. Loaded! What is he stealing? He's giving it back, isn't he? Why is he stealing? What did I tell him? I never in my life told him anything but decent things.

(HAPPY *in pajamas has come down the stairs;* WILLY *suddenly becomes aware of* HAPPY*'s presence.*)

HAPPY: Let's go now, come on.

WILLY (*Sitting down at the kitchen table*):   Huh! Why did she have to wax the floors herself? Everytime she waxes the floors she keels over. She knows that!

HAPPY: Shh! Take it easy. What brought you back tonight?

WILLY: I got an awful scare. Nearly hit a kid in Yonkers. God! Why didn't I go to Alaska with my brother Ben that time! Ben! That man was a genius, that man was success incarnate! What a mistake! He begged me to go.

HAPPY: Well, there's no use in—

WILLY: You guys! There was a man started with the clothes on his back and ended up with diamond mines!

HAPPY: Boy, someday I'd like to know how he did it.

WILLY: What's the mystery? The man knew what he wanted and went out and got it! Walked into a jungle, and comes out, the age of twenty-one, and he's rich! The world is an oyster, but you don't crack it open on a mattress!

HAPPY: Pop, I told you I'm gonna retire you for life.

WILLY: You'll retire me for life on seventy goddam dollars a week? And your women and your car and your apartment, and you'll retire me for life! Christ's sake, I couldn't get past Yonkers today! Where are you guys, where are you? The woods are burning! I can't drive a car!

(CHARLEY has appeared in the doorway. He is a large man, slow of speech, laconic, immovable. In all he says, despite what he says, there is pity, and, now, trepidation. He has a robe over pajamas, slippers on his feet. He enters the kitchen.)

CHARLEY: Everything all right?

HAPPY: Yeah, Charley, everything's . . .

WILLY: What's the matter?

CHARLEY: I heard some noise. I thought something happened. Can't we do something about the walls? You sneeze in here, and in my house hats blow off.

HAPPY: Let's go to bed, Dad. Come on.

(CHARLEY signals to HAPPY to go.)

WILLY: You go ahead, I'm not tired at the moment.

HAPPY *(To WILLY):* Take it easy, huh? *(He exits.)*

WILLY: What're you doin' up?

CHARLEY *(Sitting down at the kitchen table opposite WILLY.):* Couldn't sleep good. I had a heartburn.

WILLY: Well, you don't know how to eat.

CHARLEY: I eat with my mouth.

WILLY: No, you're ignorant. You gotta know about vitamins and things like that.

CHARLEY: Come on, let's shoot. Tire you out a little.

WILLY *(Hesitantly):* All right. You got cards?

CHARLEY *(Taking a deck from his pocket):* Yeah, I got them. Someplace. What is it with those vitamins?

WILLY *(Dealing):* They build up your bones. Chemistry.

CHARLEY: Yeah, but there's no bones in a heartburn.

WILLY: What are you talkin' about? Do you know the first thing about it?

CHARLEY: Don't get insulted.

WILLY: Don't talk about something you don't know anything about.

(They are playing. Pause.)

CHARLEY: What're you doin' home?

WILLY: A little trouble with the car.

CHARLEY: Oh. *(Pause)* I'd like to take a trip to California.

WILLY: Don't say.

CHARLEY: You want a job?

WILLY: I got a job, I told you that. *(After a slight pause)* What the hell are you offering me a job for?

CHARLEY: Don't get insulted.

WILLY: Don't insult me.

CHARLEY: I don't see no sense in it. You don't have to go on this way.

WILLY: I got a good job. *(Slight pause)* What do you keep comin' in here for?

CHARLEY: You want me to go?

WILLY *(After a pause, withering)*:   I can't understand it. He's going back to Texas again. What the hell is that?

CHARLEY: Let him go.

WILLY: I got nothin' to give him, Charley, I'm clean, I'm clean.

CHARLEY: He won't starve. None a them starve. Forget about him.

WILLY: Then what have I got to remember?

CHARLEY: You take it too hard. To hell with it. When a deposit bottle is broken you don't get your nickel back.

WILLY: That's easy enough for you to say.

CHARLEY: That ain't easy for me to say.

WILLY: Did you see the ceiling I put up in the living-room?

CHARLEY: Yeah, that's a piece of work. To put up a ceiling is a mystery to me. How do you do it?

WILLY: What's the difference?

CHARLEY: Well, talk about it.

WILLY: You gonna put up a ceiling?

CHARLEY: How could I put up a ceiling?

WILLY: Then what the hell are you bothering me for?

CHARLEY: You're insulted again.

WILLY: A man who can't handle tools is not a man. You're disgusting.

CHARLEY: Don't call me disgusting, Willy.

(UNCLE BEN, carrying a valise and an umbrella, enters the forestage from around the right corner of the house. He is a stolid man, in his sixties, with a mustache and an authoritative air. He is utterly certain of his destiny, and there is an aura of far places about him. He enters exactly as WILLY speaks.)

WILLY: I'm getting awfully tired, Ben.

(BEN's music is heard. BEN looks around at everything.)

CHARLEY: Good, keep playing; you'll sleep better. Did you call me Ben?

(BEN looks at his watch.)

WILLY: That's funny. For a second there you reminded me of my brother Ben.

BEN: I only have a few minutes. *(He strolls, inspecting the place.* WILLY *and* CHARLEY *continue playing.)*

CHARLEY: You never heard from him again, heh? Since that time?

WILLY: Didn't Linda tell you? Couple of weeks ago we got a letter from his wife in Africa. He died.

CHARLEY: That so.

BEN *(Chuckling):*   So this is Brooklyn, eh?

CHARLEY: Maybe you're in for some of his money.

WILLY: Naa, he had seven sons. There's just one opportunity I had with that man . . .

BEN: I must make a train, William. There are several properties I'm looking at in Alaska.

WILLY: Sure, sure! If I'd gone with him to Alaska that time, everything would've been totally different.

CHARLEY: Go on, you'd froze to death up there.

WILLY: What're you talking about?

BEN: Opportunity is tremendous in Alaska, William. Surprised you're not up there.

WILLY: Sure, tremendous.

CHARLEY: Heh?

WILLY: There was the only man I ever met who knew the answers.

CHARLEY: Who?

BEN: How are you all?

WILLY *(Taking a pot, smiling):*   Fine, fine.

CHARLEY: Pretty sharp tonight.

BEN: Is Mother living with you?

WILLY: No, she died a long time ago.

CHARLEY: Who?

BEN: That's too bad. Fine specimen of a lady, Mother.

WILLY *(To Charley):*   Heh?

BEN: I'd hoped to see the old girl.

CHARLEY: Who died?

BEN: Heard anything from Father, have you?

WILLY *(Unnerved):*   What do you mean, who died?

CHARLEY *(Taking a pot):*   What're you talkin' about?

BEN *(Looking at his watch):*   William, it's half-past eight!

WILLY *(As though to dispel his confusion he angrily stops* CHARLEY*'s hand):*   That's my build!

CHARLEY: I put the ace—

WILLY: If you don't know how to play the game I'm not gonna throw my money away on you!

CHARLEY *(Rising):*   It was my ace, for God's sake!

WILLY: I'm through, I'm through!

BEN: When did Mother die?

WILLY: Long ago. Since the beginning you never knew how to play cards.
CHARLEY *(Picks up the cards and goes to the door):*   All right! Next time I'll bring
   a deck with five aces.
WILLY: I don't play that kind of game!
CHARLEY *(Turning to him):*   You ought to be ashamed of yourself!
WILLY: Yeah?
CHARLEY: Yeah! *(He goes out.)*
WILLY *(Slamming the door after him):*   Ignoramus!
BEN *(As* WILLY *comes toward him through the wall-line of the kitchen):*   So you're
   William.
WILLY *(Shaking* BEN*'s hand):*   Ben! I've been waiting for you so long! What's
   the answer? How did you do it?
BEN: Oh, there's a story in that.

*(*LINDA *enters the forestage, as of old, carrying the wash basket.)*

LINDA: Is this Ben?
BEN *(Gallantly):*   How do you do, my dear.
LINDA: Where've you been all these years? Willy's always wondered why
   you—
WILLY *(Pulling* BEN *away from her impatiently):*   Where is Dad? Didn't you
   follow him? How did you get started?
BEN: Well, I don't know how much you remember.
WILLY: Well, I was just a baby, of course, only three or four years old—
BEN: Three years and eleven months.
WILLY: What a memory, Ben!
BEN: I have many enterprises, William, and I have never kept books.
WILLY: I remember I was sitting under the wagon in—was it Nebraska?
BEN: It was South Dakota, and I gave you a bunch of wild flowers.
WILLY: I remember you walking away down some open road.
BEN *(Laughing):*   I was going to find Father in Alaska.
WILLY: Where is he?
BEN: At that age I had a very faulty view of geography, William. I discovered
   after a few days that I was heading due south, so instead of Alaska, I ended
   up in Africa.
LINDA: Africa!
WILLY: The Gold Coast!
BEN: Principally diamond mines.
LINDA: Diamond mines!
BEN: Yes, my dear. But I've only a few minutes—
WILLY: No! Boys! Boys! *(*YOUNG BIFF *and* HAPPY *appear.)* Listen to this. This
   is your Uncle Ben, a great man! Tell my boys, Ben!
BEN: Why, boys, when I was seventeen I walked into the jungle, and when
   I was twenty-one I walked out. *(He laughs.)* And by God I was rich.
WILLY *(To the boys):*   You see what I been talking about? The greatest things
   can happen!

BEN *(Glancing at his watch):* I have an appointment in Ketchikan Tuesday week.

WILLY: No, Ben! Please tell about Dad. I want my boys to hear. I want them to know the kind of stock they spring from. All I remember is a man with a big beard, and I was in Mamma's lap, sitting around a fire, and some kind of high music.

BEN: His flute. He played the flute.

WILLY: Sure, the flute, that's right!

(New music is heard, a high, rollicking tune.)

BEN: Father was a very great and a very wild-hearted man. We would start in Boston, and he'd toss the whole family into the wagon, and then he'd drive the team right across the country; through Ohio, and Indiana, Michigan, Illinois, and all the Western states. And we'd stop in the towns and sell the flutes that he'd made on the way. Great inventor, Father. With one gadget he made more in a week than a man like you could make in a lifetime.

WILLY: That's just the way I'm bringing them up, Ben—rugged, well liked, all-around.

BEN: Yeah? *(To* BIFF*):* Hit that, boy—hard as you can. *(He pounds his stomach.)*

BIFF: Oh, no, sir!

BEN *(Taking boxing stance):* Come on, get to me! *(He laughs.)*

WILLY: Go to it, Biff! Go ahead, show him!

BIFF: Okay! *(He cocks his fists and starts in.)*

LINDA: *(To* WILLY*):* Why must he fight, dear?

BEN *(Sparring with* BIFF*):* Good boy! Good boy!

WILLY: How's that, Ben, heh?

HAPPY: Give him the left, Biff!

LINDA: Why are you fighting?

BEN: Good boy! *(Suddenly comes in, trips* BIFF, *and stands over him, the point of his umbrella poised over* BIFF's *eye.)*

LINDA: Look out, Biff!

BIFF: Gee!

BEN *(Patting* BIFF's *knee):* Never fight fair with a stranger, boy. You'll never get out of the jungle that way. *(Taking* LINDA's *hand and bowing)* It was an honor and a pleasure to meet you, Linda.

LINDA *(Withdrawing her hand coldly, frightened):* Have a nice—trip.

BEN *(To* WILLY*):* And good luck with your—what do you do?

WILLY: Selling.

BEN: Yes. Well . . . *(He raises his hand in farewell to all.)*

WILLY: No, Ben, I don't want you to think . . . *(He takes* BEN's *arm to show him.)* It's Brooklyn, I know, but we hunt too.

BEN: Really, now.

WILLY: Oh, sure, there's snakes and rabbits and—that's why I moved out here. Why, Biff can fell any one of these trees in no time! Boys! Go right over to where they're building the apartment house and get some sand. We're gonna rebuild the entire front stoop right now! Watch this, Ben!

BIFF: Yes, sir! On the double, Hap!

HAPPY *(As he and* BIFF *run off):* I lost weight, Pop, you notice?

*(*CHARLEY *enters in knickers, even before the boys are gone.)*

CHARLEY: Listen, if they steal any more from that building the watchman'll put the cops on them!

LINDA *(to* WILLY*):* Don't let Biff . . .

*(*BEN *laughs lustily.)*

WILLY: You shoulda seen the lumber they brought home last week. At least a dozen six-by-tens worth all kinds a money.

CHARLEY: Listen, if that watchman—

WILLY: I gave them hell, understand. But I got a couple of fearless characters there.

CHARLEY: Willy, the jails are full of fearless characters.

BEN *(Clapping* WILLY *on the back, with a laugh at* CHARLEY*):* And the stock exchange, friend!

WILLY *(Joining in* BEN*'s laughter):* Where are the rest of your pants?

CHARLEY: My wife bought them.

WILLY: Now all you need is a golf club and you can go upstairs and go to sleep. *(To* BEN*):* Great athlete! Between him and his son Bernard they can't hammer a nail!

BERNARD *(Rushing in):* The watchman's chasing Biff!

WILLY *(Angrily):* Shut up! He's not stealing anything!

LINDA *(Alarmed, hurrying off left):* Where is he? Biff, dear! *(She exits.)*

WILLY *(Moving toward the left, away from* BEN*):* There's nothing wrong. What's the matter with you?

BEN: Nervy boy. Good!

WILLY *(Laughing):* Oh, nerves of iron, that Biff!

CHARLEY: Don't know what it is. My New England man comes back and he's bleedin', they murdered him up there.

WILLY: It's contacts, Charley, I got important contacts!

CHARLEY *(Sarcastically):* Glad to hear it, Willy. Come in later, we'll shoot a little casino. I'll take some of your Portland money. *(He laughs at* WILLY *and exits.)*

WILLY *(Turning to* BEN*):* Business is bad, it's murderous. But not for me, of course.

BEN: I'll stop by on my way back to Africa.

WILLY *(Longingly):* Can't you stay a few days? You're just what I need, Ben, because I—I have a fine position here, but I—well, Dad left when I was such a baby and I never had a chance to talk to him and I still feel—kind of temporary about myself.

BEN: I'll be late for my train.

(They are at opposite ends of the stage.)

WILLY: Ben, my boys—can't we talk? They'd go into the jaws of hell for me, see, but I—

BEN: William, you're being first-rate with your boys. Outstanding, manly chaps!

WILLY *(Hanging on to his words)*:   Oh, Ben, that's good to hear! Because sometimes I'm afraid that I'm not teaching them the right kind of—Ben, how should I teach them?

BEN *(Giving great weight to each word, and with a certain vicious audacity)*:   William, when I walked into the jungle, I was seventeen. When I walked out I was twenty-one. And, by God, I was rich! *(He goes off into the darkness around the right corner of the house.)*

WILLY: . . . was rich! That's just the spirit I want to imbue them with! To walk into a jungle! I was right! I was right! I was right!

(BEN is gone, but WILLY is still speaking to him as LINDA, in nightgown and robe, enters the kitchen, glances around for WILLY, then goes to the door of the house, looks out and sees him. Comes down to his left. He looks at her.)

LINDA: Willy, dear? Willy?

WILLY: I was right!

LINDA: Did you have some cheese? *(He can't answer.)* It's very late, darling. Come to bed, heh?

WILLY *(Looking straight up)*:   Gotta break your neck to see a star in this yard.

LINDA: You coming in?

WILLY: Whatever happened to that diamond watch fob? Remember? When Ben came from Africa that time? Didn't he give me a watch fob with a diamond in it?

LINDA: You pawned it, dear. Twelve, thirteen years ago. For Biff's radio correspondence course.

WILLY: Gee, that was a beautiful thing. I'll take a walk.

LINDA: But you're in your slippers.

WILLY *(Starting to go around the house at the left)*:   I was right! I was! *(Half to LINDA, as he goes, shaking his head)* What a man! There was a man worth talking to. I was right!

LINDA *(Calling after WILLY)*:   But in your slippers, Willy!

(WILLY is almost gone when BIFF, in his pajamas, comes down the stairs and enters the kitchen.)

BIFF: What is he doing out there?

LINDA: Sh!

BIFF: God Almighty, Mom, how long has he been doing this?

LINDA: Don't, he'll hear you.

BIFF: What the hell is the matter with him?

LINDA: It'll pass by morning.

BIFF: Shouldn't we do anything?

LINDA: Oh, my dear, you should do a lot of things, but there's nothing to do, so go to sleep.

*(*HAPPY *comes down the stairs and sits on the steps.)*

HAPPY: I never heard him so loud, Mom.

LINDA: Well, come around more often; you'll hear him. *(She sits down at the table and mends the lining of* WILLY*'s jacket.)*

BIFF: Why didn't you ever write me about this, Mom?

LINDA: How would I write to you? For over three months you had no address.

BIFF: I was on the move. But you know I thought of you all the time. You know that, don't you, pal?

LINDA: I know, dear, I know. But he likes to have a letter. Just to know that there's still a possibility for better things.

BIFF: He's not like this all the time, is he?

LINDA: It's when you come home he's always the worst.

BIFF: When I come home?

LINDA: When you write you're coming, he's all smiles, and talks about the future, and—he's just wonderful. And then the closer you seem to come, the more shaky he gets, and then, by the time you get here, he's arguing, and he seems angry at you. I think it's just that maybe he can't bring himself to—to open up to you. Why are you so hateful to each other? Why is that?

BIFF *(Evasively):*   I'm not hateful, Mom.

LINDA: But you no sooner come in the door than you're fighting!

BIFF: I don't know why. I mean to change. I'm tryin', Mom, you understand?

LINDA: Are you home to stay now?

BIFF: I don't know. I want to look around, see what's doin'.

LINDA: Biff, you can't look around all your life, can you?

BIFF: I just can't take hold, Mom. I can't take hold of some kind of a life.

LINDA: Biff, a man is not a bird, to come and go with the springtime.

BIFF: Your hair . . . *(He touches her hair.)* Your hair got so gray.

LINDA: Oh, it's been gray since you were in high school. I just stopped dyeing it, that's all.

BIFF: Dye it again, will ya? I don't want my pal looking old. *(He smiles.)*

LINDA: You're such a boy! You think you can go away for a year and . . . You've got to get it into your head now that one day you'll knock on this door and there'll be strange people here—

BIFF: What are you talking about? You're not even sixty, Mom.

LINDA: But what about your father?

BIFF *(Lamely):*   Well, I meant him too.

HAPPY: He admires Pop.

LINDA: Biff, dear, if you don't have any feeling for him, then you can't have any feeling for me.

BIFF: Sure I can, Mom.

LINDA: No. You can't just come to see me, because I love him. *(With a threat, but only a threat, of tears)* He's the dearest man in the world to me, and I won't have anyone making him feel unwanted and low and blue. You've got to make up your mind now, darling, there's no leeway any more. Either he's your father and you pay him that respect, or else you're not to come here. I know he's not easy to get along with—nobody knows that better than me—but . . .

WILLY *(From the left, with a laugh):*   Hey, hey, Biffo!

BIFF *(Starting to go out after* WILLY*):*   What the hell is the matter with him? *(Happy stops him.)*

LINDA: Don't—don't go near him!

BIFF: Stop making excuses for him! He always, always wiped the floor with you. Never had an ounce of respect for you.

HAPPY: He's always had respect for—

BIFF: What the hell do you know about it?

HAPPY *(Surlily):*   Just don't call him crazy!

BIFF: He's got no character—Charley wouldn't do this. Not in his own house—spewing out that vomit from his mind.

HAPPY: Charley never had to cope with what he's got to.

BIFF: People are worse off than Willy Loman. Believe me, I've seen them!

LINDA: Then make Charley your father, Biff. You can't do that, can you? I don't say he's a great man. Willy Loman never made a lot of money. His name was never in the paper. He's not the finest character that ever lived. But he's a human being, and a terrible thing is happening to him. So attention must be paid. He's not to be allowed to fall into his grave like an old dog. Attention, attention must be finally paid to such a person. You called him crazy—

BIFF: I didn't mean—

LINDA: No, a lot of people think he's lost his—balance. But you don't have to be very smart to know what his trouble is. The man is exhausted.

HAPPY: Sure!

LINDA: A small man can be just as exhausted as a great man. He works for a company thirty-six years this March, opens up unheard-of territories to their trademark, and now in his old age they take his salary away.

HAPPY *(Indignantly):*   I didn't know that, Mom.

LINDA: You never asked, my dear! Now that you get your spending money someplace else you don't trouble your mind with him.

HAPPY: But I gave you money last—

LINDA: Christmas time, fifty dollars! To fix the hot water it cost ninety-seven fifty! For five weeks he's been on straight commission, like a beginner, an unknown!

BIFF: Those ungrateful bastards!

LINDA: Are they any worse than his sons? When he brought them business, when he was young, they were glad to see him. But now his old friends, the old buyers that loved him so and always found some order to hand him in a pinch—they're all dead, retired. He used to be able to make six, seven calls a day in Boston. Now he takes his valises out of the car and puts them back and takes them out again and he's exhausted. Instead of walking he talks now. He drives seven hundred miles, and when he gets there no one knows him any more, no one welcomes him. And what goes through a man's mind, driving seven hundred miles home without having earned a cent? Why shouldn't he talk to himself? Why? When he has to go to Charley and borrow fifty dollars a week and pretend to me that it's his pay? How long can that go on? How long? You see what I'm sitting here and waiting for? And you tell me he has no character? The man who never worked a day but for your benefit? When does he get the medal for that? Is this his reward—to turn around at the age of sixty-three and find his sons, who he loved better than his life, one a philandering bum—

HAPPY: Mom!

LINDA: That's all you are, my baby! *(To* BIFF*)* And you! What happened to the love you had for him? You were such pals! How you used to talk to him on the phone every night! How lonely he was till he could come home to you!

BIFF: All right, Mom. I'll live here in my room, and I'll get a job. I'll keep away from him, that's all.

LINDA: No, Biff. You can't stay here and fight all the time.

BIFF: He threw me out of this house, remember that.

LINDA: Why did he do that? I never knew why.

BIFF: Because I know he's a fake and he doesn't like anybody around who knows!

LINDA: Why a fake? In what way? What do you mean?

BIFF: Just don't lay it all at my feet. It's between me and him—that's all I have to say. I'll chip in from now on. He'll settle for half my pay check. He'll be all right. I'm going to bed. *(He starts for the stairs.)*

LINDA: He won't be all right.

BIFF *(Turning on the stairs, furiously)*: I hate this city and I'll stay here. Now what do you want?

LINDA: He's dying, Biff.

*(*HAPPY *turns quickly to her, shocked.)*

BIFF *(After a pause)*: Why is he dying?

LINDA: He's been trying to kill himself.

BIFF *(With great horror)*: How?

LINDA: I live from day to day.

BIFF: What're you talking about?

LINDA: Remember I wrote you that he smashed up the car again? In February?

BIFF: Well?

LINDA: The insurance inspector came. He said that they have evidence. That all these accidents in the last year—weren't—weren't—accidents.

HAPPY: How can they tell that? That's a lie.

LINDA: It seems there's a woman . . . *(She takes a breath as)*

BIFF *(Sharply but contained)*: What woman?

LINDA *(Simultaneously)*: . . . and this woman . . .

LINDA: What?

BIFF: Nothing. Go ahead.

LINDA: What did you say?

BIFF: Nothing. I just said what woman?

HAPPY: What about her?

LINDA: Well, it seems she was walking down the road and saw his car. She says that he wasn't driving fast at all, and that he didn't skid. She says he came to that little bridge, and then deliberately smashed into the railing, and it was only the shallowness of the water that saved him.

BIFF: Oh, no, he probably just fell asleep again.

LINDA: I don't think he fell asleep.

BIFF: Why not?

LINDA: Last month . . . *(With great difficulty):* Oh, boys, it's so hard to say a thing like this! He's just a big stupid man to you, but I tell you there's more good in him than in many other people. *(She chokes, wipes her eyes.)* I was looking for a fuse. The lights blew out, and I went down the cellar. And behind the fuse box—it happened to fall out—was a length of rubber pipe—just short.

HAPPY: No kidding?

LINDA: There's a little attachment on the end of it. I knew right away. And sure enough, on the bottom of the water heater there's a new little nipple on the gas pipe.

HAPPY *(Angrily):* That—jerk.

BIFF: Did you have it taken off?

LINDA: I'm—I'm ashamed to. How can I mention it to him? Every day I go down and take away that little rubber pipe. But, when he comes home, I put it back where it was. How can I insult him that way? I don't know what to do. I live from day to day, boys. I tell you, I know every thought in his mind. It sounds so old-fashioned and silly, but I tell you he put his whole life into you and you've turned your backs on him. *(She is bent over in the chair, weeping, her face in her hands.)* Biff, I swear to God! Biff, his life is in your hands!

HAPPY *(To* BIFF*):* How do you like that damned fool!

BIFF *(Kissing her):* All right, pal, all right. It's all settled now. I've been remiss. I know that, Mom. But now I'll stay, and I swear to you, I'll apply myself. *(Kneeling in front of her, in a fever of self-reproach)* It's just—you see, Mom, I don't fit in business. Not that I won't try. I'll try, and I'll make good.

HAPPY: Sure you will. The trouble with you in business was you never tried to please people.

BIFF: I know, I—

HAPPY: Like when you worked for Harrison's. Bob Harrison said you were tops, and then you go and do some damn fool thing like whistling whole songs in the elevator like a comedian.

BIFF *(Against* HAPPY*):* So what? I like to whistle sometimes.

HAPPY: You don't raise a guy to a responsible job who whistles in the elevator!

LINDA: Well, don't argue about it now.

HAPPY: Like when you'd go off and swim in the middle of the day instead of taking the line around.

BIFF *(His resentment rising):*   Well, don't you run off? You take off sometimes, don't you? On a nice summer day?

HAPPY: Yeah, but I cover myself!

LINDA: Boys!

HAPPY: If I'm going to take a fade the boss can call any number where I'm supposed to be and they'll swear to him that I just left. I'll tell you something that I hate to say, Biff, but in the business world some of them think you're crazy.

BIFF *(Angered):*   Screw the business world!

HAPPY: All right, screw it! Great, but cover yourself!

LINDA: Hap, Hap!

BIFF: I don't care what they think! They've laughed at Dad for years, and you know why? Because we don't belong in this nuthouse of a city! We should be mixing cement on some open plain, or—or carpenters. A carpenter is allowed to whistle!

(WILLY walks in from the entrance of the house, at left.)

WILLY: Even your grandfather was better than a carpenter. *(Pause. They watch him.)* You never grew up. Bernard does not whistle in the elevator, I assure you.

BIFF *(As though to laugh WILLY out of it):*   Yeah, but you do, Pop.

WILLY: I never in my life whistled in an elevator! And who in the business world thinks I'm crazy?

BIFF: I didn't mean it like that, Pop. Now don't make a whole thing out of it, will ya?

WILLY: Go back to the West! Be a carpenter, a cowboy, enjoy yourself!

LINDA: Willy, he was just saying—

WILLY: I heard what he said!

HAPPY *(Trying to quiet WILLY):*   Hey, Pop, come on now . . .

WILLY *(Continuing over HAPPY's line):*   They laugh at me, heh? Go to Filene's, go to the Hub, go to Slattery's, Boston. Call out the name Willy Loman and see what happens! Big shot!

BIFF: All right, Pop.

WILLY: Big!

BIFF: All right!

WILLY: Why do you always insult me?

BIFF: I didn't say a word. *(To LINDA)* Did I say a word?

LINDA: He didn't say anything, Willy.

WILLY *(Going to the doorway of the living-room):*   All right, good night, good night.

LINDA: Willy, dear, he just decided . . .

WILLY *(To BIFF):*   If you get tired hanging around tomorrow, paint the ceiling I put up in the living-room.

BIFF: I'm leaving early tomorrow.

HAPPY: He's going to see Bill Oliver, Pop.

WILLY *(Interestedly):*   Oliver? For what?

BIFF *(With reserve, but trying, trying):*   He always said he'd stake me. I'd like to go into business, so maybe I can take him up on it.

LINDA: Isn't that wonderful?

WILLY: Don't interrupt. What's wonderful about it? There's fifty men in the City of New York who'd stake him. *(To* BIFF*)* Sporting goods?

BIFF: I guess so. I know something about it and—

WILLY: He knows something about it! You know sporting goods better than Spalding, for God's sake! How much is he giving you?

BIFF: I don't know, I didn't even see him yet, but—

WILLY: Then what're you talkin' about?

BIFF *(Getting angry):*   Well, all I said was I'm gonna see him, that's all!

WILLY *(Turning away):*   Ah, you're counting your chickens again.

BIFF *(Starting left for the stairs):*   Oh, Jesus, I'm going to sleep!

WILLY *(Calling after him):*   Don't curse in this house!

BIFF *(Turning):*   Since when did you get so clean?

HAPPY *(Trying to stop them):*   Wait a . . .

WILLY: Don't use that language to me! I won't have it!

HAPPY *(Grabbing* BIFF, *shouts):*   Wait a minute! I got an idea. I got a feasible idea. Come here, Biff, let's talk this over now, let's talk some sense here. When I was down in Florida last time, I thought of a great idea to sell sporting goods. It just came back to me. You and I, Biff—we have a line, the Loman Line. We train a couple of weeks, and put on a couple of exhibitions, see?

WILLY: That's an idea!

HAPPY: Wait! We form two basketball teams, see? Two water-polo teams. We play each other. It's a million dollars' worth of publicity. Two brothers, see? The Loman Brothers. Displays in the Royal Palms—all the hotels. And banners over the ring and the basketball court: "Loman Brothers." Baby, we could sell sporting goods!

WILLY: That is a one-million-dollar idea!

LINDA: Marvelous!

BIFF: I'm in great shape as far as that's concerned.

HAPPY: And the beauty of it is, Biff, it wouldn't be like a business. We'd be out playin' ball again . . .

BIFF *(Enthused):*   Yeah, that's . . .

WILLY: Million-dollar . . .

HAPPY: And you wouldn't get fed up with it, Biff. It'd be the family again. There'd be the old honor, and comradeship, and if you wanted to go off for a swim or somethin'—well, you'd do it! Without some smart cooky gettin' up ahead of you!

WILLY: Lick the world! You guys together could absolutely lick the civilized world.

BIFF: I'll see Oliver tomorrow. Hap, if we could work that out . . .

LINDA: Maybe things are beginning to—

WILLY *(Wildly enthused), to* LINDA: Stop interrupting! *(To* BIFF*)* But don't wear sport jacket and slacks when you see Oliver.

BIFF: No, I'll—

WILLY: A business suit, and talk as little as possible, and don't crack any jokes.

BIFF: He did like me. Always liked me.

LINDA: He loved you!

WILLY *(To* LINDA*)*: Will you stop! *(To* BIFF*)*: Walk in very serious. You are not applying for a boy's job. Money is to pass. Be quiet, fine, and serious. Everybody likes a kidder, but nobody lends him money.

HAPPY: I'll try to get some myself, Biff. I'm sure I can.

WILLY: I see great things for you kids, I think your troubles are over. But remember, start big and you'll end big. Ask for fifteen. How much you gonna ask for?

BIFF: Gee, I don't know—

WILLY: And don't say "Gee." "Gee" is a boy's word. A man walking in for fifteen thousand dollars does not say "Gee!"

BIFF: Ten, I think, would be top though.

WILLY: Don't be so modest. You always started too low. Walk in with a big laugh. Don't look worried. Start off with a couple of your good stories to lighten things up. It's not what you say, it's how you say it—because personality always wins the day.

LINDA: Oliver always thought the highest of him—

WILLY: Will you let me talk?

BIFF: Don't yell at her, Pop, will ya?

WILLY *(Angrily):* I was talking, wasn't I?

BIFF: I don't like you yelling at her all the time, and I'm tellin' you, that's all.

WILLY: What're you, takin' over this house?

LINDA: Willy—

WILLY *(Turning on her):* Don't take his side all the time, goddammit!

BIFF *(Furiously):* Stop yelling at her!

WILLY *(Suddenly pulling on his cheek, beaten down, guilt ridden):* Give my best to Bill Oliver—he may remember me. *(He exits through the living-room doorway.)*

LINDA *(Her voice subdued):* What'd you have to start that for? *(*BIFF *turns away.)* You see how sweet he was as soon as you talked hopefully? *(She goes over to* BIFF.*)* Come up and say good night to him. Don't let him go to bed that way.

HAPPY: Come on, Biff, let's buck him up.

LINDA: Please, dear. Just say good night. It takes so little to make him happy. Come. *(She goes through the living-room doorway, calling upstairs from within the living-room.)* Your pajamas are hanging in the bathroom, Willy!

HAPPY *(Looking toward where* LINDA *went out):* What a woman! They broke the mold when they made her. You know that, Biff?

BIFF: He's off salary. My God, working on commission!

HAPPY: Well, let's face it: he's no hot-shot selling man. Except that sometimes, you have to admit, he's a sweet personality.

BIFF *(Deciding):*   Lend me ten bucks, will ya? I want to buy some new ties.

HAPPY: I'll take you to a place I know. Beautiful stuff. Wear one of my striped shirts tomorrow.

BIFF: She got gray. Mom got awful old. Gee, I'm gonna go in to Oliver tomorrow and knock him for a—

HAPPY: Come on up. Tell that to Dad. Let's give him a whirl. Come on.

BIFF *(Steamed up):*   You know, with ten thousand bucks, boy!

HAPPY *(As they go into the living-room):*   That's the talk, Biff, that's the first time I've heard the old confidence out of you! *(From within the living-room, fading off)* You're gonna live with me, kid, and any babe you want just say the word . . . *(The last lines are hardly heard. They are mounting the stairs to their parents' bedroom.)*

LINDA *(Entering her bedroom and addressing* WILLY, *who is in the bathroom. She is straightening the bed for him):*   Can you do anything about the shower? It drips.

WILLY *(From the bathroom):*   All of a sudden everything falls to pieces! Goddam plumbing, oughta be sued, those people. I hardly finished putting it in and the thing . . . *(His words rumble off.)*

LINDA: I'm just wondering if Oliver will remember him. You think he might?

WILLY *(Coming out of the bathroom in his pajamas):*   Remember him? What's the matter with you, you crazy? If he'd've stayed with Oliver he'd be on top by now! Wait'll Oliver gets a look at him. You don't know the average caliber any more. The average young man today—*(He is getting into bed.)*—is got a caliber of zero. Greatest thing in the world for him was to bum around.

*(*BIFF *and* HAPPY *enter the bedroom. Slight pause.)*

WILLY *(Stops short, looking at* BIFF*):*   Glad to hear it, boy.

HAPPY: He wanted to say good night to you, sport.

WILLY *(To* BIFF*):*   Yeah. Knock him dead, boy. What'd you want to tell me?

BIFF: Just take it easy, Pop. Good night. *(He turns to go.)*

WILLY *(Unable to resist):*   And if anything falls off the desk while you're talking to him—like a package or something—don't you pick it up. They have office boys for that.

LINDA: I'll make a big breakfast—

WILLY: Will you let me finish? *(To* BIFF*):*   Tell him you were in the business in the West. Not farm work.

BIFF: All right, Dad.

LINDA: I think everything—

WILLY *(Going right through her speech):*   And don't undersell yourself. No less than fifteen thousand dollars.

BIFF *(Unable to bear him):*   Okay. Good night, Mom. *(He starts moving.)*

WILLY: Because you got a greatness in you, Biff, remember that. You got all
kinds a greatness . . . *(He lies back, exhausted.* BIFF *walks out.)*

LINDA *(Calling after* BIFF*):* Sleep well, darling!

HAPPY: I'm gonna get married, Mom. I wanted to tell you.

LINDA: Go to sleep, dear.

HAPPY *(Going):* I just wanted to tell you.

WILLY: Keep up the good work. *(*HAPPY *exits.)* God . . . remember that
Ebbets Field game? The championship of the city?

LINDA: Just rest. Should I sing to you?

WILLY: Yeah. Sing to me. *(*LINDA *hums a soft lullaby.)* When that team came
out—he was the tallest, remember?

LINDA: Oh, yes. And in gold.

(BIFF *enters the darkened kitchen, takes a cigarette, and leaves the house. He comes
downstage into a golden pool of light. He smokes, staring at the night.)*

WILLY: Like a young god. Hercules—something like that. And the sun, the
sun all around him. Remember how he waved to me? Right up from the
field, with the representatives of three colleges standing by? And the
buyers I brought, and the cheers when he came out—Loman, Loman,
Loman! God Almighty, he'll be great yet. A star like that, magnificent, can
never really fade away!

(The light on WILLY *is fading. The gas heater begins to glow through the kitchen
wall, near the stairs, a blue flame beneath red coils.)*

LINDA *(Timidly):* Willy dear, what has he got against you?

WILLY: I'm so tired. Don't talk any more.

(BIFF *slowly returns to the kitchen. He stops, stares toward the heater.)*

LINDA: Will you ask Howard to let you work in New York?

WILLY: First thing in the morning. Everything'll be all right.

(BIFF *reaches behind the heater and draws out a length of rubber tubing. He is
horrified and turns his head toward* WILLY*'s room, still dimly lit, from which the
strains of* LINDA*'s desperate but monotonous humming rise.)*

WILLY *(Staring through the window into the moonlight):* Gee, look at the moon
moving between the buildings!

(BIFF *wraps the tubing around his hand and quickly goes up the stairs.)*

CURTAIN

ACT II

Music is heard, gay and bright. The curtain rises as the music fades away. WILLY,
in shirt sleeves, is sitting at the kitchen table, sipping coffee, his hat in his lap.
LINDA *is filling his cup when she can.*

WILLY: Wonderful coffee. Meal in itself.

LINDA: Can I make you some eggs?

WILLY: No. Take a breath.

LINDA: You look so rested, dear.

WILLY: I slept like a dead one. First time in months. Imagine, sleeping till ten on a Tuesday morning. Boys left nice and early, heh?

LINDA: They were out of here by eight o'clock.

WILLY: Good work!

LINDA: It was so thrilling to see them leaving together. I can't get over the shaving lotion in this house!

WILLY *(Smiling):* Mmm—

LINDA: Biff was very changed this morning. His whole attitude seemed to be hopeful. He couldn't wait to get downtown to see Oliver.

WILLY: He's heading for a change. There's no question, there simply are certain men that take longer to get—solidified. How did he dress?

LINDA: His blue suit. He's so handsome in that suit. He could be a—anything in that suit!

(WILLY gets up from the table. LINDA holds his jacket for him.)

WILLY: There's no question, no question at all. Gee, on the way home tonight I'd like to buy some seeds.

LINDA *(Laughing):* That'd be wonderful. But not enough sun gets back there. Nothing'll grow any more.

WILLY: You wait, kid, before it's all over we're gonna get a little place out in the country, and I'll raise some vegetables, a couple of chickens . . .

LINDA: You'll do it yet, dear.

(WILLY walks out of his jacket. LINDA follows him.)

WILLY: And they'll get married, and come for a weekend. I'd build a little guest house. 'Cause I got so many fine tools, all I'd need would be a little lumber and some peace of mind.

LINDA *(Joyfully):* I sewed the lining . . .

WILLY: I could build two guest houses, so they'd both come. Did he decide how much he's going to ask Oliver for?

LINDA *(Getting him into the jacket):* He didn't mention it, but I imagine ten or fifteen thousand. You going to talk to Howard today?

WILLY: Yeah. I'll put it to him straight and simple. He'll just have to take me off the road.

LINDA: And Willy, don't forget to ask for a little advance, because we've got the insurance premium. It's the grace period now.

WILLY: That's a hundred . . . ?

LINDA: A hundred and eight, sixty-eight. Because we're a little short again.

WILLY: Why are we short?

LINDA: Well, you had the motor job on the car . . .

WILLY: That goddam Studebaker!

LINDA: And you got one more payment on the refrigerator . . .

WILLY: But it just broke again!

LINDA: Well, it's old, dear.

WILLY: I told you we should've bought a well-advertised machine. Charley bought a General Electric and it's twenty years old and it's still good, that son-of-a-bitch.

LINDA: But, Willy—

WILLY: Whoever heard of a Hastings refrigerator? Once in my life I would like to own something outright before it's broken! I'm always in a race with the junkyard! I just finished paying for the car and it's on its last legs. The refrigerator consumes belts like a goddam maniac. They time those things. They time them so when you finally paid for them, they're used up.

LINDA *(Buttoning up his jacket as he unbuttons it):*   All told, about two hundred dollars would carry us, dear. But that includes the last payment on the mortgage. After this payment, Willy, the house belongs to us.

WILLY: It's twenty-five years!

LINDA: Biff was nine years old when we bought it.

WILLY: Well, that's a great thing. To weather a twenty-five year mortgage is—

LINDA: It's an accomplishment.

WILLY: All the cement, the lumber, the reconstruction I put in this house! There ain't a crack to be found in it any more.

LINDA: Well, it served its purpose.

WILLY: What purpose? Some stranger'll come along, move in, and that's that. If only Biff would take this house, and raise a family . . . *(He starts to go.)* Good-by, I'm late.

LINDA *(Suddenly remembering):*   Oh, I forgot! You're supposed to meet them for dinner.

WILLY: Me?

LINDA: At Frank's Chop House on Forty-eighth near Sixth Avenue.

WILLY: Is that so! How about you?

LINDA: No, just the three of you. They're gonna blow you to a big meal!

WILLY: Don't say! Who thought of that?

LINDA: Biff came to me this morning, Willy, and he said, "Tell Dad, we want to blow him to a big meal." Be there six o'clock. You and your two boys are going to have dinner.

WILLY: Gee whiz! That's really somethin'. I'm gonna knock Howard for a loop, kid. I'll get an advance, and I'll come home with a New York job. Goddammit, now I'm gonna do it!

LINDA: Oh, that's the spirit, Willy!

WILLY: I will never get behind a wheel the rest of my life!

LINDA: It's changing, Willy, I can feel it changing!

WILLY: Beyond a question. G'by, I'm late. *(He starts to go again.)*

LINDA *(Calling after him as she runs to the kitchen table for a handkerchief):*   You got your glasses?

WILLY *(Feels for them, then comes back in):*   Yeah, yeah, got my glasses.

LINDA *(Giving him the handkerchief):*   And a handkerchief.

WILLY: Yeah, handkerchief.

LINDA: And your saccharine?

WILLY: Yeah, my saccharine.

LINDA: Be careful on the subway stairs.

(She kisses him, and a silk stocking is seen hanging from her hand. Willy notices it.)

WILLY: Will you stop mending stockings? At least while I'm in the house. It gets me nervous. I can't tell you. Please.

(LINDA hides the stocking in her hand as she follows WILLY across the forestage in front of the house.)

LINDA: Remember, Frank's Chop House.

WILLY *(Passing the apron):*   Maybe beets would grow out there.

LINDA *(Laughing):*   But you tried so many times.

WILLY: Yeah. Well, don't work hard today. *(He disappears around the right corner of the house.)*

LINDA: Be careful!

(As WILLY vanishes, LINDA waves to him. Suddenly the phone rings. She runs across the stage and into the kitchen and lifts it.)

LINDA: Hello? Oh, Biff! I'm so glad you called, I just . . . Yes, sure, I just told him. Yes, he'll be there for dinner at six o'clock, I didn't forget. Listen, I was just dying to tell you. You know that little rubber pipe I told you about? That he connected to the gas heater? I finally decided to go down the cellar this morning and take it away and destroy it. But it's gone! Imagine? He took it away himself, it isn't there! *(She listens.)* When? Oh, then you took it. Oh—nothing, it's just that I'd hoped he'd taken it away himself. Oh, I'm not worried, darling, because this morning he left in such high spirits, it was like the old days! I'm not afraid any more. Did Mr. Oliver see you? . . . Well, you wait there then. And make a nice impression on him, darling. Just don't perspire too much before you see him. And have a nice time with Dad. He may have big news too! . . . That's right, a New York job. And be sweet to him tonight, dear. Be loving to him. Because he's only a little boat looking for a harbor. *(She is trembling with sorrow and joy.)* Oh, that's wonderful, Biff, you'll save his life. Thanks, darling. Just put your arm around him when he comes into the restaurant. Give him a smile. That's the boy . . . Good-by, dear. . . . You got your comb? . . . That's fine. Good-by, Biff dear.

(In the middle of her speech, HOWARD WAGNER, thirty-six, wheels on a small typewriter table on which is a wire-recording machine and proceeds to plug it in. This is on the left forestage. Light slowly fades on LINDA as it rises on HOWARD. HOWARD is intent on threading the machine and only glances over his shoulder as WILLY appears.)

WILLY: Pst! Pst!

HOWARD: Hello, Willy, come in.

WILLY: Like to have a little talk with you, Howard.

HOWARD: Sorry to keep you waiting. I'll be with you in a minute.

WILLY: What's that, Howard?

HOWARD: Didn't you ever see one of these? Wire recorder.

WILLY: Oh. Can we talk a minute?

HOWARD: Records things. Just got delivery yesterday. Been driving me crazy, the most terrific machine I ever saw in my life. I was up all night with it.

WILLY: What do you do with it?

HOWARD: I bought it for dictation, but you can do anything with it. Listen to this. I had it home last night. Listen to what I picked up. The first one is my daughter. Get this. *(He flicks the switch and "Roll out the Barrel" is heard being whistled.)* Listen to that kid whistle.

WILLY: That is lifelike, isn't it?

HOWARD: Seven years old. Get that tone.

WILLY: Ts, ts. Like to ask a little favor if you . . .

(The whistling breaks off, and the voice of HOWARD*'s daughter is heard.)*

HIS DAUGHTER: "Now you, Daddy."

HOWARD: She's crazy for me! *(Again the same song is whistled.)* That's me! Ha! *(He winks.)*

WILLY: You're very good!

(The whistling breaks off again. The machine runs silent for a moment.)

HOWARD: Sh! Get this now, this is my son.

HIS SON: "The capital of Alabama is Montgomery; the capital of Arizona is Phoenix; the capital of Arkansas is Little Rock; the capital of California is Sacramento . . ." *(and on, and on)*

HOWARD *(Holding up five fingers):* Five years old, Willy!

WILLY: He'll make an announcer some day!

HIS SON *(Continuing):* "The capital . . ."

HOWARD: Get that—alphabetical order! *(The machine breaks off suddenly.)* Wait a minute. The maid kicked the plug out.

WILLY: It certainly is a—

HOWARD: Sh, for God's sake!

HIS SON: "It's nine o'clock, Bulova watch time. So I have to go to sleep."

WILLY: That really is—

HOWARD: Wait a minute! The next is my wife.

(They wait.)

HOWARD'S VOICE: "Go on, say something." *(Pause)* "Well, you gonna talk?"

HIS WIFE: "I can't think of anything."

HOWARD'S VOICE: "Well, talk—it's turning."

HIS WIFE *(Shyly, beaten):* "Hello." *(Silence)* "Oh, Howard, I can't talk into this . . ."

HOWARD *(Snapping the machine off):*   That was my wife.

WILLY: That is a wonderful machine. Can we—

HOWARD: I tell you, Willy, I'm gonna take my camera, and my bandsaw, and all my hobbies, and out they go. This is the most fascinating relaxation I ever found.

WILLY: I think I'll get one myself.

HOWARD: Sure, they're only a hundred and a half. You can't do without it. Supposing you wanna hear Jack Benny, see? But you can't be at home at that hour. So you tell the maid to turn the radio on when Jack Benny comes on, and this automatically goes on with the radio . . .

WILLY: And when you come home you . . .

HOWARD: You can come home twelve o'clock, one o'clock, any time you like, and you get yourself a Coke and sit yourself down, throw the switch, and there's Jack Benny's program in the middle of the night!

WILLY: I'm definitely going to get one. Because lots of time I'm on the road, and I think to myself, what I must be missing on the radio!

HOWARD: Don't you have a radio in the car?

WILLY: Well, yeah, but who ever thinks of turning it on?

HOWARD: Say, aren't you supposed to be in Boston?

WILLY: That's what I want to talk to you about, Howard. You got a minute? *(He draws a chair in from the wing.)*

HOWARD: What happened? What're you doing here?

WILLY: Well . . .

HOWARD: You didn't crack up again, did you?

WILLY: Oh, no. No . . .

HOWARD: Geez, you had me worried there for a minute. What's the trouble?

WILLY: Well, tell you the truth, Howard. I've come to the decision that I'd rather not travel any more.

HOWARD: Not travel! Well, what'll you do?

WILLY: Remember, Christmas time, when you had the party here? You said you'd try to think of some spot for me here in town.

HOWARD: With us?

WILLY: Well, sure.

HOWARD: Oh, yeah, yeah, I remember. Well, I couldn't think of anything for you, Willy.

WILLY: I tell ya, Howard. The kids are all grown up, y'know. I don't need much any more. If I could take home—well, sixty-five dollars a week, I could swing it.

HOWARD: Yeah, but Willy, see I—

WILLY: I tell ya why, Howard. Speaking frankly and between the two of us, y'know—I'm just a little tired.

HOWARD: Oh, I could understand that, Willy. But you're a road man, Willy, and we do a road business. We've only got a half-dozen salesmen on the floor here.

WILLY: God knows, Howard, I never asked a favor of any man. But I was with the firm when your father used to carry you in here in his arms.

HOWARD: I know that, Willy, but—

WILLY: Your father came to me the day you were born and asked me what I thought of the name of Howard, may he rest in peace.

HOWARD: I appreciate that, Willy, but there just is no spot here for you. If I had a spot I'd slam you right in, but I just don't have a single solitary spot.

(He looks for his lighter. WILLY *has picked it up and gives it to him. Pause.)*

WILLY *(With increasing anger):*   Howard, all I need to set my table is fifty dollars a week.

HOWARD: But where am I going to put you, kid?

WILLY: Look, it isn't a question of whether I can sell merchandise, is it?

HOWARD: No, but it's a business, kid, and everybody's gotta pull his own weight.

WILLY *(Desperately):*   Just let me tell you a story, Howard—

HOWARD: 'Cause you gotta admit, business is business.

WILLY *(Angrily):*   Business is definitely business, but just listen for a minute. You don't understand this. When I was a boy—eighteen, nineteen—I was already on the road. And there was a question in my mind as to whether selling had a future for me. Because in those days I had a yearning to go to Alaska. See, there were three gold strikes in one month in Alaska, and I felt like going out. Just for the ride, you might say.

HOWARD *(Barely interested):*   Don't say.

WILLY: Oh, yeah, my father lived many years in Alaska. He was an adventurous man. We've got quite a little streak of self-reliance in our family. I thought I'd go out with my older brother and try to locate him, and maybe settle in the North with the old man. And I was almost decided to go, when I met a salesman in the Parker House. His name was Dave Singleman. And he was eighty-four years old, and he'd drummed merchandise in thirty-one states. And old Dave, he'd go up to his room, y'understand, put on his green velvet slippers—I'll never forget—and pick up his phone and call the buyers, and without ever leaving his room, at the age of eighty-four, he made his living. And when I saw that, I realized that selling was the greatest career a man could want. 'Cause what could be more satisfying than to be able to go, at the age of eighty-four, into twenty or thirty different cities, and pick up a phone, and be remembered and loved and helped by so many different people? Do you know? when he died— and by the way he died the death of a salesman, in his green velvet slippers in the smoker of the New York, New Haven and Hartford, going into Boston—when he died, hundreds of salesmen and buyers were at his funeral. Things were sad on a lotta trains for months after that. *(He stands up.* HOWARD *has not looked at him.)* In those days there was personality in it, Howard. There was respect, and comradeship, and gratitude in it. Today, it's all cut and dried, and there's no chance for bringing friendship to bear—or personality. You see what I mean? They don't know me any more.

HOWARD *(Moving away, to the right):*   That's just the thing, Willy.

WILLY: If I had forty dollars a week—that's all I'd need. Forty dollars, Howard.

HOWARD: Kid, I can't take blood from a stone, I—

WILLY *(Desperation is on him now):*   Howard, the year Al Smith was nominated, your father came to me and—

HOWARD *(Starting to go off):*   I've got to see some people, kid.

WILLY *(Stopping him):*   I'm talking about your father! There were promises made across this desk! You mustn't tell me you've got people to see—I put thirty-four years into this firm, Howard, and now I can't pay my insurance! You can't eat the orange and throw the peel away—a man is not a piece of fruit! *(After a pause)* Now pay attention. Your father—in 1928 I had a big year. I averaged a hundred and seventy dollars a week in commissions.

HOWARD *(Impatiently):*   Now, Willy, you never averaged—

WILLY *(Banging his hand on the desk):*   I averaged a hundred and seventy dollars a week in the year of 1928! And your father came to me—or rather, I was in the office here—it was right over this desk—and he put his hand on my shoulder—

HOWARD *(Getting up):*   You'll have to excuse me, Willy, I gotta see some people. Pull yourself together. *(Going out)* I'll be back in a little while.

(On HOWARD's *exit, the light on his chair grows very bright and strange.)*

WILLY: Pull myself together! What the hell did I say to him? My God, I was yelling at him! How could I! *(*WILLY *breaks off, staring at the light, which occupies the chair, animating it. He approaches this chair, standing across the desk from it.)* Frank, Frank, don't you remember what you told me that time? How you put your hand on my shoulder, and Frank . . . *(He leans on the desk and as he speaks the dead man's name he accidentally switches on the recorder, and instantly.)*

HOWARD'S SON: ". . . of New York is Albany. The capital of Ohio is Cincinnati, the capital of Rhode Island is . . ." *(The recitation continues.)*

WILLY *(Leaping away with fright, shouting):*   Ha! Howard! Howard! Howard!

HOWARD *(Rushing in):*   What happened?

WILLY *(Pointing at the machine, which continues nasally, childishly, with the capital cities):*   Shut it off! Shut it off!

HOWARD *(Pulling the plug out):*   Look, Willy . . .

WILLY *(Pressing his hands to his eyes):*   I gotta get myself some coffee. I'll get some coffee . . .

*(*WILLY *starts to walk out.* HOWARD *stops him.)*

HOWARD *(Rolling up the cord):*   Willy, look . . .

WILLY: I'll go to Boston.

HOWARD: Willy, you can't go to Boston for us.

WILLY: Why can't I go?

HOWARD: I don't want you to represent us. I've been meaning to tell you for a long time now.

WILLY: Howard, are you firing me?

HOWARD: I think you need a good long rest, Willy.

WILLY: Howard—

HOWARD: And when you feel better, come back, and we'll see if we can work something out.

WILLY: But I gotta earn money, Howard. I'm in no position to—

HOWARD: Where are your sons? Why don't your sons give you a hand?

WILLY: They're working on a very big deal.

HOWARD: This is no time for false pride, Willy. You go to your sons and you tell them that you're tired. You've got two great boys, haven't you?

WILLY: Oh, no question, no question, but in the meantime . . .

HOWARD: Then that's that, heh?

WILLY: All right, I'll go to Boston tomorrow.

HOWARD: No, no.

WILLY: I can't throw myself on my sons. I'm not a cripple!

HOWARD: Look, kid, I'm busy this morning.

WILLY *(Grasping* HOWARD's *arm):*   Howard, you've got to let me go to Boston!

HOWARD *(Hard, keeping himself under control):*   I've got a line of people to see this morning. Sit down, take five minutes, and pull yourself together, and then go home, will ya? I need the office, Willy. *(He starts to go, turns, remembering the recorder, starts to push off the table holding the recorder.)* Oh, yeah. Whenever you can this week, stop by and drop off the samples. You'll feel better, Willy, and then come back and we'll talk. Pull yourself together, kid, there's people outside.

*(*HOWARD *exits, pushing the table off left.* WILLY *stares into space, exhausted. Now the music is heard—*BEN's *music—first distantly, then closer, closer. As* WILLY *speaks,* BEN *enters from the right. He carries valise and umbrella.)*

WILLY: Oh, Ben, how did you do it? What is the answer? Did you wind up the Alaska deal already?

BEN: Doesn't take much time if you know what you're doing. Just a short business trip. Boarding ship in an hour. Wanted to say good-by.

WILLY: Ben, I've got to talk to you.

BEN *(Glancing at his watch):*   Haven't the time, William.

WILLY *(Crossing the apron to* BEN*):*   Ben, nothing's working out. I don't know what to do.

BEN: Now, look here, William. I've bought timberland in Alaska and I need a man to look after things for me.

WILLY: God, timberland! Me and my boys in those grand outdoors!

BEN: You've a new continent at your doorstep, William. Get out of these cities, they're full of talk and time payments and courts of law. Screw on your fists and you can fight for a fortune up there.

WILLY: Yes, yes! Linda, Linda!

*(*LINDA *enters as of old, with the wash.)*

LINDA: Oh, you're back?

BEN: I haven't much time.

WILLY: No, wait! Linda, he's got a proposition for me in Alaska.

LINDA: But you've got—*(To Ben)* He's got a beautiful job here.

WILLY: But in Alaska, kid, I could—

LINDA: You're doing well enough, Willy!

BEN *(To* LINDA*):* Enough for what, my dear?

LINDA *(Frightened of* BEN *and angry at him):* Don't say those things to him! Enough to be happy right here, right now. *(To* WILLY, *while* BEN *laughs)* Why must everybody conquer the world? You're well liked, and the boys love you, and someday—*(to* BEN*)*—why, old man Wagner told him just the other day that if he keeps it up he'll be a member of the firm, didn't he, Willy?

WILLY: Sure, sure. I am building something with this firm, Ben, and if a man is building something he must be on the right track, mustn't he?

BEN: What are you building? Lay your hand on it. Where is it?

WILLY *(Hesitantly):* That's true, Linda, there's nothing.

LINDA: Why? *(To* BEN*):* There's a man eighty-four years old—

WILLY: That's right, Ben, that's right. When I look at that man I say, what is there to worry about?

BEN: Bah!

WILLY: It's true, Ben. All he has to do is go into any city, pick up the phone, and he's making his living and you know why?

BEN *(Picking up his valise):* I've got to go.

WILLY *(Holding* BEN *back):* Look at this boy!

*(*BIFF, *in his high school sweater, enters carrying suitcase.* HAPPY *carries* BIFF's *shoulder guards, gold helmet, and football pants.)*

WILLY: Without a penny to his name, three great universities are begging for him, and from there the sky's the limit, because it's not what you do, Ben. It's who you know and the smile on your face! It's contacts, Ben, contacts! The whole wealth of Alaska passes over the lunch table at the Commodore Hotel, and that's the wonder, the wonder of this country, that a man can end with diamonds here on the basis of being liked! *(He turns to* BIFF.*)* And that's why when you get out on that field today it's important. Because thousands of people will be rooting for you and loving you. *(To* BEN, *who has again begun to leave)* And Ben! when he walks into a business office his name will sound out like a bell and all the doors will open to him! I've seen it, Ben, I've seen it a thousand times! You can't feel it with your hand like timber, but it's there!

BEN: Good-by, William.

WILLY: Ben, am I right? Don't you think I'm right? I value your advice.

BEN: There's a new continent at your doorstep, William. You could walk out rich. Rich! *(He is gone.)*

WILLY: We'll do it here, Ben! You hear me? We're gonna do it here!

(YOUNG BERNARD rushes in. The gay music of the Boys is heard.)

BERNARD: Oh, gee, I was afraid you left already!

WILLY: Why? What time is it?

BERNARD: It's half-past one!

WILLY: Well, come on, everybody! Ebbets Field next stop! Where's the pennants? *(He rushes through the wall-line of the kitchen and out into the living-room.)*

LINDA *(To BIFF):*   Did you pack fresh underwear?

BIFF *(Who has been limbering up):*   I want to go!

BERNARD: Biff, I'm carrying your helmet, ain't I?

HAPPY: No, I'm carrying the helmet.

BERNARD: Oh, Biff, you promised me.

HAPPY: I'm carrying the helmet.

BERNARD: How am I going to get in the locker room?

LINDA: Let him carry the shoulder guards. *(She puts her coat and hat on in the kitchen.)*

BERNARD: Can I, Biff? 'Cause I told everybody I'm going to be in the locker room.

HAPPY: In Ebbets Field it's the clubhouse.

BERNARD: I meant the clubhouse. Biff!

HAPPY: Biff!

BIFF *(Grandly, after a slight pause):*   Let him carry the shoulder guards.

HAPPY *(As he gives BERNARD the shoulder guards):*   Stay close to us now.

(WILLY rushes in with the pennants.)

WILLY *(Handing them out):*   Everybody wave when Biff comes out on the field. *(HAPPY and BERNARD run off.)* You set now, boy?

(The music has died away.)

BIFF: Ready to go, Pop. Every muscle is ready.

WILLY *(At the edge of the apron):*   You realize what this means?

BIFF: That's right, Pop.

WILLY *(Feeling BIFF's muscles):*   You're comin' home this afternoon captain of the All-Scholastic Championship Team of the City of New York.

BIFF: I got it, Pop. And remember, pal, when I take off my helmet, that touchdown is for you.

WILLY: Let's go! *(He is starting out, with his arm around BIFF, when CHARLEY enters, as of old, in knickers.)* I got no room for you, Charley.

CHARLEY: Room? For what?

WILLY: In the car.

CHARLEY: You goin' for a ride? I wanted to shoot some casino.

WILLY *(Furiously)*   Casino! *(Incredulously)* Don't you realize what today is?

LINDA: Oh, he knows, Willy. He's just kidding you.

WILLY: That's nothing to kid about!

CHARLEY: No. Linda, what's goin' on?

LINDA: He's playing in Ebbets Field.

CHARLEY: Baseball in this weather?

WILLY: Don't talk to him. Come on, come on! *(He is pushing them out.)*

CHARLEY: Wait a minute, didn't you hear the news?

WILLY: What?

CHARLEY: Don't you listen to the radio? Ebbets Field just blew up.

WILLY: You go to hell! *(*CHARLEY *laughs. Pushing them out.):* Come on, come on! We're late.

CHARLEY *(As they go):*   Knock a homer, Biff, knock a homer!

WILLY *(The last to leave, turning to* CHARLEY*):*   I don't think that was funny, Charley. This is the greatest day of his life.

CHARLEY: Willy, when are you going to grow up?

WILLY: Yeah, heh? When this game is over, Charley, you'll be laughing out of the other side of your face. They'll be calling him another Red Grange.* Twenty-five thousand a year.

CHARLEY *(Kidding):*   Is that so?

WILLY: Yeah, that's so.

CHARLEY: Well, then, I'm sorry, Willy. But tell me something.

WILLY: What?

CHARLEY: Who is Red Grange?

WILLY: Put up your hands. Goddam you, put up your hands!

*(*CHARLEY, *chuckling, shakes his head and walks away, around the left corner of the stage.* WILLY *follows him. The music rises to a mocking frenzy.)*

WILLY: Who the hell do you think you are, better than everybody else? You don't know everything, you big, ignorant, stupid . . . put up your hands!

(Light rises, on the right side of the forestage, on a small table in the reception room of CHARLEY's *office. Traffic sounds are heard.* BERNARD, *now mature, sits whistling to himself. A pair of tennis rackets and an overnight bag are on the floor beside him.)*

WILLY *(Offstage):*   What are you walking away for? Don't walk away! If you're going to say something say it to my face! I know you laugh at me behind my back. You'll laugh out of the other side of your goddam face after this game. Touchdown! Touchdown! Eighty thousand people! Touchdown! Right between the goal posts.

---

*Red Grange: Famous football player of the 1920s, running back for the University of Illinois and the Chicago Bears.

(BERNARD *is a quiet, earnest, but self-assured young man.* WILLY's *voice is coming from right upstage now.* BERNARD *lowers his feet off the table and listens.* JENNY, *his father's secretary, enters.*)

JENNY *(Distressed):*   Say, Bernard, will you go out in the hall?
BERNARD: What is that noise? Who is it?
JENNY: Mr. Loman. He just got off the elevator.
BERNARD *(Getting up):*   Who's he arguing with?
JENNY: Nobody. There's nobody with him. I can't deal with him any more, and your father gets all upset everytime he comes. I've got a lot of typing to do, and your father's waiting to sign it. Will you see him?
WILLY *(Entering):*   Touchdown! Touch—*(He sees* JENNY.*)* Jenny, Jenny, good to see you. How're ya? Workin'? Or still honest?
JENNY: Fine. How've you been feeling?
WILLY: Not much any more, Jenny. Ha, ha! *(He is surprised to see the rackets.)*
BERNARD: Hello, Uncle Willy.
WILLY *(Almost shocked):*   Bernard! Well, look who's here! *(He comes quickly, guiltily, to* BERNARD *and warmly shakes his hand.)*
BERNARD: How are you? Good to see you.
WILLY: What are you doing here?
BERNARD: Oh, just stopped by to see Pop. Get off my feet till my train leaves. I'm going to Washington in a few minutes.
WILLY: Is he in?
BERNARD: Yes, he's in his office with the accountant. Sit down.
WILLY *(Sitting down):*   What're you going to do in Washington?
BERNARD: Oh, just a case I've got there, Willy.
WILLY: That so? *(Indicating the rackets)* You going to play tennis there?
BERNARD: I'm staying with a friend who's got a court.
WILLY: Don't say. His own tennis court. Must be fine people, I bet.
BERNARD: They are, very nice. Dad tells me Biff's in town.
WILLY *(With a big smile):*   Yeah, Biff's in. Working on a very big deal, Bernard.
BERNARD: What's Biff doing?
WILLY: Well, he's been doing very big things in the West. But he decided to establish himself here. Very big. We're having dinner. Did I hear your wife had a boy?
BERNARD: That's right. Our second.
WILLY: Two boys! What do you know!
BERNARD: What kind of a deal has Biff got?
WILLY: Well, Bill Oliver—very big sporting-goods man—he wants Biff very badly. Called him in from the West. Long distance, carte blanche, special deliveries. Your friends have their own private tennis court?
BERNARD: You still with the old firm, Willy?
WILLY *(After a pause):*   I'm—I'm overjoyed to see how you made the grade, Bernard, overjoyed. It's an encouraging thing to see a young man really—

really—Looks very good for Biff—very—*(He breaks off, then)* Bernard—
(He is so full of emotion, he breaks off again.)

BERNARD: What is it, Willy?

WILLY *(Small and alone):* What—what's the secret?

BERNARD: What secret?

WILLY: How—how did you? Why didn't he ever catch on?

BERNARD: I wouldn't know that, Willy.

WILLY *(Confidentially, desperately):* You were his friend, his boyhood friend.
There's something I don't understand about it. His life ended after that
Ebbets Field game. From the age of seventeen nothing good ever hap-
pened to him.

BERNARD: He never trained himself for anything.

WILLY: But he did, he did. After high school he took so many correspondence
courses. Radio mechanics; television; God knows what, and never made
the slightest mark.

BERNARD *(Taking off his glasses):* Willy, do you want to talk candidly?

WILLY *(Rising, faces BERNARD):* I regard you as a very brilliant man, Bernard.
I value your advice.

BERNARD: Oh, the hell with the advice, Willy. I couldn't advise you. There's
just one thing I've always wanted to ask you. When he was supposed to
graduate, and the math teacher flunked him—

WILLY: Oh, that son-of-a-bitch ruined his life.

BERNARD: Yeah, but, Willy, all he had to do was go to summer school and
make up that subject.

WILLY: That's right, that's right.

BERNARD: Did you tell him not to go to summer school?

WILLY: Me? I begged him to go. I ordered him to go!

BERNARD: Then why wouldn't he go?

WILLY: Why? Why! Bernard, that question has been trailing me like a ghost
for the last fifteen years. He flunked the subject, and laid down and died
like a hammer hit him!

BERNARD: Take it easy, kid.

WILLY: Let me talk to you—I got nobody to talk to. Bernard, Bernard, was
it my fault? Y'see? It keeps going around in my mind, maybe I did
something to him. I got nothing to give him.

BERNARD: Don't take it so hard.

WILLY: Why did he lay down? What is the story there? You were his friend!

BERNARD: Willy, I remember, it was June, and our grades came out. And he'd
flunked math.

WILLY: That son-of-a-bitch!

BERNARD: No, it wasn't right then. Biff just got very angry, I remember, and
he was ready to enroll in summer school.

WILLY *(Surprised):* He was?

BERNARD: He wasn't beaten by it at all. But then, Willy, he disappeared from
the block for almost a month. And I got the idea that he'd gone up to New
England to see you. Did he have a talk with you then?

(WILLY stares in silence.)

BERNARD: Willy?

WILLY *(With a strong edge of resentment in his voice):*   Yeah, he came to Boston. What about it?

BERNARD: Well, just that when he came back—I'll never forget this, it always mystifies me. Because I'd thought so well of Biff, even though he'd always taken advantage of me. I loved him, Willy, y'know? And he came back after that month and took his sneakers—remember those sneakers with "University of Virginia" printed on them? He was so proud of those, wore them every day. And he took them down in the cellar, and burned them up in the furnace. We had a fist fight. It lasted at least half an hour. Just the two of us, punching each other down the cellar, and crying right through it. I've often thought of how strange it was that I knew he'd given up his life. What happened in Boston, Willy?

(WILLY looks at him as at an intruder.)

BERNARD: I just bring it up because you asked me.

WILLY *(Angrily):*   Nothing. What do you mean, "What happened?" What's that got to do with anything?

BERNARD: Well, don't get sore.

WILLY: What are you trying to do, blame it on me? If a boy lays down is that my fault?

BERNARD: Now, Willy, don't get—

WILLY: Well, don't—don't talk to me that way! What does that mean, "What happened?"

(CHARLEY enters. He is in his vest, and he carries a bottle of bourbon.)

CHARLEY: Hey, you're going to miss that train. *(He waves the bottle.)*

BERNARD: Yeah, I'm going. *(He takes the bottle.)* Thanks, Pop. *(He picks up his rackets and bag.)* Good-by, Willy, and don't worry about it. You know, "If at first you don't succeed . . ."

WILLY: Yes, I believe in that.

BERNARD: But sometimes, Willy, it's better for a man just to walk away.

WILLY: Walk away?

BERNARD: That's right.

WILLY: But if you can't walk away?

BERNARD *(After a slight pause):*   I guess that's when it's tough. *(Extending his hand)* Good-by, Willy.

WILLY *(Shaking BERNARD's hand):*   Good-by, boy.

CHARLEY *(An arm on BERNARD's shoulder):*   How do you like this kid? Gonna argue a case in front of the Supreme Court.

BERNARD *(Protesting):*   Pop!

WILLY *(Genuinely shocked, pained, and happy):*   No! The Supreme Court!

BERNARD: I gotta run. 'By, Dad!

CHARLEY: Knock 'em dead, Bernard!

(BERNARD goes off.)

WILLY *(As* CHARLEY *takes out his wallet):*   The Supreme Court! And he didn't even mention it!

CHARLEY *(Counting out money on the desk):*   He don't have to—he's gonna do it.

WILLY: And you never told him what to do, did you? You never took any interest in him.

CHARLEY: My salvation is that I never took any interest in anything. There's some money—fifty dollars. I got an accountant inside.

WILLY: Charley, look . . . *(With difficulty)* I got my insurance to pay. If you can manage it—I need a hundred and ten dollars.

(CHARLEY doesn't reply for a moment; merely stops moving.)

WILLY: I'd draw it from my bank but Linda would know, and I . . .

CHARLEY: Sit down, Willy.

WILLY *(Moving toward the chair):*   I'm keeping an account of everything, remember. I'll pay every penny back. *(He sits.)*

CHARLEY: Now listen to me, Willy.

WILLY: I want you to know I appreciate . . .

CHARLEY *(Sitting down on the table):*   Willy, what're you doin'? What the hell is goin' on in your head?

WILLY: Why? I'm simply . . .

CHARLEY: I offered you a job. You can make fifty dollars a week. And I won't send you on the road.

WILLY: I've got a job.

CHARLEY: Without pay? What kind of a job is a job without pay? *(He rises.)* Now, look, kid, enough is enough. I'm no genius but I know when I'm being insulted.

WILLY: Insulted!

CHARLEY: Why don't you want to work for me?

WILLY: What's the matter with you? I've got a job.

CHARLEY: Then what're you walkin' in here every week for?

WILLY *(Getting up):*   Well, if you don't want me to walk in here—

CHARLEY: I am offering you a job.

WILLY: I don't want your goddam job!

CHARLEY: When the hell are you going to grow up?

WILLY *(Furiously):*   You big ignoramus, if you say that to me again I'll rap you one! I don't care how big you are! *(He's ready to fight.)*

(Pause.)

CHARLEY *(Kindly, going to him):*   How much do you need, Willy?

WILLY: Charley, I'm strapped, I'm strapped. I don't know what to do. I was just fired.

CHARLEY: Howard fired you?

WILLY: That snotnose. Imagine that? I named him. I named him Howard.

CHARLEY: Willy, when're you gonna realize that them things don't mean anything? You named him Howard, but you can't sell that. The only thing you got in this world is what you can sell. And the funny thing is that you're a salesman, and you don't know that.

WILLY: I've always tried to think otherwise, I guess. I always felt that if a man was impressive, and well liked, that nothing—

CHARLEY: Why must everybody like you? Who liked J. P. Morgan?* Was he impressive? In a Turkish bath he'd look like a butcher. But with his pockets on he was very well liked. Now listen, Willy, I know you don't like me, and nobody can say I'm in love with you, but I'll give you a job because—just for the hell of it, put it that way. Now what do you say?

WILLY: I—I just can't work for you, Charley.

CHARLEY: What're you, jealous of me?

WILLY: I can't work for you, that's all, don't ask me why.

CHARLEY *(Angered, takes out more bills)*: You been jealous of me all your life, you damned fool! Here, pay your insurance. *(He puts the money in Willy's hand.)*

WILLY: I'm keeping strict accounts.

CHARLEY: I've got some work to do. Take care of yourself. And pay your insurance.

WILLY *(Moving to the right)*: Funny, y'know? After all the highways, and the trains, and the appointments, and the years, you end up worth more dead than alive.

CHARLEY: Willy, nobody's worth nothin' dead. *(After a slight pause)* Did you hear what I said?

(WILLY stands still, dreaming.)

CHARLEY: Willy!

WILLY: Apologize to Bernard for me when you see him. I didn't mean to argue with him. He's a fine boy. They're all fine boys, and they'll end up big—all of them. Someday they'll all play tennis together. Wish me luck, Charley. He saw Bill Oliver today.

CHARLEY: Good luck.

WILLY *(On the verge of tears)*: Charley, you're the only friend I got. Isn't that a remarkable thing? *(He goes out.)*

CHARLEY: Jesus!

(CHARLEY stares after him a moment and follows. All light blacks out. Suddenly raucous music is heard, and a red glow rises behind the screen at right. STANLEY, a young waiter, appears, carrying a table, followed by HAPPY, who is carrying two chairs.)

STANLEY *(Putting the table down)*: That's all right, Mr. Loman, I can handle it myself. *(He turns and takes the chairs from HAPPY and places them at the table.)*

HAPPY *(Glancing around)*: Oh, this is better.

*J. P. Morgan: Millionaire banker and leader of finance.

STANLEY: Sure, in the front there you're in the middle of all kinds a noise. Whenever you got a party, Mr. Loman, you just tell me and I'll put you back here. Y'know, there's a lotta people they don't like it private, because when they go out they like to see a lotta action around them because they're sick and tired to stay in the house by theirself. But I know you, you ain't from Hackensack. You know what I mean?

HAPPY *(Sitting down):*   So how's it coming, Stanley?

STANLEY: Ah, it's a dog's life. I only wish during the war they'd a took me in the Army. I coulda been dead by now.

HAPPY: My brother's back, Stanley.

STANLEY: Oh, he come back, heh? From the Far West.

HAPPY: Yeah, big cattle man, my brother, so treat him right. And my father's coming too.

STANLEY: Oh, your father too!

HAPPY: You got a couple of nice lobsters?

STANLEY: Hundred per cent, big.

HAPPY: I want them with the claws.

STANLEY: Don't worry, I don't give you no mice. *(*HAPPY *laughs.)* How about some wine? It'll put a head on the meal.

HAPPY: No. You remember, Stanley, that recipe I brought you from overseas? With the champagne in it?

STANLEY: Oh, yeah, sure. I still got it tacked up yet in the kitchen. But that'll have to cost a buck apiece anyways.

HAPPY: That's all right.

STANLEY: What'd you, hit a number or somethin'?

HAPPY: No, it's a little celebration. My brother is—I think he pulled off a big deal today. I think we're going into business together.

STANLEY: Great! That's the best for you. Because a family business, you know what I mean?—that's the best.

HAPPY: That's what I think.

STANLEY: 'Cause what's the difference? Somebody steals? It's in the family. Know what I mean? *(Sotto voce)* Like this bartender here. The boss is goin' crazy what kinda leak he's got in the cash register. You put it in but it don't come out.

HAPPY *(Raising his head):*   Sh!

STANLEY: What?

HAPPY: You notice I wasn't lookin' right or left, was I?

STANLEY: No.

HAPPY: And my eyes are closed.

STANLEY: So what's the—?

HAPPY: Strudel's comin'.

STANLEY *(Catching on, looks around):*   Ah, no, there's no—

(He breaks off as a furred, lavishly dressed girl enters and sits at the next table. Both follow her with their eyes.)

STANLEY: Geez, how'd ya know?

HAPPY: I got radar or something. *(Staring directly at her profile)* Oooooooo
    . . . Stanley.

STANLEY: I think that's for you, Mr. Loman.

HAPPY: Look at that mouth. Oh, God. And the binoculars.

STANLEY: Geez, you got a life, Mr. Loman.

HAPPY: Wait on her.

STANLEY *(Going to the girl's table):* Would you like a menu, ma'am?

GIRL: I'm expecting someone, but I'd like a—

HAPPY: Why don't you bring her—excuse me, miss, do you mind? I sell
    champagne, and I'd like you to try my brand. Bring her a champagne,
    Stanley.

GIRL: That's awfully nice of you.

HAPPY: Don't mention it. It's all company money. *(He laughs.)*

GIRL: That's a charming product to be selling, isn't it?

HAPPY: Oh, gets to be like everything else. Selling is selling, y'know.

GIRL: I suppose.

HAPPY: You don't happen to sell, do you?

GIRL: No, I don't sell.

HAPPY: Would you object to a compliment from a stranger? You ought to be
    on a magazine cover.

GIRL *(Looking at him a little archly):* I have been.

(STANLEY comes in with a glass of champagne.)

HAPPY: What'd I say before, Stanley? You see? She's a cover girl.

STANLEY: Oh, I could see, I could see.

HAPPY *(To the GIRL):* What magazine?

GIRL: Oh, a lot of them. *(She takes the drink.)* Thank you.

HAPPY: You know what they say in France, don't you? "Champagne is the
    drink of the complexion"—Hya, Biff!

(BIFF has entered and sits with HAPPY.)

BIFF: Hello, kid. Sorry I'm late.

HAPPY: I just got here. Uh, Miss—?

GIRL: Forsythe.

HAPPY: Miss Forsythe, this is my brother.

BIFF: Is Dad here?

HAPPY: His name is Biff. You might've heard of him. Great football player.

GIRL: Really? What team?

HAPPY: Are you familiar with football?

GIRL: No, I'm afraid I'm not.

HAPPY: Biff is quarterback with the New York Giants.

GIRL: Well, that is nice, isn't it? *(She drinks.)*

HAPPY: Good health.

GIRL: I'm happy to meet you.

HAPPY: That's my name. Hap. It's really Harold, but at West Point they called me Happy.

GIRL *(Now really impressed):*   Oh, I see. How do you do? *(She turns her profile.)*

BIFF: Isn't Dad coming?

HAPPY: You want her?

BIFF: Oh, I could never make that.

HAPPY: I remember the time that idea would never come into your head. Where's the old confidence, Biff?

BIFF: I just saw Oliver—

HAPPY: Wait a minute. I've got to see that old confidence again. Do you want her? She's on call.

BIFF: Oh, no. *(He turns to look at the* GIRL.*)*

HAPPY: I'm telling you. Watch this. *(Turning to the* GIRL*)* Honey? *(She turns to him.)* Are you busy?

GIRL: Well, I am . . . but I could make a phone call.

HAPPY: Do that, will you, honey? And see if you can get a friend. We'll be here for a while. Biff is one of the greatest football players in the country.

GIRL *(Standing up):* Well, I'm certainly happy to meet you.

HAPPY: Come back soon.

GIRL: I'll try.

HAPPY: Don't try, honey, try hard.

(The GIRL *exits.* STANLEY *follows, shaking his head in bewildered admiration.)*

HAPPY: Isn't that a shame now? A beautiful girl like that? That's why I can't get married. There's not a good woman in a thousand. New York is loaded with them, kid!

BIFF: Hap, look—

HAPPY: I told you she was on call!

BIFF *(Strangely unnerved):* Cut it out, will ya? I want to say something to you.

HAPPY: Did you see Oliver?

BIFF: I saw him all right. Now look, I want to tell Dad a couple of things and I want you to help me.

HAPPY: What? Is he going to back you?

BIFF: Are you crazy? You're out of your goddam head, you know that?

HAPPY: Why? What happened?

BIFF *(Breathlessly):* I did a terrible thing today, Hap. It's been the strangest day I ever went through. I'm all numb, I swear.

HAPPY: You mean he wouldn't see you?

BIFF: Well, I waited six hours for him, see? All day. Kept sending my name in. Even tried to date his secretary so she'd get me to him, but no soap.

HAPPY: Because you're not showin' the old confidence, Biff. He remembered you, didn't he?

BIFF *(Stopping* HAPPY *with a gesture):* Finally, about five o'clock, he comes out. Didn't remember who I was or anything. I felt like such an idiot, Hap.

HAPPY: Did you tell him my Florida idea?

BIFF: He walked away. I saw him for one minute. I got so mad I could've torn the walls down! How the hell did I ever get the idea I was a salesman there? I even believed myself that I'd been a salesman for him! And then he gave me one look and—I realized what a ridiculous lie my whole life has been! We've been talking in a dream for fifteen years. I was a shipping clerk.

HAPPY: What'd you do?

BIFF *(With great tension and wonder):* Well, he left, see. And the secretary went out. I was all alone in the waiting-room. I don't know what came over me, Hap. The next thing I know I'm in his office—paneled walls, everything. I can't explain it. I—Hap, I took his fountain pen.

HAPPY: Geez, did he catch you?

BIFF: I ran out. I ran down all eleven flights. I ran and ran and ran.

HAPPY: That was an awful dumb—what'd you do that for?

BIFF *(Agonized):* I don't know, I just—wanted to take something, I don't know. You gotta help me, Hap, I'm gonna tell Pop.

HAPPY: You crazy? What for?

BIFF: Hap, he's got to understand that I'm not the man somebody lends that kind of money to. He thinks I've been spiting him all these years and it's eating him up.

HAPPY: That's just it. You tell him something nice.

BIFF: I can't.

HAPPY: Say you got a lunch date with Oliver tomorrow.

BIFF: So what do I do tomorrow?

HAPPY: You leave the house tomorrow and come back at night and say Oliver is thinking it over. And he thinks it over for a couple of weeks, and gradually it fades away and nobody's the worse.

BIFF: But it'll go on forever!

HAPPY: Dad is never so happy as when he's looking forward to something!

(WILLY enters.)

HAPPY: Hello, scout!

WILLY: Gee, I haven't been here in years!

(STANLEY has followed WILLY in and sets a chair for him. STANLEY starts off but HAPPY stops him.)

HAPPY: Stanley!

(STANLEY stands by, waiting for an order.)

BIFF *(Going to WILLY with guilt, as to an invalid):* Sit down, Pop. You want a drink?

WILLY: Sure, I don't mind.

BIFF: Let's get a load on.

WILLY: You look worried.

BIFF: N-no. *(To STANLEY):* Scotch all around. Make it doubles.

STANLEY: Doubles, right. *(He goes.)*

WILLY: You had a couple already, didn't you?

BIFF: Just a couple, yeah.

WILLY: Well, what happened, boy? *(Nodding affirmatively, with a smile)* Everything go all right?

BIFF *(Takes a breath, then reaches out and grasps* WILLY's *hand):* Pal . . . *(He is smiling bravely, and* WILLY *is smiling too.)* I had an experience today.

HAPPY: Terrific, Pop.

WILLY: That so? What happened?

BIFF *(High, slightly alcoholic, above the earth):*   I'm going to tell you everything from first to last. It's been a strange day. *(Silence. He looks around, composes himself as best he can, but his breath keeps breaking the rhythm of his voice.)* I had to wait quite a while for him, and—

WILLY: Oliver?

BIFF: Yeah, Oliver. All day, as a matter of cold fact. And a lot of—instances—facts, Pop, facts about my life came back to me. Who was it, Pop? Who ever said I was a salesman with Oliver?

WILLY: Well, you were.

BIFF: No, Dad, I was a shipping clerk.

WILLY: But you were practically—

BIFF *(With determination):*   Dad, I don't know who said it first, but I was never a salesman for Bill Oliver.

WILLY: What're you talking about?

BIFF: Let's hold on to the facts tonight, Pop. We're not going to get anywhere bullin' around. I was a shipping clerk.

WILLY *(Angrily):*   All right, now listen to me—

BIFF: Why don't you let me finish?

WILLY: I'm not interested in stories about the past or any crap of that kind because the woods are burning, boys, you understand? There's a big blaze going on all around. I was fired today.

BIFF *(Shocked):*   How could you be?

WILLY: I was fired, and I'm looking for a little good news to tell your mother, because the woman has waited and the woman has suffered. The gist of it is that I haven't got a story left in my head, Biff. So don't give me a lecture about facts and aspects. I am not interested. Now what've you got to say to me?

(STANLEY enters with three drinks. They wait until he leaves.)

WILLY: Did you see Oliver?

BIFF: Jesus, Dad!

WILLY: You mean you didn't go up there?

HAPPY: Sure he went up there.

BIFF: I did. I—saw him. How could they fire you?

WILLY *(On the edge of his chair)*   What kind of a welcome did he give you?

BIFF: He won't even let you work on commission?

WILLY: I'm out! *(Driving):* So tell me, he gave you a warm welcome?

HAPPY: Sure, Pop, sure!

BIFF *(Driven):*   Well, it was kind of—

WILLY: I was wondering if he'd remember you. *(To* HAPPY*)* Imagine, man doesn't see him for ten, twelve years and gives him that kind of a welcome!

HAPPY: Damn right!

BIFF *(Trying to return to the offensive):*   Pop, look—

WILLY: You know why he remembered you, don't you? Because you impressed him in those days.

BIFF: Let's talk quietly and get this down to the facts, huh?

WILLY *(As though* BIFF *had been interrupting):*   Well, what happened? It's great news, Biff. Did he take you into his office or'd you talk in the waiting-room?

BIFF: Well, he came in, see, and—

WILLY *(With a big smile):*   What'd he say? Betcha he threw his arm around you.

BIFF: Well, he kinda—

WILLY: He's a fine man. *(To* HAPPY*)* Very hard man to see, y'know.

HAPPY *(Agreeing):*   Oh, I know.

WILLY *(To* BIFF*)*   Is that where you had the drinks?

BIFF: Yeah, he gave me a couple of—no, no!

HAPPY *(Cutting in):*   He told him my Florida idea.

WILLY: Don't interrupt. *(To* BIFF*)* How'd he react to the Florida idea?

BIFF: Dad, will you give me a minute to explain?

WILLY: I've been waiting for you to explain since I sat down here! What happened? He took you into his office and what?

BIFF: Well—I talked. And—and he listened, see.

WILLY: Famous for the way he listens, y'know. What was his answer?

BIFF: His answer was—*(He breaks off, suddenly angry.)* Dad, you're not letting me tell you what I want to tell you!

WILLY *(Accusing, angered):*   You didn't see him, did you?

BIFF: I did see him!

WILLY: What'd you insult him or something? You insulted him, didn't you?

BIFF: Listen, will you let me out of it, will you just let me out of it!

HAPPY: What the hell!

WILLY: Tell me what happened!

BIFF *(To* HAPPY*):*   I can't talk to him!

(A single trumpet note jars the ear. The light of green leaves stains the house, which holds the air of night and a dream. YOUNG BERNARD *enters and knocks on the door of the house.)*

YOUNG BERNARD *(Frantically):*   Mrs. Loman, Mrs. Loman!

HAPPY: Tell him what happened!

BIFF *(To* HAPPY*):*   Shut up and leave me alone!

WILLY: No, no! You had to go and flunk math!

BIFF: What math? What're you talking about?

YOUNG BERNARD: Mrs. Loman, Mrs. Loman!

*(*LINDA *appears in the house, as of old.)*

WILLY *(Wildly):*   Math, math, math!

BIFF: Take it easy, Pop!

YOUNG BERNARD: Mrs. Loman!

WILLY *(Furiously):*   If you hadn't flunked you'd've been set by now!

BIFF: Now, look, I'm gonna tell you what happened, and you're going to listen to me.

YOUNG BERNARD: Mrs. Loman!

BIFF: I waited six hours—

HAPPY: What the hell are you saying?

BIFF: I kept sending in my name but he wouldn't see me. So finally he . . .
(He continues unheard as light fades low on the restaurant.)

YOUNG BERNARD: Biff flunked math!

LINDA: No!

YOUNG BERNARD: Birnbaum flunked him! They won't graduate him!

LINDA: But they have to. He's gotta go to the university. Where is he? Biff! Biff!

YOUNG BERNARD: No, he left. He went to Grand Central.

LINDA: Grand—You mean he went to Boston!

YOUNG BERNARD: Is Uncle Willy in Boston?

LINDA: Oh, maybe Willy can talk to the teacher. Oh, the poor, poor boy!

(Light on house area snaps out.)

BIFF *(At the table, now audible, holding up a gold fountain pen):*   . . . so I'm washed up with Oliver, you understand? Are you listening to me?

WILLY *(At a loss):*   Yeah, sure. If you hadn't flunked—

BIFF: Flunked what? What're you talking about?

WILLY: Don't blame everything on me! I didn't flunk math—you did! What pen?

HAPPY: That was awful dumb, Biff, a pen like that is worth—

WILLY *(Seeing the pen for the first time):*   You took Oliver's pen?

BIFF *(Weakening):*   Dad, I just explained it to you.

WILLY: You stole Bill Oliver's fountain pen!

BIFF: I didn't exactly steal it! That's just what I've been explaining to you!

HAPPY: He had it in his hand and just then Oliver walked in, so he got nervous and stuck it in his pocket!

WILLY: My God, Biff!

BIFF: I never intended to do it, Dad!

OPERATOR'S VOICE: Standish Arms, good evening!

WILLY *(Shouting):*   I'm not in my room!

BIFF *(Frightened):*   Dad, what's the matter? *(He and* HAPPY *stand up.)*

OPERATOR: Ringing Mr. Loman for you!

WILLY: I'm not there, stop it!

BIFF *(Horrified, gets down on one knee before* WILLY*):*   Dad, I'll make good, I'll make good. *(*WILLY *tries to get to his feet.* BIFF *holds him down.)* Sit down now.

WILLY: No, you're no good, you're no good for anything.

BIFF: I am, Dad, I'll find something else, you understand? Now don't worry about anything. *(He holds up* WILLY's *face.)* Talk to me, Dad.

OPERATOR: Mr. Loman does not answer. Shall I page him?

WILLY *(Attempting to stand, as though to rush and silence the Operator):*   No, no, no!

HAPPY: He'll strike something, Pop.

WILLY: No, no . . .

BIFF *(Desperately, standing over* WILLY*):*   Pop, listen! Listen to me! I'm telling you something good. Oliver talked to his partner about the Florida idea. You listening? He—he talked to his partner, and he came to me . . . I'm going to be all right, you hear? Dad, listen to me, he said it was just a question of the amount!

WILLY: Then you . . . got it?

HAPPY: He's gonna be terrific, Pop!

WILLY *(Trying to stand):*   Then you got it, haven't you? You got it! You got it!

BIFF *(Agonized, holds* WILLY *down):*   No, no. Look, Pop. I'm supposed to have lunch with them tomorrow. I'm just telling you this so you'll know that I can still make an impression, Pop. And I'll make good somewhere, but I can't go tomorrow, see?

WILLY: Why not? You simply—

BIFF: But the pen, Pop!

WILLY: You give it to him and tell him it was an oversight!

HAPPY: Sure, have lunch tomorrow!

BIFF: I can't say that—

WILLY: You were doing a crossword puzzle and accidentally used his pen!

BIFF: Listen, kid, I took those balls years ago, now I walk in with his fountain pen? That clinches it, don't you see? I can't face him like that! I'll try elsewhere.

PAGE'S VOICE: Paging Mr. Loman!

WILLY: Don't you want to be anything?

BIFF: Pop, how can I go back?

WILLY: You don't want to be anything, is that what's behind it?

BIFF *(Now angry at* WILLY *for not crediting his sympathy):*   Don't take it that way! You think it was easy walking into that office after what I'd done to him? A team of horses couldn't have dragged me back to Bill Oliver!

WILLY: Then why'd you go?

BIFF: Why did I go? Why did I go! Look at you! Look at what's become of you!

(Off left, THE WOMAN *laughs.)*

WILLY: Biff, you're going to go to that lunch tomorrow, or—

BIFF: I can't go. I've got no appointment!

HAPPY: Biff, for . . . !

WILLY: Are you spiting me?

BIFF: Don't take it that way! Goddammit!

WILLY (*Strikes* BIFF *and falters away from the table*):   You rotten little louse! Are
    you spiting me?

THE WOMAN: Someone's at the door, Willy!

BIFF: I'm no good, can't you see what I am?

HAPPY (*Separating them*):   Hey, you're in a restaurant! Now cut it out, both of
    you! (*The girls enter.*) Hello, girls, sit down.

    (THE WOMAN *laughs, off left.*)

MISS FORSYTHE: I guess we might as well. This is Letta.

THE WOMAN: Willy, are you going to wake up?

BIFF (*Ignoring* WILLY):   How're ya, miss, sit down. What do you drink?

MISS FORSYTHE: Letta might not be able to stay long.

LETTA: I gotta get up very early tomorrow. I got jury duty. I'm so excited!
    Were you fellows ever on a jury?

BIFF: No, but I been in front of them! (*The girls laugh.*) This is my father.

LETTA: Isn't he cute? Sit down with us, Pop.

HAPPY: Sit him down, Biff!

BIFF (*Going to him*):   Come on, slugger, drink us under the table. To hell with
    it! Come on, sit down, pal.

    (On BIFF's *last insistence,* WILLY *is about to sit.*)

THE WOMAN (*Now urgently*):   Willy, are you going to answer the door!

    (THE WOMAN's *call pulls* WILLY *back. He starts right, befuddled.*)

BIFF: Hey, where are you going?

WILLY: Open the door.

BIFF: The door?

WILLY: The washroom . . . the door . . . where's the door?

BIFF (*Leading* WILLY *to the left*):   Just go straight down.

                            (WILLY *moves left.*)

THE WOMAN: Willy, Willy, are you going to get up, get up, get up, get up?

                                 (WILLY *exits left.*)

LETTA: I think it's sweet you bring your daddy along.

MISS FORSYTHE: Oh, he isn't really your father!

BIFF (*At left, turning to her resentfully*)   Miss Forsythe, you've just seen a prince
    walk by. A fine, troubled prince. A hardworking, unappreciated prince.
    A pal, you understand? A good companion. Always for his boys.

LETTA: That's so sweet.

HAPPY: Well, girls, what's the program? We're wasting time. Come on, Biff.
    Gather round. Where would you like to go?

BIFF: Why don't you do something for him?

HAPPY: Me!

BIFF: Don't you give a damn for him, Hap?

HAPPY: What're you talking about? I'm the one who—

BIFF: I sense it, you don't give a good goddam about him. *(He takes the rolled-up hose from his pocket and puts it on the table in front of* HAPPY.*)* Look what I found in the cellar, for Christ's sake. How can you bear to let it go on?

HAPPY: Me? Who goes away? Who runs off and—

BIFF: Yeah, but he doesn't mean anything to you. You could help him—I can't! Don't you understand what I'm talking about? He's going to kill himself, don't you know that?

HAPPY: Don't I know it! Me!

BIFF: Hap, help him! Jesus . . . help him . . . Help me, help me, I can't bear to look at his face! *(Ready to weep, he hurries out, up right.)*

HAPPY *(Starting after him):*   Where are you going?

MISS FORSYTHE: What's he so mad about?

HAPPY: Come on, girls, we'll catch up with him.

MISS FORSYTHE *(As* HAPPY *pushes her out):*   Say, I don't like that temper of his!

HAPPY: He's just a little overstrung, he'll be all right!

WILLY *(Off left, as* THE WOMAN *laughs):*   Don't answer! Don't answer!

LETTA: Don't you want to tell your father—

HAPPY: No, that's not my father. He's just a guy. Come on, we'll catch Biff, and, honey, we're going to paint this town! Stanley, where's the check! Hey, Stanley!

(They exit. STANLEY *looks toward left.)*

STANLEY *(Calling to* HAPPY *indignantly):*   Mr. Loman! Mr. Loman!

*(*STANLEY *picks up a chair and follows them off. Knocking is heard off left.* THE WOMAN *enters, laughing.* WILLY *follows her. She is in a black slip; he is buttoning his shirt. Raw, sensuous music accompanies their speech.)*

WILLY: Will you stop laughing? Will you stop?

THE WOMAN: Aren't you going to answer the door? He'll wake the whole hotel.

WILLY: I'm not expecting anybody.

THE WOMAN: Whyn't you have another drink, honey, and stop being so damn self-centered?

WILLY: I'm so lonely.

THE WOMAN: You know you ruined me, Willy? From now on, whenever you come to the office, I'll see that you go right through to the buyers. No waiting at my desk any more, Willy. You ruined me.

WILLY: That's nice of you to say that.

THE WOMAN: Gee, you are self-centered! Why so sad? You are the saddest, self-centeredest soul I ever did see-saw. *(She laughs. He kisses her.)* Come on inside, drummer boy. It's silly to be dressing in the middle of the night. *(As knocking is heard)* Aren't you going to answer the door?

WILLY: They're knocking on the wrong door.

THE WOMAN: But I felt the knocking. And he heard us talking in here. Maybe the hotel's on fire!

WILLY *(His terror rising):*   It's a mistake.

THE WOMAN: Then tell him to go away!

WILLY: There's nobody there.

THE WOMAN: It's getting on my nerves, Willy. There's somebody standing
out there and it's getting on my nerves!

WILLY *(Pushing her away from him):*   All right, stay in the bathroom here, and
don't come out. I think there's a law in Massachusetts about it, so don't
come out. It may be that new room clerk. He looked very mean. So don't
come out. It's a mistake, there's no fire.

*(The knocking is heard again. He takes a few steps away from her, and she vanishes
into the wing. The light follows him, and now he is facing* YOUNG BIFF, *who
carries a suitcase.* BIFF *steps toward him. The music is gone.)*

BIFF: Why didn't you answer?

WILLY: Biff! What are you doing in Boston?

BIFF: Why didn't you answer? I've been knocking for five minutes, I called
you on the phone—

WILLY: I just heard you. I was in the bathroom and had the door shut. Did
anything happen home?

BIFF: Dad—I let you down.

WILLY: What do you mean?

BIFF: Dad . . .

WILLY: Biffo, what's this about? *(Putting his arm around* BIFF*)* Come on, let's
go downstairs and get you a malted.

BIFF: Dad, I flunked math.

WILLY: Not for the term?

BIFF: The term. I haven't got enough credits to graduate.

WILLY: You mean to say Bernard wouldn't give you the answers?

BIFF: He did, he tried, but I only got a sixty-one.

WILLY: And they wouldn't give you four points?

BIFF: Birnbaum refused absolutely. I begged him, Pop, but he won't give me
those points. You gotta talk to him before they close the school. Because
if he saw the kind of man you are, and you just talked to him in your way,
I'm sure he'd come through for me. The class came right before practice,
see, and I didn't go enough. Would you talk to him? He'd like you, Pop.
You know the way you could talk.

WILLY: You're on. We'll drive right back.

BIFF: Oh, Dad, good work! I'm sure he'll change it for you!

WILLY: Go downstairs and tell the clerk I'm checkin' out. Go right down.

BIFF: Yes, sir! See, the reason he hates me, Pop—one day he was late for class
so I got up at the blackboard and imitated him. I crossed my eyes and
talked with a lithp.

WILLY *(Laughing):*   You did? The kids like it?

BIFF: They nearly died laughing!

WILLY: Yeah? What'd you do?

BIFF: The thquare root of thixty twee is . . . *(*WILLY *bursts out laughing;* BIFF
joins him.) And in the middle of it he walked in!

(WILLY laughs and THE WOMAN *joins in offstage.)*

WILLY *(Without hesitation):*   Hurry downstairs and—
BIFF: Somebody in there?
WILLY: No, that was next door.

(THE WOMAN laughs offstage.)

BIFF: Somebody got in your bathroom!
WILLY: No, it's the next room, there's a party—
THE WOMAN *(Enters, laughing. She lisps this):*   Can I come in? There's something in the bathtub, Willy, and it's moving!

(WILLY looks at BIFF, *who is staring open-mouthed and horrified at* THE WOMAN.)*

WILLY: Ah—you better go back to your room. They must be finished painting by now. They're painting her room so I let her take a shower here. Go back, go back . . . *(He pushes her.)*
THE WOMAN *(Resisting):*   But I've got to get dressed, Willy, I can't—
WILLY: Get out of here! Go back, go back . . . *(Suddenly striving for the ordinary)* This is Miss Francis, Biff, she's a buyer. They're painting her room. Go back, Miss Francis, go back . . .
THE WOMAN: But my clothes, I can't go out naked in the hall!
WILLY *(Pushing her offstage):*   Get outa here! Go back, go back!

(BIFF slowly sits down on his suitcase as the argument continues offstage.)

THE WOMAN: Where's my stockings? You promised me stockings, Willy!
WILLY: I have no stockings here!
THE WOMAN: You had two boxes of size nine sheers for me, and I want them!
WILLY: Here, for God's sake, will you get outa here!
THE WOMAN *(Enters holding a box of stockings):*   I just hope there's nobody in the hall. That's all I hope. *(To* BIFF) Are you football or baseball?
BIFF: Football.
THE WOMAN *(Angry, humiliated):*   That's me too. G'night. *(She snatches her clothes from* WILLY, *and walks out.)*
WILLY *(After a pause):*   Well, better get going. I want to get to the school first thing in the morning. Get my suits out of the closet. I'll get my valise. *(BIFF doesn't move.)* What's the matter? *(BIFF remains motionless, tears falling.)* She's a buyer. Buys for J. H. Simmons. She lives down the hall—they're painting. You don't imagine—*(He breaks off. After a pause)* Now listen, pal, she's just a buyer. She sees merchandise in her room and they have to keep it looking just so . . . *(Pause. Assuming command)* All right, get my suits. *(Biff doesn't move.)* Now stop crying and do as I say. I gave you an order. Biff, I gave you an order! Is that what you do when I give you an order? How dare you cry! *(Putting his arm around* BIFF) Now look, Biff, when you grow up you'll understand about these things. You mustn't—you mustn't overemphasize a thing like this. I'll see Birnbaum first thing in the morning.

BIFF: Never mind.

WILLY *(Getting down beside* BIFF*):*   Never mind! He's going to give you those points. I'll see to it.

BIFF: He wouldn't listen to you.

WILLY: He certainly will listen to me. You need those points for the U. of Virginia.

BIFF: I'm not going there.

WILLY: Heh? If I can't get him to change that mark you'll make it up in summer school. You've got all summer to—

BIFF *(His weeping breaking from him):*   Dad . . .

WILLY *(Infected by it):*   Oh, my boy . . .

BIFF: Dad . . .

WILLY: She's nothing to me, Biff. I was lonely, I was terribly lonely.

BIFF: You—you gave her Mama's stockings! *(His tears break through and he rises to go.)*

WILLY *(Grabbing for* BIFF*):*   I gave you an order!

BIFF: Don't touch me, you—liar!

WILLY: Apologize for that!

BIFF: You fake! You phony little fake! You fake! *(Overcome, he turns quickly and weeping fully goes out with his suitcase.* WILLY *is left on the floor on his knees.)*

WILLY: I gave you an order! Biff, come back here or I'll beat you! Come back here! I'll whip you!

*(*STANLEY *comes quickly in from the right and stands in front of* WILLY*.)*

WILLY *(Shouts at* STANLEY*):*   I gave you an order . . .

STANLEY: Hey, let's pick it up, pick it up, Mr. Loman. *(He helps* WILLY *to his feet.)* Your boys left with the chippies. They said they'll see you home.

(A second waiter watches some distance away.)

WILLY: But we were supposed to have dinner together.

(Music is heard, WILLY*'s theme.)*

STANLEY: Can you make it?

WILLY: I'll—sure, I can make it. *(Suddenly concerned about his clothes)* Do I—I look all right?

STANLEY: Sure, you look all right. *(He flicks a speck off* WILLY*'s lapel.)*

WILLY: Here—here's a dollar.

STANLEY: Oh, your son paid me. It's all right.

WILLY *(Putting it in* STANLEY*'s hand):*   No, take it. You're a good boy.

STANLEY: Oh, no, you don't have to . . .

WILLY: Here—here's some more, I don't need it any more. *(After a slight pause)* Tell me—is there a seed store in the neighborhood?

STANLEY: Seeds? You mean like to plant?

(As WILLY *turns,* STANLEY *slips the money back into his jacket pocket.)*

WILLY: Yes. Carrots, peas . . .

STANLEY: Well, there's hardware stores on Sixth Avenue, but it may be too late now.

WILLY *(Anxiously):* Oh, I'd better hurry. I've got to get some seeds. *(He starts off to the right.)* I've got to get some seeds, right away. Nothing's planted. I don't have a thing in the ground.

(WILLY hurries out as the light goes down. STANLEY moves over to the right after him, watches him off. The other waiter has been staring at WILLY.)

STANLEY *(To the waiter):* Well, whatta you looking at?

(The waiter picks up the chairs and moves off right. STANLEY takes the table and follows him. The light fades on this area. There is a long pause, the sound of the flute coming over. The light gradually rises on the kitchen, which is empty. HAPPY appears at the door of the house, followed by BIFF. HAPPY is carrying a large bunch of long-stemmed roses. He enters the kitchen, looks around for LINDA. Not seeing her, he turns to BIFF, who is just outside the house door, and makes a gesture with his hands, indicating "Not here, I guess." He looks into the living-room and freezes. Inside, LINDA, unseen, is seated, WILLY's coat on her lap. She rises ominously and quietly and moves toward HAPPY, who backs up into the kitchen, afraid.)

HAPPY: Hey, what're you doing up? *(LINDA says nothing but moves toward him implacably.)* Where's Pop? *(He keeps backing to the right, and now LINDA is in full view in the doorway to the living-room.)* Is he sleeping?

LINDA: Where were you?

HAPPY *(Trying to laugh it off):* We met two girls, Mom, very fine types. Here, we brought you some flowers. *(Offering them to her)* Put them in your room, Ma.

(She knocks them to the floor at BIFF's feet. He has now come inside and closed the door behind him. She stares at BIFF, silent.)

HAPPY: Now what'd you do that for? Mom, I want you to have some flowers—

LINDA *(Cutting HAPPY off, violently to BIFF):* Don't you care whether he lives or dies?

HAPPY *(Going to the stairs):* Come upstairs, Biff.

BIFF *(With a flare of disgust, to HAPPY):* Go away from me! *(To LINDA)* What do you mean, lives or dies? Nobody's dying around here, pal.

LINDA: Get out of my sight! Get out of here!

BIFF: I wanna see the boss.

LINDA: You're not going near him!

BIFF: Where is he? *(He moves into the living-room and LINDA follows.)*

LINDA *(Shouting after BIFF):* You invite him for dinner. He looks forward to it all day—*(BIFF appears in his parents' bedroom, looks around, and exits)*—and then you desert him there. There's no stranger you'd do that to!

HAPPY: Why? He had a swell time with us. Listen, when I—(LINDA *comes back into the kitchen*)—desert him I hope I don't outlive the day!

LINDA: Get out of here!

HAPPY: Now look, Mom . . .

LINDA: Did you have to go to women tonight? You and your lousy rotten whores!

(BIFF *re-enters the kitchen.*)

HAPPY: Mom, all we did was follow Biff around trying to cheer him up! *(To* BIFF*)* Boy, what a night you gave me!

LINDA: Get out of here, both of you, and don't come back! I don't want you tormenting him any more. Go on now, get your things together! *(To* BIFF*)* You can sleep in his apartment. *(She starts to pick up the flowers and stops herself.)* Pick up this stuff, I'm not your maid any more. Pick it up, you bum, you!

(HAPPY *turns his back to her in refusal.* BIFF *slowly moves over and gets down on his knees, picking up the flowers.)*

LINDA: You're a pair of animals! Not one, not another living soul would have had the cruelty to walk out on that man in a restaurant!

BIFF *(Not looking at her):* Is that what he said?

LINDA: He didn't have to say anything. He was so humiliated he nearly limped when he came in.

HAPPY: But, Mom, he had a great time with us—

BIFF *(Cutting him off violently):* Shut up!

(Without another word, HAPPY *goes upstairs.)*

LINDA: You! You didn't even go in to see if he was all right!

BIFF *(Still on the floor in front of* LINDA, *the flowers in his hand; with self-loathing):* No. Didn't. Didn't do a damned thing. How do you like that, heh? Left him babbling in a toilet.

LINDA: You louse. You . . .

BIFF: Now you hit it on the nose! *(He gets up, throws the flowers in the wastebasket.)* The scum of the earth, and you're looking at him!

LINDA: Get out of here!

BIFF: I gotta talk to the boss, Mom. Where is he?

LINDA: You're not going near him. Get out of this house!

BIFF *(With absolute assurance, determination):* No. We're gonna have an abrupt conversation, him and me.

LINDA: You're not talking to him!

(Hammering is heard from outside the house, off right. BIFF *turns toward the noise.)*

LINDA *(Suddenly pleading):* Will you please leave him alone?

BIFF: What's he doing out there?

LINDA: He's planting the garden!

BIFF *(Quietly):* Now? Oh, my God!

(BIFF moves outside, LINDA following. The light dies down on them and comes up on the center of the apron as WILLY walks into it. He is carrying a flashlight, a hoe, and a handful of seed packets. He raps the top of the hoe sharply to fix it firmly, and then moves to the left, measuring off the distance with his foot. He holds the flashlight to look at the seed packets, reading off the instructions. He is in the blue of night.)

WILLY: Carrots . . . quarter-inch apart. Rows . . . one-foot rows. *(He measures it off.)* One foot. *(He puts down a package and measures off.)* Beets. *(He puts down another package and measures again.)* Lettuce. *(He reads the package, puts it down.)* One foot—*(He breaks off as Ben appears at the right and moves slowly down to him.)* What a proposition, ts, ts. Terrific, terrific. 'Cause she's suffered, Ben, the woman has suffered. You understand me? A man can't go out the way he came in, Ben, a man has got to add up to something. You can't, you can't—*(BEN moves toward him as though to interrupt.)* You gotta consider, now. Don't answer so quick. Remember, it's a guaranteed twenty-thousand-dollar proposition. Now look, Ben, I want you to go through the ins and outs of this thing with me. I've got nobody to talk to, Ben, and the woman has suffered, you hear me?

BEN *(Standing still, considering):* What's the proposition?

WILLY: It's twenty thousand dollars on the barrelhead. Guaranteed, gilt-edged, you understand?

BEN: You don't want to make a fool of yourself. They might not honor the policy.

WILLY: How can they dare refuse? Didn't I work like a coolie to meet every premium on the nose? And now they don't pay off? Impossible!

BEN: It's called a cowardly thing, William.

WILLY: Why? Does it take more guts to stand here the rest of my life ringing up a zero?

BEN *(Yielding):* That's a point, William. *(He moves, thinking, turns.)* And twenty thousand—that *is* something one can feel with the hand, it is there.

WILLY *(Now assured, with rising power):* Oh, Ben, that's the whole beauty of it! I see it like a diamond, shining in the dark, hard and rough, that I can pick up and touch in my hand. Not like—like an appointment! This would not be another damned-fool appointment, Ben, and it changes all the aspects. Because he thinks I'm nothing, see, and so he spites me. But the funeral— *(Straightening up)* Ben, that funeral will be massive! They'll come from Maine, Massachusetts, Vermont, New Hampshire! All the old-timers with the strange license plates—that boy will be thunder-struck, Ben, because he never realized—I am known! Rhode Island, New York, New Jersey—I am known, Ben, and he'll see it with his eyes once and for all. He'll see what I am, Ben! He's in for a shock, that boy!

BEN *(Coming down to the edge of the garden):* He'll call you a coward.

WILLY (*Suddenly fearful*):   No, that would be terrible.

BEN: Yes. And a damned fool.

WILLY: No, no, he mustn't, I won't have that! (*He is broken and desperate.*)

BEN: He'll hate you, William.

(*The gay music of the Boys is heard.*)

WILLY: Oh, Ben, how do we get back to all the great times? Used to be so full of light, and comradeship, the sleigh-riding in winter, and the ruddiness on his cheeks. And always some kind of good news coming up, always something nice coming up ahead. And never even let me carry the valises in the house, and simonizing, simonizing that little red car! Why, why can't I give him something and not have him hate me?

BEN: Let me think about it. (*He glances at his watch.*) I still have a little time. Remarkable proposition, but you've got to be sure you're not making a fool of yourself.

(BEN *drifts off upstage and goes out of sight.* BIFF *comes down from the left.*)

WILLY (*Suddenly conscious of* BIFF, *turns and looks up at him, then begins picking up the packages of seeds in confusion*):   Where the hell is that seed? (*Indignantly*) You can't see nothing out here! They boxed in the whole goddam neighborhood!

BIFF: There are people all around here. Don't you realize that?

WILLY: I'm busy. Don't bother me.

BIFF (*Taking the hoe from* WILLY):   I'm saying good-by to you, Pop. (WILLY *looks at him, silent, unable to move.*) I'm not coming back any more.

WILLY: You're not going to see Oliver tomorrow?

BIFF: I've got no appointment, Dad.

WILLY: He put his arm around you, and you've got no appointment?

BIFF: Pop, get this now, will you? Everytime I've left it's been a fight that sent me out of here. Today I realized something about myself and I tried to explain it to you and I—I think I'm just not smart enough to make any sense out of it for you. To hell with whose fault it is or anything like that. (*He takes* WILLY's *arm.*) Let's just wrap it up, heh? Come on in, we'll tell Mom. (*He gently tries to pull* WILLY *to left.*)

WILLY (*Frozen, immobile, with guilt in his voice*):   No, I don't want to see her.

BIFF: Come on! (*He pulls again, and* WILLY *tries to pull away.*)

WILLY (*Highly nervous*):   No, no, I don't want to see her.

BIFF (*Tries to look into* WILLY's *face, as if to find the answer there*):   Why don't you want to see her?

WILLY (*More harshly now*):   Don't bother me, will you?

BIFF: What do you mean, you don't want to see her? You don't want them calling you yellow, do you? This isn't your fault; it's me, I'm a bum. Now come inside! (WILLY *strains to get away.*) Did you hear what I said to you?

(WILLY *pulls away and quickly goes by himself into the house.* BIFF *follows.*)

LINDA *(To* WILLY*):*   Did you plant, dear?

BIFF *(At the door, to* LINDA*):*   All right, we had it out. I'm going and I'm not writing any more.

LINDA *(Going to* WILLY *in the kitchen):*   I think that's the best way, dear. 'Cause there's no use drawing it out, you'll just never get along.

*(*WILLY *doesn't respond.)*

BIFF: People ask where I am and what I'm doing, you don't know, and you don't care. That way it'll be off your mind and you can start brightening up again. All right? That clears it, doesn't it? *(*WILLY *is silent, and* BIFF *goes to him.)* You gonna wish me luck, scout? *(He extends his hand.)* What do you say?

LINDA: Shake his hand, Willy.

WILLY *(Turning to her, seething with hurt):*   There's no necessity to mention the pen at all, y'know.

BIFF *(Gently):*   I've got no appointment, Dad.

WILLY *(Erupting fiercely):*   He put his arm around . . . ?

BIFF: Dad, you're never going to see what I am, so what's the use of arguing? If I strike oil I'll send you a check. Meantime forget I'm alive.

WILLY *(To* LINDA*):*   Spite, see?

BIFF: Shake hands, Dad.

WILLY: Not my hand.

BIFF: I was hoping not to go this way.

WILLY: Well, this is the way you're going. Good-by.

*(*BIFF *looks at him a moment, then turns sharply and goes to the stairs.)*

WILLY *(Stops him with):*   May you rot in hell if you leave this house!

BIFF *(Turning):*   Exactly what is it that you want from me?

WILLY: I want you to know, on the train, in the mountains, in the valleys, wherever you go, that you cut down your life for spite!

BIFF: No, no.

WILLY: Spite, spite, is the word of your undoing! And when you're down and out, remember what did it. When you're rotting somewhere beside the railroad tracks, remember, and don't you dare blame it on me!

BIFF: I'm not blaming it on you!

WILLY: I won't take the rap for this, you hear?

*(*HAPPY *comes down the stairs and stands on the bottom step, watching.)*

BIFF: That's just what I'm telling you!

WILLY *(Sinking into a chair at the table, with full accusation):*   You're trying to put a knife in me—don't think I don't know what you're doing!

BIFF: All right, phony! Then let's lay it on the line. *(He whips the rubber tube out of his pocket and puts it on the table.)*

HAPPY: You crazy—

LINDA: Biff! *(She moves to grab the hose, but* BIFF *holds it down with his hand.)*

BIFF: Leave it there! Don't move it!

WILLY *(Not looking at it)*: What is that?

BIFF: You know goddam well what that is.

WILLY *(Caged, wanting to escape)*: I never saw that.

BIFF: You saw it. The mice didn't bring it into the cellar! What is this supposed
to do, make a hero out of you? This supposed to make me sorry for you?

WILLY: Never heard of it.

BIFF: There'll be no pity for you, you hear it? No pity!

WILLY *(To* LINDA*)*: You hear the spite!

BIFF: No, you're going to hear the truth—what you are and what I am!

LINDA: Stop it!

WILLY: Spite!

HAPPY *(Coming down toward* BIFF*)*: You cut it now!

BIFF *(To* HAPPY*)*: The man don't know who we are! The man is gonna know!
(To WILLY*)*: We never told the truth for ten minutes in this house!

HAPPY: We always told the truth!

BIFF *(Turning on him)*: You big blow, are you the assistant buyer? You're one
of the two assistants to the assistant, aren't you?

HAPPY: Well, I'm practically—

BIFF: You're practically full of it! We all are! And I'm through with it. *(To*
WILLY*)*: Now hear this, Willy, this is me.

WILLY: I know you!

BIFF: You know why I had no address for three months? I stole a suit in Kansas
City and I was in jail. *(To* LINDA, *who is sobbing)* Stop crying. I'm through
with it.

*(*LINDA *turns away from them, her hands covering her face.)*

WILLY: I suppose that's my fault!

BIFF: I stole myself out of every good job since high school!

WILLY: And whose fault is that?

BIFF: And I never got anywhere because you blew me so full of hot air I could
never stand taking orders from anybody! That's whose fault it is!

WILLY: I hear that!

LINDA: Don't, Biff!

BIFF: It's goddam time you heard that! I had to be boss big shot in two weeks,
and I'm through with it!

WILLY: Then hang yourself! For spite, hang yourself!

BIFF: No! Nobody's hanging himself, Willy! I ran down eleven flights with
a pen in my hand today. And suddenly I stopped, you hear me? And in
the middle of that office building, do you hear this? I stopped in the middle
of that building and I saw—the sky. I saw the things that I love in this
world. The work and the food and time to sit and smoke. And I looked
at the pen and said to myself, what the hell am I grabbing this for? Why
am I trying to become what I don't want to be? What am I doing in an
office, making a contemptuous, begging fool of myself, when all I want
is out there, waiting for me the minute I say I know who I am! Why can't

I say that, Willy? *(He tries to make* WILLY *face him, but* WILLY *pulls away and moves to the left.)*

WILLY *(With hatred, threateningly):* The door of your life is wide open!

BIFF: Pop! I'm a dime a dozen, and so are you!

WILLY *(Turning on him now in an uncontrolled outburst):* I am not a dime a dozen! I am Willy Loman, and you are Biff Loman!

(BIFF *starts for* WILLY, *but is blocked by* HAPPY. *In his fury,* BIFF *seems on the verge of attacking his father.)*

BIFF: I am not a leader of men, Willy, and neither are you. You were never anything but a hard-working drummer who landed in the ash can like all the rest of them! I'm one dollar an hour, Willy! I tried seven states and couldn't raise it. A buck an hour! Do you gather my meaning? I'm not bringing home any prizes any more, and you're going to stop waiting for me to bring them home!

WILLY *(Directly to* BIFF*):* You vengeful, spiteful mutt!

(BIFF *breaks from* HAPPY. WILLY, *in fright, starts up the stairs.* BIFF *grabs him.)*

BIFF *(At the peak of his fury):* Pop, I'm nothing! I'm nothing, Pop. Can't you understand that? There's no spite in it any more. I'm just what I am, that's all.

(BIFF'*s fury has spent itself, and he breaks down, sobbing, holding on to* WILLY, *who dumbly fumbles for* BIFF'*s face.)*

WILLY *(Astonished):* What're you doing? What're you doing? *(To* LINDA*)* Why is he crying?

BIFF *(Crying, broken):* Will you let me go, for Christ's sake? Will you take that phony dream and burn it before something happens? *(Struggling to contain himself, he pulls away and moves to the stairs.)* I'll go in the morning. Put him—put him to bed. *(Exhausted,* BIFF *moves up the stairs to his room.)*

WILLY *(After a long pause, astonished, elevated):* Isn't that—isn't that remarkable? Biff—he likes me!

LINDA: He loves you, Willy!

HAPPY *(Deeply moved):* Always did, Pop.

WILLY: Oh, Biff! *(Staring wildly)* He cried! Cried to me. *(He is choking with his love, and now cries out his promise.)* That boy—that boy is going to be magnificent!

(BEN *appears in the light just outside the kitchen.)*

BEN: Yes, outstanding, with twenty thousand behind him.

LINDA *(Sensing the racing of his mind, fearfully, carefully):* Now come to bed, Willy. It's all settled now.

WILLY *(Finding it difficult not to rush out of the house):* Yes, we'll sleep. Come on. Go to sleep, Hap.

BEN: And it does take a great kind of a man to crack the jungle.

(In accents of dread, BEN*'s idyllic music starts up.)*

HAPPY *(His arm around* LINDA*):*   I'm getting married, Pop, don't forget it. I'm changing everything. I'm gonna run that department before the year is up. You'll see, Mom. *(He kisses her.)*

BEN: The jungle is dark but full of diamonds, Willy.

*(*WILLY *turns, moves, listening to* BEN*.)*

LINDA: Be good. You're both good boys, just act that way, that's all.

HAPPY: 'Night, Pop. *(He goes upstairs.)*

LINDA *(To* WILLY*):*   Come, dear.

BEN *(With greater force):*   One must go in to fetch a diamond out.

WILLY *(To* LINDA, *as he moves slowly along the edge of the kitchen, toward the door):*   I just want to get settled down, Linda. Let me sit alone for a little.

LINDA *(Almost uttering her fear):*   I want you upstairs.

WILLY *(Taking her in his arms):*   In a few minutes, Linda. I couldn't sleep right now. Go on, you look awful tired. *(He kisses her.)*

BEN: Not like an appointment at all. A diamond is rough and hard to the touch.

WILLY: Go on now. I'll be right up.

LINDA: I think this is the only way, Willy.

WILLY: Sure, it's the best thing.

BEN: Best thing!

WILLY: The only way. Everything is gonna be—go on, kid, get to bed. You look so tired.

LINDA: Come right up.

WILLY: Two minutes.

*(*LINDA *goes into the living-room, then reappears in her bedroom.* WILLY *moves just outside the kitchen door.)*

WILLY: Loves me. *(Wonderingly)* Always loved me. Isn't that a remarkable thing? Ben, he'll worship me for it!

BEN *(With promise):*   It's dark there, but full of diamonds.

WILLY: Can you imagine that magnificence with twenty thousand dollars in his pocket?

LINDA *(Calling from her room):*   Willy! Come up!

WILLY *(Calling into the kitchen):*   Yes! Yes. Coming! It's very smart, you realize that, don't you, sweetheart? Even Ben sees it. I gotta go, baby. 'By! 'By! *(Going over to* BEN, *almost dancing)* Imagine? When the mail comes he'll be ahead of Bernard again!

BEN: A perfect proposition all around.

WILLY: Did you see how he cried to me? Oh, if I could kiss him, Ben!

BEN: Time, William, time!

WILLY: Oh, Ben, I always knew one way or another we were gonna make it, Biff and I!

BEN *(Looking at his watch):*   The boat. We'll be late. *(He moves slowly off into the darkness.)*

WILLY *(Elegiacally, turning to the house):*   Now when you kick off, boy, I want a seventy-yard boot, and get right down the field under the ball, and when you hit, hit low and hit hard, because it's important, boy. *(He swings around and faces the audience.)* There's all kinds of important people in the stands, and the first thing you know . . . *(Suddenly, realizing he is alone)* Ben! Ben, where do I . . . ? *(He makes a sudden movement of search.)* Ben, how do I . . . ?

LINDA *(Calling):*   Willy, you coming up?

WILLY *(Uttering a gasp of fear, whirling about as if to quiet her):*   Sh! *(He turns around as if to find his way; sounds, faces, voices, seem to be swarming in upon him and he flicks at them, crying.)* Sh! Sh! *(Suddenly music, faint and high, stops him. It rises in intensity, almost to an unbearable scream. He goes up and down on his toes, and rushes off around the house.)* Shhh!

LINDA: Willy?

(There is no answer. LINDA waits. BIFF gets up off his bed. He is still in his clothes. HAPPY sits up. BIFF stands listening.)

LINDA *(With real fear):*   Willy, answer me! Willy!

(There is the sound of a car starting and moving away at full speed.)

LINDA: No!

BIFF *(Rushing down the stairs):*   Pop!

(As the car speeds off, the music crashes down in a frenzy of sound, which becomes the soft pulsation of a single cello string. BIFF slowly returns to his bedroom. HE and HAPPY gravely don their jackets. LINDA slowly walks out of her room. The music has developed into a dead march. The leaves of day are appearing over everything. CHARLEY and BERNARD, somberly dressed, appear and knock on the kitchen door. BIFF and HAPPY slowly descend the stairs to the kitchen as CHARLEY and BERNARD enter. All stop a moment when LINDA, in clothes of mourning, bearing a little bunch of roses, comes through the draped doorway into the kitchen. She goes to CHARLEY and takes his arm. Now all move toward the audience, through the wall-line of the kitchen. At the limit of the apron, LINDA lays down the flowers, kneels, and sits back on her heels. All stare down at the grave.)

REQUIEM

CHARLEY: It's getting dark, Linda.

(LINDA doesn't react. She stares at the grave.)

BIFF: How about it, Mom? Better get some rest, heh? They'll be closing the gate soon.

(LINDA makes no move. Pause.)

HAPPY *(Deeply angered):* He had no right to do that. There was no necessity for it. We would've helped him.

CHARLEY *(Grunting):* Hmmm.

BIFF: Come along, Mom.

LINDA: Why didn't anybody come?

CHARLEY: It was a very nice funeral.

LINDA: But where are all the people he knew? Maybe they blame him.

CHARLEY: Naa. It's a rough world, Linda. They wouldn't blame him.

LINDA: I can't understand it. At this time especially. First time in thirty-five years we were just about free and clear. He only needed a little salary. He was even finished with the dentist.

CHARLEY: No man only needs a little salary.

LINDA: I can't understand it.

BIFF: There were a lot of nice days. When he'd come home from a trip; or on Sundays, making the stoop; finishing the cellar; putting on the new porch; when he built the extra bathroom; and put up the garage. You know something, Charley, there's more of him in that front stoop than in all the sales he ever made.

CHARLEY: Yeah. He was a happy man with a batch of cement.

LINDA: He was so wonderful with his hands.

BIFF: He had the wrong dreams. All, all, wrong.

HAPPY *(Almost ready to fight* BIFF): Don't say that!

BIFF: He never knew who he was.

CHARLEY *(Stopping* HAPPY's *movement and reply. To* BIFF): Nobody dast blame this man. You don't understand: Willy was a salesman. And for a salesman, there is no rock bottom to the life. He don't put a bolt to a nut, he don't tell you the law or give you medicine. He's a man way out there in the blue, riding on a smile and a shoeshine. And when they start not smiling back—that's an earthquake. And then you get yourself a couple of spots on your hat, and you're finished. Nobody dast blame this man. A salesman is got to dream, boy. It comes with the territory.

BIFF: Charley, the man didn't know who he was.

HAPPY *(Infuriated):* Don't say that!

BIFF: Why don't you come with me, Happy?

HAPPY: I'm not licked that easily. I'm staying right in this city, and I'm gonna beat this racket! *(He looks at* BIFF, *his chin set.)* The Loman Brothers!

BIFF: I know who I am, kid.

HAPPY: All right, boy. I'm gonna show you and everybody else that Willy Loman did not die in vain. He had a good dream. It's the only dream you can have—to come out number-one man. He fought it out here, and this is where I'm gonna win it for him.

BIFF *(With a hopeless glance at* HAPPY, *bends toward his mother):* Let's go, Mom.

LINDA: I'll be with you in a minute. Go on, Charley. *(He hesitates.)* I want to, just for a minute. I never had a chance to say good-by.

(CHARLEY moves away, followed by HAPPY. BIFF remains a slight distance up and left of LINDA. She sits there, summoning herself. The flute begins, not far away, playing behind her speech.)

LINDA: Forgive me, dear. I can't cry. I don't know what it is, but I can't cry. I don't understand it. Why did you ever do that? Help me, Willy, I can't cry. It seems to me that you're just on another trip. I keep expecting you. Willy, dear, I can't cry. Why did you do it? I search and search and I search, and I can't understand it, Willy. I made the last payment on the house today. Today, dear. And there'll be nobody home. *(A sob rises in her throat.)* We're free and clear. *(Sobbing more fully, released):* We're free. *(BIFF comes slowly toward her.)* We're free . . . We're free . . .

(BIFF lifts her to her feet and moves out up right with her in his arms. LINDA sobs quietly. BERNARD and CHARLEY come together and follow them, followed by HAPPY. Only the music of the flute is left on the darkening stage as over the house the hard towers of the apartment buildings rise into sharp focus.)

THE CURTAIN FALLS

Writing Assignments for "Death of a Salesman"

I. Brief Papers: Act I

A. 1. In describing the Loman house, the playwright says, "an air of dream clings to the place, a dream rising out of reality." Make a list of the words that ascribe a dream quality to the house and setting and another list of words that suggest reality. Then write a unified paragraph that explains how the stage setting announces a conflict between dream and reality.

2. Show that in this act Willy tends to contradict himself when he is talking to or about Biff.

3. Show that Biff desires two contradictory ways of life.

4. Show that Happy desires two contradictory ways of life.

5. Contrast Willy's and Ben's ideas on what it takes to become a success.

6. Show that Willy encourages his boys to lie, cheat, and steal.

B. 1. Argue for or against the assertion that Willy is right in thinking that high school popularity is a good indication of future success.

2. Some say that Linda is just as deluded as the Loman men in believing that Oliver will back Biff and that the boys' idea of selling sporting goods is "marvelous." Others say that Linda is too level-headed to believe in the Oliver scheme but that she goes along in order to boost Willy's morale. How do you understand Linda's behavior in this scene? In developing your argument explain why the opposing position is inadequate.

3. Some say that Miller is careless or unobservant in representing Biff's popularity. They claim that star quarterbacks may have a good deal of status but that girls do not "pay for them" and their friends do not hang around like servants waiting to clean the basement. Support or attack this criticism.

C. 1. How do you respond to Willy's belief that the key to success is being well liked? How does this response affect your reading of the play?

   2. How do you respond to Happy's and Biff's plan to start a sporting goods business, and how does this response affect your reading of the play?

II. Setting in "Death of a Salesman"

Combine the following elements into a coherent paragraph that explains the function of *setting* in *Death of a Salesman*.

1. The setting is usually a clue.
2. The clue is to the subject of a play or movie.
3. The clue is to the conflict of a play or movie.

4. The subject is horror.
5. The setting is a mansion.
6. The mansion is old.
7. The mansion is run-down.
8. The setting is night.
9. The setting is stormy.
10. This is a conventional setting.
11. It is the setting for a struggle.
12. The heroine struggles.
13. She struggles with evil and monstrous forces.

14. The subject is success.
15. The setting is a skyscraper.
16. The skyscraper is gleaming.
17. The skyscraper is like the one shown in *Dallas*.
18. *Dallas* is a popular TV show.
19. The setting is appropriate.
20. There are financial schemes.
21. The schemes are made by the rich and the ambitious.

22. *Death of a Salesman* has a subject.
23. The subject is success.
24. The focus is different.
25. The focus is not on the strong and the wealthy.
26. The setting announces the focus.
27. The focus is on the weak and the low.
28. The focus is on the Loman family.

29. Willy's house is "small, fragile seeming."
30. It is illuminated by "the blue light of the sky."
31. Buildings surround the house.
32. They are "towering angular shapes."
33. They are illuminated by an "angry glow of orange."

34. We are told this.
35. Willy's house has "an air of dream."
36. It is possibly the old American dream.
37. The dream is of equality and goodness.
38. The dream is of happy families.
39. The families live among caring neighbors.
40. They live on tree-lined streets.

41. This dream is opposed.
42. It is opposed by hostile buildings.
43. The buildings seem to represent reality.
44. The reality is urban growth.
45. The reality is cutthroat competition.
46. The reality is conspicuous wealth.

47. The setting announces the play's central conflict.
48. The setting also suggests this.
49. The old dream does not have much chance.
50. It does not have much chance in modern America.
51. This goes along with the title.
52. This goes along with the opening image of the weary salesman.

III. Brief Papers: Act II and Requiem

A. 1. Why is the woman in Boston so often characterized by laughter?
   2. Show how all the young men in Act II, Howard and Bernard as well as Happy and Biff, contribute to Willy's collapse in Frank's Chop House.
   3. When Willy leaves Frank's Chop House, he says to Stanley, "I've got to get some seeds right away. Nothing's planted. I don't have a thing in the ground" (p. 1189). Show how Willy's desire to plant runs through this act and explain its relation to the central action.
   4. Near the end of this act Ben keeps saying, "The jungle is dark but full of diamonds" (p. 1196). Explain what Ben means and how this metaphor influences the action.
   5. With careful attention to the immediate context, explain what Bernard means when he says, "Sometimes it's better for a man just to walk away" (p. 1173).
   6. Explain the meaning of the expression "business is business" in the context of the play.

B. 1. In response to a question about Howard's justification for firing Willy, one student writes the following. Write a brief paper explaining why you agree or disagree with this opinion.

   > I don't feel that Howard is justified in firing Willy. Not only should Willy not be fired but he should be promoted to a desk job, at the very least. Willy has poured his heart and soul into the company for thirty-four years and has got nothing in return except a pat on the back. He has

tremendous experience and in 1928 he "averaged a hundred and seventy dollars a week in commissions." His record obviously speaks for itself, but Howard has the nerve to dismiss such an outstanding employee. Willy could only benefit the company because his presence and experience would help the younger employees to become the same kind of success. Howard, however, feels differently about the situation and lets go a hidden "gold mine" in dismissing Willy.

2. Some say that the lies Happy tells to Stanley, Letta, and Miss Forsythe are essentially harmless and amusing. These lies are part of a game that everybody plays and understands, and they do not hurt anyone. Argue for or against this view.
3. Some say the Requiem is a flaw in the play. They offer two specific objections:
   a. Charley's defense of Willy ("Nobody dast blame this man") is inconsistent with the main action and is contrary to Charley's earlier criticism of Willy.
   b. Linda's farewell is soap opera sentimentality.
   Argue for or against either objection.

C. 1. How does the demonstration with the recording machine affect your response to the scene with Howard?
   2. How does the reference to the box of stockings affect your response to the hotel scene?
   3. How do you feel about Biff's behavior after he finds the woman in Willy's room? How do you think a son should behave after such a discovery?
   4. How do you respond to Happy's decision to stay in the city, make good, and show the world that "Willy Loman did not die in vain" (p. 1198)?

IV. Music in "Death of a Salesman"

Combine the following elements into a coherent paragraph that explains the use of music in Death of a Salesman.

1. This happens in Death of a Salesman.
2. Arthur Miller uses music.
3. The music identifies characters.
4. The music establishes mood.
5. The music especially reinforces conflict.

6. This happens in the opening scene.
7. "A melody is heard, played upon a flute, small and fine, telling of grass and trees and the horizon."

8. The music seems to suggest this.
9. There is a desire for an open and natural style of life.
10. The music seems to reinforce the "air of dream."

11. The "air of dream" clings to the house.
12. The dream is opposed to the tall apartment buildings.
13. Willy says the apartment buildings have "boxed us in."

14. This happens later.
15. Flute music is associated with Willy's father.
16. Willy's father made his living traveling in a wagon.
17. Willy's father sold flutes.
18. Willy's father made the flutes himself.

19. Ben is also identified with flute music.
20. This is perhaps the reason.
21. Ben had financial success.
22. Ben reminds Willy of his own lost opportunities.

23. The flute music helps establish Willy's sense of loss.
24. The "gay and bright" music is associated with the boys.
25. The "gay and bright" music represents this.
26. Willy continually has hopes for the future.
27. Willy especially has hopes for Biff.

28. Willy remembers this.
29. Biff was a popular and brilliant quarterback.
30. The boys' music is heard.
31. The boys' music is heard again.
32. Willy thinks Biff will get a loan from Oliver.

33. There is the nostalgic flute music and the hopeful music of the boys.
34. This music is opposed to "raw and sensuous" music.
35. "Raw and sensuous" music is first associated with the woman in the Boston hotel.

36. There is a similar "raucous" music.
37. This music is heard in Frank's Chop House.
38. In Frank's Chop House the sons betray their father.
39. The Chop House scene provides a counterpoint to the hotel scene.
40. In the hotel scene Biff feels betrayed by his father.

41. This finally happens.
42. Willy dies.
43. The "music rises in intensity, almost to an unbearable scream."
44. This music is a shocking contrast.
45. It contrasts with the dreamy flute music.
46. The dreamy flute music opens the play.

V. Longer Papers

   A. Ben, Howard, and Charley are all successful capitalists. Based on a comparative analysis of their behavior, write a paper explaining the relationship between character and capitalism. Does the play suggest that you have to be ruthless and insensitive to succeed, or that business success creates insensitivity, or what?

   B. Like Ibsen's *Hedda Gabler, Death of a Salesman* belongs primarily in the tradition of nineteenth-century realism, but it employs some techniques that go beyond realism. Music is used throughout the play to identify characters and to express a certain feeling or setting: the flute music is "small and fine, telling of grass and trees and the horizon." Lighting is also used in ways that go beyond what we might expect to see in actual life. And, finally, Willy's inner conflicts are expressed by scenes which emerge, as it were, from his subconscious mind. Show how these techniques affect our understanding of the play.

   C. Some say that Willy's affair with the woman in Boston is a flaw in the play; they claim Biff's discovery is at best a secondary cause of his failure and that to make the affair seem important is to misrepresent the real cause of trouble in the Loman family. Argue for or against this assertion.

   D. Argue for or against the assertion that the play makes a convincing and coherent attack on capitalistic methods and values.

   E. Many agree with Biff in blaming Willy for the "wrong dreams" that have ruined the Loman family. But others agree with Charley that "nobody dast blame this man." Argue for one or the other of these judgments.

   F. Like much of American literature, *Death of a Salesman* is said to be antiurban and anticapitalist. City life is represented as ugly, hostile, and inhuman; money-making is represented as a tedious grind and its reward (in material luxury and playboy opportunities) provides no real satisfaction. How do you respond to this view of city life?

TOM STOPPARD
The Real Thing

Before Reading

Write for 10 minutes on one of the following questions:

1. When you call love "the real thing," do you expect it will last forever or just until you fall in love again?
2. Do you think that lovers should have exclusive sexual rights to each other?

CHARACTERS
Max, 40-ish
Charlotte, 35-ish
Henry, 40-ish

Annie, 30-ish
Billy, 22-ish
Brodie, 25

ACT 1

SCENE 1   MAX *and* CHARLOTTE.   MAX *doesn't have to be physically impressive, but you wouldn't want him for an enemy.* CHARLOTTE *doesn't have to be especially attractive, but you instantly want her for a friend.*

Living-room. Architect's drawing board, perhaps. A partly open door leads to an unseen hall and an unseen front door. One or two other doors to other rooms.

MAX *is alone, sitting in a comfortable chair, with a glass of wine and an open bottle to hand. He is using a pack of playing cards to build a pyramidical, tiered viaduct on the coffee table in front of him. He is about to add a pair of playing cards (leaning against each other to hold each other up), and the pyramid is going well. Beyond the door to the hall, the front door is heard being opened with a key. The light from there changes as the unseen front door is opened.*

MAX *does not react to the opening of the door, which is more behind him than in front of him.*

MAX: Don't slam—

(The front door slams, not violently. The viaduct of cards collapses.)

(Superfluously, philosophically.) . . . the door.

*(*CHARLOTTE, *in the hall, wearing a topcoat, looks round the door just long enough to say two words and disappears again.)*

CHARLOTTE: It's me.

THE REAL THING by Tom Stoppard (1938–   ), one of England's foremost playwrights. This play was first performed in London in 1982.

(MAX leaves the cards where they have fallen. He takes a drink from the glass. He doesn't look up at all.)

(CHARLOTTE, without the topcoat, comes back into the room carrying a small suitcase and a plastic duty-free airport bag. She puts the case down and comes up behind MAX's chair and kisses the top of his head.)

CHARLOTTE: Hello.

MAX: Hello, lover.

CHARLOTTE: That's nice. You used to call me lover.

(She drops the airport bag on his lap and returns towards the suitcase.)

MAX: Oh, it's you. I thought it was my lover. *(He doesn't look at his present. He puts the bag on the floor by his chair.)* Where is it you've been?

(The question surprises her. She is deflected from picking up her suitcase—presumably to take it into the bedroom—and the case remains where it is.)

CHARLOTTE: Well, Swittzerland, of course. Weren't you listening? *(MAX finally looks at her.)*

MAX: You look well. Done you good.

CHARLOTTE: What, since yesterday?

MAX: Well, something has. How's Ba'l?

CHARLOTTE: Who? *(MAX affects to puzzle very briefly over her answer.)*

MAX: I meant Ba'l.
Do you say 'Basel'?*
I say Ba'l.

CHARLOTTE: Oh . . . yes. I say Basel.

MAX: *(Lilts.)* "*Let's* call the whole thing *off . . .*"

(CHARLOTTE studies him briefly, quizzically.)

CHARLOTTE: Fancy a drink? *(She notes the glass, the bottle and his behaviour.)* *(Pointedly, but affectionately.)* Another drink?

(He smiles at her, empties his glass and holds it up for her. She takes the glass, finds a second glass, pours wine into both glasses and gives MAX his own glass.)

MAX: How's old Basel, then? Keeping fit?

CHARLOTTE: Are you a tiny bit sloshed?

MAX: Certainly.

CHARLOTTE: I didn't go to Basel. *(MAX is discreetly but definitely interested by that.)*

MAX: No? Where did you go, then?

CHARLOTTE: Geneva.

MAX: *(MAX is surprised. He cackles.)* Geneva! *(He drinks from his glass.)* How's old Geneva, then? Franc doing well?

CHARLOTTE: Who? *(MAX affects surprise.)*

*Basel: City in Switzerland.

MAX: The Swiss franc. Is it doing well?

CHARLOTTE: Are you all right?

MAX: Absolutely.

CHARLOTTE: How have you got on?

MAX: Not bad. My best was eleven pairs on the bottom row, but I ran out of cards.

CHARLOTTE: What about the thing you were working on? . . . What is it?

MAX: An hotel.

CHARLOTTE: Yes. You were two elevators short.

MAX: I've cracked it.

CHARLOTTE: Good.

MAX: I'm turning the whole place on its side and making it a bungalow. I still have a problem with the rooftop pool. As far as I can see, all the water is going to fall into the shallow end. How's the lake, by the way?

CHARLOTTE: What lake?

MAX: *(He affects surprise.)* Lake Geneva. You haven't been to Loch Ness, have you? Lake Geneva. It is at Geneva? It must be. They wouldn't call it Lake Geneva if it was at Ba'l or Basel. They'd call it Lake Ba'l or Basel. You know the Swiss. Utterly reliable. And they've done it without going digital, that's what I admire so much. They know it's all a snare and a delusion. I can remember digitals when they first came out. You had to give your wrist a vigorous shake like bringing down a thermometer, and the only place you could buy one was Tokyo. But it looked all over for the fifteen-jewelled movement. Men ran through the market place shouting, 'The cog is dead.' But still the Swiss didn't panic. In fact, they made a few digitals themselves, as a feint to draw the Japanese further into the mire, and got on with numbering the bank accounts. And now you see how the Japs are desperately putting hands on their digital watches. It's yodelling in the dark. They can yodel till the cows come home. The days of the digitals are numbered. The metaphor is built into them like a self-destruct mechanism. Mark my words, I was right about the skateboard, I was right about *nouvelle cuisine,* and I'll be proved right about the digital watch. Digitals have got no class, you see. They're science and technology. Makes nonsense of a decent pair of cufflinks, as the Swiss are the first to understand. Good sale? *(CHARLOTTE stares at him.)*

CHARLOTTE: What?

MAX: *(He affects surprise.)* Good sale. Was the sale good? The sale in Geneva, how was it? Did it go well in Geneva, the sale?

CHARLOTTE: What's the matter?

MAX: I'm showing an interest in your work. I thought you liked me showing an interest in your work. *My* showing. Save the gerund and screw the whale. Yes, I'm sure you do. I remember how cross you got when I said to someone, "My wife works for Sotheby's or Christie's,* I forget which." You misjudged me, as it happens. You thought I was being smart at your

*Sotheby's or Christie's: Outstanding auction houses in London.

expense. In fact, I had forgotten. How's old Christie, by the way? *(Strikes his forehead.)* There I go. How's old Sothers, by the way? Happy with the Geneva sale, I trust? *(CHARLOTTE puts her glass down and moves to stand facing him.)*

CHARLOTTE: *(To call a halt.)* All right.

MAX: Just all right? Well, that's the bloody Swiss for you. Conservative, you see. The Japs could show them a thing or two. They'd have a whaling fleet in Lake Geneva by now. How's the skiing, by the way? Plenty of snow?

CHARLOTTE: Stop it—stop it—*stop it.*
What have I done?

MAX: You forgot your passport.

CHARLOTTE: I did what?

MAX: You went to Switzerland without your passport.

CHARLOTTE: What makes you think that?

MAX: I found it in your recipe drawer.

CHARLOTTE: *(Quietly.)* Jesus God.

MAX: Quite.

(CHARLOTTE moves away and looks at him with some curiosity.)

CHARLOTTE: What were you looking for?

MAX: Your passport.

CHARLOTTE: It's about the last place I would have looked.

MAX: It was.

CHARLOTTE: Why were you looking for it?

MAX: I didn't know it was going to be your passport. If you see what I mean.

CHARLOTTE: I think I do. You go through my things when I'm away? *(Pause. Puzzled.)* Why?

MAX: I liked it when I found nothing. You should have just put it in your handbag. We'd still be an ideal couple. So to speak.

CHARLOTTE: Wouldn't you have checked to see if it had been stamped?

MAX: That's a very good point. I notice that you never went to Amsterdam when you went to Amsterdam. I must say I take my hat off to you, coming home with Rembrandt place mats for your mother. It's those little touches that lift adultery out of the moral arena and make it a matter of style.

CHARLOTTE: I wouldn't go on, if I were you.

MAX: Rembrandt place mats! I wonder who's got the originals. Some Arab, is it? 'Dinner's ready, Abdul, put the Rembrandts on the table.'

CHARLOTTE: It's like when we were burgled. The same violation. Worse.

MAX: I'm not a burglar. I'm your husband.

CHARLOTTE: As I said. Worse.

MAX: Well, I'm sorry.
I think I just apologized for finding out that you've deceived me.
Yes, I did.
How does she do it?

(She moves away, to leave the room.)

Are you going somewhere?

CHARLOTTE: I'm going to bed.

MAX: Aren't you going to tell me who it is?

CHARLOTTE: Who what is?

MAX: Your lover, lover.

CHARLOTTE: Which lover?

MAX: I assumed there'd only be the one.

CHARLOTTE: Did you?

MAX: Well, do you see them separately or both together?

Sorry, that's not fair.

Well, tell you what, nod your head if it's separately. *(She looks at him.)* Heavens.

If you have an opening free, I'm not doing much at the moment. Or is the position taken?

It is only two, is it?

Nod your head. *(She looks at him.)*

Golly, you are a dark horse. How do they all three get away at the same time? Do they work together, like the Marx Brothers?

I'm not upsetting you, I hope?

CHARLOTTE: You underestimate me.

MAX: *(Interested.)* Do I? A string quartet, you mean? That sort of thing? *(He ponders for a moment.)*

What does the fourth one do? *(She raises her hand.)*

Got it. Plays by himself.

You can slap me if you like. I won't slap you back. I abhor cliché. It's one of the things that has kept me faithful.

(CHARLOTTE returns to the hall and reappears wearing her topcoat.)

CHARLOTTE: If you don't mind, I think I will go out after all. *(She moves to close the door behind her.)*

MAX: You've forgotten your suitcase.

(Pause. She comes back and picks up the suitcase. She takes the case to the door.)

CHARLOTTE: I'm sorry if you've had a bad time. But you've done everything wrong. There's a right thing to say if you can think what it is. *(She waits a moment while MAX thinks.)*

MAX: Is it anyone I know?

CHARLOTTE: You aren't anyone I know.

(She goes out, closing the door, and then the front door is heard opening and closing.)

(MAX remains seated. After a moment he reaches down for the airport bag, puts it back on his lap and looks inside it. He starts to laugh. He withdraws from the bag a miniature Alp in a glass bowl. He gives the bowl a shake and creates a snowstorm within it. Then the snowstorm envelops the stage. Music—a pop record—makes a bridge into the next scene.)

SCENE 2   HENRY, CHARLOTTE, MAX *and* ANNIE.   HENRY *is amiable but can take care of himself.* CHARLOTTE *is less amiable and can take even better care of herself.* MAX *is nice, seldom assertive, conciliatory.* ANNIE *is very much like the woman whom* CHARLOTTE *has ceased to be.*

A living-room. A record player and shelves of records. Sunday newspapers. The music is coming from the record player.

HENRY, *with several record sleeves around him, is searching for a particular piece of music.*

There are doors to hall, kitchen, bedroom. CHARLOTTE *enters barefoot, wearing* HENRY's *dressing-gown which is too big for her. She is unkempt from sleep and seems generally disordered.*

HENRY *looks up briefly.*

HENRY: Hello.

*(*CHARLOTTE *moves forward without answering, sits down and looks around in a hopeless way.)*

CHARLOTTE: Oh, God.

HENRY: I thought you'd rather lie in. Do you want some coffee?

CHARLOTTE: I don't know. *(Possibly referring to the litter of record sleeves, wanly.)* What a mess.

HENRY: Don't worry . . . don't worry . . .

*(*HENRY *continues to search among the records.)*

CHARLOTTE: I think I'll just stay in bed.

HENRY: Actually, I phoned Max.

CHARLOTTE: What? Why?

HENRY: He was on my conscience. He's coming round.

CHARLOTTE: *(Quite strongly.)* I don't want to see *him*.

HENRY: Sorry.

CHARLOTTE: Honestly, Henry.

HENRY: Hang on—I think I've found it.

(He removes the pop record, which might have come to its natural end by now, from the record player and puts a different record on. Meanwhile—)

CHARLOTTE: Are you still doing your list?

HENRY: Mmm.

CHARLOTTE: Have you got a favourite book?

HENRY: *Finnegans Wake.* *

CHARLOTTE: Have you read it?

HENRY: Don't be silly.

(He lowers the arm on to the record and listens to a few bars of alpine Strauss—or sub-Strauss. Then he lifts the arm again.)

No . . . No . . . Damnation.

Finnegans Wake: A novel (1939) by James Joyce.

(He starts to put the record away.)

Do you remember when we were in some place like Bournemouth* or Deauville,† and there was an open-air dance floor right outside our window?

CHARLOTTE: No.

HENRY: Yes you do, I was writing my Sartre‡ play, and there was this bloody orchestra which kept coming back to the same tune every twenty minutes, so I started shouting out of the window and the hotel manager—

CHARLOTTE: That was St. Moritz.§ *(Scornfully.) Bournemouth.*

HENRY: Well, what was it?

CHARLOTTE: What was what?

HENRY: What was the tune called? It sounded like Strauss or somebody.

CHARLOTTE: How does it go?

HENRY: I don't know, do I?

CHARLOTTE: Who were you with in Bournemouth?

HENRY: Don't mess about. I'm supposed to give them my eight records tomorrow, and so far I've got five and *Finnegans Wake.*

CHARLOTTE: Well, if you don't know what it's called and you can't remember how it goes, why in Christ's name do you want it on your desert island?

HENRY: It's not supposed to be eight records you love and adore.

CHARLOTTE: Yes, it is.

HENRY: It is not. It's supposed to be eight records you associate with turning-points in your life.

CHARLOTTE: Well, I'm a turning-point in your life, and when you took me to St. Moritz your favourite record was the Ronettes doing 'Da Doo Ron Ron.'

HENRY: The Crystals. *(Scornfully.)* The Ronettes.

(CHARLOTTE gets up and during the following searches, successfully, for a record, which she ends up putting on the machine.)

CHARLOTTE: You're going about this the wrong way. Just pick your eight all-time greats and then remember what you were doing at the time. What's wrong with that?

HENRY: I'm supposed to be one of your intellectual playwrights. I'm going to look a total prick, aren't I, going on the radio to announce that while I was telling Jean-Paul Sartre that he was essentially superficial, I was spending the whole time listening to the Crystals singing 'Da Doo Ron Ron.' Look, ages ago, Debbie put on one of those classical but not too classical records—she must have been about ten or eleven, it was before she dyed her hair—and I said to you, "That's that bloody tune they were

---

*Bournemouth: A resort town in England.

†Deauville: A resort town in France.

‡Sarte: Jean-Paul Sarte (1905–1980), French philospher and the literary leader of the Existentialist movement in the post–World War II ear. Sarte was awarded, but declined, the Nobel Prize for Literature in 1964.

§St. Moritz: A resort town in Switzerland.

driving me mad with when I was trying to write 'Jean-Paul is up the Wall' in that hotel in Switzerland." Maybe *she'll* remember.

CHARLOTTE: Where is she?

(CHARLOTTE has placed the record on the machine, which now starts to play the Skater's Waltz.)

HENRY: Riding stables.
That's it! *(Triumphant and pleased, examining the record sleeve.) Skater's Waltz!* How did you know?

CHARLOTTE: They don't have open-air dance floors in the Alps in mid-winter. They have skating rinks. Now you've got six.

HENRY: Oh, I can't use that. It's so banal.

(The doorbell rings. HENRY goes to take the record off the machine.)

That's Max. Do you want to let him in?

CHARLOTTE: No. Say I'm not here.

HENRY: He knows perfectly well you're here. Where else would you be? I'll say you don't want to see him because you've seen quite enough of him. How's that?

CHARLOTTE: *(Giving up.)* Oh, I'll get dressed.

(She goes out the way she came in, towards the bedroom. HENRY goes out through another door into the hall. His voice and MAX's voice are heard, and the two men come in immediately afterwards.)

HENRY: Hello, Max. Come in.

MAX: Hello, Henry.

HENRY: *(Entering.)* It's been some time. *(MAX enters unassertively.)*

MAX: Well, you've rather been keeping out of the way, haven't you?

HENRY: Yes. I'm sorry, Max. *(Indicating the bedroom.)* Charlotte's not here. How are you?

MAX: I'm all right.

HENRY: Good.

MAX: And you?

HENRY: I'm all right.

MAX: Good.

HENRY: Well, we all seem to be all right.

MAX: Is Charlotte all right?

HENRY: I don't think she's terribly happy. Well, is it coffee or open a bottle?

MAX: Bottle, I should think.

HENRY: Hang on, then.

(HENRY goes out through the door to the kitchen. MAX turns aside and looks at a paper without interest. CHARLOTTE enters from the bedroom, having dressed without trying hard. She regards MAX, who then notices her.)

MAX: Hello, darling.

CHARLOTTE: Don't I get a day off?

MAX: *(Apologetically.)* Henry phoned . . .

CHARLOTTE: *(More kindly.)* It's all right, Max.

(HENRY enters busily from the kitchen, carrying an open champagne bottle and a jug of orange juice. Wine glasses are available in the living-room. HENRY puts himself in charge of arranging the drinks.)

HENRY: Hello, Charlotte. I was just telling Max you weren't here. So nice to see you, Max. What are you doing with yourself?

MAX: Is he joking?

HENRY: I mean apart from that. Actors are so sensitive. They feel neglected if one isn't constantly going round to the theatre to check up on them.

MAX: I was just telling Henry off for keeping out of the way.

CHARLOTTE: You'd keep out of the way if you'd written it. *(To HENRY.)* If that orange juice is for me, you can forget it.

HENRY: No, no—buck's fizz all round. I feel reckless, extravagant, famous, in love, and I'm next week's castaway on *Desert Island Discs.*

MAX: Are you really?

HENRY: Head over heels. Here you are, lover.
How was last night, by the way? *(He hands MAX and CHARLOTTE their glasses.)*

CHARLOTTE: Hopeless. I had to fake it again.

HENRY: Very witty woman, my present wife. Actually, I was talking about my play.

CHARLOTTE: Actually, so was I. I've decided it's a mistake appearing in Henry's play.

MAX: Not for me, it isn't.

CHARLOTTE: Well, of course not for you, you idiot, you're not his wife.

MAX: Oh, I see what you mean.

CHARLOTTE: Max sees what I mean. You're right, Max.

MAX: I never said anything!

HENRY: How was it really?—last night.

CHARLOTTE: Not good. The stalls had a deserted look, about two-thirds, I should think. *(With false innocence.)* Oh, sorry, darling, is that what you meant?

MAX: *(Disapproving.)* Honestly, Charlotte. It was all right, Henry, *really.* All the laughs were in place, for a Saturday night anyway, and I had someone who came round afterwards who said the reconciliation scene was extremely moving. Actually, that reminds me. They *did* say—I mean, it's a tiny thing but I thought I'd pass it on because I do feel rather the same way . . . I mean all that stuff about the Japanese and digital watches—they suddenly have no idea what I'm talking about, you see, and I thought if we could just try it one night without—*(HENRY halts him, like a traffic policeman.)*

HENRY: Excuse me, Max. *(HENRY turns to CHARLOTTE.)*
Two-thirds empty or two-thirds full? *(CHARLOTTE laughs brazenly.)*

CHARLOTTE: Hard luck, Max. *(She toasts.)* Well, here's to closing night. To the collapse of *House of Cards.*

MAX: *(Shocked.)* Charlotte!

CHARLOTTE: Well, you try playing the feed one night instead of acting Henry after a buck's fizz and two rewrites. All *his* laughs are in place all right. So's my groan. Groan, groan, they all go when they find out. Oh, *groan,* so she hasn't got a lover at all, eh? And they lose interest in me totally. I'm a victim of Henry's fantasy—a quiet, faithful bird with an interesting job, and a recipe drawer, and a stiff upper lip, and two semi-stiff lower ones all trembling for him—'I'm sorry if you've had a bad time . . . There's a right thing to say now . . .'

MAX: Jesus, Charlotte—

CHARLOTTE: *(Quite genially.)* Oh, shut up, Max. If he'd given her a lover instead of a temporary passport, we'd be in a play.

HENRY: It's a little early in the day for all this.

CHARLOTTE: No, darling, it's a little late.

MAX: Er, where's young Deborah today?

CHARLOTTE: Who?

MAX: Debbie.

CHARLOTTE: *(Baffled.)* Debbie?

MAX: Your daughter.

CHARLOTTE: Oh, daughter.

HENRY: Riding school.

CHARLOTTE: Must be some mistake. Smart talk, that's the thing. Having children is so unsmart. Endless dialogue about acne. Henry couldn't do that. He doesn't like research.

HENRY: True.

MAX: *(To* CHARLOTTE.*)* Lots of people don't have children, in real life. Me and Annie . . .

HENRY: Oh, don't—I told her once that lots of women were only good for fetching drinks, and she became quite unreasonable. *(Blithely, knowing what he is doing,* HENRY *holds his empty glass towards* CHARLOTTE.*)* Is there any more of that? *(*MAX *glances at* CHARLOTTE *and hastily tries to defuse the bomb.)*

MAX: Let me . . . *(*MAX *takes* HENRY*'s glass and fills it from the bottle and the jug.)*

CHARLOTTE: Lots of *men* are only good for fetching drinks—why don't you write about *them?* *(*MAX *hands the glass back to* HENRY.*)*

HENRY: *(Smiling up at* MAX.*)* Terribly pleased you could come round.

CHARLOTTE: Oh, yes, you owe him a drink. What an ego trip! Having all the words to come back with just as you need them. That's the difference between plays and real life—thinking time. You don't really think that if Henry caught me out with a lover, he'd sit around being witty about Rembrandt place mats? Like hell he would. He'd come apart like a pick-a-sticks. His sentence structure would go to pot, closely followed by his sphincter. You know that, don't you, Henry? Henry? No answer. Are you there, Henry? Say something witty. *(*HENRY *turns his head to her.)*

HENRY: Is it anyone I know?

MAX: *(Starting to rise.)* Well, look, thanks for the drink—

CHARLOTTE: Oh, sit down, Max, for God's sake, or he'll think it's you.

HENRY: It isn't you, is it, Max?

MAX: Oh, for Christ's sake . . . *(MAX subsides unhappily.)*

HENRY: Just kidding, Max. Badinage. You know, *dialogue. (The doorbell rings.)* See what I mean?

MAX: Annie said she'd come round if her committee finished early. She's on this Justice for Brodie Committee . . . you know . . . *(Pause.)* I'll go, should I?

HENRY: I'll go.

MAX: No, stay where you are, I'll see if it's her. *(MAX goes out to the front door.)*

CHARLOTTE: Thanks very much. Anyone else coming?

HENRY: Just give them a cheese stick. They won't stay.

CHARLOTTE: What did you phone him for in the first place?

HENRY: Well, I only have to write it once. He has to show up every night. I had a conscience.

CHARLOTTE: Do you have a conscience about me too?

HENRY: Absolutely. You can have a cheese stick.

CHARLOTTE: Well, don't ask her about Brodie.

HENRY: Right.

CHARLOTTE: If she starts on about scapegoats and cover-ups, she'll get a cheese stick up her nostril.

HENRY: Right.

CHARLOTTE: *(Enthusiastically.)* Darling! It's been ages!

(ANNIE has entered, followed by MAX. ANNIE is carrying a carrier bag loaded with greengrocery.)

ANNIE: Hello, Charlotte. This is jolly nice of you.

MAX: We can only stay a minute.

ANNIE: How are you, Henry?

HENRY: Fine.

MAX: Annie's stewarding at the protest meeting this afternoon, so we can't—

HENRY: Oh, do shut up. Don't take any notice of Max. I made him nervous.

ANNIE: What did you do to him?

HENRY: Nothing at all. I asked him if he was having an affair with Charlotte, and he was offended.

ANNIE: Was he?

HENRY: Apparently not. Been shopping?

ANNIE: Not exactly. I saw a place open on my way back and . . . Anyway, you might as well take it as an offering.

CHARLOTTE: *(Taking the bag from her and investigating it.)* Darling, there was absolutely no need to bring . . . mushrooms?

ANNIE: Yes.

CHARLOTTE: *(Not quite behaving well.)* And a turnip . . .

ANNIE: *(Getting unhappy.)* And carrots . . . Oh, dear, it must look as if—

HENRY: Where's the meat?

CHARLOTTE: Shut up.

ANNIE: I wish I'd brought flowers now.

CHARLOTTE: This is much nicer.

HENRY: So original. I'll get a vase.

ANNIE: It's supposed to be crudités.*

HENRY: Crudités! Perfect title for a pornographic revue.

CHARLOTTE: I'll make a dip.

MAX: We're not staying to eat, for heaven's sake.

HENRY: Just a quick dip.

ANNIE: Would you like *me* to?

CHARLOTTE: No, no. I know where everything is.

HENRY: Yes, Charlotte will provide dips for the crudity. She knows where everything is.

(CHARLOTTE takes charge of the vegetables. HENRY gets a fourth glass.)

Sit down, have some buck's fizz. I feel reckless, extravagant, famous, and I'm next week's castaway on *Desert Island Discs.* You can be my luxury if you like.

ANNIE: I'm not sure I'm one you can afford.

MAX: What are your eight records?

HENRY: This is the problem. I hate music.

CHARLOTTE: He likes pop music.

HENRY: You don't have to repeat everything I say.

MAX: I don't understand the problem.

CHARLOTTE: The problem is he's a snob without being an inverted snob. He's *ashamed* of liking pop music. *(CHARLOTTE takes the vegetables out into the kitchen, closing the door.)*

HENRY: This is true. The trouble is I don't like the pop music which it's all right to like. You can have a bit of Pink Floyd shoved in between your symphonies and your Dame Janet Baker—that shows a refreshing breadth of taste or at least a refreshing candour—but *I* like Wayne Fontana and the Mindbenders doing "Um Um Um Um Um Um."

MAX: Doing what?

HENRY: That's the title. *(He demonstrates it.)* "Um-Um-Um-Um-Um-Um." I like Neil Sedaka. Do you remember "Oh, Carol"?

MAX: For God's sake.

HENRY: *(Cheerfully.)* Yes, I'm not very up to date. I like Herman's Hermits, and the Hollies, and the Everly Brothers, and Brenda Lee, and the Supremes . . . I don't mean everything they did. I don't like *artists.* I like singles.

MAX: This is sheer pretension.

HENRY: *(Insistently.)* No. It *moves* me, the way people are supposed to be moved by *real* music. I was taken once to Covent Garden† to hear a

---

*crudités: Raw vegetables.

†Covent Garden: A major theater and opera house in London, the home of the Royal Ballet and the Royal Opera.

woman called Callas* in a sort of foreign musical with no dancing which people were donating kidneys to get tickets for. The idea was that I would be cured of my strange disability. As though the place were a kind of Lourdes† for the musically disadvantaged. My illness at the time took the form of believing that the Righteous Brothers' recording of "You've Lost that Lovin' Feelin' " on the London label was possibly the most haunting, the most deeply moving noise ever produced by the human spirit, and this female vocalist person was going to set me right.

MAX: No good?

HENRY: Not even close. That woman would have had a job getting into the top thirty if she were *hyped.*

MAX: You preferred the Brothers.

HENRY: I did. Do you think there's something wrong with me?

MAX: Yes. I'd say you were a moron.

HENRY: What can I do?

MAX: There's nothing you can do.

HENRY: I mean about *Desert Island Discs.*

ANNIE: You know damned well what you should do.

HENRY: Cancel?

MAX: Actually, I remember it. *(He sings, badly.)* "You've lost that lovin' feeling . . ."

HENRY: That's an idea—aversion therapy.

MAX: *(Sings.)* ". . . that lovin' feeling . . . You've lost that lovin' feeling . . ."

HENRY: I think it's working.

MAX: *(Sings.)* ". . . it's gorn, gorn, gorn . . . oh—oh—oh—yeah . . ."

HENRY: *(Happily.)* God, it's *rubbish!* You've cracked it. Now do "Oh Carol."

MAX: I don't know that one.

HENRY: I'll play it for you.

MAX: I think I'll go and help Charlotte.

ANNIE: I should go.

MAX: No. I thought of it first.

(CHARLOTTE enters, carrying a bowl.)

CHARLOTTE: One dip.

MAX: I was coming to help.

CHARLOTTE: All right, you can chop.

MAX: Fine. Chop . . .

(MAX goes out into the kitchen. CHARLOTTE places the bowl and is about to follow MAX out. HENRY dips his finger into the bowl and tastes the dip.)

*Callas: Maria Callas (1923–1977), Greek-American soprano; an outstanding opera star in the post-World War II era.
†Lourdes: A city in the south of France and the site of the famous Catholic shrine of the Blessed Virgin Mary. The waters of Lourdes are supposed to have miraculous healing power.

HENRY: It needs something.

CHARLOTTE: I beg your pardon?

HENRY: It needs something. A bit of interest. Garlic? Lemon juice? I don't know.

CHARLOTTE: *(Coldly.)* Perhaps you should employ a cook.

HENRY: Surely that would be excessive—a cook who spends all her time emptying jars of mayonnaise and adding lemon juice? What would we do with the surplus?

CHARLOTTE: Presumably put it on stage with the rest of your stuff. *(CHARLOTTE goes out into the kitchen, closing the door. Pause.)*

HENRY: Are you all right? *(ANNIE nods.)*

ANNIE: Are you all right? *(HENRY nods.)*
Touch me. *(HENRY shakes his head.)*
Touch me.

HENRY: No.

ANNIE: Come on, touch me.
Help yourself.
Touch me anywhere you like.

HENRY: No.

ANNIE: Touch me.

HENRY: No.

ANNIE: Coward.

HENRY: I love you anyway.

ANNIE: Yes, say that.

HENRY: I love you.

ANNIE: Go on.

HENRY: I love you.

ANNIE: That's it.

HENRY: I love you.

ANNIE: Touch me then. They'll come in or they won't. Take a chance. Kiss me.

HENRY: For Christ's sake.

ANNIE: Quick one on the carpet then.

HENRY: You're crackers.

ANNIE: I'm not interested in your mind.

HENRY: Yes, you are.

ANNIE: No, I'm not, I lied to you. *(Pause. HENRY smiles at her.)*
I hate Sunday.

HENRY: Thought I'd cheer you up with an obscene phone call, but Max got to it first, so I improvised.

ANNIE: I might have come round anyway. "Hello, Henry, Charlotte, just passing, long time no see."

HENRY: That would have been pushing it.

ANNIE: I'm in a mood to push it. Let's go while they're chopping turnips.

HENRY: You *are* crackers.

ANNIE: We'll go, and then it will be done. Max will suffer. Charlotte will make you suffer and get custody. You'll see Debbie on Sundays, and in three years she'll be at university not giving a damn either way.

HENRY: It's not just Debbie.

ANNIE: No, you want to give it time—

HENRY: Yes—

ANNIE: . . . time to go wrong, change, spoil. Then you'll know it wasn't the real thing.

HENRY: I don't steal other men's wives.

ANNIE: Thanks a lot.

HENRY: You know what I mean.

ANNIE: Yes, you mean you love me but you don't want it to get around. Me and the Righteous Brothers. Well, thanks a lot.

(The kitchen door is flung open and MAX *enters rather dramatically, bleeding from a cut finger.)*

MAX: Don't panic! Have you got a hankie?

ANNIE: Max?

*(*ANNIE *and* HENRY *respond appropriately, each searching for a handkerchief.* HENRY *produces one first, a clean white one, from his pocket.)*

HENRY: Here—

MAX: Thanks. No, let me—

ANNIE: Let me see.

MAX: It's all right, it's not as bad as it looks. *(To Henry.)* Typical of your bloody kitchen—all champagne and no paper towels.

ANNIE: Poor love, just hold the cut for a while.

MAX: I think I'll put it back under the tap. *(He moves towards the kitchen.)*

HENRY: Sorry about this, Max. She tried to do it to me once.

*(*MAX *leaves, leaving the door open.* HENRY *and* ANNIE*'s conversation is in no way furtive but pitched to acknowledge the open door.)*

ANNIE: I'm sorry.

HENRY: No, I'm sorry.

ANNIE: It's all right. Anything's all right. *(*HENRY *moves forward and kisses her lightly.)*

HENRY: It'll get better.

ANNIE: How?

HENRY: Maybe we'll get found out.

ANNIE: Better to tell them. Whoever comes in first, eh? If it's Max, I'll tell him. If it's Charlotte, you start.
All right?
It's easy. Like Butch Cassidy and the Sundance Kid jumping off the cliff.
It's only a couple of marriages and a child.
All right?

(CHARLOTTE enters from the kitchen, carrying a tray of chopped-up vegetables.)

(To HENRY.*)* All right?

(This is bold as brass and, consequently, safe as houses: in this way ANNIE *and* HENRY *continue to speak quite privately to each other in the interstices of the general conversation, under or over the respective preoccupations of* CHARLOTTE *and* MAX.*)*

CHARLOTTE: Did Max tell you? It's red cabbage. I've taken him off the knives. He's making another dip. He says it's Hawaiian. It's supposed to be served in an empty pineapple. We haven't got a pineapple. He's going to serve it in an empty tin of pineapple chunks. I do envy you being married to a man with a sense of humour. Henry thinks he has a sense of humour, but what he has is a joke reflex. Eh, Henry? His mind is racing. Pineapple, pineapple . . . Come on, darling.

HENRY: *(To* ANNIE.*)* No. Sorry.

ANNIE: It's all right.

CHARLOTTE: *(Busy with cutlery.)* Is Debbie expecting lunch?

HENRY: *(To* ANNIE.*)* Not really.

CHARLOTTE: What?

HENRY: No. She wants to stay out. *(*ANNIE *drinks what remains in her glass.)*

ANNIE: Where is Debbie?

HENRY: Riding school. Drink? *(*HENRY *takes her empty glass out of her hand.)*

ANNIE: Love you.

CHARLOTTE: She used to eat like a horse, till she had one. *(*HENRY *refills* ANNIE*'s glass.)*

HENRY: I'm picking her up this afternoon. *(He returns* ANNIE*'s glass.)* Buck's fizz all right?

CHARLOTTE: Picking her up?

ANNIE: I don't care.

*(*MAX *enters with the Hawaiian dip in the pineapple tin.)*

MAX: Here we are.

ANNIE: Anything's all right.

MAX: It's Hawaiian.

HENRY: You're a lovely feller.

CHARLOTTE: Well done, Max.

ANNIE: So are you.

(She meets MAX, *dips her finger into the tin and tastes the dip.)*

MAX: I hope I've got it right. What do you think?

(In his other hand MAX *has* HENRY*'s somewhat blood-stained handkerchief, which he now offers back.)*

(To Henry.) Thanks. What should I do with it?

HENRY: *(Taking it.)* It's okay, I'll take it. *(*HENRY *puts the handkerchief in his pocket.)*

ANNIE: *(To* MAX.*)* Not bad. *(To* CHARLOTTE.*)* May I?
CHARLOTTE: Feel free.
ANNIE: Hang on a sec.

(She takes the tin from MAX *and leaves the room with it, going to the kitchen.)*

CHARLOTTE: *(To* HENRY.*)* You're over-protective. She could walk it in half
    an hour.
MAX: Who, what?
CHARLOTTE: Debbie.
HENRY: By the time she finished mucking out, whatever they call it . . .
CHARLOTTE: Grooming the mount, mounting the groom . . .
HENRY: *(Unamused.)* Hilarious.
MAX: *I* wouldn't let her walk. Someone got murdered on the common not
    long ago. Mustn't put temptation in the way.
CHARLOTTE: Debbie wouldn't murder anyone. She'd just duff them up a little
    bit. I can't make her out at all.

(ANNIE *re-enters with the dip.)*

Some people have daughters who love ponies.

(Passing HENRY, ANNIE *casually puts her finger in his mouth, without pausing.)*

ANNIE: What do you think?
CHARLOTTE: Some people have daughters who go punk. We've got one who
    goes riding on Barnes Common looking like the Last of the Mohicans.
HENRY: Crackers. *(* ANNIE *delivers the dip to* CHARLOTTE.*)*
CHARLOTTE: *(To* ANNIE.*)* Is yours a case of sperm count or twisted tubes?
    Or is it that you just can't stand the little buggers?
MAX: Charlotte!
HENRY: What business is that of yours?
CHARLOTTE: He's in love with his, you know.
ANNIE: Isn't that supposed to be normal?
CHARLOTTE: No, dear, normal is the other way round.
HENRY: I say, Annie, what's this Brodie Committee all about? Charlotte was
    asking.
MAX: You know, Private Brodie.
ANNIE: It's all right.
MAX: Annie knows him.
ANNIE: I don't know him.
MAX: Tell them about meeting him on the train.
ANNIE: Yes. I met him on a train.

(Pause. But HENRY, *exhibiting avid interest, disobliges her.)*

HENRY: Yes?
ANNIE: *(Laughs uncomfortably.)* I seem to have told this story before.

HENRY: But we haven't seen you for ages.

MAX: Annie was travelling up to London from our cottage, weren't you?

HENRY: *Were* you?

ANNIE: Yes.

HENRY: *(Fascinated.)* You have a cottage in . . .?

ANNIE: Norfolk.

HENRY: Norfolk! What, up in the hills there?

ANNIE: *(Testily.) What* hills? Norfolk is absolutely—*(She brings herself up short.)*

CHARLOTTE: Oh, very funny. Stop it, Henry.

HENRY: I have no idea what you are talking about. So, you were coming up to London from your Norfolk flat—*cottage*—and you met this Private Brodie on the train.

ANNIE: Yes.

MAX: It was quite remarkable. Brodie was on his way to the anti-missiles demonstration, just like Annie.

HENRY: *Really?*

ANNIE: Yes.

HENRY: How did you know? Was he wearing a "Missiles Out" badge on his uniform?

ANNIE: He wasn't in uniform.

MAX: The guts of it, the sheer moral courage. An ordinary soldier using his weekend pass to demonstrate against their bloody missiles.

HENRY: *Their?* I thought they were ours.

MAX: No, they're American.

HENRY: Oh, yes—*their* . . .

MAX: Pure moral conscience, you see—I mean, he didn't have our motivation.

HENRY: *Our?*

MAX: Mine and Annie's. *(HENRY appears not to understand.)*
Owning property in Little Barmouth.

HENRY: Yes, of course. Private Brodie didn't own a weekend cottage in Little Barmouth, you mean.

MAX: No, he's a Scots lad. He was stationed at the camp down the road. He was practically guarding the base where these rockets are making Little Barmouth into a sitting duck for the Russian counter-attack, should it ever come to that.

HENRY: *(To* ANNIE.) I see what you mean.

ANNIE: Do you?

HENRY: Well, yes. Little Barmouth isn't going to declare war on Russia, so why should Little Barmouth be wiped out in a war not of Little Barmouth's making?

MAX: Quite.

CHARLOTTE: Shut up, Henry.

MAX: Is he being like that?

CHARLOTTE: Yes, he's being like that.

MAX: I don't see what he's got to be like that about.

HENRY: *(Capitulating enthusiastically.)* Absolutely! So you met this Private Brodie on the train, and Brodie said, "I see you're going to the demo down Whitehall." Right?

ANNIE: No. He recognized me from my children's serial. He used to watch *Rosie of the Royal Infirmary* when he was a kid.

MAX: How *about* that? It seems like the day before yesterday Annie was doing *Rosie of the Royal Infirmary.* He's *still* a kid.

ANNIE: Yes. Twenty-one.

MAX: He's a child.

HENRY: He kicked two policemen inside out, didn't he?

MAX: Piss off.
(To CHARLOTTE.*)* If you want to know what it's all about, you should come to the meeting.

CHARLOTTE: I know I should, but I like to keep my Sundays free. For entertaining friends, I mean. Fortunately, there are people like Annie to make up for people like me.

HENRY: Perhaps I'll go.

CHARLOTTE: No, you're people like me. You tell him, Annie.

ANNIE: You're picking up Debbie from riding school.

HENRY: Actually, I think I'll join the Justice for Brodie Committee. I should have thought of that before.

CHARLOTTE: They don't want dilettantes. You have to be properly motivated, like Annie.

HENRY: Brodie just wants to get out of jail. What does he care if we're motivated by the wrong reasons.

MAX: Like what?

HENRY: Perhaps one of us is worried that his image is getting a bit too right-of-centre. Another is in love with a committee member and wishes to gain her approbation . . .

CHARLOTTE: Which one are you?

HENRY: You think I'm kidding, but I'm not. Public postures have the configuration of private derangement.

MAX: Who said that?

HENRY: I did, you fool.

MAX: I mean first.

HENRY: Oh, first. *(To* ANNIE.*)* Take him off to your meeting, I'm sick of him.

ANNIE: He's not coming.

HENRY: *(Savouring it.)* You are not going to the meeting?

MAX: No, actually. Not that I wouldn't, but it would mean letting down my squash partner.

HENRY: Squash partner? An interesting moral dilemma. I wonder what Saint Augustine would have done?

MAX: I don't think Saint Augustine had a squash partner.

HENRY: I know that. Nobody would play with him. Even so. I put myself in his place. I balance a pineapple chunk on my carrot. I ponder. On the one hand, Max's squash partner. Decent chap but not a deprivation of the first magnitude. And on the other hand, Brodie, an out-and-out thug, an arsonist, vandalizer of a national shrine, *but* mouldering in jail for years to come owing, *perhaps,* to society's inability to comprehend a man divided against himself, a pacifist hooligan.

MAX: I don't condone vandalism, however idealistic. I just—

HENRY: Yes, well, as acts of vandalism go, starting a fire on a war memorial using the wreath to the Unknown Soldier as kindling scores very low on discretion. I assumed he was trying to be provocative.

MAX: Of course he was, you idiot. But he got hammered by an emotional backlash.

HENRY: No, no, you *can't*—

MAX: Yes, he bloody was!

HENRY: I mean "hammer" and "backlash." You can't *do it*!

MAX: Oh, for Christ's sake. This is your house, and I'm drinking your wine, but if you don't mind me saying so, Henry—

HENRY: *My* saying, Max.

MAX: Right. *(He puts down his glass definitively and stands up.)*
Come on, Annie.
There's something wrong with you.
You've got something missing. You may have all the words, but having all the words is not what life's about.

HENRY: I'm sorry, but it actually *hurts.*

MAX: Brodie may be no intellectual, like you, but he did march for a cause, and now he's got six years for a stupid piece of bravado and a punch-up, and he'd have been forgotten in a week if it wasn't for Annie. That's what life's about—messy bits of good and bad luck, and people caring and not necessarily having all the answers. Who the hell are you to patronize Annie? She's worth ten of you.

HENRY: I know that.

MAX: I'm sorry, Charlotte.

CHARLOTTE: Well done, Henry.

(MAX leaves towards the front door. CHARLOTTE, with a glance at HENRY, rolling her eyes in rebuke, follows him out of the room. ANNIE stands up. For the rest of the scene she is moving, hardly looking at HENRY, perhaps fetching her handbag.)

HENRY: It was just so I could look at you without it looking funny.

ANNIE: What time are you going for Debbie?

HENRY: Four o'clock. Why?

ANNIE: Three o'clock. Look for my car.

HENRY: What about Brodie?

ANNIE: Let him rot.

(ANNIE leaves, closing the door. Pop music: Herman's Hermits, "I'm Into Something Good.")

SCENE 3   MAX *and* ANNIE.   *A living-room.*

MAX *is alone, listening to a small radio, from which Herman's Hermits continue to be heard, at an adjusted level. The disposition of furniture and doors makes the scene immediately reminiscent of the beginning of Scene 1. The front door, off stage, is heard being opened with a key. The door closes.* ANNIE, *wearing a topcoat, appears briefly round the door to the hall. She is in a hurry.*

ANNIE: Have you got it on? *(She disappears and reappears without the coat.)*
    How much have I missed?
MAX: Five or ten minutes.
ANNIE: Damn. If I'd had the car, I'd have caught the beginning.
MAX: Where have you been?
ANNIE: You know where I've been. Rehearsing.

(The music ends and is followed by HENRY *being interviewed on* Desert Island Discs, *but the radio dialogue, during the few moments before* MAX *turns the sound down, is meaningless under the stage dialogue.)*

MAX: How's Julie?
ANNIE: Who?
MAX: Julie. Miss Julie. Strindberg's Miss Julie. Miss Julie by August Strindberg,* how is she?
ANNIE: Are you all right?
MAX: This probably—
ANNIE: Shush up.
MAX: This probably isn't anything, but—
ANNIE: *Max,* can I *listen?* (MAX *turns the radio sound right down.)*
    What's up? Are you cross?
MAX: This probably isn't anything, but I found this in the car, between the front seats. *(He shows her a soiled and blood-stained white handkerchief.)*
ANNIE: What is it?
MAX: Henry's handkerchief.
ANNIE: Well, give it back to him. *(She reaches for it.)*
    Here, I'll wash it and you can give it to Charlotte at the theatre.
MAX: I did give it back to him.
    When was he in the car? *(Pause.)*
    It was a clean handkerchief, apart from my blood.
    Have you got a cold?
    It looks filthy. It's dried filthy.
    You're filthy.
    You filthy cow.
    You rotten filthy—

(He starts to cry, barely audible, immobile. ANNIE *waits. He recovers his voice.)*

*Strindberg: August Strindberg (1849–1912), Swedish playwright who was a major influence on modern drama. *Miss Julie* (1888) is noted for its realistic treatment of a young woman's sexual repression and rebellion.

It's not true, is it?

ANNIE: Yes.

MAX: Oh, God. *(He stands up.)*
Why did you?

ANNIE: I'm awfully sorry, Max—

MAX: *(Interrupting, suddenly pulled together.)* All right. It happened. All right.
It didn't mean anything.

ANNIE: I'm awfully sorry, Max, but I love him.

MAX: Oh, no.

ANNIE: Yes.

MAX: Oh, *no.* You don't.

ANNIE: Yes, I do. And he loves me. That's that, isn't it? I'm sorry it's awful.
But it's better really. All that lying.

MAX: *(Breaking up again.)* Oh, Christ, Annie, stop it. I love you. Please
don't—

ANNIE: Come on, please—it doesn't have to be like this.

MAX: How long for? And *him*—oh, *God.*

(He kicks the radio savagely. The radio has gone into music again—the Righteous Brothers singing "You've Lost That Lovin' Feelin' "—and MAX's kick has the effect of turning up the volume rather loud. He flings himself upon ANNIE in something like an assault which turns immediately into an embrace. ANNIE does no more than suffer the embrace, looking over MAX's shoulder, her face blank.)

SCENE 4   HENRY *and* ANNIE.   *Living-room. Obviously temporary and makeshift quarters, divided Left and Right by a clothes rail, making two areas, "his" and "hers."* HENRY *is alone, writing at a desk.*

The disposition of door and furniture makes the scene immediately reminiscent of Scene 2. On the floor are a number of cardboard boxes containing files, papers, letters, scripts, bills . . . The pillage of a filing system. There is also a couch. The Sunday newspapers and a bound script are on or near the couch.

A radio plays pop music quietly while HENRY *writes.*

ANNIE *enters from the bedroom door, barefoot and wearing* HENRY's *robe, which is too big for her.* HENRY, *in mid-sentence, looks up briefly and looks down again.*

ANNIE: I'm not here. Promise.

(She goes to the couch and carefully opens a newspaper. HENRY *continues to write.* ANNIE *glances towards him once or twice. He takes no notice. She stands up and goes behind his chair, looking over his shoulder as he works. He takes no notice. She goes round the desk and stands in front of him. He takes no notice. She flashes open the robe for his benefit. He takes no notice. She moves round behind him again and looks over his shoulder. He turns and grabs her with great suddenness, causing her to scream and laugh. The assault turns into a standing embrace.)*

HENRY: You're a bloody nuisance.

ANNIE: Sorry, sorry, sorry. I'll be good. I'll sit and learn my script.

HENRY: No, you won't.

ANNIE: I'll go in the other room.

HENRY: This room will do.

ANNIE: No, you've got to do my play.

HENRY: I can't write it. Let me off.

ANNIE: No, you promised. It's my gift.

HENRY: All right. Stay and talk a minute. *(He turns off the radio.)* Raw material, then I'll do this page, then I'll rape you, then I'll do the page again, then I'll—Oh *(happily),* are you all right? (ANNIE *nods.)*

ANNIE: Yeah. Are you all right? *(He nods.)*
(Gleefully, self-reproachful.) Isn't it awful? Max is so unhappy while I feel so . . . *thrilled.* His misery just seems . . . not in very good taste. Am I awful? He leaves letters for me at rehearsal, you know, and gets me to come to the phone by pretending to be my agent and people. He loves me, and he wants to punish me with his pain, but I can't come up with the proper guilt. I'm sort of irritated by it. It's so *tiring* and so *uninteresting.* You never write about that, you lot.

HENRY: What?

ANNIE: Gallons of ink and miles of typewriter ribbon expended on the misery of the unrequited lover; not a word about the utter tedium of the unrequiting. It's a very interesting . . .

HENRY: Lacuna?

ANNIE: What? No, I mean it's a very interesting sort of . . .

HENRY: Prejudice?

ANNIE: It's a very interesting . . . thing.

HENRY: Yes, thing.

ANNIE: No, I mean it shows—never mind—I've lost it now.

HENRY: How are you this morning?

ANNIE: One behind. Where were you?

HENRY: You were flat out.

ANNIE: Your own fault. When I take a sleeping pill, I'm on the downhill slope. You should have come to bed when you said.

HENRY: *(Indicating his desk.)* It wasn't where I could leave it. I would have gone to sleep depressed.

ANNIE: Well, I thought, the honeymoon is over. Fifteen days and fuckless to bye-byes.

HENRY: No, actually, I managed.

ANNIE: You did not.

HENRY: Yes, I did. You were totally zonked. Only your reflexes were working.

ANNIE: Liar.

HENRY: Honestly.

ANNIE: Why didn't you wake me?

HENRY: I thought I'd try it without you talking.

Look, I'm not doing any good, why don't we—?

ANNIE: You rotter. Just for that I'm going to learn my script.

HENRY: I'll read in for you.

(She glowers at him but finds a page in the script and hands the script to him.)

ANNIE: You didn't really, did you?

HENRY: Yes. *(She "reads" without inflection.)*

ANNIE: *"Très gentil, Monsieur Jean, très gentil!"* *

HENRY: *(Reading.) "Vous voulez plaisanter, madame!"*

ANNIE: *"Et vous voulez parler français?* Where did you pick that up?"

HENRY: "In Switzerland. I worked as a waiter in one of the best hotels in Lucerne."

ANNIE: "You're quite the gentleman in that coat . . . *charmant."* You rotter.

HENRY: "You flatter me, Miss Julie."

ANNIE: "Flatter? I flatter?"

HENRY: "I'd like to accept the compliment, but modesty forbids. And, of course, my modesty entails your insincerity. Hence, you flatter me."

ANNIE: "Where did you learn to talk like that? Do you spend a lot of time at the theatre?"

HENRY: "Oh yes. I get about, you know."

ANNIE: Oh, Hen. Are you all right?

HENRY: Not really. I can't do mine. I don't know how to write love. I try to write it properly, and it just comes out embarrassing. It's either childish or it's rude. And the rude bits are absolutely juvenile. I can't use any of it. My credibility is already hanging by a thread after *Desert Island Discs.* Anyway, I'm too prudish. Perhaps I should write it completely artificial. Blank verse. Poetic imagery. Not so much of the "Will you still love me when my tits are droopy?" "Of course I will, darling, it's your bum I'm mad for," and more of the "By my troth, thy beauty makest the moon hide her radiance," do you think?

ANNIE: Not really, no.

HENRY: No. Not really. I don't know. Loving and being loved is unliterary. It's happiness expressed in banality and lust. It makes me nervous to see three-quarters of a page and no *writing* on it. I mean, I *talk* better than this.

ANNIE: You'll have to learn to do sub-text. My Strindberg is steaming with lust, but there is nothing rude on the page. We just talk round it. Then he sort of bites my finger and I do the heavy breathing and he gives me a quick feel, kisses me on the neck . . .

HENRY: Who does?

*Annie is reading Julie's part in *Miss Julie.* Henry reads the part of Jean, the servant who seduces her. Here Julie compliments Jean's appearance.

"Très gentil, Monsieur Jean, très gentil!" ("Very nice.")

"Vous voulez plaisanter, madame!" ("You wish to make jokes, madame.")

"Et vous voulez parler francais?" ("And you wish to speak French?")

ANNIE: Gerald. It's all very exciting. (HENRY *laughs, immoderately, and* ANNIE *continues coldly.)* Or amusing, of course.

HENRY: We'll do that bit . . . you breathe, I'll feel . . . *(She pushes him away.)*

ANNIE: Go away. You'll just get moody afterwards.

HENRY: When was I ever moody?

ANNIE: Whenever you get seduced from your work.

HENRY: You mean the other afternoon?

ANNIE: What other afternoon? No, I don't mean *seduced,* for God's sake. Can't you think about anything else?

HENRY: Certainly. Like what?

ANNIE: I mean "seduced," like when you're seduced by someone on the television.

HENRY: I've never been seduced on the television.

ANNIE: You were seduced by Miranda Jessop on the television.

HENRY: Professional duty.

ANNIE: If she hadn't been in it, you wouldn't have watched that play if they'd come round and done it for you on your carpet.

HENRY: Exactly. I had a postcard from her agent, would I be sure to watch her this week in *Trotsky Playhouse* or whatever they call it.

ANNIE: You only looked up when she stripped off. Think I can't see through you? That's why I took my pill. Screw you, I thought, feel free.

HENRY: You're daft. I've got to watch her if she's going to do my telly. It's just good manners.

ANNIE: *Her* tits are droopy already.

HENRY: I'm supposed to have an opinion, you see.

ANNIE: I think she's bloody overrated, as a matter of fact.

HENRY: I have to agree. I wouldn't give them more than six out of ten. *(She clouts him with her script.)*
Four. *(She clouts him again.)*
Three.

ANNIE: You think you're so bloody funny.

HENRY: What's up with you? I hardly know the woman.

ANNIE: You'll like her. She wears leopard-skin pants.

HENRY: How do you know?

ANNIE: I shared a dressing-room with her.

HENRY: I don't suppose she wears them all the time.

ANNIE: I'm bloody sure she doesn't.

HENRY: "By my troth thy beauty makest the moon—"

ANNIE: Oh, shut up.

HENRY: What are you jealous about?

ANNIE: I'm not jealous.

HENRY: All right, what are you cross about?

ANNIE: I'm not cross. Do your work.

(She makes a show of concentrating on her script. HENRY *makes a show of resuming work. Pause.)*

HENRY: I'm sorry.

ANNIE: What for?

HENRY: I don't know.

I'll have to be going out to pick up Debbie. I don't want to go if we're not friends.

Will you come, then?

ANNIE: No. It was a mistake last time. It spoils it for her, being nervous.

HENRY: She wasn't nervous.

ANNIE: Not her. You. *(Pause.)*

HENRY: Well, I'll be back around two.

ANNIE: I won't be here. *(Pause.)*

HENRY: *(Remembering.)* Oh, yes. Is it today you're going prison-visiting? You're being very—um—faithful to Brodie.

ANNIE: That surprises you, does it?

HENRY: I only mean that you haven't got much time for good causes. You haven't got a weekend cottage either.

ANNIE: You think I'm more like you.

HENRY: Yes.

ANNIE: It's just that I happen to know him.

HENRY: You don't know him. You met him on a train.

ANNIE: Well, he's the only political prisoner I've ever met on a train. He's lucky.

HENRY: Political?

ANNIE: It was a political act which got him jumped on by the police in the first place so it's . . .

HENRY: A priori?

ANNIE: No, it's—

HENRY: De facto?

ANNIE: It's common sense that resisting arrest isn't the same as a criminal doing it.

HENRY: Arson is a criminal offence.

ANNIE: Arson is burning down buildings. Setting fire to the wreath on the war memorial is a symbolic act. Surely you can see the difference?

HENRY: *(Carefully.)* Oh, yes . . . That's . . . easy to see. *(Not carefully enough. ANNIE looks at him narrowly.)*

ANNIE: And, of course, he did get hammered by an emotional backlash. *(Pause.)*

HENRY: Do you mean real leopard skin or just printed nylon? *(She erupts and assails him, shouting.)*

ANNIE: You don't love me the way I love you. I'm just a relief after Charlotte, and a novelty.

HENRY: You're a novelty all right. I never *met* anyone so silly. I love you. I don't know why you're behaving like this.

ANNIE: I'm behaving normally. It's you who's abnormal. You don't care enough to *care.* Jealousy is normal.

HENRY: I thought you said you *weren't* jealous.

ANNIE: Well, why aren't *you* ever jealous?

HENRY: Of whom?

ANNIE: Of anybody. You don't care if Gerald Jones sticks his tongue in my
ear—which, incidentally, he does whenever he gets the chance.

HENRY: Is that what this is all about?

ANNIE: It's insulting the way you just laugh.

HENRY: But you've got no interest in him.

ANNIE: I know that, but why should you assume it?

HENRY: Because you haven't. This is stupid.

ANNIE: But why don't you *mind*?

HENRY: I do.

ANNIE: No, you don't.

HENRY: That's true, I don't.
Why *is* that?
It's because I feel superior. There he is, poor bugger, picking up the odd
crumb of ear wax from the rich man's table. You're right. I don't mind.
I like it. I like the way his presumption admits his poverty. I like him,
knowing that that's all there is, because you're coming home to me and
we don't want anyone else.
I love love. I love having a lover and being one. The insularity of passion.
I love it. I love the way it blurs the distinction between everyone who isn't
one's lover.
Only two kinds of presence in the world. There's you and there's them.
I love you so.

ANNIE: I love you so, Hen.

(They kiss. The alarm on HENRY's *wristwatch goes off. They separate.)*

HENRY: Sorry.

ANNIE: Don't get kicked by the horse.

HENRY: Don't get kicked by Brodie.

*(He goes to the door to leave. At the door he looks at her and nods. She nods at
him. He leaves.)*
(ANNIE *goes slowly to* HENRY's *desk and looks at the pages on it. She turns on
the radio and turns it from pop to Bach. She goes back to the desk and, almost
absently, opens one of the drawers. Leaving it open, she goes to the door and
disappears briefly into the hall, then reappears, closing the door. She goes to one of
the cardboard boxes on the floor. She removes the contents from the box. She places
the pile of papers on the floor. Squatting down, she starts going through the pile,
methodically and unhurriedly. The radio plays on.)*

ACT 2

Scene 5   HENRY *and* ANNIE.   *Living-room/study. Three doors.*

Two years later. A different house. The two years ought to show on HENRY
and on ANNIE. *Perhaps he now uses glasses when he is reading, as he is at the*

beginning of the scene, or he may even have grown a moustache. ANNIE *may have cut her hair short. Opera (Verdi) is playing on the record player. There is a TV and video and a small radio on* HENRY*'s desk, on which there is also a typewriter.* HENRY *is alone, reading a script which consists of a sheaf of typed pages.* HENRY *reads for a few moments.*

ANNIE *enters from bedroom or kitchen and glances at* HENRY, *not casually, then sits down and watches him read for a moment. Then she looks away and listens to the music for a moment.* HENRY *glances up at her.*

ANNIE *looks at him.*

ANNIE: Well?
HENRY: Oh—um—Strauss.
ANNIE: What?
HENRY: Not Strauss.
ANNIE: I meant the play.
HENRY: *(Indicating the script.)* Ah. The play.
ANNIE: *(Scornfully.) Strauss.* How can it be Strauss? It's in Italian.
HENRY: Is it? *(He listens.)* So it is.
         Italian opera.
         One of the Italian operas.
         Verdi.
ANNIE: Which one?
HENRY: Giuseppe.

(He judges from her expression that this is not the right answer.)

         Monty?
ANNIE: I mean which *opera.*
HENRY: Ah. *(Confidently.) Madame Butterfly.*
ANNIE: You're doing it on purpose. *(She goes to the record player and stops it playing.)*
HENRY: I promise you.
ANNIE: You'd think that *something* would have sunk in after two years and a bit.
HENRY: I like it—I really do like it—quite, it's just that I can't tell them apart. Two years and a bit isn't very long when they're all going for the same sound. Actually, I've got a better ear than you—*you* can't tell the difference between the Everly Brothers and the Andrews Sisters.
ANNIE: There isn't any difference.
HENRY: Or we could split up. Can we have something decent on now?
ANNIE: No.
HENRY: All right. Put on one of your instrumental numbers. The big band sound. *(He does the opening of Beethoven's Fifth.)* Da—da—da—*dah* . . .
ANNIE: Get *on.*
HENRY: Right. *(He turns his attention to the script.)*
         Stop me if anybody has said this before, but it's interesting how many of the all time greats begin with B: Beethoven, the Big Bopper . . .

ANNIE: That's all they have in common.

HENRY: I wouldn't say that. They're both dead. The Big Bopper died in the same plane crash that killed Buddy Holly and Richie Valens, you know.

ANNIE: No, I didn't know. Have you given up on the play or what?

HENRY: Buddy Holly was twenty-two. Think of what he might have gone on to achieve. I mean, if Beethoven had been killed in a plane crash at twenty-two, the history of music would have been very different. As would the history of aviation, of course.

ANNIE: *Henry.*

HENRY: The play. *(He turns his attention back to the script.)*

ANNIE: How far have you got?

HENRY: Do you have a professional interest in this or is it merely personal?

ANNIE: Merely? *(Pause.)*

HENRY: Do you have a personal interest in this or is it merely professional?

ANNIE: Which one are you dubious about? *(Pause.)*

HENRY: Pause.

ANNIE: I could do her, couldn't I?

HENRY: Mary? Oh, sure—without make-up.

ANNIE: Well, then. *Three Sisters* * is definitely off.

HENRY: Nothing's definite with that lot.

ANNIE: The other two are pregnant.

HENRY: Half a dozen new lines could take care of that.

ANNIE: If this script could be in a fit state, say, a month from now—

HENRY: Anyway, I thought you were committing incest† in Glasgow.

ANNIE: I haven't said I'll do it.

HENRY: I think you should. It's classy stuff, Webster. I love all that Jacobean sex and violence.‡

ANNIE: It's Ford, not Webster. *And* it's Glasgow.

HENRY: Don't you work north of the West End, then?

ANNIE: I was thinking you might miss me—pardon my mistake.

HENRY: I was thinking you might like me to come with you—pardon mine.

ANNIE: You hadn't the faintest intention of coming to Glasgow for five weeks.

HENRY: That's true. I answered out of panic. Of course I'd miss you.

ANNIE: Also, it *is* somewhat north.

(HENRY "shoots" her between the eyes with his forefinger.)

HENRY: Got you. Is it rehearsing in Glasgow?

ANNIE: *(Nods.)* After the first week. *(Indicating the script.)* Where've you got to?

Three Sisters: A play (1901) by Anton Chekhov (1860–1904), Russian writer who, like Strindberg, exerted a major influence on modern realistic drama.

†commiting incest: A reference to Annie's impending role in John Ford's *'Tis Pity She's a Whore* (1633).

‡Jacobean sex and violence: The pessimistic and bloody tragedies in the early seventeenth century are called Jacobean because most were produced during the reign of James I (1603–1625).

HENRY: They're on the train.
  "You're a strange boy, Billy. How old are you?"
  "Twenty. But I've lived more than you'll ever live."
  Should I read out loud?
ANNIE: If you like.
HENRY: Give you the feel of it.
ANNIE: All right.
HENRY: I'll go back a bit . . . where they first meet. All right?

  (ANNIE *nods.* HENRY *makes train noises. She is defensive, not quite certain whether he is being wicked or not.*)

  (*Reading.*) "Excuse me, is this seat taken?"
  "No."
  "Mind if I sit down?"
  "It's a free country."
  "Thank you."
  "(He sits down opposite her. Mary carries on with reading her book.)"
  "Going far?"
  "To London."
  "So, you were saying . . . So you think it's a free country."
  "Don't you?"
  "This is it, we're all free to do as we're told. My name's Bill, by the way. What's yours?"
  "Mary."
  "I'm glad to make your acquaintance, Mary."
  "I'm glad to make yours, Bill."
  "Do you know what time this train is due to arrive in London?"
  "At about half-past one, I believe, if it is on time."
  "You put me in mind of Mussolini, Mary. Yes, you look just like him, you've got the same eyes."
ANNIE: If you're not going to read it properly, don't bother.
HENRY: Sorry.
  "At about half-past one, I believe, if it is on time."
  "You put me in mind of Mussolini, Mary. People used to say about Mussolini, he may be a Fascist, but at least the trains run on time. Makes you wonder why British Rail isn't totally on time, eh?"
  "What do you mean?"
  "I mean it's a funny thing. The Fascists are in charge but the trains are late often as not."
  "But this isn't a Fascist country."
  "Are you quite sure of that, Mary? Take the army—"
  You're not going to do this, are you?
ANNIE: Why not?
HENRY: It's no good.
ANNIE: You mean it's not literary.

HENRY: It's not literary, and it's no good. He can't write.

ANNIE: You're a snob.

HENRY: I'm a snob, and he can't write.

ANNIE: I know it's raw, but he's got something to say.

HENRY: He's got something to say. It happens to be something extremely silly and bigoted. But leaving that aside, there is still the problem that he can't write. He can burn things down, but he can't write.

ANNIE: Give it back. I shouldn't have asked you.

HENRY: For God's sake, Annie, if it wasn't Brodie you'd never have got through it.

ANNIE: But it *is* Brodie. That's the point. Two and a half years ago he could hardly put six words together.

HENRY: He still can't.

ANNIE: You *pig.*

HENRY: I'm a pig, and he can't—

ANNIE: I'll smash you one. It's you who's bigoted. You're bigoted about what writing is supposed to be like. You judge everything as though everyone starts off from the same place, aiming at the same prize. English Lit. Shakespeare out in front by a mile, and the rest of the field strung out behind trying to close the gap. You all write for people who would like to write like you if only they could write. Well, screw you, and screw English Lit.!

HENRY: Right.

ANNIE: Brodie isn't writing to compete like you. He's writing to be heard.

HENRY: Right.

ANNIE: And he's done it on his own.

HENRY: Yes. Yes . . . I can see he's done a lot of reading.

ANNIE: You can't expect it to be English Lit.

HENRY: No.

ANNIE: He's a prisoner shouting over the wall.

HENRY: Quite. Yes, I see what you mean.

ANNIE: Oh shut up! I'd rather have your sarcasm.

HENRY: Why a play? Did you suggest it?

ANNIE: Not exactly.

HENRY: Why did you?

ANNIE: The committee, what's left of it, thought . . . I mean, people have got bored with Brodie. People get bored with anything after two or three years. The campaign needs . . .

HENRY: A shot in the arm?

ANNIE: No, it needs . . .

HENRY: A kick up the arse?

ANNIE: *(Flares.)* For Christ's sake, will you stop finishing my sentences for me!

HENRY: Sorry.

ANNIE: I've lost it now.

HENRY: The campaign needs . . .

ANNIE: A writer is harder to ignore. I thought, TV plays get talked about, make some impact. Get his case reopened. Do you think? I mean, Henry, what *do* you think?

HENRY: I think it makes a lot of sense.

ANNIE: No, what do you *really* think?

HENRY: Oh, *really* think. Well, I *really* think writing rotten plays is not in itself proof of rehabilitation. Still less of wrongful conviction. But even if it were, I think that anyone who thinks that they're bored with Brodie won't know what boredom is till they've sat through his apologia. Not that anyone will get the chance, because it's half as long as *Das Kapital* and only twice as funny. I also think you should know better.

ANNIE: You arrogant bastard.

HENRY: You swear too much.

ANNIE: Roger is willing to do it, in principle.

HENRY: What Roger? Oh *Roger.* Why the hell would Roger do it?

ANNIE: He's on the committee.

(HENRY *looks at the ceiling.*)

It just needs a bit of work.

HENRY: You're all bent.

ANNIE: You're jealous.

HENRY: Of Brodie?

ANNIE: You're jealous of the idea of the writer. You want to keep it sacred, special, not something anybody can do. Some of us have it, some of us don't. *We* write, *you* get written about. What gets you about Brodie is he doesn't know his place. You say he can't write like a head waiter saying you can't come in here without a tie. Because he can't put words together. What's so good about putting words together?

HENRY: It's traditionally considered advantageous for a writer.

ANNIE: He's not a writer. He's a convict. *You're* a writer. You write *because* you're a writer. Even when you write *about* something, you have to think up something to write about just so you can keep writing. More well chosen words nicely put together. So what? Why should that be *it*? Who says?

HENRY: Nobody says. It just works best.

ANNIE: Of *course* it works. You teach a lot of people what to expect from good writing, and you end up with a lot of people saying you write well. Then somebody who isn't in on the game comes along, like Brodie, who really has something to write about, something real, and you can't get through it. Well, *he* couldn't get through *yours,* so where are you? To you, he can't write. To him, write is all you *can* do.

HENRY: Jesus, Annie, you're beginning to appal me. There's something scary about stupidity made coherent. I can deal with idiots, and I can deal with sensible argument, but I don't know how to deal with you. Where's my cricket bat?

ANNIE: Your cricket bat?

HENRY: Yes. It's a new approach.

(He heads out into the hall.)

ANNIE: Are you trying to be funny?

HENRY: No, I'm serious.

(He goes out while she watches in wary disbelief. He returns with an old cricket bat.)

ANNIE: You better not be.

HENRY: Right, you silly cow—

ANNIE: Don't you bloody dare—

HENRY: Shut up and listen. This thing here, which looks like a wooden club, is actually several pieces of particular wood cunningly put together in a certain way so that the whole thing is sprung, like a dance floor. It's for hitting cricket balls with. If you get it right, the cricket ball will travel two hundred yards in four seconds, and all you've done is give it a knock like knocking the top off a bottle of stout, and it makes a noise like a trout taking a fly . . . *(He clucks his tongue to make the noise.)* What we're trying to do is to write cricket bats, so that when we throw up an idea and give it a little knock, it might . . . *travel* . . . *(He clucks his tongue again and picks up the script.)* Now, what we've got here is a lump of wood of roughly the same shape trying to be a cricket bat, and if you hit a ball with it, the ball will travel about ten feet and you will drop the bat and dance about shouting "Ouch!" with your hands stuck into your armpits. *(Indicating the cricket bat.)* This isn't better because someone says it's better, or because there's a conspiracy by the MCC to keep cudgels off the field. It's better because it's better. You don't believe me, so I suggest you go out to bat with us and see how you get on. "You're a strange boy, Billy, how old are you?" "Twenty, but I've lived more than you'll ever live." Ooh, ouch!

(He drops the script and hops about with his hands in his armpits, going "Ouch!" ANNIE watches him expressionlessly until he desists.)

ANNIE: I hate you.

HENRY: I love you. I'm your pal. I'm your best mate. I look after you. You're the only chap.

ANNIE: Oh, Hen . . . Can't you help?

HENRY: What did you expect me to do?

ANNIE: Well . . . cut it and shape it . . .

HENRY: Cut it and shape it. Henry of Mayfair. Look—he can't write. I would have to write it for him.

ANNIE: Well, write it for him.

HENRY: I can't.

ANNIE: Why?

HENRY: Because it's *balls.* Announcing every stale revelation of the newly enlightened like stout Cortez coming upon the Pacific—war is profits, politicians are puppets, Parliament is a farce, justice is a fraud, property is theft . . . It's all here: pages and pages of it. It's like being run over very slowly by a travelling freak show of favourite simpletons, the india rubber pedagogue, the midget intellectual, the human panacea . . .

ANNIE: It's his view of the world. Perhaps from where he's standing you'd see it the same way.

HENRY: Or perhaps I'd realize where I'm standing. Or at least that I'm standing *somewhere.* There is, I suppose, a world of objects which have a certain form, like this coffee mug. I turn it, and it has no handle. I tilt it, and it has no cavity. But there is something real here which is always a mug with a handle. I suppose. But politics, justice, patriotism—they aren't even like coffee mugs. There's nothing real there separate from our perception of them. So if you try to change them as though there were something there to change, you'll get frustrated, and frustration will finally make you violent. If you know this and proceed with humility, you may perhaps alter people's perceptions so that they behave a little differently at that axis of behaviour where we locate politics or justice; but if you don't know this, then you're acting on a mistake. Prejudice is the expression of this mistake.

ANNIE: Or such is your perception.

HENRY: All right.

ANNIE: And who wrote it, why he wrote it, *where* he wrote it—none of these things count with you?

HENRY: Leave me out of it. They don't count. Maybe Brodie got a raw deal, maybe he didn't. I don't know. It doesn't count. He's a lout with language. I can't help somebody who thinks, or thinks he thinks, that editing a newspaper is censorship, or that throwing bricks is a demonstration while building tower blocks is social violence, or that unpalatable statement is provocation while disrupting the speaker is the exercise of free speech . . . Words don't deserve that kind of malarkey. They're innocent, neutral, precise, standing for this, describing that, meaning the other, so if you look after them you can build bridges across incomprehension and chaos. But when they get their corners knocked off, they're no good any more, and Brodie knocks their corners off. I don't think writers are sacred, but words are. They deserve respect. If you get the right ones in the right order, you can nudge the world a little or make a poem which children will speak for you when you're dead.

*(*ANNIE *goes to the typewriter, pulls out the page from the machine and reads it.)*

ANNIE: "Seventy-nine. Interior. Commander's capsule. From Zadok's p.o.v. we see the green glow of the laser strike-force turning towards us. BCU Zadok's grim smile. *Zadok:* 'I think it's going to work. Here they come!' *Kronk,* voice over: 'Hold your course!' *Zadok:*—"

HENRY: *(Interrupts.)* That's not words, that's pictures. The movies. Anyway, alimony doesn't count. If Charlotte made it legal with that architect she's shacked up with, I'd be writing the real stuff.

(ANNIE lets the page drop on to the typewriter.)

ANNIE: You never wrote mine.
HENRY: That's true. I didn't. I tried.
I can't remember when I last felt so depressed.
Oh yes. Yesterday.
Don't be rotten to me. I'll come to Glasgow and I'll sit in your dressing-room and I'll write Kronk and Zadok every night while you're doing *'Tis Pity She's a Whore.*
ANNIE: I'm not going to Glasgow.
HENRY: Yes, you bloody are.
ANNIE: No I'm bloody not. We'll get Brodie's play off the ground. I want to do it. *I* want to do it. Don't *I* count? Hen? *(Pause.)* Well, I can see it's difficult for a man of your fastidious tastes. Let's have some literacy. Something decent.

(ANNIE stabs her finger on to the small radio on HENRY's desk. Quietly it starts playing pop. She starts to go out of the room.)

HENRY: *(Exasperated.) Why Brodie?* Do you fancy him or what? *(She looks back at him and he sees that he has made a mistake.)* I take it back.
ANNIE: Too late.

(She leaves the room.)

SCENE 6   ANNIE *and* BILLY.   ANNIE *is sitting by the window of a moving train. She is immersed in a paperback book.*
   BILLY *walks into view and pauses, looking at her for a moment. She is unaware of his presence. He carries a zipped grip bag. He speaks with a Scottish accent.*

BILLY: Excuse me, is this seat taken? *(ANNIE hardly raises her eyes.)*
ANNIE: No.

(BILLY sits down next to or opposite her. He puts the grip on the seat next to him. He looks at her. She doesn't look up from her book. He looks at his watch and then out of the window and then back at her.)

BILLY: You'd think with all these Fascists the trains would be on time.

(ANNIE looks up at him and jumps a mile. She gives a little squeal.)

ANNIE: Jesus, you gave me a shock. *(She looks at him, pleased and amused.)*
You fool. *(BILLY drops the accent.)*
BILLY: Hello.

ANNIE: I didn't know you were on the train.

BILLY: Yes, well, there you are. How are you?

ANNIE: All right. I gather you read it, then.

BILLY: Brodie's play? Yes, I read it.

ANNIE: And?

BILLY: He can't write. *(Small pause.)*

ANNIE: I know.

I just thought it was something you'd do well.

BILLY: Oh, yes. I could do a job on it.

Are you going to do it?

ANNIE: I hope so. Not as it is, I suppose. Thank you for reading it anyway.

BILLY: Do you mind me coming to sit with you?

ANNIE: No, not at all.

BILLY: It doesn't mean we have to talk.

ANNIE: It's all right.

BILLY: How do you feel?

ANNIE: Scared. I'm always scared. I think, this is the one where I get found out.

BILLY: Well, better in Glasgow.

ANNIE: Is anyone else on this train?

BILLY: No, we're completely alone.

ANNIE: I mean any of *us,* the others.

BILLY: I don't know. Some of them are flying up, on the shuttle.

ANNIE: I fancied the train.

BILLY: I fancied it with you. *(ANNIE meets his look.)*

ANNIE: Billy . . .

BILLY: What did you think when you saw me?

ANNIE: Just now?

BILLY: No. On the first day.

ANNIE: I thought God, he's so *young.*

BILLY: *(Scottish.)* I've lived more than you'll ever live.

ANNIE: All right, all right.

BILLY: I'm the one who should be scared. You're smashing.

ANNIE: I don't feel right.

BILLY: You seem right to me.

ANNIE: I'm older than you.

BILLY: That doesn't matter.

ANNIE: I'm a lot older. I'm going to look more like your mother than your sister.

BILLY: That's all right, so long as it's incest.*Anyway, I like older women.

ANNIE: Billy, you mustn't keep flirting with me.

BILLY: Why not?

ANNIE: Well, because there's no point. Will you stop?

---

*so long as its incest: In Ford's play, *'Tis Pity She's a Whore,* Billy plays Giovanni and Annie plays Annabella, a brother and sister who have a tragic love affair.

BILLY: No. Is that all right? *(Pause.)*

ANNIE: Did you know I was going to be on this train?

BILLY: *(Nods.)* Watched you get on. I thought I'd come and find you when it got started.

ANNIE: You certainly thought about it.

BILLY: I had to wait until the inspector came round. I haven't got a first-class ticket.

ANNIE: What will you do if he comes back?

BILLY: I'll say you're my mum. How come you get a first-class ticket?

ANNIE: I don't really. I'm afraid I upped it myself.

BILLY: You approve of the class system?

ANNIE: You mean on trains or in general?

BILLY: In general. Travelling first-class.

ANNIE: There's no system. People group together when they've got something in common. Sometimes it's religion and sometimes it's, I don't know, breeding budgies or being at Eton. Big and small groups overlapping. You can't blame them. It's a cultural thing; it's not *classes* or *system.* *(She makes a connection.)* There's nothing really *there*—it's just the way you see it. Your perception.

BILLY: Bloody brilliant. There's people who've spent their lives trying to get rid of the class system, and you've done it without leaving your seat.

ANNIE: Well . . .

BILLY: The only problem with your argument is that you've got to be travelling first-class to really appreciate it.

ANNIE: I . . .

BILLY: Where do you get all that from? Did you just make it up? It's daft. I prefer Brodie. He sounds like rubbish, but you know he's right. You sound all right, but you know it's rubbish.

ANNIE: Why won't you do his play, then?

BILLY: I didn't say I wouldn't. I'll do it if you're doing it.

ANNIE: You shouldn't do it for the wrong reasons.

BILLY: Why not? Does he care?

ANNIE: You said he can't write.

BILLY: He can't write like your husband. But your husband's a first-class writer.

ANNIE: Are you being nasty about Henry?

BILLY: No. I saw *House of Cards.* I thought it was quite good.

ANNIE: He'll be relieved to hear that. *(Pause.)*

BILLY: Don't go off me.

ANNIE: If you weren't a child, you'd know that you won't get anywhere with a married woman if you're snotty about her husband. Remember that with the next one.

BILLY: I'faith, I mean no harm, sister.* I'm just scared sick of you. How is't with ye?

---

*I'faith, I mean no harm, sister: Billy begins rehearsing the role of Giovanni.

ANNIE: I am very well, brother.

BILLY: Trust me, but I am sick; I fear so sick 'twill cost my life.

ANNIE: Mercy forbid it! 'Tis not so, I hope.

BILLY: I think you love me, sister.

ANNIE: Yes, you know I do.

BILLY: I know't, indeed. You're very fair.

ANNIE: Nay, then, I see you have a merry sickness.

BILLY: That's as it proves. The poets feign, I read,
    That Juno for her forehead did exceed
    All other goddesses; but I durst swear
    Your forehead exceeds hers, as hers did theirs.

ANNIE: 'Troth, this is pretty!

BILLY: Such a pair of stars
    As are thine eyes would, like Promethean fire,
    If gently glanced, give life to senseless stones.

ANNIE: Fie upon ye!

BILLY: The lily and the rose, most sweetly strange,
    Upon your dimpled cheeks do strive for change:
    Such lips would tempt a saint; such hands as those
    Would make an anchorite lascivious.

ANNIE: O, you are a trim youth!

BILLY: Here!

(His "reading" has been getting less and less discreet. Now he stands up and opens his shirt.)

ANNIE: *(Giggling.)* Oh, leave off.

(She looks around nervously.)

BILLY: *(Starting to shout.)* And here's my breast; strike home!
    Rip up my bosom; there thou shalt behold
    A heart in which is writ the truth I speak.

ANNIE: You daft idiot.

BILLY: Yes, most earnest. You cannot love?

ANNIE: Stop it.

BILLY: My tortured soul
    Hath felt affliction in the heat of death.
    Oh, Annabella, I am quite undone!

ANNIE: Billy!

SCENE 7   HENRY *and* CHARLOTTE *and* DEBBIE.   *The living-room of Scene 2, without all the records.* CHARLOTTE *is searching through a file of newspaper cuttings and programmes. A large, loaded ruck-sack is sitting by the door.* DEBBIE *is smoking.*

Henry: Since when did you smoke?

DEBBIE: I don't know. Years. At school. Me and Terry used to light up in the boiler room.

HENRY: *I* and Terry.

DEBBIE: I and Terry. Are you sure?

HENRY: It doesn't sound right but it's correct. I paid school fees so that you wouldn't be barred by your natural disabilities from being taught Latin and learning to speak English.

CHARLOTTE: I thought it was so that she'd be a virgin a bit longer.

HENRY: It was also so that she'd speak English. *Virgo syntacta.* *

DEBBIE: You were done, Henry. Nobody left the boiler room virgo with Terry.

HENRY: I wish you'd stop celebrating your emancipation by flicking it at me like a wet towel. Did the staff know about this lout, Terry?

DEBBIE: He was on the staff. He taught Latin.

HENRY: Oh well, that's all right then.

CHARLOTTE: Apparently she'd already lost it riding anyway.

HENRY: That doesn't count.

CHARLOTTE: In the tackroom.

HENRY: God's truth. The groom.

CHARLOTTE: That's why he was bow-legged.

HENRY: I told you—I said you've got to warn her about being carried away.

DEBBIE: You don't get carried away in jodhpurs. It needs absolute determination.

HENRY: Will you stop this.

CHARLOTTE: No. I can't find it. It was yonks ago. I mean, not being catty, I was nearer the right age.

HENRY: Does it really matter who played Giovanni to your Annabella in *'Tis Pity She's a Whore?*

CHARLOTTE: I just think it's awful to have forgotten his name.

DEBBIE: Perhaps he's forgotten yours.

CHARLOTTE: But it was *my* virginity, not his.

DEBBIE: Was it actually on stage?

CHARLOTTE: Don't be silly—it was a British Council tour. No, it was in a boarding house in Zagreb.†

DEBBIE: A bawdy house?

CHARLOTTE: The British Council has a lot to answer for.

HENRY: Look, we're supposed to be discussing a family crisis.

CHARLOTTE: What's that?

HENRY: Our daughter going on the streets.

DEBBIE: On the *road,* not the streets.

CHARLOTTE: Stop being so dramatic.

HENRY: I have a right to be dramatic.

CHARLOTTE: I see what you mean.

HENRY: I'm her father.

CHARLOTTE: Oh, I see what you mean.

***Virgo syntacta:* Virgin, or pure, syntax; a play on virgo intacta, an untouched maiden.
†Zagreb: A city in Yugoslavia.

HENRY: She's too young to go off with a man.

CHARLOTTE: She's certainly too young to go off without one. It's all right. He's nice.

(CHARLOTTE has given up her search of the file and now leaves carrying the file.)

(To DEBBIE.*)* If I'm in the bath when he comes I want to see you both before you disappear.

(CHARLOTTE goes out.)

HENRY: What does he play? *(DEBBIE looks blank.)* Ma said he's a musician.

DEBBIE: Oh—um—steam organ . . .

HENRY: A travelling steam organist? *(Pause.)* He's not a musician.

DEBBIE: Fairground.

HENRY: Well, swings and roundabouts.

DEBBIE: Tunnel of love. How's Annie?

HENRY: In Glasgow.

DEBBIE: Don't worry, Henry, I'll be happy.

HENRY: Happy? What do you mean happy?

DEBBIE: Happy! Like a warm puppy.

HENRY: Dear Christ, is that what it's all come down to?—no philosophy that can't be printed on a T-shirt. You don't get visited by happiness like being lucky with the weather. The weather is the weather.

DEBBIE: And happiness?

HENRY: Happiness is . . . equilibrium. Shift your weight.

DEBBIE: Are you happy, Henry?

HENRY: I don't much like your calling me Henry. I liked being called Fa. Fa and Ma.

DEBBIE: Happy days, eh? How're the Everlys getting on? And the Searchers. How's old Elvis?

HENRY: He's dead.

DEBBIE: I did know that. I mean how's he holding up apart from that?

HENRY: I never went for him much. "All Shook Up" was the last good one. However, I suppose that's the fate of all us artists.

DEBBIE: Death?

HENRY: People saying they preferred the early stuff.

DEBBIE: Well, maybe you were better then.

HENRY: Didn't you like the last one?

DEBBIE: What, *House of Cards*? Well, it wasn't about anything, except did she have it off or didn't she? What a crisis. Infidelity among the architect class. Again.

HENRY: It was about self-knowledge through pain.

DEBBIE: No, it was about did she have it off or didn't she. As if having it off is infidelity.

HENRY: Most people think it is.

DEBBIE: Most people think *not* having it off is *fidelity.* They think all relation-ships hinge in the middle. Sex or no sex. What a fantastic range of possibili-

ties. Like an on/off switch. Did she or didn't she. By Henry Ibsen.*Why
would you want to make it such a crisis?

HENRY: I don't know, why would I?

DEBBIE: It's what comes of making such a mystery of it. When I was twelve
I was obsessed. Everything was sex. Latin was sex. The dictionary fell open
at *meretrix,* a harlot. You could feel the mystery coming off the word like
musk. *Meretrix!* This was none of your *amo, amas, amat,* this was a flash
from the forbidden planet, and it was everywhere. History was sex, French
was sex, art was sex, the Bible, poetry, penfriends, games, music, everything was sex except biology which was obviously sex but obviously not
really sex, not the one which was secret and ecstatic and wicked and a
sacrament and all the things it was supposed to be but couldn't be at one
and the same time—I got that in the boiler room and it turned out to be
biology after all. That's what free love is free of—propaganda.

HENRY: Don't get too good at that.

DEBBIE: What?

HENRY: Persuasive nonsense. Sophistry in a phrase so neat you can't see the
loose end that would unravel it. It's flawless but wrong. A perfect dud.
You can do that with words, bless 'em. How about "What free love is free
of, is love"? Another little gem. You could put a "what" on the end of
it, like Bertie Wooster, "What free love is free of is love, what?"—and
the words would go on replicating themselves like a spiral of DNA
. . . "What love is free of love?—*free* love is what love, what?—"

DEBBIE: *(Interrupting.)* Fa. You're going on.

HENRY: Yes. Well, I remember, the first time I succumbed to the sensation
that the universe was dispensable minus one lady—

DEBBIE: Don't write it, Fa. Just say it. The first time you fell in love. What?

HENRY: It's to do with knowing and being known. I remember how it stopped
seeming odd that in biblical Greek knowing was used for making love.
Whosit knew so-and-so. Carnal knowledge. It's what lovers trust each
other with. Knowledge of each other, not of the flesh but through the
flesh, knowledge of self, the real him, the real her, *in extremis,* the mask
slipped from the face. Every other version of oneself is on offer to the
public. We share our vivacity, grief, sulks, anger, joy . . . we hand it out
to anybody who happens to be standing around, to friends and family with
a momentary sense of indecency perhaps, to strangers without hesitation.
Our lovers share us with the passing trade. But in pairs we insist that we
give ourselves to each other. What selves? What's left? What else is there
that hasn't been dealt out like a deck of cards? Carnal knowledge. Personal, final, uncompromised. Knowing, being known. I revere that. Having that is being rich, you can be generous about what's shared—she
walks, she talks, she laughs, she lends a sympathetic ear, she kicks off her
shoes and dances on the tables, she's everybody's and it don't mean a

---

*Henry Ibsen: Henrik Ibsen (1828–1906), Norwegian playwright who greatly influenced modern
British drama.

thing, let them eat cake; knowledge is something else, the undealt card, and while it's held it makes you free-and-easy and nice to know, and when it's gone everything is pain. Every single thing. Every object that meets the eye, a pencil, a tangerine, a travel poster. As if the physical world has been wired up to pass a current back to the part of your brain where imagination glows like a filament in a lobe no bigger than a torch bulb. Pain. *(Pause.)*

DEBBIE: Has Annie got someone else then?

HENRY: Not as far as I know, thank you for asking.

DEBBIE: Apologies.

HENRY: Don't worry.

DEBBIE: Don't you. Exclusive rights isn't love, it's colonization.

HENRY: Christ almighty. Another *ersatz* masterpiece. Like Michelangelo working in polystyrene.

DEBBIE: Do you know what your problem is, Henry?

HENRY: What?

DEBBIE: Your Latin mistress never took you into the boiler room.

HENRY: Well, at least I passed.

DEBBIE: Only in Latin.

(Doorbell.)

Do me a favour.

HENRY: What?

DEBBIE: Stay here.

HENRY: That bad, is he?

DEBBIE: He's frightened of you.

HENRY: Jesus.

(CHARLOTTE enters in a bath robe, a towel round her hair perhaps. She carries a bunch of postcards.)

CHARLOTTE: Ten postcards—stamped and addressed. Every week I get a postcard you get ten quid. No postcards, no remittance. *(She gives DEBBIE the postcards.)*

DEBBIE: Oh—Charley—*(Kisses CHARLOTTE).*
See you, Henry.

HENRY: There; my blessing with thee. And these few precepts in thy memory . . .

DEBBIE: Too late, Fa. Love you. *(Kisses him.)*

(DEBBIE leaves with the ruck-sack followed by CHARLOTTE. HENRY waits until CHARLOTTE returns.)

CHARLOTTE: What a good job we sold the pony.

HENRY: Musician is he? She's hardly seventeen.

CHARLOTTE: I was in Zagreb when I was seventeen. *(Pause.)* How's Annie? Are you going to Glasgow for the first night?

HENRY: They don't open for a couple of weeks.

CHARLOTTE: Who's playing Giovanni?

HENRY: I don't know.

CHARLOTTE: Aren't you interested?

HENRY: Should I be?

CHARLOTTE: There's something touching about you, Henry. Everybody should be like you. Not interested. It used to bother me that you were never bothered. Even when I got talked into that dreadful nudie film because it was in Italian and Italian films were supposed to be art . . . God, that dates me, doesn't it? Debbie's into Australian films. *Australian.* Not Chips Rafferty—actual *films.*

HENRY: You've gone off again.

CHARLOTTE: Yes, well, it didn't bother you so I decided it meant you were having it off right left and centre and it wasn't supposed to matter. By the time I realized you were the last romantic it was too late. I found it *didn't* matter.

HENRY: Well, now that it doesn't . . . How many—um—roughly how many—?

CHARLOTTE: Nine. *(Pause.)*

HENRY: Gosh.

CHARLOTTE: And look what your one did compared to my nine.

HENRY: Nine?

CHARLOTTE: Feel betrayed?

HENRY: Surprised. I thought we'd made a commitment.

CHARLOTTE: There are no commitments, only bargains. And they have to be made again every day. You think making a commitment is *it.* Finish. You think it sets like a concrete platform and it'll take any strain you want to put on it. You're committed. You don't have to prove anything. In fact you can afford a little neglect, indulge in a little bit of sarcasm here and there, isolate yourself when you want to. Underneath it's concrete for life. I'm a cow in some ways, but you're an idiot. *Were* an idiot.

HENRY: Better luck next time.

CHARLOTTE: You too.
Have a drink?

HENRY: I don't think so, thank you.
How are things with your friend? An architect, isn't he?

CHARLOTTE: I had to give him the elbow. Well, he sort of left. I called him the architect of my misfortune.

HENRY: What was the matter with him?

CHARLOTTE: Very possessive type. I came home from a job, I'd been away only a couple of days, and he said, why did I take my diaphragm? He'd been through my bathroom cabinet, would you believe? And then, not finding it, he went through everything else. Can't have that.

HENRY: What did you say?

CHARLOTTE: I said, I didn't *take* my diaphragm, it just went with me. So he said, what about the tube of Duragel? I must admit he had me there.

HENRY: You should have said, "Duragel!—no wonder the bristles fell out of
    my toothbrush."
CHARLOTTE: *(Laughs.)* Cheers.
HENRY: *(Toasting with an empty hand.)* Cheers. (HENRY *stands up.*)
CHARLOTTE: Do you have to go?
HENRY: Yes, I ought to.
CHARLOTTE: You don't fancy one for the road?
HENRY: No, really.
CHARLOTTE: Or a drink?
HENRY: *(Smiles.)* No offence.
CHARLOTTE: Remember what I said.
HENRY: What was that? *(Pause.)* Oh . . . yes. No commitments. Only bargains.
    The trouble is I don't really believe it. I'd rather be an idiot. It's a kind
    of idiocy I like. I use you because you love me. I love you so use me. Be
    indulgent, negligent, preoccupied, premenstrual . . . your credit is infinite,
    I'm yours, I'm committed . . .
    It's no trick loving somebody at their *best.* Love is loving them at their
    worst. Is that romantic? Well, good.
    Everything should be romantic. Love, work, music, literature, virginity,
    loss of virginity . . .
CHARLOTTE: You've still got one to lose, Henry.

(Quiet music begins, continuing without break to the end of Scene 8.)

SCENE 8*   ANNIE *and* BILLY.   *An empty space.*
    They are kissing, embracing: wearing rehearsal clothes.

BILLY: Come, Annabella,—no more sister now,
    But love, a name more gracious,—do not blush,
    Beauty's sweet wonder, but be proud to know
    That yielding thou hast conquered, and inflamed
    A heart whose tribute is thy brother's life.
ANNIE: And mine is his. O, how these stol'n contents
    Would print a modest crimson on my cheeks,
    Had any but my heart's delight prevailed!
BILLY: I marvel why the chaster of your sex
    Should think this pretty toy called maidenhead
    So strange a loss, when, being lost, 'tis nothing,
    And you are still the same.
ANNIE: 'Tis well for you;
    Now you can talk.
BILLY: Music as well consists
    In the ear as in the playing.

*In order to accommodate a scene change, Scene 8 was spoken twice, once as a "word rehearsal"
and then again as an "acting rehearsal."

ANNIE: O, you're wanton!
   Tell on't you're best; do.
BILLY: Thou wilt chide me, then.
   Kiss me:—

(He kisses her lightly.)

ANNIE: *(Quietly.)* Billy . . .

(She returns the kiss in earnest.)

SCENE 9   HENRY *and* ANNIE.   *The living-room.* HENRY *is alone, sitting in a chair, doing nothing. It's like the beginning of Scene 1 and Scene 3.*
   ANNIE *is heard letting herself in through the front door. Then she comes in from the hall.*
   ANNIE *enters wearing a topcoat and carrying a suitcase and a small travelling bag.*

ANNIE: Hello, I'm back.

(She puts down the suitcase and the bag and goes to kiss HENRY.*)*

HENRY: Hello.

(She starts taking off her coat.)

How was it?
ANNIE: We had a good finish—a woman in the audience was sick. Billy came on with my heart skewered on his dagger and—ugh—whoops!

(She takes her coat out into the hall, reappears and goes to the travelling bag.)

HENRY: I thought you were coming back overnight.

(From the travelling bag ANNIE *takes a small, smart-looking carrier bag with handles, a purchase from a boutique.)*

ANNIE: What have you been doing? How's the film?

(She gives the present to HENRY, *kissing him lightly.)*

HENRY: I thought you were on the sleeper.
ANNIE: What's the matter?
HENRY: I was wondering what happened to you.
ANNIE: Nothing happened to me. Have you had lunch?
HENRY: No. Did you catch the early train this morning, then?
ANNIE: Yes. Scratch lunch, all right?

(She goes into the kitchen and returns after a moment.)

My God, it's all gone downhill since Sunday. Hasn't Mrs Chamberlain been?

HENRY: I phoned the hotel.

ANNIE: When?

HENRY: Last night. They said you'd checked out.

ANNIE: Did they?

(She picks up her suitcase and goes out into the bedroom. HENRY *doesn't move. A few moments later* ANNIE *reappears, without the suitcase and almost walking backwards.)*

Oh, God, Hen. Have we had burglars? What were you doing?

HENRY: Where were you?

ANNIE: On the sleeper. I don't know why I said I came down this morning. It just seemed easier. I wasn't there last night because I caught the train straight from the theatre.

HENRY: Was the train late arriving?

ANNIE: Do you want to see my ticket?

HENRY: Well, have you been to the zoo?

(She meets his look expressionlessly.)

Who were you with?

ANNIE: Don't be like this, Hen. You're not like this.

HENRY: Yes, I am.

ANNIE: I don't want you to. It's humiliating.

HENRY: I really am not trying to humiliate you.

ANNIE: For you, I mean. It's humiliating for you. *(Pause.)* I travelled down with one of the company. We had breakfast at Euston Station. He was waiting for a train. I stayed talking. Then I came home, not thinking that suddenly after two and a half years I'd be asked to account for my movements.

HENRY: You got off the sleeper and spent the morning sitting at Euston Station?

ANNIE: Yes.

HENRY: You and this actor.

ANNIE: Yes. Can I go now? *(She turns away.)*

HENRY: How did you sleep? *(She turns to look at him blankly.)*

Well, did you?

ANNIE: Did I what?

What's the point? You'd only wonder if I was lying.

HENRY: Would you lie?

ANNIE: I might.

HENRY: Did you?

ANNIE: No. You see? I'm going to tidy up and put everything back.

HENRY: Do you want to know what I was looking for?

ANNIE: No. Did you find it?

HENRY: No. *(She turns towards the bedroom.)*

HENRY: Was it Billy? *(She turns back.)*

ANNIE: Why Billy?

HENRY: I know it's him. Billy, Billy, Billy, the name keeps dropping, each time without significance, but it can't help itself. Hapless as a secret in a computer. Blip, blip. Billy, Billy. Talk to me.

I'm sorry about the bedroom.

ANNIE: You should have put everything back. Everything would be the way it was.

HENRY: You can't put things back. They won't go back. Talk to me.

I'm your chap. I know about this. We start off like one of those caterpillars designed for a particular leaf. The exclusive voracity of love. And then not. How strange that the way of things is not suspended to meet our special case. But it never is. I don't want anyone else but sometimes, surprisingly, there's someone, not the prettiest or the most available, but you know that in another life it would be her. Or him, don't you find? A small quickening. The room responds slightly to being entered. Like a raised blind. Nothing intended, and a long way from doing anything, but you catch the glint of being someone else's possibility, and it's a sort of politeness to show you haven't missed it, so you push it a little, well within safety, but there's that sense of a promise almost being made in the touching and kissing without which no one can seem to say good morning in this poncy business and one more push would do it. Billy. Right?

ANNIE: Yes.

HENRY: I love you.

ANNIE: And I you. I wouldn't be here if I didn't.

HENRY: Tell me, then.

ANNIE: I love you.

HENRY: Not that.

ANNIE: Yes, that. That's all I'd need to know.

HENRY: You'd need more.

ANNIE: No.

HENRY: I need it. I can manage knowing if you did but I can't manage not knowing if you did or not. I won't be able to work.

ANNIE: Don't blackmail.

HENRY: You'd ask me.

ANNIE: I never have.

HENRY: There's never *been* anything.

ANNIE: Dozens.

HENRY: In your head.

ANNIE: What's the difference? For the first year at least, every halfway decent looking woman under fifty you were ever going to meet.

HENRY: But you learned better.

ANNIE: No, I just learned not to care. There was nothing to keep you here so I assumed you wanted to stay. I stopped caring about the rest of it.

HENRY: I care. Tell me.

ANNIE: *(Hardening.)* I did tell you. I spent the morning talking to Billy in a station cafeteria instead of coming straight home to you and I fibbed about the train because *that* seemed like infidelity—but all you want to know is did I sleep with him first?

HENRY: Yes. Did you?

ANNIE: No.

HENRY: Did you want to?

ANNIE: Oh, for God's sake!

HENRY: You can ask me.

ANNIE: I prefer to respect your privacy.

HENRY: I have none. I disclaim it. Did you?

ANNIE: What about your dignity, then?

HENRY: Yes, you'd behave better than me. I don't believe in behaving well. I don't believe in debonair relationships. "How's your lover today, Amanda?" "In the pink, Charles. How's yours?" I believe in mess, tears, pain, self-abasement, loss of self-respect, nakedness. Not caring doesn't seem much different from not loving. Did you? You did, didn't you?

ANNIE: This isn't caring. If I had an affair, it would be out of need. Care about that. You won't play on my guilt or my remorse. I'd have none.

HENRY: Need?
       What did you talk about?

ANNIE: Brodie mostly.

HENRY: Yes. I had it coming.

ANNIE: Billy wants to do Brodie's play.

HENRY: When are you going to see Billy again?

ANNIE: He's going straight into another show. I promised to see him. I want to see him.

HENRY: Fine, when should we go? It's all right to come with you, is it?

ANNIE: Why not? Don't let me out of your sight, eh, Hen?

HENRY: When were you thinking of going?

ANNIE: I thought the weekend.

HENRY: And where is it?

ANNIE: Well, Glasgow.

HENRY: Billy travelled down with you from Glasgow and then took a train back?

ANNIE: Yes.

HENRY: And I'm supposed to score points for dignity. I don't think I can. It'll become my only thought. It'll replace thinking.

ANNIE: You mustn't do that. You have to find a part of yourself where I'm not important or you won't be worth loving. It's awful what you did to my clothes and everything. I mean what you did to yourself. It's not you. And it's you I love.

HENRY: Actually I don't think I can manage the weekend. I hope it goes well.

ANNIE: Thank you. *(She moves towards the bedroom.)*

HENRY: What does Billy think of Brodie's play?
ANNIE: He says he can't write.

(She leaves. HENRY *takes his present out of its bag. It is a tartan scarf.)*

SCENE 10 BILLY *and* ANNIE. ANNIE *sits reading on the train.*
     BILLY *approaches the seat next to* ANNIE. *He speaks with a Scottish accent. He carries a grip.*
     The dialogue is amplified through a mike.

BILLY: Excuse me, is this seat taken?
ANNIE: No.
BILLY: Mind if I sit down?
ANNIE: It's a free country. *(*BILLY *sits down.)*
BILLY: D'you reckon?
ANNIE: Sorry?
BILLY: You reckon it's a free country? *(*ANNIE *ignores him.)*
    Going far?
ANNIE: To London.
BILLY: All the way. *(*ANNIE *starts to move to an empty seat.)*
    I'll let you read.
ANNIE: Thank you. *(She sits in the empty seat.)*
BILLY: My name's Bill. *(She ignores him.)*
    Can I just ask you one question?
ANNIE: Mary.
BILLY: Can I just ask you one question, Mary?
ANNIE: One.
BILLY: Do you know what time this train is due to arrive in London?
ANNIE: At about half-past one, I believe, if it's on time.
BILLY: You put me in mind of Mussolini, Mary. People used to say about
    Mussolini, he may be a Fascist, but—
ANNIE: No—that's wrong—that's the old script—
BILLY: *(Swears under his breath.)* Sorry, Roger . . .
ROGER: *(Voice off.)* Okay, cut the tape.
ANNIE: From the top, Roger?
ROGER: *(Voice off.)* Give us a minute.

(A light change reveals that the setting is a fake, in a TV studio. ANNIE *gets up and moves away.* BILLY *joins her. They exchange a few words, and she moves back to her seat, leaving him estranged, an unhappy feeling between them. After a moment the scene fades out.)*

SCENE 11 HENRY *and* ANNIE. HENRY *is alone listening to the radio, which is playing Bach's Air on a G String.*
     ANNIE *enters from the bedroom, dressed to go out, and she is in a hurry.*

HENRY: *(Urgently, on seeing her.)* Listen—
ANNIE: I can't. I'm going to be late now.
HENRY: It's important. *Listen.*
ANNIE: What?
HENRY: *Listen. (She realizes that he means the radio. She listens for a few moments.)* What is it?
ANNIE: *(Pleased.)* Do you like it?
HENRY: I *love* it.
ANNIE: *(Congratulating him.)* It's Bach.
HENRY: The cheeky beggar.
ANNIE: What?
HENRY: He's stolen it.
ANNIE: *Bach?*
HENRY: Note for note. Practically a straight lift from Procul Harum. And he can't even get it right. Hang on. I'll play you the original.

(He moves to get the record. She, pleased by him but going, moves to him.)

ANNIE: Work well.

(She kisses him quickly and lightly but he forces the kiss into a less casual one. His voice, however, keeps its detachment.)

HENRY: You too.
ANNIE: Last day. Why don't you come? *(HENRY shrugs.)* No, all right.
HENRY: I'm only the ghost writer anyway.

(The phone rings.)

ANNIE: If that's them, say I've left.
HENRY: *(Into the phone.)* She's left . . . Oh . . . *(To* ANNIE.*)* It's your friend. *(She hesitates.)* Just go.

*(*ANNIE *takes the phone.)*

ANNIE: *(Into phone.)* Billy . . .? Yes—what?—yes, of course—I'm just late—yes—goodbye—all right . . . Yes, fine. *(She hangs up.)* I love you. Do you understand?
HENRY: No.
ANNIE: Do you think it's unfair?
HENRY: No. It's as though I've been careless, left a door open somewhere while preoccupied.
ANNIE: I'll stop.
HENRY: Not for me. I won't be the person who stopped you. I can't be that. When I got upset you said you'd stop so I try not to get upset. I don't get pathetic because when I got pathetic I could feel how tedious it was, how unattractive. Like Max, your ex. Remember Max? Love me because I'm in pain. No good. Not in very good taste. So.

Dignified cuckoldry is a difficult trick, but it can be done. Think of it as modern marriage. We have got beyond hypocrisy, you and I. Exclusive rights isn't love, it's colonization.

ANNIE: Stop it—please stop it. *(Pause.)*

HENRY: The trouble is, I can't *find* a part of myself where you're not important. I write in order to be worth your while and to finance the way I want to live with you. Not the way *you* want to live. The way *I* want to live with *you*. Without you I wouldn't care. I'd eat tinned spaghetti and put on yesterday's clothes. But as it is I change my socks, and make money, and tart up Brodie's unspeakable drivel into speakable drivel so he can be an author too, like me. Not that it seems to have done him much good. Perhaps the authorities saw that it was a touch meretricious. *Meretrix, meretricis.* Harlot.

ANNIE: You shouldn't have done it if you didn't think it was right.

HENRY: You think it's right. I can't cope with more than one moral system at a time. Mine is that what you think is right is right. What you do is right. What you want is right. There was a tribe, wasn't there, which worshipped Charlie Chaplin. It worked just as well as any other theology, apparently. They loved Charlie Chaplin. I love you.

ANNIE: So you'll forgive me anything, is that it, Hen? I'm a selfish cow but you love me so you'll overlook it, is that right? Thank you, but that's not it. I wish I felt selfish, everything would be easy. Goodbye Billy. I don't need him. How can I need someone I spend half my time telling to grow up? I'm . . .—what's a petard?,* I've often wondered.

HENRY: What?

ANNIE: A petard. Something you hoist,* is it, piece of rope?

HENRY: I don't think so.

ANNIE: Well, anyway. All right?

HENRY: All right what? I keep marrying people who suddenly lose a wheel.

ANNIE: I don't feel selfish, I feel hoist. I send out waves, you know. Not free. Not interested. He sort of got in under the radar. Acting daft on a train. Next thing I'm looking round for him, makes the day feel better, it's like love or something: no—love, absolutely, how can I say it wasn't? You weren't replaced, or even replaceable. But I liked it, being older for once, in charge, my pupil. And it was a long way north. And so on. I'm sorry I hurt you. But I meant it. It meant something. And now that it means less than I thought and I feel silly, I won't drop him as if it was nothing, a pick-up, it wasn't that, I'm not that. I just want him to stop needing me so I can stop behaving well. This is me behaving well. I have to choose who I hurt and I choose you because I'm yours. *(Pause. The phone rings.)* Maybe it's just me.

HENRY: *(Into phone.)* Roger—? She's left, about ten minutes ago—yes, I know, dear, but—don't talk to me about unprofessional, Roger—you lost

---

*petard, hoist: The allusion is to Shakespeare's *Hamlet*; "Hoist with his own petard" means he (a schemer) is blown up by a bomb intended for his enemy.

half a day shooting the war memorial with a boom shadow all over it—okay, scream at me if it makes you feel better—(ANNIE *takes the phone out of his hand.*)

ANNIE: (*Into phone.*) Keep your knickers on, it's only a bloody play. (*She hangs up and starts to go.*)
          (*Going.*) Bye.

HENRY: Annie. (*Pause.*) Yes, all right.

ANNIE: I need you.

HENRY: Yes, I know.

ANNIE: Please don't let it wear away what you feel for me. It won't, will it?

HENRY: No, not like that. It will go on or it will flip into its opposite. What time will you be back?

ANNIE: Not late.

(*He nods at her. She nods back and leaves.* HENRY *sits down in his chair. Then he gets up and starts the record playing—Procul Harum's "A Whiter Shade of Pale," which is indeed a version of Air on a G String.*
      He stands listening to it, smiling at its Bach, until the vocals start. Then the smile gets overtaken.)

HENRY: Oh, please, please, please, please, *don't.*

(*Then blackout, but the music continues.*)

SCENE 12   HENRY, ANNIE *and* BRODIE.   *In the blackout the music gives way to recorded dialogue between* ANNIE *and* BILLY, *who speaks with a Scottish accent.*

BILLY: (*Voice.*) Wait for me.

ANNIE: (*Voice.*) Yes, I will.

BILLY: (*Voice.*) Everything's got to change. Except you. Don't you change.

ANNIE: (*Voice.*) No. I won't. I'll wait for you and for everything to change.

BILLY: (*Voice.*) That could take longer. (*Laughs.*) I might have to do it myself.

(*By this time, light has appeared starting with the faint glow from the television screen.*)
(BRODIE, *alone in the living-room, is twenty-five, wearing a cheap suit. He is holding a tumbler of neat scotch, his attention engaged by the television set and particularly by the accompanying video machine. From the television the dialogue has been followed by the echoing clang of a cell door, footsteps, credit music . . .* BRODIE *turns the volume down.* HENRY *enters from the kitchen carrying a small jug of water for* BRODIE's *scotch. In the room there is wine for* HENRY *and another glass for* ANNIE.)
(BRODIE *speaks with a Scottish accent.*)

BRODIE: Very handy, these machines. When did they come out?

HENRY: Well, I suppose they were coming out about the time you were going in.

BRODIE: You can set them two weeks ahead.
HENRY: Yes.
BRODIE: How much?
HENRY: A few hundred. They vary.
BRODIE: I'll have to pinch one sometime.
HENRY: If you leave it a bit, they'll probably improve them so that you can have it recording concurrently with your sentence. (BRODIE *looks at* HENRY *without expression.*)
BRODIE: Annie looked nice. She's come on a bit since *Rosie of the Royal Infirmary.* A good-looking woman.

(HENRY *doesn't answer.* ANNIE *enters from the kitchen with a dip, peanuts, etc. on a tray. She puts the tray down.* HENRY *pours wine into a third glass.*)

Just saying you looked nice.
ANNIE: Oh, yes?
BRODIE: The pretty one was supposed to be me, was he?
ANNIE: Well . . .
BRODIE: He's not a pansy, is he?
ANNIE: I don't think so. (HENRY *hands her the glass of wine.*)
          Thank you.
HENRY: *(To* BRODIE, *indicating the TV.)* What did you think?
BRODIE: I liked it better before. You don't mind me saying?
HENRY: No.
ANNIE: It did work.
BRODIE: You mean getting me sprung?
ANNIE: No, I didn't mean that.
BRODIE: That's right. I got sprung by the militarists.
HENRY: I don't think I follow that.
BRODIE: Half a billion pounds for defence, nothing left for prisons. So you get three, four to a cell. First off, they tell the magistrates, for God's sake go easy, *fine* the bastards. But still they keep coming—four, five to a cell. Now they're frightened it's going to blow up. Even the warders are going on strike. So: "Give us the money to build more prisons!" "Can't be done, laddie, we're spending the money to keep the world free, not in prison." So they start freeing the prisoners. Get it? I'm out because the missiles I was marching against are using up the money they need for a prison to put me in. Beautiful. Can I have another?

(He holds up his empty glass for ANNIE. Slight pause. HENRY stays still.)

ANNIE: Please help yourself. (BRODIE *does so.*)
BRODIE: Early release. There was eight of us just on my corridor. *(To* HENRY.) Not one of them a controversial TV author. I don't owe you.
HENRY: Is it against your principles to say thank you for *anything,* even a drink?
BRODIE: Fair enough. You had a go. You did your best. It probably needed something, to work in with their prejudices.

HENRY: Yes, they are a bit prejudiced, these drama producers. They don't like plays which go "clunk" every time someone opens his mouth. They gang up against soap-box bigots with no idea that everything has a length. They think TV is a visual medium. *(To* ANNIE, *puzzled.)* Is this *him?*

BRODIE: Don't be clever with me, Henry, like you were clever with my play. I lived it and put my guts into it, and you came along and wrote it clever. Not for me. For her. I'm not stupid.

ANNIE: *(To* HENRY.*)* No, this isn't him.

BRODIE: Yes, it bloody is. That was me on the train, and this is me again, and I don't think you're that different either.

ANNIE: And *that* wasn't him. *(She points at the TV.)* He was helpless, like a three-legged calf, nervous as anything. A boy on the train. Chatting me up. Nice. He'd been in some trouble at the camp, some row, I forget, he was going absent without leave. He didn't know anything about a march. He didn't know anything about anything, except *Rosie of the Royal Infirmary.* By the time we got to London he would have followed me into the Ku Klux Klan. He tagged on. And when we were passing the war memorial he got his lighter out. It was one of those big chrome Zippos—click, snap. Private Brodie goes over the top to the slaughter, not an idea in his head except to impress me. What else could I do? He was my recruit.

HENRY: You should have told me. That one I would have known how to write.

ANNIE: Yes.

BRODIE: Listen—I'm still here.

ANNIE: So you are, Bill. Finish your drink, will you?

BRODIE: Why not? *(*BRODIE *finishes his drink and stands up.)*
I can come back for some dip another time.

ANNIE: No time like the present.

(ANNIE *picks up the bowl of dip and smashes it into his face. She goes to the hall door, leaving it open while she briefly disappears to get* BRODIE*'s coat.)*
(HENRY *has stood up, but* BRODIE *isn't going to do anything. He carefully wipes his face with his handkerchief.)*

HENRY: Well, it was so interesting to meet you. I'd heard so much about you.

BRODIE: I don't really blame you, Henry. The price was right. I remember the time she came to visit me. She was in a blue dress, and there was a thrill coming off her like she was back on the box, but there was no way in. It was the first time I felt I was in prison. You know what I mean.

(ANNIE *stands at the door holding* BRODIE*'s coat. He takes it from her, ignoring her as he walks out. She follows him, and the front door is heard closing.* ANNIE *returns.)*

HENRY: I don't know what it did to him, but it scared the hell out of me. Are you all right? *(She nods.)*

ANNIE: Are you all right?

(The phone rings. HENRY *picks it up.)*

HENRY: Hello. *(Into the phone, suddenly uncomfortable.)* Oh, hello. Did you want
  to speak to Annie?
ANNIE: No.
HENRY: *(Suddenly relaxes.)* Well, that's fantastic, Max!
  (To ANNIE.*)* It's your ex. He's getting married.
  (To phone.) Congratulations. Who is she?

*(*HENRY *ferries this over to* ANNIE *with an expressive look, which she returns.*
ANNIE *moves to* HENRY *and embraces his shoulders from behind. She leans on
him tiredly while he deals with the phone.)*

Oh, I think you're very wise. To marry one actress is unfortunate, to marry
two is simply asking for it.

*(*ANNIE *kisses him. He covers the mouthpiece with his hand.)*

(Into phone.) Really? Across a crowded room, eh?
ANNIE: I've had it. Look after me. *(He covers the mouthpiece.)*
HENRY: Don't worry. I'm your chap.
  (Into phone.) Well, it's very decent of you to say so, Max.
  (To ANNIE.*)* "No hard feelings?" What does he mean? If it wasn't for me,
  he wouldn't be engaged *now.*

*(*ANNIE *disengages herself from him with a smile and goes around turning out
the lights until the only light is coming from the bedroom door.)*

(Into phone.) No. I'm afraid she isn't . . . She'll be so upset when I tell her
. . . No, I mean when I tell her she missed you . . . No, she'll be delighted.
I'm delighted, Max. Isn't love wonderful?

*(*ANNIE *finishes with the lights and goes out into the bedroom.* HENRY *is being
impatiently patient with* MAX *on the phone, trying to end it.)*

HENRY: Yes, well, we look forward to meeting her. What? Oh, yes?

*(Absently he clicks on the little radio, which starts playing, softly, "I'm a Believer"
by the Monkees. He is immediately beguiled. He forgets* MAX *until the phone crackle
gets back through to him.)*

Sorry. Yes, I'm still here. *(He turns the song up slightly.)*

Writing Assignments for "The Real Thing"

I. Brief Papers: Act 1
  A. 1. Show that Max, as a character in *The House of Cards* (Scene 1), is different
       from the "real" Max, a character in *The Real Thing*.
     2. Show that in Act 1 Henry speaks and acts very much like Max does in Henry's
        play, *The House of Cards*.

3. Contrast Max's behavior in *The House of Cards* (Scene 1), when he discovers his wife's adultery, with his behavior when, in Scene 3, he discovers Annie's adultery.
4. Explain the role of Henry's handkerchief in the development of the plot.
5. Explain why Henry has trouble selecting records for his appearance on the TV show, *Desert Island Discs*?

B. Argue for or against one of the following assertions:
  1. In the scene from *The House of Cards* (Scene 1), Max is justified in accusing Charlotte of adultery.
  2. In Scene 3, Max is justified in accusing Annie of adultery.
  3. Charlotte is essentially right when she tells Henry that *The House of Cards* is unrealistic.

C. 1. In Scene 2, Annie is not afraid of revealing her love for Henry, but he wants to keep their affair a secret. Do you tend to agree with Annie or Henry?
  2. Max and Annie praise Brodie's "missile protest" as an act of "sheer moral courage." Henry, on the other hand, has little sympathy for Brodie's "vandalism." On the basis of what is revealed in Scene 2, whose opinion do you favor?
  3. Besides the vegetable snack—"crudités"—there are certain lines in Scene 2 that might also be considered crude. Select one or two of these lines and explain your response. Do you think they are in bad taste or appropriate to the occasion?
  4. What do you think Henry means when he says, "Loving and being loved is unliterary. It's happiness expressed in banality and lust"? Explain.

II. Brief Papers: Act 2

A. 1. Explain Debbie's meaning when she says that "Exclusive rights isn't love; it's colonization" (p. 1246).
  2. Show how, in Scene 6, the reading rehearsal for *'Tis Pity She's a Whore* becomes "the real thing" for Annie and Billy.
  3. At the end of the reading rehearsal in both Scene 6 and Scene 8, Annie abandons her role as Annabella speaking to Giovanni and exclaims, "Billy." Does this mean the same thing in both scenes, or does it signal some change in their relationship? Explain.
  4. At the end of the scene from *The House of Cards* (Scene 1), Max opens a present from Charlotte. At the end of Scene 9, Henry opens a present from Annie. Compare the two gifts and their effect on the two men.
  5. According to Charlotte, how did she come to believe that "it didn't matter" if she had other lovers?

B. Argue for or against one of the following assertions:
  1. Charlotte is right in saying that sexual relationships can only be a "bargain," not a "committment."
  2. Charlotte is right in calling Henry "the last romantic."

      3. Annie is justified in hitting Brodie in the face with a bowl of dip.
      4. Annie will break up with Billy and remain forever faithful to Henry.

C. 1. How do you respond to Debbie's argument that sexual love is "biology . . . free of propaganda."
    2. Do you tend to agree with Annie or Henry in their debate about what makes good writing? Explain.
    3. How do you respond to Annie's claim that Henry should "care about" her "need," even if her need is to have an affair with Billy?
    4. How does the fact that Annie is several years older than Billy affect your response to their affair?
    5. Charlotte implies that it was better that she had nine secret affairs which had no apparent effect on her marriage than that Henry had one affair (with Annie) which led to painful revelations, divorce, and the break up of his family. Do you agree with Charlotte? Explain.

III. A Modern Problem Play

Combine the following elements into a coherent paragraph that explains how *The Real Thing* is a modern problem play.

  1. This is true to a certain extent.
  2. *The Real Thing* is a modern variation.
  3. It is a variation on the nineteenth-century problem play.
  4. The problem play has a main purpose.
  5. The main purpose is to discuss a significant social issue.

  6. The problem play is unlike popular drama.
  7. The problem play does not usually have a happy ending.
  8. The problem play does not resolve conflicts.
  9. Conflicts are resolved in a way.
10. The way appeals to conventional sentiments of the audience.

11. *The Real Thing* does not come to a clear resolution.
12. *The Real Thing* makes fun of two things.
13. One thing is the conservative ideal of marriage
14. Another thing is the modern ideal of free love.

15. *The Real Thing* does not solve the marriage problem.
16. *The Real Thing* represents conflicting ideas and feelings.
17. These ideas and feeling have created this problem.

18. The problem has an origin.
19. The origin is a belief.
20. The belief is still held by most religions.
21. Marriage is monogamous and permanent.
22. Marriage should be monogamous and permanent.

23. Charlotte opposes this idea.
24. Charlotte argues this.
25. Marriage is not a commitment.
26. Marriage is not a permanent state of being.
27. Marriage is only a bargain.
28. The bargain is renewed or revoked every day.

29. Debbie speaks for many young people.
30. Debbie also attacks the conventional view.
31. The view is that lovers are sexually bound.
32. They are bound to each.
33. "Exclusive rights isn't love, it's colonization."

34. Henry consistently makes fun of modern notions.
35. Debbie and Charlotte have these notions.
36. Even Annie has modern notions.
37. Henry cannot live under the old rules.
38. The rules are fidelity and permanence.

39. Henry finds this.
40. The arguments for free love are silly and self-indulgent.
41. But Henry does this.
42. He divorces Charlotte.
43. He lives with Annie.
44. Annie has an affair with Billy.
45. Henry more or less accepts "dignified cuckoldry."

46. *The Real Thing* does not reach a clear or hopeful conclusion.
47. It provides a clear and witty exploration of new ideas.
48. These ideas could change the structure of society.
49. Some people believe this.

IV. Longer Papers

1. Argue for or against the assertion that, according to *The Real Thing,* monogamy is unrealistic and probably undesirable.
2. Debbie thinks that her father's play, *The House of Cards,* is conventional and trivial: it "wasn't about anything except did she have it off or didn't she." But Henry argues that the play is *really* about "self-knowledge through pain." We are invited to assume that the meaning of *The Real Thing* might be argued in the same way. Do you think that the play is just another treatment of infidelity among the professional classes, or is it about "self-knowledge through pain"?
3. Explain Henry's views on love and sex by showing how he tries to refute the more modern or liberal views of Charlotte, Debbie, and Annie.
4. While this play is mostly about the difficulty of defining and recognizing "the real thing" in love, it is also about the problem of defining and recognizing "the real thing" in writing. For example, both Charlotte and Debbie attack Henry's play,

The House of Cards; Henry attacks Brodie's play while Annie defends it; Annie attacks Henry's "English Lit." view of writing. With reference to these debates, and any other related matters, write a paper that shows how this problem of writing the "real stuff" is developed and resolved (or not resolved).

5. In several scenes, the characters in *The Real Thing* are acting or rehearsing other plays—*The House of Cards, Miss Julie, 'Tis Pity She's a Whore,* and Brodie's play. Discuss the various ways in which these segments of other plays contribute to our understanding of the central action and the main issues in *The Real Thing.*

6. Many people who fall in love believe (or hope) that their love is "the real thing." Has your understanding of "the real thing" been affected or modified by reading Stoppard's play? Respond to this question in a paper which, while based on your own views about "real" love, is developed and illustrated by specific reference to the ideas and incidents in *The Real Thing.*

7. Write a paper in which you agree or disagree with this criticism of *The Real Thing:*

How can anyone call Annie the *heroine* of this play? If she is, then the title should be changed to *The Real Bitch.* Early on, while she is married to Max, she seduces an ignorant young soldier, Brodie, for her own political goals, and then, instead of visiting him in jail as she promised, she sneaks off to have sex with her lover, Henry. When Henry asks, "What about Brodie?" she says, "Let him rot." Annie cares even less about Max who finds out about her adultery in a most disgusting and painful way. Annie then moves in with Henry and immediately starts nagging him to rewrite Brodie's play. In the meantime, she starts sleeping with Billy, an actor young enough to be her son. Henry is terribly hurt when he finds out about Annie and Billy, but instead of feeling sorry and apologizing, she tells Henry that he is supposed to "care about" her "need" for young lovers. If what Annie feels and wants is supposed to be "the real thing," then modern society is in very bad shape.

8. After Henry learns of Annie's continuing affair with Billy, he reflects, with some irony, on how he is supposed to accept her adultery: "Dignified cuckoldry is a difficult trick, but it can be done. Think of it as modern marriage. We have got beyond hypocrisy, you and I. Exclusive rights isn't love, it's colonization" (Scene 11, p. 1255). Argue for or against the assertion that the play supports this view of marriage.

ACKNOWLEDGMENTS

AIKEN, CONRAD: from *The Collected Short Stories* by Conrad Aiken. Reprinted by permission of Schocken Books, Inc. Copyright © 1922, 1923, 1924, 1925, 1927, 1928, 1929, 1930, 1931, 1932, 1933, 1934, 1935, 1941, 1950, 1952, 1953, 1955, 1956, 1957, 1958, 1959, 1960, 1961, 1962, 1964.

ANDERSON, SHERWOOD: Reprinted by permission of Harold Ober Associates Incorporated. Copyright © 1922 by Dial Publishing Co. Copyright renewed 1940 by Eleanor Copenhaver Anderson.

ATWOOD, MARGARET: "Against Still Life," from *The Circle Game.* Copyright © 1966 by Margaret Atwood (Toronto: House of Anansi Press, 1978). Reprinted by permission.

AUDEN, W. H.: "The Wanderer," "Lay Your Sleeping Head," from *W. H. Auden Collected Poems,* edited by Edward Mendelson. Copyright © 1934 and renewed 1962 by W. H. Auden. Reprinted by permission of Random House, Inc. and Faber and Faber Ltd.

BERRY, WENDELL: From *Openings.* Copyright © 1968 by Wendell Berry. Reprinted by permission of Harcourt Brace Jovanovich, Inc.

BRADBURY, RAY: Reprinted by permission of Don Congdon Associates, Inc. Copyright © 1950 by Ray Bradbury. Copyright renewed 1977 by Ray Bradbury.

BROOKS, GWENDOLYN: "The Mother." Copyright © 1945 Harper & Row, Publishers, Inc. Reprinted with permission.

CARVER, RAYMOND: "What We Talk About When We Talk About Love" is reprinted from *What We Talk About When We Talk About Love* by Raymond Carver. Copyright © 1981 by Raymond Carver. Reprinted by permission of Alfred A. Knopf, Inc.

CHEEVER, JOHN: Copyright © 1953, 1954, 1964 by John Cheever. Reprinted from *The Stories of John Cheever,* by permission of Alfred A. Knopf, Inc.

CLIFTON, LUCILLE: "the thirty eighth year of my life," from *An Ordinary Woman* by Lucille Clifton. Copyright © 1974 by Lucille Clifton. Reprinted by Permission of Curtis Brown, Ltd.

CUMMINGS, E. E.: Copyright © 1940 by e. e. cummings; renewed 1968 by Marion Morehouse Cummings. Reprinted by permission of Harcourt Brace Jovanovich, Inc. from *Complete Poems 1913–1962* by e. e. cummings.

DEFOE, MARK: From *Black Willow Poetry.* Reprinted by permission. Copyright © 1982 by Mark Defoe.

DICKEY, JAMES: "Adultery," copyright © 1966 by James Dickey. Reprinted from *Poems 1957– 1967;* this poem first appeared in *The Nation.* "Cherrylog Road," copyright © 1963 by James

Dickey. Reprinted from *Helmets;* this poem first appeared in *The New Yorker.* "Encounter in the Cage Country," copyright © 1966 by James Dickey. Reprinted from *Poems 1957–1967;* first appeared in *The New Yorker.* All selections reprinted by permission of Wesleyan University Press.

DICKINSON, EMILY: "Apparently With No Surprise," "The Wind Took Up the Northern Things," "One Need Not be a Chamber," "The Soul Selects Her Own Society," "Because I Could Not Stop for Death," "I Started Early—Took My Dog," "It's Easy to Invent a Life," and "I cannot live with You" reprinted by permission of the publishers and the Trustees of Amherst College from *The Poems of Emily Dickinson,* edited by Thomas H. Johnson, Cambridge, MA: The Belknap Press of Harvard University Press. Copyright © 1951, 1955, 1979, 1983 by the President and Fellows of Harvard College and from *The Complete Poems of Emily Dickinson,* edited by Thomas H. Johnson, copyright © 1929 by Martha Dickinson Bianchi; copyright renewed 1957 by Mary L. Hampson. Reprinted by permission of Little Brown and Co.

DOOLITTLE, HILDA (HD): Copyright © 1924 by Hilda Doolittle. Reprinted by permission of New Directions Publishing Corporation.

DUYN, MONA VAN: "Late Loving." Reprinted by permission of the author. Copyright, *Atlantic Monthly.*

ELIOT, T. S.: From *Collected Poems 1909–1962* by T. S. Eliot. Copyright © 1936 by Harcourt Brace Jovanovich, Inc.; copyright © 1963, 1964 by T. S. Eliot. Reprinted by permission of the publisher and Faber and Faber Ltd.

FAULKNER, WILLIAM: Copyright © 1939 and renewed 1967 by Estelle Faulkner and Jill Faulkner Summers. Reprinted from *Collected Stories of William Faulkner,* by permission of Random House, Inc.

FITZGERALD, F. SCOTT: "Winter Dreams," from *All the Sad Young Men.* Copyright © 1922 Frances Scott Fitzgerald Lanahan; copyright renewed. Reprinted with permission of Charles Scribner's Sons, an imprint of Macmillan Publishing Company. Excerpts from *The Great Gatsby,* copyright © 1925 Charles Scribner's Sons; copyright renewed 1953 Frances Scott Fitzgerald Lanahan. Reprinted with permission of Charles Scribner's Sons, an imprint of Macmillan Publishing Company.

FROST, ROBERT: "The Hill Wife," "Home Burial," from *The Poetry of Robert Frost* edited by Edward Connery Lathem. Copyright © 1916, 1930, 1939, 1969 by Holt, Rinehart and Winston. Copyright © 1944, 1958 by Robert Frost; "Design," from *The Poetry of Robert Frost* edited by Edward Connery Lathem. Copyright © 1930, 1939, 1969 by Holt, Rinehart and Winston. Copyright © 1936, 1958 by Robert Frost. Copyright © 1964, 1967 by Lesley Frost Ballantine. All selections reprinted by permission of Holt, Rinehart and Winston, Publishers.

GAINES, ERNEST J.: "The Sky is Gray" from *Bloodline* by Ernest J. Gaines. Copyright © 1963 by Ernest J. Gaines. A Dial Press Book. Reprinted by permission of Doubleday & Company, Inc.

GALLAGHER, TESS: From *Under Stars.* Reprinted by permission of The Graywolf Press.

GILMAN, CHARLOTTE PERKINS: From *The Yellow Wall-Paper.* Pantheon Books. Copyright © 1980 by Anne J. Lane.

GIOSEFFI, DANIELA: From *Eggs in the Lake.* BOA Editions. Copyright © 1979 by Daniela Gioseffi.

GLASPELL, SUSAN: Reprinted by permission of Mr. S. C. Cook.

GODWIN, GAIL: "Dream Children" reprinted from *Dream Children* by Gail Godwin. Copyright © 1976 by Gail Godwin. Reprinted by permission of Alfred Knopf, Inc.

HALL, DONALD: From *Alligator Bride: Poems New and Selected.* Copyright © 1954 by Donald Hall. Reprinted by permission.

HARDY, THOMAS. "The Darkling Thrush." From *The Complete Poems of Thomas Hardy,* edited by James Gibson. Copyright © 1978 Macmillan Publishing Company. Reprinted with permission.

HEMINGWAY, ERNEST: "Indian Camp," from *In Our Time.* Copyright © 1925 Charles Scribner's Sons; copyright renewed 1953 Ernest Hemingway. Reprinted with permission of Charles Scribner's Sons, an imprint of Macmillan Publishing Company. Excerpts from *The Sun Also Rises,* copyright © 1926 Charles Scribner's Sons; copyright renewed 1954 by Ernest Hemingway. Reprinted with the permission of Charles Scribner's Sons, an imprint of Macmillan Publishing Company.

HOPKINS, GERARD MANLEY: from *Poems of Gerard Manley Hopkins.* Copyright © 1967 by Oxford University Press.

HOUSMAN, A.E.: "To An Athlete Dying Young," "Terence, this is stupid stuff" from *The Collected Poems of A. E. Housman.* Copyright © 1939, 1940, 1965 by Holt, Rinehart and Winston, Inc. Copyright © 1967, 1968 by Robert E. Symons. Reprinted by permission of Holt, Rinehart and Winston, Publishers.

JARRELL, RANDALL: Reprinted with permission of Macmillan Publishing Company from *The Lost World* by Randall Jarrell. Copyright © Randall Jarrell 1963, 1965. Originally appeared in *The New Yorker.*

JONG, ERICA: From *Ordinary Miracles* by Erica Jong. Copyright © 1983 by Erica Jong. Reprinted by arrangement with NAL Penguin Inc., New York, NY.

JOYCE, JAMES: From *Dubliners* by James Joyce. Copyright © 1916 by B. W. Huebsch. Definitive text copyright © 1967 by the Estate of James Joyce. Reprinted by permission of Viking Penguin Inc.

KARAFEL, LORRAINE: "Heroines" from *The New Republic,* July 14–22, 1986 by Lorraine Karafel. Reprinted by the author's permission.

KINNEL, GALWAY: From *Body Rags* by Galway Kinnel. Copyright © 1967 by Galway Kinnel. Reprinted by permission of Houghton Mifflin Company.

LARKIN, PHILIP: Reprinted by permission of Faber and Faber Ltd. from *The Whitsun Weddings* by Philip Larkin.

LE GUIN, URSULA K.: "Nine Lives," copyright © 1969, 1975 by Ursula K. Le Guin; reprinted by permission of the author, and the author's agent, Virginia Kidd.

LOGAN, JOHN: "Lines to His Son on Reaching Adolescence," from *Ghosts of the Heart* by John Logan. Copyright © 1960 by John Logan. Reprinted by permissions.

LOWELL, ROBERT: "To Speak of the Woe That Is in Marriage" from *Life Studies* by Robert Lowell. Copyright © 1958, 1959 by Robert Lowell. Reprinted by permission of Farrar, Straus and Giroux, Inc.

MACLEISH, ARCHIBALD: From *Collected Poems 1917–1952* by Archibald MacLeish. Copyright © 1952 by Archibald MacLeish. Reprinted by permission of Houghton Mifflin Company.

MERWIN, W.S.: "The Salt Pond." From *The Rain in the Forest.* Copyright © 1988 Alfred A. Knopf, Inc.

MILLER, ARTHUR: *Death of a Salesman* by Arthur Miller. Copyright © 1949, renewed 1977 by Arthur Miller. Reprinted by permission of Viking Penguin, Inc. *Caution:* This play in its printed form is designed for the reading public only. All dramatic rights in it are fully protected by copyright, and no public or private performance—professional or amateur—may be given without the written permission of the author and the payment of royalty. As the courts have also ruled that the public reading of a play constitutes a public performance, no such reading may be given except under the conditions stated above. Communication should be addressed to the author's representative, International Creative Management, Inc., 40 W. 57th St., New York, NY 10019.

MOORE, MARIANNE: Reprinted with permission of Macmillan Publishing Company from *Collected Poems* by Marianne Moore. Copyright © 1941, renewed 1969 by Marianne Moore.

NISSENSON, HUGH: Reprinted by permission of Farrar, Straus and Giroux, Inc. "Forcing the End" from *In the Reign of Peace* by Hugh Nissenson. Copyright © 1968, 1969, 1970, 1972 by Hugh Nissenson.

OATES, JOYCE CAROL: Reprinted from *The Wheel of Love* by Joyce Carol Oates by permission of the publisher, Vanguard Press, Inc. Copyright © 1970, 1969, 1968, 1967, 1966, 1965, by Joyce Carol Oates.

O'CONNOR, FLANNERY: From *A Good Man is Hard to Find and Other Stories.* Copyright © 1953 by Flannery O'Connor; renewed 1981 by Mrs. Regina O'Connor. Reprinted by permission of Harcourt Brace Jovanovich, Inc.

OLSEN, TILLIE: "Tell Me a Riddle" excerpted from the book *Tell Me a Riddle* by Tillie Olsen. Copyright © 1956, 1957, 1960, 1961 by Tillie Olsen. Reprinted by permission of Delacorte Press/Seymour Lawrence.

PASTAN, LINDA: "Prosody 101" is reprinted from *A Fraction of Darkness, Poems of Linda Pastan,* by permission of W. W. Norton & Company, Inc. Copyright © 1985 by Linda Pastan.

PIERCE, CONSTANCE: "A Shift in Season," from *The Devil's Millhopper* (Spring 1982). Reprinted by permission.

PLATH, SYLVIA: "The Applicant" from *The Collected Poems of Sylvia Plath,* edited by Ted Hughes. Copyright © 1963 by Sylvia Plath. Reprinted by permission of Harper & Row, Publishers, Inc.

PORTER, KATHERINE ANNE: Copyright © 1939, 1967, by Katherine Anne Porter. Reprinted from her volume *The Leaning Tower and Other Stories* by permission of Harcourt Brace Jovanovich, Inc.

QUAMMEN, DAVID: "Walking Out" reprinted by permission of the author.

REID, ALASTAIR: From *Weathering, Poems and Translations,* E.P. Dutton, 1979. Copyright © Alastair Reid. Reprinted by permission.

REISS, JAMES: Reprinted from *Express* by James Reiss by permission of the University of Pittsburgh Press. Copyright © 1983 by James Reiss.

RICH, ADRIENNE: "Aunt Jennifer's Tigers," "White Night," "Necessities of Life," "Snapshots of a Daughter-in-law," "Diving Into the Wreck," "Living in Sin," "Trying to Talk With a Man," reprinted from *Poems, Selected and New, 1950–1974,* by Adrienne Rich, by permission of W. W. Norton & Company, Inc. Copyright © 1975, 1973, 1971, 1969, 1966 by W. W. Norton & Company, Inc. Copyright © 1967, 1963, 1962, 1961, 1960, 1959, 1958, 1957, 1956, 1955, 1954, 1953, 1952, 1951 by Adrienne Rich. "Phantasia for Elvira Shatayev" is reprinted from *The Dream of a Common Language, Poems 1974–1977,* by Adrienne Rich, by permission of W. W. Norton & Company, Inc. Copyright © 1978 by W. W. Norton & Company, Inc.

ROETHKE, THEODORE: "Elegy for Jane," copyright © 1950 by Theodore Roethke; "Dolor" copyright © 1943 by Modern Poetry Association, Inc. All selections from *The Collected Poems of Theodore Roethke* by Theodore Roethke. Reprinted by permission of Doubleday & Company, Inc.

ROMANO, TOM: From *NCTE Post Pal Postcard.* Reprinted by permission NCTE.

ROTH, PHILIP: From *Goodbye Columbus* by Philip Roth. Copyright © 1959 by Philip Roth. Reprinted by permission of Houghton Mifflin Company.

SANER, REG: Reprinted by permission of Reg Saner.

SEXTON, ANNE: "The Twelve Dancing Princesses," from *Transformations* by Anne Sexton. Copyright © 1971 by Anne Sexton. "You All Know the Story of the Other Woman," "For My Lover, Returning to His Wife," from *Love Poems* by Anne Sexton. Copyright © 1967, 1968, 1969 by Anne Sexton. All selections reprinted by permission of Houghton Mifflin Company.

SHAKESPEARE, WILLIAM: "Hamlet" is reprinted from William Shakespeare, *Hamlet, A Norton Critical Edition,* edited by Cyrus Hoy, by permission of W. W. Norton & Company, Inc. Copyright © 1963 by W. W. Norton & Company, Inc.

SHAW, IRWIN: From *Selected Stories of Irwin Shaw.* Copyright © 1939. Reprinted by permission of Irwin Shaw.

SITWELL, EDITH: From the *Collected Poems* by Edith Sitwell by permission of the publisher, Vanguard Press, Inc. Copyright © 1968 by the Vanguard Press, Inc. Copyright © 1949, 1953, 1954, 1959, 1962, 1963 by Dame Edith Sitwell. Copyrighted in Canada by Macmillan.

SNODGRASS, W. D.: "Leaving the Motel" from *After Experience* by W. D. Snodgrass. Copyright © 1966 by W.D. Snodgrass. Reprinted by permission of Harper & Row, Publishers, Inc.

SNYDER, GARY: *Myths and Texts* by Gary Snyder. Copyright © 1978 by Gary Snyder. Reprinted by permission of New Directions Publishing Corporation.

SOPHOCLES: *The Oedipus Rex of Sophocles: An English Version* by Dudley Fitts and Robert Fitzgerald is reprinted by permission of Harcourt Brace Jovanovich, Inc. Copyright © 1949 by Harcourt Brace Jovanovich, Inc.; renewed 1977 by Cornelia Fitts and Robert Fitzgerald. *Caution:* All rights, including professional, amateur, motion picture, recitation, lecturing, public reading, radio broadcasting and television, are strictly reserved. Inquiries on all rights should be addressed to Harcourt Brace Jovanovich, Inc., Copyrights and Permissions Department, Orlando, FL 32887.

SPENDER, STEPHEN: Reprinted by permission of Random House, Inc. from *Collected Poems 1928–1953* by Stephen Spender.

STAFFORD, WILLIAM: "Traveling through the Dark" from *Stories That Could be True: New and Collected Poems* by William Stafford. Copyright © 1960 by William Stafford. Reprinted by permission of Harper & Row, Publishers, Inc.

STEINBECK, JOHN: From *The Long Valley* by John Steinbeck. Copyright © 1934, renewed 1962 by John Steinbeck. Reprinted by permission of Viking Penguin, Inc.

STOPPARD, TOM: Copyright © 1982, 1983, 1984 by Tom Stoppard. Reprinted by permission of Faber and Faber, Inc.

THOMAS, DYLAN: "Do Not Go Gentle Into That Good Night," "Fern Hill," from *Poems of Dylan Thomas.* Copyright © 1945 by the Trustees for the Copyrights of Dylan Thomas. Reprinted by permission of New Directions Publishing Corporation. "In My Craft or Sullen Art" from *The Poems of Dylan Thomas.* Copyright © 1946 by New Directions Publishing Corporation.

TRILLING, LIONEL: Copyright © 1943, 1971 by Lionel Trilling. Reprinted from *Of This Time, Of That Place and Other Stories* by permission of Harcourt Brace Jovanovich, Inc.

VOIGT, ELLEN BRYANT: Copyright © 1972 by Ellen Bryant Voigt. Reprinted from *Claiming Kin* by permission of Wesleyan University Press.

WAGONER, DAVID: Copyright © 1983 by David Wagoner. "The Best Slow Dancer" first appeared in *Kayak.* "Washing a Young Rhinoceros" and "The Author of 'American Ornithology' Sketches a Bird, Now Extinct" first appeared in *The Atlantic Monthly.* Reprinted by permission of Little, Brown and Company, in association with The Atlantic Monthly Press.

WALKER, ALICE: From *Revolutionary Petunias and Other Poems.* Copyright © 1972 by Alice Walker. Reprinted by permission of Harcourt Brace Jovanovich, Inc.

WILBUR, RICHARD: "The Writer," from *The Mind-Reader.* Copyright © 1971 by Richard Wilbur. "A Late Aubade," from *Walking to Sleep.* Copyright © 1968 by Richard Wilbur. All selections reprinted by permission of Harcourt Brace Jovanovich, Inc.

WILLIAMS, WILLIAM CARLOS: "This Is Just to Say," from *Collected Earlier Poems of William Carlos Williams.* Copyright © 1938 by New Directions Publishing Corporation. "The Use of Force," from *The Farmer's Daughters.* Copyright © 1938 by William Carlos Williams. Reprinted by permission of New Directions Publishing Corporation.

WRIGHT, RICHARD: "The Man Who Lived Underground" from *Eight Men* by Richard Wright. Copyright © 1944 by L.B. Fischer Publishing Corp. Copyright © 1961 by Richard Wright. Reprinted by permission of John Hawkins & Associates, Inc.

YEATS, W.B.: "A Prayer for My Daughter," reprinted with permission of Macmillan Publishing Company from *The Poems of W. B. Yeats,* edited by Richard J. Finneran. Copyright © 1924 by Macmillan Publishing Co., Inc., renewed 1952 by Bertha Georgie Yeats: "The Wild Swans at Coole" reprinted with permission of Macmillan Publishing Company from *The Poems of W. B. Yeats,* edited by Richard J. Finneran. Copyright © 1919 by Macmillan Publishing Co., Inc., renewed 1947 by Bertha Georgie Yeats: "When You Are Old," reprinted with permission of Macmillan Publishing Company from *The Poems of W. B. Yeats,* edited by Richard J. Finneran and by permission of A. P. Watt Ltd. on behalf of Michael B. Yeats and Macmillan, London, Limited.

GLOSSARY OF
LITERARY ITEMS

This glossary provides a brief and provisional definition of the literary terms used in this text. Page numbers refer to a fuller discussion of these terms in the writing assignments and sentence-combining exercises.

Accent   A syllable which, when pronounced, receives more stress than neighboring syllables. "And as Í was gréen and cárefree, fámous amóng the bárns" ("Fern Hill"). "And hé was rích—yes, rícher thán a kíng—" ("Richard Cory"). See also *meter.*

Action   At the simplest level *action* refers to what happens in a particular narrative incident, producing a change in the fortunes of the main character. In *The Importance of Being Earnest,* Jack's proposal to Gwendolen is one such action and Lady Bracknell's refusal to permit the marriage is another. At a higher level, the *action* or *central action* is the sum of those incidents which lead to the most significant change (the climax) in the narrative. The central action of *Oedipus Rex* is the hero's search for the murderer of Laïos, leading to the hero's discovery of his own guilt. *The Importance of Being Earnest* has two important actions, Jack's courtship of Gwendolen and Algernon's courtship of Cecily, both leading to marriage. See also *plot* and *climax.*

Affirmative ending   An ending in which a sympathetic protagonist suffers pain, death, or defeat but which nevertheless suggests the triumph of values like courage, honesty, and love. The endings of "Tell Me a Riddle" and "The Sky is Gray" might be called affirmative but not happy. See also *happy ending.*

Allegory   A narrative in which characters and events are used to express an abstract meaning or doctrine. Unlike symbolic characters, who are usually psychologically complex and can be understood at many levels, allegorical characters usually represent little more than the abstract quality defined by their name—The Boss, The Flirt, The Gossip. Most stories have too many levels of meaning to be read as pure allegory. In "O Youth and Beauty!" Cash Bentley's death is foreshadowed when he meets a whore who resembles "a cartoon of Death," an allegorical figure, but the story itself resists a strict allegorical interpretation. "O Youth and Beauty!" might be read as an allegory of The Aging Athlete, but it has other levels of meaning which are more important. See also *symbol* and *parable.*

Alliteration   The repetition of initial consonant sounds, usually of accented syllables. "I have *s*een them riding *s*eaward on the waves" ("The Love Song of J. Alfred Prufrock"). See p. 614.

Allusion   A reference to characters, events, or places in history or previous literature. In "The Love Song of J. Alfred Prufrock," the line, "I am not Prince Hamlet," makes an explicit allusion to Shakespeare's play. The line, "I have seen my head [grown slightly bald] brought in upon a platter," makes an implicit allusion to the story of John the Baptist. See pp. 614 and 613.

Antagonist   Usually the character or characters who oppose the protagonist, but also any other opposing force, such as the physical environment, social or economic conditions, or a destructive force in the protagonist's nature. In "Defender of the Faith," Grossbart is the antagonist, but so is a complicated "vindictiveness" in Marx's character. See also *protagonist*.

Assonance   The repetition of vowel sounds, usually of accented syllables. In "Ulysses" Tennyson repeats long vowel sounds, *a* and *o,* to slow the rhythm of this passage: "The long day wanes; the slow moon climbs; the deep / Moans round with many voices." Here similar vowel sounds are repeated in "d*a*y" and "w*a*nes"; also in "sl*o*w" and "m*oa*ns." See p. 788.

Character   In a limited sense, character is any person in a narrative. In another sense, character is the sum of the moral, psychological, and physical qualities of this person or character. See pp. 192, 1121, and 1123.
   FLAT CHARACTER   A character in the narrative who can be summed up or characterized by one or two traits. Jelka's father (in "The Murder") is a flat character.
   ROUND CHARACTER   A character in a narrative who has depth and complexity. Hedda Gabler is a round character.
   STATIC CHARACTER   A character who does not change as a person during the course of the narrative. George Tesman (in *Hedda Gabler*) is a static character.
   DEVELOPING CHARACTER   A character who undergoes some significant change in perception or behavior. The protagonist in "Araby" is a developing character. So is Mrs. Peters in "A Jury of Her Peers."

Climax   The turning point or dramatic high point in a narrative. When Hedda Gabler burns Lövborg's manuscript, her fortune takes a decisive turn for the worse. Oedipus, on the other hand, seems doomed from the moment he begins his investigation. Each clue that brings him closer to the truth is a minor climax, leading to the ultimate climax when he discovers his true identity. See also *action* and *plot*.

Comedy   A type of drama that usually has a happy ending and that encourages laughter or at least a hopeful and light-hearted view of the human situation. Comedy is opposed to tragedy in that it usually deals with the successful struggles of ordinary men and women rather than the doomed struggles of great or noble characters. See p. 509. See also *tragedy*.

Effect   The impression, in either thought or feeling, made upon the reader by any element in a literary work—character, plot, setting, style. The *central effect* is the total impression the work makes upon the reader or audience.

Exposition   The disclosure of information not directly represented through speech or action. Exposition might be the presentation of background material in any narrative, but the term is usually applied to drama, indicating the exposure of events prior to a play's actual beginning. In *Oedipus Rex,* the chorus' memory of Oedipus' victory over the Sphinx is part of the exposition. Some say that the flashback is a form of exposition but there is a significant difference in the form of presentation. In a flashback an earlier scene is actually dramatized on stage—Biff's discovery of his father's adultery in *Death of a Salesman*—but in an exposition, the event is reported as something that has already happened. See p. 1067. See also *flashback.*

Figure of speech   A way of using language so that the words mean something other than their literal meaning. "He bought the farm" and "He kicked the bucket" are figurative ways of saying "He died." Some lines of poetry employ several different figures of speech. "Fern Hill" concludes with these lines: "Time held me green and dying / Though I sang in my chains like the sea." "Time" is a personification; "green and dying" and "in my chains" are metaphors; "like the sea" is a simile. See also *personification, metaphor, simile.*

Flashback   The direct or dramatic representation of an event that takes place in the past. *Death of a Salesman* makes extensive use of this technique. See also exposition.

Foil   A minor character who, by contrast, helps characterize a major character. In *Death of a Salesman,* Charley is a foil to Willy. See p. 1070.

Foreshadowing   An early event or speech in a story that prepares the reader for a later event. For example, Hedda Gabler plays with her father's pistols in two scenes in the early part of the play and there is also a reference to an earlier incident when she threatened to shoot Lövborg. These events and speeches foreshadow the death of both Lövborg and Hedda. See p. 892.

Free writing   Spontaneous and continuous writing without particular attention to grammar, spelling, or logical coherence—an exercise designed to generate ideas.

Happy ending   An ending of a story in which things turn out well for deserving and virtuous protagonists. There are very few happy endings in serious modern literature, and the term, *happy ending,* is usually associated with works that represent the improbable triumph of conventional virtue, that is, works tailored for the mass audience and adolescents. See also *affirmative ending.*

Imagery   The use of language to represent sense experience, either of sight, sound, smell, touch, or taste. Repeated images often take on symbolic significance, like the color *green* in "Fern Hill." At first the speaker is "happy as the grass was green," then "green and carefree," and finally "green and dying." See pp. 514 and 548.

Irony   Implies a discrepancy between what is said and what is meant (verbal irony) or between what is intended by the speaker and what is understood by the reader (dramatic irony) or between what is expected and what happens (situational irony). See pp. 45, 72, 124, 503, and 507.

VERBAL IRONY   In "Indian Camp," Uncle George calls Dr. Adams a "great man" but means something else.

DRAMATIC IRONY   Oedipus says that he is the child of fortune, but the reader knows that Oedipus will soon discover that he is the most unfortunate of men.

SITUATIONAL IRONY   In "The Murder" Jim Moore scorns Mr. Sepic's warning that his daughter will not love a man who does not beat her, but Jim finally does what his father-in-law advised.

Lyric   A type of poem in which a single speaker (the *I* of the poem) expresses personal thoughts and feelings. Many of Shakespeare's sonnets are lyrics, professing the speaker's fidelity and love. Most of the poetry in this book is lyric poetry.

Metaphor   A figure of speech in which an implicit comparison is made between two things essentially different. Metaphor is closely related to simile except that in a simile the comparison is expressed by the use of a word or phrase such as *like, as, similar to,* or *seems.* In "To His Coy Mistress" the line "My vegetable love should grow / Vaster than empires," is a metaphor implying a comparison between the growth of love and the growth of vegetables. If the comparison were expressed in a simile it might read, "My love, like a vegetable, should grow vaster than empires." See p. 687. See also *figure of speech* and *simile.*

Meter   An arrangement of language so that accented syllables occur at regularized intervals in time. Meter is a way of manipulating or intensifying the normal rhythm of speech. See also *rhythm* and *accent.*

Moral   The rule of conduct that is said to be the meaning or message of a story or poem. Although some literary works do have a specific moral purpose, most good writers try to avoid preachment and propaganda. "A Jury of Her Peers" and "The Sky is Gray" encourage the reader to a better understanding of sexism and racism, but the experience communicated in these stories can hardly be reduced to a "moral" or "lesson." See also *theme.*

Parable   A short narrative that implies a religious or moral truth: a typical Biblical model is the story of "The Prodigal Son," but stories like "The Yellow Wall-Paper" might also be read as parables. See *allegory.*

Persona   The speaker or *I* in a poem. The persona or speaker may be closely identified with the poet, as in Adrienne Rich's "Diving into the Wreck," or obviously removed from the poet, as in "Terence, This is Stupid Stuff," where Housman creates a fictional persona. See p. 562. See also *speaker.*

Personification   A figure of speech in which human attributes are given to an animal, object, or concept. In the line, "Because I could not stop for Death / He kindly stopped for me," Death is personified as a gentleman caller. See also *figure of speech* and *metaphor.*

Plot   The arrangement and representation of events in a story or narrative. In theory, the story of a play or novel begins with the earliest event known to the reader and, following a chronological sequence, ends with the last event known to the reader. The story of Oedipus begins with the prophecy to Laïos that he will be killed by his own child, but the plot of *Oedipus Rex* begins several years later with the plague in Thebes. In making plots, authors might begin in the middle or even the end of the story, or they might change the chronological sequence of events in other ways, using flashbacks or exposition to represent past episodes. Plot also determines how events are represented. In *Death of a Salesman* Willy's visit to Howard is dramatized, but Biff's visit to Oliver is related afterwards by Biff (an *exposition*). In "The Murder" the narrator describes the shooting of Jelka's lover in a direct way so that the reader is like an eyewitness. By contrast, Jim's beating of Jelka is not described directly but implied by the subsequent scene. See also *story* and *exposition.*

Point of view   The perspective from which the story is told. See pp. 249, 489, 507, and 509.

OMNISCIENT POINT OF VIEW   The narrator uses the third person and speaks as if he or she knows everything, including what all the characters think and feel, why they act as they do, and what, in a moral sense, they are worth. Most modern writers try to avoid the all-knowing air of earlier storytellers who were quick to explain and evaluate the intentions of many characters, but the term omniscient is still applied to narratives which reveal the consciousness of more than one character. In this sense, "Good Country People" is told from an omniscient point of view—first Mrs. Hopewell's and then Joy's.

LIMITED OMNISCIENT POINT OF VIEW   The narrator tells the story in the third person but tells it from the viewpoint of one character. Most third person narratives in this text have a limited omniscient point of view.

FIRST PERSON POINT OF VIEW   The narrator becomes one of the characters and tells the story in the first person. Sissy uses the first person point of view to tell her own story in "Four Summers."

OBJECTIVE POINT OF VIEW   The narrator tells the story in the third person and does not penetrate the consciousness of even the main character but simply reports what the characters do and say. This point of view is also called *dramatic* because it resembles the point of view in a play or, more nearly, a movie where point of view is determined by what the camera sees as well as what the characters say. Few narratives are purely dramatic. Even in "Indian Camp," a rigorous example of this form, the narrator reveals Nick's inner feelings in the final sentence: "He felt quite sure he would never die."

Protagonist   The principal character in a story or play. This term is better than "hero" or "heroine" because the main characters in many works are unheroic—the narrator in "I'm a Fool" or Joy/Hulga in "Good Country People." See also *antagonist*.

Realism   A term usually associated with a nineteenth-century literary movement which attempted to represent the details of ordinary life as those details might actually be observed in society. Realism sought to give the illusion of objective, well-documented social history, especially the history of everyday contemporary life. The protagonists in realistic literature often aspire to an extraordinary life, but, like Hedda Gabler, they are usually defeated by their own limitations and by the conventional forces of society.

Rhyme   The repetition of accented words with the same or nearly the same sound—*hope/ rope, love/dove* (perfect rhymes); *aisle/isle, night/knight* (identical rhymes); *abroad/ God, Queen/been* (half rhymes or slant rhymes).

Rhythm   Any wavelike recurrence of sound, usually associated with poetic speech and indicative of poetry's kinship with music and song. See also *meter*.

Setting   In a narrow sense, the place and time where the action occurs. In a broader sense, setting includes the descriptive details that determine how the reader feels about a certain place or setting. The setting of "Four Summers" is a lakeside tavern in a working-class neighborhood. Descriptive details create a setting that is dingy, vulgar, and oppressive. See p. 1200.

Simile   A figure of speech in which an explicit comparison is made between two things essentially different. A simile is like a metaphor except that in a metaphor the comparison is implied rather than expressed by a word or phrase. In "Living in Sin," the line, "no dust upon the furniture of love," is a metaphor which implies a comparison between dusting furniture and sustaining love. A later line, when the speaker feels "the daylight coming / like a relentless milkman up the stairs," is a simile which compares the coming of day with the arrival of the milkman. See p. 656. See also *figure of speech* and *metaphor.*

Sonnet A poem of fourteen lines, normally iambic pentameter, with a rhyme scheme that normally conforms to one of the two major types of sonnet—the Italian or the English/Shakespearean.

Speaker The person telling the story. In fiction, the narrator of the story, the voice the author assumes in telling the story. In poetry, the speaker is often called the *persona,* the *I* of the poem. See p. 562. See also *persona* and *point of view.*

Story A story or narrative is a general term applicable to any literary work which tells a story, including poems and novels as well as short stories. Story also refers to the sequence of events, from beginning to end, that is revealed or implied in any literary work. Although the terms *story* and *plot* are sometimes used interchangeably, story refers to a potentially unlimited sequence of events and plot refers to the way these events are selected, arranged, and presented. In a sense, then, stories provide the materials for making plots. This is especially noticeable in works that are based on history or myth, as in the case of Sophocles' plotting the story of Oedipus. See also *plot.*

Suspense The quality of a narrative that makes a reader eager to know what will happen next and how the complications in the action will be resolved.

Symbol Any concrete element—object, person, situation—that means significantly more than what it is. In *The Great Gatsby,* the green light at the end of Daisy's boat dock is, on one level of meaning, a concrete detail in the setting of the novel. But for Gatsby, the green light represents his hope for a future with Daisy and, more generally, his faith in the individual's ability to make dreams come true. Since Gatsby's faith in Daisy is based on illusion, the green light will have yet another meaning for the reader. Except in allegory, symbols tend to have multiple meanings. See pp. 95, 526, and 534. See also *allegory, imagery,* and *metaphor.*

Synaesthesia The description of one kind of sensation in terms of another in order to appeal to two or more senses at once. For instance, Edith Sitwell appeals to the visual and the tactile in the line, "a green shade in the snow."

Theme The central idea or meaning in a poem or narrative, usually the view of life that shapes the story. A theme is not the same as a "message" or "moral." "Four Summers" suggests that most people cannot escape the drab conditions of their environment, but it does not suggest a political or economic solution for the working-class society in the story. Nor does it moralize about Sissy's personal failure to escape. Even in "Good Country People," the theme of Christian love and redemption is not likely to be read as a Christian "message." See also *moral.*

Tone The attitude expressed by a writer or speaker. Tone usually expresses a feeling or emotion. The tone of "Dover Beach" is solemn and melancholy.

Tragedy A type of drama in which the protagonist, a person with a certain greatness or nobility, suffers a fall in fortune. Oedipus is generally considered a model of the tragic protagonist in spite of the fact that most tragic protagonists are far more guilty in their pride and daring. Tragedy is opposed to comedy in that comic protagonists usually overcome passion and error and make a happy adjustment to society. See p. 892. See also *comedy.*

INDEX OF AUTHORS, TITLES, AND FIRST LINES

NOTES

NOTES

NOTES

NOTES

NOTES

NOTES

NOTES

NOTES

NOTES